The Literary Experience

COMPACT SECOND EDITION

Bruce Beiderwell
University of California, Los Angeles

Jeffrey M. Wheeler
Long Beach City College

CENGAGE
Learning·

Australia • Brazil • Mexico • Singapore • United Kingdom • United States

CENGAGE
Learning

**The Literary Experience,
Compact Second Edition**
Bruce Beiderwell, Jeffrey M.
Wheeler

Product Director: Monica
Eckman

Product Team Manager:
Christopher Bennem

Product Manager: Kate Derrick

Content Developer: Megan
Garvey

Associate Content Developer:
Erin Bosco

Product Assistant: Kerry DeVito

Media Developer: Janine
Tangney

Marketing Manager: Erin
Parkins

Senior Content Project
Manager: Michael Lepera

Senior Art Director: Marissa
Falco

Manufacturing Planner: Betsy
Donaghey

IP Analyst: Ann Hoffman

IP Project Manager: Farah Fard

Production Service/Compositor:
Cenveo® Publisher Services

Text Designer: Cenveo
Publisher Services

Cover Designer: Sarah Bishins

Library of Congress Control Number: 2014946044

ISBN: 978-0-8400-3076-4

Cengage Learning
20 Channel Center Street
Boston, MA 02210
USA

Cengage Learning is a leading provider of customized learning solutions
with employees residing in nearly 40 different countries and sales in more
than 125 countries around the world. Find your local representative at
www.cengage.com

Cengage Learning products are represented in Canada by Nelson
Education, Ltd.

To learn more about Cengage Learning Solutions, visit **www.cengage.com**

Purchase any of our products at your local college store or at our preferred online store **www.cengagebrain.com**

Printed in the United States of America
Print Number: 01   Print Year: 2015

Brief Contents

Contents

2 | Scene, Episode, and Plot
What Happened? Why Do We Care?   195

Anthology

4 | Point of View
How Do We Know What We Know about What Happened?   387

Anthology

5 | Setting

*Where and When Does the Action Take Place? Why Does It Make
a Difference?*   458

Anthology

6 | Rhythm, Pace, and Rhyme
How Do Sounds Move?   535

Anthology

9 | Interruption
Where Did That Come From? Why Is This Here?   845

Anthology

10 | Tone
Did I Hear That Right?   1023

Anthology

12 | Symbolism
How Do I Know When an Event or an Image Is Supposed to Stand for Something Else?   1147

Anthology

Anthology

Preface

WHAT HASN'T CHANGED

The Literary Experience began as an anthology that sought to make critical writing central to reading—to make one active process enrich another active process. As we pointed out in the preface to the first edition, we wanted to avoid the conventional "writing about literature" approach. We felt that the preposition "about" signaled an unhealthy split between activities like reading and writing and a subject—literature. As we put it then: "The 'about' may suggest that there is some special knowledge separate from the primary texts and the immediate experience of those texts that is somehow supposed to be mastered." The way we saw it, students should write to gain understanding—not merely register their understanding. And we wanted even something more than understanding: we wanted writing to intensify the special experience that a work of art can provide.

Nothing in this second edition changes that ambitious goal, and some specific characteristics of this edition will be familiar to those who have used our book before. We didn't and still don't merely list or define critical terms. Nor do we restrict our discussions of literary terms by dividing poetry, fiction, and drama into separate realms. *The Literary Experience* invites teaching across genres. Once again, we organize reading selections and examples around elements that are common to all forms of literature, including film—elements such as plot, rhythm, character, setting, and word choice. And we introduce a specific and full critical vocabulary through grounded discussions of how those large elements function in particular stories, plays, poems, and films.

We still feel that this organization through elements of literary texts and films is more than a convenient structuring device. As before, each chapter is designed to prompt and sustain writing exercises. Focusing on point of view, for example, can help students employ an analytical framework for close and productive readings. Students will have a means—along with the command of a specialized vocabulary—to develop and organize their insights as critical writers. As the structuring element of each chapter grows less familiar (say coherence, interruption, or allusion), students are encouraged to widen their sense of possible approaches and to think of texts in new ways. With the scaffolding *The Literary Experience* provides, students will learn to apply concepts that they might not have considered in relation to literary study. That scaffolding will also help students become better readers of literary criticism. The discipline will seem less alien, for students will come to understand that arguments carried on in journals and books have often been built just as they have been building their own analyses, by focusing on a specific element within a text.

WHAT HAS CHANGED

A new opening section on writing

We felt we needed a more collected, substantial, and clearly foregrounded discussion of writing and the writing process as it relates to reading. So we've placed that discussion up front—before presenting elements and thematically clustered readings. In many textbooks designed for introduction to literature and film courses, sections on writing are presented as add-ons. Placing advice about the writing process or providing insight about what constitutes a strong paper at the end implies that understanding, learning, or the acquisition of a critical vocabulary is separate from the act of writing. Students are told, in effect, that they can become critical writers and thinkers only after mastering a body of material. Writing becomes a matter of "writing up" a subject one has mastered. Lost in such an approach is any sense of crucial givens of composition theory:

- That writing instruction centers on the process
- That writing and reading are conceptually complementary
- That writing can become a means of discovery
- That writing involves problem solving
- That writing is a social activity

Also lost is a crucial notion of reading as itself an active process that can be enriched through writing and that rewards reflection and rereading. We have sought to break down the compartmentalization of writing by aligning that activity from the outset with the whole experience of engaging a work of art and then sustaining the reading-writing connection through all the chapters that follow. The "Notes to Student Writers" (carried over from the first edition) now play back on a substantial body of examples and advice.

A new chapter arrangement

The theme chapter has been eliminated, although not of course the notion of theme itself. In this second edition, we've let concern for theme emerge from chapters on other elements. The symbolism and allegory chapters from the first edition have been collapsed into one chapter. Not only does this help keep the whole text reasonably trim, it also allows for a tighter interplay between these closely aligned notions.

We've also moved the chapter on research that appeared at the end of the first edition to the opening section on writing. By doing that we align the research process with the students' reading and writing experience. While we still provide essential information about conventions of documentation, that information now is placed more clearly in context of the ongoing conversations that are at the heart of critical writing in response to literature and film.

And most important, we've moved the genre chapter from Chapter 16 in the first edition to Chapter 1. Now this chapter leads off the text and gives us a strong thread to pull through the entire textbook. Genre becomes, along with the themes that link readings and the elements highlighted in the readings, yet another powerful lens through which to see. That is, students may gain fresh insight when they consider how one work plays out features of a larger type.

A new and distinctive use of film and film criticism

This use of genre knits film more closely into the fabric of the whole. Teachers who choose to focus exclusively on readings will find that the film references provide students a valuable grounding in relatively familiar works of art. We believe the film genres powerfully contextualize even the most challenging readings. For example, while *The Tragical History of the Life and Death of Doctor Faustus* may be no more than a distant cousin of today's popular horror films, those films do help frame productive questions about Marlowe's exploration of the boundaries between an earthly and demonic realm. And Don Lee's "The Price of Eggs in China" can hardly be understood without reflection on the assumptions about knowledge or truth that underlie the conventional detective fictions the main character, Dean, so eagerly reads.

We've also put at the start of each thematic cluster a film review that makes genre central to analysis. These reviews have been selected so that students and teachers can understand the logic of the arguments without necessarily knowing the film addressed. These reviews, by highlighting genre, are not even bound by film itself. They usefully model the sorts of essays students strive to write on poems, stories, or plays. Finally, they accent the sense we've tried to reinforce from the start that critical writing emerges from conversations about crafted works of art. And those conversations need not seem purely academic.

New selections with an accent on the contemporary

With the increased accessibility (that is, both available and free) of works in the public domain on the Web, we've decided to shift the balance of our readings toward the contemporary. While some instructors will no doubt note that a favored classic is missing, there will be other selections that offer fresh and exciting challenges. Among the stories included here that did not appear in the first edition are George Saunders's "Escape from Spiderhead," Ursula K. Le Guin's "The Wife's Story," Salman Rushdie's "The Courter," Tope Folarin's "Miracle," Jim Shepard's "Gojira, King of the Monsters," and Jennifer Egan's "Black Box"; among new plays are Václav Havel's *Temptation* and Rick Creese's *Solemn Mockeries* (newly published here); and among new poems Geoffrey Brock's "Daddy: 1933," Gwendolyn Brooks's "Sadie and Maud," Alice Walker's "Women," Yusef Komunyakaa's "A Break from the Bush," Meghan O'Rourke's "The Window at Arles," and David Shumate's "High Water Mark." All counted, more than 30 new works appear in the second edition of *The Literary Experience*.

SUPPLEMENTS

MindTap Literature, First Edition, is a highly adaptable digital solution for introduction to literature courses that gives instructors control over what students see and when, and allows them to add their favorite activities, videos, and other resources quickly and easily. Paired with the Questia online library, a rich collection of sources selected by librarians, **MindTap Literature** gives students direct links to more than 600 short stories, poems, plays, novels, and essays, as well as access to robust search tools in Questia that students can use as they do research. Comprehensive multimedia instruction in writing five major types of papers assigned in the course and supporting modules on literary terms and literary criticism provide extensive guidance for students as they learn to read and write about literature. Analytics and reports provide a snapshot of class progress, time in course, engagement, and completion rates.

QUESTIA

Questia is an online library that provides 24/7 access to the Web's premier collection of full-text books, academic journals, and periodical articles in the humanities and social sciences. As it also offers video and interactive research tutorials, it is more than a vast collection of online sources. Questia can help your students in the entire research process, from topic selection and research to organization of their notes and proper citations. Questia will help your students write better papers, providing a wider array of scholarly sources, and enabling them to organize what they've learned into a better-thought-out paper.

ACKNOWLEDGMENTS

The following reviewers have looked at different incarnations of the chapters that constitute *The Literary Experience*, both first and second editions. Their careful reading, insightful questions, and generous advice have made this book more teachable:

Donald Andrews, Chattanooga State Technical Community College
Lisa Angius, Farmingdale State College
Matthew Ayres, County College of Morris
Melissa Barth, Appalachian State University
Joseph Bathanti, Appalachian State University
Janet Beck, Appalachian State University
Betty Bettacchi, Collin County Community College
Jenny Billings Beaver, Rowan Cabarrus Community College
Jacqueline Blackwell, Thomas Nelson Community College
Amy Brazillier, Red Rocks Community College
Barbara L. Brown, San Jacinto College Central
Glenda Bryant, South Plains College, Levelland
Larry Carlson, College of Charleston
Laura Carroll, Abilene Christian University
Patricia Cearley, South Plains College, Levelland
Karen Chaffee, Ulster County Community College
Helen Chester, Milwaukee Area Technical College
Sherry Chisamore, Ulster County Community College
Basil Clark, Saginaw Valley State University
Mike Compton, University of Memphis
Denise Coulter, Atlantic Cape Community College
Marya Davis Turley, Western Kentucky University
Christy Desmet, University of Georgia
Jonathan Dewberry, New Jersey City University
Tammy DiBenedetto, Riverside Community College
Scott Douglass, Chattanooga State Technical Community College
Joy M. EichnerLynch, Contra Costa College
Jo Nell Farrar, San Jacinto College
Jane Focht-Hansen, San Antonio College
DeLisa Ging, Northern Oklahoma College
Diana Gingo, University of Texas, Dallas
Edvige Giunta, New Jersey City University
Paul Goodin, Northern Kentucky University
Joseph Granitto, Farmingdale State College
Gary Harrington, Salisbury University

Dawn Hayward, Delaware County Community College
Ana Hernandez, Miami Dade Community College
Gillian R. Hettinger, William Paterson University
Kathy Houghton, Erie Community College
Rebecca Housel, Rochester Institute of Technology
David Johansson, Brevard Community College
Ken Johnson, Georgia Perimeter College
Jan McArthur, Delgado Community College
Miles McCrimmon, J. Sargeant Reynolds Community College
Linda McGann, South Plains College, Levelland
Thomas Gerard McNamee, Eastern Oregon University
Richard Middleton-Kaplan, Harper College
Alan Mitnick, Passaic County Community College
Rod Val Moore, Los Angeles Valley College
Michael Morris, Eastfield College
Mona Narain, University of Texas, San Antonio
Jeffrey N. Nelson, University of Alabama, Huntsville
Chris Partida, North Harris Community College
Peggy Peden, Nashville State Community College
Jan Prewitt, Emporia State University
Bart Rawlinson, Mendocino College
Geri Rhodes, Albuquerque TVI Community College
Richard Rosol, Quinnipiac University
Randy Russell, Front Range Community College
Steve Sansom, North Harris Community College
Deborah Sarbin, Clarion University
Cary Ser, Miami Dade Community College
Michael Sollars, Texas Southern University
Donald R. Stinson, Northern Oklahoma College
Constance Strickland, Wesley College
Raven Sweet, University of Memphis
Andrea Kaston Tange, Eastern Michigan University
Julie Tilton, San Bernardino Valley College
Christine Grimes Topping, Jefferson Community College
Tom Treffinger, Greenville Technical College
Edward P. Walkiewicz, Oklahoma State University, Stillwater
Mark Woods, Jefferson Community College
Earl Yarington, Prince George's Community College

Finally, much of our inspiration comes from the lively and informed conversations that we have had with the faculty at UCLA's Writing Programs and in the English Department at Long Beach City College. Good colleagues make for good teaching.

It has been a great pleasure to work with the entire Cengage team on this project. In particular, we'd like to thank Megan Garvey, Managing Content Developer; Kate Derrick, Product Manager; Ann Hoffman, Intellectual Property Analyst; Farah Fard, Intellectual Property Project Manager; Michael Lepera, Content Project Manager; and Yashmita Hota, Project Manager, Cenveo® Publisher Services. We'd also like to thank those who helped us envision the project and carry it through in the first edition: Bill Brisick, Aron Keesbury, and Marita Sermolins.

Throughout the process, we have aimed to make a book worthy of the good students in our lives: Hudson Beiderwell, Charlotte Beiderwell, Flora Beiderwell, Paulo Henrique Gusmão Garcia Williams, Chloe Wheeler, and Blake Wheeler. Finally, we must thank those who have lived with this project as it has developed over both editions: Ivna Gusmão and Laura Scavuzzo Wheeler. They have heard about each idea for revision, each teaching experience with the material, and every suggestion from reviewers, and they have been our first editors and proofreaders. Their support is deeply appreciated.

Introduction: Critical Writing as Conversation

HOW DOES WRITING RELATE TO READING AND DISCUSSION?

> Imagine that you enter a parlor. You come late. When you arrive, others have long preceded you, and they are engaged in a heated discussion, a discussion too heated for them to pause and tell you exactly what it is about. . . . You listen for a while, until you decide that you have caught the tenor of the argument; then you put in your oar (from Kenneth Burke's *The Philosophy of Literary Form*).

Imagine for a moment a fairly typical movie-going experience. Assume that you've gone with a friend to see a campus screening of *Guardians of the Galaxy*. As the final credits come to a close and you begin to move toward the exit, a conversation begins with a basic question: "Did you like it?" This is an easy discussion to start and also an easy one to end if the answer is simply yes or no. But that will not be enough of an answer for anyone interested in the film or in movies in general.

Now imagine you stop at a coffee shop on campus and you find a group of friends seated around a table who have just seen the same movie. You join them and discover that they are in the midst of a lively discussion about *Guardians of the Galaxy*. You probably do more listening at first than speaking; after all, you need to know what ground they've covered and what direction they've taken. But at some point, you find an opportunity to fit your opinions into the conversation. One of the people at the table found the film "empty entertainment": "All the explosions, special effects, and big battle scenes were exciting, overblown, and silly all at once. It's just too much fantastic stuff for me. These comic book superheroes aren't real enough to be heroes. And it doesn't help that so much is played for laughs in this movie." You catch at that complaint because it allows you to pick up on an interesting point and then contribute something of your own to the conversation:

> Yeah, this movie isn't a groundbreaker. But it's better than the usual comic book stuff. Think of it this way: We don't complain about the *Odyssey* just because fantastic things happen in the story. In this movie we've got a tree

that is all about innocence and a raccoon that is totally cynical surrounded by humanoids who figure out how to live in the space in between. And I didn't have any trouble with the laughs. Some of the fun, like the 80's music on the Walkman, helped me connect with Peter Quill. And the jokes hit the right tone too. This movie has some touching scenes and some real emotions, but it never pretends to be heavy. I'm glad that it didn't try to be more than a comic book movie. I get really tired of how serious Batman and the Wolverine have become. Too much seriousness in a comic book movie really is silly.

Note that our imagined talk has moved to a point. If you are challenged to back up your interpretation, you will do so by reference to the film; you have moved beyond simply liking or disliking. You are contextualizing, putting the film into categories based on previous experience with films and with wider reading. You begin to establish criteria for further discussion. You suggest that to meet artistic standards, a good film must comment on life, and/or must imaginatively employ familiar elements (of plot, of character, of structure, and so on). As you call up these familiar categories, you are able to conduct further analysis and prompt others to continue the conversation.

This imagined coffee shop meeting links conversations with reading and writing. The talk recounted in the sample dialogue represents a process of thinking through the literary experience. Note how these few sentences begin to define and follow a point as you would do in a paper. Also see how the dialogue shows some of the rhetorical gestures common in writing; note, for example, the counterpoint starts with a concession ("yeah, this movie isn't a groundbreaker") and then moves to an assertion at the end. That strategy shows an awareness that arguments about art don't come out of nowhere—that critics respond not only to texts but also to what other people have to say about texts. The key term for both conversation and composition is *process*. As you discuss *Guardians of the Galaxy* (or any other movie, story, poem, or play) with your friends, you will likely learn something. You'll clarify—indeed—discover ideas. You'll test arguments and, when you find them weak, you'll revise or discard them. Any writing you do will grow from these sorts of discussions.

Thinking of writing as a kind of conversation will also help you factor in audience: When you write in response to a work of literature or a film, you necessarily engage with other interested readers/viewers. In this respect, critical writing represents an essential activity or ideal of college life: people share ideas and learn from others. Scholars and critics do not stop being students—and students *are* also scholars and critics. The result of critical writing is not primarily to add to a growing body of knowledge in pursuit of the perfect paper; rather, critical writing and thinking reflect a culture's continuing engagement with art and ideas. People do not read or feel Shakespeare any more deeply than the great critic Samuel Johnson read and felt Shakespeare in the eighteenth century. Fortunately, the challenge is not to surpass Johnson but to carry on the spirit of the discussions he so powerfully joined. To write in response to literature is to address readers who are genuinely interested in our subject—readers who often want to "talk back" to us.

CRITICAL WRITING AS AN EXTENSION OF READING

Many of you will resist the idea that critical writing engages readers as well as deepens the writer's own experience because such grand notions don't match your own academic experience. The fact is, critical writing is often seen from a student's perspective as merely an assignment—something to "get through," not something to grow from. But once you understand how writing takes place as part of a whole literary experience, you can begin to make writing seem less alien. Writing (like conversation) grows from alert, engaged, informed, and active reading. Literary texts ask—even demand—such a powerful idea of reading. Consider what you feel and think as you read the following short poem.

Langston Hughes (1902–1967)

Harlem (1951)

What happens to a dream deferred?

Does it dry up
like a raisin in the sun?
Or fester like a sore—
And then run?
Does it stink like rotten meat?
Or crust and sugar over—
like a syrupy sweet?

Maybe it just sags
like a heavy load.

Or does it explode?

There is no script for your response to this or any poem. You might feel anger or frustration as you read; you might sympathize with the speaker or want to argue with him. You might be confused by the questions posed. "Harlem" prompts questions, interpretations, and feelings. And whatever line of response you follow, you'll search for words to clarify and deepen the reading experience. At some point, if you wish to move forward, you should make writing part of your reading. In brief notes, journal entries, or exchanges over e-mail with other readers, you can actively seek words that register your response.

Critical writing, then, emerges from active reading; indeed, it is part of active reading. That notion applies to the experience of any work of art. You hear, you see, you feel, you think—you experience and you write. You try to enrich your response to a text (a poem, a film, a painting, a song) through your own words and explain your response to others who have read the text. When you appreciate this connection between *your* reading and *your* writing (your viewing and your writing, your seeing and your writing, your listening and your writing), you can begin to appreciate what is involved in the discipline of literary criticism and how rewarding that discipline can be.

Reading, after all, isn't just a matter of decoding letters on a page. At the broadest level, reading prompts reflection, interpretation, and discussion. People read poems and stories, of course, but people also read paintings, songs, or the look on a friend's face in a moment of crisis. The complex signals of everyday life form various sorts of "texts" to identify, organize, and set in context of related signals. Such signals become a living part of your experience and the substance of much shared experience. The act of reading and writing are vitally connected: *to write about a work of art is to extend the process that characterizes reading.*

This notion of extending reading through writing addresses a common misunderstanding and encourages a liberating vision of a student as a critical writer. We'll first take on the misunderstanding. Some of you may hate writing about a poem or a movie because you feel writing "kills" the fun of reading or viewing. This attitude lurks behind expressions like "I read for pleasure, but write for class credit"; "I view things in a creative way, but write to prove that I've understood the professor's lectures"; "I react to books and movies emotionally, but write to show my control of the structure of an essay." All of these statements suggest that reading has been divorced from writing. The notion of writing as a means of engagement with reading has been lost. Also lost is any sense that writing serves to contribute to broader, ongoing conversations with others.

But if you think of writing as an activity that deepens your understanding and communicates your distinct perspective, you will realize a broad vision of what it means to write critically and analytically. You can appreciate the importance of a specialized vocabulary. You can see how writing together with reading becomes a single creative process. You can also appreciate how writing serves to share the experience of a text in a way that may enrich the experience of others. Writing sharpens, deepens, and extends reading. In the process of production, writing helps reveal things that might have been missed. Critical writing leads to discovery and sustains an ongoing dialogue. The discoveries that you make as you write deny the possibility—even the desirability—of a single, final essay on any work of art.

This second edition of *The Literary Experience* will consistently link critical writing, critical reading, and critical conversation. It will help you write by helping you read more perceptively. It will help you read by engaging you as a writer. To this end, we'll start where most literature textbooks end: with writing. We'll first address what it means to write critically, offer practical suggestions that will help you through the task, and provide some useful information crucial for your success.

Part One

Using Writing to Think through Literature and Film

Writing as a Process

How Can I Begin to Shape Writing in Response to a Literary Text?

The complexity of the critical task and of literature itself may seem overwhelming. That complexity may prompt a desire to get grounded in some plain, practical, and productive strategies. In the sections that follow, we'll provide that grounding. And we'll address the first thing first: oftentimes the hardest thing about writing is getting started. It's something we're sure you can relate to: one line begins to crawl across the page and then seems to turn against itself. One idea seems clear, but blurs with every word that comes to your mind. After laboring for hours to make a point, the point seems to disappear. The terror of the blank screen can make you long for multiple-choice exams or true/false quizzes.

After all, the only way to get stuck on a multiple-choice exam is simply to not know the material. Such an exam asks you to apply facts in a very simple way and within a very simple structure that has been made by your professor. An essay assignment, however, shifts the creative burden. The professor in effect challenges you to establish an appropriate subject and construct an argument; you must make choices regarding organization and content; you must, at some level, *discover* something, not just know something.

This can be a scary challenge, but acknowledging the complexity of writing is the first step in overcoming common difficulties. For example, writer's block often arises from a fundamental misunderstanding. Too often students think they should be able to "read up" on a subject and then "write out" a paper in a neat, unbroken string of words. But such a notion of how a "good writer" works fosters unrealistic expectations. Student writers (or any writers for that matter) do not possess clarity so much as they achieve clarity through patient thought and reflection. And clarity is not something to achieve once and then keep; every new paper assignment creates new problems to solve.

It is essential to know that you are not doing anything wrong when you find yourself crossing out, reframing, restructuring, and revising what you write. It's more likely that you are doing something right: that you are practicing keen, self-critical skills that can ultimately be productive and rewarding. A healthy sense of the necessary messiness (as well as the real challenges) of the writer's task should be liberating at every stage of the writing process—from your early generative notes and observations, through your shaping of a topic and your testing of a thesis, and on to the drafting and redrafting of the final essay.

GETTING STARTED

The idea of writing as a process should lead us to an insight about getting started: writing is not something to do only after you've thought through a task and "know what you want to say." Writing is a tool of thought that will help you learn what it is you want to say. Writing generates more and better writing. In this section we suggest activities that anticipate and address common problems that writers encounter in the early stages of a draft. These activities should help you engage difficulties productively. The immediate goal is to help you get started; the larger goal is to keep you actively thinking throughout the writing process.

Discuss What You Read or See
Talk with peers. If a paper is to become a contribution to a conversation, you should develop a sense of what that conversation might be by using your voice and listening to the voices of others. People often think of writing as lonely work. Although it can be that, it's worth remembering that writing is also a social act; writers listen first in order to communicate with others.

Think with a Pen in Hand or at the Keyboard
The physical act of putting words on a sheet of paper or on-screen differs from mulling over an idea while you are scanning a website. We don't discourage the latter, but we insist on the former. Be sure to concentrate on a task and write out questions and thoughts as they arise. Don't censor ideas before you've had a chance to record them. Once the early energy begins to fail (this usually occurs within a half an hour), read over your entries while they are fresh and use them to generate more gathered notes. For example, you might isolate items on a list that seem worth focused consideration. Or you could arrange the list into some sort of logical sequence. If you have compiled a

string of questions, zero in on the questions that most interest you. Do those questions overlap in some way? Can you formulate a new question that brings several threads together?

Keep a Reading Response Journal to Respond to Works as You Read or View Them

Set aside about twenty minutes a few times a week to talk back to, question, organize, or summarize what you've been reading. Writing in response to reading will sharpen your engagement with the material and lead to more alert discussion of the material. It will help you identify important points and remember those points. Finally, a reading response journal will help you strengthen the link between reading and writing.

Ask "What," "Why," and "How" Questions

If you find that "freewriting" stalls you before you get started, try a more directed method: formulate and respond to questions led off by the words *what, why,* and *how.* Begin with "what" questions. That may help you get grounded in some essentials and will usually lead to a summary and description. But even though a clear command of content is important, you'll need to move beyond the summary/descriptive level if you hope to contribute to a conversation about a work of art. So move on to "why" and/or "how" questions; these questions will require an analytical response and will lead you to assess the purpose or importance of particular details. They also will prompt you to make connections among details you observe and to explain, not just describe.

Respond Directly to Remarks from Class Discussion/Lecture or to Quotations Drawn from Criticism

Some people find it productive to generate ideas in direct response to the ideas of others. So give yourself something to push against and see what happens. It's also worth noting that generating ideas through responding to others' ideas might eventually help you structure your finished essay; existing ideas can supply the context from which you work out your own ideas.

CRAFTING A FIRST FULL DRAFT

The suggestions we've offered are broadly generative. They should help you get started, but they aren't enough to lead you to a finished essay. Generative strategies should not become an end in themselves; before you get stuck with a mere list of ideas, you need to define a central issue. You must move beyond even the best sketchy thoughts. To organize and develop ideas, first you need to define a topic and a thesis.

Defining a Topic

A *topic is what a paper is about, what it addresses, what it concerns.* That sounds simple enough. But critical writing is never simple. Writers don't merely select topics, they construct them. Even in response to a specific assignment, a writer must frame a topic to help the reader appreciate the logic of the entire composition.

A good topic is

- Workable—it limits the scope of the task
- Grounded—it builds on concrete textual evidence
- Engaging—it establishes a sense of an issue or a problem that needs to be addressed

The suggestions that follow should help you define a workable and worthwhile topic. You'll note that some of the suggestions overlap from the previous section whereas others anticipate points we'll make later on when defining the thesis and revising drafts. This occasional repetition respects what we've characterized as the necessary messiness of the writing process. An overly neat, rigid, step-by-step presentation of that process would undermine the spirit of this entire book: we want to provide useful leads to work from; we don't want to impose a fixed sequence of exercises.

Be Specific

You can allow yourself the freedom to begin from a broadly defined topic, but try to narrow the topic or make it more concrete as you work. You'll eventually need a topic that limits the contract you make with readers. No critical essay "covers" everything about a text; a good essay merely covers something interesting that it has promised to cover.

Focus First on the Text(s)

We want to honor ways literature connects with life, but a critical essay on a story, poem, film, or play cannot be cast entirely as a big idea, event, or social condition that the literary work is *about.* Keep in mind an important paradox: the grandest ambitions usually result in the smallest papers. Grand ambitions are often a disguise for familiar generalities; they often stop at the level of summary or statement. The best really big ideas often grow from a specific observation, question, or insight on an aspect of a particular work.

We can most clearly illustrate the value of attending closely to the text by providing a concrete example. The following poem by Marge Piercy addresses in a very short space some very significant social issues.

Marge Piercy (1936–)

A Work of Artifice (1982)

The bonsai tree
in the attractive pot
could have grown eighty feet tall
on the side of a mountain
till split by lightning.   5
But a gardener
carefully pruned it.
It is nine inches high.
Every day as he
whittles back the branches   10
the gardener croons,
It is your nature
to be small and cozy,
domestic and weak;
how lucky, little tree,   15
to have a pot to grow in.
With living creatures
one must begin very early
to dwarf their growth:
the bound feet,   20
the crippled brain,
the hair in curlers,
the hands you
love to touch.

Piercy's poem is about the oppression of women, surely a topic worth addressing. But the compelling qualities of this poem do not reside in that topic alone. Consider this: if we register only what the poem is *about*—that is, if we merely write about what Piercy writes about—we'll find ourselves as restricted as the bonsai tree; we'll be dealing with abstract ideas and remain one step away from the poem itself. A paper that generalizes on sexual oppression in our society may fail to account for (or even address) what makes "A Work of Artifice" distinctive and special as a poem. Not only that, but such a general paper will almost certainly rehash familiar ideas; it will reduce the power of Piercy's language to the language of summary or statement.

If we go no further than to describe how women may be restricted and conclude that "oppressive male power exists in our society," we have reduced— not analyzed—Piercy's poem. But if we ask ourselves questions about the poem itself, we may press forward to a deeper level of appreciation and insight. How does Piercy project and explore a tension between the "natural self" and the artificial, constructed self she sees as a product of society? Why does she "whittle" back the lines of the poem (note that the longest line concerns the tree's potential growth)? How does she engage us in an increasingly personal and forceful relationship to the controlling metaphor of the bonsai tree? Why does she juxtapose something as ancient and debilitating as "bound feet" with the relatively familiar and seemingly innocuous "hair in curlers"?

Define Key Terms

Definition provides a way to get at a precise, yet full sense of a subject. For example, you could pause over words used in the Piercy poem (like *whittles, croons, prunes*) and consider both what those words denote (what they signify, what they mean literally) and what they connote (what they suggest, what they imply emotionally). You could also pause over the words you use or hear others use in response to the text. At times, simply modifying a word will help you establish a clearer sense of a topic. The subject of Piercy's poem, for example, is not simply "oppression." We have used the terms *sexual oppression* and *oppressive male power*. Can you press further still on this point of meaning? Sexual oppression in this poem is *insidious, subtle, deceptive, manipulative, pervasive*. Oppressive male power finds expression under the guise of *kindness, gentleness, concern*. Ironically that power is justified as *natural* whereas the entire poem accentuates its *artifice*. Such careful thinking upon the meanings of individual words can enrich your sense of the text and move you beyond overly generalized topics.

Defining a Thesis

A **thesis** is a controlling assertion. A thesis establishes a contract between writer and reader, but it is important to remember that you will not be held to this contract until you turn in the final draft of the essay. So as you begin to write, think in terms of a tentative thesis, a provisional thesis, or a hypothesis. An example from the sciences can clarify this point. A hypothesis identifies something to test; it sets forth an idea as a basis for directed study. If evidence does not bear out the hypothesis, the scientist may reformulate the idea for further testing. An experiment does not necessarily fail because the hypothesis cannot be supported. The very lack of support may provide the insight necessary for constructing a new and more useful experiment.

Without a hypothesis, there is no basis for moving forward, no purpose or direction in the collection, ordering, and testing of evidence. The experiment comes to a halt before it begins. This example suggests that writers need a thesis not only to guide readers but to guide themselves. So keep the following in mind as you begin to draft your essay:

> A provisional thesis gives you an idea to test. It provides an organizational principle, a means to evaluate evidence, a lead to pick up and develop in transitions from paragraph to paragraph. It gives you a sense of direction and purpose, but can be adjusted or completely reformulated as you explore, clarify, and enrich thoughts.

The adjusting or reformulating isn't easy, of course. Constructing a strong final thesis usually proves to be one of the most difficult tasks in writing critically in response to literature or film. Part of the difficulty concerns the nature of critical thinking. It is an easy matter to identify a position when the options are predetermined. Some questions, for example, strictly narrow the range of possible responses: Are you for or against gun control? The answer might be yes or no, but rarely in the context of college work in any field are arguments shaped by such a broad either/or question. A demanding public policy teacher would press students beyond a totalizing question to a series of more complex and specific questions: How might background checks increase or fail to increase public safety? Why are restrictions on gun types effective or ineffective in a particular state or city? How do demographic and cultural changes require us to rethink the usual terms of debate?

An argument in response to the "for or against" or "like or dislike" question would be shaped in blunt and largely personal terms. "I support" or "I oppose gun control" wouldn't lead any further than a paper that argued "I like" or "I dislike *Iron Man 3*." All of the more narrowly framed questions about gun control move away from the simple pro–con answer; these questions all focus on an aspect of a larger issue. Notice, too, that all allow for opinion without making opinion itself the ultimate point. It is impossible to challenge the statement "I oppose gun control," or for that matter "I don't like ice cream." We couldn't respond by saying, "No, you don't." But we could engage in an argument shaped from responses generated from the sorts of questions that close the previous paragraph.

We should add to our initial definition to emphasize the responsibilities that come with making an argument: *A thesis is a controlling assertion that requires and allows support.* A thesis serves as a compelling force that moves an argument forward. Defining the word *thesis* differs from actually defining a thesis. The following suggestions should help you press toward a keener sense of argument as you write a first draft.

Be Assertive, Not Descriptive

It is very common for writers to arrive at a "thesis" that is really nothing more than a preview of paragraphs to come, a list of points to be discussed. Such preliminary outlining may help you get started, but it cannot serve as an effective thesis. Consider the following example from a student paper on Stephen Crane's "An Episode of War" (a story reprinted in Chapter 2 of this book):

> To understand our reaction to the wounded lieutenant in "An Episode of War," we must consider Stephen Crane's management of plot, character, and point of view.

This may look like a thesis, but notice that there is no argumentative lead here. It previews but does not assert. We call this sort of sentence a generic thesis because we could remove the words that identify the object of attention and substitute almost any other author and title:

> To understand our reaction to X in Y, we must consider Z's management of plot, character, and point of view.

A formulaic lead like this is sure to result in an equally formulaic essay that checks off the topics for discussion in a paragraph-by-paragraph fashion without helping anyone see how the paragraphs work together. A critical writer has to do more.

Foreground Your Own Opinion or Reaction

How exactly do *you* (not *we* or some abstract *reader*) react to the wounded lieutenant in Crane's story? Why do you react in that way? How is it that Crane is able to make you respond? Questions like these might lead to a workable, argumentative, and engaging thesis as well as a richer and more coherent sense of the story's meaning. They help establish a critical issue: Crane presents the lieutenant, for the most part, from the outside. Only occasionally does Crane register experience from the lieutenant's point of view, and even then he seems to do that to provide a mere report on the surrounding scene. Such observations on the story prepare for an argument, an assertion, a thesis—they don't lead to a mere preview of topics to come. Compare the following assertion to the list-like or generic statement provided earlier:

> Crane's objective delivery intensifies sympathy for the wounded lieutenant by accenting coldly impersonal and random forces of war.

The previous sentence can't stand alone; it needs to be introduced, defended, and explained. But it wouldn't be a thesis if it didn't need to be introduced, defended, and explained.

Use Particulars to Raise Interpretive Arguments

We've already referred to the need to press from the general toward the particular. We must return to that need once again in context of highlighting an essential quality of a good thesis: a thesis demands support. You almost invariably move closer to argument as you refine the most obvious observations. Consider the following general, dull, and purely descriptive sentence:

> The lieutenant is wounded while dividing coffer for soldiers in his company.

That statement is accurate, but it's hardly a sentence to generate an analysis. It is a dead end because it's purely and broadly descriptive. But if you were to elaborate even slightly upon this core statement, you might begin to tease out argumentative possibilities:

> The major event in Crane's story—the wounding of the lieutenant—occurs in the middle of the routine task of dividing coffee.

It may not seem like much has been revised here, but the previous sentence represents a huge step forward: it can prompt us to further thought. The simple added judgment—that dividing the coffee is a "routine task"—highlights the contrast with the wounding, the "major event." Although we still don't have a thesis, we do have the basis for some interesting questions:

- Why does Crane make the wounding occur during such a routine task?
- How do other characters react to the wounding?
- What is important or odd about their reaction?
- How is the wounding of the lieutenant registered stylistically?

Once you begin to ask such questions, useful provisional or even strong final theses may take shape:

- Crane accents the randomness of fate by having the lieutenant injured during the most ordinary activity.
- Crane accents the senselessness of war by having the lieutenant's life changed in a moment during the most ordinary activity.
- Crane undercuts traditionally heroic ideas about war by having the lieutenant wounded during an ordinary activity.
- By not dramatically building up to the wounding of the lieutenant, Crane rejects the values implied by a typical war story.

Test and sharpen the tentative or working thesis against potential points of development. We suggest you write out your working thesis on an index card and keep it in plain sight while you work. As you draft the body of your essay, glance back and forth between the tentative thesis and the developing points. Use the tension between your working thesis and the analysis that follows to revise the thesis. Alternatively, cross out or adjust portions of your draft if they don't fit or follow the working thesis.

Developing Ideas

It's obvious by now that you cannot shape a topic and define a thesis without thinking ahead to the whole essay. But there are specific developmental concerns that demand attention as you move from a good idea to a good paper.

Critical writers/thinkers must cultivate a patient thoughtfulness that in many ways runs counter to the influences of everyday life. Ads, music, videos, social media, and even news features often stress speed over substance. Political campaign committees pay fortunes to media experts who reduce complex issues to sound bites. At times, you might wonder if anyone wants to follow a carefully developed analysis. No doubt, many people do not. But those people aren't likely to be teaching college courses. In college, you're presented with the challenge and the opportunity to address thoughtfully critical readers. Even a thoughtful thesis will not satisfy these readers if that thesis is followed by razor-thin paragraphs that offer few examples and no explanations.

Think of Analysis as Slow-Motion Reading

Part of the critical task is to help readers appreciate details they might have missed. Think back for a moment to Piercy's "A Work of Artifice." A reader of that poem will observe that the tree that "could" have grown eighty feet tall is imagined as dying by a dramatic and mighty act of nature—lightning. This points to an obvious meaning: it is grander for a tree to live to the size nature (not the gardener) allows. But this merely describes what most careful readers notice without a critic's help. Left undeveloped, such points compel little attention.

Things will get interesting, though, as the point is extended. By making the unpotted tree subject to nothing less than a grand force of nature, Piercy suggests the natural tree's immense potential. That very potential contextualizes the magnitude of the loss as the gardener imposes limits through his controlling art. Piercy further accentuates the tragedy apparent in this lost potential by using words such as *croons* or *whittles* to describe the gardener's voice and action. Such words suggest a quiet, unrelenting diminishment as opposed to the flash, power, and dignity inherent in death by a bolt of lightning. Men croon or whittle, but only gods throw bolts of fire.

Challenge Yourself to Explain the Significance of an Observation

Ask "So what?"—not meekly, but in the active and challenging voice of a writer who cares. Press toward the highest level of significance that your evidence allows. Underscore that significance as concretely as you can. We might observe that Piercy closely juxtaposes "bound feet" with "hair in curlers." So what? By closely following something as physically painful and debilitating as "bound feet" with something as seemingly trivial as "hair in curlers," Piercy forces us to consider how the most mundane cultural signs mark profound human losses. The reader might keep comfortably distant from the image of "bound feet" if that were the only image Piercy invoked; after all, binding the feet of young girls is a practice of another time in a distant place. Similarly, "hair in curlers" considered separately hardly strikes a heavily oppressive note. But the surprising and abrupt series of "bound feet," "crippled brain," and "hair in curlers" brings all the parts into an immediate, familiar, and unsettling new relationship. Piercy will not allow her readers to dismiss "bound feet" as entirely foreign or "hair in curlers" as entirely inconsequential.

Keep asking "how" and "why" questions at every stage of the draft. Such questions will keep you from sliding by your best ideas too quickly. For example, consider the argument that Crane's objective presentation intensifies our sympathy for the injured lieutenant. You could ask, "Why does Crane want to intensify our sympathy?" This question might encourage a substantial explanation:

> If Crane didn't make me feel for the lieutenant, I'd be left with only an intellectual understanding of his vision of war. I'd know that he sees war as chaotic and that he sees common notions of heroism or honor as meaningless in the face of large forces that operate beyond any individual's control. I'd also realize he feels there isn't any logic or justice behind specific injuries or deaths that occur in war. All of those things I can understand through the way he lays out the episode. But by making me feel for someone in particular, those ideas become more than just cynical clichés. Crane makes me feel the lieutenant's helplessness amid the large forces he is caught in.

You can see how the initial remark on Crane's "objectivity" opens possibilities for extended analysis. And you should not worry about carrying forward with such analysis at some length and in some detail. A close engagement with specifics represents your best chance to engage those who read your paper.

REVISING THE DRAFT

Once you have a solid draft in hand, you'll be tempted to get it out of hand as quickly as possible. But before you actually turn in your work as finished, consider how experienced writers work. They do not just write, they rewrite and revise. They circle back to early discovery stages as they move through final editing. They show a willingness not only to "edit" or "correct" a draft but also to rethink or refine it.

The activities suggested for creating a first full draft should help you define, develop, and organize ideas. But even a worked-over, thought-out, built-up first draft remains a draft. Important matters surely remain. Sentences can be tightened. Transitions can be made more precise in the way they signal relationships linking ideas. Points may be underscored and quotations more carefully contextualized. To write a really successful paper, you need to be sure that all the hard work and good thought you put into a first draft *shows* in the final paper.

It's easy to understand how some potentially strong papers "hide" just beneath a thin, cloudy surface. The work that goes into drafting an essay can lead you to assume far too much about how quickly a reader will pick up on your ideas. Just ask yourself two simple questions:

1. How long did I work on this paper?
2. How long will it take someone to read my paper?

A huge gap should be apparent immediately: the hours you spend writing a paper become minutes of a reader's time. This may seem a depressing observation, but this gap actually offers an advantage to any writer who appreciates the possibilities, for time spent in the writing process will show itself in the final product.

Think of it this way: readers need not know how clarity or insight resulted only after many uncertain, fuzzy, disconnected thoughts puzzled the writer along the way. Indeed, a reader may not want to be immersed in the writer's process. To put this point in context of your work in a class: instructors appreciate the results of your work, not so much the raw display of that work. So after you have produced a draft that seems finished, take the time to achieve excellence.

Clarify the Structure

Most writers achieve some feeling for the structure of the whole by the time they have worked through a complete first draft. One cannot define a topic, assert a thesis, and develop ideas without at least some idea of how everything fits together. Oftentimes, however, even a well-thought-out first draft will not show the good thought that went into it. There may be significant missteps along the way that confuse matters. It may be that the organization of the essay simply doesn't show itself. You must be sure that the paper's structure emerges clearly. The following suggestions should help.

Craft a Clear and Informative Title

This bit of advice might seem too obvious to mention, but sometimes the obvious gets overlooked amid other demands. A good title will help you orient your reader. It will announce not only your topic, but also your topic's scale. It may even suggest your attitude toward the topic. A good title will prepare your reader for what is to follow. So take time to make your title mean something. We'll list three things *not* to do as you decide on a title:

1. Never make your title a mere reference to the assignment.

    Assignment Two: English 102

2. Never make the title of the work you are writing about also the title of your paper.

    Shakespeare's *Much Ado about Nothing*

3. Never allow cleverness (or inappropriate cuteness) to lead to a cryptic or unclear title.

    Much to Do about Much Ado Be Do

If you think of a title as an opportunity to help your reader prepare for a full reading of your paper, you'll avoid the common forms of these nontitles.

Always Assume Your First Paragraph or Opening Section Needs More Work

Opening paragraphs are arguably the most important ones in an essay. Often the first paragraph prepares for everything that follows. "Good points" alone don't make a good paper. Readers need to see how insights grow from or support a main idea. So think of providing a relatively descriptive or informational opening—that is, establish context. The thesis grows out of this context. There are no fixed formulas for a good critical essay, but it's often possible to introduce the topic and deliver the thesis in a first paragraph that is no longer than half a page. If you are able to achieve such compression, the thesis should be the last sentence of the first paragraph. It will serve to press the reader forward. A thesis that appears at the start or in the middle of a paragraph (first paragraph or not) may get lost.

Outline Your Paper *After* You've Written It

Many times you can identify an organizational problem by reducing a draft to an outline. This step backward late in the writing process can reveal much. It is not easy to see your own text after you have worked a great deal to produce it. Recasting a draft into an outline form can help you take a fresh look at your work's structural logic, or expose the problems with that logic that still need to be addressed.

Build Transitions at the Start of Every Paragraph

As you read your first draft, take an especially close look at the first sentence of every paragraph in relation to the thesis and to the preceding paragraph. Does this sentence explicitly signal the relationship from one idea to another? Are key words underscored?

Inexperienced writers tend to think of organization as merely sequence. They list points, but don't think of the concepts that link points. As a result, a first draft will often leave gaps between paragraphs. If you see such gaps upon reviewing your draft, consider ways to relate, cohere, or connect ideas. Build a bridge at the *start* of every new paragraph that will allow your reader to quickly gather what has gone before, and then move forward through a purposeful argument.

The movement of a paragraph—any paragraph—should be from what is relatively familiar, general, established, or descriptive to what is relatively fresh, specific, new, or assertive. Such movement usually characterizes the first paragraph of a successful critical essay. But in subtler ways, this movement continues throughout the essay. The trick is to repeat in each paragraph without stalling, to underscore without deadening, to move back momentarily without moving in a circle.

One way to pull off this trick is to echo a crucial word or idea from the end of one paragraph in the first sentence of a new paragraph. If a paragraph moves to something important at the end, that same something can function as an established point at the beginning of the next paragraph. In other words, *what one paragraph has been working toward can become what the following paragraph works from.* You can then gracefully revise your transition sentences by repeating key words in a developing argument. Take a look at the start of this paragraph and the end of the previous paragraph. You'll see that we've employed this echoing strategy.

Read Your Draft Aloud

Hearing your own writing often helps you *see* it more plainly. A gap or an inconsistency in an argument that you do not notice in a silent reading becomes evident when you give voice to the text. Voicing a passage can also reveal stylistic problems. For example, if you are forced to pause in the middle of a sentence you've written simply because you've run out of breath, it's likely the sentence needs to be trimmed, restructured, or perhaps broken into two or three sentences.

Fully Contextualize All Quotations

Never leave a quotation unattached to your text. Remember that a quotation does not make a point for you. *You* make the point and then *use* the quotation to help back it up. Also remember that without context or lead-in, the purpose, point, or even meaning of a quotation will remain unclear. It's your job as a writer to help readers understand how quotations work in relation to the whole argument. Compare the following paired passages. The first of the pair "floats" the quotation. That is, it leaves the quotation without context. It is hard to understand in this example why the quotation appears so abruptly or how it serves to build the essay as a whole. The second, revised example introduces and follows the quotations and thereby signals how we should understand them in relation to the paper's larger purpose. Notice, too, that the second example uses a colon after the introductory sentence and before the quotation. In this case, the colon signals "as follows."

1. Mark Edmundson is interested in the many ways current fears and anxieties are expressed through Gothic stories and films. "To Hollywood, the *Frankenstein* story, whatever Mary Shelley might have thought, is all about the dangers of technology and mad professors who sin against nature, competing with its generative prowess." Dangers of overreaching come up also in Steven Spielberg's *Jurassic Park*. "*Jurassic Park* turns into something of a slasher movie, with an innocent young woman and two children, adept screamers all, careening down corridors, through dark tunnels, and (shades of *The Shining*) in and around a hotel-style kitchen."

2. Mark Edmundson is interested in the many ways current fears and anxieties are expressed through Gothic stories and films. He sees the many film versions of *Frankenstein* as centered on the anxiety born of our inability to process or control rapid developments in science and technology: "To Hollywood, the *Frankenstein* story, whatever Mary Shelley might have thought, is all about the dangers of technology and mad professors who sin against nature, competing with its generative prowess." Such themes appear in many films, and sometimes various Gothic elements are mixed together in surprising ways to voice multiple fears. For example, Edmundson interprets Steven Spielberg's *Jurassic Park* as part *Frankenstein*, part Freddy Kruger, with a little Stephen King tossed in: "*Jurassic Park* turns into something of a slasher movie, with an innocent young woman and two children, adept screamers all, careening down corridors, through dark tunnels, and (shades of *The Shining*) in and around a hotel-style kitchen." Several recent zombie films along with the television series *The Walking Dead* reveal a similar mixture of Gothic elements that register and/or process social and natural forces that many people today find scary.

Polish the Surface

When you have completed a full draft that has been revised thoughtfully in response to feedback from your peers and/or your instructor, take the time to read through once more with special attention to the sentence and word level.

In other words, once you've moved through multiple revisions and have developed a thoughtful, well-structured argument, you can focus on sentence-level editing. Most students make the mistake of jumping to this last stage too early. That mistake can be compounded by thinking of editing as merely catching mistakes. Of course, you do want to catch mistakes, but it's better to think of proofreading as a subset—or the final stage—of a larger activity. Sentence-level editing goes well beyond correctness. The best writers seek precision, economy, and force. Those qualities depend upon attention to matters of style. This book cannot fully address such matters, but we do want to highlight three specific issues that often arise for critical writers.

Use the Present Tense When Writing about the Action in a Literary Text or Film

Shakespeare wrote *Othello* early in the seventeenth century. The past tense is used in this sentence because the reference is to a historical or biographical action. But Othello *kills* Desdemona. Note the present-tense verb here, for in this case we're referring to an action within the play. The killing of Desdemona occurs every time we read or see the play. This use of the present tense may seem a small stylistic convention, but it's a convention that suggests something important: *A literary text or a film comes alive as we experience it; for that reason, the action is always present.*

Cut Unnecessary "to Be" Verbs and the Prepositional Strings That Result

Consider the following sentence:

> Woolf's *The Waves* is an example of the ideals of modernism that were dominant in the 1930s.

This sentence is neither unclear nor grammatically incorrect. But a sentence such as this—especially if it represents a broader stylistic tendency throughout the paper—will have a deadening effect. It strings parts along with no particular emphasis on any one part. The problem arises from using two "to be" verbs (*is* and *were*) and three prepositions (*of* twice and *in*). If we rewrite the sentence to eliminate both "to be" verbs and the three prepositions, we'll have something like the following:

> Woolf's *The Waves* exemplifies modernist ideals that dominated the 1930s.

We now have ten words, not seventeen; we have a tighter, more forceful sentence. More important, we've just modeled a useful revision strategy. Sometimes choosing an active verb to follow the subject not only tightens the sentence but also clarifies the meaning for both author and reader.

For Secondary Sources, Use Specific and Accurate Signal Words

If you are using secondary sources—that is, referring to what others have written about the subject you are addressing—provide essential information as efficiently as possible. The following sentence fails on all counts:

> In Jones's essay *Crane's Sense of the Dramatic*, he talks about how Crane deliberately understates the most important events in the lieutenant's story.

To begin with, we might ask, who is "he"? *He*, of course, is a pronoun, and a pronoun must refer back to a subject. The subject of the introductory clause in this example isn't Jones, but the essay by Jones. So *he* doesn't work here. In addition, if Jones's essay is an essay, the title should be in quotation marks. By convention, titles of short works that are parts of books (chapters, articles, short stories and so on) are placed within quotation marks; titles of books, magazines, or journals are italicized. So the title here should be in quotation marks. And if that simple convention is followed, the modifier *essay* becomes unnecessary. A simple revision with these points in mind might look like this:

> In "Crane's Sense of the Dramatic," Jones talks about how Crane deliberately understates the most important events in the lieutenant's story.

But we're not done yet with this sentence. "Talks about" only vaguely aligns a writer (Jones) to a subject the writer has addressed (Crane's story), but it doesn't provide any sense of the writer's attitude or tone. Think of how different the sentence becomes if it begins "Jones argues that" or "Jones suggests that" or "Jones shows how." These words all mean something specific and distinct. A critical writer should take the care to attend to choices—to register precisely what place the works of others take in the conversation. So now we can come to revisions that move well beyond the sentence we started with:

> In "Crane's Sense of the Dramatic," Jones argues that Crane deliberately understates the most important events in the lieutenant's story.

The example just shown may seem to concern only small points, but it's the one we'll close this section with for two reasons. First, this example illustrates very common problems that can easily be addressed; second, it shows how attention to details can lead to significant improvement. Putting words on paper commits us to the meaning of those words. And critics—no less than lawyers, or journalists, or poets—should appreciate the responsibility that comes with that fact.

An Orientation
to Research

How Do We Use Sources? How Do We Find Them?
What Material Do We Document?

We have maintained that critical writing involves an extension and a deepening of the literary experience. The experience starts with our reading of a literary work or our viewing of a film. But it deepens as we learn more about the work and its history and as we engage with others in conversation. When we come to class, we hear what others have been thinking and profit from what others know. We might take in some facts and ideas and make them part of our own understanding. We are often prompted to argue and through argument more clearly understand our own responses. Perhaps we modify or enlarge our sense of the text or even discover a new set of questions to ask about it. By the end of a good class discussion, our ideas about the work we are studying have become far more complex, far more interesting, and much closer to something that we might want to develop in an essay. The conversation has helped us deepen our initial response.

When we do research, we are looking for the sort of inspiration, insight, and knowledge that we get from a good class discussion. With research, though, we have more time to think about our responses and consider how they may be broadened and supported. We don't need to respond quickly in order to participate as we sometimes do in discussions. So we learn new things about the biographical or historical context of a work as we read additional *primary materials* like letters from the author, commentary from the author's peers, and other background documents from the period. Or perhaps we follow up by consulting *secondary materials*; that is, what published critics and scholars have been writing about the work we're interested in.

Like writing itself, research is an active process. Good academic writing and good scholarship demand alert, imaginative, and disciplined critical thinking. When we use primary materials, it's our responsibility to explain the relationship or relevance of those materials to insights we have. When we use secondary materials, we must affirm, modify, contest, or enlarge ideas of others very much as if we were participating thoughtfully in a class discussion. When we turn to our own writing, we seek to bring the arguments of others into the conversation we've joined. We also seek to contribute to that conversation; we often do that best through independent, creative, and thoughtful research. Research isn't simply about tagging sources onto the surface of a paper; it's having sources nourish and support the complex thinking that started with a close reading of a single text. Our discussion of research, then, should be seen as an extension of—not a break from—everything presented in this book about the literary experience.

HOW WE USE SOURCES

Some people view writing a "critical essay" as a completely different thing than writing a research paper. The critical essay is seen as the analytical response of an individual; the research essay as a compilation of opinions. This distinction, however, is much too neat. Analysis isn't done in a vacuum. And research, as we've noted, involves much more than mere data gathering.

False divisions between criticism and research lead writers to weak positions in relation to materials they gather and to clumsy use of those materials. Sometimes we hear students speak of "plugging in" quotations or "sticking in" some facts; we want to substitute words and phrases like *integrating, relating,* and *weaving in.* Good critical writers go beyond a mere display of materials; they see and use their research in the context of an argument they themselves shape. A "good" quotation, a "meaningful" summary, a "relevant" fact can only be "good," "meaningful," or "relevant" as it relates to a carefully defined point. We need to use sources to support a larger purpose we've defined; we do not want to let sources dominate us.

It's also important to think specifically about what "support" might mean. In some instances, a writer might enlist the support of a critic whose argument "backs up" the new discussion very directly. In such cases, writers essentially invoke the authority of others to confirm their own insights. But more often, writers define a particular aspect of a larger argument and apply that aspect to a point they want to make. Note how the following writer uses insights not only of those who directly address the paper's main subject—Nathanael West's *The Day of the Locust*—but of thematically relevant material from the Shakespearean critic A. C. Bradley. The writer carefully leads into and follows each reference so that none of the references feel out of place in relation to the main point of the passage. The writer has integrated, not "plugged in," research.

> With the riot at the end of the novel, West releases the potential energy and violence of a city (and perhaps a country) full of broken dreamers. The fantasy of Hollywood has been sold to them, and it has disappointed. Nasty, ugly,

and completely vacuous, Hollywood, with the machinery of its vast studios, has pushed its self-perpetuating plaster dream onto America. Kingsley Widmer examines the scope of Hollywood's failure as a dream factory and what it means for the double-crossed.[1] No one is more betrayed than one who has been cheated by false dreams. This representation of Hollywood as the purveyor of a bastardized art form that conveys powerfully corrosive effects (it even corrupts dreams!) is central to understanding West's novel. West ultimately sees Hollywood as the cheater, the force that rips off people who live there. In fact, as Lavonne Mueller notes, *The Day of the Locust* "was originally called The Cheated."[2]

When we conceptualize the novel as a story of "the cheated" rather than the story of Tod [the protagonist], *The Day of the Locust* begins to take on truly tragic proportions. The type of tragedy, however, is not traditional. As defined by A. C. Bradley, the classic Shakespearean form of tragedy "is pre-eminently the story of one person, the 'hero,' or at most of two, the 'hero' and the 'heroine.'"[3] Bradley goes on to note that the actions of this central character are the source of the tragedy. The stories of each of *The Day of the Locust's* characters are merely minor tragedies in and of themselves, and their actions have little effect on their fates; but through the patching together of a tapestry of circumstance and torment, West begins to create a sense of communal tragedy. Hollywood has seduced an enormous number of suckers with its empty dream, and the losses are measured in numerous lives wasted.

The writer of the passage has woven ideas of others into a new fabric. Sometimes such weaving in involves a deliberate kind of counterpointing. The writer uses Bradley's definition of Shakespearean tragedy to clarify a quite different kind of tragedy apparent in West's novel. In the next example, you'll note that the counterpoint is more blunt; one can support one's own idea by repudiating someone else's. Identifying and making explicit a disagreement can sharpen or emphasize a writer's contribution. Note how the writer of the following passage on H. G. Wells's *The Invisible Man* clarifies her interpretation by strongly rejecting another critic's interpretation:

> Alfred Borrello argues that the scientist Griffin represents a "god-man" in Wells's *The Invisible Man*. Borrello sees Griffin as one "dedicated to research for the good of his species but frustrated by the inability of his fellowman to accept what lies outside of the familiar."[4] Unfortunately, this interpretation completely ignores the signals Wells so carefully builds into Griffin's first person narration.

---

1. Kingsley Widmer, *Nathanael West* (Boston: Twayne, 1982).
2. David Madden, ed., *Nathanael West: The Cheaters and the Cheated: A Collection of Critical Essays* (DeLand: Everett/Edwards, 1973).
3. A. C. Bradley, *Shakespearean Tragedy: Lectures on Hamlet, Othello, King Lear, Macbeth*, 3rd rpt. (New York: Palgrave, 1992) 7.
4. Alfred Borrello, *H. G. Wells: Author in Agony* (Carbondale: Southern Illinois UP, 1972).

Griffin reveals himself as a totally selfish man. He has no feelings for his father, his fiancé, or his friends. His work absorbs him, but not for the good that work may do; in fact, Griffin never once considers the "good of his species" as Borrello mistakenly contends. On the contrary, it would seem that Griffin's disregard for the species is exactly what leads him to madness, murder, and death.

The main underlying lessons of the previous examples are (1) to always consider how a given piece may help us build our argument and (2) to always weave sources into the newly constructed fabric of ideas (that is, don't assume that the quotation will make a point for you).

A crucial part of weaving in involves using signal words that accurately represent the words and ideas of others. We need to circle back in this context to emphasize a point we made at the end of the "Polish the Surface" section. Note that the two previous passages use verbs such as *examines, defines, notes,* and *contends.* Each of these word choices helps readers understand the kind or tone of the sources used. The word choices also help clarify distinctions between the sources and the writer who is using those sources. Writers who do not employ such precise and varied signals display a less clear command of the research they've done. Contrast the following sentence with the sentence that opens the example in the previous paragraph:

Alfred Borrello talks about how the scientist Griffin represents a "god-man" in Wells's *The Invisible Man.*

"Talks about" is a very common but nearly always an inaccurate and unhelpful signal of what quality characterizes the source. Borrello isn't, after all, "talking about" a subject of interest; he *argues* for a particular interpretation of the central character in Wells's novel. Any development of the writer's objections to Borrello depends upon making the argumentative nature of Borrello's essay plain. It is hard to counterpoint a subject someone is merely "talking about." Consider the many options there are for characterizing an author's position or attitude.

analyzes	assumes	examines	insists	observes
argues	believes	explores	notes	suggests
asks	considers	implies		

Each of these words means something different and more particular than "talks about." A writer's job is to use a word that accurately represents the source referenced.

HOW TO FIND SOURCES

The writer who has a topic in mind and a sense of how to use information to explore the topic is usually the researcher who enjoys looking for sources. The search for sources is a treasure hunt—a chance to browse through libraries, archives, databases, troves of online information. But the sheer wealth of available material in even a modest library can make looking intimidating.

You might think you can avoid the library given the material available online, but as we mention in Chapter 13, online sources may have their own kinds of limits. Sometimes the limits actually arise from the enormous amount of available material. In classrooms around the world, students are generating the same sort of writing that you may be now preparing to create. In the past decade or so, students have been able to post their work online. So, too, have many others with some interest in literature and film (fans, casual readers, independent scholars, and so on). Some of this writing may be quite good, but much of it is still in a fairly early stage of the revision process, and some is quite simply not worth attention. When you do your research, try to find writing that is at least a level or two higher than you think you are able to produce. You want to learn to use materials that offer a more complex thesis than you might have thought of and more varied support than you might have considered relevant. You want research to press you to grow, not merely to provide what you already know.

Remember, too, that carefully chosen sources will help establish your authority. When using secondary sources, it is generally best to consult articles or books that have been published by a reputable press. Here are some first indicators to help you decide which presses are reputable:

- Have the books published by this press or articles from a particular journal been included on a reading list from one of your courses or in a bibliography from a book assigned by a professor?
- Is the book or journal published by a "university press" from a university you recognize (i.e., Cambridge University Press, Cornell University Press, University of Chicago Press, University of Texas Press, University of Georgia Press, etc.)?
- Have you seen books from this press on the shelves of your college bookstore or in your college library?

A yes to any of these questions would suggest that at least a few people who have professional knowledge in the matter have read the material and have acknowledged that it has some value. College libraries concentrate on acquiring these professionally reviewed materials. And even though such publications are increasingly available online, many are still only in print. In whatever form, the college library will serve as a crucial source for access.

Full access comes from learning to use your library's online catalog system as well as the best available databases. Catalog systems will differ, so take the time to become familiar with your library's setup. In general, any online search can begin by author/title searches when you happen to know the author and title. But also test out key word searches. This requires a little imagination, but you'll find the misses and hits help you sharpen ways to define your topic as well as learn ways others categorize broad topics. Most systems build upon the Library of Congress subject headings. You'll note these headings as you experiment with your own key words, but you need not rely on guessing. Most online systems have search commands that allow you to check Library of Congress headings. And don't be afraid to ask librarians for help. They will respond to your general questions and needs in terms of the specific systems in operation at your institution.

Armed with call numbers, you'll be able to find the physical book itself. Libraries of higher education generally use the Library of Congress cataloging system to organize their collections. You will find literary studies in the "P" section of the library. As you browse through the shelves, you can see how the organization works. If you look at a call number, it is fairly simple to determine some useful information about the work.

> *The Complete Works of William Shakespeare*, fourth edition, ed. David Bevington. Library of Congress call number: PR2754.B4

The "PR" indicates that this is a work of English literature. "2754" falls within the range of PR2199–3195, which contains works from the English Renaissance (1500–1640). The letter after the period indicates the last name of the author or, in this case, the editor of the text. It is not necessary to memorize any of this information, but it may be useful to have an overview of the "P" section (or languages and literature division) of this system because it is what will help you navigate the aisles in the book stacks:

P	Language and Literature
P	Linguistics
PA	Classical Philology (Greek and Latin)
PB	Modern European Languages, Celtic Languages
PC	Romance Languages
PD	Old Germanic and Scandinavian Languages
PE	English Language
PF	Dutch, Flemish, and German Languages
PG	Slavic Languages and Literature
PH	Finno-Ugrian, Basque Languages & Literature
PJ–PL	Oriental Languages
PM	American Indian and Artificial Languages
PN	Literature, Literary History and Collections
PQ	Romance Literature
PR	English Literature
PS	American Literature
PT	German Literature
PZ	Children's Literature

As you work with this system, you will find sections of the stacks relevant to your search. Browse through those shelves to find books and journals related to your

SHAKESPEARE QUARTERLY

Published for the Folger Shakespeare Library
in association with
The George Washington University
by The Johns Hopkins University Press

VOLUME 64	2013	NUMBER 4

research. Many journals specialize in literary studies. You can find journals that focus on literature in general, British literature, American literature, literature from different time periods, and literature by a specific author. If you are searching for an idea and you are writing about Shakespeare, browse through a shelf of *Shakespeare Quarterlies*. As you look through the tables of contents, you will see the vast range of articles that scholars have generated just in a single quarter on the subject of this single playwright.

A number of us use libraries that are not rich in these resources, but all schools subscribe to databases that make this library experience available anyway. Because many published articles in volumes on library shelves can be accessed online, even students at the smallest college libraries can do much research online with guidance from a librarian. In fact, we accessed the table of contents shown from a college library database. The important thing is not whether you find it online or in print, but that you've found material that has gone through a serious review process and has been published by a responsible press or organization.

As you gather materials for review, you'll need to approach them effectively. Read the writing about the literature with the same attention that you read the primary literature.

- Read for understanding—what does the work mean?
- Remember that the author is going to have some main idea—what is that idea?
- In what ways might that idea inspire controversy?
- Does the author mention any others who might disagree with the argument? (Read one or two of these other authors, if possible).
- Can you apply this argument (or an aspect of the argument) to anything beyond the work in question? For instance, can you see how the argument might apply to another work that you have been reading this term?
- To what extent does the author introduce factual information into the analysis? Does that information have any bearing on your own topic?

Often, you will not learn any new information from reading a piece of criticism. Instead, you are looking for some new insight, some different way of looking at the work that you have been reading. Many times an article will put a work into a different context that you might not have considered before you began your own writing.

GIVING APPROPRIATE CREDIT: THE ISSUE OF PLAGIARISM

We often value ideas as we value other possessions. Our society considers ownership an important aspect of our relations with things and with other people. We own electronic devices, cars, and houses, and we face anxiety because we would like to own more and don't want anyone to steal what we have. Even the less materialistic like to own the ideas that they have created. If any of us has an idea, no matter how mundane—where to go for dinner, a nice turn of phrase in conversation, a suggestion for some music that we have discovered—we know how annoying it can be to have someone else take the credit for our original thought. Most of us try to give appropriate credit whenever we can. But it is difficult to determine where any idea has been created. We have been thinking about ideas as subjects in ongoing conversations. Our ideas come from what we read, from what we watch, and from what others say. With all of these stimuli, it gets increasingly difficult to establish a clear pedigree for every idea that we put to paper. Anyone who writes, though, needs to know when it is necessary to cite sources. Sometimes the rules are pretty obvious. We all know that copying portions of someone else's work without giving proper credit is wrong.

The plainest cases of cheating fit nicely under a straightforward definition of **plagiarism**: intellectual theft—the unacknowledged (or inadequately acknowledged) use of the words and/or ideas of another. This leads to a simple moral directive: Do not steal! But like many simple directives, this one doesn't always address the real issues. Most students have no desire to steal, yet they remain confused and worried about exactly what professors expect them to document. Something beyond the demand that one do his or her own work is clearly needed, for much gray lurks about the edges of the definition offered.

We can start with some plain advice: Acknowledge sources as much as possible within your writing; don't worry about giving away your own authority. You will actually be given greater credit for tracing your ideas back to other sources than you will get for simply generating "original" ideas out of thin air. Research involves figuring out where ideas have come from, tracing conversations back to their sources, and understanding how the ideas of others can be used to build a new framework of ideas. Beyond that advice, we need to explain more fully how sources function in an academic article and what logic governs their use.

INTEGRATING SOURCES INTO WRITING: WHAT WE DOCUMENT

Accurate and full citation of sources is an essential part of writing in college. To omit or inadequately cite a source in an academic essay would be to undermine much of your own hard-earned authority. Think again of writing as conversation: a person who borrows the ideas of others without offering the slightest nod of recognition to those others will be seen at best as careless, at worst as rude and dishonest. Thoughtful citation of sources, then, should be understood not only as an ethical obligation, but as part of the entire essay's effectiveness.

All citations show our general respect for others who might be part of our conversation. First, we acknowledge our debt to someone who has introduced us to some particular idea. Second, we offer a guide to anyone who might follow to how they might have access to the thoughts that have influenced us. Precision is important so that we don't frustrate those who follow our lead. Just as we would not like to chase after some source only to find that the author we are reading was careless enough to list the wrong volume or the wrong page, or to misspell the author's name, we must do all that we can to ensure that our own bibliographic entries are accurate. Citations serve as a map to the intellectual treasure that you have discovered. Be diligent as you record the directions. You might want to come back sometime as well.

Quotation, Paraphrase, and Summary

It's an easy matter to understand that direct quotations must be written as such and cited: that is, place quotation marks around the quoted material—or block quote long passages—and note the source (specific forms will be displayed as this chapter progresses). But quotations are not the only things that must be documented: ideas require citation as well. That moves us quickly into more complicated territory. When is an idea really someone else's? If plagiarism is intellectual theft, what constitutes protected intellectual property? How much documentation does a reader expect, want, and need?

We can start by illustrating different kinds of borrowings and the credit each requires or encourages. The following passage is from "*Frankenstein* and Comedy" by Philip Stevick:

> *Frankenstein*, like early Gothic before it, like Kafka after it, and like a multitude of works of various periods, such a Melville's *Bartleby*, makes itself out of dream images told, but not fully elaborated, into rational and sequential art. The result is a narrative vehicle which allows a large measure of self-exposure, terror, pathos, and psychic pain to coexist with much absurdity, apparent ineptitude, silliness, and the risk that the whole enterprise will be brushed aside by the reader as making no claims on his mature scrutiny.[5]

Now imagine a teacher coming across the following two passages spliced into new student essays:

1. Like the Gothic novels that preceded it, like Kafka that followed it, and like many other works including Melville's *Bartleby*, Mary Shelley's *Frankenstein* builds itself from dream images that never quite get fully expressed

---

5. Philip Stevick, "*Frankenstein* and Comedy," *The Endurance of Frankenstein: Essays on Mary Shelley's Novel*, ed. George Levine and U. C. Knoepflmacher (Berkeley: U of California P, 1979), 221–39.

in an orderly or consciously controlled story. The rough narrative that results exposes private terrors of the self, psychic pain, and terror along with sheer silliness and absurdity. It is no wonder that many mature readers are tempted to dismiss *Frankenstein* as unworthy of serious scrutiny.

2. Philip Stevick maintains that *Frankenstein* seems closer to a dream than to a story. Dreams can be painfully self-revealing; but those same dreams can also be downright silly. Gothic novels and Kafka's stories share these wildly mixed qualities with Mary Shelley's work. Stevick notes that narratives such as these are sometimes difficult to take seriously (Stevick 231).

Passage 1 closely paraphrases Stevick. It follows his paragraph from start to finish and never strays far from the words he uses. It is, in fact, almost exactly the same length as the original. Yet the writer of passage 1 makes no mention of Stevick. A citation (a note or parenthetical reference) to Stevick at the close of passage 1 would be a small step in the right direction, but it would still *not* be enough. Such a note would acknowledge that the writer of the passage has used an idea of Stevick, but it would not spell out how heavily Stevick had been used. This first passage is an example of an inappropriate paraphrase; it would be considered plagiarism even though it does not use exactly the same words as the original upon which it is based.

It's useful to make a distinction between two words that are often used as synonyms: **paraphrase** and **summary**. Think of a paraphrase of another writer's text as a superficial revision of that text; the writer of a paraphrase stays close to the logic, language, and length of the original passage (as illustrated in passage 1). In contrast, think of a summary of another's text as a thorough rewriting of that text (a rewriting wholly in your own language) in as brief a form as your purpose will allow. Paraphrase as defined here should *always* be avoided. If you feel you need to stay very close to the words of your source, quote those words exactly and be sure your reader sees it as a quotation. If you do not need to stay close to the words of the original, convey as briefly as possible the essential idea and signal your debt to that idea.

Passage 2 more effectively summarizes Stevick's original paragraph. It remains close to the original, but it is tightly focused. It is not stuck on the particular words and phrases of the original (close paraphrase sometimes suggests that the writer doesn't understand the original well enough to confidently separate from it). Stevick's name also leads off passage 2 and is repeated later—a good idea when the summary runs beyond a sentence or two. The parenthetical reference at the end of this passage lets the reader know exactly where Stevick's discussion can be found. The summary is neatly framed by the first mention of Stevick and the closing parenthetical reference. A reader who came across passage 2 in a critical paper would understand the degree of indebtedness that is expressed. That reader would also be able to follow up on the topic by reading Stevick.

Distinct Insights and Common Observations

Any full summary or particular use of Stevick's insights must give credit to Stevick. But what happens when one reads Stevick, yet uses nothing in particular that would easily be identified as distinctly his? Consider this third passage that only vaguely echoes Stevick:

> 3. *Frankenstein* evokes the disturbing and mixed sensations of dreams: terror, confusion, anxiety. The most absurd images in the novel (or in a dream) must be understood as part of a wider fear.

These two sentences move far away from the original and might not seem to owe Stevick any recognition. Not only is this passage significantly shorter than the original, it is wholly rewritten. Indeed, it doesn't borrow anything from Stevick that a good reader could not get from the novel itself. If this is a summary at all, it is the barest sort. In effect, this third passage reduces the distinct contributions of Stevick to a very general, much discussed, level. Many critics before and after Stevick have associated *Frankenstein* with dreams. Why should Stevick get any special credit here for what seems a common insight? The writer has chosen to give him none.

You *must* cite distinct contributions or insights but need not credit observations that many writers have shared in common. No one would accuse the writer of the third passage of plagiarism, but you could move beyond such a grudging attention to rules and consider a more generous policy. Citations, after all, do not merely protect you from charges of plagiarism; citations have a positive purpose as well. Strange as it may seem, academic readers are interested in citations. A note at the end of the third passage would gracefully inform these readers of Stevick's article; it would display the writer's research without diminishing in any way the writer's own contribution. Indeed, if Stevick were found to be an especially significant voice in the conversation about *Frankenstein*, then the writer might want to mention him. This could be done quite easily:

> 4. Stevick observes that *Frankenstein* evokes the disturbing and mixed sensations of dreams: terror, confusion, anxiety. The most absurd images in the novel (or in a dream) must be understood as part of a wider fear (Stevick 231).

These options posed by the third and fourth examples illustrate the fact that rules cannot always suffice; good judgment about what the audience wants along with a sense of fairness come into play when deciding whether to cite a source.

Common Knowledge

You do not need to cite material that is **common knowledge**. But there may be some confusion about this deceptively simple rule, for *common knowledge* does not mean *what most people know*; in the context of academic writing, *common* *knowledge* means *knowledge that the readership could acquire or confirm from any one of several sources.* For example, most people do not know that Edith Wharton's *The Age of Innocence* won a Pulitzer Prize for Fiction in 1921, but a writer would not need to cite a source for this bit of information. Any academic reader could, if necessary, check for its accuracy without the slightest difficulty; in source after source, the information will be the same: Edith Wharton's *The Age of Innocence* did win a Pulitzer Prize for Fiction in 1921.

As always, sound judgment and good faith must help you through less clear-cut examples. For even seemingly plain facts should be cited when they invite controversy, depend upon interpretation, or are not widely established. A professor might want to know, for example, where a student discovered that the Pulitzer Prize advisory board overrode the recommendations of the nominating jury in awarding William Styron's *The Confessions of Nat Turner* the Pulitzer in 1968. This is not a disputed point, nor is it something that a particular scholar "discovered"; but not many references to Styron's award are this detailed. Such facts are not easily checked and should therefore be documented.

HOW TO CITE

Questions about the form of documentation often cause students more anxiety than the substance of their papers. This is both unfortunate and unnecessary. In literary studies, the Modern Language Association (MLA) has established guidelines for writers of research papers. With a little time and patience you can master the essential forms of citation. The following section displays model forms (based on the *MLA Handbook for Writers of Research Papers*) that you can use as checkpoints in preparing a research paper.

Parenthetical References in the Text

Debts are signaled in a text by parenthetical references (not numbered notes).[6] A sentence in a paper about Tolstoy that uses an idea from Yi-Fu Tuan's *Space and Place* might look like any one of the following:

> Yi-Fu Tuan notes that Tolstoy's sense of space subtly registers "profound political and moral commitments" (57–58).

---

6. The traditional format for citations is the footnote. The superscripted numbers, lines at the bottom of the page, and the abbreviated Latin were all part of the indoctrination process to separate true scholars from the mere dabbler. Anyone who could construct a typed manuscript that successfully accommodated a footnote deserved a higher degree. Now that we all use word processing programs that can easily create elegant footnoting for us, the practice of using a footnote for every citation has been largely abandoned, especially for the sort of academic papers that you will be producing. Generally, footnotes are places where an author can include additional informational details that are not essential to the main argument of the paper.

Tolstoy's sense of space subtly registers "profound political and moral commitments" (Tuan 57–58).

Yi-Fu Tuan claims that Tolstoy's sense of space registers deeply felt commitments (57–58).

The information within parentheses at the end of each sentence indicates that a discussion of Tolstoy's sense of space appears on pages 57 and 58 in a book or article by Tuan. Tuan's name does not appear within the parentheses in the first and third examples because the sentence itself makes it clear that Tuan is referred to. Information about Tuan's book will appear in a separate section: a Works Cited page.

The Works Cited Page

The Works Cited page starts on a separate page at the end of the essay (such a list must *not* be subdivided by theme or types of research materials). There, under "Tuan, Yi-Fu," the reader will find full bibliographic information on the work cited in the text:.

> Tuan, Yi-Fu. *Space and Place: The Perspective of Experience.* Minneapolis: U of Minnesota P, 1977. Print.

The following examples model common bibliographic forms. Note that there is an underlying structure among the entries that refer to books or parts of books. All begin with the name of the author of the piece cited (last name first). All include full titles and complete publishing information. Names of editors or translators are placed after the title and before the publishing information.

A book by a single author

> Bonca, Teddi Chichester. *Shelley's Mirrors of Love: Narcissism, Sacrifice, and Sorority.* Albany: State U of New York P, 1999. Print.

> Moore, Rod Val. *Igloo among Palms.* Iowa City: U of Iowa P, 1994. Print.

The content and order here (as in all entry forms) are the important elements. Included are the author's name (last name first), the book's title, the place of publication, the publisher (note for university presses, the abbreviations *U* and *P* are standard form), and the year of publication. On the first line, the last name is flush on the left margin, and any subsequent lines are indented five spaces. All citations in MLA format must be double-spaced.

A book by more than one author

> Gilbert, Sandra M., and Susan Gubar. *The Madwoman in the Attic: The Woman Writer and the Nineteenth-Century Literary Imagination.* New Haven: Yale UP, 1979. Print.

Note here that the second author's name is not in reverse order; there is no need to put her last name first because the listing is not alphabetized under her name.

An article in an edited collection

> Glatthaar, Joseph T. "Black Glory: The African-American Role in Union Victory." *Why the Confederacy Lost.* Ed. Gabor S. Boritt. Oxford: Oxford UP, 1992. 133–62. Print.

The author's name remains first, then the title of the article (in quotation marks), followed by the title of the book it is part of (italicized), the editor of the book, the place of publication, the publisher, and the year of publication. Note that the pages placed at the end of the entry spell out where the article begins and ends in the book. The parenthetical reference in the text of the paper itself would specify only the pages relevant to the point being made.

A translated book

> Foucault, Michel. *Discipline and Punish: The Birth of the Prison.* Trans. Alan Sheridan. New York: Pantheon, 1977. Print.

Literary texts, editions

> Dickens, Charles. *Great Expectations.* Ed. Edgar Rosenberg. New York: Norton, 1999. Print.
>
> Stein, Gertrude. "Three Portraits of Painters." *Selected Writings of Gertrude Stein.* Ed. Carl Van Vechten. New York: Vintage, 1972. 327–35. Print.
>
> Wharton, Edith. *Ethan Frome.* Intro. by Cynthia Griffin Wolff. New York: Signet, 1986. Print.
>
> Collins, Billy. "Thesaurus." *The Literary Experience.* Ed. Bruce Beiderwell and Jeffrey Wheeler. Boston: Wadsworth, 2008. 1002, Print.

Oftentimes you will not be citing a book or a part of a book but a periodical article. These entries will differ from entries for books, but the most common forms are not complicated.

An article from an academic journal

> Rader, Ralph W. "The Dramatic Monologue and Related Lyric Forms." *Critical Inquiry* 3 (1976): 131–151. Print.

The author's name is first, the title of the article next (in quotation marks), followed by the title of the journal (italicized) in which it appears, the volume number of the journal, the year of publication, and finally the inclusive pages. Most academic journals paginate continuously throughout a volume. A volume represents the collected issues of a single year (usually four issues). The first issue of the year would start on page 1. The second issue would start on whatever page the first left off, and so on throughout the year. This makes it unnecessary to note which issue the article appears in. But if each issue of a volume begins at page 1, simply cite the volume number as shown earlier, then add a period and the issue number:

> Tafoya, Eddie. "Born in East L.A.: Cheech as the Chicano Moses." *Journal of Popular Culture* 26.4 (1993): 123–29. Print.

In your research, it is very likely that you will find this information in a database rather than by looking in an actual journal. It is still essential that you record the information that we have included here, but you must also include information about the database that you have used, including the date that you accessed this information:

> Dobson, Hugh. "Mr. Sparkle Meets the Japanese Yakuza: Depictions of Japan in *The Simpsons.*" *Journal of Popular Culture* 39.1 (2006): 44–68. *Project Muse.* Web. 15 July 2014.

A newspaper article

> Heffley, Lynne. "L.A. Critics Are Crazy for *Crazy, Tavern.*" *Los Angeles Times* 8 Mar. 1994, valley ed.: F1. Print.

If a specific edition is listed in the masthead, include that after the date (not all editions of the same paper contain the same material). If no edition is listed in the masthead of the paper's first page, place the colon after the date and before the section and page number of the article cited.

An article from a monthly magazine

> Gopnik, Adam. "The Big One: Historians Rethink the War to End All Wars." *The New Yorker* 23 Aug. 2004: 78–85. Print.

Many magazines and newspapers have their own websites on which they post material that appears in their printed publications. Here is a listing for a short story that appears in this format:

> Munro, Alice. "The View from Castle Rock." *The New Yorker* 29 Aug. 2005. Web. 6 Dec. 2014.

A review

> Appelo, Tim. Rev. of *Three Tall Women* by Edward Albee. *The Nation* 14 Mar. 1994: 355–56. Print.

The previous review was not titled. Note the description of the contents in place of the missing title. Of course, if there is a title, use it. If you find the article online, include information about the database that you used to access it:

> Ebert, Roger. "Throbbing Pain Overwhelms Pleasures in *Basic Instinct 2.*" *Chicago Sun-Times* 31 Mar. 2006: NC29. *ProQuest.* Web. 23 Apr. 2014.

A film

> *The Purple Rose of Cairo*. Dir. Woody Allen. Perf. Jeff Daniels, Danny Aiello, and Mia Farrow. Orion, 1985. Film.

Inevitably, we find works that do not fit into the general categories that we have outlined here. Remember that these citation rules are entirely systematic, that it is possible to figure out the appropriate format even if your specific instance is not covered precisely.

Many databases that you will use in your school's library have a special function that will construct your Works Cited page for you. Use this feature to begin constructing your own Works Cited page, but check the format yourself. This is not like buying a paper online. Your institution subscribes to this database, and you should take advantage of its features.

Using Research to Focus Writing and Discussion

- What issues are of interest to me as I read this work?

- What ideas have I found in this article?

- How does this article point to a larger critical conversation that I might want to join?

- How have I given credit to every source I have used in this paper (and, at the same time, how have I indicated the research that I have done to develop my ideas)?

- Where have I given full and accurate citation of my sources? A writer can join a critical conversation only by acknowledging other participants in the conversation.

- Have I displayed every quotation as a quotation and cited it appropriately? Distinct ideas, contested or little-known facts, and particular insights must also be cited, even if they are cast in the writer's own words. A careless writer might mistake notes from another source as an original thought. Even though this might be an easy mistake to make, it is never acceptable.

- Have I avoided including extended paraphrases? Remember that we are writing our own papers, not summaries of articles. It is important to return again and again to our own point, to show how this outside information is relevant to the current discussion.

Part Two

The Elements of Literature

Introduction: The Elements of Literature

How Can a Specialized Vocabulary Enrich Our Experience of Literature?

THEODOTUS: The fire has spread from your ships. The first of the seven wonders of the world perishes. The library of Alexandria is in flames.

CAESAR: Is that all?

THEODOTUS: [unable to believe his senses] All! Caesar: will you go down to posterity as a barbarous soldier too ignorant to know the value of books?

CAESAR: Theodotus, I am an author myself; and I tell you it is better that the Egyptians should live their lives than dream them away with the help of books.

Caesar and Cleopatra, George Bernard Shaw

As unlikely as it might seem, the conversations that we have about literature—the very words we use to approach texts—are profoundly influenced by historical chance. Consider, for example, the book that has been among the most influential works of literary criticism in Western civilization: Aristotle's *Poetics*. The version of that work that survives is only a partial discussion. It's quite a thought: much critical thinking in the centuries since has sprung from a fragment. Perhaps we should blame Julius Caesar for what is missing: Caesar, in the midst of his affair with Cleopatra, is reputed to have ordered his troops to set a strategic fire in the port of Alexandria that spread to Alexandria's great library and destroyed its collection. One of the books that may have been in that library was the only surviving copy of Aristotle's treatise on comedy. Scholars since have bemoaned the loss of such an important text. If that treatise had survived, the shape of literary studies might be very different today.

What if Caesar had ordered his men to be more careful with their torches? We might privilege Aristophanes instead of Sophocles. Students might be more likely to read *Much Ado about Nothing* (the Shakespeare selection in the book you are now reading) than *Hamlet* (the more typical choice in most anthologies). But of course we do *not* have Aristotle's seminal text on comedy and we manage pretty well without it. That's because Aristotle wasn't scripting rules; he was providing tools. So critics (that is, interested readers) sometimes try out the terms that Aristotle uses for tragedy to see which are most useful in the discussion of comedy. We still talk about character and plot, but we modify the discussion for this other genre. In his discussion of tragedy, Aristotle suggests that in comedy character is more important than plot, but it is up to us to continue the discussion, to make sense of that claim with our own examples. And then we can try out the same notions as they might relate to fiction or poetry or film.

The methodical approach Aristotle uses to examine dramatic productions is also the approach he takes to examine organisms in the natural world, social structures, and philosophical systems. For Aristotle, everything in the world could be treated as a text to read; he did not redefine *critical thinking* as he moved from literary texts to some other subject. Thinking through a poem or a play was, then, much like thinking through a physiological process. By classifying the parts of the thing that he examines, Aristotle establishes a method of presenting his own perspective and of advancing his own argument. More important, by establishing distinct and well-defined categories, he sets up a system that others can use. Essentially, Aristotle establishes the groundwork for conversations that follow. His clear definitions of the parts of drama give us a vocabulary to talk about what we have read or seen. More than two thousand years after he set up these categories, most discussions of not only drama but also much fiction and poetry still refer to and build on Aristotle's vocabulary. And while Aristotle never had the chance to see a movie, he would recognize as his own many of the terms current film critics invoke!

DEVELOPING A FLEXIBLE CRITICAL VOCABULARY

The advantage of a specialized vocabulary is that it helps us identify parts of a whole with precision. In the study of anatomy, for instance, it is important to be able to distinguish among the various internal organs; the lungs, heart, and liver may all work together, but they serve very different functions. Creating a vocabulary makes it possible to see and to discuss the intricacies of a subject. But the vocabulary isn't the thing itself; it is a means to help us understand the thing—the object of our study. You may have heard the expression "use the right tool for the right job" on a home improvement show; we think that expression applies equally well to the task of criticism.

Because Aristotle gave us an especially rich and useful vocabulary, we often look for complications and moments of discovery when we begin to analyze a work of literature or a film, just as we locate the heart and lungs when we think about anatomy. But having such a perceptive guide may blind us to other aspects of a work of art. We might find the parts of the play that Aristotle points out because we have words to describe them; we might miss parts of the play that Aristotle's vocabulary doesn't address. That said, we could argue that the loss of Aristotle's treatise on comedy helps us push the boundaries that his terms set for us. After all, we should not employ any term (or any tool) without exercising judgment. Nor should we be content with only the vocabulary Aristotle has given us. As we define elements of comedy, we develop a process to identify the elements of any play, poem, story, or film that we might want to analyze.

In this book, we foreground the process through which we approach literary texts and the literary experience. Because Aristotle's text is so old and so well established, it is easy to think about his elements of poetics as absolute and complete rather than arbitrary and useful. But systems of thought come alive only when we realize they are both arbitrary *and* useful. The words that Aristotle uses to describe the elements of drama are the ones we begin with when we describe any expressive art, yet when we discuss particular plays, stories, poems, or films, we discover that we need to adapt, elaborate, and invent. As we describe "new" elements, we develop a fuller vocabulary to describe general elements like word choice, point of view, or rhythm.

To understand that each of these elements is a tool for articulating the complex ideas presented in expressive arts, we find it useful to break the traditional boundaries of fiction, poetry, drama, and film that most textbooks impose. Using a symbol like a flag, for instance, to represent something other than itself (a country, a cause, patriotism, warmongering) is something that teachers may highlight in the study of poetry because poets often compress and concentrate meaning through symbols. But it's obvious that symbols are not found only in poems. Isolating a discussion of symbols in a "poetry unit" distorts and limits how we approach the larger subject of literature and literary analysis. To put it simply: a screenplay and a sonnet may well share common elements. We believe that by examining a single element across genres, readers and writers can learn to manipulate key terms more effectively and to use those terms outside the confines of this textbook.

Also, by concentrating on a particular literary element when engaging with a text, students have a strategy to use as they write. This approach encourages students to focus narrowly on specific details within the text that contribute to the element under consideration and to explore how that element is significant to their understanding of the larger text. In each chapter of this book, we provide examples of these writing strategies, modeling attention to elements as a strategy to develop analysis. Students who practice these writing (and thinking) exercises develop focused analysis that becomes easier and more natural to them as they progress through the various elements that are presented throughout this book.

The goal of *The Literary Experience* is to help each of you engage in conversations with anyone who has ever been interested in discussing responses to a work of art. Furthermore, it seeks to enable you to express yourself when you read a book or see a film that moves you in some way. When you contribute to this discussion, others should be able to pick up the threads of your ideas to continue weaving further discussions. So we do not want to reduce literary study to a vocabulary lesson, but we do want you to acquire a vocabulary that helps you read and respond to texts, that helps you say something important about texts, that enables others to respond to your reading. We want you to discover the value of particular words as you experience a poem, play, story, or film.

1 Genre

How Do Our Expectations Impact Our Literary Experience?

How Are Those Expectations Formed?

If you've grown up in the United States, it's likely you think of an avocado as a salad vegetable or salad fruit. If you've grown up in Brazil, it's likely you think of the avocado as a dessert fruit. Neither way of classifying arises from what an avocado "really" is; nor are categories like "appetizers," "salads," "main courses," "desserts"—even "fruits" and "vegetables"—universally fixed. Custom and use guide our understanding. In the United States, we see avocados sliced over lettuce and added to sandwiches with onions and tomatoes; avocados are served before or with the main meal. We don't think of ordering an avocado milk shake for a snack or enjoying a frothy avocado mousse after dinner. But in Brazil, an avocado is customarily prepared as a sweet, as a dessert; avocados come after the meal or altogether separate from it.

Of course, there is nothing wrong with either way of looking at the avocado—that is, as long as the way of looking allows you to enjoy avocados. If you've grown to love them in a salad, try them with arugula or watercress. If you've grown accustomed to thinking of them as dessert, feel free to make an avocado cake. But in either case, it's good to know that the avocado doesn't have to be one type of food or the other, because if you are locked into a single way of using an avocado, you'll probably find variations distasteful or strange. If you are an adventurous diner, you might want to try both American and Brazilian ways of preparing an avocado, or you might thoroughly rethink the categories or even discard categories altogether to consider the avocado purely as an avocado.

A work of art, like an avocado, can be grouped according to custom and use. A work of art, also like an avocado, can be moved from one group to another. And the groups themselves may be redefined or discarded. Determinations of kind or type along with decisions about what individual items belong to those types are variable; they are not absolute, not unchanging. With literature and film, we often find ourselves adjusting the basis upon which distinctions of kind are made. This ever-shifting way of defining a category and what belongs in a category is what makes the concept of genre such a tricky subject.

WHAT IS GENRE?

Genre is defined most broadly as a literary/artistic type or kind; it suggests the grouping of individual works into larger categories. That grouping can be made in various ways. Genres are commonly defined by reference to fairly basic **expectations** an audience brings to a work. Some of the most basic expectations have long been observed: a **tragedy** ends in death, a **comedy** ends in marriage. To expand upon that distinction slightly, we expect tragedies to concern grand failures—a powerful sense of lost promise is crucial. We expect comedies to offer some sense of fulfillment, albeit oftentimes of a small sort. Characters in comedies overcome misunderstandings and limitations to achieve their fair share of happiness.

There are, of course, different kinds of comedies and tragedies. There are additional terms that register more specific expectations. A **farce** (a form of **low comedy**) sustains no tension that arises from complexities of character. Consequently, a farce builds upon silly actions that require only superficial resolution (there may be situational complexities in farce, but not emotional ones). The pleasure of watching *Seinfeld* depends largely on how cleverly episode after episode adds up to nothing. In contrast to such light entertainments, **high comedy** delivers the emotional substance of complex people. For example, the lovers in Shakespeare's *Much Ado about Nothing* face very hard obstacles created by ill will, anger, pride, and jealousy. They also suffer for the mistakes they make. And partly because of this capacity to suffer, they can appreciate the happiness they finally achieve.

Although it is important to know key terms that are commonly used to identify elements of a genre, it is more important still to understand how identifying those elements helps us appreciate an individual text. A good critic must do more than merely name genres or provide information *about* genres. Shakespeare's foolish busybody Polonius from *Hamlet* takes the naming approach, and it leads him to a long and ultimately pointless list: "tragedy, comedy, history, pastoral, pastoral-comical, historical pastoral, tragical-historical, tragical-comical-historical-pastoral." Polonius does not understand that a genre is something to explore and test, not merely label and list. The study of genre demands that we reflect upon categories we identify and name. We must consider what we have been taught to expect from a particular kind of work as well as ask ourselves what those expectations signify:

- Creative works of art precede the critical discussion of those works as representative of a type or kind. Aristotle wouldn't have written about tragedy as a genre if he had not viewed many plays that he felt shared essential characteristics. (You wouldn't consider an avocado a salad fruit if you had not grown up eating avocados in salads.)

- Defining a genre does not fix the characteristics of a genre permanently in place. Aristotle was a brilliant critic, but his description of tragedy should not be taken as a set of rules all tragedies must follow. (Even if you think of avocados only as a salad fruit, there remain many inventive ways to use avocados in a great variety of salads.)

- If it doesn't help you to think of a particular work existing within a particular genre, don't hesitate to move that work into another genre, or redefine the genre, or dismiss the notion of genre. (If you are tired of avocados in salads, try an avocado dessert, or make an avocado main dish, or just eat the avocado plain.)

CONVENTIONS

Elements that have become familiar through our reading/viewing experience are called **conventions** (**formula** is a related, although somewhat stricter, word). Without conventions, there can be no genre. Our recognition of conventions becomes the basis upon which we construct a sense of genre. Often conventions emerge in elements of plot. In teen horror films (like *Halloween* or *Nightmare on Elm Street*), our viewing experience leads us to expect a crazed killer to attack the young lovers who have sneaked off to make out. In courtroom dramas (like *A Few Good Men*), we learn to expect an explosive confrontation between a defense lawyer and a difficult witness that will reveal the truth that has been hidden. In romantic comedies (like *My Best Friend's Wedding* or *Silver Linings Playbook*), we learn to expect the leading male and female characters to stumble over a series of misunderstandings before they discover that they are meant for each other. We often take satisfaction in such familiar genre stories because they at some level provide reassurance. They confirm unspoken beliefs or underscore common wisdom: that young couples shouldn't sneak around to make out, that false accusations will not be sustained in our courts, that true love always finds a way.

Conventions, of course, don't take shape only in elements of a story line. Anything our reading/viewing experience has taught us to expect as essential to a type can trigger our identification of a genre. A dark and stormy night serves as a conventional setting for certain types of gothic fiction. A guy sporting a straggly mustache and a black hat instantly signals a threat in the world of the western. A pairing of unlike personalities in a shared endeavor becomes the basis for dozens of buddy films. And the mood or tone of reflective sadness over the death of a promising youth marks the conventional tone and subject of the elegy. We begin to respond to many individual works in context of a body of expectations we have acquired in our past reading and viewing.

Experiencing Literature through Genre

Ghost stories often begin by establishing a tension between rational skepticism and unexplained, disturbing occurrences. The initial tension acknowledges our resistance to tales of the supernatural to lure us in. Readers are, in effect, moved from their mundane lives into fictional worlds where anything can happen. Consider how quickly Charlotte Riddell (a nineteenth-century writer of supernatural tales) invokes basic generic conventions in the opening paragraphs of one of her many ghost stories. We are introduced to a no-nonsense narrator and his more vulnerable family. As you read, think of how this opening relates to familiar elements in ghost stories you may have heard or of horror films you have seen.

Charlotte Riddell (1832–1906)

from Nut Bush Farm (1882)

When I entered upon the tenancy of Nut Bush Farm almost the first piece of news which met me, in the shape of a whispered rumour, was that "something" had been seen in the "long field."

Pressed closely as to what he meant, my informant reluctantly stated that the "something" took the "form of a man," and that the wood and the path leading thereto from Whittleby were supposed to be haunted.

Now, all this annoyed me exceedingly. I do not know when I was more put out than by this intelligence. It is unnecessary to say I did not believe in ghosts or anything of that kind, but my wife being a very nervous, impressionable woman, and our only child a delicate weakling, in the habit of crying himself into fits if left alone at night without a candle, I really felt at my wits' end to imagine what I should do if a story of this sort reached their ears. ❖

This narrator represents a kind of commonsense approach to the world, but he does not seem at the outset a very sympathetic figure. We're hardly surprised or disappointed to see this narrator shaken progressively from his confident faith in the material reality of everyday life. We expect and want ghost stories to shake up hardheaded skeptics. That is what ghost stories do. Significantly, by the end of this tale, we have the same tension we had at the start. But now it is the narrator who is shaken and the people who surround him who are the skeptics. We're now able to align ourselves with the narrator against all those sensible fools who refuse to accept a reality that lies outside the ordinary. Note how the essential dynamic has been repeated and yet revised in the closing lines from "Nut Bush Farm."

My brother took Nut Bush Farm off my hands. He says the place never was haunted—that I never saw Mr. Hascot except in my own imagination—that the whole thing originated in a poor state of health and a too credulous disposition!

I leave the reader to judge between us. ❖

We may well end "Nut Bush Farm" still thinking of ghosts as existing only in stories, but the generic elements evident in the passage are clearly intended to help us accept *in the reading of the story* an alternative belief.

DISRUPTIONS

Genres depend upon our recognition of familiar features. But it would be a mistake to assume a genre piece never veers from the expected. Genres aren't absolutely fixed or altogether predictable. A deviation from an established convention—a surprise that results from breaking an expectation—is called a **disruption**. The familiar element is revised or even reversed. A disruption can be thought of as a specific kind of interruption (see Chapter 9, p. 845)—one that challenges thematic implications of a genre. Disruptions in a genre piece may call into question the beliefs that lie behind the conventions. If the sexually eager young couple we think is doomed in a horror movie turn out to have a good (and safe) time together, maybe we shouldn't worry so much about young couples sneaking off; if the defense lawyer in a courtroom drama can't break through what we see as a tissue of lies, maybe our legal system doesn't work as well as we like to think; if the "right couple" in what appeared to be a conventional romantic comedy turns out to be very wrong together, maybe our notions of "true love" need to be rethought. Whereas conventions reassure, disruptions challenge and upset. Mixing familiar conventions that do not normally appear together is a common mode of disruption.

Experiencing Literature through Genre

A famous example of generic mixing occurs in Shakespeare's *Macbeth*. Just after the king has been assassinated, just as Macbeth and Lady Macbeth begin to feel the terrible weight of what they have done, a foulmouthed drunken Porter arrives at the castle and seeks entrance. He knocks at the gate. He speaks (to himself, Macduff, the audience, and anyone who will listen from within the castle walls) about subjects that hardly seem fitting in context of the grand tragedy that has begun to unfold. He punctuates his rambling bawdy soliloquy with continued knocking at the gate. As you read the following dialogue, keep in mind that it is placed just after the murder of the king and just before the general discovery of the murder. Some of the grandest and most intense lines in the play bracket the lowly dialogue we've reprinted here. For example, just before the entrance of the Porter, Macbeth reflects upon his act:

William Shakespeare (1564–1616)

from Macbeth (1607)

To know my deed, 'twere best not know myself.
(*Knock*)
Wake Duncan with thy knocking! I would thou couldst.

And shortly after the Porter's final line, we have Macduff's announcement upon finding the king slain:

Confusion now hath made his masterpiece:
Most sacrilegious murder hath broke ope
The Lord's anointed temple and stole thence
The life of th' building!

In the middle of such lines the Porter's speech might seem out of place. In his speech, the Porter alludes to serious matters (the Jesuits tried for political conspiracies against the crown were considered by protestants to be "equivocators"), but immediately turns such serious matters to bawdy jokes on how drink makes him both sexually aroused and sexually incapable. The low comic tone clashes greatly with the tragic weight and dignity of the surrounding text.

Some critics call this kind of mixing **comic relief**, but that term hardly fits this instance. In this case, Shakespeare is clarifying and intensifying—not undercutting—the tragedy of *Macbeth*. The knocking-at-the-gate scene provokes at most uncomfortable laughter; the wrongness of the deed has thrown everything out of synch. The Porter's incessant pounding at the gate intensifies the horror of what has occurred within the gates. Macbeth's treasonous and brutal act has undermined the stability and integrity of his world. The breakdown of generic categories through the mixing of the high and the low complements the moral breakdown that results from the murder.

DISPLACEMENT AND PARODY

A **displacement** of one genre for another or a complete **blending** of genres extends mixing to its furthest limit. Joss Whedon's television series *Buffy the Vampire Slayer* places conventional high school coming-of-age stories in context of the horror genre. Comedy blends with terror; the mundane ("does this boy/girl like me?")

ZUMA Press, Inc./Alamy

The demon here (in the lower left corner of the publicity poster) is dressed and posed very much like a conventional song-and-dance man, but he has a demon's face and does pose a threat to Buffy and her sister.

blends with the cosmic ("the end of the world is upon us"). We come to understand that the comic is at times horrific or that the mundane can feel cosmic (a breakup in a serious relationship may indeed seem like the end of the world). Once Whedon establishes the ongoing generic blend, he can overlay still more generic elements as he wishes in individual episodes. A particularly striking instance is the musical episode "Once More, with Feeling" (2001). In that episode, a particularly inventive singing demon gains power over residents of Sunnydale (the town's name, of course, is part of the generic fusion). People burst into song and dance, very much in the fashion of standard Broadway musicals. The catch is that they must sing the feelings that best remain private. Eventually, they burst not just into song but into flames. The lightness of a conventional musical takes a bitter and genuinely dangerous edge. The various genres merge together as something new and provocative.

Perhaps the most radical disruption involves mockery; the very elements that had been established as meaningful in a genre become the subject of ridicule. Such sustained comic imitation of a serious work is called **parody**. Although parody is sometimes thought to mark the death of a genre, it's perhaps more accurate and useful to consider it a form of revision. If the genre really were dead, the parody wouldn't be funny and it wouldn't serve any purpose. Why laugh at something that no one cares about? Occasionally, critics will use the term **self-parody**. Whereas a parody is a controlled work of satire, a purposeful diminishment of a work or works taken by some as serious, a self-parody is an unintentional revelation of empty and tired formulas. Self-parody results from a genre writer/director who fails to infuse conventions with meaning or life; the result of such a failure is often that we laugh at the conventions rather than respond to them in ways we are "supposed" to respond. Think of a spy film, for example, that tries very hard to be sexy and suspenseful, but turns out to be so clichéd that it becomes funny. Or a horror movie that guarantees everyone scares and frights, but delivers its "shockers" so lamely that the audience responds only with laughter.

Mark Twain's "Ode to Stephen Dowling Bots, Dec'd" shows that it is possible to parody a type of work that has already diminished itself by numerous uninspired formulaic pieces. Twain is motivated not so much by the badness of a kind of work but by the widespread acceptance of that bad work. He suggests that our culture produces and praises a ponderous and polite literature that needs to be seen for what it is—fake, empty, cliché ridden, and dishonest. It's worth noting that the conventions of an **ode** (a lyrical form in which an inspired poet describes someone or something that has provided that inspiration) have in the last century become less conventions of form and more conventions of mood and subject. That is, odes were once structured in three parts that reflected their origins as public poems, performed by a chorus that moved in one direction as it delivered the first part (the **strophe**), the opposite direction as it voiced the second part (the **antistrophe**), and stood still as it came to the final section (the **epode**). Now we may think of odes as substantial poems of a meditative cast. They normally sustain a tone of dignity, high seriousness, and calm dispassion in dealing with a public matter. These conventions, although broadly defined, may be considered a basis for thinking of the ode in terms of genre. But Twain wants to explode what he sees as stifling conventions of propriety that keep people distant from real feelings. In his parody, he calls attention to our low expectations by meeting them only too well.

Mark Twain (1835–1910)

Ode to Stephen Dowling Bots, Dec'd

(from *Adventures of Huckleberry Finn*, 1884)

And did young Stephen sicken,
    And did young Stephen die?
And did the sad hearts thicken,
    And did the mourners cry?

No; such was not the fate of   5
    Young Stephen Dowling Bots;
Though sad hearts round him thickened,
    'Twas not from sickness' shots.

No whooping-cough did rack his frame,
    Nor measles drear, with spots;   10
Not these impaired the sacred name
    Of Stephen Dowling Bots.

Despised love struck not with woe
    That head of curly knots,
Not stomach troubles laid him low;   15
    Young Stephen Dowling Bots.

O no. Then list with tearful eye,
    Whilst I his fate do tell.
His soul did from this cold world fly,
    By falling down a well.   20

They got him out and emptied him;
    Alas it was too late;
His spirit was gone for to sport aloft
    In the realms of the good and the great.

Making Connections

An allusion calls to mind ideas or associations that a reader has acquired from previous reading experience (see Chapter 14, p. 1366). A writer's purposeful use of genre also demands prior experience from the reader. It might seem, then, that a heavily allusive text is essentially the same as a genre work. Although there may be overlap, it is useful to make a distinction. An allusion casts the reader back on a particular text or type of text at a particular place in a text. There may be many allusions in a single work, and those allusions might be drawn from many different texts. Each allusion demands particular consideration in the context of its specific occurrence. Genre works ask us to think in more general terms of patterns, types, or kinds. That is, we're asked to think of how shared features work similarly in different texts.

After reading Twain's parody, we're likely to be very careful about the ways we speak or write about death in formal or public occasions. The last thing we'll want to do is trust too much in the most common of generic expressions. In this case, the conventions have been so overused that the poem loses any authentic relationship to the individual supposedly being honored.

GENRE AND POPULAR CULTURE

When we think hard about genre, we learn about the culture that produces the genre. Conventions embody values, wishes, and fears. For example, until the late 1960s, the western was among the most clearly established film genres and a popular genre of fiction as well. Many children growing up in the United States of the 1950s had thoroughly internalized the western's conventions. Television stories, dime novels, Saturday matinees had laid down the guidelines. Boys especially learned to recognize and employ all the necessary elements.

At left, very young boys who grew up in the 1950s learned to mimic the gestures of their western heroes. At right, Gary Cooper in *High Noon* (1952).

American children of this generation had no difficulty recognizing a western. Although they had no critical consciousness of genre, their expectations were easily put into play. When they saw the quiet stranger ride into town, they knew much of what was to follow. The stranger would befriend a weak person. He would stand tall against a threatening bad guy (usually a braggart). He would resist "gunplay," but after many provocations he would enter and win a shootout. He would then ride off into the sunset while a grateful town would watch him go. All had seen that story many times in various forms. Good and bad were black and white. Good guys didn't want to fight, yet they always won the fights they entered—at least the fight that really counted, the decisive shoot-out at the climax. Civilization, peace, and stability were at stake at the opening of the film and were accomplished facts by the end. Of course, the real world of the 1950s was not so simple. No period of history is ever simple. But the highly conventionalized westerns of that time may have signaled a desire for clarity or perhaps a denial of complexity.

Experiencing Film through Genre

Popular movies provide especially clear illustrations of how genres take shape and change to reflect the mood of the times. Film and television are, after all, the most widely shared forms of artistic expression in our culture. We sit with others to watch a movie; we see and hear how others respond as we respond. We come to build a shared knowledge of scenes, characters, images, and plots that we bring to each movie we see, and that we add to with each movie we see. We can all readily identify a wealth of types: screwball comedies, combat films, horror films, musicals, gangster movies, buddy movies, and so on. Thinking about three western movies from three different periods can help us see how—and to what end—conventions take shape and are disrupted as social and political attitudes shift.

Shane (1953) has been called the "perfect" western, and to the extent that it embodies key elements of the classic western it may well be. Based on a 1949 novel of the same title by Jack Schaefer, *Shane* evokes a myth of growth and opportunity that had a powerful hold on the United States just after World War II. The country had come out of the Depression and a war. Men were coming back to start careers. Women were sometimes forced to leave careers to make room for those men. Tract homes were laid down, marriages made, children born, schools built. It's this cultural context that gives rise to *Shane*. The main action of *Shane* deals with the threat to the Starrett family and resolves itself in the defense of that family. Joe (Van Heflin), Marian (Jean Arthur), and their son (Brandon De Wilde) are the idealized ancestors of people going to the movies in 1953. Those moviegoers appreciated the conventions that both tested and rewarded the Starretts' hard work, honesty, determination, and decency. They felt that they had inherited the world that Shane and the Starretts had labored for and fought to secure.

By the mid- to late 1960s, the western's myth of progress seemed too accepting of conventional roles and rules and too optimistic about what violence could achieve. *Shane* had been one of the most popular films of its day, but by 1970, straightforward westerns had nearly disappeared. In fact, one of the biggest box office hits of 1974 was *Blazing Saddles*—a western made to ridicule westerns. In this film, director Mel Brooks shrewdly plays a fairly common strategy: when a genre becomes over worn or out of touch, it is ripe for satire. The values that once gave it force become subject to dismissal. In *Blazing Saddles*, the western's conventions are wildly disrupted. The main result is a kind of low humor: cowboys noisily fart around the campfire after eating beans; the bar maid (Madeline Kahn) enjoys decidedly phallic sausages at dinner with the new sheriff (Cleavon Little). In the more serious parts of the general fun, Brooks pokes holes in racial and gender assumptions built into conventional westerns: a crooked politician (Harvey Korman) appoints an African American man sheriff because he knows that the racist townspeople won't accept the rule of law from a man they consider inferior. By mocking most everything that was presented seriously in *Shane*, *Blazing Saddles* signaled a new perspective on earlier notions of social progress. A popular genre, along with the beliefs that the genre supported, seemed almost laughed out of existence.

The western, however, was too much a part of the general culture to die out completely. Even if people could no longer accept conventions of the western uncritically, they could still be trusted to recognize those conventions and the values they once encoded. In *Unforgiven* (1992), director Clint Eastwood found ways to use the audience's knowledge of genre in serious and unsettling ways. Working from a screenplay by David Webb Peoples, Eastwood created a film that subtly disrupted the conventional western point by point. *Unforgiven* makes us reflect upon the significance of the expectations shaped by classic westerns like *Shane*. Will Munny (played by Eastwood)—a man of notorious temper and character—has been "reformed" by the love of a woman. This seems to begin where Shane wanted to end, but *Unforgiven* opens with Munny digging his wife's grave. Although Munny had become a hardworking family man, he finds the farm and the children offer little satisfaction. To make matters worse, Munny's pigs have the fever. As he labors to separate those infected from the few that remain healthy, Munny is literally dragged through the mud and excrement. Conventionalized scenes of work in *Shane* had idealized the healthiness and productivity of hard work.

Paramount/The Kobal Collection

Shane (1953)

Warner Bros/The Kobal Collection

Unforgiven (1992)

Munny soon receives an offer to join in the contract killing of two cowboys who "cut up a woman." So, like Shane, he finds himself returning to his violent past; unlike Shane, however, Munny's return to type begins, not ends, the story. Even though Munny at first says the cowboys "deserve" killing, it quickly becomes clear that "deserve has nothing to do with it" (a point made explicit at the end).

More recently, the western has enjoyed a resurgence among directors who made their names in other genres. The films display the familiar conventions, but any faith in the western mythology has changed significantly. The Coen brothers, who as filmmakers are known for their ability to create films that epitomize the technical aspects of whatever genre they happen to be working in and, often, to simultaneously tweak those conventions, created a remarkably straight remake of *True Grit* (2010). Quentin Tarantino brought his characteristic blend of cinematic ingenuity and violence to the west in *Django Unchained* (2012). Interestingly, both of these films were recognized for their artistry: their camera work, their direction, and their acting. Jon Favreau, better known for *Elf* and *Iron Man*, created *Cowboys and Aliens* (2011) in which he blends elements of the western and the science fiction film. Gore Verbinski went from *The Pirates of the Caribbean* to the animated *Rango* (2011), starring Johnny Depp as a gun-slinging chameleon. For each of these filmmakers, the western genre seems to be an artistic challenge—how can I work within this traditional genre before I go on to do something else?

A Note to Student Writers: Academic Genres

Genres aren't identifiable only in stories, poems, films, and plays. Academic essays also develop generic characteristics. Although it is important to understand that conventions of form, tone, argument, and presentation do operate in critical essays of various types, far too often academic genres are reduced to one overly simple and severely limited formula: "five-paragraph essay." This formula is sometimes presented (or understood) as a fixed model. Students are taught that they *must* introduce a topic and assert a thesis in the first paragraph, follow the thesis with three supporting points (a paragraph for each point), and conclude in a final paragraph. More generous, but still cramped, lessons allow for a slight expansion of the same basic model (that is, students are allowed an additional paragraph or two in the body for more supporting points). If we understand the teaching of such models as intended to communicate very basic ideas about structure (that papers should have a beginning, middle, and end), there is little harm done. But it is very important to realize that not all "good writing" about any subject can be neatly contained by an inflexible organizational formula.

Perhaps the biggest problem with working from any set model is that such a practice makes the formula the primary thing. In other words, the structure doesn't allow for ideas to grow. It imposes limits upon any complex thoughts we may discover or hope to explore. A careful reading of most any good essay will reveal that one point need not be contained by one paragraph, that there is no "right" number of paragraphs. Writers don't "fill in" a preset number of paragraphs; they develop paragraphs as their ideas unfold and as the argument demands. We suggest that you remember that academic genres, like literary genres, are multiple and are subject to change. Most important, remember that genres function to shape and express meaning, not to box in meaning.

MODELING CRITICAL ANALYSIS: TOM STOPPARD, THE FIFTEEN MINUTE HAMLET

Tom Stoppard's *The Fifteen Minute Hamlet* presents much of the action of the original play: the ghost of Hamlet's father comes and asks for revenge; Hamlet rebukes his mother; Hamlet kills Polonius; Claudius sends him away; Ophelia goes mad, dies, and is buried; Laertes mourns. Laertes strikes Hamlet with a poison-tipped foil; Hamlet cuts Laertes with the same; Gertrude drinks unknowingly from a poisoned cup; Hamlet stabs Claudius. All die. Fontinbras arrives and acknowledges Hamlet's nobility. Surely all that death adds up to tragedy—or surely not. Stoppard's radical cutting disrupts any sense of tragedy. Aristotle defined tragedy as an imitation of a profound action that an audience could identify with and through that identification achieve a kind of release, what Aristotle termed **catharsis**. Stoppard keeps a distance from reality; he imitates only a play. We're conscious from the start of gaps in character development as his version of *Hamlet* rockets forward. Because we're not given any reason to care about the characters, we cannot react emotionally to their fates. In fact, we have no reason to think of these characters as having any existence off the stage. The artifice of it all is made especially apparent by the fact that in this fifteen-minute version, everyone dies twice—once in the main body of the play and once in the still more radically abbreviated encore.

By racing through Shakespeare's *Hamlet* and grabbing tiny bits of memorable lines and key scenes, Stoppard asks us to consider what constitutes the play and the genre. We know this is not *Hamlet*, and yet we recognize much of *Hamlet* in it. Whatever made that play a tragedy gets left out. What is left in moves us to a very different genre. Imagine how this play would be performed. The speed would lend it many of the characteristics of a slapstick comedy or farce (a physical comedy): characters in *The Fifteen Minute Hamlet* charge about, rush on stage and off stage, deliver lines without context, fall down dead, get up, and fall down dead again before getting up once more to welcome the cheers of the audience. The audience at a well-done production of *The Fifteen Minute Hamlet* will be laughing throughout.

Stoppard may also be asking us to reflect back seriously on Shakespeare's play and on the way we may diminish tragedies. It's possible his reduction serves as a comment on a common resistance to really experiencing literature. Do we engage great works of art directly or look for shortcuts (study guides, for example) that allow us to display knowledge (on tests or in social situations) about great works? Do we too often substitute secondhand representations of literature in place of literature itself? Do we learn "about" literature or do we read and respond? Stoppard reminds us that *Hamlet* isn't just a matter of what happens that anyone might summarize for us. And if we've read it only for what happens, we've written our own fifteen-minute version without knowing it. If that were the case, the laugh would be on us.

Tom Stoppard (1937–   )

The Fifteen Minute Hamlet (1976)

CHARACTERS

MARCELLUS, BERNARDO, LAERTES, HORATIO *(Scenes 1, 3, and encore)*
FRANCISCO, OSRIC, FORTINBRAS, GRAVEDIGGER, GHOST, HORATIO *(Scene 1)*
OPHELIA
GERTRUDE
HAMLET
SHAKESPEARE, CLAUDIUS, POLONIUS
TIME AND SCENE: *The action takes place at a shortened version of Elsinore Castle.*

Scene 1

A castle battlement. Thunder and wind. Two guards, BERNARDO/MARCELLUS
and FRANCISCO/HORATIO, *enter.*

BERNARDO/MARCELLUS: Who's there?

FRANCISCO/HORATIO: Nay, answer me.

BERNARDO/MARCELLUS: Long live the King. Get thee to bed.

FRANCISCO/HORATIO: For this relief, much thanks.

BERNARDO/MARCELLUS: What, has this thing appeared again tonight?   5

FRANCISCO/HORATIO: Peace, break thee off: look where it comes again.
    (He points off left.)

BERNARDO/MARCELLUS: Looks it not like the King?

FRANCISCO/HORATIO: By heaven, I charge thee, speak!

BERNARDO/MARCELLUS *(He points and looks left.)*: 'Tis here.

FRANCISCO/HORATIO *(He points and looks centre.)*: 'Tis there.   10

BERNARDO/MARCELLUS *(He looks right.)*: 'Tis gone.

FRANCISCO/HORATIO: But look, the morn in russet mantle clad
    Walks o'er the dew of yon high eastern hill.

BERNARDO/MARCELLUS: Let us impart what we have seen tonight
    Unto young Hamlet.   15

(They exit.)

Scene 2

A room of state within the castle. A flourish of trumpets as CLAUDIUS *and*
GERTRUDE *enter.*

CLAUDIUS: Though yet of Hamlet our dear brother's death
The memory be green

*(*HAMLET *enters.)*

    our sometime sister, now our Queen,
    Have we taken to wife.
    But now, my cousin Hamlet, and my son—   5

HAMLET: A little more than kin, and less than kind.

*(*CLAUDIUS *and* GERTRUDE *exit.)*

    O that this too too solid flesh would melt!
    That it should come to this—but two months dead!
    So loving to my mother: Frailty, thy name is woman!
    Married with mine uncle, my father's brother.   10
    The funeral baked meats did coldly furnish forth
    The marriage tables.

*(*HORATIO *rushes on.)*

HORATIO: My lord, I think I saw him yesternight—
    The King, your father—upon the platform where we watched.

HAMLET: 'Tis very strange.   15

HORATIO: Armed, my lord—
 A countenance more in sorrow than in anger.
HAMLET: My father's spirit in arms? All is not well.
 Would the night were come!
(HAMLET and HORATIO exit to the parapet.)

Scene 3

The castle battlements at night. There is the noise of carousing, cannon, fireworks.
HORATIO *and* HAMLET *appear on the parapet.*
HAMLET: The King doth wake tonight and takes his rouse.
 Though I am native here and to the manner born,
 It is a custom more honoured in the breach
 Than in the observance.
 (There is the sound of wind.)
HORATIO: Look, my lord, it comes. *(He points.)*   5
(The GHOST *enters.)*
HAMLET: Angels and ministers of grace defend us!
 Something is rotten in the state of Denmark!
 Alas, poor ghost.
GHOST: I am thy father's spirit.
 Revenge his foul and most unnatural murder.   10
HAMLET: Murder?
GHOST: The serpent that did sting thy father's life
 Now wears his crown.
HAMLET: O my prophetic soul! Mine uncle?
(The GHOST *exits.)*
(To HORATIO.*)* There are more things in heaven and earth   15
 Than are dreamt of in your philosophy.
(HORATIO exits.)
 Hereafer I shall think meet
 To put an antic disposition on.
 The time is out of joint. O cursed spite
 That ever I was born to set it right!   20
(HAMLET exits.)

Scene 4

A room within the castle. There is a flourish of trumpets, leading into flute and harpsichord music. POLONIUS *enters and immediately* OPHELIA *rushes on.*
POLONIUS: How now, Ophelia, what's the matter?
OPHELIA: My lord, as I was sewing in my chamber, Lord Hamlet with his 5
 doublet all unbraced, no hat upon his head, pale as his shirt, his knees
 knocking each other, and with a look so piteous, he comes before me.

POLONIUS: Mad for thy love?
    I have found the very cause of Hamlet's lunacy.
    (HAMLET *enters as* OPHELIA *exits.*)
    Look where sadly the poor wretch comes reading.
    What do you read, my lord?
HAMLET: Words, words, words.   10
POLONIUS: Though this be madness, yet there is method in it.
HAMLET: I am but mad north northwest: when the wind is southerly! I know a
    hawk from a handsaw.
POLONIUS: The actors are come hither, my lord. *(He goes.)*
HAMLET: We'll hear a play tomorrow.   15
    I have heard that guilty creatures sitting at a play
    Have by the very cunning of the scene
    Been struck so to the soul that presently
    They have proclaimed their malefactions.
    I'll have these players play something   20
    Like the murder of my father before mine uncle.
    If he but blench, I know my course,
    The play's the thing
    Wherein I'll catch the conscience of the King.
    (Pause.)
    To be, or not to be *(He puts a dagger to his heart.)*   25
    (CLAUDIUS *and* OPHELIA *enter.*)
    that is the question.
OPHELIA: My lord—
HAMLET: Get thee to a nunnery!
(OPHELIA *and* HAMLET *exit.*)
CLAUDIUS: Love? His affections do not that way tend
    There's something in his soul   30
    O'er which his melancholy sits on brood.
    He shall with speed to England.
(CLAUDIUS *exits.*)

Scene 5
A hall within the castle. A flourish of trumpets heralds the entrance of HAMLET
and OPHELIA, MARCELLUS *and* HORATIO *who are joking together,* CLAUDIUS *and*
GERTRUDE.
HAMLET *(to imaginary players.)*: Speak the speech, I pray you, as I pronounced it
    to you; tripplingly on the tongue. Hold, as t'were, the mirror up to nature.
(Everyone sits to watch imaginary play. Masque music is heard.)
    (to GERTRUDE.*)* Madam, how like you the play?
GERTRUDE: The lady doth protest too much, methinks.   5

HAMLET: He poisons him in the garden for his estate. You shall see anon how the murderer gets the love of Gonzago's wife.

(CLAUDIUS *rises.*)

The King rises!

(*Music stops, hubbub noise starts.*)

What, frighted with false fire?

(CLAUDIUS *exits; re-enters at side as* POLONIUS.*)*

ALL: Give o'er the play.   10

HAMLET: Lights! Lights! Lights! I'll take the ghost's word for a thousand pounds!

(*Exeunt all except polonius.*)

POLONIUS (*standing at side.*): He's going to his mother's closet. Behind the arras I'll convey myself to hear the process.

Scene 6

The QUEEN'S *apartment.* POLONIUS *slips behind the arras as it is raised. Lute music is heard.* HAMLET *and* GERTRUDE *enter.*

HAMLET: Now, Mother, what's the matter?

GERTRUDE: Hamlet, thou hast thy father much offended.

HAMLET: Mother, you have my father much offended. (*He holds her.*)

GERTRUDE: What wilt thou do? Thou wilt not murder me? Help! Help! Ho!

POLONIUS (*behind arras.*): Help!   5

HAMLET: How now? A rat? (*He stabs* POLONIUS.*)* Dead for a ducat, dead!

GERTRUDE: O me, what has thou done?

HAMLET: Nay, I know not.

GERTRUDE: Alas, he's mad.

HAMLET: I must be cruel only to be kind. Good night, Mother.   10

(HAMLET *exits dragging* POLONIUS. GERTRUDE *exits, sobbing. The arras is dropped.*)

Scene 7

Another room in the castle. Flourish of trumpets as CLAUDIUS *and* HAMLET *enter.*

CLAUDIUS: Now, Hamlet, where's Polonius?

HAMLET: At supper.

CLAUDIUS: Hamlet, this deed must send thee hence.

Therefore prepare thyself,

Everything is bent for England.   5

(HAMLET *exits.*)

And England, if my love thou holds't at aught, Thou mayst not coldly set our sov'reign process, The present death of Hamlet. Do it, England!

(CLAUDIUS *exits.*)

Interlude

At sea. Sea music. HAMLET *enters on parapet, swaying as if on a ship's bridge. Sea music ends.* HAMLET *exits.*

Scene 8

Yet another room in the castle. Flourish of trumpets as CLAUDIUS *and* LAERTES *enter.*

LAERTES: Where is my father?

CLAUDIUS: Dead.

(OPHELIA *enters in mad trance, singing. Lute music is heard.*)

OPHELIA: They bore him barefaced on the bier,
  Hey nonny nonny, hey nonny.
  And on his grave rained many a tear . . .   5

LAERTES: O heat dry up my brains—O kind Sister,
  (OPHELIA *falls to ground.*)
  Had'st thou thy wits, and did'st persuade revenge
  It could not move thus.

CLAUDIUS: And where the offence is, let the great axe fall.

(CLAUDIUS *and* LAERTES *exit. Gravestone rises to hide* OPHELIA. *Bell tolls four times.*)

Scene 9

A churchyard. A GRAVEDIGGER *and* HAMLET *enter.*

HAMLET: Ere we were two days old at sea, a pirate of very warlike appointment gave us
  chase. In the grapple I boarded them. On the instant they got clear of our ship;
  so I alone became their prisoner. They have dealt with me like thieves of mercy.

GRAVEDIGGER: What is he that builds stronger than either the mason, the   5
  shipwright or the carpenter?

HAMLET: A gravemaker. The houses he makes will last till Doomsday.
  (GRAVEDIGGER *gives skull to* HAMLET.)
  Whose was it?

GRAVEDIGGER: This same skull, Sir, was Yorick's skull, the King's jester.

HAMLET: Alas, poor Yorick. (*He returns skull to* GRAVEDIGGER.)   10
  But soft—that is Laertes. (*He withdraws to side.*)

(LAERTES *enters.*)

LAERTES: What ceremony else?
  Lay her in the earth,
  And from her fair and unpolluted flesh
  May violets spring. I tell thee, churlish priest,   15
  (CLAUDIUS *and* GERTRUDE *enter.*)
  A ministering angel shall my sister be
  When thou liest howling.

HAMLET (*offstage.*): What, the fair Ophelia?

LAERTES: O treble woe. Hold off the earth awhile,
  Till I have caught her once more in my arms.   20

HAMLET (*re-entering acting area.*):
  What is he whose grief bears such an emphasis?
  This is I, Hamlet the Dane!

LAERTES: The devil take thy soul.
(*They grapple.*)
HAMLET: Away thy hand!
(CLAUDIUS *and* GERTRUDE *pull them apart.*)
CLAUDIUS AND GERTRUDE: Hamlet! Hamlet! (*speaking together.*)   25
HAMLET: I loved Ophelia. What wilt thou do for her?
GERTRUDE: O he is mad, Laertes!
(CLAUDIUS, GERTRUDE *and* LAERTES *exit.*)
HAMLET: The cat will mew, and dog will have his day!
(*He exits. Gravestone is dropped.*)

Scene 10
A Hall in the castle. A flourish of trumpets as HAMLET *enters.*
HAMLET: There's a divinity that shapes our ends, rough hew them how
   we will. But thou would'st not think how ill all's here about my
   heart. But 'tis no matter. We defy augury. There is a special providence in
   the fall of a sparrow. If it be now, 'tis not to come; If it be
   not to come, it will be now; it if be not now yet it will come. The   5
   readiness is all.
      (LAERTES *enters with* OSRIC *bearing swords followed by* CLAUDIUS *and* GERTRUDE
      with goblets.)
      Come on, Sir!
LAERTES: Come, my lord.
(*Fanfare of trumpets.* LAERTES *and* HAMLET *draw swords and duel.*)
HAMLET: One.   10
LAERTES: No.
HAMLET: Judgement?
OSRIC: A hit, a very palpable hit.
CLAUDIUS: Stay, give me a drink.
      Hamlet, this pearl is thine, here's to thy health.
(*He drops pearl in goblet.*) Give him the cup.   15
GERTRUDE: The Queen carouses to thy fortune, Hamlet.
(GERTRUDE *takes the cup.*)
CLAUDIUS: Gertrude, do not drink!
GERTRUDE: I will, my lord. (*She drinks.*)
LAERTES: My lord, I'll hit him now.
      Have at you, now!   20
(HAMLET *and* LAERTES *grapple and fight.*)
CLAUDIUS: Part them, they are incensed.
      They bleed on both sides.
(OSRIC *and* CLAUDIUS *part them.* OSRIC *exits.*)
LAERTES: I am justly killed by my own treachery. (*He falls.*)

GERTRUDE: The drink, the drink! I am poisoned! *(She dies.)*
HAMLET: Treachery! Seek it out.   25
(FORTINBRAS enters.)
LAERTES: It is here, Hamlet. Hamlet thou art slain.
    Lo, here I lie, never to rise again.
    The King, the King's to blame.
HAMLET: The point envenomed too?
    Then venom to thy work. *(He kills CLAUDIUS.)*   30
LAERTES: Exchange forgiveness with me, noble Ha . . . m . . . *(He dies.)*
HAMLET: I follow thee.
    I cannot live to hear the news from England.
    The rest is silence. *(He dies.)*
FORTINBRAS: Goodnight sweet prince,   35
    And flights of angels sing thee to thy rest.
    (He turns to face away from audience.)
    Go, bid the soldiers shoot.
    (Four shots heard from off stage. All stand, bow once and exit.)
END

The Encore
A stagehand enters with a placard bearing the legend "Encore." He parades across the stage and exits. A flourish of trumpets. CLAUDIUS *and* GERTRUDE *enter.*
CLAUDIUS: Our sometime sister, now our Queen,
    (HAMLET enters.)
    have we taken to wife.
HAMLET: That it should come to this!
(CLAUDIUS and GERTRUDE exit. Sound of wind. HORATIO enters.)
HORATIO: My lord. I saw him yesternight—
    The King, your father.   5
HAMLET: Angels and ministers of grace defend us! *(He exits, running,*
    through rest of speech.) Something is rotten in the state of Denmark.
(GHOST enters above.)
GHOST: I am thy father's spirit.
    The serpent that did sting thy father's life.
(HAMLET enters above.)
    Now wears his crown .   10
HAMLET: O my prophetic soul!
    Hereafter I shall think meet
    To put an antic disposition on.
(They exit. Short flourish of trumpets. Enter POLONIUS below, running.)

POLONIUS: Look where sadly the poor wretch comes.

(POLONIUS *exits, running.* HAMLET *enters.*)

HAMLET: I have heard that guilty creatures sitting at a play   15
Have by the very cunning of the scene been struck.

(*Enter* CLAUDIUS, GERTRUDE, OPHELIA, MARCELLUS *and* HORATIO *joking. All sit to watch imaginary play.*)

If he but blench, I know my course.

(*Masque music.* CLAUDIUS *rises.*)

The King rises!

ALL: Give o'er the play!

(*Exeunt* ALL *except* GERTRUDE *and* HAMLET.)

HAMLET: I'll take the ghost's word for a thousand pounds.   20

(POLONIUS *enters, goes behind arras. Short flourish of trumpets.*)

Mother, you have my father much offended.

GERTRUDE: Help!

POLONIUS: Help, Ho!

HAMLET (*He stabs* POLONIUS.): Dead for a ducat, dead!

(POLONIUS *falls dead off stage.* GERTRUDE *and* HAMLET *exit. Short flourish of trumpets.* CLAUDIUS *enters followed by* HAMLET.)

CLAUDIUS: Hamlet, this deed must send thee hence.   25

(HAMLET *exits.*)

Do it, England.

(CLAUDIUS *exits.* OPHELIA *enters and falls to the ground. Gravestone rises to hide her. Bell tolls twice.* GRAVEDIGGER *and* HAMLET *enter.*)

HAMLET: A pirate gave us chase. I alone became their prisoner. (*He takes skull from* GRAVEDIGGER.) Alas poor Yorick—but soft (*He returns skull to* GRAVEDIGGER.)—This is I, Hamlet the Dane!

(GRAVEDIGGER *exits.* LAERTES *enters.*)

LAERTES: The devil take thy soul!   30

(*They grapple, then break. Enter* OSRIC *between them with swords. They draw. Enter* CLAUDIUS *and* GERTRUDE *with goblets.*)

HAMLET: Come on, Sir!

(LAERTES *and* HAMLET *fight. Pause.*)

OSRIC: A hit, a very palpable hit

CLAUDIUS: Give him the cup. Gertrude, do not drink!

GERTRUDE: I am poisoned? (*She dies.*)

LAERTES: Hamlet, thou art slain? (*He dies.*)   35

HAMLET: Then venom to thy work! (*He kills* CLAUDIUS.)
The rest is silence. (*He dies.*)

(*Two shots off stage.*)

Using Genre to Focus Writing and Discussion

To write about any genre, we must establish the characteristics that define it. Remember that in most cases, the label of "genre" comes after the creation of the text. The generic label is a critical tool that we can use to group similar works together, and it is quite appropriate to consider a single work in multiple generic categories.

- To define the genre, first consider which specific works we have grouped together. What common elements do these works share? What is the rationale for this particular grouping?

- How important are these particular elements to understanding each work?

- How do we understand each of the works better because we have grouped them in this manner?

- To what extent is our definition of this genre something that the authors themselves are conscious of? How can you demonstrate this consciousness? For instance, are there allusions to other works within the genre or discussions of conventions within the work itself or disruptions of the generic conventions within the work?

- What aspects of the work does our attention to genre keep us from considering?

- What other genres might we use to group any of the works that we have gathered here?

- Considerations of genre are often fairly clear in the field of film. Think of a recent film that you think belongs to a well-established genre. What would you call the genre? What elements are repeated? What expectations are invoked? Does this film disrupt any conventions? How would you describe the disruption? What is the effect of both the conventions and the disruptions?

Anthology

HORROR: A CRITIC WRITES ABOUT THE HORROR GENRE

One of the most recognizable genres in film is the horror film in which vampires, zombies, aliens, demons, ghosts, serial killers, or some other monstrous incarnations of evil disrupt the tranquility of the real world, or at least the real world as it is presented in the opening scenes of the film. This genre has often been put down as less serious, less worthy of consideration than other films, but it is a genre that has long been popular enough that its conventions are familiar.

Thinking about categories is a useful strategy for beginning your own analysis of any film or work of literature. As you put multiple works together into a single category, you establish a set of attributes that these works share. The act of classifying itself is analysis—what differences are significant enough that they might require a new category. As you classify, you must consistently test and apply the standards that you have developed, and if you are to present your category to anyone else, you must explain what elements you have used to define this group and to illustrate how this group is distinct from other groups.

In this section, we have included Paulo Hudson's 2009 review of Rob Zombie's *Halloween II*, not because we expect anyone to have seen this particular iteration of this horror franchise but because, in his review, Hudson situates the film within the horror genre and shows how horror itself is a reflection of the society that produces and consumes it. As you read Hudson's essay, pay close attention to his techniques.

- *Definition:* What are the specific conventions of the horror genre that Hudson lists (for instance, "purposeful illogic" and "resistance to solutions")? Are there conventions of the horror genre that he has left out? How do you know about these? Why does he focus on those that he has chosen? Are there any aspects of this particular film that might not fit into the definition that he has presented here?
- *Thesis:* What is Hudson's thesis in this essay? Does he recommend the film? What is his main point in the essay?
- *Summary:* How much of the plot does Hudson present?
- *Other film examples:* How does Hudson use examples of other films or directors to define what constitutes a horror film or a tradition within horror films?
- *Analysis:* Find specific moments in the essay where Hudson presents his own analysis of the genre (for example, "defying logic is an essential part of the nightmare quality"). How does this analysis relate to his purpose in this essay?

As you look at the works in this section, begin to refine your own definition of the genre of horror. To what extent does each of the works included here fit the definition that you have created?

"In the Black Mill" is a work that self-consciously adopts the conventions of pulp fiction. This short story may include every element that is required within the horror genre. Although the story was written by Michael Chabon, he has created a fictional narrator "August Van Zorn" to present this genre work. The young archeologist defies numerous warnings to study ancient tribal rituals outside an insular industrial town and the mysterious mill at its center. The language of the entire story is not at all natural—it echoes the stilted artificiality of early-twentieth-century genre fiction: "I immediately noted the one structure that, while it did nothing to elevate my opinion of my new hometown, altered the humdrum aspect of Plunkettsburg sufficiently to make it remarkable, and also sinister." The adjectives alone promise that all is not as it seems in this mill town.

George R. R. Martin's *Sandkings* begins with Simon Kress (on planet Baldur) undisturbed by the legal restrictions that might prevent his purchase of exotic creatures. He ignores the instructions of the pet trader who sells him a sandking colony, and Kress provokes the creatures to fight with one another.

Christopher Marlowe's *The Tragical History of the Life and Death of Doctor Faustus* may seem an unlikely choice to include within the horror genre. This play was written about four hundred years before the short stories that we have included here. It is a play rather than a short story. Its subjects appear, on the surface, to adhere to a religious ideology far removed from the planet Baldur or the industrial town of Plunkettsburg. But when Faustus opens the forbidden book of spells to summon Mephistopheles, how different are his actions from those of the teenagers in just about any horror film who leave the safety of their cabin to go into the woods (or anywhere they have been warned against going)? Yes, of course there are differences, but once we set the stories within the same category, we can begin to explore how and why these differences are interesting. One observation might be that the actions that take place in *Faustus* seem more real and that the consequences seem more serious. We might say that it is a story about morality. Are the other stories here as well as the genre of the horror film also morality tales? Is the horror that we feel at the end of the play any more terrifying than what we experience at the end of one of the other stories? How might we relate this observation to Hudson's observation of the audience at *Halloween II* that was watching to laugh at the horror?

Consider our choices in this section (and throughout this book) as the beginning of a conversation. What aspects of a particular work do we emphasize because we have placed it within this particular genre? How is that emphasis appropriate to our understanding of that work? What aspects of the work don't seem to fit into this genre? Or where do we see tension between our understanding of that work and our understanding of the genre? Remember that, for our writing, tension is helpful—if we need to resolve tension, we have something to write about.

REVIEW

Paulo Hudson (1984–   )

Here We Go Again: the Latest Entry in the *Halloween* Franchise (2009)

Michael Myers, the demonic character at the center of the *Halloween* franchise, is a hard man to kill. Over the course of ten films, he has been shot, stabbed, tumbled to the depths of an open mine, injected with acid, burned, beaten, and beheaded. The list could go on. The franchise itself seems nearly as durable. It has been critically panned, copied, parodied, and "re-booted." But Michael Myers and the films he inhabits do carry on, most recently in director Rob Zombie's *Halloween II*.

The "II" calls for attention. The oddity of this being a second *Halloween II* (the first arrived in theaters in the fall of 1981) makes the title seem a joke. But in the mind of the all too serious Zombie, there is more likely a bold statement intended—a claim that he has dismissed excess narrative baggage and started fresh with the two films he has written and directed. Originality may be his first line of defense against those inclined to dismiss the project as commercial and dramatic overkill. To his credit, Zombie does indeed give us new story elements that accent the psychology of his main characters; he cleverly integrates popular songs to underscore the tension between the mundane and the macabre; and on occasion he pauses amidst the frenzied bloody action scenes to provide gauzy atmospheric and symbolic dream images that cast us back to who-knows-what primal traumas. Zombie possesses a creative quality well suited to the demands of the horror film: he embraces weirdness without reservation.

But I still left the theater wondering: is there anything new under the sun—or in this case, moon—for those who squeal or suffer through the *Halloween II* of Rob Zombie? The stuff of the modern horror film remains the stuff of the gothic—that is to say, the nightmares of adolescence. The genre long ago settled into a very deep groove. Any one of the ten *Halloween* movies (or any of *The Nightmare on Elm Street* movies, or the *Friday the 13ᵗʰ* movies, and so on) pits an old evil against young people. Those young people may represent innocence, or they may express feelings of entitlement that come with early sexual experience. Either way, the Michaels, Jasons, or Freddys of the dark side will have nothing of it. They attack the very idea of life.

More specifically, they attack settled notions of normal life. The Haddonfield of the Halloween movies is a decidedly ordinary midwestern town. Sheriff Brakett (Brad Dourif) is a regular guy with a conventionally pretty daughter, Annie (Danielle Harris). It's not a stretch to think of them as living on Elm Street, or having extended family living out west in the Sunnydale of TV's

Buffy, the Vampire Slayer. The routines of middle class life are essential to the fabric of these movies, because it's just these routines that have to be violated.

There are of course other recurring features. How often do we see in horror films characters doing exactly what they should not do? Laurie Strode (the prime target played gamely by Scout Taylor-Compton) learns that she is Michael's sister, Angel Myers; that grim revelation drives her to seek solace at a party with friends. Anyone who watches the film knows that that party won't end well; Laurie should surely know thatl! But she somehow doesn't and her friends die horribly and she is captured. Then, when Michael carries Laurie away to an abandoned warehouse, Dr. Loomis (played wearily by Malcolm McDowell) chooses to enter the warehouse in order to talk Michael into letting Laurie go. So much for Dr. Loomis's psychiatric acumen. But such "what are they thinking" moments shouldn't be dismissed as clumsy storytelling; defying logic is an essential part of the nightmare quality at the core of this and every slasher movie. As we all know, in nightmares things do *not* make sense.

The purposeful illogic of all such unaccountable actions is typically complemented in horror films by foregrounding the futility of explanations. From the start of the *Halloween* series, Dr. Loomis was doing what he could to stop Michael by understanding him. In some horror movies, a detective takes on the role of the failed rationalist. And in others, professional experts on the paranormal step in to help and do not (think, for example, of the well-intended but ultimately hapless academics enlisted by the family in *Poltergeist*). If someone was able to pull things together and explain everything, we'd achieve a sense of closure and peace that has no place in a horror film.

And this resistance to solutions brings us back to the fact that you just can't keep a demon killer buried, at least not for long. Taylor Mane, the actor with the thankless task of playing the killer behind the mask, may not be back, but Michael Myers will be, in some form at least. At the end of this latest *Halloween II*, it appears that Sherriff Brackett has finally killed Michael. This time, Michael Myers really must be dead as his bullet-riddled body falls upon the sharp blades of farm equipment. But we don't have to wait long to learn that he is more displaced than dead. As the film nears the final credits, we see Laurie Strode emerge from the burning warehouse. She wears her brother's mask and behind it perhaps a wicked smile. She is Angel Myer, Michael's double. I'm sure we'll see her again.

FICTION

Michael Chabon (1963–)

Michael Chabon grew up in Pittsburgh, Pennsylvania, and Columbia, Maryland. He studied at Carnegie Mellon University and graduated from the University of Pittsburgh. He earned an MFA from the University of California, Irvine. Chabon's first novel was *The Mysteries of Pittsburgh* (1988). His second, *Wonder Boys* (1995), was adapted for the screen. His novel *The Adventures of Kavalier and Clay* (2000) won the Pulitzer Prize for Fiction. He has also published nonfiction works such as *Manhood for Amateurs: The Pleasures and Regrets of a Husband, Father, and Son* (2009). Chabon is a staunch defender of genre fiction, especially of the primacy of plot within novels. In addition to supporting others who write such fiction, he has written in the fantasy and detective genres. The "narrator" of the story is fictional author August Van Zorn who appears in other works by Chabon and for whom Chabon has constructed a fictional bibliography.

In the Black Mill (1999)

By August Van Zorn

In the fall of 1948, when I arrived in Plunkettsburg to begin the fieldwork I hoped would lead to a doctorate in archaeology, there were still a good number of townspeople living there whose memories stretched back to the time, in the final decade of the previous century, when the soot-blackened hills that encircle the town fairly swarmed with savants and mad diggers. In 1892 the discovery, on a hilltop overlooking the Miskahannock River, of the burial complex of a hitherto-unknown tribe of Mound Builders had set off a frenzy of excavation and scholarly poking around that made several careers, among them that of the aged hero of my profession who was chairman of my dissertation committee. It was under his redoubtable influence that I had taken up the study of the awful, illustrious Miskahannocks, with their tombs and bone pits, a course that led me at last, one gray November afternoon, to turn my overladen fourthhand Nash off the highway from Pittsburgh to Morgantown, and to navigate, tightly gripping the wheel, the pitted ghost of a roadbed that winds up through the Yuggogheny Hills, then down into the broad and gloomy valley of the Miskahannock.

As I negotiated that endless series of hairpin and blind curves, I was afforded an equally endless series of dispiriting partial views of the place where I would spend the next ten months of my life. Like many of its neighbors in that iron-veined country, Plunkettsburg was at first glance unprepossessing—a low, rusting little city, with tarnished onion domes and huddled houses, drab as an armful of dead leaves strewn along the ground. But as I left the last hill behind me and got my first unobstructed look, I immediately noted the one structure that, while it did nothing to elevate my opinion of my new home, altered the humdrum aspect of Plunkettsburg sufficiently to make it remarkable, and also sinister. It stood off to the east of town, in a zone of weeds and rust-colored earth, a vast, black box, bristling with spiky chimneys, extending over some five acres or more, dwarfing everything around it. This was, I knew at once, the famous Plunkettsburg Mill. Evening was coming on, and in the half-light its windows winked and flickered with inner fire, and its towering stacks vomited smoke into the autumn twilight. I shuddered, and then cried out. So intent had I been on the ghastly black apparition of the mill that I had nearly run my car off the road.

" 'Here in this mighty fortress of industry,' " I quoted aloud in the tone of a newsreel narrator, reassuring myself with the ironic reverberation of my voice, " 'turn the great cogs and thrust the relentless pistons that forge the pins and trusses of the American dream.' " I was recalling the words of a chamber of commerce brochure I had received last week from my hosts, the antiquities department of Plunkettsburg College, along with particulars of my lodging and library privileges. They were anxious to have me; it had been many years since the publication of my chairman's *Miskahannock Surveys* had effectively settled all answerable questions—save, I hoped, one—about the vanished tribe and consigned Plunkettsburg once again to the mists of academic oblivion and the thick black effluvia of its satanic mill.

"So what is there left to say about that pointy-toothed crowd?" said Carlotta Brown-Jenkin, draining her glass of brandy. The chancellor of Plunkettsburg College and chairwoman of the antiquities department had offered to stand me to dinner on my first night in town. We were sitting in the Hawaiian-style dining room of a Chinese restaurant downtown. Brown-Jenkin was herself appropriately antique, a gaunt old girl in her late seventies, her nearly hairless scalp worn and yellowed, the glint of her eyes, deep within their cavernous sockets, like that of ancient coins discovered by torchlight. "I quite thought that your distinguished mentor had revealed all their bloody mysteries."

"Only the women filed their teeth," I reminded her, taking another swal- 5
low of Indian Ring beer, the local brew, which I found to possess a dark, not entirely pleasant savor of autumn leaves or damp earth. I gazed around the low room with its ersatz palm thatching and garlands of wax orchids. The only other people in the place were a man on wooden crutches with a pinned-up trouser leg and a man with a wooden hand, both of them drinking Indian Ring, and the bartender, an extremely fat woman in a thematically correct but hideous red muumuu. My hostess had assured me, without a great deal of enthusiasm, that we were about to eat the best-cooked meal in town.

"Yes, yes," she recalled, smiling tolerantly. Her particular field of study was great Carthage, and no doubt, I thought, she looked down on my unlettered band of savages. "They considered pointed teeth to be the essence of female beauty."

"That is, of course, the theory of my distinguished mentor," I said, study-ing the label on my beer bottle, on which there was printed Thelder's 1894 engraving of the Plunkettsburg Ring, which was also reproduced on the cover of *Miskahannock Surveys*.

"You do not concur?" said Brown-Jenkin.

"I think that there may in fact be other possibilities."

"Such as?"   10

At this moment the waiter arrived, bearing a tray laden with plates of unidentifiable meats and vegetables that glistened in garish sauces the colors of women's lipstick. The steaming dishes emitted an overpowering blast of vinegar, as if to cover some underlying stench. Feeling ill, I averted my eyes from the food and saw that the waiter, a thickset, powerful man with bland Slavic features, was missing two of the fingers on his left hand. My stomach revolted. I excused myself from the table and ran directly to the bathroom.

"Nerves," I explained to Brown-Jenkin when I returned, blushing, to the table. "I'm excited about starting my research."

"Of course," she said, examining me critically. With her napkin she wiped a thin red dribble of sauce from her chin. "I quite understand."

"There seem to be an awful lot of missing limbs in this room," I said, trying to lighten my mood. "Hope none of them ended up in the food."

The chancellor stared at me, aghast.   15

"A very bad joke," I said. "My apologies. My sense of humor was not, I'm afraid, widely admired back in Boston, either."

"No," she agreed, with a small, unamused smile. "Well." She patted the long, thin strands of yellow hair atop her head. "It's the *mill*, of course."

"Of course," I said, feeling a bit dense for not having puzzled this out myself. "Dangerous work they do there, I take it."

"The mill has taken a piece of half the men in Plunkettsburg," Brown-Jenkin said, sounding almost proud. "Yes, its terribly dangerous work." There had crept into her voice a boosterish tone of admiration that could not fail to remind me of the chamber of commerce brochure. "*Important* work."

"Vitally important," I agreed, and to placate her I heaped my plate with   20
colorful, luminous, indeterminate meat, a gesture for which I paid dearly through all the long night that followed.

I took up residence in Murrough House, just off the campus of Plunkettsburg College. It was a large, rambling structure, filled with hidden passages, queerly shaped rooms, and staircases leading nowhere, built by the notorious lady magnate, "the Robber Baroness," Philippa Howard Murrough, founder of the college, noted spiritualist and author and dark genius of the Plunkettsburg Mill. She had spent the last four decades of her life, and a considerable part of her manufacturing fortune, adding to, demolishing, and rebuilding her home. On her death the resultant warren, a chimera of brooding Second Empire gables, peaked Victorian turrets, and baroque porticoes with a coat of glossy black ivy, passed into the hands of the private girls' college she had endowed, which converted it to a faculty club and lodgings for visiting scholars. I had a round turret room on the fourth and uppermost floor. There were no other visiting scholars in the house and, according to the porter, this had been the case for several years.

Old Halicek, the porter, was a bent, slow-moving fellow who lived with his daughter and grandson in a suite of rooms somewhere in the unreachable lower regions of the house. He too had lost a part of his body to the great mill in his youth—his left ear. It had been reduced, by a device that Halicek called a Dodson line extractor, to a small pink ridge nestled in the lee of his bushy white sideburns. His daughter, Mrs. Eibonas, oversaw a small staff of two maids and a waiter and did the cooking for the dozen or so faculty members who took their lunches at Murrough House every day. The waiter was Halicek's grandson, Dexter Eibonas, an earnest, good-looking, affable redhead of seventeen who was a favorite among the college faculty. He was intelligent, curious, widely if erratically read. He was always pestering me to take him out to dig in the mounds, and while I would not have been averse to his pleasant company, the terms of my agreement with the board of the college, who were the trustees of the site, expressly forbade the recruiting of local workmen. Nevertheless I gave him books on archaeology and kept him abreast of my discoveries, such as they were. Several of the Plunkettsburg professors, I learned, had also taken an interest in the development of his mind.

"They sent me up to Pittsburgh last winter," he told me one evening about a month into my sojourn, as he brought me a bottle of Ring and a plate of Mrs. Eibonas's famous kielbasa with sauerkraut. Professor Brown-Jenkin had been much mistaken, in my opinion, about the best-laid table in town. During the most tedious, chilly, and profitless stretches of my scratchings-about in the bleak, flinty Yuggoghenies, I was often sustained solely by thoughts of Mrs. Eibonas's homemade sausages and cakes. "I had an interview with the dean of engineering at Tech. Professor Collier even paid for a hotel for Mother and me."

"And how did it go?"

"Oh, it went fine, I guess," said Dexter. "I was accepted."   25

"Oh," I said, confused. The autumn semester at Carnegie Tech, I imagined, would have been ending that very week.

"Have you—have you deferred your admission?"

"Deferred it indefinitely, I guess. I told them no thanks." Dexter had, in an excess of nervous energy, been snapping a tea towel back and forth. He stopped. His normally bright eyes took on a glazed, I would almost have said a dreamy, expression. "I'm going to work in the mill."

"The *mill*?" I said, incredulous. I looked at him to see if he was teasing me, but at that moment he seemed to be entertaining only the pleasantest imaginings of his labors in that fiery black castle. I had a sudden vision of his pleasant face rendered earless, and looked away. "Forgive my asking, but why would you want to do that?"

"My father did it," said Dexter, his voice dull. "His father, too. I'm on the   30 hiring list." The light came back into his eyes, and he resumed snapping the towel. "Soon as a place opens up, I'm going in."

He left me and went back into the kitchen, and I sat there shuddering. *I'm going in.* The phrase had a heroic, doomed ring to it, like the pronounce-ment of a fireman about to enter his last burning house. Over the course of the previous month I'd had ample opportunity to observe the mill and its effect on the male population of Plunkettsburg. Casual observation, in local markets and bars, in the lobby of the Orpheum on State Street, on the side-walks, in Birch's general store out on Gray Road where I stopped for coffee and cigarettes every morning on my way up to the mound complex, had led me to estimate that in truth, fully half of the townsmen had lost some visible portion of their anatomies to Murrough Manufacturing, Inc. And yet all my attempts to ascertain how these often horribly grave accidents had befallen their bent, maimed, or limping victims were met, invariably, with an explanation at once so detailed and so vague, so rich in mechanical jargon and yet so free of actual information, that I had never yet succeeded in producing in my mind an adequate picture of the incident in question, or, for that matter, of what kind of deadly labor was performed in the black mill.

What, precisely, was manufactured in that bastion of industrial democ-racy and fount of the Murrough millions? I heard the trains come sighing and moaning into town in the middle of the night, clanging as they were shunted into the mill sidings. I saw the black diesel trucks, emblazoned with the crim-son initial M, lumbering through the streets of Plunkettsburg on their way to and from the loading docks. I had two dozen conversations, over endless mugs of Indian Ring, about shift schedules and union activities (invariably quashed) and company picnics, about ore and furnaces, metallurgy and turbines. I heard the resigned, good-natured explanations of men sliced open by Rawlings diva-gators, ground up by spline presses, mangled by steam sorters, half-decapitated by rolling Hurley plates. And yet after four months in Plunkettsburg I was no closer to understanding the terrible work to which the people of that town sac-rificed, with such apparent goodwill, the bodies of their men.

I took to haunting the precincts of the mill in the early morning as the six o'clock shift was coming on and late at night as the graveyard men streamed through the iron gates, carrying their black lunch pails. The fence, an elaborate Victorian confection of wickedly tipped, thick iron pikes trailed with iron ivy, enclosed the mill yard at such a distance from the mountainous factory itself that it was impossible for me to get near enough to see anything but the glow of huge fires through the begrimed mesh windows. I applied at the company offices in town for admission, as a visitor, to the plant but was told by the receptionist, rather rudely, that the Plunkettsburg Mill was not a tourist facility. My fascination with the place grew so intense and distracting that I neglected my work; my wanderings through the abandoned purlieus of the savage Miska-hannocks grew desultory and ruminative, my discoveries of artifacts, never frequent, dwindled to almost nothing, and I made fewer and fewer entries in my journal. Finally, one exhausted morning, after an entire night spent lying in my bed at Murrough House staring out the leaded window at a sky that was bright orange with the reflected fire of the mill, I decided I had had enough.

I dressed quickly, in plain tan trousers and a flannel work shirt. I went down to the closet in the front hall, where I found a drab old woolen coat and a watch cap that I pulled down over my head. Then I stepped outside. The terrible orange flashes had subsided and the sky was filled with stars. I hurried across town to the east side, to Stan's Diner on Mill Street, where I knew I would find the day shift wolfing down ham and eggs and pancakes. I slipped between two large men at the long counter and ordered coffee. When one of my neighbors got up to go to the toilet, I grabbed his lunch pail, threw down a handful of coins, and hurried over to the gates of the mill, where I joined the crowd of men. They looked at me oddly, not recognizing me, and I could see them murmuring to one another in puzzlement. But the earliness of the morning or an inherent reserve kept them from saying anything. They figured, I suppose, that whoever I was, I was somebody else's problem. Only one man, tall, with thinning yellow hair, kept his gaze on me for more than a moment. His eyes, I was surprised to see, looked very sad.

"You shouldn't be here, buddy," he said, not unkindly.   35

I felt myself go numb. I had been caught.

"What? Oh, no, I–I–"

The whistle blew. The crowd of men, swelled now to more than a hundred, jerked to life and waited, nervous, on the balls of their feet, for the gates to open. The man with the yellow hair seemed to forget me. In the distance an equally large crowd of men emerged from the belly of the mill and headed toward us. There was a grinding of old machinery, the creak of stressed iron, and then the ornamental gates rolled away. The next instant I was caught up in the tide of men streaming toward the mill, borne along like a cork. Halfway there our group intersected with the graveyard shift and in the ensuing chaos of bodies and hellos I was sure my plan was going to work. I was going to see, at last, the inside of the mill.

I felt something, someone's fingers, brush the back of my neck, and then I was yanked backward by the collar of my coat. I lost my footing and fell to the ground. As the changing shifts of workers flowed around me I looked up and saw a huge man standing over me, his arms folded across his chest. He was wearing a black jacket emblazoned on the breast with a large M. I tried to stand, but he pushed me back down.

"You can just stay right there until the police come," he said.   40

"Listen," I said. My research, clearly, was at an end. My scholarly privileges would be revoked. I would creep back to Boston, where, of course, my committee and, above all, my chair would recommend that I quit the department. "You don't have to do that."

Once more I tried to stand, and this time the company guard threw me back to the ground so hard and so quickly that I couldn't break my fall with my hands. The back of my head slammed against the pavement. A passing worker stepped on my outstretched hand. I cried out.

"Hey," said a voice. "Come on, Moe. You don't need to treat him that way."

It was the sad-eyed man with the yellow hair. He interposed himself between me and my attacker.

"Don't do this, Ed," said the guard. "I'll have to write you up."   45

I rose shakily to my feet and started to stumble away, back toward the gates. The guard tried to reach around Ed, to grab hold of me. As he lunged forward, Ed stuck out his foot, and the guard went sprawling.

"Come on, professor," said Ed, putting his arm around me. "You better get out of here."

"Do I know you?" I said, leaning gratefully on him.

"No, but you know my nephew, Dexter. He pointed you out to me at the pictures one night."

"Thank you," I said, when we reached the gate. He brushed some dust   50
from the back of my coat, handed me the knit stocking cap, then took a black bandanna from the pocket of his dungarees. He touched a corner of it to my mouth, and it came away marked with a dark stain.

"Only a little blood," he said. "You'll be all right. You just make sure to stay clear of this place from now on." He brought his face close to mine, filling my nostrils with the sharp medicinal tang of his aftershave. He lowered his voice to a whisper. "And stay off the beer."

"What?"

"Just stay off it." He stood up straight and returned the bandanna to his back pocket. "I haven't taken a sip in two weeks." I nodded, confused. I had been drinking two, three, sometimes four bottles of Indian Ring every night, finding that it carried me effortlessly into profound and dreamless sleep.

"Just tell me one thing," I said.

"I can't say nothing else, professor."   55

"It's just—what is it you do, in there?"

"Me?" he said, pointing to his chest. "I operate a sprue extruder."

"Yes, yes," I said, "but what does a sprue extruder *do?* What is it *for?*"

He looked at me patiently but a little remotely, a distracted parent with an inquisitive child.

"It's for extruding sprues," he said. "What else?" Thus repulsed, humili-   60
ated, and given good reason to fear that my research was in imminent jeopardy of being brought to an end, I resolved to put the mystery of the mill out of my mind once and for all and get on with my real business in Plunkettsburg. I went out to the site of the mound complex and worked with my brush and little hand spade all through that day, until the light failed. When I got home,

exhausted, Mrs. Eibonas brought me a bottle of Indian Ring and I gratefully
drained it before I remembered Ed's strange warning. I handed the sweating
bottle back to Mrs. Eibonas. She smiled.

"Can I bring you another, professor?" she said.

"No, thank you," I said. Her smile collapsed. She looked very disappointed. "All right," she said. For some reason the thought of disappointing
her bothered me greatly, so I told her, "Maybe one more."

I retired early and dreamed dreams that were troubled by the scratching of
iron on earth and by a clamoring tumult of men. The next morning I got up
and went straight out to the site again.

For it was going to take work, a lot of work, if my theory was ever going to
bear fruit. During much of my first several months in Plunkettsburg I had been
hampered by snow and by the degree to which the site of the Plunkettsburg
Mounds—a broad plateau on the eastern slope of Mount Orrert, on which
there had been excavated, in the 1890s, thirty-six huge molars of packed earth,
each the size of a two-story house—had been picked over and disturbed by that
early generation of archaeologists. Their methods had not in every case been as
fastidious as one could have hoped. There were numerous areas of old digging
where the historical record had, through carelessness, been rendered illegible.
Then again, I considered, as I gazed up at the ivy-covered flank of the ancient,
artificial hillock my mentor had designated B-3, there was always the possibility
that my theory was wrong.

Like all the productions of academe, I suppose, my theory was composed   65
of equal parts of indebtedness and spite. I had formulated it in a kind of rebellion against that grand old man of the field, my chairman, the very person who
had inculcated in me a respect for the deep, subtle savagery of the
Miskahannock Indians. His view—the standard one—was that the culture of the
builders of the Plunkettsburg Mounds, at its zenith, had expressed, to a degree
unequaled in the Western Hemisphere up to that time, the aestheticizing of
the nihilist impulse. They had evolved all the elaborate social structures—texts,
rituals, decorative arts, architecture—of any of the worlds great religions:
dazzling feats of abstract design represented by the thousands of baskets, jars,
bowls, spears, tablets, knives, flails, axes, codices, robes, and so on that were
housed and displayed with such pride in the museum of my university, back in
Boston. But the Miskahannocks, insofar as anyone had ever been able to determine (and many had tried), worshiped nothing, or, as my teacher would have
it, Nothing. They acknowledged neither gods nor goddesses, conversed with no
spirits or familiars. Their only purpose, the focus and the pinnacle of their
artistic genius, was the killing of men. Nobody knew how many of the unfortunate males of the neighboring tribes had fallen victim to the Miskahannocks'
delicate artistry of torture and dismemberment. In 1903 Professor William
Waterman of Yale discovered fourteen separate ossuary pits along the banks of

the river, not far from the present site of the mill. These had contained enough bones to frame the bodies of seven thousand men and boys. And nobody knew why they had died. The few tattered, fragmentary blood-on-tanbark texts so far discovered concerned themselves chiefly with the recurring famines that plagued Miskahannock civilization and, it was generally theorized, had been responsible for its ultimate collapse. The texts said nothing about the sacred arts of killing and torture. There was, my teacher had persuasively argued, one reason for this. The deaths had been purposeless; their justification, the cosmic purposelessness of life itself.

Now, once I had settled myself on spiteful rebellion, as every good pupil eventually must, there were two possible paths available to me. The first would have been to attempt to prove beyond a doubt that the Miskahannocks had, in fact, worshiped some kind of god, some positive, purposive entity, however bloodthirsty. I chose the second path. I accepted the godlessness of the Miska-hannocks. I rejected the refined, reasoning nihilism my mentor had postulated (and to which, as I among very few others knew, he himself privately subscribed). The Miskahannocks, I hoped to prove, had had another motive for their killing: They were hungry; according to the tattered scraps of the Plunkettsburg Codex, very hungry indeed. The filed teeth my professor subsumed to the larger aesthetic principles he elucidated thus had, in my view, a far simpler and more utilitarian purpose. Unfortunately, the widespread incidence of cannibalism among the women of a people vanished four thousand years since was proving rather diffi-cult to establish. So far, in fact, I had found no evidence of it at all.

I knelt to untie the canvas tarp I had stretched across my digging of the previous day. I was endeavoring to take an inclined section of B-3, cutting a passage five feet high and two feet wide at a 30-degree angle to the horizontal. This endeavor in itself was a kind of admission of defeat, since B-3 was one of two mounds, the other being its neighbor B-5, designated a "null mound" by those who had studied the site. It had been thoroughly pierced and penetrated and found to be utterly empty; reserved, it was felt, for the mortal remains of a dynasty that failed. But I had already made careful searches of the thirty-four other tombs of the Miskahannock queens. The null mounds were the only ones remaining. If, as I anticipated, I found no evidence of anthropophagy, I would have to give up on the mounds entirely and start looking elsewhere. There were persistent stories of other bone pits in the pleats and hollows of the Yuggoghenies. Perhaps I could find one, a fresh one, one not trampled and cor-rupted by the primitive methods of my professional forebears.

I peeled back the sheet of oiled canvas I had spread across my handiwork and received a shock. The passage, which over the course of the previous day I had managed to extend a full four feet into the side of the mound, had been completely filled in. Not merely filled in; the thick black soil had been tamped down and a makeshift screen of ivy had been drawn across it. I took a step back and looked around the site, certain all at once that I was being observed. There were only the crows in the treetops. In the distance I could hear the Murrough trucks on the tortuous highway, grinding gears as they climbed up out of the valley. I looked down at the ground by my feet and saw the faint imprint of a foot smaller than my own. A few feet from this, I found another. That was all.

I ought to have been afraid, I suppose, or at the least concerned, but at this point, I confess, I was only angry. The site was heavily fenced and posted with NO TRESPASSING signs, but apparently some local hoodlums had come up in the night and wasted all of the previous day's hard work. The motive for this vandalism eluded me, but I supposed that a lack of any discernible motive was in the nature of vandalism itself. I picked up my hand shovel and started in again on my doorway into the mound. The fifth bite I took with the little iron tooth brought out something strange. It was a black bandanna, twisted and soiled. I spread it out across my thigh and found the small, round trace of my own blood on one corner. I was bewildered, and again I looked around to see if someone was watching me. There were only the laughter and ragged fingers of the crows. What was Ed up to? Why would my rescuer want to come up onto the mountain and ruin my work? Did he think he was protecting me? I shrugged, stuffed the bandanna into a pocket, and went back to my careful digging. I worked steadily throughout the day, extending the tunnel six inches nearer than I had come yesterday to the heart of the mound, then drove home to Murrough House, my shoulders aching, my fingers stiff. I had a long, hot soak in the big bathtub down the hall from my room, smoked a pipe, and read, for the fifteenth time at least, the section in *Miskahannock Surveys* dealing with B-3. Then at 6:30 I went downstairs to find Dexter Eibonas waiting to serve my dinner, his expression blank, his eyes bloodshot. I remember being surprised that he didn't immediately demand details of my day on the dig. He just nodded, retreated into the kitchen, and returned with a heated can of soup, half a loaf of white bread, and a bottle of Ring. Naturally after my hard day I was disappointed by this fare, and I inquired as to the whereabouts of Mrs. Eibonas.

"She had some family business, professor," Dexter said, rolling up his   70
hands in his tea towel, then unrolling them again. "Sad business."

"Did somebody—die?"

"My uncle Ed," said the boy, collapsing in a chair beside me and covering his twisted features with his hands. "He had an accident down at the mill, I guess. Fell headfirst into the impact mold."

"What?" I said, feeling my throat constrict. "My God, Dexter! Something has to be done! That mill ought to be shut down!"

Dexter took a step back, startled by my vehemence. I had thought at once, of course, of the black bandanna, and now I wondered if I was not somehow responsible for Ed Eibonas's death. Perhaps the incident in the mill yard the day before, his late-night digging in the dirt of B-3 in some kind of misguided effort to help me, had left him rattled, unable to concentrate on his work, prey to accidents.

"You just don't understand," said Dexter. "It's our way of life here. There 75 isn't anything for us but the mill." He pushed the bottle of Indian Ring toward me. "Drink your beer, professor."

I reached for the glass and brought it to my lips but was swept by a sudden wave of revulsion like that which had overtaken me at the Chinese restaurant on my first night in town. I pushed back from the table and stood up, my violent start upsetting a pewter candelabra in which four tapers burned. Dexter lunged to keep it from falling over, then looked at me, surprised. I stared back, chest heaving, feeling defiant without being sure of what exactly I was defying.

"I am not going to touch another drop of that beer!" I said, the words sounding petulant and absurd as they emerged from my mouth.

Dexter nodded. He looked worried.

"All right, professor," he said, obligingly, as if he thought I might have become unbalanced. "You just go on up to your room and lie down. I'll bring you your food a little later. How about that?" The next day I lay in bed, aching, sore, and suffering from that peculiar brand of spiritual depression born largely of suppressed fear. On the following morning I roused myself, shaved, dressed in my best clothes, and went to the Church of St. Stephen, on Nolt Street, the heart of Plunkettsburg's Estonian neighborhood, for the funeral of Ed Eibonas. There was a sizable turnout, as was always the case, I was told, when there had been a death at the mill. Such deaths were reportedly uncommon; the mill was a cruel and dangerous but rarely fatal place. At Dexter's invitation I went to the dead man's house to pay my respects to the widow, and two hours later I found myself, along with most of the other male mourners, roaring drunk on some kind of fruit brandy brought out on special occasions. It may have been that the brandy burned away the jitters and anxiety of the past two days; in any case the next morning I went out to the mounds again, with a tent and a cookstove and several bags of groceries. I didn't leave for the next five days.

My hole had been filled in again, and this time there was no clue to the 80 identity of the filler, but I was determined not to let this spook me, as the saying goes. I simply dug. Ordinarily I would have proceeded cautiously, carrying the dirt out by thimblefuls and sifting each one, but I felt my time on the site growing short. I often saw cars on the access road by day, and headlight beams by night, slowing down as if to observe me. Twice a day a couple of sheriff's deputies would pull up to the Ring and sit in their car, watching. At first whenever they appeared, I stopped working, lit a cigarette, and waited for them to arrest me. But when after the first few times nothing of the sort occurred, I relaxed a little and kept on with my digging for the duration of their visit.

I was resigned to being prevented from completing my research, but before this happened I wanted to get to the heart of B-3.

On the fourth day, when I was halfway to my goal, George Birch drove out from his general store, as I had requested, with cans of stew, bottles of soda pop, and cigarettes. He was normally a dour man, but on this morning his face seemed longer than ever. I inquired if there was anything bothering him.

"Carlotta Brown-Jenkin died last night," he said. "Friend of my mother's. Tough old lady." He shook his head. "Influenza. Shame."

I remembered that awful, Technicolored meal so many months before, the steely glint of her eyes in their cavernous sockets. I did my best to look properly sympathetic.

"That is a shame," I said.

He set down the box of food and looked past me at the entrance to my 85 tunnel. The sight of it seemed to disturb him.

"You sure you know what you're doing?" he said.

I assured him that I did, but he continued to look skeptical.

"I remember the last time you archaeologist fellows came to town, you know," he said. As a matter of fact I did know this, since he told me almost every time I saw him. "I was a boy. We had just got electricity in our house."

"Things must have changed a great deal since then," I said.

"Things haven't changed at all," he snapped. He was never a cheerful man, 90 George Birch. He turned, hitching up his trousers, and limped on his wooden foot back to his truck.

That night I lay in my bedroll under the canvas roof of my tent, watching the tormented sky. The lantern hissed softly beside my head; I kept it burning low, all night long, advertising my presence to any who might seek to come and undo my work. It had been a warm, springlike afternoon, but now a cool breeze was blowing in from the north, stirring the branches of the trees over my head. After a while I drowsed a little; I fancied I could hear the distant fluting of the Miskahannock flowing over its rocky bed and, still more distant the low, insistent drumming of the machine heart in the black mill. Suddenly I sat up: The music I had been hearing, of breeze and river and far-off machinery, seemed at once very close and not at all metaphoric. I scrambled out of my bedroll and tent and stood, taut, listening, at the edge of Plunkettsburg Ring. It *was* music I heard, strange music, and it seemed to be issuing, impossibly, from the other end of the tunnel I had been digging and redigging over the past two weeks—from within mound B-3, the null mound!

I have never, generally, been plagued by bouts of great courage, but I do suffer from another vice whose outward appearance is often indistinguishable from that of bravery: I am pathologically curious. I was not brave enough, in that eldritch moment, actually to approach B-3, to investigate the source of the music I was hearing; but though every primitive impulse urged me to flee,

I stood there, listening, until the music stopped, an hour before dawn. I heard sorrow in the music, and mourning, and the beating of many small drums. And then in the full light of the last day of April, emboldened by bright sunshine and a cup of instant coffee, I made my way gingerly toward the mound. I picked up my shovel, lowered my foolish head into the tunnel, and crept carefully into the bowels of the now-silent mound. Seven hours later I felt the shovel strike something hard, like stone or brick. Then the hardness gave way, and the shovel flew abruptly out of my hands. I had reached, at last, the heart of mound B-3.

And it was not empty; oh no, not at all. There were seven sealed tombs lining the domed walls, carved stone chambers of the usual Miskahannock type, and another ten that were empty, and one, as yet unsealed, that held the unmistakable, though withered, yellow, naked, and eternally slumbering form of Carlotta Brown-Jenkin. And crouched on her motionless chest, as though prepared to devour her throat, sat a tiny stone idol, hideous, black, brandishing a set of wicked ivory fangs.

Now I gave in to those primitive impulses; I panicked. I tore out of the burial chamber as quickly as I could and ran for my car, not bothering to collect my gear. In twenty minutes I was back at Murrough House. I hurried up the front steps, intending only to go to my room, retrieve my clothes and books and papers, and leave behind Plunkettsburg forever. But when I came into the foyer I found Dexter, carrying a tray of eaten lunches back from the dining room to the kitchen. He was whistling light-heartedly and when he saw me he grinned. Then his expression changed.

"What is it?" he said, reaching out to me. "Has something happened?"   95

"Nothing," I said, stepping around him, avoiding his grasp. The streets of Plunkettsburg had been built on evil ground, and now I could only assume that every one of its citizens, even cheerful Dexter, had been altered by the years and centuries of habitation. "Everything's fine. I just have to leave town."

I started up the wide, carpeted steps as quickly as I could, mentally packing my bags and boxes with essentials, loading the car, twisting and backtracking up the steep road out of this cursed valley.

"My name came up," Dexter said. "I start tomorrow at the mill."

Why did I turn? Why did I not keep going down the long, crocked hallway and carry out my sensible, cowardly plan?

"You can't do that," I said. He started to smile, but there must have been   100 something in my face. The smile fizzed out. "You'll be killed. You'll be mangled. That good-looking mug of yours will be hideously deformed."

"Maybe," he said, trying to sound calm, but I could see that my own agitation was infecting him. "Maybe not."

"It's the women. The queens. They're alive."

"The queens are alive? What are you talking about, professor? I think you've been out on the mountain too long."

"I have to go, Dexter," I said. "I'm sorry. I can't stay here anymore. But if you have any sense at all, you'll come with me. I'll drive you to Pittsburgh. You can start at Tech. They'll help you. They'll give you a job. . . ." I could feel myself starting to babble.

Dexter shook his head. "Can't," he said. "My name came up! Shoot, I've 105 been waiting for this all my life."

"Look," I said. "All right. Just come with me, out to the Ring." I looked at my watch. "We've got an hour until dark. Just let me show you something I found out there, and then if you still want to go to work in that infernal factory, I'll shake your hand and bid you farewell."

"You'll really take me out to the site?"

I nodded. He set the tray on a deal table and untied his apron.

"Let me get my jacket," he said.

I packed my things and we drove in silence to the necropolis. I was filled 110 with regret for this course of action, with intimations of disaster. But I felt I couldn't simply leave town and let Dexter Eibonas walk willingly into that fiery eructation of the evil genius, the immemorial accursedness, of his drab Pennsylvania hometown. I couldn't leave that young, unmarked body to be broken and split on the horrid machines of the mill. As for why Dexter wasn't talking, I don't know; perhaps he sensed my mounting despair, or perhaps he was simply lost in youthful speculation on the unknown vistas that lay before him, subterranean sights forbidden and half-legendary to him since he had first come to consciousness of the world. As we turned off Gray Road onto the access road that led up to the site, he sat up straight and looked at me, his face grave with the consummate adolescent pleasure of violating rules.

"There," I said. I pointed out the window as we crested the rise. The Plunkettsburg Ring lay spread out before us, filled with jagged shadows, in the slanting, rust red light of the setting sun. From this angle the dual circular plan of the site was not apparent, and the thirty-six mounds appeared to stretch from one end of the plateau to the other, like a line of uneven teeth studding an immense, devouring jawbone.

"Let's make this quick," I said, shuddering. I handed him a spare lantern from the trunk of the Nash, and then we walked to the edge of the aboriginal forest that ran upslope from the plateau to the wind-shattered precincts of Mount Orrert's sharp peak. It was here, in the lee of a large maple tree, that I had set up my makeshift camp. At the time the shelter of that homely tree had seemed quite inviting, but now it appeared to me that the forest was the source of all the lean shadows reaching their ravening fingers across the plateau. I ducked quickly into my tent to retrieve my lantern and then hurried back to

rejoin Dexter. I thought he was looking a little uneasy now. His gait slowed
as we approached B-3. When we trudged around to confront the raw earthen
mouth of the passage I had dug, he came to a complete stop.

"We're not going inside there," he said in a monotone. I saw come into
his eyes the dull, dreamy look that was there whenever he talked about going to
work in the mill. "It isn't allowed."

"It's just for a minute, Dexter. That's all you'll need."

I put my hands on his shoulders and gave him a push, and we stumbled   115
through the dank, close passage, the light from our lanterns veering wildly
around us. Then we were in the crypt.

"No," Dexter said. The effect on him of the sight of the time-ravaged
naked body of Carlotta Brown- Jenkin, of the empty tombs, the hideous idol,
the outlandish ideograms that covered the walls, was everything I could have
hoped for. His jaw dropped, his hands clenched and unclenched, he took a
step backward. "She just died!"

"Yesterday," I agreed, trying to allay my own anxiety with a show of ironic
detachment.

"But what . . . what's she doing out here?" He shook his head quickly, as
though trying to clear it of smoke or spiderwebs.

"Don't you know?" I asked him, for I still was not completely certain of
his or any townsman's uninvolvement in the evil, at once ancient and machine-
age, that was evidently the chief business of Plunkettsburg.

"No! God, no!" He pointed to the queer, fanged idol that crouched with a   120
hungry leer on the late chancellor's hollow bosom. "God, what is that thing?"

I went over to the tomb and cautiously, as if the figure with its enormous,
obscene tusks might come to life and rip off a mouthful of my hand, picked up
the idol. It was as black and cold as space, and so heavy that it bent my hand
back at the wrist as I hefted it. With both hands I got a firm grip on it and
turned it over. On its pedestal were incised three symbols in the spiky, complex
script of the Miskahannocks, unrelated to any other known human language
or alphabet. As with all of the tribe's inscriptions, the characters had both a
phonetic and a symbolic sense. Often these were quite independent of one
another.

"Yu . . . yug . . . gog," I read, sounding it out carefully. Yuggog.

"What does that mean?"

"It doesn't mean anything, as far as I know. But it can be read another way.
It's trickier. Here's tooth . . . gut—that's hunger—and this one—" I held up the
idol toward him. He shied away. His face had gone completely pale, and there
was a look of fear in his eyes, of awareness of evil, that I found, God forgive me,
strangely gratifying. "This is a kind of general intensive, I believe. Making this
read, loosely rendered, hunger . . . itself. How odd."

"Yuggog," Dexter said softly, a thin strand of spittle joining his lips.   125

"Here," I said cruelly, tossing the heavy thing toward him. Let him go into the black mill now, I thought, after he's seen *this*. Dexter batted at the thing, knocking it to the ground. There was a sharp, tearing sound like matchwood splitting. For an instant Dexter looked utterly, cosmically startled. Then he, and the idol of Yuggog, disappeared. There was a loud thud, and a clatter, and I heard him groan. I picked up the splintered halves of the carved wooden trapdoor Dexter had fallen through and gazed down into a fairly deep, smooth-sided hole. He lay crumpled at the bottom, about eight feet beneath me, in the light of his overturned lantern.

"My God! I'm sorry! Are you all right?"

"I think I sprained my ankle," he said. He sat up and raised his lantern. His eyes got very wide. "Professor, you have to see this."

I lowered myself carefully into the hole and stared with Dexter into a great round tunnel, taller than either of us, paved with crazed human bones, stretching far beyond the pale of our lanterns.

"A tunnel," he said. "I wonder where it goes." 130

"I can only guess," I said. "And that's never good enough for me."

"Professor! You aren't—"

But I had already started into the tunnel, a decision that I attributed not to courage, of course, but to my far greater vice. I did not see that as I took those first steps into the tunnel I was in fact being bitten off, chewed, and swallowed, as it were, by the very mouth of the Plunkettsburg evil. I took small, queasy steps along the horrible floor, avoiding insofar as I could stepping on the outraged miens of human skulls, searching the smoothed, plastered walls of the tunnel for ideograms or other hints of the builders of this amazing structure. The tunnel, or at least this version of it, was well built, buttressed regularly by sturdy iron piers and lintels, and of chillingly recent vintage. Only great wealth, I thought, could have managed such a feat of engineering. A few minutes later I heard a tread behind me and saw the faint glow of a lantern. Dexter joined me, favoring his right ankle, his lantern swinging as he walked.

"We're headed northwest," I said. "We must be under the river by now."

"Under the river?" he said. "Could Indians have built a tunnel like this?" 135

"No, Dexter, they could not."

He didn't say anything for a moment as he took this information in.

"Professor, we're headed for the mill, aren't we?"

"I'm afraid we must be," I said.

We walked for three quarters of an hour, until the sound of pounding 140 machinery became audible, grew gradually unbearable, and finally exploded directly over our heads. The tunnel had run out. I looked up at the trapdoor above us. Then I heard a muffled scream. To this day I don't know if the screamer was one of the men up on the floor of the factory or Dexter Eibonas, a massive hand clapped brutally over his mouth, because the next instant, at the back of my head, a supernova bloomed and flared brightly.

I wake in an immense room, to the idiot pounding of a machine. The walls are sheets of fire flowing upward like inverted cataracts; the ceiling is lost in shadow from which, when the flames flare brightly, there emerges the vague impression of a steely web of girders among which dark things ceaselessly creep. Thick coils of rope bind my arms to my sides, and my legs are lashed at the ankles to those of the plain pine chair in which I have been propped.

It is one of two dozen chairs in a row that is one of a hundred, in a room filled with men, the slumped, crew-cut, big-shouldered ordinary men of Plunkettsburg and its neighboring towns. We are all waiting, and watching, as the women of Plunkettsburg, the servants of Yuggog, pass noiselessly among us in their soft, horrible cloaks stitched from the hides of dead men, tapping on the shoulder of now one fellow, now another. None of my neighbors, however, appears to have required the use of strong rope to conjoin him to his fate. Without a word the designated men, their blood thick with the dark earthen brew of the Ring witches, rise and follow the skins of miscreant fathers and grandfathers down to the ceremonial altar at the heart of the mill, where the priestesses of Yuggog throw oracular bones and, given the result, take hold of the man's ear, his foot, his fingers. A yellow snake, its venom presumably anesthetic, is applied to the fated extremity. Then the long knife is brought to bear, and the vast, immemorial hunger of the god of the Miskahannocks is assuaged for another brief instant. In the past three hours on this Walpurgis Night, nine men have been so treated; tomorrow, people in this bewitched town that, in a reasonable age, has learned to eat its men a little at a time, will speak, I am sure, of a series of horrible accidents at the mill. The women came to take Dexter Eibonas an hour ago. I looked away as he went under the knife, but I believe he lost the better part of his left arm to the god. I can only assume that very soon now I will feel the tap on my left shoulder of the fingers of the town librarian, the grocer's wife, of Mrs. Eibonas herself. I am guiltier by far of trespass than Ed Eibonas and do not suppose I will survive the procedure.

Strange how calm I feel in the face of all this; perhaps there remain traces of the beer in my veins, or perhaps in this hellish place there are other enchantments at work. In any case, I will at least have the satisfaction of seeing my theory confirmed, or partly confirmed, before I die, and the concomitant satisfaction, so integral to my profession, of seeing my teacher's theory cast in the dustbin. For, as I held, the Miskahannocks hungered; and hunger, black, primordial, unstanchable hunger itself, was their god. It was indeed the misguided scrambling and digging of my teacher and his colleagues, I imagine, that awakened great Yuggog from its four-thousand-year slumber. As for the black mill that fascinated me for so many months, it is a sham. The single great machine to my left takes in no raw materials and emits no ingots or sheets. It is simply an immense piston, endlessly screaming and pounding like the skin of an immense drum the ground that since the days of the Miskahannocks has been the sacred precinct of the god. The flames that flash through the windows and the smoke that proceeds from the chimneys are bits of trickery, mechanical contrivances devised, I suppose, by Philippa Howard Murrough herself, in the days when the revived spirit of Yuggog first whispered to her of its awful, eternal appetite for the flesh of men. The sole industry of Plunkettsburg is carnage, scarred and mangled bodies the only product.

One thought disturbs the perfect, poison calm with which I am suffused—the trucks that grind their way in and out of the valley, the freight trains that come clanging in the night. What cargo, I wonder, is unloaded every morning at the docks of the Plunkettsburg Mill? What burden do those trains bear away?

- How do we know that August Van Zorn is not the real author of this story?
- What aspects of his character are important to maintaining the horror genre?
- How do other characters allow Van Zorn to present his particular story?
- What details accumulate to suggest that the Black Mill is ominous?
- Collect specific examples of stilted language throughout the story.
- What is the goal of this story? Does it frighten? Does it convey a moral? Does it evoke some particular feeling?

George R. R. Martin (1948–)

Born in New Jersey, George R. R. Martin began writing at an early age. Some of his early stories are about a mythical world for his pet turtles, and he developed an early interest in comics. Martin earned degrees in journalism from Northwestern University in Illinois. His most famous works began with the novel *A Game of Thrones* (1996), the first book in the saga *A Song of Ice and Fire*. Five of the planned seven books in the series have been published at this time. Martin also writes for television and has written scripts for and co-produced the HBO series based on his books.

Sandkings (1979)

Simon Kress lived alone in a sprawling manor house among the dry, rocky hills fifty kilometers from the city. So, when he was called away unexpectedly on business, he had no neighbors he could conveniently impose on to take his pets. The carrion hawk was no problem; it roosted in the unused belfry and customarily fed itself anyway. The shambler Kress simply shooed outside and left to fend for itself; the little monster would gorge on slugs and birds and rockjocks. But the fish tank, stocked with genuine Earth piranha, posed a difficulty. Kress finally just threw a haunch of beef into the huge tank. The piranha could always eat each other if he were detained longer than expected. They'd done it before. It amused him. Unfortunately, he was detained much longer than expected this time. When he finally returned, all the fish were dead. So was the carrion hawk. The shambler had climbed up to the belfry and eaten it. Simon Kress was vexed. The next day he flew his skimmer to Asgard, a journey of some two hundred kilometers. Asgard was Baldur's largest city and boasted the oldest and largest starport as well. Kress liked to impress his friends with animals that were unusual, entertaining, and expensive; Asgard was the place to buy them. This time, though, he had poor luck. Xenopets had closed its doors, t'Etherane the Petseller tried to foist another carrion hawk off on him, and Strange Waters offered nothing more exotic than piranha, glowsharks, and spider-squids. Kress had had all those; he wanted something new. Near dusk, he found himself walking down the Rainbow Boulevard, looking for places he had not patronized before. So close to the starport, the street was lined by importers' marts. The big corporate emporiums had impressive long windows, where rare and costly alien artifacts reposed on felt cushions against dark drapes that made the interiors of the stores a mystery. Between them were the junk shops—narrow, nasty little places whose display areas were crammed with all manner of offworld bric-a-brac. Kress tried both kinds of shops, with equal dissatisfaction. Then he came across a store that was different. It was quite close to the port. Kress had never been there before. The shop occupied a small, single-story building of moderate size, set between a euphoria bar and a temple-brothel of the Secret Sisterhood. Down this far, the Rainbow Boulevard grew tacky. The shop itself was unusual. Arresting. The windows were full of mist; now a pale red, now the gray of true fog, now sparkling and golden. The mist swirled and eddied and glowed faintly from within. Kress glimpsed objects in the window—machines, pieces of art, other things he could not recognize— but he could not get a good look at any of them. The mists flowed sensuously around them, displaying a bit of first one thing and then another, then cloaking all. It was intriguing. As he watched, the mist began to form letters. One word at a time. Kress stood and read:

WO AND SHADE IMPORTERS ARTIFACTS ART LIFEFORMS
AND MISC

The letters stopped. Through the fog, Kress saw something moving. That was enough for him, that and the word "Lifeforms" in their advertisement. He swept his walking cloak over his shoulder and entered the store.

Inside, Kress felt disoriented. The interior seemed vast, much larger than he would have guessed from the relatively modest frontage. It was dimly lit, peaceful.

The ceiling was a starscape, complete with spiral nebulae, very dark and realistic, very nice. The counters all shone faintly, the better to display the merchandise within. The aisles were carpeted with ground fog. In places, it came almost to his knees and swirled about his feet as he walked.

"Can I help you?" 5

She seemed almost to have risen from the fog. Tall and gaunt and pale, she wore a practical gray jumpsuit and a strange little cap that rested well back on her head.

"Are you Wo or Shade?" Kress asked. "Or only sales help?"

"Jala Wo, ready to serve you," she replied. "Shade does not see customers. We have no sales help."

"You have quite a large establishment," Kress said. "Odd that I have never heard of you before."

"We have only just opened this shop on Baldur," the woman said. "We 10 have franchises on a number of other worlds, however. What can I sell you? Art, perhaps? You have the look of a collector. We have some fine Nor T'alush crystal carvings."

"No," Simon Kress said. "I own all the crystal carvings I desire. I came to see about a pet."

"A lifeform?"

"Yes."

"Alien?"

"Of course." 15

"We have a mimic in stock. From Celia's World. A clever little simian. Not only will it learn to speak, but eventually it will mimic your voice, inflections, gestures, even facial expressions."

"Cute," said Kress. "And common. I have no use for either, Wo. I want something exotic. Unusual. And not cute. I detest cute animals. At the moment I own a shambler. Imported from Cotho, at no mean expense. From time to time I feed him a litter of unwanted kittens. That is what I think of cute. Do I make myself understood?"

Wo smiled enigmatically. "Have you ever owned an animal that worshiped you?" she asked.

Kress grinned. "Oh, now and again. But I don't require worship, Wo. Just entertainment."

"You misunderstand me," Wo said, still wearing her strange smile. "I 20 meant worship literally."

"What are you talking about?"

"I think I have just the thing for you," Wo said. "Follow me."

She led Kress between the radiant counters and down a long, fog-shrouded aisle beneath false starlight. They passed through a wall of mist into another section of the store, and stopped before a large plastic tank. An aquarium, thought Kress.

Wo beckoned. He stepped closer and saw that he was wrong. It was a terrarium. Within lay a miniature desert about two meters square. Pale sand bleached scarlet by wan red light. Rocks: basalt and quartz and granite. In each corner of the tank stood a castle.

Kress blinked, and peered, and corrected himself; actually only three castles stood. The fourth leaned; a crumbled, broken ruin. The other three were crude but intact, carved of stone and sand. Over their battlements and through their rounded porticoes, tiny creatures climbed and scrambled. Kress pressed his face against the plastic. "Insects?" he asked.   25

"No," Wo replied. "A much more complex lifeform. More intelligent as well. Considerably smarter than your shambler. They are called sandkings."

"Insects," Kress said, drawing back from the tank. "I don't care how complex they are." He frowned. "And kindly don't try to gull me with this talk of intelligence. These things are far too small to have anything but the most rudimentary brains."

"They share hiveminds," Wo said. "Castle minds, in this case. There are only three organisms in the tank, actually. The fourth died. You see how her castle has fallen."

Kress looked back at the tank. "Hiveminds, eh? Interesting." He frowned again. "Still, it is only an oversized ant farm. I'd hoped for something better."

"They fight wars."   30

"Wars? Hmmm." Kress looked again.

"Note the colors, if you will," Wo told him. She pointed to the creatures that swarmed over the nearest castle. One was scrabbling at the tank wall. Kress studied it. It still looked like an insect to his eyes. Barely as long as his fingernail, six-limbed, with six tiny eyes set all around its body. A wicked set of mandibles clacked visibly, while two long, fine antennae wove patterns in the air. Antennae, mandibles, eyes, and legs were sooty black, but the dominant color was the burnt orange of its armor plating. "It's an insect," Kress repeated.

"It is not an insect," Wo insisted calmly. "The armored exoskeleton is shed when the sandking grows larger. If it grows larger. In a tank this size, it won't." She took Kress by the elbow and led him around the tank to the next castle. "Look at the colors here."

He did. They were different. Here the sandkings had bright red armor; antennae, mandibles, eyes, and legs were yellow. Kress glanced across the tank. The denizens of the third live castle were off-white, with red trim. "Hmmm," he said.

"They war, as I said," Wo told him. "They even have truces and alliances.   35
It was an alliance that destroyed the fourth castle in this tank. The blacks were getting too numerous, so the others joined forces to destroy them."

Kress remained unconvinced. "Amusing, no doubt. But insects fight wars too."

"Insects do not worship," Wo said.

"Eh?"

Wo smiled and pointed at the castle. Kress stared. A face had been carved into the wall of the highest tower. He recognized it. It was Jala Wo's face. "How. . . ?"

"I projected a holograph of my face into the tank, kept it there for a few   40
days. The face of god, you see? I feed them; I am always close. The sandkings have a rudimentary psionic sense. Proximity telepathy. They sense me, and worship me by using my face to decorate their buildings. All the castles have them, see." They did.

On the castle, the face of Jala Wo was serene and peaceful, and very life-like. Kress marveled at the workmanship. "How do they do it?"

"The foremost legs double as arms. They even have fingers of a sort; three small, flexible tendrils. And they cooperate well, both in building and in battle. Remember, all the mobiles of one color share a single mind."

"Tell me more," Kress said.

Wo smiled. "The maw lives in the castle. Maw is my name for her. A pun, if you will; the thing is mother and stomach both. Female, large as your fist, immobile. Actually, sandking is a bit of a misnomer. The mobiles are peasants and warriors, the real ruler is a queen. But that analogy is faulty as well. Considered as a whole, each castle is a single hermaphroditic creature."

"What do they eat?"   45

"The mobiles eat pap—predigested food obtained inside the castle. They get it from the maw after she has worked on it for several days. Their stomachs can't handle anything else, so if the maw dies, they soon die as well. The maw . . . the maw eats anything. You'll have no special expense there. Table scraps will do excellently."

"Live food?" Kress asked.

Wo shrugged. "Each maw eats mobiles from the other castles, yes."

"I am intrigued," he admitted. "If only they weren't so small."

"Yours can be larger. These sandkings are small because their tank is small.   50
They seem to limit their growth to fit available space. If I moved these to a larger tank, they'd start growing again."

"Hmmmm. My piranha tank is twice this size, and vacant. It could be cleaned out, filled with sand. . . ."

"Wo and Shade would take care of the installation. It would be our pleasure."

"Of course," said Kress, "I would expect four intact castles."

"Certainly," Wo said. They began to haggle about the price.

* * *

Three days later Jala Wo arrived at Simon Kress' estate, with dormant sandk-   55
ings and a work crew to take charge of the installation. Wo's assistants were aliens unlike any Kress was familiar with—squat, broad bipeds with four arms

and bulging, multifaceted eyes. Their skin was thick and leathery, twisted into horns and spines and protrusions at odd spots upon their bodies. But they were very strong, and good workers. Wo ordered them about in a musical tongue that Kress had never heard.

In a day it was done. They moved his piranha tank to the center of his spacious living room, arranged couches on either side of it for better viewing, scrubbed it clean, and filled it two-thirds of the way up with sand and rock. Then they installed a special lighting system, both to provide the dim red illumination the sandkings preferred and to project holographic images into the tank. On top they mounted a sturdy plastic cover, with a feeder mechanism built in. "This way you can feed your sandkings without removing the top of the tank," Wo explained. "You would not want to take any chances on the mobiles escaping."

The cover also included climate control devices, to condense just the right amount of moisture from the air. "You want it dry, but not too dry," Wo said.

Finally one of the four-armed workers climbed into the tank and dug deep pits in the four corners. One of his companions handed the dormant maws over to him, removing them one by one from their frosted cryonic traveling cases. They were nothing to look at. Kress decided they resembled nothing so much as a mottled, half-spoiled chunk of raw meat. With a mouth.

The alien buried them, one in each corner of the tank. Then they sealed it all up and took their leave.

"The heat will bring the maws out of dormancy," Wo said. "In less than a 60 week, mobiles will begin to hatch and burrow to the surface. Be certain to give them plenty of food. They will need all their strength until they are well established. I would estimate that you will have castles rising in about three weeks."

"And my face? When will they carve my face?"

"Turn on the hologram after about a month," she advised him. "And be patient. If you have any questions, please call. Wo and Shade are at your service." She bowed and left.

Kress wandered back to the tank and lit a joy-stick. The desert was still and empty. He drummed his fingers impatiently against the plastic, and frowned.

* * *

On the fourth day, Kress thought he glimpsed motion beneath the sand, subtle subterranean stirrings.

On the fifth day, he saw his first mobile, a lone white. 65

On the sixth day, he counted a dozen of them, whites and reds and blacks. The oranges were tardy. He cycled through a bowl of half-decayed table scraps. The mobiles sensed it at once, rushed to it, and began to drag pieces back to their respective corners. Each color group was very organized. They did not fight. Kress was a bit disappointed, but he decided to give them time.

The oranges made their appearance on the eighth day. By then the other sandkings had begun to carry small stones and erect crude fortifications. They still did not war. At the moment they were only half the size of those he had seen at Wo and Shade's, but Kress thought they were growing rapidly.

The castles began to rise midway through the second week. Organized battalions of mobiles dragged heavy chunks of sandstone and granite back to their corners, where other mobiles were pushing sand into place with mandibles and tendrils. Kress had purchased a pair of magnifying goggles so he could watch them work, wherever they might go in the tank. He wandered around and around the tall plastic walls, observing. It was fascinating. The castles were a bit plainer than Kress would have liked, but he had an idea about that. The next day he cycled through some obsidian and flakes of colored glass along with the food. Within hours, they had been incorporated into the castle walls.

The black castle was the first completed, followed by the white and red fortresses. The oranges were last, as usual. Kress took his meals into the living room and ate seated on the couch, so he could watch. He expected the first war to break out any hour now.

He was disappointed. Days passed; the castles grew taller and more grand, and Kress seldom left the tank except to attend to his sanitary needs and answer critical business calls. But the sandkings did not war. He was getting upset. 70

Finally, he stopped feeding them.

Two days after the table scraps had ceased to fall from their desert sky, four black mobiles surrounded an orange and dragged it back to their maw. They maimed it first, ripping off its mandibles and antennae and limbs, and carried it through the shadowed main gate of their miniature castle. It never emerged. Within an hour, more than forty orange mobiles marched across the sand and attacked the blacks' corner. They were outnumbered by the blacks that came rushing up from the depths. When the fighting was over, the attackers had been slaughtered. The dead and dying were taken down to feed the black maw.

Kress, delighted, congratulated himself on his genius.

When he put food into the tank the following day, a three-cornered battle broke out over its possession. The whites were the big winners.

After that, war followed war. 75

* * *

Almost a month to the day after Jala Wo had delivered the sandkings, Kress turned on the holographic projector, and his face materialized in the tank. It turned, slowly, around and around, so his gaze fell on all four castles equally. Kress thought it rather a good likeness—it had his impish grin, wide mouth, full cheeks. His blue eyes sparkled, his gray hair was carefully arrayed in a fashionable sidesweep, his eyebrows were thin and sophisticated.

Soon enough, the sandkings set to work. Kress fed them lavishly while his image beamed down at them from their sky. Temporarily, the wars stopped. All activity was directed towards worship.

His face emerged on the castle walls.

At first all four carvings looked alike to him, but as the work continued and Kress studied the reproductions, he began to detect subtle differences in technique and execution. The reds were the most creative, using tiny flakes of slate to put the gray in his hair. The white idol seemed young and mischievous to him, while the face shaped by the blacks—although virtually the same, line for line—struck him as wise and beneficent. The orange sandkings, as ever, were last and least. The wars had not gone well for them, and their castle was sad compared to the others. The image they carved was crude and cartoonish, and they seemed to intend to leave it that way.

When they stopped work on the face, Kress grew quite piqued with them, 80 but there was really nothing he could do.

When all the sandkings had finished their Kress-faces, he turned off the holograph and decided that it was time to have a party. His friends would be impressed. He could even stage a war for them, he thought. Humming happily to himself, he began to draw up a guest list.

* * *

The party was a wild success.

Kress invited thirty people: a handful of close friends who shared his amusements, a few former lovers, and a collection of business and social rivals who could not afford to ignore his summons. He knew some of them would be discomfited and even offended by his sandkings. He counted on it. Simon Kress customarily considered his parties a failure unless at least one guest walked out in high dudgeon.

On impulse he added Jala Wo's name to his list. "Bring Shade if you like," he added when dictating her invitation.

Her acceptance surprised him just a bit. "Shade, alas, will be unable to 85 attend. He does not go to social functions," Wo added. "As for myself, I look forward to the chance to see how your sandkings are doing."

Kress ordered them up a sumptuous meal. And when at last the conversation had died down, and most of his guests had gotten silly on wine and joysticks, he shocked them by personally scraping their table leavings into a large bowl. "Come, all of you," he told them.

"I want to introduce you to my newest pets." Carrying the bowl, he conducted them into his living room.

The sandkings lived up to his fondest expectations. He had starved them for two days in preparation, and they were in a fighting mood. While the guests ringed the tank, looking through the magnifying glasses Kress had thoughtfully provided, the sandkings waged a glorious battle over the scraps. He counted almost sixty dead mobiles when the struggle was over. The reds and whites, who had recently formed an alliance, emerged with most of the food.

"Kress, you're disgusting," Cath m'Lane told him. She had lived with him for a short time two years before, until her soppy sentimentality almost drove him mad. "I was a fool to come back here. I thought perhaps you'd changed, wanted to apologize." She had never forgiven him for the time his shambler had eaten an excessively cute puppy of which she had been fond. "Don't ever invite me here again, Simon." She strode out, accompanied by her current lover and a chorus of laughter.

His other guests were full of questions. 90

Where did the sandkings come from?, they wanted to know. "From Wo and Shade, Importers," he replied, with a polite gesture towards Jala Wo, who had remained quiet and apart through most of the evening.

Why did they decorate their castles with his likeness? "Because I am the source of all good things. Surely you know that?" That brought a round of chuckles.

Will they fight again? "Of course, but not tonight. Don't worry. There will be other parties." Jad Rakkis, who was an amateur xenologist, began talking about other social insects and the wars they fought. "These sandkings are amusing, but nothing really. You ought to read about Terran soldier ants, for instance."

"Sandkings are not insects," Jala Wo said sharply, but Jad was off and running, and no one paid her the slightest attention. Kress smiled at her and shrugged.

Malada Blane suggested a betting pool the next time they got together to 95 watch a war, and everyone was taken with the idea. An animated discussion about rules and odds ensued. It lasted for almost an hour. Finally the guests began to take their leave.

Jala Wo was the last to depart. "So," Kress said to her when they were alone, "it appears my sandkings are a hit."

"They are doing well," Wo said. "Already they are larger than my own."

"Yes," Kress said, "except for the oranges."

"I had noticed that," Wo replied. "They seem few in number, and their castle is shabby."

"Well, someone must lose," Kress said. "The oranges were late to emerge 100 and get established. They have suffered for it."

"Pardon," said Wo, "but might I ask if you are feeding your sandkings sufficiently?"

Kress shrugged. "They diet from time to time. It makes them fiercer."

She frowned. "There is no need to starve them. Let them war in their own time, for their own reasons. It is their nature, and you will witness conflicts

that are delightfully subtle and complex. The constant war brought on by
hunger is artless and degrading." Simon Kress repaid Wo's frown with interest.
"You are in my house, Wo, and here I am the judge of what is degrading. I fed
the sandkings as you advised, and they did not fight."

"You must have patience."

"No," Kress said. "I am their master and their god, after all. Why should I 105
wait on their impulses? They did not war often enough to suit me. I corrected
the situation."

"I see," said Wo. "I will discuss the matter with Shade."

"It is none of your concern, or his," Kress snapped.

"I must bid you good night, then," Wo said with resignation. But as she
slipped into her coat to depart, she fixed him with a final disapproving stare.
"Look to your faces, Simon Kress," she warned him. "Look to your faces."

Puzzled, he wandered back to the tank and stared at the castles after she
had taken her departure. His faces were still there, as ever. Except—he snatched
up his magnifying goggles and slipped them on. Even then it was hard to make
out. But it seemed to him that the expression on the face of his images had
changed slightly, that his smile was somehow twisted so that it seemed a touch
malicious.

But it was a very subtle change, if it was a change at all. Kress finally put it 110
down to his suggestibility, and resolved not to invite Jala Wo to any more of his
gatherings.

* * *

Over the next few months, Kress and about a dozen of his favorites got
together weekly for what he liked to call his "war games."

Now that his initial fascination with the sandkings was past, Kress spent
less time around his tank and more on his business affairs and his social life,
but he still enjoyed having a few friends over for a war or two. He kept the com-
batants sharp on a constant edge of hunger. It had severe effects on the orange
sandkings, who dwindled visibly until Kress began to wonder if their maw was
dead. But the others did well enough.

Sometimes at night, when he could not sleep, Kress would take a bottle
of wine into the darkened living room, where the red gloom of his miniature
desert was the only light. He would drink and watch for hours, alone. There
was usually a fight going on somewhere, and when there was not he could easily start one by dropping in some small morsel of food.

They took to betting on the weekly battles, as Malada Blane had suggested. Kress won a good amount by betting on the whites, who had become
the most powerful and numerous colony in the tank, with the grandest castle.
One week he slid the corner of the tank top aside, and dropped the food close
to the white castle instead of on the central battleground as usual, so that the

others had to attack the whites in their stronghold to get any food at all. They tried. The whites were brilliant in defense. Kress won a hundred standards from Jad Rakkis.

Rakkis, in fact, lost heavily on the sandkings almost every week. He pre-   115 tended to a vast knowledge of them and their ways, claiming that he had studied them after the first party, but he had no luck when it came to placing his bets. Kress suspected that Jad's claims were empty boasting. He had tried to study the sandkings a bit himself, in a moment of idle curiosity, tying in to the library to find out to what world his pets were native. But there was no listing for them. He wanted to get in touch with Wo and ask her about it, but he had other concerns, and the matter kept slipping his mind. Finally, after a month in which his losses totalled more than a thousand standards, Jad Rakkis arrived at the war games carrying a small plastic case under his arm. Inside was a spiderlike thing covered with fine golden hair.

"A sand spider," Rakkis announced. "From Cathaday. I got it this afternoon from t'Etherane the Petseller. Usually they remove the poison sacs, but this one is intact. Are you game, Simon? I want my money back. I'll bet a thousand standards, sand spider against sandkings."

Kress studied the spider in its plastic prison. His sandkings had grown—they were twice as large as Wo's, as she'd predicted—but they were still dwarfed by this thing. It was venomed, and they were not. Still, there were an awful lot of them. Besides, the endless sandking wars had begun to grow tiresome lately. The novelty of the match intrigued him. "Done," Kress said. "Jad, you are a fool. The sandkings will just keep coming until this ugly creature of yours is dead."

"You are the fool, Simon," Rakkis replied, smiling. "The Cathadayn sand spider customarily feeds on burrowers that hide in nooks and crevices and—well, watch—it will go straight into those castles, and eat the maws."

Kress scowled amid general laughter. He hadn't counted on that. "Get on with it," he said irritably. He went to freshen his drink.

The spider was too large to cycle conveniently through the food chamber.   120 Two of the others helped Rakkis slide the tank top slightly to one side, and Malada Blane handed him up his case. He shook the spider out. It landed lightly on a miniature dune in front of the red castle, and stood confused for a moment, mouth working, legs twitching menacingly.

"Come on," Rakkis urged. They all gathered round the tank. Simon Kress found his magnifiers and slipped them on. If he was going to lose a thousand standards, at least he wanted a good view of the action.

The sandkings had seen the invader. All over the castle, activity had ceased. The small scarlet mobiles were frozen, watching.

The spider began to move toward the dark promise of the gate. On the tower above, Simon Kress' countenance stared down impassively.

At once there was a flurry of activity. The nearest red mobiles formed themselves into two wedges and streamed over the sand toward the spider. More warriors erupted from inside the castle and assembled in a triple line to guard the approach to the underground chamber where the maw lived. Scouts came scuttling over the dunes, recalled to fight.

Battle was joined.   125

The attacking sandkings washed over the spider. Mandibles snapped shut on legs and abdomen, and clung. Reds raced up the golden legs to the invader's back. They bit and tore. One of them found an eye, and ripped it loose with tiny yellow tendrils. Kress smiled and pointed.

But they were small, and they had no venom, and the spider did not stop. Its legs flicked sandkings off to either side. Its dripping jaws found others, and left them broken and stiffening. Already a dozen of the reds lay dying. The sand spider came on and on. It strode straight through the triple line of guardians before the castle. The lines closed around it, covered it, waging desperate battle. A team of sandkings had bitten off one of the spider's legs, Kress saw. Defenders leaped from atop the towers to land on the twitching, heaving mass.

Lost beneath the sandkings, the spider somehow lurched down into the darkness and vanished.

Jad Rakkis let out a long breath. He looked pale. "Wonderful," someone else said. Malada Blane chuckled deep in her throat.

"Look," said Idi Noreddian, tugging Kress by the arm.   130

They had been so intent on the struggle in the corner that none of them had noticed the activity elsewhere in the tank. But now the castle was still, the sands empty save for dead red mobiles, and now they saw.

Three armies were drawn up before the red castle. They stood quite still, in perfect array, rank after rank of sandkings, orange and white and black. Waiting to see what emerged from the depths.

Simon Kress smiled. "A cordon sanitaire," he said. "And glance at the other castles, if you will, Jad."

Rakkis did, and swore. Teams of mobiles were sealing up the gates with sand and stone. If the spider somehow survived this encounter, it would find no easy entrance at the other castles. "I should have brought four spiders," Jad Rakkis said. "Still, I've won. My spider is down there right now, eating your damned maw."

Kress did not reply. He waited. There was motion in the shadows.   135

All at once, red mobiles began pouring out of the gate. They took their positions on the castle, and began repairing the damage the spider had wrought. The other armies dissolved and began to retreat to their respective corners. "Jad," said Simon Kress, "I think you are a bit confused about who is eating who."

* * * *

The following week Rakkis brought four slim silver snakes. The sandkings dispatched them without much trouble.

Next he tried a large black bird. It ate more than thirty white mobiles, and its thrashing and blundering virtually destroyed their castle, but ultimately its wings grew tired, and the sandkings attacked in force wherever it landed.

After that it was a case of insects, armored beetles not too unlike the sandkings themselves. But stupid, stupid. An allied force of oranges and blacks broke their formation, divided them, and butchered them.

Rakkis began giving Kress promissory notes.   140

It was around that time that Kress met Cath m'Lane again, one evening when he was dining in Asgard at his favorite restaurant. He stopped at her table briefly and told her about the war games, inviting her to join them. She flushed, then regained control of herself and grew icy. "Someone has to put a stop to you, Simon. I guess it's going to be me," she said. Kress shrugged and enjoyed a lovely meal and thought no more about her threat.

Until a week later, when a small, stout woman arrived at his door and showed him a police wristband. "We've had complaints," she said. "Do you keep a tank full of dangerous insects, Kress?"

"Not insects," he said, furious. "Come, I'll show you."

When she had seen the sandkings, she shook her head. "This will never do. What do you know about these creatures, anyway? Do you know what world they're from? Have they been cleared by the ecological board? Do you have a license for these things? We have a report that they're carnivores, possibly dangerous. We also have a report that they are semi-sentient. Where did you get these creatures, anyway?"

"From Wo and Shade," Kress replied.   145

"Never heard of them," the woman said. "Probably smuggled them in, knowing our ecologists would never approve them. No, Kress, this won't do. I'm going to confiscate this tank and have it destroyed. And you're going to have to expect a few fines as well."

Kress offered her a hundred standards to forget all about him and his sandkings.

She tsked. "Now I'll have to add attempted bribery to the charges against you."

Not until he raised the figure to two thousand standards was she willing to be persuaded. "It's not going to be easy, you know," she said. "There are forms to be altered, records to be wiped. And getting a forged license from the ecologists will be time-consuming. Not to mention dealing with the complainant. What if she calls again?"

"Leave her to me," Kress said. "Leave her to me."   150

* * *

He thought about it for a while. That night he made some calls.

First he got t'Etherane the Petseller. "I want to buy a dog," he said, "A puppy."

The round-faced merchant gawked at him. "A puppy? That is not like you, Simon. Why don't you come in? I have a lovely choice."

"I want a very specific kind of puppy," Kress said. "Take notes. I'll describe to you what it must look like." Afterward he punched for Idi Noreddian. "Idi," he said, "I want you out here tonight with your holo equipment. I have a notion to record a sandking battle. A present for one of my friends."

* * *

The night after they made the recording, Simon Kress stayed up late. He 155 absorbed a controversial new drama in his sensorium, fixed himself a small snack, smoked a joy-stick or two, and broke out a bottle of wine. Feeling very happy with himself, he wandered into the living room, glass in hand.

The lights were out. The red glow of the terrarium made the shadows flushed and feverish. He walked over to look at his domain, curious as to how the blacks were doing in the repairs on their castle. The puppy had left it in ruins.

The restoration went well. But as Kress inspected the work through his magnifiers, he chanced to glance closely at the face. It startled him.

He drew back, blinked, took a healthy gulp of wine, and looked again.

The face on the walls was still his. But it was all wrong, all twisted. His cheeks were bloated and piggish, his smile was a crooked leer. He looked impossibly malevolent.

Uneasy, he moved around the tank to inspect the other castles. They were 160 each a bit different, but ultimately all the same.

The oranges had left out most of the fine detail, but the result still seemed monstrous, crude—a brutal mouth and mindless eyes.

The reds gave him a satanic, twitching kind of smile. His mouth did odd, unlovely things at its corners.

The whites, his favorites, had carved a cruel idiot god. Simon Kress flung his wine across the room in rage. "You dare," he said under his breath. "Now you won't eat for a week, you damned. . ." His voice was shrill. "I'll teach you." He had an idea. He strode out of the room, and returned a moment later with an antique iron throwing-sword in his hand. It was a meter long, and the point was still sharp. Kress smiled, climbed up and moved the tank cover aside just enough to give him working room, opening one corner of the desert. He leaned down, and jabbed the sword at the white castle below him. He waved it back and forth, smashing towers and ramparts and walls. Sand and stone collapsed, burying the scrambling mobiles. A flick of his wrist obliterated the features of the insolent, insulting caricature the sandkings had made of his

face. Then he poised the point of the sword above the dark mouth that opened
down into the maw's chamber, and thrust with all his strength. He heard a
soft, squishing sound, and met resistance. All of the mobiles trembled and collapsed. Satisfied, Kress pulled back.

He watched for a moment, wondering whether he'd killed the maw. The
point of the throwing-sword was wet and slimy. But finally the white sandkings
began to move again. Feebly, slowly, but they moved.

He was preparing to slide the cover back in place and move on to a second 165
castle when he felt something crawling on his hand.

He screamed and dropped the sword, and brushed the sandking from his
flesh. It fell to the carpet, and he ground it beneath his heel, crushing it thoroughly long after it was dead. It had crunched when he stepped on it. After that,
trembling, he hurried to seal the tank up again, and rushed off to shower and
inspect himself carefully. He boiled his clothing. Later, after several fresh glasses
of wine, he returned to the living room. He was a bit ashamed of the way the
sandking had terrified him. But he was not about to open the tank again. From
now on, the cover stayed sealed permanently. Still, he had to punish the others.

Kress decided to lubricate his mental processes with another glass of wine.
As he finished it, an inspiration came to him. He went to the tank smiling, and
made a few adjustments to the humidity controls.

By the time he fell asleep on the couch, his wine glass still in his hand, the
sand castles were melting in the rain.

* * *

Kress woke to angry pounding on his door. 170

He sat up, groggy, his head throbbing. Wine hangovers were always the
worst, he thought. He lurched to the entry chamber.

Cath m'Lane was outside. "You monster," she said, her face swollen and
puffy and streaked by tears. "I cried all night, damn you. But no more, Simon,
no more."

"Easy," he said, holding his head. "I've got a hangover."

She swore and shoved him aside and pushed her way into his house. The
shambler came peering round a corner to see what the noise was. She spat at
it and stalked into the living room, Kress trailing ineffectually after her. "Hold
on," he said, "where do you . . . you can't. . . ." He stopped, suddenly horror-
struck. She was carrying a heavy sledgehammer in her left hand. "No," he said.

She went directly to the sandking tank. "You like the little charmers so 175
much, Simon? Then you can live with them."

"Cath!" he shrieked. Gripping the hammer with both hands, she swung as
hard as she could against the side of the tank. The sound of the impact set his
head to screaming, and Kress made a low blubbering sound of despair. But the
plastic held.

She swung again. This time there was a crack, and a network of thin lines sprang into being.

Kress threw himself at her as she drew back her hammer for a third swing. They went down flailing, and rolled. She lost her grip on the hammer and tried to throttle him, but Kress wrenched free and bit her on the arm, drawing blood. They both staggered to their feet, panting.

"You should see yourself, Simon," she said grimly. "Blood dripping from your mouth. You look like one of your pets. How do you like the taste?"

"Get out," he said. He saw the throwing-sword where it had fallen the 180 night before, and snatched it up. "Get out," he repeated, waving the sword for emphasis. "Don't go near that tank again."

She laughed at him. "You wouldn't dare," she said. She bent to pick up her hammer.

Kress shrieked at her, and lunged. Before he quite knew what was happening, the iron blade had gone clear through her abdomen.

Cath m'Lane looked at him wonderingly, and down at the sword. Kress fell back whimpering. "I didn't mean . . . I only wanted . . ."

She was transfixed, bleeding, dead, but somehow she did not fall. "You monster," she managed to say, though her mouth was full of blood. And she whirled, impossibly, the sword in her, and swung with her last strength at the tank. The tortured wall shattered, and Cath m'Lane was buried beneath an avalanche of plastic and sand and mud.

Kress made small hysterical noises and scrambled up on the couch. 185

Sandkings were emerging from the muck on his living room floor. They were crawling across Cath's body. A few of them ventured tentatively out across the carpet. More followed.

He watched as a column took shape, a living, writhing square of sandkings, bearing something, something slimy and featureless, a piece of raw meat big as a man's head. They began to carry it away from the tank. It pulsed.

That was when Kress broke and ran.

* * *

It was late afternoon before he found the courage to return.

He had run to his skimmer and flown to the nearest city, some fifty kilo- 190 meters away, almost sick with fear. But once safely away, he had found a small restaurant, put down several mugs of coffee and two anti-hangover tabs, eaten a full breakfast, and gradually regained his composure.

It had been a dreadful morning, but dwelling on that would solve nothing. He ordered more coffee and considered his situation with icy rationality.

Cath m'Lane was dead at his hand. Could he report it, plead that it had been an accident? Unlikely. He had run her through, after all, and he had already told that policer to leave her to him. He would have to get rid of the evidence, and hope that she had not told anyone where she was going this morning. That was probable. She could only have gotten his gift late last night. She said that she had cried all night, and she had been alone when she arrived. Very well; he had one body and one skimmer to dispose of.

That left the sandkings. They might prove more of a difficulty. No doubt they had all escaped by now. The thought of them around his house, in his bed and his clothes, infesting his food—it made his flesh crawl. He shuddered and overcame his revulsion. It really shouldn't be too hard to kill them, he reminded himself. He didn't have to account for every mobile. Just the four maws, that was all. He could do that. They were large, as he'd seen. He would find them and kill them.

Simon Kress went shopping before he flew back to his home. He bought a set of skinthins that would cover him from head to foot, several bags of poison pellets for rockjock control, and a spray cannister of illegally strong pesticide. He also bought a magnalock towing device.

When he landed, he went about things methodically. First he hooked 195
Cath's skimmer to his own with the magnalock. Searching it, he had his first piece of luck. The crystal chip with Idi Noreddian's holo of the sandking fight was on the front seat. He had worried about that.

When the skimmers were ready, he slipped into his skinthins and went inside for Cath's body.

It wasn't there.

He poked through the fast-drying sand carefully, but there was no doubt of it; the body was gone. Could she have dragged herself away? Unlikely, but Kress searched. A cursory inspection of his house turned up neither the body nor any sign of the sandkings. He did not have time for a more thorough investigation, not with the incriminating skimmer outside his front door. He resolved to try later.

Some seventy kilometers north of Kress' estate was a range of active volcanoes. He flew there, Cath's skimmer in tow. Above the glowering cone of the largest, he released the magnalock and watched it vanish in the lava below.

It was dusk when he returned to his house. That gave him pause. Briefly 200
he considered flying back to the city and spending the night there. He put the thought aside. There was work to do. He wasn't safe yet. He scattered the poison pellets around the exterior of his house. No one would find that suspicious. He'd always had a rockjock problem. When that task was completed, he primed the cannister of pesticide and ventured back inside.

Kress went through the house room by room, turning on lights everywhere he went until he was surrounded by a blaze of artificial illumination. He paused to clean up in the living room, shoveling sand and plastic fragments back into the broken tank. The sandkings were all gone, as he'd feared. The castles were shrunken and distorted, slagged by the watery bombardment Kress had visited upon them, and what little remained was crumbling as it dried.

He frowned and searched on, the cannister of pest spray strapped across his shoulders.

Down in his deepest wine cellar, he came upon Cath m'Lane's corpse.

It sprawled at the foot of a steep flight of stairs, the limbs twisted as if by a fall. White mobiles were swarming all over it, and as Kress watched, the body moved jerkily across the hard-packed dirt floor. He laughed, and twisted the illumination up to maximum. In the far corner, a squat little earthen castle and a dark hole were visible between two wine racks. Kress could make out a rough outline of his face on the cellar wall.

The body shifted once again, moving a few centimeters towards the castle. 205 Kress had a sudden vision of the white maw waiting hungrily. It might be able to get Cath's foot in its mouth, but no more. It was too absurd. He laughed again, and started down into the cellar, finger poised on the trigger of the hose that snaked down his right arm. The sandkings—hundreds of them moving as one—deserted the body and formed up battle lines, a field of white between him and their maw.

Suddenly Kress had another inspiration. He smiled and lowered his firing hand. "Cath was always hard to swallow," he said, delighted at his wit. "Especially for one your size. Here, let me give you some help. What are gods for, after all?"

He retreated upstairs, returning shortly with a cleaver. The sandkings, patient, waited and watched while Kress chopped Cath m'Lane into small, easily digestible pieces.

* * *

Simon Kress slept in his skinthins that night, the pesticide close at hand, but he did not need it. The whites, sated, remained in the cellar, and he saw no sign of the others.

In the morning he finished the clean-up of the living room. After he was through, no trace of the struggle remained except for the broken tank.

He ate a light lunch, and resumed his hunt for the missing sandkings. In 210 full daylight, it was not too difficult. The blacks had located in his rock garden, and built a castle heavy with obsidian and quartz. The reds he found at the bottom of his long-disused swimming pool, which had partially filled with wind-blown sand over the years. He saw mobiles of both colors ranging about his grounds, many of them carrying poison pellets back to their maws. Kress decided his pesticide was unnecessary. No use risking a fight when he could just let the poison do its work. Both maws should be dead by evening.

That left only the burnt orange sandkings unaccounted for. Kress circled his estate several times, in ever-widening spirals, but found no trace of them. When he began to sweat in his skinthins—it was a hot, dry day—he decided it was not important. If they were out here, they were probably eating the poison pellets along with the reds and blacks.

He crunched several sandkings underfoot, with a certain degree of satisfaction, as he walked back to the house. Inside, he removed his skinthins, settled down to a delicious meal, and finally began to relax. Everything was under control. Two of the maws would soon be defunct, the third was safely located where he could dispose of it after it had served his purposes, and he had no doubt that he would find the fourth. As for Cath, all trace of her visit had been obliterated.

His reverie was interrupted when his viewscreen began to blink at him. It was Jad Rakkis, calling to brag about some cannibal worms he was bringing to the war games tonight.

Kress had forgotten about that, but he recovered quickly. "Oh, Jad, my pardons. I neglected to tell you. I grew bored with all that, and got rid of the sandkings. Ugly little things. Sorry, but there'll be no party tonight."

Rakkis was indignant. "But what will I do with my worms?"   215

"Put them in a basket of fruit and send them to a loved one," Kress said, signing off. Quickly he began calling the others. He did not need anyone arriving at his doorstep now, with the sandkings alive and infesting the estate.

As he was calling Idi Noreddian, Kress became aware of an annoying oversight. The screen began to clear, indicating that someone had answered at the other end. Kress flicked off.

Idi arrived on schedule an hour later. She was surprised to find the party cancelled, but perfectly happy to share an evening alone with Kress. He delighted her with his story of Cath's reaction to the holo they had made together. While telling it, he managed to ascertain that she had not mentioned the prank to anyone. He nodded, satisfied, and refilled their wine glasses. Only a trickle was left. "I'll have to get a fresh bottle," he said. "Come with me to my wine cellar, and help me pick out a good vintage. You've always had a better palate than I."

She came along willingly enough, but balked at the top of the stairs when Kress opened the door and gestured for her to precede him. "Where are the lights?" she said. "And that smell—what's that peculiar smell, Simon?"

When he shoved her, she looked briefly startled. She screamed as she   220 tumbled down the stairs. Kress closed the door and began to nail it shut with the boards and airhammer he had left for that purpose. As he was finishing, he heard Idi groan. "I'm hurt," she called. "Simon, what is this?" Suddenly she squealed, and shortly after that the screaming started.

It did not cease for hours. Kress went to his sensorium and dialed up a saucy comedy to blot it out of his mind.

When he was sure she was dead, Kress flew her skimmer north to the volcanoes and discarded it. The magnalock was proving a good investment.

* * *

Odd scrabbling noises were coming from beyond the wine cellar door the next morning when Kress went down to check it out. He listened for several uneasy moments, wondering if Idi Noreddian could possibly have survived, and was now scratching to get out. It seemed unlikely; it had to be the sandkings. Kress did not like the implications of that. He decided that he would keep the door sealed, at least for the moment, and went outside with a shovel to bury the red and black maws in their own castles.

He found them very much alive.

The black castle was glittering with volcanic glass, and sandkings were all 225 over it, repairing and improving. The highest tower was up to his waist, and on it was a hideous caricature of his face. When he approached, the blacks halted in their labors, and formed up into two threatening phalanxes. Kress glanced behind him and saw others closing off his escape. Startled, he dropped the shovel and sprinted out of the trap, crushing several mobiles beneath his boots.

The red castle was creeping up the walls of the swimming pool. The maw was safely settled in a pit, surrounded by sand and concrete and battlements. The reds crept all over the bottom of the pool. Kress watched them carry a rockjock and a large lizard into the castle. He stepped back from the poolside, horrified, and felt something crunch. Looking down, he saw three mobiles climbing up his leg. He brushed them off and stamped them to death, but others were approaching quickly. They were larger than he remembered. Some were almost as big as his thumb.

He ran. By the time he reached the safety of the house, his heart was racing and he was short of breath. The door closed behind him, and Kress hurried to lock it. His house was supposed to be pest-proof. He'd be safe in here.

A stiff drink steadied his nerve. So poison doesn't faze them, he thought. He should have known. Wo had warned him that the maw could eat anything. He would have to use the pesticide. Kress took another drink for good measure, donned his skinthins, and strapped the cannister to his back. He unlocked the door.

Outside, the sandkings were waiting.

Two armies confronted him, allied against the common threat. More than 230 he could have guessed. The damned maws must be breeding like rockjocks. They were everywhere, a creeping sea of them.

Kress brought up the hose and flicked the trigger. A gray mist washed over the nearest rank of sandkings. He moved his hand from side to side.

Where the mist fell, the sandkings twitched violently and died in sudden spasms. Kress smiled. They were no match for him. He sprayed in a wide arc before him and stepped forward confidently over a litter of black and red bodies. The armies fell back. Kress advanced, intent on cutting through them to their maws. All at once the retreat stopped. A thousand sandkings surged toward him. Kress had been expecting the counterattack. He stood his ground, sweeping his misty sword before him in great looping strokes. They came at him and died. A few got through; he could not spray everywhere at once. He felt them climbing up his legs, sensed their mandibles biting futilely at the reinforced plastic of his skinthins. He ignored them, and kept spraying.

Then he began to feel soft impacts on his head and shoulders.

Kress trembled and spun and looked up above him. The front of his house was alive with sandkings. Blacks and reds, hundreds of them. They were launching themselves into the air, raining down on him. They fell all around him. One landed on his faceplate, its mandibles scraping at his eyes for a terrible second before he plucked it away.

He swung up his hose and sprayed the air, sprayed the house, sprayed until 235 the airborne sandkings were all dead and dying. The mist settled back on him, making him cough. He coughed, and kept spraying. Only when the front of the house was clean did Kress turn his attention back to the ground.

They were all around him, on him, dozens of them scurrying over his body, hundreds of others hurrying to join them. He turned the mist on them. The hose went dead. Kress heard a loud hiss, and the deadly fog rose in a great cloud from between his shoulders, cloaking him, choking him, making his eyes burn and blur. He felt for the hose, and his hand came away covered with dying sandkings. The hose was severed; they'd eaten it through. He was surrounded by a shroud of pesticide, blinded. He stumbled and screamed, and began to run back to the house, pulling sandkings from his body as he went.

Inside, he sealed the door and collapsed on the carpet, rolling back and forth until he was sure he had crushed them all. The cannister was empty by then, hissing feebly. Kress stripped off his skinthins and showered. The hot spray scalded him and left his skin reddened and sensitive, but it made his flesh stop crawling.

He dressed in his heaviest clothing, thick workpants and leathers, after shaking them out nervously. "Damn," he kept muttering, "damn." His throat was dry. After searching the entry hall thoroughly to make certain it was clean, he allowed himself to sit and pour a drink. "Damn," he repeated. His hand shook as he poured, slopping liquor on the carpet.

The alcohol settled him, but it did not wash away the fear. He had a second drink, and went to the window furtively. Sandkings were moving across the thick plastic pane. He shuddered and retreated to his communications console. He had to get help, he thought wildly. He would punch through a call to the authorities, and policers would come out with flamethrowers and. . . .

Simon Kress stopped in mid-call, and groaned. He couldn't call in the 240 police. He would have to tell them about the whites in his cellar, and they'd find the bodies there. Perhaps the maw might have finished Cath m'Lane by now, but certainly not Idi Noreddian. He hadn't even cut her up. Besides, there would be bones. No, the police could be called in only as a last resort.

He sat at the console, frowning. His communications equipment filled a whole wall; from here he could reach anyone on Baldur. He had plenty of money, and his cunning—he had always prided him self on his cunning. He would handle this somehow.

He briefly considered calling Wo, but soon dismissed the idea. Wo knew too much, and she would ask questions, and he did not trust her. No, he needed someone who would do as he asked without questions.

His frown faded, and slowly turned into a smile. Simon Kress had contacts. He put through a call to a number he had not used in a long time.

A woman's face took shape on his viewscreen: white-haired, bland of expression, with a long hook nose. Her voice was brisk and efficient. "Simon," she said. "How is business?"

"Business is fine, Lissandra," Kress replied. "I have a job for you."   245

"A removal? My price has gone up since last time, Simon. It has been ten years, after all."

"You will be well paid," Kress said. "You know I'm generous. I want you for a bit of pest control."

She smiled a thin smile. "No need to use euphemisms, Simon. The call is shielded."

"No, I'm serious. I have a pest problem. Dangerous pests. Take care of them for me. No questions. Understood?"

"Understood."   250

"Good. You'll need . . . oh, three or four operatives. Wear heat-resistant skinthins, and equip them with flamethrowers, or lasers, something on that order. Come out to my place. You'll see the problem. Bugs, lots and lots of them. In my rock garden and the old swimming pool you'll find castles. Destroy them, kill everything inside them. Then knock on the door, and I'll show you what else needs to be done. Can you get out here quickly?" Her face was impassive. "We'll leave within the hour."

* * *

Lissandra was true to her word. She arrived in a lean black skimmer with three operatives. Kress watched them from the safety of a second-story window. They were all faceless in dark plastic skinthins. Two of them wore portable flamethrowers, a third carried lasercannon and explosives. Lissandra carried nothing; Kress recognized her by the way she gave orders.

Their skimmer passed low overhead first, checking out the situation. The sandkings went mad. Scarlet and ebony mobiles ran everywhere, frenetic. Kress could see the castle in the rock garden from his vantage point. It stood tall as a man. Its ramparts were crawling with black defenders, and a steady stream of mobiles flowed down into its depths.

Lissandra's skimmer came down next to Kress' and the operatives vaulted out and unlimbered their weapons. They looked inhuman, deadly.

The black army drew up between them and the castle. The reds—Kress suddenly realized that he could not see the reds. He blinked. Where had they gone? 255

Lissandra pointed and shouted, and her two flamethrowers spread out and opened up on the black sandkings.

Their weapons coughed dully and began to roar, long tongues of blue-and-scarlet fire licking out before them. Sandkings crisped and blackened and died. The operatives began to play the fire back and forth in an efficient, interlocking pattern. They advanced with careful, measured steps.

The black army burned and disintegrated, the mobiles fleeing in a thousand different directions, some back toward the castle, others toward the enemy. None reached the operatives with the flamethrowers. Lissandra's people were very professional.

Then one of them stumbled.

Or seemed to stumble. Kress looked again, and saw that the ground had given way beneath the man. Tunnels, he thought with a tremor of fear—tunnels, pits, traps. The flamer was sunk in sand up to his waist, and suddenly the ground around him seemed to erupt, and he was covered with scarlet sandkings. He dropped the flamethrower and began to claw wildly at his own body. His screams were horrible to hear. 260

His companion hesitated, then swung and fired. A blast of flame swallowed human and sandkings both. The screaming stopped abruptly. Satisfied, the second flamer turned back to the castle and took another step forward, and recoiled as his foot broke through the ground and vanished up to the ankle. He tried to pull it back and retreat, and the sand all around him gave way. He lost his balance and stumbled, flailing, and the sandkings were everywhere, a boiling mass of them, covering him as he writhed and rolled. His flamethrower was useless and forgotten.

Kress pounded wildly on the window, shouting for attention. "The castle! Get the castle!"

Lissandra, standing back by her skimmer, heard and gestured. Her third operative sighted with the lasercannon and fired. The beam throbbed across the grounds and sliced off the top of the castle. He brought it down sharply, hacking at the sand and stone parapets. Towers fell. Kress' face disintegrated. The laser bit into the ground, searching round and about. The castle crumbled; now it was only a heap of sand. But the black mobiles continued to move. The maw was buried too deeply; they hadn't touched her.

Lissandra gave another order. Her operative discarded the laser, primed an explosive, and darted forward. He leaped over the smoking corpse of the first flamer, landed on solid ground within Kress' rock garden, and heaved.

The explosive ball landed square atop the ruins of the black castle. White-hot
light seared Kress' eyes, and there was a tremendous gout of sand and rock and
mobiles. For a moment dust obscured everything. It was raining sandkings and
pieces of sandkings.

Kress saw that the black mobiles were dead and unmoving.   265

"The pool," he shouted down through the window. "Get the castle in the
pool."

Lissandra understood quickly; the ground was littered with motionless
blacks, but the reds were pulling back hurriedly and re-forming. Her operative
stood uncertain, then reached down and pulled out another explosive ball. He
took one step forward, but Lissandra called him and he sprinted back in her
direction.

It was all so simple then. He reached the skimmer, and Lissandra took him
aloft. Kress rushed to another window in another room to watch. They came
swooping in just over the pool, and the operative pitched his bombs down at
the red castle from the safety of the skimmer. After the fourth run, the castle
was unrecognizable, and the sandkings stopped moving.

Lissandra was thorough. She had him bomb each castle several additional
times. Then he used the lasercannon, crisscrossing methodically until it was
certain that nothing living could remain intact beneath those small patches of
ground. Finally they came knocking at his door. Kress was grinning manically
when he let them in. "Lovely," he said.

Lissandra pulled off the mask of her skinthins. "This will cost you, Simon.   270
Two operatives gone, not to mention the danger to my own life."

"Of course," Kress blurted. "You'll be well paid, Lissandra. Whatever you
ask, just so you finish the job."

"What remains to be done?"

"You have to clean out my wine cellar," Kress said. "There's another castle
down there. And you'll have to do it without explosives. I don't want my house
coming down around me."

Lissandra motioned to her operative. "Go outside and get Rajk's flamethrower. It should be intact."

He returned armed, ready, silent. Kress led them down to the wine cellar.   275
The heavy door was still nailed shut, as he had left it. But it bulged outward slightly, as if warped by some tremendous pressure. That made Kress
uneasy, as did the silence that held reign about them. He stood well away from
the door as Lissandra's operative removed his nails and planks. "Is that safe in
here?" he found himself muttering, pointing at the flamethrower. "I don't want
a fire, either, you know."

"I have the laser," Lissandra said. "We'll use that for the kill. The flamethrower probably won't be needed. But I want it here just in case. There are
worse things than fire, Simon."

He nodded.

The last plank came free of the cellar door. There was still no sound from below. Lissandra snapped an order, and her underling fell back, took up a position behind her, and leveled the flamethrower square at the door. She slipped her mask back on, hefted the laser, stepped forward, and pulled open the door.

No motion. No sound. It was dark down there.   280

"Is there a light?" Lissandra asked.

"Just inside the door," Kress said. "On the right hand side. Mind the stairs, they're quite steep."

She stepped into the door, shifted the laser to her left hand, and reached up with her right, fumbling inside for the light panel. Nothing happened. "I feel it," Lissandra said, "but it doesn't seem to . . ."

Then she was screaming, and she stumbled backward. A great white sandking had clamped itself around her wrist. Blood welled through her skinthins where its mandibles had sunk in. It was fully as large as her hand.

Lissandra did a horrible little jig across the room and began to smash her   285
hand against the nearest wall. Again and again and again. It landed with a heavy, meaty thud. Finally the sandking fell away. She whimpered and fell to her knees. "I think my fingers are broken," she said softly. The blood was still flowing freely. She had dropped the laser near the cellar door.

"I'm not going down there," her operative announced in clear firm tones.

Lissandra looked up at him. "No," she said. "Stand in the door and flame it all. Cinder it. Do you understand?"

He nodded.

Simon Kress moaned. "My house," he said. His stomach churned. The white sandking had been so large. How many more were down there? "Don't," he continued. "Leave it alone. I've changed my mind. Leave it alone."

Lissandra misunderstood. She held out her hand. It was covered with   290
blood and greenish-black ichor. "Your little friend bit clean through my glove, and you saw what it took to get it off. I don't care about your house, Simon. Whatever is down there is going to die."

Kress hardly heard her. He thought he could see movement in the shadows beyond the cellar door. He imagined a white army bursting forth, all as large as the sandking that had attacked Lissandra. He saw himself being lifted by a hundred tiny arms, and dragged down into the darkness where the maw waited hungrily. He was afraid. "Don't," he said.

They ignored him.

Kress darted forward, and his shoulder slammed into the back of Lissandra's operative just as the man was bracing to fire. He grunted and unbalanced and pitched forward into the black. Kress listened to him fall down the stairs. Afterward there were other noises—scuttlings and snaps and soft squishing sounds.

Kress swung around to face Lissandra. He was drenched in cold sweat, but a sickly kind of excitement was on him. It was almost sexual.

Lissandra's calm cold eyes regarded him through her mask. "What are you 295 doing?" she demanded as Kress picked up the laser she had dropped. "Simon!"

"Making a peace," he said, giggling. "They won't hurt god, no, not so long as god is good and generous. I was cruel. Starved them. I have to make up for it now, you see." "You're insane," Lissandra said. It was the last thing she said. Kress burned a hole in her chest big enough to put his arm through. He dragged the body across the floor and rolled it down the cellar stairs. The noises were louder—chitinous clackings and scrapings and echoes that were thick and liquid. Kress nailed up the door once again.

As he fled, he was filled with a deep sense of contentment that coated his fear like a layer of syrup. He suspected it was not his own.

* * *

He planned to leave his home, to fly to the city and take a room for a night, or perhaps for a year. Instead Kress started drinking. He was not quite sure why. He drank steadily for hours, and retched it all up violently on his living room carpet. At some point he fell asleep. When he woke, it was pitch dark in the house.

He cowered against the couch. He could hear noises. Things were moving in the walls. They were all around him. His hearing was extraordinarily acute. Every little creak was the footstep of a sandking. He closed his eyes and waited, expecting to feel their terrible touch, afraid to move lest he brush against one.

Kress sobbed, and was very still for a while, but nothing happened. 300

He opened his eyes again. He trembled. Slowly the shadows began to soften and dissolve. Moonlight was filtering through the high windows. His eyes adjusted.

The living room was empty. Nothing there, nothing, nothing. Only his drunken fears.

Simon Kress steeled himself, and rose, and went to a light. Nothing there. The room was quiet, deserted.

He listened. Nothing. No sound. Nothing in the walls. It had all been his imagination, his fear.

The memories of Lissandra and the thing in the cellar returned to him 305 unbidden. Shame and anger washed over him. Why had he done that? He could have helped her burn it out, kill it. Why . . . he knew why. The maw had done it to him, put fear in him. Wo had said it was psionic, even when it was small. And now it was large, so large. It had feasted on Cath, and Idi, and now it had two more bodies down there. It would keep growing. And it had learned to like the taste of human flesh, he thought.

He began to shake, but he took control of himself again and stopped. It wouldn't hurt him. He was god. The whites had always been his favorites.

He remembered how he had stabbed it with his throwing-sword. That was before Cath came. Damn her anyway.

He couldn't stay here. The maw would grow hungry again. Large as it was, it wouldn't take long. Its appetite would be terrible. What would it do then? He had to get away, back to the safety of the city while it was still contained in his wine cellar. It was only plaster and hard-packed earth down there, and the mobiles could dig and tunnel. When they got free. . . . Kress didn't want to think about it.

He went to his bedroom and packed. He took three bags. Just a single change of clothing, that was all he needed; the rest of the space he filled with his valuables, with jewelry and art and other things he could not bear to lose. He did not expect to return.

His shambler followed him down the stairs, staring at him from its baleful 310 glowing eyes. It was gaunt. Kress realized that it had been ages since he had fed it. Normally it could take care of itself, but no doubt the pickings had grown lean of late. When it tried to clutch at his leg, he snarled at it and kicked it away, and it scurried off, offended.

Kress slipped outside, carrying his bags awkwardly, and shut the door behind him.

For a moment he stood pressed against the house, his heart thudding in his chest. Only a few meters between him and his skimmer. He was afraid to cross them. The moonlight was bright, and the front of his house was a scene of carnage. The bodies of Lissandra's two flamers lay where they had fallen, one twisted and burned, the other swollen beneath a mass of dead sandkings. And the mobiles, the black and red mobiles, they were all around him. It was an effort to remember that they were dead. It was almost as if they were simply waiting, as they had waited so often before.

Nonsense, Kress told himself. More drunken fears. He had seen the castles blown apart. They were dead, and the white maw was trapped in his cellar. He took several deep and deliberate breaths, and stepped forward onto the sandkings. They crunched. He ground them into the sand savagely. They did not move.

Kress smiled, and walked slowly across the battleground, listening to the sounds, the sounds of safety.

Crunch. Crackle. Crunch. 315

He lowered his bags to the ground and opened the door to his skimmer.

Something moved from shadow into light. A pale shape on the seat of his skimmer. It was as long as his forearm. Its mandibles clacked together softly, and it looked up at him from six small eyes set all around its body.

Kress wet his pants and backed away slowly.

There was more motion from inside the skimmer. He had left the door open. The sandking emerged and came toward him, cautiously. Others followed. They had been hiding beneath his seats, burrowed into the upholstery. But now they emerged. They formed a ragged ring around the skimmer.

Kress licked his lips, turned, and moved quickly to Lissandra's skimmer.   320
He stopped before he was halfway there. Things were moving inside that one too. Great maggoty things, half-seen by the light of the moon.

Kress whimpered and retreated back toward the house. Near the front door, he looked up.

He counted a dozen long white shapes creeping back and forth across the walls of the building. Four of them were clustered close together near the top of the unused belfry where the carrion hawk had once roosted. They were carving something. A face. A very recognizable face.

Simon Kress shrieked and ran back inside.

* * *

A sufficient quantity of drink brought him the easy oblivion he sought. But   325
he woke. Despite everything, he woke. He had a terrific headache, and he smelled, and he was hungry. Oh so very hungry. He had never been so hungry.

Kress knew it was not his own stomach hurting.

A white sandking watched him from atop the dresser in his bedroom, its antennae moving faintly. It was as big as the one in the skimmer the night before. He tried not to shrink away. "I'll . . . I'll feed you," he said to it. "I'll feed you." His mouth was horribly dry, sandpaper dry. He licked his lips and fled from the room.

The house was full of sandkings; he had to be careful where he put his feet. They all seemed busy on errands of their own. They were making modifications in his house, burrowing into or out of his walls, carving things. Twice he saw his own likeness staring out at him from unexpected places. The faces were warped, twisted, livid with fear.

He went outside to get the bodies that had been rotting in the yard, hoping to appease the white maw's hunger. They were gone, both of them. Kress remembered how easily the mobiles could carry things many times their own weight.

It was terrible to think that the maw was still hungry after all of that.   330
When Kress re-entered the house, a column of sandkings was wending its way down the stairs. Each carried a piece of his shambler. The head seemed to look at him reproachfully as it went by.

Kress emptied his freezers, his cabinets, everything, piling all the food in the house in the center of his kitchen floor. A dozen whites waited to take it away. They avoided the frozen food, leaving it to thaw in a great puddle, but they carried off everything else.

When all the food was gone, Kress felt his own hunger pangs abate just a bit, though he had not eaten a thing. But he knew the respite would be short-lived. Soon the maw would be hungry again. He had to feed it.

Kress knew what to do. He went to his communicator. "Malada," he began casually when the first of his friends answered, "I'm having a small party tonight. I realize this is terribly short notice, but I hope you can make it. I really do."

He called Jad Rakkis next, and then the others. By the time he had fin-   335
ished, nine of them had accepted his invitation. Kress hoped that would be enough.

* * *

Kress met his guests outside—the mobiles had cleaned up remarkably quickly, and the grounds looked almost as they had before the battle—and walked them to his front door. He let them enter first. He did not follow.

When four of them had gone through, Kress finally worked up his courage. He closed the door behind his latest guest, ignoring the startled exclamations that soon turned into shrill gibbering, and sprinted for the skimmer the man had arrived in. He slid in safely, thumbed the startplate, and swore. It was programmed to lift only in response to its owner's thumbprint, of course.

Jad Rakkis was the next to arrive. Kress ran to his skimmer as it set down, and seized Rakkis by the arm as he was climbing out. "Get back in, quickly," he said, pushing. "Take me to the city. Hurry, Jad. Get out of here!"

But Rakkis only stared at him, and would not move. "Why, what's wrong, Simon? I don't understand. What about your party?"

And then it was too late, because the loose sand all around them was stir-   340
ring, and the red eyes were staring at them, and the mandibles were clacking. Rakkis made a choking sound, and moved to get back in his skimmer, but a pair of mandibles snapped shut about his ankle, and suddenly he was on his knees. The sand seemed to boil with subterranean activity. Jad thrashed and cried terribly as they tore him apart. Kress could hardly bear to watch.

After that, he did not try to escape again. When it was all over, he cleaned out what remained in his liquor cabinet, and got extremely drunk. It would be the last time he would enjoy that luxury, he knew. The only alcohol remaining in the house was stored down in the wine cellar.

Kress did not touch a bite of food the entire day, but he fell asleep feeling bloated, sated at last, the awful hunger vanquished. His last thoughts before the nightmares took him were of whom he could ask out tomorrow.

* * *

Morning was hot and dry. Kress opened his eyes to see the white sandking on his dresser again. He shut them again quickly, hoping the dream would leave him.

It did not, and he could not go back to sleep. Soon he found himself staring at the thing.

He stared for almost five minutes before the strangeness of it dawned on him; the sandking was not moving.

The mobiles could be preternaturally still, to be sure. He had seen them   345
wait and watch a thousand times. But always there was some motion about them—the mandibles clacked, the legs twitched, the long fine antennae stirred and swayed.

But the sandking on his dresser was completely still.

Kress rose, holding his breath, not daring to hope. Could it be dead? Could something have killed it? He walked across the room.

The eyes were glassy and black. The creature seemed swollen, somehow, as if it were soft and rotting inside, filling up with gas that pushed outward at the plates of white armor. Kress reached out a trembling hand and touched it.

It was warm—hot even—and growing hotter. But it did not move.

He pulled his hand back, and as he did, a segment of the sandking's white   350
exoskeleton fell away from it. The flesh beneath was the same color, but softer-looking, swollen and feverish. And it almost seemed to throb.

Kress backed away, and ran to the door.

Three more white mobiles lay in his hall. They were all like the one in his bedroom.

He ran down the stairs, jumping over sandkings. None of them moved. The house was full of them, all dead, dying, comatose, whatever. Kress did not care what was wrong with them. Just so they could not move.

He found four of them inside his skimmer. He picked them up one by one, and threw them as far as he could. Damned monsters. He slid back in, on the ruined half-eaten seats, and thumbed the startplate.

Nothing happened.   355

Kress tried again, and again. Nothing. It wasn't fair. This was his skimmer, it ought to start, why wouldn't it lift, he didn't understand. Finally he got out and checked, expecting the worst. He found it. The sandkings had torn apart his gravity grid. He was trapped. He was still trapped.

Grimly, Kress marched back into the house. He went to his gallery and found the antique axe that had hung next to the throwing- sword he had used on Cath m'Lane. He set to work. The sandkings did not stir even as he chopped them to pieces. But they splattered when he made the first cut, the bodies almost bursting. Inside was awful; strange half-formed organs, a viscous reddish ooze that looked almost like human blood, and the yellow ichor.

Kress destroyed twenty of them before he realized the futility of what he was doing. The mobiles were nothing, really. Besides, there were so many of them. He could work for a day and night and still not kill them all.

He had to go down into the wine cellar and use the axe on the maw.

Resolute, he started down. He got within sight of the door, and stopped.   360
It was not a door any more. The walls had been eaten away, so that the
hole was twice the size it had been, and round. A pit, that was all. There was
no sign that there had ever been a door nailed shut over that black abyss.

A ghastly, choking, fetid odor seemed to come from below.

And the walls were wet and bloody and covered with patches of white
fungus.

And worst, it was breathing.

Kress stood across the room and felt the warm wind wash over him as it   365
exhaled, and he tried not to choke, and when the wind reversed direction, he
fled.

Back in the living room, he destroyed three more mobiles, and collapsed.
What was happening? He didn't understand.

Then he remembered the only person who might understand. Kress went
to his communicator again, stepping on a sandking in his haste, and prayed
fervently that the device still worked. When Jala Wo answered, he broke down
and told her everything.

She let him talk without interruption, no expression save for a slight frown
on her gaunt, pale face. When Kress had finished, she said only, "I ought to
leave you there."

Kress began to blubber. "You can't. Help me. I'll pay. . . ."

"I ought to," Wo repeated, "but I won't."   370

"Thank you," Kress said. "Oh, thank. . . ."

"Quiet," said Wo. "Listen to me. This is your own doing. Keep your
sandkings well, and they are courtly ritual warriors. You turned yours into
something else, with starvation and torture. You were their god. You made
them what they are. That maw in your cellar is sick, still suffering from the
wound you gave it. It is probably insane. Its behavior is . . . unusual.

"You have to get out of there quickly. The mobiles are not dead, Kress.
They are dormant. I told you the exoskeleton falls off when they grow larger.
Normally, in fact, it falls off much earlier. I have never heard of sandkings
growing as large as yours while still in the insectoid stage. It is another result of
crippling the white maw, I would say. That does not matter.

"What matters is the metamorphosis your sandkings are now undergoing.
As the maw grows, you see, it gets progressively more intelligent. Its psionic
powers strengthen, and its mind becomes more sophisticated, more ambitious.
The armored mobiles are useful enough when the maw is tiny and only semi-
sentient, but now it needs better servants, bodies with more capabilities. Do
you understand? The mobiles are all going to give birth to a new breed of sandking. I can't say exactly what it will look like. Each maw designs its own, to fit
its perceived needs and desires. But it will be biped, with four arms, and oppos-
able thumbs. It will be able to construct and operate advanced machinery. The

individual sandkings will not be sentient. But the maw will be very sentient indeed." Simon Kress was gaping at Wo's image on the viewscreen. "Your workers," he said, with an effort. "The ones who came out here . . . who installed the tank. . . ."

Jala Wo managed a faint smile. "Shade," she said.   375

"Shade is a sandking," Kress repeated numbly. "And you sold me a tank of . . . of . . . infants, ah. . . ."

"Do not be absurd," Wo said. "A first-stage sandking is more like a sperm than an infant. The wars temper and control them in nature. Only one in a hundred reaches second stage. Only one in a thousand achieves the third and final plateau, and becomes like Shade. Adult sandkings are not sentimental about the small maws. There are too many of them, and their mobiles are pests." She sighed. "And all this talk wastes time. That white sandking is going to waken to full sentience soon. It is not going to need you any longer, and it hates you, and it will be very hungry. The transformation is taxing. The maw must eat enormous amounts both before and after. So you have to get out of there. Do you understand?"

"I can't," Kress said. "My skimmer is destroyed, and I can't get any of the others to start. I don't know how to reprogram them. Can you come out for me?"

"Yes," said Wo. "Shade and I will leave at once, but it is more than two hundred kilometers from Asgard to you, and there is equipment we will need to deal with the deranged sandking you've created. You cannot wait there. You have two feet. Walk. Go due east, as near as you can determine, as quickly as you can. The land out there is pretty desolate. We can find you easily with an aerial search, and you'll be safely away from the sandking. Do you understand?"

"Yes," said Simon Kress. "Yes, oh, yes."   380

They signed off, and he walked quickly toward the door. He was halfway there when he heard the noise—a sound halfway between a pop and a crack.

One of the sandkings had split open. Four tiny hands covered with pinkish-yellow blood came up out of the gap and began to push the dead skin aside.

Kress began to run.

* * *

He had not counted on the heat.

The hills were dry and rocky. Kress ran from the house as quickly as he   385
could, ran until his ribs ached and his breath was coming in gasps. Then he walked, but as soon as he had recovered he began to run again. For almost an hour he ran and walked, ran and walked, beneath the fierce hot sun. He sweated freely, and wished that he had thought to bring some water. He watched the sky in hopes of seeing Wo and Shade.

He was not made for this. It was too hot, and too dry, and he was in no condition. But he kept himself going with the memory of the way the maw had breathed, and the thought of the wriggling little things that by now were surely crawling all over his house. He hoped Wo and Shade would know how to deal with them.

He had his own plans for Wo and Shade. It was all their fault, Kress had decided, and they would suffer for it. Lissandra was dead, but he knew others in her profession. He would have his revenge. He promised himself that a hundred times as he struggled and sweated his way east.

At least he hoped it was east. He was not that good at directions, and he wasn't certain which way he had run in his initial panic, but since then he had made an effort to bear due east, as Wo had suggested.

When he had been running for several hours, with no sign of rescue, Kress began to grow certain that he had gone wrong.

When several more hours passed, he began to grow afraid. What if Wo and Shade could not find him? He would die out here. He hadn't eaten in two days; he was weak and frightened; his throat was raw for want of water. He couldn't keep going. The sun was sinking now, and he'd be completely lost in the dark. What was wrong? Had the sandkings eaten Wo and Shade? The fear was on him again, filling him, and with it a great thirst and a terrible hunger. But Kress kept going. He stumbled now when he tried to run, and twice he fell. The second time he scraped his hand on a rock, and it came away bloody. He sucked at it as he walked, and worried about infection.

The sun was on the horizon behind him. The ground grew a little cooler, for which Kress was grateful. He decided to walk until last light and settle in for the night. Surely he was far enough from the sandkings to be safe, and Wo and Shade would find him come morning.

When he topped the next rise, he saw the outline of a house in front of him.

It wasn't as big as his own house, but it was big enough. It was habitation, safety. Kress shouted and began to run toward it. Food and drink, he had to have nourishment, he could taste the meal now. He was aching with hunger. He ran down the hill towards the house, waving his arms and shouting to the inhabitants. The light was almost gone now, but he could still make out a half-dozen children, playing in the twilight. "Hey there," he shouted. "Help, help."

They came running toward him.

Kress stopped suddenly. "No," he said, "oh, no. Oh, no." He backpedaled, slipped on the sand, got up and tried to run again. They caught him easily. They were ghastly little things with bulging eyes and dusky orange skin. He struggled, but it was useless. Small as they were, each of them had four arms, and Kress had only two.

They carried him toward the house. It was a sad, shabby house built of crumbling sand, but the door was quite large, and dark, and it breathed. That was terrible, but it was not the thing that set Simon Kress to screaming. He screamed because of the others, the little orange children who came crawling out from the castle, and watched impassively as he passed.

All of them had his face.

- Does this story seem to have a moral? How important is this moral to our experience of the story? Or is there some other element of the story that seems to be more significant?
- The story relies upon a number of imaginary features—what are these? How does Martin present them?
- How does our understanding of sandkings develop through the story?
- Whose point of view do we get throughout this story?

Charlotte Perkins Gilman (1860–1935)

Charlotte Perkins Gilman was born in Hartford, Connecticut. Gilman's upbringing and first marriage were far from easy: her father deserted his family and was only in sporadic contact with his daughter, her mother was emotionally distant, and Gilman herself experienced a deep depression after giving birth. This depression, difficult though it was, proved to be a turning point for her. Following her recovery and her subsequent divorce, she began to establish herself as a feminist activist and writer. Gilman wrote in a number of genres, producing poems, political tracts, and novels, but she is best remembered for a semiautobiographical work of short fiction, "The Yellow Wallpaper," which she published in 1899. Though the techniques for treating depression described in the story are no longer in use, "The Yellow Wallpaper" remains a powerful indictment of the ways in which women can be smothered by relationships.

The Yellow Wallpaper (1892)

It is very seldom that mere ordinary people like John and myself secure ancestral halls for the summer.

A colonial mansion, a hereditary estate, I would say a haunted house and reach the height of romantic felicity—but that would be asking too much of fate!

Still I will proudly declare that there is something queer about it.

Else, why should it be let so cheaply? And why have stood so long untenanted?

John laughs at me, of course, but one expects that in marriage.   5

John is practical in the extreme. He has no patience with faith, an intense horror of superstition, and he scoffs openly at any talk of things not to be felt and seen and put down in figures.

John is a physician, and *perhaps*—(I would not say it to a living soul, of course, but this is dead paper and a great relief to my mind)—*perhaps* that is one reason I do not get well faster.

You see, he does not believe I am sick!

And what can one do?

If a physician of high standing, and one's own husband, assures friends   10 and relatives that there is really nothing the matter with one but temporary nervous depression—a slight hysterical tendency—what is one to do?

My brother is also a physician, and also of high standing, and he says the same thing.

So I take phosphates or phosphites—whichever it is, and tonics, and journeys, and air, and exercise, and am absolutely forbidden to "work" until I am well again.

Personally, I disagree with their ideas.

Personally, I believe that congenial work, with excitement and change, would do me good.

But what is one to do?   15

I did write for a while in spite of them; but it *does* exhaust me a good deal—having to be so sly about it, or else meet with heavy opposition.

I sometimes fancy that in my condition if I had less opposition and more society and stimulus—but John says the very worst thing I can do is to think about my condition, and I confess it always makes me feel bad.

So I will let it alone and talk about the house.

The most beautiful place! It is quite alone, standing well back from the road, quite three miles from the village. It makes me think of English places that you read about, for there are hedges and walls and gates that lock, and lots of separate little houses for the gardeners and people.

There is a *delicious* garden! I never saw such a garden—large and shady,   20 full of box-bordered paths, and lined with long grape-covered arbors with seats under them.

There were greenhouses, too, but they are all broken now.

There was some legal trouble, I believe, something about the heirs and co-heirs; anyhow, the place has been empty for years.

That spoils my ghostliness, I am afraid, but I don't care—there is something strange about the house—I can feel it.

I even said so to John one moonlight evening, but he said what I felt was a *draught*, and shut the window.

I get unreasonably angry with John sometimes. I'm sure I never used to   25
be so sensitive. I think it is due to this nervous condition.

But John says if I feel so, I shall neglect proper self-control; so I take pains
to control myself—before him, at least, and that makes me very tired.

I don't like our room a bit. I wanted one downstairs that opened onto the
piazza and had roses all over the window, and such pretty old-fashioned chintz
hangings! but John would not hear of it.

He said there was only one window and not room for two beds, and no
near room for him if he took another.

He is very careful and loving, and hardly lets me stir without special direction.

I have a schedule prescription for each hour in the day; he takes all   30
care from me, and so I feel basely ungrateful not to value it more.

He said we came here solely on my account, that I was to have perfect rest
and all the air I could get. "Your exercise depends on your strength, my dear,"
said he, "and your food somewhat on your appetite; but air you can absorb all
the time." So we took the nursery at the top of the house.

It is a big, airy room, the whole floor nearly, with windows that look all
ways, and air and sunshine galore. It was nursery first and then playroom and
gymnasium, I should judge; for the windows are barred for little children, and
there are rings and things in the walls.

The paint and paper look as if a boys' school had used it. It is stripped
off—the paper—in great patches all around the head of my bed, about as far as I
can reach, and in a great place on the other side of the room low down. I never
saw a worse paper in my life.

One of those sprawling flamboyant patterns committing every artistic sin.

It is dull enough to confuse the eye in following, pronounced enough to   35
constantly irritate and provoke study, and when you follow the lame uncertain
curves for a little distance they suddenly commit suicide—plunge off at outrageous angles, destroy themselves in unheard of contradictions.

The color is repellant, almost revolting; a smouldering unclean yellow,
strangely faded by the slow-turning sunlight.

It is a dull yet lurid orange in some places, a sickly sulphur tint in others.

No wonder the children hated it! I should hate it myself if I had to live in
this room long.

There comes John, and I must put this away,—he hates to have me write
a word.

We have been here two weeks, and I haven't felt like writing before,   40
since that first day.

I am sitting by the window now, up in this atrocious nursery, and there is
nothing to hinder my writing as much as I please, save lack of strength.

John is away all day, and even some nights when his cases are serious.

I am glad my case is not serious!

But these nervous troubles are dreadfully depressing.

John does not know how much I really suffer. He knows there is   45
no *reason* to suffer, and that satisfies him.

Of course it is only nervousness. It does weigh on me so not to do my
duty in any way!

I meant to be such a help to John, such a real rest and comfort, and
here I am a comparative burden already!

Nobody would believe what an effort it is to do what little I am able,—to
dress and entertain, and order things.

It is fortunate Mary is so good with the baby. Such a dear baby!

And yet I cannot be with him, it makes me so nervous.   50

I suppose John never was nervous in his life. He laughs at me so about
this wallpaper!

At first he meant to repaper the room, but afterward he said that I was
letting it get the better of me, and that nothing was worse for a nervous
patient than to give way to such fancies.

He said that after the wallpaper was changed it would be the heavy bedstead, and then the barred windows, and then that gate at the head of the
stairs, and so on.

"You know the place is doing you good," he said, "and really, dear, I
don't care to renovate the house just for a three months' rental."

"Then do let us go downstairs," I said, "there are such pretty rooms   55
there."

Then he took me in his arms and called me a blessed little goose, and
said he would go down cellar, if I wished, and have it whitewashed into the
bargain.

But he is right enough about the beds and windows and things.

It is an airy and comfortable room as anyone need wish, and, of course,
I would not be so silly as to make him uncomfortable just for a whim.

I'm really getting quite fond of the big room, all but that horrid paper.

Out of one window I can see the garden, those mysterious deep-shaded   60
arbors, the riotous old-fashioned flowers, and bushes and gnarly trees.

Out of another I get a lovely view of the bay and a little private wharf
belonging to the estate. There is a beautiful shaded lane that runs down there
from the house. I always fancy I see people walking in these numerous paths
and arbors, but John has cautioned me not to give way to fancy in the least.
He says that with my imaginative power and habit of story-making, a nervous
weakness like mine is sure to lead to all manner of excited fancies, and that
I ought to use my will and good sense to check the tendency. So I try.

I think sometimes that if I were only well enough to write a little it would
relieve the press of ideas and rest me.

But I find I get pretty tired when I try.

It is so discouraging not to have any advice and companionship about my work. When I get really well, John says we will ask Cousin Henry and Julia down for a long visit; but he says he would as soon put fireworks in my pillowcase as to let me have those stimulating people about now.

I wish I could get well faster.   65

But I must not think about that. This paper looks to me as if it *knew* what a vicious influence it had!

There is a recurrent spot where the pattern lolls like a broken neck and two bulbous eyes stare at you upside down.

I get positively angry with the impertinence of it and the everlastingness. Up and down and sideways they crawl, and those absurd, unblinking eyes are everywhere. There is one place where two breadths didn't match, and the eyes go all up and down the line, one a little higher than the other.

I never saw so much expression in an inanimate thing before, and we all know how much expression they have! I used to lie awake as a child and get more entertainment and terror out of blank walls and plain furniture than most children could find in a toy-store.

I remember what a kindly wink the knobs of our big, old bureau used   70
to have, and there was one chair that always seemed like a strong friend.

I used to feel that if any of the other things looked too fierce I could always hop into that chair and be safe.

The furniture in this room is no worse than inharmonious, however, for we had to bring it all from downstairs. I suppose when this was used as a playroom they had to take the nursery things out, and no wonder! I never saw such ravages as the children have made here.

The wallpaper, as I said before, is torn off in spots, and it sticketh closer than a brother—they must have had perseverance as well as hatred.

Then the floor is scratched and gouged and splintered, the plaster itself is dug out here and there, and this great heavy bed, which is all we found in the room, looks as if it had been through the wars.

But I don't mind it a bit—only the paper.   75

There comes John's sister. Such a dear girl as she is, and so careful of me! I must not let her find me writing.

She is a perfect and enthusiastic housekeeper, and hopes for no better profession. I verily believe she thinks it is the writing which made me sick!

But I can write when she is out, and see her a long way off from these windows.

There is one that commands the road, a lovely shaded winding road, and one that just looks off over the country. A lovely country, too, full of great elms and velvet meadows.

This wallpaper has a kind of sub-pattern in a different shade, a par-   80
ticularly irritating one, for you can only see it in certain lights, and not
clearly then.

But in the places where it isn't faded and where the sun is just so—I can
see a strange, provoking, formless sort of figure, that seems to skulk about
behind that silly and conspicuous front design.

There's sister on the stairs!

Well, the Fourth of July is over! The people are all gone, and I am tired out.
John thought it might do me good to see a little company, so we just had
mother and Nellie and the children down for a week.

Of course I didn't do a thing. Jennie sees to everything now.

But it tired me all the same.   85

John says if I don't pick up faster he shall send me to Weir Mitchell in
the fall.

But I don't want to go there at all. I had a friend who was in his hands
once, and she says he is just like John and my brother, only more so!

Besides, it is such an undertaking to go so far.

I don't feel as if it was worthwhile to turn my hand over for anything,
and I'm getting dreadfully fretful and querulous.

I cry at nothing, and cry most of the time.   90

Of course I don't when John is here, or anybody else, but when I am
alone.

And I am alone a good deal just now. John is kept in town very often by
serious cases, and Jennie is good and lets me alone when I want her to.

So I walk a little in the garden or down that lovely lane, sit on the
porch under the roses, and lie down up here a good deal.

I'm getting really fond of the room in spite of the wallpaper. Perhaps
because of the wallpaper.

It dwells in my mind so!   95

I lie here on this great immovable bed—it is nailed down, I believe—and
follow that pattern about by the hour. It is as good as gymnastics, I assure
you. I start, we'll say, at the bottom, down in the corner over there where it
has not been touched, and I determine for the thousandth time that I *will*
follow that pointless pattern to some sort of a conclusion.

I know a little of the principle of design, and I know this thing was not
arranged on any laws of radiation, or alternation, or repetition, or symmetry, or anything else that I ever heard of.

It is repeated, of course, by the breadths, but not otherwise.

Looked at in one way each breadth stands alone, the bloated curves and
flourishes—a kind of "debased Romanesque" with *delirium tremens*—go waddling up and down in isolated columns of fatuity.

But, on the other hand, they connect diagonally, and the sprawling 100
outlines run off in great slanting waves of optic horror, like a lot of wallowing seaweeds in full chase.

The whole thing goes horizontally, too, at least it seems so, and
I exhaust myself in trying to distinguish the order of its going in that
direction.

They have used a horizontal breadth for a frieze, and that adds wonderfully to the confusion.

There is one end of the room where it is almost intact, and there,
when the crosslights fade and the low sun shines directly upon it, I can
almost fancy radiation after all,—the interminable grotesques seem to
form around a common centre and rush off in headlong plunges of equal
distraction.

It makes me tired to follow it. I will take a nap, I guess.

I don't know why I should write this. 105
    I don't want to.
    I don't feel able.
And I know John would think it absurd. But I *must* say what I feel
and think in some way—it is such a relief!
But the effort is getting to be greater than the relief.
Half the time now I am awfully lazy, and lie down ever so much. 110
John says I mustn't lose my strength, and has me take cod liver
oil and lots of tonics and things, to say nothing of ale and wine and
rare meat.
Dear John! He loves me very dearly, and hates to have me sick.
I tried to have a real earnest reasonable talk with him the other day,
and tell him how I wish he would let me go and make a visit to Cousin
Henry and Julia.
But he said I wasn't able to go, nor able to stand it after I got there;
and I did not make out a very good case for myself, for I was crying before
I had finished.
It is getting to be a great effort for me to think straight. Just this nerv-
ous weakness I suppose.
And dear John gathered me up in his arms, and just carried me upstairs 115
and laid me on the bed, and sat by me and read to me till it tired my head.
He said I was his darling and his comfort and all he had, and that I
must take care of myself for his sake, and keep well.
He says no one but myself can help me out it, that I must use my will
and self-control and not let any silly fancies run away with me.
There's one comfort, the baby is well and happy, and does not have
to occupy this nursery with the horrid wallpaper.

If we had not used it, that blessed child would have! What a fortunate escape! Why, I wouldn't have a child of mine, an impressionable little thing, live in such a room for worlds.

I never thought of it before, but it is lucky that John kept me here after all, I can stand it so much easier than a baby, you see. 120

Of course I never mention it to them any more—I am too wise, but I keep watch of it all the same.

There are things in the wallpaper that nobody knows but me, or ever will.

Behind that outside pattern the dim shapes get clearer every day.

It is always the same shape, only very numerous.

And it is like a woman stooping down and creeping about behind that pattern. I don't like it a bit. I wonder—I begin to think—I wish John would take me away from here! 125

It is so hard to talk with John about my case, because he is so wise, and because he loves me so.

But I tried it last night.

It was moonlight. The moon shines in all around just as the sun does.

I hate to see it sometimes, it creeps so slowly, and always comes in by one window or another.

John was asleep and I hated to waken him, so I kept still and watched the moonlight on that undulating wallpaper till I felt creepy. 130

The faint figure behind seemed to shake the pattern, just as if she wanted to get out.

I got up softly and went to feel and see if the paper *did* move, and when I came back John was awake.

"What is it, little girl?" he said. "Don't go walking about like that—you'll get cold."

I thought it was a good time to talk, so I told him that I really was not gaining here, and that I wished he would take me away.

"Why, darling!" said he, "our lease will be up in three weeks, and I can't see how to leave before. 135

"The repairs are not done at home, and I cannot possibly leave town just now. Of course if you were in any danger, I could and would, but you really are better, dear, whether you can see it or not. I am a doctor, dear, and I know. You are gaining flesh and color, your appetite is better, I feel really much easier about you."

"I don't weigh a bit more," said I, "nor as much; and my appetite may be better in the evening when you are here but it is worse in the morning when you are away!"

"Bless her little heart!" said he with a big hug, "she shall be as sick as she pleases! But now let's improve the shining hours by going to sleep, and talk about it in the morning!"

"And you won't go away?" I asked gloomily.

"Why, how can I, dear? It is only three weeks more and then we will take a nice little trip of a few days while Jennie is getting the house ready. Really dear you are better!"

"Better in body perhaps—" I began, and stopped short, for he sat up straight and looked at me with such a stern, reproachful look that I could not say another word.

"My darling," said he, "I beg you, for my sake and for our child's sake, as well as for your own, that you will never for one instant let that idea enter your mind! There is nothing so dangerous, so fascinating, to a temperament like yours. It is a false and foolish fancy. Can you trust me as a physician when I tell you so?"

So of course I said no more on that score, and we went to sleep before long. He thought I was asleep first, but I wasn't, and lay there for hours trying to decide whether that front pattern and the back pattern really did move together or separately.

On a pattern like this, by daylight, there is a lack of sequence, a defiance of law, that is a constant irritant to a normal mind.

The color is hideous enough, and unreliable enough, and infuriating enough, but the pattern is torturing.

You think you have mastered it, but just as you get well underway in following, it turns a back-somersault and there you are. It slaps you in the face, knocks you down, and tramples upon you. It is like a bad dream.

The outside pattern is a florid arabesque, reminding one of a fungus. If you can imagine a toadstool in joints, an interminable string of toadstools, budding and sprouting in endless convolutions—why, that is something like it.

That is, sometimes!

There is one marked peculiarity about this paper, a thing nobody seems to notice but myself, and that is that it changes as the light changes.

When the sun shoots in through the east window—I always watch for that first long, straight ray—it changes so quickly that I never can quite believe it.

That is why I watch it always.

By moonlight—the moon shines in all night when there is a moon—I wouldn't know it was the same paper.

At night in any kind of light, in twilight, candlelight, lamplight, and worst of all by moonlight, it becomes bars! The outside pattern I mean, and the woman behind it is as plain as can be.

I didn't realize for a long time what the thing was that showed behind, that dim sub-pattern, but now I am quite sure it is a woman.

By daylight she is subdued, quiet. I fancy it is the pattern that keeps   155
her so still. It is so puzzling. It keeps me quiet by the hour.

I lie down ever so much now. John says it is good for me, and to sleep all I can.

Indeed he started the habit by making me lie down for an hour after each meal.

It is a very bad habit I am convinced, for you see I don't sleep.

And that cultivates deceit, for I don't tell them I'm awake—O, no!

The fact is I am getting a little afraid of John.   160

He seems very queer sometimes, and even Jennie has an inexplicable look.

It strikes me occasionally, just as a scientific hypothesis,—that perhaps it is the paper!

I have watched John when he did not know I was looking, and come into the room suddenly on the most innocent excuses, and I've caught him several times *looking at the paper*! And Jennie too. I caught Jennie with her hand on it once.

She didn't know I was in the room, and when I asked her in a quiet, a very quiet voice, with the most restrained manner possible, what she was doing with the paper—she turned around as if she had been caught stealing, and looked quite angry—asked me why I should frighten her so!

Then she said that the paper stained everything it touched, that she had   165
found yellow smooches on all my clothes and John's, and she wished we would be more careful!

Did not that sound innocent? But I know she was studying that pattern, and I am determined that nobody shall find it out but myself!

Life is very much more exciting now than it used to be. You see I have something more to expect, to look forward to, to watch. I really do eat better, and am more quiet than I was.

John is so pleased to see me improve! He laughed a little the other day, and said I seemed to be flourishing in spite of my wallpaper.

I turned it off with a laugh. I had no intention of telling him it was *because* of the wallpaper—he would make fun of me. He might even want to take me away.

I don't want to leave now until I have found it out. There is a week   170
more, and I think that will be enough.

I'm feeling ever so much better! I don't sleep much at night, for it is so interesting to watch developments; but I sleep a good deal in the daytime.

In the daytime it is tiresome and perplexing.

There are always new shoots on the fungus, and new shades of yellow all over it. I cannot keep count of them, though I have tried conscientiously.

It is the strangest yellow, that wallpaper! It makes me think of all the yellow things I ever saw—not beautiful ones like buttercups, but old foul, bad yellow things.

But there is something else about that paper—the smell! I noticed it the   175
moment we came into the room, but with so much air and sun it was not bad.
Now we have had a week of fog and rain, and whether the windows are open or not, the smell is here.

It creeps all over the house.

I find it hovering in the dining-room, skulking in the parlor, hiding in the hall, lying in wait for me on the stairs.

It gets into my hair.

Even when I go to ride, if I turn my head suddenly and surprise it— there is that smell!

Such a peculiar odor, too! I have spent hours in tying to analyze it, to   180
find what it smelled like.

It is not bad—at first, and very gentle, but quite the subtlest, most enduring odor I ever met.

In this damp weather it is awful, I wake up in the night and find it hanging over me.

It used to disturb me at first. I thought seriously of burning the house—to reach the smell.

But now I am used to it. The only thing I can think of that it is like is the *color* of the paper! A yellow smell.

There is a very funny mark on this wall, low down, near the mopboard. 185
A streak that runs round the room. It goes behind every piece of furniture, except the bed, a long, straight, even *smooch*, as if it had been rubbed over and over.

I wonder how it was done and who did it, and what they did it for. Round and round and round—round and round and round—it makes me dizzy!

I really have discovered something at last.

Through watching so much at night, when it changes so, I have finally found out.

The front pattern *does* move—and no wonder! The woman behind shakes it!

Sometimes I think there are a great many women behind, and sometimes   190
only one, and she crawls around fast, and her crawling shakes it all over.

Then in the very bright spots she keeps still, and in the very shady spots she just takes hold of the bars and shakes them hard.

And she is all the time trying to climb through. But nobody could climb through that pattern—it strangles so; I think that is why it has so many heads.

They get through, and then the pattern strangles them off and turns them upside down, and makes their eyes white!

If those heads were covered or taken off it would not be half so bad.

I think that woman gets out in the daytime!

And I'll tell you why—privately—I've seen her!

I can see her out of every one of my windows!

It is the same woman, I know, for she is always creeping, and most women do not creep by daylight.

I see her in that long shaded lane, creeping up and down. I see her in those dark grape arbors, creeping all around the garden.

I see her on that long road under the trees, creeping along, and when a 200 carriage comes she hides under the blackberry vines.

I don't blame her a bit. It must be very humiliating to be caught creeping by daylight!

I always lock the door when I creep by daylight. I can't do it at night, for I know John would suspect something at once.

And John is so queer now, that I don't want to irritate him. I wish he would take another room! Besides, I don't want anybody to get that woman out at night but myself.

I often wonder if I could see her out of all the windows at once.

But, turn as fast as I can, I can only see out of one at one time. 205

And though I always see her, she *may* be able to creep faster than I can turn!

I have watched her sometimes away off in the open country, creeping as fast as a cloud shadow in a high wind.

If only that top pattern could be gotten off from the under one! I mean to try it, little by little.

I have found out another funny thing, but I shan't tell it this time! It does not do to trust people too much.

There are only two more days to get this paper off, and I believe John is 210 beginning to notice. I don't like the look in his eyes.

And I heard him ask Jennie a lot of professional questions, about me. She had a very good report to give.

She said I slept a good deal in the daytime.

John knows I don't sleep very well at night, for all I'm so quiet!

He asked me all sorts of questions too, and pretended to be very loving and kind.

As if I couldn't see through him! 215

Still, I don't wonder he acts so, sleeping under this paper for three months.

It only interests me, but I feel sure John and Jennie are secretly affected by it.

Hurrah! This is the last day, but it is enough. John to stay in town over night, and won't be out until this evening.

Jennie wanted to sleep with me—the sly thing! But I told her I should undoubtedly rest better for a night all alone.

That was clever, for really I wasn't alone a bit! As soon as it was moon- 220
light and that poor thing began to crawl and shake the pattern, I got up and
ran to help her.

I pulled and she shook, I shook and she pulled, and before morning we
had peeled off yards of that paper.

A strip about as high as my head and half around the room.

And then when the sun came and that awful pattern began to laugh at me,
I declared I would finish it today!

We go away tomorrow, and they are moving all my furniture down again
to leave things as they were before.

Jennie looked at the wall in amazement, but I told her merrily that 225
I did it out of pure spite at the vicious thing.

She laughed and said she wouldn't mind doing it herself, but I must not
get tired.

How she betrayed herself that time!

But I am here, and no person touches this paper but me,—not *alive*!

She tried to get me out of the room—it was too patent! But I said it was so
quiet and empty and clean now that I believed I would lie down again and sleep
all I could, and not to wake me even for dinner—I would call when I woke.

So now she is gone, and the servants are gone, and the things are gone, 230
and there is nothing left but that great bedstead nailed down, with the canvas
mattress we found on it.

We shall sleep downstairs tonight, and take the boat home tomorrow.

I quite enjoy the room, now it is bare again.

How those children did tear about here!

This bedstead is fairly gnawed!

But I must get to work. 235

I have locked the door and thrown the key down into the front path.

I don't want to go out, and I don't want to have anybody come in, till
John comes.

I want to astonish him.

I've got a rope up here that even Jennie did not find. If that woman does
get out, and tries to get away, I can tie her!

But I forgot I could not reach far without anything to stand on! 240

This bed will *not* move!

I tried to lift and push it until I was lame, and then I got so angry I bit off
a little piece at one corner—but it hurt my teeth.

Then I peeled off all the paper I could reach standing on the floor. It
sticks horribly and the pattern just enjoys it! All those strangled heads and
bulbous eyes and waddling fungus growths just shriek with derision!

I am getting angry enough to do something desperate. To jump out of the
window would be admirable exercise, but the bars are too strong even to try.

Besides I wouldn't do it. Of course not. I know well enough that a step 245
like that is improper and might be misconstrued.

I don't like to *look* out of the windows even—there are so many of those
creeping women, and they creep so fast.

I wonder if they all come out of that wallpaper as I did?

But I am securely fastened now by my well-hidden rope—you don't get
me out in the road there!

I suppose I shall have to get back behind the pattern when it comes night,
and that is hard!

It is so pleasant to be out in this great room and creep around as I please! 250

I don't want to go outside. I won't, even if Jennie asks me to.

For outside you have to creep on the ground, and everything is green
instead of yellow.

But here I can creep smoothly on the floor, and my shoulder just fits in
that long smooch around the wall, so I cannot lose my way.

Why, there's John at the door!

It is no use, young man, you can't open it! 255

How he does call and pound!

Now he's crying for an axe.

It would be a shame to break down that beautiful door!

"John dear!" said I in the gentlest voice, "the key is down by the front
steps, under a plantain leaf!"

That silenced him for a few moments. 260

Then he said—very quietly indeed, "Open the door, my darling!"

"I can't," said I. "The key is down by the front door under a plantain leaf!"

And then I said it again, several times, very gently and slowly, and said
it so often that he had to go and see, and he got it of course, and came in.
He stopped short by the door.

"What is the matter?" he cried. "For God's sake, what are you doing!"

I kept on creeping just the same, but I looked at him over my shoulder. 265

"I've got out at last," said I, "in spite of you and Jane. And I've pulled off
most of the paper, so you can't put me back!"

Now why should that man have fainted? But he did, and right across my
path by the wall, so that I had to creep over him every time!

■ What do we learn about the nature of the wallpaper in the room? Why are these
details important? How does this attention to the wallpaper give us insight into
the psychological state of the narrator? Locate specific instances where her
observations about the wallpaper indicate some change in her state of mind.

■ How does the narrator present her husband? In what ways are our perceptions of her husband different from what she tells us?

POETRY

Robert Browning (1812–1889)

Porphyria's Lover (1842)

The rain set early in to-night,
    The sullen wind was soon awake,
It tore the elm-tops down for spite,
    And did its worst to vex the lake:
    I listened with heart fit to break.   5
When glided in Porphyria; straight
    She shut the cold out and the storm,
And kneeled and made the cheerless grate
    Blaze up, and all the cottage warm;
    Which done, she rose, and from her form   10
Withdrew the dripping cloak and shawl,
    And laid her soiled gloves by, untied
Her hat and let the damp hair fall,
    And, last, she sat down by my side
    And called me. When no voice replied,   15
She put my arm about her waist,
    And made her smooth white shoulder bare,
And all her yellow hair displaced,
    And, stooping, made my cheek lie there,
    And spread, o'er all, her yellow hair,   20
Murmuring how she loved me—she
    Too weak, for all her heart's endeavour,
To set its struggling passion free
    From pride, and vainer ties dissever,
    And give herself to me for ever.   25
But passion sometimes would prevail,
    Nor could to-night's gay feast restrain
A sudden thought of one so pale
    For love of her, and all in vain:
    So, she was come through wind and rain.   30
Be sure I looked up at her eyes
    Happy and proud; at last I knew
Porphyria worshipped me; surprise
    Made my heart swell, and still it grew
    While I debated what to do.   35

That moment she was mine, mine, fair,
   Perfectly pure and good: I found
A thing to do, and all her hair
   In one long yellow string I wound
   Three times her little throat around,   40
And strangled her. No pain felt she;
   I am quite sure she felt no pain.
As a shut bud that holds a bee,
   I warily oped her lids: again
   Laughed the blue eyes without a stain.   45
And I untightened next the tress
   About her neck; her cheek once more
Blushed bright beneath my burning kiss:
   I propped her head up as before,
   Only, this time my shoulder bore   50
Her head, which droops upon it still:
   The smiling rosy little head,
So glad it has its utmost will,
   That all it scorned at once is fled,
   And I, its love, am gained instead!   55
Porphyria's love: she guessed not how
   Her darling one wish would be heard.
And thus we sit together now,
   And all night long we have not stirred,
   And yet God has not said a word   60

- Compare Porphyria's treatment of the narrator in the first half of the poem to the narrator's treatment of Porphyria at the end of the poem. What significance might these parallels have?

- How might this story be interpreted as an allegory about the nature of love? How might you challenge such an allegorical reading?

Carolyn Forché (1950–   )

The Colonel (1978)

What you have heard is true. I was in his house. His wife carried a tray of coffee and sugar. His daughter filed her nails, his son went out for the night. There were daily papers, pet dogs, a pistol on the cushion beside him. The moon swung bare on its black cord over the house. On the television was a cop show.

It was in English. Broken bottles were embedded in the walls around the house to scoop the kneecaps from a man's legs or cut his hands to lace. On the windows there were gratings like those in liquor stores. We had dinner, rack of lamb, good wine, a gold bell was on the table for calling the maid. The maid brought green mangoes, salt, a type of bread. I was asked how I enjoyed the country. There was a brief commercial in Spanish. His wife took everything away. There was some talk then of how difficult it had become to govern. The parrot said hello on the terrace. The colonel told it to shut up, and pushed himself from the table. My friend said to me with his eyes: say nothing. The colonel returned with a sack used to bring groceries home. He spilled many human ears on the table. They were like dried peach halves. There is no other way to say this. He took one of them in his hands, shook it in our faces, dropped it into a water glass. It came alive there. I am tired of fooling around he said. As for the rights of anyone, tell your people they can go fuck themselves. He swept the ears to the floor with his arm and held the last of his wine in the air. Something for your poetry, no? he said. Some of the ears on the floor caught this scrap of his voice. Some of the ears on the floor were pressed to the ground.

- How does the description of the house prepare us for the ears that the colonel pours out on the table?
- How does the colonel's question "Something for your poetry, no?" change the nature of the description that the remainder of the poem presents?

William Butler Yeats (1865–1939)

Leda and the Swan (1918)

A sudden blow: the great wings beating still
Above the staggering girl, her thighs caressed
By the dark webs, her nape caught in his bill,
He holds her helpless breast upon his breast.

How can those terrified vague fingers push   5
The feathered glory from her loosening thighs?
And how can body, laid in that white rush,
But feel the strange heart beating where it lies?

A shudder in the loins engenders there
The broken wall, the burning roof and tower   10
And Agamemnon dead.

> Being so caught up,
> So mastered by the brute blood of the air,
> Did she put on his knowledge with his power
> Before the indifferent beak could let her drop?   15

- The god Zeus, disguised in the form of a swan, raped Leda. One of their offspring was Helen, the Greek beauty whose abduction by Paris set off the Trojan War. Helen's sister, Clytemnestra, shared her mother's womb, though she had a different father. Clytemnestra killed her own husband, Agamemnon, when he returned from leading the Greek forces to victory in the Trojan War. What are the different boundaries that are broken by this rape (and acknowledged in this poem)?
- How does the poem depict the relation between the rape and subsequent history?

Linda Pastan (1932–   )

Ethics (1980)

In ethics class so many years ago
our teacher asked this question every fall:
if there were a fire in a museum
which would you save, a Rembrandt painting
or an old woman who hadn't many   5
years left anyhow? Restless on hard chairs
caring little for pictures or old age
we'd opt one year for life, the next for art
and always half-heartedly. Sometimes
the woman borrowed my grandmother's face   10
leaving her usual kitchen to wander
some drafty, half imagined museum.
One year, feeling clever, I replied
why not let the woman decide herself?
Linda, the teacher would report, eschews   15
the burdens of responsibility.
This fall in a real museum I stand
before a real Rembrandt, old woman,
or nearly so, myself. The colors
within this frame are darker than autumn,   20

darker even than winter—the browns of earth,
though earth's most radiant elements burn
through the canvas. I know now that woman
and painting and season are almost one
and all beyond saving by children.   25

- How has the theoretical question from ethics class changed for the poet?
- How has her answer changed?

Christina Rossetti (1830–1894)

Goblin Market (1862)

Morning and evening
Maids heard the goblins cry:
"Come buy our orchard fruits,
Come buy, come buy:
Apples and quinces,   5
Lemons and oranges,
Plump unpeck'd cherries,
Melons and raspberries,
Bloom-down-cheek'd peaches,
Swart-headed mulberries,   10
Wild free-born cranberries,
Crab-apples, dewberries,
Pine-apples, blackberries,
Apricots, strawberries;—
All ripe together   15
In summer weather,—
Morns that pass by,
Fair eves that fly;
Come buy, come buy:
Our grapes fresh from the vine,   20
Pomegranates full and fine,
Dates and sharp bullaces,
Rare pears and greengages,
Damsons and bilberries,
Taste them and try: 25
Currants and gooseberries,
Bright-fire-like barberries,

Figs to fill your mouth,
Citrons from the South,
Sweet to tongue and sound to eye; 30
Come buy, come buy."

Evening by evening
Among the brookside rushes,
Laura bow'd her head to hear,
Lizzie veil'd her blushes: 35
Crouching close together
In the cooling weather,
With clasping arms and cautioning lips,
With tingling cheeks and finger tips.
"Lie close," Laura said, 40
Pricking up her golden head:
"We must not look at goblin men,
We must not buy their fruits:
Who knows upon what soil they fed
Their hungry thirsty roots?" 45
"Come buy," call the goblins
Hobbling down the glen.

"Oh," cried Lizzie, "Laura, Laura,
You should not peep at goblin men."
Lizzie cover'd up her eyes, 50
Cover'd close lest they should look;
Laura rear'd her glossy head,
And whisper'd like the restless brook:
"Look, Lizzie, look, Lizzie,
Down the glen tramp little men. 55
One hauls a basket,
One bears a plate,
One lugs a golden dish
Of many pounds weight.
How fair the vine must grow 60
Whose grapes are so luscious;
How warm the wind must blow
Through those fruit bushes."
"No," said Lizzie, "No, no, no;
Their offers should not charm us, 65
Their evil gifts would harm us."
She thrust a dimpled finger

In each ear, shut eyes and ran:
Curious Laura chose to linger
Wondering at each merchant man.   70
One had a cat's face,
One whisk'd a tail,
One tramp'd at a rat's pace,
One crawl'd like a snail,
One like a wombat prowl'd obtuse and furry,   75
One like a ratel tumbled hurry skurry.
She heard a voice like voice of doves
Cooing all together:
They sounded kind and full of loves
In the pleasant weather.   80

Laura stretch'd her gleaming neck
Like a rush-imbedded swan,
Like a lily from the beck,
Like a moonlit poplar branch,
Like a vessel at the launch   85
When its last restraint is gone.

Backwards up the mossy glen
Turn'd and troop'd the goblin men,
With their shrill repeated cry,
"Come buy, come buy."   90
When they reach'd where Laura was
They stood stock still upon the moss,
Leering at each other,
Brother with queer brother;
Signalling each other,   95
Brother with sly brother.
One set his basket down,
One rear'd his plate;
One began to weave a crown
Of tendrils, leaves, and rough nuts brown   100
(Men sell not such in any town);
One heav'd the golden weight
Of dish and fruit to offer her: 105
"Come buy, come buy," was still their cry.
Laura stared but did not stir,
Long'd but had no money:
The whisk-tail'd merchant bade her taste

In tones as smooth as honey,   110
The cat-faced purr'd,
The rat-faced spoke a word
Of welcome, and the snail-paced even was heard;
One parrot-voiced and jolly
Cried "Pretty Goblin" still for "Pretty Polly;"—   115
One whistled like a bird.

But sweet-tooth Laura spoke in haste:
"Good folk, I have no coin;
To take were to purloin:
I have no copper in my purse,   120
I have no silver either,
And all my gold is on the furze
That shakes in windy weather
Above the rusty heather."
"You have much gold upon your head,"   125
They answer'd all together:
"Buy from us with a golden curl."
She clipp'd a precious golden lock,
She dropp'd a tear more rare than pearl,
Then suck'd their fruit globes fair or red: 130
Sweeter than honey from the rock,
Stronger than man-rejoicing wine,
Clearer than water flow'd that juice;
She never tasted such before,
How should it cloy with length of use?   135
She suck'd and suck'd and suck'd the more
Fruits which that unknown orchard bore;
She suck'd until her lips were sore;
Then flung the emptied rinds away
But gather'd up one kernel stone,   140
And knew not was it night or day
As she turn'd home alone.

Lizzie met her at the gate
Full of wise upbraidings:
"Dear, you should not stay so late,   145
Twilight is not good for maidens;
Should not loiter in the glen
In the haunts of goblin men.
Do you not remember Jeanie,

How she met them in the moonlight,   150
Took their gifts both choice and many,
Ate their fruits and wore their flowers
Pluck'd from bowers
Where summer ripens at all hours?
But ever in the noonlight   155
She pined and pined away;
Sought them by night and day,
Found them no more, but dwindled and grew grey;
Then fell with the first snow,
While to this day no grass will grow   160
Where she lies low:
I planted daisies there a year ago
That never blow.
You should not loiter so."
"Nay, hush," said Laura: 165
"Nay, hush, my sister:
I ate and ate my fill,
Yet my mouth waters still;
To-morrow night I will
Buy more;" and kiss'd her: 170
"Have done with sorrow;
I'll bring you plums to-morrow
Fresh on their mother twigs,
Cherries worth getting;
You cannot think what figs   175
My teeth have met in,
What melons icy-cold
Piled on a dish of gold
Too huge for me to hold,
What peaches with a velvet nap,   180
Pellucid grapes without one seed:
Odorous indeed must be the mead
Whereon they grow, and pure the wave they drink
With lilies at the brink,
And sugar-sweet their sap."   185

Golden head by golden head,
Like two pigeons in one nest
Folded in each other's wings,
They lay down in their curtain'd bed:
Like two blossoms on one stem,   190

Like two flakes of new-fall'n snow,
Like two wands of ivory
Tipp'd with gold for awful kings.
Moon and stars gaz'd in at them,
Wind sang to them lullaby,   195
Lumbering owls forbore to fly,
Not a bat flapp'd to and fro
Round their rest:
Cheek to cheek and breast to breast
Lock'd together in one nest.   200

Early in the morning
When the first cock crow'd his warning,
Neat like bees, as sweet and busy,
Laura rose with Lizzie:
Fetch'd in honey, milk'd the cows,   205
Air'd and set to rights the house,
Kneaded cakes of whitest wheat,
Cakes for dainty mouths to eat,
Next churn'd butter, whipp'd up cream,
Fed their poultry, sat and sew'd;   210
Talk'd as modest maidens should:
Lizzie with an open heart,
Laura in an absent dream,
One content, one sick in part;
One warbling for the mere bright day's delight,   215
One longing for the night.

At length slow evening came:
They went with pitchers to the reedy brook;
Lizzie most placid in her look,
Laura most like a leaping flame.   220
They drew the gurgling water from its deep;
Lizzie pluck'd purple and rich golden flags,
Then turning homeward said: "The sunset flushes
Those furthest loftiest crags;
Come, Laura, not another maiden lags.   225
No wilful squirrel wags,
The beasts and birds are fast asleep."
But Laura loiter'd still among the rushes
And said the bank was steep.

And said the hour was early still   230
The dew not fall'n, the wind not chill;
Listening ever, but not catching
The customary cry,
"Come buy, come buy,"
With its iterated jingle   235
Of sugar-baited words:
Not for all her watching
Once discerning even one goblin
Racing, whisking, tumbling, hobbling;
Let alone the herds   240
That used to tramp along the glen,
In groups or single,
Of brisk fruit-merchant men.

Till Lizzie urged, "O Laura, come;
I hear the fruit-call but I dare not look: 245
You should not loiter longer at this brook:
Come with me home.
The stars rise, the moon bends her arc,
Each glowworm winks her spark,
Let us get home before the night grows dark: 250
For clouds may gather
Though this is summer weather,
Put out the lights and drench us through;
Then if we lost our way what should we do?"

Laura turn'd cold as stone   255
To find her sister heard that cry alone,
That goblin cry,
"Come buy our fruits, come buy."
Must she then buy no more such dainty fruit?   260
Must she no more such succous pasture find,
Gone deaf and blind?
Her tree of life droop'd from the root:
She said not one word in her heart's sore ache;
But peering thro' the dimness, nought discerning,   265
Trudg'd home, her pitcher dripping all the way;
So crept to bed, and lay
Silent till Lizzie slept;
Then sat up in a passionate yearning,

And gnash'd her teeth for baulk'd desire, and wept   270
As if her heart would break.

Day after day, night after night,
Laura kept watch in vain
In sullen silence of exceeding pain.
She never caught again the goblin cry: 275
"Come buy, come buy;"—
She never spied the goblin men
Hawking their fruits along the glen:
But when the noon wax'd bright
Her hair grew thin and grey;   280
She dwindled, as the fair full moon doth turn
To swift decay and burn
Her fire away.

One day remembering her kernel-stone
She set it by a wall that faced the south;   285
Dew'd it with tears, hoped for a root,
Watch'd for a waxing shoot,
But there came none;
It never saw the sun,
It never felt the trickling moisture run: 290
While with sunk eyes and faded mouth
She dream'd of melons, as a traveller sees
False waves in desert drouth
With shade of leaf-crown'd trees,
And burns the thirstier in the sandful breeze.   295

She no more swept the house,
Tended the fowls or cows,
Fetch'd honey, kneaded cakes of wheat,
Brought water from the brook:
But sat down listless in the chimney-nook   300
And would not eat.

Tender Lizzie could not bear
To watch her sister's cankerous care
Yet not to share.
She night and morning   305
Caught the goblins' cry:
"Come buy our orchard fruits,

Come buy, come buy;"—
Beside the brook, along the glen,
She heard the tramp of goblin men,   310
The yoke and stir
Poor Laura could not hear;
Long'd to buy fruit to comfort her,
But fear'd to pay too dear.
She thought of Jeanie in her grave,   315
Who should have been a bride;
But who for joys brides hope to have
Fell sick and died
In her gay prime,
In earliest winter time,   320
With the first glazing rime,
With the first snow-fall of crisp winter time.

Till Laura dwindling
Seem'd knocking at Death's door:
Then Lizzie weigh'd no more   325
Better and worse;
But put a silver penny in her purse,
Kiss'd Laura, cross'd the heath with clumps of furze
At twilight, halted by the brook:
And for the first time in her life   330
Began to listen and look.

Laugh'd every goblin
When they spied her peeping:
Came towards her hobbling,
Flying, running, leaping,   335
Puffing and blowing,
Chuckling, clapping, crowing,
Clucking and gobbling,
Mopping and mowing,
Full of airs and graces,   340
Pulling wry faces,
Demure grimaces,
Cat-like and rat-like,
Ratel- and wombat-like,
Snail-paced in a hurry,   345
Parrot-voiced and whistler,
Helter skelter, hurry skurry,

Chattering like magpies,
Fluttering like pigeons,
Gliding like fishes,—   350
Hugg'd her and kiss'd her:
Squeez'd and caress'd her:
Stretch'd up their dishes,
Panniers, and plates:
"Look at our apples   355
Russet and dun,
Bob at our cherries,
Bite at our peaches,
Citrons and dates,
Grapes for the asking,   360
Pears red with basking
Out in the sun,
Plums on their twigs;
Pluck them and suck them,
Pomegranates, figs."—   365

"Good folk," said Lizzie,
Mindful of Jeanie:
"Give me much and many: —
Held out her apron,
Toss'd them her penny.   370
"Nay, take a seat with us,
Honour and eat with us,"
They answer'd grinning:
"Our feast is but beginning.
Night yet is early,   375
Warm and dew-pearly,
Wakeful and starry:
Such fruits as these
No man can carry:
Half their bloom would fly,   380
Half their dew would dry,
Half their flavour would pass by.
Sit down and feast with us,
Be welcome guest with us,
Cheer you and rest with us."—   385
"Thank you," said Lizzie: "But one waits
At home alone for me:
So without further parleying,

If you will not sell me any
Of your fruits though much and many,   390
Give me back my silver penny
I toss'd you for a fee."—
They began to scratch their pates,
No longer wagging, purring,
But visibly demurring,   395
Grunting and snarling.
One call'd her proud,
Cross-grain'd, uncivil;
Their tones wax'd loud,
Their looks were evil.   400
Lashing their tails
They trod and hustled her,
Elbow'd and jostled her,
Claw'd with their nails,
Barking, mewing, hissing, mocking,   405
Tore her gown and soil'd her stocking,
Twitch'd her hair out by the roots,
Stamp'd upon her tender feet,
Held her hands and squeez'd their fruits
Against her mouth to make her eat.   410

White and golden Lizzie stood,
Like a lily in a flood,—
Like a rock of blue-vein'd stone
Lash'd by tides obstreperously,—
Like a beacon left alone   415
In a hoary roaring sea,
Sending up a golden fire,—
Like a fruit-crown'd orange-tree
White with blossoms honey-sweet
Sore beset by wasp and bee,—   420
Like a royal virgin town
Topp'd with gilded dome and spire
Close beleaguer'd by a fleet
Mad to tug her standard down.   425

One may lead a horse to water,
Twenty cannot make him drink.
Though the goblins cuff'd and caught her,
Coax'd and fought her,   430

Bullied and besought her,
Scratch'd her, pinch'd her black as ink,
Kick'd and knock'd her,
Maul'd and mock'd her,   435
Lizzie utter'd not a word;
Would not open lip from lip
Lest they should cram a mouthful in:
But laugh'd in heart to feel the drip
Of juice that syrupp'd all her face,   440
And lodg'd in dimples of her chin,
And streak'd her neck which quaked like curd.
At last the evil people,
Worn out by her resistance,
Flung back her penny, kick'd their fruit   445
Along whichever road they took,
Not leaving root or stone or shoot;
Some writh'd into the ground,
Some div'd into the brook
With ring and ripple,   450
Some scudded on the gale without a sound,
Some vanish'd in the distance.

In a smart, ache, tingle,
Lizzie went her way;
Knew not was it night or day;   455
Sprang up the bank, tore thro' the furze,
Threaded copse and dingle,
And heard her penny jingle
Bouncing in her purse,—
Its bounce was music to her ear.   460
She ran and ran
As if she fear'd some goblin man
Dogg'd her with gibe or curse
Or something worse: 465
But not one goblin scurried after,
Nor was she prick'd by fear;
The kind heart made her windy-paced
That urged her home quite out of breath with haste
And inward laughter.   470

She cried, "Laura," up the garden,
"Did you miss me?
Come and kiss me.

Never mind my bruises,
Hug me, kiss me, suck my juices   475
Squeez'd from goblin fruits for you,
Goblin pulp and goblin dew.
Eat me, drink me, love me;
Laura, make much of me;
For your sake I have braved the glen   480
And had to do with goblin merchant men."

Laura started from her chair,
Flung her arms up in the air,
Clutch'd her hair:
"Lizzie, Lizzie, have you tasted   485
For my sake the fruit forbidden?
Must your light like mine be hidden,
Your young life like mine be wasted,
Undone in mine undoing,
And ruin'd in my ruin,   490
Thirsty, canker'd, goblin-ridden?"—
She clung about her sister,
Kiss'd and kiss'd and kiss'd her: 495
Tears once again
Refresh'd her shrunken eyes,
Dropping like rain
After long sultry drouth;
Shaking with aguish fear, and pain,   500
She kiss'd and kiss'd her with a hungry mouth.

Her lips began to scorch,
That juice was wormwood to her tongue,
She loath'd the feast:
Writhing as one possess'd she leap'd and sung,   505
Rent all her robe, and wrung
Her hands in lamentable haste,
And beat her breast.
Her locks stream'd like the torch
Borne by a racer at full speed,   510
Or like the mane of horses in their flight,
Or like an eagle when she stems the light
Straight toward the sun,
Or like a caged thing freed,
Or like a flying flag when armies run.   515

Swift fire spread through
her veins, knock'd at her heart,
Met the fire smouldering there
And overbore its lesser flame;
She gorged on bitterness without a name: 520
Ah! fool, to choose such part
Of soul-consuming care!
Sense fail'd in the mortal strife:
Like the watch-tower of a town
Which an earthquake shatters down,   525
Like a lightning-stricken mast,
Like a wind-uprooted tree
Spun about,
Like a foam-topp'd waterspout
Cast down headlong in the sea,   530
She fell at last;
Pleasure past and anguish past,
Is it death or is it life?

Life out of death.
That night long Lizzie watch'd by her,   535
Counted her pulse's flagging stir,
Felt for her breath,
Held water to her lips, and cool'd her face
With tears and fanning leaves:
But when the first birds chirp'd about their eaves,   540
And early reapers plodded to the place
Of golden sheaves,
And dew-wet grass
Bow'd in the morning winds so brisk to pass,
And new buds with new day   545
Open'd of cup-like lilies on the stream,
Laura awoke as from a dream,
Laugh'd in the innocent old way,
Hugg'd Lizzie but not twice or thrice;
Her gleaming locks show'd not one thread of grey,   550
Her breath was sweet as May
And light danced in her eyes.

Days, weeks, months, years
Afterwards, when both were wives
With children of their own;   555

Their mother-hearts beset with fears,
Their lives bound up in tender lives;
Laura would call the little ones
And tell them of her early prime,
Those pleasant days long gone   560
Of not-returning time:
Would talk about the haunted glen,
The wicked, quaint fruit-merchant men,
Their fruits like honey to the throat
But poison in the blood;   565
(Men sell not such in any town):
Would tell them how her sister stood
In deadly peril to do her good,
And win the fiery antidote:
Then joining hands to little hands   570
Would bid them cling together,
"For there is no friend like a sister
In calm or stormy weather;
To cheer one on the tedious way,   575
To fetch one if one goes astray,
To lift one if one totters down,
To strengthen whilst one stands."

■ Look carefully at the presentation of the "goblins." To what does the poet
   compare them? What verbs are used to describe their actions? Compare the
   verbs used in their confrontation with Lizzie to those that appear when they
   confront Laura. Notice any other sequences of verbs in the poem.

DRAMA

Christopher Marlowe (1564–1593)

Christopher Marlowe was born in Canterbury, England. He attended Cambridge
University; while a student there, he apparently undertook a number of missions
on behalf of the Protestant queen, Elizabeth. His role as a secret agent (or double agent) remains unclear. In any case, within a year of receiving his MA from
Cambridge, two of his plays were produced in London. The remainder of his short
life was colorful. He was arrested on a number of occasions for fighting, once on

charges of atheism, but was never imprisoned, and he likely continued to act in dangerous political intrigues. He died of knife wounds suffered in a fight in a tavern (recent scholarship suggests that the fight may have been manufactured to cover Marlowe's assassination). Marlowe was unquestionably a great dramatist, and he wrote a number of dramatic and lyric poems in addition to his plays. One of these, the lyric beginning "Come live with me and be my love," is among the best-known poems of the English language, one that has prompted responses from a number of other poets over the centuries.

The Tragical History of the Life and Death of Doctor Faustus (ca. 1593)

CHARACTERS

THE POPE
CARDINAL OF LORRAIN
EMPEROR OF GERMANY
DUKE OF VANHOLT
FAUSTUS
VALDES *and* CORNELIUS, *friends to* FAUSTUS
WAGNER, *servant to* FAUSTUS
CLOWN
ROBIN
RALPH
VINTNER
HORSE-COURSER
KNIGHT
OLD MAN
SCHOLARS, FRIARS, *and* ATTENDANTS
DUCHESS OF VANHOLT
LUCIFER
BELZEBUB
MEPHISTOPHILIS
GOOD ANGEL
EVIL ANGEL
THE SEVEN DEADLY SINS
DEVILS
SPIRITS *in the shape of* ALEXANDER THE GREAT, *of his* PARAMOUR, *and of* HELEN OF TROY
CHORUS
(*Enter* CHORUS.)

CHORUS: Not marching now in fields of Thrasimene,
    Where Mars did mate° the Carthaginians;
    Nor sporting in the dalliance of love,
    In courts of kings where state is overturn'd;
    Nor in the pomp of proud audacious deeds,   5
    Intends our Muse to vaunt his heavenly verse:
    Only this, gentlemen,—we must perform
    The form of Faustus' fortunes, good or bad.
    To patient judgments we appeal our plaud°
    And speak for Faustus in his infancy.   10
    Now is he born, his parents base of stock,
    In Germany, within a town call'd Rhodes°
    Of riper years to Wittenberg he went,
    Whereas his kinsmen chiefly brought him up.
    So soon he profits in divinity,   15
    The fruitful plot of scholarism grac'd,°
    That shortly he was grac'd with doctor's name,
    Excelling all whose sweet delight disputes
    In heavenly matters of theology;
    Till swollen with cunning,° of a self-conceit,   20
    His waxen wings° did mount above his reach,
    And, melting, Heavens conspir'd his overthrow;
    For, falling to a devilish exercise,
    And glutted [more] with learning's golden gifts,
    He surfeits upon cursed necromancy.   25
    Nothing so sweet as magic is to him,
    Which he prefers before his chiefest bliss.
    And this the man that in his study sits!
(*Exit.*)

Scene 1

(*Enter* FAUSTUS *in his Study.*)
FAUSTUS: Settle my studies, Faustus, and begin
    To sound the depth of that thou wilt profess;°
    Having commenc'd, be a divine in show.
    Yet level° at the end of every art,

---

2. mate: Confound. But Hannibal was victorious at Lake Trasumennus, B.C. 217. **9. plaud:** For applause. **12. Rhodes:** Roda, in the Duchy of Saxe-Altenburg, near Jena. **16. fruitful plot . . . grac'd:** The garden of scholarship being adorned by him. **20. cunning:** Knowledge. **21. His waxen wings:** An allusion to the myth of Icarus, who flew too near the sun. **2. profess:** teach publicly. **4. level:** aim.

And live and die in Aristotle's works.   5
Sweet Analytics,° 'tis thou hast ravish'd me,
Bene disserere est finis logices.
Is to dispute well logic's chiefest end?
Affords this art no greater miracle?
Then read no more, thou hast attain'd the end;   10
A greater subject fitteth Faustus' wit.
Bid ὂν καὶ μὴ ὂν° farewell; Galen° come,
Seeing *Ubi desinit Philosophus, ibi incipit Medicus*°
Be a physician, Faustus, heap up gold,
And be eternis'd for some wondrous cure.   15
Summum bonum medicinæ sanitas,°
"The end of physic is our body's health."
Why, Faustus, hast thou not attain'd that end?
Is not thy common talk sound Aphorisms?°
Are not thy bills° hung up as monuments,   20
Whereby whole cities have escap'd the plague,
And thousand desperate maladies been eas'd?
Yet art thou still but Faustus and a man.
Wouldst thou make men to live eternally,
Or, being dead, raise them to life again?   25
Then this profession were to be esteem'd.
Physic, farewell.—Where is Justinian?
(Reads.)
Si una eademque res legatur duobus, alter rem, alter valorem rei, &c.°
A pretty case of paltry legacies!
(Reads.)
Exhæreditare filium non potest pater nisi, &c.°   30
Such is the subject of the Institute°
And universal Body of the Law.
His° study fits a mercenary drudge,
Who aims at nothing but external trash;
Too servile and illiberal for me.   35
When all is done, divinity is best;

---

6. **Analytics:** Logic. 12. ὂν καὶ μὴ ὂν°: The Aristotelian phrase for "being and not being." 12. **Galen:** Greek physician whose theories were highly regarded in the Middle Ages. 13. **Ubi . . . Medicus:** "Where the philosopher leaves off, there the physician begins." 16. **Summum . . . sanitas:** This and the previous quotation are from Aristotle. 19. **Aphorisms:** Medical maxims. 20. **bills:** Announcements. 28. **Si una eademque . . . &c.:** "If one and the same thing is bequeathed to two persons, one gets the thing and the other the value of the thing." 30. **Exhæreditare lium . . . &c.:** "A father cannot disinherit the son except," etc. 31. **Institute:** Of Justinian, under whom the Roman law was codified. 33. **His:** Its.

Jerome's Bible°, Faustus, view it well.
(*Reads.*)
Stipendium peccati mors est. Ha! *Stipendium, &c.*
"*The reward of sin is death.*" That's hard,
(*Reads.*)
Si peccasse negamus, fallimur, et nulla est in nobis veritas.   40
"If we say that we have no sin we deceive ourselves, and there's no truth in
us." Why then, belike we must sin and so consequently die. Ay, we must
die an everlasting death.
What doctrine call you this, *Che sera sera,*
"What will be shall he?" Divinity, adieu!   45
These metaphysics of magicians
And necromantic books are heavenly;
Lines, circles, scenes, letters, and characters,
Ay, these are those that Faustus most desires.
O what a world of profit and delight,   50
Of power, of honour, of omnipotence
Is promis'd to the studious artisan!
All things that move between the quiet poles
Shall be at my command. Emperors and kings
Are but obeyed in their several provinces,   55
Nor can they raise the wind or rend the clouds;
But his dominion that exceeds° in this
Stretcheth as far as doth the mind of man.
A sound magician is a mighty god:
Here, Faustus, try thy, brains to gain a deity.   60
Wagner!
(*Enter* WAGNER.)
                    Commend me to my dearest friends,
The German Valdes and Cornelius;
Request them earnestly to visit me.
WAG I will, sir.
(*Exit.*)
FAUSTUS: Their conference will be a greater help to me   65
         Than all my labours, plod I ne'er so fast.
(*Enter* GOOD ANGEL *and* EVIL ANGEL.)
         G. ANG: O Faustus! lay that damned book aside,
         And gaze not upon it lest it tempt thy soul,
         And heap God's heavy wrath upon thy head.
         Read, read the Scriptures: that is blasphemy.   70

---

37. Jerome's Bible: The Vulgate. **57. exceeds:** Excels.

E. ANG: Go forward, Faustus, in that famous art,
    Wherein all Nature's treasure is contain'd:
    Be thou on earth as Jove is in the sky,
    Lord and commander of these elements.
(*Exeunt* ANGELS.)
FAUSTUS: How am I glutted with conceit° of this!   75
    Shall I make spirits fetch me what I please,
    Resolve me of all ambiguities,
    Perform what desperate enterprise I will?
    I'll have them fly to India for gold,
    Ransack the ocean for orient pearl,   80
    And search all corners of the new-found world
    For pleasant fruits and princely delicates;
    I'll have them read me strange philosophy
    And tell the secrets of all foreign kings;
    I'll have them wall all Germany with brass,   85
    And make swift Rhine circle fair Wittenberg;
    I'll have them fill the public schools with silk,
    Wherewith the students shall be bravely clad;
    I'll levy soldiers with the coin they bring,
    And chase the Prince of Parma from our land,°   90
    And reign sole king of all the provinces;
    Yea, stranger engines for the brunt of war
    Than was the fiery keel° at Antwerp's bridge,
    I'll make my servile spirits to invent.
    Come, German Valdes and Cornelius,   95
    And make me blest with your sage conference.
    (*Enter* VALDES *and* CORNELIUS.)°
    Valdes, sweet Valdes, and Cornelius,
    Know that your words have won me at the last
    To practise magic and concealed arts:
    Yet not your words only, but mine own fantasy,   100
    That will receive no object, for my head
    But ruminates on necromantic skill.
    Philosophy is odious and obscure,
    Both law and physic are for petty wits;
    Divinity is basest of the three,   105
    Unpleasant, harsh, contemptible, and vile:

---

75. conceit: Idea. **90. our land:** The Netherlands, over which Parma re-established the Spanish dominion. **93. fiery keel:** A ship filled with explosives used to blow up a bridge built by Parma in 1585 at the
siege of Antwerp. °**Valdes and Cornelius:** The famous Cornelius Agrippa. German Valdes is not known.

'Tis magic, magic, that hath ravish'd me.
Then, gentle friends, aid me in this attempt;
And I that have with concise syllogisms
Gravell'd the pastors of the German church,   110
And made the flow'ring pride of Wittenberg
Swarm to my problems, as the infernal spirits
On sweet Musæus,° when he came to hell,
Will be as cunning as Agrippa was,
Whose shadows made all Europe honour him.   115
VALD: Faustus, these books, thy wit, and our experience
Shall make all nations to canonise us.
As Indian Moors° obey their Spanish lords,
So shall the subjects of every element
Be always serviceable to us three;   120
Like lions shall they guard us when we please;
Like Almain rutters° with their horsemen's staves,
Or Lapland giants, trotting by our sides;
Sometimes like women or unwedded maids,
Shadowing more beauty in their airy brows   125
Than have the white breasts of the queen of love:
From Venice shall they drag huge argosies,
And from America the golden fleece
That yearly stuffs old Philip's treasury;
If learned Faustus will be resolute.   130
FAUSTUS: Valdes, as resolute am I in this
As thou to live; therefore object it not.
CORN: The miracles that magic will perform
Will make thee vow to study nothing else.
He that is grounded in astrology,   135
Enrich'd with tongues, well seen° in minerals,
Hath all the principles magic doth require.
Then doubt not, Faustus, but to be renown'd,
And more frequented for this mystery
Than heretofore the Delphian Oracle.   140
The spirits tell me they can dry the sea,
And fetch the treasure of all foreign wracks,
Ay, all the wealth that our forefathers hid
Within the massy entrails of the earth;
Then tell me, Faustus, what shall we three want?   145

---

113. Musæus: Cf. Virgil, *Aeneid*, vi. 667. **118. Indian Moors:** Americans Indians. **122. Almain rutters:** Troopers. Germ. *Reiters*. **136. seen:** Versed.

FAUSTUS: Nothing, Cornelius! O this cheers my soul!
    Come show me some demonstrations magical,
    That I may conjure in some lusty grove,
    And have these joys in full possession.

VALD: Then haste thee to some solitary grove   150
    And bear wise Bacon's° and Albanus'° works,
    The Hebrew Psalter and New Testament;
    And whatsoever else is requisite
    We will inform thee ere our conference cease.

CORN: Valdes, first let him know the words of art;   155
    And then, all other ceremonies learn'd,
    Faustus may try his cunning by himself.

VALD: First I'll instruct thee in the rudiments.
    And then wilt thou be perfecter than I.

FAUSTUS: Then come and dine with me, and after meat,   160
    We'll canvass every quiddity° thereof;
    For ere I sleep I'll try what I can do:
    This night I'll conjure though I die therefore.

(*Exeunt.*)

Scene 2
Before Faustus' House

(*Enter two* SCHOLARS.)

1 SCHOL: I wonder what's become of Faustus that was wont to make our
    schools ring with *sic probo*?°

2 SCHOL: That shall we know, for see here comes his boy.

(*Enter* WAGNER.)

1 SCHOL: How now, sirrah! Where's thy master?

WAG: God in heaven knows!   5

2 SCHOL: Why, dost not thou know?

WAG: Yes, I know. But that follows not.

1 SCHOL: Go to, sirrah! Leave your jesting, and tell us where he is.

WAG: That follows not necessary by force of argument, that you, being licentiate,
    should stand upon't: therefore, acknowledge your error and be attentive.   10

2 SCHOL: Why, didst thou not say thou knew'st?

WAG: Have you any witness on't?

1 SCHOL: Yes, sirrah, I heard you.

WAG: Ask my fellow if I be a thief.   15

---

151. Bacon's: Roger Bacon. **151. Albanus':** Perhaps Pietro d'Abano, a medieval alchemist; perhaps a misprint for Albertus (Magnus), the great schoolman. **161. quiddity:** Fine point. **2. *sic probo*:** "Thus I prove"—a common formula in scholastic discussions.

2 SCHOL: Well, you will not tell us?

WAG: Yes, sir, I will tell you; yet if you were not dunces, you would never
ask me such a question; for is not he *corpus naturale?*° and is not that
mobile? Then wherefore should you ask me such a question? But that I
am by nature phlegmatic, slow to wrath, and prone to lechery (to love,   20
I would say), it were not for you to come within forty foot of the place
of execution, although I do not doubt to see you both hang'd the next
sessions. Thus having triumph'd over you, I will set my countenance
like a precisian,° and begin to speak thus:—Truly, my dear brethren,
my master is within at dinner, with Valdes and Cornelius, as this wine,   25
if it could speak, would inform your worships; and so the Lord bless
you, preserve you, and keep you, my dear brethren, my dear brethren.

(*Exit.*)

1 SCHOL: Nay, then, I fear he has fallen into that damned Art, for which
they two are infamous through the world.

2 SCHOL: Were he a stranger, and not allied to me, yet should I grieve for   30
him. But come, let us go and inform the Rector, and see if he by his
grave counsel can reclaim him.

1 SCHOL: O, I fear me nothing can reclaim him.

2 SCHOL: Yet let us try what we can do.

(*Exeunt.*)

Scene 3
A Grove

(*Enter* FAUSTUS *to conjure.*)

FAUSTUS: Now that the gloomy shadow of the earth
   Longing to view Orion's drizzling look,
   Leaps from th' antarctic world unto the sky,
   And dims the welkin with her pitchy breath,
   Faustus, begin thine incantations,   5
   And try if devils will obey thy hest,
   Seeing thou hast pray'd and sacrific'd to them.
   Within this circle is Jehovah's name,
   Forward and backward anagrammatis'd,
   The breviated names of holy saints,
   Figures of every adjunct° to the Heavens,   10
   And characters of signs and erring stars,°

---

18. *corpus naturale:* '*Corpus naturale seu mobile*' (literally, "natural or movable body") was the scholastic
expression for the subject matter of Physics. **24. precisian:** Puritan. **11. every adjunct:** Every star
belonging to. **12. erring stars:** Planets.

By which the spirits are enforc'd to rise:
Then fear not, Faustus, but be resolute,
And try the uttermost magic can perform.   15
Sint mihi Dei Acherontis propitii! Valeat numen triplex Jehovae! Ignei,
aerii, aquatani spiritus, salvete! Orientis princeps Belzebub, inferni ardentis
monarcha, et Demogorgon, propitiamus vos, ut appareat et surgat Mephi-
stophilis. Quid tu moraris? Per Jehovam, Gehennam, et consecratum
aquam quam nunc spargo, signumque crucis quod nunc facio, et per vota   20
nostra, ipse nunc surgat nobis dicatus Mephistophilis!°
(*Enter* MEPHISTOPHILIS, *a* DEVIL.)
I charge thee to return and change thy shape;
Thou art too ugly to attend on me.
Go, and return an old Franciscan friar;
That holy shape becomes a devil best.   25
(*Exit* DEVIL.)
I see there's virtue in my heavenly words;
Who would not be proficient in this art?
How pliant is this Mephistophilis,
Full of obedience and humility!
Such is the force of magic and my spells.   30
[Now,] Faustus, thou art conjuror laureate,
Thou canst command great Mephistophilis:
Quin regis Mephistophilis fratris imagine.°
(*Re-enter* MEPHISTOPHILIS, *like a Franciscan Friar.*)
MEPH: Now, Faustus, what would'st thou have me do?
FAUSTUS: I charge thee wait upon me whilst I live,   35
To do whatever Faustus shall command,
Be it to make the moon drop from her sphere,
Or the ocean to overwhelm the world.
MEPH: I am a servant to great Lucifer,
And may not follow thee without his leave;   40
No more than he commands must we perform.
FAUSTUS: Did he not charge thee to appear to me?
MEPH: No, I came hither of mine own accord.
FAUSTUS: Did not my conjuring speeches raise thee? Speak:

16–21. *Sint mihi ... Mephistophilis!:* "Be propitious to me, gods of Acheron! May the triple deity
of Jehovah prevail! Spirits of fire, air, water, hail! Belzebub, Prince of the East, monarch of burning hell, and Demogorgon, we propitiate ye, that Mephistophilis may appear and rise. Why dost
thou delay? By Jehovah, Gehenna, and the holy water which now I sprinkle, and the sign of the
cross which now I make, and by our prayer, may Mephistophilis now summoned by us arise!"
33. *Quin regis ... imagine:* "For indeed thou hast power in the image of thy brother Mephistophilis."

MEPH: That was the cause, but yet *per accidens*;   45
    For when we hear one rack° the name of God,
    Abjure the Scriptures and his Saviour Christ,
    We fly in hope to get his glorious soul;
    Nor will we come, unless he use such means
    Whereby he is in danger to be damn'd: 50
    Therefore the shortest cut for conjuring
    Is stoutly to abjure the Trinity,
    And pray devoutly to the Prince of Hell.
FAUSTUS: So Faustus hath
    Already done; and holds this principle,
    There is no chief but only Belzebub,   55
    To whom Faustus doth dedicate himself.
    This word "damnation" terrifies not him,
    For he confounds hell in Elysium°
    His ghost be with the old philosophers!   60
    But, leaving these vain trifles of men's souls,
    Tell me what is that Lucifer thy lord?
MEPH: Arch-regent and commander of all spirits.
FAUSTUS: Was not that Lucifer an angel once?
MEPH: Yes, Faustus, and most dearly lov'd of God.   65
FAUSTUS: How comes it then that he is Prince of devils?
MEPH: O, by aspiring pride and insolence;
    For which God threw him from the face of Heaven.
FAUSTUS: And what are you that you live with Lucifer?
MEPH: Unhappy spirits that fell with Lucifer,   70
    Conspir'd against our God with Lucifer,
    And are for ever damn'd with Lucifer.
FAUSTUS: Where are you damn'd?
MEPH: In hell.
FAUSTUS: How comes it then that thou art out of hell?   75
MEPH: Why this is hell, nor am I out of it.
    Think'st thou that I who saw the face of God,
    And tasted the eternal joys of Heaven,
    Am not tormented with ten thousand hells,
    In being depriv'd of everlasting bliss?   80
    O Faustus! leave these frivolous demands,
    Which strike a terror to my fainting soul.

---

46. rack: Twist in anagrams. **59. he confounds hell in Elysium:** Heaven and hell are indifferent to him.

FAUSTUS: What, is great Mephistophilis so passionate°
    For being depriv'd of the joys of Heaven?
    Learn thou of Faustus manly fortitude,   85
    And scorn those joys thou never shalt possess.
    Go bear these tidings to great Lucifer:
    Seeing Faustus hath incurr'd eternal death
    By desperate thoughts against Jove's deity,
    Say he surrenders up to him his soul,   90
    So he will spare him four and twenty years,
    Letting him live in all voluptuousness;
    Having thee ever to attend on me;
    To give me whatsoever I shall ask,
    To tell me whatsoever I demand,
    To slay mine enemies, and aid my friends,   95
    And always be obedient to my will.
    Go and return to mighty Lucifer,
    And meet me in my study at midnight,
    And then resolve° me of thy master's mind.   100
MEPH: I will, Faustus.
(*Exit.*)
FAUSTUS: Had I as many souls as there be stars,
    I'd give them all for Mephistophilis.
    By him I'll be great Emperor of the world,
    And make a bridge through the moving air,   105
    To pass the ocean with a band of men;
    I'll join the hills that bind the Afric shore,
    And make that [country] continent to Spain,
    And both contributory to my crown.
    The Emperor shall not live but by my leave,   110
    Nor any potentate of Germany.
    Now that I have obtain'd what I desire,
    I'll live in speculation° of this art
    Till Mephistophilis return again.
(*Exit.*)

Scene 4
A Street

(*Enter* WAGNER *and the* CLOWN.)
WAG: Sirrah, boy, come hither.

---

83. passionate: Sorrowful. **100. resolve:** Inform. **113. speculation:** Study.

CLOWN: How, boy! Swowns, boy! I hope you have seen many boys with
such pickadevaunts° as I have. Boy, quotha!

WAG: Tell me, sirrah, hast thou any comings in?

CLOWN: Ay, and goings out too. You may see else.   5

WAG: Alas, poor slave! See how poverty jesteth in his nakedness! The villain is
bare and out of service, and so hungry that I know he would give his soul
to the devil for a shoulder of mutton, though it were blood-raw.

CLOWN: How? My soul to the Devil for a shoulder of mutton, though 'twere
blood-raw! Not so, good friend. By'r Lady, I had need have it well   10
roasted and good sauce to it, if I pay so dear.

WAG: Well, wilt thou serve me, and I'll make thee go like *Qui mihi discipulus?*°

CLOWN: How, in verse?

WAG: No, sirrah; in beaten silk and stavesacre.°

CLOWN: How, how, Knave's acre!° Ay, I thought that was all the land his   15
father left him. Do you hear? I would be sorry to rob you of your living.

WAG: Sirrah, I say in stavesacre.

CLOWN: Oho! Oho! Stavesacre! Why, then, belike if I were your man I should
be full of vermin.

WAG: So thou shalt, whether thou beest with me or no. But, sirrah, leave   20
your jesting, and bind yourself presently unto me for seven years, or
I'll turn all the lice about thee into familiars, and they shall tear thee
in pieces.

CLOWN: Do you hear, sir? You may save that labour; they are too familiar
with me already. Swowns! they are as bold with my flesh as if they   25
had paid for [their] meat and drink.

WAG: Well, do you hear, sirrah? Hold, take these guilders. (*Gives money.*)

CLOWN: Gridirons! what be they?

WAG: Why, French crowns.

CLOWN: Mass, but for the name of French crowns, a man were as good   30
have as many English counters. And what should I do with these?

WAG: Why, now, sirrah, thou art at an hour's warning, whensoever and
wheresoever the Devil shall fetch thee.

CLOWN: No, no. Here, take your gridirons again.

WAG: Truly I'll none of them.   35

CLOWN: Truly but you shall.

WAG: Bear witness I gave them him.

CLOWN: Bear witness I give them you again.

---

3. pickadevaunts: Beards cut to a sharp point (Fr. *pic-à-devant*). **12. *Qui mihi discipulus:*** "Whoever
is my disciple," the first words of W. Lily's "*Ad discipulos carmen de moribus*" (Ode to His Disciples on
Morality). **14. stavesacre:** A kind of larkspur, used for destroying lice. **15. Knave's acre:** A mean
street in London.

WAG: Well, I will cause two devils presently to fetch thee away—Baliol
    and Belcher.   40

CLOWN: Let your Baliol and your Belcher come here, and I'll knock them,
    they were never so knockt since they were devils. Say I should kill one of
    them, what would folks say? "Do you see yonder tall fellow in the round
    slop°?—he has kill'd the devil." So I should be call'd Kill-devil all the
    parish over.   45

(Enter two DEVILS: the CLOWN runs up and down crying.)

WAG: Baliol and Belcher! Spirits, away! *(Exeunt DEVILS.)*

CLOWN: What, are they gone? A vengeance on them, they have vile long
    nails! There was a he-devil, and a she-devil! I'll tell you how you shall
    know them: all he-devils has horns, and all she-devils has clifts and
    cloven feet.   50

WAG: Well, sirrah, follow me.

CLOWN: But, do you hear—if I should serve you, would you teach me to raise up
    Banios and Belcheos?

WAG: I will teach thee to turn thyself to anything; to a dog, or a cat, or a
    mouse, or a rat, or anything.   55

CLOWN: How! a Christian fellow to a dog or a cat, a mouse or a rat! No, no,
    sir. If you turn me into anything, let it be in the likeness of a little pretty
    frisky flea, that I may be here and there and everywhere. Oh, I'll tickle
    the pretty wenches' plackets; I'll be amongst them, i' faith.

WAG: Well, sirrah, come.   60

CLOWN: But, do you hear, Wagner?

WAG: How!—Baliol and Belcher!

CLOWN: O Lord! I pray, sir, let Banio and Belcher go sleep.

WAG: Villain—call me Master Wagner, and let thy left eye be diametarily°
    fixt upon my right heel, with *quasi vestigias nostras insistere.*°   65

(Exit.)

CLOWN: God forgive me, he speaks Dutch fustian. Well, I'll follow him,
    I'll serve him, that's flat.

(Exit.)

Scene 5

(Enter FAUSTUS in his study.)

FAUSTUS: Now, Faustus, must
    Thou needs be damn'd, and canst thou not be sav'd:
    What boots it then to think of God or Heaven?
    Away with such vain fancies, and despair:

---

44. round slop: Short wide breeches. **64. diametarily:** For *diametrically.* **65. *quasi . . . insistere:*** "As if
to tread in my tracks."

Despair in God, and trust in Belzebub.   5
Now go not backward: no, Faustus, be resolute.
Why waverest thou? O, something soundeth in mine ears
"Abjure this magic, turn to God again!"
Ay, and Faustus will turn to God again.
To God?—He loves thee not—   10
The God thou serv'st is thine own appetite,
Wherein is fix'd the love of Belzebub;
To him I'll build an altar and a church,
And offer lukewarm blood of new-born babes.
(*Enter* GOOD ANGEL *and* EVIL ANGEL.)
G. ANG: Sweet Faustus, leave that execrable art.   15
FAUSTUS: Contrition, prayer, repentance! What of them?
G. ANG: O, they are means to bring thee unto Heaven.
E. ANG: Rather illusions, fruits of lunacy,
      That makes men foolish that do trust them most.
G. ANG: Sweet Faustus, think of Heaven, and heavenly things.   20
E. ANG: No, Faustus, think of honour and of wealth.
(*Exeunt* ANGELS.)
FAUSTUS: Of wealth!
      Why, the signiory of Emden° shall be mine.
      When Mephistophilis shall stand by me,
      What God can hurt thee, Faustus? Thou art safe;   25
      Cast no more doubts. Come, Mephistophilis,
      And bring glad tidings from great Lucifer;—
      Is't not midnight? Come, Mephistophilis;
      Veni, veni, Mephistophile!
      (*Enter* MEPHISTOPHILIS.)
      Now tell me, what says Lucifer thy lord?   30
MEPH: That I shall wait on Faustus whilst he lives,
      So he will buy my service with his soul.
FAUSTUS: Already Faustus hath hazarded that for thee.
MEPH: But, Faustus, thou must bequeath it solemnly,
      And write a deed of gift with thine own blood,   35
      For that security craves great Lucifer.
      If thou deny it, I will back to hell.
FAUSTUS: Stay, Mephistophilis! and tell me what good
      Will my soul do thy Lord.
MEPH: Enlarge his kingdom.   40

---

23. Emden: Emden, near the mouth of the river Ems, was an important commercial town in
Elizabethan times.

FAUSTUS: Is that the reason why he tempts us thus?
MEPH: *Solamen miseris socios habuisse doloris.*°
FAUSTUS: Why, have you any pain that torture others?
MEPH: As great as have the human souls of men.
But tell me, Faustus, shall I have thy soul?   45
And I will be thy slave, and wait on thee,
And give thee more than thou hast wit to ask.
FAUSTUS: Ay, Mephistophilis, I give it thee.
MEPH: Then Faustus, stab thine arm courageously.
And bind thy soul that at some certain day   50
Great Lucifer may claim it as his own;
And then be thou as great as Lucifer.
FAUSTUS (*Stabbing his arm.*): Lo, Mephistophilis, for love of thee
I cut mine arm, and with my proper blood
Assure my soul to be great Lucifer's,   55
Chief lord and regent of perpetual night!
View here the blood that trickles from mine arm.
And let it be propitious for my wish.
MEPH: But, Faustus, thou must
Write it in manner of a deed of gift.   60
FAUSTUS: Ay, so I will. (*Writes.*) But, Mephistophilis,
My blood congeals, and I can write no more.
MEPH: I'll fetch thee fire to dissolve it straight.
(*Exit.*)
FAUSTUS: What might the staying of my blood portend?
Is it unwilling I should write this bill?   65
Why streams it not that I may write afresh?
Faustus gives to thee his soul. Ah, there it stay'd.
Why should'st thou not? Is not thy soul thine own?
Then write again, *Faustus gives to thee his soul.*
(*Re-enter* MEPHISTOPHILIS *with a chafer of coals.*)
MEPH: Here's fire. Come, Faustus, set it on.   70
FAUSTUS: So now the blood begins to clear again;
Now will I make an end immediately. (*Writes.*)
MEPH (*Aside.*): O what will not I do to obtain his soul.
FAUSTUS: *Consummatum est:*° this bill is ended,
And Faustus hath bequeath'd his soul to Lucifer—   75
But what is this inscription on mine arm?
Homo, fuge!° Whither should I fly?

---

42. *Solamen . . . doloris:* "Misery loves company." **74.** *Consummatum est:* "It is finished." **77.** *Homo, fuge!:* "Man, fly!"

If unto God, he'll throw me down to hell.
My senses are deceiv'd; here's nothing writ:—
I see it plain; here in this place is writ   80
Homo, fuge! Yet shall not Faustus fly.
MEPH: I'll fetch him somewhat to delight his mind.
(Exit.)
(Re-enter MEPHISTOPHILIS *with* DEVILS, *giving crowns and rich apparel to*
FAUSTUS, *and dance, and then depart.)*
FAUSTUS: Speak, Mephistophilis, what means this show?
MEPH: Nothing, Faustus, but to delight thy mind withal,
And to show thee what magic can perform.   85
FAUSTUS: But may I raise up spirits when I please?
MEPH: Ay, Faustus, and do greater things than these.
FAUSTUS: Then there's enough for a thousand souls.
Here, Mephistophilis, receive this scroll,
A deed of gift of body and of soul: 90
But yet conditionally that thou perform
All articles prescrib'd between us both.
MEPH: Faustus, I swear by hell and Lucifer
To effect all promises between us made.
FAUSTUS: Then hear me read them: *On these conditions following. First, that*   95
Faustus may be a spirit in form and substance. Secondly, that Mephistophilis
shall be his servant, and at his command. Thirdly, that Mephistophilis shall do
for him and bring him whatsoever [he desires]. Fourthly, that he shall be in his
chamber or house invisible. Lastly, that he shall appear to the said John Faustus,
at all times, in what form or shape soever he pleases. I, John Faustus, of   100
Wittenberg, Doctor, by these presents do give both body and soul to Lucifer,
Prince of the East, and his minister, Mephistophilis; and furthermore grant
unto them, that twenty-four years being expired, the articles above written
inviolate, full power to fetch or carry the said John Faustus, body and soul,
flesh, blood, or goods, into their habitation wheresoever. By me, John Faustus.   105
MEPH: Speak, Faustus, do you deliver this as your deed?
FAUSTUS: Ay, take it, and the Devil give thee good on't.
MEPH: Now, Faustus, ask what thou wilt.
FAUSTUS: First will I question with thee about hell.
Tell me where is the place that men call hell?   110
MEPH: Under the heavens.
FAUSTUS: Ay, but whereabout?
MEPH: Within the bowels of these elements,
Where we are tortur'd and remain for ever;
Hell hath no limits, nor is circumscrib'd   115
In one self place; for where we are is hell,

And where hell is there must we ever be:
And, to conclude, when all the world dissolves,
And every creature shall be purified,
All places shall be hell that is not Heaven.   120
FAUSTUS: Come, I think hell's a fable.
MEPH: Ay, think so still, till experience change thy mind.
FAUSTUS: Why, think'st thou then that Faustus shall be damn'd?
MEPH: Ay, of necessity, for here's the scroll
    Wherein thou hast given thy soul to Lucifer.   125
FAUSTUS: Ay, and body too; but what of that?
    Think'st thou that Faustus is so fond° to imagine
    That, after this life, there is any pain?
    Tush; these are trifles, and mere old wives' tales.
MEPH: But, Faustus, I am an instance to prove the contrary,   130
    For I am damned, and am now in hell.
FAUSTUS: How! now in hell!
    Nay, an this be hell, I'll willingly be damn'd here;
    What? walking, disputing, &c.?
    But, leaving off this, let me have a wife,   135
    The fairest maid in Germany;
    For I am wanton and lascivious,
    And cannot live without a wife.
MEPH: How—a wife?
    I prithee, Faustus, talk not of a wife.   140
FAUSTUS: Nay, sweet Mephistophilis, fetch me one, for I will have one.
MEPH: Well—thou wilt have one. Sit there till I come:
    I'll fetch thee a wife in the Devil's name.
(Exit.)
(Re-enter MEPHISTOPHILIS *with a* DEVIL *dressed like a woman, with fireworks.)*
MEPH: Tell [me,] Faustus, how dost thou like thy wife?
FAUSTUS: A plague on her for a hot whore!   145
MEPH: Tut, Faustus,
    Marriage is but a ceremonial toy;
    And if thou lovest me, think no more of it.
    I'll cull thee out the fairest courtesans,
    And bring them every morning to thy bed;   150
    She whom thine eye shall like, thy heart shall have,
    Be she as chaste as was Penelope,
    As wise as Saba,° or as beautiful
    As was bright Lucifer before his fall.

---

127. fond: Foolish. **153. Saba:** The Queen of Sheba.

Here, take this book, peruse it thoroughly: 155
(*Gives a book.*)
The iterating° of these lines brings gold;
The framing of this circle on the ground
Brings whirlwinds, tempests, thunder and lightning;
Pronounce this thrice devoutly to thyself,
And men in armour shall appear to thee,   160
Ready to execute what thou desir'st.
FAUSTUS: Thanks, Mephistophilis; yet fain would I have a book wherein
   I'might behold all spells and incantations, that I might raise up spirits
   when I please.
MEPH: Here they are, in this book. (*Turns to them.*)   165
FAUSTUS: Now would I have a book where I might see all characters and planets
   of the heavens, that I might know their motions and dispositions.
MEPH: Here they are too.
(*Turns to them.*)
FAUSTUS: Nay, let me have one book more,—and then I have done,—wherein
   I might see all plants, herbs, and trees that grow upon the earth.   170
MEPH: Here they be.
FAUSTUS: O, thou art deceived.
MEPH: Tut, I warrant thee. *Turns to them.*
(*Exeunt.*)

Scene 6
The Same

(*Enter* FAUSTUS *and* MEPHISTOPHILIS.)
FAUSTUS: When I behold the heavens, then I repent,
   And curse thee, wicked Mephistophilis,
   Because thou hast depriv'd me of those joys.
MEPH: Why, Faustus,
   Thinkest thou Heaven is such a glorious thing?   5
   I tell thee 'tis not half so fair as thou,
   Or any man that breathes on earth.
FAUSTUS: How provest thou that?
MEPH: 'Twas made for man, therefore is man more excellent.
FAUSTUS: If it were made for man, 'twas made for me;   10
   I will renounce this magic and repent.
(*Enter* GOOD ANGEL *and* EVIL ANGEL.)
G. ANG: Faustus, repent; yet God will pity thee.

---

156. iterating: Repeating.

E. ANG: Thou art a spirit; God cannot pity thee.

FAUSTUS: Who buzzeth in mine ears I am a spirit?
   Be I a devil, yet God may pity me;   15
   Ay, God will pity me if I repent.

E. ANG: Ay, but Faustus never shall repent.

(*Exeunt* ANGELS.)

FAUSTUS: My heart's so hard'ned I cannot repent.
   Scarce can I name salvation, faith, or heaven,
   But fearful echoes thunder in mine ears   20
   "Faustus, thou art damn'd!" Then swords and knives,
   Poison, gun, halters, and envenom'd steel
   Are laid before me to despatch myself,
   And long ere this I should have slain myself,
   Had not sweet pleasure conquer'd deep despair.   25
   Have I not made blind Homer sing to me
   Of Alexander's love and Œnon's death?
   And hath not he that built the walls of Thebes
   With ravishing sound of his melodious harp,
   Made music with my Mephistophilis?   30
   Why should I die then, or basely despair?
   I am resolv'd: Faustus shall ne'er repent.
   Come, Mephistophilis, let us dispute again,
   And argue of divine astrology
   Tell me, are there many heavens above the moon?   35
   Are all celestial bodies but one globe,
   As is the substance of this centric earth?

MEPH: As are the elements, such are the spheres
   Mutually folded in each other's orb,
   And, Faustus,
   All jointly move upon one axletree   40
   Whose terminine is term'd the world's wide pole;
   Nor are the names of Saturn, Mars, or Jupiter
   Feign'd, but are erring stars.

FAUSTUS: But tell me, have they all one motion, both *situ et tempore?*°   45

MEPH: All jointly move from east to west in twenty-four hours upon
   the poles of the world; but differ in their motion upon the poles
   of the zodiac.

FAUSTUS: Tush!
   These slender trifles Wagner can decide;   50
   Hath Mephistophilis no greater skill?

---

45. *situ et tempore:* "In direction and in time?"

Who knows not the double motion of the planets?
The first is finish'd in a natural day;
The second thus: as Saturn in thirty years; Jupiter in twelve; Mars in
four; the Sun, Venus, and Mercury in a year; the moon in twenty-eight   55
days. Tush, these are freshmen's suppositions. But tell me, hath every
sphere a dominion or *intelligentia?*

MEPH: Ay.

FAUSTUS: How many heavens, or spheres, are there?

MEPH: Nine: the Seven planets, the firmament, and the empyreal heaven.   60

FAUSTUS: Well, resolve me in this question: Why have we not conjunctions,
oppositions, aspects, eclipses, all at one time, but in some years we have
more, in some less?

MEPH: *Per inæqualem motum respecta totius.*°

FAUSTUS: Well, I am answered. Tell me who made the world.   65

MEPH: I will not.

FAUSTUS: Sweet Mephistophilis, tell me.

MEPH: Move me not, for I will not tell thee.

FAUSTUS: Villain, have I not bound thee to tell me anything?

MEPH: Ay, that is not against our kingdom; but this is.   70
Think thou on hell, Faustus, for thou art damn'd.

FAUSTUS: Think, Faustus, upon God that made the world.

MEPH: Remember this.

FAUSTUS: Ay, go, accursed spirit, to ugly hell.
'Tis thou hast damn'd distressed Faustus' soul.   75
Is't not too late?

(Re-enter GOOD ANGEL *and* EVIL ANGEL.)

E. ANG: Too late.

G. ANG: Never too late, if Faustus can repent.

E. ANG: If thou repent, devils shall tear thee in pieces.

G. ANG: Repent, and they shall never raze thy skin.   80

(Exeunt ANGELS.)

FAUSTUS: Ah, Christ, my Saviour,
Seek to save distressed Faustus' soul.

(Enter LUCIFER, BELZEBUB, *and* MEPHISTOPHILIS.)

LUC: Christ cannot save thy soul, for he is just;
There's none but I have interest in the same.

FAUSTUS: O, who art thou that look'st so terrible?   85

LUC: I am Lucifer,
And this is my companion-prince in hell.

FAUSTUS: O Faustus! they are come to fetch away thy soul!

---

64. *Per . . . totius:* "On account of their unequal motion in relation to the whole."

LUC: We come to tell thee thou dost injure us;
    Thou talk'st of Christ contrary to thy promise;   90
    Thou should'st not think of God: think of the Devil,
    And of his dam, too.
FAUSTUS: Nor will I henceforth: pardon me in this,
    And Faustus vows never to look to Heaven,
    Never to name God, or to pray to him,   95
    To burn his Scriptures, slay his ministers,
    And make my spirits pull his churches down.
LUC: Do so, and we will highly gratify thee. Faustus, we are come from hell
    to show thee some pastime. Sit down, and thou shalt see all the Seven
    Deadly Sins appear in their proper shapes.   100
FAUSTUS: That sight will be pleasing unto me, As Paradise was to Adam
    the first day
    Of his creation.
LUC: Talk not of Paradise nor creation, but mark this show: talk of the
    Devil, and nothing else.—Come away!   115
(*Enter the* SEVEN DEADLY SINS.)
    Now, Faustus, examine them of their several names and dispositions.
FAUSTUS: What art thou—the first?
PRIDE: I am Pride. I disdain to have any parents. I am like to Ovid's flea: I can
    creep into every corner of a wench; sometimes, like a periwig, I sit
    upon her brow; or like a fan of feathers, I kiss her lips; indeed   115
    I do—what do I not? But, fie, what a scent is here! I'll not speak another
    word, except the ground were perfum'd, and covered with cloth of arras.
FAUSTUS: What art thou—the second?
COVET: I am Covetousness, begotten of an old churl in an old leathern bag;
    and might I have my wish I would desire that this house and all the   115
    people in it were turn'd to gold, that I might lock you up in my good
    chest. O, my sweet gold!
FAUSTUS: What art thou—the third?
WRATH: I am Wrath. I had neither father nor mother: I leapt out of a lion's
    mouth when I was scarce half an hour old; and ever since I have run up   120
    and down the world with this case° of rapiers wounding myself when I
    had nobody to fight withal. I was born in hell; and look to it, for some
    of you shall be my father.
FAUSTUS: What art thou—the fourth?
ENVY: I am Envy, begotten of a chimney sweeper and an oyster-wife. I cannot   125
    read, and therefore wish all books were burnt. I am lean with seeing
    others eat. O that there would come a famine through all the world, that

---

121. case: Pair.

all might die, and I live alone! then thou should'st see how fat I would
be. But must thou sit and I stand! Come down with a vengeance!   130
FAUSTUS: Away, envious rascal! What art thou—the fifth?
GLUT: Who, I, sir? I am Gluttony. My parents are all dead, and the devil a
penny they have left me, but a bare pension, and that is thirty meals a
day and ten bevers°—a small trifle to suffice nature. O, I come of a
royal parentage! My grandfather was a Gammon of Bacon, my grandmother a Hogshead of Claret-wine; my godfathers were these, Peter   135
Pickleherring, and Martin Martlemas-beef.° O, but my godmother, she
was a jolly gentlewoman, and well beloved in every good town and city;
her name was Mistress Margery Marchbeer. Now, Faustus, thou hast
heard all my progeny, wilt thou bid me to supper?
FAUSTUS: No, I'll see thee hanged: thou wilt eat up all my victuals.   140
GLUT: Then the Devil choke thee!
FAUSTUS: Choke thyself, glutton! Who art thou—the sixth?
SLOTH: I am Sloth. I was begotten on a sunny bank, where I have lain ever
since; and you have done me great injury to bring me from thence: let
me be carried thither again by Gluttony and Lechery. I'll not speak   145
another word for a king's ransom.
FAUSTUS: What are you, Mistress Minx, the seventh and last?
LECH: Who, I, sir? I am one that loves an inch of raw mutton better than
an ell of fried stockfish; and the first letter of my name begins with
Lechery.   150
LUC: Away to hell, to hell! (*Exeunt the* SINS.)
      —Now, Faustus, how dost thou like this?
FAUSTUS: O, this feeds my soul!
LUC: Tut, Faustus, in hell is all manner of delight.
FAUSTUS: O might I see hell, and return again.   155
      How happy were I then!
LUC: Thou shalt; I will send for thee at midnight.
      In meantime take this book; peruse it throughly,
      And thou shalt turn thyself into what shape thou wilt.
FAUSTUS: Great thanks, mighty Lucifer!   160
      This will I keep as chary as my life.
LUC: Farewell, Faustus, and think on the Devil.
FAUSTUS: Farewell, great Lucifer! Come, Mephistophilis.
(*Exeunt omnes.*)
(*Enter* WAGNER.)

---

132. bevers: Refreshments between meals. **136. Martin Martlemas-beef:** Martlemas or Martinmas
was the customary time for hanging up provisions to dry which had been salted for the winter.

WAG: Learned Faustus,
　　To know the secrets of astronomy,　　　　　　　　　165
　　Graven in the book of Jove's high firmament,
　　Did mount himself to scale Olympus' top,
　　Being seated in a chariot burning bright,
　　Drawn by the strength of yoky dragons' necks.
　　He now is gone to prove cosmography,　　　　　　　170
　　And, as I guess, will first arrive at Rome,
　　To see the Pope and manner of his court,
　　And take some part of holy Peter's feast,
　　That to this day is highly solemnis'd.
(Exit.)

Scene 7
The Pope's Privy-Chamber

(*Enter* FAUSTUS *and* MEPHISTOPHILIS.)
FAUSTUS: Having now, my good Mephistophilis,
　　Past with delight the stately town of Trier,°
　　Environ'd round with airy mountain-tops,
　　With walls of flint, and deep entrenched lakes,
　　Not to be won by any conquering prince;　　　　　　5
　　From Paris next, coasting the realm of France,
　　We saw the river Maine fall into Rhine,
　　Whose banks are set with groves of fruitful vines;
　　Then up to Naples, rich Campania,
　　Whose buildings fair and gorgeous to the eye,　　　　10
　　The streets straight forth, and pav'd with finest brick,
　　Quarter the town in four equivalents.
　　There saw we learned Maro's° golden tomb,
　　The way he cut, an English mile in length,
　　Thorough a rock of stone in one night's space;　　　15
　　From thence to Venice, Padua, and the rest,
　　In one of which a sumptuous temple stands,
　　That threats the stars with her aspiring top,
　　Thus hitherto has Faustus spent his time:
　　But tell me, now, what resting-place is this?　　　　20
　　Hast thou, as erst I did command,
　　Conducted me within the walls of Rome?

---

2. **Trier:** Treves. 13. **Maro's:** Virgil, who was reputed a magician in the Middle Ages, was buried at Naples.

MEPH: Faustus, I have; and because we will not be unprovided, I have taken
   up° his Holiness' privy-chamber for our use.

FAUSTUS: I hope his Holiness will bid us welcome.   25

MEPH: Tut, 'tis no matter, man, we'll be bold with his good cheer.
   And now, my Faustus, that thou may'st perceive
   What Rome containeth to delight thee with,
   Know that this city stands upon seven hills
   That underprop the groundwork of the same.   30
   [Just through the midst runs flowing Tiber's stream,
   With winding banks that cut it in two parts:]
   Over the which four stately bridges lean,
   That make safe passage to each part of Rome:
   Upon the bridge call'd Ponto Angelo   35
   Erected is a castle passing strong,
   Within whose walls such store of ordnance are,
   And double cannons, fram'd of carved brass,
   As match the days within one cómplete year;
   Besides the gates and high pyramides,   40
   Which Julius Cæsar brought from Africa.

FAUSTUS: Now by the kingdoms of infernal rule,
   Of Styx, of Acheron, and the fiery lake
   Of ever-burning Phlegethon, I swear
   That I do long to see the monuments   45
   And situation of bright-splendent Rome:
   Come therefore, let's away.

MEPH: Nay, Faustus, stay; I know you'd fain see the Pope,
   And take some part of holy Peter's feast,
   Where thou shalt see a troop of bald-pate friars,   50
   Whose *summum bonum* is in belly-cheer.

FAUSTUS: Well, I'm content to compass then some sport,
   And by their folly make us merriment.
   Then charm me, [Mephistophilis,] that I
   May be invisible, to do what I please   55
   Unseen of any whilst I stay in Rome.

(MEPHISTOPHILIS *charms him.*)

MEPH: So, Faustus, now
   Do what thou wilt, thou shalt not be discern'd.

(*Sound a sennet.*° *Enter the* POPE *and the* CARDINAL *of* LORRAIN *to the banquet,*
   with FRIARS *attending.*)

23–24. taken up: Engaged. °**sennet:** A particular set of notes on the trumpet or cornet different from
a flourish.

POPE: My Lord of Lorrain, wilt please you draw near?

FAUSTUS: Fall to, and the devil choke you an° you spare!   60

POPE: How now! Who's that which spake?—Friars, look about.

1 FRIAR: Here's nobody, if it like your Holiness.

POPE: My lord, here is a dainty dish was sent me from the Bishop of Milan.

FAUSTUS: I thank you, sir. (*Snatches it.*)

POPE: How now! Who's that which snatch'd the meat from me? Will no   65
    man look? My Lord, this dish was sent me from the Cardinal of Florence.

FAUSTUS: You say true; I'll ha't. (*Snatches it.*)

POPE: What, again! My lord, I'll drink to your Grace.

FAUSTUS: I'll pledge your Grace. (*Snatches the cup.*)   70

C. OF LOR: My lord, it may be some ghost newly crept out of purgatory,
    come to beg a pardon of your Holiness.

POPE: It may be so. Friars, prepare a dirge to lay the fury of this ghost. Once
    again, my lord, fall to. (*The* POPE *crosseth himself.*)

FAUSTUS: What, are you crossing of yourself? Well, use that trick no more   75
    I would advise you.
    (*The* POPE *crosses himself again.*)
    Well, there's the second time. Aware the third, I give you fair warning.
    (*The* POPE *crosses himself again, and* FAUSTUS *hits him a box of the ear; and*
    they all run away.)
    Come on, Mephistophilis, what shall we do?

MEPH: Nay, I know not. We shall be curs'd with bell, book, and candle.

FAUSTUS: How! bell, book, and candle,—candle, book, and bell,   80
    Forward and backward to curse Faustus to hell!
    Anon you shall hear a hog grunt, a calf bleat, and an ass bray,
    Because it is Saint Peter's holiday.
(*Re-enter all the* FRIARS *to sing the Dirge.*)

1 FRIAR: Come, brethren, let's about our business with good devotion.
    (*They sing:*)
    Cursed be he that stole away his Holiness' meat from the table!   85
    Maledicat Dominus!°
    Cursed be he that struck his Holiness a blow on the face! *Maledicat Dominus!*
    Cursed be he that took Friar Sandelo a blow on the pate! *Maledicat*
    Dominus!   90
    Cursed be he that disturbeth our holy dirge! *Maledicat Dominus!*
    Cursed be he that took away his Holiness' wine! *Maledicat Dominus!*
    Et omnes sancti!° Amen!
    (MEPHISTOPHILIS *and* FAUSTUS *beat the* FRIARS, *and fling fireworks among them,*
    and so exeunt.)

---

60. an: If. **86.** *Maledicat Dominus!:* "May the Lord curse him." **93.** *Et omnes sancti!:* "And all the saints."

(*Enter* CHORUS.)

CHORUS: When Faustus had with pleasure ta'en the view
　　Of rarest things, and royal courts of kings,　　　　　　　　95
　　He stay'd his course, and so returned home;
　　Where such as bear his absence but with grief,
　　I mean his friends, and near'st companions,
　　Did gratulate his safety with kind words,
　　And in their conference of what befell,　　　　　　　　100
　　Touching his journey through the world and air,
　　They put forth questions of Astrology,
　　Which Faustus answer'd with such learned skill,
　　As they admir'd and wond'red at his wit.
　　Now is his fame spread forth in every land;　　　　　　　　105
　　Amongst the rest the Emperor is one,
　　Carolus the Fifth, at whose palace now
　　Faustus is feasted 'mongst his noblemen.
　　What there he did in trial of his art,
　　I leave untold—your eyes shall see perform'd.　　　　　　　　110
(*Exit.*)

Scene 8
An Inn-yard

(*Enter* ROBIN *the Ostler with a book in his hand.*)

ROBIN: O, this is admirable! here I ha' stolen one of Dr. Faustus' conjuring
　　books, and i' faith I mean to search some circles for my own use. Now will
　　I make all the maidens in our parish dance at my pleasure, stark naked
　　before me; and so by that means I shall see more than e'er I felt or saw yet.

(*Enter* RALPH *calling* ROBIN.)

RALPH: Robin, prithee come away; there's a gentleman tarries to have his　　5
　　horse, and he would have his things rubb'd and made clean. He keeps
　　such a chafing with my mistress about it; and she has sent me to look
　　thee out. Prithee come away.

ROBIN: Keep out, keep out, or else you are blown up; you are dismemb'red,
　　Ralph: keep out, for I am about a roaring piece of work.　　10

RALPH: Come, what dost thou with that same book? Thou canst not read.

ROBIN: Yes, my master and mistress shall find that I can read, he for his
　　forehead, she for her private study; she's born to bear with me, or else
　　my art fails.

RALPH: Why, Robin, what book is that?　　15

ROBIN: What book! Why, the most intolerable book for conjuring that e'er
　　was invented by any brimstone devil.

RALPH: Canst thou conjure with it?

ROBIN: I can do all these things easily with it: first, I can make thee drunk
    with ippocras° at any tabern in Europe for nothing; that's one of my   20
    conjuring works.

RALPH: Our Master Parson says that's nothing.

ROBIN: True, Ralph; and more, Ralph, if thou hast any mind to Nan Spit,
    our kitchenmaid, then turn her and wind her to thy own use as often as
    thou wilt, and at midnight.   25

RALPH: O brave Robin, shall I have Nan Spit, and to mine own use? On that
    condition I'll feed thy devil with horsebread as long as he lives, of free cost.

ROBIN: No more, sweet Ralph: let's go and make clean our boots, which lie
    foul upon our hands, and then to our conjuring in the Devil's name.   30

(*Exeunt.*)

Scene 9
An Inn

(*Enter* ROBIN *and* RALPH *with a silver goblet.*)

ROBIN: Come, Ralph, did not I tell thee we were for ever made by this Doctor
    Faustus' book? *Ecce signum,*° here's a simple purchase° for horse-keepers;
    our horses shall eat no hay as long as this lasts.

(*Enter the* VINTNER.)

RALPH: But, Robin, here comes the Vintner.

ROBIN: Hush! I'll gull him supernaturally. Drawer, I hope all is paid: 5
    God be with you. Come, Ralph.

VINT: Soft, sir; a word with you. I must yet have a goblet paid from you, ere
    you go.

ROBIN: I, a goblet, Ralph; I, a goblet! I scorn you, and you are but a° &c. I,
    a goblet! search me.   10

VINT: I mean so, sir, with your favour. (*Searches him.*)

ROBIN: How say you now?

VINT: I must say somewhat to your fellow. You, sir!

RALPH: Me, sir! me, sir! search your fill. (VINTNER *searches him.*)
    Now, sir, you may be ashamed to burden honest men with a matter of
    truth.   15

VINT: Well, t' one of you hath this goblet about you.

ROBIN (*Aside.*): You lie, drawer, 'tis afore me.—Sirrah you, I'll teach ye to
    impeach honest men; stand by;—I'll scour you for a goblet!—stand
    aside you had best, I charge you in the name of Belzebub.
    (*Aside to* RALPH.) Look to the goblet, Ralph.   20

VINT: What mean you, sirrah?

---

20. **ippocras:** Wine mixed with sugar and spices. **2. *Ecce signum:*** "Behold the sign." **2. purchase:**
Gain. **9. you are but a:** The abuse was left to the actor's inventiveness.

ROBIN: I'll tell you what I mean. *(Reads from a book.)* Sanctobulorum, Periphrasticon—Nay, I'll tickle you, Vintner. *(Aside to RALPH.)* Look to the goblet, Ralph. *(Reads.)* Polypragmos Belseborams framanto pacostiphos tostu, Mephistophilis, &c.   25

(Enter MEPHISTOPHILIS, sets squibs at their backs, and then exit. They run about.)

VINT: O nomine Domini!° what meanest thou, Robin? Thou hast no goblet.

RALPH: Peccatum peccatorum!° Here's thy goblet, good vintner. *(Gives the goblet to VINTNER, who exits.)*

ROBIN: Misericordia pro nobis!° What shall I do? Good Devil, forgive me now, and I'll never rob thy library more.

(Re-enter to them MEPHISTOPHILIS.)

MEPH: Monarch of hell, under whose black survey   30
    Great potentates do kneel with awful fear,
    Upon whose altars thousand souls do lie,
    How am I vexed with these villains' charms?
    From Constantinople am I hither come
    Only for pleasure of these damned slaves.   35

ROBIN: How from Constantinople? You have had a great journey. Will you take sixpence in your purse to pay for your supper, and begone?

MEPH: Well, villains, for your presumption, I transform thee into an ape, and thee into a dog; and so begone.

(Exit.)

ROBIN: How, into an ape? That's brave! I'll have fine sport with the boys.   40
    I'll get nuts and apples enow.

RALPH: And I must be a dog.

ROBIN: I' faith thy head will never be out of the pottage pot.

(Exeunt.)

Scene 10
The Court of the Emperor

(Enter EMPEROR, FAUSTUS, and a KNIGHT with ATTENDANTS.)

EMP: Master Doctor Faustus, I have heard strange report of thy knowledge in the black art, how that none in my empire nor in the whole world can compare with thee for the rare effects of magic; they say thou hast a familiar spirit, by whom thou canst accomplish what thou list. This, therefore, is my request, that thou let me see some proof of thy skill   5
that mine eyes may be witnesses to confirm what mine ears have heard reported; and here I swear to thee by the honour of mine imperial

---

26. *O nomine Domini!*: "In the name of the Lord." **27. *Peccatum peccatorum!*:** "Sin of sins." **28. *Misericordia pro nobis!*:** "Mercy on us."

crown, that, whatever thou doest, thou shalt be no ways prejudiced or
endamaged.

KNIGHT *(Aside.)*: I' faith he looks much like a conjuror.   10

FAUSTUS: My gracious sovereign, though I must confess myself far inferior
to the report men have published, and nothing answerable° to the honour
of your imperial majesty, yet for that love and duty binds me thereunto, I
am content to do whatsoever your majesty shall command me.

EMP: Then, Doctor Faustus, mark what I shall say.   15
As I was sometime solitary set
Within my closet, sundry thoughts arose
About the honour of mine ancestors,
How they had won by prowess such exploits,
Got such riches, subdued so many kingdoms,   20
As we that do succeed, or they that shall
Hereafter possess our throne, shall
(I fear me) ne'er attain to that degree
Of high renown and great authority;
Amongst which kings is Alexander the Great,   25
Chief spectacle of the world's pre-eminence,
The bright shining of whose glorious acts
Lightens the world with his° reflecting beams,
As, when I heard but motion° made of him,
It grieves my soul I never saw the man.   30
If, therefore, thou by cunning of thine art
Canst raise this man from hollow vaults below,
Where lies entomb'd this famous conqueror,
And bring with him his beauteous paramour,
Both in their right shapes, gesture, and attire   35
They us'd to wear during their time of life,
Thou shalt both satisfy my just desire,
And give me cause to praise thee whilst I live.

FAUSTUS: My gracious lord, I am ready to accomplish your request so far
forth as by art, and power of my Spirit, I am able to perform.   40

KNIGHT *(Aside.)*: I' faith that's just nothing at all.

FAUSTUS: But, if it like your Grace, it is not in my ability to present before
your eyes the true substantial bodies of those two deceased princes,
which long since are consumed to dust.

KNIGHT *(Aside.)*: Ay, marry, Master Doctor, now there's a sign of grace in   45
you, when you will confess the truth.

---

12. answerable: Proportionate. **28. his:** Its. **29. motion:** Mention.

FAUSTUS: But such spirits as can lively resemble Alexander and his paramour
shall appear before your Grace in that manner that they best liv'd in,
in their most flourishing estate; which I doubt not shall sufficiently
content your imperial majesty.   50

EMP: Go to, Master Doctor, let me see them presently.

KNIGHT: Do you hear, Master Doctor? You bring Alexander and his paramour
before the Emperor!

FAUSTUS: How then, sir?

KNIGHT: I' faith that's as true as Diana turn'd me to a stag!   55

FAUSTUS: No, sir, but when Actæon died, he left the horns for you.
Mephistophilis, begone.

(*Exit* MEPHISTOPHILIS.)

KNIGHT: Nay, an you go to conjuring, I'll begone.

(*Exit.*)

FAUSTUS: I'll meet with you anon for interrupting me so. Here they are, my
gracious lord.   60

(*Re-enter* MEPHISTOPHILIS *and* SPIRITS *in the shape of* ALEXANDER *and his* PARAMOUR.)

EMP: Master Doctor, I heard this lady while she liv'd had a wart or mole in her
neck: how shall I know whether it be so or no?

FAUSTUS: Your Highness may boldly go and see.

(*Exeunt Spirits.*)

EMP: Sure these are no spirits, but the true substantial bodies of those two
deceased princes.   65

FAUSTUS: Will't please your Highness now to send for the Knight that was so
pleasant with me here of late?

EMP: One of you call him forth.

(*Exit Attendant.*)

(*Re-enter the* KNIGHT *with a pair of horns on his head.*)

How now, sir Knight! why I had thought thou had'st been a bachelor,
but now I see thou hast a wife, that not only gives thee horns, but   70
makes thee wear them. Feel on thy head.

KNIGHT: Thou damned wretch and execrable dog,
Bred in the concave of some monstrous rock,
How darest thou thus abuse a gentleman?
Villain, I say, undo what thou hast done!   75

FAUSTUS: O, not so fast, sir; there's no haste; but, good, are you rememb'red
how you crossed me in my conference with the Emperor? I think I have
met with you for it.

EMP: Good Master Doctor, at my entreaty release him; he hath done penance
sufficient.   80

FAUSTUS: My gracious lord, not so much for the injury he off'red me here in
your presence, as to delight you with some mirth, hath Faustus worthily

requited this injurious Knight; which, being all I desire, I am content
to release him of his horns: and, sir Knight, hereafter speak well of
scholars. Mephistophilis, transform him straight. (MEPHISTOPHILIS   85
removes the horns.) Now, my good lord, having done my duty I humbly
take my leave.

EMP: Farewell, Master Doctor; yet, ere you go,
Expect from me a bounteous reward.

(*Exeunt.*)

Scene 11
A Green; Afterwards, The House of Faustus

(*Enter* FAUSTUS *and* MEPHISTOPHILIS.)

FAUSTUS: Now, Mephistophilis, the restless course
That Time doth run with calm and silent foot,
Short'ning my days and thread of vital life,
Calls for the payment of my latest years;
Therefore, sweet Mephistophilis, let us   5
Make haste to Wittenberg.

MEPH: What, will you go on horseback or on foot?

FAUSTUS: Nay, till I'm past this fair and pleasant green.
I'll walk on foot.

(*Enter a* HORSE-COURSER.)

HORSE-C: I have been all this day seeking one Master Fustian: mass,   10
see where he is! God save you, Master Doctor!

FAUSTUS: What, horse-Courser! You are well met.

HORSE-C: Do you hear, sir? I have brought you forty dollars for your horse.

FAUSTUS: I cannot sell him so: if thou likest him for fifty, take him.

HORSE-C: Alas, sir, I have no more.—I pray you speak for me.   15

MEPH: I pray you let him have him: he is an honest fellow, and he has a
great charge, neither wife nor child.

FAUSTUS: Well, come, give me your money. (HORSE-COURSER *gives* FAUSTUS
the money.) My boy will deliver him to you. But I must tell you one
thing before you have him; ride him not into the water at any hand.   20

HORSE-C: Why, sir, will he not drink of all waters?

FAUSTUS: O yes, he will drink of all waters, but ride him not into the water: ride
him over hedge or ditch, or where thou wilt, but not into the water.

HORSE-C: Well, sir.—Now I am made man forever. I'll not leave my horse
for forty. (*Aside.*) If he had but the quality of hey-ding-ding, hey-ding-   25
ding, I'd make a brave living on him: he has a buttock as slick as an eel.
Well, God b' wi'ye, sir, your boy will deliver him me: but hark ye, sir; if my
horse be sick or ill at ease, if I bring his water to you, you'll tell me what it is?

(*Exit* HORSE-COURSER.)

FAUSTUS: Away, you villain; what, dost think I am a horse-doctor?   30
What art thou, Faustus, but a man condemn'd to die?
Thy fatal time doth draw to final end;
Despair doth drive distrust unto my thoughts:
Confound these passions with a quiet sleep:
Tush, Christ did call the thief upon the cross;   35
Then rest thee, Faustus, quiet in conceit. (*Sleeps in his chair.*)
(*Re-enter* HORSE-COURSER, *all wet, crying.*)
HORSE-C: Alas, alas! Doctor Fustian, quotha? Mass, Doctor Lopus° was never
such a doctor. Has given me a purgation has purg'd me of forty dollars;
I shall never see them more. But yet, like an ass as I was, I would not
be ruled by him, for he bade me I should ride him into no water. Now   40
I, thinking my horse had had some rare quality that he would not have
had me known of, I, like a venturous youth, rid him into the deep
pond at the town's end. I was no sooner in the middle of the pond, but
my horse vanish'd away, and I sat upon a bottle of hay, never so near
drowning in my life. But I'll seek out my Doctor, and have my forty   45
dollars again, or I'll make it the dearest horse!—O, yonder is his snipper-
snapper.—Do you hear? You hey-pass,° where's your master?
MEPH: Why, sir, what would you? You cannot speak with him.
HORSE-C: But I will speak with him.
MEPH: Why, he's fast asleep. Come some other time.   50
HORSE-C: I'll speak with him now, or I'll break his glass windows about his ears.
MEPH: I tell thee he has not slept this eight nights.
HORSE-C: An he have not slept this eight weeks, I'll speak with him.
MEPH: See where he is, fast asleep.
HORSE-C: Ay, this is he. God save you, Master Doctor! Master Doctor,   55
Master Doctor Fustian!—Forty dollars, forty dollars for a bottle of hay!
MEPH: Why, thou seest he hears thee not.
HORSE-C: So ho, ho!—so, ho, ho! (*Hollas in his ear.*) No, will you not wake?
I'll make you wake ere I go. (*Pulls* FAUSTUS *by the leg, and pulls it away.*)
Alas, I am undone! What shall I do?   60
FAUSTUS: O my leg, my leg! Help, Mephistophilis! call the officers. My leg,
my leg!
MEPH: Come, villain, to the constable.
HORSE-C: O lord, sir, let me go, and I'll give you forty dollars more.
MEPH: Where be they?   65
HORSE-C: I have none about me. Come to my ostry° and I'll give them you.

---

37. Doctor Lopus: Dr. Lopez, physician to Queen Elizabeth, hanged in 1594 on the charge of conspiring to poison the Queen. **47. hey-pass:** A juggler's term, like "presto, fly!" Here applied to the juggler himself. **66. ostry:** Inn.

MEPH: Begone quickly.

(HORSE-COURSER *runs away.*)

FAUSTUS: What, is he gone? Farewell he! Faustus has his leg again, and the
horse-courser, I take it, a bottle of hay for his labour. Well, this trick shall
cost him forty dollars more.   70

(*Enter* WAGNER.) How now, Wagner, what's the news with thee?

WAG: Sir, the Duke of Vanholt doth earnestly entreat your company.

FAUSTUS: The Duke of Vanholt! an honourable gentleman, to whom I must
be no niggard of my cunning. Come, Mephistophilis, let's away to him.

(*Exeunt.*)

Scene 12
The Court of the Duke of Vanholt

(*Enter the* DUKE *of* VANHOLT, *the* DUCHESS, FAUSTUS, *and* MEPHISTOPHILIS.)

DUKE: Believe me, Master Doctor, this merriment hath much pleased me.

FAUSTUS: My gracious lord, I am glad it contents you so well.—But it may
be, madam, you take no delight in this. I have heard that great-bellied
women do long for some dainties or other. What is it, madam? Tell me,
and you shall have it.   5

DUCHESS: Thanks, good Master Doctor; and for I see your courteous intent
to pleasure me, I will not hide from you the thing my heart desires; and
were it now summer, as it is January and the dead time of the winter, I
would desire no better meat than a dish of ripe grapes.

FAUSTUS: Alas, madam, that's nothing! Mephistophilis, begone.   10

(*Exit* MEPHISTOPHILIS.)

Were it a greater thing than this, so it would content you, you should
have it.

(*Re-enter* MEPHISTOPHILIS *with the grapes.*)

Here they be, madam; wilt please you taste on them?

DUKE: Believe me, Master Doctor, this makes me wonder above the rest,
that being in the dead time of winter, and in the month of January,   15
how you should come by these grapes.

FAUSTUS: If it like your Grace, the year is divided into two circles over the
whole world, that, when it is here winter with us, in the contrary circle
it is summer with them, as in India, Saba, and farther countries in the
East; and by means of a swift spirit that I have, I had them brought   20
hither, as ye see.—How do you like them, madam; be they good?

DUCHESS: Believe me, Master Doctor, they be the best grapes that I e'er
tasted in my life before.

FAUSTUS: I am glad they content you so, madam.

DUKE: Come, madam, let us in, where you must well reward this learned   25
man for the great kindness he hath show'd to you.

DUCHESS: And so I will, my lord; and whilst I live, rest beholding for this courtesy.
FAUSTUS: I humbly thank your Grace.
DUKE: Come, Master Doctor, follow us and receive your reward.   30
(*Exeunt.*)

Scene 13
A Room in the House of Faustus

(*Enter* WAGNER, *solus.*)
WAG: I think my master means to die shortly,
For he hath given to me all his goods;
And yet, methinks, if that death were near,
He would not banquet and carouse and swill
Amongst the students, as even now he doth,   5
Who are at supper with such belly-cheer
As Wagner ne'er beheld in all his life.
See where they come! Belike the feast is ended.
(*Enter* FAUSTUS, *with two or three* SCHOLARS *and* MEPHISTOPHILIS.)
1 SCHOL: Master Doctor Faustus, since our conference about fair ladies,
which was the beautifullest in all the world, we have determined with   10
ourselves that Helen of Greece was the admirablest lady that ever
lived: therefore, Master Doctor, if you will do us that favour, as to let us
see that peerless dame of Greece, whom all the world admires for majesty,
we should think ourselves much beholding unto you.
FAUSTUS: Gentlemen,   15
For that I know your friendship is unfeigned,
And Faustus' custom is not to deny
The just requests of those that wish him well,
You shall behold that peerless dame of Greece,
No otherways for pomp and majesty   20
Than when Sir Paris cross'd the seas with her,
And brought the spoils to rich Dardania.
Be silent, then, for danger is in words.
(*Music sounds, and* HELEN *passeth over the stage.*)
2 SCHOL: Too simple is my wit to tell her praise,
Whom all the world admires for majesty.   25
3 SCHOL: No marvel though the angry Greeks pursu'd
With ten years' war the rape of such a queen,
Whose heavenly beauty passeth all compare.
1 SCHOL: Since we have seen the pride of Nature's works,
And only paragon of excellence,   30
(*Enter an* OLD MAN.) Let us depart; and for this glorious deed
Happy and blest be Faustus evermore.

FAUSTUS: Gentlemen, farewell—the same I wish to you.
(*Exeunt* SCHOLARS *and* WAGNER.)
OLD MAN: Ah, Doctor Faustus, that I might prevail
 To guide thy steps unto the way of life,   35
 By which sweet path thou may'st attain the goal
 That shall conduct thee to celestial rest!
 Break heart, drop blood, and mingle it with tears,
 Tears falling from repentant heaviness
 Of thy most vile and loathsome filthiness,   40
 The stench whereof corrupts the inward soul
 With such flagitious crimes of heinous sins
 As no commiseration may expel,
 But mercy, Faustus, of thy Saviour sweet,
 Whose blood alone must wash away thy guilt.   45
FAUSTUS: Where art thou, Faustus? Wretch, what hast thou done?
 Damn'd art thou, Faustus, damn'd; despair and die!
 Hell calls for right, and with a roaring voice
 Says "Faustus! come! thine hour is (almost) come!"
 And Faustus (now) will come to do thee right.   50
 (MEPHISTOPHILIS *gives him a dagger.*)
OLD MAN: Ah stay, good Faustus, stay thy desperate steps!
 I see an angel hovers o'er thy head,
 And, with a vial full of precious grace,
 Offers to pour the same into thy soul:
 Then call for mercy, and avoid despair.   55
FAUSTUS: Ah, my sweet friend, I feel
 Thy words do comfort my distressed soul.
 Leave me a while to ponder on my sins.
OLD MAN: I go, sweet Faustus, but with heavy cheer,
 Fearing the ruin of thy hopeless soul.   60
(*Exit.*)
FAUSTUS: Accursed Faustus, where is mercy now?
 I do repent; and yet I do despair;
 Hell strives with grace for conquest in my breast:
 What shall I do to shun the snares of death?
MEPH: Thou traitor, Faustus, I arrest thy soul   65
 For disobedience to my sovereign lord;
 Revolt, or I'll in piecemeal tear thy flesh.
FAUSTUS: Sweet Mephistophilis, entreat thy lord
 To pardon my unjust presumption,
 And with my blood again I will confirm   70
 My former vow I made to Lucifer.

MEPH: Do it now then quickly, with unfeigned heart,
　　　 Lest danger do attend thy drift.
(FAUSTUS *stabs his arm and writes on a paper with his blood.*)
FAUSTUS: Torment, sweet friend, that base and crooked age,°
　　　 That durst dissuade me from my Lucifer,　　　　　75
　　　 With greatest torments that our hell affords.
MEPH: His faith is great, I cannot touch his soul;
　　　 But what I may afflict his body with
　　　 I will attempt, which is but little worth.
FAUSTUS: One thing, good servant, let me crave of thee,　80
　　　 To glut the longing of my heart's desire,—
　　　 That I might have unto my paramour
　　　 That heavenly Helen, which I saw of late,
　　　 Whose sweet embracings may extinguish clean
　　　 These thoughts that do dissuade me from my vow,　85
　　　 And keep mine oath I made to Lucifer.
MEPH: Faustus, this or what else thou shalt desire
　　　 Shall be perform'd in twinkling of an eye.
　　　 (*Re-enter* HELEN.)
FAUSTUS: Was this the face that launch'd a thousand ships,
　　　 And burnt the topless° towers of Ilium?　　　　　90
　　　 Sweet Helen, make me immortal with a kiss.
　　　 (*Kisses her.*)
　　　 Her lips suck forth my soul; see where it flies!—
　　　 Come, Helen, come, give me my soul again.
　　　 Here will I dwell, for Heaven be in these lips,
　　　 And all is dross that is not Helena.　　　　　　　95
(*Enter* OLD MAN.)
　　　 I will be Paris, and for love of thee,
　　　 Instead of Troy, shall Wittenberg be sack'd;
　　　 And I will combat with weak Menelaus,
　　　 And wear thy colours on my plumed crest;
　　　 Yea, I will wound Achilles in the heel,　　　　　100
　　　 And then return to Helen for a kiss.
　　　 Oh, thou art fairer than the evening air
　　　 Clad in the beauty of a thousand stars;
　　　 Brighter art thou than flaming Jupiter
　　　 When he appear'd to hapless Semele:　　　　　　105
　　　 More lovely than the monarch of the sky

---

74. base and crooked age: Old Man. **90. topless:** Unsurpassed in height.

In wanton Arethusa's azur'd arms:
And none but thou shalt be my paramour.
(*Exeunt.*)

OLD MAN: Accursed Faustus, miserable man,
That from thy soul exclud'st the grace of Heaven,   110
And fly'st the throne of his tribunal seat!

(*Enter* DEVILS.)

Satan begins to sift me with his pride:
As in this furnace God shall try my faith,
My faith, vile hell, shall triumph over thee.
Ambitious fiends! see how the heavens smiles   115
At your repulse, and laughs your state to scorn!
Hence, hell! for hence I fly unto my God. *Exeunt.*

Scene 14
The Same

(*Enter* FAUSTUS *with the* SCHOLARS.)

FAUSTUS: Ah, gentlemen!

1 SCHOL: What ails Faustus?

FAUSTUS: Ah, my sweet chamber-fellow, had I lived with thee, then had I
lived still! but now I die eternally. Look, comes he not, come he not?

2 SCHOL: What means Faustus?   5

3 SCHOL: Belike he is grown into some sickness by being over solitary.

1 SCHOL: If it be so, we'll have physicians to cure him. 'Tis but a surfeit.
Never fear, man.

FAUSTUS: A surfeit of deadly sin that hath damn'd both body and soul.

2 SCHOL: Yet, Faustus, look up to Heaven; remember God's mercies are 10
infinite.

FAUSTUS: But Faustus' offences can never be pardoned: the serpent that
tempted Eve may be sav'd, but not Faustus. Ah, gentlemen, hear me
with patience, and tremble not at my speeches! Though my heart pants
and quivers to remember that I have been a student here these thirty   15
years, oh, would I had never seen Wittenberg, never read book! And
what wonders I have done, all Germany can witness, yea, the world;
for which Faustus hath lost both Germany and the world, yea Heaven
itself, Heaven, the seat of God, the throne of the blessed, the kingdom of
joy; and must remain in hell for ever, hell, ah, hell, for ever! Sweet   20
friends! what shall become of Faustus being in hell for ever?

3 SCHOL: Yet, Faustus, call on God.

FAUSTUS: On God, whom Faustus hath abjur'd! on God, whom Faustus
hath blasphemed! Ah, my God, I would weep, but the Devil draws in
my tears. Gush forth blood instead of tears! Yea, life and soul! Oh, he   25

stays my tongue! I would lift up my hands, but see, they hold them, they hold them!

ALL: Who, Faustus?

FAUSTUS: Lucifer and Mephistophilis. Ah, gentlemen, I gave them my soul for my cunning!   30

ALL: God forbid!

FAUSTUS: God forbade it indeed; but Faustus hath done it. For vain pleasure of twenty-four years hath Faustus lost eternal joy and felicity. I writ them a bill with mine own blood: the date is expired; the time will come, and he will fetch me.   35

1 SCHOL: Why did not Faustus tell us of this before, that divines might have prayed for thee?

FAUSTUS: Oft have I thought to have done so; but the Devil threat'ned to tear me in pieces if I nam'd God; to fetch both body and soul if I once gave ear to divinity: and now 't is too late. Gentlemen, away! lest you   40 perish with me.

2 SCHOL: Oh, what shall we do to save Faustus?

FAUSTUS: Talk not of me, but save yourselves, and depart.

3 SCHOL: God will strengthen me. I will stay with Faustus.

1 SCHOL: Tempt not God, sweet friend; but let us into the next room, and   45 there pray for him.

FAUSTUS: Ay, pray for me, pray for me! and what noise soever ye hear, come not unto me, for nothing can rescue me.

2 SCHOL: Pray thou, and we will pray that God may have mercy upon thee.

FAUSTUS: Gentlemen, farewell! If I live till morning I'll visit you: if not—   50 Faustus is gone to hell.

ALL: Faustus, farewell!

(Exeunt SCHOLARS. The clock strikes eleven.)

FAUSTUS: Ah, Faustus,
    Now hast thou but one bare hour to live,
    And then thou must be damn'd perpetually!
    Stand still, you ever-moving spheres of Heaven,   55
    That time may cease, and midnight never come;
    Fair Nature's eye, rise, rise again and make
    Perpetual day; or let this hour be but
    A year, a month, a week, a natural day,   60
    That Faustus may repent and save his soul!
    O lente, lente, currite noctis equi!°
    The stars move still,° time runs, the clock will strike,

---

62. O lente . . . equi!: "Run softly, softly, horses of the night"—Ovid's *Amores*, i. 13. **63. still:** Without ceasing.

The Devil will come, and Faustus must be damn'd.
O, I'll leap up to my God! Who pulls me down?   65
See, see where Christ's blood streams in the firmament!
One drop would save my soul—Half a drop: ah, my Christ!
Ah, rend not my heart for naming of my Christ!
Yet will I call on him: O spare me, Lucifer!—
Where is it now? 'Tis gone; and see where God   70
Stretcheth out his arm, and bends his ireful brows!
Mountain and hills come, come and fall on me,
And hide me from the heavy wrath of God!
No! no!
Then will I headlong run into the earth;   75
Earth gape! O no, it will not harbour me!
You stars that reign'd at my nativity,
Whose influence hath allotted death and hell,
Now draw up Faustus like a foggy mist
Into the entrails of yon labouring clouds,   80
That when they vomit forth into the air,
My limbs may issue from their smoky mouths,
So that my soul may but ascend to Heaven.
(The watch strikes the half hour.)
Ah, half the hour is past! 'Twill all be past anon!
O God!   85
If thou wilt not have mercy on my soul,
Yet for Christ's sake whose blood hath ransom'd me,
Impose some end to my incessant pain;
Let Faustus live in hell a thousand years—
A hundred thousand, and at last be sav'd!   90
O, no end is limited to damned souls!
Why wert thou not a creature wanting soul?
Or why is this immortal that thou hast?
Ah, Pythagoras' metempsychosis! were that true,
This soul should fly from me, and I be chang'd   95
Unto some brutish beast! All beasts are happy,
For, when they die,
Their souls are soon dissolv'd in elements;
But mine must live, still to be plagu'd in hell.
Curst be the parents that engend'red me!   100
No, Faustus: curse thyself: curse Lucifer
That hath depriv'd thee of the joys of Heaven.
(The clock striketh twelve.)
O, it strikes, it strikes! Now, body, turn to air,
Or Lucifer will bear thee quick to hell.

(Thunder and lightning.)
O soul, be chang'd into little water-drops,   105
And fall into the ocean—ne'er be found.
My God! my God! look not so fierce on me!
(Enter DEVILS.*)*
Adders and serpents, let me breathe awhile!
Ugly hell, gape not! come not, Lucifer!
I'll burn my books!—Ah Mephistophilis!   110
(Exeunt DEVILS *with* FAUSTUS. *Enter* CHORUS.*)*
[CHO.]: Cut is the branch that might have grown full straight,
And burned is Apollo's laurel bough,
That sometimes grew within this learned man,
Faustus is gone; regard his hellish fall,
Whose fiendful fortune may exhort the wise   115
Only to wonder at unlawful things,
Whose deepness doth entice such forward wits
To practise more than heavenly power permits.
(Exit.)

Terminat hora diem, terminat author opus.°

- In this play, some characters, rather than being fully developed, represent particular ideas. Identify such characters.
- What are the functions of the good angel and the bad angel in the play?
- In what ways is Mephistopheles the most admirable character in the play?
- How do the antics of Robin, Ralph, and the clown relate to the actions of Faustus?
- What does Faustus achieve by selling his soul?
- How do his actions compare to his initial plans?
- How well does Mephistopheles satisfy the requests that Faustus makes?

Experiencing Literature through Writing

1. The previous works are included in this section because they help us define the horror genre. Use at least three of the works that we have included to construct your own definition of this genre. It may be most interesting to look at the works that have the *least* in common.

---

119. Terminat . . . *opus:* "The hour ends the day, the author ends his work."

a. Begin by reviewing Paulo Hudson's definition of the genre. What does he establish as conventions within the genre?

b. Try to distinguish techniques that you define as being representative of the horror genre, from specific allusions to other works. What are specific formal devices that you see repeated in the works in this section? How do authors share a common use of language? How do they construct their poetry in a similar way? How do they structure their plays along similar lines?

c. Explain how two works that seem quite different actually belong in the same category.

d. How is your definition of the horror genre useful to your understanding of each of the works that you have chosen? How does it help you develop your analysis of each?

2. Compare the texts in this anthology with those in the section on the war film. Compare specific texts to explain whether or not it is appropriate to group all of these works within the same genre. How would you define this genre? Why is inclusion or exclusion from this grouping useful to our understanding of these particular texts?

2

Scene, Episode, and Plot

At some level, we're all storytellers. We have a need and a desire to give meaning to the raw experience of our lives by selecting and arranging details. When we recount something that happens to us, we're likely to leave out things that don't quite fit. We may even slightly modify what did happen in order to achieve a truth or power that goes beyond plain facts. We're attentive to dramatic design. We lead into our stories, build to a point of crisis, and finish forcefully. Our motives for crafting stories are complex and varied. We might want to give a satisfying close to a difficult period of our lives so that we can "move on"; in this respect, we are often the audience for our own stories. On other occasions, we want to make sure actions add up to some clear message or moral for the person we're speaking to (think of a parent telling a child a story that begins, "when I was your age..."). There is also a great pleasure in putting a string of events together so that those events become a unified story—a skillfully constructed work of art.

The drive to give artistic shape to experience is so strong that it often works with very little prompting. Much conversation involves exchanging stories. We listen to a friend tell a story and then tell another in response. Our intense need for—as well as our deep pleasure in—stories shows in the fact that we build them from the slightest bits of raw material that come our way: a small incident at work, a disagreement with a friend, an observed odd behavior of a stranger in line at a convenience store. We can even work something up from a single image. In fact, we often do work from something that small. A photograph, for example, captures feelings of a particular moment, but that moment often suggests to our imaginations a time before and a time after. We'll often build a narrative from the evidence a single picture provides, despite the obvious limitations of

Paramount/The Kobal Collection/Picture Desk

Breakfast at Tiffany's (1961)

that evidence. This building involves both our creative and our critical intelligence. We assess how details fit together to suggest actions that surround the picture. For example, look closely at the film still from *Breakfast at Tiffany's*.

It's quite possible to tell a very brief story "around" this picture. Some obvious questions may come quickly to mind that force us to respond in terms of narrative. What has brought this woman to the store? What is happening at the moment caught by the camera? What will unfold? How does the story end? We can't, of course, *know* the answers, but the film still offers specific features that prompt us to speculate. Consider, for example, the woman's expression and body language. She stands out on the street, but her sunglasses hide her eyes from us. She is elegantly dressed as she stands outside, holding her cup and bag. Notice, too, the contrast between the elaborate chandeliers hanging inside the window and the more mundane cars and crowd in the outside world behind her. What story do you make from such observations?

INCIDENT, SCENE, AND SEQUENCE

In the brief discussion of the film still, we've touched upon the notions of incident and scene. **Incident** suggests a specific, small action. **Scene** is a word closely related to but more expansive than incident. In a dramatic work, a scene might be understood simply as the entrance and/or exit of important characters from the stage. A scene may also be defined by mood (a crying scene, a comic scene, a revenge scene), function (a transitional scene, an expository scene, and anticipatory scene), or even place (an outdoor scene, a bedroom scene, a courtyard scene). But the term is usually employed more broadly still and is not limited to dramatic productions. A scene may be thought of as a coherent action within a larger structure of action. In this sense, a scene should convey a particular conflict that is subordinate to some larger conflict.

Incidents and scenes (if left to stand alone) are fragments. They are the bits and pieces that can be arranged to build a plot. **Plot** refers to the meaningful fabric of action. It suggests structure. At the most basic level, this means that a plot has a beginning, middle, and end; it represents a whole action. More specifically, an author provides **exposition** (context), then conveys **rising action** (action that leads to a decisive point), a **climax** (the decisive point), **falling action,** and **resolution** or **denouement** (a French word meaning "the untying of a knot"). Plots, then, are usually highly crafted actions. The **sequence** of scenes that make up a plot is not a random sequence or a mere series of conflicts. It's a carefully laid-out set of scenes that grow from **conflict** and make sense together. Perhaps one action causes another, or relates thematically to another, or counterpoints another. The author's careful arrangement of action in plot may be especially evident in **foreshadowing** (preparing the reader for action that is to come) and **flashback** (a return to past action). Both of these strategies illustrate how plot requires that we think of scenes in relation to one another.

Experiencing Literature through Plot

To sharpen our sense of plot's importance and meaning, we'll examine two brief pieces that upset or cut short our expectations. The two poems that follow ask us to consider what meaning we draw from plots by refusing to give us any plot in the usual sense. Both ask us to be self-conscious about the degree to which we actively shape stories. Can any significant piece of life be contained by a well-thought-out story? Can we assign a beginning, middle, and end to experience? Are lives as neat as that? Do we (as natural storytellers) impose order on chaos? If that is so, are stories a way to make experience significant? Robert Pinsky's "Poem with Lines in Any Order" centers us on these problems. Pinsky makes us think about many things, including our own active, participatory role in giving shape and meaning to events. Are we all plot makers in a world that has no master plot?

Robert Pinsky (1940–)

Poem with Lines in Any Order (2004)

Sonny said, *Then he shouldn't have given Molly the two more babies.*
Dave's sister and her husband adopted the baby, and that was Babe.
You can't live in the past.
Sure he was a tough guy but he was no hero.
Sonny and Toots went to live for a while with the Braegers.   5
It was a time when it seemed like everybody had a nickname.
Nobody can live in the future.
When Rose died having Babe, Dave came after the doctor with a gun.
Toots said, *What would you expect, he was a young man and there she was.*
Sonny still a kid himself when Dave moved out on Molly.   10
The family gave him Rose's cousin Molly to marry so she could raise the
    children.
There's no way to just live in the present.
In their eighties Toots and Sonny still arguing about their father.
Dave living above the bar with Della and half the family.

The first thing most readers do once they finish this poem is to go back
and play with the sequence of lines to make something more satisfying.
But is this what Pinsky is asking for? His title might encourage us to take
the lines (and the experiences they represent) as truly random. Is it possible that Pinsky is asking us to accept chaos and reflect upon our tendencies to give
events a beginning, middle, and end? Or perhaps he is suggesting that plots split
up into as many shapes as there are people to give them shape. Then again, maybe
these lines aren't really random at all. There is a thread woven through the poem

> **Making Connections**
>
> Szymborska's "ABC" and Pinsky's "Poem with Lines in Any Order" also inevitably raise questions about "character." Who are the characters here? Our sense of character arises largely out of seeing characters behave in the context of meaningfully ordered events. As you read about character in Chapter 3, think back on these two poems and ask yourself how much your sense of character depends upon plot.

that makes us think about how we relate (or fail to relate) the story to actual
experience: "You can't live in the past" (line 3). "Nobody can live in the
future" (line 7). "There's no way to just live in the present" (line 12). That
is, there is no way to live if we accept everything as a jumbled mess of random signals and fail to give shape and meaning to the events that happen
around us: we seek some order in order to live.

Wislawa Szymborska also deftly toys with notions of sequence in "ABC"—a poem that reminds us of how artificial and arbitrary our storytelling can be. Szymborska doesn't present lines "in any order" as Pinsky does, but by making the order unfold in alphabetical sequence, we're left struck by a sense of arbitrariness; the sequence is played out on a grid that has no necessary or organic relationship to experience. Szymborska is also blunt in marking off the limits of what we know or can know. If, like the narrators of the poem, we can't "find out" about things that are important to us, can we create richly interwoven plots? Can we find meaning?

Wislawa Szymborska (1923–   )

ABC (Stanislaw Baranczak and Clare Cavanagh, trans.; 2004)

I'll never find out now
what A. thought of me.
If B. ever forgave me in the end.
Why C. pretended everything was fine.
What part D. played in E.'s silence.   5
What F. had been expecting, if anything.
Why G. forgot when she knew perfectly well.
What H. had to hide.
What I. wanted to add.
If my being around   10
meant anything
to J. and K. and the rest of the alphabet.

EPISODE, IMPRESSION, AND FRAGMENT

Some important thematic implications of a fully developed, carefully designed plot are challenged by writers with simple strategies of abbreviation. If a writer thinks that the real world can't be captured within a traditional plot, then some reduced form of narration becomes an attractive choice. An **episode** suggests a single, continuous, and brief action that stands alone. An episode within a large story or novel refers to a specific action that could be detached from the larger plot. Some novels are built from a string of episodes. This tumbled-out-one-thing-after-another sequence of actions constitutes an **episodic narrative** or an **episodic novel**. Episodic narratives tend to be open as opposed to closed. An **open ending** is one that leaves essential matters largely unresolved. Mark Twain's *Adventures of Huckleberry Finn* nicely illustrates an episodic and open narrative. Huck recounts a string of adventures and at the end "lights out" to the territory ahead for what will be further adventures. Any sequel (and Twain did write one for Huck) will add episodes but will never "wrap up" Huck's experience. The reader may be left unsure about what happens to important characters, or about what significance to draw from the action, or about how "whole" the action was. A **closed ending** more aggressively wraps up the various strands of action. It communicates a relatively final conclusion. Popular detective stories are probably the clearest example of strongly closed fictions.

An episode can be thought of as a means to purposefully abbreviate plot. Plot, as we've mentioned, involves both writer and reader in a careful putting together of incidents and scenes. It challenges us to find patterns, discover relationships, and distinguish primary from secondary. Some modern writers, wary of the control implied by fully developed plots (as some painters are wary of fully realized representations of objects), deliberately cut stories short; they may feel that the **fragment** they offer readers more honestly represents the confusing, unstable world in which we live. Or at least they believe the fragment more accurately registers the way we experience life. A deliberate emphasis on episode as opposed to plot is related to the notion of an **impression**. It's useful to think about what we mean by that word and by **impressionism** or **impressionist**. An impression brings us back to the immediate feeling created by a picture or a painting.

When critics first labeled the painter Claude Monet an "impressionist," they were not praising him. Many early viewers felt Monet failed to make complete sense of—or achieve an ideal vision of—the subjects he painted. For example, some critics complained that Monet diminished his subjects by attending so closely to the particular qualities of light (conditioned by weather, the time of day, the season) that surrounded the subjects: "Why is he painting the fog when he should be painting the church?" We could imagine Monet answering, "Because it was foggy on the day that I sat before the church" or "Fog is the main thing I saw when I painted that day" or "Because I wished to capture the ephemeral nature of fog." Monet might have asked his own questions in response to the complaint: "Why should I paint something that supposedly lies behind what I *actually* see at a particular moment? Why do you assume the church and not the fog is the real subject of my painting?"

There is an important idea here that relates very much to the vision of artists working with other materials (words, film, sound). An impression is of the moment. It is bound by time, subject to changing conditions. An impression is essentially subjective. It registers what an individual saw or felt at a single moment. It is a sensation—something seen, felt, smelled. An impression is not a statement or an ideal; nor is it an absolute, fixed eternal truth. It is not a generalization. And it is *not* a plot.

Claude Monet, *Portal of Rouen Cathedral in Morning Light* (1894)

Erich Lessing/Art Resource, NY

Experiencing Literature through Impression and Episode

What Monet was doing with paint meshes with what Stephen Crane oftentimes did with words. Crane didn't believe that the world he knew allowed for long, carefully wrought, richly plotted fictions. He worked in short forms and often deliberately reduced his sense of scale. He registered impressions through the experiences of individual characters and believed that those subjective impressions were as close as he could get to "truth." The title of the story that follows deliberately announces his sense of limits. Crane uses the indefinite article *an*, not the definite article *the*. He promises to deliver a single fragment of experience, one bit from many that could have been selected. He also explicitly presents an "episode." We don't expect great length. We don't expect a complex weaving together of incidents. Because of his title, we don't seek to make this one episode more than a particular episode that occurs at a particular time and place. The life of the main character before the episode or after isn't really Crane's interest. Yet the shock of loss one feels upon reading this work is sufficient to justify it as art.

Stephen Crane (1871–1900)

An Episode of War (1899)

The lieutenant's rubber blanket lay on the ground, and upon it he had poured the company's supply of coffee. Corporals and other representatives of the grimy and hot-throated men who lined the breastwork had come for each squad's portion.

The lieutenant was frowning and serious at this task of division. His lips pursed as he drew with his sword various crevices in the heap, until brown squares of coffee, astoundingly equal in size, appeared on the blanket. He was on the verge of a great triumph in mathematics, and the corporals were thronging forward, each to reap a little square, when suddenly the lieutenant cried out and looked quickly at a man near him as if he suspected it was a case of personal assault. The others cried out also when they saw blood upon the lieutenant's sleeve.

He had winced like a man stung, swayed dangerously, and then straightened. The sound of his hoarse breathing was plainly audible. He looked sadly, mystically, over the breastwork at the green face of a wood, where now were many puffs of white smoke. During this moment the men about him gazed statue-like and silent, astonished and awed by this catastrophe which happened when catastrophes were not expected—when they had leisure to observe it.

As the lieutenant stared at the wood, they too swung their heads, so that for another instant all hands, still silent, contemplated the distant forest as if their minds were fixed upon the mystery of a bullet's journey.

The officer had, of course, been compelled to take his sword into his left hand. He did not hold it by the hilt. He gripped it at the middle of the blade, awkwardly. Turning his eyes from the wood, he looked at the sword as he held it there, and seemed puzzled as to what to do with it. In short, this weapon had all of a sudden become a strange thing to him. He looked at it in a kind of stupefaction, as if he had been endowed with a trident, a scepter, or a spade.

Finally he tried to sheathe it. To sheathe a sword held by the left hand, at the middle of the blade, in a scabbard hung at the left hip, is a feat worthy of a sawdust ring. This wounded officer engaged in a desperate struggle with the sword and the wobbling scabbard, and during the time of it he breathed like a wrestler.

But at this instant the men, spectators, awoke from their stone-like poses and crowded forward sympathetically. The orderly-sergeant took the sword and tenderly placed it in the scabbard. At the time, he leaned nervously backward, and did not allow even his finger to brush the body of the lieutenant.

A wound gives strange dignity to him who bears it. Well men shy from this new and terrible majesty. It is as if the wounded man's hand is upon the curtain which hangs before the revelations of all existence—the meaning of ants, potentates, wars, cities, sunshine, snow, a feather dropped from a bird's wing; and the power of it sheds radiance upon a bloody form, and makes the other men understand sometimes that they are little. His comrades look at him with large eyes thoughtfully. Moreover, they fear vaguely that the weight of a finger upon him might send him headlong, precipitate the tragedy, hurl him at once into the dim, gray unknown. And so the orderly-sergeant, while sheathing the sword, leaned nervously backward.

There were others who proffered assistance. One timidly presented his shoulder and asked the lieutenant if he cared to lean upon it, but the latter waved him away mournfully. He wore the look of one who knows he is the victim of a terrible disease and understands his helplessness. He again stared over the breastwork at the forest, and then, turning, went slowly rearward. He held his right wrist tenderly in his left hand as if the wounded arm was made of brittle glass.

And the men in silence stared at the woods, then at the departing lieutenant; then at the wood, then at the lieutenant.

As the wounded officer passed from the line of battle, he was enabled to see many things which as a participant in the fight were unknown to him. He saw a general on a black horse gazing over the lines of blue infantry at the green woods which veiled his problems. An aide galloped furiously, dragged his horse suddenly to a halt, saluted, and presented a paper. It was, for a wonder, precisely like an historical painting.

To the rear of the general and his staff a group, composed of a bugler, two or three orderlies, and the bearer of the corps standard, all upon maniacal horses, were working like slaves to hold their ground, preserve their respectful interval, while the shells boomed in the air about them, and caused their chargers to make furious quivering leaps.

A battery, a tumultuous and shining mass, was swirling toward the right. The wild thud of hoofs, the cries of the riders, shouting blame and praise, menace and encouragement, and, last, the roar of the wheels, the slant of the glistening guns, brought the lieutenant to an intent pause. The battery swept in curves that stirred the heart; it made halts as dramatic as the crash of a wave on the rocks, and when it fled onward this aggregation of wheels, levers, motors had a beautiful unity, as if it were a missile. The sound of it was a war chorus that reached into the depths of man's emotion.

The lieutenant, still holding his arm as if it were of glass, stood watching this battery until all detail of it were lost, save the figures of the riders, which rose and fell and waved lashes over the black mass.

Later, he turned his eyes toward the battle, where the shooting some-times crackled like bush-fires, sometimes sputtered with exasperating irregu-larity, and sometimes reverberated like the thunder. He saw the smoke rolling upward and saw crowds of men who ran and cheered, or stood and blazed away at the inscrutable distance.

He came upon some stragglers, and they told him how to find the field hospital. They described its exact location. In fact, these men, no longer hav-ing part in the battle, knew more of it than the others. They told the per-formance of every corps, every division, the opinion of every general. The lieutenant, carrying his wounded arm rearward, looked upon them with wonder.

At the roadside a brigade was making coffee and buzzing with talk like a girl's boarding school. Several officers came out to him and inquired concern-ing things of which he knew nothing. One, seeing his arm, began to scold. "Why, man, that's no way to do. You want to fix that thing." He appropriated the lieutenant and the lieutenant's wound. He cut the sleeve and laid bare the arm, every nerve of which softly fluttered under his touch. He bound his handkerchief over the wound, scolding away in the meantime. His tone allowed one to think that he was in the habit of being wounded every day. The lieutenant hung his head, feeling, in this presence, that he did not know how to be correctly wounded.

The low white tents of the hospital were grouped around an old school-house. There was here a singular commotion. In the foreground two ambu-lances interlocked wheels in the deep mud. The drivers were tossing the blame of it back and forth, gesticulating and berating, while from the ambu-lances, both crammed with wounded, there came an occasional groan. An interminable crowd of bandaged men were coming and going. Great num-bers sat under the trees nursing heads or arms or legs. There was a dispute of some kind raging on the steps of the schoolhouse. Sitting with his back against a tree a man with a face as gray as a new army blanket was serenely smoking a corncob pipe. The lieutenant wished to rush forward and inform him that he was dying.

A busy surgeon was passing near the lieutenant. "Good morning," he said, with a friendly smile. Then he caught sight of the lieutenant's arm, and his face at once changed. "Well, let's have a look at it." He seemed possessed suddenly of a great contempt for the lieutenant. This wound evidently placed the latter on a very low social plane. The doctor cried out impatiently: "What mutton-head had tied it up that way anyhow?"

The lieutenant answered, "Oh a man."

When the wound was disclosed the doctor fingered it disdainfully. "Humph," he said. "You come along with me and I'll 'tend to you." His voice contained the same scorn as if he were saying: "You will have to go to jail."

The lieutenant had been very meek, but now his face flushed, and he looked into the doctor's eyes. "I guess I won't have it amputated," he said.

"Nonsense, man!" Nonsense! Nonsense!" cried the doctor. "Come along, now. I won't amputate it. Come along. Don't be a baby."

"Let go of me," said the lieutenant, holding back wrathfully, his glance fixed upon the door of the old school house, as sinister to him as the portals of death.

And this is the story of how the lieutenant lost his arm. When he reached home, his sisters, his mother, his wife, sobbed for a long time at the sight of the flat sleeve. "Oh, well," he said, standing shamefaced amid these tears, "I don't suppose it matters so much as all that." ❖

The main action of Crane's "An Episode of War" occurs out of the blue. The soldiers are *not* in the midst of battle. They are in the midst of the most mundane of activities: rationing out the company's supply of coffee. The bullet comes as a surprise. The men don't spring into action in response. They gawk, feel awkward, seem a little awed that one among them has been injured. The wounding doesn't fit into a larger action—it is a random event, a horrifying reminder that danger is ever present and that the most momentous events are not scripted. When life does match up with art, it seems almost ridiculously accidental: "An aide galloped furiously, dragged his horse suddenly to a halt, saluted, and presented a paper. It was, for a wonder, precisely like a historical painting." It seems appropriate that Crane leaves his story open at the end. We have a strong impression of the moment he returns home, but a limited sense of how that moment will be played out in his family life ahead. By not attempting to strongly close the story, Crane suggests the most solid truths are limited ones.

MOMENTUM OF PLOT: TENSION, RELEASE, RISING ACTION, CLIMAX AND RESOLUTION

At some level, a grandly plotted story is like a great musical piece: it builds tension, releases tension, and achieves resolution. Or as we noted earlier, authors establish necessary background (exposition), create narrative momentum from some conflict (rising action) to a climax, and then more or less pull things together (resolution). The careful working together of various strands may lend a narrative great emotional force. Plots involve us in actions and in the fates of characters; plots encourage us to keep turning the pages. Plot can also help communicate a compelling worldview by giving larger shape, meaning, or purpose to action. But short of such grand effects, plot offers the sheer pleasure of artful management. We appreciate the craft involved in a well-made story.

Arthur Conan Doyle's Sherlock Holmes stories have long offered readers pleasure in the plot. Michael Chabon, a contemporary novelist, writes that "Conan Doyle found a way to fold several stories, and the proper means of telling them, over and over into a tightly compacted frame, with a proportionate gain in narrative power. [The Sherlock Holmes stories] are storytelling engines, steam driven, brass-fitted, but among the most efficient narrative apparatuses the world has ever seen. After all these years, they still run remarkably well." "A Scandal in Bohemia" (included in the anthology for this chapter) is one of these smooth-running engines. As you read that story, consider the distinction Holmes makes between "seeing" and "observing." For him, seeing is a mere matter of physical perception. Observing, though, is making sure that what we see registers fully. It is a neat distinction for a detective, and one that works well for a literary critic, too.

Doyle's "A Scandal in Bohemia" gives us an especially good chance to consider the point Chabon makes about Doyle's folding several stories together. The "folding" is what distinguishes a plot from a mere string of events. We're left with a strong sense of unity and closure with the Doyle story, because all the parts mesh so well. As Chabon points out, the meshing is so fine that we might not notice that Doyle has several stories working together. The King initially tells a story to Holmes: Irene Adler has a compromising picture that may influence world events. Holmes later tells a story to Watson: The detective went in disguise to Adler's neighborhood and became a participant in her elopement and marriage to Godfrey Norton. Watson recounts to us the trick Holmes pulls to uncover the picture's hiding place (after Holmes had spelled out to Watson what was to occur): the false injury, the smoke bomb, the cry of fire. Irene Adler tells a story to Holmes in her remaining letter: She was (despite forewarnings) taken in by him but saw through his deception just in time. And Watson again reports to us on how Holmes and the King respond to Adler's poise. All of these stories work together to give us a sense of a unified action that begins, builds, and closes. We have one plot woven of many incidents told from multiple perspectives and aimed at (seemingly) different audiences. Observing all of this complexity in "A Scandal in Bohemia" prepares us well for how subtly plots may operate.

MULTIPLE AND REFLEXIVE PLOTS

The layers that make up a Sherlock Holmes story suggest a number of fresh possibilities for constructing plots. The layers can be more than an efficient engine; they can suggest the complex textures of "real" life. Nor do the layers need to add up to a unified story. We often discover that as a single work unfolds, we process multiple stories or **multiple plots**. We get a sense in many narratives that plots are there for us to discover, to construct. A cliché like "there are always two sides to a story" becomes inadequate because we realize that two sides are hardly enough to account for the complexity we routinely contend with in both life and art. We're often prompted to consider how one story becomes something quite different if we simply shift a point of emphasis.

A number of writers, particularly more recent writers, convey a high degree of self-consciousness in their work. That is, they are aware of, as well as interested in, the philosophical, psychological, and dramatic potential inherent in plot. Such self-consciousness can become a kind of strategy; readers are reminded as they read to think about the plot as a plot. We sometimes call such plots **reflexive plots**; the way in which a story is constructed becomes the very thing we are forced to think about, to reflect upon.

Memento, a film directed in 2000 by Christopher Nolan who later updated the Batman film franchise, is an exceptionally good example of a **reflexive** or **self-conscious narrative**. Nolan (working from "Memento Mori," a short story by his brother, Jonathan Nolan) literally runs his plot backward. The main character—Leonard Shelby (played by Guy Pearce)—is a man who has no short-term memory as a result of a blow to his head. He remembers who he is (his name, his family, his life before his injury) but cannot hold in his mind the simplest moment-to-moment experiences. Leonard forgets not only his keys,

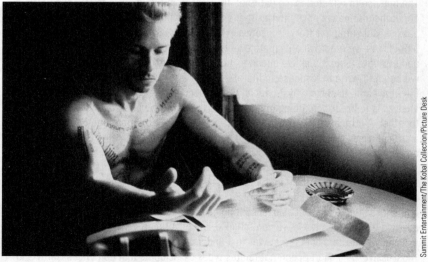

In *Memento* (2000), Leonard Shelby (Guy Pearce) develops a system of using notes, Polaroid pictures, and tattoos to help him remember crucial information.

but his car. He forgets people he has met within minutes of leaving their presence; he forgets where he lives or how he got to whatever place he happens to be; he forgets why he is doing what he is doing and he forgets very quickly what he has just done.

Nolan gives us the last action first—a brutal killing—and then moves backward to help us understand how and why things came to that end. Shelby, despite his forgetfulness, is motivated by revenge. He seeks to kill the man who raped and murdered his wife and who took his memory. His detective work can move forward only through a painstaking process of note taking. Because he cannot remember any clue he comes across, he must write down everything. He tattoos crucial information on his own skin. And of course, once he consults these notes, the situations that prompted the writing have been forgotten. By telling the story in this fashion, Nolan demands that the viewers put many of the pieces together for themselves. He also makes us aware that the main character has fashioned a rather different plot than the actual truth. We're then left to think about truth, about limits, about motives, about not just "what" happens, but why a "what" happened. In a sense, the plot in this case is the meaning or theme of the story.

A Note to Student Writers: Critical Reading and Understanding

The impulse to tell stories isn't all that different from the impulse to talk and write about the stories we encounter as readers and viewers. Critical reading isn't just passively absorbing a story; it involves participating in the creation of the story as it unfolds. As we read, we anticipate events and link incidents. We discuss, interpret, and evaluate. Sometimes we question, complain, and even "fix" the story. When we begin to write in response to literature, we press such impulses forward more forcefully still. In some ways, critical writing becomes its own kind of narrative. To analyze is to break something into pieces so that we can understand how it all fits together. A critical essay involves this breaking down and fitting together. Writing a critical essay makes a story *ours*. The process of writing critically forces us to understand what happens and why.

One seemingly simple thing you can do to get a grip on essential features of a text is to summarize the action that unfolds in a work you are reading. You'll find it is often a helpful exercise. Summary forces you to read closely and shrink the text to the barest essentials. Such a basic recounting can oftentimes open up what might seem puzzling works. Even when we don't think of a work primarily in terms of events, there is usually some core action that we must understand. For example, Sharon Olds's "Possessive" is a short poem that relates types of incidents that don't necessarily add up to a fully realized story. The poem's total effect might seem to convey a mood (loss and warmongering) and an appeal (how can this have happened to my daughter!).

But neither the mood nor the appeal will make much sense if we can't recount what happens in the poem.

Sharon Olds (1942–   )

The Possessive (1980)

My daughter—as if I
owned her—that girl with the
hair wispy as a frayed bellpull
has been to the barber, that knife grinder,
and had the edge of her hair sharpened.   5
Each strand now cuts
both ways. The blade of new bangs
hangs over her red-brown eyes
like carbon steel.
All the little   10
spliced ropes are sliced. The curtain of
dark paper-cuts veils the face that
started from next to nothing in my body—
My body. My daughter. I'll have to find
another word. In her bright helmet   15
she looks at me as if across a
great distance. Distant fires can be
glimpsed in the resin lights of her eyes:
the watch fires of an enemy, a while before
the war starts.   20

The daughter has had her hair cut, and the change in her appearance provides an image that propels this poem, but there is more here than just a haircut. That trip to the barber sets up a succession of incidents that create a category of experience more than a single action. But Olds gives us many particulars to work with. The hair is sharpened, each strand cuts, the blade of bangs hangs like carbon steel: in each image, the hair is a weapon. We get quick hints of larger incidents that we need to flesh out for ourselves. The daughter "started from next to nothing in my body" but has now changed into something else. As the poem progresses, we see the distance that has developed between the mother and daughter. Olds suggests that by cutting the hair that she recognizes, her daughter has become a different person; this superficial change has made her alien to her own mother. The poem's most basic action might be summarized as follows: This daughter has grown suddenly into someone the author hardly recognizes, someone who is strong, independent of, and potentially hostile to her mother.

MODELING CRITICAL ANALYSIS: JAMAICA KINCAID, GIRL

Jamaica Kincaid's "Girl" hardly seems to have a plot. Plots are, after all, made up of incidents and scenes that work together. A plot isn't a list of observations, but a carefully arranged sequence of events. "Girl" for the most part seems to "list" demands an older woman (a mother?) makes on a young girl: do this, don't do that, do things this way, don't do things that way. And "Girl" packs everything into one very long sentence. How can a single sentence, however long, develop a plot?

Jamaica Kincaid (1949–   )

Girl (1983)

Wash the white clothes on Monday and put them on the stone heap; wash the color clothes on Tuesday and put them on the clothesline to dry; don't walk barehead in the hot sun; cook pumpkin fritters in very hot sweet oil; soak your little cloths right after you take them off; when buying cotton to make yourself a nice blouse, be sure that it doesn't have gum on it, because that way it won't hold up well after a wash; soak salt fish overnight before you cook it; is it true that you sing benna in Sunday school?; always eat your food in such a way that it won't turn someone else's stomach; on Sundays try to walk like a lady and not like the slut you are so bent on becoming; don't sing benna in Sunday school; you mustn't speak to wharf-rat boys, not even to give directions; don't eat fruits on the street—flies will follow you; *but I don't sing benna on Sundays at all and never in Sunday school*; this is how to sew on a button; this is how to make a buttonhole for the button you have just sewed on; this is how to hem a dress when you see the hem coming down and so to prevent yourself from looking like the slut I know you are so bent on becoming; this is how you iron your father's khaki shirt so that it doesn't have a crease; this is how you iron your father's khaki pants so that they don't have a crease; this is how you grow okra—far from the house, because okra tree harbors red ants; when you are growing dasheen, make sure it gets plenty of water or else it makes your throat itch when you are eating it; this is how you sweep a corner; this is how you sweep a whole house; this is how you sweep a yard; this is how you smile to someone you don't like too much; this is how you smile to someone you don't like at all; this is how you smile to someone you like completely; this is how you set a table for tea; this is how you set a table for dinner; this is how you set a table for dinner with an important guest; this is how you set a table for lunch; this is how you set a table for breakfast; this is how to behave in the presence of men who don't know you very well, and this way they won't recognize immediately the slut I have warned you against becoming; be sure to wash every day, even if it is with your own spit; don't squat down to play marbles—you are not a boy, you know; don't pick people's flowers—you might catch something; don't throw stones at blackbirds, because it might not be a blackbird at all; this is how to make a bread pudding; this is how to make doukona; this is how to make pepper pot; this is how to make a good medicine for a cold; this is how to make a good medicine to throw away a child before it even becomes a child; this is how to catch a fish; this is how to throw back a fish you don't like, and that way something bad won't fall on you; this is how to bully a man; this is how a man bullies you; this is how to love a man, and if this doesn't work there are other ways, and if they don't work don't feel too bad about giving up; this is how to spit up in the air if you feel like it, and this is how to move quick so that it doesn't fall on you; this is how to make ends meet; always squeeze bread to make sure it's fresh; *but what if the baker won't let me feel the bread?*; you mean to say that after all you are really going to be the kind of woman who the baker won't let near the bread? ❖

It is useful to think of the many stories, the many plots, suggested by Kincaid's list of impressions, memories, and incidents. Kincaid triggers multiple associations about growing up that readers can fill in, indeed must fill in. She seems to depend upon the reader's ability to elaborate on the smallest hints and create full scenes or even stories. We can imagine how thickly textured the girl's life is with reprimands. For example, if she joins other children for a game of marbles, she can be scolded for squatting like a boy. Such gender lessons of course are part of larger assumptions about status and power. The girl is not a boy and must always remember what that fact means. It means that any sign of independence quickly becomes a marker of moral or social inadequacy. It means that the girl must control signs because she controls little else: how to "behave in the presence of men," how to hide who she is, how to "make good medicine to throw away a child before it even becomes a child."

Kincaid gives readers some means to structure the whole. If we look at "Girl" carefully, we'll note some important interruptions and repetitions. On two occasions, we have a break in the voice—the person on the receiving end of all the instructions speaks for herself. The first time this happens (about a third of the way into the piece) the woman steams ahead without a pause. The girl has spoken, but the woman hasn't listened or hasn't thought any back talk is worth responding to. The second break (marked by italics, as the first is) occurs at the end of the piece. Here the girl questions the real-world application of the advice: *"what if the baker won't let me feel the bread."* The older woman's response returns again the strategy of diminishment that has been part of the whole story: What kind of woman is this girl bent on becoming? The older woman sees nothing but bad ahead, but readers are more likely to imagine her youthful independence more than any presumed natural deficiency.

Using Plot to Focus Writing and Discussion

- What happens over the course of the text?
- How have things changed from the opening scene?
- What events lead to this conclusion?
- Is this a conclusion that you expected? What led you to this expectation? What details in the opening of the text shape your expectations?
- Why do events unfold here in the order that they do? Is this a chronological account of events, or is there some other ordering principle?
- Are there events that we do not learn about? How are these undiscovered details significant?
- How has the author made this story interesting?

Anthology

DETECTIVE WORK: A CRITIC WRITES ABOUT THE DETECTIVE PLOT

Detective work is, among other things, a professional activity. In "A Scandal in Bohemia," Holmes is presented a problem and is asked to solve it for a fee. We would like, in this anthology, to apply the notion of detective work to your role as an active, engaged reader. Although we include Doyle's classic detective story along with modern variants of the form, we haven't restricted the following readings to a specific type of story. We'd like to use the image and activity of the detective to suggest something larger: We're using the activity of the detective to suggest a way of reading and writing.

Doyle has his detective draw a distinction between "seeing" and "observing." For Holmes, "seeing" is a purely physical act; Watson sees as well as Holmes. "Observing" takes the physical sensations the eye processes and subjects those sensations to reflection and analysis in relation to other available experiences or information. We often think of "evidence" as some tangible thing, but we need to remember that *proving* is an intellectual activity. A hammer is just a hammer; it becomes evidence only if one can place the hammer in context of a complex body of information and make it support an interpretation.

Don Lee's "The Price of Eggs in China" is a detective story with some element of who-dun-it. But that seems only a slight element. "The Price of

Basil Rathbone played a traditional Sherlock Holmes in films that ran from 1939 to 1946.

Benedict Cumberbatch as the detective in the contemporary BBC adaptation *Sherlock*

Eggs in China" is also a love story, a revenge story, a psychological study, a reflection upon art and the creative process. It's all of these things because it invites us to think about not just the story that Don Lee tells but also about the stories that the different characters construct. As in the film *Memento*, we're left to question the "truth" of the various stories as well as question the motives that lie behind the telling. We need to observe in the Holmesian sense of the word all the available material. We need to see details as clues to meaning. The fact that Dean, one of the main characters in "The Price of Eggs in China," is an avid reader of detective stories contributes to the self-conscious feel of the whole story. Dean becomes, quite literally, a plotter; he sets up evidence so that it will be read in a particular way. And, of course, the three main characters (Dean, Caroline, and Marcella) are all artists. Perhaps Lee is suggesting that artists are inevitably plotters. Or to put it a slightly different way, maybe we all have to engage life as detectives encountering deep and dangerous mysteries.

Poems, too, involve narrative. Events unfold in a carefully (if minutely) plotted manner. But even when plot is not an issue, you'll need to pay close attention to what we might call "the facts" of a specific case. For example, you'll need to keep the seeing/observing distinction in mind as you read Emily Dickinson's "I like to see it lap the Miles" and "A Route of Evanescence." If these two poems seem puzzling, it's because they are puzzles—or what are called **riddle poems**. Dickinson gives us descriptions without ever directly telling us what she is describing. We're left to identify the missing subject. Dickinson's playful poetic game suggests that she sees readers as having an important role. In some ways, we might think of ourselves as co-creating these poems with Dickinson. All the pieces in each poem will snap together as a coherent work of art only when we identify the subject Dickinson has left unnamed.

Few people think first of detection in regard to *Oedipus Rex*. But this great play certainly builds on riddles solved and, more crucially, unsolved. The inability of Oedipus to appreciate the deepest mysteries of his own life moves the tragedy forward. Sophocles plots the action in a way that engages us in the forces that undo his protagonist. You'll note in this case a clear distinction between story and plot. The plot of the play centers on the quest to discover who murdered King Laius of Thebes. The story of Oedipus begins before his birth, with the prophecy that a son of Jocasta and Laius will kill the father. The story continues with the birth of Oedipus; the order for his death; the smuggling of the infant away from danger; his growth to adulthood as (he believes) the son of the King and Queen of Corinth; his departure from Corinth upon learning of the prophecy, his violent encounter with a group of travelers that (unknown to him) fulfills the prophecy; his return to Thebes; his solving of the riddle; his coronation as King; his marriage to Jocasta; his long reign; his investigation into the long unsolved murder of Laius; his discovery of the truth; and his self-blinding and banishment.

We could go on, because this story continues into the next generation. But the way we've just related the events do not match well with the way Sophocles arranges (that is, plots) actions. The play *Oedipus Rex* begins very near to the end of the long list of events that we've noted. Much that is crucial to the story has no part in the action of the play itself (although everything we've listed can operate as a knowledge base the audience brings to the theater). The plot of *Oedipus* moves both forward and backward in time and allows us to experience the whole action in ways a reductive story line cannot communicate. The address Oedipus offers his citizens/suppliants to open the play establishes for the audience Oedipus as King. He is at the height of his powers, a proud and respected monarch. The forces that conspire to undo him have collected over his whole life, but will be unleashed only in the compressed few hours of life to follow. We get, then, an intense experience of how complex events may link together to bring about the fall of a noble subject. The plot of *Oedipus Rex* puts us in the role of a seeker—looking for clues to meaning and significance. When we closely engage with a work of art, that role seems unavoidable. In the readings that follow, you can test a hypothesis: Reading is always a form of detective work.

Note how, in his review, Sragow focuses on the filmic problem of representing the ordering of the plot. We often think of narrative as occurring in a natural order—it is just the way that events unfold—but as the detective genre highlights for us, plotting, as the name suggests, rarely occurs naturally at all. Each plot point (or clue within this genre) must be meticulously collected and ordered for the story to make sense, for the detective to present a coherent narrative that solves the mystery. The plot is something that must be invented, investigated, and imagined. When Sherlock Holmes is represented on film, it is easy to lose his thought process, and this is one of the aspects of the BBC drama that Sragow applauds as it makes Sherlock's mind the place where so much of the story's action unfolds.

REVIEW

Michael Sragow (1952–   )

Getting Sherlock Holmes Right Onscreen (2012)

If you click on the special features of the just-released DVD of "Sherlock Holmes: Game of Shadows," you'll find a short tribute to something called "Holmesavision." It turns out to be the name given to the director Guy Ritchie's method of turning every quasi-Holmesian deduction or confrontation into an action sequence. Using variable speeds and quick cutting to illustrate Holmes's turns of mind twist by twist—usually before the Master commits himself to an action or solution, but sometimes long afterward—Ritchie makes sure he won't leave behind the slowest member of the audience while pretending that he's honoring his hero's greased-lightning illuminations.

These sequences quickly become annoying and repetitive. Instead of bringing you inside Holmes's racing brain and clicking synapses, they simply make his mental feints as easy to follow as the words in a sing-along. The payoff in Ritchie's first Sherlock Holmes movie was supposed to be the adrenaline rush of seeing Holmes execute a fight strategy or a mental trap exactly as he envisioned it. The payoff in "Game of Shadows" is meant to be the fun of seeing fate and a wily adversary toss grit into Holmes's intellectual cogs, and match his every calculation.

But even if you buy into Ritchie's substitution of kinetic thrills for cumulative mystery and suspense, the film has a been-there, thought-that feel to it. Robert Downey Jr. doesn't completely lose his verve and dash as Holmes, and Jude Law never overdraws on his air of put-upon gallantry as Dr. Watson, but the series has romped prematurely into camp. It was easier to take Downey's Holmes as a daredevil in the first film—in this one, he comes perilously close to being an eternal imp. It's a shame, because Downey, as he shows even in the boisterous "The Avengers," has a gift for balancing knowing patter with big emotions like self-sacrifice. I've often thought he'd be a great Sydney Carton in a new "A Tale of Two Cities."

The most worthy item on the "Game of Shadows" disc may be an advertisement for the second season of "Sherlock," which came out on DVD two weeks ago. The BBC series, a string of three ninety-minute films per season, achieves in modern dress what the Ritchie film attempts in fancy Edwardian costume. It makes Sherlock Holmes exciting and accessible by finding contemporary analogies to Arthur Conan Doyle's conundrums. The series employs just as many flashy tricks as Ritchie's movie, but here they work for a reason: they mesh with the narrative instead of sticking out from it. The filmmakers are offhand with their virtuosity, whether they're printing text messages on the screen as Sherlock reads them, or chalking in his observations on top of a man's suit, or replicating the combination of imagined details and facts that he sees while he visualizes a crime scene (to the extent of re-creating studio sets in open landscapes). They're simply keeping us up to speed with Sherlock (barely), not explaining everything away for us. In this series' canny update of "The Hound of the Baskervilles" (it involves chemical mind control and an espionage agency), the Master tests the theory that will assuage his own fears and doubts by retreating into a memory plane dubbed "The Mind Palace." In a way, half the series is set in Holmes's mind palace.

"Brainy is the new sexy" says this series' Irene Adler (Lara Pulver). It's an on-the-nose line that plays exactly right—both because Irene is here a domina-trix, always manipulating everyone, and because Benedict Cumberbatch's sub-limely elusive Sherlock shakes it off. Cumberbatch first won wide attention by playing a rotter in "Atonement" with pitiless intelligence and intensity. After the first season of "Sherlock," he was impressive in alternating turns as the title character and the monster in Danny Boyle's stage "Frankenstein." His mad doctor was spookily cerebral, his monster magnificently primal (and heartbreaking and lyrical, too). 5

He's perfect for the Sherlock that Steven Moffat and Mark Gatiss have created, with equal cunning and affection. Cumberbatch sometimes plays the hero as a villain, but mostly for effect. When he denies that he's a psychopath and tells reporters that he's instead a "highly functioning sociopath," he presents the press with an image they can lock onto, not an advertisement for himself. What limits the phenomenally talented Downey from plumbing depths as Sherlock is that everything in Ritchie's showy production is extroverted and theatrical. Even in our much more public era, Cumberbatch's Sherlock keeps key aspects of his personality private—except from his partner Watson, and from Irene Adler and, sadly, the arch-villain Moriarty. For the other half of the series takes place in what we'd call "the Heart Palace" of Martin Freeman's Dr. John Watson. We see the crimes from Sherlock's perspective, but we see Sherlock from Watson's. Freeman's Watson (like the original, a veteran of a war in Afghanistan) persuasively embodies Watson's own appetite for risk-taking. He creates an intelligent, sometimes puckish, and often questioning foil to Cumberbatch's brilliant brand of cheek. Most important, he communicates his empathy for a man who really does act, sometimes, like a sociopath.

In the DVD extras for the first season of "Sherlock," we learn that creators Moffatt and Gattis consider the best prior adaptations of Conan Doyle to be the Hollywood movies starring Basil Rathbone and Nigel Bruce. You can see how right they are on the "Complete Sherlock Holmes Collection," containing the fourteen Sherlock Holmes features that starred Rathbone and defined the Great Detective for generations. In 1939, Rathbone and Bruce starred for Twentieth Century Fox in a solid "Hound of the Baskervilles," and an even better "Adventures of Sherlock Holmes." They're at full throttle in the latter—a breathless tale of Professor Moriarty's attempt to exploit the restlessness of Holmes's intelligence. The arch-villain Moriarty (George Zucco) sends the sleuth on a wild-albatross chase while the evil genius himself schemes to make off with the crown jewels. Rathbone seizes the chance to celebrate and satirize—simultaneously—Holmes's peripatetic brilliance. Bruce's Watson never makes the Ed McMahon–like error of applauding Holmes's cleverness too loudly; he's more like a genteel Sancho Panza, suspicious of his pal's fantastic rationality. The result is everything a civilized thriller should be: witty, playful, and exciting. And Ida Lupino brings a hint of sexuality into Holmes's hermetic universe. She's refreshingly fervid—you can feel the heart of a dame beating within the damsel in distress.

After their stint at Fox, Rathbone and Bruce did a dozen quickies for Universal, starting in 1942. The set contains beautiful restorations of all twelve. Set in the nineteen-forties instead of the nineteenth century, they resemble lively, literate Saturday-matinée serials—but they were the best inspiration of all to the makers of "Sherlock," because they brought Homes and Watson into the Second World War era with confidence and brio.

What "Sherlock Holmes and the Secret Weapon" shares with the credited Arthur Conan Doyle source story, "The Adventure of the Dancing Men," is a code in which the figures of dancing men in different positions stand for the letters of the alphabet. "Secret Weapon" surrounds it with an espionage tale about a Swiss scientist (William Post, Jr.) who invents a sophisticated bombsight and escapes the Nazis en route to London—only to fall prey to Moriarty (Lionel Atwill). There are entertaining bursts of deduction, along with a nod to Poe's "The Purloined Letter," and a climax wherein Holmes shrewdly comes up with the slowest, cruellest way for Moriarty to finish him off—and Moriarty takes him up on it.

"The Woman in Green" offers more traditional sleuthing shenanigans   10
in the series' modern but still fog-shrouded London (actually the backlot at
Universal). This time, Rathbone's Holmes and Bruce's Watson crack the
mystery of why the corpses of several young women are found with one finger
amputated. Is it the work of a compulsive serial killer? Or just another
dastardly scheme by Moriarty? High points are the florid banter of the title
villainess (a hypnotist played by Hillary Brooke) and a classic ploy involving
the bust of Caesar at 221-B Baker Street.

The main reason the Rathbone-Bruce movies endure is the way that
they capture the tinge of romance that Holmes so wisely accused Watson
of injecting in his stories. Rathbone was born to wear Holmes's cape and
deerstalker cap, to smoke his old brier-root pipe, and to rattle off his rati-
ocinations with merry hubris. His perfect wedge of a profile slices through
the London fog, and he uses his imposing brow to signal one idea while his
glinting eyes intimate another. He and Bruce develop a rapport that is sometimes as vaudevillian, but also as close, as Hope and Crosby's. At their best,
they make you laugh and cheer.

FICTION

Arthur Conan Doyle (1859–1930)

Arthur Conan Doyle is one of the most widely read authors in English, and his
character Sherlock Homes one of the most recognized characters in English
literature. Born in Edinburgh, Scotland, Doyle worked as a physician before
becoming a professional writer, and he returned to this profession during the
Boer War (1899–1902) when he served as a field surgeon. Doyle wrote every
kind of literature, from poetry to books on spiritualism to a political pamphlet in
defense of British conduct during the Boer War (for which he was knighted). But
his detective fiction is the work for which he is chiefly remembered. The character of Sherlock Homes, the utterly rational detective, has remained popular up
to the present day and has been the subject of numerous books, plays, films, and
television shows. Though Doyle once killed the character off, Holmes's enormous popularity (and the attendant money) made him reconsider.

A Scandal in Bohemia (1891)

To Sherlock Holmes she is always *the* woman. I have seldom heard him mention
her under any other name. In his eyes she eclipses and predominates the whole
of her sex. It was not that he felt any emotion akin to love for Irene Adler.

All emotions, and that one particularly, were abhorrent to his cold, precise but admirably balanced mind. He was, I take it, the most perfect reasoning and observing machine that the world has seen, but as a lover he would have placed himself in a false position. He never spoke of the softer passions, save with a gibe and a sneer. They were admirable things for the observer—excellent for drawing the veil from men's motives and actions. But for the trained reasoner to admit such intrusions into his own delicate and finely adjusted temperament was to introduce a distracting factor which might throw a doubt upon all his mental results. Grit in a sensitive instrument, or a crack in one of his own high-power lenses, would not be more disturbing than a strong emotion in a nature such as his. And yet there was but one woman to him, and that woman was the late Irene Adler, of dubious and questionable memory.

I had seen little of Holmes lately. My marriage had drifted us away from each other. My own complete happiness, and the home-centred interests which rise up around the man who first finds himself master of his own establishment, were sufficient to absorb all my attention, while Holmes, who loathed every form of society with his whole Bohemian soul, remained in our lodgings in Baker Street, buried among his old books, and alternating from week to week between cocaine and ambition, the drowsiness of the drug, and the fierce energy of his own keen nature. He was still, as ever, deeply attracted by the study of crime, and occupied his immense faculties and extraordinary powers of observation in following out those clues, and clearing up those mysteries which had been abandoned as hopeless by the official police. From time to time I heard some vague account of his doings: of his summons to Odessa in the case of the Trepoff murder, of his clearing up of the singular tragedy of the Atkinson brothers at Trincomalee, and finally of the mission which he had accomplished so delicately and successfully for the reigning family of Holland. Beyond these signs of his activity, however, which I merely shared with all the readers of the daily press, I knew little of my former friend and companion.

One night—it was on the twentieth of March, 1888—I was returning from a journey to a patient (for I had now returned to civil practice), when my way led me through Baker Street. As I passed the well-remembered door, which must always be associated in my mind with my wooing, and with the dark incidents of the *Study in Scarlet*, I was seized with a keen desire to see Holmes again, and to know how he was employing his extraordinary powers. His rooms were brilliantly lit, and, even as I looked up, I saw his tall, spare figure pass twice in a dark silhouette against the blind. He was pacing the room swiftly, eagerly, with his head sunk upon his chest and his hands clasped behind him. To me, who knew his every mood and habit, his attitude and manner told their own story. He was at work again. He had risen out of his drug-created dreams and was hot upon the scent of some new problem. I rang the bell and was shown up to the chamber which had formerly been in part my own.

His manner was not effusive. It seldom was; but he was glad, I think, to see me. With hardly a word spoken, but with a kindly eye, he waved me to an armchair, threw across his case of cigars, and indicated a spirit case and a gasogene in the corner. Then he stood before the fire and looked me over in his singular introspective fashion.

"Wedlock suits you," he remarked. "I think, Watson, that you have put on seven and a half pounds since I saw you." 5

"Seven!" I answered.

"Indeed, I should have thought a little more. Just a trifle more, I fancy, Watson. And in practice again, I observe. You did not tell me that you intended to go into harness."

"Then, how do you know?"

"I see it, I deduce it. How do I know that you have been getting yourself very wet lately, and that you have a most clumsy and careless servant girl?"

"My dear Holmes," said I, "this is too much. You would certainly 10 have been burned, had you lived a few centuries ago. It is true that I had a country walk on Thursday and came home in a dreadful mess, but as I have changed my clothes I can't imagine how you deduce it. As to Mary Jane, she is incorrigible, and my wife has given her notice; but there, again, I fail to see how you work it out."

He chuckled to himself and rubbed his long, nervous hands together.

"It is simplicity itself," said he; "my eyes tell me that on the inside of your left shoe, just where the firelight strikes it, the leather is scored by six almost parallel cuts. Obviously they have been caused by someone who has very carelessly scraped round the edges of the sole in order to remove crusted mud from it. Hence, you see, my double deduction that you had been out in vile weather, and that you had a particularly malignant boot-slitting specimen of the London slavery. As to your practice, if a gentleman walks into my rooms smelling of iodoform, with a black mark of nitrate of silver upon his right forefinger, and a bulge on the right side of his top-hat to show where he has secreted his stethoscope, I must be dull, indeed, if I do not pronounce him to be an active member of the medical profession."

I could not help laughing at the ease with which he explained his process of deduction. "When I hear you give your reasons," I remarked, "the thing always appears to me to be so ridiculously simple that I could easily do it myself, though at each successive instance of your reasoning I am baffled until you explain your process. And yet I believe that my eyes are as good as yours."

"Quite so," he answered, lighting a cigarette, and throwing himself down into an armchair. "You see, but you do not observe. The distinction is clear. For example, you have frequently seen the steps which lead up from the hall to this room."

"Frequently." 15
"How often?"
"Well, some hundreds of times."
"Then how many are there?"
"How many? I don't know."
"Quite so! You have not observed. And yet you have seen. That is just 20
my point. Now, I know that there are seventeen steps, because I have both
seen and observed. By the way, since you are interested in these little problems, and since you are good enough to chronicle one or two of my trifling
experiences, you may be interested in this." He threw over a sheet of thick,
pink-tinted note-paper which had been lying open upon the table. "It came
by the last post," said he. "Read it aloud."

The note was undated, and without either signature or address.

There will call upon you to-night, at a quarter to eight o'clock [it said], a
gentleman who desires to consult you upon a matter of the very deepest
moment. Your recent services to one of the royal houses of Europe have
shown that you are one who may safely be trusted with matters which
are of an importance which can hardly be exaggerated. This account of
you we have from all quarters received. Be in your chamber then at that
hour, and do not take it amiss if your visitor wears a mask.

"This is indeed a mystery," I remarked. "What do you imagine that it
means?"

"I have no data yet. It is a capital mistake to theorize before one has
data. Insensibly one begins to twist facts to suit theories, instead of theories
to suit facts. But the note itself. What do you deduce from it?"

I carefully examined the writing, and the paper upon which it was
written.

"The man who wrote it was presumably well to do," I remarked, endea- 25
vouring to imitate my companion's processes. "Such paper could not be
bought under half a crown a packet. It is peculiarly strong and stiff."

"Peculiar—that is the very word," said Holmes. "It is not an English
paper at all. Hold it up to the light."

I did so, and saw a large "E" with a small "g," a "P," and a large "G"
with a small "t" woven into the texture of the paper.

"What do you make of that?" asked Holmes.

"The name of the maker, no doubt; or his monogram, rather."

"Not at all. The 'G' with the small 't' stands for 'Gesellschaft,' which is 30
the German for 'Company.' It is a customary contraction like our 'Co.' 'P,'
of course, stands for 'Papier.' Now for the 'Eg.' Let us glance at our Continental Gazetteer." He took down a heavy brown volume from his shelves.

"Eglow, Eglonitz—here we are, Egria. It is in a German-speaking country—in
Bohemia, not far from Carlsbad. 'Remarkable as being the scene of the
death of Wallenstein, and for its numerous glass-factories and paper-mills.'
Ha, ha, my boy, what do you make of that?" His eyes sparkled, and he sent
up a great blue triumphant cloud from his cigarette.

"The paper was made in Bohemia," I said.

"Precisely. And the man who wrote the note is a German. Do you note
the peculiar construction of the sentence—'This account of you we have
from all quarters received.' A Frenchman or Russian could not have written
that. It is the German who is so uncourteous to his verbs. It only remains,
therefore, to discover what is wanted by this German who writes upon
Bohemian paper and prefers wearing a mask to showing his face. And here
he comes, if I am not mistaken, to resolve all our doubts."

As he spoke there was the sharp sound of horses' hoofs and grating wheels against the curb, followed by a sharp pull at the bell. Holmes
whistled.

"A pair, by the sound," said he. "Yes," he continued, glancing out of the
window. "A nice little brougham and a pair of beauties. A hundred and fifty
guineas apiece. There's money in this case, Watson, if there is nothing else."

"I think that I had better go, Holmes."   35

"Not a bit, Doctor. Stay where you are. I am lost without my Boswell.
And this promises to be interesting. It would be a pity to miss it."

"But your client——"

"Never mind him. I may want your help, and so may he. Here he
comes. Sit down in that armchair, Doctor, and give us your best attention."

A slow and heavy step, which had been heard upon the stairs and in
the passage, paused immediately outside the door. Then there was a loud
and authoritative tap.

"Come in!" said Holmes.   40

A man entered who could hardly have been less than six feet six inches
in height, with the chest and limbs of a Hercules. His dress was rich with
a richness which would, in England, be looked upon as akin to bad taste.
Heavy bands of astrakhan were slashed across the sleeves and fronts of his
double-breasted coat, while the deep blue cloak which was thrown over his
shoulders was lined with flame-coloured silk and secured at the neck with
a brooch which consisted of a single flaming beryl. Boots which extended
halfway up his calves, and which were trimmed at the tops with rich brown
fur, completed the impression of barbaric opulence which was suggested by
his whole appearance. He carried a broad-brimmed hat in his hand, while he
wore across the upper part of his face, extending down past the cheekbones,
a black vizard mask, which he had apparently adjusted that very moment, for
his hand was still raised to it as he entered. From the lower part of the face

he appeared to be a man of strong character, with a thick, hanging lip, and a long, straight chin suggestive of resolution pushed to the length of obstinacy.

"You had my note?" he asked with a deep harsh voice and a strongly marked German accent. "I told you that I would call." He looked from one to the other of us, as if uncertain which to address.

"Pray take a seat," said Holmes. "This is my friend and colleague, Dr. Watson, who is occasionally good enough to help me in my cases. Whom have I the honour to address?"

"You may address me as the Count Von Kramm, a Bohemian nobleman. I understand that this gentleman, your friend, is a man of honour and discretion, whom I may trust with a matter of the most extreme importance. If not, I should much prefer to communicate with you alone."

I rose to go, but Holmes caught me by the wrist and pushed me back into my chair. "It is both, or none," said he. "You may say before this gentleman anything which you may say to me." 45

The Count shrugged his broad shoulders. "Then I must begin," said he, "by binding you both to absolute secrecy for two years; at the end of that time the matter will be of no importance. At present it is not too much to say that it is of such weight it may have an influence upon European history."

"I promise," said Holmes.

"And I."

"You will excuse this mask," continued our strange visitor. "The august person who employs me wishes his agent to be unknown to you, and I may confess at once that the title by which I have just called myself is not exactly my own."

"I was aware of it," said Holmes drily. 50

"The circumstances are of great delicacy, and every precaution has to be taken to quench what might grow to be an immense scandal and seriously compromise one of the reigning families of Europe. To speak plainly, the matter implicates the great House of Ormstein, hereditary kings of Bohemia."

"I was also aware of that," murmured Holmes, settling himself down in his armchair and closing his eyes.

Our visitor glanced with some apparent surprise at the languid, lounging figure of the man who had been no doubt depicted to him as the most incisive reasoner and most energetic agent in Europe. Holmes slowly reopened his eyes and looked impatiently at his gigantic client.

"If your Majesty would condescend to state your case," he remarked, "I should better able to advise you."

The man sprang from his chair and paced up and down the room in uncontrollable agitation. Then, with a gesture of desperation, he tore the mask from his face and hurled it upon the ground. "You are right," he cried; "I am the King. Why should I attempt to conceal it?" 55

"Why, indeed?" murmured Holmes. "Your Majesty had not spoken before I was aware that I was addressing Wilhelm Gottsreich Sigismond von Orm-stein, Grand Duke of Cassel-Felstein, and hereditary King of Bohemia."

"But you can understand," said our strange visitor, sitting down once more and passing his hand over his high white forehead, "you can understand that I am not accustomed to doing such business in my own person. Yet the matter was so delicate that I could not confide it to an agent without putting myself in his power. I have come incognito from Prague for the purpose of consulting you."

"Then, pray consult," said Holmes, shutting his eyes once more.

"The facts are briefly these: Some five years ago, during a lengthy visit to Warsaw, I made the acquaintance of the well-known adventuress, Irene Adler. The name is no doubt familiar to you."

"Kindly look her up in my index, Doctor," murmured Holmes without 60 opening his eyes. For many years he had adopted a system of docketing all paragraphs concerning men and things, so that it was difficult to name a subject or a person on which he could not at once furnish information. In this case I found her biography sandwiched in between that of a Hebrew rabbi and that of a staff-commander who had written a monograph upon the deep-sea fishes.

"Let me see!" said Holmes. "Hum! Born in New Jersey in the year 1858. Contralto—hum! La Scala, hum! Prima donna Imperial Opera of Warsaw—yes! Retired from operatic stage—ha! Living in London—quite so! Your Majesty, as I understand, became entangled with this young person, wrote her some compromising letters, and is now desirous of getting those letters back."

"Precisely so. But how——"

"Was there a secret marriage?"

"None."

"No legal papers or certificates?" 65

"None."

"Then I fail to follow your Majesty. If this young person should produce her letters for blackmailing or other purposes, how is she to prove their authenticity?"

"There is the writing."

"Pooh, pooh! Forgery."

"My private note-paper." 70

"Stolen."

"My own seal."

"Imitated."

"My photograph."

"Bought." 75

"We were both in the photograph."

"Oh, dear! That is very bad! Your Majesty has indeed committed an indiscretion."

"I was mad—insane."

"You have compromised yourself seriously."

"I was only Crown Prince then. I was young. I am but thirty now." 80

"It must be recovered."

"We have tried and failed."

"Your Majesty must pay. It must be bought."

"She will not sell."

"Stolen, then." 85

"Five attempts have been made. Twice burglars in my pay ransacked her house. Once we diverted her luggage when she traveled. Twice she has been waylaid. There has been no result."

"No sign of it?"

"Absolutely none."

Holmes laughed. "It is quite a pretty little problem," said he.

"But a very serious one to me," returned the King reproachfully. 90

"Very, indeed. And what does she propose to do with the photograph?"

"To ruin me."

"But how?"

"I am about to be married."

"So I have heard." 95

"To Clotilde Lothman von Saxe-Meningen, second daughter of the King of Scandinavia. You may know the strict principles of her family. She is herself the very soul of delicacy. A shadow of a doubt as to my conduct would bring the matter to an end."

"And Irene Adler?"

"Threatens to send them the photograph. And she will do it. I know that she will do it. You do not know her, but she has a soul of steel. She has the face of the most beautiful of women, and the mind of the most resolute of men. Rather than I should marry another woman, there are no lengths to which she would not go—none."

"You are sure that she has not sent it yet?"

"I am sure." 100

"And why?"

"Because she has said that she would send it on the day when the betrothal was publicly proclaimed. That will be next Monday."

"Oh, then we have three days yet," said Holmes with a yawn. "That is very fortunate, as I have one or two matters of importance to look into just at present. Your Majesty will, of course, stay in London for the present?"

"Certainly. You will find me at the Langham under the name of the Count Von Kramm."

"Then I shall drop you a line to let you know how we progress." 105

"Pray do so. I shall be all anxiety."

"Then, as to money?"

"You have carte blanche."

"Absolutely?"

"I tell you that I would give one of the provinces of my kingdom to   110
have that photograph."

"And for present expenses?"

The King took a heavy chamois leather bag from under his cloak and
laid it on the table.

"There are three hundred pounds in gold and seven hundred in notes,"
he said.

Holmes scribbled a receipt upon a sheet of his note-book and handed
it to him.

"And Mademoiselle's address?" he asked.   115

"Is Briony Lodge, Serpentine Avenue, St. John's Wood."

Holmes took a note of it. "One other question," said he. "Was the photograph a cabinet?"

"It was."

"Then, good-night, your Majesty, and I trust that we shall soon have
some good news for you. And good-night, Watson," he added, as the
wheels of the royal brougham rolled down the street. "If you will be good
enough to call tomorrow afternoon at three o'clock I should like to chat
this little matter over with you."

2

At three o'clock precisely I was at Baker Street, but Holmes had not yet   120
returned. The landlady informed me that he had left the house shortly
after eight o'clock in the morning. I sat down beside the fire, however, with
the intention of awaiting him, however long he might be. I was already
deeply interested in his inquiry, for, though it was surrounded by none of
the grim and strange features which were associated with the two crimes
which I have already recorded, still, the nature of the case and the exalted
station of his client gave it a character of its own. Indeed, apart from
the nature of the investigation which my friend had on hand, there was
something in his masterly grasp of a situation, and his keen, incisive reasoning, which made it a pleasure to me to study his system of work, and
to follow the quick, subtle methods by which he disentangled the most
inextricable mysteries. So accustomed was I to his invariable success that
the very possibility of his failing had ceased to enter into my head.

It was close upon four before the door opened, and a drunken-looking
groom, ill-kempt and side-whiskered, with an inflamed face and disreputable
clothes, walked into the room. Accustomed as I was to my friend's amazing
powers in the use of disguises, I had to look three times before I was certain
that it was indeed he. With a nod he vanished into the bedroom, whence

he emerged in five minutes tweed-suited and respectable, as of old. Putting his hands into his pockets, he stretched out his legs in front of the fire and laughed heartily for some minutes.

"Well, really!" he cried, and then he choked and laughed again until he was obliged to lie back, limp and helpless, in the chair.

"What is it?"

"It's quite too funny. I am sure you could never guess how I employed my morning, or what I ended by doing."

"I can't imagine. I suppose that you have been watching the habits, and perhaps the house, of Miss Irene Adler."

"Quite so; but the sequel was rather unusual. I will tell you, however. I left the house a little after eight o'clock this morning in the character of a groom out of work. There is a wonderful sympathy and freemasonry among horsy men. Be one of them, and you will know all that there is to know. I soon found Briony Lodge. It is a *bijou* villa, with a garden at the back, but built out in front right up to the road, two stories. Chubb lock to the door. Large sitting-room on the right side, well furnished, with long windows almost to the floor, and those preposterous English window fasteners which a child could open. Behind there was nothing remarkable, save that the passage window could be reached from the top of the coach-house. I walked round it and examined it closely from every point of view, but without noting anything else of interest.

"I then lounged down the street and found, as I expected, that there was a mews in a lane which runs down by one wall of the garden. I lent the ostlers a hand in rubbing down their horses, and received in exchange twopence, a glass of half and half, two fills of shag tobacco, and as much information as I could desire about Miss Adler, to say nothing of half a dozen other people in the neighbourhood in whom I was not in the least interested, but whose biographies I was compelled to listen to."

"And what of Irene Adler?" I asked.

"Oh, she has turned all the men's heads down in that part. She is the daintiest thing under a bonnet on this planet. So say the Serpentine-mews, to a man. She lives quietly, sings at concerts, drives out at five every day, and returns at seven sharp for dinner. Seldom goes out at other times, except when she sings. Has only one male visitor, but a good deal of him. He is dark, handsome, and dashing, never calls less than once a day, and often twice. He is a Mr. Godfrey Norton, of the Inner Temple. See the advantages of a cabman as a confidant. They had driven him home a dozen times from Serpentine-mews, and knew all about him. When I had listened to all they had to tell, I began to walk up and down near Briony Lodge once more, and to think over my plan of campaign.

"This Godfrey Norton was evidently an important factor in the matter. He was a lawyer. That sounded ominous. What was the relation between them, and what the object of his repeated visits? Was she his client, his friend, or

125

130

his mistress? If the former, she had probably transferred the photograph to his keeping. If the latter, it was less likely. On the issue of this question depended whether I should continue my work at Briony Lodge, or turn my attention to the gentleman's chambers in the Temple. It was a delicate point, and it widened the field of my inquiry. I fear that I bore you with these details, but I have to let you see my little difficulties, if you are to understand the situation."

"I am following you closely," I answered.

"I was still balancing the matter in my mind when a hansom cab drove up to Briony Lodge, and a gentleman sprang out. He was a remarkably handsome man, dark, aquiline, and moustached—evidently the man of whom I had heard. He appeared to be in a great hurry, shouted to the cabman to wait, and brushed past the maid who opened the door with the air of a man who was thoroughly at home.

"He was in the house about half an hour, and I could catch glimpses of him in the windows of the sitting-room, pacing up and down, talking excitedly, and waving his arms. Of her I could see nothing. Presently he emerged, looking even more flurried than before. As he stepped up to the cab, he pulled a gold watch from his pocket and looked at it earnestly, 'Drive like the devil,' he shouted, 'first to Gross & Hankey's in Regent Street, and then to the Church of St. Monica in the Edgeware Road. Half a guinea if you do it in twenty minutes!'

"Away they went, and I was just wondering whether I should not do well to follow them when up the lane came a neat little landau, the coachman with his coat only half-buttoned, and his tie under his ear, while all the tags of his harness were sticking out of the buckles. It hadn't pulled up before she shot out of the hall door and into it. I only caught a glimpse of her at the moment, but she was a lovely woman, with a face that a man might die for.

"'The Church of St. Monica, John,' she cried, 'and half a sovereign if 135 you reach it in twenty minutes.'

"This was quite too good to lose, Watson. I was just balancing whether I should run for it, or whether I should perch behind her landau when a cab came through the street. The driver looked twice at such a shabby fare, but I jumped in before he could object. 'The Church of St. Monica,' said I, 'and half a sovereign if you reach it in twenty minutes.' It was twenty-five minutes to twelve, and of course it was clear enough what was in the wind.

"My cabby drove fast. I don't think I ever drove faster, but the others were there before us. The cab and the landau with their steaming horses were in front of the door when I arrived. I paid the man and hurried into the church. There was not a soul there save the two whom I had followed and a surpliced clergyman, who seemed to be expostulating with them. They were all three standing in a knot in front of the altar. I lounged up the side aisle like any other idler who has dropped into a church. Suddenly, to my surprise, the three at the altar faced round to me, and Godfrey Norton came running as hard as he could towards me.

"'Thank God,' he cried. 'You'll do. Come! Come!'

"'What then?' I asked.

"'Come, man, come, only three minutes, or it won't be legal.' 140

"I was half-dragged up to the altar, and before I knew where I was I found myself mumbling responses which were whispered in my ear, and vouching for things of which I knew nothing, and generally assisting in the secure tying up of Irene Adler, spinster, to Godfrey Norton, bachelor. It was all done in an instant, and there was the gentleman thanking me on the one side and the lady on the other, while the clergyman beamed on me in front. It was the most preposterous position in which I ever found myself in my life, and it was the thought of it that started me laughing just now. It seems that there had been some informality about their license, that the clergyman absolutely refused to marry them without a witness of some sort, and that my lucky appearance saved the bridegroom from having to sally out into the streets in search of a best man. The bride gave me a sovereign, and I mean to wear it on my watch-chain in memory of the occasion."

"This is a very unexpected turn of affairs," said I; "and what then?"

"Well, I found my plans very seriously menaced. It looked as if the pair might take an immediate departure, and so necessitate very prompt and energetic measures on my part. At the church door, however, they separated, he driving back to the Temple, and she to her own house. 'I shall drive out in the park at five as usual,' she said as she left him. I heard no more. They drove away in different directions, and I went off to make my own arrangements."

"Which are?"

"Some cold beef and a glass of beer," he answered, ringing the bell. 145 "I have been too busy to think of food, and I am likely to be busier still this evening. By the way, Doctor, I shall want your coöperation."

"I shall be delighted."

"You don't mind breaking the law?"

"Not in the least."

"Nor running a chance of arrest?"

"Not in a good cause." 150

"Oh, the cause is excellent!"

"Then I am your man."

"I was sure that I might rely on you."

"But what is it you wish?"

"When Mrs. Turner has brought in the tray I will make it clear to you. 155 Now," he said as he turned hungrily on the simple fare that our landlady had provided, "I must discuss it while I eat, for I have not much time. It is nearly five now. In two hours we must be on the scene of action. Miss Irene, or Madame, rather, returns from her drive at seven. We must be at Briony Lodge to meet her."

"And what then?"

"You must leave that to me. I have already arranged what is to occur. There is only one point on which I must insist. You must not interfere, come what may. You understand?"

"I am to be neutral?"

"To do nothing whatever. There will probably be some small unpleasantness. Do not join in it. It will end in my being conveyed into the house. Four or five minutes afterwards the sitting-room window will open. You are to station yourself close to that open window."

"Yes."   160

"You are to watch me, for I will be visible to you."

"Yes."

"And when I raise my hand—so—you will throw into the room what I give you to throw, and will, at the same time, raise the cry of fire. You quite follow me?"

"Entirely."

"It is nothing very formidable," he said, taking a long cigar-shaped roll   165
from his pocket. "It is an ordinary plumber's smoke-rocket, fitted with a cap at either end to make it self-lighting. Your task is confined to that. When you raise your cry of fire, it will be taken up by quite a number of people. You may then walk to the end of the street, and I will rejoin you in ten minutes. I hope that I have made myself clear?"

"I am to remain neutral, to get near the window, to watch you, and at the signal to throw in this object, then to raise the cry of fire, and to wait you at the corner of the street."

"Precisely."

"Then you may entirely rely on me."

"That is excellent. I think, perhaps, it is almost time that I prepare for the new role I have to play."

He disappeared into his bedroom and returned in a few minutes in   170
the character of an amiable and simple-minded Nonconformist clergyman. His broad black hat, his baggy trousers, his white tie, his sympathetic smile, and general look of peering and benevolent curiosity were such as Mr. John Hare alone could have equalled. It was not merely that Holmes changed his costume. His expression, his manner, his very soul seemed to vary with every fresh part that he assumed. The stage lost a fine actor, even as science lost an acute reasoner, when he became a specialist in crime.

It was a quarter past six when we left Baker Street, and it still wanted ten minutes to the hour when we found ourselves in Serpentine Avenue. It was already dusk, and the lamps were just being lighted as we paced up and down in front of Briony Lodge, waiting for the coming of its occupant. The house was just such as I had pictured it from Sherlock Holmes's succinct description, but the locality appeared to be less private than I expected. On the contrary, for a small street in a quiet neighbourhood, it was remarkably animated. There was a group of shabbily dressed men smoking and laughing in a corner, a scissors-grinder with his wheel, two guardsmen who were flirting with a nurse-girl, and several well-dressed young men who were lounging up and down with cigars in their mouths.

"You see," remarked Holmes, as we paced to and fro in front of the house, "this marriage rather simplifies matters. The photograph becomes a double-edged weapon now. The chances are that she would be as averse to its being seen by Mr. Godfrey Norton, as our client is to its coming to the eyes of his princess. Now the question is, Where are we to find the photograph?"

"Where, indeed?"

"It is most unlikely that she carries it about with her. It is cabinet size. Too large for easy concealment about a woman's dress. She knows that the King is capable of having her waylaid and searched. Two attempts of the sort have already been made. We may take it, then, that she does not carry it about with her."

"Where, then?"   175

"Her banker or her lawyer. There is that double possibility. But I am inclined to think neither. Women are naturally secretive, and they like to do their own secreting. Why should she hand it over to anyone else? She could trust her own guardianship, but she could not tell what indirect or political influence might be brought to bear upon a business man. Besides, remember that she had resolved to use it within a few days. It must be where she can lay her hands upon it. It must be in her own house."

"But it has twice been burgled."

"Pshaw! They did not know how to look."

"But how will you look?"

"I will not look."   180

"What then?"

"I will get her to show me."

"But she will refuse."

"She will not be able to. But I hear the rumble of wheels. It is her carriage. Now carry out my orders to the letter."

As he spoke the gleam of the side-lights of a carriage came round the   185
curve of the avenue. It was a smart little landau which rattled up to the door of Briony Lodge. As it pulled up, one of the loafing men at the corner dashed forward to open the door in the hope of earning a copper, but was elbowed away by another loafer, who had rushed up with the same intention. A fierce quarrel broke out, which was increased by the two guardsmen, who took sides with one of the loungers, and by the scissors-grinder, who was equally hot upon the other side. A blow was struck, and in an instant

the lady, who had stepped from her carriage, was the centre of a little knot of flushed and struggling men, who struck savagely at each other with their fists and sticks. Holmes dashed into the crowd to protect the lady; but just as he reached her he gave a cry and dropped to the ground, with the blood running freely down his face. At his fall the guardsmen took to their heels in one direction and the loungers in the other, while a number of better-dressed people, who had watched the scuffle without taking part in it, crowded in to help the lady and to attend to the injured man. Irene Adler, as I will still call her, had hurried up the steps; but she stood at the top with her superb figure outlined against the lights of the hall, looking back into the street.

"Is the poor gentleman much hurt?" she asked.

"He is dead," cried several voices.

"No, no, there's life in him!" shouted another. "But he'll be gone before you can get him to hospital."

"He's a brave fellow," said a woman. "They would have had the lady's purse and watch if it hadn't been for him. They were a gang, and a rough one, too. Ah, he's breathing now."

"He can't lie in the street. May we bring him in, marm?" 190

"Surely. Bring him into the sitting-room. There is a comfortable sofa. This way, please!"

Slowly and solemnly he was borne into Briony Lodge and laid out in the principal room, while I still observed the proceedings from my post by the window. The lamps had been lit, but the blinds had not been drawn, so that I could see Holmes as he lay upon the couch. I do not know whether he was seized with compunction at that moment for the part he was playing, but I know that I never felt more heartily ashamed of myself in my life than when I saw the beautiful creature against whom I was conspiring, or the grace and kindliness with which she waited upon the injured man. And yet it would be the blackest treachery to Holmes to draw back now from the part which he had intrusted to me. I hardened my heart, and took the smoke-rocket from under my ulster. After all, I thought, we are not injuring her. We are but preventing her from injuring another.

Holmes had sat up upon the couch, and I saw him motion like a man who is in need of air. A maid rushed across and threw open the window. At the same instant I saw him raise his hand, and at the signal I tossed my rocket into the room with a cry of "Fire!" The word was no sooner out of my mouth than the whole crowd of spectators, well dressed and ill—gentlemen, ostlers, and servant-maids—joined in a general shriek of "Fire!" Thick clouds of smoke curled through the room and out at the open window. I caught a glimpse of rushing figures, and a moment later the voice of Holmes from within assuring them that it was a false alarm. Slipping through the shouting crowd I made my way to the corner of the street, and in ten minutes was rejoiced to find my friend's arm in mine, and to get away from the scene of uproar. He walked swiftly and in silence for some few minutes until we had turned down one of the quiet streets which lead towards the Edgeware Road.

"You did it very nicely, Doctor," he remarked. "Nothing could have been better. It is all right."

"You have the photograph?"

195

"I know where it is."

"And how did you find out?"

"She showed me, as I told you she would."

"I am still in the dark."

"I do not wish to make a mystery," said he, laughing. "The matter was perfectly simple. You, of course, saw that everyone in the street was an accomplice. They were all engaged for the evening."

200

"I guessed as much."

"Then, when the row broke out, I had a little moist red paint in the palm of my hand. I rushed forward, fell down, clapped my hand to my face, and became a piteous spectacle. It is an old trick."

"That also I could fathom."

"Then they carried me in. She was bound to have me in. What else could she do? And into her sitting-room, which was the very room which I suspected. It lay between that and her bedroom, and I was determined to see which. They laid me on a couch, I motioned for air, they were compelled to open the window, and you had your chance."

"How did that help you?"

205

"It was all-important. When a woman thinks that her house is on fire, her instinct is at once to rush to the thing which she values most. It is a perfectly over-powering impulse, and I have more than once taken advantage of it. In the case of the Darlington substitution scandal it was of use to me, and also in the Arnsworth Castle business. A married woman grabs at her baby; an unmarried one reaches for her jewel-box. Now it was clear to me that our lady of to-day had nothing in the house more precious to her than what we are in quest of. She would rush to secure it. The alarm of fire was admirably done. The smoke and shouting were enough to shake nerves of steel. She responded beautifully. The photograph is in a recess behind a sliding panel just above the right bell-pull. She was there in an instant, and I caught a glimpse of it as she half-drew it out. When I cried out that it was a false alarm, she replaced it, glanced at the rocket, rushed from the room, and I have not seen her since. I rose, and, making my excuses, escaped from the house. I hesitated whether to attempt to secure the photograph at once; but the coachman had come in, and as he was watching me narrowly it seemed safer to wait. A little over-precipitance may ruin all."

"And now?" I asked.

"Our quest is practically finished. I shall call with the King to-morrow, and with you, if you care to come with us. We will be shown into the sitting-room to wait for the lady, but it is probable that when she comes she may find neither us nor the photograph. It might be a satisfaction to his Majesty to regain it with his own hands."

"And when will you call?"

"At eight in the morning. She will not be up, so that we shall have a 210 clear field. Besides, we must be prompt, for this marriage may mean a complete change in her life and habits. I must wire to the King without delay."

We had reached Baker Street and had stopped at the door. He was searching his pockets for the key when someone passing said:

"Good-night, Mister Sherlock Holmes."

There were several people on the pavement at the time, but the greeting appeared to come from a slim youth in an ulster who had hurried by.

"I've heard that voice before," said Holmes, staring down the dimly lit street. "Now, I wonder who the deuce that could have been."

3

I slept at Baker Street that night, and we were engaged upon our toast and 215 coffee in the morning when the King of Bohemia rushed into the room.

"You have really got it!" he cried, grasping Sherlock Holmes by either shoulder and looking eagerly into his face.

"Not yet."

"But you have hopes?"

"I have hopes."

"Then, come. I am all impatience to be gone." 220

"We must have a cab."

"No, my brougham is waiting."

"Then that will simplify matters." We descended and started off once more for Briony Lodge.

"Irene Adler is married," remarked Holmes. 225

"Married! When?"

"Yesterday."

"But to whom?"

"To an English lawyer named Norton."

"But she could not love him."

"I am in hopes that she does." 230

"And why in hopes?"

"Because it would spare your Majesty all fear of future annoyance. If the lady loves her husband, she does not love your Majesty. If she does not love your Majesty, there is no reason why she should interfere with your Majesty's plan."

Don Lee (1959–   )

Don Lee, a third-generation Korean American, was born in Tokyo, Japan, where Lee's father was serving in the American foreign service. The family then moved to a military base in Seoul, South Korea, before returning to Japan during Lee's teenage years. Lee attended the University of California Los Angeles and majored in engineering, but while there he decided to become a writer instead. It is perhaps not surprising, given his background, that the work he has published so far has been preoccupied with questions of identity. Lee has received a number of awards for his writing, which includes a book of short stories, *Yellow*, and a novel, *Country of Origin*. He has taught at Emerson College, and since 1988 he has edited *Ploughshares*, the school's literary journal.

The Price of Eggs in China (2001)

It was noon when Dean Kaneshiro arrived at Oriental Hair Poet No. 2's house, and as she opened the door, she said, blinking, "Hello. Come in. I'm sorry. I'm not quite awake."

He carried his measuring rig through the living room, noting the red birch floor, the authentic Stickley, the Nakashima table, the Maloof credenza—good craftsmanship, carefully selected, this poet, Marcella Ahn, was a woman who knew wood.

"When you called," she said in her study, "I'd almost forgotten. It's been over two years! I hope I wasn't too difficult to track down."

Immediately Dean was annoyed. When she had ordered the chair, he had been clear about his backlog, and today was the exact date he'd given her for the fitting. And she *had* been difficult to track down, despite his request, two years ago, that she notify him of any changes of address. Her telephone number in San Francisco had been disconnected, and he had had to find her book in the library, then call her publisher in New York, then her agent, only to learn that Marcella Ahn had moved an hour south of San Francisco to the very town, Rosarita Bay, where he himself lived. Never mind that he should have figured this out, having overheard rumors of yet another Asian poet in town with spectacular long hair, rumors which had prompted the references to her and Caroline Yip, his girlfriend of eight months, as the Oriental Hair Poets.

He adjusted his rig. Marcella Ahn was thin and tall, but most of   5
her height was in her torso, not her legs—typical of Koreans. She wore tight midnight-blue velvet pants, lace-up black boots, and a flouncy white Victorian blouse, her tiny waist cinched by a thick leather belt.

"Sit, please," he said. She settled into the measuring rig. He walked around her twice, then said, "Stand up, please." After she got up, he fine-tuned the back supports and armrests and shortened the legs. "Again, please."

She sat down. "Oh, that's much better, infinitely better," she said. "You can do that just by looking?"

Now came the part that Dean always hated. He could use the rig to custom-fit his chairs for every part of the body except for one. "Could you turn around, please?"

"Sorry?"

"Could you turn around? For the saddling of the seat?" 10

Marcella Ahn's eyes lighted, and the whitewash of her foundation and powder was suddenly broken by the mischievous curl of her lips, which were painted a deep claret. "You mean you want to examine... my *buttocks?*"

He could feel sweat popping on his forehead. "Please."

Still smirking, she raised her arms, the ruffled cuffs of her blouse dropping away, followed by the jangling release of two dozen silver bracelets on each wrist. There were silver rings on nearly every digit, too, and with her exquisitely lacquered fingers, she slowly gathered her hair—straight and lambent and hanging to midthigh—and raked it over one shoulder so it lay over her breast. Then she pivoted on her toe, turned around, and daintily lifted the tail of her blouse to expose her butt.

He squatted behind her and stared at it for a full ten seconds. It was a good butt, a firm, StairMastered butt, a shapely, surprisingly protuberant butt.

She peeked over her shoulder. "Need me to bend over a little?" she 15 asked.

He bounced up and moved across the room and pretended to jot down some notes, then looked around. More classic modern furniture, very expensive. And the place was neat, obsessive-compulsive neat. He pointed to her desk. "You'll be using the chair here?"

"Yes."

"To do your writing?"

"Uh-huh."

"I'll watch you, then. For twenty minutes, please." 20

"What? Right now?"

"It'll help me to see you work, how you sit, maybe slouch."

"It's not that simple," she said.

"No?"

"Of course not. Poets can't write on demand. You know nothing about 25 poetry, do you?"

"No, I don't," Dean said. All he ever read, in fact, were mystery novels. He went through three or four of them a week—anything with a crime, an investigation. He was now so familiar with forensic techniques, he could predict almost any plot twist, but his head still swam in delight at the first hint of a frame-up or double-cross.

He glanced out the window. Marcella Ahn lived off Skyview Ridge Road, which crested the rolling foothills, and she had one of the few panoramic views of Rosarita Bay—the harbor to the north, the marsh to the south, the town in the middle, and, everywhere beyond, the vast Pacific.

Marcella Ahn had her hands on her hips. "And I don't slouch," she said.

Eventually he did convince her to sit in her present desk chair, an ugly vinyl contraption with pneumatic levers and bulky ergonomic pads. She opened a bound notebook and uncapped a fountain pen, and hovered over the blank page for what seemed like a long time. Then she abruptly set everything aside and booted up her laptop computer. "What do you do with clients who aren't within driving distance?"

"I ask for a videotape, and I talk to their tailor. Try to work, please. Then   30 I'll be out of your way."

"I feel so silly."

"Just pretend I'm not here," he said.

Marcella Ahn continued to stare at the computer screen. She shifted, crossed her legs, and tucked them underneath her. Finally, she set her fingers on the keys and tapped out three words—all she could manage, apparently. She exhaled heavily. "When will the chair be ready?"

"I'll start on it next month, on April twentieth, then three weeks, so May eleventh," he told her, though he required only half that time. He liked to plan for contingencies, and he knew his customers wanted to believe—especially with the prices they were paying—that it took him longer to make the chairs.

"Can I visit your studio?" she asked.   35

"No, you cannot."

"Ah, you see, you can dish it—"

"It would be very inconvenient."

"For twenty minutes."

"Please don't," he said.   40

"Seriously. I can't swing by for a couple of minutes?"

"No."

Marcella Ahn let out a dismissive puff. "Artists," she said.

Oriental Hair Poet No. 1 was a slob. Caroline Yip lived in an apartment above the R. B. Feed & Hardware store, one small room with a Pullman kitchen, a cramped bathroom, and no closets. Her only furnishings were a futon, a boom box, and a coffee table, and the floor was littered with clothes, CDs, shoes, books, newspapers, bills, and magazines. There was a thick layer of grease on the stovetop, dust and hair and curdled food on every other surface, and the bathroom was clogged with sixty-two bottles of shampoo and conditioner, some half-filled, most of them empty.

Dean had stayed in the apartment only once—the first time they had   45 slept together. He had lain naked on her futon, and Caroline had inspected his erection, baldly surveying it from different angles. "Your penis looks like a fire hydrant," she had said. "Everything about you is short, squat, and thick." It was true. Dean was an avid weightlifter, not an ounce of fat on him, but his musculature was broad and tumescent, absent of definition. His forearms were pickle jars, almost as big as his thighs, and his crewcutted head sat on his shoulders without the relief of a neck. "What am I doing with you?" Caroline said. "This is what it's come down to, this is how far I've sunk. I'm about to fuck a Nipponese fire hydrant with the verbal capacity of tap water."

There were other peculiarities. She didn't sleep well, although she had done almost everything possible short of psychotherapy—which she didn't believe in—to alleviate her insomnia and insistent stress: acupuncture, herbs, yoga, homeopathy, tai chi. She ran five miles a day, and she meditated for twenty minutes each morning and evening, beginning her sessions by trying to relax her face, stretching and contorting it, mouth yowling open, eyes bulging—it was a horrific sight.

Even when she did sleep, it was fitful. Because she ground her teeth, she wore a plastic mouthpiece to bed, and she bit down so hard on it during the night, she left black spots where her fillings were positioned. She had nightmares, a recurring nightmare, of headless baby chickens chasing after her, hundreds of decapitated little chicks tittering in rabid pursuit.

The nightmares, however, didn't stop her from eating chicken, or anything else, for that matter. She was a waif, five-two, barely a hundred pounds. Her hair—luxuriant, butt-length, and naturally kinky, a rarity among Asians—seemed to weigh more than she did. Yet she had a ravenous appetite. She was constantly asking for seconds, picking off Dean's plate. "Where does it all go?" he asked over dinner one night, a month into their courtship.

"What?"

"The food." 50

"I have a very fast metabolism. You're not going to finish that?"

He scraped the rest of his portion into her bowl, and he watched her eat. He had surprised himself by how fond he'd become of her. He was a disciplined man, one with solitary and fastidious habits, yet Caroline's idiosyncrasies were endearing to him. Maybe this was the true measure of love, he thought—when you willingly tolerate behavior that, in anyone else, would be annoying, even abhorrent to you. Without thinking, he blurted out, "I love you."

"Yikes," Caroline said. She put her chopsticks down and wiped her mouth. "You are the sweetest man I know, Dean. But I worry about you. You're so innocent. Didn't anyone let you out of the house when you were young? Don't you know you're not supposed to say things like that so soon?"

"Do you love me?"

She sighed. "I don't right now," she said. Then she laid her hands 55 on top of his head and shook it. "But I think I will. Okay, you big boob?"

It took her two more months to say that she might, maybe, be a little bit in love with him, too. "Despite everything, I guess I'm still a romantic," she said. "I will never learn."

They were both reclusive by nature, and most of the time were content to sequester themselves in Dean's house, which was tucked in a canyon in the coastal mountains. They watched videos, read, cooked Japanese dishes: *tonkatsu, oyako donburi, tempura, unagi*. It was a quiet life, free of catastrophe, and it had lulled Dean into thinking that there would be no harm in telling her about his encounter with Oriental Hair Poet No. 2.

"That cunt!" Caroline said. "That conniving Korean cunt! She's moved here on purpose!"

It was all she could talk about for three days. Caroline Yip and Marcella Ahn, it turned out, had a history. They had both lived in Cambridge, Massachusetts, in their twenties, and for several years they had been the best of friends—inseparable, really. But then their first books came out at the same time, Marcella's from a major New York publisher, Caroline's from a small, albeit respected press. Both had very similar jacket photos, the two women looking solemn and precious, hair flowing in full regalia. An unfortunate coincidence. Critics couldn't resist reviewing them together, mocking the pair, even then, as "The Oriental Hair Poets," "The Braids of the East," and "The New Asian Poe-tresses."

But Marcella came away from these barbs relatively unscathed. Her book, 60 *Speak to Desire*, was taken seriously, compared to Marianne Moore and Emily Dickinson. Her poetry was highly erudite, usually beginning with mundane observations about birds or plant life, then slipping into long, abstract meditations on entropy and inertia, the Bible, evolution, and death, punctuated by the briefest mention of personal deprivations—anorexia, depression, abandonment. Or so the critics said. Dean still had the book from the library, but he couldn't make heads or tails of it.

In contrast, Caroline's book, *Chicks of Chinese Descent*, had been skewered. She wrote in a slangy, contemporary voice, full of topical, pop culture allusions. She wrote about masturbation and Marilyn Monroe, about tampons and *moo goo gai pan*, about alien babies and chickens possessed by the devil. She was roundly dispatched as a mediocre talent.

Worse, Caroline said, was what happened afterward. Marcella began to thwart her at every turn. Teaching jobs, coveted magazine publications, awards, residencies, fellowships—everything Caroline applied for, Marcella got. It didn't hurt that Marcella was a shameless schmoozer, flirting and networking with anyone who might be of use. Yet, the fact was, Marcella was rich. Her father was a shipping tycoon, and she had a trust fund in the millions. She didn't need any of these pitifully small sinecures which would have meant a livelihood to Caroline, and it became obvious that the only reason Marcella was pursuing them at all was to taunt her.

"She's a vulture, a vampire," Caroline told Dean. "You know she won't go out in the light of day? She stays up until four, five in the morning and doesn't wake up until past noon."

And then there was the matter of Evan Paviromo, the English-Italian editor of a literary journal whom Caroline had dated for seven years, waiting patiently for them to get married and have children. He broke it off one day without explanation. She dogged him. Why? Why was he ending it? She refused to let him go without some sort of answer. Finally he complied. "It's something Marcella said," he admitted.

At first Caroline feared they were having an affair, but the truth was more   65 vicious. "Marcella told me she admired me," Evan said, "that I was far more generous than she could ever be. She said she just wouldn't be able to stay with someone whose work she didn't really respect. I thought about that, and I decided I'm not that generous. It's something that would eat away at me, that's bothered me all along. It's something I can't abide."

Caroline fled to California, eventually landing in Rosarita Bay. She completely disengaged herself from the poetry world. She was still writing every day, excruciating as it was for her, but she had not attempted to publish anything in six years. She was thirty-seven now, and a waitress—the breakfast shift at a diner, the dinner shift at a barbecue joint. Her feet had grown a full size from standing so much, and she was broke. But she had started to feel like her old self again, healthier, more relaxed, sleeping better. Dean had a lot to do with it, she said. She was happy—or as happy as it was possible for a poet to be. Until now. Until Marcella Ahn suddenly arrived.

"She's come to torment me," Caroline said. "Why else would she move to Rosarita Bay?"

"It's not such a bad place to live."

"Oh, please."

Dean supposed she was right. On the surface, Rosarita Bay looked like   70 a nice seaside town, a rural sanctuary between San Francisco and Santa Cruz. It billed itself as the pumpkin capital of the world, and it had a Main Street lined with gas street lamps and old-time, clapboarded, saltbox shops and restaurants. Secluded and quiet, it felt like genuine small-town America, and most of the eight thousand residents preferred it that way, voting down every development plan that came down the pike.

Yet the things that gave Rosarita Bay its charm were also killing it. There were only two roads into town, Highway 1 on the coast and Highway 71 through the San Vicente Mountains, both of them just two lanes and prone to landslides. The fishing and farming industries were drying up, there were no new jobs, and, for those who worked in San Francisco or "over the hill" in San Vicente, it was a murderous, traffic-choked commute. The weather was also terrible, rain-soaked and wave-battered in the winter, wind-beaten in the spring, and fog-shrouded all summer long, leaving basically two good months—September and October.

In theory quaint and pretty, Rosarita Bay was actually a no-man's-land, a sleepy, slightly seedy backwater with the gray air of anonymity. People stuck to themselves, as if shied by failure and missed opportunities. You could get lost here, forgotten. It was, when all was said and done, a place of exile. It was not a place for a wealthy, jet-setting artiste and bon vivant like Marcella Ahn. But to come here because of Caroline? No. Dean could not believe it.

"How could she have even known you were here?" he asked Caroline.

"You said you're not in touch with any of those people anymore."

"She probably hired a detective."

"Come on."

"You don't understand. I suppose you think if anyone's looking for   75
revenge, it'd be me, that I can't be a threat to her because I'm such a loser."

"I wish you'd stop putting yourself down all the time. You're not a loser."

"Yes, I am. You're just too polite to say so. You're so fucking Japanese."
Early on, she had given him her book to read, and he had told her he liked
it. But when pressed, he'd had to admit that he didn't really understand the
poems. He was not an educated man, he had said.

"You pass yourself off as this simple chairmaker," Caroline said. "You   80
were practically monosyllabic when we began seeing each other. But I know
you're not the gallunk you make yourself out to be."

"I think you're talented. I think you're very talented." How could he
explain it to her? Something had happened as he'd read her book. The poems,
confusing as they were, had made his skin prickle, his throat thicken, random
images and words—*kiwi, quiver, belly, maw*—wiggling into his head and taking
residence.

"Are you attracted to her?" Caroline asked.

"What?"

"You're not going to make the chair for her, are you?"

"I have to."   85

"You don't have a contract."

"No, but—"

"You still think it's all a coincidence."

"She ordered the chair *sixteen months* before I met you."

"You see how devious she is?"   90

Dean couldn't help himself. He laughed.

"She has some sick bond to me," Caroline said. "In all this time, she
hasn't published another book, either. She *needs* me. She *needs* my misery.
You think I'm being hysterical, but you wait."

It began with candy and flowers, left anonymously behind the hardware store,
on the stairs that led up to Caroline's apartment. Dean had not sent them.

"It's her," Caroline said.

The gifts continued, every week or so, then every few days. Chocolates,   95
carnations, stuffed animals, scarves, hairbrushes, barrettes, lingerie. Caroline,

increasingly anxious, moved in with Dean, and quickly came down with a horrendous cold.

Hourly he would check on her, administering juice, echinacea, or antihistamines, then would go back to the refuge of his workshop. It was where he was most comfortable—alone with his tools and wood, making chairs that would last hundreds of years. He made only armchairs now, one chair, over and over, the Kaneshiro Chair. Each one was fashioned out of a single board of *keyaki*, Japanese zelkova, and was completely handmade. From the logging to the tung oil finish, the wood never touched a power tool. All of Dean's saws and chisels and planes were hand-forged in Japan, and he shunned vises and clamps of any kind, sometimes holding pieces between his feet to work on them.

On first sight, the chair's design wasn't that special—blocky right angles, thick Mission-style slats—but its beauty lay in the craftsmanship. Dean used no nails or screws, no dowels or even glue. Everything was put together by joints, forty-four delicate, intricate joints, modeled after a traditional method of Japanese joinery dating to the seventeenth century, called *sashimono*. Once coupled, the joints were tenaciously, permanently locked. They would never budge, they would never so much as squeak.

What's more, every surface was finished with a hand plane. Dean would not deign to have sandpaper in his shop. He had apprenticed for four years with a master carpenter in the city of Matsumoto, in Nagano prefecture, spending the first six months just learning how to sharpen his tools. When he returned to California, he could pull a block plane over a board and produce a continuous twelve-foot-long shaving, without a single skip or dig, that was less than a tenth of a millimeter thick—so thin you could read a newspaper through it.

Dean aimed for perfection with each chair. With the first kerf of his *dozuki* saw, with the initial chip of a chisel, he was committed to the truth of the cut. Tradition dictated that any errors could not be repaired, but had to remain untouched to remind the woodworker of his humble nature. More and more, Dean liked to challenge himself. He no longer used a level, square, or marking gauge, relying on his eye, and soon he planned to dispense with rulers altogether, maybe even with pencils and chalk. He wanted to get to the point where he could make a Kaneshiro Chair blindfolded.

But he had a problem. Japanese zelkova, the one- to two-thousand-year-old variety he needed, was rare and very expensive—amounting to over $150 a pound. There were only three traditional woodcutters left in Japan, and Dean's sawyer, Hayashi Kota, was sixty-nine. Hayashi-san's intuition was irreplaceable. So much of the work was in reading the trees and determining where to begin sawing to reveal the best figuring and grain—like cutting diamonds. Afraid the sawyer might die soon, Dean had begun stockpiling wood five years ago. In his lumber shed, which was climate-controlled to keep the

100

wood at a steady thirty-seven percent humidity, was about two hundred thousand dollars' worth of zelkova. Hayashi-san cut the logs through and through and air-dried them in Japan for a year, and after two weeks of kiln heat, the boards were shipped to Dean, who stacked them on end in *boule* order. When he went into the shed to select a new board, he was always overcome by the beauty of the wood, the smell of it. He'd run his hand over the boards—hardly a check or crack on them—and would want to weep.

Given the expense of the wood and the precision his chairs required, anyone seeing Dean in his shop would have been shocked by the rapidity with which he worked. He never hesitated. He *attacked* the wood, chips flying, shavings whirling into the air, sawdust piling at his feet. He could sustain this ferocity for hours, never letting his concentration flag. No wonder, then, that it took him a few moments to hear the knocking on the door late that afternoon. It took him even longer to comprehend why anyone would be disturbing him in his workshop, his *sanctum sanctorum*.

Caroline swung open the door and stepped inside, looking none too happy. "You have a visitor," she said.

Marcella Ahn sidled past her. "Hello!"

Dean almost dropped his *ryoba* saw.

"Is that my chair?" she asked, pointing to the stack of two-by-twos on his bench. "I know, I know, you told me not to come, but I had to. You won't hold it against me, will you?"

Without warning, Caroline let out a violent sneeze, her hair whiplashing forward.

"Bless you," Dean and Marcella said at the same time.

Caroline snorted up a long string of snot, glaring at Oriental Hair Poet No. 2. They were a study in contrasts, Marcella once again decked out as an Edwardian whore: a corset and bodice, miniskirt and high heels, full makeup, hair glistening. Caroline was wearing her usual threadbare cardigan and flannel shirt, pajama bottoms, and flip-flops. She hadn't bathed in two days, sick in bed the entire time.

"When you get over this cold," Marcella said to her, "we'll have to get together and catch up. I just can't get over seeing you here."

"It *is* incredible, isn't it?" Caroline said. "It must defy all the laws of probability." She walked to the wall and lifted a mortise chisel from the rack. "The chances of your moving here, when you could live anywhere in the world, it's probably more likely for me to shit an egg for breakfast. Why *did* you move here?"

"Pure chance," Marcella told her cheerily. "I happened to stop for coffee on my way to Aptos, and I saw one of those real estate circulars for this house. It looked like an unbelievable bargain. Beautiful woodwork. I thought, What the hell, I might as well see it while I'm here. I was tired of living in cities."

105

110

"What have you been doing since you got to town? Buying lots of gifts?" Dean watched her dig the chisel blade into a piece of scrap. He wished she would put the chisel down. It was very sharp.

Marcella appeared confused. "Gifts? No. Well, unless you count Mr. Kaneshiro's chair as a gift. To myself. You don't have a finished one here? I've actually never seen one except in the Museum of Modern Art."

"Sorry," he told her, nervous now, hoping it would slip by Caroline.   115 But it did not. "The Museum of Modern Art?" she asked. "In New York?"

Marcella nodded. She absently flicked her hair back with her hand, and one of her bracelets flew off her wrist, pinging against the window and landing on some wood chips.

Caroline speared it up with the chisel and dangled it in front of Marcella, who slid it off somewhat apprehensively. Caroline then turned to Dean. "Your chairs are in the Museum of Modern Art in New York?"

He shrugged. "Just one."

"You didn't know?" Marcella asked Caroline, plainly pleased she didn't.   120 "Your boyfriend's quite famous."

"How famous?"

"I would like to get back to work now," Dean said.

"He's in Cooper-Hewitt's permanent collection, the M.F.A. in Boston, the American Craft Museum."

"I need to work, please."

"Don't you have a piece in the White House?"   125

"Time is late, please."

"Can I ask you some questions about your process?"

"No." He grabbed the chisel out of Caroline's hand before she could react and ushered Marcella Ahn to the door. "Okay, thank you. Goodbye."

"Caroline, when do you want to get together? Maybe for tea?"

"She'll call you," Dean said, blocking her way back inside.   130

"You'll give her my number?"

"Yes, yes, thank you," he said, and shut the door.

Caroline was sitting on his planing bench, looking gaunt and exhausted. Through the window behind her, Dean saw it was nearing dusk, the wind calming down, the trees quiet. Marcella Ahn was out of view, but he could hear her starting her car, then driving away. He sat down next to Caroline and rubbed her back. "You should go back to bed. Are you hungry? I could make you something."

"Is there anything else about you I should know? Maybe you've taught at Yale or been on the Pulitzer committee? Maybe you've won a few genius grants?"

He wagged his head. "Just one."   135

"What?"

He told her everything. Earlier in his career, he had done mostly conceptual woodwork, more sculpture than furniture. His father was indeed a fifth-generation Japanese carpenter, as he'd told her, but Dean had broken with tradition, leaving his family's cabinetmaking business in San Luis Obispo to study studio furniture at the Rhode Island School of Design. After graduating, he had moved to New York, where he was quickly declared a phenomenon, a development that baffled him. People talked about his work with terms like "verticality" and "negation of ego" and "primal tension," and they might as well have been speaking Farsi. He rode it for all it was worth, selling pieces at a record clip. But eventually, he became bored. He didn't experience any of the rivalries that Caroline had, nor was he too bothered by the egos and fatuity that abounded in the art world. He just didn't believe in what he was doing anymore, particularly after his father died of a sudden stroke. Dean wanted to return to the pure craftsmanship and functionality of woodworking, building something people could actually *use*. So he dropped everything to apprentice in Japan. Afterward, he distilled all of his knowledge into the Kaneshiro Chair, which was regarded as significant a landmark as Frank Lloyd Wright's Willits Chair. Ironically, his work was celebrated anew. He received a five-year genius grant that paid him an annual $50,000, all of which he had put into hoarding the zelkova in his shed.

"How much do you get a chair?" Caroline asked.

"Ten thousand."

"God, you're only thirty-eight."   140

"It's an inflated market."

"And you never thought to tell me any of this in the eight months we've been going out? I thought you were barely getting by. You live in this crappy little house with cheap furniture, your pickup is ten years old, you never take vacations. I thought it was because you weren't very savvy about your business, making one chair at a time, no advertising or catalogue or anything, no store lines. I thought you were *clueless*."

"It's not important."

"Not important? Are you insane? Not important? It changes everything."

"Why?"   145

"You know why, or you wouldn't have kept this secret from me."

"It was an accident. I didn't set out to be famous. It just happened. I'm ashamed of it."

"You should be. You're either pathologically modest, or you were afraid I'd be repelled by how successful you are, compared to me. But you should have told me."

"I just make chairs now," Dean said. "I'm just like you with your poetry. I work hard like you. I don't do it for the money or the fame or to be popular with the critics."

"It's just incidental that you've gotten all of those things without   150
even trying."

"Let's go in the house. I'll make you dinner."

"No. I have to go home. I can't be with you anymore."

"Caroline, please."

"You must think I'm pathetic, you must pity me," she said. "You're not
like me at all. You're just like Marcella."

They had fights before, puzzling affairs where she would walk out in a huff,   155
incensed by an innocuous remark he'd made, a mysterious gaffe he'd committed. A day or two would go by, then she would talk to him, peevishly at first,
ultimately relenting after she had dressed him down with a pointed lecture on
his need to be more sensitive, more supportive, more complimentary, more
assertive, more emotive, more sympathetic, above all, more *communicative*. Dean
would listen without protest, and, newly educated and humbled, he would
always be taken back. But not this time. This time was different. On the telephone the next day, Caroline was cool and resolute—no whining or nagging, no
histrionics or ultimatums or room for negotiation. "It's over, Dean," she said.

The following afternoon, he went to her apartment with a gallon of *miso*
soup. "For your cold," he said.

She looked down at the tub in his hands. "I'm fine now. I don't need the
soup. The cold's gone."

They were standing outside on the stairway landing. "You're not going to
let me in?" he asked.

"Dean, didn't you hear what I said yesterday?"

"Just tell me how I should change. I'll change."   160

"It's not like that."

"What's it like, then? Tell me what you want me to do."

"Nothing," she said. "You can't fix this. Don't come by again, don't call,
okay? It'll be easier if we just break it off clean."

He tried to leave her alone, but none of it made any sense to him. Why
was she ending it? What had he done wrong? It had to be one of her mood
swings, a little hormonal blip, a temporary synaptic disruption, all of which
he'd witnessed and weathered before. It had to be more about Marcella Ahn
than him. She couldn't really be serious. The best course of action seemed
to be to wait it out, while at the same time being solicitous and attentive. So
he called—not *too* frequently, maybe once a day or so—and since she wouldn't
pick up her phone, he left messages: "I just wanted to see how you're doing.
I miss you." He drove to her apartment and knocked on her door, and since
she wouldn't answer it, he left care packages: macadamia nuts, coffee, cream,
filters, toilet paper, sodas, granola bars, springwater, toothpaste—the everyday
staples she always forgot to buy.

Five days passed, and she didn't appear to be weakening. A little des-   165
perate, he decided to go to Rae's Diner. When Caroline came out of the
kitchen and saw him sitting in her station, she didn't seem surprised, but
she was angry. She wouldn't acknowledge him, wouldn't come to his table.
After twenty minutes, Dean flagged down Rae, the owner. "Could you tell
Caroline to take my order?" he asked.

Rae, a lanky, middle-aged brunette with a fierce sunlamp tan, studied him,
then Caroline. "If you two are having a fight, I'm not going to be in the middle
of it. You want to stay, you'll have to pay."

"That's what I'm trying to do. She won't take my order."

"Why don't you just move to another station?"

"There aren't any other tables."

"The counter, then."   170

"I'm a paying customer, I should be able to sit where I want."

Rae shook her head. "Any screaming, one little commotion, and you're
out of here. And no dawdling over a cup of coffee, either. The minute your
table's cleared, you go."

She had a brief conference with Caroline, who began arguing with her,
but in the end Rae won out, and Caroline marched over to Dean's table. She
didn't look well—pale and baggy-eyed. She wasn't sleeping or eating much, it
was clear. He tried to make pleasantries. "How have you been?" he asked her.
She would not say a word, much less look at him. She waited for his order,
ballpoint poised over her pad. A few minutes later, when his food was ready,
she clattered the plate in front of him and walked away. When he raised
his coffee cup for a refill, she slopped the pot, spilling coffee over the brim,
almost scorching his crotch. He left her a generous tip.

He came to a similar arrangement with the manager of Da Bones, the
barbecue restaurant where Caroline worked nights—as long as he paid, he
could stay. He ate meals at every one of Caroline's shifts for a week, at the end
of which he had gained eight pounds and was popping antacids as if they were
gumballs. It was greasy, artery-busting food. A typical breakfast now consisted
of six eggs over easy, sausage, hash browns, blueberry flapjacks, coffee, orange
juice, biscuits, and milk gravy. Dinner was the hungry man combo—beef bris-
ket, half a rack of baby backs, kielbasa, blackened chicken, rice, beans, slaw,
and cornbread—accompanied by a side of mashed and two plates of conch
fritters. But it was worth it. Caroline's resolve, he could tell, was beginning
to crack (although the same could be said about her health; she looked
awful). One night, as he asked for his fifth glass of water, she actually said
something. She said, "You are getting to be a real pain in the ass," and she
almost smiled. He was getting to her.

But two days later, he received a strange summons. A sergeant from the   175
sheriff's office, Gene Becklund, requested he come down for a talk concerning

Caroline. Mystified, Dean drove over to the sheriff's office on Highway 1 and was escorted into an interrogation room. Gene Becklund was a tall, soft-spoken man with prematurely gray hair. He opened the conversation by saying, "You've been going over to your ex-girlfriend's apartment a lot, dropping off little presents? Even though she told you not to call or visit?"

Unsettled, Dean nodded yes.

"You've also been bothering her at her workplace nearly every day?"

"'Bothering'?"

"And you've been leaving a lot of messages on her machine, haven't you?"

"We haven't really broken up," Dean said. "We're just having a fight."   180

"Uh-huh."

"I'm not harassing her or anything."

"Okay."

"Did she say I was harassing her?"

"Why don't we listen to something," Becklund said, and turned on   185
a cassette player. On the tape was a garbled, robotic, unidentifiable voice, reciting the vile, evil things that would be done to Caroline—anal penetration, disembowelment. "You think you can treat people the way you've treated me, Miss Mighty High?" the voice said. "Think again. I'm going to enjoy watching you die."

"Jesus," Dean said.

Becklund clicked off the tape. "That's just a sample. There have been other calls—very ugly. The voice is disguised. It's hard to even know whether it's a man or a woman."

"The caller used a voice changer."

"You're familiar with them?"

"I read a lot of crime novels."   190

"I was surprised how cheap the things are. You can get them off the Internet," Becklund said. "The calls were made from various pay phones, mostly between two and four in the morning. Ms. Yip asked the phone company to begin tracing incoming calls a couple of weeks ago. We can trace where they're being made, but not who's making them." Almost as an afterthought, he asked, "You're not making them, are you?"

"No. Is that what Caroline thinks?"

"Here's what I never understand. She *should* think that, everything in my experience says so, but she doesn't. She thinks it's this woman, Marcella Ahn. I've talked to her, too, but she claims she's only left a couple of messages to invite Ms. Yip to tea, and to see if she would do a poetry reading with her at Beryl's Bookstore."

Dean had never really believed it was Marcella Ahn who was leaving the gifts. Maybe an enamored restaurant customer, or the pimply clerk in the hardware store, but not Marcella. Now he reconsidered. "Maybe it's not all a coincidence," he said. "Maybe it is her." Suddenly it almost made sense. "I think it might really be her."

"Maybe," Becklund said. "But my money's on you. Unfortunately, I   195
can't get a restraining order issued without Ms. Yip's cooperation. But I can do this. I can tell you that all the things you did before—the presents, the calls, the workplace visits—weren't prosecutable under the anti-stalking laws until you made a physical threat. You crossed the line with the physi-cal threat. From now on, you make one little slip-up, I can arrest you." He tapped the tabletop with his fingertip. "I suggest you stay away from her."

Dean ignored Becklund. He was frightened for Caroline, and he would do all he could to protect her. The next morning, he waited across the street from the diner for Caroline's shift to finish. When she came outside, he didn't recognize her at first. She had cut off all her hair.

She was walking briskly, carrying a Styrofoam food container, and he had to sprint to catch up to her. "Caroline, please talk to me," he said. "Will you talk to me? Sergeant Becklund told me about the messages."

She stopped but did not turn around. As he stepped in front of her, he saw she was crying. Her hair was shorn to no more than an inch, matted in clumps and tufts, exposing scalp in some places. Evidently she had chopped it off herself in a fit of self-immolation. "Oh, baby," he said, "what have you done?"

She dropped the container, splattering egg salad onto the sidewalk, and collapsed into him. "Do you believe me now?" she asked. "Do you believe it's her?"

"Yes. I do."   200

"What makes one person want to destroy another?" she asked. "For what? The pettiness, the backstabbing, the meanness—what's the point? Is it fun? She has everything. What more does she want? Why is she doing this to me?"

Dean held her. "I don't know."

"It's such a terrible world, Dean. You can't trust anyone. No matter where you go, there's always someone wishing you ill will. You think they're your friends, and then they're smearing you, trying to ruin you. I can't take this anymore. Why can't she just go away? Can't you make her go away?"

"Is that what you want?"

"Yes," Caroline said.   205

It was all Dean needed to hear. He took her to his house, put her to bed, and got to work.

It didn't take long to learn her routine. Caroline had been right: Marcella Ahn never left her house until near sunset, when she would go to the newly renovated Y.M.C.A. to attend a cardioboxing class, topped off with half an hour on the StairMaster. She usually didn't shower at the Y, but would go straight home in her workout clothes. At nine or so, she might emerge and drive to Beryl's Bookstore & Café in town for a magazine and a cappuccino. Once, she went to the Moonside Trading Post for a video. Another time, the Safeway on Highway 71 at two A.M. She had one guest, a male, dressed in a suit, an O.B./G.Y.N. at a San Francisco hospital, according to the parking sticker on his BMW. He spent the night. She didn't go anywhere near Caroline's apartment or make any clandestine calls from pay phones.

Dean didn't try to conceal his stakeouts from Caroline, but he misled her into thinking he wanted to catch Marcella in the act. He had no such expectations. By this time, Marcella had to know that she was—however removed—a suspect, that she might be watched. Dean had an entirely different agenda.

One afternoon, he interrupted his surveillance to go to a spy hobbyist shop in San Francisco. He had found it through the Internet on the Rosarita Bay Library computer—Sergeant Becklund had given him the idea. At the store, he bought a lock pick set, $34.95, and a portable voice changer, $29.95. (The clerk also tried to sell him a 200,000-volt stun gun, on sale for $119.95.) Dean paid cash—no credit card records or bank statements to implicate him later.

In the dead of night, he made a call from a pay phone in the neighboring 210 town of Miramar to his own answering machine, imitating the taunts he'd heard in the sheriff's office with the voice changer. "Hey, Jap boyfriend, you're back together with her, are you? Well, fear not, I know where you live." Before leaving the house, he had switched off his telephone's ringer and turned down the volume on the answering machine. He didn't want to scare Caroline, even though she was likely asleep, knocked out by the sleeping pills prescribed by a doctor he'd taken her to see at the town clinic. Still, in the morning, he had no choice but to play the message for her. Otherwise, she wouldn't have called Becklund in a panic, imploring him to arrest Marcella Ahn. "She's insane," Caroline told him. "She's trying to drive me crazy. She's going to try to kill me. You have to do something."

Becklund came to Dean's house, listened to the tape, and appeared to have a change of heart. Dean and Caroline had reconciled. There was no reason to suspect him anymore. Becklund had to look elsewhere. "Keep your doors and windows locked," he told Dean.

After that, the only question was when. It couldn't be too soon, but each day of waiting became more torturous.

The following Wednesday, before her dinner shift, he drove Caroline to Rummy Creek and parked on the headlands overlooking the ocean. It was another miserable, gray, windy day, Dean's truck buffeted by gusts. Rummy Creek was world famous for its big waves, and there was supposed to be a monster swell approaching, but the water was flat, a clump of surfers in the distance bobbing gently on the surface like kelp.

"There haven't been any phone calls all week," Caroline said inside his truck.

"I know. Maybe she's decided to stop."   215

"No," Caroline said, "she'd never stop. Something's going to happen. I can feel it. I'm scared, Dean."

He dropped her off at Da Bones, then drove up Skyview Ridge Road and nestled in the woods outside Marcella's house. On schedule, she left for the Y.M.C.A. at six P.M. After a few minutes, he strolled to the door as casually as possible. She didn't have a neighbor within a quarter mile, but he worried about the unforeseen—the gynecologist lover, a UPS delivery, Becklund deciding belatedly to serve a restraining order. Wearing latex surgical gloves, Dean inserted a lock pick and tension bar into the keyhole on the front door. The deadbolt opened within twenty seconds. Thankfully she had not installed an alarm system yet. He took off his shoes and walked through the kitchen into the garage. This was the biggest variable in his plan. If he didn't find what he needed there, none of it would work. But to his relief, Marcella Ahn had several cans of motor oil on the shelf, as well as some barbecue lighter fluid—it wasn't gasoline, but it would do. In the recycle bin, there were four empty bottles of pinot grigio. In the kitchen, a funnel and a dishrag. He poured one part motor oil and one part lighter fluid into a bottle, a Molotov cocktail recipe provided by the Internet. In her bedroom, he pulled several strands of hair from her brush, pocketed one of her bracelets, and grabbed a pair of platform-heeled boots from her closet. Then he was out, and he sped to his house in Vasquez Canyon. All he had to do was press in some bootprints in the dirt in front of the lumber shed, but he was running out of time. He drove back to Marcella's, hurriedly washed the soles of the boots in the kitchen sink, careful to leave a little mud, replaced the boots in the closet, checked through the house, and locked up. Then he went to Santa Cruz and tossed the lock pick set and voice changer into a dumpster.

He did nothing more until three A.M. By then, Caroline was unconscious from the sleeping pills. Dean drove to Marcella Ahn's again. He had to make sure she was home, and alone. He walked around her house, peeking into the windows. She was in her study, sitting at her desk in front of her laptop computer. She had her head in her hands, and she seemed to be quietly weeping. Dean was overcome with misgivings for a moment. He had to remind himself that she was at fault here, that she deserved what was coming to her.

He returned to his own property. Barefoot and wearing only the latex gloves and his underwear, he snagged the strands of Marcella's hair along the doorframe of the lumber shed. He threw the bracelet toward the driveway. He twisted the dishrag into the mouth of the wine bottle, then tilted it from side to side to mix the fluids and soak the rag. He started to flick his lighter, but then hesitated, once more stalled by doubt. Were those mystery novels he read really that accurate? Would the Hair & Fiber and Latent Prints teams be deceived at all? Was he being a fool—a complete amateur who would be ferreted out with ease? He didn't know. All he knew was that he loved Caroline, and he had to take this risk for her. If something wasn't done, he was certain he would lose her. He lit the rag and smashed the bottle against the first stack of zelkova inside the shed. The fire exploded up the boards. He shut the door and ran back into the house and climbed into bed beside Caroline. In a matter of seconds, the smoke detectors went off. The shed was wired to the house, and the alarm in the hallway rang loud enough to wake Caroline. "What's going on?" she asked.

Dean peered out the window. "I think there's a fire," he said. He pulled   220 on his pants and shoes and ran to the shed. When he kicked open the door, the heat blew him back. Flames had already engulfed three *boules* of wood, the smoke was thick and black, the fire was spreading. Something had gone wrong. The sprinkler system—his expensive, state-of-the-art, dry-pipe sprinkler system—had not activated. He had not planned to sacrifice this much wood, one or two stacks at most, and now he was in danger of losing the entire shed.

There was no investigation, per se. Two deputies took photographs and checked for fingerprints, but that was about all. Dean asked Becklund, "Aren't you going to call the crime lab unit?" and Becklund said, "This is it."

It was simple enough for the fire department to determine that it was arson, but not who set it. The insurance claims adjuster was equally lackadaisical. Within a few days, he signed off for Dean to receive a $75,000 check. Dean and Caroline had kept the blaze contained with extinguishers and garden hoses for the twenty-two minutes it took for the fire trucks to arrive, but nearly half of Dean's wood supply had been consumed, the rest damaged by smoke and water.

No charges were filed against Marcella Ahn. After talking to Becklund and a San Vicente County assistant district attorney, though, she agreed—on the advice of counsel—to move out of Rosarita Bay, which was hardly a great inconvenience for her, since she owned five other houses and condos. Caroline never heard from her again, and, as far as they knew, she never published another book—a one-hit wonder.

Caroline, on the other hand, finally submitted her second book to a publisher. Dean was relentless about making her do so. The book was accepted right away, and when it came out, it caused a brief sensation. Great reviews. Awards and fellowships. Dozens of requests for readings and appearances. Caroline couldn't be bothered. By then, she and Dean had had their first baby, a girl, Anna, and Caroline wanted more children, a baker's dozen if possible. She was transformed. No more nightmares, and she could nap standing up (house-keeping remained elusive). In relation to motherhood, to the larger joys and tragedies that befell people, the poetry world suddenly seemed silly, insignificant. She would continue to write, but only, she said, when she had the time and will. Of course, she ended up producing more than ever.

Marcella Ahn's chair was the last Dean made from the pristine zelkova. He would dry and clean up the boards that were salvageable, and when he exhausted that supply, he would switch to English walnut, a nice wood—pretty, durable, available.   225

He delivered the chair to Marcella just before she left town, on May 11, as scheduled. She was surprised to see him and the chair, but a promise was a promise. He had never failed to deliver an order, and she had prepaid for half of it.

He set the chair down in the living room—crowded with boxes and crates— and she sat in it. "My God," she said, "I didn't know it would be this comfortable. I could sit here all day."

"I'd like to ask you for a favor," Dean said as she wrote out a check for him. He held an envelope in his hand.

"A favor?"

"Yes. I'd like you to read Caroline's new poems and tell me if they're good."   230

"You must be joking. After everything she's done?"

"I don't know poetry. You're the only one who can tell me. I need to know."

"Do you realize I could have been sent to state prison for two years? For a crime I didn't commit?"

"It would've never gone to trial. You would've gotten a plea bargain—a suspended sentence and probation."

"How do you know?" Marcella asked. "Your girlfriend is seriously deranged. I only wanted to be her friend, and she devised this insidious plot to frame me and run me out of town. She's diabolical."

"You stalked her."   235

"I did no such thing. Don't you get it? She faked it. She set me up. *She* was the stalker. Hasn't that occurred to you? Hasn't that gotten through that thick, dim-witted skull of yours? She burned your *wood*."

"You're lying. You're very clever, but I don't believe you," Dean said. And he didn't, although she made him think for a second. He pulled out the book manuscript from the envelope. "Are you going to read the poems or not?"

"No."

"Aren't you curious what she's been doing for the past six years?" Dean asked. "Isn't this what you came here to find out?"   240

Marcella slowly hooked her hair behind her ears and took her time to respond. "Give it to me," she finally said.

For the next half hour, she sat in his chair in the living room, flipping through the seventy-one pages, and Dean watched her. Her expression was unyielding and contemptuous at first, then it went utterly slack, then taut again. She breathed quickly through her nose, her jaw clamped, her eyes blinked.

"Are they good?" Dean asked when she finished.

She handed the manuscript back to him. "They're pedestrian. They're clunky. There's no music to the language."

"They're good," Dean told her.   245

"I didn't say that."

"You don't have to. I saw it in your face." He walked to the door and let himself out.

"I didn't say they were good!" Marcella Ahn screamed after him. "Do you hear me? I didn't say that. I didn't say they were good!"

Dean never told Caroline about his last visit with Marcella Ahn, nor did he ever ask her about the stalking, although he was tempted at times. One spring afternoon, they were outside on his deck, Caroline leaning back in the rocker he'd made for her, her eyes closed to the sun, Anna asleep in her lap. It had rained heavily that winter, and the eucalyptus and pine surrounding the house were now in full leaf. They sat silently and listened to the wind bending through the trees. He had rarely seen her so relaxed.

Anna, still asleep, lolled her head, her lips pecking the air in steady   250
rhythm—an infant soliloquy.

"Caroline," he said.

"Hm?"

"What do you think she's dreaming about?"

Caroline looked down at Anna. "Your guess is as good as mine," she said. "Maybe she has a secret. Can babies have secrets?" She ran her hand through her hair, which she had kept short, and she smiled at Dean.

Was it possible that Caroline had fabricated everything about Marcella Ahn? He did not want to know. She would, in turn, never question him about the fire. The truth wouldn't have mattered. They had each done what was necessary to be with the other. Such was the price of love among artists, such was the price of devotion.

■ The story is a detective story with some element of who-dun-it. But that seems only a slight element. How is "The Price of Eggs in China" also a love story, a revenge story, a psychological study, and a reflection upon art and the creative process?

■ How do the different characters construct their own different stories?

■ Why is it significant that Dean, one of the main characters, is an avid reader of detective stories?

■ The three main characters (Dean, Caroline, and Marcella) are all artists. How is this fact significant to our reading of their stories?

POETRY

Emily Dickinson (1830–1886)

[A Route of Evanescence] (#1463) (1879)

A Route of Evanescence°
With a revolving Wheel—
A Resonance of Emerald—
A Rush of Cochineal°
And every Blossom on the Bush   5
Adjusts its tumbled Head—
The mail from Tunis, probably,
An easy Morning's Ride—

Emily Dickinson (1830–1886)

[I like to see it lap the Miles] (#585) (1862)

I like to see it lap the Miles—
And lick the Valleys up—
And stop to feed itself at Tanks—
And then—prodigious step

Around a Pile of Mountains—   5
And supercilious peer
In Shanties—by the sides of Roads—
And then a Quarry pare

To fit its sides
And crawl between   10
Complaining all the while
In horrid—hooting stanza—
Then chase itself down Hill—

And neigh like Boanerges—
Then—prompter than a Star   15

---

1. Evanescence: the tendency to vanish away. **4. Cochineal:** a brilliant scarlet dye.

Stop—docile and omnipotent
At its own stable door—

- In these two poems, Dickinson offers us two different riddles. When we look closely at each of the details she has listed, what figure does she describe in each poem?
- In "A Route of Evanescence," the detail about "the mail from Tunis" appears not to fit with the other details. How can you account for the detail? Is there any similar detail in "I like to see it lap the Miles—"?

E. A. Robinson (1869–1935)

Richard Cory (1897)

Whenever Richard Cory went down town,
We people on the pavement looked at him:
He was a gentleman from sole to crown,
Clean favored, and imperially slim.

And he was always quietly arrayed,   5
And he was always human when he talked;
But still he fluttered pulses when he said,
"Good-morning," and he glittered when he walked.

And he was rich—yes, richer than a king—   10
And admirably schooled in every grace:
In fine, we thought that he was everything
To make us wish that we were in his place.

So on we worked, and waited for the light,   15
And went without the meat, and cursed the bread;
And Richard Cory, one calm summer night,
Went home and put a bullet through his head.

- How does the final line of the poem challenge the appearances that the town has long accepted?
- What were Cory's greatest strengths? How does their presentation in the poem create a dramatic impact?

William Stafford (1914–1993)

Traveling through the Dark (1962)

Traveling through the dark I found a deer
dead on the edge of the Wilson River road.
It is usually best to roll them into the canyon:
that road is narrow; to swerve might make more dead.

By glow of the tail-light I stumbled back of the car   5
and stood by the heap, a doe, a recent killing;
she had stiffened already, almost cold.
I dragged her off; she was large in the belly.

My fingers touching her side brought me the reason—
her side was warm; her fawn lay there waiting,   10
alive, still, never to be born.

Beside that mountain road I hesitated.
The car aimed ahead its lowered parking lights;
under the hood purred the steady engine.
I stood in the glare of the warm exhaust turning red;   15
around our group I could hear the wilderness listen

I thought hard for us all—my only swerving—
then pushed her over the edge into the river.

■ In Stafford's poem, the narrator describes a pause in his usual routine.
   What is this routine? How does the narrator decide to go on?

Aron Keesbury (1971–   )

On the Robbery across the Street (1998)

(*An eyewitness to the Brinks heist*)

I tell them, look. Sure, I was around.
The tenant from four
come down to the store
that night to see can he get a cat.

Tony or Jimmy, his name is.   5
Henry maybe. Mike? Joe?
Maybe Jimmy. Look, I don't know
but he's a nice boy anyway. Wears specs,

you know. He come down
asks me, says can I get a cat   10
upstairs? I says sure. Keep that
sandy crap out of the drains, though—

clogs them all up, you know.
Then I got to get all new pipes.
So he runs upstairs. He's all hyped   15
up like I ain't seen the cat he's got

already. Maybe two,
three weeks he's got a cat up there.
These kids. Jazzing all around, I swear,
think they can get away with murder.   20

But he's a nice boy and I tell the cops,
I say, look. I been in this store here
for thirty-seven years.
Thirty-seven years in this store.

I tell them sure. I say, look.   25
I was here, I was around
that night. I been in this town
thirty-seven years.
And I don't see nothing.

- What details in the poem give us information about the 1950 Brinks robbery in Boston?

- This robbery in which nearly $3 million was stolen was famously difficult to solve. How does this poem illustrate that aspect of the heist?

Muriel Rukeyser (1913–1980)

Myth (1973)

Long afterward, Oedipus, old and blinded, walked the
roads. He smelled a familiar smell. It was the Sphinx.
Oedipus said, "I want to ask one question. Why didn't
I recognize my mother?" "You gave the wrong answer,"
said the Sphinx. "But that was what made everything   5
possible," said Oedipus. "No," she said. "When I asked,
What walks on four legs in the morning, two at noon,
and three in the evening, you answered,

Man. You didn't say anything about woman."
"When you say Man," said Oedipus, "you include   10
women too. Everyone knows that." She said,
"That's what you think."

■ How is "You gave the wrong answer" stunning to both Oedipus and to those
of us who are familiar with his story?

■ How does Rukeyser's final line bring a modern sensibility to the Oedipus myth?

DRAMA

Sophocles (497–406 BCE)

Because ancient biographies are so often unreliable, it is difficult to know much
about Sophocles with any certainty. Literary historians generally accept, however,
that he was the son of a businessman; he was a gifted singer; his first victory in the
principal dramatic festival, the Greater Dionysia, occurred in 468 BC; and he never
won less than second prize and came in first on at least eighteen occasions. He
also served as treasurer, senator, and general in Athens. His plays that have survived to the present day, including *Oedipus Rex* (*Oedipus the King*) and Antigone,
are among the undisputed classics of world literature.

Oedipus Rex (George Young, trans.; ca. 430 BCE)

CHARACTERS

OEDIPUS, *King of Thebes.*
PRIEST *of Zeus.*
CREON, *brother to Jocasta the Queen.*
TIRESIAS, *a Prophet, with the title of King.*
A Messenger from Corinth.
An old Shepherd.
A Second Messenger, servant of Oedipus' household.
JOCASTA *the Queen, wife to Oedipus, formerly married to Laius, the last King.*

ANTIGONE,
ISMENE, } *daughters to Oedipus and Jocasta.*

The CHORUS *is composed of Senators of Thebes.*
Inhabitants of Thebes, Attendants.
A Boy leading Tiresias.

Scene, before the Royal Palace at Thebes. Enter OEDIPUS; *to him the Priest of Zeus, and Inhabitants of Thebes.*

OEDIPUS: Children, you modern brood of Cadmus[1] old,
　　　What mean you, sitting in your sessions here,
　　　High-coronalled with votive olive-boughs,
　　　While the whole city teems with incense-smoke,
　　　And paean hymns, and sounds of woe the while?　　　5
　　　Deeming unmeet, my children, this to learn
　　　From others, by the mouth of messengers,
　　　I have myself come hither, Oedipus,
　　　Known far and wide by name. Do thou old man,
　　　Since 'tis thy privilege to speak for these,　　　10
　　　Say in what case ye stand; if of alarm,
　　　Or satisfaction with my readiness
　　　To afford all aid; hard-hearted must I be,
　　　Did I not pity such petitioners.
PRIEST: Great Oedipus, my country's governor,　　　15
　　　Thou seest our generations, who besiege
　　　Thy altars here; some not yet strong enough
　　　To flutter far; some priests, with weight of years
　　　Heavy, myself of Zeus; and these, the flower
　　　Of our young manhood; all the other folk　　　20
　　　Sit, with like branches, in the market-place,
　　　By the Ismenian hearth oracular[2]
　　　And the twin shrines of Pallas.[3] Lo, the city
　　　Labours—thyself art witness—over-deep
　　　Already, powerless to uprear her head　　　25
　　　Out of the abysses of a surge of blood;
　　　Stricken in the budding harvest of her soil,
　　　Stricken in her pastured herds, and barren travail
　　　Of women; and He, the God with spear of fire,
　　　Leaps on the city, a cruel pestilence,　　　30
　　　And harries it; whereby the Cadmean home
　　　Is all dispeopled, and with groan and wail
　　　The blackness of the Grave made opulent.
　　　Not that we count thee as the peer of Heaven,
　　　I, nor these children, seat us at thy hearth;　　　35

---

1. Founder of Thebes.
2. Referring to Ismene, a legendary Theban woman.
3. Athena.

But as of men found foremost in affairs,
Chances of life and shifts of Providence;
Whose coming to our Cadmean town released
The toll we paid, of a hard Sorceress,[4]
And that, without instruction or advice   40
Of our imparting; but of Heaven it came
Thou art named, and known, our life's establishes
Thee therefore, Oedipus, the mightiest head
Among us all, all we thy supplicants
Implore to find some way to succour us,   45
Whether thou knowest it through some voice from heaven,
Or, haply of some man; for I perceive
In men experienced that their counsels best
Find correspondence in things actual.
Haste thee, most absolute sir, be the state's builder!   50
Haste thee, look to it; doth not our country now
Call thee deliverer, for thy zeal of yore?
Never let us remember of thy rule
That we stood once erectly, and then fell;
But build this city in stability!   55
With a fair augury didst thou shape for us
Our fortune then; like be thy prowess now!
If thou wilt rule this land (which thou art lord of),
It were a fairer lordship filled with folk
Than empty; towers and ships are nothingness,   60
Void of our fellow men to inhabit them.

OEDIPUS: Ah my poor children, what you come to seek
Is known already—not unknown to me.
You are all sick, I know it; and in your sickness
There is not one of you so sick as I.   65
For in your case his own particular pain
Comes to each singly; but my heart at once
Groans for the city, and for myself, and you.
Not therefore as one taking rest in sleep
Do you uprouse me; rather deem of me   70
As one that wept often, and often came
By many ways through labyrinths of care;
And the one remedy that I could find
By careful Seeking—I supplied it. Creon,

---

4. The Sphinx, whose riddle Oedipus guessed.

Menoeceu's son, the brother of my queen,   75
I sent to Pytho, to Apollo's house,
To ask him by what act or word of mine
I might redeem this city; and the hours
Already measured even with today
Make me solicitous how he has sped;   80
For he is longer absent than the time
Sufficient, which is strange. When he shall come,
I were a wretch did I not then do all
As the God shews.
PRIEST: In happy time thou speak'st;   85
As these, who tell me Creon is at hand.
OEDIPUS: Ah King Apollo, might he but bring grace,
Radiant in fortune, as he is in face!
PRIEST: I think he comes with cheer; he would not, else,
Thus be approaching us with crown on brow,   90
All berries of the bay.
OEDIPUS: We shall know soon;
He is within hearing.

Enter CREON *, attended.*

                                    My good lord and cousin,   95
Son of Menoeceus,
What answer of the God have you brought home?
CREON: Favourable; I mean, even what sounds ominously,
If it have issue in the way forthright,
May all end well.   100
OEDIPUS: How runs the oracle?
I am not confident, nor prone to fear
At what you say, so far.
CREON: If you desire
To hear while these stand near us, I am ready   105
To speak at once—or to go in with you.
OEDIPUS: "Speak before all! My heavy load of care
More for their sake than for my own I bear.
CREON: What the God told me, that will I declare.
Phoebus our Lord gives us express command   110
To drive pollution, bred within this land,
Out of the country, and not cherish it
Beyond the power of healing.
OEDIPUS: By what purge?
What is the tenor of your tragedy?   115

CREON: Exile, or recompense of death for death;
    Since 'tis this blood makes winter to the city.
OEDIPUS: Whose fate is this he signifies?
CREON: My liege,
    We had a leader, once, over this land,   120
    Called Laius—ere you held the helm of state.
OEDIPUS: So I did hear; I never saw the man.
CREON: The man is dead; and now, we are clearly bidden
    To bring to account certain his murderers.
OEDIPUS: And where on earth are they? Where shall be found   125
    This dim-seen track-mark of an ancient crime?
CREON: "Within this land," it ran. That which is sought,
    That may be caught. What is unheeded scapes us.
OEDIPUS: Was it at home, afield, or anywhere
    Abroad, that Laius met this violent end?   130
CREON: He went professedly on pilgrimage;
    But since he started, came back home no more.
OEDIPUS: Nor any messenger nor way-fellow
    Looked on, from whom one might have learnt his story
    And used it?   135
CREON: No, they perished, all but one;
    He fled affrighted; and of what he saw
    Had but one thing to say for certain.
OEDIPUS: Well,
    And what was that? one thing might be the means   140
    Of our discovering many, could we gain
    Some narrow ground for hope.
CREON: Robbers, he said,
    Met them, and slew him; by no single strength,
    But multitude of hands.   145
OEDIPUS: How could your robber
    Have dared so far—except there were some practice
    With gold from hence?
CREON: Why, it seemed probable.
    But, Laius dead, no man stood up to help   150
    Amid our ills.
OEDIPUS: What ill was in the way,
    Which, when a sovereignty had lapsed like this,
    Kept you from searching of it out?
CREON: The Sphinx   155
    With her enigma forced us to dismiss
    Things out of sight, and look to our own steps.

OEDIPUS: Well, I will have it all to light again.
Right well did Phoebus, yea and well may you
Insist on this observance toward the dead;   160
So shall you see me, as of right, with you,
Venging this country and the God together.
Why, 'tis not for my neighbours' sake, but mine,
I shall dispel this plague-spot; for the man,
Whoever it may be, who murdered him,   165
Lightly might hanker to serve me the same.
I benefit myself in aiding him.
Up then, my children, straightway, from the floor;
Take up your votive branches; let some other
Gather the tribes of Cadmus hitherward;   170
Say, I will make clean work. Please Heaven, our state
Shall soon appear happy, or desperate.

PRIEST: Come children, let us rise; it was for this,
Which he himself proclaims, that we came hither.
Now may the sender of these oracles,   175
In saving and in plague-staying, Phoebus, come!

> *Exeunt* CREON, PRIEST *and* THEBANS.
> OEDIPUS: *retires.*

Enter THEBAN SENATORS, *as Chorus.*

Chorus.

I. 1.

O Prophecy of Jove, whose words are sweet,
With what doom art thou sent
To glorious Thebes, from Pytho's gilded seat?
I am distraught with fearful wonderment,
I thrill with terror, and wait reverently—   5
Yea, Io Paean, Delian lord,[5] on thee!
What matter thou wilt compass—either strange,
Or once again recurrent as the seasons change,
Offspring of golden Hope, immortal Oracle,
Tell me, O tell!   10

---

5. Apollo.

I. 2.

Athena first I greet with invocation,
Daughter of Jove, divine!
Next Artemis thy sister, of this nation
Keeper, high seated in the encircling shrine,
Filled with her praises, of our market-place,   5
And Phoebus, shooting arrows far through space;
Appear ye Three, the averters of my fate!
If e'er before, when mischief rose upon the state,
Ye quenched the flames of evil, putting them away,
Come—come to-day!   10

II. 1.

Woe, for unnumbered are the ills we bear!
Sickness pervades our hosts;
Nor is there any spear of guardian care,
Wherewith a man might save us, found in all our coasts.
For all the fair soil's produce now no longer springs;   5
Nor women from the labour and loud cries
Of their child-births arise;
And you may see, flying like a bird with wings,
One after one, outspeeding the resistless brand,
Pass—to the Evening Land.   10

II. 2.

In countless hosts our city perisheth.
Her children on the plain
Lie all unpitied—pitiless—breeding death.
Our wives meanwhile, and white-haired mother's in their train,
This way and that, suppliant, along the altar-side   5
Sit, and bemoan their doleful maladies;
Like flame their paeans rise,
With wailing and lament accompanied;
For whose dear sake O Goddess, O Jove's golden child,
Send Help with favour mild!   10

III. 1.

And Ares the Destroyer, him who thus—
Not now in harness of brass shields, as wont—
Ringed round with clamour, meets us front to front
And fevers us,
O banish from our country! Drive him back,   5
With winds upon his track,

On to the chamber vast of Amphitrite,[6]
Or that lone anchorage, the Thracian main;
For now, if night leave bounds to our annoy,
Day levels all again;   10
Wherefore, O father, Zeus, thou that dost wield the might
Of fire-fraught light,
Him with thy bolt destroy!

III. 2.

Next, from the bendings of thy golden string
I would see showered thy artillery
Invincible, marshalled to succour me,
Lycean King![7]
Next, those flame-bearing beams, arrows most bright,   5
Which Artemis by night
Through Lycian highlands speeds her scattering;
Thou too, the Evian, with thy Maenad band,
Thou golden-braided patron of this land
Whose visage glows with wine,   10
O save us from the god whom no gods honour! Hear,
Bacchus! Draw near,
And light thy torch of pine!

Enter OEDIPUS, *attended.*

OEDIPUS: You are at prayers; but for your prayers' intent
You may gain help, and of your ills relief,
if you will minister to the pestilence,
And hearken and receive my words, which I—
A stranger to this tale, and to the deed   5
A stranger—shall pronounce; for of myself
I could not follow up the traces far,
Not having any key. But, made since then
A fellow-townsman to the townsmen here,
To all you Cadmeans I thus proclaim;   10
Whichever of you knows the man, by whom
Laius the son of Labdacus was slain,
Even if he is afraid, seeing he himself
Suppressed the facts that made against himself,

---

6. The sea.
7. Apollo.

I bid that man shew the whole truth to me;   15
For he shall suffer no disparagement,
Except to quit the land, unscathed. Again,
If any knows another—say some stranger
To have been guilty, let him not keep silence;
For I will pay him the reward, and favour   20
Shall be his due beside it. But again,
If you will hold your peace, and any man
From self or friend in terror shall repel
This word of mine, then—you must hear me say
What I shall do. Whoe'er he be, I order   25
That of this land, whose power and throne are mine,
None entertain him, none accost him, none
Cause him to share in prayers or sacrifice
Offered to Heaven, or pour him lustral wave,
But all men from their houses banish him;   30
Since it is he contaminates us all,
Even as the Pythian oracle divine
Revealed but now to me. Such is my succour
Of him that's dead, and of the Deity.
And on the guilty head I imprecate   35
That whether by himself he has lain covert,
Or joined with others, without happiness,
Evil, in evil, he may pine and die.
And for myself I pray, if with my knowledge
He should become an inmate of my dwelling,   40
That I may suffer all that I invoked
On these just now. Moreover all these things
I charge you to accomplish, in behalf
Of me, and of the God, and of this land,
So ruined, barren and forsaken of Heaven.   45
For even though the matter were not now
By Heaven enjoined you, 'twas unnatural
For you to suffer it to pass uncleansed,
A man most noble having been slain, a king too!
Rather, you should have searched it out; but now,   50
Since I am vested with the government
Which he held once, and have his marriage-bed,
And the same wife; and since our progeny—
If his had not miscarried—had sprung from us
With common ties of common motherhood—   55
Only that Fate came heavy upon his head—

On these accounts I, as for my own father,
Will fight this fight, and follow out every clue,
Seeking to seize the author of his murder—
The scion of Labdacus and Polydore   60
And earlier Cadmus and Agenor old;
And such as disobey—the Gods I ask
Neither to raise them harvest from the ground
Nor children from the womb, but that they perish
By this fate present, and yet worse than this;   65
While you, the other Cadmeans, who approve,
May succouring Justice and all Gods in heaven
Accompany for good for evermore!

1 SENATOR: Even as thou didst adjure me, so, my king, .
I will reply. I neither murdered him,   70
Nor can point out the murderer. For the quest—
To tell us who on earth has done this deed
Belonged to Phoebus, by whose word it came.

OEDIPUS: Your words are just; but to constrain the Gods
To what they will not, passes all men's power.   75

1 SENATOR: I would say something which appears to me
The second chance to this.

OEDIPUS: And your third, also—
If such you have—by all means tell it.

1 SENATOR: Sir,   80
Tiresias above all men, I am sure,
Ranks as a seer next Phoebus, king with king;
Of him we might enquire and learn the truth
With all assurance.

OEDIPUS: That is what I did;   85
And with no slackness; for by Creon's advice
I sent, twice over; and for some time, now,.
'Tis strange he is not here.

1 SENATOR: Then all the rest
Are but stale words and dumb.   90

OEDIPUS: What sort of words?
I am weighing every utterance.

1 SENATOR: He was said
To have been killed by footpads.

OEDIPUS: So I heard;   95
But he who saw it is himself unseen.

1 SENATOR: Well, if his bosom holds a grain of fear,
Curses like yours he never will abide!

OEDIPUS: Whom the doing awes not, speaking cannot scare.

1 SENATOR: Then there is one to expose him: here they come,   100
    Bringing the godlike seer, the only man
    Who has in him the tongue that cannot lie.

Enter TIRESIAS, *led by a boy.*

OEDIPUS: Tiresias, thou who searchest everything,
    Communicable or nameless, both in heaven   105
    And on the earth—thou canst not see the city,
    But knowest no less w'hat pestilence visits it,
    Wherefrom our only saviour and defence
    We find, sir king, in thee. For Phoebus—if
    Thou dost not know it from the messengers—   110
    To us, who sent to ask him, sent word back,
    That from this sickness no release should come,
    Till we had found and slain the men who slew
    Laius, or driven them, banished, from the land.
    Wherefore do thou—not sparing augury,   115
    Either through birds, or any other way
    Thou hast of divination—save thyself,
    And save the city, and me; save the whole mass
    By this dead corpse infected; for in thee
    Stands our existence; and for men, to help   120
    With might and main is of all tasks the highest.

TIRESIAS: Alas! How terrible it is to know,
    Where no good comes of knowing! Of these matters
    I was full well aware, but let them slip me;
    Else I had not come hither.   125

OEDIPUS: But what is it?
    How out of heart thou hast come!

TIRESIAS: Let me go home;
    So shalt thou bear thy load most easily—
    If thou wilt take my counsel—and I mine.   130

OEDIPUS: Thou hast not spoken loyally, nor friendly
    Toward the State that bred thee, cheating her
    Of this response!

TIRESIAS: Because I do not see
    Thy words, not even thine, going to the mark;   135
    So, not to be in the same plight—

1 SENATOR: For Heaven's sake,
    If thou hast knowledge, do not turn away,
    When all of us implore thee suppliant!

TIRESIAS: Ye   140
  Are all unknowing; my say, in any sort,
  I will not say, lest I display thy sorrow.

OEDIPUS: What, you do know, and will not speak? Your mind
  Is to betray us, and destroy the city?

TIRESIAS: I will not bring remorse upon myself   145
  And upon you. Why do you search these matters?
  Vain, vain! I will not tell you.

OEDIPUS: Worst of traitors!
  For you would rouse a very stone to wrath—
  Will you not speak out ever, but stand thus   150
  Relentless and persistent?

TIRESIAS: My offence
  You censure; but your own, at home, you see not,
  And yet blame me!

OEDIPUS: Who would not take offence,   155
  Hearing the words in which you flout the city?

TIRESIAS: Well, it will come, keep silence as I may.

OEDIPUS: And what will come should I not hear from you?

TIRESIAS: I will declare no further. Storm at this,
  If't please you, to the wildest height of anger!   160

OEDIPUS: At least I will not, being so far in anger,
  Spare anything of what is clear to me:
  Know, I suspect you joined to hatch the deed;
  Yea, did it—all but slaying with your own hands;
  And if you were not blind, I should aver   165
  The act was your work only!

TIRESIAS: Was it so?
  I charge you to abide by your decree
  As you proclaimed it; nor from this day forth
  Speak word to these, or me; being of this land   170
  Yourself the abominable contaminator!

OEDIPUS: So shamelessly set you this story on foot,
  And think, perhaps, you shall go free?

TIRESIAS: I am
  Free! for I have in me the strength of truth.   175

OEDIPUS: Who prompted you? for from your art it was not!

TIRESIAS: Yourself! You made me speak, against my will.

OEDIPUS: Speak! What? Repeat, that I may learn it better!

TIRESIAS: Did you not understand me at first hearing,
  Or are you tempting me, when you say "Speak!"   180

OEDIPUS: Not so to say for certain; speak again.

TIRESIAS: I say that you are Laius' murderer—
   He whom you seek.
OEDIPUS: Not without chastisement
   Shall you, twice over, utter wounds!   185
TIRESIAS: Then shall I
   Say something more, that may incense you further?
OEDIPUS: Say what you please; it will be said in vain.
TIRESIAS: I say you know not in what worst of shame
   You live together with those nearest you,   190
   And see not in what evil plight you stand.
OEDIPUS: Do you expect to go on revelling
   In utterances like this?
TIRESIAS: Yes, if the truth
   Has any force at all.   195
OEDIPUS: Why so it has,
   Except for you; it is not so with you;
   Blind as you are in eyes, and ears, and mind!
TIRESIAS: Fool, you reproach me as not one of these
   Shall not reproach you, soon!   200
OEDIPUS: You cannot hurt me,
   Nor any other who beholds the light,
   Your life being all one night.
TIRESIAS: Nor is it fated
   You by my hand should fall; Apollo is   205
   Sufficient; he will bring it all to pass.
OEDIPUS: Are these inventions Creon's work, or yours?
TIRESIAS: Your bane is no-ways Creon, but your own self.
OEDIPUS: O riches, and dominion, and the craft
   That excels craft, and makes life enviable,   210
   How vast the grudge that is nursed up for you,
   When for this sovereignty, which the state
   Committed to my hands, unsought-for, free,
   Creon, the trusty, the familiar friend,
   With secret mines covets to oust me from it,   215
   And has suborned a sorcerer like this,
   An engine-botching crafty cogging knave,
   Who has no eyes to see with, but for gain,
   And was born blind in the art! Why, tell me now,
   How stand your claims to prescience? How came it,   220
   When the oracular monster was alive,
   You said no word to set this people free?
   And yet it was not for the first that came

To solve her riddle; sooth was needed then,
Which you could not afford; neither from birds,   225
Nor any inspiration; till I came,
The unlettered Oedipus, and ended her,
By sleight of wit, untaught of augury—
I whom you now seek to cast out, in hope
To stand upon the steps of Creon's throne!   230
You and the framer of this plot methinks
Shall rue your purge for guilt! Dotard you seem,
Else by experience you had come to know
What thoughts these are you think!

1 SENATOR: As we conceive,   235
His words appear (and, Oedipus, your own,)
To have been said in anger; now not such
Our need, but rather to consider this—
How best to interpret the God's oracle.

TIRESIAS: King as you are, we must be peers at least 240
In argument; I am your equal, there;
For I am Loxias'[8] servant, and not yours;
So never need be writ of Creons train.
And since you have reproached me with my blindness,
I say—you have your sight, and do not see   245
What evils are about you, nor with whom,
Nor in what home you are dwelling. Do you know
From whom you are? Yea, you are ignorant
That to your own you are an enemy,
Whether on earth, alive, or under it.   250
Soon from this land shall drive you, stalking grim,
Your mother's and your father's two-edged curse,
With eyes then dark, though they look proudly now.
What place on earth shall not be harbour, then,
For your lamenting? What Cithaeron-peak[9]   255
Shall not be resonant soon, when you discern
What hymen-song was that, which wafted you
On a fair voyage, to foul anchorage
Under yon roof? and multitudes besides
Of ills you know not of shall level you   260
Down to your self—down to your children! Go,
Trample on Creon, and on this mouth of mine;

---

8. Apollo's.
9. Mountain associated with many myths; see also page 292.

But know, there is not one of all mankind
That shall be bruised more utterly than you.

OEDIPUS: Must I endure to hear all this from him?   265
Hence, to perdition! quickly hence! begone
Back from these walls, and turn you home again.

TIRESIAS: But that you called me, I had not come hither.

OEDIPUS: I did not know that you would utter folly;
Else I had scarce sent for you, to my house.   270

TIRESIAS: Yea, such is what we seem, foolish to you,
And to your fathers, who begat you, wise.

OEDIPUS: What fathers? Stop! Who was it gave me being?

TIRESIAS: This day shall give you birth and death in one.

OEDIPUS: How all too full of riddles and obscure   275
Is your discourse!

TIRESIAS: Were you not excellent
At solving riddles?

OEDIPUS: Ay, cast in my teeth
Matters in which you must allow my greatness!   280

TIRESIAS: And yet this very fortune was your ruin!

OEDIPUS: Well, if I saved this city, I care not.

TIRESIAS: Well,
I am going; and you, boy, take me home.

OEDIPUS: Ay, let him.   285
Your turbulence impedes us, while you stay;
When you are gone, you can annoy no more.

                                             [Retires.

TIRESIAS: I go, having said that I came to say;
Not that I fear your frown; for you possess
No power to kill me; but I say to you—   290
The man you have been seeking, threatening him,
And loud proclaiming him for Laius' murder,
That man is here; believed a foreigner
Here sojourning; but shall be recognized
For Theban born hereafter; yet not pleased   295
In the event; for blind instead of seeing,
And poor for wealthy, to a foreign land,
A staff to point his footsteps, he shall go.
Also to his own sons he shall be found
Related as a brother, though their sire,   300
And of the woman from whose womb he came
Both son and spouse; one that has raised up seed
To his own father, and has murdered him.

Now get you in, and ponder what I say;
And if you can detect me in a lie,   305
Then come and say that I am no true seer.

[Exeunt TIRESIAS *and Boy.*

Chorus.

I 1.

Who is he, who was said
By the Delphian soothsaying rock
To have wrought with hands blood-red
Nameless unspeakable deeds?
Time it were that he fled   5
Faster than storm-swift steeds!
For upon him springs with a shock,
Armed in thunder and fire,
The Child of Jove, at the head
    Of the Destinies dread,   10
That follow, and will not tire.

I. 2.

For a word but now blazed clear
From Parnassus' snow-covered mound,[10]
To hunt down the Unknown!
He, through the forest drear,
By rocks, by cavernous ways,   5
Stalks, like a bull that strays,
Heartsore, footsore, alone;
Flying from Earth's central seat,
Flying the oracular sound
    That with swift wings' beat   10
For ever circles him round.

II. 1.

Of a truth dark thoughts, yea dark and fell,
    The augur wise doth arouse in me,
        Who neither assent, nor yet gainsay;
And what to affirm, I cannot tell;
        But I flutter in hope, unapt to see   5
            Things of to-morrow, or to-day.

---

10 Mount Parnassus is also associated with Apollo.

Why in Polybus' son[11] they should find a foe,
   Or he in the heirs of Labdacus,
      I know no cause, or of old, or late,
In test whereof I am now to go   10
   Against the repute of Oedipus,
      To avenge a Labdakid's unknown fate.

I 2.

True, Zeus indeed, and Apollo, are wise,
   And knowers of what concerns mankind;
      But that word of a seer, a man like me,
Weighs more than mine, for a man to prize,
   Is all unsure. Yea, one man's mind   5
      May surpass another's in subtlety;

But never will I, till I see the rest,
   Assent to those who accuse him now.
      I saw how the air-borne Maiden came
Against him, and proved him wise, by the test,   10
   And good to the state; and for this, I trow,
      He shall not, ever, be put to shame.

Enter CREON.

CREON: I am come hither, fellow citizens,
   Having been told that Oedipus the king
   Lays grievous accusations to my charge,
   Which I will not endure. For if he fancies
   He in our present troubles has endured   5
   Aught at my hands, either in word or deed,
   Tending to harm him, I have no desire
   My life should be prolonged, bearing this blame.
   The injury that such a word may do
   Is no mere trifle, but inore vast than any,   10
   If I am to be called a criminal
   Here in the town, and by my friends, and you.
1 SENATOR: Nay, the reproach, it may be, rather came
   Through stress of anger, than advisedly.
CREON: But it was plainly said, by my advice   15
   The prophet gave false answers.
1 SENATOR: It was said;
   But how advised I know not.

11 Oedipus.

CREON: Was this charge
 Of a set mind, and with set countenance   20
 Imputed against me?
1 SENATOR: I do not know.
 I have no eyes for what my masters do.
 But here he comes, himself, forth of the palace.

Enter OEDIPUS.

OEDIPUS: Fellow, how cam'st thou hither? Dost thou boast 25
 So great a front of daring, as to come
 Under my roof, the assassin clear of me,
 And manifest pirate of my royalty?
 Tell me, by heaven, did you detect in me
 The bearing of a craven, or a fool,   30
 That you laid plans to do it; or suppose
 I should not recognize your work in this,
 Creeping on slily, and defend myself?
 Is it not folly, this attempt of yours,
 Without a following, without friends, to hunt 35
 After a throne, a thing which is achieved
 By aid of followers and much revenue?
CREON: Do me this favour; hear me say as much
 As you have said; and then, yourself decide.
OEDIPUS: You are quick to talk, but I am slow to learn 40
 Of you; for I have found you contrary
 And dangerous to me.
CREON: Now, this same thing
 First hear, how I shall state it.
OEDIPUS: This same thing 45
 Do not tell me—that you are not a villain!
CREON: If you suppose your arrogance weighs aught
 Apart from reason, you are much astray.
OEDIPUS: If you suppose you can escape the pain
 Due for a kinsman's wrong, you are astray! 50
CREON: You speak with justice; I agree! But tell me,
 How is it that you say I injured you?
OEDIPUS: Did you persuade me that I ought to send
 To fetch that canting soothsayer, or no?
CREON: Why yes, and now, I am of the same mind, still. 55
OEDIPUS: How long is it since Laius—
CREON: What? I know not.
OEDIPUS: Died—disappeared, murdered by violence?

CREON: Long seasons might be numbered, long gone by.
OEDIPUS: Well, did this seer then practise in the craft?   60
CREON: Yes, just as wise, and just as much revered.
OEDIPUS: And did he at that time say one word of me?
CREON: Well, nowhere in my presence, anyhow.
OEDIPUS: But did not you hold inquest for the dead?
CREON: We did, of course; and got no evidence.   65
OEDIPUS: Well then, how came it that this wiseacre
    Did not say these things then?
CREON: I do not know.
    In matters where I have no cognizance
    I hold my tongue.   70
OEDIPUS: This much, at least, you know,
    And if you are wise, will say!
CREON: And what is that?
    For if I know it, I shall not refuse.
OEDIPUS: Why, that unless he had conspired with you   75
    He never would have said that Laiu's murder
    Was of my doing!
CREON: If he says so, you know.
    Only I claim to know that first from you,
    Which you put now to me.   80
OEDIPUS: Learn anything!
    For I shall not be found a murderer.
CREON: Well then; you have my sister to your wife?
OEDIPUS: There's no denying that question.
CREON: And with her   85
    Rule equal, and in common hold the land?
OEDIPUS: All she may wish for she obtains of me.
CREON: And make I not a third, equal with you?
OEDIPUS: Ay, there appears your friendship's falsity.
CREON: Not if you reason with yourself, as I.   90
    And note this first; if you can think that any
    Would rather choose a sovereignty, with fears,
    Than the same power, with undisturbed repose?
    Neither am I, by nature, covetous
    To be a king, rather than play the king,   95
    Nor any man who has sagacity.
    Now I have all things, without fear, from you;
    Reigned I myself, I must do much I hated.
    How were a throne, then, pleasanter for me
    Than painless empire and authority?   100

I am not yet so blinded as to wish
For honour, other than is joined with gain.
Now am I hail-fellow-well-met with all;
Now every man gives me good-morrow; now
The waiters on your favour fawn on me;   105
For all their prospering depends thereby.
Then how should I exchange this lot for yours?
A mind well balanced cannot turn to crime.
I neither am in love with this design,
Nor, in a comrade, would I suffer it.   110
For proof of which, first, go to Pytho; ask
For the oracles, if I declared them truly;
Next, if you can detect me in the act
Of any conjuration with the seer,
Then, by a double vote, not one alone,   115
Mine and your own, take me, and take my life;
But do not, on a dubious argument,
Charge me beside the facts. For just it is not,
To hold bad men for good, good men for bad,
To no good end; nay, 'twere all one to me   120
To throw away a friend, a worthy one,
And one's own life, which most of all one values.
Ah well; in time, you will see these things plainly;
For time alone shews a man's honesty,
But in one day you may discern his guilt.   125

1 SENATOR: His words sound fair—to one who fears to fall;
For swift in counsel is unsafe, my liege.

OEDIPUS: When he who plots against me in the dark
Comes swiftly on, I must be swift in turn.
If I stay quiet, his ends will have been gained,   130
And mine all missed.

CREON: What is it that you want?
To expel me from the country?

OEDIPUS: Not at all.
Your death I purpose, not your banishment.   135

CREON: Not without shewing, first, what a thing is jealousy!

OEDIPUS: You talk like one who will not yield, nor heed.

CREON: Because I see you mean injuriously.

OEDIPUS: Not to myself!

CREON: No more you ought to me!   140

OEDIPUS: You are a traitor!

CREON: What if you are no judge?

OEDIPUS: I must be ruler.
CREON: Not if you rule badly.
OEDIPUS: City, my city!   145
CREON: The city is mine too,
    And not yours only.
1 SENATOR: Good my lords, have done,
    Here is Jocasta; in good time, I see her
    Come to you from the palace; with her aid   150
    'Twere meet to appease your present difference.

Enter JOCASTA

JOCASTA: Unhappy men, what was it made you raise
    This senseless broil of words? Are you not both
    Ashamed of stirring private grievances,
    The land being thus afflicted? Get you in—   155
    And, Creon, do you go home; push not mere nothing
    On to some terrible calamity!
CREON: Sister, your husband Oedipus thinks fit
    To treat me villainously; choosing for me
    Of two bad things, one; to expatriate me,   160
    Or seize and kill me.
OEDIPUS: I admit it, wife;
    For I have found him out in an offence
    Against my person, joined with treachery.
CREON: So may I never thrive, but perish, banned   165
    Of Heaven, if I have done a thing to you
    Of what you charge against me!
JOCASTA: Oedipus!
    O in Heavens name believe it! Above all
    Revere this oath in heaven; secondly   170
    Myself, and these, who stand before you here.
1 SENATOR: Hear her, my king! With wisdom and goodwill I pray you hear!
OEDIPUS: What would you have me grant?
1 SENATOR: Respect his word; no bauble, heretofore;
    And by this oath made weighty.   175
OEDIPUS: Do you know
    For what you ask?
1 SENATOR: I do.
OEDIPUS: Say what you mean, then!
1 SENATOR: That you expel not, ever, with disgrace,   180
    The friend, who has abjured it, on a charge
    Void of clear proof.

OEDIPUS: Now, understand it well;
    Seek this, you seek my death or exile!
1 SENATOR: Nay,   185
    By the Sun-god, first of all Gods in heaven!
    So may I perish, to the uttermost,
    Cut off from Heaven, without the help of men,
    If I have such a thought! But the land's waste
    Will break my heart with grief—and that this woe,   190
    Your strife, is added to its former woe.
OEDIPUS: Well, let him go, though I get slain outright,
    Or thrust by force, dishonoured, from the land;
    Your voice, not his, makes me compassionate,
    Pleading for pity; he, where'er he be,   195
    Shall have my hatred.
CREON: You display your spleen
    In yielding; but, when your wrath passes bound,
    Are formidable! Tempers such as yours
    Most grievous are to their own selves to bear,   200
    Not without justice.
OEDIPUS: Leave me; get you gone!
CREON: I go; you know me not; these know me honest.

                                                    [*Exit.*

1 SENATOR: Lady, what hinders you from taking him
    Into the house?   205
JOCASTA: I would know how this happened.
1 SENATOR: A blind surmise arose, out of mere babble;
    But even what is unjust inflicts a sting.
JOCASTA: On part of both?
1 SENATOR: Yes truly.   210
JOCASTA: And what was said?
1 SENATOR: Enough it seems, enough it seems to me,
    Under the former trouble of the land,
    To leave this where it lies.
OEDIPUS: Do you perceive   215
    How far you are carried—a well-meaning man!
    Slurring my anger thus, and blunting it?
1 SENATOR: I said it, O my king, not once alone—
    But be assured, I should have shewn myself
    Robbed of my wits, useless for work of wit,   220
    Renouncing thee! who didst impel the sails
    Of my dear land, baffled mid straits, right onward,

And it may be, wilt waft her safely now!
JOCASTA: For Heaven's sake tell me too, my lord, what was it
    Caused you so deep an anger?   225
OEDIPUS: I will tell you;
    For I respect you, lady, more than these;
    'Twas Creon—at plots which he has laid for me.
JOCASTA: If you will charge the quarrel in plain terms,
    Why speak!   230
OEDIPUS: He says that I am Laius' slayer.
JOCASTA: Of his own knowledge, or on hearsay?
OEDIPUS: Nay,
    But by citation of a knavish seer;
    As for himself, he keeps his words blame-free.   235
JOCASTA: Now set you free from thought of that you talk of;
    Listen and learn, nothing in human life
    Turns on the soothsayer's art. Tokens of this
    I'll show you in few words. To Laius once
    There came an oracle, I do not say   240
    From Phoebus' self, but from his ministers,
    That so it should befall, that he should die
    By a son's hands, whom he should have by me.
    And him—the story goes—robbers abroad
    Have murdered, at a place where three roads meet;   245
    While from our son's birth not three days went by
    Before, with ankles pinned, he cast him out,
    By hands of others, on a pathless moor.
    And so Apollo did not bring about
    That he should be his father's murderer;   250
    Nor yet that Laius should endure the stroke
    At his son's hands, of which he was afraid.
    This is what came of soothsayers' oracles;
    Whereof take thou no heed. That which we lack,
    If a God seek, himself will soon reveal.   255
OEDIPUS: What perturbation and perplexity
    Take hold upon me, woman, hearing you!
JOCASTA: What stress of trouble is on you, that you say so?
OEDIPUS: I thought I heard you say Laius was slain
    Where three roads meet!   260
JOCASTA: Yes, so the rumour ran,
    And so runs still.
OEDIPUS: And where might be the spot
    Where this befell?

JOCASTA: Phocis the land is named;   265
    There are two separate roads converge in one
    From Daulia and Delphi.
OEDIPUS: And what time
    Has passed since then?
JOCASTA: It was but just before   270
    You were installed as ruler of the land,
    The tidings reached the city.
OEDIPUS: God of Heaven!
    What would st thou do unto me!
JOCASTA: Oedipus,   275
    What is it on your mind?
OEDIPUS: Ask me not yet.
    But Laius—say, what was he like? what prime
    Of youth had he attained to?
JOCASTA: He was tall;   280
    The first white flowers had blossomed in his hair;
    His figure was not much unlike your own.
OEDIPUS: Me miserable! It seems I have but now
    Proffered myself to a tremendous curse
    Not knowing!   285
JOCASTA: How say you? I tremble, O my lord,
    To gaze upon you!
OEDIPUS: I am sore afraid
    The prophet was not blind; but you will make
    More certain, if you answer one thing more.   290
JOCASTA: Indeed I tremble; but the thing you ask
    I'll answer, when I know it.
OEDIPUS: Was he going
    Poorly attended, or with many spears
    About him, like a prince?   295
JOCASTA: But five in all;
    One was a herald; and one carriage held
    Laius himself,
OEDIPUS: O, it is plain already!
    Woman, who was it told this tale to you?   300
JOCASTA: A servant, who alone came safe away.
OEDIPUS: Is he perchance now present, in the house?
JOCASTA: Why no; for after he was come from thence,
    And saw you governing, and Laius dead,
    He came and touched my hand, and begged of me   305
    To send him to the fields and sheep-meadows,

So he might be as far as possible
From eyesight of the townsmen; and I sent him;
For he was worthy, for a slave, to obtain
Even greater favours.   310
OEDIPUS: Could we have him back
     Quickly?
JOCASTA: We could. But why this order?
OEDIPUS: Wife,
     I fear me I have spoken far too much;   315
     Wherefore I wish to see him.
JOCASTA: He shall come!
     But I am worthy, in my turn, to know
     What weighs so heavily upon you, Sir?
OEDIPUS: And you shall know; since I have passed so far   320
     The bounds of apprehension. For to whom
     Could I impart, passing through such a need,
     Greater in place—if that were all—than you?
     —I am the son of Polybus of Corinth,
     And of a Dorian mother, Merope.   325
     And I was counted most preëminent
     Among the townsmen there; up to the time
     A circumstance befell me, of this fashion—
     Worthy of wonder, though of my concern
     Unworthy. At the board a drunken fellow   330
     Over his cups called me a changeling;
     And I, being indignant—all that day
     Hardly refrained—but on the morrow went
     And taxed my parents with it to their face;
     Who took the scandal grievously, of him   335
     Who launched the story. Well, with what they said
     I was content; and yet the thing still galled me;
     For it spread far. So without cognizance
     Of sire or mother I set out to go
     To Pytho.[12] Phoebus sent me of my quest   340
     Bootless away; but other terrible
     And strange and lamentable things revealed,
     Saying I should wed my mother, and produce
     A race intolerable for men to see,
     And be my natural father's murderer.   345
     When I heard that, measuring where Corinth stands

---

12 The Pythian oracle at Delphi.

Even thereafter by the stars alone,
Where I might never think to see fulfilled
The scandals of ill prophecies of me,
I fled, an exile. As I journeyed on,   350
I found myself upon the self-same spot
Where, you say, this king perished. In your ears,
Wife, I will tell the whole. When in my travels
I was come near this place where three roads meet,
There met me a herald, and a man that rode   355
In a colt-carriage, as you tell of him,
And from the track the leader, by main force,
And the old man himself, would thrust me. I,
Being enraged, strike Kim who jostled me—
The driver—and the old man, when he saw it,   360
Watching as I was passing, from the carf
With his goad's fork smote me upon the head.
He paid, though! duly I say not; but in brief,
Smitten by the staff in this right hand of mine,
Out of the middle of the carriage straight   365
He rolls down headlong; and I slay them all!
But if there be a semblance to connect
This nameless man with Laius, who is now
More miserable than I am? Who on earth
Could have been born with more of hate from heaven?   370
Whom never citizen or stranger may
Receive into their dwellings, or accost,
But must thrust out of doors; and 'tis no other
Laid all these curses on myself, than I!
Yea, with embraces of the arms whereby   375
He perished, I pollute my victim's bed!
Am I not vile? Am I not all unclean?
If I must fly, and flying, never can
See my own folk, or on my native land
Set foot, or else must with my mother wed,   380
And slay my father Polybus, who begat
And bred me? Would he not speak truly of me
Who judged these things sent by some barbarous Power?
Never, you sacred majesties of Heaven,
Never may I behold that day; but pass   385
Out of men's sight, ere I shall see myself
Touched by the stain of such a destiny!
1 SENATOR: My liege, these things affect us grievously;

Still, dll you hear his story who was by,
 Do not lose hope!   390
OEDIPUS: Yea, so much hope is left,
 Merely to wait for him, the herdsman.
JOCASTA: Well,
 Suppose him here, what do you want of him?
OEDIPUS: I'll tell you; if he should be found to say   395
 Just what you said, I shall be clear from harm.
JOCASTA: What did you hear me say, that did not tally?
OEDIPUS: You were just telling me that he made mention
 Of "robbers"—"men"—as Laius' murderers.
 Now if he shall affirm their number still,
 I did not slay him. One cannot be the same   400
 As many. But if he shall speak of one—
 One only, it is evident this deed
 Already will have been brought home to me.
JOCASTA: But be assured, that was the word, quite plainly!   405
 And now he cannot blot it out again.
 Not I alone, but the whole city heard it.
 Then, even if he shift from his first tale,
 Not so, my lord, will he at all explain
 The death of Laius, as it should have been,   410
 Whom Loxias declared my son must slay!
 And after all, the poor thing never killed him,
 But died itseif before! so that henceforth
 I do not mean to look to left or right
 For fear of soothsaying!   415
OEDIPUS: You are well advised,
 Still, send and fetch the labourer; do not miss it.
JOCASTA: I will send quickly. Now let us go within.
 I would do nothing that displeases you.

[Exeunt OEDIPUS *and* JOCASTA.

Chorus.

I. 1.

 Let it be mine to keep
The holy purity of word and deed
 Foreguided all by mandates from on high
 Born in the ethereal region of the sky,
Their only sire Olympus; them nor seed   5

Of mortal man brought forth, nor Lethe cold
     Shall ever lay to sleep;
In them Deity is great, and grows not old.

I. 2.

     Pride is the germ of kings;
Pride, when puffed up, vainly, with many things
    Unseasonable, unfitting, mounts the wall,
    Only to hurry to that fatal fall,
Where feet are vain to serve her. But the task   5
Propitious to the city GOD I ask
     Never to take away!
GOD I will never cease to hold my stay.

II. 1.

     But if any man proceed
     Insolently in word or deed,
     Without fear of right, or care
     For the seats where Virtues are,
     Him, for his ill-omened pride,   5
     Let an evil death betide!
If honestly his gear he will not gain,
    Nor keep himself from deeds unholy,
Nor from inviolable things abstain,
     Blinded by folly.   10
In such a course, what mortal from his heart
     Dart upon dart
    Can hope to avert of indignation?
Yea, and if acts like these are held in estimation,
     Why dance we here our part?   15

II. 2.

     Never to the inviolate hearth
     At the navel of the earth,[13]
     Nor to Abae's fane, in prayer,
     Nor the Olympian, will I fare,
     If it shall not so befall   5
     Manifestly unto all.
But O our king—if thou art named aright—
    Zeus, that art Lord of all things ever,
Be this not hid from Thee, nor from Thy might

---

13 The oracle at Delphi.

Which endeth never.   10
For now already men invalidate
    The dooms of Fate
  Uttered for Laius, fading slowly;
Apollo's name and rites are nowhere now kept holy;
    Worship is out of date.   15

                                  [*Enter* JOCASTA, *attended.*

JOCASTA: Lords of the land, it came into my heart
  To approach the temples of the Deities,
  Taking in hand these garlands, and this incense;
  For Oedipus lets his mind float too light
  Upon the eddies of all kinds of grief;   20
  Nor will he, like a man of soberness,
  Measure the new by knowledge of the old,
  But is at mercy of whoever speaks,
  If he but speak the language of despair.
  I can do nothing by exhorting him.   25
  Wherefore, Lycean Phoebus, unto thee—
  For thou art very near us—I am come.
  Bringing these offerings, a petitioner
  That thou afford us fair deliverance;
  Since now we are all frighted, seeing him—   30
  The vessel's pilot, as 'twere—panic-stricken.

Enter a Messenger.

MESSENGER: Sirs, might I learn of you, where is the palace
  Of Oedipus the King? or rather, where
  He is himself, if you know, tell me.
1 SENATOR: Stranger,   35
  This is his dwelling, and he is within;
  This lady is his children's mother, too.
MESSENGER: A blessing ever be on hers and her,
  Who is, in such a perfect sort, his wife!
JOCASTA: The like be with you too, as you deserve,   40
  Sir, for your compliment. But say what end
  You come for, and what news you wish to tell.
MESSENGER: Good to the house, and to your husband, lady.
JOCASTA: Of what sort? and from whom come you?
MESSENGER: From Corinth.   45
  In that which I am now about to say
  May you find pleasure! and why not? And yet
  Perhaps you may be sorry.

JOCASTA: But what is it? How can it carry such ambiguous force?
MESSENGER: The dwellers in the land of Isthmia,   50
    As was there said, intend to appoint him king.
JOCASTA: What! Is not Polybus, the old prince, still reigning?
MESSENGER: No, truly; he is Death's subject, in the grave.
JOCASTA: How say you, father? Is Polybus no more?
MESSENGER: I stake my life upon it, if I lie!   55
JOCASTA: Run, girl, and tell your master instantly.

[Exit an attendant.

    O prophecies of Gods, where are you now!
    Oedipus fled, long since, from this man's presence,
    Fearing to kill him; and now he has died
    A natural death, not by his means at all!   60

Enter OEDIPUS.

OEDIPUS: O my most dear Jocasta, wife of mine,
    Why did you fetch me hither from the house?
JOCASTA: Hear this man speak! Listen and mark, to what
    The dark responses of the God are come!
OEDIPUS: And who is this? What says he?   65
JOCASTA: He's from Corinth,
    To tell us that your father Polybus
    Lives no more, but is dead!
OEDIPUS: What say you, sir?
    Tell your own tale yourself.   70
MESSENGER: If first of all
    I must deliver this for certainty,
    Know well, that he has gone the way of mortals.
OEDIPUS: Was it by treason, or some chance disease?
MESSENGER: A little shock prostrates an aged frame!   75
OEDIPUS: Sickness, you mean, was my poor father's end?
MESSENGER: Yes, and old age; his term of life was full.
OEDIPUS: Heigh ho! Why, wife! why should a man regard
    The oracular hearth of Pytho, or the birds
    Cawing above us, by whose canons I   80
    Was to have slain my father? He is dead,
    And buried out of sight; and here am I,
    Laying no finger to the instrument,
    (Unless, indeed, he pined for want of me,
    And so, I killed him!) Well, Polybus is gone;   85
    And with him all those oracles of ours
    Bundled to Hades, for old songs, together!

JOCASTA: Did I not say so all along?

OEDIPUS: You did;
  But I was led astray by fear.   90

JOCASTA: Well, now
  Let none of these predictions any more
  Weigh on your mind!

OEDIPUS: And how can I help dreading
  My mother's bed?   95

JOCASTA: But why should men be fearful,
  O'er whom Fortune is mistress, and foreknowledge
  Of nothing sure? Best take life easily,
  As a man may. For that maternal wedding,
  Have you no fear; for many men ere now   100
  Have dreamed as much; but he who by such dreams
  Sets nothing, has the easiest life of it.

OEDIPUS: All these things would have been well said of you,
  Were not my mother living still; but now,
  She being alive, there is all need of dread;   105
  Though you say well.

JOCASTA: And yet your father's burial
  Lets in much daylight!

OEDIPUS: I acknowledge, much.
  Still, her who lives I fear.   110

MESSENGER: But at what woman
  Are you dismayed?

OEDIPUS: At Merope, old man,
  The wife of Polybus.

MESSENGER: And what of her   115
  Causes you terror?

OEDIPUS: A dark oracle,
  Stranger, from heaven.

MESSENGER: May it be put in words?
  Or is it wrong another man should know it?   120

OEDIPUS: No, not at all. Why, Loxias declared
  That I should one day marry my own mother,
  And with my own hands shed my father's blood.
  Wherefore from Corinth I have kept away
  Far, for long years; and prospered; none the less   125
  It is most sweet to see one's parents' face.

MESSENGER: And in this apprehension you became
  An emigrant from Corinth?

OEDIPUS: And, old man,
    Desiring not to be a parricide.   130
MESSENGER: Why should I not deliver you, my liege—
    Since my intent in coming here was good—
    Out of this fear?
OEDIPUS: Indeed you would obtain
    Good guerdon from me.   135
MESSENGER: And indeed for this
    Chiefest I came, that upon your return
    I might in some sort benefit.
OEDIPUS: But I Will never go, to meet my parents there!
MESSENGER: O son, 'tis plain you know not what you do!   140
OEDIPUS: How so, old man? in Heavens name tell me!
MESSENGER: If on this account you shun the journey home!
OEDIPUS: Of course I fear lest Phoebus turn out true.
MESSENGER: Lest through your parents you incur foul stain?
OEDIPUS: Yes, father, yes; that is what always scares me.   145
MESSENGER: Now do you know you tremble, really, at nothing?
OEDIPUS: How can that be, if I was born their child?
MESSENGER: Because Polybus was nought akin to you!
OEDIPUS: What, did not Polybus beget me?
MESSENGER: No,   150
    No more than I did; just so much as I!
OEDIPUS: How, my own sire no more than—nobody?
MESSENGER: But neither he begat you, nor did I.
OEDIPUS: Then from what motive did he call me son?
Messenger: Look here; he had you as a gift from me.   155
OEDIPUS: And loved me then, so much, at second hand?
MESSENGER: Yes, his long childlessness prevailed on him.
OEDIPUS: And did you find or purchase me, to give him?
MESSENGER: I found you in Cithaeron's wooded dells.
OEDIPUS: How came you to be journeying in these parts?   160
MESSENGER: I tended flocks upon the mountains here.
OEDIPUS: You were a shepherd, and you ranged for hire?
MESSENGER: But at the same time your preserver, son!
OEDIPUS: You found me in distress? What was my trouble?
MESSENGER: Your ankle joints may witness.   165
OEDIPUS: O, why speak you
    Of that old evil?
MESSENGER: I untied you, when
    You had the soles of both your feet bored through.

OEDIPUS: A shameful sort of swaddling bands were mine.   170
MESSENGER: Such, that from them you had the name you bear.[14]
OEDIPUS: Tell me, by heaven! at sire's or mother's hand—
MESSENGER: I know not: he who gave you knows of that
    Better than I.
OEDIPUS: You got me from another?   175
    You did not find me?
MESSENGER: No, another shepherd
    gave you to me.
OEDIPUS: Who was he? are you able
    To point him out?   180
MESSENGER: They said that he was one
    Of those who followed Laius, whom you know.
OEDIPUS: Him who was once the monarch of this land?
MESSENGER: Precisely! This man was his herdsman.
OEDIPUS: Now is this man still alive for me to see?   185
MESSENGER: You must know best, the people of the place.
OEDIPUS: Is any here among you bystanders,
    Who knows the herdsman whom he tells us of,
    From seeing him, either in the fields or here?
    Speak! it were time that this had been cleared up.   190
1 SENATOR: I think he is no other than that peasant
    Whom you were taking pains to find, before;
    But she could say as well as any one—
    Jocasta.
OEDIPUS: Lady, you remember him   195
    Whose coming we were wishing for but now;
    Does he mean him?
JOCASTA: Why ask who 'twas he spoke of?
    Nay, never mind—never remember it—
    'Twas idly spoken!,   200
OEDIPUS: Nay, it cannot be
    That having sugh a clue I should refuse
    To solve the mystery of my parentage!
JOCASTA: For Heaven's sake, if you care for your own life,
    Don't seek it! I am sick, and that's enough!   205
OEDIPUS: Courage! At least, if I be thrice a slave,
    Born so three-deep, it cannot injure you!

---

14 By a folk etymology, the name Oedipus is taken to mean "swollen feet."

JOCASTA: But I beseech you, hearken! Do not do it!

OEDIPUS: I will not hearken—not to know the whole.

JOCASTA: I mean well; and I tell you for the best!   210

OEDIPUS: What you call best is an old sore of mine.

JOCASTA: Wretch, what thou art O might'st thou never know!

OEDIPUS: Will some one go and fetch the herdsman hither?
    She is welcome to her gilded lineage!

JOCASTA: O   215
    Woe, woe, unhappy! This is all I have
    To say to thee, and no word more, for ever!

                              [Exit.

1 SENATOR: Why has the woman vanished, Oedipus,
    Driven so wild with grief? I am afraid
    Out of her silence will break forth some trouble.   220

OEDIPUS: Break out what will, I shall not hesitate,
    Low though it be, to trace the source of me.
    But she, perhaps, being, as a woman, proud,
    Of my unfit extraction is ashamed.
    —I deem myself the child of Fortune! I   225
    Shall not be shamed of her, who favours me;
    Seeing I have her for mother; and for kin
    The limitary Moons, that found me small,
    That fashioned me for great! Parented thus,
    How could I ever in the issue prove   230
    Other—that I should leave my birth unknown?

Chorus

1.

    If I am a true seer,
    My mind from error clear,
Tomorrow's moon shall not pass over us,
    Ere, O Cithaeron, we
    Shall magnify in thee   5
The land, the lap, the womb of Oedipus;
And we shall hymn thy praises, for good things
Of thy bestowing, done unto our kings.
Yea, Phoebus, if thou wilt, amen, so might it be!

2.

    Who bare thee? Which, O child,
    Over the mountain-wild
Sought to by Pan of the immortal Maids?

Or Loxias—was he
    The sire who fathered thee?   5
For dear to him are all the upland glades.
Was it Cyllene's lord[15] acquired a son,
    Or Bacchus, dweller on the heights, from one
Of those he liefest loves, Oreads[16] of Helicon?

Enter Attendants with an Old Man, a Shepherd.

OEDIPUS: If I may guess, who never met with him,   10
    I think I see that herdsman, Senators,
    We have long been seeking; for his ripe old age
    Harmoniously accords with this man's measure;
    Besides, I recognize the men who bring him
    As of my household; but in certainty   15
    You can perhaps exceed me, who beheld
    The herdsman formerly.

1 SENATOR: Why, to be sure,
    I recognize him; for he was a man
    Trusty as any Laius ever had   20
    About his pastures.

OEDIPUS: You I ask the first,
    The Corinthian stranger; do you speak of him?

MESSENGER: Yes, him you see;

OEDIPUS: Sirrah, old man, look here;   25
    Answer my questions. Were you Laiu's man?

OLD MAN: Truly his thrall; not bought, but bred at home.

OEDIPUS: Minding what work, or in what character?

OLD MAN: Most of my time I went after the flocks.

OEDIPUS: In what directions, chiefly, were your folds?   30

OLD MAN: There was Cithaeron; and a bit near by.

OEDIPUS: Do you know this man, then? Did you see him there?

OLD MAN: Him? After what? What man do you mean?

OEDIPUS: This fellow
    Here present; did you ever meet with him?   35

OLD MAN: Not so to say off-hand, from memory.

MESSENGER: And that's no wonder, sir; but beyond doubt
    I will remind him, though he has forgotten,
    I am quite sure he knows, once on a time,
    When in the bit about Cithaeron there—   40

---

15 Hermes.
16 Mountain nymphs.

He with two flocks together, I with one—
I was his neighbour for three whole half years
From spring-tide onward to the Bear-ward's[17] day;
And with the winter to my folds I drove,
And he to Laius' stables. Are these facts,   45
Or are they not—what I am saying?

OLD MAN: Yes,
You speak the truth; but it was long ago.

MESSENGER: Come, say now, don't you mind that you then gave me
A baby boy to bring up for my own?   50

OLD MAN: What do you mean? Why do you ask it me?

MESSENGER: This is the man, good fellow; who was then
A youngling!

OLD MAN: Out upon you! Hold your peace!

OEDIPUS: Nay, old man, do not chide him; for your words   55
Deserve a chiding rather than his own!

OLD MAN: O best of masters, what is my offence?

OEDIPUS: Not telling of that boy he asks about.

OLD MAN: He says he knows not what! He is all astray!

OEDIPUS: You will not speak of grace—you shall perforce!   60

OLD MAN: Do not for God's sake harm me, an old man!

OEDIPUS: Quick, some one, twist his hands behind him!

OLD MAN: Wretch,
What have I done? What do you want to know?

OEDIPUS: Did you give him that boy he asks about?   65

OLD MAN: I gave it him. Would I had died that day!

OEDIPUS: Tell the whole truth, or you will come to it!

OLD MAN: I am undone far more, though, if I speak!

OEDIPUS: The man is trifling with us, I believe.

OLD MAN: No, no; I said I gave it, long ago!   70

OEDIPUS: Where did you get it? At home, or from some other?

OLD MAN: It was not mine; another gave it me.

OEDIPUS: Which of these citizens? and from what roof?

OLD MAN: Don't, master, for God's sake, don't ask me more!

OEDIPUS: You are a dead man, if I speak again!   75

OLD MAN: Then—'twas a child—of Laius' household.

OEDIPUS: What,
Slave-born? or one of his own family?

OLD MAN: O, I am at the horror, now, to speak!

OEDIPUS: And I to hear. But I must hear—no less.   80

---

17 The constellation Bootes.

OLD MAN: Truly it was called his son; but she within,
  Your lady, could best tell you how it was.

OEDIPUS: Did she then give it you?

OLD MAN: My lord, even so.

OEDIPUS: For what?   85

OLD MAN: For me to make away with it.

OEDIPUS: Herself the mother? miserable!

OLD MAN: In dread
  Of evil prophecies—

OEDIPUS: What prophecies?   90

OLD MAN: That he should kill his parents, it was said.

OEDIPUS: How came you then to give it to this old man?

OLD MAN: For pity, O my master! thinking he
  Would carry it away to other soil,
  From whence he came; but he to the worst of harms   95
  Saved it! for if thou art the man he says,
  Sure thou wast born destined to misery!

OEDIPUS: Woe! woe! It is all plain, indeed! O Light,
  This be the last time I shall gaze on thee,
  Who am revealed to have been born of those   100
  Of whom I ought not—to have wedded whom
  I ought not—and slain whom I might not slay!

                                                              [*Exit.*

Chorus.

I. 1.

O generations of mankind!
    How do I find
    Your lives nought worth at all!
For who is he—what state
Is there, more fortunate   5
Than only to seem great,
    And then, to fall?
I having thee for pattern, and thy lot—
Thine, O poor Oedipus—I envy not
    Aught in mortality;   10
      For this is he

I. 2.

Who, shooting far beyond the rest,
    Won wealth all-blest,
    Slaying, Zeus, thy monster-maid,

Crook-taloned, boding; and
Who did arise and stand 5
Betwixt death and our land,
 A tower of aid;
Yea for this cause thou hast been named our king,
And honoured in the highest, governing
  The city of Thebae great 10
   In royal state.

II. 1.

And now, who lives more utterly undone?
 Who with sad woes, who with mischances rude
  Stands closer yoked by life's vicissitude?
  O honoured head of Oedipus, for whom
  Within the same wide haven there was room 5
  To come—child, to the birth—
   Sire, to the nuptial bower,
 How could the furrows of thy parent earth—
How could they suffer thee, O hapless one,
  In silence, to this hour? 10

II. 2.

Time found thee out—Time who sees everything—
 Unwittingly guilty; and arraigns thee now
  Consort ill-sorted, unto whom are bred
  Sons of thy getting, in thine own birth-bed.
   O scion of Laius' race, 5
   Would I had never never seen thy face!
 For I lament, even as from lips that sing
 Pouring a dirge; yet verily it was thou
  Gav'st me to rise
 And breathe again, and close my watching eyes. 10

Enter a second MESSENGER.

2 MESSENGER: O you most honoured ever of this land,
  What deeds have you to hear, what sights to see,
  What sorrow to endure, if you still cherish
  The house of Labdacus with loyalty?
  For Ister[18] I suppose or Phasis'[19] wave 15
  Never could purge this dwelling from the ills

---

18 The Danube.
19 A river emptying into the Black Sea.

It covers—or shall instantly reveal,
Invited, not inflicted; of all wounds,
Those that seem wilful are the worst to bear.
1 SENATOR: There was no lack, in what we knew before, 20
Of lamentable; what have you more to say?
2 MESSENGER: The speediest of all tales to hear and tell;
The illustrious Jocasta is no more.
1 SENATOR: Unhappy woman! From what cause?
2 MESSENGER: Self-slain. 25
Of what befell the saddest part is spared;
For you were not a witness. None the less
So far as I can tell it you shall hear
Her miserable story. When she passed
So frantically inside the vestibule, 30
She went straight onward to the bed-chamber,
With both her hands tearing her hair; the doors
She dashed to as she entered, crying out
On Laius, long since dead, calling to mind
His fore-begotten offspring, by whose hands 35
He, she said, died, and left to his own seed
Its mother's most unnatural bearing-bed.
Nor did she not bewail that nuptial-couch
Where she brought forth, unhappy, brood on brood,
Spouse to her spouse, and children to her child. 40
And then—I know no further how she perished;
For Oedipus brake in, crying aloud;
For whom it was impossible to watch
The ending of her misery; but on him
We gazed, as he went raging all about, 45
Beseeching us to furnish him a sword
And say where he could find his wife—no wife,
Rather the mother-soil both of himself
And children; and, as he raved thus, some Power
Shews him—at least, none of us present did. 50
Then, shouting loud, he sprang upon the doors
As following some guide, and burst the bars
Out of their sockets, and alights within.
There we beheld his wife hanging, entwined
In a twined noose. He seeing her, with a groan 55
Looses the halter; then, when on the ground
Lay the poor wretch, dreadful it was to see
What followed; snatching from her dress gold pins

Wherewith she was adorned, he lifted them,
And smote the nerves of his own eyeballs, saying   60
Something like this—that they should see no more
Evils like those he had endured or wrought;
Darkling, thereafter, let them gaze on forms
He might not see, and fail to recognize
The faces he desired! Chanting this burden,   65
Not once, but many times, he raised his hand
And stabbed his eyes; so that from both of them
The blood ran down his face, not drop by drop,
But all at once, in a dark shower of gore.
—These are the ills that from a two-fold source,   70
Not one alone, but in both wife and spouse,
Mingled together, have burst forth at once.
Their former pristine happiness indeed
Was happiness before; but in this hour
Shame—lamentation—Atè[20]—death—of all   75
That has a name of evil, nought's away!
1 SENATOR: And does he stand in any respite now
   Of misery, poor soul?
2 MESSENGER: He calls aloud
   For some one to undo the bolts, and shew   80
   To all the Cadmeans him, his father's slayer—
   His mother's—uttering words unhallowed—words
   I may not speak; that he will cast himself
   Forth of the land, abide no more at home
   Under the curse of his own cursing. Nay,   85
   But he lacks force, and guidance; for his sickness
   Is more than man can bear. See for yourself;
   For these gates open, and you will straight behold
   A sight—such as even he that loathes must pity!

Enter OEDIPUS *blind.*
                              Chorus.
   O sorrow, lamentable for eyes to see!
   Sorest of all past ills encountering me!
   What frenzy, O wretch, is this, that came on thee?

   What Deity was it that with a leap so great—
   Farther than farthest—sprang on thy sad fate?   5
   Woe is me, woe is me for thee—unfortunate!

---

20 Doom caused by guilt and ignorance.

Fain would I gaze at thee, would ask thee much,
Many things learn of thee, wert thou not such
As I may not even behold, as I shudder to touch.

OEDIPUS: Me miserable! Whither must I go?   10
Ah whither flits my voice, borne to and fro?
Thou Power unseen, how hast thou brought me low!

1 SENATOR: To ills, intolerable to hear or see.

OEDIPUS: Thou horror of thick darkness overspread,
Thou shadow of unutterable dread   15
Not to be stemmed or stayed, fallen on my head—
Woe's me once more! How crowd upon my heart
Stings of these wounds, and memories of woe!

1 SENATOR: No marvel if thou bear a double smart
And writhe, so stricken, with a two-fold throe!   20

OEDIPUS: Still art thou near me—ready still to tend
And to endure me, faithful to the end,
Blind as I am, with kindness, O my friend!
For strange thou art not; but full well I know
That voice of thine, all darkling though I be.   25

1 SENATOR: Rash man, how could'st thou bear to outrage so
Thine eyes? What Power was it, that wrought on thee?

OEDIPUS: Apollo, Apollo fulfils,
O friends, my measure of ills—
Fills my measure of woe;   30
Author was none, but I,
None other, of the blow;
For why was I to see,
When to descry
No sight on earth could have a charm for me?   35

1 SENATOR: It was even as thou sayest.

OEDIPUS: What was there left for sight?
What, that could give delight?
Or whose address,
O friends, could I still hear with happiness?   40
Lead me to exile straight;

Lead me, O my friends, the worst
Of murderers, of mortals most accurst,
Yea and to Gods chief object of their hate.

1 SENATOR: Of cunning hapless, as of hapless fate,   45
I would that I had never known thy name!

OEDIPUS: May he perish, whoe'er 'twas drew me
Out of the cruel gyve
That bound my feet, on the lea!
He who saved me alive,   50
Who rescued me from fate,
Shewing no kindness to me!
Sorrow so great,
Had I died then, had spared both mine and me.

1 SENATOR: Fain were I too it had been so.   55

OEDIPUS: Not then had I become
My father's murderer,
Nor wedded her I have my being from:
Whom now no God will bless,
Child of incestuousness   60
In her that bare me, being the spouse of her;
Yea if aught ill worse than all ill be there,
That Oedipus must bear.

1 SENATOR: I know not how to say thou hast done well;
For it were better for thee now to die,   65
Than to live on in blindness.

OEDIPUS: Tell me not—
Give me no counsel now, that what is done
Has not been done thus best. I know not how
With seeing eyes I could have looked upon   70
My father—coming to the under-world,
Or my poor mother, when against them both
I have sinned sins, worse than a halter's meed.
Or do you think that children were a sight
Delectable for me to gaze at, born   75
As they were born? Never with eyes of mine!
No, nor the city, nor the citadel,
Nor consecrated shrines of deities,

From which, to my most utter misery,
I, of all other men in Thebes the man   80
Most bravely nurtured, cut myself away,
And of my own mouth dictated to all
To thrust out me, the impious—me, declared
Abominable of Heaven, and Laius' son.
Was I, who in myself made evident   85
So dark a stain, with unaverted eyes
To look on these? That least of all! Nay rather,
If there were any way to choke the fount
Of hearing, through my ears, I would have tried
To seal up all this miserable frame   90
And live blind, deaf to all things; sweet it were
To dwell in fancy, out of reach of pain.
—Cithaeron! wherefore didst thou harbour me!
Why not at once have slain me? Never then
Had I displayed before the face of men   95
Who and from whom I am! O Polybus,
And Corinth, and the old paternal roof
I once called mine, with what thin film of honour,
Corruption over-skinned, you fostered me,
Found ill myself, and from ill parents, now!   100
O you, the three roads, and the lonely brake,
The copse, and pass at the divided way,
Which at my hands drank blood that was my own—
My father's—do you keep in memory
What in your sight I did, and how again   105
I wrought, when I came hither? Wedlock, wedlock,
You gave me being, you raised up seed again
To the same lineage, and exhibited
In one incestuous flesh son—brother—sire,
Bride, wife and mother; and all ghastliest deeds   110
Wrought among men! But O, ill done, ill worded!
In Heaven's name hide me with all speed away,
Or slay me, or send adrift upon some sea
Where you may look on me no longer! Come,
Touch, if you will, a miserable man;   115
Pray you, fear nothing; for my misery
No mortal but myself can underbear.

1 SENATOR: Creon is at hand; he is the man you need,
       Who must decide and do; being, after you,
       The sole protector left us, for the land.   120
OEDIPUS: Ah Heaven, what language shall I hold to him?
       What rightful credit will appear in me?
       For I have been found wholly in the wrong
       In all that passed between us heretofore!

Enter CREON.
CREON: Not as a mocker come I, Oedipus,   125
       Nor to reproach for any former pain.
       But you—even if you reverence no more
       Children of men,—at least so far revere
       The royal Sun-god's all-sustaining fire,
       Not to parade, thus flagrant, such a sore   130
       As neither earth nor day can tolerate,
       Nor dew from Heaven! Take him in instantly!
       That kindred only should behold and hear
       The griefs of kin, fits best with decency.
OEDIPUS: In Heaven's name, seeing that you transported me   135
       Beyond all hope, coming, the first of men,
       To me the last of men, grant me one boon!
       'Tis for your good, not for my own, I say it.
CREON: What is it that you crave so eagerly?
OEDIPUS: Out of this country cast me with all speed,   140
       Where I may pass without accost of men.
CREON: So had I done, be sure, had I not wished
       To learn our duty, first, at the God's mouth.
OEDIPUS: Surely his oracle was all made plain,
       Me, the profane, the parricide, to slay!   145
CREON: So was it said; but in our present need
       'Tis better to enquire what we must do.
OEDIPUS: Will ye seek answer for a wretch like me?
CREON: Even you might trust what the God answers, now.
OEDIPUS: Ay, and I charge thee, and will beg of thee,   150
       order thyself such burial as thou wilt,
       For her who lies within; seeing it is meet
       Thou do so, for thine own. But never more
       Be this my native town burdened with me
       For living inmate; rather suffer me   155
       To haunt the mountains—where my mountain is,
       Cithaeron, which my mother and my sire,

Living, appointed for my sepulchre,
That as they meant, my slayers, I may expire.
Howbeit this much I know, neither disease   160
Nor aught beside can kill me; never else
Had I been rescued from the brink of death,
But for some dire calamity. Ah well,
Let our own fate wag onward as it may;
And for my sons, Creon, take thou no care   165
Upon thee; they are men, so that they never
Can lack the means to live, where'er they be;
But my two girls, wretched and pitiable,
For whose repast was never board of mine
Ordered apart, without me, but in all   170
That I partook they always shared with me,
Take care of them; and let me, above all else,
Touch them with hands, and weep away my troubles!
Pardon, my lord; pardon, illustrious sir;
If but my hands could feel them, I might seem   175
To have them still, as when I still could see.

ANTIGONE *and* ISMENE *are brought in.*

—What do I say? In Heaven's name, do I not
Hear my two darlings, somewhere shedding tears?
And can it be that Creon, pitying me,
Sends me my dearest, my two daughters, hither?   180
Is it so indeed?
CREON: Yes, it is I vouchsafed this boon, aware
What joy you have and long have had of them.
OEDIPUS: Why then, good luck go with thee, and Providence
Be guardian to thee, better than to me,   185
In payment for their coming!—Children dear,
Where are you? Come, come hither to my arms—
To these brotherly arms—procurers that
The eyes—that were your sire's—once bright—should see
Thus! who am shewn, O children, to have been   190
Author of you—unseeing—unknowing—in
Her bed, whence I derived my being! You
I weep for; for I cannot gaze on you;
Knowing what is left of bitter in the life
Which at men's hands you needs must henceforth live. 195
For to what gatherings of the citizens
Will you resort, or to what festivals,

Whence you will not, in place of holiday,
Come home in tears? Or when you shall have grown
To years of marriage, who—ah, who will be   100
The man to abide the hazard of disgrace
Such as must be the bane, both of my sons,
And you as well? For what reproach is lacking?
Your father slew his father, and became
Father of you—by her who bare him. So   105
Will they reproach you; who will wed you then?
No one, my children; but you needs must Wither,
Barren—unwed. But thou, Menoeceus' son,
Since thou art all the father these have left them,
For we, the two that were their parents, now   110
Are both undone, do not thou suffer them
To wander, vagabond and husband-less,
Being of thy kin; nor let them fall so low
As are my fortunes; but have pity on them,
Seeing them so tender, and so desolate   115
Of all friends, but for thee. Give me thy hand,
Good sir, and promise this—To you, my girls,
If you were old enough to understand,
I should have much to say; but as it is,
This be your prayer; in some permitted place   120
That you may breathe; and have your lot in life
Happier than his, who did engender you.

CREON: Get thee in; thou hast bewailed thee enough, in reason.

OEDIPUS: Though it be bitter, I must do it.

CREON: All's good, in good season.   125

OEDIPUS: Do you know how to make me?

CREON: Say on, and I shall know.

OEDIPUS: Banish me from this country.

CREON: That must the God bestow.

OEDIPUS: But to Gods, above all men, I am a mark for hate. 130

CREON: And for that same reason you will obtain it straight.

OEDIPUS: Say you so?

CREON: Yes truly, and I mean what I say.

OEDIPUS: Lead me hence then, quickly.

CREON: Go; but let the children stay.   135

OEDIPUS: Do not take them from me!

CREON: Think not to have all at thy pleasure;
    For what thou didst attain to far outwent thy measure.

CREON, *the Children, etc. retire.* OEDIPUS *is led in.*

Chorus.

Dwellers in Thebes, behold this Oedipus,
The man who solved the riddle marvellous,
A prince of men,
Whose lot what citizen
Did not with envy see,   5
How deep the billows of calamity
    Above him roll.
        Watch therefore and regard that supreme day;
        And of no mortal say
        "That man is happy," till   10
        Vexed by no grievous ill
        He pass Life's goal.

[Exeunt omnes.]

- How does Oedipus act as a detective? What crime is it that he is trying to solve? How does he collect clues to help him learn the truth about this past event?

- When does the action of this play take place? How does Sophocles introduce historical information into the plot?

- When does Jocasta realize the truth about her situation?

- How does Oedipus learn about his true history? Describe the specific scene where this information is broken to him.

- How does Oedipus fulfill his initial promise to the town of Thebes once he has learned the truth about his own identity?

Experiencing Literature through Writing

1. Select a single work from this chapter. As you consider what happened in that text, explain how the progress of events is interesting. As you write about the plot, don't just summarize. Begin by describing a specific incident that seems surprising or unusual within the story. Explain why it stands out in this way. Then think about whether the surrounding events prepare us adequately for this aspect of the plot. Most important, explain why this aspect of the plot is significant to our understanding of the larger text.

2. The readings in this chapter focus on the role of detection. Discuss a single work from the chapter. Explore the ways in which that particular

text is a detective story. How does this larger label help us give significance to the work in question?

3. The readings in this chapter appear under the title "Detective Work." Pick one work from this chapter and discuss the ways in which it is inappropriate to label it as a detective story. Explain why it is interesting to make this distinction.

4. Michael Chabon points to the ingenious plotting strategies that Arthur Conan Doyle uses in the Sherlock Holmes stories. His analysis of the stories focuses narrowly on the packaging of plot, about the many different layers of narration that Doyle uses to present these stories. Dr. Watson narrates, but he is often recounting a narrative that Holmes has given to him. Dr. Watson and Holmes discuss published versions of Watson's own stories, some of them stories that Doyle actually published, others that are fictional works. In the work that you are reading, what different strategies does the author use to package the plot to tell the story?

3

Character

At the end of Homer's epic *Odyssey*, Odysseus returns home to Ithaca after twenty years away. The entire narrative has been building to this moment, and once it arrives, we realize his terrible problem: Odysseus has been gone so long, will anyone recognize him? The story provides different answers to this question. His faithful dog Argos recognizes him by smell because apparently the many adventures that he has been through have not changed this essential identifying feature. Odysseus's smell is inherent to his person, but none of the humans in the story have such a fine sense of smell. Eurycleia, the woman who nursed Odysseus as a child, recognizes a scar left above his knee by an injury in a boar hunt. The woman who nursed him through this injury recognizes this distinctive physical mark. But the other characters, even his wife Penelope who has been waiting loyally for his return, cannot see that it is Odysseus without a series of tests. It's a powerful moment in the story because it captures a sense of helpless loneliness, of profound disconnection. At some level, we recognize the uncomfortable truth that none of us know for certain who other people are (how they feel or why they act as they do). That fact suggests the frightening thought that none of us really *know* other people.

It's a thought everyone confronts and almost no one fully accepts. We stubbornly seek to break from the boundaries of self and understand people around us. We observe mannerisms and vocal tones. We "put ourselves in another person's shoes." We think about how our individual experience fits larger patterns of behavior. We use our own experience and our own feelings as a checkpoint against what we see in others. All of these efforts to realize how "other people are" demand much of our imaginative intelligence; we exercise close observation, shrewd analysis, and patient reflection. Such exercise reminds us that literary experience *is* experience; to put it another way, there is no need to distinguish literary experience from "life experience." Our fascination with stories is strongly rooted in our everyday desire to know people, to understand the motives that underlie action, or to grasp the feelings that show in words and gestures. Odysseus left home when his son Telemachus was just a baby, so the boy knows his father only from the stories that others have told him. To introduce himself to his son, Odysseus has to show that his story is the same story that Telemachus has been hearing about his father his whole life. Persuading his wife that he is Odysseus is the final, and most difficult, moment in his homecoming. His physical appearance has changed in twenty years, so she cannot identify him by sight alone. The fact that he can wield Odysseus's bow is not enough to convince her of his identity. The public stories are not sufficient. He must demonstrate some intimate knowledge that only he and Penelope share.

BUILDING CHARACTER

In describing their own creative process, some writers make **character** (quite simply, people or figures in a story) a primary force. Vividly imagined characters can, in effect, speak to the writers who create them. A turn in a plot might result from an author's sense that a main character demanded that turn. Did Caroline Yip in Don Lee's "The Price of Eggs in China" (Chapter 2) leave her lover, Dean, simply because the author needed to create a fight between the two that would set up their later actions? Or was Lee compelled to let Caroline leave because the insecure Caroline he had come to know could not stay with a man she learns is a tremendously successful artist—not the moderately accomplished craftsman she had thought he was? To put it another way, did Lee's characters emerge from the story, or did the story emerge from the characters?

We would need to ask Don Lee about his writing process, but it's certainly clear that characters can come alive for authors as well as readers. Experiencing a literary text, whether we are reading it or writing it, involves a close engagement with characters outside ourselves. This experience makes our world bigger. If we do not (as readers or writers) conceive of characters as people we can know, these characters will seem artificial, unconvincing, and uninteresting.

Of course, we must also imagine situations (usually points of conflict) that define characters. Usually, those situations involve some clear point of conflict. In fact, the word **protagonist** (the main or leading character) comes from the Greek phrase for "the first one to battle." If the battle is against another character, the opponent is the **antagonist.** These words, because they capture a crucial defining tension, are in some ways more useful than terms such as *main* and *secondary character.* It's also important to remember that although a protagonist is usually the hero or heroine and the antagonist may be a villain, the terms are not synonymous because a hero or heroine may not be the central actor in a narrative. We could easily imagine a story with both a hero and a heroine, but not a story with two protagonists. **Hero** and **heroine** also introduce, in common usage, positive moral or social qualities (just as villain suggests evil or malice). *Protagonist* and *antagonist*, strictly speaking, center us on how characters function in a narrative action, not how they affirm the author's values.

Experiencing Literature through Character

Michael Chabon's highly regarded novel *The Amazing Adventures of Kavalier & Clay* gives us two vividly realized characters who need to create a character of their own. Sammy and Joe (Chabon's main characters) have a contract to produce a comic book; in the following scene, they begin, understandably enough, by trying to imagine a new superpower upon which to build a new superhero. But this line of thinking goes nowhere: Sammy and Joe get stuck on the wrong questions. Only when they change their approach to building character does their project come alive.

Michael Chabon (1963–)

from The Amazing Adventures of Kavalier & Clay (2000)

"Who is he," Joe said.

"Who is he, and what does he do?"

"He flies."

Sammy shook his head. "Superman flies."

"So ours does not?"

"I just think I'd ..."

"To be original."

"If we can. Try to do it without flying, at least. No flying, no strength of a
hundred men, no bulletproof skin."

"Okay," Joe said. The humming seemed to recede a little. "And some
others, they do what?"

"Well, Batman—"

"He flies, like a bat."

"No, he doesn't fly."

"But he is blind."

"No, he only dresses like a bat. He has no batlike qualities at all. He uses only his fists."

"That sounds dull."

"Actually, it's spooky. You'd like it."

"Maybe another animal."

"Uh, well, yeah. Okay. A hawk. Hawkman."

"Hawk, yes, okay. But that one must fly."

"Yeah, you're right. Scratch the bird family. The, uh, the Fox. The Shark."

"A swimming one."

"Maybe a swimming one. Actually, no, I know a guy works in the Chesler shop, he said they're already doing a guy who swims. For Timely."

"A lion?"

"Lion. The Lion. Lionman."

"He could be strong. He roars very loud."

"He has a super roar."

"It strikes fear."

"It breaks dishes."

"The bad guys go deaf."

They laughed. Joe stopped laughing.

"I think we have to be serious," he said.

"You're right," said Sammy. "The Lion, I don't know. Lions are lazy. How about the Tiger. Tigerman. No, no. Tigers are killers. Shit. Let's see."

They began to go through the rolls of the animal kingdom, concentrating naturally on the predators: Catman, Wolfman, the Owl, the Panther, the Black Bear. They considered the primates: the Monkey, Gorillaman, the Gibbon, the Ape, the Mandrill with his multicolored wonder ass that he used to bedazzle opponents.

"Be serious," Joe chided again.

"I'm sorry, I'm sorry. Look, forget animals. Everybody's going to be thinking of animals. In two months, I'm telling you, by the time our guy hits the stands, there's going to be guys running around dressed like every damn animal in the zoo. Birds. Bugs. Underwater guys. And I'll bet you anything there's going to be five guys who are really strong, and invulnerable, and can fly."

"If he goes as fast as the light," Joe suggested.

"Yeah, I guess it's good to be fast."

"Or if he can make a thing burn up. If he can—listen! If he can, you know. Shoot the fire, with his eyes!"

"His eyeballs would melt."

"Then with his hands. Or, yes, he turns into a fire!"

"Timely's doing that already, too. They got the fire guy and the water guy."

"He turns into *ice*. He makes the ice everywhere."

"Crushed or cubes?"

"Not good?"

Sammy shook his head. "Ice," he said. "I don't see a lot of stories in ice."

"He turns into electricity?" Joe tried. "He turns into acid?" "He turns into gravy. He turns into an enormous hat. Look, stop. Stop. Just stop."

They stopped in the middle of the sidewalk, between Sixth and Seventh avenues, and that was when Sam Clay experienced a moment of global vision, one which he would afterward come to view as the one undeniable brush against the diaphanous, dollar-colored hem of the Angel of New York to be vouchsafed to him in his lifetime.

"This is not the question," he said. "If he's like a cat or a spider or a fucking wolverine, if he's huge, if he's tiny, if he can shoot flames or ice or death rays or Vat 69, if he turns into fire or water or stone or India rubber. He could be a Martian, he could be a ghost, he could be a god or a demon or a wizard or monster. Okay? It doesn't *matter*, because right now, see, at this very moment, we have a bandwagon rolling. I'm telling you. Every little skinny guy like me in New York who believes there's life on Alpha Centauri and got the shit kicked out of him in school and can smell a dollar is out there right this minute trying to jump into it, walking around with a pencil in his shirt pocket, saying, 'He's like a falcon, no, he's like a tornado, no, he's like a goddamned wiener dog.' Okay?"

"Okay."

"And no matter what we come up with, and how we dress him, some other character with the same shtick, with the same style of boots and the same little doodad on his chest, is already out there, or is coming out tomorrow, or is going to be knocked off from our guy inside a week and a half."

Joe listened patiently, awaiting the point of this peroration, but Sammy seemed to have lost the thread. Joe followed his cousin's gaze along the sidewalk but saw only a pair of what looked to be British sailors lighting their cigarettes off a single shielded match.

"So..." Sammy said. "So..."

"So that is not the question." Joe prompted.

"That's what I'm saying."

"Continue."

They kept walking.

"How? is not the question. What? is not the question," Sammy said.

"The question is why."

"The question is *why*."

"Why," Joe repeated.

"Why is he doing it?"

"Doing what?"

"Dressing up like a monkey or an ice cube or a can of fucking corn."

"To fight crime, isn't it?"

"Well, yes, to fight crime. To fight evil. But that's all any of these guys are doing. That's as far as they ever go. They just...you know, it's the right thing to do, so they do it. How interesting is that?"

"I see."

"Only Batman, you know...see, yeah, that's good. That's what makes Batman good, and not dull at all, even though he's just a guy who dresses up like a bat and beats people up."

"What is the reason for Batman? The why?"

"His parents were killed, see? In cold blood. Right in front of his eyes, when he was a kid. By a robber."

"It's revenge."

"That's interesting." Sammy said. "See?"

"And he was driven mad."

"Well..."

"And that's why he puts on bat's clothes."

"Actually, they don't go as far as to say that," Sammy said. "But I guess it's there between the lines."

"So we need to figure out what is the why."

"What is the why?" Sammy agreed. ❖

Chabon does double duty in this wonderfully vivid scene. He's telling us something about the creation of character; he's letting us into a secret of his art. Building character isn't about mere features or characteristics; it's about the underlying *why* that makes the choice of features or characteristics apt. To use Chabon's (or Sammy's) own example, Batman isn't a compelling, dark, and menacing hero simply because black bat suits and ominous stares are cool, but because this character's outfit and bearing express the barely controlled rage that resides within him. The *what* (the bat) builds from the *why* (a brutalizing childhood experience). Maybe Christopher Nolan, the director of *Memento*, read Chabon's book: In the latest movie version of the Batman story, Nolan makes *why* the film's premise. The film's title underscores the point: *Batman Begins.* Nolan has been quoted as saying that Batman was interesting largely because he isn't, in the usual sense, a superhero; he's just a "guy who does a lot of push-ups." But what is really interesting is that he is driven to do those push-ups. The motivation—the why—is generative. Nolan, like Sammy, believes the beginning provides the why that gives emotional substance to the costumes and toys that took over some of the earlier, less successful versions of the character.

PRESENTING CHARACTER

Chabon has a second thing going in the previous excerpt: He is building two richly imagined and freshly presented new characters—Sammy and Joe. Chabon's method of **characterization** (the technique of creating a sense of character) seems almost invisible; it is as if he simply allows the characters to present themselves. Sammy and Joe come alive primarily from **dialogue;** we hear them speak and observe them interacting. Chabon resists, for the most part, the temptation to swoop in like some authorial superhero and tell us everything about these characters directly. We're allowed to listen in and observe things for ourselves, much as we do when we watch a play. We might notice that Sammy consistently takes the lead in this conversation. He's the one dissatisfied with the usual run of superheroes. He's the one who, in his frustration of not breaking from the superficial formulas, presses boring ideas to ridiculous conclusions (for example, Lionman's "super roar" breaks dishes). Sammy is the one who is more drenched in comic-book lore and knowledge of comic-book competitors. Sammy fills Joe in on the essentials about Batman. He knows what's going on in the business—what the rivals are working on. He is also the one who first grasps the basic problem. Sammy realizes that they need to change the question. Joe speaks less, but Chabon manages to make him come alive too. Joe may not be so thoroughly versed in comic book heroes, but he is persistent (he's the one who keeps bringing Sammy back by telling him to "be serious"). And he is smart enough to listen to his cousin and not allow the flash of insight to get away. He prods him just as it seems that Sammy's moment of inspiration dims. He first comes up with the crucial word *why*, even if he doesn't fully grasp its importance.

A Note to Student Writers: Leading Questions

Sammy's insight is one that critical writers would do well to consider. A "what" question could be a good starting place for description and summary, but "whats" don't lead easily into analysis. "Why" questions lead more powerfully into developing ideas. They help us think through distinctions, explain impressions, and support assertions. So when you feel stuck on "what," try formulating critical questions around "why" and see if those questions help you press your ideas forward. And although Sammy insists that "how," like "what," is "not the question," critical writers may generate a great deal from "how" questions that turn attention to the artist's craft as opposed to the character's behavior.

Making Connections

Consider how we often read character in everyday life through specific observation of things the person owns or buys. For example, we might speculate about the person in front of us at the grocery store on the basis of items that person has in the shopping cart. If we notice that same person a few minutes later in the parking lot, our first impression might be reinforced or revised by the car the person drives. Writers manage such impressions very carefully. Remember that they are really the ones who choose the groceries and the cars for their characters.

PICTURING CHARACTER

Listening in on a conversation, catching a tone of voice or a turn of phrase, helps us know Sammy and Joe. But we can see character emerge as a physical presence and through gestures as well. We interpret character from a dense fabric of visual clues: clothes, posture, facial expressions, physical size, age, and so on. We must also consider how those clues fit with other elements within our field of vision. Where is a scene taking place? What seems to be the situation? How do the characters interact?

Experiencing Film and Literature through Character

The film still shown here from *Gone with the Wind* (1939) catches a moment when Mammy (played by Hattie McDaniel) is helping the heroine, Scarlett O'Hara (Vivien Leigh), dress. It's a picture loaded with information that helps us understand character. Of course, there is the obvious: Mammy is a servant (a slave actually, although we wouldn't necessarily know that if we had only this photograph); Scarlett is the served. Mammy is black; Scarlett, white. Mammy is enormous; Scarlett, trim. The clothes accent the size differences: Mammy's bluntly cut and buttoned-up housemaid's uniform contrasts sharply with Scarlett's elaborate yet delicate underclothes. The size difference is underscored further by the fact that Mammy is tightening a corset on the already very slender Scarlett. There can't be any doubt who sleeps in the bed. Scarlett quite literally owns this world.

The various bits of information from the photograph, along with the most minimal background information (the names of the two characters and knowledge that the scene is set in the pre–Civil War South), might lead us to fairly simple insights about these characters if it weren't for some subtler signals. However subservient Mammy must ultimately be, subservience isn't what comes through here. Mammy is talking in an animated manner, and Scarlett is listening, even though she hardly seems happy with what she is hearing. Furthermore, Hattie McDaniel's Mammy is not just big—she's substantial. She fills more than a large physical space within the frame. She expresses authority and strength. Scarlett, for her part, is hardly compliant. Vivien Leigh communicates Scarlett's impetuous willfulness. The way she

Vivien Leigh and Hattie McDaniel in *Gone with the Wind* (1939)

holds the bedpost against Mammy's tug on her corset strings suggests the force-ful push–pull nature of her complex relationship with human "property."

The role that Hattie McDaniel played was, at the time of the film in 1939, one of a very narrow range of roles available for black actresses. That contemporary social reality lends further, troubling, dimensions to the picture. McDaniel was to become the target of some who felt that her portrayal too expertly realized the essentially racist vision of the book and film. It's certainly a sad note that no black actor or actress from the film could attend the premiere in Atlanta, Georgia, with the rest of the principal actors. And to enlarge the affront, McDaniel's photograph was deleted from a publicity program to be distributed at that grand event (her prominence in that program insulted some local officials). Yet she won an Academy Award for her portrayal of Mammy (a first for an African American); she also had the satisfaction of knowing that playing a servant paid much better than actually working as one (McDaniel was a maid not long before coming to Hollywood).

The complexities of the situation that Hattie McDaniel finds herself in provide the African American poet Rita Dove a rich study in character. What does it feel like to be oversized but invisible? An award winner who cannot be a "star"? An actress who must play only the limited roles she has tried

Hattie McDaniel accepting her Academy Award at
the Coconut Grove in 1940

to escape with mixed success in life? The poem "Hattie McDaniel Arrives
at the Coconut Grove" pictures the night of the Academy Awards in 1940
with greater complexity than the photograph of Hattie McDaniel could
possibly capture. We see in Dove's poem a method of characterization that
builds from the outside (from what we see around the character, not from
what the character says). We get only one line from McDaniel herself amid
much description; Dove sets the scene and helps us see McDaniel the actress
dressed very unlike Mammy the film character. We also get some relevant
cultural, historical, and biographical information. Finally, we get the poet's
reflections on Hattie McDaniel: questions, speculation, identification, and
finally, judgment.

Rita Dove (1952–)

Hattie McDaniel Arrives at the Coconut Grove (2004)

late, in aqua and ermine, gardenias
scaling her left sleeve in a spasm of scent,
her gloves white, her smile chastened, purse giddy
with stars and rhinestones clipped to her brilliantined hair,
on her free arm that fine Negro   5
Mr. Wonderful Smith.

It's the day that isn't, February 29th,
at the end of the shortest month of the year—
and the shittiest, too, everywhere
except Hollywood, California,   10

where the maid can wear mink and still be a maid,
bobbing her bandaged head and cursing
the white folks under her breath as she smiles
and shoos their silly daughters
in from the night dew... What can she be   15
thinking of, striding into the ballroom
where no black face has ever showed itself
except above a serving tray?

Hi-Hat Hattie, Mama Mac, Her Haughtiness,
the "little lady" from Showboat whose name   20
Bing forgot, Beulah & Bertha & Malena
& Carrie & Violet & Cynthia & Fidelia,
one half of the Dark Barrymores—
dear Mammy we can't help but hug you crawl into
your generous lap tease you   25
with arch innuendo so we can feel that
much more wicked and youthful
and sleek but oh what

we forgot: the four husbands, the phantom
pregnancy, your famous parties, your celebrated   30
ice box cake. Your giggle above the red petticoat's rustle,
black girl and white girl walking hand in hand
down the railroad tracks
in Kansas City, six years old.
The man who advised you, now   35
that you were famous, to "begin eliminating"
your more "common" acquaintances
and your reply (catching him square
in the eye): "That's a good idea.
I'll start right now by eliminating you."   40

Is she or isn't she? Three million dishes,
a truckload of aprons and headrags later, and here
you are: poised, between husbands
and factions, no corset wide enough
to hold you in, your face a dark moon split   45
by that spontaneous smile—your trademark,
your curse. No matter, Hattie: it's a long, beautiful walk
into that flower-smothered standing ovation,
so go on

and make them wait. 50

Dove's final lines suggest a deep appreciation and sympathy for Hattie McDaniel. The great smile was both a "trademark" and a "curse." But Dove's speaker doesn't end on that note of ambivalence. Hattie is to enjoy her moment, and Dove wants the reader to enjoy it with her.

FEELING FOR CHARACTER

The desire to know something about others isn't built on an abstract curiosity. We must *want* to know about a character. A character must matter to us. If Sammy felt that the *why* of Batman didn't justify the *what*, he would likely have found the character unbalanced (too violent) or just plain silly (bat suits and bat gadgets). He wouldn't think of Batman as a creative touchstone. Of course, we don't usually need to accept the kind of unlikely *what* that comes with a superhero. Most artists build from more mundane materials; many artists work from subjects quite literally close to home: family, friends, jobs, and so on. The simplest *whys* can lead to a rich and deeply involving sense of character: Why did she ask him to lunch? Why did he behave so coldly? Why did they eat so little? Why did she insist on paying the bill?

Experiencing Literature through Character

Concern for character often grows from immediate personal concerns. Cathy Song in the poem "Picture Bride" reflects on the distant past of a grandmother. How can the younger woman, the poem's speaker, connect with a grandmother over time and dramatically changed circumstances? How does the old woman encompass for the speaker a still-living history? Why is it important to rescue a sense of the older woman's past? Everything in the poem is driven by a powerful sense of **identification.** The grandmother was a year younger than the poet when she moved from home to a new land and an arranged marriage. The poet realizes the profundity of that move. She sorts through her own feelings, her own situation, and wonders how that young woman (that young woman who became the old woman who is the poet's grandmother) must have felt when she—at the poet's age—came to an unfamiliar land and looked in the face of a stranger she knew was to be her husband. This act of imagining also lends weight to the poem's speaker. It is not just the grandmother whom we meet in this poem. The speaker becomes a character as well.

Cathy Song (1955–)

Picture Bride (1983)

She was a year younger
than I,
twenty-three when she left Korea.
Did she simply close
the door of her father's house   5
and walk away. And
was it a long way
through the tailor shops of Pusan
to the wharf where the boat
waited to take her to an island   10
whose name she had only recently learned,
on whose shore
a man waited,
turning her photograph
to the light when the lanterns   15
in the camp outside
Waialua Sugar Mill were lit
and the inside of his room
grew luminous
from the wings of moths   20
migrating out of the cane stalks?
What things did my grandmother
take with her? And when
she arrived to look
into the face of the stranger   25
who was her husband,
thirteen years older than she,
did she politely untie
the silk bow of her jacket,
her tent-shaped dress   30
filling with the dry wind
that blew from the surrounding fields
where the men were burning cane?

Song suggests the character of both the grandmother and the granddaughter
through questions. Perhaps she cannot cross a gulf between past and present
with flat statements. Too much specific knowledge has been lost over the

years; the grandmother's youth has become too distant. But enough detail remains to give substance to the questions. And the speaker of the poem can identify closely because the speaker is what the grandmother once was: a young woman.

Robert Hayden also reflects on family in "Those Winter Sundays." His speaker concretely remembers his father and doesn't need to imagine or project from bits of information others have collected. Nor does he ask questions about what his father felt or who he was; his knowledge is limited but firm. Hayden tells a brief story that unfolds a sense of a quiet, uncomplaining man who expresses feelings through hard work and everyday acts of attention. The picture of the father comes through clearly. We get a sketch of a character who is defined by his steadiness. At the end we're left thinking of the second character in the poem. The question that rounds off Hayden's poem is self-reflective. It causes us to think of the son who only as an adult begins to appreciate the depth of his father's love.

Robert Hayden (1913–1980)

Those Winter Sundays (1966)

Sundays too my father got up early
and put his clothes on in the blueblack cold,
then with cracked hands that ached
from labor in the weekday weather made
banked fires blaze. No one ever thanked him.   5

I'd wake and hear the cold splintering, breaking.
When the rooms were warm, he'd call,
and slowly I would rise and dress,
fearing the chronic angers of that house,
Speaking indifferently to him,   10
who had driven out the cold
and polished my good shoes as well.
What did I know, what did I know
of love's austere and lonely offices?

The father and son in Hayden's poem introduce in miniature a broad distinction critics often make between character types in novels and plays: static and dynamic. **Static characters** do not change in the course of the story; **dynamic characters** do change. It is useful to further distinguish character types within these categories. Some static characters become objects of criticism; they foolishly resist what seems an appropriate or necessary change. Hayden's father is not this sort of static character. He is unchanging in a way that suggests steadiness, firmness of purpose, and clarity of essential values. The father's static quality results from the unrelentingly hard world he must deal with; it's not a personality defect. Some dynamic characters change as a result of specific knowledge; they simply adjust behavior on the basis of new information. Other dynamic characters change at the deepest level of being; they undergo a revolution in their way of seeing and approaching the world. "Those Winter Sundays" is too brief a piece to communicate a full sense of what knowledge the son comes to, but it does suggest a profound insight on the nature of mature love that could hardly leave the son unchanged.

CHARACTER AND FUNCTION

So far, we've discussed character in terms of knowing or understanding others. We've used words like *motivation, sympathy,* and *identification.* The assumption is that we engage with characters as we engage with people. But we need to acknowledge that characters in literary texts serve a wide range of functions; they are not always in a work for us to "know" as we might hope to know a person.

Many people take the lead of the novelist E. M. Forster and distinguish between **round characters** and **flat characters.** Round characters (according to Forster) possess a complex psychology—layers of complex and perhaps even conflicting motivations. Flat characters are one-dimensional; they may possess a vivid trait but not a substantial identity. These terms can sometimes be useful in making broad distinctions among character types, but *round* and *flat* will be misleading words if we use them to signal a fixed artistic value. It would be a mistake, for example, to assume that round characters are "well drawn" and flat characters are "poorly conceived."

Characters must always be viewed in relation to a whole work. We don't ask only who they are but how they function. For example, we recognize many characters for roles that have become familiar over innumerable works (the shady gambler, the annoying little brother, the meddlesome mother-in-law). Such **stock characters** (the flattest of the flat) do not demand much of us, nor do they leave us with a feeling that we've enlarged our range of experience. But this is not to say that they are, from an artistic standpoint, failures. In such cases, the character's complexity is not the issue; what matters is, does the character fit within a plan for the whole? A stock character might be used to help move a plot forward or perhaps provide a bit of information necessary for a larger purpose. Some simple characters bring out qualities in major characters; they act as **foils** that show off the relatively complex dimensions others possess.

More important still, we must remember that psychological insight isn't the only means to depth or the only type of depth. Some characters embody ideas (or ideals) more than recognizable behaviors. They may seem more satiric than realistic, more fanciful than grounded, more mythic than human. Distinctions such as these are about kind, not quality. A flat character may actually allow us (in some works at least) to access profound feelings. Occasionally, the character's supposed "narrowness" or one-dimensionality may be better described as intensely concentrated.

The father in Judith Ortiz Cofer's "My Father in the Navy: A Childhood Memory" isn't "real" in the same sense that a fully realized independent character is real. In the mind of the speaker, the father possesses no psychological depth or even independent existence. In this poem, that is hardly a problem, for the speaker's father, the angel who appears magically to herald a new day, helps us appreciate the longings of the child—the child's desire for a family's wholeness, for a strongly reassuring presence. The father is beautifully realized, not as a person but as an image a child holds. If the poet chose to give him "depth," the poem's subject would shift: it would no longer be the same intensely felt "childhood memory."

Judith Ortiz Cofer (1952–)

My Father in the Navy: A Childhood Memory (1987)

Stiff and immaculate
in the white cloth of his uniform
and a round cap on his head like a halo,
he was an apparition on leave from a shadow-world
and only flesh and blood when he rose from below   5
the waterline where he kept watch over the engines
and dials making sure the ship parted the waters
on a straight course.
Mother, brother and I kept vigil
on the nights and dawns of his arrivals,   10
watching the corner beyond the neon sign of a quasar
for the flash of white our father like an angel
heralding a new day.
His homecomings were the verses
we composed over the years making up   15
the siren's song that kept him coming back
from the bellies of iron whales
and into our nights
like the evening prayer.

The character who is most "rounded" here is the speaker. We feel and understand the rich desire of the child for the father. We can also appreciate the great power that the child feels the father possesses. If we complain that Cofer has not developed the father's character, we've missed what Cofer *has* accomplished in the character of the daughter.

MODELING CRITICAL ANALYSIS: JAMAICA KINCAID, GIRL

We mentioned in the last chapter that Jamaica Kincaid's "Girl" (p. 210) defies any easy discussion of plot; it would seem that the story is more purely a character sketch. But a moment's reflection raises interesting critical issues. The title directs us to the girl as a point of focus, as the main character. But the story itself is almost entirely delivered by the woman who orders and instructs the girl. Only two short lines are spoken directly by the girl. Much of what we actually read isn't about the girl at all. It is about behaviors and duties that are pressed upon her. How is it that her character emerges? Is the girl the main character?

From the very start Kincaid opens with commands. Having the speaker aggressively load on obligations puts the reader, in effect, in the same position as the girl: we are at the receiving end of all the orders. One result is that we can sympathize with the girl. We can feel the weight of being a girl in a culture that is both demanding and restrictive. A sense of character then emerges not from a look inside the girl or from the girl's words but from a visceral understanding of how outside forces (social rules, customs, and expectations) control the girl's experience of the world.

It is in that context that we may see her brief interruptions as admirable—perhaps even heroic. The main speaker projects an identity upon the girl, but the girl resists. She doesn't, she objects, sing *"benna on Sundays"*; she does question an order that does not match her own understanding of the way the world works. Of course, the question she asks at the story's end—*"what if the baker won't let me feel the bread?"*—is quickly thrown back against her: "you mean . . . you are really going to be the kind of woman who the baker won't let near the bread?" This question rhetorically functions more as an accusation or as a judgment upon the girl. But as strongly as we might feel its sting, we hold steady and have some reason to think the girl will too. The girl is one who claims some sense of self against the identity put upon her from the outside.

It's also important to note that the girl is not the only character we get to know. The older woman who acts as mentor, boss, judge, and mother has internalized the many lessons that she gives so readily. The fact that she knows how to wash, sew, plant, cook, nurse, iron, and so on suggests that hers has been a life spent doing things for others. But she hasn't accepted a life lived wholly at the whims of those more powerful than she. She knows how to use the few powers she has: "this is how you smile to someone you don't like too much; this is how you smile to someone you don't like at all; this is how you smile to someone you like completely." She knows how to "bully" a man and how it can happen that a man bullies her. She is a character who has managed to achieve some independence in a highly restricted world. For example, near the end, she tells the girl how to love a man but also tells her to not feel too bad if those instructions don't work. It seems that the woman acknowledges limitations built into her society but finds ways to circumvent some of those limitations. And it seems she wants the girl to have that survivor's knowledge too.

Using Character to Focus Writing and Discussion

- Who are the characters in the story?
- How is each introduced? What are their names?
- What are their physical characteristics? What are their personalities?
- What details help us identify a particular character even when that character is not identified by name?
- Which characters (if any) are better developed than other characters in the text?
- What changes (if any) do we see in the characters?
- What contrasts or tensions, if any, do we see among characters?
- Which character gains our sympathy or support within the narrative? Does this sympathy lead us to feel unsympathetic for any other character?
- How do the characters function within the narrative? How important is any single character to moving the plot forward? How important is any single character to our knowledge of other characters within the narrative?
- How does any single character exhibit a value system that influences the ways that we receive the narrative?

Anthology

FOLKLORE: A CRITIC WRITES ABOUT CHARACTER WITHIN THE FOLKLORE GENRE

Folklore often refers to a genre of stories that are passed down orally. The performance of the story is as important as the story itself in passing down the beliefs, values, and traditions of a particular society: By repeating a story within a family or within some other cultural group, the storyteller reaffirms the values of that group. The story of some individual character represents the larger concerns and interests of the group as a whole.

In his *Morphology of the Folk Tale*, Vladimir Propp argues that heroes within the world's folklore share recurring characteristics. The hero is often introduced as an ordinary person in a home environment that has been disrupted by the villain or villainous forces. The hero must leave home. The hero receives guidance, often in some magical form from some helpful agent. The hero is tested, and returns (unrecognized) to engage in direct combat with the villain. When the hero succeeds, the hero will often be transfigured with new garments and a new identity, and the villain will be punished.

In her review of *Maleficent*, Joan Acocella reviews important Sleeping Beauty stories from three centuries—a fairy tale, a ballet, and an animated feature. She underscores what all those versions share in common in order to explain how and to what purpose a new film version starring Angelina Jolie fundamentally changes things. In revising the Sleeping Beauty story, Jolie, along with the director Robert Stromberg and screenwriter Linda Woolveton, do more than tweak an old favorite. *Maleficent* thoughtfully reflects upon some of the fundamental dynamics Propp had identified as central to the folk tale. We now have a heroine and not a hero. And the final transformation of that heroine—not new garments, or even new wings, but a re-appropriation of wings—doesn't perfectly align with a strict formula. Still, as Acocella makes clear, it's important to know the tradition if we are to appreciate what is meaningful about the new.

"Everyday Use" by Alice Walker presents three African American women—a mother and her two daughters—who represent contrasting reactions to their contemporary American experience. The story echoes the New Testament parable of the prodigal son (Luke 15:11-32) in which a father welcomes home the son who has wasted his inheritance while the loyal son looks on. In Walker's update of the story, the prodigal daughter comes home transfigured by the many trappings of her sophistication—an education, new clothes, and a new name. These mark her as different from the sister she left behind. Dee returns home to claim elements of her cultural identity that she values very differently from her mother and sister. She might be seen as a folkloric hero who has gone out into the world and is now returning home in triumph. Dee seems to think of herself in these terms, but her mother offers another interpretation.

Notice that, beginning with the title, Alice Munro's "How I Met My Husband" sets itself into the oral tradition that is so often associated with folklore. This is a familiar narrative act: The narrator is describing a history that explains how she arrived at her current status with which they are presumably familiar.

Through the story, we learn how the characters we know emerged from those of history.

Contrast this style of storytelling with that in Jhumpa Lahiri's "This Blessed House" where a newly married couple in contemporary Boston wrestle with their connections to traditional Indian and Hindi culture and the Christian artifacts that some previous occupant has left throughout the house that the couple has just purchased. Lahiri explores the avenues by which culture is transmitted in contemporary society.

The poems in the cluster provide many additional angles on family culture and probe richly varied feelings in common human experience. Robert Frost's "Home Burial" dramatizes the shattering effects of the death of a child. We see unfold in subtle gestures how the surviving parents are painfully separated by their differing ways of responding to tragedy. Edgar Lee Masters probes the power of secrets and the pressures of reputation. His short poems quickly sketch a master emotion (fears, resentment, regret, and so on) that brings individual characters alive from the graveyard. Sylvia Plath dives deeply into childhood pains that do not relent in adulthood. She becomes the main character of her own poetry. In all of the readings that follow here, characters emerge for us to know. They engage us in a broad, yet intense human experience.

REVIEW

Joan Acocella (1945–   )

Love's True Kiss:
Maleficent's Complex Sexual Politics (2014)

The sexual politics of Disney's *Maleficent* are a complicated business. The most important thing, or at least the basic thing, is that the moviemakers took a villainess and turned her into a sympathetic character. "Maleficent" is an update of "The Sleeping Beauty," which, to name the three versions especially relevant to the new movie, is a seventeenth-century tale by Charles Perrault; a nineteenth-century Russian ballet—probably the most honored of all nineteenth-century ballets—choreographed by Marius Petipa to a score by Tchaikovsky; and a 1959 Disney animated feature. Unsurprisingly, since these renditions come from different centuries and different media, they vary in many details (I will favor the details of the ballet in its modern versions), but on one point they emphatically agree: an innocent princess, Aurora (her name means "sunrise"), is condemned to death, or to a permanent coma, by an evil fairy, supposedly because, by mistake, the fairy was not invited to the princess's christening party. A lot of readers and movie- and ballet-watchers will notice that, at the party, the invited guests are all dressed in pretty clothes and have nice manners, while the evil fairy wears a slick black garment, simultaneously deluxe and sinister, and arrives at the palace in a carriage drawn by rats or the like—circumstances that raise a doubt as to whether her exclusion was, in fact, due to a clerical error. Might she not be a reiteration of an old trope: Eris, the goddess of discord, who threw the golden apple, thereby precipitating the Trojan War? Might she not be that thing we've all been told about, the thing than which Hell hath no greater fury: a woman scorned?

In the new movie, the fairy's wrath is given a backstory. We meet two children. One is Stefan, a regular country boy. The other is a girl he has encountered in the woods: Maleficent, with a sweet, round, normal face but also, curiously, wings. The wings are not dainty little things, like something on an Advent card. They are big and brown, and, as I remember, they are taller than Maleficent. She zooms around on them wildly. She is not vain about them, however; she thinks they are just part of her body. To us, on the other hand, they are magical, making her both beautiful and weird. Her name (invented for the 1959 animated movie) is another double message. It means "evil-doer"—a prophecy of what will happen in the film—but many people will associate it with some pretty, old-fashioned girl's name, such as Millicent or, more likely, with "magnificent."

Maleficent and Stefan are friends. But the king of the territories neighboring Maleficent's goes to war with her and loses, whereupon he declares that whoever can kill her will succeed him as king. Stefan goes to visit Maleficent and brings his dagger, but he can't bring himself to murder her. (Think of Snow White and the huntsman.) So he does something almost worse: he drugs her and cuts off her wings. Blessedly, we don't see this happen. We only hear, once Maleficent awakens, her horrible cries—low, guttural, unstoppable—rising out of the woods. Angelina Jolie, who plays the adult Maleficent, has said that it was clear to her and to the writer that the removal of the wings was an image of rape. I am certain that someone involved must also have had clitoridectomy in mind. A piece of the girl's body, and a source of power and happiness, has been sliced off. The wings are taken to the castle and hung in a glass case, like a display in the Museum of Natural History.

Stefan, as promised, becomes king. He and his queen produce Princess Aurora (Elle Fanning), and then begins the real story, the story of Maleficent's emotional life. (Reportedly, fifteen minutes were cut from the beginning of the movie in order to get to this business faster.) Frightened by a death curse that Maleficent has laid on the baby, King Stefan sends Aurora away, to be reared by three fairies, lovable but silly old ladies. While they are off doing whatever they do, Aurora is watched over by—yes—Maleficent. Maleficent didn't mean to get involved in this. Early on, she says to one of the cute little girls who plays the young Aurora, "I do not like children." This is a meta joke. First of all, the child actress whom Jolie is speaking to is her own five-year-old daughter, Vivienne Jolie-Pitt. Second, Jolie demonstrably does like children. She and her mate, Brad Pitt, are famous philoprogenitives. They have six children, three of them adopted, and she has been a leader in international child-protection movements.

From another angle, too, she has a special relationship to motherhood. 5
As she explained on the Op-Ed page of the *Times* last year, she recently had a double mastectomy, because she had learned from genetic testing that she was at a very high risk for breast cancer. A big-time, gorgeous movie star, announcing that she has had both of her breasts removed: Is this something that Marilyn Monroe would have done? It is not.

Which brings us to the next point. Jolie, who often plays a sexy little item—in several of her early movies she was one of those "Nikita" types, with the short skirt and the lethal weapon—becomes, in *Maleficent*, the very opposite, a mater dolorosa. The evil spell hanging over Aurora is such that, if she is pricked by a spindle, she will fall into a deep sleep and will revive only by "love's true kiss." Maleficent, now fond of Aurora, tries to get every spindle in the kingdom removed from Aurora's reach. When that doesn't work—Aurora is pricked, and she succumbs—Maleficent gets in touch with Prince Phillip, a nice young man from a neighboring kingdom. He and Aurora met once before, and they liked each other. Now here he comes again; he kisses her, and we await the promised result. Her eyelashes will flutter, her bosom will rise and fall. But they don't. This is the film's wittiest and most politically forthright moment: kiss, wait, wait, nothing. Maleficent gives up. Clearly, Aurora will sleep forever. Before leaving to return to the woods, Maleficent leans over the body of the sleeping girl and plants a farewell kiss on her brow. And Aurora wakes up! That is "love's true kiss": not romantic love, the thunderbolt, but a steady, daily love. And not necessarily from a man, who you think will magically save you, but from a woman, who perhaps will unmagically save you just by having loved you, quietly, for a long time.

It is to Jolie's enormous credit that she is able to put this wholesome revisionist message across without righteousness or sentimentality. Her performance is less a matter of words than of small physical details: tilts of her lovely head, topped, here, with a pair of Minoan-bull-type horns; gleams of the eyes, plunging to great, green depths; and, of course, adjustments of the famous Duchampian cheekbones, whose angularity was greatly enhanced for the occasion by the Disney makeup people. Jolie manages to be both soft and sharp, poignant and yet still a little slithery. (Those horns are covered in black leather, or something close.) This is quite a trick, but perhaps not for Jolie. In her early years, she was a wild thing. She told interviewers that she had tried every drug she could find, that she was bisexual, that she was interested in B.D.S.M., and so on. She showed off her many tattoos. Now, at thirty-nine, she is a special envoy for the United Nations High Commissioner for Refugees. Perhaps it wasn't so hard for her, in *Maleficent*, to be both a badass and a paragon.

The film's moral tolerance extends to its other characters. The treatment of the men is especially interesting. King Stefan falls to his death from one of the castle's high parapets, but, God knows, he had it coming. As for the rather goofy Prince Phillip, his ineffectual kiss is not laughed at, and when we last see him and Aurora they seem to be happily getting to know each other. In the meantime, Maleficent has acquired a sort of lieutenant, Diaval, who is a shape-shifter. His default position is as a raven, but he can pretty much be whatever she needs: a dragon, etc. In the end, Maleficent's wings are restored—they sense her presence in the castle and escape from their vitrine to reattach themselves to her—whereupon she and Diaval zoom off, pulsing, into a white sky. God bless them! Above all, God bless Maleficent, who wasn't sure, until the end, that she wanted to do all those good deeds.

FICTION

Alice Munro (1931–)

Award-winning short story writer Alice Munro was born in 1931 in Ontario, Canada. She received her BA from the University of Western Ontario in 1952. Munro was artist-in-residence at the University of Western Ontario from 1974 to 1975 and at the University of British Columbia in 1980. She has received numerous awards for her writing, including the Governor General's Literary Award for *Dance of the Happy Shades* (1969), *Who Do You Think You Are?: Stories* (1978), *The Beggar Maid: Stories of Flo and Rose* (1979), and *The Progress of Love* (1987). Her collection of stories, *Runaway,* was published in October 2004. In 2013, Munro was honored for her lifetime achievement with the Nobel Prize in Literature.

How I Met My Husband (1974)

We heard the plane come over at noon, roaring through the radio news, and we were sure it was going to hit the house, so we all ran out into the yard. We saw it come in over the treetops, all red and silver, the first close-up plane I ever saw. Mrs. Peebles screamed.

"Crash landing," their little boy said. Joey was his name.

"It's okay," said Dr. Peebles. "He knows what he's doing." Dr. Peebles was only an animal doctor, but had a calming way of talking, like any doctor.

This was my first job—working for Dr. and Mrs. Peebles, who had bought an old house out on the Fifth Line, about five miles out of town. It was just when the trend was starting of town people buying up old farms, not to work them but to live on them.

We watched the plane land across the road, where the fairgrounds used to be. It did make a good landing field, nice and level for the old race track, and the barns and display sheds torn down now for scrap lumber so there was nothing in the way. Even the old grandstand bays had burned.

"All right," said Mrs. Peebles, snappy as she always was when she got over her nerves. "Let's go back in the house. Let's not stand here gawking like a set of farmers."

She didn't say that to hurt my feelings. It never occurred to her.

I was just setting the dessert down when Loretta Bird arrived, out of breath, at the screen door.

"I thought it was going to crash into the house and kill youse all!"

She lived on the next place and the Peebleses thought she was a countrywoman, they didn't know the difference. She and her husband didn't farm, he worked on the roads and had a bad name for drinking. They had seven children and couldn't get credit at the HiWay Grocery. The Peebleses made her welcome, not knowing any better, as I say, and offered her dessert.

Dessert was never anything to write home about, at their place. A dish of Jell-O or sliced bananas or fruit out of a tin. "Have a house without a pie, be ashamed until you die," my mother used to say, but Mrs. Peebles operated differently.

Loretta Bird saw me getting the can of peaches.

"Oh, never mind," she said. "I haven't got the right kind of a stomach to trust what comes out of those tins, I can only eat home canning."

I could have slapped her. I bet she never put down fruit in her life.

"I know what he's landed here for," she said. "He's got permission to use the fairgrounds and take people up for rides. It costs a dollar. It's the same fellow who was over at Palmerston last week and was up the lakeshore before that. I wouldn't go up, if you paid me."

"I'd jump at the chance," Dr. Peebles said. "I'd like to see this neighborhood from the air."

Mrs. Peebles said she would just as soon see it from the ground. Joey said he wanted to go and Heather did, too. Joey was nine and Heather was seven.

"Would you, Edie?" Heather said.

I said I didn't know. I was scared, but I never admitted that, especially in front of children I was taking care of.

5

10

15

"People are going to be coming out here in their cars raising dust and   20
trampling your property, if I was you I would complain," Loretta said. She
hooked her legs around the chair rung and I knew we were in for a lengthy
visit. After Dr. Peebles went back to his office or out on his next call and
Mrs. Peebles went for her nap, she would hang around me while I was trying to do the dishes. She would pass remarks about the Peebleses in their
own house.

"She wouldn't find time to lay down in the middle of the day, if she
had seven kids like I got."

She asked me did they fight and did they keep things in the dresser
drawer not to have babies with. She said it was a sin if they did. I pretended
I didn't know what she was talking about.

I was fifteen and away from home for the first time. My parents had
made the effort and sent me to high school for a year, but I didn't like it.
I was shy of strangers and the work was hard, they didn't make it nice for
you or explain the way they do now. At the end of the year the averages
were published in the paper, and mine came out at the very bottom, 37
percent. My father said that's enough and I didn't blame him. The last
thing I wanted, anyway, was to go on and end up teaching school. It happened the very day the paper came out with my disgrace in it, Dr. Peebles
was staying at our place for dinner, having just helped one of our cows
have twins, and he said I looked smart to him and his wife was looking for
a girl to help. He said she felt tied down, with the two children, out in the
country. I guess she would, my mother said, being polite, though I could
tell from her face she was wondering what on earth it would be like to
have only two children and no barn work, and then to be complaining.

When I went home I would describe to them the work I had to do, and
it made everybody laugh. Mrs. Peebles had an automatic washer and dryer,
the first I ever saw. I have had those in my own home for such a long time
now it's hard to remember how much of a miracle it was to me, not having
to struggle with the wringer and hang up and haul down. Let alone not having to heat water. Then there was practically no baking. Mrs. Peebles said
she couldn't make pie crust, the most amazing thing I ever heard a woman
admit. I could, of course, and I could make light biscuits and a white cake
and dark cake, but they didn't want it, she said they watched their figures.
The only thing I didn't like about working there, in fact, was feeling half
hungry a lot of the time. I used to bring back a box of doughnuts made
out at home, and hide them under my bed. The children found out, and I
didn't mind sharing, but I thought I better bind them to secrecy.

The day after the plane landed Mrs. Peebles put both children in   25
the car and drove over to Chesley, to get their hair cut. There was a good
woman then at Chesley for doing hair. She got hers done at the same place,

Mrs. Peebles did, and that meant they would be gone a good while. She had to pick a day Dr. Peebles wasn't going out into the country, she didn't have her own car. Cars were still in short supply then, after the war.

I loved being left in the house alone, to do my work at leisure. The kitchen was all white and bright yellow, with fluorescent lights. That was before they ever thought of making the appliances all different colors and doing the cupboards like dark old wood and hiding the lighting. I loved light. I loved the double sink. So would anybody new-come from washing dishes in a dishpan with a rag-plugged hole on an oilcloth-covered table by light of a coal-oil lamp.

I kept everything shining.

The bathroom too. I had a bath in there once a week. They wouldn't have minded if I took one oftener, but to me it seemed like asking too much, or maybe risking making it less wonderful. The basin and the tub and the toilet were all pink, and there were glass doors with flamingoes painted on them, to shut off the tub. The light had a rosy cast and the mat sank under your feet like snow, except that it was warm. The mirror was three-way. With the mirror all steamed up and the air like a perfume cloud, from things I was allowed to use, I stood up on the side of the tub and admired myself naked, from three directions. Sometimes I thought about the way we lived out at home and the way we lived here and how one way was so hard to imagine when you were living the other way. But I thought it was still a lot easier, living the way we lived at home, to picture something like this, the painted flamingoes and the warmth and the soft mat, than it was anybody knowing only things like this to picture how it was the other way. And why was that?

I was through my jobs in no time, and had the vegetables peeled for supper and sitting in cold water besides. Then I went into Mrs. Peebles' bedroom. I had been in there plenty of times, cleaning, and I always took a good look in her closet, at the clothes she had hanging there. I wouldn't have looked in her drawers, but a closet is open to anybody. That's a lie. I would have looked in drawers, but I would have felt worse doing it and been more scared she could tell.

Some clothes in her closet she wore all the time, I was quite familiar with them. Others she never put on, they were pushed to the back. I was disappointed to see no wedding dress. But there was one long dress I could just see the skirt of, and I was hungering to see the rest. Now I took note of where it hung and lifted it out. It was satin, a lovely weight on my arm, light bluish-green in color, almost silvery. It had a fitted, pointed waist and a full skirt and an off-the-shoulder fold hiding the little sleeves.

Next thing was easy. I got out of my own things and slipped it on. I was slimmer at fifteen than anybody would believe who knows me now and the 30 fit was beautiful. I didn't, of course, have a strapless bra on, which was what it needed, I just had to slide my straps down my arms under the material. Then I tried pinning up my hair, to get the effect. One thing led to another. I put on rouge and lipstick and eyebrow pencil from her dresser. The heat of the day and the weight of the satin and all the excitement made me thirsty, and I went out to the kitchen, got-up as I was, to get a glass of ginger ale with ice cubes from the refrigerator. The Peebleses drank ginger ale, or fruit drinks, all day, like water, and I was getting so I did too. Also there was no limit on ice cubes, which I was so fond of I would even put them in a glass of milk.

I turned from putting the ice tray back and saw a man watching me through the screen. It was the luckiest thing in the world I didn't spill the ginger ale down the front of me then and there.

"I never meant to scare you. I knocked but you were getting the ice out, you didn't hear me."

I couldn't see what he looked like, he was dark the way somebody is pressed up against a screen door with the bright daylight behind them. I only knew he wasn't from around here.

"I'm from the plane over there. My name is Chris Watters and what I was wondering was if I could use that pump."

There was a pump in the yard. That was the way the people used to get 35 their water. Now I noticed he was carrying a pail.

"You're welcome," I said. "I can get it from the tap and save you pumping." I guess I wanted him to know we had piped water, didn't pump ourselves.

"I don't mind the exercise." He didn't move, though, and finally he said, "Were you going to a dance?"

Seeing a stranger there had made me entirely forget how I was dressed.

"Or is that the way ladies around here generally get dressed up in the afternoon?"

I didn't know how to joke back then. I was too embarrassed.   40

"You live here? Are you the lady of the house?"

"I'm the hired girl."

Some people change when they find that out, their whole way of looking at you and speaking to you changes, but his didn't.

"Well, I just wanted to tell you you look very nice. I was so surprised when I looked in the door and saw you. Just because you looked so nice and beautiful."

I wasn't even old enough then to realize how out of the common it is, 45 for a man to say something like that to a woman, or somebody he is treating like a woman. For a man to say a word like *beautiful*. I wasn't old enough to realize or to say anything back, or in fact to do anything but wish he would go away. Not that I didn't like him, but just that it upset me so, having him look at me, and me trying to think of something to say.

He must have understood. He said good-bye, and thanked me, and went and started filling his pail from the pump. I stood behind the Venetian blinds in the dining room, watching him. When he had gone, I went into the bedroom and took the dress off and put it back in the same place. I dressed in my own clothes and took my hair down and washed my face, wiping it on Kleenex, which I threw in the wastebasket.

The Peebleses asked me what kind of man he was. Young, middle-aged, short, tall? I couldn't say.

"Good-looking?" Dr. Peebles teased me.

I couldn't think a thing but that he would be coming to get his water again, he would be talking to Dr. or Mrs. Peebles, making friends with them, and he would mention seeing me that first afternoon, dressed up. Why not mention it? He would think it was funny. And no idea of the trouble it would get me into.

After supper the Peebleses drove into town to go to a movie. She   50
wanted to go somewhere with her hair fresh done. I sat in my bright kitchen wondering what to do, knowing I would never sleep. Mrs. Peebles might not fire me, when she found out, but it would give her a different feeling about me altogether. This was the first place I ever worked but I already had picked up things about the way people feel when you are working for them. They like to think you aren't curious. Not just that you aren't dishonest, that isn't enough. They like to feel you don't notice things, that you don't think or wonder about anything but what they liked to eat and how they liked things ironed, and so on. I don't mean they weren't kind to me, because they were. They had me eat my meals with them (to tell the truth I expected to, I didn't know there were families who don't) and sometimes they took me along in the car. But all the same.

I went up and checked on the children being asleep and then I went out. I had to do it. I crossed the road and went in the old fairgrounds gate. The plane looked unnatural sitting there, and shining with the moon. Off at the far side of the fairgrounds, where the bush was taking over, I saw his tent.

He was sitting outside it smoking a cigarette. He saw me coming.

"Hello, were you looking for a plane ride? I don't start taking people up till tomorrow." Then he looked again and said, "Oh, it's you. I didn't know you without your long dress on."

My heart was knocking away, my tongue was dried up. I had to say something. But I couldn't. My throat was closed and I was like a deaf-and-dumb.

"Did you want a ride? Sit down. Have a cigarette."   55

I couldn't even shake my head to say no, so he gave me one.

"Put it in your mouth or I can't light it. It's a good thing I'm used to shy ladies."

I did. It wasn't the first time I had smoked a cigarette, actually. My girl-friend out home, Muriel Lowe, used to steal them from her brother.

"Look at your hand shaking. Did you just want to have a chat, or what?"

In one burst I said, "I wisht you wouldn't say anything about that dress."   60

"What dress? Oh, the long dress."

"It's Mrs. Peebles'."

"Whose? Oh, the lady you work for? Is that it? She wasn't home so you got dressed up in her dress, eh? You got dressed up and played queen. I don't blame you. You're not smoking the cigarette right. Don't just puff. Draw it in. Did anybody ever show you how to inhale? Are you scared I'll tell on you? Is that it?"

I was so ashamed at having to ask him to connive this way I couldn't nod. I just looked at him and he saw *yes*.

"Well I won't. I won't in the slightest way mention it or embarrass you.   65
I give you my word of honor."

Then he changed the subject, to help me out, seeing I couldn't even thank him.

"What do you think of this sign?"

It was a board sign lying practically at my feet.

SEE THE WORLD FROM THE SKY. ADULTS $1.00, CHILDREN 50¢. QUALIFIED PILOT.

"My old sign was getting pretty beat up, I thought I'd make a new one.   70
That's what I've been doing with my time today."

The lettering wasn't all that handsome, I thought. I could have done a better one in half an hour.

"I'm not an expert at sign making."

"It's very good," I said.

"I don't need it for publicity, word of mouth is usually enough. I turned away two carloads tonight. I felt like taking it easy. I didn't tell them ladies were dropping in to visit me."

Now I remembered the children and I was scared again, in case one of   75
them had waked up and called me and I wasn't there.

"Do you have to go so soon?"

I remembered some manners. "Thank you for the cigarette."

"Don't forget. You have my word of honor."

I tore off across the fairgrounds, scared I'd see the car heading home from town. My sense of time was mixed up, I didn't know how long I'd been out of the house. But it was all right, it wasn't late, the children were asleep. I got in bed myself and lay thinking what a lucky end to the day, after all, and among things to be grateful for I could be grateful Loretta Bird hadn't been the one who caught me.

The yard and borders didn't get trampled, it wasn't as bad as that. All   80
the same it seemed very public, around the house. The sign was on the
fairgrounds gate. People came mostly after supper but a good many in the
afternoon, too. The Bird children all came without fifty cents between them
and hung on the gate. We got used to the excitement of the plane coming
in and taking off, it wasn't excitement anymore. I never went over, after that
one time, but would see him when he came to get his water. I would be out
on the steps doing sitting-down work, like preparing vegetables, if I could.

"Why don't you come over? I'll take you up in my plane."

"I'm saving my money," I said, because I couldn't think of anything else.

"For what? For getting married?"

I shook my head.

"I'll take you up for free if you come sometime when it's slack. I   85
thought you would come, and have another cigarette."

I made a face to hush him, because you never could tell when the
children would be sneaking around the porch, or Mrs. Peebles herself listening in the house. Sometimes she came out and had a conversation with
him. He told her things he hadn't bothered to tell me. But then I hadn't
thought to ask. He told her he had been in the war, that was where he
learned to fly a plane, and now he couldn't settle down to ordinary life,
this was what he liked. She said she couldn't imagine anybody liking such
a thing. Though sometimes, she said, she was almost bored enough to try
anything herself, she wasn't brought up to living in the country. It's all my
husband's idea, she said. This was news to me.

"Maybe you ought to give flying lessons," she said.

"Would you take them?"

She just laughed.

Sunday was a busy flying day in spite of it being preached against from   90
two pulpits. We were all sitting out watching. Joey and Heather were over
on the fence with the Bird kids. Their father had said they could go, after
their mother saying all week they couldn't.

A car came down the road past the parked cars and pulled up right in
the drive. It was Loretta Bird who got out, all importance, and on the driver's
side another woman got out, more sedately. She was wearing sunglasses.

"This is a lady looking for the man that flies the plane," Loretta Bird said.

"I heard her inquire in the hotel coffee shop where I was having a Coke
and I brought her out."

"I'm sorry to bother you," the lady said. "I'm Alice Kelling, Mr. Watters'
fiancée."

This Alice Kelling had on a pair of brown and white checked slacks and
a yellow top. Her bust looked to me rather low and bumpy. She had a worried face. Her hair had had a permanent, but had grown out, and she wore

a yellow band to keep it off her face. Nothing in the least pretty or even young-looking about her. But you could tell from how she talked she was from the city, or educated, or both.

Dr. Peebles stood up and introduced himself and his wife and me and asked her to be seated. 95

"He's up in the air right now, but you're welcome to sit and wait. He gets his water here and he hasn't been yet. He'll probably take his break about five."

"That is him, then?" said Alice Kelling, wrinkling and straining at the sky.

"He's not in the habit of running out on you, taking a different name?" Dr. Peebles laughed. He was the one, not his wife, to offer iced tea. Then she sent me into the kitchen to fix it. She smiled. She was wearing sunglasses too.

"He never mentioned his fiancée," she said.

I loved fixing iced tea with lots of ice and slices of lemon in tall glasses. 100 I ought to have mentioned before, Dr. Peebles was an abstainer, at least around the house, or I wouldn't have been allowed to take the place. I had to fix a glass for Loretta Bird too, though it galled me, and when I went out she had settled in my lawn chair, leaving me the steps.

"I knew you was a nurse when I first heard you in that coffee shop."

"How would you know a thing like that?"

"I get my hunches about people. Was that how you met him, nursing?"

"Chris? Well yes. Yes, it was."

"Oh, were you overseas?" said Mrs. Peebles. 105

"No, it was before he went overseas. I nursed him when he was stationed at Centralia and had a ruptured appendix. We got engaged and then he went overseas. My, this is refreshing, after a long drive."

"He'll be glad to see you," Dr. Peebles said. "It's a rackety kind of life, isn't it, not staying one place long enough to really make friends."

"Youse've had a long engagement," Loretta Bird said.

Alice Kelling passed that over. "I was going to get a room at the hotel, but when I was offered directions I came on out. Do you think I could phone them?"

"No need," Dr. Peebles said. "You're five miles away from him if you 110 stay at the hotel. Here, you're right across the road. Stay with us. We've got rooms on rooms, look at this big house."

Asking people to stay, just like that, is certainly a country thing, and maybe seemed natural to him now, but not to Mrs. Peebles, from the way she said, oh yes, we have plenty of room. Or to Alice Kelling, who kept protesting, but let herself be worn down. I got the feeling it was a temptation to her, to be that close. I was trying for a look at her ring. Her nails were painted red, her fingers were freckled and wrinkled. It was a tiny stone. Muriel Lowe's cousin had one twice as big.

Chris came to get his water, late in the afternoon just as Dr. Peebles had predicted. He must have recognized the car from a way off. He came smiling.

"Here I am chasing after you to see what you're up to," called Alice Kelling. She got up and went to meet him and they kissed, just touched, in front of us.

"You're going to spend a lot on gas that way," Chris said.

Dr. Peebles invited Chris to stay for supper, since he had already 115
put up the sign that said: NO MORE RIDES TILL 7 P.M. Mrs. Peebles wanted it served in the yard, in spite of the bugs. One thing strange to anybody from the country is this eating outside. I had made a potato salad earlier and she had made a jellied salad, that was one thing she could do, so it was just a matter of getting those out, and some sliced meat and cucumbers and fresh leaf lettuce. Loretta Bird hung around for some time saying, "Oh, well, I guess I better get home to those yappers," and, "It's so nice just sitting here, I sure hate to get up," but nobody invited her, I was relieved to see, and finally she had to go.

That night after rides were finished Alice Kelling and Chris went off somewhere in her car. I lay awake till they got back. When I saw the car lights sweep my ceiling I got up to look down on them through the slats of my blind. I don't know what I thought I was going to see. Muriel Lowe and I used to sleep on her front veranda and watch her sister and her sister's boy friend saying good night. Afterward we couldn't get to sleep, for longing for somebody to kiss us and rub up against us and we would talk about suppose you were out in a boat with a boy and he wouldn't bring you in to shore unless you did it, or what if somebody got you trapped in a barn, you would have to, wouldn't you, it wouldn't be your fault. Muriel said her two girl cousins used to try with a toilet paper roll that one of them was a boy. We wouldn't do anything like that; just lay and wondered.

All that happened was that Chris got out of the car on one side and she got out on the other and they walked off separately—him toward the fairgrounds and her toward the house. I got back in bed and imagined about me coming home with him, not like that.

Next morning Alice Kelling got up late and I fixed a grapefruit for her the way I had learned and Mrs. Peebles sat down with her to visit and have another cup of coffee. Mrs. Peebles seemed pleased enough now, having company. Alice Kelling said she guessed she better get used to putting in a day just watching Chris take off and come down, and Mrs. Peebles said she didn't know if she should suggest it because Alice Kelling was the one with the car, but the lake was only twenty-five miles away and what a good day for a picnic.

Alice Kelling took her up on the idea and by eleven o'clock they were in the car, with Joey and Heather and a sandwich lunch I had made. The only thing was that Chris hadn't come down, and she wanted to tell him where they were going.

"Edie'll go over and tell him," Mrs. Peebles said. "There's no problem."   120
Alice Kelling wrinkled her face and agreed.

"Be sure and tell him we'll be back by five!"

I didn't see that he would be concerned about knowing this right away, and I thought of him eating whatever he ate over there, alone, cooking on his camp stove, so I got to work and mixed up a crumb cake and baked it, in between the other work I had to do; then, when it was a bit cooled, wrapped it in a tea towel. I didn't do anything to myself but take off my apron and comb my hair. I would like to have put some makeup on, but I was too afraid it would remind him of the way he first saw me, and that would humiliate me all over again.

He had come and put another sign on the gate: NO RIDES THIS P.M. APOL-OGIES. I worried that he wasn't feeling well. No sign of him outside and the tent flap was down. I knocked on the pole.

"Come in," he said, in a voice that would just as soon have said *Stay out*.   125
I lifted the flap.

"Oh, it's you. I'm sorry. I didn't know it was you."

He had been just sitting on the side of the bed, smoking. Why not at least sit and smoke in the fresh air?

"I brought a cake and hope you're not sick," I said.

"Why would I be sick? Oh—that sign. That's all right. I'm just tired of   130
talking to people. I don't mean you. Have a seat." He pinned back the tent flap. "Get some fresh air in here."

I sat on the edge of the bed, there was no place else. It was one of those fold-up cots, really: I remembered and gave him his fiancée's message.

He ate some of the cake. "Good."

"Put the rest away for when you're hungry later."

"I'll tell you a secret. I won't be around here much longer."

"Are you getting married?"   135

"Ha ha. What time did you say they'd be back?"

"Five o'clock."

"Well, by that time this place will have seen the last of me. A plane can get further than a car." He unwrapped the cake and ate another piece of it, absent-mindedly.

"Now you'll be thirsty."

"There's some water in the pail."   140

"It won't be very cold. I could bring some fresh. I could bring some ice from the refrigerator."

"No," he said. "I don't want you to go. I want a nice long time of saying good-bye to you."

He put the cake away carefully and sat beside me and started those little kisses, so soft, I can't ever let myself think about them, such kindness in his face and lovely kisses, all over my eyelids and neck and ears, all over, then me kissing back as well as I could (I had only kissed a boy on a dare before, and kissed my own arms for practice) and we lay back on the cot and pressed together, just gently, and he did some other things, not bad things or not in a bad way. It was lovely in the tent, that smell of grass and hot tent cloth with the sun beating down on it, and he said, "I wouldn't do you any harm for the world." Once, when he had rolled on top of me and we were sort of rocking together on the cot, he said softly, "Oh, no," and freed himself and jumped up and got the water pail. He splashed some of it on his neck and face, and the little bit left, on me lying there.

"That's to cool us off, miss."

When we said good-bye I wasn't at all sad, because he held my face and   145
said "I'm going to write you a letter. I'll tell you where I am and maybe you can come and see me. Would you like that? Okay then. You wait." I was really glad I think to get away from him, it was like he was piling presents on me I couldn't get the pleasure of till I considered them alone.

No consternation at first about the plane being gone. They thought he had taken somebody up, and I didn't enlighten them. Dr. Peebles had phoned he had to go to the country, so there was just us having supper, and then Loretta Bird thrusting her head in the door and saying, "I see he's took off."

"What?" said Alice Kelling, and pushed back her chair.

"The kids come and told me this afternoon he was taking down his tent. Did he think he'd run through all the business there was around here? He didn't take off without letting you know, did he?"

"He'll send me word," Alice Kelling said. "He'll probably phone tonight. He's terribly restless, since the war."

"Edie, he didn't mention to you, did he?" Mrs. Peebles said, "When   150
you took over the message?"

"Yes," I said. So far so true.

"Well why didn't you say?" All of them were looking at me. "Did he say where he was going?"

"He said he might try Bayfield," I said. What made me tell such a lie? I didn't intend it.

"Bayfield, how far is that?" said Alice Kelling.

Mrs. Peebles said, "Thirty, thirty-five miles."   155

"That's not far. Oh, well, that's really not far at all. It's on the lake, isn't it?" You'd think I'd be ashamed of myself, setting her on the wrong track. I did it to give him more time, whatever time he needed. I lied for him, and also, I have to admit, for me. Women should stick together and not do things like that. I see that now, but didn't then. I never thought of myself as being in any way like her, or coming to the same troubles, ever.

She hadn't taken her eyes off me. I thought she suspected my lie.

"When did he mention this to you?"

"Earlier."   160

"When you were over at the plane?"

"Yes."

"You must've stayed and had a chat." She smiled at me, not a nice smile. "You must've stayed and had a little visit with him."

"I took a cake," I said, thinking that telling some truth would spare me telling the rest.

"We didn't have a cake," said Mrs. Peebles rather sharply. 165

"I baked one."

Alice Kelling said, "That was very friendly of you."

"Did you get permission," said Loretta Bird. "You never know what these girls'll do next," she said. "It's not they mean harm so much, as they're ignorant."

"The cake is neither here nor there," Mrs. Peebles broke in. "Edie, I wasn't aware you knew Chris that well."

I didn't know what to say. 170

"I'm not surprised," Alice Kelling said in a high voice. "I knew by the look of her as soon as I saw her. We get them at the hospital all the time." She looked hard at me with her stretched smile. "Having their babies. We have to put them in a special ward because of their diseases. Little country tramps. Fourteen and fifteen years old. You should see the babies they have, too."

"There was a bad woman here in town had a baby that pus was running out of its eyes," Loretta Bird put in.

"Wait a minute," said Mrs. Peebles. "What is this talk? Edie. What about you and Mr. Watters? Were you intimate with him?"

"Yes," I said. I was thinking of us lying on the cot and kissing, wasn't that intimate? And I would never deny it.

They were all one minute quiet, even Loretta Bird. 175

"Well," said Mrs. Peebles. "I am surprised. I think I need a cigarette. This is the first of any such tendencies I've seen in her," she said, speaking to Alice Kelling, but Alice Kelling was looking at me.

"Loose little bitch." Tears ran down her face. "Loose little bitch, aren't you? I knew as soon as I saw you. Men despise girls like you. He just made use of you and went off, you know that, don't you? Girls like you are just nothing, they're just public conveniences, just filthy little rags!"

"Oh, now," said Mrs. Peebles.

"Filthy," Alice Kelling sobbed. "Filthy little rags!"

"Don't get yourself upset," Loretta Bird said. She was swollen up with 180 pleasure at being in on this scene. "Men are all the same."

"Edie, I'm very surprised," Mrs. Peebles said. "I thought your parents were so strict. You don't want to have a baby, do you?"

I'm still ashamed of what happened next. I lost control, just like a six-year-old, I started howling. "You don't get a baby from just doing that!"

"You see. Some of them are that ignorant," Loretta Bird said.

But Mrs. Peebles jumped up and caught my arms and shook me.

"Calm down. Don't get hysterical. Calm down. Stop crying. Listen to   185
me. Listen. I'm wondering, if you know what being intimate means. Now
tell me. What did you think it meant?"

"Kissing," I howled.

She let go. "Oh, Edie. Stop it. Don't be silly. It's all right. It's all a misunderstanding. Being intimate means a lot more than that. Oh, I *wondered*."

"She's trying to cover up, now," said Alice Kelling. "Yes. She's not so
stupid. She sees she got herself in trouble."

"I believe her," Mrs. Peebles said. "This is an awful scene."

"Well there is one way to find out," said Alice Kelling, getting up. "After   190
all, I am a nurse."

Mrs. Peebles drew a breath and said, "No. No. Go to your room, Edie.
And stop that noise. This is too disgusting."

I heard the car start in a little while. I tried to stop crying, pulling back each
wave as it started over me. Finally I succeeded, and lay heaving on the bed.

Mrs. Peebles came and stood in the doorway.

"She's gone," she said. "That Bird woman too. Of course, you know
you should never have gone near that man and that is the cause of all this
trouble. I have a headache. As soon as you can, go and wash your face in
cold water and get at the dishes and we will not say any more about this."

Nor we didn't. I didn't figure out till years later the extent of what I   195
had been saved from. Mrs. Peebles was not very friendly to me afterward,
but she was fair. Not very friendly is the wrong way of describing what she
was. She had never been very friendly. It was just that now she had to see
me all the time and it got on her nerves, a little.

As for me, I put it all out of my mind like a bad dream and concentrated
on waiting for my letter. The mail came every day except Sunday, between
one-thirty and two in the afternoon, a good time for me because Mrs. Peebles
was always having her nap. I would get the kitchen all cleaned and then go
up to the mailbox and sit in the grass, waiting. I was perfectly happy, waiting,
I forgot all about Alice Kelling and her misery and awful talk and Mrs. Peebles
and her chilliness and the embarrassment of whether she told Dr. Peebles
and the face of Loretta Bird, getting her fill of other people's troubles. I was
always smiling when the mailman got there, and continued smiling even
after he gave me the mail and I saw today wasn't the day. The mailman was a
Carmichael. I knew by his face because there are a lot of Carmichaels living
out by us and so many of them have a sort of sticking-out top lip. So I asked
his name (he was a young man, shy, but good-humored, anybody could ask
him anything) and then I said, "I knew by your face!" He was pleased by that
and always glad to see me and got a little less shy. "You've got the smile I've
been waiting on all day!" he used to holler out the car window.

It never crossed my mind for a long time a letter might not come. I believed in it coming just like I believed the sun would rise in the morning. I just put off my hope from day to day, and there was the goldenrod out around the mailbox and the children gone back to school, and the leaves turning, and I was wearing a sweater when I went to wait. One day walking back with the hydro bill stuck in my hand, that was all, looking across at the fairgrounds with the full-blown milkweed and dark teasels, so much like fall, it just struck me: *No letter was ever going to come.* It was an impossible idea to get used to. No, not impossible. If I thought about Chris's face when he said he was going to write to me, it was impossible, but if I forgot that and thought about the actual tin mailbox, empty, it was plain and true. I kept on going to meet the mail, but my heart was heavy now like a lump of lead. I only smiled because I thought of the mailman counting on it, and he didn't have an easy life, with the winter driving ahead.

Till it came to me one day there were women doing this with their lives all over. There were women just waiting and waiting by mailboxes for one letter or another. I imagined me making this journey day after day and year after year, and my hair starting to go gray, and I thought, I was never made to go on like that. So I stopped meeting the mail. If there were women all through life waiting, and women busy and not waiting, I knew which I had to be. Even though there might be things the second kind of women have to pass up and never know about, it still is better.

I was surprised when the mailman phoned the Peebleses' place in the evening and asked for me. He said he missed me. He asked if I would like to go to Goderich, where some well-known movie was on, I forget now what. So I said yes, and I went out with him for two years and he asked me to marry him, and we were engaged a year more while I got my things together, and then we did marry. He always tells the children the story of how I went after him by sitting by the mailbox every day, and naturally I laugh and let him, because I like for people to think what pleases them and makes them happy.

- As readers, we know more about Edie than the other characters in the story. Find a specific scene in which this extra knowledge is important and explain its significance.

- Does the narrator use any consistent strategies to describe Chris in this story? How does Edie's presentation of Chris compare with that of any of the other characters she encounters?

- What are Edie's relations with her employers? How does this relationship help define Edie's character?

- How did Edie meet her husband?

- How is the title of this work an appropriate description of the story it contains?

Jhumpa Lahiri (1967–   )

Jhumpa Lahiri was born in London, England. Lahiri, the daughter of Bengali parents, grew up in Rhode Island but made many family visits to Calcutta, India. She received her BA from Barnard College and an MA and PhD from Boston University. Lahiri currently lives in New York City. Lahiri's debut story collection, *Interpreter of Maladies* (1999), was a critical success and received the O. Henry Award in 1999 and the Pulitzer Prize in fiction in 2000. In 1999, Lahiri was named one of the twenty best young fiction writers in America by the *New Yorker*. Her novel, *The Namesake*, was published in 2003.

This Blessed House (1999)

They discovered the first one in a cupboard above the stove, beside an unopened bottle of malt vinegar.

"Guess what I found." Twinkle walked into the living room, lined from end to end with taped-up packing boxes, waving the vinegar in one hand and a white porcelain effigy of Christ, roughly the same size as the vinegar bottle, in the other.

Sanjeev looked up. He was kneeling on the floor, marking, with ripped bits of a Post-it, patches on the baseboard that needed to be retouched with paint. "Throw it away."

"Which?"

"Both."   5

"But I can cook something with the vinegar. It's brand-new."

"You've never cooked anything with vinegar."

"I'll look something up. In one of those books we got for our wedding."

Sanjeev turned back to the baseboard, to replace a Post-it scrap that had fallen to the floor. "Check the expiration. And at the very least get rid of that idiotic statue."

"But it could be worth something. Who knows?" She turned it upside   10 down, then stroked, with her index finger, the minuscule frozen folds of its robes. "It's pretty."

"We're not Christian," Sanjeev said. Lately he had begun noticing the need to state the obvious to Twinkle. The day before he had to tell her that if she dragged her end of the bureau instead of lifting it, the parquet floor would scratch.

She shrugged. "No, we're not Christian. We're good little Hindus." She planted a kiss on top of Christ's head, then placed the statue on top of the fireplace mantel, which needed, Sanjeev observed, to be dusted.

By the end of the week the mantel had still not been dusted; it had, however, come to serve as the display shelf for a sizable collection of Christian paraphernalia. There was a 3-D postcard of Saint Francis done in four colors, which Twinkle had found taped to the back of the medicine cabinet, and a wooden cross key chain, which Sanjeev had stepped on with bare feet as he was installing extra shelving in Twinkle's study. There was a framed paint-by-number of the three wise men, against a black velvet background, tucked in the linen closet. There was also a tile trivet depicting a blond, un-bearded Jesus, delivering a sermon on a mountaintop, left in one of the drawers of the built-in china cabinet in the dining room.

"Do you think the previous owners were born-agains?" asked Twinkle, making room the next day for a small plastic snow-filled dome containing a miniature Nativity scene, found behind the pipes of the kitchen sink.

Sanjeev was organizing his engineering texts from MIT in alphabetical   15
order on a bookshelf, though it had been several years since he had needed to consult any of them. After graduating, he moved from Boston to Connecticut, to work for a firm near Hartford, and he had recently learned that he was being considered for the position of vice president. At thirty-three he had a secretary of his own and a dozen people working under his supervision who gladly supplied him with any information he needed. Still, the presence of his college books in the room reminded him of a time in his life he recalled with fondness, when he would walk each evening across the Mass. Avenue bridge to order Mughlai chicken with spinach from his favorite Indian restaurant on the other side of the Charles, and return to his dorm to write out clean copies of his problem sets.

"Or perhaps it's an attempt to convert people," Twinkle mused.

"Clearly the scheme has succeeded in your case."

She disregarded him, shaking the little plastic dome so that the snow swirled over the manger.

He studied the items on the mantel. It puzzled him that each was in its own way so silly. Clearly they lacked a sense of sacredness. He was further puzzled that Twinkle, who normally displayed good taste, was so charmed. These objects meant something to Twinkle, but they meant nothing to him. They irritated him. "We should call the Realtor. Tell him there's all this nonsense left behind. Tell him to take it away."

"Oh, Sanj." Twinkle groaned. "Please. I would feel terrible throwing   20
them away. Obviously they were important to the people who used to live here. It would feel, I don't know, sacrilegious or something."

"If they're so precious, then why are they hidden all over the house? Why didn't they take them with them?

"There must be others," Twinkle said. Her eyes roamed the bare off-white walls of the room, as if there were other things concealed behind the plaster. "What else do you think we'll find?"

But as they unpacked their boxes and hung up their winter clothes and the silk paintings of elephant processions bought on their honeymoon in Jaipur, Twinkle, much to her dismay, could not find a thing. Nearly a week had passed before they discovered, one Saturday afternoon, a larger-than-life-sized watercolor poster of Christ, weeping translucent tears the size of peanut shells and sporting a crown of thorns, rolled up behind a radiator in the guest bedroom. Sanjeev had mistaken it for a window shade.

"Oh, we must, we simply must put it up. It's too spectacular." Twinkle lit a cigarette and began to smoke it with relish, waving it around Sanjeev's head as if it were a conductor's baton as Mahler's Fifth Symphony roared from the stereo downstairs.

"Now, look. I will tolerate, for now, your little biblical menagerie in the living room. But I refuse to have this," he said, flicking at one of the painted peanut-tears, "displayed in our home."   25

Twinkle stared at him, placidly exhaling, the smoke emerging in two thin blue streams from her nostrils. She rolled up the poster slowly, securing it with one of the elastic bands she always wore around her wrist for tying back her thick, unruly hair, streaked here and there with henna. "I'm going to put it in my study," she informed him. "That way you don't have to look at it."

"What about the housewarming? They'll want to see all the rooms. I've invited people from the office."

She rolled her eyes. Sanjeev noted that the symphony, now in its third movement, had reached a crescendo, for it pulsed with the telltale clashing of cymbals.

"I'll put it behind the door," she offered. "That way, when they peek in, they won't see. Happy?"

He stood watching her as she left the room, with her poster and her cigarette; a few ashes had fallen to the floor where she'd been standing. He   30 bent down, pinched them between his fingers, and deposited them in his cupped palm. The tender fourth movement, the *adagietto*, began. During breakfast, Sanjeev had read in the liner notes that Mahler had proposed to his wife by sending her the manuscript of this portion of the score. Although there were elements of tragedy and struggle in the Fifth Symphony, he had read, it was principally music of love and happiness.

He heard the toilet flush. "By the way," Twinkle hollered, "if you want to impress people, I wouldn't play this music. It's putting me to sleep."

Sanjeev went to the bathroom to throw away the ashes. The cigarette butt still bobbed in the toilet bowl, but the tank was refilling, so he had to wait a moment before he could flush it again. In the mirror of the medicine cabinet he inspected his long eyelashes—like a girl's, Twinkle liked to tease. Though he was of average build, his cheeks had a plumpness to them; this, along with the eyelashes, detracted, he feared, from what he hoped was a distinguished profile. He was of average height as well, and had wished ever since he had stopped growing that he were just one inch taller. For this reason it irritated him when Twinkle insisted on wearing high heels, as she had done the other night when they ate dinner in Manhattan. This was the first weekend after they'd moved into the house; by then the mantel had already filled up considerably, and they had bickered about it in the car on the way down. But then Twinkle had drunk four glasses of whiskey in a nameless bar in Alphabet City, and forgot all about it. She dragged him to a tiny bookshop on St. Mark's Place, where she browsed for nearly an hour, and when they left she insisted that they dance a tango on the sidewalk in front of strangers.

Afterward, she tottered on his arm, rising faintly over his line of vision, in a pair of suede three-inch leopard-print pumps. In this manner they walked the endless blocks back to a parking garage on Washington Square, for Sanjeev had heard far too many stories about the terrible things that happened to cars in Manhattan. "But I do nothing all day except sit at my desk," she fretted when they were driving home, after he had mentioned that her shoes looked uncomfortable and suggested that perhaps she should not wear them. "I can't exactly wear heels when I'm typing." Though he abandoned the argument, he knew for a fact that she didn't spend all day at her desk; just that afternoon, when he got back from a run, he found her inexplicably in bed, reading. When he asked why she was in bed in the middle of the day she told him she was bored. He had wanted to say to her then, You could unpack some boxes. You could sweep the attic. You could retouch the paint on the bathroom windowsill, and after you do it you could warn me so that I don't put my watch on it. They didn't bother her, these scattered, unsettled matters. She seemed content with whatever clothes she found at the front of the closet, with whatever magazine was lying around, with whatever song was on the radio—content yet curious. And now all of her curiosity centered around discovering the next treasure.

A few days later when Sanjeev returned from the office, he found Twinkle on the telephone, smoking and talking to one of her girlfriends in California even though it was before five o'clock and the long-distance rates were at their peak. "Highly devout people," she was saying, pausing every now and then to exhale. "Each day is like a treasure hunt. I'm serious. This you won't believe. The switch plates in the bedrooms were decorated with scenes from the Bible. You know, Noah's Ark and all that. Three bedrooms, but one is my study. Sanjeev went to the hardware store right away and replaced them, can you imagine, he replaced every single one."

Now it was the friend's turn to talk. Twinkle nodded, slouched on the floor in front of the fridge, wearing black stirrup pants and a yellow chenille sweater, groping for her lighter. Sanjeev could smell something aromatic on

35

the stove, and he picked his way carefully across the extra-long phone cord tangled on the Mexican terra-cotta tiles. He opened the lid of a pot with some sort of reddish brown sauce dripping over the sides, boiling furiously.

"It's a stew made with fish. I put the vinegar in it," she said to him, interrupting her friend, crossing her fingers. "Sorry, you were saying?" She was like that, excited and delighted by little things, crossing her fingers before any remotely unpredictable event, like tasting a new flavor of ice cream, or dropping a letter in a mailbox. It was a quality he did not understand. It made him feel stupid, as if the world contained hidden wonders he could not anticipate, or see. He looked at her face, which, it occurred to him, had not grown out of its girlhood, the eyes untroubled, the pleasing features unfirm, as if they still had to settle into some sort of permanent expression. Nicknamed after a nursery rhyme, she had yet to shed a childhood endearment. Now, in the second month of their marriage, certain things nettled him—the way she sometimes spat a little when she spoke, or left her undergarments after removing them at night at the foot of their bed rather than depositing them in the laundry hamper.

They had met only four months before. Her parents, who lived in California, and his, who still lived in Calcutta, were old friends, and across continents they had arranged the occasion at which Twinkle and Sanjeev were introduced—a sixteenth birthday party for a daughter in their circle— when Sanjeev was in Palo Alto on business. At the restaurant they were seated side by side at a round table with a revolving platter of spareribs and egg rolls and chicken wings, which, they concurred, all tasted the same. They had concurred too on their adolescent but still persistent fondness for Wodehouse novels, and their dislike for the sitar, and later Twinkle confessed that she was charmed by the way Sanjeev had dutifully refilled her teacup during their conversation.

And so the phone calls began, and grew longer, and then the visits, first he to Stanford, then she to Connecticut, after which Sanjeev would save in an ashtray left on the balcony the crushed cigarettes she had smoked during the weekend—saved them, that is, until the next time she came to visit him, and then he vacuumed the apartment, washed the sheets, even dusted the plant leaves in her honor. She was twenty-seven and recently abandoned, he had gathered, by an American who had tried and failed to be an actor; Sanjeev was lonely, with an excessively generous income for a single man, and had never been in love. At the urging of their matchmakers, they married in India, amid hundreds of well-wishers whom he barely remembered from his childhood, in incessant August rains, under a red and orange tent strung with Christmas tree lights on Mandeville Road.

"Did you sweep the attic?" he asked Twinkle later as she was folding paper napkins and wedging them by their plates. The attic was the only part of the house they had not yet given an initial cleaning.

"Not yet. I will, I promise. I hope this tastes good," she said, planting 40
the steaming pot on top of the Jesus trivet. There was a loaf of Italian bread
in a little basket, and iceberg lettuce and grated carrots tossed with bottled
dressing and croutons, and glasses of red wine. She was not terribly ambitious in the kitchen. She bought preroasted chickens from the supermarket
and served them with potato salad prepared who knew when, sold in little
plastic containers. Indian food, she complained, was a bother; she detested
chopping garlic, and peeling ginger, and could not operate a blender, and
so it was Sanjeev who, on weekends, seasoned mustard oil with cinnamon
sticks and cloves in order to produce a proper curry.

He had to admit, though, that whatever it was that she had cooked today,
it was unusually tasty, attractive even, with bright white cubes of fish, and
flecks of parsley, and fresh tomatoes gleaming in the dark brown-red broth.

"How did you make it?"

"I made it up."

"What did you do?"

"I just put some things into the pot and added the malt vinegar at the end." 45

"How much vinegar?"

She shrugged, ripping off some bread and plunging it into her bowl.

"What do you mean you don't know? You should write it down. What
if you need to make it again, for a party or something?"

"I'll remember," she said. She covered the bread basket with a
dishtowel that had, he suddenly noticed, the Ten Commandments printed
on it. She flashed him a smile, giving his knee a little squeeze under the
table. "Face it. This house is blessed."

The housewarming party was scheduled for the last Saturday in October, and 50
they had invited about thirty people. All were Sanjeev's acquaintances, people from the office, and a number of Indian couples in the Connecticut area,
many of whom he barely knew, but who had regularly invited him, in his
bachelor days, to supper on Saturdays. He often wondered why they included
him in their circle. He had little in common with any of them, but he always
attended their gatherings, to eat spiced chickpeas and shrimp cutlets, and
gossip and discuss politics, for he seldom had other plans. So far, no one had
met Twinkle; back when they were still dating, Sanjeev didn't want to waste
their brief weekends together with people he associated with being alone.
Other than Sanjeev and an ex-boyfriend who she believed worked in a pot-
tery studio in Brookfield, she knew no one in the state of Connecticut. She
was completing her master's thesis at Stanford, a study of an Irish poet whom
Sanjeev had never heard of.

Sanjeev had found the house on his own before leaving for the wedding,
for a good price, in a neighborhood with a fine school system. He was

impressed by the elegant curved staircase with its wrought-iron banister, and the dark wooden wainscoting, and the solarium overlooking rhododendron bushes, and the solid brass 22, which also happened to be the date of his birth, nailed impressively to the vaguely Tudor facade. There were two working fireplaces, a two-car garage, and an attic suitable for converting into extra bedrooms if, the Realtor mentioned, the need should arise. By then Sanjeev had already made up his mind, was determined that he and Twinkle should live there together, forever, and so he had not bothered to notice the switch plates covered with biblical stickers, or the transparent decal of the Virgin on the half shell, as Twinkle liked to call it, adhered to the window in the master bedroom. When, after moving in, he tried to scrape it off, he scratched the glass.

The weekend before the party they were raking the lawn when he heard Twinkle shriek. He ran to her, clutching his rake, worried that she had discovered a dead animal, or a snake. A brisk October breeze stung the tops of his ears as his sneakers crunched over brown and yellow leaves. When he reached her, she had collapsed on the grass, dissolved in nearly silent laughter. Behind an overgrown forsythia bush was a plaster Virgin Mary as tall as their waists, with a blue painted hood draped over her head in the manner of an Indian bride. Twinkle grabbed the hem of her T-shirt and began wiping away the dirt staining the statue's brow.

"I suppose you want to put her by the foot of our bed," Sanjeev said. She looked at him, astonished. Her belly was exposed, and he saw that there were goose bumps around her navel. "What do you think? Of course we can't put this in our bedroom."

"We can't?"   55

"No, silly Sanj. This is meant for outside. For the lawn."

"Oh God, no. Twinkle, no."

"But we must. It would be bad luck not to."

"All the neighbors will see. They'll think we're insane."

"Why, for having a statue of the Virgin Mary on our lawn? Every   60 other person in this neighborhood has a statue of Mary on the lawn. We'll fit right in."

"We're not Christian."

"So you keep reminding me." She spat onto the tip of her finger and started to rub intently at a particularly stubborn stain on Mary's chin. "Do you think this is dirt, or some kind of fungus?"

He was getting nowhere with her, with this woman whom he had known for only four months and whom he had married, this woman with whom he now shared his life. He thought with a flicker of regret of the snapshots his mother used to send him from Calcutta, of prospective brides

who could sing and sew and season lentils without consulting a cookbook.
Sanjeev had considered these women, had even ranked them in order of
preference, but then he had met Twinkle. "Twinkle, I can't have the people
I work with see this statue on my lawn."

"They can't fire you for being a believer. It would be discrimination."

"That's not the point."   65

"Why does it matter to you so much what other people think?"

"Twinkle, please." He was tired. He let his weight rest against his rake as
she began dragging the statue toward an oval bed of myrtle, beside the lamp-
post that flanked the brick pathway. "Look, Sanj. She's so lovely."

He returned to his pile of leaves and began to deposit them by hand-
fuls into a plastic garbage bag. Over his head the blue sky was cloudless.
One tree on the lawn was still full of leaves, red and orange, like the tent in
which he had married Twinkle.

He did not know if he loved her. He said he did when she had first
asked him, one afternoon in Palo Alto as they sat side by side in a darkened,
nearly empty movie theater. Before the film, one of her favorites, something
in German that he found extremely depressing, she had pressed the tip
of her nose to his so that he could feel the flutter of her mascara-coated
eyelashes. That afternoon he had replied, yes, he loved her, and she was
delighted, and fed him a piece of popcorn, letting her finger linger an instant
between his lips, as if it were his reward for coming up with the right answer.

Though she did not say it herself, he assumed then that she loved   70
him too, but now he was no longer sure. In truth, Sanjeev did not know
what love was, only what he thought it was not. It was not, he had decided,
returning to an empty carpeted condominium each night, and using only
the top fork in his cutlery drawer, and turning away politely at those weekend dinner parties when the other men eventually put their arms around
the waists of their wives and girlfriends, leaning over every now and again
to kiss their shoulders or necks. It was not sending away for classical music
CDs by mail, working his way methodically through the major composers
that the catalogue recommended, and always sending his payments in on
time. In the months before meeting Twinkle, Sanjeev had begun to realize this. "You have enough money in the bank to raise three families," his
mother reminded him when they spoke at the start of each month on the
phone. "You need a wife to look after and love." Now he had one, a pretty
one, from a suitably high caste, who would soon have a master's degree.
What was there not to love?

That evening Sanjeev poured himself a gin and tonic, drank it and
most of another during one segment of the news, and then approached
Twinkle, who was taking a bubble bath, for she announced that her limbs
ached from raking the lawn, something she had never done before. He

didn't knock. She had applied a bright blue mask to her face, was smoking and sipping some bourbon with ice and leafing through a fat paperback book whose pages had buckled and turned gray from the water. He glanced at the cover; the only thing written on it was the word "Sonnets" in dark red letters. He took a breath, and then he informed her very calmly that after finishing his drink he was going to put on his shoes and go outside and remove the Virgin from the front lawn.

"Where are you going to put it?" she asked him dreamily, her eyes closed. One of her legs emerged, unfolding gracefully, from the layer of suds. She flexed and pointed her toes.

"For now I am going to put it in the garage. Then tomorrow morning on my way to work I am going to take it to the dump."

"Don't you dare." She stood up, letting the book fall into the water, bubbles dripping down her thighs. "I hate you," she informed him, her eyes narrowing at the word "hate." She reached for her bathrobe, tied it tightly about her waist, and padded down the winding staircase, leaving sloppy wet footprints along the parquet floor. When she reached the foyer, Sanjeev said, "Are you planning on leaving the house that way?" He felt a throbbing in his temples, and his voice revealed an unfamiliar snarl when he spoke.

"Who cares? Who cares what way I leave this house?"   75

"Where are you planning on going at this hour?"

"You can't throw away that statue. I won't let you." Her mask, now dry, had assumed an ashen quality; and water from her hair dripped onto the caked contours of her face.

"Yes I can. I will."

"No," Twinkle said, her voice suddenly small. "This is our house. We own it together. The statue is a part of our property." She had begun to shiver. A small pool of bathwater had collected around her ankles. He went to shut a window, fearing that she would catch cold. Then he noticed that some of the water dripping down her hard blue face was tears.

"Oh God, Twinkle, please, I didn't mean it." He had never seen her cry   80
before, had never seen such sadness in her eyes. She didn't turn away or try to stop the tears; instead she looked strangely at peace. For a moment she closed her lids, pale and unprotected compared to the blue that caked the rest of her face. Sanjeev felt ill, as if he had eaten either too much or too little.

She went to him, placing her damp toweled arms about his neck, sobbing into his chest, soaking his shirt. The mask flaked onto his shoulders.

In the end they settled on a compromise: the statue would be placed in a recess at the side of the house, so that it wasn't obvious to passersby, but was still clearly visible to all who came.

The menu for the party was fairly simple: there would be a case of champagne, and samosas from an Indian restaurant in Hartford, and big trays of rice with chicken and almonds and orange peels, which Sanjeev had spent the greater part of the morning and afternoon preparing. He had never entertained on such a large scale before and, worried that there would not be enough to drink, ran out at one point to buy another case of champagne just in case. For this reason he burned one of the rice trays and had to start it over again. Twinkle swept the floors and volunteered to pick up the samosas; she had an appointment for a manicure and a pedicure in that direction, anyway. Sanjeev had planned to ask if she would consider clearing the menagerie off the mantel, if only for the party, but she left while he was in the shower. She was gone for a good three hours, and so it was Sanjeev who did the rest of the cleaning. By five-thirty the entire house sparkled, with scented candles that Twinkle had picked up in Hartford illuminating the items on the mantel, and slender stalks of burning incense planted into the soil of potted plants. Each time he passed the mantel he winced, dreading the raised eyebrows of his guests as they viewed the flickering ceramic saints, the salt and pepper shakers designed to resemble Mary and Joseph. Still, they would be impressed, he hoped, by the lovely bay windows, the shining parquet floors, the impressive winding staircase, the wooden wainscoting, as they sipped champagne and dipped samosas in chutney.

Douglas, one of the new consultants at the firm, and his girlfriend Nora were the first to arrive. Both were tall and blond, wearing matching wire-rimmed glasses and long black overcoats. Nora wore a black hat full of sharp thin feathers that corresponded to the sharp thin angles of her face. Her left hand was joined with Douglas's. In her right hand was a bottle of cognac with a red ribbon wrapped around its neck, which she gave to Twinkle.

"Great lawn, Sanjeev," Douglas remarked. "We've got to get that rake   85
out ourselves, sweetie. And this must be..."

"My wife. Tanima."

"Call me Twinkle."

"What an unusual name," Nora remarked.

Twinkle shrugged. "Not really. There's an actress in Bombay named Dimple Kapadia. She even has a sister named Simple."

Douglas and Nora raised their eyebrows simultaneously, nodding slowly,   90
as if to let the absurdity of the names settle in. "Pleased to meet you, Twinkle."

"Help yourself to champagne. There's gallons."

"I hope you don't mind my asking," Douglas said, "but I noticed the statue outside, and are you guys Christian? I thought you were Indian."

"There are Christians in India," Sanjeev replied, "but we're not."

"I love your outfit," Nora told Twinkle.

"And I adore your hat. Would you like the grand tour?"   95

The bell rang again, and again and again. Within minutes, it seemed, the house had filled with bodies and conversations and unfamiliar fragrances. The women wore heels and sheer stockings, and short black dresses made of crepe and chiffon. They handed their wraps and coats to Sanjeev, who draped them carefully on hangers in the spacious coat closet, though Twinkle told people to throw their things on the ottomans in the solarium. Some of the Indian women wore their finest saris, made with gold filigree that draped in elegant pleats over their shoulders. The men wore jackets and ties and citrus-scented aftershaves. As people filtered from one room to the next, presents piled onto the long cherry-wood table that ran from one end of the downstairs hall to the other.

It bewildered Sanjeev that it was for him, and his house, and his wife, that they had all gone to so much care. The only other time in his life that something similar had happened was his wedding day, but somehow this was different, for these were not his family, but people who knew him only casually, and in a sense owed him nothing. Everyone congratulated him. Lester, another coworker, predicted that Sanjeev would be promoted to vice president in two months maximum. People devoured the samosas, and dutifully admired the freshly painted ceilings and walls, the hanging plants, the bay windows, the silk paintings from Jaipur. But most of all they admired Twinkle, and her brocaded *salwar-kameez*, which was the shade of a persimmon with a low scoop in the back, and the little string of white rose petals she had coiled cleverly around her head, and the pearl choker with a sapphire at its center that adorned her throat. Over hectic jazz records, played under Twinkle's supervision, they laughed at her anecdotes and observations, forming a widening circle around her, while Sanjeev replenished the samosas that he kept warming evenly in the oven, and getting ice for people's drinks, and opening more bottles of champagne with some difficulty, and explaining for the fortieth time that he wasn't Christian. It was Twinkle who led them in separate groups up and down the winding stairs, to gaze at the back lawn, to peer down the cellar steps. "Your friends adore the poster in my study," she mentioned to him triumphantly, placing her hand on the small of his back as they, at one point, brushed past each other.

Sanjeev went to the kitchen, which was empty, and ate a piece of chicken out of the tray on the counter with his fingers because he thought no one was looking. He ate a second piece, then washed it down with a gulp of gin straight from the bottle.

"Great house. Great rice." Sunil, an anesthesiologist, walked in, spooning food from his paper plate into his mouth. "Do you have more champagne?"

"Your wife's wow," added Prabal, following behind. He was an unmarried professor of physics at Yale. For a moment Sanjeev stared at him blankly, then blushed; once at a dinner party Prabal had pronounced that Sophia Loren was wow, as was Audrey Hepburn. "Does she have a sister?" 100

Sunil picked a raisin out of the rice tray. "Is her last name Little Star?"

The two men laughed and started eating more rice from the tray, plowing through it with their plastic spoons. Sanjeev went down to the cellar for more liquor. For a few minutes he paused on the steps, in the damp, cool silence, hugging the second crate of champagne to his chest as the party drifted above the rafters. Then he set the reinforcements on the dining table.

"Yes, everything, we found them all in the house, in the most unusual places," he heard Twinkle saying in the living room. "In fact we keep finding them."

"No!"

"Yes! Every day is like a treasure hunt. It's too good. God only knows   105
what else we'll find, no pun intended."

That was what started it. As if by some unspoken pact, the whole party joined forces and began combing through each of the rooms, opening closets on their own, peering under chairs and cushions, feeling behind curtains, removing books from bookcases. Groups scampered, giggling and swaying, up and down the winding staircase.

"We've never explored the attic," Twinkle announced suddenly, and so everybody followed.

"How do we get up there?"

"There's a ladder in the hallway, somewhere in the ceiling."

Wearily Sanjeev followed at the back of the crowd, to point out the   110
location of the ladder, but Twinkle had already found it on her own. "Eureka!" she hollered.

Douglas pulled the chain that released the steps. His face was flushed and he was wearing Nora's feather hat on his head. One by one the guests disappeared, men helping women as they placed their strappy high heels on the narrow slats of the ladder, the Indian women wrapping the free ends of their expensive saris into their waistbands. The men followed behind, all quickly disappearing, until Sanjeev alone remained at the top of the winding staircase. Footsteps thundered over his head. He had no desire to join them. He wondered if the ceiling would collapse, imagined, for a split second, the sight of all the tumbling drunk perfumed bodies crashing, tangled, around him. He heard a shriek, and then rising, spreading waves of laughter in discordant tones. Something fell, something else shattered. He could hear them babbling about a trunk. They seemed to be struggling to get it open, banging feverishly on its surface.

He thought perhaps Twinkle would call for his assistance, but he was not summoned. He looked about the hallway and to the landing below, at the champagne glasses and half-eaten samosas and napkins smeared with lipstick abandoned in every corner, on every available surface. Then he noticed that Twinkle, in her haste, had discarded her shoes altogether, for they lay by the foot of the ladder, black patent-leather mules with heels like golf tees, open toes, and slightly soiled silk labels on the instep where her soles had rested. He placed them in the doorway of the master bedroom so that no one would trip when they descended.

He heard something creaking open slowly. The strident voices had subsided to an even murmur. It occurred to Sanjeev that he had the house all to himself. The music had ended and he could hear, if he concentrated, the hum of the refrigerator, and the rustle of the last leaves on the trees outside, and the tapping of their branches against the windowpanes. With one flick of his hand he could snap the ladder back on its spring into the ceiling, and they would have no way of getting down unless he were to pull the chain and let them. He thought of all the things he could do, undisturbed. He could sweep Twinkle's menagerie into a garbage bag and get in the car and drive it all to the dump, and tear down the poster of weeping Jesus, and take a hammer to the Virgin Mary while he was at it. Then he would return to the empty house; he could easily clear up the cups and plates in an hour's time, and pour himself a gin and tonic, and eat a plate of warmed rice and listen to his new Bach CD while reading the liner notes so as to understand it properly. He nudged the ladder slightly, but it was sturdily planted against the floor. Budging it would require some effort.

"My God, I need a cigarette," Twinkle exclaimed from above.

Sanjeev felt knots forming at the back of his neck. He felt dizzy. He 115 needed to lie down. He walked toward the bedroom, but stopped short when he saw Twinkle's shoes facing him in the doorway. He thought of her slipping them on her feet. But instead of feeling irritated, as he had ever since they'd moved into the house together, he felt a pang of anticipation at the thought of her rushing unsteadily down the winding staircase in them, scratching the floor a bit in her path. The pang intensified as he thought of her rushing to the bathroom to brighten her lipstick, and eventually rushing to get people their coats, and finally rushing to the cherry-wood table when the last guest had left, to begin opening their housewarming presents. It was the same pang he used to feel before they were married, when he would hang up the phone after one of their conversations, or when he would drive back from the airport, wondering which ascending plane in the sky was hers.

"Sanj, you won't believe this."

She emerged with her back to him, her hands over her head, the tops of her bare shoulder blades perspiring, supporting something still hidden from view.

"You got it, Twinkle?" someone asked.

"Yes, you can let go."

Now he saw that her hands were wrapped around it: a solid silver bust 120 of Christ, the head easily three times the size of his own. It had a patrician bump on its nose, magnificent curly hair that rested atop a pronounced collarbone, and a broad forehead that reflected in miniature the walls and doors and lampshades around them. Its expression was confident, as if assured of its devotees, the unyielding lips sensuous and full. It was also sporting Nora's feather hat. As Twinkle descended, Sanjeev put his hands around her waist to balance her, and he relieved her of the bust when she had reached the ground. It weighed a good thirty pounds. The others began lowering themselves slowly, exhausted from the hunt. Some trickled downstairs in search of a fresh drink.

She took a breath, raised her eyebrows, crossed her fingers. "Would you mind terribly if we displayed it on the mantel? Just for tonight? I know you hate it."

He did hate it. He hated its immensity, and its flawless, polished surface, and its undeniable value. He hated that it was in his house, and that he owned it. Unlike the other things they'd found, this contained dignity, solemnity, beauty even. But to his surprise these qualities made him hate it all the more. Most of all he hated it because he knew that Twinkle loved it.

"I'll keep it in my study from tomorrow," Twinkle added. "I promise."

She would never put it in her study, he knew. For the rest of their days together she would keep it on the center of the mantel, flanked on either side by the rest of the menagerie. Each time they had guests Twinkle would explain how she had found it, and they would admire her as they listened. He gazed at the crushed rose petals in her hair, at the pearl and sapphire choker at her throat, at the sparkly crimson polish on her toes. He decided these were among the things that made Prabal think she was wow. His head ached from gin and his arms ached from the weight of the statue. He said, "I put your shoes in the bedroom."

"Thanks. But my feet are killing me." Twinkle gave his elbow a little squeeze and headed for the living room.   125

Sanjeev pressed the massive silver face to his ribs, careful not to let the feather hat slip, and followed her.

- Look at the description of the Christian objects that appear throughout the house. How does each object emerge? Where do you see the different descriptions? How do Sanjeev and Twinkle interpret each of these objects? How does each of these interpretations reflect and define the character that we see in this story?

- How do Sanjeev and Twinkle define their own identity in relation to one another, to their cultural community with which they identify, and to the communities in which they live and work?

- How do details about each character's understanding of their house and its contents demonstrate that character's values?

Alice Walker (1944–)

Alice Walker was born in Eatonton, Georgia. She enrolled at Spelman College in Atlanta, Georgia, in 1961 and transferred to Sarah Lawrence College in New York in 1963. After receiving her BA from Sarah Lawrence in 1965, Walker moved to Mississippi to teach and promote civil rights. Her career also includes cofounding a publishing company and writing poetry, essays, short stories, novels, and literary criticism. Walker's southern roots and womanist beliefs have greatly influenced her writing. Her works often take place in rural settings and explore the historical and present-day struggles of African Americans, particularly African American women. Walker has received many awards for her work, including the 1974 American Academy and Institute of Arts and Letters Award for *In Love and Trouble: Stories of Black Women* (1973) and both the 1983 Pulitzer Prize and 1983 National Book Award for her fifth novel, *The Color Purple* (1982).

Everyday Use (1973)

for your grandmama

I will wait for her in the yard that Maggie and I made so clean and wavy yesterday afternoon. A yard like this is more comfortable than most people know. It is not just a yard. It is like an extended living room. When the hard clay is swept clean as a floor and the fine sand around the edges lined with tiny, irregular grooves, anyone can come and sit and look up into the elm tree and wait for the breezes that never come inside the house.

Maggie will be nervous until after her sister goes: she will stand hopelessly in corners, homely and ashamed of the burn scars down her arms and legs, eyeing her sister with a mixture of envy and awe. She thinks her sister has held life always in the palm of one hand, that "no" is a word the world never learned to say to her.

You've no doubt seen those TV shows where the child who has "made it" is confronted, as a surprise, by her own mother and father, tottering in weakly from backstage. (A pleasant surprise, of course: What would they do if parent and child came on the show only to curse out and insult each other?) On TV mother and child embrace and smile into each other's faces. Sometimes the mother and father weep, the child wraps them in her arms and leans across the table to tell how she would not have made it without their help. I have seen these programs.

Sometimes I dream a dream in which Dee and I are suddenly brought together on a TV program of this sort. Out of a dark and soft-seated limousine I am ushered into a bright room filled with many people. There I meet a smiling, gray, sporty man like Johnny Carson who shakes my hand and tells me what a fine girl I have. Then we are on the stage and Dee is embracing me with tears in her eyes. She pins on my dress a large orchid, even though she has told me once that she thinks orchids are tacky flowers.

In real life I am a large, big-boned woman with rough, man-working 5 hands. In the winter I wear flannel nightgowns to bed and overalls during the day. I can kill and clean a hog as mercilessly as a man. My fat keeps me hot in zero weather. I can work outside all day, breaking ice to get water for washing; I can eat pork liver cooked over the open fire minutes after it comes steaming from the hog. One winter I knocked a bull calf straight in the brain between the eyes with a sledge hammer and had the meat hung up to chill before nightfall. But of course all this does not show on television. I am the way my daughter would want me to be: a hundred pounds lighter, my skin like an uncooked barley pancake. My hair glistens in the hot bright lights. Johnny Carson has much to do to keep up with my quick and witty tongue.

But that is a mistake. I know even before I wake up. Who ever knew a Johnson with a quick tongue? Who can even imagine me looking a strange white man in the eye? It seems to me I have talked to them always with one foot raised in flight, with my head turned in whichever way is farthest from them. Dee, though. She would always look anyone in the eye. Hesitation was no part of her nature.

"How do I look, Mama?" Maggie says, showing just enough of her thin body enveloped in pink skirt and red blouse for me to know she's there, almost hidden by the door.

"Come out into the yard," I say.

Have you ever seen a lame animal, perhaps a dog run over by some careless person rich enough to own a car, sidle up to someone who is ignorant enough to be kind to him? That is the way my Maggie walks. She has been like this, chin on chest, eyes on ground, feet in shuffle, ever since the fire that burned the other house to the ground.

Dee is lighter than Maggie, with nicer hair and a fuller figure. She's a 10 woman now, though sometimes I forget. How long ago was it that the other house burned? Ten, twelve years? Sometimes I can still hear the flames and feel Maggie's arms sticking to me, her hair smoking and her dress falling off her in little black papery flakes. Her eyes seemed stretched open, blazed open by the flames reflected in them. And Dee. I see her standing off under the sweet gum tree she used to dig gum out of; a look of concentration on her face as she watched the last dingy gray board of the house fall in toward the red-hot brick chimney. Why don't you do a dance around the ashes? I'd wanted to ask her. She had hated the house that much.

I used to think she hated Maggie, too. But that was before we raised the money, the church and me, to send her to Augusta to school. She used to read to us without pity; forcing words, lies, other folks' habits, whole lives upon us two, sitting trapped and ignorant underneath her voice. She washed us in a river of make-believe, burned us with a lot of knowledge we didn't necessarily need to know. Pressed us to her with the serious way she read, to shove us away at just the moment, like dimwits, we seemed about to understand.

Dee wanted nice things. A yellow organdy dress to wear to her graduation from high school; black pumps to match a green suit she'd made from an old suit somebody gave me. She was determined to stare down any disaster in her efforts. Her eyelids would not flicker for minutes at a time. Often I fought off the temptation to shake her. At sixteen she had a style of her own and knew what style was.

I never had an education myself. After second grade the school was closed down. Don't ask me why: in 1927 colored asked fewer questions than they do now. Sometimes Maggie reads to me. She stumbles along good-naturedly but can't see well. She knows she is not bright. Like good looks and money, quickness passed her by. She will marry John Thomas (who has mossy teeth in an earnest face) and then I'll be free to sit here and I guess just sing church songs to myself. Although I never was a good singer. Never could carry a tune. I was always better at a man's job. I used to love to milk till I was hooked in the side in '49. Cows are soothing and slow and don't bother you, unless you try to milk them the wrong way.

I have deliberately turned my back on the house. It is three rooms, just like the one that burned, except the roof is tin; they don't make shingle roofs any more. There are no real windows, just some holes cut in the sides, like the portholes in a ship, but not round and not square, with rawhide holding the shutters up on the outside. This house is in a pasture, too, like the other one. No doubt when Dee sees it she will want to tear it down. She wrote me once that no matter where we "choose" to live, she will manage to come see us. But she will never bring her friends. Maggie and I thought about this and Maggie asked me, "Mama, when did Dee ever *have* any friends?"

She had a few. Furtive boys in pink shirts hanging about on washday 15 after school. Nervous girls who never laughed. Impressed with her they worshiped the well-turned phrase, the cute shape, the scalding humor that erupted like bubbles in lye. She read to them.

When she was courting Jimmy T she didn't have much time to pay to us, but turned all her faultfinding power on him. He *flew* to marry a cheap gal from a family of ignorant flashy people. She hardly had time to recompose herself.

When she comes I will meet—but there they are!

Maggie attempts to make a dash for the house, in her shuffling way, but I stay her with my hand. "Come back here," I say. And she stops and tries to dig a well in the sand with her toe.

It is hard to see them clearly through the strong sun. But even the first glimpse of leg out of the car tells me it is Dee. Her feet were always neat-looking, as if God himself had shaped them with a certain style. From the other side of the car comes a short, stocky man. Hair is all over his head a foot long and hanging from his chin like a kinky mule tail. I hear Maggie suck in her breath. "Uhnnnh," is what it sounds like. Like when you see the wriggling end of a snake just in front of your foot on the road. "Uhnnnh."

Dee next. A dress down to the ground, in this hot weather. A dress so 20 loud it hurts my eyes. There are yellows and oranges enough to throw back the light of the sun. I feel my whole face warming from the heat waves it throws out. Earrings gold, too, and hanging down to her shoulders. Bracelets dangling and making noises when she moves her arm up to shake the folds of the dress out of her armpits. The dress is loose and flows, and as she walks closer, I like it. I hear Maggie go "Uhnnnh" again. It is her sister's hair. It stands straight up like the wool on a sheep. It is black as night and around the edges are two long pigtails that rope about like small lizards disappearing behind her ears.

"Wa-su-zo-Tean-o!" she says, coming on in that gliding way the dress makes her move. The short stocky fellow with the hair to his navel is all grinning and he follows up with "Asalamalakim, my mother and sister!" He moves to hug Maggie but she falls back, right up against the back of my chair. I feel her trembling there and when I look up I see the perspiration falling off her chin.

"Don't get up," says Dee. Since I am stout it takes something of a push. You can see me trying to move a second or two before I make it. She turns, showing white heels through her sandals, and goes back to the car. Out she peeks next with a Polaroid. She stoops down quickly and lines up picture after picture of me sitting there in front of the house with Maggie cowering behind me. She never takes a shot without making sure the house is included. When a cow comes nibbling around the edge of the yard she snaps it and me and Maggie *and* the house. Then she puts the Polaroid in the back seat of the car, and comes up and kisses me on the forehead.

Meanwhile Asalamalakim is going through the motions with Maggie's hand. Maggie's hand is as limp as a fish, and probably as cold, despite the sweat, and she keeps trying to pull it back. It looks like Asalamalakim wants to shake hands but wants to do it fancy. Or maybe he don't know how people shake hands. Anyhow, he soon gives up on Maggie.

"Well," I say. "Dee."

"No, Mama," she says. "Not 'Dee,' Wangero Leewanika Kemanjo!" 25

"What happened to 'Dee'?" I wanted to know.

"She's dead," Wangero said. "I couldn't bear it any longer being named after the people who oppress me."

"You know as well as me you was named after your aunt Dicie," I said. Dicie is my sister. She named Dee. We called her "Big Dee" after Dee was born.

"But who was *she* named after?" asked Wangero.

"I guess after Grandma Dee," I said.   30

"And who was she named after?" asked Wangero.

"Her mother," I said, and saw Wangero was getting tired. "That's about as far back as I can trace it," I said. Though, in fact, I probably could have carried it back beyond the Civil War through the branches.

"Well," said Asalamalakim, "there you are."

"Uhnnnh," I heard Maggie say.

"There I was not," I said, "before 'Dicie' cropped up in our family, so   35
why should I try to trace it that far back?"

He just stood there grinning, looking down on me like somebody inspecting a Model A car. Every once in a while he and Wangero sent eye signals over my head.

"How do you pronounce this name?" I asked.

"You don't have to call me by it if you don't want to," said Wangero.

"Why shouldn't I?" I asked. "If that's what you want us to call you, we'll call you."

"I know it might sound awkward at first," said Wangero.   40

"I'll get used to it," I said. "Ream it out again."

Well, soon we got the name out of the way. Asalamalakim had a name twice as long and three times as hard. After I tripped over it two or three times he told me to just call him Hakim-a-barber. I wanted to ask him was he a barber, but I didn't really think he was, so I didn't ask.

"You must belong to those beef-cattle peoples down the road," I said. They said "Asalamalakim" when they met you, too, but they didn't shake hands. Always too busy: feeding the cattle, fixing the fences, putting up salt-lick shelters, throwing down hay. When the white folks poisoned some of the herd the men stayed up all night with rifles in their hands. I walked a mile and a half just to see the sight.

Hakim-a-barber said, "I accept some of their doctrines, but farming and raising cattle is not my style." (They didn't tell me, and I didn't ask, whether Wangero (Dee) had really gone and married him.)

We sat down to eat and right away he said he didn't eat collards and   45
pork was unclean. Wangero, though, went on through the chitlins and corn bread, the greens and everything else. She talked a blue streak over the sweet potatoes. Everything delighted her. Even the fact that we still used the benches her daddy made for the table when we couldn't afford to buy chairs.

"Oh, Mama!" she cried. Then turned to Hakim-a-barber. "I never knew how lovely these benches are. You can feel the rump prints," she said, running her hands underneath her and along the bench. Then she gave a sigh and her hand closed over Grandma Dee's butter dish. "That's it!" she said. "I knew there was something I wanted to ask you if I could have." She jumped up from the table and went over in the corner where the churn stood, the milk in it clabber by now. She looked at the churn and looked at it.

"This churn top is what I need," she said. "Didn't Uncle Buddy whittle it out of a tree you all used to have?"

"Yes," I said.

"Uh huh," she said happily. "And I want the dasher, too."

"Uncle Buddy whittle that, too?" asked the barber.   50

Dee (Wangero) looked up at me.

"Aunt Dee's first husband whittled the dash," said Maggie so low you almost couldn't hear her. "His name was Henry, but they called him Stash."

"Maggie's brain is like an elephant's," Wangero said, laughing. "I can use the churn top as a centerpiece for the alcove table," she said, sliding a plate over the churn, "and I'll think of something artistic to do with the dasher."

When she finished wrapping the dasher the handle stuck out. I took it for a moment in my hands. You didn't even have to look close to see where hands pushing the dasher up and down to make butter had left a kind of sink in the wood. In fact, there were a lot of small sinks; you could see where thumbs and fingers had sunk into the wood. It was beautiful light yellow wood, from a tree that grew in the yard where Big Dee and Stash had lived.

After dinner Dee (Wangero) went to the trunk at the foot of my bed   55
and started rifling through it. Maggie hung back in the kitchen over the dishpan. Out came Wangero with two quilts. They had been pieced by Grandma Dee and then Big Dee and me had hung them on the quilt frames on the front porch and quilted them. One was in the Lone Star pattern. The other was Walk Around the Mountain. In both of them were scraps of dresses Grandma Dee had worn fifty and more years ago. Bits and pieces of Grandpa Jarrell's Paisley shirts. And one teeny faded blue piece, about the size of a penny matchbox, that was from Great Grandpa Ezra's uniform that he wore in the Civil War.

"Mama," Wangero said sweet as a bird. "Can I have these old quilts?"

I heard something fall in the kitchen, and a minute later the kitchen door slammed.

"Why don't you take one or two of the others?" I asked. "These old things was just done by me and Big Dee from some tops your grandma pieced before she died."

"No," said Wangero. "I don't want those. They are stitched around the borders by machine."

"That'll make them last better," I said.   60

"That's not the point," said Wangero. "These are all pieces of dresses Grandma used to wear. She did all this stitching by hand. Imagine!" She held the quilts securely in her arms, stroking them.

"Some of the pieces, like those lavender ones, come from old clothes her mother handed down to her," I said, moving up to touch the quilts. Dee (Wangero) moved back just enough so that I couldn't reach the quilts. They already belonged to her.

"Imagine!" she breathed again, clutching them closely to her bosom.

"The truth is," I said, "I promised to give them quilts to Maggie, for when she marries John Thomas."

She gasped like a bee had stung her.   65

"Maggie can't appreciate these quilts!" she said. "She'd probably be backward enough to put them to everyday use."

"I reckon she would," I said. "God knows I been saving 'em for long enough with nobody using 'em. I hope she will!" I didn't want to bring up how I had offered Dee (Wangero) a quilt when she went away to college. Then she had told me they were old-fashioned, out of style.

"But they're *priceless*!" she was saying now, furiously; for she has a temper.

"Maggie would put them on the bed and in five years they'd be in rags. Less than that!"

"She can always make some more," I said. "Maggie knows how to quilt."

Dee (Wangero) looked at me with hatred. "You just will not under-   70
stand. The point is these quilts, *these* quilts!"

"Well," I said, stumped. "What would *you* do with them?"

"Hang them," she said. As if that was the only thing you *could* do with quilts.

Maggie by now was standing in the door. I could almost hear the sound her feet made as they scraped over each other.

"She can have them, Mama," she said, like somebody used to never winning anything, or having anything reserved for her. "I can 'member Grandma Dee without the quilts."

I looked at her hard. She had filled her bottom lip with checkerberry   75
snuff and it gave her face a kind of dopey, hangdog look. It was Grandma Dee and Big Dee who taught her how to quilt herself. She stood there with her scarred hands hidden in the folds of her skirt. She looked at her sister with something like fear but she wasn't mad at her. This was Maggie's portion. This was the way she knew God to work.

When I looked at her like that something hit me in the top of my head and ran down to the soles of my feet. Just like when I'm in church and the spirit of God touches me and I get happy and shout. I did something I never had done before: hugged Maggie to me, then dragged her on into the room, snatched the quilts out of Miss Wangero's hands and dumped them into Maggie's lap. Maggie just sat there on my bed with her mouth open.

"Take one or two of the others," I said to Dee.

But she turned without a word and went out to Hakim-a-barber.

"You just don't understand," she said, as Maggie and I came out to the car.

"What don't I understand?" I wanted to know.　　　　　　　　　　　80

"Your heritage," she said. And then she turned to Maggie, kissed her, and said, "You ought to try to make something of yourself, too, Maggie. It's really a new day for us. But from the way you and Mama still live you'd never know it."

She put on some sunglasses that hid everything above the tip of her nose and her chin.

Maggie smiled; maybe at the sunglasses. But a real smile, not scared. After we watched the car dust settle I asked Maggie to bring me a dip of snuff. And then the two of us sat there just enjoying, until it was time to go in the house and go to bed.

- Go back to the first two paragraphs of this story. Notice that they are written in the future tense. How do these paragraphs set up the story that follows?

- Look at the description of how Maggie walks. What details do we learn about her relation to the narrator?

- What does the narrator tell us about her own background?

- How does Dee's new name, Wangero Leewanika Kemanjo, define her character within this story?

- How does the exchange with the quilt address Dee's claim that her mother and sister "just don't understand" their heritage?

POETRY

Eavan Boland (1944–   )

The Pomegranate (1994)

The only legend I have ever loved is
the story of a daughter lost in hell.
And found and rescued there.
Love and blackmail are the gist of it.
Ceres and Persephone the names.　　　　　　　　　　　5

And the best thing about the legend is
I can enter it anywhere. And have.
As a child in exile in
a city of fogs and strange consonants,
I read it first and at first I was   10
an exiled child in the crackling dusk of
the underworld, the stars blighted. Later
I walked out in a summer twilight
searching for my daughter at bedtime.
When she came running I was ready   15
to make any bargain to keep her.
I carried her back past whitebeams
and wasps and honey-scented buddleias.
But I was Ceres then and I knew
winter was in store for every leaf   20
On every tree on that road.
Was inescapable for each one we passed.
And for me.

      It is winter
and the stars are hidden.
I climb the stairs and stand where I can see   25
my child asleep beside her teen magazines,
Her can of Coke, her plate of uncut fruit.
The pomegranate! How did I forget it?
She could have come home and been safe
and ended the story and all   30
our heartbroken searching but she reached
out a hand and plucked a pomegranate.
She put out her hand and pulled down
the French sound for apple and
the noise of stone and the proof   35
that even in the place of death,
at the heart of legend, in the midst
of rocks full of unshed tears
ready to be diamonds by the time
the story was told, a child can be   40
hungry. I could warn her. There is still a chance.
The rain is cold. The road is flint-coloured.
The suburb has cars and cable television.
The veiled stars are above ground.
It is another world. But what else   45

can a mother give her daughter but such
beautiful rifts in time?
If I defer the grief I will diminish the gift.
The legend will be hers as well as mine.
She will enter it. As I have.   50
She will wake up. She will hold
the papery, flushed skin in her hand.
And to her lips. I will say nothing.

■ Ceres was the goddess of the earth and harvest. Her daughter, Persephone,
   was kidnapped by Hades, the god of the underworld. When her mother
   came to rescue her, Persephone could not leave because she had eaten a
   pomegranate seed there. Ceres and Hades agreed to share Persephone,
   each for half of the year. When she is in the underworld, the earth goes
   dormant with fall and winter. How does the story of Persephone describe
   the relationship between this mother and her daughter?

Billy Collins (1941–   )

Lanyard (2005)

The other day I was ricocheting slowly
off the blue walls of this room,
bouncing from typewriter to piano,
from bookshelf to an envelope lying on the floor,
when I found myself in the L section of the dictionary   5
where my eyes fell upon the word *lanyard*.

No cookie nibbled by a French novelist
could send one more suddenly into the past—
a past where I sat at a workbench at a camp
by a deep Adirondack lake   10
learning how to braid thin plastic strips
into a lanyard, a gift for my mother.

I had never seen anyone use a lanyard
or wear one, if that's what you did with them,
but that did not keep me from crossing   15
strand over strand again and again
until I had made a boxy
red and white lanyard for my mother.

She gave me life and milk from her breasts,
and I gave her a lanyard. 20
She nursed me in many a sick room,
lifted spoons of medicine to my lips,
laid cold face-cloths on my forehead,
and then led me out into the airy light

and taught me to walk and swim, 25
and I, in turn, presented her with a lanyard.
Here are thousands of meals, she said,
and here is clothing and a good education.
And here is your lanyard, I replied,
which I made with a little help from a counselor. 30

Here is a breathing body and a beating heart,
strong legs, bones and teeth,
and two clear eyes to read the world, she whispered,
and here, I said, is the lanyard I made at camp.
And here, I wish to say to her now, 35
is a smaller gift—not the archaic truth

that you can never repay your mother,
but the rueful admission that when she took
the two-tone lanyard from my hands,
I was as sure as a boy could be 40
that this useless, worthless thing I wove
out of boredom would be enough to make us even.

■ How does the absurdity of the lanyard allow the poet to move beyond the "worn truth / that you can never repay your mother"?

Robert Frost (1874–1963)

Home Burial (1914)

He saw her from the bottom of the stairs
Before she saw him. She was starting down,
Looking back over her shoulder at some fear.
She took a doubtful step and then undid it
To raise herself and look again. He spoke 5
Advancing toward her: "What is it you see
From up there always—for I want to know."

She turned and sank upon her skirts at that,
And her face changed from terrified to dull.
He said to gain time: "What is it you see,"   10
Mounting until she cowered under him.
"I will find out now—you must tell me, dear."
She, in her place, refused him any help
With the least stiffening of her neck and silence.
She let him look, sure that he wouldn't see,   15
Blind creature; and awhile he didn't see.
But at last he murmured, "Oh," and again, "Oh."

"What is it—what?" she said.
                              "Just that I see."

"You don't," she challenged. "Tell me what it is."

"The wonder is I didn't see at once.   20
I never noticed it from here before.
I must be wonted to it—that's the reason.
The little graveyard where my people are!
So small the window frames the whole of it.
Not so much larger than a bedroom, is it?   25
There are three stones of slate and one of marble,
Broad-shouldered little slabs there in the sunlight
On the sidehill. We haven't to mind *those*.
But I understand; it is not the stones,
But the child's mound—"   30
                    "Don't, don't, don't, don't," she cried.
She withdrew, shrinking from beneath his arm
That rested on the banister, and slid downstairs;
And turned on him with such a daunting look,
He said twice over before he knew himself:
"Can't a man speak of his own child he's lost?"   35

"Not you!—Oh, where's my hat? Oh, I don't need it!
I must get out of here, I must get air.
I don't know rightly whether any man can"

"Amy! Don't go to someone else this time.
Listen to me. I won't come down the stairs."   40
He sat and fixed his chin between his fists.
"There's something I should like to ask you, dear."

"You don't know how to ask it."
                              "Help me, then."

Her fingers moved the latch for all reply.
"My words are nearly always an offense.   45
I don't know how to speak of anything
So as to please you. But I might be taught,
I should suppose. I can't say I see how.
A man must partly give up being a man
With women-folk. We could have some arrangement   50
By which I'd bind myself to keep hands off
Anything special you're a-mind to name.
Though I don't like such things 'twixt those that love.
Two that don't love can't live together without them.
But two that do can't live together with them."   55
She moved the latch a little, "Don't—don't go.
Don't carry it to someone else this time.
Tell me about it if it's something human.
Let me into your grief. I'm not so much
Unlike other folks as your standing there   60
Apart would make me out. Give me my chance.
I do think, though, you overdo it a little.
What was it brought you up to think it the thing
To take your mother-loss of a first child
So inconsolably—in the face of love.   65
You'd think his memory might be satisfied—"

"There you go sneering now!"

                              "I'm not, I'm not!

You make me angry. I'll come down to you.
God, what a woman! And it's come to this,
A man can't speak of his own child that's dead."   70

"You can't because you don't know how to speak.
If you had any feelings, you that dug
With your own hand—how could you?—his little grave;
I saw you from that very window there,
Making the gravel leap and leap in air,   75
Leap up, like that, like that, and land so lightly
And roll back down the mound beside the hole.
I thought, Who is that man? I didn't know you.
And I crept down the stairs and up the stairs
To look again, and still your spade kept lifting.
Then you came in. I heard your rumbling voice   80

Out in the kitchen, and I don't know why,
But I went near to see with my own eyes.
You could sit there with the stains on your shoes
Of the fresh earth from your own baby's grave   85
And talk about your everyday concerns.
You had stood the spade up against the wall
Outside there in the entry, for I saw it."

"I shall laugh the worst laugh I ever laughed.
I'm cursed. God, if I don't believe I'm cursed."   90

"I can repeat the very words you were saying:
'Three foggy mornings and one rainy day
Will rot the best birch fence a man can build.'
Think of it, talk like that at such a time!
What had how long it takes a birch to rot   95
To do with what was in the darkened parlor?
You *couldn't* care! The nearest friends can go
With anyone to death, comes so far short
They might as well not try to go at all.
No, from the time when one is sick to death,   100
One is alone, and he dies more alone.
Friends make pretense of following to the grave,
But before one is in it, their minds are turned
And making the best of their way back to life   105
And living people, and things they understand.
But the world's evil. I won't have grief so
If I can change it. Oh, I won't, I won't!"

"There, you have said it all and you feel better.
You won't go now. You're crying. Close the door.
The heart's gone out of it: why keep it up?   110
Amy! There's someone coming down the road!"
"*You*—oh, you think the talk is all. I must go—
Somewhere out of this house. How can I make you—"
"If—you—do!" She was opening the door wider.
"Where do you mean to go? First tell me that.   115
I'll follow and bring you back by force. I *will!*—"

■ How are the two characters who are speaking to each other in this poem
   related? Where do they disagree? Why is discussion of a rotting birch fence
   significant to their conversation? What are they really talking about?

Audre Lorde (1934–1992)

Now That I Am Forever with Child (1963)

How the days went
while you were blooming within me
I remember   each upon each
the swelling changed planes of my body

how you first fluttered   then jumped   5
and I thought it was my heart.

How the days wound down
and the turning of winter
I recall   you
growing heavy against the wind.   10
I thought now her hands
are formed her hair
has started to curl
now her teeth are done
now she sneezes.   15
Then the seed opened
I bore you one morning
just before spring
my head rang like a fiery piston
my legs were towers between which   20
a new world was passing.

Since then
I can only distinguish
one thread within running hours
you   flowing through selves
toward You.

■ How is "I thought it was my heart" significant to the relationship that the
   narrator describes?

Edgar Lee Masters (1869–1950)

Elsa Wertman (1915)

I was a peasant girl from Germany,
Blue-eyed, rosy, happy and strong.
And the first place I worked was at Thomas Greene's.

On a summer's day when she was away
He stole into the kitchen and took me   5
Right in his arms and kissed me on my throat,
I turning my head. Then neither of us
Seemed to know what happened.
And I cried for what would become of me.   10
And cried and cried as my secret began to show.
One day Mrs. Greene said she understood,
And would make no trouble for me,
And, being childless, would adopt it.
(He had given her a farm to be still.)
So she hid in the house and sent out rumors,   15
As if it were going to happen to her.
And all went well and the child was born—They were so kind to me.
Later I married Gus Wertman, and years passed.
But—at political rallies when sitters-by thought I was crying
At the eloquence of Hamilton Greene—   20
That was not it.
No! I wanted to say:
That's my son! That's my son!

Edgar Lee Masters (1869–1950)

Hamilton Greene (1915)

I was the only child of Frances Harris of Virginia
And Thomas Greene of Kentucky,
Of valiant and honorable blood both.
To them I owe all that I became,
Judge, member of Congress, leader in the State.
From my mother I inherited
Vivacity, fancy, language;
From my father will, judgment, logic.
All honor to them
For what service I was to the people!

■   These two poems come from a collection in which Masters imagines the
lives of people buried together in a fictional small-town cemetery. They
each speak about their lives with an honesty that they could not have
employed during their lives. How is it possible for both of the characters in
this particular pairing to be honest yet to offer such different accounts of
the same story?

Sylvia Plath (1932–1963)

Daddy (1962)

You do not do, you do not do
Any more, black shoe
In which I have lived like a foot
For thirty years, poor and white,
Barely daring to breathe or Achoo.   5

Daddy, I have had to kill you.
You died before I had time—
Marble-heavy, a bag full of God,
Ghastly statue with one gray toe
Big as a Frisco seal   10

And a head in the freakish Atlantic
Where it pours bean green over blue
In the waters off the beautiful Nauset.
I used to pray to recover you.
Ach, du.   15

In the German tongue, in the Polish town
Scraped flat by the roller
Of wars, wars, wars.
But the name of the town is common.
My Polack friend   20

Says there are a dozen or two.
So I never could tell where you
Put your foot, your root,
I never could talk to you.
The tongue stuck in my jaw.   25

It stuck in a barb wire snare.
Ich, ich, ich, ich,
I could hardly speak.
I thought every German was you.
And the language obscene   30

An engine, an engine,
Chuffing me off like a Jew.
A Jew to Dachau, Auschwitz, Belsen.
I began to talk like a Jew.
I think I may well be a Jew.   35

The snows of the Tyrol, the clear beer of Vienna
Are not very pure or true.
With my gypsy ancestress and my weird luck
And my Taroc pack and my Taroc pack
I may be a bit of a Jew.   40

I have always been scared of you,
With your Luftwaffe, your gobbledygoo.
And your neat mustache
And your Aryan eye, bright blue.
Panzer-man, panzer-man, O You—   45

Not God but a swastika
So black no sky could squeak through.
Every woman adores a Fascist,
The boot in the face, the brute
Brute heart of a brute like you.   50

You stand at the blackboard, daddy,
In the picture I have of you,
A cleft in your chin instead of your foot
But no less a devil for that, no not
Any less the black man who   55

Bit my pretty red heart in two.
I was ten when they buried you.
At twenty I tried to die
And get back, back, back to you.
I thought even the bones would do.   60

But they pulled me out of the sack,
And they stuck me together with glue.
And then I knew what to do.
I made a model of you,
A man in black with a Meinkampf look   65

And a love of the rack and the screw.
And I said I do, I do.
So daddy, I'm finally through.
The black telephone's off at the root,
The voices just can't worm through.   70

If I've killed one man, I've killed two—
The vampire who said he was you

And drank my blood for a year,
Seven years, if you want to know.
Daddy, you can lie back now.   75

There's a stake in your fat black heart
And the villagers never liked you.
They are dancing and stamping on you.
They always knew it was you.
Daddy, daddy, you bastard, I'm through.   80

■ Why does she need to kill Daddy? What is her relationship with her father?

■ How does a review of his heritage help her put the "stake in your fat black heart"?

Geoffrey Brock (1964–   )

Daddy: 1933 (2008)

If one takes
a walk on a clear sunny
day in April,

when the first
willows are in bloom,   5
one may often see

young bumblebee queens
eagerly sipping
nectar from the catkins—

thus begins   10
the one book written
by Otto Emil Plath.

It is a delightful thing
to pause and watch
these queens, clad   15

in their costumes of rich
velvet, their wings
not yet torn—

he wrote it the year after
Sylvia was born—   20
by the long foraging

flights which they will be obliged
to take later.

■ Does Brock's appropriation of Otto Emil Plath's words affect your reading of
   Plath's "Daddy"?

■ How do you interpret Brock's attitude towards his subject given that he
   offers very few words of his own?

Gary Soto (1952–   )

Black Hair (1985)

At eight I was brilliant with my body.
In July, that ring of heat
We all jumped through, I sat in the bleachers
Of Romain Playground, in the lengthening
Shade that rose from our dirty feet.   5
The game before us was more than baseball.
It was a figure—Hector Moreno
Quick and hard with turned muscles,
His crouch the one I assumed before an altar
Of worn baseball cards, in my room.   10

I came here because I was Mexican, a stick
Of brown light in love with those
Who could do it—the triple and hard slide,
The gloves eating balls into double plays.
What could I do with 50 pounds, my shyness,   15
My black torch of hair, about to go out?
Father was dead, his face no longer
Hanging over the table or our sleep,
And mother was the terror of mouths
Twisting hurt by butter knives.   20
In the bleachers I was brilliant with my body,
Waving players in and stomping my feet,
Growing sweaty in the presence of white shirts.
I chewed sunflower seeds. I drank water

And bit my arm through the late innings.   25
When Hector lined balls into deep
Center, in my mind I rounded the bases
With him, my face flared, my hair lifting
Beautifully, because we were coming home
To the arms of brown people.   30

■ What sort of role model does Hector provide for the narrator?
■ Why is the poem titled "Black Hair"?

Kitty Tsui (1953–   )

A Chinese Banquet (1994)

for the one who was not invited

it was not a very formal affair but
all the women over twelve
wore long gowns and a corsage,
except for me.

it was not a very formal affair, just   5
the family getting together,
poa poa, kuw fu without *kuw mow*
(her excuse this year is a headache).

aunts and uncles and cousins,
the grandson who is a dentist,   10
the one who drives a mercedes benz,
sitting down for shark's fin soup.

they talk about buying a house and
taking a two-week vacation in beijing.
i suck on shrimp and squab,   15
dreaming of the cloudscape in your eyes.

my mother, her voice beaded with sarcasm:
you're twenty-six and not getting younger.
it's about time you got a decent job.
she no longer asks when i'm getting married.   20

you're twenty-six and not getting younger.
what are you doing with your life?

you've got to make a living.
why don't you study computer programming?

she no longer asks when i'm getting married.   25
one day, wanting desperately to
bridge the boundaries that separate us,
wanting desperately to touch her,

tell her: mother, I'm gay,
mother i'm gay and so happy with her.   30
but she will not listen,
she shakes her head.

she sits across from me,
emotions invading her face.
her eyes are wet but   35
she will not let tears fall.

mother, i say,
you love a man.
i love a woman.
it is not what she wants to hear.   40

aunts and uncles and cousins,
very much a family affair.
but you are not invited,
being neither my husband nor my wife.

aunts and uncles and cousins   45
eating longevity noodles
fragrant with ham inquire:
sold that old car of yours yet?

i want to tell them: my back is healing,
i dream of dragons and water.   50
my home is in her arms,
our bedroom ceiling the wide open sky.

■ How do repeated phrases and images help establish characters within this
   poem?
■ How does the description of the banquet change the second time we
   read it?

Michael Lassell (1947–   )

How to Watch Your Brother Die (1985)

For Carl Morse

When the call comes, be calm.
Say to your wife, "My brother is dying. I have to fly
to California."
Try not to be too shocked that he already looks like
a cadaver.   5
Say to the young man sitting by your brother's side,
"I'm his brother."
Try not to be shocked when the young man says,
"I'm his lover. Thanks for coming."

Listen to the doctor with a steel face on.   10
Sign the necessary forms.
Tell the doctor you will take care of everything.
Wonder why doctors are so remote.

Watch the lover's eyes as they stare into
your brother's eyes as they stare into   15
space.
Wonder what they see there.
Remember the time he was jealous and
opened your eyebrow with a sharp stick.
Forgive him out loud   20
even if he can't
understand you.
Realize the scar will be
all that's left of him.

Over coffee in the hospital cafeteria   25
say to the lover, "You're an extremely good-looking
young man."
Hear him say,
"I never thought I was good enough looking to
deserve your brother."   30

Watch the tears well up in his eyes. Say,
"I'm sorry. I don't know what it means to be

the lover of another man."
Hear him say,
"It's just like a wife, only the commitment is   35
deeper because the odds against you are so much
greater."
Say nothing, but
take his hand like a brother's.

Drive to Mexico for unproven drugs that might   40
help him live longer.
Explain what they are to the border guard.
Fill with rage when he informs you,
"You can't bring those across."
Begin to grow loud.   45
Feel the lover's hand on your arm
restraining you. See in the guard's eye
how much a man can hate another man.
Say to the lover, "How can you stand it?"
Hear him say, "You get used to it."   50
Think of one of your children getting used to
another man's hatred.

Call your wife on the telephone. Tell her,
"He hasn't much time.
I'll be home soon." Before you hang up say,   55
"How could anyone's commitment be deeper than
a husband and wife?" Hear her say,
"Please. I don't want to know the details."
When he slips into an irrevocable coma,
hold his lover in your arms while he sobs,   60
no longer strong. Wonder how much longer
you will be able to be strong.
Feel how it feels to hold a man in your arms
whose arms are used to holding men.
Offer God anything to bring your brother back.   65
Know you have nothing God could possibly want.
Curse God, but do not
abandon Him.

Stare at the face of the funeral director
when he tells you he will not   70

embalm the body for fear of
contamination. Let him see in your eyes
how much a man can hate another man.
Stand beside a casket covered in flowers,
white flowers. Say,   75
"Thank you for coming," to each of the several
hundred men
who file past in tears, some of them
holding hands. Know that your brother's life
was not what you imagined. Overhear two   80
mourners say, "I wonder who'll be next?" and
"I don't care anymore,
as long as it isn't you."

Arrange to take an early flight home.
His lover will drive you to the airport.   85
When your flight is announced say,
awkwardly, "If I can do anything, please
let me know." Do not flinch when he says,
"Forgive yourself for not wanting to know him
after he told you. He did."   90
Stop and let it soak in. Say,
"He forgave me, or he knew himself?"
"Both," the lover will say, not knowing what else
to do. Hold him like a brother while he
kisses you on the cheek. Think that   95
you haven't been kissed by a man since
your father died. Think,
"This is no moment not to be strong."
Fly first class and drink Scotch. Stroke
your split eyebrow with a finger and   100
think of your brother alive. Smile
at the memory and think
how your children will feel in your arms,
warm and friendly and without challenge.

- What impact does the scar have upon the narrator?
- Find the moments in the poem where the narrator contrasts his growing
  understanding of both love and hate.

Gwendolyn Brooks (1917–2000)

Sadie and Maud (1945)

Maud went to college.
Sadie stayed at home.
Sadie scraped life
With a fine-tooth comb.

She didn't leave a tangle in.   5
Her comb found every strand.
Sadie was one of the livingest chits
In all the land.

Sadie bore two babies
Under her maiden name.   10
Maud and Ma and Papa
Nearly died of shame.

When Sadie said her last so-long
Her girls struck out from home.
(Sadie had left as heritage   15
Her fine-tooth comb.)

Maud, who went to college,
Is a thin brown mouse.
She is living all alone
In this old house.   20

- How does Brooks contrast the sisters? Which one appears to have done better in this narrative?
- What is the significance of the "fine-tooth comb"?

Sharon McCartney (1959–   )

After the Chuck Jones Tribute on Teletoon (2002)

Swan-diving off the crewcut mesas of Monument Valley
in an Icarus contraption of fluff and paste, roadrunner
bull's-eyed far below, coyote can't help it—it's an addiction,
a disease, beyond his control. He's resigned to pain,
the blacksmith's anvil stuka-ing his skull, the Sisyphean boulder   5

snowballing down each time he shoulders it upward,
his crabbed frame of bones and hide steamrollered, accordion-
folded or simply incinerated. *Hope is the thing with feathers,*
he grumbles but he can't get Prometheus out of his craw;
his scrawny belly cringes under the eagle's talons, cold avian   10
claws on his abdomen. He paws the packed earth of the river
gorge, fear and sorrow a garment he can't shed, a raiment,
his scratchy winter coat. What else is there to do in the desert?
Experience tells him he can't win and yet he persists.
Who can predict the actions of the Gods? The chances   15
are slim but statistics mean nothing to the one who succeeds.
He splashes a false horizon on sandstone, sets the sun
precariously low, dots the vanishing point, steps three paces
back with his Picasso beret and palette, thumb up to correct
the perspective, and plummets off the predictable cliff.   20

- The poet describes the actions of the cartoon characters Coyote and Roadrunner in terms of characters in classical mythology. How are such allusions appropriate? How do they impact our understanding of the cartoon actions?

Experiencing Literature through Writing

1. Select a single character in one of the works from this chapter. How has the author made this character seem real? Explain what qualities stand out in this character and how those qualities are significant to the larger story.

   a. What specific details do we learn about the character?
   b. In what context do these details appear?
   c. Are there any apparent contradictions within the character? Identify any and explain how the author resolves or makes use of these contradictions.

2. The readings in this chapter focus on relationships among people. In many of these relationships, it is clear that the characters within the relationship do not share the same views of that relationship. Describe how one character uses the relationship in this work for self-definition.

3. Characters rarely exist isolated from events. Their characteristics often become more apparent as we see them engaged, in action or with other characters. Find a specific description of a character acting in a specific scene. Explain how specific details of that action reveal the character.

4 Point of View

How Do We Know What We Know about What Happened?

We may say that a storyteller *relates* a story to us. That verb helps us think about how any narration of a story not only adds coherence to a series of random events but also gives the audience a relationship to the events, a position in relation to what has happened.

Anyone who has ever experienced some sort of misunderstanding among friends or family members is quite aware of the significance of perspective. Everyone involved has a different version of the events. We spend much time recounting each of our individual perspectives; comparing what we perceived with what someone else saw; searching for the source of the problem within these narratives; and hoping that by unfolding our different narratives, we might bring ourselves back to some semblance of the harmony that existed before the misunderstanding. It is often the person who wasn't there who gets to hear all of the accounts and to judge the merits of the different perspectives. This form of storytelling can be quite tense, and the implications can be far-reaching precisely because everyone involved has some relation to the story. Authors frequently take advantage of the intensity of feeling that comes with a particular point of view: perspective is always part of a narrative.

PERSPECTIVE

Point of view is a term that comes from the study of art and from an interest in making figures on a page seem lifelike. The point of view refers to an actual point or hole that is used to establish the position of objects within a composition. The Dürer woodcut depicts two artists who are using a mechanical method

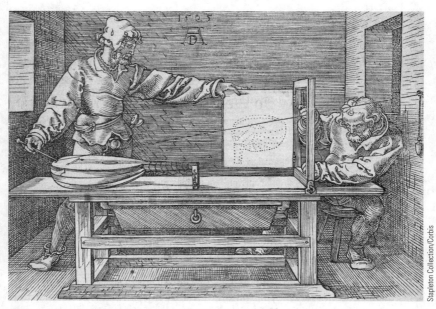

Albrecht Dürer, *Working on Perspective* (1525)

to establish point of view. They have fixed their point to the wall on the right. By stretching a string from that point to the lute that they are about to draw, the artists note where the string passes through the frame of the picture to determine precisely where the object should appear when they swing their white canvas back into the frame.

The artists depicted in the woodcut will make the scene seem real by setting all objects onto the canvas in strict relation to the viewpoint that they have arbitrarily selected. In Western art, the movement to utilize and to codify theories of perspective came during the fifteenth century, when there was a great interest in humanism and the general acknowledgment that human observations tend not to be objective; we notice things that interest us, and we define them not as they actually are but in relation to ourselves.

In a two-dimensional work of art, the sense of depth that perspective gives is an illusion. The artist distorts the objects within the field of vision to make the scene appear just as it would to that single eye "seeing" the picture. The most common "trick" in representing perspective is to make parallel lines converge as they move away from the vantage point. For instance, in the Dürer woodcut, we know that the walls of the room are parallel; the fact that they come together behind our artists is a trick of perspective to indicate increasing distance from our point of view.

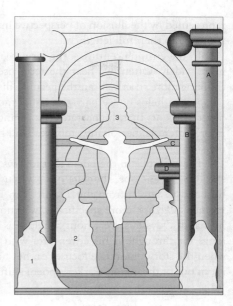

Masaccio, *Trinity* (1427–1428)

Erich Lessing/Art Resource, NY

Artists of the Renaissance made much more elaborate versions of Dürer's simple exercise. They constructed mathematical models to create the illusion of depth, such as Masaccio creates in *Trinity*. On the left, you can see his completed painting with lines drawn in to illustrate Dürer's strings and the distortions that come with perspective. On the right is a sketch of the side view (or depth) that is

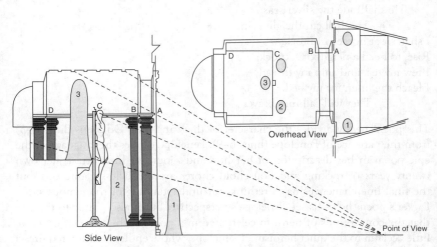

Plan and elevation of Masaccio's *Trinity* according to Piero Sanpaolesi's *Brunelleschi*

represented by the illusion of perspective in Masaccio's painting, with the strings stretched to their full length.

In the ensuing centuries, the term *point of view* has come to be used much more widely. Often, we hear the term used to mean simply an opinion. But thinking more strictly about the peculiar distortions that come from any specific perspective helps us see narrative issues more clearly. It helps us go beyond the order of events that the narrator has arranged for us and consider how the narrator's interests, personality, motives, and background are an important part of the story.

For example, in the poem that follows, Dorothy Parker writes from the perspective of Penelope, the wife of Odysseus, who waits for twenty years for her husband to return from the Trojan War. Penelope is a literary character from Homer's *Odyssey*; more specifically, we know her from the point of view of her husband, Odysseus, for whom Penelope is symbolic of the stable home that he longs for throughout his adventures with warriors, gods, and monsters. Even when the story's narrative focuses on her house, Penelope is generally up in her room out of the action. Parker's poem shifts this focus.

Dorothy Parker (1893–1967)

Penelope (1928)

In the pathway of the sun,
In the footsteps of the breeze,
Where the world and sky are one,
    He shall ride the silver seas,
        He shall cut the glittering wave.   5
I shall sit at home, and rock;
Rise, to heed a neighbor's knock;
Brew my tea, and snip my thread;
Bleach the linen for my bed.
        They will call him brave.   10

This poem neatly divides the character of the wandering Odysseus (lines 1–5) from the patience of Penelope (lines 6–9). Penelope echoes the language of the epic poem in her description of her husband's journey. In contrast, her own twenty years of rocking and household chores are much less glamorous, but the final line challenges us to rethink our understanding of the famous story. Parker's poem helps us see Penelope's perspective, but it also points to the fact that the conventions of heroism celebrated in a poem such as the *Odyssey* give little acclaim to the quiet heroism of Penelope, whose endless waiting requires a formidable endurance without the grand adventures that Odysseus enjoys.

A Note to Student Writers: Distinguishing Author from Speaker

You must accurately signal perspective in the narratives you analyze. Although an author of a poem or story may on occasion speak directly from personal feelings and convictions, it is generally best to distinguish the **poet** or **author** from the **speaker**. Although Parker is the author of "Penelope," she is not the speaker. Authors imagine, create, and give life to speakers. Authors use speakers to achieve particular effects. Notice that the previous paragraph refers to "Parker's poem" but highlights Penelope as the speaker. In some cases, this distinction is absolutely necessary (an author who relates a story through a cruel and manipulative speaker wouldn't like to be identified as one with the speaker).

THE NARRATIVE EYE

In 1818, Casper David Friedrich created two paintings that work together as a pair. Their contrasts are pronounced. One uses cool blue colors; the other uses warm oranges. In one, a man stands on top of rugged rocks; in the other, a woman stands amid softer vegetation. But the composition of the two paintings is quite similar. At the center of each, Friedrich gives us the back of a single

Caspar David Friedrich, *Wanderer above the Sea of Fog* (1818)

© Foto Marburg/Art Resource, NY

Caspar David Friedrich, *Woman in the Morning Light* (1818)

character: we share something of the characters' point of view. In one picture, we see rocks, mountains, and fog. In the other, we see a brilliant sunrise at daybreak. But we also see the characters who stand before these landscapes. By placing people in the foreground of the pictures, Friedrich changes everything. Each landscape is significant because of the character who experiences that landscape and who, therefore, defines it for us. Without the human figures, there would be scant connection between Friedrich's fog and his morning light. And we would not have some important interpretive clues. For example, we would not be prompted to think of how Friedrich defines masculine and feminine in terms of nature.

These paintings remind us again of issues vital both to visual arts and to literary texts in general. The people from whose points of view we are seeing are fictions created by artists. As much as we feel that we are getting the man's or the woman's **perspective,** that we see from their vantage point, in Friedrich's paintings we are actually standing behind each of them. Our perspective is the artist's perspective, but the artist makes us feel empathy for these characters in the foreground, and thus we forget that the artist is manipulating our reaction. In addition, it is clear that there is no getting around point of view in a work of art. Even if Friedrich removed the man and the woman from his paintings, we'd still be seeing from a perspective the artist has controlled. So always ask yourself as you read literature: Through whose eyes do I see? How might that point of view influence what I'm seeing and hearing? How does perspective shape my understanding of events?

RELIABLE AND UNRELIABLE NARRATORS

As readers, we must think hard about point of view because it strongly shapes the meaning, authority, and power we draw from fiction. We often cannot understand stories unless we understand how they are told. What is the source of a story? What prompts its telling? How much does the teller know? Can the narrator be trusted? We can begin to respond to such questions by broadly classifying narrative points of view as either third-person or first-person narration.

Third-Person Narrators

In **third-person narration,** the narrator is outside the story and refers to all characters by name or as "he," "she," or "they." An **omniscient narrator** moves freely about in time and space. In many cases, an omniscient narrator may move freely in and out of the minds of the characters. A narrator that breaks into a story to guide the reader's judgment is called an **intrusive narrator.**

At the beginning of *A Christmas Carol*, Charles Dickens employs a narrator who can't quite let the story get going. This narrator digresses upon conventions of language (why do we use "door-nail" to epitomize death?) and conventions in literature (what makes Hamlet's father a remarkable character in Shakespeare's play?) as he strives to convey the simple fact that Scrooge's partner, Marley, is dead.

Charles Dickens (1812–1870)

from A Christmas Carol (1843)

Marley was dead: to begin with. There is no doubt whatever about that. The register of his burial was signed by the clergyman, the clerk, the undertaker, and the chief mourner. Scrooge signed it. And Scrooge's name was good upon 'Change, for anything he chose to put his hand to. Old Marley was as dead as a door-nail.

Mind! I don't mean to say that I know, of my own knowledge, what there is particularly dead about a door-nail. I might have been inclined, myself, to regard a coffin-nail as the deadest piece of ironmongery in the trade. But the wisdom of our ancestors is in the simile; and my unhallowed hands shall not disturb it, or the Country's done for. You will therefore permit me to repeat, emphatically, that Marley was as dead as a door-nail.

Scrooge knew he was dead? Of course he did. How could it be otherwise? Scrooge and he were partners for I don't know how many years. Scrooge was his sole executor, his sole administrator, his sole assign, his sole residuary legatee, his sole friend, and sole mourner. And even Scrooge was not so dreadfully cut up by the sad event, but that he was an excellent man of business on the very day of the funeral, and solemnized it with an undoubted bargain.

The mention of Marley's funeral brings me back to the point I started from. There is no doubt that Marley was dead. This must be distinctly understood, or nothing wonderful can come of the story I am going to relate. If we were not perfectly convinced that Hamlet's Father died before the play began, there would be nothing more remarkable in his taking a stroll at night, in an easterly wind, upon his own ramparts, than there would be in any other middle-aged gentleman rashly turning out after dark in a breezy spot—say Saint Paul's Churchyard for instance—literally to astonish his son's weak mind. ❖

This intrusive narrator stands outside the action and refers to Scrooge in the third person but is also aware of Scrooge's thoughts (Scrooge is aware of Marley's death but not "dreadfully cut up by the sad event"). This narrator guides the reader's judgment by talking about the convention of ghost stories, pointing out to the reader that the story that follows will fit into that tradition. This narrator establishes a presence as a chatty and personable companion to lead us through a story about a character who is altogether less humane than our guide.

An author who restricts the third-person narration to the consciousness of one or more characters employs a **limited narrator** or **limited omniscient narrator**. An **objective narrator** reports, records, or shows only what could be seen or heard by an outside observer. Authors who use an objective narrator do not comment on the action. Neither do they get inside the minds of any of the characters (at least not directly). Many of Ernest Hemingway's short stories use an objective narrator. An objective narrator is sometimes called an **impersonal narrator**. The following excerpt from Hemingway's "Hills Like White Elephants" serves as a good example of objective or impersonal narration:

> The hills across the valley of the Ebro were long and white. On this side there was no shade and no trees and the station was between two lines of rails in the sun. Close against the side of the station there was the warm shadow of the building and a curtain, made of strings of bamboo beads, hung across the open door into the bar, to keep out flies. The American and the girl with him sat at a table in the shade, outside the building. It was very hot and the express from Barcelona would come in forty minutes. It stopped at this junction for two minutes and went on to Madrid. ❖

In this account, in stark contrast to the selection from Dickens, the narrator offers only facts that anyone might observe about this scene. There are no excursions into the peculiarities of the English language or thoughts about the way these characters might think about each other. Especially after reading Dickens, we might say that this narrator has no personality, but the sparse descriptive style that Hemingway uses here has its own peculiarities. What does the narrator notice?

The hills, the lack of shade, the string of beads to keep out the flies, and the train schedule. These are all things that any observer might see, but look carefully at another detail. The first character is called "the American." There is not a name, just the nationality. The second character is "the girl"—again no name, and now only a vague indicator of age. How can this objective narrator tell that this is an American rather than someone from somewhere else? Is "girl" the same as "woman"? And what does the narrator fail to describe? The time of day, the relation between these two people, what they are wearing, why they are here. The few details that the narrator has chosen to notice discreetly lends a personality to this impersonal voice and helps us see that even objectivity comes from a particular point of view.

First-Person Narrators

Such particularity is easy to note in some cases. A **first-person narrator** speaks from within the story and can know only what the imagined "I" knows ("I looked back just as he rounded the corner and saw him pick up the wallet"). Just like a jury member who decides how much to value the testimony of an eyewitness, readers of first-person narratives consider evidence of reliability. Ultimately, readers must define where the author stands in relation to the events the author's narrator recounts.

In the Sherlock Holmes stories, Dr. Watson faithfully chronicles the adventures of the detective. His characteristics as Holmes's audience and as the self-conscious recorder of what happens influence what we get to see of Holmes. We see only what Watson sees. He may be on the scene (sometimes performing some duty to help Holmes solve the crime), or he may have to trust the account that Holmes gives him. He acts as an appreciative audience to Holmes's theatrical deductive work, and we have to wonder whether his admiration of Holmes might ever make him change the scene to Holmes's advantage or to interpret events in complementary ways. Still, all in all, we accept him as a **reliable narrator** within his limits.

An author may, of course, speak directly through a character to register his or her own deepest values. But first-person narrators often express an author's moral perspective indirectly or ironically. For example, the first-person narrator could be a child who reports "facts" without understanding them. Or the first-person narrator could even be a dishonest, self-serving, cruel character. Such narrators are **unreliable narrators**. To further complicate matters, readers must also consider how involved a first-person narrator is in the story. Some first-person narrators are **detached observers** (perhaps Nick Carraway in *The Great Gatsby*); others play the central role in the story they will tell (Huck in *Adventures of Huckleberry Finn*). Sometimes, instead of hearing the polished version of a story that such a narrator might deliver to an audience, the narrative appears to be a **stream of consciousness**; we hear it as though it were the narrator's own often rambling, jumbled thoughts (Bloom in James Joyce's *Ulysses*).

Experiencing Literature through Point of View

In "The Vacation," Wendell Berry describes a video camera as an objective narrative instrument, but he also suggests the limits of such an apparatus.

Wendell Berry (1934–   )

The Vacation (1997)

Once there was a man who filmed his vacation.
He went flying down the river in his boat
with his video camera to his eye, making
a moving picture of the moving river
upon which his sleek boat moved swiftly   5
toward the end of his vacation. He showed
his vacation to his camera, which pictured it,
preserving it forever: the river, the trees,
the sky, the light, the bow of his rushing boat
behind which he stood with his camera   10
preserving his vacation even as he was having it
so that after he had had it he would still
have it. It would be there. With a flick
of a switch, there it would be. But he
would not be in it. He would never be in it.   15

This poem is about narration: Berry tells the tale of a man who can see his vacation only through the point of view of his camera. But this poem about narration is also narrated. What sort of narrator does Berry use? Berry's narrator tells a story. The narrator is not a person in the story but does have access to the thoughts of the man with the camera, as well as to knowledge that the man does not have and to a future that the man is not anticipating. Berry uses this narrator to judge the man and to comment on the problem of allowing a recording device to substitute for actual experience. Without directly stating so, Berry's narrator suggests that the man pays a price for trying so hard not to lose any of his vacation.

Making Connections

An author uses a variety of techniques to give us a character who seems real and consistent, even in inconsistencies. Character is discussed in Chapter 3. It is important to note that the narrator of a work can be considered another character, but this character may seem to be hidden, especially if the character speaks as "I."

FILM FOCUS AND ANGLES

A film also expresses a narrative voice—a point of view. The building block of any film is the smallest element: the single **frame**. In analyzing the **composition** of a painting or of a single frame, we can learn something about point of view by considering how the characters and all of the other elements are arranged within the frame. The objects in the **foreground** will demand special attention. A foregrounded subject can be further prioritized by **shallow focus**, a technique that brings a specific plane into clear focus and leaves the rest of the picture out of focus.

In this frame from *The Lone Ranger*, Tonto (Johnny Depp) commands our attention, and the rest of the scene is apparently less important. The shot itself focuses on his head rather than on anything else in the scene. It is clear that there is something else going on, but the shot indicates that whatever this other activity may be, it is not central to this scene. In **deep focus**, objects remain clear as they grow more distant; in deep focus, the cinematographer achieves a greater **depth of field** and forgoes concentration on a specific subject.

In the film still from *Hunger Games*, we can see part of the effect that director Gary Ross has achieved by focusing on Katniss Everdeen (Jennifer Lawrence) within the crowd that is waiting to hear whose name will be drawn for the "Hunger Games." By blurring the other figures in the crowd, we see that Katniss is a member of that crowd, but it is clear that she is the character we are meant to follow throughout the scene.

The angle from which a picture is taken also contributes to the overall impression we get when we see a scene. A **high-angle shot** (a picture taken from above the subject) may communicate a sweeping feel or may place the viewer in a strong position in relation to the subject.

In this frame from the film *Captain Phillips*, the high angle of the shot emphasizes the small scale of three Somali pirates in the boat even as they are menacing

The Lone Ranger (2013)

Jerry Bruckheimer Films/The Kobal Collection/Picture Desk

Lionsgate/The Kobal Collection/Picture Desk

Hunger Games (2012)

with their pointed guns. We see the scene from the point of view of the captain up on the much larger cargo ship that the pirates are about to board. These effects can be exaggerated by the degree of the angle (an **extreme high-level shot** or an **aerial view**). In the following frame, we look down on the dancing figures from *The Great Gatsby*; the camera angle contributes to the presentation of the

Michael de Luca Productions/The Kobal Collection/Picture Desk

Captain Phillips (2013)

The Great Gatsby (2013)

Bazmark Films/The Kobal Collection/Picture Desk

sumptuous setting of this film. It is a scene of excess, and the shot complements the music and the swirl of dancing and color that opens the film.

An **eye-level shot** (camera and subject at the same height) generally suggests greater immediacy by putting the viewer right with the subject. A **low-angle shot** (the camera set below the subject) may lend the subject of the picture power over the viewer.

© PRANA-FILM/The Kobal Collection

Nosferatu (1922)

For example, we look up to the hunchback in the film *Nosferatu*. Of course, the degree of the angle is important here as well. In this case it emphasizes the deformity of the figure. Just as a filmmaker or a painter must choose where to place the camera or where to stand when making a painting, an author must choose where to stand to transfer perceived reality into words. This decision impacts our perception of the entire narrative as we read.

Henry Taylor's poem "After a Movie" uses the cinematic motif to show the point of view of a person who leaves a movie and looks at the world with an eye still used to the dark world of the movie theater. Notice how the person sees real scenes as though they were frames from a film.

Henry Taylor (1942–   )

After a Movie (1996)

The last small credits fade
as house lights rise. Dazed in that radiant instant
of transition, you dwindle through the lobby
and out to curbside, pulling on a glove
with the decisive competence   5
of the scarred detective

or his quarry. Scanning
the rainlit street for taxicabs, you visualize,
without looking, your image in the window
of the jeweler's shop, where white hands hover   10
above the string of luminous pearls
on a faceless velvet bust.

Someone across the street
enters a bar, leaving behind a charged vacancy
in which you cut to the dim booth inside,   15
where you are seated, glancing at the door.
You lift an eyebrow, recognizing
the unnamed colleague

who will conspire with you
against whatever the volatile script provides....   20
A cab pulls up. You stoop into the dark
and settle toward a version of yourself.
Your profile cruises past the city
on a home-drifting stream

through whose surface, sometimes,   25
you glimpse the life between the streambed and the ripples,
as, when your gestures are your own again,
your fingers lift a cup beyond whose rim
a room bursts into clarity
and light falls on all things.   30

The character in this poem views the world as though he were one of the characters in the film that has just ended: "the scarred detective/or his quarry." He sees the world as if it were carefully arranged for this scene. He is not an actor who knows ahead of time what the "volatile script provides." But he has adopted the consciousness of the fictional character who works within the conventions of film. Instead of just looking across the street, his eyes work like a camera, "Scanning / the rainlit street." In a jeweler's shop window, his own reflection shows in the foreground, but the character sees like a camera through that reflection to focus on the string of pearls. Not until the final lines of the poem is the character able to regain his natural point of view when "a room bursts into clarity / and light falls on all things."

Experiencing Film through Point of View

Alfred Hitchcock dramatizes the problem of limited point of view in *Rear Window* (1954), the story of photographer L. B. Jefferies (Jimmy Stewart), who is confined to his apartment as he recuperates from a broken leg. To pass the time, Jefferies looks out his window into the windows of the apartments that face his, and he sees scenes from the lives of his neighbors. He would seem to be an impartial observer, and he believes that he is detached from the lives that he is observing; these are not people he knows. But as he watches, he becomes involved in the stories that unfold. He becomes a narrator creating his own order from the fragmented scenes that he observes. As the film progresses, Hitchcock suggests that Jefferies may have become more involved in these stories than in his own life.

While looking out over his neighborhood, Jefferies comes to believe that the man in an opposing apartment has killed his wife and somehow disposed of the body. Jefferies's suspicion arises only from odd things that he sees from his window, yet he eventually draws his nurse, Stella (Thelma Ritter), and his girlfriend, Lisa Fremont (Grace Kelly), into his obsession. Jefferies also calls in his friend Doyle (a police detective played by Wendell Corey) to check out the "evidence," but Doyle dismisses Jefferies's theories. The pursuit of the murderer is left to a man who can't get out of his apartment, a beautiful society woman, and a plainspoken practical nurse.

© Bettmann/CORBIS

Rear Window (1954)

Rear Window is very cleverly scripted, but its pleasures cannot be expressed by a summary of action. Hitchcock establishes in the film's opening shot what becomes the film's essential dynamic. The audience looks from an apartment window across to adjacent apartments; the audience, in effect, inhabits the apartment from which the view is shot. After the camera pans over the neighborhood, it turns back to reveal the viewer we have already been linked to (we have seen through his eyes): L. B. Jefferies, broken leg and all. The exchange between looking at and being looked at will underlie everything that follows.

Hitchcock highlights the particularity of point of view in this film by carefully framing individual shots. The border that the camera (and screen) establishes includes the very window frames that Jefferies sees through (both his own windows and his neighbors'). By calling attention to frames, Hitchcock suggests that we always shape what we see. In other words, we construct reality much like we compose a picture; we arrange what we perceive so that it fits together or "adds up" in a way that makes sense to us. Such thoughts lead us to realize that no person's vision is complete; therefore, no person's interpretation of actions can be absolutely trustworthy. Much of the suspense of *Rear Window* arises from the thought that Jefferies may not be seeing all that he needs to see. Perhaps truth requires that he see the very things the frames cut off.

Hitchcock's specific emphasis on window frames keeps us particularly aware that we are not only looking from one apartment but also peering into the private apartments of others. Frames in this respect can be seen as boundaries we are not supposed to cross. Note, for example, that Jefferies is a bit disappointed when the newlywed wife thinks to close the blinds to her bedroom window. If Jefferies is a "Peeping Tom," as his nurse at first claims, we who watch movies (at least this movie) seem no better; we, after all, are eager to see everything he sees across the square. Therefore, the thrill Jefferies and the audience get from discovery is compromised by the knowledge that the thrill does not arise from a praiseworthy pursuit of truth and justice. We all become fascinated by seeing things others would choose to hide from us.

SHIFTING PERSPECTIVES

The medium of film offers a ready alternative to the problem of a limited perspective. Almost every film offers a variety of camera angles to give us a sense that we see what is really happening. When a television network covers a sporting event, it places cameras around the arena to offer some sense of full coverage of the event. When a referee in a football game makes a call, he does so from his unique place on the field, from his observation of that play, and from his memory of what he has observed. He might confer with the other referees to confirm his call; meanwhile, the network will quickly review the play from each of its cameras, and those of us who are watching may feel as though we have a better idea of what really happened than those who have made the official call. There is a sense that the more one sees, the more likely one is to see things "correctly," but every person has a different interpretation of events; the person who hears all the different stories may or may not feel better informed than those who were actually there. The pursuit of "correctness" gives way to an interest in exploring the different approaches made possible by each point of view. Each new view deepens the experience, even if it does not resolve anything.

Just as camera angles alter the way an event is perceived, authors shift the perspective within a narrative to give particular depth to the story. In Stevie Smith's "Not Waving but Drowning," the poem shifts from an objective narrator to the voice of a dead man to those who are watching and back again to the dead man.

Stevie Smith (1902–1971)

Not Waving but Drowning (1957)

Nobody heard him, the dead man,
But still he lay moaning:
I was much further out than you thought
And not waving but drowning.

Poor chap, he always loved larking   5
And now he's dead
It must have been too cold for him his heart gave way,
They said.

Oh, no no no, it was too cold always
(Still the dead one lay moaning)   10
I was much too far out all my life
And not waving but drowning.

A central image of the poem is the difficulty posed by different perspectives: what might have looked like playful waving was actually a cry for help. The tragedy within this image is that the observers, who are aware of the man and his waving, might have offered help, but they were unable to interpret his gesture. As we hear from the man, we learn that there was a much larger communication problem. The observers characterize him as one who enjoys "larking," and even after his death, they assume that the cause of death was cold water. The dead man is still trying to correct their misperception—his "no no no" desperately tries to shake the survivors out of the nearly comical rhythm of the poem and of their confidently wrong explanations. He claims to have been "too far out" all of his life. The image of the drowned man trying to talk with those who get to interpret his life could stand for anyone in any sort of circumstance who has gotten "too far out."

Experiencing Literature through Perspective

In Frank Gaspar's poem "It Is the Nature of the Wing," the narrator strives to become conscious of multiple perspectives and is fully aware of the fragmentary nature of each one. Yet the narrator sees every distraction as potentially enlightening.

Frank X. Gaspar (1946–   )

It Is the Nature of the Wing (2004)

The problem is being a fragment trying to live out a whole life.
From this, everything follows. Or the problem is being
fractured and preoccupied with one's own mending, which
lasts as long as you do and comes with its legion of distractions.
Just now, when a lovely-throated motor comes gliding up   5
the street to one driveway or another, I can tell you
there is a certain kind of safety in a fact like that. It is so
solid you can lean on it in your bad hours. It can lift you, too,
from your despair, which is of no consequence, which can
be measured against the dropping flowers of the wisteria,   10
which fall because of their nature and essence, and stain
the redwood planks of the small deck in the back of the house.
That doesn't mean those used-up blossoms feel at home
under everyone's feet or at the mercy of my stiffened broom.
Didn't Plato say it is the nature of the wing to lift what is heavy?   15
He was speaking of love again, I can remember that much, and
then love was a ladder, too, but lifting again, always upward.
Then it is possible to love Plato for his faith, which is so strong
he becomes difficult and obdurate in the late nights. He is
hardly distracted by a passing car. He is fixed on something   20
beautiful, and why not? When I step out onto the porch, there
is nothing shining in the sky. Oh, and the wisteria blooms have
fallen some more and are like a sad carpet. And some small
insects are dancing in the garage's yellow lamp. They don't hear
the little bats squeaking. It's all right. You could even say they   25
look happy, they look joyful. Surely they are beautiful in their
ignorance and danger. See how they hold your head and command
your eye? Looking upward? Looking toward that homely light?

The narrator begins by noticing the unconsciousness of machinery, the motor
(a fragment of the car that is actually moving up the street). He moves on to
grasp at the perspective of wisteria blossoms (which may not feel at home
under our feet), Plato (an attempt to understand the line that Gaspar uses as
his title), and insects by the garage. The narrator simultaneously fails in his
quest not to be distracted from the larger questions that consume him and
succeeds by using these seemingly distracting perspectives to help him look
"upward" toward some larger philosophical understanding of unattainable
ideas such as love and faith.

An awareness of perspective helps us as readers see how authors manipulate our attention. Point of view controls the degree of sympathy we may have toward a character; it guides our judgment of the actions of characters and contributes to our interpretation of the whole work. An awareness of technique gives us a greater appreciation of the craft that goes into the literary production and enriches our conversations about what we are reading.

MODELING CRITICAL ANALYSIS: ROBERT BROWNING, MY LAST DUCHESS

One of the most famous first-person narrators in poetry is the duke who tells the story of his late wife in Robert Browning's "My Last Duchess." The poem takes place in the ducal palace of Ferrara, Italy, during the Renaissance. The duke is speaking admiringly about a painting of his wife (now deceased) that he commissioned the artist "Frà Pandolf" to paint. Through the duke's description of the painting and the manner in which the image was painted, we begin to learn something of the character of this "last Duchess" and of the duke himself. We gradually learn that the duke is speaking to an emissary for the man whose daughter might become the next duchess.

Robert Browning (1812–1889)

My Last Duchess (1842)

FERRARA

That's my last Duchess painted on the wall,
Looking as if she were alive. I call
That piece a wonder, now: Frà Pandolf's hands
Worked busily a day, and there she stands.
Will't please you sit and look at her? I said   5
"Frà Pandolf" by design, for never read
Strangers like you that pictured countenance,
The depth and passion of its earnest glance,
But to myself they turned (since none puts by
The curtain I have drawn for you, but I)   10
And seemed as they would ask me, if they durst,
How such a glance came there; so, not the first
Are you to turn and ask thus. Sir, 'twas not
Her husband's presence only, called that spot

Of joy into the Duchess' cheek: perhaps   15
Frà Pandolf chanced to say "Her mantle laps
Over my Lady's wrist too much," or "Paint
Must never hope to reproduce the faint
Half-flush that dies along her throat": such stuff
Was courtesy, she thought, and cause enough   20
For calling up that spot of joy. She had
A heart—how shall I say?—too soon made glad,
Too easily impressed; she liked whate'er
She looked on, and her looks went everywhere.
Sir, 'twas all one! My favour at her breast,   25
The dropping of the daylight in the West,
The bough of cherries some officious fool
Broke in the orchard for her, the white mule
She rode with round the terrace—all and each
Would draw from her alike the approving speech,   30
Or blush, at least. She thanked men,—good! but thanked
Somehow—I know not how—as if she ranked
My gift of a nine-hundred-years-old name
With anybody's gift. Who'd stoop to blame
This sort of trifling? Even had you skill   35
In speech—which I have not—to make your will
Quite clear to such an one, and say, "Just this
Or that in you disgusts me; here you miss,
Or there exceed the mark"—and if she let
Herself be lessoned so, nor plainly set   40
Her wits to yours, forsooth, and made excuse,
—E'en then would be some stooping, and I choose
Never to stoop. Oh sir, she smiled, no doubt,
Whene'er I passed her; but who passed without
Much the same smile? This grew; I gave commands;   45
Then all smiles stopped together. There she stands
As if alive. Will't please you rise? We'll meet
The company below, then. I repeat,
The Count your master's known munificence
Is ample warrant that no just pretense   50
Of mine for dowry will be disallowed;
Though his fair daughter's self, as I avowed
At starting, is my object. Nay, we'll go
Together down, sir. Notice Neptune, though,
Taming a sea-horse, thought a rarity,   55
Which Claus of Innsbruck cast in bronze for me!

Browning presents the poem as a speech from the duke. That speech is never interrupted by a question or a response. The duke has something to say but has no interest in hearing from someone else. In showing his gallery, the duke offers a self-portrait, perhaps a calculated self-portrait. It's essential to note that the "I" of "My Last Duchess" is emphatically not Robert Browning. Author and speaker must be kept distinct. As the speaker's conversation unfolds, so do his relations with the scene itself. He tells about "my last Duchess" and the artist who rendered her, and in so doing, the duke reveals much about himself. We pick up on his jealousy and his unrestrained frustration at what he perceives to be the lack of respect that his dead wife showed to him. As the duke finishes talking about this painting (in the middle of line 47) and moves on to the next artwork in his collection, we get the poetic equivalent of a widening shot so that we can suddenly see the audience listening to the talking duke. In this revelation, we learn more about the duke's sense of morality. He feels no qualms about having given "commands" that stopped "all smiles" from his wife. Whether he means to warn his future wife of his intolerance for any sort of indiscretion, whether he is simply brutally honest about his past, or whether he is so self-involved as to be unaware of the repugnance of his attitudes and actions, we cannot help feeling that the emissary would be wrong to let the next marriage go forward.

By creating this account from the perspective of the duke, Browning also puts us into the position of the emissary who is gradually discovering the character of a potential future member of the family. Though we begin by appreciating art and the duke's storytelling, we ultimately realize that the seemingly learned man who is talking about art is, at best, a boor, and, at worst, a murderer without a conscience.

Using Point of View to Focus Writing and Discussion

- Who is speaking? How do we know?
- How does this speaker's position influence our view of events?
- If the narrator is not a character in the action, whose point of view influences our understanding of events?
- What values or limitations impact this narrator's presentation?
- How many, if any, of these limitations did the author intend to include? For instance, we may see limitations such as a view of women's place in society that indicate the author's cultural bias rather than something that the author created as part of a character in the story.
- How do we encounter any other point of view in this narrative?
- What details in the narrative help us understand the speaker?
- What, if anything, can we see that contradicts the account that we hear from our narrator?

Anthology

MYTHOPOEIA

Characteristics of the Genre of Mythopoeia

In this genre of literature, authors create their own, often densely layered, mythologies. Rather than alluding to existing cultures and mythic stories, these works imitate traditional mythologies but have created whole worlds and cultures in which they situate these myths. Among the authors whose work is often described as fitting within this genre are J. R. R. Tolkien, C. S. Lewis, H. P. Lovecraft, and George R. R. Martin. Their stories are often illustrated with elaborate maps. The details on these maps point to complex fantastic worlds beyond what we are able to read. It is a fiction that suggests that there are layers upon layers of additional stories within this fantastic world and that what we are reading is only a limited selection.

The selections in this section illustrate the importance of perspective in shaping the reactions of the characters to a scene and the action itself. The main character in "Janus" is a real-estate agent who attributes her own success to her ability to see her properties from the perspective of her prospective clients and who works to manipulate how they see these houses. The world of this story is highly realistic, yet her special bowl makes it intriguing to think about the depths of the mythology that she has created within her world. We might look at her as both author of and participant in this mythology. What are we to do with her unwillingness to share her mythology with others?

A CRITIC WRITES ABOUT POINT OF VIEW

In his review of David O. Russell's *American Hustle*, David Denby shows how a film about greedy, manipulative, and deeply cynical characters can also be large spirited and generous. More particularly, he shows how we can sympathize—maybe even like—people we could never trust with our money. By alternating between the point of view of the two main swindlers, Irving and Sydney, Russell encourages us to not only see, but feel what drives them. We come to understand that their greatest scams don't overcome all their human feelings. Indeed, we understand that basic feelings we can all appreciate motivate behaviors we can never condone. Seen only from the outside, it would be hard to conjure up any concern for the fate of these calculating misfits, but Russell throws us fully into the high energy, on the edge lives of his characters. We don't have the time or the inclination to judge them and, as Denby makes clear, that makes for an exhilarating movie experience. Instead of a somber lesson on the corruption of the American Dream, we get vivid sense of what makes that myth compelling.

The narrator of a work of mythopoeia has a delicate task of presenting the fantastic world as though it were a real world, yet showing us the remarkable features that set it apart from the world we know. One strategy to achieve this effect is to have a character travel from our world to the fantasy world (a convenient wardrobe that transports its occupants to Narnia). Another is to present a narrator who seems altogether familiar but who reveals himself or herself as a citizen of this other world. Ursula K. Le Guin's "The Wife's Story" tells a simple domestic story, but to understand the significance of the story, we must learn the identity of the narrator.

The readings in this section illustrate the importance of perspective in shaping the reactions of the characters to a scene and the action itself. We see a particular sort of conflict with two sides of the same story in the poems by William Carlos Williams and Erica-Lynn Gambino. With the second voice, a more recent poet creates a tension and a relationship that depends upon the first voice but is not evident in the initial narrative.

These added perspectives also lead us to challenge our own capacity as readers. Generally we trust the narratives we hear, but as soon as we hear another version of events, we begin to doubt our confidence in that first version. If one perspective is distorted, how are we to know whether or not all perspectives are similarly flawed? Is there a "true" objective version of events? Would such a version be interesting?

REVIEW

David Denby (1943–)

Grand Scam (2013)

David O. Russell's "American Hustle," an intentionally overripe comedy about corruption, duplicity, loyalty, and love, is a series of astonishments. Russell, rewriting a script developed by Eric Singer, takes off from the Abscam affair—the bizarre criminal investigation of the nineteen-seventies in which the F.B.I. called on a swindler named Mel Weinberg to help ensnare public officials. (Six congressmen and a senator were among those ultimately convicted.) The bureau's elaborate sting involved two "Arab sheikhs" (both F.B.I. employees) eager to invest in Atlantic City's nascent casino industry and willing to bribe officials in order to procure operating licenses. ("Abscam" was short for "Abdul scam.") Russell has both simplified and juiced a tale that is already close to preposterous; he has created a fantasia told from the point of view of two con artists, a man and a woman (based loosely on Weinberg's mistress). Not just the crooks but virtually everyone in the movie seems slightly crazed by ambition. The one person who's ordinary in temperament, an F.B.I. supervisor played by Louis C.K., could be a member of a different species. We seem to have stepped into the magical sphere—Shakespeare rules over it and Ernst Lubitsch and Preston Sturges are denizens—where profound human foolishness becomes a form of grace.

Christian Bale, bearded and forty pounds heavier, with a complex and unreliable hairpiece (parts of it come loose at unsuitable moments), is Irving Rosenfeld, who owns a chain of dry cleaners in New York and sells forged and stolen art on the side. Like all successful con men, Irving has a serene understanding of deception: most people, he's sure, will believe what they want to believe. He's deeply dishonest but not, in most ways, a terrible man. Irving wants things to work out for people; his half-goodness is part of the expanding joke of the movie. During a winter indoor-pool party at a friend's house on Long Island, he meets an ambitious young woman, Sydney Prosser (Amy Adams), a former stripper, who is alarmingly intelligent and deter-mined to make something of herself. She and Irving bond over a mutual love of Duke Ellington and begin an affair. Sydney also joins Irving's scams, posing as a British aristocrat with banking connections; she wears dresses cleaved to the waist and boldly stares everyone down while quaking in her high heels. When the pair are caught by a high-strung F.B.I. agent, Richie DiMaso (Bradley Cooper), they wind up working for the bureau, carrying out Richie's big-time sting. Racing around New York, Irving occasionally goes home to his luscious nutbrain wife, Rosalyn (Jennifer Lawrence), who has a habit of blundering into his arrangements at exactly the wrong time. The movie evokes such classics as "Married to the Mob," "Goodfellas," and "Prizzi's Honor," but it has a fizziness all its own and a pell-mell but lucid storytelling strategy that is one of the most impressive achievements in recent filmmaking.

Like "Goodfellas," this movie uses voice-over to swing us into the action, offering first Irving's view of the world, then Sydney's, then the two in alterna-tion, as the characters expound on their up-from-the-bottom ethos of survival. They are matched in avidity by Richie, who lives at home with his mother and sets his straight hair with curlers so that he can look sexy-Italian. His desire for Sydney is aroused so quickly that he tries to pry her loose from Irving even as he's arresting her. She flirts with him and maybe falls for him, but, in any case, she's determined to use him. Currents of love and jealousy electrify the convoluted, many-faceted operation that the three pull off. In Russell's "Silver Linings Playbook," Cooper's patented anxiety—the burning blue eyes and the motormouth feverishness—nagged and clogged the early scenes. But here his rapid-fire attack is comically just right. Richie isn't as bright as he thinks he is; his mind works erratically, and Russell leaves some air around Cooper's lines, many of which take startlingly odd turns. Sprucing up like John Travolta getting ready for the disco in "Saturday Night Fever" (which came out in the same period in which this movie is set), Cooper wears a medallion on his exposed chest. His night on the disco floor with Amy Adams is the dreamiest of consummations—they're both great dancers.

One of Irving and Sydney's swindles involves loans that are promised but never paid. It's the only serious plot mistake that Russell makes—as portrayed, it's flatly unconvincing—but you pass over it, because the momentum of the story is irresistible. Working with the cinematographer Linus Sandgren, Russell takes the camera smoothly and rapidly through offices, restaurants, and parties, feeding one episode into the next, and linking them with movement or narration, like sustained musical phrases. In a few scenes, a character silently mouths the words of the song playing on the soundtrack, as if propelled by the beat in his head. The movie has a ceaseless flow, the music of greed never stops.

Richie summons a New Jersey politician, Carmine Polito (Jeremy Renner,   5 with a serious pompadour), to the Plaza Hotel and offers him a suitcase full of money to help clear the way for the casinos. Carmine refuses and leaves, but Irving chases him down in front of the hotel, and makes a personal connection with him. A true artist must keep things moving toward the instant of seduction, and Irving and Carmine, partying with their wives, become friends. The suborning of public officials requires drink, music, and long nights in restaurants, and "American Hustle" is rich in jubilant sociability. "Always take the favor over money," Irving advises Carmine, which is an outrageous thing to say, since he has just successfully bribed him. At another level, though, Irving means it, as he guiltily begins to do favors for the man he has trapped. Carmine wants to get the casinos going so that his constituents can find jobs, and Irving's attempt to protect him becomes a complicating and moving strain in the movie. "American Hustle" is built around many acts of cynical manipulation, but it is generous, even kindly, in spirit. Corruption and con artistry, in this telling, are mutually dependent, and not always evil. The single truly malevolent figure is a Mafia boss from Miami (played by Robert De Niro), whose sinister jokes make Irving and Richie panic at the thought of what they have got into.

Some of the behavior onscreen is so outlandish that you wonder, at times, if the entire movie isn't a put-on, but then a surge of feeling, or an idiosyncratic moment, brings you back to the common ground of devotion and to the mysteries of human character. Russell has finally reached the kind of sustained heightened excitement that he has been working toward ever since he directed the satirical "Flirting with Disaster," in 1996. (He reached it in parts of "The Fighter.") What he puts on the screen here is faster than life and more volatile than common realism, but it's definitely not farce. His characters act stupidly because they want something desperately, and his actors, all of them taking enormous risks, form an ensemble that is the equal of anything from Hollywood's golden age.

Jennifer Lawrence's needy stay-at-home wife has buttery golden looks and piled-up blond hair—she's a vulgar beauty with a bedroom voice. Lawrence doesn't project; she *pours*, passing without hesitation from teasing sensuality to strident bitchiness and abject anger. Amy Adams has played nice ("Junebug," "Doubt"), and she has played hard ("The Master"); this movie allows her to pull the two together, and she's remarkably vivid in scene after scene. Sydney vamps Irving in one of his dry-cleaning establishments wearing his customers' fancy clothes. (In a dizzying touch, suits hanging on a garment conveyor whirl past them as they kiss.) She grabs at a chance for the good life, even in borrowed dresses, and Adams, throwing back her head in triumph, captures the spirit of American drive. When Adams and Lawrence, playing rivals for Irving's affection, meet at last, it's literally a face-off, strength against strength at a distance of a few inches, and the screen explodes. The object of this war is an unlikely prize, but Bale makes shrewdness sexy. A Welsh actor playing Bronx Jewish in a sludgy voice, Bale is funny from the first scene, but he doesn't try for laughs—a man with a hairpiece needs to stay in control. The real Mel Weinberg is still alive, somewhere in Florida, and Bale persuades you that his character is tough enough to live forever.

"Inside Llewyn Davis" and "Nebraska" are the current standards of what a serious Hollywood movie looks like. "American Hustle" offers so many easy pleasures that people may not think of it as a work of art, but it is. In the world that Russell has created, if you don't come to play you're not fully alive. An art devoted to appetite has as much right to screen immortality as the most austere formal invention. ❖

FICTION

Ann Beattie (1947–   )

Ann Beattie was born in 1947 in Washington, D.C. Though a poor student in high school, she earned a BA from American University and an MA from the University of Connecticut. Her first published works were short stories, which began appearing regularly in *The New Yorker*. Soon thereafter she published her first novel, *Chilly Scenes of Winter*, and she has alternated ever since between the short- and

long-fiction formats. Beattie has received considerable critical acclaim for her portraits of characters belonging to her own generation, a generation at once excited
and bewildered by the social upheavals of the 1960s. These characters are typically
adrift in a world from which any certainty of value or meaning has been removed.
Initially described as a "minimalist," a label she never accepted, Beattie has developed over time a more richly descriptive style.

Janus (1986)

The bowl was perfect. Perhaps it was not what you'd select if you faced a
shelf of bowls, and not the sort of thing that would inevitably attract a lot
of attention at a crafts fair, yet it had real presence. It was as predictably
admired as a mutt who has no reason to suspect he might be funny. Just
such a dog, in fact, was often brought out (and in) along with the bowl.

Andrea was a real-estate agent, and when she thought that some prospective buyers might be dog lovers, she would drop off her dog at the same
time she placed the bowl in the house that was up for sale. She would put a
dish of water in the kitchen for Mondo, take his squeaking plastic frog out
of her purse and drop it on the floor. He would pounce delightedly, just as
he did every day at home, batting around his favorite toy. The bowl usually
sat on a coffee table, though recently she had displayed it on top of a pine
blanket chest and on a lacquered table. It was once placed on a cherry table
beneath a Bonnard still life, where it held its own.

Everyone who has purchased a house or who has wanted to sell a house
must be familiar with some of the tricks used to convince a buyer that the
house is quite special: a fire in the fireplace in early evening; jonquils in a
pitcher on the kitchen counter, where no one ordinarily has space to put
flowers; perhaps the slight aroma of spring, made by a single drop of scent
vaporizing from a lamp bulb.

The wonderful thing about the bowl, Andrea thought, was that it was
both subtle and noticeable—a paradox of a bowl. Its glaze was the color of
cream and seemed to glow no matter what light it was placed in. There
were a few bits of color in it—tiny geometric flashes—and some of these were
tinged with flecks of silver. They were as mysterious as cells seen under a
microscope; it was difficult not to study them, because they shimmered,
flashing for a split second, and then resumed their shape. Something about
the colors and their random placement suggested motion. People who liked
country furniture always commented on the bowl, but then it turned out
that people who felt comfortable with Biedermeier loved it just as much.
But the bowl was not at all ostentatious, or even so noticeable that anyone
would suspect that it had been put in place deliberately. They might notice
the height of the ceiling on first entering a room, and only when their eye

moved down from that, or away from the refraction of sunlight on a pale wall, would they see the bowl. Then they would go immediately to it and comment. Yet they always faltered when they tried to say something. Perhaps it was because they were in the house for a serious reason, not to notice some object.

Once Andrea got a call from a woman who had not put in an offer   5
on a house she had shown her. That bowl, she said—would it be possible to find out where the owners had bought that beautiful bowl? Andrea pretended that she did not know what the woman was referring to. A bowl, somewhere in the house? Oh, on a table under the window. Yes, she would ask, of course. She let a couple of days pass, then called back to say that the bowl had been a present and the people did not know where it had been purchased.

When the bowl was not being taken from house to house, it sat on Andrea's coffee table at home. She didn't keep it carefully wrapped (although she transported it that way, in a box); she kept it on the table, because she liked to see it. It was large enough so that it didn't seem fragile or particularly vulnerable if anyone sideswiped the table or Mondo blundered into it at play. She had asked her husband to please not drop his house key in it. It was meant to be empty.

When her husband first noticed the bowl, he had peered into it and smiled briefly. He always urged her to buy things she liked. In recent years, both of them had acquired many things to make up for all the lean years when they were graduate students, but now that they had been comfortable for quite a while, the pleasure of new possessions dwindled. Her husband had pronounced the bowl "pretty," and he had turned away without picking it up to examine it. He had no more interest in the bowl than she had in his new Leica.

She was sure that the bowl brought her luck. Bids were often put in on houses where she had displayed the bowl. Sometimes the owners, who were always asked to be away or to step outside when the house was being shown, didn't even know that the bowl had been in their house. Once—she could not imagine how—she left it behind, and then she was so afraid that something might have happened to it that she rushed back to the house and sighed with relief when the woman owner opened the door. The bowl, Andrea explained—she had purchased a bowl and set it on the chest for safekeeping while she toured the house with the prospective buyers, and she.... She felt like rushing past the frowning woman and seizing her bowl. The owner stepped aside, and it was only when Andrea ran to the chest that the lady glanced at her a little strangely In the few seconds before Andrea picked up the bowl, she realized that the owner must have just seen that it had been perfectly placed, that the sunlight struck the bluer part of it.

Her pitcher had been moved to the far side of the chest, and the bowl predominated. All the way home, Andrea wondered how she could have left the bowl behind. It was like leaving a friend at an outing—just walking off. Sometimes there were stories in the paper about families forgetting a child somewhere and driving to the next city. Andrea had only gone a mile down the road before she remembered.

In time, she dreamed of the bowl. Twice, in a waking dream—early in the morning, between sleep and a last nap before rising—she had a clear vision of it. It came into sharp focus and startled her for a moment—the same bowl she looked at every day.

She had a very profitable year selling real estate. Word spread, and   10
she had more clients than she felt comfortable with. She had the foolish thought that if only the bowl were an animate object she could thank it. There were times when she wanted to talk to her husband about the bowl. He was a stockbroker, and sometimes told people that he was fortunate to be married to a woman who had such a fine aesthetic sense and yet could also function in the real world. They were a lot alike, really—they had agreed on that. They were both quiet people—reflective, slow to make value judgments, but almost intractable once they had come to a conclusion. They both liked details, but while ironies attracted her, he was more impatient and dismissive when matters became many sided or unclear. They both knew this, and it was the kind of thing they could talk about when they were alone in the car together, coming home from a party or after a weekend with friends. But she never talked to him about the bowl. When they were at dinner, exchanging their news of the day, or while they lay in bed at night listening to the stereo and murmuring sleepy disconnections, she was often tempted to come right out and say that she thought that the bowl in the living room, the cream-colored bowl, was responsible for her success. But she didn't say it. She couldn't begin to explain it. Sometimes in the morning, she would look at him and feel guilty that she had such a constant secret.

Could it be that she had some deeper connection with the bowl—a relationship of some kind? She corrected her thinking: How could she imagine such a thing, when she was a human being and it was a bowl? It was ridiculous. Just think of how people lived together and loved each other.... But was that always so clear, always a relationship? She was confused by these thoughts, but they remained in her mind. There was something within her now, something real, that she never talked about.

The bowl was a mystery, even to her. It was frustrating, because her involvement with the bowl contained a steady sense of unrequited good fortune; it would have been easier to respond if some sort of demand were made in return. But that only happened in fairy tales. The bowl was just a bowl.

She did not believe that for one second. What she believed was that it was something she loved.

In the past, she had sometimes talked to her husband about a new property she was about to buy or sell—confiding some clever strategy she had devised to persuade owners who seemed ready to sell. Now she stopped doing that, for all her strategies involved the bowl. She became more delib-erate with the bowl, and more possessive. She put it in houses only when no one was there, and removed it when she left the house. Instead of just moving a pitcher or a dish, she would remove all the other objects from a table. She had to force herself to handle them carefully, because she didn't really care about them. She just wanted them out of sight.

She wondered how the situation would end. As with a lover, there was no exact scenario of how matters would come to a close. Anxiety became the operative force. It would be irrelevant if the lover rushed into someone else's arms, or wrote her a note and departed to another city. The horror was the possibility of the disappearance. That was what mattered.

She would get up at night and look at the bowl. It never occurred to her that she might break it. She washed and dried it without anxiety, and she moved it often, from coffee table to mahogany corner table or wherever, without fearing an accident. It was clear that she would not be the one who would do anything to the bowl. The bowl was only handled by her, set safely on one surface or another; it was not very likely that anyone would break it. A bowl was a poor conductor of electricity: it would not be hit by light-ning. Yet the idea of damage persisted. She did not think beyond that—to what her life would be without the bowl. She only continued to fear that some accident would happen. Why not, in a world where people set plants where they did not belong, so that visitors touring a house would be fooled into thinking that dark corners got sunlight—a world full of tricks?

She had first seen the bowl several years earlier, at a crafts fair she had visited half in secret, with her lover. He had urged her to buy the bowl. She didn't *need* any more things, she told him. But she had been drawn to the bowl, and they had lingered near it. Then she went on to the next booth, and he came up behind her, tapping the rim against her shoulder as she ran her fingers over a wood carving. "You're still insisting that I buy that?" she said. "No," he said. "I bought it for you." He had bought her other things before this—things she liked more, at first—the child's ebony-and-turquoise ring that fitted her little finger; the wooden box, long and thin, beautifully dovetailed, that she used to hold paper clips; the soft gray sweater with a pouch pocket. It was his idea that when he could not be there to hold her hand she could hold her own—clasp her hands inside the lone pocket that stretched across the front. But in time she became more attached to the bowl than to any of his other presents. She tried to talk herself out of it.

15

She owned other things that were more striking or valuable. It wasn't an object whose beauty jumped out at you; a lot of people must have passed it by before the two of them saw it that day.

Her lover had said that she was always too slow to know what she really loved. Why continue with her life the way it was? Why be two-faced, he asked her. He had made the first move toward her. When she would not decide in his favor, would not change her life and come to him, he asked her what made her think she could have it both ways. And then he made the last move and left. It was a decision meant to break her will, to shatter her intransigent ideas about honoring previous commitments.

Time passed. Alone in the living room at night, she often looked at the bowl sitting on the table, still and safe, unilluminated. In its way, it was perfect: the world cut in half, deep and smoothly empty. Near the rim, even in dim light, the eye moved toward one small flash of blue, a vanishing point on the horizon.

- How do we learn about the significance of the bowl? Trace the specific details to their specific position within the story.
- Who narrates this story? How much does the narrator know? How does this narrator impact our experience of the story? To what extent does the narrator question Andrea's perceptions of the world?
- What happens in this story? How does the story end? What changes over the course of the narrative?

Ursula K. Le Guin (1929–)

The Wife's Story

Ursula Kroeber Le Guin was born in Berkeley, California. As the daughter of an anthropologist, she was frequently exposed to a variety of international and ethnic customs. When she was a child, she particularly enjoyed Norse mythology and Native American tales; these legends later influenced her fantasy and science fiction writings. Le Guin earned her bachelor's degree from Radcliffe College in 1951 and completed her MA one year later at Columbia University. *Rocannon's World* (1966), Le Guin's first published novel, was the beginning of a series of books set on the fictitious planet Hain. As the books grew increasingly popular with audiences, Le Guin was encouraged to write for young adults, and the Earthsea series was created. Le Guin's work has been popular with critics, and her numerous honors and awards include the 1970 International Science

Fiction Association's Nebula and Hugo Awards for *The Left Hand of Darkness,* the 1972 National Book Award for Children's Literature for *The Tombs of Atuan,* and the 1995 World Fantasy Convention's Lifetime Achievement Award.

He was a good husband, a good father. I don't understand it. I don't believe in it. I don't believe that it happened. I saw it happen but it isn't true. It can't be. He was always gentle. If you'd have seen him playing with the children, anybody who saw him with the children would have known that there wasn't any bad in him, not one mean bone. When I first met him he was still living with his mother, over near Spring Lake, and I used to see them together, the mother and the sons, and think that any young fellow that was that nice with his family must be one worth knowing. Then one time when I was walking in the woods I met him by himself coming back from a hunting trip. He hadn't got any game at all, not so much as a field mouse, but he wasn't cast down about it. He was just larking along enjoying the morning air. That's one of the things I first loved about him. He didn't take things hard, he didn't grouch and whine when things didn't go his way. So we got to talking that day. And I guess things moved right along after that, because pretty soon he was over here pretty near all the time. And my sister said—see, my parents had moved out the year before and gone south, leaving us the place—my sister said, kind of teasing but serious, "Well! If he's going to be here every day and half the night, I guess there isn't room for me!" And she moved out—just down the way. We've always been real close, her and me. That's the sort of thing doesn't ever change. I couldn't ever have got through this bad time without my sis.

Well, so he come to live here. And all I can say is, it was the happy year of my life. He was just purely good to me. A hard worker and never lazy, and so big and fine-looking. Everybody looked up to him, you know, young as he was. Lodge Meeting nights, more and more often they had him to lead the singing. He had such a beautiful voice, and he'd lead off strong, and the others following and joining in, high voices and low. It brings the shivers on me now to think of it, hearing it, nights when I'd stayed home from meeting when the children was babies—the singing coming up through the trees there, and the moonlight, summer nights, the full moon shining. I'll never hear anything so beautiful. I'll never know a joy like that again.

It was the moon, that's what they say. It's the moon's fault, and the blood. It was in his father's blood. I never knew his father, and now I wonder what become of him. He was from up Whitewater way, and had no kin around here. I always thought he went back there, but now I don't know. There was some talk about him, tales, that come out after what happened to my husband. It's something runs in the blood, they say, and it may never come out, but if it does, it's the change of the moon that does it. Always it happens in the dark of the moon. When everybody's home and asleep. Something comes over the one that's got the curse in his blood, they say, and he gets up because he can't sleep, and goes out into the glaring sun, and goes off all alone—drawn to find those like him.

And it may be so, because my husband would do that. I'd half rouse and say, "Where you going to?" and he'd say, "Oh, hunting, be back this evening," and it wasn't like him, even his voice was different. But I'd be so sleepy, and not wanting to wake the kids, and he was so good and responsible, it was no call of mine to go asking "Why?" and "Where?" and all like that.

So it happened that way maybe three times or four. He'd come back   5
late and worn out, and pretty near cross for one so sweet-tempered—not wanting to talk about it. I figured everybody got to bust out now and then, and nagging never helped anything. But it did begin to worry me. Not so much that he went, but that he come back so tired and strange. Even, he smelled strange. It made my hair stand up on end. I could not endure it and I said, "What is that—those smells on you? All over you!" And he said, "I don't know," real short, and made like he was sleeping. But he went down when he thought I wasn't noticing, and washed and washed himself. But those smells stayed in his hair, and in our bed, for days.

And then the awful thing. I don't find it easy to tell about this. I want to cry when I have to bring it to my mind. Our youngest, the little one, my baby, she turned from her father. Just overnight. He come in and she got scared-looking, stiff, with her eyes wide, and then she begun to cry and try to hide behind me. She didn't yet talk plain but she was saying over and over, "Make it go away! Make it go away!"

The look in his eyes, just for one moment, when he heard that. That's what I don't want ever to remember. That's what I can't forget. The look in his eyes looking at his own child.

I said to the child, "Shame on you, what's got into you!"—scolding, but keeping her right up close to me at the same time, because I was frightened, too. Frightened to shaking.

He looked away then and said something like, "Guess she just waked up dreaming," and passed it off that way. Or tried to. And so did I. And I got real mad with my baby when she kept on acting crazy scared of her own dad. But she couldn't help it and I couldn't change it.

He kept away that whole day. Because he knew, I guess. It was just   10
beginning dark of the moon.

It was hot and close inside, and dark, and we'd all been asleep some while, when something woke me up. He wasn't there beside me. I heard a little stir in the passage, when I listened. So I got up, because I could bear it no longer. I went out into the passage, and it was light there, hard sunlight coming in from the door. And I saw him standing just outside, in the tall grass by the entrance. His head was hanging. Presently he sat down, like he felt weary, and looked down at his feet. I held still, inside, and watched—I didn't know what for.

And I saw what he saw. I saw the changing. In his feet, it was, first. They got long, each foot got longer, stretching out, the toes stretching out and the foot getting long, and fleshy, and white. And no hair on them. The hair begun to come away all over his body. It was like his hair fried away in the sunlight and was gone. He was white all over then, like a worm's skin. And he turned his face. It was changing while I looked, it got flatter and flatter, the mouth flat and wide, and the teeth grinning flat and dull, and the nose just a knob of flesh with nostril holes, and the ears gone, and the eyes gone blue—blue, with white rims around the blue—staring at me out of that flat, soft, white face.

He stood up then on two legs.

I saw him, I had to see him. My own dear love, turned into the hateful one.

I couldn't move, but as I crouched there in the passage staring out into 15
the day I was trembling and shaking with a growl that burst out into a crazy, awful howling. A grief howl and a terror howl and a calling howl. And the others heard it, even sleeping, and woke up.

It stared and peered, that thing my husband had turned into, and shoved its face up to the entrance of our house. I was still bound by mortal fear, but behind me the children had waked up, and the baby was whimpering. The mother anger come into me then, and I snarled and crept forward.

The man thing looked around. It had no gun, like the ones from the man places do. But it picked up a heavy fallen tree branch in its long white foot, and shoved the end of that down into our house, at me. I snapped the end of it in my teeth and started to force my way out, because I knew the man would kill our children if it could. But my sister was already coming. I saw her running at the man with her head low and her mane high and her eyes yellow as the winter sun. It turned on her and raised up that branch to hit her. But I come out of the doorway, mad with the mother anger, and the others all were coming answering my call, the whole pack gathering, there in that blind glare and heat of the sun at noon.

The man looked round at us and yelled out loud, and brandished the branch it held. Then it broke and ran, heading for the cleared fields and plowlands, down the mountainside. It ran, on two legs, leaping and weaving, and we followed it.

I was last, because love still bound the anger and the fear in me. I was running when I saw them pull it down. My sister's teeth were in its throat.

I got there and it was dead. The others were drawing back from the kill, because of the taste of the blood, and the smell. The younger ones were cowering and some crying, and my sister rubbed her mouth against her forelegs over and over to get rid of the taste. I went up close because I thought if the thing was dead the spell, the curse must be done, and my husband could come back—alive, or even dead, if I could only see him, my true love, in his true form, beautiful. But only the dead man lay there white and bloody. We drew back and back from it, and turned and ran, back up into the hills, back to the woods of the shadows and the twilight and the blessed dark.

- What do we know about the narrator of the story? Note where we learn each of these significant details.

- Where does our understanding of the story shift? Now, go back through the earlier parts of this narrative and note how we understand details differently now.

- What assumptions do we bring to our reading? How has Le Guin exposed these assumptions?

POETRY

Sylvia Plath (1932–1963)

Mirror (1963)

I am silver and exact. I have no preconceptions.
Whatever I see I swallow immediately
Just as it is, unmisted by love or dislike.
I am not cruel, only truthful—
The eye of a little god, four-cornered.   5
Most of the time I meditate on the opposite wall.
It is pink, with speckles. I have looked at it so long
I think it is a part of my heart. But it flickers.
Faces and darkness separate us over and over.

Now I am a lake. A woman bends over me,   10
Searching my reaches for what she really is.
Then she turns to those liars, the candles or the moon.

I see her back, and reflect it faithfully.
She rewards me with tears and an agitation of hands.
I am important to her. She comes and goes.   15
Each morning it is her face that replaces the darkness.
In me she has drowned a young girl, and in me an old woman
Rises toward her day after day, like a terrible fish.

■ In this poem the speaker is an inanimate object that takes on personal
  characteristics. Find specific images that describe what a mirror does but
  that add feeling or personal characteristics to the otherwise unfeeling
  operation of the mirror.

■ Why has Plath divided the poem into two parts? What distinguishes the first
  from the second? How is the lake distinct from the "silver and exact" mirror
  of the first stanza?

William Carlos Williams (1883–1963)

This Is Just to Say (1934)

I have eaten
the plums
that were in
the icebox

and which   5
you were probably
saving
for breakfast

Forgive me
they were delicious   10
so sweet
and so cold

■ How does Williams divide the poem? Label the content of each stanza.

■ What perspective do we get in this poem?

■ What sensations does the poem convey?

Erica-Lynn Gambino (1969–)

This Is Just to Say (1997)

(for William Carlos Williams)

I have just
asked you to
get out of my
apartment

even though   5
you never
thought
I would

Forgive me
you were   10
driving
me insane

- How does this poem ask us to reread the Williams poem?
- Look at each stanza. How does each compare to the Williams stanzas?
- In what ways can this poem stand on its own?

Edna St. Vincent Millay (1892–1950)

Childhood Is the Kingdom Where Nobody Dies (1937)

Childhood is not from birth to a certain age and at a certain age
The child is grown, and puts away childish things.
Childhood is the kingdom where nobody dies.
Nobody that matters, that is. Distant relatives of course
Die, whom one never has seen or has seen for an hour,   5
And they gave one candy in a pink-and-green stripéd bag,
    or a jack-knife,
And went away, and cannot really be said to have lived at all.

And cats die. They lie on the floor and lash their tails,
And their reticent fur is suddenly all in motion

With fleas that one never knew were there,   10
Polished and brown, knowing all there is to know,
Trekking off into the living world.
You fetch a shoe-box, but it's much too small, because she won't
     curl up now:
So you find a bigger box, and bury her in the yard, and weep.
But you do not wake up a month from then, two months   15
A year from then, two years, in the middle of the night
And weep, with your knuckles in your mouth, and say Oh, God! Oh, God!
Childhood is the kingdom where nobody dies that matters,
     —mothers and fathers don't die.
And if you have said, "For heaven's sake, must you always
     be kissing a person?"
Or, "I do wish to gracious you'd stop tapping on the window   20
     with your thimble!"
Tomorrow, or even the day after tomorrow if you're busy having fun,
Is plenty of time to say, "I'm sorry, mother."

To be grown up is to sit at the table with people who have died,
     who neither listen nor speak;
Who do not drink their tea, though they always said
Tea was such a comfort.   25

Run down into the cellar and bring up the last jar of raspberries;
     they are not tempted.
Flatter them, ask them what was it they said exactly
That time, to the bishop, or to the overseer, or to Mrs. Mason;
They are not taken in.
Shout at them, get red in the face, rise,   30
Drag them up out of their chairs by their stiff shoulders and
     shake them and yell at them;
They are not startled, they are not even embarrassed; they slide
     back into their chairs.

Your tea is cold now.
You drink it standing up,
And leave the house.   35

- The perspective of the child is a particularly rich subject for poetry. How
  does Millay define the difference between the perspective of the child and
  of the adult?

- Compare the images that she uses to illustrate this difference.

Adrienne Rich (1953–)

Living in Sin (1955)

She had thought the studio would keep itself,
no dust upon the furniture of love.
Half heresy, to wish the taps less vocal,
the panes relieved of grime. A plate of pears,
a piano with a Persian shawl, a cat   5
stalking the picturesque amusing mouse
had risen at his urging.
Not that at five each separate stair would writhe
under the milkman's tramp; that morning light
so coldly would delineate the scraps   10
of last night's cheese and three sepulchral bottles;
that on the kitchen shelf among the saucers
a pair of beetle-eyes would fix her own—
envoy from some black village in the mouldings...
Meanwhile, he, with a yawn,   15
sounded a dozen notes upon the keyboard,
declared it out of tune, shrugged at the mirror,
rubbed at his beard, went out for cigarettes;
while she, jeered by the minor demons,
pulled back the sheets and made the bed and found   20
a towel to dust the table-top,
and let the coffee-pot boil over on the stove.
By evening she was back in love again,
though not so wholly but throughout the night
she woke sometimes to feel the daylight coming   25
like a relentless milkman up the stairs.

■ Look at each of the descriptions of the appearance of the studio. Which
descriptors have negative connotations? To what extent does the progress
of the poem erase these negative feelings? Can you find any specific place
where a negative is replaced by a positive idea?

Theodore Roethke (1908–1963)

Elegy for Jane (1953)

My student, thrown by a horse

I remember the neckcurls, limp and damp as tendrils;
And her quick look, a sidelong pickerel smile;

And how, once startled into talk, the light syllables leaped for her,
And she balanced in the delight of her thought,

A wren, happy, tail into the wind,   5
Her song trembling the twigs and small branches.
The shade sang with her;
The leaves, their whispers turned to kissing;
And the mold sang in the bleached valleys under the rose.

Oh, when she was sad, she cast herself down into such a pure depth,   10
Even a father could not find her:
Scraping her cheek against straw;
Stirring the clearest water.

My sparrow, you are not here,
Waiting like a fern, making a spiny shadow.   15
The sides of wet stones cannot console me,
Nor the moss, wound with the last light.

If only I could nudge you from this sleep,
My maimed darling, my skittery pigeon.
Over this damp grave I speak the words of my love: 20
I, with no rights in this matter,
Neither father nor lover.

■ In the final lines, the poet admits that he has "no rights in this matter."
How does the poem prove that, in spite of conventions, he does have a
right to feel grief? How is the question of propriety here both similar to
and different from the question as it arises in so many of the works in this
section?

H. D. (1886–1961)

Helen (1924)

All Greece hates
the still eyes in the white face,
the lustre as of olives
where she stands,
and the white hands.   5

All Greece reviles
the wan face when she smiles,
hating it deeper still
when it grows wan and white,
remembering past enchantments   10
and past ills.

Greece sees unmoved,
God's daughter, born of love,
the beauty of cool feet
and slenderest knees,   15
could love indeed the maid,
only if she were laid,
white ash amid funereal cypresses.

■ Helen is traditionally described as the most beautiful woman of all time.
   Hers is the "face that launched a thousand ships" to fight the Trojan War.
   What evidence do we get of that beauty in this poem?

Alice Walker (1944–   )

Women (1981)

They were women then
My mama's generation
Husky of voice—Stout of
Step
With fists as well as   5
Hands
How they battered down
Doors
And ironed
Starched white   10
Shirts
How they led
Armies
Head dragged Generals
Across mined   15
Fields
Booby-trapped
Ditches

To discover books
Desks   20
A place for us
How they knew what we
Must know
Without knowing a page
Of it   25
Themselves.

- What does the poet suggest when she asserts that these women had "fists as well as / Hands"?

- How does the war imagery in this poem lead to a different conclusion from that of "The Possessive"?

DRAMA

Richard Creese (1951–   )

Creese earned his BA at the University of Colorado at Boulder and his PhD at UCLA where he currently teaches. He wrote and produced the 2002 documentary *The Man Who Lost the Civil War* about Confederate General Henry Hopkins Sibley and his little-known 1862 campaign in New Mexico. He works closely with the Independent Shakespeare Company in Los Angeles, which has staged his most recent play *Dora and Me/Yo Soy Dora*. His one-man play, *Solemn Mockeries,* draws from historical documents to present the astonishing testimony of William-Henry Ireland (1775–1835) and his account of forging a "lost" Shakespeare play called *Vortigern.*

Solemn Mockeries

ACT I

Scene 1
(*Enter William-Henry Ireland, on the edge of middle age but still boyish. The year is 1816. He wears the fashion of the day, but his clothes are threadbare. He has fallen on hard times.*)
(*The set includes a large desk which is littered with old books and papers, in no apparent order. Upstage is a platform that can suggest a stage. Posters for 18th-century plays decorate the back wall.*)

WILLIAM-HENRY: Ladies and gentlemen, yes, I am the notorious
   William-Henry Ireland. First and foremost, allow me to swear that
   I have never killed a man. I have never misbehaved myself in the
   presence of a lady, whether matron or maiden. I have never injured
   or even frightened a child. Never have I burned down a church. Never   5
   unpeopled a marketplace with cannon fire. And yet here I stand, over
   twenty years an exile. A pariah. A leper.
   For I have committed the LITERARY CRIME OF THE CENTURY.
   As one witty fellow put it, I have "seized the Chalice from the Altar of
   English Literature—and pissed therein."   10

(Pause.)

WILLIAM-HENRY: But now, man by man, woman by woman, audience by
   audience, I shall tell my story and I shall be understood. And I shall be
   forgiven.

(WILLIAM-HENRY produces an aged letter from the desk.)

WILLIAM-HENRY: Let us begin with this. As a school boy at the Academy
   at Ealing, I was considered "not over-bright." As the Headmaster put it   15
   in this letter which I once bore home for the vacation.

*(Here and elsewhere, when a character's name is given, William-Henry will perform
that character.)*

HEADMASTER: *(Frank and grave.)*
We regret to inform you that your son, Master William-Henry, is so stupid
   as to be a disgrace to his school. We would much prefer that he did
   not return to Ealing; for we conceive that <u>that</u> would be no better   20
   than robbing you of your money."

(William-Henry tosses the letter aside.)

WILLIAM-HENRY: Although I was unteachable in many ways, I was ever fond
   of making pasteboard theaters and other theatrical pursuits. My father,
   Mr. Samuel Ireland, was a friend of the proprietor of the Drury Lane
   Theater, where my sisters and I ran free. Joyful little theater rats, we   25
   scampered above, behind, beneath, and around every nook and cranny
   of the Old Drury. And the best moment of my young life was as a boy
   player in a performance at the mansion of Mr. Richard Brinsley Sheridan
   himself. Yes, <u>that</u> Mr. Sheridan! The author of *The School for Scandal*.

(Pause.)

WILLIAM-HENRY: We were theatrical in other ways, my family—my father,   30
   Mr. Ireland; my two sisters; Mrs. Freeman my, uh, our, uh, "Housekeeper"; and myself. We spent at least four nights of every week reading
   aloud from the plays of Shakespeare. Mr. Ireland would cast himself in

all the great roles, pausing often to expound on the passages that
struck his fancy.   35

MR. IRELAND: (*Earnest but tedious.*)
"O, pardon me, you poor, bleeding piece of earth!" Can you not feel
the very blood that Caesar bled? And the metaphor! Not "piece of
flesh," but "piece of earth"! In the crucible of Shakespeare's genius,
flesh magically transmogrified to earth!   40

WILLIAM-HENRY: Evenings could be quite long at the Ireland Household.
But we had a more curious literary habit. Often we read from that
sensational novel *Love and Madness*. Do you remember it? Based on
the true story of the murder of a young woman? The mistress of that
notorious rake, The Earl of Sandwich?   45

(*Pause.*)

Let us pause for an audience quiz. What famous eating device was
invented by the Earl of Sandwich? Well done. Good show. But have
you ever wondered about it? On that fateful night, at the gaming
table. He was hungry but he didn't want to leave his cards or his dice
or whatever—But what did he ask for? And didn't he have the perfect   50
name for it? What if he'd been the Earl of <u>Shitterton</u>?

(*Short pause.*)

WILLIAM-HENRY: (*cont'd*)
But I digress. We were talking about *Love and Madness*—or, rather, the
real history on which the novel was based.
As I was saying, the Earl of Sandwich had a mistress, and naturally   55
she was a raving beauty. And naturally, an unfortunate young man, a
Lieutenant Hackman, went raving mad over her. As who wouldn't?

WILLIAM-HENRY: When she refused him, he lay in wait outside the Covent
Garden Theater with two pistols and shot one bullet into her lovely
head. He then fired a second bullet into his own overheated brain.   60
Fortunately, he survived. Unfortunately, only long enough to be hanged.
Rather strange reading for a respectable family. Don't you think?

(*William-Henry finds* Love and Madness *among the other books.*)

WILLIAM-HENRY: How Mr. Ireland would throw his whole being into this
story! What sentiment! How sublime! Moving himself to tears.

MR. IRELAND: (*Reading*)   65
"The hand of Nature heaped up every species of combustible in my bosom.
The torch of Love has set the heap on fire. I must perish in the flames."

WILLIAM-HENRY: Enigmatically, Mrs. Freeman would glare icicles at him, as
if the entire novel were a weapon aimed at her. And when she read her
part, it seemed a means of revenge. On someone: 70

MRS. FREEMAN: (*Reading.*)
    "Better all should be discovered, than suffer what I suffer."

(*Uneasy pause.*)

WILLIAM-HENRY: Right. Well, this <u>is</u> a kind of confession, so I will disclose
    that Mrs. Freeman had, in fact, once been the mistress of the libertine
    Earl of Sandwich! Not the mistress who got shot outside the theater,   75
    a different one. Apparently, the Earl had wearied of Mrs. Freeman
    and had looked for a <u>decent</u> means to end their <u>indecent</u> relationship.
    Enter, the respectable Mr. Ireland, who agreed to take the lady in as his
    "Housekeeper."

(*More*)

WILLIAM-HENRY: (*cont'd*)   80
    And was paid 12,000 pounds for his compassion.
    At times, one could discern the shameless coquette who had once
    entertained the lecherous Sandwich. I can remember the ghastly
    sounds, from behind closed doors, when she would squeal, "Oh, Mr.
    Ireland! Truly, Mr. Ireland!"   85

(*A shivering pause.*)

WILLIAM-HENRY: Actually, having not yet awakened to the stirrings of man-
    hood, I had no interest in the illicit goings-on of Lord Sandwich and
    his mistresses. What fired my imagination was the long digression in
    the novel to the life of Thomas Chatterton. Young Chatterton, the
    forger of "medieval" poems on ancient parchment. The inventor of   90
    "Rowley" the poet-hyphen-monk. Until he was exposed as a fraud and
    he rabbited for London.

(*A thoughtful pause.*)

WILLIAM-HENRY: (*cont'd*)
    In London he attempted to live the life of a literary man. But, finding
    not fame and honor, but infamy and hunger, he came to a realization: 95
    He would be more satisfied, happier, altogether better off—if he were
    dead. To that end, he ingested arsenic and, true to his word, he was
    soon quite dead.

(*Depressive pause.*)

    I often envied him his fate. To end my existence in a similar cause. I
    did not go through with it. Alas. But I wrote my first poem about poor   100
    Chatterton.

(*He searches among the books and papers and produces his poem.*)

WILLIAM-HENRY: (*Reading sentimentally.*)
Comfort and joy's forever fled:

He ne'er will warble more!
Ah me! The sweetest youth is dead   105
  That e'er tuned reed before.
The hand of Misery bowed him low;
  E'en Hope forsook his brain:
Relentless man contemned his woe:
  To you he sighed in vain.   110
Oppressed with want, in wild despair he cried
"No more I'll live!" Swallowed the draught, and died.

(Having brought himself to tears, he takes a moment to regain control.)

WILLIAM-HENRY: And so I became a poet. I rushed into my father's shop
   and presented him with my first poem. But Mr. Ireland only snorted
   and ran his eyes over it, and said nothing. Like many men of the last   115
   century, Mr. Ireland believed that all the great poetry had already been
   written.

(Pause.)

WILLIAM-HENRY: Stunned, I even appealed to the icy Mrs. Freeman. Do
   you remember the sad case of the unlucky altar boy? He was passing
   beneath the bell tower of Saint Mary Woolnoth one deadly winter day   120
   when an enormous icicle fell from the tower, struck him between his
   neck and shoulder blade, and plunged into his heart? Mrs. Freeman
   was the icicle in my heart. Like the red sky of the low winter noon, her
   painted cheeks brought color but no warmth.

MRS. FREEMAN: You! A poet! Ha!   125

WILLIAM-HENRY: Was I wrong to believe that this was unnatural behavior for
   a mother?

(He realizes that he has let it slip out.)

WILLIAM-HENRY: All right, Mrs. Freeman was rather more than our
   "Housekeeper." Every indication—except her complete lack of maternal
   instincts—suggests that she was my mother. That Mr. Ireland was my   130
   <u>father</u> is far less certain. He sometimes hinted that some day, when I
   came of age, he would astonish me with a certain revelation. But he
   never did. Am I the son of the Earl of Sandwich? At least that would
   mean I am of noble blood.
   And it might explain Mr. Ireland's reserve in his interactions with   135
   me. And perhaps Mrs. Freeman, hating the Earl for essentially bribing
   Mr. Ireland to take her off his hands—

(Pause. William-Henry needs a deep drink and takes one.)

WILLIAM-HENRY: Though rarely if ever did I call Mr. Ireland "Father,"
   certainly not "Papa," you will not understand this tale of woe unless

you believe that no son ever loved father more. What an enthusiast   140
he was! Not only about Shakespeare but historical relics of any kind.

MR. IRELAND: This is the pinked leather shoe worn by Lady Lovelace of
Charles the First's court. This velvet purse given by Henry the Eighth
to Ann Boleyn. Sir Philip Sidney's jacket. An emblazoned banner of
Shakespeare's patron, the Earl of Southampton. The vestment of John   145
Wycliff, translator of the Bible. From Egypt, the seer cloth of a phar-
aoh's mummy. And from the estate of that literary lion Mr. Joseph
Addison—a fruit knife.

WILLIAM-HENRY: Now, you cannot imagine Mr. Ireland's enthusiasm
when, in the summer of 1793, he and his Unpromising Son arrived in   150
Stratford-upon-Avon. And it was with great joy that a Mr. George spotted us climbing down from the coach. He knew a good mark when he
saw one.

MR. GEORGE: Would you be needing a guide, sir? I can show you the true
and authentic Stratford-upon-Avon—not the springes to catch wood-   155
cocks and tourists in. My own great, great, great grandfather—Julius
George, his name was—happened to be a mate of the Bard's brother.
The character of Julius Caesar was based on him, on my ancestor: The
Good God's Truth, that is. Wouldn't you like to see New Place? The
Immortal Poet's home?   160

WILLIAM-HENRY: Naturally, it was determined that the knowledgeable Mr.
George <u>must</u> be our guide. He led us along a winding route past brows-
ing herds of Bardolaters. At last we came to the site of New Place.
Frankly, I was rather disappointed to learn that the actual house had
been razed many years before. But Mr. Ireland stood transfixed for   165
several minutes, as if the image <u>behind</u> his eyeballs were all he needed.

MR. GEORGE: And there, sir, once stood the famous mulberry tree. The very
tree planted by William Shakespeare. I know because my great, great,
great grandfather lent him the spade and sold him the manure.

MR. IRELAND: But what happened to the famous mulberry?   170

MR. GEORGE: Oh, sir! What a tale of villainy that is. The evilest man ever to
walk this green earth, he must have been. That Reverend Mr. Gastrell
who wearied of all the tourists embracing the mulberry—practically
trying to start a family with it, if you take my meaning! So in a fit of
pique, he chopped it down.   175

MR. IRELAND: What villainy, indeed! Does any poor remnant remain?

MR. GEORGE: Now there, sir, you are in luck.

WILLIAM-HENRY: So he led us to the "Shakespeare Curiosity Shop" where the
wood of the ill-fated mulberry had produced a vast collection of relics.
Thousands of relics! What a monstrously large tree that mulberry   180

must have been! Mr. Ireland snatched up a wooden goblet carved from
the very tree.

MR. IRELAND: A toothpick case cut with Shakespeare's coat of arms.
Tobacco stoppers, wafer seals...

WILLIAM-HENRY: Every sort of wooden bagatelle, joined his collection.   185

MR. GEORGE: And now, sir, it would be a crime, a mortal sin, to come
all the way to Stratford-upon-Avon and <u>not</u> see Anne Hathaway's Cottage.
My great, great aunt Gemma was a neighbor of the Hathaways. Lived to be
107 and kept all her wits and all her teeth besides. It took a runaway horse
to finally pop her off, it did. And rumor has it that Old Auntie Gemma was   190
the model for the Shrew in that play what's called "Taming a Shrew." Could
be true, I don't know. But it is an indisputable fact that she knew young
Willie Shakespeare when he came a-wooing the delectable Miss Hathaway.
(*Pause.*)

WILLIAM-HENRY: So our Mr. George led us to the Cottage where we found
an old chair that he said had long been known as...   195

MR. GEORGE: "Shakespeare's courting chair." In this very chair, sir, the Bard
would sit and bounce his bonny Anne upon his knee.

WILLIAM-HENRY: How could Fate be so kind to one man? For two
hundred years the Courting Chair had escaped the notice of
collectors. Until now. Until Mr. Ireland. <u>And</u> it was for sale!   200
Mr. Ireland pronounced a poetic speech and pressed his obeisant lips
to the oaken seat. Then he reached his hand into his trembling purse,
and the Courting Chair was ours.

MR. GEORGE: Do you know about Clopton House, sir? And the Ghost of
Charlotte Clopton?   205

MR. IRELAND: Actually, we've only come about the Bard.

MR. GEORGE: This <u>is</u> about the Bard, sir. Indirectly. You, see, the Bard
would have walked by that house and heard the wailing of the poor
lady. It had been a plague year, you see, and perhaps you know that
sometimes the plague can mimic the symptoms of death. Many a live   210
burial in those days, sir. Far too many, in my opinion. Poor Charlotte
was one of them. Imagine her ghastly cries, sir. As she attempted to
claw her way out of that marble tomb. It was from that very episode
that Shakespeare took the story of Juliet waking up in her own tomb.

MR. IRELAND: (*totally uninterested*)   215
How interesting.

MR. GEORGE: More to the point, sir, were Master Shakespeare's papers.

MR. IRELAND: Papers? What papers?

MR. GEORGE: As I was saying, sir, Shakespeare's home at New Place
burned to the ground in the Great Conflagration. But certain citizens of   220

the town—including my great, great grandfather—rushed into the flames to
rescue many arms full of the Late Bard's papers. From there they conveyed
them to Clopton House. And to this day Clopton House still stands.

WILLIAM-HENRY: For some reason, upon our arrival at the aforesaid house,
Mr. George then took his leave of us. After being generously paid, of   225
course. Clopton House was now owned by a Farmer Williams whom
we first spotted tending to a ridiculously large cow. Mr. Ireland immediately accosted the man.

MR. IRELAND: Now see here, if you have in your possession any papers per
taining to Shakespeare the Poet, you must show them to us at once.   230

WILLIAM-HENRY: It would seem that in the Midlands it is considered the
height of discourtesy to accost one while one is milking one's cow. For
Farmer Williams seemed to take an immediate disliking to us.

FARMER WILLIAMS: (*Still milking.*)
By God, I wish you had arrived a little sooner! Why, it isn't a   235
fortnight since I removed some baskets of letters and papers, in order
to clear a small chamber for some young partridges which I wished to
bring up alive! Do you like partridges, sir?

MR. IRELAND: Damn the partridges, man?! Where are Shakespeare's papers!

FARMER WILLIAMS: (*sadistically lying*)   240
Oh, I recall many a bundle with that name wrote upon them. But
being that it was a cold day, I placed them in the fireplace and I made
a roaring fire of them.

WILLIAM-HENRY: Poor Mr. Ireland! Quite gray with grief, he sank to his
knees and pulled his coat up over his head. When he could regain his   245
feet and his ability to speak, he demanded to see the partridge room,
as if some scrap of Shakespeariana might have survived. Alas, the partridge room contained nothing but underfed partridges.

(*Pause.*)

WILLIAM-HENRY: Mr. Ireland did not speak again until our coach was
approaching London.   250

MR. IRELAND: Oh, Sam, my lad.

WILLIAM-HENRY: He called me "Sam."

(*He considers telling us why, then decides not to.*)

MR. IRELAND: Oh, Sam, I would give all that I possess for even one
scrap of parchment on which the Immortal Shakespeare had signed
his name.   255

WILLIAM-HENRY: How trivial can seem the moment that destroys a life. I
silently vowed that I would be the one to present Mr. Ireland with an
authentic autograph by the Bard. From that day on, I would prowl the
book stalls and shops of London and sometimes discover an ancient relic.

Proudly, I would present it to Mr. Ireland, and for a moment he would   260
acknowledge me, sometimes even shake my hand.

MR. IRELAND: Good show, Sam. A very tangible find.

WILLIAM-HENRY: And he would find a place among the shelves for my
prize, organized as they were by Mr. Ireland's eccentric system:
All books arranged not by subject or date, but by color.   265

(Thoughtful pause.)

WILLIAM-HENRY: I should perhaps explain why he called me "Sam."

(More)

WILLIAM-HENRY: *(cont'd)*
Mr. Ireland's Christian name was Samuel and he gave that name to
the first born of twins. I was the second and the sickliest, but alas, the
only twin to survive. Yes, it is difficult to be addressed in one's youth   270
by the name of a dead baby, but you must understand that Mr. Ireland
spoke the name with affection. It was nothing for a sensitive boy to feel
slighted by or upset about.

(Long Pause.)

Scene 2

WILLIAM-HENRY: Being considered a "boy of no parts" had its advantages.
Nothing was expected of me, so I lived like a newborn puppy,
chasing butterflies and toys. Into my seventeenth year, I lived mostly
inside my own head. How often I sighed to be the inmate of some
gloomy mansion or dreary heath or enchanted castle. I collected   5
ancient armor—helmets, breastplates, gorgets, cuisses. And when
the moon shone upon my private armory, I would sit upright in bed
and picture scenes from the old romances. I considered a career as a
knight-errant.
Alas! Then it all ended without warning when Mr. Ireland pronounced   10
a kind of death sentence:

MR. IRELAND: Sam, it is high time for you to enter a profession. I have
arranged for you to be articled to a conveyancer in chancery.

WILLIAM-HENRY: No evil wizard in a romance ever uttered a curse more
ruinous: "Articled to a conveyancer in chancery"? In plain English,   15
it meant the death of my delicate soul. My body, meanwhile, for the
next fifty or sixty years, would be employed in writing and rewriting
contracts for the conveyance of property in a windowless tomb that
reeked of dead paper.
The only relief from that torment was Montague Talbot, who worked   20
nearby and who immediately appointed himself my "only friend."
Talbot was about thirty and a would-be actor who greeted every

eventuality—disappointment, grief, amusement, all—with the same
braying laugh.

TALBOT: We're nothing but pit ponies, Ireland. Have you seen them?   25
Poor innocent beasts that descend into the black mines, where they
live out their days in coal dust and darkness. Farewell forever,
O Golden Sun. O good, green earth, adieu. That's the life of a
conveyancer—if you call it being alive.

WILLIAM-HENRY: Talbot was a bit of an ass, but he was right about our   30
occupation. Luckily, I was left alone in chambers much of the time,
and I would amuse myself with ancient deeds with their musty parchment and their wax seals. I hoped that Fortune would throw some
document my way which bore the autograph of William Shakespeare.
But after six dismal months, I came to a fatal realization: If I wanted   35
Good Fortune, I would have to fabricate it for myself.

(Pause.)

WILLIAM-HENRY: I had seen facsimiles of Shakespeare's signatures and
for Mr. Ireland's sake I began to trace them and to imitate the Bard's
hand. Day after day, I perfected my craft, and eventually could sign
his autograph better than my own. I watered down some modern ink   40
and wrote on the flyleaf of an Elizabethan book. But the ink appeared
obviously modern. How could one imitate that brown patina so
distinctive of ancient documents?
I laughingly showed my first forgery to a bookbinder named Laurie
and announced that I had produced it. He seemed unconcerned, as if   45
forgery were the common practice.

MR. LAURIE: (Unconcerned)
A goodly hand, sir. It appears to be from many years back. But the
color, sir, is all wrong, isn't it?

WILLIAM-HENRY: Then one of the journeymen gave me some fatal advice.   50

JOURNEYMAN: (Low-class London accent)
Here's the man for the job, sir. You take these here phials, these three,
which we use for marbling the covers of our calf bindings, see? And you
shake them together all frothy-like and this produces a kind of fermen-
tation, doesn't it? And, look ye, that lovely, antique brown color you   55
find not in the ink of your modern age.

WILLIAM-HENRY: And so he wrote with the concoction on a scrap of paper.
But the writing was too dim to be legible. And I said so.

JOURNEYMAN: Naturally, it would be dim, sir. That's why you take your
manuscript and you hold it up to your roaring fire. And the writing   60
darkens, as if with the centuries, and no one is the wiser.

WILLIAM-HENRY: If only I had walked away from that bookbinder's shop
and left that phial of ink on the counter! Instead, I produced a

mortgage deed, signed William Shakespeare. Trembling with hope
and dread, I presented it to Mr. Ireland. "Sir, what do you think   65
of this?" At first he only mumbled and sighed, as if it were only
another of my attempts at poetry. But then he focused his
eyes and they grew wide and a vein stood out on his forehead, and
he spoke to me:

MR. IRELAND: Sam, my boy. My dear, dear boy. By God! I have now held   70
in my hands an autograph of Shakespeare. I can die a happy man.

WILLIAM-HENRY: But Mr. Ireland did not die. Nor did he remain happy
for long. Soon, he began to covet more relics of the same nature.
Which, since I had wisely purchased a large phial of the guilty ink,
I quickly produced. I forged a note to Shakespeare's fellow player,   75
John Heminges; a letter of thanks to the Earl of Southampton;
then the Earl's gracious reply to the Bard; and several other legal
and business papers—all of which Mr. Ireland swallowed like a wolf.
Then I took a creative leap. Mr. Ireland had often worried about
Shakespeare's religion: 80

MR. IRELAND: They say that he "died a Papist," Sam. And what woeful
tidings those would be. The noblest soul of all time and ages, lost
in the darkness of superstition and idolatry!

WILLIAM-HENRY: So I fabricated a Profession of Faith, obviously written
by a Protestant. And Mr. Ireland was giddy with reverence and relief.   85
And naturally he could not resist the pleasure of showing off my
"discoveries" to two eminent experts of the day.
You cannot imagine the very picnic of panic that <u>that</u> induced in my
young nerves! Mr. Joseph Wharton: The author of that great treatise,
The Essay on Pope! And Dr. Samuel Parr, the famous Headmaster at   90
Harrow. A renowned classical scholar known as the hardest flogger
ever to haunt a school! And both were in a carriage, now, as we spoke,
riding to pronounce me a fraud and a fabricator.

(Fearful pause.)

WILLIAM-HENRY: I confess that I had never felt so much terror. My skin
crawled and tingled under the heat of the anticipated flogging. The   95
two scholars arrived and trained their intelligence on Mr. Ireland as
he read aloud my forged Profession of Faith:

MR. IRELAND: Forgive, O Lord, all our sins. And with thy great goodness
take us all to thy breast. O cherish us like the Sweet Chicken that
under the covert of her spreading wings receives her little brood   100
and hovering over them keeps them harmless and in safety. Signed:
William Shakespeare.

WILLIAM-HENRY: There was an eternal wait for Dr. Parr to pronounce his
sentence.

DOCTOR PARR: (*Gravely.*)   105
Sir, we have many very fine passages in our church service, and our litany abounds with beauties; but here, sir, <u>here</u> is a man who has out-distanced us all!

WILLIAM-HENRY: What I felt! What jaw-dropping joy! I did not dare even smile, let alone cry out like a young wolf at his first kill. "Outdistanced" 110 them all! <u>My</u> writings taken for those of the Matchless Bard? Mine! Contrary to all opinion, I was not half-witted, after all! I was fired with the discovery of my own genius.

(*Pause.*)

WILLIAM-HENRY: Oh, those were halcyon days, when I was the new light in my father's eye. I would awake joyfully, often before dawn, spring   115 from my bed, eager for the new day's adventure, the new day's forgery. Now, Mr. Ireland would often sit in "Shakespeare's Courting Chair," an imaginary Anne Hathaway on his knee, and lament the fact that we knew nothing of their courtship. So I fabricated a letter from the Bard to his future Bride full of all the sentiments my father could wish for.   120 How Mr. Ireland savored it as he read.

MR. IRELAND: "O, Anne! I cherish thee in my heart for thou art as a tall cedar stretching forth its branches and succoring smaller plants from the nipping winter or the boisterous winds!"

WILLIAM-HENRY: Mr. Ireland was a worshiper at the shrine of the the True   125 Faith, but he was not above making a guinea or two off the pilgrims. He scheduled viewings of the Relics for Mondays, Wednesdays, and Fridays from noon until three in the afternoon. And the admission fee was a not inconsiderable ten shillings, sixpence.
On the day when Mr. Ireland displayed the letter to Anne Hathaway   130 there appeared my self-appointed "only friend," Montague Talbot, barely stifling his braying laugh. I knew he could not afford the price of admission so he must have talked his way past Mr. Ireland. During the intermission in the viewing—during which we sold refreshments— Talbot accosted me, a drink in each hand.   135

TALBOT: Well, well, my little pit pony, gulling the Eminent Literati of London, are we?

WILLIAM-HENRY: (*to Talbot*)
"Gulling" has nothing to do with it. Who let you in? And who gave you those drinks?   140

TALBOT: Well, I am known in London, aren't I?

WILLIAM-HENRY: (*to the Audience*)
It was almost as if he had guessed my secret. But how could he? He was an ass. And he was an actor!

TALBOT: Those wax seals, William-Henry. They seem so genuine.   145

WILLIAM-HENRY: Of course they're genuine. And you're drunk.

TALBOT: They remind me of something. Oh, yes, the bluish-green seals on the de Farnham documents. You know, the ones that went missing.

WILLIAM-HENRY: You talk too much, Talbot. And you don't know a bloody thing. I'll have you thrown out of here.   150

TALBOT: What a way to talk to your Only Friend!

WILLIAM-HENRY: So Talbot handed me his two empty glasses and sidled off somewhere. Probably to finish off the cucumber Shittertons.

(Pause.)

WILLIAM-HENRY: Meanwhile, the Eminent Literati continued to praise my work. And why not? The sentiments expressed were exactly what they   155
all wished Shakespeare <u>had</u> expressed—though he never had. Then, upon learning that Talbot was an actor, Mr. Ireland awarded him the honor of reading from the tender poem to Anne Hathaway which I had forged and attached to the letter.

TALBOT: *(Reading, over-acting.)*   160
Is there in heaven aught more rare
Than thou sweet Nymph of Avon fair.
Is there on Earth a Man more true
Than Willy Shakespeare is to you.

Since then nor fortune, death nor Age   165
Can faithful Willy's love assuage,
Then do I live and die for you,
Thy Willy sincere and most true.

(Pause.)

WILLIAM-HENRY: Now it had never occurred to me that I would also have to fabricate a history to account for the fabrications themselves.   170

WILLIAM-HENRY: When suddenly demanded, I stammered out a lame tale of a Mr. H., a gentleman of fortune whom I had met in a coffeehouse. He had invited me to his palatial home, where he happened to have "many old papers" from his ancestors. Being a man of uncommon generosity, he made a present of the papers to me.   175
I blundered on that the gentleman, being possessed of a large fortune, did not think it fit to subject himself to impertinent questions. That was the best I could do on the spur of the moment.
But there was no respite from Mr. Ireland's daily insistence that he meet Mr. H. and see for himself the magical trunk which I had   180
invented to hold the Shakespearean treasures. All I could do was distract him by promising more and greater treasures. For example, the original manuscript of *King Lear*. Mr. Ireland had often lamented Shakespeare's lack of decorum.

MR. IRELAND: I tell you, Sam: The licentious passages were added by the   185
licentious players!

WILLIAM-HENRY: So, for my next over-reaching undertaking I decided to
   rewrite in the old hand a manuscript of *King Lear*. Why didn't anyone
   notice that I was essentially forging on demand? I was like a waiter in a
   chop house. "Yes, sir, <u>yours</u> I believe was the mutton. And for you, sir,   190
   the manuscript of *King Lear*." I set to work improving that immortal
   tragedy. This was Shakespeare true to himself, as his self should have
   been. I was not rewriting so much as <u>recovering</u> the real Shakespeare.

(He finds a manuscript among the books and papers.)

WILLIAM-HENRY: I am especially proud of this augmentation I made to
   Kent's last lines in the tragedy. He says: 195
   I have a journey sir, shortly to go,
   My master calls, and I must not say no.

Really? Is that the best the Immortal Bard could do? I improved it in
the following manner:

   Thanks, Sir, but I go to that unknown Land   200
   That chains each pilgrim fast within its Soil,
   By living men most shunned, most dreaded;
   Still, my good master this same Journey took,
   He calls me, I am content and straight obey.
   Then farewell World, the busy Scene is done.   205
   Kent lived most true. Kent dies most like a man.

WILLIAM-HENRY: It was while I was forging that particular manuscript
   that Talbot surprised me in the act.

TALBOT: I've caught you, William-Henry Ireland. In flagrante delicto!
   I knew what you were up to with those papers. A blind man could   210
   see it. "Out! Out! Vile jelly!" Indeed!

WILLIAM-HENRY: It was almost a relief to confess my crimes. I begged him,
   for the sake of my father, not to reveal my secrets.

TALBOT: *(A long conspiratorial laugh.)*
   Reveal them? Why would I reveal such a source of fun? Oh, how   215
   you've netted me, William-Henry, and hauled me onto your Ship
   of Corruption. As the Bard says, "The fraud of England hath now
   entrapped the noble-minded Talbot."

WILLIAM-HENRY: *(to Talbot)*
   Certainly not—   220

TALBOT: It's not like your Only Friend would blackmail you, is it? But
   perhaps I <u>could</u> take just one little document. Say, this letter?

(Talbot grabs a paper.)

   Well, well, my lucky day, isn't it? From Queen Elizabeth. To Master
   Shakespeare, c/o the Globe. Oughta be worth a fiver, anyway.

WILLIAM-HENRY: (*to the audience*)   225
    I hated to part with even one of my creations, but if it would buy my
    "only Friend's" silence, so be it.
(*to Talbot*)
    Take it, Talbot, and go away.
TALBOT: Oh, I shall go away, all right. I shall go on the stage. Not here in
    London, in this graveyard of talent. But to that small pond wherein   230
    I shall be a mighty whale. To Dublin! Only remember, Ireland, you've
    promised me half.
WILLIAM-HENRY: Half? Half of what?
TALBOT: Half of your illicit gains, of course.
WILLIAM-HENRY: (*to the audience*)   235
    Since I had given everything to my father and therefore expected no
    gains at all, I gladly promised him half.
(*to Talbot*)
    That's more than fair, Talbot. Give my regards to Peters Street.
    Remember me to Merrion Square.
TALBOT: One more thing, William-Henry. Consider the dangers of some   240
    true or fraudulent descendent of Shakespeare's jumping out of the
    family tree? He could claim all of <u>our</u> papers as his own.
WILLIAM-HENRY: I immediately hated the fact that he now referred to the
    papers as our papers, but I let it go, concerned only with getting him
    on his way.   245
TALBOT: Look to it, William-Henry. Adieu, adieu. Remember me.
WILLIAM-HENRY: Alas, Talbot had a point: I needed an ancestor. And fast.
    So, contrary to the usual course of Nature, I conceived one. I gave
    him the name "Ireland," and went perhaps too far when I named
    him after myself. I invented a "Deed of Gift" from William Shake-   250
    speare to an Elizabethan William-Henry Ireland:
    "Whereas on or about the third day of the last month, being August,
    having with my good friend Master William-Henry Ireland and others
    taken boat, we did purpose going up Thames; but some, being much
    too merry with liquor, did upset our aforesaid barque."   255
    Etcetera, etcetera. The gist of which being that my ancestor had saved
    him from drowning. The grateful Shakespeare concluded, "And
    for the which, I do hereby give him as followeth: My written plays
    Henry IV, *Henry V*, and *King Lear*. And I do also give unto the aforesaid
    William-Henry Ireland my never yet imprinted play *Vortigern*."   260
(*Pause.*)

WILLIAM-HENRY: But what, you wonder, is this *Vortigern*? In the soaring
    pride of those days, fanned by the uplifting winds of my father's

praise, I decided to write my own Shakespearean play. Or rather, the
tragedy that Shakespeare <u>would</u> have written if he'd lived in times less
benighted than his own.   265

My play, *Vortigern*, was conceived—as are we all—as the result of the
frenzied motions of a father. It happened that Mr. Ireland's fingers
had become entangled in my lapels.

MR. IRELAND: (*Angrily shaking William-Henry*)

By God, Sam, I will meet your mysterious Mr. H., or by God, sir,   270
I will die in the attempt!

WILLIAM-HENRY: As he shook me, I contemplated the painting of King
Vortigern which had long hung in my father's study. With my usual
impetuosity, I made a sudden announcement: "I have seen in that
trunk a manuscript. An unknown play by William Shakespeare!"   275
At once, the image of King Vortigern was still again. And again I saw
that expression of warmth in my father's eyes that said, "Yes, this is my
son after all." And then he spoke to me.

MR. IRELAND: My dear Sam. Have you? Is it possible?

WILLIAM-HENRY: (*Aside, cocky*)   280

Oh, yes. That very night I set to work composing Shakespeare's lost
play: *Vortigern*! <u>My</u> *Vortigern*! But that will be the subject of Act II.
Let us pause for refreshment and an intermission. Who's for the bar?!

(*Exit.*)

ACT II

Scene 1
(*Enter William-Henry.*)

WILLIAM-HENRY: Ladies and Gentlemen, you cannot imagine my joy as I
accompanied Mr. Ireland to the Drury Lane Theater to negotiate for the
representation of *Vortigern*!

I remembered those carefree days, my sisters and I skittering above,
behind, and below that very stage. And suddenly there I was, with my   5
father, in the presence of Mr. Richard Brinsley Sheridan, Esq. How
mannerly he was! How cordial. They said of him that his glance was
so masterly, his speech so captivating, that visitors often forgot what
they had come for—and they went away before they could ask him for
anything. As if they had come only to <u>gaze</u> at the great man.   10
Our case was better. For Mr. Sheridan—without the benefit of having
read the play—immediately claimed the first rights to produce *Vortigern*!
<u>My</u> *Vortigern*! At Drury Lane, the finest theater in London.

WILLIAM-HENRY: What's more, the title role would be played by none other
than Mr. John Philip Kemble, the actor-manager at Old Drury and the   15
finest tragedian of the age. You must remember his immortal Hamlet

of 1783, the performance that made the role <u>his</u>, forever. And now I had
composed an even greater role: Vortigern.

KEMBLE: (*grandly acting.*)

Now is the cup of my ambition full!   20
And by this rising tempest in my blood
I feel the fast approach of greatness which
E'en like a peasant stoops for my acceptance.

WILLIAM-HENRY: Not terribly bad, is it? And what an opportunity for an
actor! Not to mention the actor's sister. For Kemble's sister was the   25
magnificent Mrs. Sarah Siddons, famous forever for her Lady Macbeth.
For her I wrote the part of Edmunda, Vortigern's all-suffering wife.
Have you seen her portrait? Sir Joshua Reynolds himself painted her
as "The Tragic Muse."

(*He sits and demonstrates Mrs. Siddons' pose as the Tragic Muse.*)

MRS. SIDDONS: (*Still posing*)   30
O! heavens in your great mercy aid me now.
My brain grows hot! I can no longer bear it.
Forbid his presence too. O! I am distracted!

WILLIAM-HENRY: Notice how masterfully I insert the "O's"! It's the "O's"
that give the play its distinctive emotional flavor.   35

MRS. SIDDONS: O! I have need of medicine and of comfort;
Again my wits do wander, I'll retire.
And let the bleak winds battle with my head,
I'll to my couch and lay me on its pillow.

WILLIAM-HENRY: You can see why I was so confident of success. But even   40
better, the part of Flavia would be played by the beautiful, the enchanting
Mrs. Jordan! It was said that to hear Mrs. Jordan laugh was to drink nectar.

(*He demonstrates her nectar-like laugh.*)

WILLIAM-HENRY: And I ask you gentlemen, is there anything in this wide
world so alluring as a gorgeous, voluptuous woman dressed as a boy?
I had seen her do Rosalind in *As You Like It* and I must confess that   45
naked Master Cupid had shot into my heart <u>not</u> an arrow but a
thunderbolt.

WILLIAM-HENRY: And the most amorous moment of my young life
suddenly occurred.

(*To Mrs. Jordan*)

May I, Mrs. Jordan, have the honor of presenting you with my part.   50
Er, may I honor your parts....

(He plays Mrs. Jordan doing her nectar-drinking laugh.)

WILLIAM-HENRY: I mean, of course, my part I wrote for . . . That is, that
   Shakespeare wrote for you.

MRS. JORDAN: No, my dear young man. The honor is all mine.

WILLIAM-HENRY: And then I said: Er. Um. I. . . . Or words to that effect.   55
   All right, the dialogue wasn't quite "Romeo and Juliet"—except in my
   own young heart.

(Pause.)

WILLIAM-HENRY: By the way, "Mrs. Jordan" was only a stage name, the
   "Mrs." attached to discourage cads and bounders—not that such a
   thing would discourage a cad or a bounder. In any case, accompanied   60
   by the loyal Fool, Flavia escapes the evil court—dressed as a boy. Very
   Shakespearean, that.
   Alas, although she was not married, she was already spoken for by the
   Duke of Clarence. His mistress, in fact. The future mother of his
   children. Yes, that Duke of Clarence, who God willing shall become   65
   the King of England, William the Fourth of that name. Bad news for
   my marriage hopes. But excellent news for *Vortigern*. For Mrs. Jordan
   had quickly won over the Duke as a supporter of the papers and the
   play. And his regal status gave him authority. He pronounced:

DUKE OF CLARENCE:

(Quite taffy-nosed)

   I do deem these documents authentic and the play *Vortigern* beyond   70
   a doubt the work of Our Great Author Shakespeare and by far his
   greatest tragedy.

WILLIAM-HENRY: So, now I know what you are thinking. With such a cast
   and such a script, what could possibly go wrong? In reality, I was a
   knight errant and *Vortigern* was my steed. And we were in a terrible   75
   race against an ogre. No, I do not exaggerate. The race was to get my
   play onstage, where it could be judged on its own merits. Once I was
   established at the theater, if the papers were exposed as forgeries, no
   one would mind so much a minor literary hoax. I'd be seen as another
   Chatterton, young, brilliant, and easy to forgive. Unless—   80

(He rummages among the books and pulls out Malone's tome.)

WILLIAM-HENRY: Unless this malicious tome appeared before my play.
   Written by that self-appointed "scholar" Edmond Malone. Malone,
   the murderer of the brilliant and sensitive Thomas Chatterton. Yes,
   madam, murderer! It was my word. For it was Malone who exposed
   poor Chatterton's poems as forgeries. Malone killed him as surely as   85
   did the arsenic. So as you hear of my heroic quest to bring my poor

play to the stage in time, you must imagine Malone like an ogre
in his lair. Whence the hideous sounds: Malone gnawing on poor
Chatterton's bones.

(He tosses the tome away.)

WILLIAM-HENRY: Much against <u>my</u> wishes, Mr. Ireland determined that   90
he would publish *The Miscellaneous Papers of William Shakespeare.*
As things were, visitors could look at but not touch samples of the
ancient relics. But if we published the papers Malone could have
his cruel way with them, and all would be lost.
Mr. Sheridan had given us his assurance that the play would be   95
performed by December 15th, 1795, which would be just in time;
for Mr. Ireland planned to publish the *Miscellaneous Papers* later
in that same month. My play would be judged by its own beauties,
unsullied by doubts about the papers.

(Pause.)

WILLIAM-HENRY: But the odious Malone leaked out his commentary   100
about certain details he had gathered from those who had seen the
papers. For example, in my letter from Queen Elizabeth, I had made
a small error. It was addressed to "Master Shakespeare at the Globe"
and dated 1588. I hadn't realized that the Globe had not been built
until 1599.   105
And the "Deed of Gift," dated 1604, which gave my imaginary ancestor the rights to *King Lear*, neglected to explain what <u>that</u> play—which
had not been written yet—was doing in <u>this</u> deed. That was the kind
of trivia that the pernickety Mr. Malone trafficked in.

(Pause.)

WILLIAM-HENRY: And there were other setbacks. One day during rehearsal   110
my father appeared, his face quite fishified, and he announced:
MR. IRELAND: The Lord Chamberlain has banned the play because of the
regicide in Act I.
WILLIAM-HENRY: In the era of the French Revolution, of course, regicide
was considered a rather disagreeable topic. So my father began the   115
tedious process of rewriting, for which he had no talent whatsoever.
And now, a busy spider in my own tangled web, I had to wait until
Mr. Ireland retired for the night, then retrieve from their hiding
place his inept "improvements"; then I had to forge <u>his</u> handwriting
and before dawn sneak my own rewrites back into <u>his</u> papers.   120
Somehow, I managed it, and the Lord Chamberlain was mollified
and *Vortigern* was back on course. Then Mr. Ireland brought some
wonderful news:

MR. IRELAND: My dear Sam, Mr. John Henry Pye himself has been to
    Norfolk Street.   125

(*More*)

MR. IRELAND (*cont'd*):   Mr. Pye, the Poet Laureate! And he has shed tears
    over *Vortigern* and sworn that he had not been so affected by a play in
    all his years. And best of all, he's agreed to write the Prologue.

WILLIAM-HENRY: Back in the 90s the Prologue was as necessary to a play
    as the corkscrew was to the wine. And though the Poet Laureate   130
    had received his laurels for political <u>obedience</u> rather than poetical
    <u>excellence</u>, he <u>was</u> the Poet Laureate.

(*Pause.*)

WILLIAM-HENRY: Then something else happened that threatened my play.
    One night in my bedchamber, I was polishing my neglected armor
    when suddenly a full suit clanged to the floor. Greatly alarmed,   135
    I grabbed a sword and backed into a corner. Then, stepping out of
    the darkness, enflamed with resentment and drink, appeared my
    "only friend" Montague Talbot.

TALBOT: (*Drunk and angry*)
    So there you are, Judas Iscariot!   140

WILLIAM-HENRY: Talbot? What the devil are you on about?

TALBOT: The play! <u>Our</u> play, you bloody renegade. You'd promised me half
    the profits, then you didn't even write to inform me about *Vortigoon*.

WILLIAM-HENRY: *Vortigern*.

TALBOT: I had to read about it in the bloody Dublin papers. I'll ruin you,   145
    Ireland. I shall become the town crier of Drury Lane and expose you
    naked to the world.

WILLIAM-HENRY: I wouldn't advise that, Talbot. I wrote the title role just
    for <u>you</u>.

TALBOT: What? I, the title role? I, Vortigoon?   150

WILLIAM-HENRY: The newspapers were wrong, Talbot. *Vortigern* opens in
    the summer. I shall send you the script the moment it is finished. We
    shall begin rehearsals next spring. And you shall stay here with us, of
    course. As our guest.

TALBOT: Forgive me, William-Henry. I'd no idea—I'm so embarrassed!   155

WILLIAM-HENRY: (*Back to the audience.*)
    I had been perpetuating fraud for so long that lying had become second
    nature. And I'd been around actors enough to know that if you say
    you've written a part just for them, they'll eat out of your hand. So for
    a few minutes Montague Talbot was a gigantic parrot nibbling nuts and   160
    seeds from my generous palm. Then he returned to Dublin.

(*Pause.*)

WILLIAM-HENRY: Soon, December came and there were still many delays. Mr. Sheridan had lost enthusiasm for the play—now that he had read it. And now he seemed unwilling to expend funds for new scenery or costumes. Mr. Ireland was incensed: 165

MR. IRELAND: By God, Sam! I shall not see our priceless manuscript treated like an old rag. I'll be damned before I approve revamped scenery.

WILLIAM-HENRY: With Mr. Malone's meaty breath already warming our necks, I believed that revamped scenery would be quite good enough. But we remained in limbo all through December. And on Christmas   170
Eve *Miscellaneous Papers* was published. And someone tossed a copy into Malone's filthy lair. Then in January there was more bad news, this time delivered by the enchanting Mrs. Jordan.

MRS. JORDAN: Mrs. Siddons has abandoned the play! She claims, "Vortigern is an impostor."   175

WILLIAM-HENRY: And soon Mr. Ireland confirmed the awful news.

MR. IRELAND: Sam, there's mutiny afoot! The theater people are conspiring to sabotage the play!

WILLIAM-HENRY: Surely this was more of his usual nonsense. Wasn't it? Mr. John Philip Kemble managed the theater like a ship's captain: 180
with a strong hand and a backbone of steel. Surely he would not allow mere actors to wreck his opportunity to play the role of a lifetime. To play Vortigern!
Still, at times I did not quite understand our captain's thinking.

(*More*)

WILLIAM-HENRY (*cont'd*):   For example, his choice of the comedy to play on   185
the same bill as *Vortigern*: Why would he choose a farce about an art collector who deals in forgeries? And was it wise to schedule opening night for April Fool's Day? But more evil tidings burst in with my father's next announcement.

MR. IRELAND: We've lost the Poet Laureate!   190

WILLIAM-HENRY: Mr. Pye, hacking through his mediocre Prologue, had been accosted by the Malone faction. And Mr. Pye, who like every fool in London, happened to have a play perfect for Drury Lane, did not want to sully his meager reputation.
All the while, the poisonous Mr. Malone held back his own pub-   195
lication. Obviously, he planned to publish on the eve of *Vortigern*, when there would be no time for us to reply before the performance. Finally, only two days before the performance, there appeared Malone's vicious growling:

EDMOND MALONE: (*with stupefying authority*)   200

The fabrication of these manuscripts, by whomsoever made, has accordingly betrayed himself in every line; so as to show beyond a possibility of doubt, that not a single piece in this collection was the production of Shakespeare.

WILLIAM-HENRY: Stupefying! I am certain that no man could have read all   205
four hundred and twenty-four pages and lived. Still, the venomous volume sold out within hours and the talk of London was of nothing but of my creations. And when that fateful April morning dawned, the words of Chatterton jumped to my mind:

King Edward saw the ruddy streaks   210
  Of light eclipse the gray:
And heard the raven's croaking throat
  Proclaim the fated day.
    I, a boy of not yet 19, was to see his own play represented at Drury
    Lane. Let us take a moment to allow that boy to contemplate with   215
    ecstasy the night to come.
(*Long pause.*)

Scene 2

WILLIAM-HENRY: During the 1790s to many a denizen of London there
was no more pleasant diversion than to riot at a theater. The custom
was for the fate of the play to be decided not by its own merits but by
how many allies the playwright could bring to the theater, preferably
well-armed.   5
    On the fated night, Mr. Ireland had done his best to fortify the theater
with Believers. And in a central box, alongside Mr. Ireland, was the
comforting Eminence of the Duke of Clarence. In the pit, our best
ally was Mr. Charles Sturt, Minister of Parliament, armed with his
famous roaring voice. Obviously, however, it was to be a Battle Royal, as   10
Malone's Minions grabbed their seats, armed with fruit and vegetables
that they had no intention of eating.
(*Pause.*)

WILLIAM-HENRY: Never before had Drury Lane seen such a crowd, at least
2500 paid, not to mention those who overwhelmed the ushers and
treated themselves to a gratis performance. Many persons who had   15
paid the box prices found all the seats taken. So they dropped down
from the boxes into the pit and grabbed their seats there.
    Awaiting my Destiny, I could not bear to sit idly in the box, so
I moved backstage, where I talked with the lovely Mrs. Jordan.
    Mr. Sheridan was a caged bird in the wings, gazing at the sky of the   20
expected box office, and yet knowing what a riotous mob could do
to a theater.

He must have been thinking of the Covent Garden riot of '63 when
a mob stormed the theater like a pack of laughing hyenas. They tore
up all the benches in the boxes and the pit. They broke the glasses   25
of every chandelier. They slashed the linings of the boxes to tatters,
to very rags. And not satisfied with their nihilistic revels, they
began to hack away at the wooden pillars that held up the galleries.
Oh, yes, a theater riot! What a marvelous pastime!

WILLIAM-HENRY: At long last it was time for the Prologue, which had been   30
hacked together by a friend of my father's who unfortunately was not
a poet. His name...has been justly forgotten. But the actor was
the nervous Mr. Whitfield. Amidst the hissing and shouting poor
Whitfield froze at his post and could not remember his lines. The
would-be rioters vacillated between violence and compassion. But   35
compassion won out and finally they urged the pathetic actor onward.
He remembered his speech.

MR. WHITFIELD: No common cause your verdict now demands,
Before the court immortal Shakespeare stands.

WILLIAM-HENRY: I retreated further, to the green room where the sweet   40
and sympathetic Mrs. Jordan kept me apprised. And now the crowd
had turned our way! And dear Mrs. Jordan, upon the completion
of Act II, congratulated me on my success. Alas, she knew not of
Mr. Kemble's inexplicable casting. What, I wondered, was this man
thinking?   45
My Second Baron spoke of the trumpets: "Nay, stop not there, but
let them bellow on, / Till with their clamorous noise they shame
the thunder." A fine line, <u>that</u>, I still insist. But not as delivered by
Mr. Dignum! Mr. Dignum, known for his high, guttural, and funny
voice and his clownish antics in many a silly comedy! Beholding   50
that gentleman strut forth in a tragedy set the whole house to peals
of laughter. "Let them bellow on!" he squeaked. And no wit in the
audience could resist repeating one last time, in the Dignum style,
"Let them bellow on!"
Our ally, Mr. Sturt, M.P., had imbibed rather freely by then, and he   55
roared like a drunken lion from his stage box, "Give the thing a fair
trial!" And his authority, and his brazen lungs, lulled the storm of
laughter for a moment.

(*Pause.*)

WILLIAM-HENRY: I had written a fine part in the Saxon General Horsus,
but again I wondered what Mr. Kemble had been thinking. Why cast   60
Mr. Phillimore in that role. You remember the late Mr. Phillimore,
don't you, most famous for his enormous nose? And of course at
the time there was the vulgar superstition that an enormous nose

corresponded with an enormous "manhood." And every wag in the pit had to remind the audience of that correspondence. An occupational hazard, I suppose, but why place Mr. Phillimore so that his elephantine profile could command the stage at all times? 65

(Pause.)

WILLIAM-HENRY: And in Act IV, General Horsus died in combat. Upon receiving the fatal wound, his unfortunate carcass fell on the curtain line. As the act ended, and the curtain fell, he was literally divided 70 between the audience and his comrades in costume.
Tragic laughter erupted from the pit to the top gallery. And, as the wooden roller at the bottom of the curtain was quite heavy, the "dead" General Horsus out-echoed the laughter with his yelps of pain. The Duke of Clarence rose in his box and proclaimed, "This will not do. 75 It will not."

(More)

WILLIAM-HENRY *(cont'd)*:   Mr. Sturt, M.P., drunkenly sprang from his seat and attempted to haul the fallen actor from under the curtain and off the stage. On the other side, the actors grabbed the "dead" man's legs and hoisted him in the other direction. Finally, the late General resur- 80 rected himself and broke free on the public side of the curtain and made a dash for the exit—to the merriment of the multitude.
Could things get any worse? In Act V I had composed a marvelous speech for the tragic hero, Vortigern, which concluded with these moving lines: 85

KEMBLE: And when this solemn mockery is o'er,
With icy hand thou tak'st him by the feet,
And upward, so, till thou dost reach the heart,
And wrap him in the cloak of lasting night.

WILLIAM-HENRY: My most poetical phrase, "when this solemn mockery is 90 o'er," was the "watchword" agreed upon by the Malone faction for the general howl. When Mr. Kemble spoke the phrase with that bloody peculiar emphasis of his— "this solemn mockery"—fiendish laughter echoed from the pit, not to subside for ten minutes at least.
And finally I knew that Kemble had not been the captain of a 95 mutinous ship but rather the head mutineer. Malone must have gotten to him. Why else would Kemble sabotage his own starring role? Much later, when welcome silence had returned at last, Mr. Kemble redelivered, with comic butchery, "this solemn mockery." And Chaos was come again. Cataracts and hurricanos of laughter threatened the 100 very foundation of the theater. Mr. Sturt, M.P., and other members of our faction tried to silence the riot. The Duke of Clarence took his

valor with him as he fled the box, fearing for his safety.
And soon the air itself was many-colored with pelted fruit. And
Vortigern, in a dark sea of laughter, was pulled under and drowned.   105
And thus my career as a playwright came to an end.

(*Long pause.*)

Scene 3

WILLIAM-HENRY: Tragedy requires that a good man, not knowing the
terrible consequences of his actions, make an outright charge onto
the battlefield of the unknown and thereby destroy not only himself
but his army, his kingdom, or his people.

WILLIAM-HENRY: My unintended consequence was that for <u>my</u> Crimes   5
Against the National Literature poor Mr. Ireland bore the full outrage.
I knew at once that I must confess to my crimes and rescue him from
persecution. First, however, I must tell him the truth. I fortified myself
with tea, then with brandy, and hat-in-hand I approached him. But he
had his own agenda.   10

MR. IRELAND: Sam, you must turn over to me, at once, all of the remaining
papers and manuscripts that you have promised me. I demand that
trunk.

WILLIAM-HENRY: (*to the audience*)
Poor Mr. Ireland. He seemed to believe that he had only to produce   15
more fraudulent papers to prove the validity of the rest. As if a cage
full of sparrows, taken by weight, could add up to an eagle. I began to
sputter out my full confession. Or tried. But he interrupted me with a
new appeal.

MR. IRELAND: Surely, Sam, if there is a person for whom you can feel   20
affection, it must be that father who has never ceased to render you
every comfort and attention, from your earliest moment of existence
until now.

WILLIAM-HENRY: Again I attempted my confession, but again he grabbed the
reins of the conversation.   25

MR. IRELAND: If you cannot think of <u>me</u> as a friend, Sam, I fear you will
be deceived in all friendships that you may in future form. I do not
recollect in any of my conduct towards you anything other than that
of a friend, of a companion.

WILLIAM-HENRY: As you may have guessed, I did not get much confessing   30
done that day. None. Then Mr. Ireland escaped London and went to
stay with old friends in Berkshire.

WILLIAM-HENRY: I had been marooned, for two years and more, in a game
of charades in which there were no rules and no apparent end-game.
Finally, I confessed it all to my sister Jane.   35

(*More*)

WILLIAM-HENRY (*cont'd*):   Her eyes had always been bright, for she was a
     painter, but every one of my revelations dimmed them. I saw late
     afternoon, then dusk, then moonless night fall in my sister's eyes.
     She opened her lips, now and again, as if to speak. But she could only
     tremble and sigh, "Poor Mr. Ireland. How will you ever tell him?"   40

(*Pause.*)

WILLIAM-HENRY: That was indeed the question. In desperation, I appealed
     to that most February of women, Mrs. Freeman. I hoped that, if she
     <u>was</u> my mother, perhaps my desperate state would thaw her heart.
     Her response quickly proved that in appealing to her maternal instincts
     I had been madly optimistic: 45

MRS. FREEMAN: You worthless puppy! His Grace the Duke of Clarence has
     declared the papers genuine! Only <u>you</u> would be stupid enough to
     think that by confessing to a fabrication you would be thought a genius!

WILLIAM-HENRY: What does one do when a mother's love fails? One
     turns to one's lawyer. Our Mr. Wallis had been one of the most   50
     loyal of the Believers. So he was infinitely astonished by my
     revelations. All he could utter between his fidgets and flinches,
     his attempts to re-light his already glowing pipe, was "No,
     William-Henry. No. No. No." Then I handed over my "antique"
     ink, my flyleaves, and my endpapers. And I wrote for him in my   55
     Shakespearean hand and browned it by the fire. Being a lawyer, his
     first impulse was extreme caution. Rather than the confession that
     might relieve my soul, he urged silence.

(*Pause.*)

WILLIAM-HENRY: Some time later, Mr. Ireland returned from Berkshire,
     not refreshed and recovered but rather more anxious than ever.   60
     Anxiety had only worn him down and reduced him to silence.
     Within that silence, through which I swear a high wind was ever
     blowing, I told him: "Mr. Ireland, it was me. I fabricated the play,
     Vortigern, the papers, everything. Forgive me, father. It was me."

MR. IRELAND: You? You?   65

WILLIAM-HENRY: How many months had I dwelt in mortal fear of being
     discovered as the author of the manuscripts! Finally it was time for my
     just punishment. And what punishment did the literary harpies have in
     store for me? Worse than I could have imagined. Mr. Ireland refused to
     believe me!   70

MR. IRELAND: Nonsense. You haven't the talent! You never had.

WILLIAM-HENRY: And he not only insulted me to my face but he published his
     opinions in the press.

MR. IRELAND: It is my firm belief that there is not a word of truth in Sam's confession. I still believe the papers genuine. And I am as convinced   75
as I am of my own existence that the boy had no hand in these manuscripts.

(*Pause.*)

WILLIAM-HENRY: I made one last appeal to Mr. Ireland: "If the writer of the Papers shows any spark of genius and deserves honor, I, Sir, your son, am that person. And if I live but a little longer, I will live to prove it."   80

MR. IRELAND: If you would have honor, Sam, then introduce me to your Mr. H. Or be gone. And be damned.

(*Pause.*)

WILLIAM-HENRY: I quitted his house that night and never returned. In exile from my family, in disgrace, with no prospects of raising the means to keep myself decently housed or fed, I resolved to marry.   85
Miss Alice Crudge accepted my proposal and we were wed in July. Crudge. The only woman in the Commonwealth who could change her name to the notorious "Ireland" and feel that she'd gotten a bargain.

I also resolved to publish a pamphlet, in which I laid out the whole   90
story of my forgeries. Five hundred copies were quickly bought up at a shilling. If only I had speculated in some copies! For a few years later one sold for a guinea. Mr. Ireland's response: he doubted that I had the brains to write even the pamphlet.

(*Pause.*)

WILLIAM-HENRY: My father and I met only once more. It was a cold and shame-   95
ful affair. Mr. Ireland could only affirm once more that he would die believing the papers were by Shakespeare and by no other man. Stunned and angry, I refused to tip my hat to him or even shake his hand. I never saw him again.

WILLIAM-HENRY: In the days to come, Mr. Ireland's business failed, as how   100
could it not? No one trusted in the validity of any book or paper that he might sell. Undaunted, in 1799, a full three years after the debacle at Drury Lane, he published *Vortigern*, "written by William Shakespeare," elegantly bound in "russia and green Morocco cases." And the next year he died. He mentioned me in his will: 105

MR. IRELAND: I give to my son William-Henry Ireland the repeating watch I have generally worn. And as I wish to die in peace and good will with all mankind, I hereby freely and sincerely forgive my son for having made me the innocent agent of mischief and imposition.

WILLIAM-HENRY: Since that time I and my small family have lived hand-   110
to-mouth. It seems my credibility in literary matters is a bit wanting.

But I have published dozens of pamphlets, poetry, histories, even
novels—some under my own name. Some "by the author of the
Shakespearean Manuscripts." My most <u>profitable</u> work was entitled *The Public and Private Life of that Celebrated Actress Mrs. Jordan.* 115
Profitable because the Duke of Clarence paid me handsomely <u>not</u> to
publish it.
And no, sirs, I did not revert to forgery ever again.
Well, all right, with one exception. For whatever reason, there was a
demand for my original forgeries, I suppose as historical curiosities. 120
So I sold them. Then to others who requested them, I reproduced and
sold them again. Several times. But we are left with the philosophical
question: Can one forge one's own forgeries? Would that not suggest a
logical impossibility?: "A genuine forgery"?

(Pause.)

WILLIAM-HENRY: As you exit tonight, you shall see my various publications 125
displayed in the book stall. They are for sale.

(fade to black.)

WILLIAM-HENRY: Would anyone like to buy a courting chair?

Experiencing Literature through Writing

1. Select a single work from this chapter (or any other). Identify the point
   of view that guides us through this story. Explain why that point of view
   is significant to our understanding of the text. As you write, consider the
   following questions:
   a. What specific details in the work help you determine the point of
      view in this work?
   b. What details in the work make this point of view particularly interest-
      ing? For instance, are there parts of this story that no one else would
      be able to experience?
   c. How does the author use point of view to influence our sympathies
      within the story?
   d. Are there details within this work in which point of view does not
      seem significant? Can you explain how your comments about point
      of view have some bearing on these details?
2. In each reading selection in this section, the author uses the perspective
   of a character to tell the story in a particular way. Discuss the manipulation of our sympathies through point of view in one or more of these
   works. How does the author make us trust (or doubt) the characters
   through whom we hear each of these stories? How do we get to know the

characters? How much of that knowledge comes from what the characters tell us? How much comes from other sources?

3. The issue of perspective within literary works is tied closely to character, but it also determines how we receive the plot of the story. We make sense of a point of view because we understand the character who is standing in that position, and we make sense of what is happening because of our position in relation to events. Pick one work, and discuss the impact of perspective upon our understanding of that work's plot.

5

Setting

Where and When Does the Action Take Place?
Why Does It Make a Difference?

Setting may be thought of in narrow terms as the physical and temporal **background** to a story. In the theater, the word *setting* refers specifically to how items are arranged on a stage. Actors, of course, move about the stage in relation to these items. Normally, our attention is focused primarily on the actors. There is nothing wrong with such restrictive ideas of the word when one wants a restricted idea, but this chapter defines **setting** more expansively as the total environment within which narrative actions take place. The characters' general living conditions as well as the time and place in which they live constitute setting.

Such a broad use of the word setting also *suggests* its great importance. Reflect for a moment on an especially powerful event in your life. It's likely that you remember that event not only as an action, but as an action grounded in a particular time and place. It would be hard to narrate the action without describing where and when the action unfolded. Or put the case in reverse: Reflect for a moment on a significant place in your life. It's likely that that place will provoke you to feel, to remember, to tell stories. Setting is then not merely background—or at least not necessarily only background. Setting can function as part of a literary text's whole effect.

PLACE AND TIME

Place and time function together in our lives as well as in literary texts. We often anticipate the importance of our memories by taking pictures of grand occasions (graduation, birthdays, moving to a new home, and so on). Most of us strive to

Caroline Purser/Photographer's Choice/Getty Images

A postcard of London is held in what seems to be the exact location from where the photograph was originally taken, giving off an eerie sense of time and place.

record images not only of people, but also of the physical environments closely tied to these people's experience. One traditional negotiation between action and setting can be seen in the action of a vacationer writing a message on a postcard.

The front of the postcard shows an idealized picture of the place where the writer is visiting; the back of the card allows the writer to insert herself into that setting, by reporting on what has happened to her in that place. Even though the results are often banal ("The weather is beautiful; wish you were here"), the linking of action and character with setting allows the receiver to locate a loved one in a familiar, though faraway, place. The modern equivalent of this locating happens when the traveler takes a self-portrait, usually in front of some iconic scenery, and posts that image with a descriptor of a few characters. Skilled authors who can take us fully into another place or time offer far deeper pleasures.

In his famous personal essay "Once More to the Lake," E. B. White shows what it is like to recall old events through the act of revisiting a place. A complex sense of time past, present, and (through the son) future emerges from the description. White registers specific details and makes it clear those details count for something. He writes of how similar the lake (where he had vacationed with his father) still is when he returns years later with his son, but he also comments on the differences that have come about due to progress: "[T]he road under our sneakers was only a two-track road. The middle track was missing, the one with the marks of the hooves and the splotches of dried, flaky manure. There had always been three tracks to choose from in choosing which track to walk in; now the choice was narrowed down to two." The distinction here between trails carved by horses and trails kept clear by automobiles is subtle, but White uses the difference in the place to help him describe the narrowing options of his own life as he has grown older. The most disconcerting difference for him is the fact that his son has now taken his place, performing his role in the memories that White associates with the lake.

White's setting is hardly mere background; it is an integral part of the meaning that unfolds in the narrative. It exerts a power over the action of the story. The nature of the place is dynamic; it changes over time in ways that chart White's own progress through life. An appeal of setting within fiction is that, as in White's memoir, it brings the past to life—it makes the past meaningful to the present moment.

A Note to Student Writers: Descriptive Summaries

E. B. White is coauthor with Richard Strunk of a classic writing guide still widely used. In *Elements of Style*, Strunk and White emphasize the importance of concrete, specific images to vivid descriptive writing. In the previous passage, White wants to be sure we see the tracks cut in the dirt road, for he knows that if we don't get a solid feel for the reality of the place, none of the ideas or emotions that have grown from the place will be compelling. Readers need something they can access through touch, sight, and sound.

Critical writers can learn something from this emphasis on the concrete. It's important to establish a very clear sense of a text to be analyzed before jumping into an analysis. We've said that "why" and "how" questions help one think analytically, but it's worth remembering that a simple "what" question often needs to come first. A "what" question won't likely lead you to a thesis, but it may help you clarify your sense of a topic. It's useful to think of summary as a kind of description. And like any good description, summary must build on well-selected and clearly presented details that can be checked against the reader's or viewer's own experience.

Experiencing Literature through Setting

Sometimes setting makes other elements of narrative (character and action) decidedly secondary; setting can be the primary force of meaning and emotional effect. In "February Evening in New York," Denise Levertov embeds a brief scene involving two characters in the middle of a richly textured impression of a specific place and time. We're forced to read character and incident in context of feelings created by the enormous energy of city life in New York.

Denise Levertov (1923–   )

February Evening in New York (1959)

As the stores close, a winter light
  opens air to iris blue,
  glint of frost through the smoke,
  grains of mica, salt of the sidewalk.
As the buildings close, released autonomous   5
  feet pattern the streets
  in hurry and stroll; balloon heads
  drift and dive above them; the bodies
  aren't really there.
As the lights brighten, as the sky darkens,   10
  a woman with crooked heels says to another woman
  while they step along at a fair pace,
  "You know, I'm telling you, what I love best
  is life. I love life! Even if I ever get
  to be old and wheezy—or limp! You know?   15
  Limping along?—I'd still . . ." Out of hearing.
To the multiple disordered tones
  of gears changing, a dance
  to the compass points, out, four-way river.
  Prospect of sky   20
  wedged into avenues, left at the ends of streets,
  west sky, east sky: more life tonight! A range
  of open time at winter's outskirts.

Notice that Levertov hasn't double spaced after any of the syntactical breaks in her lines. Everything crowds together as we read, just as the New York sidewalks grow packed as stores close and people are "released." The sentences that begin with "as" also grow progressively longer (four lines, five lines, then seven lines). Impressions pile upon impressions. The importance of setting to this poem is so great that Levertov has the setting reflected in the poem's structure. In the density of this poem's impressions, we're encouraged to read the lines of the "woman with crooked heels" as indicative of a larger encompassing energy that subsumes even the sky that is barely "wedged into avenues" for the viewer who looks to the ends of the streets.

Setting can also take a central function in sections of extended narratives. The following passage is taken from Theodore Drieser's *Sister Carrie*, a very long novel published in 1900 and acknowledged for its groundbreaking **realism**—a mode of depiction that builds on close, accurate attention to specific historical and social settings. In this selection, eighteen-year-old Carrie Meeber has arrived alone in Chicago, and, through her eyes, we see a place that is as unfamiliar to us (as a modern audience) as it is to her, a newcomer to the city. The narrator is telling us about Carrie and about the Chicago that she sees. This narrator reveals the social pressures that work upon Carrie through a description of the department store she moves through. As you read, note the ways in which the setting is essential to our understanding of Carrie's character.

Theodore Dreiser (1871–1945)

from Sister Carrie (1900)

At that time the department store was in its earliest form of successful operation, and there were not many. The first three in the United States, established about 1884, were in Chicago. Carrie was familiar with the names of several through the advertisements in the "Daily News," and now proceeded to seek them. The words of Mr. McManus had somehow managed to restore her courage, which had fallen low, and she dared to hope that this new line would offer her something. Some time she spent in wandering up and down, thinking to encounter the buildings by chance, so readily is the mind, bent upon prosecuting a hard but needful errand, eased by that self-deception which the semblance of search, without the reality, gives. At last she inquired of a police officer, and was directed to proceed "two blocks up," where she would find "The Fair."

The nature of these vast retail combinations, should they ever permanently disappear, will form an interesting chapter in the commercial history of our nation. Such a flowering out of a modest trade principle the world had never witnessed up to that time. They were along the line of the most effective retail organisation, with hundreds of stores coordinated into one and laid out upon the most imposing and economic basis. They were handsome, bustling, successful affairs, with a host of clerks and a swarm of patrons. Carrie passed along the busy aisles, much affected by the remarkable displays of trinkets, dress goods, stationery, and jewelry. Each separate counter was a show place of dazzling interest and attraction. She could not help feeling the claim of each trinket and valuable upon her personally, and yet she did not stop. There was nothing there which she could not have used—nothing which she did not long to own. The dainty slippers and stockings, the delicately frilled skirts and petticoats, the laces, ribbons, hair-combs, purses, all touched her with individual desire, and she felt keenly the fact that not any of these things were in the range of her purchase. She was a work-seeker, an outcast without employment, one whom the average employee could tell at a glance was poor and in need of a situation.

It must not be thought that any one could have mistaken her for a nervous, sensitive, high-strung nature, cast unduly upon a cold, calculating, and unpoetic world. Such certainly she was not. But women are peculiarly sensitive to their adornment.

Not only did Carrie feel the drag of desire for all which was new and pleasing in apparel for women, but she noticed too, with a touch at the heart, the fine ladies who elbowed and ignored her, brushing past in utter disregard of her presence, themselves eagerly enlisted in the materials which the store contained. Carrie was not familiar with the appearance of her more fortunate sisters of the city. Neither had she before known the nature and appearance of the shop girls with whom she now compared poorly. They were pretty in the main, some even handsome, with an air of independence and indifference which added, in the case of the more favoured, a certain piquancy. Their clothes were neat, in many instances fine, and wherever she encountered the eye of one it was only to recognize in it a keen analysis of her own position—her individual shortcomings of dress and that shadow of manner which she thought must hang about her and make clear to all who and what she was. A flame of envy lighted in her heart. She realised in a dim way how much the city held—wealth, fashion, ease—every adornment for women, and she longed for dress and beauty with a whole heart.

On the second floor were the managerial offices, to which, after some inquiry, she was now directed. There she found other girls ahead of her, applicants like herself, but with more of that self-satisfied and independent air which experience of the city lends; girls who scrutinised her in a painful manner. After a wait of perhaps three-quarters of an hour, she was called in turn. ❖

The place in this instance defines the character. We understand and feel Carrie's insecurity through the environment within which she lives. Her excitement, fear, envy, ambition, as well as her social status and educational background all become apparent as things we not only know, but experience through her engagement with the department store and all it contains.

THE ROLE OF PHYSICAL OBJECTS

Objects can also serve as props to activate the memory and retrieve the past. Well-chosen details can bring alive the social and emotional conditions of a character's environment. In Kazuo Ishiguro's novel *Remains of the Day* (1989), the narrator is Mr. Stevens, a butler whose identity is linked to the prestigious house that he has long served; however, Stevens has had the misfortune to move through his career as the upper class declines both economically and morally. In one scene, while on a journey away from Darlington Hall (the place he has spent almost all of his adult life), Stevens considers taking a side trip to the English village of Mursden. Because his entire life is bound within a very narrow social world, he assumes that the reader is as fluent in the details of butlery as he is. The fact that we are not so fluent contributes to our understanding of how contained a life Stevens has led. Note the ways in which Ishiguro's butler, addressing the reader directly, evokes a sense of place and time through describing household details.

Kazuo Ishiguro (1954–   )

from Remains of the Day (1989)

Perhaps "Mursden" will ring a bell for you, as it did for me upon my first spotting it on the road atlas yesterday. In fact, I must say I was tempted to make a slight detour from my planned route just to see the village. Mursden, Somerset, was where the firm of Giffen and Co. was once situated, and it was to Mursden one was required to dispatch one's order for a supply of Giffen's dark candles of polish, "to be flaked, mixed into wax and applied by hand." For some time, Giffen's was undoubtedly the finest silver polish available, and it was only the appearance of new chemical substances on the market shortly before the war that caused the demand for this impressive product to decline.

As I remember, Giffen's appeared at the beginning of the twenties, and I am sure I am not alone in closely associating its emergence with that change of mood within our profession—that change which came to push the polishing of silver to the position of central importance it still by and large maintains today. This shift was, I believe, like so many other major shifts around this period, a generational matter; it was during these years that our generation of butlers "came of age," and figures like Mr. Marshall, in particular, played a crucial part in making silver-polishing so central. This is not to suggest, of course, that the polishing of silver—particularly those items that would appear at table—was not always regarded a serious duty. But it would not be unfair to suggest that many butlers of, say, my father's generation did not consider the matter such a key one, and this is evidenced by the fact that in those days, the butler of a household rarely supervised the polishing of silver directly, being content to leave it to, say, the under-butler's whims, carrying out inspections only intermittently. It was Mr. Marshall, it is generally agreed, who was the first to recognize the full significance of silver—namely, that no other objects in the house were likely to come under such intimate scrutiny from outsiders as was silver during a meal, and as such, it served as a public index of a house's standards. And Mr. Marshall it was who first caused stupefaction amongst ladies and gentlemen visiting Charleville House with displays of silver polished to previously unimagined standards. Very soon, naturally, butlers up and down the country, under pressure from their employers, were focusing their minds on the question of silver-polishing. There quickly sprang up, I recall, various butlers, each claiming to have discovered methods by which they could surpass Mr. Marshall—methods they made a great show of keeping secret, as though they were French chefs guarding their recipes. But I am confident—as I was then—that the sorts of elaborate and mysterious processes performed by someone like Mr. Jack Neighbours had little or no discernible effect on the end result. As far as I was concerned, it was a simple enough matter: one used good polish, and one supervised closely. Giffen's was the polish ordered by all discerning butlers of the time, and if this product was used correctly, one had no fear of one's silver being second best to anybody's.

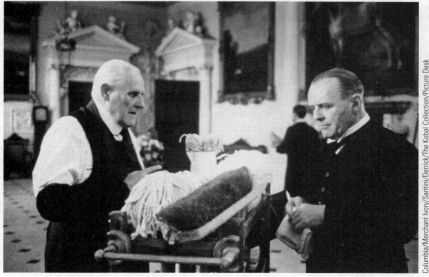

Remains of the Day (1993)

I am glad to be able to recall numerous occasions when the silver at Darlington Hall had a pleasing impact upon observers. For instance, I recall Lady Astor remarking, not without a certain bitterness, that our silver "was probably unrivalled." I recall also watching Mr. George Bernard Shaw, the renowned playwright, at dinner one evening, examining closely the dessert spoon before him, holding it up to the light and comparing its surface to that of a nearby platter, quite oblivious to the company around him. ❖

The claim that something as mundane as silver polish might be as significant as our narrator suggests would seem preposterous until we see how much this particular product had an impact upon the work that Stevens did. Inspired by an obscure place-name that is familiar to him only from its association with a household product, Stevens tells us much about a time and a social condition that is unfamiliar to us. The idea that butlers might share the social pretensions of their master, the fact that there was competition among household staffs, and the possibility that it might play out in the glow of silver all help put us into another world. That world becomes more grounded in reality through Stevens's reflections upon a specific consumer product.

> **Making Connections**
>
> In Chapter 4 we considered point of view. In this passage from *Remains of the Day*, Ishiguro develops a distinct point of view through the voice of his narrator. He uses Stevens's lengthy reflections on silver polish to create for us a certain view of class and propriety. We see the setting from the perspective of the butler and we understand that what Stevens reports is controlled by his years of service to the upper class.

This element of setting also contributes to our understanding of the delicate psychological state Mr. Stevens is in throughout his journey. The imaginative "detour" he takes to Mursden is clearly motivated by his need to find a stable reference point. Stevens's car trip from one part of England to another moves him far from his sense of home. Coming upon a town associated with something he knows well helps him maintain some sense of comfort and confidence amid an unfamiliar place. Reflecting so much on this particular commercial product makes him feel that he has in fact been connected to this new, wider world—even if he hasn't *lived* in that world.

Stevens's silver polish is real enough, but it's hardly familiar to us. The fact that we don't know anything about the product contributes to our sense that that world he inhabits is passing. When a product mentioned or shown in a narrative *is* familiar to us, we may grow suspicious: we might dismiss a scene that includes a brand-name item as mere product placement—an advertisement embedded in the work. Although we are often right to be cynical (corporations routinely pay to have their products show up in movies, for example), we should not fail to see how everyday products can be integrated meaningfully into a narrative and may contribute significantly to the way setting functions. Movies illustrate the point nicely. For example, think of the ways familiar items scattered over a tabletop might function in relation to a larger action within a film. In a horror movie, the familiarity might help us identify with the world presented and therefore make impending disasters feel more threatening. In a domestic drama, we might define our relation to characters through the items on the tabletop: a can of Mountain Dew would say one thing, an open bottle of Jack Daniels another, and a Perrier still another. If a character in a comedy pulls a shiny late-model Mercedes SUV into a McDonald's drive-thru and orders a Diet Coke, Big Mac, and fries—supersized, we'll pick up a general satiric comment on contemporary American culture. If a character in a detective story parks his 1962 Chevy Impala in front of a Foster's Freeze (a California chain particularly popular in the early days of fast food), we'll be located in a very specific *milieu*—a French word that literally means center or middle and is used to designate particular social, temporal, and physical surroundings. The Harvard student who runs through the Boston winter in a GAP sweatshirt and sandals evokes a particular time as well as a certain brand of nonconformity within the stratified system of dining clubs that he is not invited to join.

Mise-en-scène (another important French term) suggests what is quite literally put into the scene. It originally referred to the staging of plays: the arrangement and inclusion of furniture, backdrops, stray items, and props that make up the environment within which characters act. In a similar fashion, film critics

Product placement in *The Social Network* (2010)

Columbia Pictures/The Kobal Collection/Picture Desk

use the term *mise-en-scène* to describe what is captured within a shot. The concept applies to any constructed work of art that places objects in a scene. It is useful to remember that details of setting are selected, framed, foregrounded with a purpose in mind. Objects don't just happen to be part of a setting.

IMAGINARY PLACES

Art is always about bringing imagination to life. So far, we've treated setting in terms of how artists lull us into accepting a setting as real—as identifying it as a place and time we can recognize and relate to. On some occasions, setting functions much differently. In Edgar Allan Poe's "Ulalume—a Ballad" we quickly get lost in both time and space. Even the place-names we have are confusing: "It was hard by the dim lake of Auber, / In the misty mid region of Weir." You can scan a map very closely and not find Auber or Weir. Poe hasn't consulted an atlas, for he doesn't so much want to identify his setting as to use setting to evoke a sensation. Auber and Weir are the names of two landscape painters of the period. Poe is not asking us to accept the reality of these places, he is asking that we associate his poem with feelings we might have in relation to other artistic works. Here, as is often the case in Gothic pieces, **atmosphere** (feelings evoked in the reader through setting) prevails over concrete matters of time and space. Poe's setting radically disconnects us from everyday life.

Many other works seek to create through setting an interplay between the real and the fanciful. This problem becomes interesting in the directions that a playwright gives to describe the setting of a play. Unlike fiction where the entire setting appears in the text of the story, the play provides only the dialogue. To produce a play, set designers, who follow the instructions that the playwright gives in the introduction to the play, build the actual stages on which the actors will perform. They make the imaginary setting described in the printed play into some realized place. In *The Glass Menagerie*, for example, Tennessee Williams describes specific realistic features of the Wingfield apartment, where the play takes place, including a fire escape that is a part of the set. But that detail, which is a rather straightforward instruction for a set designer, is interesting to Williams because it is "a structure whose name is a touch of accidental poetic truth, for all of these huge buildings are always burning with the slow and implacable fires of human desperation." He describes a real object that a stage carpenter might build as he shows that his interest is in the meanings that he finds in that object. He sets the action in a specific, real place, but his explanation is of its symbolic value rather than of its real details. To describe the setting, he insists that this play is set in "memory and is therefore nonrealistic. Memory takes a lot of poetic license. It omits some details, others are exaggerated, according to the emotional value of the articles it touches, for memory is seated predominantly in the heart. The interior is therefore rather dim and poetic." *Dim* is an adjective that is instructive for those who try to translate these directions into a real stage; *poetic* is a bit more problematic and open to a far greater range of possible meanings. This playwright emphasizes the imaginary nature of the real place that is to be created on the stage.

Movies again may illustrate the effect. The level of planning that goes into each frame of film (and every aspect of setting) becomes clear when we look at the storyboards that directors draw long before they begin to shoot a film. Because filming requires so many artists working together, the director will plan out each shot in advance. To tell the story, the director determines where the action will take place and what camera angles will be necessary to track that action. Looking at the storyboards helps us appreciate the tremendous planning and work that often goes into creating everything we see. Initial storyboards quite literally sketch the basic elements of a setting. By the time we see the final product, the production team has fleshed out that sketch to give it exactly the desired look and feel.

Experiencing Film through Setting

The following sequence includes an early sketch, a more detailed sketch from the storyboards and the actual shot from two scenes of Jean-Pierre Jeunet's *Amélie* (2001). Jeunet is known to be one of the most conscientious planners in the film business; these sequences demonstrate that planning a film consists of far more than just writing dialogue. Look at the director's evolving ideas about the angles from which we see the characters. Notice that the director has an idea (especially in the scene on the left) of how the details of the set should emphasize the action. As you look at the details of each shot, describe the setting. When does the action take place? What sorts of places are these? How do the details that we see here suggest a set of larger details that we cannot see?

Amélie is a film that creates a distinct world that is real in all of its details but does not quite feel like any real world we know. Even in these two shots, one can see something of this effect. The yellow quality of the lighting suggests that the scenes are set in some past time. The serious girl who is examining the stuffed monster is working in an environment that helps emphasize her young professionalism. The woman sits in a bath that is at once elegant enough to have come out of the latest design catalog and the careful arrangement of light and flowers are at odds with her ordinary appearance. Jeunet seems to want us to look at the world with a fresh perspective—to observe subtle beauties that are somehow obscured by their familiarity. The little things that don't quite mesh catch our attention and make us see in unaccustomed ways.

Sketch by Luc Desportes, used with permission; sketch and film still reproduced with the permission of Jean-Pierre Jeunet

Sketch by Luc Desportes, used with permission; sketch and film still reproduced with the permission of Jean-Pierre Jeunet

Storyboards and film stills from *Amélie* (2001)

Babe: Pig in the City (1998)

Universal/Mill film/The Kobal Collection/Picture Desk

Jeunet's sort of visual playfulness is pressed to a further extreme in *Babe: Pig in the City* (George Miller, 1998). Miller and his team create a city skyline for Babe to look out upon that is a composite of the world's most famous cities. The setting here is a wildly inventive mixture or blending of images that are simultaneously familiar and disorienting. Take a look at the still from the film and try to identify as many famous structures as you can. What have the set designers done to make the buildings fit together in this particular cityscape? What sort of effect does this cityscape achieve? To what extent does it seem real? Where does the fantastic aspect begin? Why would the filmmakers favor a composite skyline over a real one?

Also consider the effect on the audience of framing the shot with the back of Babe's (the pig's) head looking out at the city. The main character is in the position (along with the audience) of taking it all in. We suggest you take a look back to the Friedrich paintings in Chapter 4. It may seem strange to set this movie still in comparison to famous nineteenth-century paintings, but Miller here is employing a similar technique. Setting is felt not only as a place, but as a particular character's experience of place. The audience joins in that experience by looking, in effect, over the shoulder of the character. Setting isn't just background.

A Note to Student Writers: Paying Attention to Details

The first step to writing about setting is to notice details. As you read, don't focus only on the action. Look around the characters to see where they are standing, what is in the background, and what objects they are holding as the action goes on around them. Your goal here is to freeze the frame of the narrative and to compile lists of the surrounding details. As you develop your thoughts about setting, you must do something with that list. It is never enough just to list, but as you start to talk about a detail or two that you find particularly interesting, you will probably begin to see connections between that detail and other details of the setting. Ask yourself which details are most significant, explain why, and justify your rankings. Notice how these details have been presented and think about how they contribute to the action that you were focused on before you began to focus closely on setting. When you write about setting, you will quickly discover that the setting is significant precisely because of the insight that it gives you about character or plot or some other element of the story. None of these elements exist in isolation, but the exercise of noticing setting helps a reader pay attention to details of all sorts.

MODELING CRITICAL ANALYSIS: ROBERT BROWNING, MY LAST DUCHESS

Robert Browning's "My Last Duchess" is a **dramatic monologue**—a poem in which a single speaker addresses an audience within a dramatic situation. We can start by thinking here of setting in specifically theatrical terms. To imagine in our mind's eye how Browning sets his stage we need a chair that is positioned in front of the painting. And of course we need the painting as well as the drawn curtain to the side of it. We also need some objects of art about the room to indicate the material grandeur of the place and a stairwell that suggests the two are in private quarters above the "company" on the main floor who likely await news of the negotiation. This need not be a very elaborately set stage, but each item and its placement is important.

Once the scene is set, some interpretive possibilities become clearer. For example, it's possible we can learn something of the power relationship between the duke and the envoy by the position of the chair. Note that the duke seems to orchestrate things throughout. He moves the envoy in position in front of the painting and asks (directs?) him to sit and look carefully. The curtain is normally drawn, so it would seem the duke has a deliberate purpose in placing the envoy before his "last Duchess." Once seated, the duke recounts her story and her fate. She displeased him; she is dead. Once the duchess's story is told, the duke asks the envoy to rise from the chair. He makes his claim on a generous dowry from the prospective duchess's family. He is ready to return to the company. And as he invites (orders?) the envoy to go downstairs with him, he calls attention to a statue that depicts Neptune "Taming a sea-horse." Through that statue, Browning underscores the duke's obsession with control evident from the very start in the way he positioned the chair to direct the envoy's attention.

The specifically dramatic setting of "My Last Duchess" functions as part of the whole action, but it is not the only setting Browning employs. The duke's speech in effect also moves us offstage and conjures images of very different places. The duchess is recalled outdoors in an orchard relating to other people than the duke. We see her riding a mule about the terrace. The setting in which the meeting between the duke and envoy occurs grows still colder when contrasted to the vivacity of a life that was not bound by the walls of his house.

Anthology

DYSTOPIA

In 1761, Giovanni Piranesi published *Imaginary Prisons*, a book of etchings that depict imaginary interiors of places of torture and confinement. His work as an artist of architecture and as a stage designer is evident in the image that is presented here from that book. This unreal space has depth, texture, and levels of detail that make it seem entirely real. In addition, this place conveys a mood: it feels oppressive, confusing, and unpleasant. The vaulted ceilings in

pgFR58dxJPdbfw at Google Cultural Institute

Giovanni Piranesi, from *Imaginary Prisons* (1761)

the background look much like what we would expect to see in a cathedral, but here the shadows, the network of stairs and bridges, the hanging chains, the projecting beams, and the imposing grillwork make the structure seem more subterranean than soaring. Piranesi's etching provides a useful reminder of the ways in which setting can evoke a mood and suggest a story, even without character or action.

A CRITIC WRITES ABOUT DYSTOPIA AS SETTING

Laura Miller discusses dystopian fiction by contrasting the fictions aimed at an adult audience with those aimed at a young adult audience. As she established the general characteristics of this genre—the elaborately imagined worlds in which things have gone terribly wrong—she challenges the assumption that the purpose of these stories is to warn us. Unlike the totalitarian society that is imagined in *1984*, the dystopias that we find in young adult literature such as *The Hunger Games* are more significant for their settings. "It's not about persuading the reader to stop something terrible from happening—it's about what's happening, right this minute, in the stormy psyche of the adolescent reader." Miller argues that these settings are reflections of the lives of contemporary young adults whose prisons are such places as the social world of high schools where the rules seem as arbitrary and ruthless as any dystopian world imaginable. As you read the works in this section, consider how they fit the criteria that Miller sets out in her essay.

Some are closely related to the Piranesi etching—vaguely old but without any referent to signal a specific time. These settings often feel dark without necessarily being night. And they can be weird. Samuel Taylor Coleridge's "Kubla Khan" (written, Coleridge insists, directly from dream imagery) also creates a setting that functions not to ground us in reality, but to displace us from the real—to break down familiar ways of knowing and feeling. In these works, atmosphere associated with place is as important as anything that might happen in the narrative.

We've also included in this section stories and poems that depend upon detailed renderings of recognizable places. The poems by Gary Soto and Chitra Banerjee Divakaruni, and the fiction of Salman Rushdie, for example, locate us in specifically defined times and places; such settings relate to the experience of people we might know. The apt detail, the keen eye for specifics makes the ordinary meaningful in works like these. They ground us in the situations of the characters.

Still other works in this cluster ground us in reality but keep pressing us with the sense that reality is what many people seek to escape or transcend.

Using Setting to Focus Writing and Discussion

- Collect the details that the author offers about the setting. In any constructed world, whether that world in on film or in text, every detail of setting has been created by the artist. Look at the details that we might think of as mundane or insignificant—how do these relate to the rest of the work?

- Where does the author describe the setting? Is it all in one place or dispersed throughout the text?

- Whose voice gives us this setting? In what ways is this fact significant?

- Which does the author describe first, the setting or the character? In what ways does the description of one influence the description of the other?

- To what extent does the setting determine how the characters act or think?

- To what extent is there some contrast, or even conflict, between the characters in the text and the setting that they occupy?

- If there are different settings within the work, how are these differences articulated and how do the different settings play different roles in the text?

- In what way does the setting help establish a tone in this work?

REVIEW

Laura Miller (1960–   )

Fresh Hell (2010)

Rebecca Stead chose to set her children's novel "When You Reach Me"—winner of the 2010 Newbery Medal—in nineteen-seventies New York partly because that's where she grew up, but also, as she told one interviewer, because she wanted "to show a world of kids with a great deal of autonomy." Her characters, middle-class middle-school students, routinely walk around the Upper West Side by themselves, a rare freedom in today's city, despite a significant drop in New York's crime rate since Stead's footloose youth. The world of our hovered-over teens and preteens may be safer, but it's also less conducive to adventure, and therefore to adventure stories.

Perhaps that's why so many of them are reading "The Hunger Games," a trilogy of novels by Suzanne Collins, which take place at an unspecified time in North America's future. Her heroine, Katniss Everdeen, lives in one of twelve numbered districts dominated by a decadent, exploitative central city called the Capitol. Every year, two children from each district are drafted by lottery to compete in a televised gladiatorial contest, the Hunger Games, which are held in a huge outdoor arena. The winner is the last child left alive. The fervently awaited third installment in the trilogy, "Mockingjay," will be published by Scholastic in August, and there are currently in print more than 2.3 million copies of the previous two books, "The Hunger Games" and "Catching Fire."

Collins's trilogy is only the most visible example of a recent boom in dystopian fiction for young people. Many of these books come in series, spinning out extended narratives in intricately imagined worlds. In Scott Westerfeld's popular "Uglics" series, for example, all sixteen- year-olds undergo surgery to conform to a universal standard of prettiness determined by evolutionary biology; in James Dashner's "The Maze Runner," teen-age boys awaken, all memories of their previous lives wiped clean, in a walled compound surrounded by a monster-filled labyrinth. The books tend to end in cliff-hangers that provoke their readers to post half-mocking protestations of agony ("SUZANNE, ARE YOU PURPOSELY TORTURING YOUR FANS!?!?!?") on Internet discussion boards.

Publishers have signed up dozens of similar titles in the past year or two, and, as with any thriving genre, themes and motifs get swapped around from other genres and forms. There are, or will soon be, books about teen-agers slotted into governmentally arranged professions and marriages or harvested for spare parts or genetically engineered for particular skills or brainwashed by subliminal messages embedded in music or outfitted with Internet connections in their brains. Then, there are the post-apocalyptic scenarios in which humanity is reduced to subsistence farming or neo-feudalism, stuck in villages ruled by religious fanatics or surrounded by toxic wastelands, predatory warlords, or flesh-eating zombie hordes. An advantage to having young readers is that most of this stuff is fresh to them. They aren't going to sniff at a premise repurposed from an old "Twilight Zone" episode or mutter that the villain is an awful lot like the deranged preacher Robert Mitchum plays in "The Night of the Hunter." To thrill them, a story doesn't have to be unprecedented. It just has to be harrowing.

Dystopian novels for middle-grade and young-adult readers (M.G. and   5
Y.A., respectively, in publishing-industry lingo) have been around for decades. Readers of a certain age may remember having their young minds blown by William Sleator's "House of Stairs," the story of five teenagers imprisoned in a seemingly infinite M. C. Escher-style network of staircases that ultimately turns out to be a gigantic Skinner box designed to condition their behavior. John Christopher's "The White Mountains," in which alien overlords install mind-control caps on the heads of all those over the age of thirteen, tore through my own sixth-grade classroom like a wicked strain of the flu. Depending on the anxieties and preoccupations of its time, a dystopian Y.A. novel

might speculate about the aftermath of nuclear war (Robert C. O'Brien's "Z for Zachariah") or the drawbacks of engineering a too harmonious social order (Lois Lowry's "The Giver") or the consequences of resource exhaustion (Saci Lloyd's "The Carbon Diaries 2015"). And, of course, most American school-children are at some point also assigned to read one of the twentieth century's dystopian classics for adults, such as "Brave New World" or "1984."

The youth-centered versions of dystopia part company with their adult predecessors in some important respects. For one thing, the grownup ones are grimmer. In an essay for the 2003 collection "Utopian and Dystopian Writing for Children and Young Adults," the British academic Kay Sambell argues that "the narrative closure of the protagonist's final defeat and failure is absolutely crucial to the admonitory impulse of the classic adult dystopia." The adult dysto-pia extrapolates from aspects of the present to show readers how terrible things will become if our deplorable behavior continues unchecked. The more utterly the protagonist is crushed, the more urgent and forceful the message. Because authors of children's fiction are "reluctant to depict the extinction of hope within their stories," Sambell writes, they equivocate when it comes to deliver-ing a moral. Yes, our errors and delusions may lead to catastrophe, but if—as usually happens in dystopian novels for children—a new, better way of life can be assembled from the ruins would the apocalypse really be such a bad thing?

Sambell's observation implies that dystopian stories for adults and chil-dren have essentially the same purpose—to warn us about the dangers of some current trend. That's certainly true of books like "1984" and "Brave New World"; they detail the consequences of political authoritarianism and feckless hedonism. This is what will happen if we don't turn back now, they scold, and scolding makes sense when your readers have a shot at getting their hands on the wheel.

Children, however, don't run the world, and teen-agers, especially, feel the sting of this. "The Hunger Games" could be taken as an indictment of reality TV, but only someone insensitive to the emotional tenor of the story could regard social criticism as the real point of Collins's novel. "The Hunger Games" is not an argument. It operates like a fable or a myth, a story in which outlandish and extravagant figures and events serve as conduits for universal experiences. Dystopian fiction may be the only genre written for children that's routinely *less* didactic than its adult counterpart. It's not about persuading the reader to stop something terrible from happening—it's about what's happening, right this minute, in the stormy psyche of the adolescent reader. "The success of 'Uglies,'" Westerfeld once wrote in his blog, "is partly thanks to high school being a dystopia."

Take the Hunger Games themselves. In the first book of Collins's tril-ogy, Katniss explains that the games are a "punishment" for a failed uprising against the Capitol many years earlier, and they're meant to be "humiliating as well as torturous." The twenty-four child contestants, called tributes, are compelled to participate, and the people of their districts must watch the televised bloodbath. Yet residents of the richer districts (District 12, Katniss's home, is a hardscrabble mining province) regard competing as "a huge honor," and some young people, called Career Tributes, train all their lives for the games. When Katniss herself becomes a tribute (she volunteers, in order to save her younger sister), she's taken to the Capitol and given a glamorous makeover and a wardrobe custom-designed for her by her own personal fashion maestro. She's cheered by crowds, feted at galas, interviewed on national television, fed sumptuous meals, and housed in a suite filled with wondrous devices. She's forced to live every teenage girl's dream. (Her professed claim to hate it all is undermined by the loving detail with which she describes every last goody.)

As a tool of practical propaganda, the games don't make much sense. They lack that essential quality of the totalitarian spectacle: ideological coherence. You don't demoralize and dehumanize a subject people by turning them into celebrities and coaching them on how to craft an appealing persona for a mass audience. ("Think of yourself among friends," Katniss's media handler urges.) Are the games a disciplinary measure or an extreme sporting event? A beauty pageant or an exercise in despotic terror? Given that the winning tribute's district is "showered with prizes, largely consisting of food," why isn't it the poorer, hungrier districts that pool their resources to train Career Tributes, instead of the wealthier ones? And the practice of carrying off a population's innocent children and commanding their parents to watch them be slaughtered for entertainment—wouldn't that do more to provoke a rebellion than to head one off?

If, on the other hand, you consider the games as a fever-dream allegory of the adolescent social experience, they become perfectly intelligible. Adults dump teenagers into the viper pit of high school, spouting a lot of sentimental drivel about what a wonderful stage of life it's supposed to be. The rules are arbitrary, unfathomable, and subject to sudden change. A brutal social hierarchy prevails, with the rich, the good-looking, and the athletic lording their advantages over everyone else. To survive you have to be totally fake. Adults don't seem to understand how high the stakes are; your whole life could be over, and they act like it's just some "phase"! Everyone's always watching you, scrutinizing your clothes or your friends and obsessing over whether you're having sex or taking drugs or getting good enough grades, but no one cares who you really are or how you really feel about anything.

The typical arc of the dystopian narrative mirrors the course of adolescent disaffection. First, the fictional world is laid out. It may seem pleasant enough. Tally, the heroine of "Uglies" (and its two sequels), looks forward to the surgery that will transform her into a Pretty and allow her to move to the party enclave of New Pretty Town. Eleven-year-old Jonas, in "The Giver," has no problem with the blandly tranquil community where he grows up. Then somebody new, a misfit, turns up, or the hero stumbles on an incongruity. A crack opens in the façade. If the society is a false utopia, the hero discovers the lie at its very foundation: the Pretties are lobotomized when they receive their plastic surgery, the residents of Jonas's community have been drained of all passion. If the society is frankly miserable or oppressive, the hero will learn that, contrary to what he's been told, there may be an alternative out there, somewhere. Conditions at home become more and more unbearable until finally the hero, alone or with a companion, decides to make a break for it, heading out across dangerous terrain.

Because these new dystopias follow a logic more archetypal than rational, many of them don't even attempt to abide by the strictures of science fiction. Or perhaps they care only about the third of Arthur C. Clarke's famous three rules of prediction: "Any sufficiently advanced technology is indistinguishable from magic." In her rooms in the Capitol, Katniss, who has previously spent her days poaching in the woods with a bow and arrow, finds she can "program the closet for an outfit to my taste. The windows zoom in and out on parts of the city at my command. You only need to whisper a type of food from a gigantic menu into a mouthpiece and it appears, hot and steamy, before you in less than a minute." She might as well be living in a fairy-tale castle, dining off enchanted golden plates that refill themselves every evening.

The snow-globe timelessness of these novels doesn't prevent them from incorporating the particular flavor of contemporary kid culture. Waking up in a hostile, confined place without an identity or any notion of what you're supposed to do or how you can get out—as Thomas, the hero of "The Maze Runner," does— is a scenario often found in video games. So are the rings that give their possessors more lives in Catherine Fisher's "Incarceron," where the characters are confined to a prison as big as a small country, complete with cities and metal forests. Like "The Maze Runner," "Catching Fire" features a moment in which the desperate players must picture the geography around them as seen from above, like a game board or puzzle in whose pattern can be found a crucial clue. There's more hand-to-hand combat in these dystopias than there was in the books of thirty years ago, and it's more important to the stories, which frequently culminate in a showdown resembling the climax of an action movie. Carrie Ryan's "The Forest of Hands and Teeth" takes an insular, vaguely medieval community reminiscent of the town in the M. Night Shyamalan film "The Village," subjects it to George Romero-style zombie attacks, and then throws in a love quadrangle with enough emo angst to rival "Twilight."

The experience of growing up under nearly continuous adult supervision—the circumstances that made writing about autonomous contemporary sixth-graders so difficult for Rebecca Stead—has tinged these novels as

15

well. The protagonists in the technological dystopias of earlier generations frequently contended with surveilling cameras, hoping to either elude or defy them. Face-offs between the human eye and a soulless lens still occur, the teen hacker who narrates Cory Doctorow's "Little Brother," a privacy-rights anthem set in near-future San Francisco, provides helpful instructions on how to make a concealed-camera detector out of a toilet-paper tube and a handful of spare L.E.D. lights. Often, however, the attitude is sullen resignation; in "Incarceron," the hero, Finn, can do no more than note the small red lights of the prison's ubiquitous "Eyes" staring down at him from the rafters. When Katniss is finally delivered into the Hunger Games arena, a tract of forest, she never even bothers to look around for the cameras; she knows they're embedded everywhere. "It has probably been difficult for the cameras to get a good shot of me," she thinks as she climbs down from a tree. "I know they must be tracking me now though. The minute I hit the ground, I'm guaranteed a close-up." In "The Hunger Games," surveillance is ambient.

The Internet plays a less important role in these novels than you might expect. One notable exception, M. T. Anderson's merciless and very clever satire of late-capitalist complacency, "Feed," has information (mostly advertising) piped right into people's brains; the novel's narrator thinks of the laptop era as being "like if you carried your lungs in a briefcase and opened it to breathe." ("Feed" is one of the few Y.A. dystopias in which adolescence doesn't confer any special immunity to the Big Lie. It's a lot closer to "Brave New World" than to "The Hunger Games," and its ending is notably downbeat.) In perhaps the most impressive of the recent crop, "The Knife of Never Letting Go," by Patrick Ness, the Internet appears metaphorically, in the form of a virus that causes people's thoughts to be broadcast into the minds of all those around them. "Information is absolutely everywhere today," Ness has explained, "texts and emails and messaging—so much it feels like you can't get away from it."

Todd, the novel's narrator, is a post-apocalyptic Huck Finn, the youngest resident of an all-male frontier town (the women have been killed off by the virus), where he's bombarded by mental "Noise," a cacophony of impressions and ideas, rendered at one point as a web of overlapping scrawls. Todd prefers to hang out in the nearby swamp, which is also Noisy, because the virus broadcasts animals' thoughts, too, but less intrusively so:

> The loud is a different kind of loud, because swamp loud is just curiosity, creachers figuring out who you are and if yer a threat. Whereas the town knows all about you already and wants to know more and wants to beat you with what it knows till how can you have any of yerself left at all?

The young readers of "The Knife of Never Letting Go" may feel the same way about their overscrutinized, information- flooded lives, or maybe that's just how Ness thinks he'd feel if he were them. It somehow fits the paranoid spirit of these novels that adults are the ones who write them, publish them, stock them in stores and libraries, assign them in classes, and decide which ones win prizes. (Most of the reader reviews posted online seem to be written by adults as well.) But kids do read the books, and some of them will surely grow up to write dystopian tales of their own, incited by technologies or social trends we have yet to conceive. By then, reality TV and privacy on the Internet may seem like quaint, outdated problems. But the part about the world being broken or intolerable, about the need to sweep away the past to make room for the new? That part never gets old.

FICTION

George Saunders (1958–   )

George Saunders studied engineering at the Colorado School of Mines and initially worked as a technical writer and geophysical engineer. He has published in *The New Yorker, Harper's, McSweeney's,* and *GQ.* His first collection of stories, *CivilWarLand in Bad Decline,* was published in 1996. He is on the faculty of Syracuse University. In 2006, Saunders was awarded the MacArthur "genius" fellowship. His fiction often satirizes contemporary culture, especially consumerism and the place of corporations and the media within culture. He also writes fiction for children, including *The Very Persistent Gappers of Frip* (2000), and has published collections of his essays, *The Brain-Dead Megaphone* (2007). This short story comes from his 2013 collection titled *Tenth of December.*

Escape from Spiderhead (2010)

Drip on?" Abnesti said over the P. A.

"What's in it?" I said.

"Hilarious," he said.

"Acknowledge," I said.

Abnesti used his remote. My MobiPak™ whirred. Soon the Interior   5
Garden looked really nice. Everything seemed super-clear.

I said out loud, as I was supposed to, what I was feeling.

"Garden looks nice," I said. "Super-clear."

Abnesti said, "Jeff, how about we pep up those language centers?"

"Sure," I said.

"Drip on?" he said.   10

"Acknowledge," I said.

He added some Verbaluce™ to the drip, and soon I was feeling the same things but saying them better. The garden still looked nice. It was like the bushes were so tight-seeming and the sun made everything stand out? It was like any moment you expected some Victorians to wander in with their cups of tea. It was as if the garden had become a sort of embodiment of the domestic dreams forever intrinsic to human consciousness. It was as if I could suddenly discern, in this contemporary vignette, the ancient corollary through which Plato and some of his contemporaries might have strolled; to wit, I was sensing the eternal in the ephemeral.

I sat, pleasantly engaged in these thoughts, until the Verbaluce™ began to wane. At which point the garden just looked nice again. It was something about the bushes and whatnot? It made you just want to lay out there and catch rays and think your happy thoughts. If you get what I mean.

Then whatever else was in the drip wore off, and I didn't feel much about the garden one way or the other. My mouth was dry, though, and my gut had that post-Verbaluce™ feel to it.

"What's going to be cool about that one?" Abnesti said. "Is, say a guy   15
has to stay up late guarding a perimeter. Or is at school waiting for his kid and gets bored. But there's some nature nearby? Or say a park ranger has to work a double shift?"

"That will be cool," I said.

"That's ED763," he said. "We're thinking of calling it NatuGlide. Or maybe ErthAdmire."

"Those are both good," I said,

"Thanks for your help, Jeff," he said.

Which was what he always said.   20

"Only a million years to go," I said.

Which was what I always said.

Then he said, "Exit the Interior Garden now, Jeff, head over to Small Workroom 2."

II

Into Small Workroom 2 they sent this pale tall girl.

"What do you think?" Abnesti said over the P. A.

"Me?" I said. "Or her?"

"Both," Abnesti said.

"Pretty good," I said.   5

"Fine, you know," she said. "Normal."

Abnesti asked us to rate each other more quantifiably, as per pretty, as per sexy.

It appeared we liked each other about average, i.e., no big attraction or revulsion either way.

Abnesti said, "Jeff, drip on?"

"Acknowledge," I said.   10

"Heather, drip on?" he said.

"Acknowledge," Heather said.

Then we looked at each other like, What happens next?

What happened next was, Heather soon looked super-good. And I could tell she thought the same of me. It came on so sudden we were like laughing. How could we not have seen it, how cute the other one was? Luckily there was a couch in the Workroom. It felt like our drip had, in addition to whatever they were testing, some ED556 in it, which lowers your shame level to like niL Because soon, there on the couch, off we went. It was super-hot between us. And not merely in a hondog way. Hot, yes, but also just right. Like if you'd dreamed of a certain girl all your life and all of a sudden there she was, in your Domain.

"Jeff," Abnesti said. "I'd like your permission to pep up your language   15
centers."

"Go for it," I said, under her now.

"Drip on?" he said.

"Acknowledge," I said.

"Me, too?" Heather said.

"You got it," Abnesti said, with a laugh. "Drip on?"   20

"Acknowledge," she said, all breathless.

Soon, experiencing the benefits of the flowing Verbaluce™ in our drips, we were not only fucking really well but also talking pretty great. Like, instead of just saying the sex-type things we had been saying (such as "wow" and "oh God" and "hell yes" and so forth), we now began freestyling re our sensations and thoughts, in elevated diction, with eighty-per-cent increased vocab, our well-articulated thoughts being recorded for later analysis.

For me, the feeling was, approximately; Astonishment at the dawning realization that this woman was being created in real time, directly from my own mind, per my deepest longings. Finally, after all these years (was my thought), I had found the precise arrangement of body/face/mind that personified all that was desirable. The taste of her mouth, the look of that halo of blondish hair spread out around her cherubic yet naughty-looking face (she was beneath me now, legs way up), even (not to be crude or dishonor the exalted feelings I was experiencing) the sensations her vagina was producing along the length of my thrusting penis were precisely those I had always hungered for, though I had never, before this instant, realized that I so ardently hungered for them.

That is to say: a desire would arise and, concurrently, the satisfaction of that desire would also arise. It was as if (a) I longed for a certain (heretofore untasted) taste until (b) said longing became nearly unbearable, at which time (c) I found a morsel of food with that exact taste already in my mouth, perfectly satisfying my longing.

Every utterance, every adjustment of posture bespoke the same thing: 25
we had known each other forever, were soul mates, had met and loved in numerous preceding lifetimes, and would meet and love in many subsequent lifetimes, always with the same transcendently stupefying results.

Then there came a hard-to-describe but very real drifting-off into a number of sequential reveries that might best be described as a type of nonnarrative mind scenery, i.e., a series of vague mental images of places I had never been (a certain pine-packed valley in high white mountains, a chalet-type house in a cul-de-sac, the yard of which was overgrown with wide, stunted Seussian trees), each of which triggered a deep sentimental longing, longings that coalesced into, and were soon reduced to, one central longing, i.e., an intense longing for Heather and Heather alone.

This mind-scenery phenomenon was strongest during our third (!) bout of lovemaking. (Apparently, Abnesti had included some Vivistif™ in my drip.)

Afterward, our protestations of love poured forth simultaneously, linguistically complex and metaphorically rich: I daresay we had become poets. We were allowed to lie there, limbs intermingled, for nearly an hour. It was bliss. It was perfection. It was that impossible thing: happiness that does not wilt to reveal the thin shoots of some new desire rising from within it.

We cuddled with a fierceness/focus that rivalled the fierceness/focus with which we had fucked. There was nothing *less* about cuddling vis-à-vis fucking, is what I mean to say. We were all over each other in the super-friendly way of puppies, or spouses meeting for the first time after one of them has undergone a close brush with death. Everything seemed moist, permeable, *sayable*.

Then something in the drip began to wane. I think Abnesti had shut   30
off the Verbaluce™? Also the shame reducer? Basically, everything began to *dwindle*. Suddenly we felt shy. But still loving. We began the process of trying to talk après Verbaluce™: always awkward.

Yet I could see in her eyes that she was still feeling love for me.

And I was definitely still feeling love for her.

Well, why not? We had just fucked three times! Why do you think they call it "making love"? That was what we had just made three times: love.

Then Abnesti said, "Drip on?"

We had kind of forgotten he was even there, behind his one-way mirror.   35

I said, "Do we have to? We are really liking this right now."

"We're just going to try to get you guys back to baseline," he said. "We've got more to do today."

"Shit," I said.

"Rats," she said.

"Drip on?" he said.

40

"Acknowledge," we said.

Soon something began to change. I mean, she was fine. A handsome pale girl. But nothing special. And I could see that she felt the same re me, i.e., what had all that fuss been about just now?

Why weren't we dressed? We real quick got dressed.

Kind of embarrassing.

Did I love her? Did she love me?

45

Ha.

No.

Then it was time for her to go. We shook hands.

Out she went.

Lunch came in. On a tray. Spaghetti with chicken chunks.

50

Man, was I hungry.

I spent all lunchtime thinking. It was weird. I had the memory of fucking Heather, the memory of having felt the things I'd felt for her, the memory of having said the things I'd said to her. My throat was like raw from how much I'd said and how fast I'd felt compelled to say it. But in terms of feelings? I basically had nada left.

Just a hot face and some shame re having fucked three times in front of Abnesti.

III

After lunch in came another girl. About equally so-so. Dark hair. Average build. Nothing special, just like, upon first entry, Heather had been nothing special.

"This is Rachel," Abnesti said on the PA. "This is Jeff."

"Hi, Rachel," I said.

"Hi, Jeff," she said.

"Drip on?" Abnesti said.

5

We Acknowledged.

Something seemed very familiar about the way I now began feeling. Suddenly Rachel looked super-good. Abnesti requested permission to pep up our language centers via Verbaluce™. We Acknowledged. Soon we, too, were fucking like bunnies. Soon we, too, were talking like articulate maniacs re our love. Once again certain sensations were arising to meet my concurrently arising desperate hunger for just those sensations. Soon my memory of the perfect taste of Heather's mouth was being overwritten by the current taste of Rachel's mouth, so much more the taste I now desired. I was feeling unprecedented emotions, even though those unprecedented emotions were (I discerned somewhere in my consciousness) exactly the same emotions I had felt earlier, for that now unworthy-seeming vessel Heather. Rachel was, I mean to say, *it*. Her lithe waist, her voice, her hungry mouth/hands/loins—they were all *it*.

I just loved Rachel so much.

Then came the sequential geographic reveries (see above): same pine-packed valley, same chalet-looking house, accompanied by that same longing-for-place transmuting into a longing for (this time) Rachel. While continuing to enact a level of sexual strenuousness that caused what I would describe as a gradually tightening, chest-located, sweetness rubber band to both connect us and compel us onward, we whispered feverishly (precisely, poetically) about how long we felt we had known each other, i.e., forever.

Again the total number of times we made love was three. 10

Then, like before, came the dwindling. Our talking became less excellent. Words were fewer, our sentences shorter. Still, I loved her. Loved Rachel Everything about her just seemed *perfect*: her cheek mole, her black hair, the little butt-squirm she did now and then, as if to say, Mmm-mmm, was that ever good.

"Drip on?" Abnesti said. "We are going to try to get you both back to baseline."

"Acknowledge," she said.

"Well, hold on," I said.

"Jeff," Abnesti said, irritated, as if trying to remind me that I was here not 15 by choice but because I had done my crime and was in the process of doing my time.

"Acknowledge," I said. And gave Rachel one last look of love, knowing (as she did not yet know) that this would be the last look of love I would be giving her.

Soon she was merely fine to me, and I merely fine to her. She looked, as had Heather, embarrassed, as in, What was up with that just now? Why did I just go so overboard with Mr. Average here?

Did I love her? Or her me?

No.

When it was time for her to go, we shook hands. 20

The place where my MobiPak™ was surgically joined to my lower back was sore from all our positional changes. Plus I was way tired. Plus I was feeling so sad. Why sad? Was I not a dude? Had I not just fucked two different girls, for a total of six times, in one day?

Still, honestly, I felt sadder than sad.

I guess I was sad that love was not real? Or not all that real, anyway? I guess I was sad that love could feel so real and the next minute be gone, and all because of something Abnesti was doing.

IV

After Snack Abnesti called me into Control. Control being like the head of a spider. With its various legs being our Workrooms. Sometimes we were called upon to work alongside Abnesti in the head of the spider. Or, as we termed it: the Spiderhead.

"Sit," he said. "Look into Large Workroom 1."

In Large Workroom 1 were Heather and Rachel, side by side.

"Recognize them?" he said.

"Ha," I said.

"Now," Abnesti said. "I'm going to present you with a choice, Jeff. This is what we're playing at here. See this remote? Let's say you can hit *this* button and Rachel gets some Darkenfloxx™. Or you can hit *this* button and Heather gets the Darkenfloxx™. See? You choose."

"They've got Darkenfloxx™ in their MobiPaks™?" I said.

"You've all got have Darkenfloxx™ in your MobiPaks™, dummy," Abnesti said affectionately. "Verlaine put it there Wednesday. In anticipation of this very study."

Well, that made me nervous.

Imagine the worst you have ever felt, times ten. That does not even come close to how bad you feel on Darkenfloxx™. The time it was administered to us in Orientation, briefly, for demo purposes, at one-third the dose now selected on Abnesti's remote? I have never felt so terrible. All of us were just moaning, heads down, like, How could we ever have felt life was worth living?

I do not even like to think about that time.

"What's your decision, Jeff?" Abnesti said. "Is Rachel getting the Darkenfloxx™? Or Heather?"

"I can't say," I said.

"You have to," he said.

"I can't," I said. "It would be like random."

"You feel your decision would be random," he said.

"Yes," I said.

And that was true. I really didn't care. It was like if I put *you* in the Spiderhead and gave you the choice: which of these two strangers would you like to send into the shadow of the valley of death?

"Ten seconds," Abnesti said. "What we're testing for here is any residual fondness."

It wasn't that I liked them both. I honestly felt completely neutral toward both. It was exactly as if I had never seen, much less fucked, either one. (They had really succeeded in taking me back to baseline, I guess I am saying.)

But, having once been Darkenfloxxed™, I just didn't want to do that to anyone. Even if I didn't like the person very much, even if I hated the person, I still wouldn't want to do it.

"Five seconds," Abnesti said.

"I can't decide," I said. "It's random."

"Truly random?" he said. "O.K. I'm giving the Darkenfloxx™ to Heather."

I just sat there.   25

"No, actually," he said. "I'm giving it to Rachel."

Just sat there.

'Jeff,' he said. 'You have convinced me. It would, to you, be random. You truly have no preference. I can see that. And therefore I don't have to do it. See what we just did? With your help? For the first time? Via the ED289/290 suite? Which is what we've been testing today? You have to admit it: you were in love. Twice. Right?"

"Yes," I said.

"Very much in love," he said. "Twice."   30

"I said yes," I said.

"But you just now expressed no preference," he said. "Ergo, no trace of either of those great loves remains. You are totally cleansed. We brought you high, laid you low, and now here you sit, the same emotionwise as before our testing even began. That is powerful. That is killer. We have unlocked a mysterious eternal secret. What a fantastic game-changer! Say someone can't love? Now he or she can. We can make him. Say someone loves too much? Or loves someone deemed unsuitable by his or her caregiver? We can tone that shit right down. Say someone is blue, because of true love? We step in, or his or her caregiver does: blue no more. No longer, in terms of emotional controllability, are we ships adrift. No one is. We see a ship adrift, we climb aboard, install a rudder. Guide him/her toward love. Or away from it. You say, 'All you need is love'? Look, here comes ED289/290. Can we stop war? We can sure as heck slow it down! Suddenly the soldiers on both sides start fucking. Or, at low dosage, feeling super-fond. Or say we have two rival dictators in a death grudge. Assuming ED289/290 develops nicely in pill form, allow me to slip each dictator a mickey. Soon their tongues are down each other's throats and doves of peace are pooping on their epaulets. Or, depending on the dosage, they may just be hugging. And who helped us do that? You did."

All this time, Rachel and Heather had just been sitting there in Large Workroom 1.

"That's it, gals, thanks," Abnesti said on the P. A.

And they left, neither knowing how close they had come to getting   35
Darkenfloxxed™ out their wing-wangs.

Verlaine took them out the back way, i.e., not through the Spiderhead but via the Back Alley. Which is not really an alley, just a carpeted hallway leading back to our Domain Cluster.

"Think, Jeff," Abnesti said. "Think if you'd had the benefit of ED289/290 on your fateful night."

Tell the truth, I was getting kind of sick of him always talking about my fateful night.

I'd been sorry about it right away and had got sorrier about it ever since, and was now so sorry about it that him rubbing it in my face did not make me one bit sorrier, it just made me think of him as being kind of a dick.

"Can I go to bed now?" I said.   40

"Not yet," Abnesti said. "It is hours to go before you sleep."

Then he sent me into Small Workroom 3, where some dude I didn't know was sitting.

V

Rogan," the dude said.

"Jeff," I said.

"What's up?" he said.

"Not much," I said.

We sat tensely for a long time, not talking. Maybe ten minutes passed.   5

We got some rough customers in here. I noted that Rogan had a tattoo of a rat on his neck, a rat that had just been knifed and was crying. But even through its tears it was knifing a smaller rat, who just looked surprised.

Finally Abnesti came on the P. A.

"That's it, guys, thanks," he said.

"What the fuck was that about?" Rogan said.

Good question, Rogan, I thought. Why had we been left just sitting   10
there? In the same manner that Heather and Rachel had been left just sitting there? Then I had a hunch. To test my hunch, I did a sudden lurch into the Spider- head. Which Abnesti always made a point of not keeping locked, to show how much he trusted and was unafraid of us.

And guess who was in there?

"Hey, Jeff," Heather said.

"Jeff, get out," Abnesti said.

"Heather, did Mr. Abnesti just now make you decide which of us, me or Rogan, to give some Darkenfloxx™ to?" I said.

"Yes," Heather said. She must have been on some VeriTalk™, because   15
she spoke the truth in spite of Abnesti's withering silencing glance.

"Did you recently fuck Rogan, Heather?" I said. "In addition to me? And also fall in love with him, as you did with me?"

"Yes," she said.

"Heather, honestly," Abnesti said. "Put a sock in it."

Heather looked around for a sock, VeriTalk™ making one quite literal.

Back in my Domain, I did the math: Heather had fucked me three 20
times. Heather had probably also fucked Rogan three times, since, in the
name of design consistency, Abnesti would have given Rogan and me equal
relative doses of Vivistif™.

And yet, speaking of design consistency, there was still one shoe to
drop, if I knew Abnesti, always a stickler in terms of data symmetry, which
was: wouldn't Abnesti also need Rachel to decide who to Darkenfloxx™,
i.e., me or Rogan?

After a short break, my suspicions were confirmed: I found myself
again sitting in Small Workroom 3 with Rogan!

Again we sat not talking for a long time. Mostly he picked at the
smaller rat and I tried to watch without him seeing.

Then, like before, Abnesti came on the P. A. and said, "That's it, guys,
thanks."

"Let me guess," I said. "Rachel's in there with you." 25

"Jeff, if you don't stop doing that, I swear," Abnesti said.

"And she just declined to Darkenfloxx™ either me or Rogan?" I said.

"Hi, Jeff!" Rachel said. "Hi, Rogan!"

"Rogan," I said. "Did you by any chance fuck Rachel earlier today?"

"Pretty much," Rogan said. 30

My mind was like reeling. Rachel had fucked me plus Rogan? Heather
had fucked me plus Rogan? And everyone who had fucked anyone had
fallen in love with that person, then out of it?

What kind of crazy-ass Project Team was this?

I mean, I had been on some crazy-ass Project Teams in my time, such as
one where the drip had something in it that made hearing music exquisite,
and hence when some Shostakovich was piped in actual bats seemed to circle
my Domain, or the one where my legs became totally numb and yet I found
I could still stand fifteen straight hours at a fake cash register, miraculously
suddenly able to do extremely hard long-division problems in my mind.

But of all my crazy-ass Project Teams this was by far the most crazy-assed.

I could not help but wonder what tomorrow would bring. 35

VI

Except today wasn't even over.

I was again called into Small Workroom 3. And was sitting there when
this unfamiliar guy came in.

"I'm Keith!" he said, rushing over to shake my hand.

He was a tall Southern drink of water, all teeth and wavy hair.

"Jeff," I said. 5

"Really nice meeting you!" he said.

Then we sat there not talking. Whenever I looked over at Keith, he would gleam his teeth at me and shake his head all wry, as if to say, "Odd job of work, isn't it?"

"Keith," I said. "Do you by any chance know two chicks named Rachel and Heather?"

"I sure as heck do," Keith said. And suddenly his teeth had a leering quality to them.

"Did you by any chance have sex with both Rachel and Heather earlier   10 today, three times each?" I said.

"What are you, man, a dang psychic?" Keith said. "You're blowing my mind, I admit, it!"

"Jeff, you're totally doinking with our experimental design integrity," Abnesti said.

"So either Rachel or Heather is sitting in the Spiderhead right now," I said. "Trying to decide."

"Decide what?" Keith said.

"Which of us to Darkenfloxx™," I said.   15

"Eek," Keith said. And now his teeth looked scared.

"Don't worry," I said. "She won't do it."

"Who won't?" Keith said.

"Whoever's in there," I said.

"That's it, guys, thanks," Abnesti said.   20

Then, after a short break, Keith and I were once again brought into Small Workroom 3, where once again we waited as, this time, Heather declined to Darkenfloxx™ either one of us.

Back in my Domain, I constructed a who-had-fucked-whom chart, which went like this:

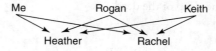

Abnesti came in.

"Despite all your shenanigans," he said, "Rogan and Keith had exactly the same reaction as you did. And as Rachel and Heather did. None of you, at the critical moment, could decide whom to Darkenfloxx™. Which is super. What does that mean? Why is it super? It means that ED289/290 is the real deal. It can make love, it can take love away. I'm almost inclined to start the naming process."

'Those girls did it nine times each today?" I said.   25

"Peace4All," he said. "Luvlnclyned. You seem pissy. Are you pissy?"

"Well, I feel a little jerked around," I said.

"Do you feel jerked around because you still have feelings of love for one of the girls?" he said. "That would need to be noted. Anger? Possessiveness? Residual sexual longing?"

"No," I said.

"You honestly don't feel miffed that a girl for whom you felt love was then 30 funked by two other guys, and, not only that, she then felt exactly the same quality/quantity of love for those guys as she had felt for you, or, in the case of Rachel, was about to feel for you, at the time that she funked Rogan? I think it was Rogan. She may have funked Keith first. Then you, penultimately. I'm vague on the order of operations. I could look it up. But think deeply on this."

I thought deeply on it.

"Nothing," I said.

"Well, it's a lot to sort through," he said. "Luckily it's night. Our day is done. Anything else you want to talk about? Anything else you're feeling?"

"My penis is sore," I said.

"Well, no surprise there," he said. "Think how those girls must feel. 35 I'll send Verlaine in with some cream."

Soon Verlaine came in with some cream.

"Hi, Verlaine," I said.

"Hi, Jeff," he said. "You want to put this on yourself or want me to do it?"

"I'll do it," I said.

"Cool," he said. 40

And I could tell he meant it.

"Looks painful," he said.

"It really is," I said.

"Must have felt pretty good at the time, though?" he said.

His words seemed to be saying he was envious, but I could see in his 45 eyes, as they looked at my penis, that he wasn't envious at all.

Then I slept the sleep of the dead.

As they say.

VII

Next morning I was still asleep when Abnesti came on the P. A.

"Do you remember yesterday?" he said.

"Yes," I said.

"When I asked which gal you'd like to see on the Darkenfloxx™?" he said. "And you said neither?"

"Yes," I said. 5

"Well, that was good enough for me," he said. "But apparently not good enough for the Protocol Committee. Not good enough for the Three Horsemen of Anality. Come in here. Let's get started—we're going to need to do a kind of Confirmation Trial. Oh, this is going to stink."

I entered the Spiderhead.

Sitting in Small Workroom 2 was Heather.

"So this time," Abnesti said, "per the Protocol Committee, instead of me asking you which girl to give the Darkenfloxx™ to, which the Prot-Comm felt was too subjective, we're going to give this girl the Darken-floxx™ no matter what you say. Then see what you say. Like yesterday, we're going to put you on a drip of—Verlaine? Verlaine? Where are you? Are you there? What is it again? Do you have the project order?"

"Verbaluce™, VeriTalk™, Chat-Ease™," Verlaine said over the P. A.   10

"Right," Abnesti said. "And did you refresh his MobiPak™? Are his quantities good?"

"I did it," Verlaine said. "I did it while he was sleeping. Plus I already told you I already did it."

"What about her?" Abnesti said. "Did you refresh her MobiPak™? Are her quantities good?"

"You stood right there and watched me, Ray," Verlaine said.

"Jeff, sorry," Abnesti said to me. "We're having a little tension in here   15 today. Not an easy day ahead."

"I don't want you to Darkenfloxx™ Heather," I said.

"Interesting," he said. "Is that because you love her?"

"No," I said. "I don't want you to Darkenfloxx™ anybody."

"I know what you mean," he said. "That is so sweet. Then again: is this Confirmation Trial about what you want? Not so much. What it's about is us recording what you say as you observe Heather getting Darkenfloxxed™. For five minutes. Five-minute trial. Here we go. Drip on?"

I did not say "Acknowledge."   20

"You should feel flattered," Abnesti said. "Did we choose Rogan? Keith? No. We deemed your level of speaking more commensurate with our data needs."

I did not say "Acknowledge."

"Why so protective of Heather?" Abnesti said. "One would almost think you loved her."

"No," I said.

"Do you even know her story?" he said. "You don't. You legally can't.   25 Does it involve whiskey, gangs, infanticide? I can't say. Can I imply, some-what peripherally, that her past, violent and sordid, did not exactly include a dog named Lassie and a lot of family talks about the Bible while Grammy sat doing macramé, adjusting her posture because the quaint fireplace was so sizzling? Can I suggest that, if you knew what I know about Heather's past, making Heather briefly sad, nauseous, and/or horrified might not seem like the worst idea in the world? No, I can't."

"All right, all right," I said.

"You know me," he said. "How many kids do I have?"

"Five," I said.

"What are their names?" he said.

"Mick, Todd, Karen, Lisa, Phoebe," I said.   30

"Am I a monster?" he said. "Do I remember birthdays around here? When a certain individual got athlete's foot on his groin on a Sunday, did a certain other individual drive over to Rexall and pick up a prescription, paying for it with his own personal money?"

That was a nice thing he'd done, but it seemed kind of unprofessional to bring it up now.

"Jeff," Abnesti said. "What do you want me to say here? Do you want me to say that your Fridays are at risk? I can easily say that."

Which was cheap. My Fridays meant a lot to me, and he knew that. Fridays I got to Skype Mom.

"How long do we give you?" Abnesti said.   35

"Five minutes," I said.

"How about we make it ten?" Abnesti said.

Mom always looked heartsick when our time was up. It had almost killed her when they arrested me. The trial had almost killed her. She'd spent her savings to get me out of real jail and in here. When I was a kid, she had long brown hair, past her waist. During the trial she cut it. Then it went gray. Now it was just a white poof about the size of a cap.

"Drip on?" Abnesti said.

"Acknowledge," I said.   40

"O.K. to pep up your language centers?" he said.

"Fine," I said.

"Heather, hello?" he said.

"Good morning!" Heather said.

"Drip on?" he said.   45

"Acknowledge," Heather said.

Abnesti used his remote.

The Darkenfloxx™ started flowing. Soon Heather was softly crying. Then was up and pacing. Then jaggedly crying. A little hysterical, even.

"I don't like this," she said, in a quaking voice.

Then she threw up in the trash can.   50

"Speak, Jeff," Abnesti said to me. "Speak a lot, speak in detail. Let's make something useful of this, shall we?"

Everything in my drip felt Grade A. Suddenly I was waxing poetic. I was waxing poetic re what Heather was doing, and waxing poetic re my feelings about what Heather was doing. Basically, what I was feeling was: Every human is born of man and woman. Every human, at birth, is, or at least has the potential to be, beloved of his/her mother/father. Thus every human is worthy of love. As I watched Heather suffer, a great tenderness suffused my body, a tenderness hard to distinguish from a sort of vast existential nausea; to wit, why are such beautiful beloved vessels made slaves to so much pain? Heather presented as a bundle of pain receptors. Heather's mind was fluid and could be ruined (by pain, by sadness). Why? Why was she made this way? Why so fragile?

Poor child, I was thinking, poor girl. Who loved you? Who loves you?

"Hang in there, Jeff," Abnesti said. "Verlaine! What do you think? Any vestige of romantic love in Jeff's Verbal Commentary?"

"I'd say no," Verlaine said over the P. A. "That's all just pretty much basic human feeling right there."   55

"Excellent," Abnesti said. "Time remaining?"

"Two minutes," Verlaine said.

I found what happened next very hard to watch. Under the influence of the Verbaluce™, the VeriTalk™, and the ChatEase™, I also found it impossible not to narrate.

In each Workroom was a couch, a desk, and a chair, all, by design, impossible to disassemble. Heather now began disassembling her impossible-to-disassemble chair. Her face was a mask of rage. She drove her head into the wall. Like a wrathful prodigy, Heather, beloved of someone, managed, in her great sadness-fuelled rage, to disassemble the chair while continuing to drive her head into the wall.

"Jesus," Verlaine said.   60

"Verlaine, buck up," Abnesti said. "Jeff, stop crying. Contrary to what you might think, there's not much data in crying. Use your words. Don't make this in vain."

I used my words. I spoke volumes, was precise. I described and redescribed what I was feeling as I watched Heather do what she now began doing, intently, almost beautifully, to her face/head with one of the chair legs.

In his defense, Abnesti was not in such great shape himself: breathing hard, cheeks candy-red, as he tapped the screen of his iMac non-stop with a pen, something he did when stressed.

"Time," he finally said, and cut the Darkenfloxx™ off with his remote. "Fuck. Get in there, Verlaine. Hustle it."

Verlaine hustled into Small Workroom 2.   65

"Talk to me, Sammy," Abnesti said.

Verlaine felt for Heather's pulse, then raised his hands, palms up, so that he looked like Jesus, except shocked instead of beatific, and also he had his glasses up on top of his head.

"Are you *kidding* me?" Abnesti said.

"What now?" Verlaine said. "What do I—"

"Are you fricking *kidding* me?" Abnesti said.   70

Abnesti burst out of his chair, shoved me out of the way, and flew through the door into Small Workroom 2.

VIII

I returned to my Domain.

At three, Verlaine came on the P. A. "Jeff," he said. "Please return to the Spiderhead."

I returned to the Spiderhead.

"We're sorry you had to see that, Jeff," Abnesti said.

"That was unexpected," Verlaine said.   5

"Unexpected plus unfortunate," Abnesti said. "And sorry I shoved you."

"Is she dead?" I said.

"Well, she's not the best," Verlaine said.

"Look, Jeff, these things happen," Abnesti said. "This is science. In science we explore the unknown. It was unknown what five minutes on Darkenfloxx™ would do to Heather. Now we know. The other thing we know, per Verlaine's assessment of your commentary, is that you really, for sure, do not harbor any residual romantic feelings for Heather. That's a big deal, Jeff. A beacon of hope at a sad time for all. Even as Heather was, so to speak, going down to the sea in her ship, you remained totally unwavering in terms of continuing to not romantically love her. My guess is ProtComm's going to be like, 'Wow, Utica's really leading the pack in terms of providing some mind-blowing new data on ED289/290.'"

It was quiet in the Spiderhead.   10

"Verlaine, go out," Abnesti said. "Go do your bit. Make things ready."

Verlaine went out.

"Do you think I liked that?" Abnesti said.

"You didn't seem to," I said.

"Well, I didn't," Abnesti said. "I hated it. I'm a person. I have feelings.   15
Still, personal sadness aside, that was good. You did terrific over all. We all did terrific. Heather especially did terrific. I honor her. Let's just—let's see this thing through, shall we? Let's complete it. Complete the next portion of our Confirmation Trial."

Into Small Workroom 4 came Rachel.

IX

Are we going to Darkenfloxx™ Rachel now?" I said.

"Think, Jeff," Abnesti said. "How can we know that you love neither Rachel nor Heather if we only have data regarding your reaction to what just now happened to Heather? Use your noggin. You are not a scientist, but Lord knows you work around scientists all day. Drip on?"

I did not say "Acknowledge."

"What's the problem, Jeff?" Abnesti said.

"I don't want to kill Rachel," I said.

"Well, who does?" Abnesti said. "Do I? Do you, Verlaine?"   5

"No," Verlaine said over the P. A.

"Jeff, maybe you're overthinking this," Abnesti said. "Is it possible the Darkenfloxx™ will kill Rachel? Sure. We have the Heather precedent. On the other hand, Rachel may be stronger. She seems a little larger."

"She's actually a little smaller," Verlaine said.

"Well, maybe she's tougher," Abnesti said.   10

"We're going to weight-adjust her dosage," Verlaine said. "So."

"Thanks, Verlaine," Abnesti said. "Thanks for clearing that up."

"Maybe show him the file," Verlaine said.

Abnesti handed me Rachel's file.

Verlaine came back in.   15

"Read it and weep," he said.

Per Rachel's file, she had stolen jewelry from her mother, a car from her father, cash from her sister, statues from their church. She'd gone to jail for drugs. After four times in jail for drugs, she'd gone to rehab for drugs, then to rehab for prostitution, then to what they call rehab-refresh, for people who've been in rehab so many times they are basically immune. But she must have been immune to the rehab-refresh, too, because after that came her biggie: a triple murder—her dealer, the dealer's sister, the dealer's sister's boyfriend.

Reading that made me feel a little funny that we'd fucked and I'd loved her.

But I still didn't want to kill her.

"Jeff," Abnesti said. "I know you've done a lot of work on this with   20
Mrs. Lacey. On killing and so forth. But this is not you. This is us."

"It's not even us," Verlaine said. "It's science."

"The mandates of science," Abnesti said. "Plus the dictates."

"Sometimes science sucks," Verlaine said.

"On the one hand, Jeff," Abnesti said, "a few minutes of unpleasantness for Heather—"

"Rachel," Verlaine said.   25

"A few minutes of unpleasantness for Rachel," Abnesti said, "years of relief for literally tens of thousands of underloving or overloving folks."

"Do the math, Jeff," Verlaine said.

"Being good in small ways is easy," Abnesti said. "Doing the huge good things, that's harder."

"Drip on?" Verlaine said. "Jeff?"

I did not say "Acknowledge."   30

"Fuck it, enough," Abnesti said. "Verlaine, what's the name of that one? The one where I give him an order and he obeys it?"

"Docilryde™," Verlaine said.

"Is there Docilryde™ in his MobiPak™?" Abnesti said.

"There's Docilryde™ in every MobiPak™," Verlaine said.   35

"Does he need to say 'Acknowledge'?" Abnesti said.

"Docilryde™'s a Class C, so—" Verlaine said.

"See, that, to me, makes zero sense," Abnesti said. "What good's an obedience drug if we need his permission to use it?"

"We just need a waiver," Verlaine said.

"How long does that shit take?" Abnesti said.   40

"We fax Albany, they fax us back," Verlaine said.

"Come on, come on, make haste," Abnesti said, and they went out, leaving me alone in the Spiderhead.

X

It was sad. It gave me a sad, defeated feeling to think that soon they'd be back and would Docilryde™ me, and I'd say "Acknowledge," smiling agreeably the way a person smiles on Docilryde™, and then the Darkenfloxx™ would flow, into Rachel, and I would begin describing, in that rapid, robotic way one describes on Verbaluce™/ VeriTalk™/ChatEase™, the things Rachel would, at that time, begin doing to herself.

It was like all I had to do to be a killer again was sit there and wait.

Which was a hard pill to swallow, after my work with Mrs. Lacey.

"Violence finished, anger no more," she'd make me say, over and over. Then she'd have me do a Detailed Remembering re my fateful night.

I was nineteen. Mike Appel was seventeen. We were both wasto. All   5
night he'd been giving me grief. He was smaller, younger, less popular. Then we were out front of Frizzy's, rolling around on the ground. He was quick. He was mean. I was losing. I couldn't believe it. I was bigger, older, yet losing? Around us, watching, was basically everybody we knew. Then he had me on my back. Someone laughed. Someone said, "Shit, poor Jeff." Nearby was a brick. I grabbed it, glanced Mike in the head with it. Then was on top of him.

Mike gave. That is, there on his back, scalp bleeding, he gave, by shooting me a certain look, like, Dude, come on, we're not all that serious about this, are we?

We were.

I was.

I don't even know why I did it.

It was like, with the drinking and the being a kid and the nearly losing,   10
I'd been put on a drip called, like, Temper Berst or something.

InstaRaje.

LifeRooner.

"Hey, guys, hello!" Rachel said. "What are we up to today?"

There was her fragile head, her undamaged face, one arm lifting a hand
to scratch a cheek, legs bouncing with nerves, peasant skirt bouncing, too,
clogged feet crossed under the hem.

Soon all that would be just a lump on the floor.   15

I had to think.

Why were they going to Darkenfloxx™ Rachel? So they could hear me
describe it. If I wasn't here to describe it, they wouldn't do it. How could
I make it so I wouldn't be here? I could leave. How could I leave? There
was only one door out of the Spiderhead, which was autolocked, and on
the other side was either Barry or Hans, with that electric wand called the
DisciStick™. Could I wait until Abnesti came in, wonk him, try to race past
Barry or Hans, make a break for the Main Door?

Any weapons in the Spiderhead? No, just Abnesti's birthday mug, a
pair of running shoes, a roll of breath mints, his remote.

His remote?

What a dope. That was supposed to be on his belt at all times. Other-   20
wise one of us might help ourselves to whatever we found, via Inventory
Directory, in our MobiPaks™: some Bonviv™, maybe, some BlissTyme™,
some SpeedErUp™.

Some Darkenfloxx™.

Jesus. That was one way to leave.

Scary, though.

Just then, in Small Workroom 4, Rachel, I guess thinking the Spiderhead
empty, got up and did this happy little shuffle, like she was some cheerful
farmer chick who'd just stepped outside to find the hick she was in love
with coming up the road with a calf under his arm or whatever.

Why was she dancing? No reason.   25

Just alive, I guess.

Time was short.

The remote was well labelled.

Good old Verlaine.

I used it, dropped it down the heat vent, in case I changed my mind,   30
then stood there like, I can't believe I just did that.

My MobiPak™ whirred.

The Darkenfloxx™ flowed.

Then came the horror: worse than I'd ever imagined. Soon my arm was
about a mile down the heat vent. Then I was staggering around the Spiderhead, looking for something, anything. In the end, here's how bad it got: I
used a corner of the desk.

What's death like?

You're briefly unlimited.   35

I sailed right out through the roof.

And hovered above it, looking down. Here was Rogan, checking his neck in the mirror. Here was Keith, squat-thrusting in his underwear. Here was Ned Riley, here was B. Troper, here was Gail Orley, Stefan DeWitt, killers all, all bad, I guess, although, in that instant, I saw it differently. At birth, they'd been charged by God with the responsibility of growing into total fuck-ups. Had they chosen this? Was it their fault, as they tumbled out of the womb? Had they aspired, covered in placental blood, to grow into harmers, dark forces, life-enders? In that first holy instant of breath/awareness (tiny hands clutching and unclutching), had it been their fondest hope to render (via gun, knife, or brick) some innocent family bereft? No; and yet their crooked destinies had lain dormant within them, seeds awaiting water and light to bring forth the most violent, life-poisoning flowers, said water/light actually being the requisite combination of neurological tendency and environmental activation that would transform them (transform us!) into earth's offal, murderers, and foul us with the ultimate, unwashable transgression.

Wow, I thought, was there some Verbaluce™ in that drip or what?

But no.

This was all me now.   40

I got snagged, found myself stuck on a facility gutter, and squatted there like an airy gargoyle. I was there but was also everywhere. I could see it all: a clump of leaves in the gutter beneath my see-through foot; Mom, poor Mom, at home in Rochester, scrubbing the shower, trying to cheer herself via thin hopeful humming; a deer near the dumpster, suddenly alert to my spectral presence; Mike Appel's mom, also in Rochester, a bony, distraught checkmark occupying a slender strip of Mike's bed; Rachel below in Small Workroom 4, drawn to the oneway mirror by the sounds of my death; Abnesti and Verlaine rushing into the Spiderhead; Verlaine kneeling to begin CPR.

Night was falling. Birds were singing. Birds were, it occurred to me to say, enacting a frantic celebration of day's end. They were manifesting as the earth's bright-colored nerve endings, the sun's descent urging them into activity, filling them individually with life-nectar, the life-nectar then being passed into the world, out of each beak, in the form of that bird's distinctive song, which was, in turn, an accident of beak shape, throat shape, breast configuration, brain chemistry: some birds blessed in voice, others cursed; some squawking, others rapturous.

From somewhere, something kind asked, *Would you like to go back? It's completely up to you. Your body appears salvageable.*

No, I thought, no, thanks, I've had enough.

My only regret was Mom. I hoped someday, in some better place, I'd   45
get a chance to explain it to her, and maybe she'd be proud of me, one last
time, after all these years.

From across the woods, as if by common accord, birds left their trees
and darted upward. I joined them, flew among them, they did not recognize
me as something apart from them, and I was happy, so happy, because for
the first time in years, and forevermore, I had not killed, and never would.

- This story may not include any elaborate descriptions of the world in which
  it takes place, but the actions suggest that it is an unfamiliar setting. Collect
  details that suggest a contrast between this fictional world and more
  familiar settings.

- Note the places where you do find specific descriptions of scenery. What is
  the purpose of these moments in the story?

- Why might this story be described as dystopian fiction? What fantastical
  elements does the story present? How is that fantasy blunted by the progress
  of the story?

Salman Rushdie (1947–   )

Born in Bombay, India, Salman Rushdie studied history at Cambridge before working as a copywriter for an advertising firm in Britain. While working there, he wrote
Midnight's Children, the novel that earned him the Booker Prize in 1981 and that was
named the Best of the Bookers in 2008. Like much of his fiction, the novel concerns
the migration of people, of language, of ideas, and of culture back and forth between
East and West. He published his most notorious novel *The Satanic Verses* in 1988,
and it was banned in many conservative Muslim countries because of what they
perceived as an irreverent depiction of the prophet Muhammad. Ayatollah Khomeini,
the spiritual leader of Iran, issued a *fatwa* calling for Rushdie's execution. In 1989 as
a result of this controversy, the United Kingdom and Iran broke off diplomatic relations. Rushdie lived in hiding for nearly a decade, but he has continued to write and
to publish novels, short stories, and essays. He now lives in New York.

The Courter (2008)

I

Certainly-Mary was the smallest woman Mixed-Up the hall porter had come across,
dwarfs excepted, a tiny sixty-year-old Indian lady with her greying hair tied behind
her head in a neat bun, hitching up her red-hemmed white sari in the front and

negotiating the apartment block's front steps as if they were Alps. "No," he said aloud, furrowing his brow. What would be the right peaks. Ah, good, that was the name. "Ghats," he said proudly. Word from a schoolboy atlas long ago, when India felt as far away as Paradise. (Nowadays Paradise seemed even further away but India, and Hell, had come a good bit closer.) "Western Ghats, Eastern Ghats, and now Kensington Ghats," he said, giggling. "Mountains."

She stopped in front of him in the oak-panelled lobby. "But ghats in India are also stairs," she said. "Yes yes certainly. For instance in Hindu holy city of Varanasi, where the Brahmins sit taking the filgrims' money is called Dasashwamedh-ghat. Broad-broad staircase down to River Ganga. O, most certainly! Also Manikarnika-ghat. They buy fire from a house with a tiger leaping from the roof—yes certainly, a statue tiger, coloured by Technicolor, what are you thinking?—and they bring it in a box to set fire to their loved ones' bodies. Funeral fires are of sandal. Photographs not allowed; no, certainly not."

He began thinking of her as Certainly-Mary because she never said plain yes or no; always this O-yes-certainly or no-certainly-not. In the confused circumstances that had prevailed ever since his brain, his one sure thing, had let him down, he could hardly be certain of anything any more; so he was stunned by her sureness, first into nostalgia, then envy, then attraction. And attraction was a thing so long forgotten that when the churning started he thought for a long time it must be the Chinese dumplings he had brought home from the High Street carry-out.

English was hard for Certainly-Mary, and this was a part of what drew damaged old Mixed-Up towards her. The letter p was a particular problem, often turning into an f or a c; when she proceeded through the lobby with a wheeled wicker shopping basket, she would say, "Going shocking," and when, on her return, he offered to help lift the basket up the front ghats, she would answer, "Yes, fleas." As the elevator lifted her away, she called through the grille: "Oé, courter! Thank you, courter. O, yes, certainly." (In Hindi and Konkani, however, her p's knew their place.)

So: thanks to her unexpected, somehow stomach-churning magic, he was no longer porter, but courter. "Courter," he repeated to the mirror when she had gone. His breath made a little dwindling picture of the word on the glass. "Courter courter caught." Okay. People called him many things, he did not mind. But this name, this courter, this he would try to be.

5

2

For years now I've been meaning to write down the story of Certainly-Mary, our ayah, the woman who did as much as my mother to raise my sisters and me, and her great adventure with her "courter" in London, where we all lived for a time in the early Sixties in a block called Waverley House; but what with one thing and another I never got round to it.

Then recently I heard from Certainly-Mary after a longish silence. She wrote to say that she was ninety-one, had had a serious operation, and would I kindly send her some money, because she was embarrassed that her niece, with whom she was now living in the Kurla district of Bombay, was so badly out of pocket.

I sent the money, and soon afterwards received a pleasant letter from the niece, Stella, written in the same hand as the letter from "Aya"—as we had always called Mary, palindromically dropping the "h." Aya had been so touched, the niece wrote, that I remembered her after all these years. "I have been hearing the stories about you folks all my life," the letter went on, "and I think of you a little bit as family. Maybe you recall my mother, Mary's sister. She unfortunately passed on. Now it is I who write Mary's letters for her. We all wish you the best."

This message from an intimate stranger reached out to me in my enforced exile from the beloved country of my birth and moved me, stirring things that had been buried very deep. Of course it also made me feel guilty about having done so little for Mary over the years. For whatever reason, it has become more important than ever to set down the story I've been carrying around unwritten for so long, the story of Aya and the gentle man whom she renamed—with unintentional but prophetic overtones of romance—"the courter." I see now that it is not just their story, but ours, mine, as well.

3

His real name was Mecir: you were supposed to say Mishirsh because it had invisible accents on it in some Iron Curtain language in which the accents had to be invisible, my sister Durré said solemnly, in case somebody spied on them or rubbed them out or something. His first name also began with an m but it was so full of what we called Communist consonants, all those z's and c's and w's walled up together without vowels to give them breathing space, that I never even tried to learn it.

At first we thought of nicknaming him after a mischievous little comic-book character, Mr. Mxyztplk from the Fifth Dimension, who looked a bit like Elmer Fudd and used to make Superman's life hell until ole Supe could trick him into saying his name backwards, Klptzyxm, whereupon he disappeared back into the Fifth Dimension; but because we weren't too sure how to say Mxyztplk (not to mention Klptzyxm) we dropped that idea. "We'll just call you Mixed-Up," I told him in the end, to simplify life. "Mishter Mikshed-Up Mishirsh." I was fifteen then and bursting with unemployed cock and it meant I could say things like that right into people's faces, even people less accommodating than Mr. Mecir with his stroke.

What I remember most vividly are his pink rubber washing-up gloves, which he seemed never to remove, at least not until he came calling for Certainly-Mary...At any rate, when I insulted him, with my sisters Durré and Muneeza cackling in the lift, Mecir just grinned an empty good-natured grin, nodded, "You call me what you like, okay," and went back to buffing and polishing the brasswork. There was no point teasing him if he was going to be like that, so I got into the lift and all the way to the fourth floor we sang *I Can't Stop Loving You* at the top of our best Ray Charles voices, which were pretty awful. But we were wearing our dark glasses, so it didn't matter.

4

It was the summer of 1962, and school was out. My baby sister Scheherazade was just one year old. Durré was a beehived fourteen; Muneeza was ten, and already quite a handful. The three of us—or rather Durré and me, with Muneeza trying desperately and unsuccessfully to be included in our gang—would stand over Scheherazade's cot and sing to her. "No nursery rhymes," Durré had decreed, and so there were none, for though she was a year my junior she was a natural leader. The infant Scheherazade's lullabies were our cover versions of recent hits by Chubby Checker, Neil Sedaka, Elvis and Pat Boone.

"Why don't you come home, Speedy Gonzales?" we bellowed in sweet disharmony: but most of all, and with actions, we would jump down, turn around and pick a balé of cotton. We would have jumped down, turned around and picked those bales all day except that the Maharaja of B—in the flat below complained, and Aya Mary came in to plead with us to be quiet.

"Look, see, it's Jumble-Aya who's fallen for Mixed-Up," Durré shouted, and Mary blushed a truly immense blush. So naturally we segued right into a quick me-oh-my-oh; son of a gun, we had big fun. But then the baby began to yell, my father came in with his head down bull-fashion and steaming from both ears, and we needed all the good luck charms we could find.

I had been at boarding school in England for a year or so when Abba took the decision to bring the family over. Like all his decisions, it was neither explained to nor discussed with anyone, not even my mother. When they first arrived he rented two adjacent flats in a seedy Bayswater mansion block called Graham Court, which lurked furtively in a nothing street that crawled along the side of the ABC Queensway cinema towards the Porchester Baths. He commandeered one of these flats for himself and put my mother, three sisters and Aya in the other; also, on school holidays, me. England, where liquor was freely available, did little for my father's *bonhomie*, so in a way it was a relief to have a flat to ourselves.

Most nights he emptied a bottle of Johnnie Walker Red Label and a soda-siphon. My mother did not dare to go across to "his place" in the evenings. She said: "He makes faces at me."   5

Aya Mary took Abba his dinner and answered all his calls (if he wanted anything, he would phone us up and ask for it). I am not sure why Mary was spared his drunken rages. She said it was because she was nine years his senior, so he could tell him to show due respect.

After a few months, however, my father leased a three- bedroom fourth-floor apartment with a fancy address. This was Waverley House in Kensington Court, W8. Among its other residents were not one but two Indian Maharajas, the sporting Prince P— as well as the old B— who has already been mentioned. Now we were jammed in together, my parents and Baby Scare-zade (as her siblings had affectionately begun to call her) in the master bedroom, the three of us in a much smaller room, and Mary, I regret to admit, on a straw mat laid on the fitted carpet in the hall. The third bedroom became my father's office, where he made phone-calls and kept his *Encyclopaedia Britannica*, his *Reader's Digests*, and (under lock and key) the television cabinet. We entered it at our peril. It was the Minotaur's lair.

One morning he was persuaded to drop in at the corner pharmacy and pick up some supplies for the baby. When he returned there was a hurt, schoolboyish look on his face that I had never seen before, and he was pressing his hand against his cheek.

"She hit me," he said plaintively.

"Hai! Allah-tobah! Darling!" cried my mother, fussing. "Who hit you? Are you injured? Show me, let me see."   10.

"I did nothing," he said, standing there in the hall with the pharmacy bag in his other hand and a face as pink as Mecir's rubber gloves. "I just went in with your list. The girl seemed very helpful. I asked for baby compound, Johnson"s powder, teething jelly, and she brought them out. Then I asked did she have any nipples, and she slapped my face."

My mother was appalled. "Just for that?" And Certainly-Mary backed her up. "What is this nonsense?" she wanted to know. "I have been in that chemist's shock, and they have flenty nickels, different sizes, all on view."

Durré and Muneeza could not contain themselves. They were rolling round on the floor, laughing and kicking their legs in the air.

"You both shut your face at once," my mother ordered. "A madwoman has hit your father. Where is the comedy?"

"I don't believe it," Durré gasped. "You just went up to that girl and said," and here she fell apart again, stamping her feet and holding her stomach, " '*have you got any nipples?*' "   15

My father grew thunderous, empurpled. Durré controlled herself. "But Abba," she said, at length, "here they call them teats."

Now my mother's and Mary's hands flew to their mouths, and even my father looked shocked. "But how shameless!" my mother said. "The same word as for what's on your bosoms?" She coloured, and stuck out her tongue for shame.

"These English," sighed Certainly-Mary. "But aren't they the limit? Certainly-yes; they are."

I remember this story with delight, because it was the only time I ever saw my father so discomfited, and the incident became legendary and the girl in the pharmacy was installed as the object of our great veneration. (Durré and I went in there just to take a look at her—she was a plain, short girl of about seventeen, with large, unavoidable breasts—but she caught us whispering and glared so fiercely that we fled.) And also because in the general hilarity I was able to conceal the shaming truth that I, who had been in England for so long, would have made the same mistake as Abba did.

It wasn't just Certainly-Mary and my parents who had trouble with the   20
English language. My schoolfellows tittered when in my Bombay way I said "brought-up" for upbringing (as in "where was your brought-up?") and "thrice" for three times and "quarter-plate" for side- plate and "macaroni" for pasta in general. As for learning the difference between nipples and teats, I really hadn't had any opportunities to increase my word power in that area at all.

5

So I was a little jealous of Certainly-Mary when Mixed- Up came to call. He rang our bell, his body quivering with deference in an old suit grown too loose, the trousers tightly gathered by a belt; he had taken off his rubber gloves and there were roses in his hand. My father opened the door and gave him a withering look. Being a snob, Abba was not pleased that the flat lacked a separate service entrance, so that even a porter had to be treated as a member of the same universe as himself.

"Mary," Mixed-Up managed, licking his lips and pushing back his floppy white hair. "I, to see Miss Mary, come, am."

"Wait on," Abba said, and shut the door in his face.

Certainly-Mary spent all her afternoons off with old Mixed-Up from then on, even though that first date was not a complete success. He took her "up West" to show her the visitors' London she had never seen, but at the top of an up escalator at Piccadilly Circus, while Mecir was painfully enunciating the words on the posters she couldn't read—*Unzip a banana*, and *Idris when I's dri*—she got her sari stuck in the jaws of the machine, and as the escalator pulled at the garment it began to unwind. She was forced to spin round and round like a top, and screamed at the top of her voice, "O BAAP!   BAAPU-RÉ!   BAAP-RÉ-BAAP-RÉ-BAAP!" It was Mixed-Up who saved her by pushing the emergency-stop button before the sari was completely unwound and she was exposed in her petticoat for all the world to see.

"O, courter!" she wept on his shoulder. "O, no more escaleater, courter, nevermore, surely not!"   5

My own amorous longings were aimed at Durré's best friend, a Polish girl called Rozalia, who had a holiday job at Faiman's shoe shop on Oxford Street. I pursued her pathetically throughout the holidays and, on and off, for the next two years. She would let me have lunch with her sometimes and buy her a Coke and a sandwich, and once she came with me to stand on the terraces at White Hart Lane to watch Jimmy Greaves's first game for the Spurs. "Come on you whoi-oites," we both shouted dutifully. "Come on you *Lily-whoites*." After that she even invited me into the back room at Faiman's, where she kissed me twice and let me touch her breast, but that was as far as I got.

And then there was my sort-of-cousin Chandni, whose mother's sister had married my mother's brother, though they had since split up. Chandni was eighteen months older than me, and so sexy it made you sick. She was training to be an Indian classical dancer, Odissi as well as Natyam, but in the meantime she dressed in tight black jeans and a clinging black polo-neck jumper and took me, now and then, to hang out at Bunjie's, where she knew most of the folk-music crowd that frequented the place, and where she answered to the name of Moonlight, which is what *chandni* means. I chainsmoked with the folkies and then went to the toilet to throw up.

Chandni was the stuff of obsessions. She was a teenage dream, the Moon River come to Earth like the Goddess Ganga, dolled up in slinky black. But for her I was just the young greenhorn cousin to whom she was being nice because he hadn't learned his way around.

She-E-rry, won't you come out tonight? yodelled the Four Seasons. I knew exactly how they felt. *Come, come, come out toni-yi-yight.* And while you're at it, love me do.

6

They went for walks in Kensington Gardens. "Pan," Mixed-Up said, pointing at a statue. "Los' boy. Nev' grew up." They went to Barkers and Pontings and Derry & Toms and picked out furniture and curtains for imaginary homes. They cruised supermarkets and chose little delicacies to eat. In Mecir's cramped lounge they sipped what he called "chimpanzee tea" and toasted crumpets in front of an electric bar fire.

Thanks to Mixed-Up, Mary was at last able to watch television. She liked children's programmes best, especially *The Flintstones*. Once, giggling at her daring, Mary confided to Mixed-Up that Fred and Wilma reminded her of her Sahib and Begum Sahiba upstairs; at which the courter, matching her audaciousness, pointed first at Certainly-Mary and then at himself, grinned a wide gappy smile and said, "Rubble."

Later, on the news, a vulpine Englishman with a thin moustache and mad eyes declaimed a warning about immigrants, and Certainly-Mary flapped her hand at the set: "Khali-pili bom marta," she objected, and then, for her host's benefit translated: "For nothing he is shouting shouting. Bad life! Switch it off."

They were often interrupted by the Maharajas of B— and P—, who came downstairs to escape their wives and ring other women from the call-box in the porter's room.

"Oh, baby, forget that guy," said sporty Prince P—, who seemed to spend all his days in tennis whites, and whose plump gold Rolex was almost lost in the thick hair on his arm. "I'll show you a better time than him, baby; step into my world."   5

The Maharaja of B— was older, uglier, more matter-of-fact. "Yes, bring all appliances. Room is booked in name of Mr Douglas Home. Six forty-five to seven fifteen. You have printed rate card? Please. Also a two-foot ruler, must be wooden. Frilly apron, plus."

This is what has lasted in my memory of Waverley House, this seething mass of bad marriages, booze, philanderers and unfulfilled young lusts; of the Maharaja of P— roaring away towards London's casinoland every night, in a red sports car with fitted blondes, and of the Maharaja of B— skulking off to Kensington High Street wearing dark glasses in the dark, and a coat with the collar turned up even though it was high summer; and at the heart of our little universe were Certainly-Mary and her courter, drinking chimpanzee tea and singing along with the national anthem of Bedrock.

But they were not really like Barney and Betty Rubble at all. They were formal, polite. They were . . . courtly. He courted her, and, like a coy, ringleted ingénue with a fan, she inclined her head, and entertained his suit.

7

I spent one half-term weekend in 1963 at the home in Beccles, Suffolk of Field Marshal Sir Charles Lutwidge-Dodgson, an old India hand and a family friend who was supporting my application for British citizenship. "The Dodo," as he was known, invited me down by myself, saying he wanted to get to know me better.

He was a huge man whose skin had started hanging too loosely on his face, a giant living in a tiny thatched cottage and forever bumping his head. No wonder he was irascible at times; he was in Hell, a Gulliver trapped in that rose-garden Lilliput of croquet hoops, church bells, sepia photographs and old battle-trumpets.

The weekend was fitful and awkward until the Dodo asked if I played chess. Slightly awestruck at the prospect of playing a Field Marshal, I nodded; and ninety minutes later, to my amazement, won the game.

I went into the kitchen, strutting somewhat, planning to boast a little to the old soldier's long-time housekeeper, Mrs Liddell. But as soon as I entered she said: "Don't tell me. You never went and won?"

"Yes," I said, affecting nonchalance. "As a matter of fact, yes, I did."   5

"Gawd," said Mrs Liddell. "Now there'll be hell to pay. You go back in there and ask him for another game, and this time make sure you lose."

I did as I was told, but was never invited to Beccles again.

Still, the defeat of the Dodo gave me new confidence at the chessboard, so when I returned to Waverley House after finishing my O levels, and was at once invited to play a game by Mixed-Up (Mary had told him about my victory in the Battle of Beccles with great pride and some hyperbole), I said: "Sure, I don't mind." How long could it take to thrash the old duffer, after all?

There followed a massacre royal. Mixed-Up did not just beat me; he had me for breakfast, over easy. I couldn't believe it—the canny opening, the fluency of his combination play, the force of his attacks, my own impossibly cramped, strangled positions—and asked for a second game. This time he tucked into me even more heartily. I sat broken in my chair at the end, close to tears. *Big girls don't cry*, I reminded myself, but the song went on playing in my head: *That's just an alibi.*

"Who are you?" I demanded, humiliation weighing down every syllable.   10
"The devil in disguise?"

Mixed-Up gave his big, silly grin. "Grand Master," he said. "Long time. Before head."

*   *   *

"You're a Grand Master," I repeated, still in a daze. Then in a moment of horror I remembered that I had seen the name Mecir in books of classic games. "Nimzo-Indian," I said aloud. He beamed and nodded furiously.

"That Mecir?" I asked wonderingly.

"That," he said. There was saliva dribbling out of a corner of his sloppy old mouth. This ruined old man was in the books. He was in the books. And even with his mind turned to rubble he could still wipe the floor with me.

"Now play lady," he grinned. I didn't get it. "Mary lady," he said. "Yes   15
yes certainly."

She was pouring tea, waiting for my answer. "Aya, you can't play," I said, bewildered.

"Learning, baba," she said. "What is it, na? Only a game."

And then she, too, beat me senseless, and with the black pieces, at that. It was not the greatest day of my life.

8

From *100 Most Instructive Chess Games* by Robert Reshevsky, 1961:

M. Mecir—M. Najdorf

Dallas 1950, Nimzo-Indian Defense

The attack of a tactician can be troublesome to meet—that of a strategist even more so. Whereas the tactician's threats may be unmistakable, the strategist confuses the issue by keeping things in abeyance. He threatens to threaten!

Take this game for instance: Mecir posts a Knight at Q6 to get a grip on   5
the center. Then he establishes a passed Pawn on one wing to occupy his opponent on the Queen side. Finally he stirs up the position on the King- side. What does the poor bewildered opponent do? How can he defend everything at once? Where will the blow fall?

Watch Mecir keep Najdorf on the run, as he shifts the attack from side to side!

Chess had become their private language. Old Mixed-Up, lost as he was for words, retained, on the chessboard, much of the articulacy and subtlety which had vanished from his speech. As Certainly-Mary gained in skill—and she had learned with astonishing speed, I thought bitterly, for someone who couldn't read or write or pronounce the letter p—she was better able to understand, and respond to, the wit of the reduced maestro with whom she had so unexpectedly forged a bond.

He taught her with great patience, showing-not-telling, repeating openings and combinations and endgame techniques over and over until she began to see the meaning in the patterns. When they played, he handicapped himself, he told her her best moves and demonstrated their consequences, drawing her, step by step, into the infinite possibilities of the game.

Such was their courtship. "It is like an adventure, baba," Mary once tried to explain to me. "It is like going with him to his country, you know? What a place, baap-ré! Beautiful and dangerous and funny and full of fuzzles. For me it is a big-big discovery. What to tell you? I go for the game. It is a wonder."

I understood, then, how far things had gone between them. Certainly-   10
Mary had never married, and had made it clear to old Mixed-Up that it was too late to start any of that monkey business at her age. The courter was

a widower, and had grown-up children somewhere, lost long ago behind the ever-higher walls of Eastern Europe. But in the game of chess they had found a form of flirtation, an endless renewal that precluded the possibility of boredom, a courtly wonderland of the ageing heart.

What would the Dodo have made of it all? No doubt it would have scandalised him to see chess, chess of all games, the great formalisation of war, transformed into an art of love.

As for me: my defeats by Certainly-Mary and her courter ushered in further humiliations. Durré and Muneeza went down with the mumps, and so, finally, in spite of my mother's efforts to segregate us, did I. I lay terrified in bed while the doctor warned me not to stand up and move around if I could possibly help it. "If you do," he said, "your parents won't need to punish you. You will have punished yourself quite enough."

I spent the following few weeks tormented day and night by visions of grotesquely swollen testicles and a subsequent life of limp impotence—finished before I'd even started, it wasn't fair!—which were made much worse by my sisters' quick recovery and incessant gibes. But in the end I was lucky; the illness didn't spread to the deep South. "Think how happy your hundred and one girlfriends will be, bhai," sneered Durré, who knew all about my continued failures in the Rozalia and Chandni departments.

On the radio, people were always singing about the joys of being sixteen years old. I wondered where they were, all those boys and girls of my age having the time of their lives. Were they driving around America in Studebaker convertibles? They certainly weren't in my neighbourhood. London, W8 was Sam Cooke country that summer. *Another Saturday night . . .* There might be a mop-top love-song stuck at number one, but I was down with lonely Sam in the lower depths of the charts, how-I-wishing I had someone, etc., and generally feeling in a pretty goddamn dreadful way.

9

"Baba, come quick."

It was late at night when Aya Mary shook me awake. After many urgent hisses, she managed to drag me out of sleep and pull me, pajama'ed and yawning, down the hall. On the landing outside our flat was Mixed-Up the courter, huddled up against a wall, weeping. He had a black eye and there was dried blood on his mouth.

"What happened?" I asked Mary, shocked.

"Men," wailed Mixed-Up. "Threaten. Beat."

He had been in his lounge earlier that evening when the sporting Maharaja of P— burst in to say, "If anybody comes looking for me, okay, any tough-guy type guys, okay, I am out, okay? Oh you tea. Don't let them go upstairs, okay? Big tip, okay?"

5

A short time later, the old Maharaja of B— also arrived in Mecir's lounge, looking distressed.

"Suno, listen on," said the Maharaja of B—. "You don't know where I am, samajh liya? Understood? Some low persons may inquire. You don't know. I am abroad, achha? On extended travels abroad. Do your job, porter. Handsome recompense."

Late at night two tough-guy types did indeed turn up. It seemed the hairy Prince P— had gambling debts. "Out," Mixed-Up grinned in his sweetest way. The tough-guy types nodded, slowly. They had long hair and thick lips like Mick Jagger's. "He's a busy gent. We should of made an appointment," said the first type to the second. "Didn't I tell you we should of called?"

"You did," agreed the second type. "Got to do these things right, you said, he's royalty. And you was right, my son, I put my hand up, I was dead wrong. I put my hand up to that."

"Let's leave our card," said the first type. "Then he'll know to expect us."   10

"Ideal," said the second type, and smashed his fist into old Mixed-Up's mouth. "You tell him," the second type said, and struck the old man in the eye. "When he's in. You mention it."

He had locked the front door after that; but much later, well after midnight, there was a hammering. Mixed-Up called out, "Who?"

"We are close friends of the Maharaja of B—" said a voice. "No, I tell a lie. Acquaintances."

"He calls upon a lady of our acquaintance," said a second voice. "To be precise."

"It is in that connection that we crave audience," said the first voice.   15

"Gone," said Mecir. "Jet plane. Gone."

There was a silence. Then the second voice said, "Can't be in the jet set if you never jump on a jet, eh? Biarritz, Monte, all of that."

"Be sure and let His Highness know," said the first voice, "that we eagerly await his return."

"With regard to our mutual friend," said the second voice. "Eagerly."

What does the poor bewildered opponent do? The words from the chess book   20
popped unbidden into my head. *How can he defend everything at once? Where will the blow fall? Watch Mecir keep Najdorf on the run, as he shifts the attack from side to side!*

Mixed-Up returned to his lounge and on this occasion, even though there had been no use of force, he began to weep. After a time he took the elevator up to the fourth floor and whispered through our letterbox to Certainly-Mary sleeping on her mat.

"I didn't want to wake Sahib," Mary said. "You know his trouble, na? And Begum Sahiba is so tired at end of the day. So now you tell, baba, what to do?"

What did she expect me to come up with? I was sixteen years old. "Mixed-Up must call the police," I unoriginally offered.

"No, no, baba," said Certainly-Mary emphatically. "If the courter makes a scandal for Maharaja-log, then in the end it is the courter only who will be out on his ear."

I had no other ideas. I stood before them feeling like a fool, while they   25 both turned upon me their frightened, supplicant eyes.

"Go to sleep," I said. "We'll think about it in the morning." *The first pair of thugs were tacticians, I was thinking. They were troublesome to meet. But the second pair were scarier; they were strategists. They threatened to threaten.*

Nothing happened in the morning, and the sky was clear. It was almost impossible to believe in fists, and menacing voices at the door. During the course of the day both Maharajas visited the porter's lounge and stuck five-pound notes in Mixed-Up's waistcoat pocket. "Held the fort, good man," said Prince P—, and the Maharaja of B— echoed those sentiments: "Spot on. All handled now, achha? Problem over."

The three of us—Aya Mary, her courter, and me—held a council of war that afternoon and decided that no further action was necessary. The hall porter was the front line in any such situation, I argued, and the front line had held. And now the risks were past. Assurances had been given. End of story.

"End of story," repeated Certainly-Mary doubtfully, but then, seeking to reassure Mecir, she brightened. "Correct," she said. "Most certainly! All-done, finis." She slapped her hands against each other for emphasis. She asked Mixed-Up if he wanted a game of chess; but for once the courter didn't want to play.

10

After that I was distracted, for a time, from the story of Mixed-Up and Certainly-Mary by violence nearer home.

My middle sister Muneeza, now eleven, was entering her delinquent phase a little early. She was the true inheritor of my father's black rage, and when she lost control it was terrible to behold. That summer she seemed to pick fights with my father on purpose; seemed prepared, at her young age, to test her strength against his. (I intervened in her rows with Abba only once, in the kitchen. She grabbed the kitchen scissors and flung them at me. They cut me on the thigh. After that I kept my distance.)

As I witnessed their wars I felt myself coming unstuck from the idea of family itself. I looked at my screaming sister and thought how brilliantly self-destructive she was, how triumphantly she was ruining her relations with the people she needed most.

And I looked at my choleric, face-pulling father and thought about British citizenship. My existing Indian passport permitted me to travel only to a very few countries, which were carefully listed on the second right-hand page. But I might soon have a British passport and then, by hook or by crook, I would get away from him. I would not have this face-pulling in my life.

At sixteen, you still think you can escape from your father. You aren't   5
listening to his voice speaking through your mouth, you don't see how your gestures already mirror his; you don't see him in the way you hold your body, in the way you sign your name. You don't hear his whisper in your blood.

On the day I have to tell you about, my two-year-old sister Chhoti Scheherazade, Little Scare-zade, started crying as she often did during one of our family rows. Amma and Aya Mary loaded her into her push-chair and made a rapid getaway. They pushed her to Kensington Square and then sat on the grass, turned Scheherazade loose and made philosophical remarks while she tired herself out. Finally, she fell asleep, and they made their way home in the fading light of the evening. Outside Waverley House they were approached by two well-turned-out young men with Beatle haircuts and the buttoned-up, collarless jackets made popular by the band. The first of these young men asked my mother, very politely, if she might be the Maharani of B—.

"No," my mother answered, flattered.

"Oh, but you are, madam," said the second Beatle, equally politely. "For you are heading for Waverley House and that is the Maharaja's place of residence."

"No, no," my mother said, still blushing with pleasure. "We are a different Indian family."

"Quite so," the first Beatle nodded understandingly, and then, to my   10
mother's great surprise, placed a finger alongside his nose, and winked. "Incognito, eh. Mum's the word."

"Now excuse us," my mother said, losing patience. "We are not the ladies you seek."

The second Beatle tapped a foot lightly against a wheel of the push-chair. "Your husband seeks ladies, madam, were you aware of that fact? Yes, he does. Most assiduously, may I add;"

"Too assiduously," said the first Beatle, his face darkening.

"I tell you I am not the Maharani Begum," my mother said, growing suddenly alarmed. "Her business is not my business. Kindly let me pass."

The second Beatle stepped closer to her. She could feel his breath,   15
which was minty. "One of the ladies he sought out was our ward, as you might say," he explained. "That would be the term. Under our protection, you follow. Us, therefore, being responsible for her welfare."

"Your husband," said the first Beatle, showing his teeth in a frightening way, and raising his voice one notch, "damaged the goods. Do you hear me, Queenie? He damaged the fucking goods."

"Mistaken identity, fleas," said Certainly-Mary. "Many Indian residents in Waverley House. We are decent ladies; *fleas*."

The second Beatle had taken out something from an inside pocket. A blade caught the light. "Fucking wogs," he said. "You fucking come over here, you don't fucking know how to fucking behave. Why don't you fucking fuck off to fucking Wogistan? Fuck your fucking wog arses. Now then," he added in a quiet voice, holding up the knife, "unbutton your blouses."

* * *

Just then a loud noise emanated from the doorway of Waverley House. The two women and the two men turned to look, and out came Mixed-Up, yelling at the top of his voice and windmilling his arms like a mad old loon.

"Hullo," said the Beatle with the knife, looking amused. "Who's this, then? Oh oh fucking seven?"

Mixed-Up was trying to speak, he was in a mighty agony of effort, but all that was coming out of his mouth was raw, unshaped noise. Scheherazade woke up and joined in. The two Beatles looked displeased. But then something happened inside old Mixed-Up; something popped, and in a great rush he gabbled, "Sirs sirs no sirs these not B— women sirs B— women upstairs on floor three sirs Maharaja of B— also sirs God's truth mother's grave swear."

It was the longest sentence he had spoken since the stroke that had broken his tongue long ago.

And what with his torrent and Scheherazade's squalls there were suddenly heads poking out from doorways, attention was being paid, and the two Beatles nodded gravely. "Honest mistake," the first of them said apologetically to my mother, and actually bowed from the waist. "Could happen to anyone," the knife-man added, ruefully. They turned and began to walk quickly away. As they passed Mecir, however, they paused. "I know you, though," said the knife-man. " '*Jet plane. Gone.*' " He made a short movement of the arm, and then Mixed-Up the courter was lying on the pavement with blood leaking from a wound in his stomach. "All okay now," he gasped, and passed out.

11

He was on the road to recovery by Christmas; my mother's letter to the landlords, in which she called him a "knight in shining armour," ensured that he was well looked after, and his job was kept open for him. He continued to live in his little ground-floor cubby-hole, while the hall porter's duties were carried out by shift-duty staff. "Nothing but the best for our very own hero," the landlords assured my mother in their reply.

The two Maharajas and their retinues had moved out before I came home for the Christmas holidays, so we had no further visits from the Beatles or the Rolling Stones. Certainly-Mary spent as much time as she could with Mecir; but it was the look of my old Aya that worried me more than poor Mixed-Up. She looked older, and powdery, as if she might crumble away at any moment into dust.

"We didn't want to worry you at school," my mother said. "She has been having heart trouble. Palpitations. Not all the time, but."

Mary's health problems had sobered up the whole family. Muneeza's tantrums had stopped, and even my father was making an effort. They had put up a Christmas tree in the sitting-room and decorated it with all sorts of baubles. It was so odd to see a Christmas tree at our place that I realised things must be fairly serious.

On Christmas Eve my mother suggested that Mary might like it if we all   5
sang some carols. Amma had made song-sheets, six copies, by hand. When we did *O come, all ye faithful* I showed off by singing from memory in Latin. Everybody behaved perfectly. When Muneeza suggested that we should try *Swinging on a Star* or *I Wanna Hold Your Hand* instead of this boring stuff, she wasn't really being serious. So this is family life, I thought. This is it.

But we were only play-acting.

A few weeks earlier, at school, I'd come across an American boy, the star of the school's Rugby football team, crying in the Chapel cloisters. I asked him what the matter was and he told me that President Kennedy had been assassinated. "I don't believe you," I said, but I could see that it was true. The football star sobbed and sobbed. I took his hand.

"When the President dies, the nation is orphaned," he eventually said, broken-heartedly parroting a piece of cracker-barrel wisdom he'd probably heard on Voice of America.

"I know how you feel," I lied. "My father just died, too."

Mary's heart trouble turned out to be a mystery; unpredictably it came and   10
went. She was subjected to all sorts of tests during the next six months, but each time the doctors ended up by shaking their heads: they couldn't find anything wrong with her. Physically, she was right as rain; except that there were these periods when her heart kicked and bucked in her chest like the wild horses in *The Misfits*, the ones whose roping and tying made Marilyn Monroe so mad.

Mecir went back to work in the spring, but his experience had knocked the stuffing out of him. He was slower to smile, duller of eye, more inward. Mary, too, had turned in upon herself. They still met for tea, crumpets and *The Flintstones*, but something was no longer quite right.

At the beginning of the summer Mary made an announcement.

"I know what is wrong with me," she told my parents, out of the blue. "I need to go home."

"But, Aya," my mother argued, "homesickness is not a real disease."

"God knows for what-all we came over to this country," Mary said. "But   15 I can no longer stay. No. Certainly not." Her determination was absolute.

So it was England that was breaking her heart, breaking it by not being India. London was killing her, by not being Bombay. And Mixed-Up? I wondered. Was the courter killing her, too, because he was no longer himself? Or was it that her heart, roped by two different loves, was being pulled both East and West, whinnying and rearing, like those movie horses being yanked this way by Clark Gable and that way by Montgomery Clift, and she knew that to live she would have to choose?

"I must go," said Certainly-Mary. "Yes, certainly. *Bas.* Enough."

That summer, the summer of '64, I turned seventeen. Chandni went back to India. Durré's Polish friend Rozalia informed me over a sandwich in Oxford Street that she was getting engaged to a "real man," so I could forget about seeing her again, because this Zbigniew was the jealous type. Roy Orbison sang *It's Over* in my ears as I walked away to the Tube, but the truth was that nothing had really begun.

Certainly-Mary left us in mid-July. My father bought her a one-way ticket to Bombay, and that last morning was heavy with the pain of ending. When we took her bags down to the car, Mecir the hall porter was nowhere to be seen. Mary did not knock on the door of his lounge, but walked straight out through the freshly polished oak-panelled lobby, whose mirrors and brasses were sparkling brightly; she climbed into the back seat of our Ford Zodiac and sat there stiffly with her carry-on grip on her lap, staring straight ahead. I had known and loved her all my life. *Never mind your damned courter*, I wanted to shout at her, *what about me?*

As it happened, she was right about the homesickness. After her return to   20 Bombay, she never had a day's heart trouble again; and, as the letter from her niece Stella confirmed, at ninety-one she was still going strong.

Soon after she left, my father told us he had decided to "shift location" to Pakistan. As usual, there were no discussions, no explanations, just the simple fiat. He gave up the lease on the flat in Waverley House at the end of the summer holidays, and they all went off to Karachi, while I went back to school.

I became a British citizen that year. I was one of the lucky ones, I guess, because in spite of that chess game I had the Dodo on my side. And the passport did, in many ways, set me free. It allowed me to come and go, to make choices that were not the ones my father would have wished. But I, too, have ropes around my neck, I have them to this day, pulling me this way and that, East and West, the nooses tightening, commanding, *choose, choose.*

I buck, I snort, I whinny, I rear, I kick. Ropes, I do not choose between you. Lassoes, lariats, I choose neither of you, and both. Do you hear? I refuse to choose.

A year or so after we moved out I was in the area and dropped in at Waverley House to see how the old courter was doing. Maybe, I thought, we could have a game of chess, and he could beat me to a pulp. The lobby was empty, so I knocked on the door of his little lounge. A stranger answered.

"Where's Mixed-Up?" I cried, taken by surprise. I apologised at once, 25 embarrassed. "Mr Mecir, I meant, the porter."

'I'm the porter, sir,' the man said. "I don't know anything about any mix-up.'

- Rushdie presents us with images of London at a very specific time. How do his references to advertising images and to popular music contribute to your sense of place in the story?

- Explain why Mecir, "old Mixed-Up," has a decidedly different view of London than the narrator's father.

- How does the language that the characters construct within this story come out of their interactions with elements of setting?

POETRY

Samuel Taylor Coleridge (1792–1834)

Kubla Khan; or, a Vision in a Dream (1798)

In Xanadu did Kubla Khan
A stately pleasure-dome decree:
Where Alph, the sacred river, ran
Through caverns measureless to man
   Down to a sunless sea.   5
So twice five miles of fertile ground
With walls and towers were girdled round:
And here were gardens bright with sinuous rills
Where blossomed many an incense-bearing tree;
And there were forests ancient as the hills,   10
Enfolding sunny spots of greenery.

But oh! that deep romantic chasm which slanted
Down the green hill athwart a cedarn cover!
A savage place! as holy and enchanted
As e'er beneath a waning moon was haunted   15
By woman wailing for her demon-lover!
And from this chasm, with ceaseless turmoil seething,
As if this earth in fast thick pants were breathing,
A mighty fountain momently was forced,
Amid whose swift half-intermitted burst   20
Huge fragments vaulted like rebounding hail,
Of chaffy grain beneath the thresher's flail:
And 'mid these dancing rocks at once and ever
It flung up momently the sacred river.
Five miles meandering with a mazy motion   25
Through wood and dale the sacred river ran,
Then reached the caverns measureless to man,
And sank in tumult to a lifeless ocean:
And 'mid this tumult Kubla heard from far
Ancestral voices prophesying war!   30
  The shadow of the dome of pleasure
  Floated midway on the waves;
  Where was heard the mingled measure
  From the fountain and the caves.
It was a miracle of rare device,   35
A sunny pleasure-dome with caves of ice!
  A damsel with a dulcimer
  In a vision once I saw:
  It was an Abyssinian maid,
  And on her dulcimer she played,   40
  Singing of Mount Abora.
  Could I revive within me
  Her symphony and song,
  To such a deep delight 'twould win me,
That with music loud and long,   45
I would build that dome in air,
That sunny dome! those caves of ice!
And all who heard should see them there,
And all should cry, Beware! Beware!
His flashing eyes, his floating hair!   50
Weave a circle round him thrice,
And close your eyes with holy dread,
For he on honey-dew hath fed,
And drunk the milk of Paradise.

- How does the language in this poem describe the contrast between the "pleasure-dome" and the "caves of ice"?
- What is the relation between this place and the prophecy?

Edgar Allan Poe (1809–1849)

The Raven (1844)

Once upon a midnight dreary, while I pondered, weak and weary,
Over many a quaint and curious volume of forgotten lore,
While I nodded, nearly napping, suddenly there came a tapping,
As of some one gently rapping, rapping at my chamber door.
"'Tis some visitor," I muttered, "tapping at my chamber door—   5
              Only this, and nothing more."

Ah, distinctly I remember it was in the bleak December,
And each separate dying ember wrought its ghost upon the floor.
Eagerly I wished the morrow;—vainly I had sought to borrow
From my books surcease of sorrow—sorrow for the lost Lenore—   10
For the rare and radiant maiden whom the angels name Lenore—
              Nameless here for evermore.

And the silken sad uncertain rustling of each purple curtain
Thrilled me—filled me with fantastic terrors never felt before;
So that now, to still the beating of my heart, I stood repeating   15
"'Tis some visitor entreating entrance at my chamber door;—
Some late visitor entreating entrance at my chamber door;
              This it is, and nothing more."

Presently my soul grew stronger; hesitating then no longer,
"Sir," said I, "or Madam, truly your forgiveness I implore;   20
But the fact is I was napping, and so gently you came rapping,
And so faintly you came tapping, tapping at my chamber door,
That I scarce was sure I heard you"—here I opened wide the door;—
              Darkness there, and nothing more.

Deep into that darkness peering, long I stood there wondering, fearing,   25
Doubting, dreaming dreams no mortal ever dared to dream before;
But the silence was unbroken, and the darkness gave no token,

And the only word there spoken was the whispered word, "Lenore!"
This I whispered, and an echo murmured back the word, "Lenore!"—
        Merely this, and nothing more.   30

Back into the chamber turning, all my soul within me burning,
Soon I heard again a tapping somewhat louder than before.
"Surely," said I, "surely that is something at my window lattice;
Let me see, then, what thereat is, and this mystery explore—
Let my heart be still a moment and this mystery explore;—   35
        'Tis the wind and nothing more!"

Open here I flung the shutter, when, with many a flirt and flutter,
In there stepped a stately raven of the saintly days of yore;
Not the least obeisance made he; not an instant stopped or stayed he;
But, with mien of lord or lady, perched above my chamber door—   40
Perched upon a bust of Pallas just above my chamber door—
        Perched, and sat, and nothing more.

Then this ebony bird beguiling my sad fancy into smiling,
By the grave and stern decorum of the countenance it wore,
"Though thy crest be shorn and shaven, thou," I said, "art sure no craven,   45
Ghastly grim and ancient raven wandering from the Nightly shore—
Tell me what thy lordly name is on the Night's Plutonian shore!"
        Quoth the raven, "Nevermore."

Much I marvelled this ungainly fowl to hear discourse so plainly,
Though its answer little meaning—little relevancy bore,   50
For we cannot help agreeing that no living human being
Ever yet was blessed with seeing bird above his chamber door—
Bird or beast upon the sculptured bust above his chamber door,
        With such name as "Nevermore."

But the raven, sitting lonely on the placid bust, spoke only   55
That one word, as if his soul in that one word he did outpour.
Nothing farther then he uttered—not a feather then he fluttered—
Till I scarcely more than muttered "Other friends have flown before—
On the morrow *he* will leave me, as my hopes have flown before."
        Then the bird said "Nevermore."   60

Startled at the stillness broken by reply so aptly spoken,
"Doubtless," said I, "what it utters is its only stock and store
Caught from some unhappy master whom unmerciful Disaster
Followed fast and followed faster till his songs one burden bore—
Till the dirges of his Hope that melancholy burden bore   65
        Of 'Never—nevermore.'"

But the raven still beguiling all my sad soul into smiling,
Straight I wheeled a cushioned seat in front of bird and bust and door;
Then, upon the velvet sinking, I betook myself to linking
Fancy unto fancy, thinking what this ominous bird of yore— 70
What this grim, ungainly, ghastly, gaunt, and ominous bird of yore
        Meant in croaking "Nevermore."

This I sat engaged in guessing, but no syllable expressing
To the fowl whose fiery eyes now burned into my bosom's core;
This and more I sat divining, with my head at ease reclining 75
On the cushion's velvet lining that the lamplight gloated o'er,
But whose velvet violet lining with the lamplight gloating o'er,
        She shall press, ah, nevermore!

Then, methought, the air grew denser, perfumed from an unseen censer
Swung by angels whose faint foot-falls tinkled on the tufted floor. 80
"Wretch," I cried, "thy God hath lent thee—by these angels he hath sent thee
Respite—respite and nepenthe from thy memories of Lenore!
Quaff, oh quaff this kind nepenthe and forget this lost Lenore!"
        Quoth the raven, "Nevermore."

"Prophet!" said I, "thing of evil!—prophet still, if bird or devil!— 85
Whether Tempter sent, or whether tempest tossed thee here ashore,
Desolate, yet all undaunted, on this desert land enchanted—
On this home by Horror haunted—tell me truly, I implore—
Is there—*is* there balm in Gilead?—tell me—tell me, I implore!"
        Quoth the raven, "Nevermore." 90

"Prophet!" said I, "thing of evil—prophet still, if bird or devil!
By that Heaven that bends above us—by that God we both adore—
Tell this soul with sorrow laden if, within the distant Aidenn,
It shall clasp a sainted maiden whom the angels name Lenore—
Clasp a rare and radiant maiden whom the angels name Lenore." 95
        Quoth the raven, "Nevermore."

"Be that word our sign of parting, bird or fiend!" I shrieked upstarting—
"Get thee back into the tempest and the Night's Plutonian shore!
Leave no black plume as a token of that lie thy soul hath spoken!
Leave my loneliness unbroken!—quit the bust above my door! 100
Take thy beak from out my heart, and take thy form from off my door!"
        Quoth the raven, "Nevermore."

And the raven, never flitting, still is sitting, still is sitting
On the pallid bust of Pallas just above my chamber door;
And his eyes have all the seeming of a demon's that is dreaming, 105

And the lamp-light o'er him streaming throws his shadow on the floor;
And my soul from out that shadow that lies floating on the floor
>   Shall be lifted—nevermore!

- Locate the specific words in each stanza that describe the setting. How does this setting lend to the tone of the poem?

- What details of this setting seem supernatural? How many of them have a rational explanation?

Dudley Randall (1914–2000)

Ballad of Birmingham (1969)

(On the bombing of a church in Birmingham, Alabama, 1963)

"Mother dear, may I go downtown
Instead of out to play,
And march the streets of Birmingham
In a Freedom March today?"

"No, baby, no, you may not go,   5
For the dogs are fierce and wild,
And clubs and hoses, guns and jails
Aren't good for a little child."

"But, mother, I won't be alone.
Other children will go with me,   10
And march the streets of Birmingham
To make our country free."

"No, baby, no you may not go,
For I fear those guns will fire.
But you may go to church instead   15
And sing in the children's choir."

She has combed and brushed her night-dark hair,
And bathed rose petal sweet.
And drawn white gloves on her small brown hands,
And white shoes on her feet.   20

The mother smiled to know her child
Was in the sacred place,

But that smile was the last smile
To come upon her face.

For when she heard the explosion,   25
Her eyes grew wet and wild.
She raced through the streets of Birmingham
Calling for her child.

She clawed through bits of glass and brick,
Then lifted out a shoe.   30
"Oh, here's the shoe my baby wore,
But, baby, where are you?"

- The poem contrasts the perceived dangers of a civil rights march with the safety of a church. How do the events of the poem turn that world upside down?

- What impact does the poem's simple rhyming form have on the story that it tells?

Langston Hughes (1902–1967)

Night Funeral in Harlem (1967)

Night funeral
    In Harlem:

> Where did they get
> Them two fine cars?

Insurance man, he did not pay—   5
His insurance lapsed the other day—
Yet they got a satin box
For his head to lay.

    Night funeral
    In Harlem: 10

> Who was it sent
> That wreath of flowers?

Them flowers came
from that poor boy's friends—

They'll want flowers, too,   15
When they meet their ends.

  Night funeral
  in Harlem:

  Who preached that
  Black boy to his grave?   20
Old preacher-man
Preached that boy away—
Charged Five Dollars
His girl friend had to pay.

  Night funeral   25
  In Harlem:

When it was all over
And the lid shut on his head
and the organ had done played
and the last prayers been said   30
and six pallbearers
Carried him out for dead
And off down Lenox Avenue
That long black hearse done sped,
  The street light   35
  At his corner
  Shined just like a tear—
That boy that they was mournin'
Was so dear, so dear
To them folks that brought the flowers,   40
To that girl who paid the preacher-man—
It was all their tears that made
  That poor boy's
  Funeral grand.

  Night funeral   45
  In Harlem.

■ The poem uses a pattern of questions and answers to describe the nature
   of this funeral. From what perspective do we hear this particular narrative?
   Where is the grief in this poem? How does the grief function differently
   than in the previous poems?

Gary Soto (1952–   )

Braly Street (1977)

Every summer
The asphalt softens
Giving under the edge
Of boot heels and the trucks
That caught radiators   5
Of butterflies.
Bottle caps and glass
Of the '40s and '50s
Hold their breath
Under the black earth   10
Of asphalt and are silent
Like the dead whose mouths
Have eaten dirt and bermuda.
Every summer I come
To this street   15
Where I discovered ants bit,
Matches flare,
And pinto beans unraveled
Into plants; discovered
Aspirin will not cure a dog   20
Whose fur twitches.

It's sixteen years
Since our house
Was bulldozed and my father
Stunned into a coma...   25
Where it was,
An oasis of chickweed
And foxtails.
Where the almond tree stood
There are wine bottles   30
Whose history
Is a liver. The long caravan
Of my uncle's footprints
Has been paved
With dirt. Where my father   35
Cemented a pond
There is a cavern of red ants

Living on the seeds
The wind brings
And cats that come here   40
To die among
The browning sage.

It's sixteen years
Since bottle collectors
Shoveled around   45
The foundation
And the almond tree
Opened its last fruit
To the summer.
The houses are gone,   50
The Molinas, Morenos,
The Japanese families
Are gone, the Okies gone
Who moved out at night
Under a canopy of   55
Moving stars.

In '57 I sat
On the porch, salting
Slugs that came out
After the rain,   60
While inside my uncle
Weakened with cancer
And the blurred vision
Of his hands
Darkening to earth.   65
In '58 I knelt
Before my father
Whose spine was pulled loose.
Before his face still
Growing a chin of hair,   70
Before the procession
Of stitches behind
His neck, I knelt
And did not understand.

Braly Street is now   75
Tin ventilators

On the warehouses, turning
Our sweat
Towards the yellowing sky;
Acetylene welders   80
Beading manifolds,
Stinging the half-globes
Of retinas. When I come
To where our house was,
I come to weeds   85
And a sewer line tied off
Like an umbilical cord;
To the chinaberry
Not pulled down
And to its rings   90
My father and uncle
Would equal, if alive.

■ Locate instances where the poet describes specific objects as if they had
the lives that he is describing here.

Gary Soto (1952–)

Kearney Park (1985)

True Mexicans or not, let's open our shirts
And dance, a spark of heels
Chipping at the dusty cement. The people
Are shiny like the sea, turning
To the clockwork of *rancheras*,   5
The accordion wheezing, the drum-tap
Of work rising and falling.
Let's dance with our hats in hand.
The sun is behind the trees,
Behind my stutter of awkward steps   10
With a woman who is a brilliant arc of smiles,
An armful of falling water. Her skirt
Opens and closes. My arms
Know no better but to flop
On their own, and we spin, dip   15
And laugh into each other's faces—

Faces that could be famous
On the coffee table of my *abuelita*.
But grandma is here, at the park, with a beer
At her feet, clapping   20
And shouting, "Dance, hijo, dance!"
Laughing, I bend, slide, and throw up
A great cloud of dust,
Until the girl and I are no more.

■ How do the actions of the people in this poem help establish this setting?

Chitra Banerjee Divakaruni (1957–   )

Indian Movie, New Jersey (1990)

Not like the white filmstars, all rib
and gaunt cheekbone, the Indian sex-goddess
smiles plumply from behind a flowery
branch. Below her brief red skirt, her thighs
are satisfying-solid, redeeming   5
as tree trunks. She swings her hips
and the men-viewers whistle. The lover-hero
dances in to a song, his lip-sync
a little off, but no matter, we
know the words already and sing along.   10
It is safe here, the day
golden and cool so no one sweats,
roses on every bush and the Dal Lake
clean again.
                    The sex-goddess switches
to thickened English to emphasize   15
a joke. We laugh and clap. Here
we need not be embarrassed by words
dropping like lead pellets into foreign ears.
The flickering movie-light
wipes from our faces years of America, sons   20
who want mohawks and refuse to run
the family store, daughters who date
on the sly.
                    When at the end the hero

dies for his friend who also
loves the sex-goddess and now can marry her,   25
we weep, understanding. Even the men
clear their throats to say, "What *qurbani*!
What *dosti*!" After, we mill around
unwilling to leave, exchange greetings
and good news: a new gold chain, a trip   30
to India. We do not speak
of motel raids, canceled permits, stones
thrown through glass windows, daughters and sons
raped by Dotbusters.
                                    In this dim foyer
we can pull around us the faint, comforting smell   35
of incense and *pakoras*, can arrange
our children's marriages with hometown boys and girls,
open a franchise, win a million
in the mail. We can retire
in India, a yellow two-storied house   40
with wrought-iron gates, our own
Ambassador car. Or at least
move to a rich white suburb, Summerfield
or Fort Lee, with neighbors that will
talk to us. Here while the film-songs still echo   45
in the corridors and restrooms, we can trust
in movie truths: sacrifice, success, love and luck,
the America that was supposed to be.

- What place does this poem describe?
- How does the fantasy world of the movie create a specific community
  among those who watch it?

Christina Rossetti (1830–1894)

Cobwebs (1890)

It is a land with neither night nor day,
   Nor heat nor cold, nor any wind, nor rain,
   Nor hills nor valleys; but one even plain
Stretches thro' long unbroken miles away:
While thro' the sluggish air a twilight grey   5

Broodeth; no moons or seasons wax and wane,
No ebb and flow are there among the main,
No bud-time no leaf-falling there for aye,
No ripple on the sea, no shifting sand,
No beat of wings to stir the stagnant space,   10
No pulse of life thro' all the loveless land:
And loveless sea; no trace of days before.
No guarded home, no toil-won restingplace
No future hope no fear forevermore.

■ Most of the descriptions here are given in the negative. From these
descriptions, what is this place like?

■ How many of these descriptions offer us a real place? How many describe
reactions to, or impressions of, the place?

Oscar Wilde (1854–1900)

The Harlot's House (1885)

We caught the tread of dancing feet,
We loitered down the moonlit street,
And stopped beneath the harlot's house.

Inside, above the din and fray,
We heard the loud musicians play   5
The "Treues Liebes Herz" of Strauss.

Like strange mechanical grotesques,
Making fantastic arabesques,
The shadows raced across the blind.

We watched the ghostly dancers spin   10
To sound of horn and violin,
Like black leaves wheeling in the wind.

Like wire-pulled automatons,
Slim silhouetted skeletons
Went sidling through the slow quadrille,   15

Then took each other by the hand,
And danced a stately saraband;
Their laughter echoed thin and shrill.

Sometimes a clockwork puppet pressed
A phantom lover to her breast,   20
Sometimes they seemed to try to sing.

Sometimes a horrible marionette
Came out, and smoked its cigarette
Upon the steps like a live thing.

Then, turning to my love, I said,   25
"The dead are dancing with the dead,
The dust is whirling with the dust."

But she—she heard the violin,
And left my side, and entered in:
Love passed into the house of lust.   30

Then suddenly the tune went false,
The dancers wearied of the waltz,
The shadows ceased to wheel and whirl.

And down the long and silent street,
The dawn, with silver-sandalled feet,   35
Crept like a frightened girl.

- Compare the setting here with that presented in "Kearney Park" (p. 528). How do they use similar setting elements differently?

- What impact does the title of this poem have upon our understanding of the setting? What about the place is real? What is imaginary?

William Blake (1757–1827)

London (1794)

I wander thro each chartered street,
Near where the charter'd Thames does flow,
And mark in every face I meet
Marks of weakness, marks of woe.

In every cry of every Man,   5
In every Infant's cry of fear,
In every voice, in every ban,
The mind-forg'd manacles I hear.

How the Chimney-sweeper's cry
Every blackning Church appalls;   10
And the hapless Soldier's sigh
Runs in blood down Palace walls.

But most through midnight streets I hear
How the youthful Harlot's curse
Blasts the new-born Infant's tear,   15
And blights with plagues the Marriage hearse.

- What are the specific images that Blake "reads" in London's streets? Is the
  poet a visitor to the city or a resident?
- What is the connection that Blake establishes among each of these images
  and the conclusions that he draws at the end of each stanza?

William Wordsworth (1770–1850)

London, 1802 (1807)

Milton! thou should'st be living at this hour:
England hath need of thee: she is a fen
Of stagnant waters: altar, sword, and pen,
Fireside, the heroic wealth of hall and bower,
Have forfeited their ancient English dower   5
Of inward happiness. We are selfish men;
Oh! raise us up, return to us again;
And give us manners, virtue, freedom, power.
Thy soul was like a star, and dwelt apart:
Thou hadst a voice whose sound was like the sea: 10
Pure as the naked heavens, majestic, free,
So didst thou travel on life's common way,
In cheerful godliness; and yet thy heart
The lowliest duties on herself did lay.

- What is the difference between the images that Wordsworth lists in lines 2–4
  and those that appear in lines 9–10? How are these images related to the
  qualities listed in line 8?
- Why might Milton be helpful?

Experiencing Literature through Writing

1. Select a single work from this chapter (or any other). Identify a significant setting within that work. Explain why that setting is significant to our understanding of the text. As you write, consider the following questions:

   a. What specific details in the work help you recognize the setting in this work?
   b. What details in the work make this setting particularly interesting?
   c. Are there multiple settings in the work? Does the author develop some contrast among these settings?
   d. Are there details within this work that do not seem attached to any setting? How is the setting significant if these details do not seem to be related to the setting?

2. In the works in this chapter, we get details that help us see some places that seem very real and some that seem much less substantial. Compare two works that allow you to explore this contrast. What makes one seem like a familiar place and the other mysterious?

3. Discuss the relation between the details about setting that we get in one work and the point of view that reveals those details to us. For instance, we might get the details through the eyes of a child. How does knowledge of the viewpoint influence our reading of those details? To what extent is our understanding of the setting a function of the point of view?

6

Rhythm, Pace, and Rhyme

How Do Sounds Move?

Usually, when we think of rhythm we think first of music. It's easy to understand why. We take in and express rhythms physically. We hear; we feel; we dance. Artists and critics together have created a rich technical language to analyze, describe, and appreciate the sensations music inspires. We can speak of a bass line as that which establishes something for all the other players to follow (clumsy dancers sometimes move to a song's melody or tune and disregard the deeper rhythms that melody is built upon). Rhythm is the pulse that undergirds everything; if the pulse grows faint, the entire composition can become vague or listless. If the pulse becomes irregular, the composition can become confusing, disturbing, challenging, annoying, or even comedic.

Many terms rooted in the study of music (*counterpoint/contrapuntal, amplification, cadence, measure, motif,* etc.) carry over easily to literary study—especially to the study of poetry. Poetry has always been music's close relative. And it is certainly true that poets attend strictly to lines (the way every word is sounded in every line and every line is arranged on every page) in a way that doesn't necessarily concern novelists, essayists, filmmakers, or most dramatists. But that said, it's also clear that poets aren't the only artists who care about rhythm. The pulse that constitutes rhythm isn't something felt only in music and poetry—or experienced exclusively through sound. Even to use the word *pulse* tells us something: the beating of our hearts is the ultimate rhythmic touchstone. It shouldn't be surprising that a quality so basic to our very existence is accessed as well as expressed in a variety of ways; we hear, see, and feel rhythms.

In this chapter, we'll consider rhythm in the broadest—and most liberating—sense of the word. We'll think of rhythm along with related elements of sound like the speed or pace of delivery. We'll also consider distinct qualities of sound like rhyme in its various forms. We'll press further still to address visual and filmic rhythm. And we'll see how rhythms of sound enrich the texture of any kind of writing—not just poetry. In taking such an approach, we'll suggest ways to open up the word *rhythm* and understand more fully how deeply rhythm infuses works of art. We'll also encourage a flexible use of a technical, critical vocabulary without diminishing the precision of that vocabulary. Through it all, we will not neglect traditional metrical concerns centered on the study of poetry. Putting all of these elements in a larger context, we'll demonstrate how even the most highly specialized point of focus relates to vital critical concerns that cross familiar boundaries. We'll start by crossing a boundary that is often strongly marked: the one that separates sound from sight.

FILMIC RHYTHM

Vladimir Nabokov has said that a good critic reads with his backbone. T. S. Eliot once noted that great art is felt before it is understood. Emily Dickinson was perhaps getting at the same thing when she said that she didn't know how to define "poetry" but knew a poem when she felt it take off the top of her head. These kinds of physical responses register a fine appreciation for rhythm. They also mark what for some people characterizes an essential dimension of the filmgoing experience. We take in the sensory impressions of film at an extraordinarily rapid pace—not too rapid to process through our backbones, but much too fast to immediately sort out intellectually. We know a film has an impact well before we appreciate exactly what that impact involves or how it was achieved. Accounting for the feeling, as we've noted before, is the job of the critic. This process of accounting through discussion and writing can send us back to the film (or other films) more receptive, more alert, and more alive to film's possibilities.

In a film, the illusion of movement is created by running a series of still frames rapidly by a viewer: movies are moving pictures. The component of film beyond the individual **frame**, then, is the **shot**—a single length of film that communicates a continuous action on the screen. This length of film can, of course, be cut at any frame (that is, it can be a brief glimpse or a view that unfolds over many minutes). The joining or splicing (as well as the arranging or organizing) of shots is a function of **editing** (see Chapter 9 for a more complete discussion). The relationship among shots (among varying lengths of film/varying lengths of time that pass from one shot to another) creates a rhythmic sense that can convey extraordinary depth of feeling.

It's important here to distinguish pace from rhythm. **Pace** indicates the relative speed of an unfolding action or the variety of actions that unfold within a defined space of time. We might speak of a story or film as fast or slow paced based upon the number of incidents that are packed into our reading or viewing experience. Whereas pace involves relatively simple standards of fast or slow narratives, **filmic rhythm** involves *patterns* of movement, composition, and sound. **Shot analysis** is a means to comprehend how a film (or section of film) communicates meaning and power. In shot analysis, one breaks down a film and assesses the relationship of shot to shot, the rhythms that are created, and the effects of the whole. Although such analysis ultimately involves more than simply measuring the length of each shot, that measurement is important in understanding filmic rhythm.

Experiencing Film through Rhythm

If you've seen the popular classic *Jaws* (1975), there is a good chance you remember the opening scene very well. That opening demonstrates Steven Spielberg's command of a film's rhythm.

Universal/The Kobal Collection/Picture Desk

Universal/The Kobal Collection/ Goldman,Louis/Picture Desk

Louis Goldman/Universal/The Kobal Collection/Picture Desk

Universal/The Kobal Collection/ Goldman,Louis/Picture Desk

Jaws (1975) The film itself never shows the image that appeared in its advertising campaign. In this scene, the viewer sees only the girl and the ocean, not the shark.

Students off for summer vacations are partying at the beach after dark—and the party is at the sit-around-the-fire, drink-a-little-beer stage. Spielberg opens with a patient shot that slowly pans across the scene and pauses only to center us on one character—a young man who gazes across at a girl. A few brief shots move us back and forth between the boy and the girl who has caught his eye. Spielberg continues to cut fairly quickly, but in an evenly spaced way, between shots of the boy and the girl as they break from the group and run along the beach, undressing as they run. The lines of dialogue, if read separately from the images, convey nothing beyond the most minimal exposition of character and action:

SCENE: *Beach*

CASSIDY: What's your name again?

CHRISSIE WATKINS: Chrissie!

CASSIDY: Where are we going?

CHRISSIE: Swimming!

CASSIDY: Slow up, slow down! I'm not drunk! Slow down! Wait I'm coming! I'm coming! I'm definitely coming! Wait, slow up! I can swim—just can't walk or dress myself.

CHRISSIE: Come on in the water!

CASSIDY: Take it easy. Take it easy.

CHRISSIE: Oh! God help me! God! Argh! God help!

CASSIDY: I'm coming . . . I'm coming.

CHRISSIE: It hurts! It hurts! Oh my god! God help me! God please help!

This hardly seems inspired writing, but of course, words alone don't make up the movie. The whole *viewing* experience is terrifying. We see the unfortunate girl get to the water. The boy stumbles, falls on the sand, and goes to sleep. Spielberg again slows the exchange from shot to shot once the boy is out of the action; now the movement builds **tension** as Spielberg moves from a shot of the girl at the surface enjoying the water to a shot of equal length taken beneath from the perspective of the shark hunting for food, to a single brief shot of the boy asleep on the beach. Once the shark attacks, Spielberg holds the shot on the girl at the surface for what seems an excruciatingly long time. He wants to establish her (and our) helplessness in relation to this creature. He does this not by showing the creature itself, but by showing what can happen to the people who enter its realm. After the girl is finally pulled under and quiet returns, Spielberg returns to a shot of the boy: silent, unknowing, oblivious to the world and all its dangers. The horror is established in context of the sleepy vacation town and the pleasures of beach life. The opposition finds expression largely through Spielberg's mastery of film's rhythmic possibilities.

POETIC RHYTHM

Shot analysis in film involves closely observing and describing relationships among shots that function thematically and emotionally. It is useful to think of metrical analysis of poetry as in some fundamental way related to shot analysis (or the other way around, of course). A filmmaker arranges and organizes a series of shots into a whole that expresses a pattern of movement—moments of stress and of relief. A poet arranges and organizes a pattern of sounds that reinforce or create meaning, that suggest feeling behind meaning.

In the analysis of poetry, **meter** refers to a regular (therefore discernable) rhythmic pattern of sounds that is charted line by line; in the analysis of film, a pattern of unfolding action is charted shot by shot. At some point, the analogy between film analysis and the analysis of a poem's meter breaks down (as analogies usually do), but we can think of the poetic foot as the element that most closely corresponds to the frame (in that it is the smallest building block). A poetic **foot** is the combination of one stressed syllable with one or more unstressed syllables that constitutes the recurring rhythmic unit within the larger pattern of a poetic line or of any given stretch of text.

There are five standard units (feet) in English poetry:

- The **iambic** foot (the most common in English poetry) consists of two syllables, the first unstressed and the second stressed (toDAY, but WHY? inSPIRE). Any pattern that moves from unstressed to stressed syllables is sometimes called **rising meter.**
- The **trochaic** foot consists of two syllables, the first stressed and the second unstressed (TRAVel, STANdard). Any pattern that moves from stressed to unstressed syllables is sometimes called **falling meter.**
- The **anapestic** foot consists of three syllables, the first two unstressed and the third stressed (anyMORE).
- The **dactylic** foot consists of three syllables, the first stressed and the last two unstressed (FInally).
- The **spondaic**, which consists of two consecutive stressed syllables (HOT DOG, OH MY!), and the **pyrrhic**, which consists of two consecutive unstressed syllables, are considered **variants** (or **substitutions**) of standard feet. That is, a spondee or a pyrrhic can break a prevailing pattern, but spondees and pyrrhics cannot make up a pattern (a line cannot be composed of all stressed syllables or all unstressed syllables because one quality can be defined only in relation to the other).

A **metric line** of poetry is measured by the number of feet that it comprises. The most common lines are **trimeter** (three feet), **tetrameter** (four feet), **pentameter** (five feet), and **hexameter** (six feet).

If we extend our analogy to film a bit further here, we can think of a metric line of poetry as a shot; for example, a line of **iambic pentameter** (the prevailing rhythm of much English poetry—"oh, GENtle FAUstus, LEAVE this DAMnéd ART"—and a natural speech pattern) could be seen as analogous to a single length of film, a shot. Poetic lines may be organized in larger patterns still by rhyme schemes (arrangements of rhyming words), line length, or more complex metrical forms. These larger patterns are called **stanzas**—a verse paragraph. Lines make up stanzas much as shots can be grouped as scenes. The following examples are common stanzaic forms:

- **couplet** (two lines)
  Early to bed and early to rise
  Makes a man healthy, wealthy, and wise.

- **tercet** (three lines)
  The winged seeds, where they lie cold and low,
  Each like a corpse within its grave, until
  Thine azure sister of the Spring shall blow.
  —Percy Bysshe Shelley, from "Ode to the West Wind"

- **quatrain** (four lines)
  When the voices of children are heard on the green
  And laughing is heard on the hill,
  My heart is at rest within my breast
  And everything else is still
  —William Blake, from "Nurse's Song"

There are, of course, other forms, most notably the **octave** (eight lines) and **sestet** (six lines) (see the discussion of the sonnet in Chapter 8).

Experiencing Literature through Rhythm

Rhythm in much poetry in English must be charted by attention to both syllables and stresses. Such attention to the metrical shape of a poem is called **prosody**. To **scan** a line of poetry or any text is to define the rhythmic pattern. Such analysis, or **scansion**, must remain fairly rough (in this book, stressed syllables are shown in all uppercase letters, and unstressed syllables, in all lowercase letters). Syllables are, after all, pronounced with a wide and flexible range of emphases; marking every syllable either stressed (´) or unstressed (˘) cannot register that range with great precision. But judicious metrical analysis can help us describe what rhythms we hear and may also help deepen our appreciation of the writer's craft. Poets can achieve emphasis through meter; they can make us notice a key word or idea. And as the two following works make clear, a poet may even fuse meter and meaning.

Herman Melville (1819–1891)

The Maldive Shark (1888)

About the Shark, phlegmatical one,
Pale sot of the Maldive sea,
The sleek little pilot-fish, azure and slim,
How alert in attendance be.
From his saw-pit of mouth, from his charnel of maw,   5
They have nothing of harm to dread,
But liquidly glide on his ghastly flank
Or before his Gorgonian head;
Or lurk in the port of serrated teeth
In white triple tiers of glittering gates,   10
And there find a haven when peril's abroad,
An asylum in jaws of the Fates!
They are friends; and friendly they guide him to prey,
Yet never partake of the treat—
Eyes and brains to the dotard lethargic and dull,   15
Pale ravener of horrible meat.

William Blake (1757–1827)

Nurse's Song (1789)

When the voices of children are heard on the green,
And laughing is heard on the hill,
My heart is at rest within my breast,
    And every thing else is still.

"Then come home my children, the sun is gone down,   5
And the dews of the night arise;
Come, come, leave off play, and let us away
Till the morning appears in the skies."

"No, no, let us play, for it is yet day,
And we cannot go to sleep;   10
Besides, in the sky, the little birds fly,
And the hills are all cover'd with sheep."

"Well, well, go & play till the light fades away,
And then go home to bed."
The little ones leaped & shouted & laugh'd   15
    And all the hills ecchoed

Read "The Maldive Shark" and "Nurse's Song" aloud several times and you'll begin to hear a lilting, rather fast meter. It is a rhythm like one you have probably heard before in poems for children or comic verse. The strongly marked rhythm results from the repeated use of trisyllabic feet. In the first line of "Nurse's Song," anapests prevail:

When the voices of children are heard on the green...
(when the VOIces of CHILdren are HEARD on the GREEN)

In "The Maldive Shark," the opening line closes with an anapest, and anapests and dactyls generally prevail throughout:

About the Shark, phlegmatical one...
(aBOUT the SHARK, phlegMATical ONE)

In Blake's poem, the anapests seem clearly appropriate: "Nurse's Song" is (at least on the surface) a song of innocence. The poem centers mainly on the power of children's play and joy to transform the spirit of the speaker. But note how Melville uses rhythms similar to Blake's to create a troubling thematic undercurrent. The trisyllabic feet in "The Maldive Shark" do not function to reinforce themes like innocence, childhood, and peace. The lilting quality of Melville's meter starkly contrasts with images of death and blunt power that are associated with the shark. The apparent split between form and content suggests that things are not what they seem. A similar, complex mixed signal is evident in the construction of the poem's first sentence. The first *line* seems to announce the shark as subject of the poem (this is a poem "about the shark"), but if we pay attention to the whole sentence, which ends with line 4, we note the focus has shifted: the shark isn't even the grammatical subject. The poem actually centers on the pilot fish that swim "about the shark."

The sleek, intelligent, quick, alert, attractive pilot-fish are set before us in the rhythm of the poem; visual images of the heavy, dumb, slow, uncaring, repellent shark move powerfully through this rhythm. The implication of this contrast is that what we sometimes assume to be good or innocent often operates together with what we see as evil or corrupt. In other words, what seems not to go together goes together all too well. The pilot-fish lead the shark to its prey so that they may be safe from its hunger. Melville's play with meter challenges conventional and comfortable notions of morality and order. His poem helps us understand that meter is not mere decoration.

Melville and Blake make meter central to the meaning of these two poems, but meter can be worth attending to even when it is not the central critical matter of the entire work. Note, for example, how Stephen Crane's opening sentences from his short story "A Bride Comes to Yellow Sky" rhythmically convey a sense of a train's relentless movement westward (and with the train's movement, the rolling influence of an entire culture):

The Great Pullman was whirling onward with such dignity of motion that a glance from the window seemed simply to prove that the plains of Texas were pouring eastward. Vast flats of green grass, dull-hued spaces of mesquite and cactus, little groups of frame houses, woods of light and tender trees, all were sweeping into the east, sweeping over the horizon, a precipice. ❖

Interpretations of a line's rhythm are subject to debate—as is any kind of interpretation—but a good case could be made here for breaking the last sentence into poetic lines for the sake of directing an oral reading:

Vast flats of green grass,
Dull-hued spaces of mesquite and cactus,
Little groups of frame houses,
Woods of light and tender trees
All were sweeping into the east,   5
Sweeping over the horizon
A precipice.

The opening line employs spondees; and trochees, not the more common iambs, prevail in the next three lines. It seems that Crane is both describing and embodying the train's movement along the tracks west. The fourth and fifth lines, though, break that pattern midline. But it's not just a shift to iambs in line 5; rather, in the middle of line 6 and the start of the final line, Crane substitutes pyrrhic feet (the two consecutive unstressed syllables) or perhaps anapests (two unaccented followed by an accented syllable). The effect of the unaccented syllables run together is that his sentence gathers speed as it moves to the precipice. The old West, as we'll come to learn in the story, is falling over that precipice into a more "civilized" (more domesticated, tame) East.

Granted, these changes would fundamentally alter what Crane wrote. Crane didn't arrange his lines as we have. And his story could not reward from beginning to end the attention to rhythmic patterns we've devoted to this sentence. Still, it is worth remembering that Crane was a poet as well as a short story writer (and a journalist, too), and it's plain that in this passage he creates effects partly through his attention to sound as well as sense. So the altering of the text is not an attempt to make it something it is not; rather, it is a way of revealing what we hear and feel, but imperfectly appreciate. From the perspective of a critical writer, attention to meter in a text may yield fresh insights as to how that text achieves meaning and power.

THE RHYTHM OF PAUSES

Scansion can reveal much of a writer's art, but obviously there are rhythmic effects that are not accounted for by marking poetic feet (just as shot analysis alone cannot account for all aspects of a film's rhythm). Artists in various mediums manage pauses of various weights to effect interpretation; much meaning or emotion can be conveyed by pauses (or by the lack of pause). An artist can hold an audience's/reader's attention on a word or image, or make the audience/reader wait just a moment before delivering something profound.

The **caesura** is a pause *within* a line of poetry (sometimes called an **extrametrical** effect and charted by a double slash [//] between words at the point of pause). A full stop at the end of a line is an **end stop**. A line that "strides over" into the next line without a pause is **enjambed** (the poet has employed **enjambment**). Although *caesura, end stop,* and *enjambment* are terms that apply specifically to the analysis of poetry (how pauses are managed within and between lines), many powerful effects in any piece of writing or film result from the careful management of pauses. A pause at the right time can anticipate a sudden turn; it can allow one to absorb an emotional effect; it can draw attention to what precedes or follows. It can accentuate a rhythmic quality of a text, or it can make us keenly aware of rhythm by breaking the pattern (if something is too regular, we may hardly notice).

Experiencing Literature through Rhythm

Samuel Johnson employs a carefully measured rhythm for thematic purpose. "On the Death of Dr. Robert Levet" is about a man who had a long and well-used life. Levet cut no great figure in terms of what the world values, but Johnson sees Levet's modest accomplishments as deserving real praise. In the context of the hard surrounding world (Johnson casts all humankind as workers in "Hope's delusive mine"), Levet toils faithfully in service to those who seek his help. Death, in Johnson's view, ends that difficult service and brings the aged Levet to his Maker.

Samuel Johnson (1709–1784)

On the Death of Dr. Robert Levet (1783)

Condemn'd to Hope's delusive mine,
    As on we toil from day to day,
By sudden blasts, or slow decline,
    Our social comforts drop away.

Well tried through many a varying year,   5
    See Levet to the grave descend;
Officious, innocent, sincere,
    Of every friendless name the friend.

Yet still he fills affection's eye,
    Obscurely wise and coarsely kind;   10
Nor, letter'd Arrogance, deny
    Thy praise to merit unrefined.

When fainting nature called for aid,
    And hovering death prepared the blow,
His vigorous remedy display'd   15
    The power of art without the show.

In misery's darkest cavern known,
    His useful care was ever nigh,
Where hopeless Anguish pour'd his groan,
    And lonely want retired to die.   20

No summons mock'd by chill delay,
    No petty gain disdained by pride,
The modest wants of every day
    The toil of every day supplied.

His virtues walked their narrow round,   25
    Nor made a pause, nor left a void;
And sure the eternal Master found
    The single talent well employ'd.

The busy day, the peaceful night,
    Unfelt, uncounted, glided by;   30
His frame was firm, his powers were bright,
    Though now his eightieth year was nigh.

Then with no throbbing fiery pain,
    No cold gradations of decay,
Death broke at once the vital chain,   35
    And freed his soul the nearest way.

The feeling in this poem is not narrowly for Levet's death. Indeed, Levet's sudden death is cast as a release. Whatever hardship one faces in this life, Johnson suggests, can be placed in a broader and well-ordered picture. The measured pauses within the lines enforce this sense of balance. Whatever our lot on earth, Johnson seems to say, God has structured a coherent master plan within which we can work. Note the clear midline pauses in lines 3 ("By sudden blasts, // or slow decline"), 10 ("Obscurely wise // and coarsely kind"), 26, 29, and 31. Many other lines convey a much less distinct, but still arguably evident pause in the middle of the line. Consider, for example, lines 2 ("As on we toil // from day to day"), 14 ("And hovering death // prepared the blow"), 16, 20, and 28. When caesuras do not so evenly divide a line in half, they still evenly divide the line, as in line 7 ("Officious, // innocent, // sincere") and 30 ("Unfelt, // uncounted, // glided by"). Johnson's phrasing suggests the steadiness he wishes to maintain in reflecting upon the life and death of his friend.

We could further note here that Johnson maintains this steadiness through his management of the entire stanza. He gives us no metrical surprises, no pronounced breaks from the prevailing iambic tetrameter (a line of four iambic feet). He brings most lines to a full stop or end stop. Every quatrain (poetic paragraph of four lines) closes a complete thought and enforces a pronounced pause. The pace of the poem, the phrases so carefully balanced by caesuras, the structural clarity and consistency—all suggest a poet in command of his message and confident in his faith.

Ben Jonson feels no such emotional balance or spiritual assurance as he struggles to write about a very different sort of death. "On My First Son" expresses an intensely personal loss. Obviously, one's own seven-year-old child cannot serve as a point of reflection on a life well used and kindly ended—the kind of reflection that prevails in Samuel Johnson's tribute to his old friend Dr. Levet. The intense pain Ben Jonson feels cannot lead him to feel grateful that his son escaped pain by dying young. The grieving father is angry, confused, and hurt. Given such feelings, any measured, balanced, regular rhythm would seem strangely controlled. Not surprisingly, we do not get that steady rhythm.

Ben Jonson (1572–1637)

On My First Son (1616)

Farewell, thou child of my right hand, and joy;
My sin was too much hope of thee, loved boy:
Seven years thou wert lent to me, and I thee pay,
Exacted by thy fate, on the just day.
O could I lose all father now! for why   5
Will man lament the state he should envy,
To have soon 'scaped world's and flesh's rage,
And, if no other misery, yet age?
Rest in soft peace, and asked, say, "Here doth lie
Ben Jonson his best piece of poetry."   10
For whose sake henceforth all his vows be such
As what he loves may never like too much.

Much of Jonson's unresolved emotional torment is conveyed by the sudden, irregularly placed caesuras (the pauses in this poem fall near the beginning or the end of several lines, but not in the middle). It is as if in the first four lines the speaker makes a tentative, reluctant attempt to say goodbye. This attempt is broken by a rush of feeling that stalls just before the end of the fifth line. At that point, Jonson forces us to rush ahead without stop from the end of line 5 clear through line 6:

O could I lose all father now! // for why
Will man lament the state he should envy.

The enjambment here suggests that emotions cannot be bound by the constraints of line. Again, rhythm relates to sense; it is part of the critic's job to help readers see that relationship.

A Note to Student Writers: Commanding Attention

Clearly, pauses aren't the sole property of poets. Sentences, just like lines of poems, build and release tension in any number of ways. Good writers in any mode want to signal pace and emphasis for their readers. Readers need help sometimes in noticing what is really important. A carefully placed pause, a balanced series, an emphatic turn or break from a prevailing pattern—all can bring home a point. We suggest that you bring this insight into your own writing. You, like any writer, must find ways to make readers concentrate attention on the words that need or demand attention. One way of doing this (as we've mentioned before in other contexts) is to read your own work aloud periodically as you draft and revise. Reading aloud will not only help make you conscious of rhythmic effects in works of art, it will lead you to appreciate how many of those effects play out in your own prose. In short, we want you to be alert to how rhythmic effects are deeply part of almost any carefully constructed text—including the texts you construct.

THE RHYTHM OF SOUNDS

The quality of sounds strongly influences the weight and stress we sense that falls on individual words. Sounds also influence the way we speak words in sequence—sounds of individual words influence the rhythm we feel arise from a group of words. And, of course, sounds of individual words must be spoken and heard in relation to other words. People do not pronounce words in isolation (such tonelessness is for machines: consider the phonetic, word-by-word correctness of the mechanically generated voices you hear on phone message systems). We pronounce words in ways that mesh with how those words unfold in a line or a sentence as well as how they balance, contrast, or echo one another.

Rhyme serves as an especially powerful means of achieving such balance, contrast, or echo. **Full** or **perfect rhyme** consists of the similarity of sounds in accented vowels and any consonants that follow (*date, fate*). In a **masculine rhyme**, the stress is on the final syllable of the words (*clown, renown*). A **feminine rhyme** is one in which the final two syllables rhyme; the first rhyming syllable is stressed, and the final syllable is unstressed (*buckle, knuckle*). **Assonance** also consists of a similarity in vowel sounds, but the consonants that follow differ (*date, lake*). **Consonance** strikes a similarity in the sounds of the final stressed consonant; it is the preceding vowel that differs (*date, rite*). Words that echo sounds in these ways are sometimes called **slant rhymes** or **off-rhymes**. **Alliteration** refers to the repetition of initial sounds in words (*date, dud*). All of these terms concerns sounds, but rhyme generally refers to similar sounds that occur at corresponding places in a line of poetry. Assonance, consonance, and alliteration may be employed at various intervals throughout any given passage of poetry or prose. Rhymes in the middle of a line are called **internal rhymes**; those at the end of a line, **end rhymes**.

Rhyme is so strongly part of the way we voice a word that it sometimes overcomes other rhythmic signals and distorts the way we deliver a line. Think, for example, of the times you feel prompted to pause at the end of a rhymed line of poetry despite the syntactical demand to move forward. Small children will normally pause very heavily after every rhyme, and in a sense that tendency reflects a good impulse even if it is ultimately misguided. Of course, the sounds of words also have much to do with the rhythm and pace of a line. The running together of hard consonants will usually force readers to slow down; one simply can't perfectly pronounce passages full of *p* sounds without pausing and allowing each word to have some space. Other sounds glide together very easily and greatly speed rhythm. Alexander Pope's famous lines from his "Essay on Criticism" illustrate perfectly how slowness and speed can be suggested by sounds:

> When Ajax strives some rock's vast weight to throw,
> The line too labors, and the words move slow;
> Not so when swift Camilla scours the plain,
> Flies o'er the unbending corn, and skims along the main.

We also hear sounds differently depending on meaning and context. For example, one might think that the sibilants (*s* sounds) that dominate lines from Alfred, Lord Tennyson's "The Lotus Eaters" (1842) convey softness, easiness, and sleepiness:

> There is sweet music here that softer falls
> Than petals from blown roses on the grass,
> Or night-dews on still waters between walls
> Of Shadowy granite, in a gleaming pass;

> Music that gentlier on the spirit lies,
> Than tired eyelids upon tired eyes;
> Music that brings sweet sleep down from the blissful skies.

We can use the terms **euphony** (to describe pleasing, soothing sounds) and **cacophony** (to describe harsh, unpleasant sounds), but we do not hear the sounds as soothing purely because of the sounds themselves. There is nothing inherently soothing in the sound of the letter *s* (think of the hissing of a snake). Tennyson's meaning directs us to inflect these particular words with a particular languor. So this section ends with a warning: Avoid arguing a point from sound alone.

> **Making Connections**
>
> Sound and rhythm can have importance even when they have no apparent meaning. Consider, for example, how music functions in a film or a play. Even when you are absorbed by the action, the rhythmic unfolding of that action may be led by background music you don't consciously notice. Also consider the way sounds and rhythms can serve as a kind of incantation—sounds can weave a spell. Such atmospheric effects are (as discussed in Chapter 5) very important to Gothic works.

Be sure that you are attentive to sound in relation to all the other evidence you gather to explain how a given work communicates.

Experiencing Literature through Rhythm and Rhyme

As powerful as rhymes may be in the effect of the whole work, they may function in very subtle ways. In the short poem that follows, upon first reading you will probably feel the matter-of-fact finality of Randall Jarrell's closing line.

Randall Jarrell (1914–1965)

The Death of the Ball Turret Gunner (1945)

> From my mother's sleep I fell into the State,
> And I hunched in its belly till my wet fur froze.
> Six miles from earth, loosed from its dream of life,
> I woke to black flak and the nightmare fighters.
> When I died they washed me out of the turret with a hose.   5

You might not notice, however, that that feeling is enforced by a rhyme: "hose" rhymes perfectly with "froze." Jarrell's poem does not have the metrical regularity that often leads us to anticipate a rhyme. Nor does the

Making Connections

Rhyme does more than accentuate rhythmic elements; rhyme can be a structuring device—a means to highlight a central meaning or problem (see the discussion of Millay's "I, Being Born a Woman and Distressed" in Chapter 8). Robert Frost's "Fire and Ice" is tightly structured around three rhymes (A/B/A/A/B/C/B/C/B). The "A" rhymes set one side of an elemental opposition: fire and the emotion of desire; the "B" rhymes center around a feeling associated with "ice." The "C" rhymes identify that cold feeling: hate.

Frost's word choice (especially at the poem's finish) is also striking. *Suffice* hardly seems the word one would expect in wrapping up a thought about a power great enough to end the world. But the particular quality of hatred that Frost expresses needs to find expression in such a tightly limited, proper little word (for more on word choice, see Chapter 11).

rhyme follow very closely: "froze" ends line 2; "hose" ends line 5. Yet this rather distant rhyme accounts in part for the sudden, forceful finish. The life of the gunner is absolutely over, and so is the poem; the rhyme accentuates the finish of both. It closes off this brief monologue.

Jarrell also employs internal rhymes (rhymes within the line instead of at the end of lines) and consonance to suggest the sensory assault of enemy gunfire that awakens the ball-turret gunner to the nightmare of life: "woke to black flak." The sounds communicate experience as well as meaning; confusion and terror mark that experience. The hardness of the sounds in context of the meaning aggressively presses upon us as we read. The example here illustrates **onomatopoeia**—the sounds of the words replicate the meaning they convey.

Robert Frost (1874–1963)

Fire and Ice (1923)

Some say the world will end in fire,
Some say in ice.
From what I've tasted of desire
I hold with those who favor fire.
But if it had to perish twice,   5
I think I know enough of hate
To say that for destruction ice
Is also great
And would suffice.

MODELING CRITICAL ANALYSIS:
ROBERT BROWNING, MY LAST DUCHESS

Robert Browning's "My Last Duchess" (p. 406) reads very much like the one-way conversation Browning intends it to be. We hear a man, the duke, *speaking* to another man, the envoy. His delivery might be rather formal in places, but he is a duke after all—one with a "nine-hundred-years-old name." What most readers sense is the naturalness of his style.

Ralph Rader, a literary critic whose reading of this poem has influenced ours, suggests we should not be taken in by the duke's tone. Rader points to something very obvious that few people notice: this poem is written in rhymed couplets throughout. In fact, the rhymes are full or perfect end rhymes; the lines themselves are of iambic pentameter. Something must be amiss: how can we read as speech language that is so clearly crafted? How is it that anyone could read a poem and not notice that it is rhymed so regularly? Not notice that it is so carefully measured rhythmically?

One level of answers to such questions requires attention to Browning's technique. We don't pick up on the rhymes or the accentual/syllabic regularity of lines because Browning hides them. He employs caesuras at various points within the lines; he regularly enjambs lines; and he keeps the structure of his sentences (syntax) out of synch with the arrangement of his poetic lines. For example, notice how the full pause near the end of line 2 comes at the end of a sentence. The line, though, continues briefly after that pause and moves forward without a break into line 3 which then "strides over" into line 4. As a result, any good dramatic reading will not make us *hear* the end rhyme that is there if we *look* (*wall, call*).

So we are led to another question: Why should Browning bother to come up with perfect rhymes and then go to the trouble of making us *not* notice them? The answer, Rader suggests, is that Browning (the poet) wants readers to see how duplicitous the duke (the speaker) is. In other words, the duke only pretends to be casual and spontaneous. He only claims to be a man who has "no skill in speech." A careful reading of the poem—especially to rhythms and rhymes that are at once transparent and hidden—reveals a duke who knows exactly what message he wants to send to the envoy, yet also knows not to send that message directly. To put it another way, Browning has built into the poem evidence of how crafty the duke is. What is the duke's message? Rader argues that the duke wants to make it clear that he expects the next wife to know exactly what is expected of her. He also wants everyone involved in the negotiation to know what the consequences of not meeting those expectations will be. Most readers see the duke as unintentionally revealing himself as cruel—indeed murderous. Rader looks to the rhythms and rhymes of Browning's poem to argue that the duke is in full, conscious control of his terrible message.

Using Rhythm, Pace, and Rhyme to Focus Writing and Discussion
■ To locate rhythms, we must look at individual words and at sentence structures within the text.
■ What words or sounds are repeated within the text?
■ What patterns govern these repetitions?
■ What characteristics can we ascribe to the sounds of this text? Are they soothing? Harsh? How do these sounds correspond to the literal meaning of the text?
■ Is there some contrast in rhythms? For instance, does the text set up a pattern and then break it? If so, what is the effect?
■ What sentence patterns do we find in this work? Does the author use consistently short sentences? Long sentences? Any consistent variety?
■ Are there different characters who speak with different rhythms in the text? How are these differences related to the role of the characters in the text?

Anthology

FARCE: A CRITIC WRITES ABOUT RHYTHM AND FARCE

Farce is generally defined as the comedy that results when stereotyped characters are thrown together in improbable situations. Because this particular genre generally does not have a sophisticated plot (though it might be convoluted) or complex characters, it often depends upon rhythm to sustain it. Penelope Gilliatt points out that misunderstanding is at the center of the comedy throughout the film *The Return of the Pink Panther* (1975). Specifically, the central character, the hapless Inspector Clouseau (played by Peter Sellers), lacks any instinct that might make him a good detective. He has an air of official competence that belies his actual abilities. He is incapable of making himself understood and fails to observe the immediate world. Clouseau's peculiar innocence and profound incompetence at dealing with the world around him put him into situations that result in the movie's humor. Peter Sellers creates a character who maintains his own peculiar rhythm at odds with everything that is going on around him, and Blake Edwards choreographs each scene so that Clouseau's self-confident bumbling results in the most ridiculous chaos. In her analysis of the film, Gilliatt presents details of plot and character that help us understand the rhythm of the film that Sellers and Edwards have created.

Students are sometimes frustrated when they try to make sense of "A Very Old Man with Enormous Wings: A Tale for Children" by examining the plot or the characters. The plot can seem like a series of disconnected episodes; the characters can seem like stereotypes. One way to grapple with the story is to think of it in symbolic terms: What does the old man represent? What do the crabs signify? But staying on the surface of the story can also yield provocative insights. What if we were to analyze this story as an example of farce? After all, the title character seems out of synch with what happens around him. Some of the descriptors that Gilliatt used in her analysis of Clouseau's awkwardness might apply.

The title character, the "very old man," drops clumsily out of the sky and is never an active or effective agent in the story. He is not even an attractive presence. Apart from his wings, he doesn't appear to have any special qualities. He is unable to express himself, and he seems nearly oblivious to the concerns of other characters. Yet the townspeople assume that he must be an angel with all of the magical abilities that such a being possesses. Gilliatt observes that a fundamental misunderstanding in farce is between plot and character, that "narrative and character live separate lives." That split can be observed in this case. The "very old man" lives separately from the rest of the story; we never learn where he came from; his character does not have any complex emotions or any psychological depth that we can observe. In fact, the narrative itself seems to generate its own misunderstanding. A line from the first paragraph reads: "The world had been sad since Tuesday." The words are straightforward, but what does it mean to say that the world is "sad" or to define the title character as simply "very old"? There are narrative forms that would use specific detail to show us the qualities that are presented here in these abstract adjectives, but these simple declarations of a quality or emotion give the story its distinct rhythm; the tale is from the start halting and jumpy. The only order to be found in this world is sequential: one thing happens after another. But there are no logical connections that tie the accumulated things together. Perhaps the farce here is not one to laugh at. The disjunctive rhythm of this tale might help us define this sadness that hangs over all from the start. Much of the action of the story comes in the form of characters looking for explanations, for logical connections, for understanding, but their search is frustrated by the very object that inspired it. The "very old man" doesn't do anything. Throughout the work he remains innocent (even oblivious) to the desires that surround him.

Some form of innocence characterizes most of the selections in this section. Although farce doesn't always result, we might say innocence dances in an uneasy rhythm with experience. The poems selected from William Blake's *Songs of Innocence* and *Songs of Experience* provide the thematic keynote. Blake, as we pointed out in the discussion of the "Nurse's Song" earlier, matches rhythmic features of his poems with the "contrary states of the human soul" he seeks to express. As you read these poems, be sure to think of each as part of a larger fabric of poems. Compare the different rhythmic effects Blake achieves in regard to the same subject (the two views of the chimney sweep, the two views of a Holy Thursday) or of paired subjects (the lamb and the tiger). You'll find that any discussion of meaning or theme in these poems requires attention to rhythm and sounds.

But one shouldn't be too quick to simply divide innocence from experience in Blake's poetry. The difference is finally a matter of perspective: there is, after all, profound and terrible experience in poems of innocence (suffering children, repressive authority figures, and so on). The tension between the "contrary states" often exists within a single poem. Such complexity is very much a part of James Baldwin's classic story "Sonny's Blues." Baldwin gives us a narrator who might seem "innocent" in comparison to the brother whose story he tells. But as we get into the story, the word *innocent* grows complex. Does it mean "good" in comparison to "bad"? Or does Baldwin suggest that the narrator's innocence is a way to mask pain and suffering—to deny feelings? Is it possible that the brother who experiences so much trouble is more innocent in the headlong way he seeks to live through his art? And that art, of course, is music. Baldwin builds his story to a climax that plays out in context of the journey Sonny takes with his band. The narrator says he knows that "not many people ever really hear" music. Only on occasion do sounds touch us powerfully. The narrator also believes that the musician hears, creates, struggles with, and achieves something deeper and more lasting. As you read the story, think of the meaning of the rhythmic dialogue that goes on between Sonny and the bass player that closes the story.

Like Baldwin, Suzan-Lori Parks puts specific, individual questions about innocence and experience in context of a rich and complicated history. In *Topdog/Underdog*, she also gives us a story of two brothers. These brothers seem condemned to act within and act out a terrible, repetitive dynamic that has been shaped by past collective experience—an enormous haunting national tragedy. The situation of the play is improbable: The black man named Lincoln, who puts on whiteface to play Lincoln at the local boardwalk, comes home to the brother named Booth who wants desperately to be Lincoln (the one-time king of a shell game who is trying to go straight). If that sounds confusing, it is—sort of. In fact, the inner workings of *Topdog/Underdog* sometimes take on characteristics of farce, although here the misunderstandings are great in both scale and depth. But once you get into the play, you will find it develops a powerful logic that moves purposefully to the end. You'll also see how the rhythms of the shell game (rhythms intended to disrupt attention and keep people from seeing accurately) are integrated into the rich texture of the whole play.

REVIEW

Penelope Gilliatt (1932–1993)

Peter Sellers in the Pink (1975)

The uncovetable hard-boiled egg of a diamond that is the prize of Blake Edwards' "The Return of the Pink Panther" has a flaw that conjures up the image of a pink panther when the jewel is held to the light. The French cop who is brought in to find the invaluable ovoid after it has been brilliantly thieved also has a flaw. It is the flaw of being completely unfitted to be a cop. Called Inspector Clouseau, as he was in "The Pink Panther" and "A Shot in the Dark" (both 1964), he is rampant again in the subtle comic person of Peter Sellers, who has refined a beautiful and infant clarity about slapstick humor as he has grown older. The detective superficially exudes all the apt professional virtues—grasp, alertness, authority—but the impression turns out to be delusory. Under Clouseau's stoic mask of lofty exemption from fluster, which is much like the expression worn in a honking traffic jam by the one driver who happens not to be in a hurry, his cast of thought is impractical, errant, and bashful. He is unobservant of the immediate world and of its mundane ordering of cause and effect—of the fact that a door banged against the head of a man behind it will have the consequence of bruises, for instance—to a point that might indicate genius if this attribute were to occur in an abstract thinker. In a detective, it has the result of removing him from an actuality that proves to be crucial. Clouseau finds himself forced into unkind collision with the thingness of things. The sense of the concrete expected of a police inspector is of too high a sort for this mooner. It is like asking Simone Weil to bottle gooseberries. He might well turn out to be much gifted in realms not yet dreamed of—composing for a massed band of nose flutes, discovering that cats live outside the space-time continuum—but his career as a cop does not expend his talents, whatever they are. And, whatever they are, they exact much fortitude from others. Peter Sellers' performance is one of the most delicately cataclysmic studies in accident-proneness since the silents. Even when he is simply strolling along a busy French street, with his accustomed look of official purposefulness, he pokes his own baton painfully in his eye. Rounding a corner and acknowledging the door of a bank with an oblivious little gesture of politesse, he tries to convince a begging street musician with a monkey that begging is forbidden without a license. Typically, edict degenerates into argument, and meanwhile the monkey amiably nibbles the baton. As the dispute goes on, the bank is smoothly robbed behind Clouseau's back. The gangsters seem overjoyed at their luck. To be happened upon by a *flic's* uniform filled by someone as hopeless at his job as Inspector Clouseau would be any criminal's dream. Even Clouseau's capacity for making himself understood is fragile. His French-accented English is very peculiar, very contagious. The consonants mostly stay in place, but the vowels go haywire. He tells the befuddled musician and what he briskly calls the minkey that it is against the low to be begging without a lissance. The musician, quickly catching the disease, blames everything on the minkey, who is holding the capful of cash. It is the minkey who is the business-man, says the beggar. He, the beggar, is only a musician and certainly doesn't know what the minkey does with the money. The minkey looks blameless, and absorbed by the bank heist.

When Clouseau has to explain in higher places why he didn't twig what was going on, he does it in the huffy mood of a waitress saying she hasn't got two pairs of hands. He says he did not nu the bank was being rubed. It is this attitude that drives his superior officer mad. The boss, wittily played by a Herbert Lom newborn in comedy, goes downhill in a swift spiral. He begins suavely, sitting behind a very executive-looking desk. It holds not only a real gun but also an executive-looking joke present, from his wife: a gunshaped ciga-rette lighter. We begin to sense that this chief inspector is an executive on the brink, an executive in desperate need of worry beads. The source of the need is the torment of employing Clouseau, a wreaker of havoc about whom the chief inspector says that Attila the Hun is a Red Cross volunteer by comparison. Clouseau's presence in the office gives the chief inspector a nervous tic, and goes on to cause a serious halving of the nose, the chief inspector shooting off the end with his own gun when he is meaning to light a sedating cigarette in aid of recovery from a visit by Clouseau. Before this, Clouseau has brought his enragingly calm powers of disapproval to bear on the deliberate efforts of the chief inspector to get the real gun to work on Clouseau himself. Surveying things with the particular sourness of the mechanically inept watching mechan-ical ineptitude in others, he is never in any doubt that the weapon is the ciga-rette lighter. The murder in the chief inspector's heart is quite hidden from his slumberous but testy underling. "Probably out of fluid," advises Clouseau expertly, driving the chief inspector beyond his limits. And "You need a new flint." Exit. Mania. Bang. Self-inflicted end of a perfectly good half-nose. The chief inspector's mind is eventually so disarrayed by dreams of killing Clouseau that he illustratively strangles a psycho-analyst who has been trying to get him to put his dreams into mere words.

"The Pink Panther" was very good slapstick; "The Return of the Pink Panther" is slapstick carried to the most shapely and reckless degree. Peter Sellers does some beautiful things in this matured portrait of Clouseau. The detective has become an exquisite study in disgruntlement. When he is sum-moned to the mythical Arab country of Lugash to inspect the site of the famous diamond's theft—an act we have seen being committed by a darkly disguised burglar equipped with an aerosol spray to detect protective radar equipment; wax to butter a floor so that the burglar can slide in the direction of the Pink Panther's plinth; a mechanism that looks like an astronaut's idea of a Plantagenet longbow; and a couple of pairs of extensible pincers that operate in the questing manner of lobster claws—the Sellers character looks at the scene of the crime in the spirit of some bored and quite unqualified dentist contemplating a foray into the molars. He trudges about in mild discontent, uttering something between a "Hum" and a "Tsk," emptying a flurry of what looks like talcum powder to detect fingerprints, and attempting aplomb to override the fact that the lens has fallen out of his Holmes-style magnifying glass. He decides instantly that the culprit is the mysterious Phantom, perhaps because the Phantom is the only criminal whom this ill-read amateur has heard of. Pouncing as if on an original thought, he arrives at the idea long held by everyone before him in the world police force: that the Phantom is Sir Charles Litton (played by Christopher Plummer, who is a good sardonic actor but not pliant or funny in the context of this peculiarly well-characterized custard-pie larkiness). Clouseau announces triumphantly that the dastardly job is the work of Sir Sharles Phantom, the notorious Litton. The search for corroborative clues takes the inspector in directions too idiosyncratic for the plot to be troubled with. In this film, as in many of the best comedies, narrative and character live separate lives. The plot here proceeds on its own way while Clouseau proceeds on his. He asks, with a look of intense craftiness, if Sir Sharles has a swimming pull. The question has no bearing on anything, but never mind. Then he dresses up, variously. And then he plunges into another swimming pull twice, at the wheel of a van of one kind or another that has gone out of control because Clouseau has irritably removed any clutch, brake, or accelerator that has got in his way. This is his approach to all engineering questions. When a device offends him, he plucks it out. Disguised as a telephone engineer outside a grand villa in Nice, he hygienically pulls out the innards of a severe case of stuck doorbell, and informs a jealous escort of the giggling Lady Litton (Catherine Schell), as he winds yards of wire around the doorbell plate, "I have fixed your doorbell from the ringing." Disguised as a hotel cleaner in Lady Litton's hotel suite in Gstaad, he gets waylaid by his own interest in a faulty lamp, which he inspects by the method of putting his finger into the naked socket and getting a colossal electric shock.

For the benefit of children, to whom the picture is joy, it should perhaps be said that some of the best moments include the sticking of a brocaded seat cover to Clouseau's trousers, a sauna bath sequence that he plays disguised as a towel hook, the ingestion of a know-all parrot into the huge sucking fitment of a hotel-sized vacuum cleaner, and a magnified reaction by the same fitment to the bosom of a very large German-Swiss masseuse. For adults, there is funniness of the most copious and delicately built sort in the temperament of the hero of this screenplay, by Frank Waldman and Blake Edwards. Clouseau belongs to the type of the obsessive *manque*. His job is a detective's, but his real happiness lies in a secret life of speechless practical jokes that he shares with his Oriental manservant, a tongue-tied but spry fanatic of farce who will hide in places like the deep-freeze when the master is expected home, or serve his own surprise Chinese fortune cookies in a Japanese restaurant. Sellers is now in a fine period of taking his own grave and low-key time, and he is working here at his best. He seems to have perfected his gift for depicting minor bureaucratic disaffection in the souls of extraordinary and earnest men. This Clouseau—following from the earlier ones, and from the Indian in "The Party," the Italian in "After the Fox," and the Los Angeles lawyer in "I Love You, Alice B. Toklas!"—is the funniest, most sober, and most tenderly observed man Sellers has created since his famous Bombay Indian on a gramophone record of long ago, who answered the condescension of a BBC interviewer about an Indian production of "My Fair Lady" with a puzzlement much more august. Sellers makes of hidden tentativeness in aliens an eloquent substitute for the unctuous sexual timidity affected lately in a lot of showbiz comedy, and in his shy characters' flashes of contempt for doggedly functioning civilization there is a noble comic riposte to the put-upon gags of the myriad jokesters who specialize in small-scale middle-class blues.

FICTION

James Baldwin (1924–1987)

James Baldwin was born in Harlem, New York, in 1924. One of nine children, he was profoundly influenced by his father, a preacher and a strict, demanding man who was eventually incarcerated for mental illness. Soon after graduating from high school, Baldwin was determined to become a professional writer. Discouraged by the racial climate in the United States, he moved to France, where he experienced a creative flowering. Gaining fame as both a novelist and essayist, he was soon recognized as one of the most perceptive observers and critics of America and its racial discontents. Much of his work concerns a search for identity and an attempt to reconcile apparently conflicting elements—black–white, heterosexual–homosexual, American–European. Among his best-known works are the novel *Go Tell It on the Mountain* and the collection of essays *The Fire Next Time*.

Sonny's Blues (1957)

I read about it in the paper, in the subway, on my way to work. I read it, and I couldn't believe it, and I read it again. Then perhaps I just stared at it, at the newsprint spelling out his name, spelling out the story. I stared at it in the swinging lights of the subway car, and in the faces and bodies of the people, and in my own face, trapped in the darkness which roared outside.

It was not to be believed and I kept telling myself that, as I walked from the subway station to the high school. And at the same time I couldn't doubt it. I was scared, scared for Sonny. He became real to me again. A great block of ice got settled in my belly and kept melting there slowly all day long, while I taught my classes algebra. It was a special kind of ice. It kept melting, sending trickles of ice water all up and down my veins, but it never got less. Sometimes it hardened and seemed to expand until I felt my guts were going to come spilling out or that I was going to choke or scream. This would always be at a moment when I was remembering some specific thing Sonny had once said or done.

When he was about as old as the boys in my classes his face had been bright and open, there was a lot of copper in it; and he'd had wonderfullydirect brown eyes, and great gentleness and privacy. I wondered what he looked like now. He had been picked up, the evening before, in a raid on an apartment downtown, for peddling and using heroin.

I couldn't believe it: but what I mean by that is that I couldn't find any room for it anywhere inside me. I had kept it outside me for a long time. I hadn't wanted to know. I had had suspicions, but I didn't name them, I keptputting them away. I told myself that Sonny was wild, but he wasn't crazy. And he'd always been a good boy, he hadn't ever turned hard or evil or disrespectful, the way kids can, so quick, so quick, especially in Harlem. I didn't want to believe that I'd ever see my brother going down, coming to nothing, all that light in his face gone out, in the condition I'd already seen so many others. Yet it had happened and here I was, talking about algebra to a lot of boys who might, every one of them for all I knew, be popping off needles every time they went to the head. Maybe it did more for them than algebra could.

I was sure that the first time Sonny had ever had horse, he couldn't have been much older than these boys were now. These boys, now, were living as we'd been living then, they were growing up with a rush and their heads bumped abruptly against the low ceiling of their actual possibilities. They were filled with rage. All they really knew were two darknesses, the darkness of their lives, which was now closing in on them, and the darkness of the movies, which had blinded them to that other darkness, and in which they now, vindictively, dreamed, at once more together than they were at any other time, and more alone.

When the last bell rang, the last class ended, I let out my breath. It seemed I'd been holding it for all that time. My clothes were wet—I may have looked as though I'd been sitting in a steam bath, all dressed up, all afternoon. I sat alone in the classroom a long time. I listened to the boys

5

outside, downstairs, shouting and cursing and laughing. Their laughter struck me for perhaps the first time. It was not the joyous laughter which—God knows why—one associates with children. It was mocking and insular, its intent was to denigrate. It was disenchanted, and in this, also, lay the authority of their curses. Perhaps I was listening to them because I was thinking about my brother and in them I heard my brother. And myself.

One boy was whistling a tune, at once very complicated and very simple, it seemed to be pouring out of him as though he were a bird, and it sounded very cool and moving through all that harsh, bright air, only just holding its own through all those other sounds.

I stood up and walked over to the window and looked down into the courtyard. It was the beginning of the spring and the sap was rising in the boys. A teacher passed through them every now and again, quickly, as though he or she couldn't wait to get out of that courtyard, to get those boys out of their sight and off their minds. I started collecting my stuff. I thought I'd better get home and talk to Isabel.

The courtyard was almost deserted by the time I got downstairs. I saw this boy standing in the shadow of a doorway, looking just like Sonny. I almost called his name. Then I saw that it wasn't Sonny, but somebody we used to know, a boy from around our block. He'd been Sonny's friend. He'd never been mine, having been too young for me, and, anyway, I'd never liked him. And now, even though he was a grown-up man, he still hung around that block, still spent hours on the street corners, was always high and raggy. I used to run into him from time to time and he'd often work around to asking me for a quarter or fifty cents. He always had some real good excuse, too, and I always gave it to him. I don't know why.

But now, abruptly, I hated him. I couldn't stand the way he looked at   10
me, partly like a dog, partly like a cunning child. I wanted to ask him what the hell he was doing in the school courtyard.

He sort of shuffled over to me, and he said, "I see you got the papers. So you already know about it."

"You mean about Sonny? Yes, I already know about it. How come they didn't get you?"

He grinned. It made him repulsive and it also brought to mind what he'd looked like as a kid. "I wasn't there. I stay away from them people."

"Good for you." I offered him a cigarette and I watched him through the smoke. "You come all the way down here just to tell me about Sonny?"

"That's right." He was sort of shaking his head and his eyes looked   15
strange, as though they were about to cross. The bright sun deadened his damp dark brown skin and it made his eyes look yellow and showed up the dirt in his kinked hair. He smelled funky. I moved a little away from him and I said, "Well, thanks. But I already know about it and I got to get home."

"I'll walk you a little ways," he said. We started walking. There were a couple of kids still loitering in the courtyard and one of them said goodnight to me and looked strangely at the boy beside me.

"What're you going to do?" he asked me. "I mean, about Sonny?"

"Look. I haven't seen Sonny for over a year, I'm not sure I'm going to do anything. Anyway, what the hell can I do?"

"That's right," he said quickly, "ain't nothing you can do. Can't much help old Sonny no more, I guess."

It was what I was thinking and so it seemed to me he had no right to say it.   20

"I'm surprised at Sonny, though," he went on—he had a funny way of talking, he looked straight ahead as though he were talking to himself—"I thought Sonny was a smart boy, I thought he was too smart to get hung."

"I guess he thought so too," I said sharply, "and that's how he got hung. And how about you? You're pretty goddamn smart, I bet."

Then he looked directly at me, just for a minute. "I ain't smart," he said. "If I was smart, I'd have reached for a pistol a long time ago."

"Look. Don't tell me your sad story, if it was up to me, I'd give you one." Then I felt guilty—guilty, probably, for never having supposed that the poor bastard had a story of his own, much less a sad one, and I asked, quickly, "What's going to happen to him now?"

He didn't answer this. He was off by himself some place.   25

"Funny thing," he said, and from his tone we might have been discussing the quickest way to get to Brooklyn, "when I saw the papers this morning, the first thing I asked myself was if I had anything to do with it. I felt sort of responsible."

I began to listen more carefully. The subway station was on the corner, just before us, and I stopped. He stopped, too. We were in front of a bar and he ducked slightly, peering in, but whoever he was looking for didn't seem to be there. The juke box was blasting away with something black and bouncy and I half watched the barmaid as she danced her way from the juke box to her place behind the bar. And I watched her face as she laughingly responded to something someone said to her, still keeping time to the music. When she smiled one saw the little girl, one sensed the doomed, still-struggling woman beneath the battered face of the semiwhore.

"I never *give* Sonny nothing," the boy said finally, "but a long time ago I come to school high and Sonny asked me how it felt." He paused, I couldn't bear to watch him, I watched the barmaid, and I listened to the music which seemed to be causing the pavement to shake. "I told him it felt great." The music stopped, the barmaid paused and watched the juke box until the music began again. "It did."

All this was carrying me some place I didn't want to go. I certainly didn't want to know how it felt. It filled everything, the people, the houses, the music, the dark, quicksilver barmaid, with menace; and this menace was their reality.

"What's going to happen to him now?" I asked again.   30

"They'll send him away some place and they'll try to cure him." He shook his head. "Maybe he'll even think he's kicked the habit. Then they'll let him loose"—he gestured, throwing his cigarette into the gutter. "That's all."

"What do you mean, that's *all*?"

But I knew what he meant.

"I *mean*, that's *all*." He turned his head and looked at me, pulling down the corners of his mouth. "Don't you know what I mean?" he asked, softly.

"How the hell *would* I know what you mean?" I almost whispered it,   35 I don't know why.

"That's right," he said to the air, "how would *he* know what I mean?" He turned toward me again, patient and calm, and yet I somehow felt him shaking, shaking as though he were going to fall apart. I felt that ice in my guts again, the dread I'd felt all afternoon; and again I watched the barmaid, moving about the bar, washing glasses, and singing. "Listen. They'll let him out and then it'll just start all over again. That's what I mean."

"You mean—they'll let him out. And then he'll just start working his way back in again. You mean he'll never kick the habit. Is that what you mean?"

"That's right," he said, cheerfully. "*You* see what I mean."

"Tell me," I said at last, "why does he want to die? He must want to die, he's killing himself, why does he want to die?"

He looked at me in surprise. He licked his lips. "He don't want to die.   40 He wants to live. Don't nobody want to die, ever."

Then I wanted to ask him—too many things. He could not have answered, or if he had, I could not have borne the answers. I started walking.

"Well, I guess it's none of my business."

"It's going to be rough on old Sonny," he said. We reached the subway station.

"This is your station?" he asked. I nodded. I took one step down. "Damn!" he said, suddenly. I looked up at him. He grinned again. "Damn it if I didn't leave all my money home. You ain't got a dollar on you, have you? Just for a couple of days, is all."

All at once something inside gave and threatened to come pouring out   45 of me. I didn't hate him any more. I felt that in another moment I'd start crying like a child.

"Sure," I said. "Don't sweat." I looked in my wallet and didn't have a dollar, I only had a five. "Here," I said. "That hold you?"

He didn't look at it—he didn't want to look at it. A terrible, closed look came over his face, as though he were keeping the number on the bill a secret from him and me. "Thanks," he said, and now he was dying to see me go. "Don't worry about Sonny. Maybe I'll write him or something."

"Sure," I said. "You do that. So long."

"Be seeing you," he said. I went on down the steps.

And I didn't write Sonny or send him anything for a long time. When I   50
finally did, it was just after my little girl died, and he wrote me back a letter which made me feel like a bastard.

Here's what he said:

Dear brother,

You don't know how much I needed to hear from you. I wanted to write you many a time but I dug how much I must have hurt you and so I didn't write. But now I feel like a man who's been trying to climb up out of some deep, real deep and funky hole and just saw the sun up there, outside. I got to get outside.

I can't tell you much about how I got here. I mean I don't know how to tell you. I guess I was afraid of something or I was trying to escape from something and you know I have never been very strong in the head (smile). I'm glad Mama and Daddy are dead and can't see what's happened to their son and I swear if I'd known what I was doing I would never have hurt you so, you and a lot of other fine people who were nice to me and who believed in me.

I don't want you to think it had anything to do with me being a musi-   55
cian. It's more than that. Or maybe less than that. I can't get anything straight in my head down here and I try not to think about what's going to happen to me when I get outside again. Sometime I think I'm going to flip and *never* get outside and sometime I think I'll come straight back. I tell you one thing, though, I'd rather blow my brains out than go through this again. But that's what they all say, so they tell me. If I tell you when I'm coming to New York and if you could meet me, I sure would appreciate it. Give my love to Isabel and the kids and I was sure sorry to hear about little Gracie. I wish I could be like Mama and say the Lord's will be done, but I don't know it seems to me that trouble is the one thing that never does get stopped and I don't know what good it does to blame it on the Lord. But maybe it does some good if you believe it.

> Your brother,
> Sonny

Then I kept in constant touch with him and I sent him whatever I could and I went to meet him when he came back to New York. When I saw him

many things I thought I had forgotten came flooding back to me. This was
because I had begun, finally, to wonder about Sonny, about the life that
Sonny lived inside. This life, whatever it was, had made him older and thin-
ner and it had deepened the distant stillness in which he had always moved.
He looked very unlike my baby brother. Yet, when he smiled, when we
shook hands, the baby brother I'd never known looked out from the depths
of his private life, like an animal waiting to be coaxed into the light.

"How you been keeping?" he asked me.

"All right. And you?"

"Just fine." He was smiling all over his face. "It's good to see you again."

"It's good to see you."   60

The seven years' difference in our ages lay between us like a chasm: I
wondered if these years would ever operate between us as a bridge. I was
remembering, and it made it hard to catch my breath, that I had been there
when he was born; and I had heard the first words he had ever spoken.
When he started to walk, he walked from our mother straight to me. I
caught him just before he fell when he took the first steps he ever took in
this world.

"How's Isabel?"

"Just fine. She's dying to see you."

"And the boys?"

"They're fine, too. They're anxious to see their uncle."   65

"Oh, come on. You know they don't remember me."

"Are you kidding? Of course they remember you."

He grinned again. We got into a taxi. We had a lot to say to each other,
far too much to know how to begin.

As the taxi began to move, I asked, "You still want to go to India?"

He laughed. "You still remember that. Hell, no. This place is Indian   70
enough for me."

"It used to belong to them," I said.

And he laughed again. "They damn sure knew what they were doing
when they got rid of it."

Years ago, when he was around fourteen, he'd been all hipped on the
idea of going to India. He read books about people sitting on rocks, naked,
in all kinds of weather, but mostly bad, naturally, and walking barefoot
through hot coals and arriving at wisdom. I used to say that it sounded to
me as though they were getting away from wisdom as fast as they could.
I think he sort of looked down on me for that.

"Do you mind," he asked, "if we have the driver drive alongside the
park? On the west side—I haven't seen the city in so long."

"Of course not," I said. I was afraid that I might sound as though   75
I were humoring him, but I hoped he wouldn't take it that way.

So we drove along, between the green of the park and the stony, lifeless elegance of hotels and apartment buildings, toward the vivid, killing streets of our childhood. These streets hadn't changed, though housing projects jutted up out of them now like rocks in the middle of a boiling sea. Most of the houses in which we had grown up had vanished, as had the stores from which we had stolen, the basements in which we had first tried sex, the rooftops from which we had hurled tin cans and bricks. But houses exactly like the houses of our past yet dominated the landscape, boys exactly like the boys we once had been found themselves smothering in these houses, came down into the streets for light and air and found themselves encircled by disaster. Some escaped the trap, most didn't. Those who got out always left something of themselves behind, as some animals amputate a leg and leave it in the trap. It might be said, perhaps, that I had escaped, after all, I was a school teacher; or that Sonny had, he hadn't lived in Harlem for years. Yet, as the cab moved uptown through streets which seemed, with a rush, to darken with dark people, and as I covertly studied Sonny's face, it came to me that what we both were seeking through our separate cab windows was that part of ourselves which had been left behind. It's always at the hour of trouble and confrontation that the missing member aches.

We hit 110th Street and started rolling up Lenox Avenue. And I'd known this avenue all my life, but it seemed to me again, as it had seemed on the day I'd first heard about Sonny's trouble, filled with a hidden menace which was its very breath of life.

"We almost there," said Sonny.

"Almost." We were both too nervous to say anything more.

We live in a housing project. It hasn't been up long. A few days after it   80
was up it seemed uninhabitably new, now, of course, it's already rundown. It looks like a parody of the good, clean, faceless life—God knows the people who live in it do their best to make it a parody. The beat-looking grass lying around isn't enough to make their lives green, the hedges will never hold out the streets, and they know it. The big windows fool no one, they aren't big enough to make space out of no space. They don't bother with the windows, they watch the TV screen instead. The playground is most popular with the children who don't play at jacks, or skip rope, or roller skate, or swing, and they can be found in it after dark. We moved in partly because it's not too far from where I teach, and partly for the kids; but it's really just like the houses in which Sonny and I grew up. The same things happen, they'll have the same things to remember. The moment Sonny and I started into the house I had the feeling that I was simply bringing him back into the danger he had almost died trying to escape.

Sonny has never been talkative. So I don't know why I was sure he'd be dying to talk to me when supper was over the first night. Everything went fine, the oldest boy remembered him, and the youngest boy liked him, and Sonny had remembered to bring something for each of them; and Isabel, who is really much nicer than I am, more open and giving, had gone to a lot of trouble about dinner and was genuinely glad to see him. And she's always been able to tease Sonny in a way that I haven't. It was nice to see her face so vivid again and to hear her laugh and watch her make Sonny laugh. She wasn't, or, anyway, she didn't seem to be, at all uneasy or embarrassed. She chatted as though there were no subject which had to be avoided and she got Sonny past his first, faint stiffness. And thank God she was there, for I was filled with that icy dread again. Everything I did seemed awkward to me, and everything I said sounded freighted with hidden meaning. I was trying to remember everything I'd heard about dope addiction and I couldn't help watching Sonny for signs. I wasn't doing it out of malice. I was trying to find out something about my brother. I was dying to hear him tell me he was safe.

"Safe!" my father grunted, whenever Mama suggested trying to move to a neighborhood which might be safer for children. "Safe, hell! Ain't no place safe for kids, nor nobody."

He always went on like this, but he wasn't, ever, really as bad as he sounded, not even on weekends, when he got drunk. As a matter of fact, he was always on the lookout for "something a little better," but he died before he found it. He died suddenly, during a drunken weekend in the middle of the war, when Sonny was fifteen. He and Sonny hadn't ever got on too well. And this was partly because Sonny was the apple of his father's eye. It was because he loved Sonny so much and was frightened for him, that he was always fighting with him. It doesn't do any good to fight with Sonny. Sonny just moves back, inside himself, where he can't be reached. But the principal reason that they never hit it off is that they were so much alike. Daddy was big and rough and loud-talking, just the opposite of Sonny, but they both had— that same privacy.

Mama tried to tell me something about this, just after Daddy died. I was home on leave from the army.

This was the last time I ever saw my mother alive. Just the same, this picture gets all mixed up in my mind with pictures I had of her when she was younger. The way I always see her is the way she used to be on a Sunday afternoon, say, when the old folks were talking after the big Sunday dinner. I always see her wearing pale blue. She'd be sitting on the sofa. And my father would be sitting in the easy chair, not far from her. And the living room would be full of church folks and relatives. There they sit, in chairs all around the living room, and the night is creeping up outside, but nobody knows it yet. You can see the darkness growing against the windowpanes and you hear

85

the street noises every now and again, or maybe the jangling beat of a tambourine from one of the churches close by, but it's real quiet in the room. For a moment nobody's talking, but every face looks darkening, like the sky outside. And my mother rocks a little from the waist, and my father's eyes are closed. Everyone is looking at something a child can't see. For a minute they've forgotten the children. Maybe a kid is lying on the rug, half asleep. Maybe somebody's got a kid in his lap and is absentmindedly stroking the kid's head. Maybe there's a kid, quiet and big-eyed, curled up in a big chair in the corner. The silence, the darkness coming, and the darkness in the faces frighten the child obscurely. He hopes that the hand which strokes his forehead will never stop—will never die. He hopes that there will never come a time when the old folks won't be sitting around the living room, talking about where they've come from, and what they've seen, and what's happened to them and their kinfolk.

But something deep and watchful in the child knows that this is bound to end, is already ending. In a moment someone will get up and turn on the light. Then the old folks will remember the children and they won't talk any more that day. And when light fills the room, the child is filled with darkness. He knows that every time this happens he's moved just a little closer to that darkness outside. The darkness outside is what the old folks have been talking about. It's what they've come from. It's what they endure. The child knows that they won't talk any more because if he knows too much about what's happened to *them*, he'll know too much too soon, about what's going to happen to *him*.

The last time I talked to my mother, I remember I was restless. I wanted to get out and see Isabel. We weren't married then and we had a lot to straighten out between us.

There Mama sat, in black, by the window. She was humming an old church song, *Lord, you brought me from a long ways off*. Sonny was out somewhere. Mama kept watching the streets.

"I don't know," she said, "if I'll ever see you again, after you go off from here. But I hope you'll remember the things I tried to teach you."

"Don't talk like that," I said, and smiled. "You'll be here a long time yet." 90

She smiled, too, but she said nothing. She was quiet for a long time. And I said, "Mama, don't you worry about nothing. I'll be writing all the time, and you be getting the checks...."

"I want to talk to you about your brother," she said, suddenly. "If anything happens to me he ain't going to have nobody to look out for him."

"Mama," I said, "ain't nothing going to happen to you or Sonny. Sonny's all right. He's a good boy and he's got good sense."

"It ain't a question of his being a good boy," Mama said, "nor of his having good sense. It ain't only the bad ones, nor yet the dumb ones that gets sucked under." She stopped, looking at me. "Your Daddy once had a

brother," she said, and she smiled in a way that made me feel she was in
pain. "You didn't never know that, did you?"

"No," I said, "I never knew that," and I watched her face.   95

"Oh, yes," she said, "your Daddy had a brother." She looked out of the
window again. "I know you never saw your Daddy cry. But *I* did—many a
time, through all these years."

I asked her, "What happened to his brother? How come nobody's ever
talked about him?"

This was the first time I ever saw my mother look old.

"His brother got killed," she said, "when he was just a little younger
than you are now. I knew him. He was a fine boy. He was maybe a little full
of the devil, but he didn't mean nobody no harm."

Then she stopped and the room was silent, exactly as it had sometimes   100
been on those Sunday afternoons. Mama kept looking out into the streets.

"He used to have a job in the mill," she said, "and, like all young folks,
he just liked to perform on Saturday nights. Saturday nights, him and your
father would drift around to different places, go to dances and things like
that, or just sit around with people they knew, and your father's brother
would sing, he had a fine voice, and play along with himself on his guitar.
Well, this particular Saturday night, him and your father was coming home
from some place, and they were both a little drunk and there was a moon
that night, it was bright like day. Your father's brother was feeling kind of
good, and he was whistling to himself, and he had his guitar slung over his
shoulder. They was coming down a hill and beneath them was a road that
turned off from the highway. Well, your father's brother, being always kind
of frisky, decided to run down this hill, and he did, with that guitar banging
and clanging behind him, and he ran across the road, and he was making
water behind a tree. And your father was sort of amused at him and he was
still coming down the hill, kind of slow. Then he heard a car motor and
that same minute his brother stepped from behind the tree, into the road,
in the moonlight. And he started to cross the road. And your father started
to run down the hill, he says he don't know why. This car was full of white
men. They was all drunk, and when they seen your father's brother they let
out a great whoop and holler and they aimed the car straight at him. They
was having fun, they just wanted to scare him, the way they do sometimes,
you know. But they was drunk. And I guess the boy, being drunk, too, and
scared, kind of lost his head. By the time he jumped it was too late. Your
father says he heard his brother scream when the car rolled over him, and
he heard the wood of that guitar when it give, and he heard them strings go
flying, and he heard them white men shouting, and the car kept on a-going
and it ain't stopped till this day. And, time your father got down the hill, his
brother weren't nothing but blood and pulp."

Tears were gleaming on my mother's face. There wasn't anything I could say.

"He never mentioned it," she said, "because I never let him mention it before you children. Your Daddy was like a crazy man that night and for many a night thereafter. He says he never in his life seen anything as dark as that road after the lights of that car had gone away. Weren't nothing, weren't nobody on that road, just your Daddy and his brother and that busted guitar. Oh, yes. Your Daddy never did really get right again. Till the day he died he weren't sure but that every white man he saw was the man that killed his brother."

She stopped and took out her handkerchief and dried her eyes and looked at me.

"I ain't telling you all this," she said, "to make you scared or bitter or to make you hate nobody. I'm telling you this because you got a brother. And the world ain't changed." 105

I guess I didn't want to believe this. I guess she saw this in my face. She turned away from me, toward the window again, searching those streets.

"But I praise my Redeemer," she said at last, "that He called your Daddy home before me. I ain't saying it to throw no flowers at myself, but, I declare, it keeps me from feeling too cast down to know I helped your father get safely through this world. Your father always acted like he was the roughest, strongest man on earth. And everybody took him to be like that. But if he hadn't had me there—to see his tears!"

She was crying again. Still, I couldn't move. I said, "Lord, Lord, Mama, I didn't know it was like that."

"Oh, honey," she said, "there's a lot that you don't know. But you are going to find out." She stood up from the window and came over to me. "You got to hold on to your brother," she said, "and don't let him fall, no matter what it looks like is happening to him and no matter how evil you gets with him. You going to be evil with him many a time. But don't you forget what I told you, you hear?"

"I won't forget," I said. "Don't you worry, I won't forget. I won't let nothing happen to Sonny." 110

My mother smiled as though she was amused at something she saw in my face. Then, "You may not be able to stop nothing from happening. But you got to let him know you's *there*."

Two days later I was married, and then I was gone. And I had a lot of things on my mind and I pretty well forgot my promise to Mama until I got shipped home on a special furlough for her funeral.

And, after the funeral, with just Sonny and me alone in the empty kitchen, I tried to find out something about him.

"What do you want to do?" I asked him.

"I'm going to be a musician," he said. 115

For he had graduated, in the time I had been away, from dancing to the juke box to finding out who was playing what, and what they were doing with it, and he had bought himself a set of drums.

"You mean, you want to be a drummer?" I somehow had the feeling that being a drummer might be all right for other people but not for my brother Sonny.

"I don't think," he said, looking at me very gravely, "that I'll ever be a good drummer. But I think I can play a piano."

I frowned. I'd never played the role of the oldest brother quite so seriously before, had scarcely ever, in fact, *asked* Sonny a damn thing. I sensed myself in the presence of something I didn't really know how to handle, didn't understand. So I made my frown a little deeper as I asked: "What kind of musician do you want to be?"

He grinned. "How many kinds do you think there are?"   120

"Be *serious*," I said.

He laughed, throwing his head back, and then looked at me. "I *am* serious."

"Well, then, for Christ's sake, stop kidding around and answer a serious question. I mean, do you want to be a concert pianist, you want to play classical music and all that, or—or what?" Long before I finished he was laughing again. "For Christ's *sake*, Sonny!"

He sobered, but with difficulty. "I'm sorry. But you sound so—*scared*!" and he was off again.

"Well, you may think it's funny now, baby, but it's not going to be so   125
funny when you have to make your living at it, let me tell you *that*." I was furious because I knew he was laughing at me and I didn't know why.

"No," he said, very sober now, and afraid, perhaps, that he'd hurt me, "I don't want to be a classical pianist. That isn't what interests me. I mean"—he paused, looking hard at me, as though his eyes would help me to understand, and then gestured helplessly, as though perhaps his hand would help—"I mean, I'll have a lot of studying to do, and I'll have to study *everything*, but, I mean, I want to play *with*—jazz musicians." He stopped. "I want to play jazz," he said.

Well, the word had never before sounded as heavy, as real, as it sounded that afternoon in Sonny's mouth. I just looked at him and I was probably frowning a real frown by this time. I simply couldn't see why on earth he'd want to spend his time hanging around nightclubs, clowning around on bandstands, while people pushed each other around a dance floor. It seemed—beneath him, somehow. I had never thought about it before, had never been forced to, but I suppose I had always put jazz musicians in a class with what Daddy called "good-time people."

"Are you *serious*?"

"Hell, *yes*, I'm serious."

He looked more helpless than ever, and annoyed, and deeply hurt.   130

I suggested, helpfully: "You mean—like Louis Armstrong?"

His face closed as though I'd struck him. "No. I'm not talking about none of that old-time, down home crap."

"Well, look, Sonny, I'm sorry, don't get mad. I just don't altogether get it, that's all. Name somebody—you know, a jazz musician you admire."

"Bird."

"Who?"   135

"Bird! Charlie Parker! Don't they teach you nothing in the goddamn army?"

I lit a cigarette. I was surprised and then a little amused to discover that I was trembling. "I've been out of touch," I said. "You'll have to be patient with me. Now. Who's this Parker character?"

"He's just one of the greatest jazz musicians alive," said Sonny, sullenly, his hands in his pockets, his back to me. "Maybe *the* greatest," he added, bitterly, "that's probably why *you* never heard of him."

"All right," I said, "I'm ignorant. I'm sorry. I'll go out and buy all the cat's records right away, all right?"

"It don't," said Sonny, with dignity, "make any difference to me.   140
I don't care what you listen to. Don't do me no favors."

I was beginning to realize that I'd never seen him so upset before. With another part of my mind I was thinking that this would probably turn out to be one of those things kids go through and that I shouldn't make it seem important by pushing it too hard. Still, I didn't think it would do any harm to ask: "Doesn't all this take a lot of time? Can you make a living at it?"

He turned back to me and half leaned, half sat, on the kitchen table. "Everything takes time," he said, "and—well, yes, sure, I can make a living at it. But what I don't seem to be able to make you understand is that it's the only thing I want to do."

"Well, Sonny," I said gently, "you know people can't always do exactly what they *want* to do—"

"*No*, I don't know that," said Sonny, surprising me. "I think people *ought* to do what they want to do, what else are they alive for?"

"You getting to be a big boy," I said desperately, "it's time you started   145
thinking about your future."

"I'm thinking about my future," said Sonny, grimly. "I think about it all the time."

I gave up. I decided, if he didn't change his mind, that we could always talk about it later. "In the meantime," I said, "you got to finish school." We had already decided that he'd have to move in with Isabel and her folks. I knew this wasn't the ideal arrangement because Isabel's folks are inclined to be dicty and they hadn't especially wanted Isabel to marry me. But I didn't know what else to do. "And we have to get you fixed up at Isabel's."

There was a long silence. He moved from the kitchen table to the window. "That's a terrible idea. You know it yourself."

"Do you have a *better* idea?"

He just walked up and down the kitchen for a minute. He was as tall as 150 I was. He had started to shave. I suddenly had the feeling that I didn't know him at all.

He stopped at the kitchen table and picked up my cigarettes. Looking at me with a kind of mocking, amused defiance, he put one between his lips. "You mind?"

"You smoking already?"

He lit the cigarette and nodded, watching me through the smoke. "I just wanted to see if I'd have the courage to smoke in front of you." He grinned and blew a great cloud of smoke to the ceiling. "It was easy." He looked at my face. "Come on, now. I bet you was smoking at my age, tell the truth."

I didn't say anything but the truth was on my face, and he laughed. But now there was something very strained in his laugh. "Sure. And I bet that ain't all you was doing."

He was frightening me a little. "Cut the crap," I said. "We already 155 decided that you was going to go and live at Isabel's. Now what's got into you all of a sudden?"

"*You* decided it," he pointed out. "*I* didn't decide nothing." He stopped in front of me, leaning against the stove, arms loosely folded. "Look, brother. I don't want to stay in Harlem no more, I really don't." He was very earnest. He looked at me, then over toward the kitchen window. There was something in his eyes I'd never seen before, some thoughtfulness, some worry all his own. He rubbed the muscle of one arm. "It's time I was getting out of here."

"Where do you want to *go*, Sonny?"

"I want to join the army. Or the navy, I don't care. If I say I'm old enough, they'll believe me."

Then I got mad. It was because I was so scared. "You must be crazy. You goddamn fool, what the hell do you want to go and join the *army* for?"

"I just told you. To get out of Harlem." 160

"Sonny, you haven't even finished *school*. And if you really want to be a musician, how do you expect to study if you're in the *army*?"

He looked at me, trapped, and in anguish. "There's ways. I might be able to work out some kind of deal. Anyway, I'll have the G.I. Bill when I come out."

"*If* you come out." We stared at each other. "Sonny, please. Be reasonable. I know the setup is far from perfect. But we got to do the best we can."

"I ain't learning nothing in school," he said. "Even when I go." He turned away from me and opened the window and threw his cigarette out into the narrow alley. I watched his back. "At least, I ain't learning nothing you'd want me to learn." He slammed the window so hard I thought the glass would fly out, and turned back to me. "And I'm sick of the stink of these garbage cans!"

"Sonny," I said, "I know how you feel. But if you don't finish school   165
now, you're going to be sorry later that you didn't." I grabbed him by the shoulders. "And you only got another year. It ain't so bad. And I'll come back and I swear I'll help you do *whatever* you want to do. Just try to put up with it till I come back. Will you please do that? For me?"

He didn't answer and he wouldn't look at me.

"Sonny. You hear me?"

He pulled away. "I hear you. But you never hear anything *I* say."

I didn't know what to say to that. He looked out of the window and then back at me. "OK," he said, and sighed. "I'll try."

Then I said, trying to cheer him up a little, "They got a piano at   170
Isabel's. You can practice on it."

And as a matter of fact, it did cheer him up for a minute. "That's right," he said to himself. "I forgot that." His face relaxed a little. But the worry, the thoughtfulness, played on it still, the way shadows play on a face which is staring into the fire.

But I thought I'd never hear the end of that piano. At first, Isabel would write me, saying how nice it was that Sonny was so serious about his music and how, as soon as he came in from school, or wherever he had been when he was supposed to be at school, he went straight to that piano and stayed there until suppertime. And, after supper, he went back to that piano and stayed there until everybody went to bed. He was at the piano all day Saturday and all day Sunday. Then he bought a record player and started playing records. He'd play one record over and over again, all day long sometimes, and he'd improvise along with it on the piano. Or he'd play one section of the record, one chord, one change, one progression, then he'd do it on the piano. Then back to the record. Then back to the piano.

Well, I really don't know how they stood it. Isabel finally confessed that it wasn't like living with a person at all, it was like living with sound. And the sound didn't make any sense to her, didn't make any sense to any of them—naturally. They began, in a way, to be afflicted by this presence that was living in their home. It was as though Sonny were some sort of god, or monster. He moved in an atmosphere which wasn't like theirs at all. They fed him and he ate, he washed himself, he walked in and out of their door; he certainly wasn't nasty or unpleasant or rude, Sonny isn't any of those things; but it was as though he were all wrapped up in some cloud, some fire, some vision all his own; and there wasn't any way to reach him.

At the same time, he wasn't really a man yet, he was still a child, and they had to watch out for him in all kinds of ways. They certainly couldn't throw him out. Neither did they dare to make a great scene about that piano because even they dimly sensed, as I sensed, from so many thousands of miles away, that Sonny was at that piano playing for his life.

But he hadn't been going to school. One day a letter came from the   175
school board and Isabel's mother got it—there had, apparently, been other letters but Sonny had torn them up. This day, when Sonny came in, Isabel's mother showed him the letter and asked where he'd been spending his time. And she finally got it out of him that he'd been down in Greenwich Village, with musicians and other characters, in a white girl's apartment. And this scared her and she started to scream at him and what came up, once she began—though she denies it to this day—was what sacrifices they were making to give Sonny a decent home and how little he appreciated it.

Sonny didn't play the piano that day. By evening, Isabel's mother had calmed down but then there was the old man to deal with, and Isabel herself. Isabel says she did her best to be calm but she broke down and started crying. She says she just watched Sonny's face. She could tell, by watching him, what was happening with him. And what was happening was that they penetrated his cloud, they had reached him. Even if their fingers had been a thousand times more gentle than human fingers ever are, he could hardly help feeling that they had stripped him naked and were spitting on that nakedness. For he also had to see that his presence, that music, which was life or death to him, had been torture for them and that they had endured it, not at all for his sake, but only for mine. And Sonny couldn't take that. He can take it a little better today than he could then but he's still not very good at it and, frankly, I don't know anybody who is.

The silence of the next few days must have been louder than the sound of all the music ever played since time began. One morning, before she went to work, Isabel was in his room for something and she suddenly realized that all of his records were gone. And she knew for certain that he was gone. And he was. He went as far as the navy would carry him. He finally sent me a postcard from some place in Greece and that was the first I knew that Sonny was still alive. I didn't see him any more until we were both back in New York and the war had long been over.

He was a man by then, of course, but I wasn't willing to see it. He came by the house from time to time, but we fought almost every time we met. I didn't like the way he carried himself, loose and dreamlike all the time, and I didn't like his friends, and his music seemed to be merely an excuse for the life he led. It sounded just that weird and disordered.

Then we had a fight, a pretty awful fight, and I didn't see him for months. By and by I looked him up, where he was living, in a furnished room in the Village, and I tried to make it up. But there were lots of other people in the room and Sonny just lay on his bed, and he wouldn't come downstairs with me, and he treated these other people as though they were his family and I weren't. So I got mad and then he got mad, and then I told him that he might just as well be dead as live the way he was living. Then he stood up and he told me not to worry about him any more in life, that he *was* dead as far as I was concerned. Then he pushed me to the door and the other people looked on as though nothing were happening, and he slammed the door behind me. I stood in the hallway, staring at the door. I heard somebody laugh in the room and then the tears came to my eyes. I started down the steps, whistling to keep from crying, I kept whistling to myself, *You going to need me, baby, one of these cold, rainy days.*

I read about Sonny's trouble in the spring. Little Grace died in the fall. 180 She was a beautiful little girl. But she only lived a little over two years. She died of polio and she suffered. She had a slight fever for a couple of days, but it didn't seem like anything and we just kept her in bed. And we would certainly have called the doctor, but the fever dropped, she seemed to be all right. So we thought it had just been a cold. Then, one day, she was up, playing, Isabel was in the kitchen fixing lunch for the two boys when they'd come in from school, and she heard Grace fall down in the living room. When you have a lot of children you don't always start running when one of them falls, unless they start screaming or something. And, this time, Gracie was quiet. Yet, Isabel says that when she heard that *thump* and then that silence, something happened to her to make her afraid. And she ran to the living room and there was little Grace on the floor, all twisted up, and the reason she hadn't screamed was that she couldn't get her breath. And when she did scream, it was the worst sound, Isabel says, that she'd ever heard in all her life, and she still hears it sometimes in her dreams. Isabel will sometimes wake me up with a low, moaning, strangling sound and I have to be quick to awaken her and hold her to me and where Isabel is weeping against me seems a mortal wound.

I think I may have written Sonny the very day that little Grace was buried. I was sitting in the living room in the dark, by myself, and I suddenly thought of Sonny. My trouble made his real.

One Saturday afternoon, when Sonny had been living with us, or anyway, been in our house, for nearly two weeks, I found myself wandering aimlessly about the living room, drinking from a can of beer, and trying to work up courage to search Sonny's room. He was out, he was usually out whenever I was home, and Isabel had taken the children to see their grandparents. Suddenly I was standing still in front of the living room window, watching Seventh

Avenue. The idea of searching Sonny's room made me still. I scarcely dared to admit to myself what I'd be searching for. I didn't know what I'd do if I found it. Or if I didn't.

On the sidewalk across from me, near the entrance to a barbecue joint, some people were holding an old-fashioned revival meeting. The barbecue cook, wearing a dirty white apron, his conked hair reddish and metallic in the pale sun, and a cigarette between his lips, stood in the doorway, watching them. Kids and older people paused in their errands and stood there, along with some older men and a couple of very tough-looking women who watched everything that happened on the avenue, as though they owned it, or were maybe owned by it. Well, they were watching this, too. The revival was being carried on by three sisters in black, and a brother. All they had were their voices and their Bibles and a tambourine. The brother was testifying and while he testified two of the sisters stood together, seeming to say, amen, and the third sister walked around with the tambourine outstretched and a couple of people dropped coins into it. Then the brother's testimony ended and the sister who had been taking up the collection dumped the coins into her palm and transferred them to the pocket of her long black robe. Then she raised both hands, striking the tambourine against the air, and then against one hand, and she started to sing. And the two other sisters and the brother joined in.

It was strange, suddenly, to watch, though I had been seeing these meetings all my life. So, of course, had everybody else down there. Yet, they paused and watched and listened and I stood still at the window. "*'Tis the old ship of Zion*," they sang, and the sister with the tambourine kept a steady, jangling beat, "*it has rescued many a thousand!*" Not a soul under the sound of their voices was hearing this song for the first time, not one of them had been rescued. Nor had they seen much in the way of rescue work being done around them. Neither did they especially believe in the holiness of the three sisters and the brother, they knew too much about them, knew where they lived, and how. The woman with the tambourine, whose voice dominated the air, whose face was bright with joy, was divided by very little from the woman who stood watching her, a cigarette between her heavy, chapped lips, her hair a cuckoo's nest, her face scarred and swollen from many beatings, and her black eyes glittering like coal. Perhaps they both knew this, which was why, when, as rarely, they addressed each other, they addressed each other as Sister. As the singing filled the air the watching, listening faces underwent a change, the eyes focusing on something within; the music seemed to soothe a poison out of them; and time seemed, nearly, to fall away from the sullen, belligerent, battered faces, as though they were fleeing back to their first condition, while dreaming of their last. The bar-becue cook half shook his head and smiled, and dropped his cigarette and disappeared into his joint. A man fumbled in his pockets for change and stood holding it in his hand impatiently, as though he had just remembered a pressing appointment further up the avenue. He looked furious. Then I saw Sonny, standing on the edge of the crowd. He was carrying a wide, flat notebook with a green cover, and it made him look, from where I was standing, almost like a schoolboy. The coppery sun brought out the copper in his skin, he was very faintly smiling, standing very still. Then the singing stopped, the tambourine turned into a collection plate again. The furious man dropped in his coins and vanished, so did a couple of the women, and Sonny dropped some change in the plate, looking directly at the woman with a little smile. He started across the avenue, toward the house. He has a slow, loping walk, something like the way Harlem hipsters walk, only he's imposed on this his own half-beat. I had never really noticed it before.

I stayed at the window, both relieved and apprehensive. As Sonny   185 disappeared from my sight, they began singing again. And they were still singing when his key turned in the lock.

"Hey," he said.

"Hey, yourself. You want some beer?"

"No. Well, maybe." But he came up to the window and stood beside me, looking out. "What a warm voice," he said.

They were singing *If I could only hear my mother pray again!*

"Yes," I said, "and she can sure beat that tambourine."   190

"But what a terrible song," he said, and laughed. He dropped his notebook on the sofa and disappeared into the kitchen. "Where's Isabel and the kids?"

"I think they went to see their grandparents. You hungry?"

"No." He came back into the living room with his can of beer. "You want to come some place with me tonight?"

I sensed, I don't know how, that I couldn't possibly say no. "Sure. Where?"

He sat down on the sofa and picked up his notebook and started   195 leafing through it. "I'm going to sit in with some fellows in a joint in the Village."

"You mean, you're going to play, tonight?"

"That's right." He took a swallow of his beer and moved back to the window. He gave me a sidelong look. "If you can stand it."

"I'll try," I said.

He smiled to himself and we both watched as the meeting across the way broke up. The three sisters and the brother, heads bowed, were singing *God be with you till we meet again.* The faces around them were very quiet. Then the song ended. The small crowd dispersed. We watched the three women and the lone man walk slowly up the avenue.

"When she was singing before," said Sonny, abruptly, "her voice 200
reminded me for a minute of what heroin feels like sometimes—when it's in
your veins. It makes you feel sort of warm and cool at the same time. And
distant. And—and sure." He sipped his beer, very deliberately not looking at
me. I watched his face. "It makes you feel—in control. Sometimes you've got
to have that feeling."

"Do you?" I sat down slowly in the easy chair.

"Sometimes." He went to the sofa and picked up his notebook again.
"Some people do."

"In order," I asked, "to play?" And my voice was very ugly, full of
contempt and anger.

"Well"—he looked at me with great, troubled eyes, as though, in fact,
he hoped his eyes would tell me things he could never otherwise say— "they
think so. And *if* they think so—!"

"And what do *you* think?" I asked. 205

He sat on the sofa and put his can of beer on the floor. "I don't know,"
he said, and I couldn't be sure if he were answering my question or pursuing his thoughts. His face didn't tell me. "It's not so much to *play*. It's to
stand it, to be able to make it at all. On any level." He frowned and smiled:
"In order to keep from shaking to pieces."

"But these friends of yours," I said, "they seem to shake themselves to
pieces pretty goddamn fast."

"Maybe." He played with the notebook. And something told me that I
should curb my tongue, that Sonny was doing his best to talk, that I should
listen. "But of course you only know the ones that've gone to pieces. Some
don't—or at least they haven't *yet* and that's just about all *any* of us can say."
He paused. "And then there are some who just live, really, in hell, and they
know it and they see what's happening and they go right on. I don't know."
He sighed, dropped the notebook, folded his arms. "Some guys, you can
tell from the way they play, they on something *all* the time. And you can
see that, well, it makes something real for them. But of course," he picked
up his beer from the floor and sipped it and put the can down again, "they
want to, too, you've got to see that. Even some of them that say they don't—
some, not all."

"And what about you?" I asked—I couldn't help it. "What about you?
Do *you* want to?"

He stood up and walked to the window and I remained silent for a 210
long time. Then he sighed. "Me," he said. Then: "While I was downstairs
before, on my way here, listening to that woman sing, it struck me all of a
sudden how much suffering she must have had to go through—to sing like
that. It's *repulsive* to think you have to suffer that much."

I said: "But there's no way not to suffer—is there, Sonny?"

"I believe not," he said and smiled, "but that's never stopped anyone from trying." He looked at me. "Has it?" I realized, with this mocking look, that there stood between us, forever, beyond the power of time or forgiveness, the fact that I had held silence—so long!—when he had needed human speech to help him. He turned back to the window. "No, there's no way not to suffer. But you try all kinds of ways to keep from drowning in it, to keep on top of it, and to make it seem—well, like you. Like you did something, all right, and now you're suffering for it. You know?" I said nothing. "Well you know," he said, impatiently, "why do people suffer? Maybe it's better to do something to give it a reason, *any* reason."

"But we just agreed," I said, "that there's no way not to suffer. Isn't it better, then, just to—take it?"

"But nobody just takes it," Sonny cried, "that's what I'm telling you! *Everybody* tries not to. You're just hung up on the *way* some people try—it's not *your* way!"

The hair on my face began to itch, my face felt wet. "That's not true,"   215
I said, "that's not true. I don't give a damn what other people do, I don't even care how they suffer. I just care how *you* suffer." And he looked at me. "Please believe me," I said, "I don't want to see you—die—trying not to suffer."

"I won't," he said flatly, "die trying not to suffer. At least, not any faster than anybody else."

"But there's no need," I said, trying to laugh, "is there? in killing yourself."

I wanted to say more, but I couldn't. I wanted to talk about will power and how life could be—well, beautiful. I wanted to say that it was all within; but was it? or, rather, wasn't that exactly the trouble? And I wanted to promise that I would never fail him again. But it would all have sounded— empty words and lies.

So I made the promise to myself and prayed that I would keep it.

"It's terrible sometimes, inside," he said, "that's what's the trouble.   220
You walk these streets, black and funky and cold, and there's not really a living ass to talk to, and there's nothing shaking, and there's no way of getting it out—that storm inside. You can't talk it and you can't make love with it, and when you finally try to get with it and play it, you realize *nobody's* listening. So *you've* got to listen. You got to find a way to listen."

And then he walked away from the window and sat on the sofa again, as though all the wind had suddenly been knocked out of him. "Sometimes you'll do *anything* to play, even cut your mother's throat." He laughed and looked at me. "Or your brother's." Then he sobered. "Or your own." Then: "Don't worry. I'm all right now and I think I'll *be* all right. But I can't forget—where I've been. I don't mean just the physical place I've been, I mean where I've *been*. And *what* I've been."

"What have you been, Sonny?" I asked.

He smiled—but sat sideways on the sofa, his elbow resting on the back, his fingers playing with his mouth and chin, not looking at me. "I've been something I didn't recognize, didn't know I could be. Didn't know anybody could be." He stopped, looking inward, looking helplessly young, looking old. "I'm not talking about it now because I feel *guilty* or anything like that—maybe it would be better if I did, I don't know. Anyway, I can't really talk about it. Not to you, not to anybody," and now he turned and faced me. "Sometimes, you know, and it was actually when I was most out of the world, I felt that I was in it, that I was *with* it, really, and I could play or I didn't really have to *play*, it just came out of me, it was there. And I don't know how I played, thinking about it now, but I know I did awful things, those times, sometimes, to people. Or it wasn't that I *did* anything to them—it was that they weren't real." He picked up the beer can; it was empty; he rolled it between his palms: "And other times—well, I needed a fix, I needed to find a place to lean, I needed to clear a space to *listen*—and I couldn't find it, and I—went crazy, I did terrible things to *me*, I was terrible *for* me." He began pressing the beer can between his hands, I watched the metal begin to give. It glittered, as he played with it like a knife, and I was afraid he would cut himself, but I said nothing. "Oh well. I can never tell you. I was all by myself at the bottom of something, stinking and sweating and crying and shaking, and I smelled it, you know? *my* stink, and I thought I'd die if I couldn't get away from it and yet, all the same, I knew that everything I was doing was just locking me in with it. And I didn't know," he paused, still flattening the beer can, "I didn't know, I still *don't* know, something kept telling me that maybe it was good to smell your own stink, but I didn't think that *that* was what I'd been trying to do—and—who can stand it?" and he abruptly dropped the ruined beer can, looking at me with a small, still smile, and then rose, walking to the window as though it were the lodestone rock. I watched his face, he watched the avenue. "I couldn't tell you when Mama died—but the reason I wanted to leave Harlem so bad was to get away from drugs. And then, when I ran away, that's what I was running from—really. When I came back, nothing had changed, *I* hadn't changed, I was just—older." And he stopped, drumming with his fingers on the windowpane. The sun had vanished, soon darkness would fall. I watched his face. "It can come again," he said, almost as though speaking to himself. Then he turned to me. "It can come again," he repeated. "I just want you to know that."

"All right," I said, at last. "So it can come again. All right."

He smiled, but the smile was sorrowful. "I had to try to tell you," he said.

"Yes," I said. "I understand that."

225

"You're my brother," he said, looking straight at me, and not smiling
at all.

"Yes," I repeated, "yes. I understand that."

He turned back to the window, looking out. "All that hatred down
there," he said, "all that hatred and misery and love. It's a wonder it doesn't
blow the avenue apart."

We went to the only nightclub on a short, dark street, downtown. We   230
squeezed through the narrow, chattering, jampacked bar to the entrance of
the big room, where the bandstand was. And we stood there for a moment,
for the lights were very dim in this room and we couldn't see. Then, "Hello,
boy," said the voice and an enormous black man, much older than Sonny or
myself, erupted out of all that atmospheric lighting and put an arm around
Sonny's shoulder. "I been sitting right here," he said, "waiting for you."

He had a big voice, too, and heads in the darkness turned toward us.

Sonny grinned and pulled a little away, and said, "Creole, this is my
brother. I told you about him."

Creole shook my hand. "I'm glad to meet you, son," he said, and it was
clear that he was glad to meet me *there*, for Sonny's sake. And he smiled,
"You got a real musician in *your* family," and he took his arm from Sonny's
shoulder and slapped him, lightly, affectionately, with the back of his hand.

"Well. Now I've heard it all," said a voice behind us. This was another
musician, and a friend of Sonny's, a coal-black, cheerful-looking man, built
close to the ground. He immediately began confiding to me, at the top of
his lungs, the most terrible things about Sonny, his teeth gleaming like a
lighthouse and his laugh coming up out of him like the beginning of an
earthquake. And it turned out that everyone at the bar knew Sonny, or
almost everyone; some were musicians, working there, or nearby, or not
working, some were simply hangers-on, and some were there to hear Sonny
play. I was introduced to all of them and they were all very polite to me.
Yet, it was clear that, for them, I was only Sonny's brother. Here, I was in
Sonny's world. Or, rather: his kingdom. Here, it was not even a question
that his veins bore royal blood.

They were going to play soon and Creole installed me, by myself, at a 235
table in a dark corner. Then I watched them, Creole, and the little black
man, and Sonny, and the others, while they horsed around, standing just
below the bandstand. The light from the bandstand spilled just a little
short of them and, watching them laughing and gesturing and moving
about, I had the feeling that they, nevertheless, were being most careful
not to step into that circle of light too suddenly; that if they moved into
the light too suddenly, without thinking, they would perish in flame.
Then, while I watched, one of them, the small black man, moved into

the light and crossed the bandstand and started fooling around with
his drums. Then—being funny and being, also, extremely ceremonious—
Creole took Sonny by the arm and led him to the piano. A woman's voice
called Sonny's name and a few hands started clapping. And Sonny, also
being funny and being ceremonious, and so touched, I think, that he
could have cried, but neither hiding it nor showing it, riding it like a man,
grinned, and put both hands to his heart and bowed from the waist.

Creole then went to the bass fiddle and a lean, very bright-skinned
brown man jumped up on the bandstand and picked up his horn. So
there they were, and the atmosphere on the bandstand and in the room
began to change and tighten. Someone stepped up to the microphone and
announced them. Then there were all kinds of murmurs. Some people at
the bar shushed others. The waitress ran around, frantically getting in the
last orders, guys and chicks got closer to each other, and the lights on the
bandstand, on the quartet, turned to a kind of indigo. Then they all looked
different there. Creole looked about him for the last time, as though he
were making certain that all his chickens were in the coop, and then he—
jumped and struck the fiddle. And there they were.

All I know about music is that not many people ever really hear it.
And even then, on the rare occasions when something opens within, and
the music enters, what we mainly hear, or hear corroborated, are personal, private, vanishing evocations. But the man who creates the music is
hearing something else, is dealing with the roar rising from the void and
imposing order on it as it hits the air. What is evoked in him, then, is of
another order, more terrible because it has no words, and triumphant,
too, for that same reason. And his triumph, when he triumphs, is ours.
I just watched Sonny's face. His face was troubled, he was working hard,
but he wasn't with it. And I had the feeling that, in a way, everyone on
the bandstand was waiting for him, both waiting for him and pushing him
along. But as I began to watch Creole, I realized that it was Creole who
held them all back. He had them on a short rein. Up there, keeping the
beat with his whole body, wailing on the fiddle, with his eyes half closed,
he was listening to everything, but he was listening to Sonny. He was having a dialogue with Sonny. He wanted Sonny to leave the shoreline and
strike out for the deep water. He was Sonny's witness that deep water and
drowning were not the same thing—he had been there, and he knew. And
he wanted Sonny to know. He was waiting for Sonny to do the things on
the keys which would let Creole know that Sonny was in the water.

And, while Creole listened, Sonny moved, deep within, exactly like
someone in torment. I had never before thought of how awful the relationship must be between the musician and his instrument. He has to fill it,
this instrument, with the breath of life, his own. He has to make it do what

he wants it to do. And a piano is just a piano. It's made out of so much wood and wires and little hammers and big ones, and ivory. While there's only so much you can do with it, the only way to find this out is to try; to try and make it do everything.

And Sonny hadn't been near a piano for over a year. And he wasn't on much better terms with his life, not the life that stretched before him now. He and the piano stammered, started one way, got scared, stopped; started another way, panicked, marked time, started again; then seemed to have found a direction, panicked again, got stuck. And the face I saw on Sonny I'd never seen before. Everything had been burned out of it, and, at the same time, things usually hidden were being burned in, by the fire and fury of the battle which was occurring in him up there.

Yet, watching Creole's face as they neared the end of the first set,   240
I had the feeling that something had happened, something I hadn't heard. Then they finished, there was scattered applause, and then, without an instant's warning, Creole started into something else, it was almost sardonic, it was *Am I Blue*. And, as though he commanded, Sonny began to play. Something began to happen. And Creole let out the reins. The dry, low, black man said something awful on the drums, Creole answered, and the drums talked back. Then the horn insisted, sweet and high, slightly detached perhaps, and Creole listened, commenting now and then, dry, and driving, beautiful and calm and old. Then they all came together again, and Sonny was part of the family again. I could tell this from his face. He seemed to have found, right there beneath his fingers, a damn brand-new piano. It seemed that he couldn't get over it. Then, for a while, just being happy with Sonny, they seemed to be agreeing with him that brand-new pianos certainly were a gas.

Then Creole stepped forward to remind them that what they were playing was the blues. He hit something in all of them, he hit something in me, myself, and the music tightened and deepened, apprehension began to beat the air. Creole began to tell us what the blues were all about. They were not about anything very new. He and his boys up there were keeping it new, at the risk of ruin, destruction, madness, and death, in order to find new ways to make us listen. For, while the tale of how we suffer, and how we are delighted, and how we may triumph is never new, it always must be heard. There isn't any other tale to tell, it's the only light we've got in all this darkness.

And this tale, according to that face, that body, those strong hands on those strings, has another aspect in every country, and a new depth in every generation. Listen, Creole seemed to be saying, listen. Now these are Sonny's blues. He made the little black man on the drums know it, and the bright, brown man on the horn. Creole wasn't trying any longer to get Sonny in the water. He was wishing him Godspeed. Then he stepped back, very slowly, filling the air with the immense suggestion that Sonny speak for himself.

Then they all gathered around Sonny and Sonny played. Every now and again one of them seemed to say, amen. Sonny's fingers filled the air with life, his life. But that life contained so many others. And Sonny went all the way back, he really began with the spare, flat statement of the opening phrase of the song. Then he began to make it his. It was very beautiful because it wasn't hurried and it was no longer a lament. I seemed to hear with what burning he had made it his, and what burning we had yet to make it ours, how we could cease lamenting. Freedom lurked around us and I understood, at last, that he could help us to be free if we would listen, that he would never be free until we did. Yet, there was no battle in his face now, I heard what he had gone through, and would continue to go through until he came to rest in earth. He had made it his: that long line, of which we knew only Mama and Daddy. And he was giving it back, as everything must be given back, so that, passing through death, it can live forever. I saw my mother's face again, and felt, for the first time, how the stones of the road she had walked on must have bruised her feet. I saw the moonlit road where my father's brother died. And it brought something else back to me, and carried me past it, I saw my little girl again and felt Isabel's tears again, and I felt my own tears begin to rise. And I was yet aware that this was only a moment, that the world waited outside, as hungry as a tiger, and that trouble stretched above us, longer than the sky.

Then it was over. Creole and Sonny let out their breath, both soaking wet, and grinning. There was a lot of applause and some of it was real. In the dark, the girl came by and I asked her to take drinks to the bandstand. There was a long pause, while they talked up there in the indigo light and after awhile I saw the girl put a Scotch and milk on top of the piano for Sonny. He didn't seem to notice it, but just before they started playing again, he sipped from it and looked toward me, and nodded. Then he put it back on top of the piano. For me, then, as they began to play again, it glowed and shook above my brother's head like the very cup of trembling.

- Notice the different sections in this story. Use specific details from each to explain the significance of each different rhythm. For instance, in the opening section, look at the series of short sentences. How do these sentences help set up the story?

- Find the specific places in the story where sounds (or silences) are described. How does Baldwin use a rhythm of language to evoke these sounds?

■ There is a clear contrast between the lives of the two brothers here. Which one is innocent? Which is experienced? Use specific details to defend your answers.

Gabriel García Márquez (1928–2014)

Gabriel García Márquez was born in Aracataca, Colombia. He attended the Universidad Nacional de Colombia from 1947 to 1948 and Universidad de Cartagena from 1948 to 1949. He worked as a reporter for newspapers in Colombia, France, England, Venezuela, and Cuba. García Márquez often combines his journalistic skills with elements of fantasy. The mixture results in what many English-speaking critics have called "magical realism," but García Márquez has himself resisted that term. He believes that the poverty, instability, and violence of much modern life defy conventional realistic treatment. García Márquez has expressed a special affinity for William Faulkner among North American writers. A prolific and flexible writer, García Márquez has published novellas, novels, short story collections, plays, screenplays, film scripts, children's books, essays, and journalistic pieces. His novel *One Hundred Years of Solitude* has gained popularity with critics around the world. The Chilean poet Pablo Neruda called it "the greatest revelation in the Spanish language since the *Don Quixote* of Cervantes." García Márquez's other award-winning works include *Love in the Time of Cholera*. In 1982, García Márquez received the Nobel Prize in literature.

A Very Old Man with Enormous Wings: A Tale for Children (1955)

Translated by Gregory Rabassa

On the third day of rain they had killed so many crabs inside the house that Pelayo had to cross his drenched courtyard and throw them into the sea, because the newborn child had a temperature all night and they thought it was due to the stench. The world had been sad since Tuesday. Sea and sky were a single ash-gray thing and the sands of the beach, which on March nights glimmered like powdered light, had become a stew of mud and rotten shellfish. The light was so weak at noon that when Pelayo was coming back to the house after throwing away the crabs, it was hard for him to see what it was that was moving and groaning in the rear of the courtyard. He had to go very close to see that it was an old man, a very old man, lying face down in the mud, who, in spite of his tremendous efforts, couldn't get up, impeded by his enormous wings.

Frightened by that nightmare, Pelayo ran to get Elisenda, his wife, who was putting compresses on the sick child, and he took her to the rear of the courtyard. They both looked at the fallen body with mute stupor. He was dressed like a ragpicker. There were only a few faded hairs left on his bald skull and very few teeth in his mouth, and his pitiful condition of a drenched great-grandfather had taken away any sense of grandeur he might have had. His huge buzzard wings, dirty and half-plucked, were forever entangled in the mud. They looked at him so long and so closely that Pelayo and Elisenda very soon overcame their surprise and in the end found him familiar. Then they dared speak to him, and he answered in an incomprehensible dialect with a strong sailor's voice. That was how they skipped over the inconvenience of the wings and quite intelligently concluded that he was a lonely castaway from some foreign ship wrecked by the storm. And yet, they called in a neighbor woman who knew everything about life and death to see him, and all she needed was one look to show them their mistake.

"He's an angel," she told them. "He must have been coming for the child, but the poor fellow is so old that the rain knocked him down."

On the following day everyone knew that a flesh-and-blood angel was held captive in Pelayo's house. Against the judgment of the wise neighbor woman, for whom angels in those times were the fugitive survivors of a celestial conspiracy, they did not have the heart to club him to death. Pelayo watched over him all afternoon from the kitchen, armed with his bailiff's club, and before going to bed he dragged him out of the mud and locked him up with the hens in the wire chicken coop. In the middle of the night, when the rain stopped, Pelayo and Elisenda were still killing crabs. A short time afterward the child woke up without a fever and with a desire to eat. Then they felt magnanimous and decided to put the angel on a raft with fresh water and provisions for three days and leave him to his fate on the high seas. But when they went out into the courtyard with the first light of dawn, they found the whole neighborhood in front of the chicken coop having fun with the angel, without the slightest reverence, tossing him things to eat through the openings in the wire as if he weren't a supernatural creature but a circus animal.

Father Gonzaga arrived before seven o'clock, alarmed at the strange news. By that time onlookers less frivolous than those at dawn had already arrived and they were making all kinds of conjectures concerning the captive's future. The simplest among them thought that he should be named mayor of the world. Others of sterner mind felt that he should be promoted to the rank of five-star general in order to win all wars. Some visionaries hoped that he could be put to stud in order to implant on earth a race of winged wise men who could take charge of the universe. But Father Gonzaga, before becoming a priest, had been a robust woodcutter. Standing by the wire, he reviewed his catechism in an instant and asked them to open the door so that he could take a close look at that pitiful man who looked more like a huge decrepit hen among the fascinated chickens. He was lying in a corner drying his open wings in the sunlight among the fruit peels and breakfast leftovers that the early risers had thrown him. Alien to the impertinences of the world, he only lifted his antiquarian eyes and murmured something in his dialect when Father Gonzaga went into the chicken coop and said good morning to him in Latin. The parish priest had his first suspicion of an impostor when he saw that he did not understand the language of God or know how to greet His ministers. Then he noticed that seen close up he was much too human: he had an unbearable smell of the outdoors, the back side of his wings were strewn with parasites and his main feathers had been mistreated by terrestrial winds, and nothing about him measured up to the proud dignity of angels. Then he came out of the chicken coop and in a brief sermon warned the curious against the risks of being ingenuous. He reminded them that the devil had the bad habit of making use of carnival tricks in order to confuse the unwary. He argued that if wings were not the essential element in determining the difference between a hawk and an airplane, they were even less so in the recognition of angels. Nevertheless, he promised to write a letter to his bishop so that the latter would write to his primate so that the latter would write to the Supreme Pontiff in order to get the final verdict from the highest courts.

His prudence fell on sterile hearts. The news of the captive angel spread with such rapidity that after a few hours the courtyard had the bustle of a marketplace and they had to call in troops with fixed bayonets to disperse the mob that was about to knock the house down. Elisenda, her spine all twisted from sweeping up so much marketplace trash, then got the idea of fencing in the yard and charging five cents admission to see the angel.

The curious came from far away. A traveling carnival arrived with a flying acrobat who buzzed over the crowd several times, but no one paid any attention to him because his wings were not those of an angel but, rather, those of a sidereal bat. The most unfortunate invalids on earth came in search of health: a poor woman who since childhood had been counting her heartbeats and had run out of numbers; a Portuguese man who couldn't sleep because the noise of the stars disturbed him; a sleepwalker who got up at night to undo the things he had done while awake; and many others with less serious ailments. In the midst of that shipwreck disorder that made the earth tremble, Pelayo and Elisenda were happy with fatigue, for in less than a week they had crammed their rooms with money and the line of pilgrims waiting their turn to enter still reached beyond the horizon.

The angel was the only one who took no part in his own act. He spent his time trying to get comfortable in his borrowed nest, befuddled by the hellish heat of the oil lamps and sacramental candles that had been placed along the wire. At first they tried to make him eat some mothballs, which, according to the wisdom of the wise neighbor woman, were the food prescribed for angels. But he turned them down, just as he turned down the papal lunches that the penitents brought him, and they never found out whether it was because he was an angel or because he was an old man that in the end ate nothing but eggplant mush. His only supernatural virtue seemed to be patience. Especially during the first days, when the hens pecked at him, searching for the stellar parasites that proliferated in his wings, and the cripples pulled out feathers to touch their defective parts with, and even the most merciful threw stones at him, trying to get him to rise so they could see him standing. The only time they succeeded in arousing him was when they burned his side with an iron for branding steers, for he had been motionless for so many hours that they thought he was dead. He awoke with a start, ranting in his hermetic language and with tears in his eyes, and he flapped his wings a couple of times, which brought on a whirlwind of chicken dung and lunar dust and a gale of panic that did not seem to be of this world. Although many thought that his reaction had been one not of rage but of pain, from then on they were careful not to annoy him, because the majority understood that his passivity was not that of a hero taking his ease but that of a cataclysm in repose.

Father Gonzaga held back the crowd's frivolity with formulas of maidservant inspiration while awaiting the arrival of a final judgment on the nature of the captive. But the mail from Rome showed no sense of urgency. They spent their time finding out if the prisoner had a navel, if his dialect had any connection with Aramaic, how many times he could fit on the head of a pin, or whether he wasn't just a Norwegian with wings. Those meager letters might have come and gone until the end of time if a providential event had not put an end to the priest's tribulations.

It so happened that during those days, among so many other carnival 10 attractions, there arrived in town the traveling show of the woman who had been changed into a spider for having disobeyed her parents. The admission to see her was not only less than the admission to see the angel, but people were permitted to ask her all manner of questions about her absurd state and to examine her up and down so that no one would ever doubt the truth of her horror. She was a frightful tarantula the size of a ram and with the head of a sad maiden. What was most heart-rending, however, was not her outlandish shape but the sincere affliction with which she recounted the details of her misfortune. While still practically a child she had sneaked out of her parents' house to go to a dance, and while she was coming back through the woods after having danced all night without permission, a fearful thunderclap rent the sky in two and through the crack came the lightning bolt of brimstone that changed her into a spider. Her only nourishment came from the meatballs that charitable souls chose to toss into her mouth. A spectacle like that, full of so much human truth and with such a fearful lesson, was bound to defeat without even trying that of a haughty angel who scarcely deigned to look at mortals. Besides, the few miracles attributed to the angel showed a certain mental disorder, like the blind man who didn't recover his sight but grew three new teeth, or the paralytic who didn't get to walk but almost won the lottery, and the leper whose sores sprouted sunflowers. Those consolation miracles, which were more like mocking fun, had already ruined the angel's reputation when the woman who had been changed into a spider finally crushed him completely. That was how Father Gonzaga was cured forever of his insomnia and Pelayo's courtyard went back to being as empty as during the time it had rained for three days and crabs walked through the bedrooms.

The owners of the house had no reason to lament. With the money they saved they built a two-story mansion with balconies and gardens and high netting so that crabs wouldn't get in during the winter, and with iron bars on the windows so that angels wouldn't get in. Pelayo also set up a rabbit warren close to town and gave up his job as bailiff for good, and Elisenda bought some satin pumps with high heels and many dresses of iridescent silk, the kind worn on Sunday by the most desirable women in those times. The chicken coop was the only thing that didn't receive any attention. If they washed it down with Creolin and burned tears of myrrh inside it every so often, it was not in homage to the angel but to drive away the dungheap stench that still hung everywhere like a ghost and was turning the new house into an old one. At first, when the child learned to walk, they were careful that he not get too close to the chicken coop. But then they began to lose their fears and got used to the smell, and before the child got his second teeth he'd gone inside the chicken coop to play, where the wires were falling apart. The angel was no less standoffish with him than with other mortals, but he tolerated the most ingenious infamies with the patience of a dog who had no illusions. They both came down with chicken pox at the same time. The doctor who took care of the child couldn't resist the temptation to listen to the angel's heart, and he found so much whistling in the heart and so many sounds in his kidneys that it seemed impossible for him to be alive. What surprised him most, however, was the logic of his wings. They seemed so natural on that completely human organism that he couldn't understand why other men didn't have them too.

When the child began school it had been some time since the sun and rain had caused the collapse of the chicken coop. The angel went dragging himself about here and there like a stray dying man. They would drive him out of the bedroom with a broom and a moment later find him in the kitchen. He seemed to be in so many places at the same time that they grew to think that he'd been duplicated, that he was reproducing himself all through the house, and the exasperated and unhinged Elisenda shouted that it was awful living in that hell full of angels. He could scarcely eat and his antiquaria eyes had also become so foggy that he went about bumping into posts. All he had left were the bare cannulae of his last feathers. Pelayo threw a blanket over him and extended him the charity of letting him sleep in the shed, and only then did they notice that he had a temperature at night, and was delirious with the tongue twisters of an old Norwegian. That was one of the few times they became alarmed, for they thought he was going to die and not even the wise neighbor woman had been able to tell them what to do with dead angels.

And yet he not only survived his worst winter, but seemed improved with the first sunny days. He remained motionless for several days in the farthest corner of the courtyard, where no one would see him, and at the beginning of December some large, stiff feathers began to grow on his wings, the feathers of a scarecrow, which looked more like another misfortune of decrepitude. But he must have known the reason for those changes, for he was quite careful that no one should notice them, that no one should hear the sea chanteys that he sometimes sang under the stars. One morning Eliseda was cutting some bunches of onions for lunch when a wind that seemed to come from the high seas blew into the kitchen. Then she went to the window and caught the angel in his first attempts at flight. They were so clumsy that his fingernails opened a furrow in the vegetable patch and he was on the point of knocking the shed down with the ungainly flapping that slipped on the light and couldn't get a grip on the air. But he did manage to gain altitude. Elisenda let out a sigh of relief, for herself and for him, when she saw him pass over the last houses, holding himself up in some way with the risky flapping of a senile vulture. She kept watching him even when she was through cutting the onions and she kept on watching until it was no longer possible for her to see him, because then he was no longer an annoyance in her life but an imaginary dot on the horizon of the sea.

- This story is labeled as "A Tale for Children." In what specific instances in the story does this label seem appropriate? In what instances does it seem to be something else?
- Father Gonzaga attempts to place the mysterious "very old man" into the symbolic systems with which he is familiar. Find the specific passages where he draws his conclusions, trace his reasoning, and discuss its limits.

- When the "very old man" flies away, why does Elisund "let out a sigh of relief"? How has the "very old man" impacted the life that she had established with Pelayo?
- How does García Márquez depict the community that receives the "very old man"? Locate specific details to describe his attitude toward this group.
- Explore the various misunderstandings that fill this story. In what ways are these characters presented farcically?

Oluwabusayo Temitope "Tope" Folarin (1982–)

Born in Ogden, Utah, Folarin graduated from Morehouse College in Atlanta, Georgia, and earned master's degrees in African studies and comparative social policy while studying as a Rhodes Scholar at Cambridge University. He lives in Washington, D.C., and has not returned to his parents' Nigerian homeland since he was about one year old. In his writing, he addresses the fact that Nigeria is at once a country he hardly knows and one he knows intimately. The story that appears here was awarded the Caine Prize for African Writing in 2013 and is part of a novel set in an evangelical Nigerian church located in Texas.

Miracle (2012)

Our heads move simultaneously, and we smile at the tall, svelte man who strides purposefully down the aisle to the pulpit. Once there, he raises both of his hands then lowers them slightly. He raises his chin and says *let us pray.*

"Dear Father, we come to you today, on the occasion of this revival, and we ask that you bless us abundantly, we who have made it to America, because we know we are here for a reason. We ask for your blessings because we are not here alone. Each of us represents dozens, sometimes hundreds of people back home. So many lives depend on us Lord, and the burden on our shoulders is great. Jesus, bless this service, and bless us. We ask that we will not be the same people at the end of the service as we were at the beginning. All this we ask of you, our dear savior, Amen."

The pastor sits, and someone bolts from the front row to the piano and begins to play. The music we hear is familiar and at the same time new; the bandleader punches up a pre-programmed beat on the cheap electronic piano and plays a few Nigerian gospel songs to get us in the mood for revival. We sing along, though we have to wait a few moments at the beginning of each song to figure out what he's playing. We sing joyful songs to the Lord, then songs of redemption, and then we sing songs of hope, hope that tomorrow will be better than today, hope that, one day soon, our lives will begin to resemble the dreams that brought us to America.

The tinny Nigerian gospel music ends when the pastor stands, and he
prays over us again. He prays so long and so hard that we feel the weight of
his words pressing down on us. His prayer is so insistent, so sincere, that
his words emerge from the dark chrysalis of his mouth as bright, fluttering
prophesies. In our hearts we stop asking if and begin wondering when our
deeply held wishes will come true. After his sweating and shaking and cajoling he shouts another *Amen*, a word that now seems defiant, not pleading.
We echo his defiance as loudly as we can, and when we open our eyes we
see him pointing to the back of the church.

Our eyes follow the line of his finger, and we see the short old man   5
hunched over in the back, two men on either side of him. Many of us have
seen him before, in this very space; we've seen the old man perform miracles that were previously only possible in the pages of our Bibles. We've
seen him command the infirm to be well, the crippled to walk, the poor to
become wealthy. Even those of us who are new, who know nothing of him,
can sense the power emanating from him.

We have come from all over North Texas to see him. Some of us have
come from Oklahoma, some of us from Arkansas, a few of us from Louisiana and a couple from New Mexico. We own his books, his tapes, his holy
water, his anointing oil. We know that he is an instrument of God's will,
and we have come because we need miracles.

We need jobs. We need good grades. We need green cards. We need
American passports. We need our parents to understand that we are Americans. We need our children to understand they are Nigerians. We need new
kidneys, new lungs, new limbs, new hearts. We need to forget the harsh rigid-
ity of our lives, to remember why we believe, to be beloved, and to hope.

We need miracles.

We murmur as the two men help him to the front, and in this
charged atmosphere everything about him makes sense, even the irony of
his blindness, his inability to see the wonders that God performs through
his hand. His blindness is a confirmation of his power. It's the burden
he bears on our behalf; his residence in a space of perpetual darkness has
only sharpened his spiritual vision over the years. He can see more than
we will ever see.

When the old man reaches the pulpit his attendants turn him around   10
so he's facing us. He's nearly bald—a few white hairs cling precariously to the
sides of his shining head—and he's wearing a large pair of black sunglasses.
A bulky white robe falls from his neck to the floor. Beneath, he's wearing a
flowing white *agbada*.

He remains quiet for a few moments—we can feel the anticipation
building, breath by breath, in the air. He smiles. Then he begins to hum.
A haunting, discordant melody. The bandleader tries to find the tune

among the keys of his piano, but the old man slaps the air and the bandleader allows the searching music to die.

He continues to hum and we listen to his music. Suddenly he turns to our left and points to a space somewhere on the ceiling:

"I DEMAND YOU TO LEAVE THIS PLACE!" he screams, and we know there is something malevolent in our midst. We search the area his sightless eyes are probing, somewhere in the open space above our heads. We can't see anything, but we raise our voices in response to the prophet's call. Soon our voices are a cacophonous stew of Yoruba and English, shouting and singing, spitting and humming, and the prophet from Nigeria speaks once more:

"We must continue to pray ladies and gentlemen! There are forces here that do not wish for this to be a successful service. If we are successful in our prayers that means they have failed! They do not wish to fail! So we cannot expect that our prayers will simply come true; we must fight!"

We make our stew thicker; we throw in more screams and prayers until   15
we can no longer distinguish one voice from another. Finally, after several long minutes, the prophet raises his hands:

"We are finished. It is done."

And we begin to celebrate, but our celebration lacks conviction—we haven't yet received what we came here for.

The prophet sways to the beat of our tepid praise. The man on his left stands and dabs his forehead. The prophet clears his throat and reaches forward with his right hand until he finds the microphone. He grabs it, leans into it.

"I have been in the U.S. for two months now…" he begins, rhythmically moving his head left and right, "I have been to New York, to Delaware, to Philadelphia, to Washington, to Florida, to Atlanta, to Minnesota, to Kansas, to Oklahoma, and now, finally, I have arrived here."

We cheer loudly.   20

"I will visit Houston and San Antonio before I leave here, and then I will go to Nevada, and then California. I will travel all over this country for the next month, visiting Nigerians across this great land, but I feel in my spirit that the most powerful blessings will happen *here*."

We holler and whoop and hug each other, for his words are confirmation of the feelings we've been carrying within ourselves since the beginning of the service.

"The reason I am saying that the most powerful blessings will happen here is because God has told me that you have been the most faithful of his flock in the U.S. You haven't forgotten your people back home. You haven't forgotten your parents and siblings who sent you here, who pray for you every day. You have remained disciplined and industrious in this place, the

land of temptation. And for all your hard work, for your faithfulness, God is
going to reward you today."

Some of us raise our hands and praise the Father. A few of us bow our
heads, a few of us begin to weep with happiness.

"But in order for your blessings to be complete, you will have to pray   25
today like you have never prayed before. You will have to believe today like
you have never believed before. The only barrier to your blessing is the
threshold of your belief. Today the only thing I will be talking about is
belief. If I have learned anything during my visits to this country, it is that
belief is only possible for those who have dollars. I am here to tell you that
belief comes *before* dollars. If you have belief, then the dollars will follow."

Silence again. We search our hearts for the seedlings of doubt that
reside there. Many of us have to cut through thickets of doubt before we can
find our own hearts again. We use the silence to uproot our doubt and we
pray that our hearts will remain pure for the remainder of the service.

"Let me tell you, great miracles will be performed here today. People
will be talking about this day for years and years to come. And the only
thing that will prevent you from receiving your share is your unbelief..."

At this moment he begins to cough violently, and the man on his right
rushes forward with a handkerchief. He places the handkerchief in the
prophet's hand, and the prophet coughs into it for a few seconds, and then
he wipes his mouth. We wait anxiously for him to recover.

He laughs. "I am an old man now. You will have to excuse me. Just pray
for me!"

"We will pray for you Prophet!" we yell in response.   30

"Yes, just pray for me, and I will continue to pray for you."

"Thank you Prophet! Amen! Amen!"

"And because you have been faithful, God will continue to bless you,
he will anoint you, he will appoint you!"

"Amen!"

"Now God is telling me that there is someone here who is struggling   35
with something big, a handicap that has lasted for many, many years."

We fall quiet because we know he is talking about us.

"He's telling me that you have been suffering in silence with this problem, and that you have come to accept the problem as part of yourself."

We nod in agreement. How many indignities have we accepted as a
natural part of our lives?

"The purpose of my presence in your midst is to let you know that
you should no longer accept the bad things that have become normal
in your lives. America is trying to teach you to accept your failures, your
setbacks. Now is the time to reject them! To claim the success that is right-
fully yours!"

His sunglasses fall from his face, and we see the brilliant white orbs   40
quivering frantically in their sockets, two full moons that have forgotten
their roles in the drama of the universe. His attendants lunge to the floor to
recover them, and together they place the glasses back on his ancient face.
The prophet continues as if nothing happened.

"I do not perform these miracles because I wish to be celebrated. I
perform these miracles because God works through me, and he has given
me the grace to show all of you what is possible in your *physical* and *spiritual*
lives. And now God is telling me; you, come up here."

We remain standing because we don't know to whom he is referring.

"YOU! You! You! YOU! Come up here!"

We begin to walk forward, shyly, slowly. I turn around suddenly, and I
realize I'm no longer a part of the whole. I notice, then, that the lights are
too bright, and the muggy air in the room settles, fog-like, on my face. Now
I am in the aisle, and I see the blind old man pointing at me.

"You, young man. Come here. Come up here for your miracle!"   45

I just stand there, and I feel something red and frightening bubbling
within me. I stand there as the prophet points at me, and I feel hands pushing me, forcing me to the front. I don't have enough time to wrap up my
unbelief and tuck it away.

Then I'm standing on the stage, next to the prophet.

The prophet moves closer to me and places a hand on top of my head.
He presses down until I'm kneeling before him. He rocks my head back and
forth.

"Young man, you have great things ahead of you, but I can sense that
something is ailing you. There is some disease, some disorder that has colo-
nized your body, and it is threatening to colonize your soul. Tell me, are you
having problems breathing?"

I find myself surprised at his indirect reference to my asthma. But now   50
the doubts are bombarding me from every direction. Maybe he can hear my
wheezing? It's always harder for me to breathe when I'm nervous, and I'm
certainly nervous now.

"Yes sir," I reply.

"Ah, you do not need to confirm. I now have a fix on your soul, and
the Holy Spirit is telling me about the healings you need." He brushes his
fingers down my face, and my glasses fall to the ground. Everything becomes
dim.

"How long have you been wearing glasses my son?"

"Since I was five, sir."

"And tell me, how bad is your vision?"   55

Really bad. I have the thickest lenses in school, the kind that make my
eyes seem like two giant fish floating in blurry, separate ponds.

"It's bad sir."

The prophet removes his hand from my head and I can feel him thrashing about, as if he's swimming in air, until an attendant thrusts a microphone into his groping hand.

"As you guys can see, I know a little about eye problems," he booms, and although it sounds like he's attempting a joke, no one laughs, and his words crash against the back wall and wash over us a second time, and then a third.

"And no one this young should be wearing glasses that are so thick!" 60
The congregation cheers in approval. I hear a whispered *yes prophet*.

"I can already tell that you have become too comfortable with your handicap," he roars, "and that is one of the main problems in this country. Handicaps have become *normal* here." I see the many heads nodding in response. "People accept that they are damaged in some fashion, and instead of asking God to intervene, they accept the fact that they are broken!"

More head nodding, more *Amens*.

"Let me tell you something," he continues. He's sweating profusely; some of it dribbles onto my head. My scalp is burning. "God gives us these ailments so that we are humbled, so that we are forced to build a relationship with him. That is why all of us, in some way or another, are damaged. And the reason they have come to accept handicaps in this country is because these Americans do not want to build a relationship with God. They want to remain forever disconnected from His grace, and you can already see what is happening to this country."

The *Amens* explode from many mouths; some louder, some softer, some gruff, some pleading.

"So the first step to getting closer to God, to demonstrating that you 65 are a serious Christian, is declaring to God all of your problems and ailments, and asking him to heal you."

A few *Amens* from the back overwhelm everything. I squint to see if I can connect the praise to the faces, but I can only see the featureless faces swathed in fog.

"So now I'm going to ask God to heal this young man who has become accustomed to his deformity. But before I touch you, before I ask the Holy Spirit to do its work, I must ask you, before everyone here—are you ready for your miracle?"

I stare at the congregation. I see some nodding. I've never thought of a life without glasses, but now my head is filled with visions of perfect clarity. I can see myself playing basketball without the nerdy, annoying straps that I always attach to my glasses so they won't fall off my face. I imagine evenings without headaches, headaches that come after hours spent peering through lenses that give me sight while rejecting my eyes.

"Are you ready?" he asks again, and I can feel the openness in the air that exists when people are waiting for a response. I know I'm waiting for my response as well.

"I'm ready." 70

"Amen!"

"AMEN! AMEN!" Their *Amens* batter me; I bow beneath the harsh blows of their spiritual desperation.

"My son, you are ready to receive your gift from God."

His two attendants scramble from his side, drag me to my feet, and bring me down to the floor. One positions himself next to me, the other behind me. When I look over my shoulder I see the attendant standing there with his arms extended before him.

"I feel something very powerful coursing through my spirit," the 75 prophet yells. "This is going to be a big miracle. Bring me to the boy!"

The attendant beside me strides up to the stage and helps the prophet down the steps. He positions the prophet before me, and I notice that the prophet seems even shorter than before. He is only a few inches taller than me. His hot breath causes my eyes to water; I resist the urge to reach up and rub them.

The prophet suddenly pulls off his sunglasses. He stares at me with his sightless eyes. I become uncomfortable, so I lean slightly to the right and his face follows. I lean slightly to the left and his face does the same. A sly smile begins to unfurl itself across his face. My heart begins to beat itself to death.

"Do not be frightened. I can see you through my spiritual eyes," he says. "And after this miracle, if you are a diligent Christian, you will be able to do the same."

Before I can respond, his right hand shoots forward, and he presses my temples. I stumble backwards but maintain my balance. I turn to gaze at all the people in front of me, and though I can't see individual faces I see befuddlement in its many, various forms. I see random expressions contort themselves into a uniform expression of confusion. I actually manage to separate my brother from the masses because his presence is the only on in the room that seems to match my own. We're both confused, but our confusion isn't laced with fear.

The prophet presses my temples again, and again, and each time I 80 regain my balance. His attendants are ignoring me now. They're both looking down at the prophet, inquiring with their eyes about something. I'm not sure what. Then I hear the shuffling feet, and I know that the people are becoming restless.

"The spirit of bad sight is very strong in him, and it won't let go," the prophet yells.

Life returns to the church like air filling up a balloon. I see the prophet's attendants nod, and the new *Amens* that tunnel into my ears all have an
edge of determination.

"This healing will require special Holy Ghost healing power. Come,
take my robe!" The attendant closest to me pulls the robe from his back,
and the prophet stands before me even smaller and less imposing than
before. "While I am working on this spirit everyone in this room must pray.
You must pray that I will receive the power I need to overcome this spirit
within him!"

I see many heads moving up and down in prayer, and I hear loud pleading, and snapping, and impassioned howling.

"That is very good!"   85

The prophet steps forward and blows in my eyes, and then he rubs
my temples. I remain standing. He blows and rubs again. The same. He
does it again, and again, and each time the praying grows louder and
more insistent. The prophet moves even closer to me, and this time
when he presses my temples he does not let go. He shoves my head
back until I fall, and the attendant behind me eases me to the floor. I
finally understand. I remain on the floor while his attendants cover
me with a white sheet. Above, I hear the prophet clapping his hands,
and I know that he's praying. The fluorescent lights on the ceiling are
shining so brightly that the light seems to be huddling in the sheet
with me. I hug the embodied light close.

After a few minutes the prophet stops clapping.

"It is finished! Pick the young man up."

His attendants grab my arms and haul me up. I hear a cheer building
up in the crowd, gaining form and weight, but the prophet cuts everything
off with a loud grunt.

"Not yet. It is too soon. And young man, keep your eyes closed." I   90
realize that my eyes are still closed, and I wonder how he knows.

I begin to believe in miracles. I realize that many miracles have
already happened; the old prophet can see me even though he's blind,
and my eyes feel different somehow, huddled beneath their thin lids.
I think about the miracle of my family, the fact that we've remained
together despite the terror of my mother's abrupt departure, and I even
think about the miracle of my presence in America. My father reminds
my brother and me almost every day how lucky we are to be living in
poverty in America, he claims that all of our cousins in Nigeria would
die for the chance, but his words were meaningless before. Compared
to what I have already experienced in life, compared to the tribulations
that my family has already weathered, the matter of my eyesight seems
almost insignificant. *Of course I can be healed! This is nothing. God has*

already done more for me than I can imagine. This healing isn't even for me. It
is to show others, who believe less, whose belief requires new fuel, that God is
still working in our lives.

Then the Prophet yells in my ear: OPEN YOUR EYES.

My lids slap open, and I see the same fog as before. The disembodied heads are swelling with unreleased joy. I know what I have to do.

"I can see!" I cry, and the loud cheers and sobbing are like new clothing.

"We must test his eyes, just to make sure! We are not done yet!" yells   95
the prophet, and nervousness slowly creeps up my spine like a centipede. "We have to confirm so the doubters in here and the doubters in the world can know that God's work is real!"

One of his attendants walks a few feet in front of me and holds up a few fingers. I squint and lean forward. I pray I get it right.

"Three!" I yell, and the crowd cheers more loudly than before.

"Four!" I scream, and the cheers themselves gain sentience. They last long after mouths have closed.

"One!" I cry, and the mouths open again, to give birth to new species of joy.

*   *   *

This is what I learned during my first visit to a Nigerian church: that a   100
community is made up of truths and lies. Both must be cultivated in order for the community to survive.

The prophet performed many more miracles that day. My father beamed all the way home, and I felt that I had been healed, in a way, even if my eyes were the same as before.

That evening, after tucking my brother and me in, my father dropped my glasses into a brown paper bag, and he placed the bag on the nightstand by
my bed.

"You should keep this as evidence, so that you always remember the power of God," he whispered in my ear.

The next morning, when I woke up, I opened my eyes, and I couldn't see a thing. I reached into the bag and put on my glasses without thinking. My sight miraculously returned.

■ The story presents the rhythm of a church service and the interaction of members of the congregation with the church's pastor. Make a list of specific details that convey the service's rhythm. Is there any point at which this rhythm is interrupted?

- How do the words spoken at the service contrast with the thoughts of those in the congregation?
- How is the main character both part of and separate from this congregation?
- Would you describe the main character as innocent? What is your rationale for your answer?
- Comment on what he claims he learned that day "that a community is made up of truths and lies." How does he participate in this community?

POETRY

Ogden Nash (1902–1971)

Kind of an Ode to Duty (1935)

O Duty,
Why hast thou not the visage of a sweetie or a cutie?
Why displayest thou the countenance of the kind of conscientious
    organizing spinster
That the minute you see her you are aginster?
Why glitter thy spectacles so ominously?   5
Why art thou clad so abominously?
Why are thou so different from Venus
And why do thou and I have so few interests mutually in common
    between us?
Why art thou fifty per cent martyr
And fifty-one per cent Tartar?   10
Why is it thy unfortunate wont
To try to attract people by calling on them either to leave undone the
    deeds they like, or to do the deeds they don't?
Why art thou so like an April postmortem
Or something that died in the ortumn?
Above all, why dost thou continue to hound me?   15
Why art thou always albatrossly hanging around me?
Thou so ubiquitous,
And I so iniquitous,
I seem to be the one person in the world thou art perpetually
    preaching at who or to who;

Whatever looks like fun, there art thou standing between me and it,   20
    calling "you-hoo."
O Duty, Duty!
How noble a man should I be hadst thou the visage of a sweetie
    or a cutie! Wert thou but houri instead of hag
Then would my halo indeed be in the bag!
But as it is thou art so much forbiddinger than a Wodehouse hero's   25
    forbiddingest aunt
That in the words of the poet, When Duty whispers low, "Thou must,"
    this erstwhile youth replies, "I just can't."

- In spite of the poem's tone, what images of duty here seem to be descriptions that might be appropriate in any context?
- What does the poet achieve by portraying Duty as an allegorical figure? Locate specific instances where Duty takes on these characteristics.

Amiri Baraka (1934– 2014)

In Memory of Radio (1961)

Who has ever stopped to think of the divinity of Lamont Cranston?
(Only Jack Kerouac, that I know of: & me.
The rest of you probably had on WCBS and Kate Smith,
Or something equally unattractive.)

What can I say?   5
It is better to have loved and lost
Than to put linoleum in your living rooms?
Am I a sage or something?
Mandrake's hypnotic gesture of the week?
(Remember, I do not have the healing powers of Oral Roberts. . .   10
I cannot, like F. J. Sheen, tell you how to get saved & rich!
I cannot even order you to the gaschamber satori like Hitler or Gody
    Knight.

& Love is an evil word.
Turn it backwards/see, see what I mean?
An evol word. & besides   15
who understands it?
I certainly wouldn't like to go out on that kind of limb.

Saturday mornings we listened to the *Red Lantern* & his undersea folk.
At 11, *Let's Pretend*
& we did   20
& I, the poet, still do, Thank God!

What was it he used to say (after the transformation when he was safe
& invisible & the unbelievers couldn't throw stones?) "Heh, heh, heh,
Who knows what evil lurks in the hearts of men? The Shadow knows."

O, yes he does   25
O, yes he does.
An evil word it is,
This Love.

- How does the poet contrast the lives of normal listeners with the sorts of stories that they heard on their radios?
- This poem is recalling an early time when storytelling took a different form. The poet in 1961 is recalling the radio programs that dominated his childhood. How does the poet suggest that this particular medium worked in a different way from the storytelling that replaced it?

Langston Hughes (1902–1967)

Dream Boogie (1951)

Good morning, daddy!
Ain't you heard

The boogie-woogie rumble
Of a dream deferred?

Listen closely: 5
You'll hear their feet
Beating out and beating out a —

 You think
 It's a happy beat?

Listen to it closely: 10
Ain't you heard
something underneath
like a —

 What did I say?

Sure,   15
I'm happy!
Take it away!

> *Hey, pop!*
> *Re-bop!*
> *Mop!*
>
> *Y-e-a-h!*

■ How does Hughes use the rhythm of "boogie-woogie" to drown out the
   disappointment of "a dream deferred"?

Langston Hughes (1902–1967)

The Negro Speaks of Rivers (1921)

I've known rivers:
I've known rivers ancient as the world and older than the
    flow of human blood in human veins.

My soul has grown deep like the rivers.
I bathed in Euphrates when dawns were young.
I built my hut near the Congo and it lulled me to sleep.   5
I looked upon the Nile and raised the pyramids above it.
I heard the singing of the Mississippi when Abe Lincoln went down to
    New Orleans, and I've seen its muddy bosom turn all golden in the sunset.

I've known rivers:
Ancient, dusky rivers.

My soul has grown deep like the rivers.   10

■ How does the poet use repeated phrases and sentence patterns to develop
   the idea "my soul has grown deep like the rivers"?

Theodore Roethke (1908–1963)

My Papa's Waltz (1940)

The whiskey on your breath
Could make a small boy dizzy;
But I hung on like death:
Such waltzing was not easy.

We romped until the pans   5
Slid from the kitchen shelf;
My mother's countenance
Could not unfrown itself.

The hand that held my wrist
Was battered on one knuckle;   10
At every step you missed
My right ear scraped a buckle.

You beat time on my head
With a palm caked hard by dirt,
Then waltzed me off to bed   15
Still clinging to your shirt.

■ In "My Papa's Waltz," the poet establishes a clear rhythm that lasts
  throughout the poem. How does this rhythm compare to or contrast with the
  action described? How does rhythm suggest the poet's feelings in regard to
  the father's rough behavior?

Lawrence Ferlinghetti (1919–   )

Constantly risking absurdity (1958)

Constantly risking absurdity
                              and death
      whenever he performs
                      above the heads
                              of his audience   5
the poet like an acrobat
              climbs on rime
                      to a high wire of his own making
and balancing on eyebeams
                      above a sea of faces   10
        paces his way
                  to the other side of day
performing entrechats
                  and sleight-of-foot tricks
and other high theatrics   15
                  and all without mistaking
        any thing
                  for what it may not be
      For he's the super realist
                      who must perforce perceive   20

> taut truth
>   before the taking of each stance or step
>   in his supposed advance
>   toward that still higher perch
>   where Beauty stands and waits   25
>   with gravity
>   to start her death-defying leap
>   And he
>   a little charleychaplin man
>   who may or may not catch   30
>   her fair eternal form
>   spreadeagled in the empty air
>   of existence

- According to the poem, how do poets take risks?
- What specific images does the poet use to connect the act of writing poetry to the performance of an acrobat? How does this specific analogy help elaborate the meaning of the poem's title?

William Blake (1757–1827)

The Chimney Sweeper (Innocence) (1789)

When my mother died I was very young,
And my father sold me while yet my tongue
Could scarcely cry "'weep! 'weep! 'weep! 'weep!"°
So your chimneys I sweep, & in soot I sleep.

There's little Tom Dacre, who cried when his head   5
That curl'd like a lamb's back, was shav'd: so I said.
"Hush Tom! never mind it, for when your head's bare,
You know that the soot cannot spoil your white hair."

And so he was quiet, & that very night,
As Tom was a-sleeping he had such a sight!—   10
That thousands of sweepers Dick, Joe, Ned, & Jack,
Were all of them lock'd up in coffins of black.

And by came an Angel who had a bright key
And he open'd the coffins & set them all free.

---

3. **'weep:** the child's lisping way of uttering his cry through the streets, "sweep, sweep"

Then down a green plain leaping, laughing, they run,   15
And wash in a river, and shine in the Sun.

Then naked & white, all their bags left behind,
They rise upon clouds, and sport in the wind;
And the Angel told Tom, if he'd be a good boy,
He'd have God for his father, & never want joy.   20

And so Tom awoke; and we rose in the dark
And got with our bags & our brushes to work.
Tho' the morning was cold, Tom was happy & warm
So if all do their duty, they need not fear harm.

William Blake (1757–1827)

Holy Thursday (Innocence) (1789)

'Twas on a Holy Thursday, their innocent faces clean
The children walking two & two, in red & blue & green
Grey headed beadles walkd before with wands as white as snow,
Till into the high dome of Pauls they like Thames waters flow.

O what a multitude they seemd, these flowers of London town!   5
Seated in companies they sit with radiance all their own.
The hum of multitudes was there but multitudes of lambs,
Thousands of little boys & girls raising their innocent hands.

Now like a mighty wind they raise to heaven the voice of song,
Or like harmonious thunderings the seats of heaven among.   10
Beneath them sit the agéd men, wise guardians of the poor;
Then cherish pity, lest you drive an angel from your door.

William Blake (1757–1827)

Holy Thursday (Experience) (1794)

Is this a holy thing to see,
In a rich and fruitful land,
Babes reducd to misery,
Fed with cold and usurous hand?

Is that trembling cry a song?   5
Can it be a song of joy?
And so many children poor?
It is a land of poverty!

And their sun does never shine,
And their fields are bleak & bare,   10
And their ways are fill'd with thorns;
It is eternal winter there.

For where-e'er the sun does shine,
And where-e'er the rain does fall,
Babe can never hunger there,   15
Nor poverty the mind appall.

William Blake (1757–1827)

The Chimney Sweeper (Experience) (1794)

A little black thing among the snow,
Crying "'weep! 'weep!" in notes of woe!
"Where are thy father & mother? say?"
"They are both gone up to the church to pray."

"Because I was happy upon the heath,   5
And smil'd among the winter's snow,
They clothed me in the clothes of death,
And taught me to sing the notes of woe.

"And because I am happy & dance & sing,
They think they have done me no injury,   10
And are gone to praise God & his Priest & King,
Who make up a heaven of our misery."

- Look at the Blake poems as pairs. First are poems of innocence. Second are poems of experience. What differences are there in the rhythms of each pair? Are there any rhythmic consistencies among the experience poems or innocence poems?

- How do their rhythms reflect the different approach to the same subject matter that we see in these pairs?

Gwendolyn Brooks (1917–2000)

We Real Cool (1960)

THE POOL PLAYERS.
SEVEN AT THE GOLDEN SHOVEL.

We real cool. We
Left school. We

Lurk late. We
Strike straight. We

Sing sin. We   5
Thin gin. We

Jazz June. We
Die soon.

- What is the effect of the fact that the subject of every sentence (except the first) is not attached to its predicate?
- Compare "We Real Cool" to "Dream Boogie" (p. 603). How do both poems use their rhythms to imitate the social forces that the poems challenge?

Sharon Olds (1942–   )

I Go Back to May 1937 (1997)

I see them standing at the formal gates of their colleges,
I see my father strolling out
under the ochre sandstone arch, the
red tiles glinting like bent
plates of blood behind his head, I   5
see my mother with a few light books at her hip
standing at the pillar made of tiny bricks with the
wrought-iron gate still open behind her, its
sword-tips black in the May air,
they are about to graduate, they are about to get married,   10
they are kids, they are dumb, all they know is they are
innocent, they would never hurt anybody.
I want to go up to them and say Stop,
don't do it—she's the wrong woman,

he's the wrong man, you are going to do things   15
you cannot imagine you would ever do,
you are going to do bad things to children,
you are going to suffer in ways you never heard of,
you are going to want to die. I want to go
up to them there in the late May sunlight and say it,   20
her hungry pretty blank face turning to me,
her pitiful beautiful untouched body,
his arrogant handsome blind face turning to me,
his pitiful beautiful untouched body,
but I don't do it. I want to live. I   25
take them up like the male and female
paper dolls and bang them together
at the hips like chips of flint as if to
strike sparks from them, I say
Do what you are going to do, and I will tell about it.   30

■ In Olds's poem, what images serve the poet in her descriptions of innocence and of experience?

■ Look carefully at the long listing sentences that are central to the poem: lines 1–12, 13–19, 19–25. What is the impact of these almost breathless lists? Whose experience does each describe?

Heather McHugh (1948–   )

Past All Understanding (1998)

Gasworks Park, 1996

A woman there was balancing her baby
back-to-back. They held each other's hands,
did tilts and bends and teeter-totters on
each other's inclinations, making
casual covalency into   5
a human ideogram,
spontaneous Pilobolus—
a spectacle at which
the estimable Kooch
(half Border and half Lab)   10

began to bark. He wouldn't stop. The child slid off
the woman's back; now they were two
who scowled and stared. You looked.
I started to explain, like one
big oddity to him. (They weren't appeased.) He barks at!   15
crippled people too. (Now they were horrified.) Meanwhile a wind

rose at the kiosk, stapled with yard jobs, sub-clubs, bands somebody-
    named
for animals. The whole park fluttered up and flailed, and Kooch.
    unquenchable,
perceived the higher truth. By now the uproar was enough
to make the bicyclists bypassing (bent beneath their packs),   20
an assortment of teaching assistants (harried, earnest, hardly earning)—
and even some white-haired full professorships all come to a halt
in the wake of the wave of their tracks.
What brouhahas! What flaps!
To Kooch's mind, if you   25
could call it that,
the worst was
yet to come—

for looming overhead, a host of red and yellow kites appeared
intent on swooping even to the cowlicks of the humans—Were   30
these people blind—the woman in pink, the man in blue, who paused
    there
in his purview, stupidly, to shake their heads? He thinks
we're in danger, I tried again
to reason with my fellow-man
But now the dog   35

was past all understanding, he was uncontainable. He burst
into a pure fur paroxysm, blaming the sky for all that we
were worth, holding his ground with four feet braced
against an over-turning earth....

■ What is the significance of the passages in parentheses? Is there any
  pattern to these lines? Trace the specific words that suggest a building of
  energy throughout the poem.

DRAMA

Suzan-Lori Parks (1964–   )

Suzan-Lori Parks was born in 1964 in Fort Knox, Kentucky, the child of an army officer whose family had to move frequently as a result of his work. Parks went to high school in West Germany, then attended Mount Holyoake College, where she worked with the writer James Baldwin, who encouraged her to write plays. Parks rapidly achieved acclaim for her dramatic works, and the second of her plays won the Obie Award as the best Off-Broadway play of 1989. In 2002 she achieved even greater success when her play *Topdog/Underdog* was awarded the Pulitzer Prize for Drama. Parks's drama and fiction have been praised for the ways in which they examine African American life and the legacies of slavery and racism.

Topdog/Underdog (2002)

Author's notes: From the "Elements of Style"
I'm continuing the use of my slightly unconventional theatrical elements. Here's a road map.

- *(Rest)*
  Take a little time, a pause, a breather; make a transition.
- A Spell
  An elongated and heightened *(Rest)*. Denoted by repetition of figures' names with no dialogue. Has sort of an architectural look:

  Lincoln
  Booth
  Lincoln
  Booth

  This is a place where the figures experience their pure true simple state. While no action or stage business is necessary, directors should fill this moment as they best see fit.
- [Brackets in the text indicate optional cuts for production.]
- (Parentheses around dialogue indicate softly spoken passages (asides; sotto voce)).

Scene 1
Thursday evening. A seedily furnished rooming house room. A bed, a reclining chair, a small wooden chair, some other stuff but not much else. BOOTH, *a black man in his early 30s, practices his 3-card monte scam on the classic setup: 3 playing cards and the cardboard playing board atop 2 mismatched milk crates. His moves and accompanying patter are for the most part, studied and awkward.*

BOOTH: Watch me close watch me close now: who-see-thuh-red-card-who-see-thuh-red-card? I-see-thuh-red-card. Thuh-red-card-is-thuh-winner. Pick-thuh-red-card-you-pick-uh-winner. Pick-uh-black-card-you-pick-uh-loser. Theres-thuh-loser, yeah, theres-thuh-black-card, theres-thuh-other-loser-and-theres-thuh-red-card, thuh-winner. 5
(Rest.)
Watch me close watch me close now: 3-Card-throws-thuh-cards-lightning-fast. 3-Card-thats-me-and-Ima-last. Watch-me-throw-cause-here-I-go. One-good-pickll-get-you-in, 2-good-picks-and-you-gone-win. See-thuh-red-card-see-thuh-red-card-who-see-thuh-red-card?
(Rest.)
Dont touch my cards, man, just point to thuh one you want. You-pick- 10
that-card-you-pick-a-loser, yeah, that-cards-a-loser. You-pick-that-card-thats-thuh-other-loser. You-pick-that-card-you-pick-a-winner. Follow that card. You gotta chase that card. You-pick-thuh-dark-deuce-thats-a-loser-other-dark-deuces-thuh-other-loser, red-deuce, thuh-deuce-of-heartsll-win-it-all. Follow thuh red card. 15
(Rest.)
Ima show you thuh cards: 2 black cards but only one heart. Now watch me now. Who-sees-thuh-red-card-who-knows-where-its-at? Go on, man, point to thuh card. Put yr money down cause you aint no clown.
No? Ah you had thuh card, but you didnt have thuh heart.
(Rest.)
You wanna bet? 500 dollars? Shoot. You musta been watching 3-Card 20
real close. Ok. Lay the cash in my hand cause 3-Cards thuh man.
Thank you, mister. This card you say?
(Rest.)
Wrong! Sucker! Fool! Asshole! Bastard! I bet yr daddy heard how stupid you was and drank himself to death just cause he didnt wanna have nothing to do witchu! I bet yr mama seen you when you was born and 25
she wished she was dead, sucker! Ha Ha Ha! And 3-Card, once again, wins all thuh money!!
(Rest.)
What? Cops looking my way? Fold up thuh game, and walk away. Sneak outa sight. Set up on another corner.
(Rest.)
Yeah. 30
(Rest.)
(Having won the imaginary loot and dodged the imaginary cops, BOOTH *sets up his equipment and starts practicing his scam all over again.* LINCOLN *comes in quietly. He is a black man in his later 30s. He is dressed in an antique frock coat and wears a top hat and fake beard, that is, he is dressed to look like Abraham Lincoln. He surreptitiously*

walks into the room to stand right behind BOOTH, *who, engrossed in his cards, does not notice* LINCOLN *right away.)*

BOOTH: Watch me close watch me close now: who-see-thuh-red-card-who-see-thuh-red-card? I-see-thuh-red-card. Thuh-red-card-is-thuh-winner. Pick-thuh-red-card-you-pick-uh-winner. Pick-uh-black-card-you-pick-uh-loser. Theres-thuh-loser-yeah-theres-thuh-black-card, theres-thuh-other-loser-and-theres-thuh-red-card, thuh-winner. Don't touch my cards, man, don't—   35
(Rest.)
Dont do that shit. Dont do that shit. Dont do that shit!

*(*BOOTH, *sensing someone behind him, whirls around, pulling a gun from his pants. While the presence of* LINCOLN *doesnt surprise him, the Lincoln costume does.)*

BOOTH: And woah, man dont *ever* be doing that shit! Who thuh fuck you think you is coming in my shit all spooked out and shit. You pull that one more time I'll shoot you!
LINCOLN: I only had a minute to make the bus.   40
BOOTH: Bullshit.
LINCOLN: Not completely. I mean, its either bull or shit, but not a complete lie so it aint bullshit, right?
(Rest.)
Put yr gun away.
BOOTH: Take off the damn hat at least.   45
*(*LINCOLN *takes off the stovepipe hat.)*
*(*BOOTH *puts his gun away.)*
LINCOLN: Its cold out there. This thing kept my head warm.
BOOTH: I dont like you wearing that bullshit, that shit that bull that disguise that getup that motherdisfuckinguise anywhere in the daddy-dick-sticking vicinity of my humble abode.
*(*LINCOLN *takes off the beard.)*
LINCOLN: Better?   50
BOOTH: Take off the damn coat too. Damn, man. Bad enough you got to wear that shit all day you come up in here wearing it. What my women gonna say?
LINCOLN: What women?
BOOTH: I got a date with Grace tomorrow. Shes in love with me again but   55
she dont know it yet. Aint no man can love her the way I can. She sees you in that getup its gonna reflect bad on me. She coulda seen you coming down the street. Shit. Could be standing outside right now taking her ring off and throwing it on the sidewalk.
*(*BOOTH *takes a peek out the window.)*
BOOTH: I got her this ring today. Diamond. Well, diamond-esque, but it looks   60
just as good as the real thing. Asked her what size she wore. She say 7 so I

go boost a size 6 and a half, right? Show it to her and she loves it and
I shove it on her finger and its a tight fit right, so she cant just take it off
on a whim, like she did the last one I gave her. Smooth, right?

(BOOTH *takes another peek out the window.*)

LINCOLN: She out there?   65

BOOTH: Nope. Coast is clear.

LINCOLN: You boosted a ring?

BOOTH: Yeah. I thought about spending my inheritance on it but—take off
    that damn coat, man, you make me nervous standing there looking like
    a spook, and that damn face paint, take it off. You should take all of it   70
    off at work and leave it there.

LINCOLN: I dont bring it home someone might steal it.

BOOTH: At least *take it off* there, then.

LINCOLN: Yeah.

(*Rest.*)

(LINCOLN *takes off the frock coat and applies cold cream, removing the whiteface.*)

LINCOLN: I was riding the bus. Really I only had a minute to make my bus   75
    and I was sitting in the arcade thinking, should I change into my street
    clothes or should I make the bus? Nobody was in there today anyway.
    Middle of the week middle of winter. Not like on weekends. Weekends
    the place is packed. So Im riding the bus home. And this kid asked
    me for my autograph. I pretended I didnt hear him at first. I'd had a   80
    long day. But he kept asking. Theyd just done Lincoln in history class
    and he knew all about him, he'd been to the arcade but, I dunno, for
    some reason he was tripping cause there was Honest Abe right beside
    him on the bus. I wanted to tell him to go fuck hisself. But then I got
    a look at him. A little rich kid. Born on easy street, you know the type.   85
    So I waited until I could tell he really wanted it, the autograph, and I
    told him he could have it for 10 bucks. I was gonna say 5, cause of the
    Lincoln connection but something in me made me ask for 10.

BOOTH: But he didnt have a 10. All he had was a penny. So you took the
    penny.   90

LINCOLN: All he had was a 20. So I took the 20 and told him to meet me on
    the bus tomorrow and Honest Abe would give him the change.

BOOTH: Shit.

LINCOLN: Shit is right.

(*Rest.*)

BOOTH: Whatd you do with thuh 20?   95

LINCOLN: Bought drinks at Luckys. A round for everybody. They got a kick out
    of the getup.

BOOTH: You shoulda called me down.

LINCOLN: Next time, bro.

(Rest.)

LINCOLN: You making bookshelves? With the milk crates, you making   100
bookshelves?

BOOTH: Yeah, big bro, Im making bookshelves.

LINCOLN: Whats the cardboard part for?

BOOTH: Versatility.

LINCOLN: Oh.   105

BOOTH: I was thinking we dont got no bookshelves we dont got no dining
room table so Im making a sorta modular unit you put the books in the
bottom and the table top on top. We can eat and store our books. We
could put the photo album in there.

(BOOTH gets the raggedy family photo album and puts it in the milk crate.)

BOOTH: Youd sit there, I'd sit on the edge of the bed. Gathered around the   110
dinner table. Like old times.

LINCOLN: We just gotta get some books but thats great, Booth, thats real great.

BOOTH: Dont be calling me Booth no more, K?

LINCOLN: You changing yr name?

BOOTH: Maybe.   115

LINCOLN

BOOTH

LINCOLN: What to?

BOOTH: Im not ready to reveal it yet.

LINCOLN: You already decided on something?   120

BOOTH: Maybe.

LINCOLN: You gonna call yrself something african? That be cool. Only pick
something thats easy to spell and pronounce, man, cause you know, some
of them african names, I mean, ok, Im down with the power to the people
thing, but, no ones gonna hire you if they cant say yr name. And some   125
of them fellas who got they african names, no one can say they names
and they cant say they names neither. I mean, you dont want yr new
handle to obstruct yr employment possibilities.

BOOTH

LINCOLN   130

BOOTH: You bring dinner?

LINCOLN: "Shango" would be a good name. The name of the thunder god.
If you aint decided already Im just throwing it in the pot. I brought
chinese.

BOOTH: Lets try the table out.   135

LINCOLN: Cool.

(They both sit at the new table. The food is far away near the door.)

LINCOLN

BOOTH

LINCOLN: I buy it you set it up. Thats the deal. Thats the deal, right?

BOOTH: You like this place?   140

LINCOLN: Ssallright.

BOOTH: But a little cramped sometimes, right?

LINCOLN: You dont hear me complain. Although that recliner sometimes
    Booth, man—no Booth, right—man, Im too old to be sleeping in that chair.

BOOTH: Its my place. You dont got a place. Cookie, she threw you out.   145
    And you cant seem to get another woman. Yr lucky I let you stay.

LINCOLN: Every Friday you say *mi casa es su casa.*

BOOTH: Every Friday you come home with yr paycheck. Today is Thursday and
    I tell you brother, its a long way from Friday to Friday. All kinds of things
    can happen. All kinds of bad feelings can surface and erupt while yr   150
    little brother waits for you to bring in yr share.
    (Rest.)
    I got my Thursday head on, Link. Go get the food.

(LINCOLN *doesnt budge.*)

LINCOLN: You dont got no running water in here, man.

BOOTH: So?

LINCOLN: You dont got no toilet you dont got no sink.   155

BOOTH: Bathrooms down the hall.

LINCOLN: You living in thuh Third World, fool! Hey, I'll get thuh food.

(LINCOLN *goes to get the food. He sees a stray card on the floor and examines it
without touching it. He brings the food over, putting it nicely on the table.*)

LINCOLN: You been playing cards?

BOOTH: Yeah.

LINCOLN: Solitaire?   160

BOOTH: Thats right. Im getting pretty good at it.

LINCOLN: Thats soup and thats sauce. I got you the meat and I got me the
    skrimps.

BOOTH: I wanted the skrimps.

LINCOLN: You said you wanted the meat. This morning when I left you said   165
    you wanted the meat.
    (Rest.)
    Here man, take the skrimps. No sweat.

(*They eat. Chinese food from styrofoam containers, cans of soda, fortune cookies.*
LINCOLN *eats slowly and carefully,* BOOTH *eats ravenously.*)

LINCOLN: Yr getting good at solitaire?

BOOTH: Yeah. How about we play a hand after eating?

LINCOLN: Solitaire?   170

BOOTH: Poker or rummy or something.

LINCOLN: You know I dont touch thuh cards, man.

BOOTH: Just for fun.

LINCOLN: I dont touch thuh cards.

BOOTH: How about for money?   175

LINCOLN: You dont got no money. All the money you got I bring in here.

BOOTH: I got my inheritance.

LINCOLN: Thats like saying you dont got no money cause you aint never gonna
   do nothing with it so its like you dont got it.

BOOTH: At least I still got mines. You blew yrs.   180

LINCOLN

BOOTH

LINCOLN: You like the skrimps?

BOOTH: Ssallright.

LINCOLN: Whats yr fortune?   185

BOOTH: "Waste not want not." Whats yrs?

LINCOLN: "Your luck will change!"

(BOOTH *finishes eating. He turns his back to* LINCOLN *and fiddles around with the
cards, keeping them on the bed, just out of* LINCOLNS *sight. He mutters the 3-card
patter under his breath. His moves are still clumsy. Every once and a while he darts
a look over at* LINCOLN *who does his best to ignore* BOOTH.)

BOOTH: ((((Watch me close watch me close now: who-see-thuh-red-card- who-
   see-thuh-red-card? I-see-thuh-red-card. Thuh-red-card-is-thuh-winner. Pick-
   thuh-red-card-you-pick-uh-winner. Pick-uh-black-card-and-you-pick-uh-   190
   loser. Theres-thuh-loser, yeah, theres-thuh-black-card, theres-thuh-other-
   loser-and-theres-thuh-red-card, thuh-winner! Cop C, STICK, Cop C!
   Go on—))))

LINCOLN: ((Shit.))

BOOTH: (((((((One-good-pickll-get-you-in, 2-good-picks-and-you-gone-win.   195
   Dont touch my cards, man, just point to thuh one you want. You-pick-
   that- card-you-pick-uh-loser, yeah, that-cards-uh-loser. You-pick-that-card-
   thats-thuh-other-loser. You-pick-that-card-you-pick-uh-winner. Follow-that-
   card. You-gotta-chase-that-card!)))))))

LINCOLN: You wanna hustle 3-card monte, you gotta do it right, you gotta   200
   break it down. Practice it in smaller bits. Yr trying to do the whole thing
   at once thats why you keep fucking it up.

BOOTH: Show me.

LINCOLN: No. Im just saying you wanna do it you gotta do it right and
   if you gonna do it right you gotta work on it in smaller bits, thatsall.   205

BOOTH: You and me could team up and do it together. We'd clean up, Link.

LINCOLN: I'll clean up—bro.

(LINCOLN *cleans up. As he clears the food,* BOOTH *goes back to using the "table" for
its original purpose.)

BOOTH: My new names 3-Card. 3-Card, got it? You wanted to know it so now
    you know it. 3-card monte by 3-Card. Call me 3-Card from here on out.
LINCOLN: 3-Card. Shit. 210
BOOTH: Im getting everybody to call me 3-Card. Grace likes 3-Card better
    than Booth. She says 3-Cards got something to it. Anybody not calling
    me 3-Card gets a bullet.
LINCOLN: Yr too much, man.
BOOTH: Im making a point. 215
LINCOLN: Point made, 3-Card. Point made.
(LINCOLN *picks up his guitar. Plays at it.*)
BOOTH: Oh, come on, man, we could make money you and me. Throwing
    down the cards. 3-Card and Link: look out! We could clean up you
    and me. You would throw the cards and I'd be yr Stickman. The one
    in the crowd who looks like just an innocent passerby, who looks like 220
    just another player, like just another customer, but who gots intimate
    connections with you, the Dealer, the one throwing the cards, the main
    man. I'd be the one who brings in the crowd, I'd be the one who makes
    them want to put they money down, you do yr moves and I do mines.
    You turn yr head and I turn the card— 225
LINCOLN: It aint as easy as all that. Theres—
BOOTH: We could be a team, man. Rake in the money! Sure thered be some
    cats out there with fast eyes, some brothers and sisters who would
    watch real close and pick the right card, and so thered be some days
    when we would lose money, but most of the days we would come out 230
    on top! Pockets bulging, plenty of cash! And the ladies would be thrill-
    ing! You could afford to get laid! Grace would be all over me again.
LINCOLN: I thought you said she was all over you.
BOOTH: She is she is. Im seeing her tomorrow but today we gotta solidify the
    shit twixt you and me. Big brother Link and little brother Booth— 235
LINCOLN: 3-Card.
BOOTH: Yeah. Scheming and dreaming. No one throws the cards like you,
    Link. And with yr moves and my magic, and we get Grace and a girl for
    you to round out the posse. We'd be golden, bro! Am I right?
LINCOLN 240
LINCOLN
BOOTH: Am I right?
LINCOLN: I dont touch thuh cards, 3-Card. I dont touch thuh cards no more.
LINCOLN
BOOTH 245
LINCOLN
BOOTH

BOOTH: You know what Mom told me when she was packing to leave? You
was at school motherfucker you was at school. You got up that morning
and sat down in yr regular place and read the cereal box while Dad read 250
the sports section and Mom brought you yr dick toast and then you got
on the damn school bus cause you didnt have the sense to do nothing
else you was so into yr own shit that you didnt have the sense to feel
nothing else going on. I had the sense to go back cause I was feeling
something going on man, I was feeling something changing. So I—   255

LINCOLN: Cut school that day like you did almost every day—

BOOTH: She was putting her stuff in bags. She had all them nice suitcases but
she was putting her stuff in bags.
(Rest.)
Packing up her shit. She told me to look out for you. I told her I was
the little brother and the big brother should look out after the little   260
brother. She just said it again. That I should look out for you. Yeah.
So who gonna look out for me. Not like you care. Here I am interested
in an economic opportunity, willing to work hard, willing to take risks
and all you can say you shiteating motherfucking pathetic limpdick
uncle tom, all you can tell me is how you dont do no more what I be   265
wanting to do. Here I am trying to earn a living and you standing in my
way. YOU STANDING IN MY WAY, LINK!

LINCOLN: Im sorry.

BOOTH: Yeah, you sorry all right.

LINCOLN: I cant be hustling no more, bro.   270

BOOTH: What you do all day aint no hustle?

LINCOLN: Its honest work.

BOOTH: Dressing up like some crackerass white man, some dead president and
letting people shoot at you sounds like a hustle to me.

LINCOLN: People know the real deal. When people know the real deal it aint   275
a hustle.

BOOTH: We do the card game people will know the real deal. Sometimes we
will win sometimes they will win. They fast they win, we faster we win.

LINCOLN: I aint going back to that, bro. I aint going back.

BOOTH: You play Honest Abe. You aint going back but you going all the way   280
back. Back to way back then when folks was slaves and shit.

LINCOLN: Dont push me.

BOOTH

LINCOLN

BOOTH: You gonna have to leave.   285

LINCOLN: I'll be gone tomorrow.

BOOTH: Good. Cause this was only supposed to be a temporary arrangement.

LINCOLN: I will be gone tomorrow.

BOOTH: Good.

(BOOTH *sits on his bed.* LINCOLN, *sitting in his easy chair with his guitar, plays and sings.*)

LINCOLN: My dear mother left me, my fathers gone away   290
 My dear mother left me and my fathers gone away
 I dont got no money, I dont got no place to stay.

 My best girl, she threw me out into the street
 My favorite horse, they ground him into meat
 Im feeling cold from my head down to my feet   295

 My luck was bad but now it turned to worse
 My luck was bad but now it turned to worse
 Dont call me up a doctor, just call me up a hearse.

BOOTH: You just made that up?

LINCOLN: I had it in my head for a few days.   300

BOOTH: Sounds good.

LINCOLN: Thanks.
 (*Rest.*)
 Daddy told me once why we got the names we do.

BOOTH: Yeah?

LINCOLN: Yeah.   305
 (*Rest.*)
 He was drunk when he told me, or maybe I was drunk when he told
 me. Anyway he told me, may not be true, but he told me. Why he
 named us both. Lincoln and Booth.

BOOTH: How come. How come, man?

LINCOLN: It was his idea of a joke.   310

(*Both men relax back as the lights fade.*)

Scene 2

Friday evening. The very next day. BOOTH *comes in looking like he is bundled up against the cold. He makes sure his brother isnt home, then stands in the middle of the room. From his big coat sleeves he pulls out one new shoe then another, from another sleeve come two more shoes. He then slithers out a belt from each sleeve. He removes his coat. Underneath he wears a very nice new suit. He removes the jacket and pants revealing another new suit underneath. The suits still have the price tags on them. He takes two neckties from his pockets and two folded shirts from the back of his pants. He pulls a magazine from the front of his pants. Hes clearly had a busy day of shoplifting. He lays one suit out on* LINCOLN'S *easy chair. The other he lays out on his own bed. He goes out into the hall returning with a folding screen which*

he sets up between the bed and the recliner creating 2 separate spaces. He takes out
a bottle of whiskey and two glasses, setting them on the two stacked milk crates.
He hears footsteps and sits down in the small wooden chair reading the magazine.
LINCOLN, *dressed in street clothes, comes in.*

LINCOLN: Taaaaadaaaaaaaa!

BOOTH: Lordamighty, Pa, I smells money!

LINCOLN: Sho nuff, Ma. Poppas brung home thuh bacon.

BOOTH: Bringitherebringitherebringithere.

(*With a series of very elaborate moves* LINCOLN *brings the money over to* BOOTH.)

BOOTH: Put it in my hands, Pa!   5

LINCOLN: I want ya tuh smells it first, Ma!

BOOTH: Put it neath my nose then, Pa!

LINCOLN: Take yrself a good long whiff of them greenbacks.

BOOTH: Oh lordamighty Ima faint, Pa! Get me muh med-sin!

(LINCOLN *quickly pours two large glasses of whiskey.*)

LINCOLN: Dont die on me, Ma!   10

BOOTH: Im fading fast, Pa!

LINCOLN: Thinka thuh children, Ma! Thinka thuh farm!

BOOTH: 1-2-3.

(*Both men gulp down their drinks simultaneously.*)

LINCOLN AND BOOTH: AAAAAAAAAAAAAAAAAAAAAH!

(*Lots of laughing and slapping on the backs.*)

LINCOLN: Budget it out man budget it out.   15

BOOTH: You in a hurry?

LINCOLN: Yeah. I wanna see how much we got for the week.

BOOTH: You rush in here and dont even look around. Could be a fucking
    A-bomb in the middle of the floor you wouldnt notice. Yr wife, Cookie—

LINCOLN: X-wife—   20

BOOTH: —could be in my bed you wouldnt notice—

LINCOLN: She was once—

BOOTH: Look the fuck around please.

(LINCOLN *looks around and sees the new suit on his chair.*)

LINCOLN: Wow.

BOOTH: Its yrs.   25

LINCOLN: Shit.

BOOTH: Got myself one too.

LINCOLN: Boosted?

BOOTH: Yeah, I boosted em. Theys stole from a big-ass department store. That
    store takes in more money in one day than we will in our whole life. I stole   30
    and I stole generously. I got one for me and I got one for you. Shoes belts
    shirts ties socks in the shoes and everything. Got that screen too.

LINCOLN: You all right, man.

BOOTH: Just cause I aint good as you at cards dont mean I cant do nothing.

LINCOLN: Lets try em on.   35

(They stand in their separate sleeping spaces, BOOTH near his bed, LINCOLN near his recliner, and try on their new clothes.)

BOOTH: Ima wear mine tonight. Gracell see me in this and *she* gonna ask me
   tuh marry *her*.
   (Rest.)
   I got you the blue and I got me the brown. I walked in there and walked
   out and they didnt as much as bat an eye. Thats how smooth lil bro be,
   Link.   40

LINCOLN: You did good. You did real good, 3-Card.

BOOTH: All in a days work.

LINCOLN: They say the clothes make the man. All day long I wear that
   getup. But that dont make me who I am. Old black coat not even real
   old just fake old. Its got worn spots on the elbows, little raggedy places   45
   thatll break through into holes before the winters out. Shiny strips
   around the cuffs and the collar. Dust from the cap guns on the left
   shoulder where they shoot him, where they shoot me I should say but I
   never feel like they shooting me. The fella who had the gig before I had
   it wore the same coat. When I got the job they had the getup hanging   50
   there waiting for me. Said thuh fella before me just took it off one day
   and never came back.
   (Rest.)
   Remember how Dads clothes used to hang in the closet?

BOOTH: Until you took em outside and burned em.
   (Rest.)
   He had some nice stuff. What he didnt spend on booze he spent on   55
   women. What he didnt spend on them two he spent on clothes. He had
   some nice stuff. I would look at his stuff and calculate thuh how long it
   would take till I was big enough to fit it. Then you went and burned it
   all up.

LINCOLN: I got tired of looking at em without him in em.   60
   (Rest.)
   They said thuh fella before me—he took off the getup one day, hung it
   up real nice, and never came back. And as they offered me thuh job,
   saying of course I would have to wear a little makeup and accept less
   than what they would offer a—another guy—

BOOTH: Go on, say it. "White." Theyd pay you less than theyd pay a white guy.   65

LINCOLN: I said to myself thats exactly what I would do: wear it out and then
   leave it hanging there and not come back. But until then, I would make
   a living at it. But it dont make me. Worn suit coat, not even worn by

the fool that Im supposed to be playing, but making fools out of all
those folks who come crowding in for they chance to play at something 70
great. Fake beard. Top hat. Dont make me into no Lincoln. I was
Lincoln on my own before any of that.

(*The men finish dressing. They style and profile.*)

BOOTH: Sharp, huh?

LINCOLN: Very sharp.

BOOTH: You look sharp too, man. You look like the real you. Most of the 75
time you walking around all bedraggled and shit. You look good. Like
you used to look back in thuh day when you had Cookie in love with
you and all the women in the world was eating out of yr hand.

LINCOLN: This is real nice, man. I dont know where Im gonna wear it but its
real nice. 80

BOOTH: Just wear it around. Itll make you feel good and when you feel good
yll meet someone nice. Me I aint interested in meeting no one nice,
I mean, I only got eyes for Grace. You think she'll go for me in this?

LINCOLN: I think thuh tie you gave me'll go better with what you got on.

BOOTH: Yeah? 85

LINCOLN: Grace likes bright colors dont she? My ties bright, yrs is too
subdued.

BOOTH: Yeah. Gimmie yr tie.

LINCOLN: You gonna take back a gift?

BOOTH: I stole the damn thing didnt I? Gimmie yrs! I'll give you mines. 90

(*They switch neckties.* BOOTH *is pleased.* LINCOLN *is more pleased.*)

LINCOLN: Do thuh budget.

BOOTH: Right. Ok lets see: we got 314 dollars. We put 100 aside for the rent.
100 a week times 4 weeks makes the rent and—

LINCOLN AND BOOTH: —we dont want thuh rent spent.

BOOTH: That leaves 214. We put aside 30 for the electric leaving 184. We put 95
aside 50 for thuh phone leaving 134.

LINCOLN: We dont got a phone.

BOOTH: We pay our bill theyll turn it back on.

LINCOLN: We dont need no phone.

BOOTH: How you gonna get a woman if you dont got a phone? Women these 100
days are more cautious, more whaddacallit, more circumspect. You go
into a club looking like a fast daddy, you get a filly to give you her numer-
ophono and gone is the days when she just gives you her number and
dont ask for yrs.

LINCOLN: Like a woman is gonna call me. 105

BOOTH: She dont wanna call you she just doing a preliminary survey of the
property. Shit, Link, you dont know nothin no more.

(*Rest.*)

She gives you her number and she asks for yrs. You give her yr number. The phone number of yr home. Thereby telling her 3 things: 1) you got a home, that is, you aint no smooth talking smooth dressing homeless   110 joe; 2) that you is in possession of a telephone and a working telephone number which is to say that you got thuh cash and thuh wherewithal to acquire for yr self the worlds most revolutionary communication apparatus and you together enough to pay yr bills!

LINCOLN: Whats 3?   115

BOOTH: You give her yr number you telling her that its cool to call if she should so please, that is, that you aint got no wife or wife approxima-tion on the premises.

(Rest.)

50 for the phone leaving 134. We put aside 40 for "med-sin."

LINCOLN: The price went up. 2 bucks more a bottle.   120

BOOTH: We'll put aside 50, then. That covers the bills. We got 84 left. 40 for meals together during the week leaving 44. 30 for me 14 for you. I got a woman I gotta impress tonight.

LINCOLN: You didnt take out for the phone last week.

BOOTH: Last week I was depressed. This week things is looking up. For both   125 of us.

LINCOLN: Theyre talking about cutbacks at the arcade. I only been there 8 months, so—

BOOTH: Dont sweat it man, we'll find something else.

LINCOLN: Not nothing like this. I like the job. This is sit down, you know,   130 easy work. I just gotta sit there all day. Folks come in kill phony Honest Abe with the phony pistol. I can sit there and let my mind travel.

BOOTH: Think of women.

LINCOLN: Sometimes.

(Rest.)

All around the whole arcade is buzzing and popping. Thuh whirring   135 of thuh duckshoot, baseballs smacking the back wall when someone misses the stack of cans, some woman getting happy cause her fella just won the ring toss. The Boss playing the barker talking up the fake freaks. The smell of the ocean and cotton candy and rat shit. And in thuh middle of all that, I can just sit and let my head go quiet. Make up   140 songs, make plans. Forget.

(Rest.)

You should come down again.

BOOTH: Once was plenty, but thanks.

(Rest.)

Yr Best Customer, he come in today?

LINCOLN: Oh, yeah, he was there.   145

BOOTH: He shoot you?

LINCOLN: He shot Honest Abe, yeah.

BOOTH: He talk to you?

LINCOLN: In a whisper. Shoots on the left whispers on the right.

BOOTH: Whatd he say this time? 150

LINCOLN: "Does thuh show stop when no ones watching or does thuh show go on?"

BOOTH: Hes getting deep.

LINCOLN: Yeah.

BOOTH: Whatd he say, that one time? "Yr only yrself—" 155

LINCOLN: "—when no ones watching," yeah.

BOOTH: Thats deep shit.

(Rest.)

Hes a brother, right?

LINCOLN: I think so.

BOOTH: He know yr a brother? 160

LINCOLN: I dunno.

BOOTH: Hes a *deep* black brother.

LINCOLN: Yeah. He makes the day interesting.

BOOTH (Rest.): Thats a fucked-up job you got.

LINCOLN: Its a living. 165

BOOTH: But you aint living.

LINCOLN: Im alive aint I?

(Rest.)

One day I was throwing the cards. Next day Lonny died. Somebody shot him. I knew I was next, so I quit. I saved my life.

(Rest.)

The arcade gig is the first lucky break Ive ever had. And Ive actually 170 grown to like the work. And now theyre talking about cutting me.

BOOTH: You was lucky with thuh cards.

LINCOLN: Lucky? Aint nothing lucky about cards. Cards aint luck. Cards is work. Cards is skill. Aint never nothing lucky about cards.

(Rest.)

I dont wanna lose my job. 175

BOOTH: Then you gotta jazz up yr act. Elaborate yr moves, you know. You was always too stiff with it. You cant just sit there! Maybe, when they shoot you, you know, leap up flail yr arms then fall down and wiggle around and shit so they gotta shoot you more than once. Blam Blam Blam! Blam! 180

LINCOLN: Help me practice. I'll sit here like I do at work and you be like one of the tourists.

BOOTH: No thanks.

LINCOLN: My paychecks on the line, man.

BOOTH: I got a date. Practice on yr own.   185

    (*Rest.*)

    I got a rendezvous with Grace. Shit she so sweet she makes my teeth hurt.

    (*Rest.*) Link, uh, howbout slipping me an extra 5 spot. Its the biggest

    night of my life.

LINCOLN

BOOTH   190

(LINCOLN *gives* BOOTH *a 5er.*)

BOOTH: Thanks.

LINCOLN: No sweat.

BOOTH: Howabout I run through it with you when I get back. Put on yr

    getup and practice till then.

LINCOLN: Sure.   195

(BOOTH *leaves.* LINCOLN *stands there alone. He takes off his shoes, giving them
a shine. He takes off his socks and his fancy suit, hanging it neatly over the little
wooden chair. He takes his getup out of his shopping bag. He puts it on, slowly,
like an actor preparing for a great role: frock coat, pants, beard, top hat, necktie.
He leaves his feet bare. The top hat has an elastic band which he positions securely
underneath his chin. He picks up the white pancake makeup but decides against it.
He sits. He pretends to get shot, flings himself on the floor and thrashes around. He
gets up, considers giving the new moves another try, but instead pours himself a big
glass of whiskey and sits there drinking.*)

Scene 3

*Much later that same Friday evening. The recliner is reclined to its maximum hori-
zontal position and* LINCOLN *lies there asleep. He wakes with a start. He is horrific,
bleary eyed and hungover, in his full Lincoln regalia. He takes a deep breath, realizes
where he is and reclines again, going back to sleep.* BOOTH *comes in full of swagger.
He slams the door trying to wake his brother who is dead to the world. He opens
the door and slams it again. This time* LINCOLN *wakes up, as hungover and horrid
as before.* BOOTH *swaggers about, his moves are exaggerated, roosterlike. He walks
round and round* LINCOLN *making sure his brother sees him.*

LINCOLN: You hurt yrself?

BOOTH: I had me "an evening to remember."

LINCOLN: You look like you hurt yrself.

BOOTH: Grace Grace Grace. *Grace.* She wants me back. She wants me back

    so bad she wiped her hand over the past where we wasnt together just   5

    so she could say we aint never been apart. She wiped her hand over our

    breakup. She wiped her hand over her childhood, her teenage years,

    her first boyfriend, just so she could say that she been mine since the

    dawn of time.

LINCOLN: Thats great, man.   10

BOOTH: And all the shit I put her through: she wiped it clean. And the
    women I saw while I was seeing her—

LINCOLN: Wiped clean too?

BOOTH: Mister Clean, Mister, Mister Clean!

LINCOLN: Whered you take her?   15

BOOTH: We was over at her place. I brought thuh food. Stopped at the best
    place I could find and stuffed my coat with only the best. We had the
    music we had the candlelight we had—

LINCOLN: She let you do it?

BOOTH: Course she let me do it.   20

LINCOLN: She let you do it without a rubber?

BOOTH: —Yeah.

LINCOLN: Bullshit.

BOOTH: I put my foot down—and she melted. And she was—huh—she was
    something else. I dont wanna get you jealous, though.   25

LINCOLN: Go head, I dont mind.

BOOTH (*Rest.*): Well, you know what she looks like.

LINCOLN: She walks on by and the emergency room fills up cause all the guys
    get whiplash from lookin at her.

BOOTH: Thats right thats right. Well—she comes to the door wearing   30
    nothing but her little nightie, eats up the food I'd brought like there
    was no tomorrow and then goes and eats on me.

(*Rest.*)

LINCOLN: Go on.

BOOTH: I dont wanna make you feel bad, man.

LINCOLN: Ssallright. Go on.   35

BOOTH (*Rest.*): Well, uh, you know what shes like. Wild. Goodlooking. So
    sweet my teeth hurt.

LINCOLN: A sexmachine.

BOOTH: Yeah.

LINCOLN: A hotsy-totsy.   40

BOOTH: Yeah.

LINCOLN: Amazing Grace.

BOOTH: Amazing Grace! Yeah. Thats right. She let me do her how I wanted.
    And no rubber.

    (*Rest.*)

LINCOLN: Go on.   45

BOOTH: You dont wanna hear the mushy shit.

LINCOLN: Sure I do.

BOOTH: You hate mushy shit. You always hated thuh mushy shit.

LINCOLN: Ive changed. Go head. You had "an evening to remember,"

remember? I was just here alone sitting here. Drinking. Go head. Tell   50
Link thuh stink.
(*Rest.*)
Howd ya do her?
BOOTH: Dogstyle.
LINCOLN: Amazing Grace.
BOOTH: In front of a mirror.   55
LINCOLN: So you could see her. Her face her breasts her back her ass. Graces
   got a great ass.
BOOTH: Its all right.
LINCOLN: Amazing Grace!
(BOOTH *goes into his bed area and takes off his suit, tossing the clothes on the floor.*)
BOOTH: She said next time Ima have to use a rubber. She let me have my way   60
   this time but she said that next time I'd have to put my boots on.
LINCOLN: Im sure you can talk her out of it.
BOOTH: Yeah.
   (*Rest.*)
   What kind of rubbers you use, I mean, when you was with Cookie.
LINCOLN: We didnt use rubbers. We was married, man.   65
BOOTH: Right. But you had other women on the side. What kind you use
   when you was with them?
LINCOLN: Magnums.
BOOTH: Thats thuh kind I picked up. For next time. Grace was real strict
   about it. Magnums.   70
(*While* BOOTH *sits on his bed fiddling with his box of condoms,* LINCOLN *sits in his chair and resumes drinking.*)
LINCOLN: Theyre for "the larger man."
BOOTH: Right. Right.
(LINCOLN *keeps drinking as* BOOTH, *sitting in the privacy of his bedroom, fiddles with the condoms, perhaps trying to put one on.*)
LINCOLN: Thats right.
BOOTH: Graces real different from them fly-by-night gals I was making do with.
   Shes in school. Making something of herself. Studying cosmetology. You   75
   should see what she can do with a womans hair and nails.
LINCOLN: Too bad you aint a woman.
BOOTH: What?
LINCOLN: You could get yrs done for free, I mean.
BOOTH: Yeah. She got this way of sitting. Of talking. That. Everything she   80
   does is. Shes just so hot.
   (*Rest.*)
   We was together 2 years. Then we broke up. I had my little employment
   difficulty and she needed time to think.

LINCOLN: And shes through thinking now.

BOOTH: Thats right. 85

LINCOLN

BOOTH

LINCOLN: Whatcha doing back there?

BOOTH: Resting. That girl wore me out.

LINCOLN: You want some med-sin? 90

BOOTH: No thanks.

LINCOLN: Come practice my moves with me, then.

BOOTH: Lets hit it tomorrow, K?

LINCOLN: I been waiting. I got all dressed up and you said if I waited up— come on, man, they gonna replace me with a wax dummy. 95

BOOTH: No shit.

LINCOLN: Thats what theyre talking about. Probably just talk, but—come on, man, I even lent you 5 bucks.

BOOTH: Im tired.

LINCOLN: You didnt get shit tonight. 100

BOOTH: You jealous, man. You just jail-us.

LINCOLN: You laying over there yr balls blue as my boosted suit. Laying over there waiting for me to go back to sleep or black out so I wont hear you rustling thuh pages of yr fuck book.

BOOTH: Fuck you, man. 105

LINCOLN: I was over there looking for something the other week and theres like 100 fuck books under yr bed and theyre matted together like a bad fro, bro, cause you spunked in the pages and didnt wipe them off.

BOOTH: Im hot. I need constant sexual release. If I wasnt taking care of myself by myself I would be out there running around on thuh town 110 which costs cash that I dont have so I would be doing worse: I'd be out there doing who knows what, shooting people and shit. Out of a need for unresolved sexual release. I'm a hot man. I aint apologizing for it. When I dont got a woman, I gotta make do. Not like you, Link. When you dont got a woman you just sit there. Letting yr shit fester. Yr dick, 115 if it aint falled off yet, is hanging there between yr legs, little whiteface shriveled-up blank-shooting grub worm. As goes thuh man so goes thuh mans dick. Thats what I say. Least my shits intact.

(Rest.)

You a limp dick jealous whiteface motherfucker whose wife dumped him cause he couldnt get it up and she told me so. Came crawling to me cause 120 she needed a man.

(Rest.)

I gave it to Grace good tonight. So goodnight.

LINCOLN (Rest.): Goodnight.

LINCOLN
BOOTH   125
LINCOLN
BOOTH
LINCOLN
BOOTH

(LINCOLN *sitting in his chair.* BOOTH *lying in bed. Time passes.* BOOTH *peeks out to see if* LINCOLN *is asleep.* LINCOLN *is watching for him.*)

LINCOLN: You can hustle 3-card monte without me you know.   130
BOOTH: Im planning to.
LINCOLN: I could contact my old crew. You could work with them. Lonny
    aint around no more but theres the rest of them. Theyre good.
BOOTH: I can get my own crew. I dont need yr crew. Buncha has-beens.
    I can get my own crew.   135
LINCOLN: My crews experienced. We usedta pull down a thousand a day.
    Thats 7 G a week. That was years ago. They probably do twice, 3 times
    that now.
BOOTH: I got my own connections, thank you.
LINCOLN: Theyd take you on in a heartbeat. With my say. My say still   140
    counts with them. They know you from before, when you tried to
    hang with us but—wernt ready yet. They know you from then, but I'd
    talk you up. I'd say yr my bro, which they know, and I'd say youd been
    working the west coast. Little towns. Mexican border. Taking tourists.
    I'd tell them you got moves like I dreamed of having. Meanwhile youd   145
    be working out yr shit right here, right in this room, getting good and
    getting better every day so when I did do the reintroductions youd have
    some marketable skills. Youd be passable.
BOOTH: I'd be more than passable, I'd be the be all end all.
LINCOLN: Youd be the be all end all. And youd have my say. If yr interested.   150
BOOTH: Could do.
LINCOLN: Youd have to get a piece. They all pack pistols, bro.
BOOTH: I *got* a piece.
LINCOLN: Youd have to be packing something more substantial than that pop
    gun, 3-Card. These hustlers is upper echelon hustlers they pack upper   155
    echelon heat, not no Saturday night shit, now.
BOOTH: Whata you know of heat? You aint hung with those guys for 6, 7
    years. You swore off em. Threw yr heat in thuh river and you "Dont
    touch thuh cards." I know more about heat than you know about
    heat.   160
LINCOLN: Im around guns every day. At the arcade. Theyve all been reworked
    so they only fire caps but I see guns every day. Lots of guns.
BOOTH: What kinds?

LINCOLN: You been there, you seen them. Shiny deadly metal each with their own deadly personality. 165

BOOTH: Maybe I *could* visit you over there. I'd boost one of them guns and rework it to make it shoot for real again. What kind you think would best suit my personality?

LINCOLN: You aint stealing nothing from the arcade.

BOOTH: I go in there and steal if I want to go in there and steal I go in there 170 and steal.

LINCOLN: It aint worth it. They dont shoot nothing but blanks.

BOOTH: Yeah, like you. Shooting blanks.

   (Rest.)
   (Rest.)

You ever wonder if someones gonna come in there with a real gun? A real gun with real slugs? Someone with uh axe tuh grind or something? 175

LINCOLN: No.

BOOTH: Someone who hates you come in there and guns you down and gets gone before anybody finds out.

LINCOLN: I dont got no enemies.

BOOTH: Yr X. 180

LINCOLN: Cookie dont hate me.

BOOTH: Yr Best Customer? Some miscellaneous stranger?

LINCOLN: I cant be worrying about the actions of miscellaneous strangers.

BOOTH: But there they come day in day out for a chance to shoot Honest Abe. 185

   (Rest.)

Who are they mostly?

LINCOLN: I dont really look.

BOOTH: You must see something.

LINCOLN: Im supposed to be staring straight ahead. Watching a play, like Abe was. 190

BOOTH: All day goes by and you never ever take a sneak peek at who be pulling the trigger.

(Pulled in by his own curiosity, BOOTH *has come out of his bed area to stand on the dividing line between the two spaces.)*

LINCOLN: Its pretty dark. To keep thuh illusion of thuh whole thing.

   (Rest.)

But on thuh wall opposite where I sit theres a little electrical box, like a fuse box. Silver metal. Its got uh dent in it like somebody hit it with 195 they fist. Big old dent so everything reflected in it gets reflected upside down. Like yr looking in uh spoon. And thats where I can see em. The assassins.

   (Rest.)

Not behind me yet but I can hear him coming. Coming in with his gun in hand, thuh gun he already picked out up front when he paid his fare. Coming on in. But not behind me yet. His dress shoes making too much noise on the carpet, the carpets too thin, Boss should get a new one but hes cheap. Not behind me yet. Not behind me yet. Cheap lightbulb just above my head. 200

(Rest.)

And there he is. Standing behind me. Standing in position. Standing upside down. Theres some feet shapes on the floor so he knows just where he oughta stand. So he wont miss. Thuh gun is always cold. Winter or summer thuh gun is always cold. And when the gun touches me he can feel that Im warm and he knows Im alive. And if Im alive then he can shoot me dead. And for a minute, with him hanging back there behind me, its real. Me looking at him upside down and him looking at me looking like Lincoln. Then he shoots. 210 215

(Rest.)

I slump down and close my eyes. And he goes out thuh other way. More come in. Uh whole day full. Bunches of kids, little good for noth ings, in they school uniforms. Businessmen smelling like two for one martinis. Tourists in they theme park t-shirts trying to catch it on film. Housewives with they mouths closed tight, shooting more than once. 220

(Rest.)

They all get so into it. I do my best for them. And now they talking bout cutting me, replacing me with uh wax dummy.

BOOTH: You just gotta show yr boss that you can do things a wax dummy cant do. You too dry with it. You gotta add spicy shit. 225

LINCOLN: Like what.

BOOTH: Like when they shoot you, I dunno, scream or something.

LINCOLN: Scream?

(BOOTH plays the killer without using his gun.)

BOOTH: Try it. I'll be the killer. Bang! 230

LINCOLN: Aaaah!

BOOTH: Thats good.

LINCOLN: A wax dummy can scream. They can put a voicebox in it and make it like its screaming.

BOOTH: You can curse. Try it. Bang! 235

LINCOLN: Motherfucking cocksucker!

BOOTH: Thats good, man.

LINCOLN: They aint going for that, though.

BOOTH: You practice rolling and wiggling on the floor?

LINCOLN: A little. 240

BOOTH: Lemmie see. Bang!

(LINCOLN *slumps down, falls on the floor and silently wiggles around.*)

BOOTH: You look more like a worm on the sidewalk. Move yr arms. Good.
Now scream or something.

LINCOLN: Aaaah! Aaaaah! Aaaah!

BOOTH: A little tougher than that, you sound like yr fucking.   245

LINCOLN: Aaaaaah!

BOOTH: Hold yr head or something, where I shotcha. Good. And look at me!
I am the assassin! *I am Booth!!* Come on man this is life and death! Go all
out!

(LINCOLN *goes all out!*)

BOOTH: Cool, man thats cool. Thats enough.   250

LINCOLN: Whatdoyathink?

BOOTH: I dunno, man. Something about it. I dunno. It was looking too real
or something.

LINCOLN: Goddamn you! They dont want it looking too real. I'd scare the
customers. Then I'd be out for sure. Yr trying to get me fired.   255

BOOTH: Im trying to help. Cross my heart.

LINCOLN: People are funny about they Lincoln shit. Its historical. People
like they historical shit in a certain way. They like it to unfold the way
they folded it up. Neatly like a book. Not raggedy and bloody and
screaming. You trying to get me fired.   260
(*Rest.*)
I am uh brother playing Lincoln. Its uh stretch for anyones imagination. And it aint easy for me neither. Every day I put on that shit, I
leave my own shit at the door and I put on that shit and I go out there
and I make it work. I make it look easy but its hard. That shit is hard.
But it works. Cause I work it. And you trying to get me fired.   265
(*Rest.*)
I swore off them cards. Took nowhere jobs. Drank. Then Cookie threw
me out. What thuh fuck was I gonna do? I seen that "Help Wanted"
sign and I went up in there and I looked good in the getup and agreed
to the whiteface and they really dug it that me and Honest Abe got the
same name.   270
(*Rest.*)
Its a sit down job. With benefits. I dont wanna get fired. They wont
give me a good reference if I get fired.

BOOTH: Iffen you was tuh get fired, then, well—then you and me could—
hustle the cards together. We'd have to support ourselves somehow.
(*Rest.*)
Just show me how to do the hook part of the card hustle, man. The part   275
where the Dealer looks away but somehow he sees—

LINCOLN: I couldnt remember if I wanted to.

BOOTH: Sure you could.
LINCOLN: No.
   (*Rest.*)
   Night, man.   280
BOOTH: Yeah.

(LINCOLN *stretches out in his recliner.* BOOTH *stands over him waiting for him to get up, to change his mind. But* LINCOLN *is fast asleep.* BOOTH *covers him with a blanket then goes to his bed, turning off the lights as he goes. He quietly rummages underneath his bed for a girlie magazine which, as the lights fade, he reads with great interest.*)

Scene 4
Saturday. *Just before dawn.* LINCOLN *gets up. Looks around.* BOOTH *is fast asleep, dead to the world.*

LINCOLN: No fucking running water.

(*He stumbles around the room looking for something which he finally finds: a plastic cup, which he uses as a urinal. He finishes peeing and finds an out of the way place to stow the cup. He claws at his Lincoln getup, removing it and tearing it in the process. He strips down to his t-shirt and shorts.*)

LINCOLN: Hate falling asleep in this damn shit. Shit. Ripped the beard. I
   can just hear em tomorrow. Busiest day of the week. They looking me
   over to make sure Im presentable. They got a slew of guys working
   but Im the only one they look over every day. "Yr beards ripped, pal.   5
   Sure, we'll getcha new one but its gonna be coming outa yr pay." Shit.
   I should quit right then and there. I'd yank off the beard, throw it on
   the ground and stomp it, then go strangle the fucking boss. Thatd be
   good. My hands around his neck and his bug eyes bugging out. You
   been ripping me off since I took this job and now Im gonna have to   10
   take it outa yr pay, motherfucker. Shit.
   (*Rest.*)
   Sit down job. With benefits.
   (*Rest.*)
   Hustling. Shit, I was good. I was great. Hell I was the be all end all. I
   was throwing cards like throwing cards was made for me. Made for me
   and me alone. I was the best anyone ever seen. Coast to coast. Every-   15
   body said so. And I never lost. Not once. Not one time. Not never.
   Thats how much them cards was mines. I was the be all end all. I was
   that good.
   (*Rest.*)
   Then you woke up one day and you didnt have the taste for it no more.
   Like something in you knew—. Like something in you knew it was time   20
   to quit. Quit while you was still ahead. Something in you was telling

you—. But hells no. Not Link thuh stink. So I went out there and threw
one more time. What thuh fuck. And Lonny died.
(Rest.)
Got yrself a good job. And when the arcade lets you go yll get another
good job. I dont gotta spend my whole life hustling. Theres more to   25
Link than that. More to me than some cheap hustle. More to life than
cheating some idiot out of his paycheck or his life savings.
(Rest.)
Like that joker and his wife from out of town. Always wanted to see
the big city. I said you could see the bigger end of the big city with a
little more cash. And if they was fast enough, faster than me, and here I   30
slowed down my moves I slowed em way down and my Lonny, my right
hand, my Stickman, Lonny could draw a customer in like nothing else,
Lonny could draw a fly from fresh shit, he could draw Adam outa Eve
just with that look he had, Lonny always got folks playing.
(Rest.)
Somebody shot him. They dont know who. Nobody knows nobody cares.   35
(Rest.)
We took that man and his wife for hundreds. No, thousands. We took
them for everything they had and everything they ever wanted to have.
We took a father for the money he was gonna get his kids new bike
with and he cried in the street while we vanished. We took a mothers
welfare check, she pulled a knife on us and we ran. She threw it but her   40
aim werent shit. People shopping. Greedy. Thinking they could take me
and they got took instead.
(Rest.)
Swore off thuh cards. Something inside me telling me—. But I was good.
LINCOLN
LINCOLN   45

*(He sees a packet of cards. He studies them like an alcoholic would study a drink.
Then he reaches for them, delicately picking them up and choosing 3 cards.)*

LINCOLN: Still got my moves. Still got my touch. Still got my chops. Thuh
    feel of it. And I aint hurting no one, God. Link is just here hustling
    hisself.
    (Rest.)
    Lets see whatcha got.

*(He stands over the monte setup. Then he bends over it placing the cards down and
moving them around. Slowly at first, aimlessly, as if hes just making little ripples in
water. But then the game draws him in. Unlike* BOOTH, LINCOLN'S *patter and moves
are deft, dangerous, electric.)*

LINCOLN: (((Lean in close and watch me now: who see thuh black card who see   50
    thuh black card I see thuh black card black cards thuh winner pick thuh

black card thats thuh winner pick thuh red card thats thuh loser pick
thuh other red card thats thuh other loser pick thuh black card you
pick thuh winner. Watch me as I throw thuh cards. Here we go.)))
(*Rest.*)

(((Who see thuh black card who see thuh black card? You pick thuh red   55
card you pick a loser you pick that red card you pick a loser you pick
thuh black card thuh deuce of spades you pick a winner who sees thuh
deuce of spades thuh one who sees it never fades watch me now as I
throw thuh cards. Red losers black winner follow thuh deuce of spades
chase thuh black deuce. Dark deuce will get you thuh win.)))   60
(*Even though* LINCOLN *speaks softly,* BOOTH *wakes and, unbeknownst to* LINCOLN,
listens intently.)
(*Rest.*)

LINCOLN: ((10 will get you 20, 20 will get you 40.))
(*Rest.*)
((Ima show you thuh cards: 2 red cards but only one spade. Dark
winner in thuh center and thuh red losers on thuh sides. Pick uh red
card you got a loser pick thuh other red card you got a loser pick thuh
black card you got a winner. One good pickll get you in, 2 good picks   65
and you gone win. Watch me come on watch me now.))
(*Rest.*)
((Who sees thuh winner who knows where its at? You do? You sure?
Go on then, put yr money where yr mouth is. Put yr money down you
aint no clown. No? Ah, you had thuh card but you didnt have thuh
heart.))   70
(*Rest.*)
((Watch me now as I throw thuh cards watch me real close. Ok, man,
you know which card is the deuce of spades? Was you watching Links
lighting fast express? Was you watching Link cause he the best? So you
sure, huh? Point it out first, then place yr bet and Linkll show you yr
winner.))   75
(*Rest.*)
((500 dollars? You thuh man of thuh hour you thuh man with thuh
power. You musta been watching Link real close. You must be thuh
man who know thuh most. Ok. Lay the cash in my hand cause Link
the man. Thank you, mister. This card you say?))
(*Rest.*)
((Wrong! Ha!))   80
(*Rest.*)
((Thats thuh show. We gotta go.))
(LINCOLN *puts the cards down. He moves away from the monte setup. He sits on the
edge of his easy chair, but he can't take his eyes off the cards.*)

INTERMISSION

Scene 5

Several days have passed. Its now Wednesday night. BOOTH *is sitting in his brand-new*
suit. The monte setup is nowhere in sight. In its place is a table with two nice chairs.
The table is covered with a lovely tablecloth and there are nice plates, silverware,
champagne glasses and candles. All the makings of a very romantic dinner for
two. The whole apartment in fact takes its cue from the table. Its been cleaned up
considerably.
New curtains on the windows, a doily-like object on the recliner. BOOTH *sits at*
the table darting his eyes around, making sure everything is looking good.

BOOTH: Shit.

(He notices some of his girlie magazines visible from underneath his bed. He goes
over and nudges them out of sight. He sits back down. He notices that theyre still
visible. He goes over and nudges them some more, kicking at them finally. Then he
takes the spread from his bed and pulls it down, hiding them. He sits back down. He
gets up. Checks the champagne on much melted ice. Checks the food.)

BOOTH: Foods getting cold, Grace!! Dont worry man, she'll get here, she'll
   get here.

(He sits back down. He goes over to the bed. Checks it for springiness. Smoothes
down the bedspread. Double-checks 2 matching silk dressing gowns, very expensive,
marked "His" and "Hers." Lays the dressing gowns across the bed again. He sits
back down. He cant help but notice the visibility of the girlie magazines again. He
goes to the bed, kicks them fiercely, then on his hands and knees shoves them. Then
he begins to get under the bed to push them, but he remembers his nice clothing and
takes off his jacket. After a beat he removes his pants and, in this half-dressed way,
he crawls under the bed to give those telltale magazines a good and final shove.
LINCOLN *comes in. At first* BOOTH, *still stripped down to his underwear, thinks its his*
date. When he realizes its his brother, he does his best to keep LINCOLN *from entering*
the apartment. LINCOLN *wears his frock coat and carries the rest of his getup in a*
plastic bag.)

LINCOLN: You in the middle of it?
BOOTH: What the hell you doing here?   5
LINCOLN: If yr in thuh middle of it I can go. Or I can just be real quiet and
   just—sing a song in my head or something.
BOOTH: The casas off limits to you tonight.
LINCOLN: You know when we lived in that 2-room place with the cement
   backyard and the frontyard with nothing but trash in it, Mom and Pops   10
   would do it in the middle of the night and I would always hear them
   but I would sing in my head, cause, I dunno, I couldnt bear to listen.

BOOTH: You gotta get out of here.

LINCOLN: I would make up all kinds of songs. Oh, sorry, yr all up in it. No
    sweat, bro. No sweat. Hey, Grace, howyadoing?!   15

BOOTH: She aint here yet, man. Shes running late. And its a good thing too
    cause I aint all dressed yet. Yr gonna spend thuh night with friends?

LINCOLN: Yeah.

(BOOTH *waits for* LINCOLN *to leave.* LINCOLN *stands his ground.*)

LINCOLN: I lost my job.

BOOTH: Hunh.   20

LINCOLN: I come in there right on time like I do every day and that motherfucker
    gives me some song and dance about cutbacks and too many folks complaining.

BOOTH: Hunh.

LINCOLN: Showd me thuh wax dummy—hes buying it right out of a catalog.
    (*Rest.*)
    I walked out still wearing my getup.   25
    (*Rest.*)
    I could go back in tomorrow. I could tell him I'll take another pay cut.
    Thatll get him to take me back.

BOOTH: Link. Yr free. Dont go crawling back. Yr free at last! Now you can do
    anything you want. Yr not tied down by that job. You can—you can do
    something else. Something that pays better maybe.   30

LINCOLN: You mean Hustle.

BOOTH: Maybe. Hey, Graces on her way. You gotta go.

(LINCOLN *flops into his chair.* BOOTH *is waiting for him to move.* LINCOLN *doesnt
budge.*)

LINCOLN: I'll stay until she gets here. I'll act nice. I wont embarrass you.

BOOTH: You gotta go.

LINCOLN: What time she coming?   35

BOOTH: Shes late. She could be here any second.

LINCOLN: I'll meet her. I met her years ago. I'll meet her again.
    (*Rest.*)
    How late is she?

BOOTH: She was supposed to be here at 8.

LINCOLN: Its after 2 A.M. Shes—shes late.   40
    (*Rest.*)
    Maybe when she comes you could put the blanket over me and
    I'll just pretend like Im not here.
    (*Rest.*)
    I'll wait. And when she comes I'll go. I need to sit down. I been walking
    around all day.

BOOTH   45
LINCOLN

(BOOTH *goes to his bed and dresses hurriedly.*)

BOOTH: Pretty nice, right? The china thuh silver thuh crystal.

LINCOLN: Its great.

    (*Rest.*)

    Boosted?

BOOTH: Yeah.   50

LINCOLN: Thought you went and spent yr inheritance for a minute, you
    had me going I was thinking shit, Booth—3-Card—that 3-Cards gone
    and spent his inheritance and the gal is—late.

BOOTH: Its boosted. Every bit of it.

    (*Rest.*)

    Fuck this waiting bullshit.   55

LINCOLN: She'll be here in a minute. Dont sweat it.

BOOTH: Right.

(BOOTH *comes to the table. Sits. Relaxes as best he can.*)

BOOTH: How come I got a hand for boosting and I dont got a hand for
    throwing cards? Its sorta the same thing—you gotta be quick—and slick.
    Maybe yll show me yr moves sometime.   60

LINCOLN
BOOTH
LINCOLN
BOOTH

LINCOLN: Look out the window. When you see Grace coming, I'll go.   65

BOOTH: Cool. Cause youd jinx it, youd really jinx it. Maybe you being
    here has jinxed it already. Naw. Shes just a little late. You aint jinxed
    nothing.

(BOOTH *sits by the window, glancing out, watching for his date.* LINCOLN *sits in his
recliner. He finds the whiskey bottle, sips from it. He then rummages around, finding
the raggedy photo album. He looks through it.*)

LINCOLN: There we are at that house. Remember when we moved in?

BOOTH: No.   70

LINCOLN: You were 2 or 3.

BOOTH: I was 4.

LINCOLN: I was 9. We all thought it was the best fucking house in the world.

BOOTH: Cement backyard and a frontyard full of trash, yeah, dont be
    going down memory lane man, yll jinx thuh vibe I got going in   75
    here. Gracell be walking in here and wrinkling up her nose cause
    you done jinxed up thuh joint with yr raggedy recollections.

LINCOLN: We had some great times in that house, bro. Selling lemonade on
thuh corner, thuh treehouse out back, summers spent lying in thuh
grass and looking at thuh stars.   80
BOOTH: We never did none of that shit.
LINCOLN: But we had us some good times. That row of nails I got you to
line up behind Dads car so when he backed out the driveway to work—
BOOTH: He came back that night, only time I ever seen his face go red, 4 flat
tires and yelling bout how thuh white man done sabotaged him again.   85
LINCOLN: And neither of us flinched. Neither of us let on that itd been us.
BOOTH: It was at dinner, right? What were we eating?
LINCOLN: Food.
BOOTH: We was eating pork chops, mashed potatoes and peas. I remember
cause I had to look at them peas real hard to keep from letting on. And 90
I would glance over at you, not really glancing not actually turning my
head, but I was looking at you out thuh corner of my eye. I was sure he
was gonna find us out and then he woulda whipped us good. But
I kept glancing at you and you was cool, man. Like nothing was
going on. You was cooooool.   95
   (Rest.)
What time is it?
LINCOLN: After 3.
   (Rest.)
You should call her. Something mighta happened.
BOOTH: No man, Im cool. She'll be here in a minute. Patience is a virtue.
She'll be here.   100
LINCOLN: You look sad.
BOOTH: Nope. Im just, you know, Im just—
LINCOLN: Cool.
BOOTH: Yeah. Cool.
(BOOTH *comes over, takes the bottle of whiskey and pours himself a big glassful.* 105
   He returns to the window looking out and drinking.)
BOOTH: They give you a severance package, at thuh job?
LINCOLN: A weeks pay.
BOOTH: Great.
LINCOLN: I blew it. Spent it all.   110
BOOTH: On what?
LINCOLN: —. Just spent it.
   (Rest.)
It felt good, spending it. Felt really good. Like back in thuh day when
I was really making money. Throwing thuh cards all day and strutting
and rutting all night. Didnt have to take no shit from no fool, didnt   115

have to worry about getting fired in favor of some damn wax dummy.
I was thuh shit and they was my fools.

(Rest.)

Back in thuh day.

(Rest.)

(Rest.)

Why you think they left us, man?

BOOTH: Mom and Pops? I dont think about it too much.   120

LINCOLN: I dont think they liked us.

BOOTH: Naw. That aint it.

LINCOLN: I think there was something out there that they liked more than
they liked us and for years they was struggling against moving towards
that more liked something. Each of them had a special something that   125
they was struggling against. Moms had hers. Pops had his. And they
was struggling. We moved out of that nasty apartment into a house. A
whole house. It wernt perfect but it was a house and theyd bought it
and they brought us there and everything we owned, figuring we could
be a family in that house and them things, them two separate things   130
each of them was struggling against, would just leave them be. Them
things would see thuh house and be impressed and just leave them be.
Would see thuh job Pops had and how he shined his shoes every night
before he went to bed, shining them shoes whether they needed it or
not, and thuh thing he was struggling against would see all that and   135
just let him be, and thuh thing Moms was struggling against, it would
see the food on the table every night and listen to her voice when she'
read to us sometimes, the clean clothes, the buttons sewed on all right
and it would just let her be. Just let us all be, just regular people living
in a house. That wernt too much to ask.   140

BOOTH: Least we was grown when they split.

LINCOLN: 16 and 11 aint grown.

BOOTH: 16s grown. Almost. And I was ok cause you were there.

(Rest.)

Shit man, it aint like they both one day both, together packed all they
shit up and left us so they could have fun in thuh sun on some tropical   145
island and you and me would have to grub in thuh dirt forever. They
didnt leave together. That makes it different. She left. 2 years go by.
Then he left. Like neither of them couldnt handle it no more. She split
then he split. Like thuh whole family mortgage bills going to work thing
was just too much. And I dont blame them. You dont see me holding   150
down a steady job. Cause its bullshit and I know it. I seen how it
cracked them up and I aint going there.

(Rest.)

It aint right me trying to make myself into a one woman man just
because she wants me like that. One woman rubber-wearing motherfucker. Shit. Not me. She gonna walk in here looking all hot and shit   155
trying to see how much she can get me to sweat, how much she can get
me to give her before she gives me mines. Shit.

LINCOLN

BOOTH

LINCOLN: Moms told me I shouldnt never get married.   160

BOOTH: She told me thuh same thing.

LINCOLN: They gave us each 500 bucks then they cut out.

BOOTH: Thats what Im gonna do. Give my kids 500 bucks then cut out.
Thats thuh way to do it.

LINCOLN: You dont got no kids.   165

BOOTH: Im gonna have kids then Im gonna cut out.

LINCOLN: Leaving each of yr offspring 500 bucks as yr splitting.

BOOTH: Yeah.

(Rest.)

Just goes to show Mom and Pops had some agreement between them.

LINCOLN: How so.   170

BOOTH: Theyd stopped talking to eachother. Theyd stopped screwing
eachother. But they had an agreement. Somewhere in there when it
looked like all they had was hate they sat down and did thuh "split"
budget.

(Rest.)

When Moms splits she gives me 5 hundred-dollar bills rolled up and   175
tied up tight in one of her nylon stockings. She tells me to put it in
a safe place, to spend it only in case of an emergency, and not to tell
nobody I got it, not even you. 2 years later Pops splits and before he
goes—

LINCOLN: He slips me 10 fifties in a clean handkerchief: "Hide this some-   180
wheres good, dont go blowing it, dont tell no one you got it, especially
that Booth."

BOOTH: Theyd been scheming together all along. They left separately but
they was in agreement. Maybe they arrived at the same place at the
same time, maybe they renewed they wedding vows, maybe they got   185
another family.

LINCOLN: Maybe they got 2 new kids. 2 boys. Different than us, though.
Better.

BOOTH: Maybe.

(*Their glasses are empty. The whiskey bottle is empty too.* BOOTH *takes the champagne
bottle from the ice tub. He pops the cork and pours drinks for his brother and himself.*)

BOOTH: I didnt mind them leaving cause you was there. Thats why Im   190
    hooked on us working together. If we could work together it would be
    like old times. They split and we got that room downtown. You was
    done with school and I stopped going. And we had to run around
    doing odd jobs just to keep the lights on and the heat going and thuh
    child protection bitch off our backs. It was you and me against thuh   195
    world, Link. It could be like that again.

LINCOLN

BOOTH

LINCOLN

BOOTH   200

LINCOLN: Throwing thuh cards aint as easy as it looks.

BOOTH: I aint stupid.

LINCOLN: When you hung with us back then, you was just on thuh sidelines.
    Thuh perspective from thuh sidelines is thuh perspective of a customer.
    There was all kinds of things you didnt know nothing about.   205

BOOTH: Lonny would entice folks into thuh game as they walked by. Thuh 2
    folks on either side of ya looked like they was playing but they
    was only pretending tuh play. Just tuh generate excitement. You was
    moving thuh cards as fast as you could hoping that yr hands would be
    faster than yr customers eyes. Sometimes you won sometimes you lost   210
    what else is there to know?

LINCOLN: Thuh customer is actually called the "Mark." You know why?

BOOTH: Cause hes thuh one you got yr eye on. You mark him with yr eye.

LINCOLN

LINCOLN   215

BOOTH: Im right, right?

LINCOLN: Lemmie show you a few moves. If you pick up these yll have a
    chance.

BOOTH: Yr playing.

LINCOLN: Get thuh cards and set it up.   220

BOOTH: No shit.

LINCOLN: Set it up set it up.

(In a flash, BOOTH *clears away the romantic table setting by gathering it all up in the tablecloth and tossing it aside. As he does so he reveals the "table" underneath: the 2 stacked monte milk crates and the cardboard playing surface.* LINCOLN *lays out the cards. The brothers are ready.* LINCOLN *begins to teach* BOOTH *in earnest.)*

LINCOLN: Thuh deuce of spades is thuh card tuh watch.

BOOTH: I work with thuh deuce of hearts. But spades is cool.

LINCOLN: Theres thuh Dealer, thuh Stickman, thuh Sides, thuh Lookout and 225
    thuh Mark. I'll be thuh Dealer.

BOOTH: I'll be thuh Lookout. Lemmie be thuh Lookout, right? I'll keep an
    eye for thuh cops. I got my piece in my pants.

LINCOLN: You got it on you right now?

BOOTH: I always carry it.   230

LINCOLN: Even on a date? In yr own home?

BOOTH: You never know, man.

    (*Rest.*)

    So Im thuh Lookout.

LINCOLN: Gimmie yr piece.

(BOOTH *gives* LINCOLN *his gun.* LINCOLN *moves the little wooden chair to face right
in front of the setup. He then puts the gun on the chair.*)

LINCOLN: We dont need nobody standing on the corner watching for cops   235
    cause there aint none. Thatll be the lookout.

BOOTH: I'll be thuh Stickman, then.

LINCOLN: Stickman knows the game inside out. You aint there yet. But
    you will be. You wanna learn good, be my Sideman. Playing along with
    the Dealer, moving the Mark to lay his money down. You wanna learn,   240
    right?

BOOTH: I'll be thuh Side.

LINCOLN: Good.

    (*Rest.*)

    First thing you learn is what is. Next thing you learn is what aint. You
    dont know what is you dont know what aint, you dont know shit.   245

BOOTH: Right.

LINCOLN

BOOTH

BOOTH: Whatchu looking at?

LINCOLN: Im sizing you up.   250

BOOTH: Oh yeah?!

LINCOLN: Dealer always sizes up thuh crowd.

BOOTH: Im yr Side, Link, Im on yr team, you dont go sizing up yr own team.
    You save looks like that for yr Mark.

LINCOLN: Dealer always sizes up thuh crowd. Everybody out there is part   255
    of the crowd. His crew is part of the crowd, he himself is part of the
    crowd. Dealer always sizes up thuh crowd.

(LINCOLN *looks* BOOTH *over some more then looks around at an imaginary crowd.*)

BOOTH: Then what then what?

LINCOLN: Dealer dont wanna play.

BOOTH: Bullshit man! Come on you promised!   260

LINCOLN: Thats thuh Dealers attitude. He *acts* like he dont wanna play. He
    holds back and thuh crowd, with their eagerness to see his skill and
    their willingness to take a chance, and their greediness to win his cash,

the larceny in their hearts, all goad him on and push him to throw his
cards, although of course the Dealer has been wanting to throw his 265
cards all along. Only he dont never show it.

BOOTH: Thats some sneaky shit, Link.

LINCOLN: It sets thuh mood. You wanna have them in yr hand before you
deal a hand, K?

BOOTH: Cool. —K. 270

LINCOLN: Right.

LINCOLN

BOOTH

BOOTH: You sizing me up again?

LINCOLN: Theres 2 parts to throwing thuh cards. Both parts are fairly com- 275
plicated. Thuh moves and thuh grooves, thuh talk and thuh walk,
thuh patter and thuh pitter pat, thuh flap and thuh rap: what yr doing
with yr mouth and what yr doing with yr hands.

BOOTH: I got thuh words down pretty good.

LINCOLN: You need to work on both. 280

BOOTH: K.

LINCOLN: A goodlooking walk and a dynamite talk captivates their entire
attention. The Mark focuses with 2 organs primarily: his eyes and his
ears. Leave one out you lose yr shirt. Captivate both, yr golden.

BOOTH: So them times I seen you lose, them times I seen thuh Mark best 285
you, that was a time when yr hands werent fast enough or yr patter
werent right.

LINCOLN: You could say that.

BOOTH: So, there was plenty of times—

(LINCOLN *moves the cards around.*)

LINCOLN: You see what Im doing? Dont look at my hands, man, look at my 290
eyes. Know what is and know what aint.

BOOTH: What is?

LINCOLN: My eyes.

BOOTH: What aint?

LINCOLN: My hands. Look at my eyes not my hands. And you standing there 295
thinking how thuh fuck I gonna learn how tuh throw thuh cards if I
be looking in his eyes? Look into my eyes and get yr focus. Dont think
about learning how tuh throw thuh cards. Dont think about nothing.
Just look into my eyes. Get yr focus.

BOOTH: Theyre red. 300

LINCOLN: Look into my eyes.

BOOTH: You been crying?

LINCOLN: Just look into my eyes, fool. Now. Look down at thuh cards. I
been moving and moving and moving them around. Ready?

BOOTH: Yeah.   305

LINCOLN: Ok, Sideman, thuh Marks got his eye on you. Yr gonna show him
  its easy.

BOOTH: K.

LINCOLN: Pick out thuh deuce of spades. Dont pick it up just point to it.

BOOTH: This one, right?   310

LINCOLN: Dont ask thuh Dealer if yr right, man, point to yr card with
  confidence.

(BOOTH *points.*)

BOOTH: That one.

  (*Rest.*)

  Flip it over, man.

(LINCOLN *flips over the card. It is in fact the deuce of spades.* BOOTH *struts around
gloating like a rooster.* LINCOLN *is mildly crestfallen.*)

BOOTH: Am I right or am I right?! Make room for 3-Card! Here comes thuh champ!   315

LINCOLN: Cool. Stay focused. Now we gonna add the second element. Listen.
  LINCOLN *moves the cards and speaks in a low hypnotic voice.*

LINCOLN: Lean in close and watch me now: who see thuh black card who
  see thuh black card I see thuh black card black cards thuh winner pick
  thuh black card thats thuh winner pick thuh red card thats thuh loser   320
  pick thuh other red card thats thuh other loser pick thuh black card
  you pick thuh winner. Watch me as I throw thuh cards. Here we go.
  (*Rest.*)
  Who see thuh black card who see thuh black card? You pick thuh red
  card you pick a loser you pick that red card you pick a loser you pick
  thuh black card thuh deuce of spades you pick a winner who sees thuh   325
  deuce of spades thuh one who sees it never fades watch me now as I
  throw thuh cards. Red losers black winner follow thuh deuce of spades
  chase thuh black deuce. Dark deuce will get you thuh win. One good
  pickll get you in 2 good picks you gone win. 10 will get you 20, 20 will
  get you 40.   330
  (*Rest.*)
  Ima show you thuh cards: 2 red cards but only one spade. Dark winner
  in thuh center and thuh red losers on thuh sides. Pick uh red card you
  got a loser pick thuh other red card you got a loser pick thuh black card
  you got a winner. Watch me watch me watch me now.
  (*Rest.*)
  Ok, 3-Card, you know which cards thuh deuce of spades?   335

BOOTH: Yeah.

LINCOLN: You sure? Yeah? You sure you sure or you just think you sure? Oh
  you sure you sure huh? Was you watching Links lighting fast express?

Was you watching Link cause he the best? So you sure, huh? Point it
out. Now, place yr bet and Linkll turn over yr card.   340

BOOTH: What should I bet?

LINCOLN: Dont bet nothing man, we just playing. Slap me 5 and point out
thuh deuce.

(BOOTH *slaps* LINCOLN *5, then points out a card which* LINCOLN *flips over. It is in
fact again the deuce of spades.*)

BOOTH: Yeah, baby! 3-Card got thuh moves! You didnt know lil bro had
thuh stuff, huh? Think again, Link, think again.   345

LINCOLN: You wanna learn or you wanna run yr mouth?

BOOTH: Thought you had fast hands. Wassup? What happened tuh "Links-
Lightning Fast Express"? Turned into uh local train looks like tuh me.

LINCOLN: Thats yr whole motherfucking problem. Yr so busy running yr
mouth you aint never gonna learn nothing! You think you something   350
but you aint shit.

BOOTH: I aint shit, I am _The_ Shit. Shit. Wheres thuh dark deuce? Right
there! Yes, baby!

LINCOLN: Ok, 3-Card. Cool. Lets switch. Take thuh cards and show me
whatcha got. Go on. Dont touch thuh cards too heavy just—its a light   355
touch. Like yr touching Graces skin. Or, whatever, man, just a light
touch. Like uh whisper.

BOOTH: Like uh whisper.

(BOOTH *moves the cards around, in an awkward imitation of his brother.*)

LINCOLN: Good.

BOOTH: Yeah. All right. Look into my eyes.   360

(BOOTH'S *speech is loud and his movements are jerky. He is doing worse than when
he threw the cards at the top of the play.*)

BOOTH: Watch-me-close-watch-me-close-now: who-see-thuh-black-card-
who-see-thuh-black-card? I-see-thuh-black-card. Here-it-is. Thuh-black-
card-is-thuh-winner. Pick-thuh-black-card-and-you-pick-uh-winner.
Pick-uh-red-card-and-you-pick-uh-loser. Theres-thuh-loser-yeah-theres-
thuh-red-card, theres-thuh-other-loser-and-theres-thuh-black-card,   365
thuh-winner. Watch-me-close-watch-me-close-now: 3-Card-throws-thuh-
cards-lightning-fast. 3-Card-thats-me-and-Ima-last. Watch-me-throw-
cause-here-I-go. See thuh black card? Yeah? Who see I see you see thuh
black card?

LINCOLN: Hahahahhahahahahahahah!   370

(LINCOLN *doubles over laughing.* BOOTH *puts on his coat and pockets his gun.*)

BOOTH: What?

LINCOLN: Nothing, man, nothing.

BOOTH: *What?!*

LINCOLN: Yr just, yr just a little wild with it. You talk like that on thuh street
cards or no cards and theyll lock you up, man. Shit. Reminds me of   375
that time when you hung with us and we let you try being thuh Stick
cause you wanted to so bad. Thuh hustle was so simple. Remember? I
told you that when I put my hand in my left pocket you was to get
thuh Mark tuh pick thuh card on that side. You got to thinking something like Links left means my left some dyslexic shit and turned thuh   380
wrong card. There was 800 bucks on the line and you fucked it up.
(Rest.)
But it was cool, little bro, cause we made the money back. It worked
out cool.
(Rest.)
So, yeah, I said a light touch, little bro. Throw thuh cards light. Like uh
whisper.   385

BOOTH: Like Graces skin.

LINCOLN: Like Graces skin.

BOOTH: What time is it?

(LINCOLN holds up his watch. BOOTH takes a look.)

BOOTH: Bitch. *Bitch!* She said she was gonna show up around 8.
8-a-fucking-clock.   390

LINCOLN: Maybe she meant 8 A.M.

BOOTH: Yeah. She gonna come all up in my place talking bout how she *love*
me. How she cant stop *thinking* bout me. Nother mans shit up in her
nother mans thing in her nother mans dick on her breath.

LINCOLN: Maybe something happened to her.   395

BOOTH: Something happened to her all right. She trying to make a chump
outa me. I aint her chump. I aint nobodys chump.

LINCOLN: Sit. I'll go to the payphone on the corner. I'll—

BOOTH: Thuh world puts its foot in yr face and you dont move. You tell thuh
world tuh keep on stepping. But Im my own man, Link. I aint you.   400

(BOOTH goes out, slamming the door behind him.)

LINCOLN: You got that right.

(After a moment LINCOLN picks up the cards. He moves them around fast, faster, faster.)

Scene 6

*Thursday night. The room looks empty, as if neither brother is home. LINCOLN comes
in. Has high on liquor. He strides in, leaving the door slightly ajar.*

LINCOLN: Taaadaaaa!
(Rest.)

(*Rest.*)
Taadaa, motherfucker. Taadaa!
(*Rest.*)
Booth—uh, 3-Card—you here? Nope. Good. Just as well. Ha Ha
Ha Ha Ha!

(*He pulls an enormous wad of money from his pocket. He counts it, slowly and luxuriously, arranging and smoothing the bills and sounding the amounts under his breath.
He neatly rolls up the money, secures it with a rubber band and puts it back in his
pocket. He relaxes in his chair. Then he takes the money out again, counting it all
over again, but this time quickly, with the touch of an expert hustler.*)

LINCOLN: You didnt go back, Link, you got back, you got it back you got yr
    shit back in thuh saddle, man, you got back in business. Walking in   5
    Luckys and you seen how they was looking at you? Lucky starts pour-
    ing for you when you walk in. And the women. You see how they
    was looking at you? Bought drinks for everybody. Bought drinks for
    Lucky. Bought drinks for Luckys damn dog. Shit. And thuh women be
    hanging on me and purring. And I be feeling that old call of thuh wild   10
    calling. I got more phone numbers in my pockets between thuh time I
    walked out that door and thuh time I walked back in than I got in my
    whole life. Cause my shit is back. And back better than it was when it
    left too. Shoot. Who thuh man? Link. Thats right. Purrrrring all up on
    me and letting me touch them and promise them shit. 3 of them sweet-   15
    hearts in thuh restroom on my dick all at once and I was there my shit
    was there. And Cookie just went out of my mind which is cool which
    is very cool. 3 of them. Fighting over it. Shit. Cause they knew I'd been
    throwing thuh cards. Theyd seen me on thuh corner with thuh old
    crew or if they aint seed me with they own eyes theyd heard word. Links   20
    thuh stink! Theyd heard word and they seed uh sad face on some poor
    sucker or a tear in thuh eye of some stupid fucking tourist and they
    figured it was me whod just took thuh suckers last dime, it was me who
    had all thuh suckers loot. They knew. They knew.

(BOOTH *appears in the room. He was standing behind the screen, unseen all this
    time. He goes to the door, soundlessly, just stands there.*)

LINCOLN: And they was all in Luckys. Shit. And they was waiting for me to   25
    come in from my last throw. Cant take too many fools in one day, its
    bad luck, Link, so they was all waiting in there for me to come in thuh
    door and let thuh liquor start flowing and thuh music start going and
    let thuh boys who dont have thuh balls to get nothing but a regular job
    and uh weekly paycheck, let them crowd around and get in somehow   30
    on thuh excitement, and make way for thuh ladies, so they can run they
    hands on my clothes and feel thuh magic and imagine thuh man,

with plenty to go around, living and breathing underneath.
(Rest.)
They all thought I was down and out! They all thought I was some No-
Count HasBeen LostCause motherfucker. But I got my shit back. Thats   35
right. They stepped on me and kept right on stepping. Not no more.
Who thuh man?! Goddamnit, who thuh—

(BOOTH *closes the door.*)

LINCOLN

BOOTH

(Rest.)

LINCOLN: Another evening to remember, huh?   40

BOOTH *(Rest.)*: Uh—yeah, man, yeah. Thats right, thats right.

LINCOLN: Had me a memorable evening myself.

BOOTH: I got news.
    (Rest.)
    What you been up to?

LINCOLN: Yr news first.   45

BOOTH: Its good.

LINCOLN: Yeah?

BOOTH: Yeah.

LINCOLN: Go head then.

BOOTH *(Rest.)*: Grace got down on her knees. Down on her knees, man.   50
    Asked *me* tuh marry *her.*

LINCOLN: Shit.

BOOTH: Amazing Grace!

LINCOLN: Lucky you, man.

BOOTH: And guess where she was, I mean, while I was here waiting for her.   55
    She was over at her house watching tv. I'd told her come over Thursday
    and I got it all wrong and was thinking I said Wednesday and here
    I was sitting waiting my ass off and all she was doing was over at her
    house just watching tv.

LINCOLN: Howboutthat.   60

BOOTH: She wants to get married right away. Shes tired of waiting. Feels her
    clock ticking and shit. Wants to have my baby. But dont look so glum
    man, we gonna have a boy and we gonna name it after you.

LINCOLN: Thats great, man. Thats really great.

BOOTH   65

LINCOLN

BOOTH: Whats yr news?

LINCOLN *(Rest.)*: Nothing.

BOOTH: Mines good news, huh?

LINCOLN: Yeah. Real good news, bro.   70

BOOTH: Bad news is—well, shes real set on us living together. And she always did like this place.
    (Rest.)
    Yr gonna have to leave. Sorry.
LINCOLN: No sweat.
BOOTH: This was only a temporary situation anyhow.   75
LINCOLN: No sweat man. You got a new life opening up for you, no sweat.
    Graces moving in today? I can leave right now.
BOOTH: I dont mean to put you out.
LINCOLN: No sweat. I'll just pack up.
(LINCOLN rummages around finding a suitcase and begins to pack his things.)
BOOTH: Just like that, huh? "No sweat"?! Yesterday you lost yr damn job.   80
    You dont got no cash. You dont got no friends, no nothing, but you
    clearing out just like that and its "no sweat"?!
LINCOLN: Youve been real generous and you and Grace need me gone and its
    time I found my own place.
BOOTH: No sweat.   85
LINCOLN: No sweat.
    (Rest.)
    K. I'll spill it. I got another job, so getting my own place aint gonna be
    so bad.
BOOTH: You got a new job! Doing what?
LINCOLN: Security guard.   90
BOOTH *(Rest.)*: Security guard. Howaboutthat.
(LINCOLN continues packing the few things he has. He picks up a whiskey bottle.)
BOOTH: Go head, take thuh med-sin, bro. You gonna need it more than me.
    I got, you know, I got my love to keep me warm and shit.
LINCOLN: You gonna have to get some kind of work, or are you gonna let
    Grace support you?   95
BOOTH: I got plans.
LINCOLN: She might want you now but she wont want you for long if you
    dont get some kind of job. Shes a smart chick. And she cares about
    you. But she aint gonna let you treat her like some pack mule while
    shes out working her ass off and yr laying up in here scheming and   100
    dreaming to cover up thuh fact that you dont got no skills.
BOOTH: Grace is very cool with who I am and where Im at, thank you.
LINCOLN: It was just some advice. But, hey, yr doing great just like yr doing.
LINCOLN
BOOTH   105
LINCOLN
BOOTH
BOOTH: When Pops left he didnt take nothing with him. I always thought
    that was fucked-up.

LINCOLN: He was a drunk. Everything he did was always half regular and 110
half fucked-up.

BOOTH: Whyd he leave his clothes though? Even drunks gotta wear clothes.

LINCOLN: Whyd he leave his clothes whyd he leave us? He was uh drunk, bro.
He—whatever, right? I mean, you aint gonna figure it out by thinking
about it. Just call it one of thuh great unsolved mysteries of existence. 115

BOOTH: Moms had a man on thuh side.

LINCOLN: Yeah? Pops had side shit going on too. More than one. He would
take me with him when he went to visit them. Yeah.
(Rest.)
Sometimes he'd let me meet the ladies. They was all very nice. Very
polite. Most of them real pretty. Sometimes he'd let me watch. Most of 120
thuh time I was just outside on thuh porch or in thuh lobby or in
thuh car waiting for him but sometimes he'd let me watch.

BOOTH: What was it like?

LINCOLN: Nothing. It wasnt like nothing. He made it seem like it was this big
deal this great thing he was letting me witness but it wasnt like nothing. 125
(Rest.)
One of his ladies liked me, so I would do her after he'd done her. On
thuh sly though. He'd be laying there, spent and sleeping and snoring
and her and me would be sneaking it.

BOOTH: Shit.

LINCOLN: It was alright. 130

BOOTH

LINCOLN

(LINCOLN *takes his crumpled Abe Lincoln getup from the closet. Isnt sure what to do
with it.)*

BOOTH: Im gonna miss you—coming home in that getup. I dont even got a
picture of you in it for the album.

LINCOLN: *(Rest.):* Hell, I'll put it on. Get thuh camera get thuh camera. 135

BOOTH: Yeah?

LINCOLN: What thuh fuck, right?

BOOTH: Yeah, what thuh fuck.

(BOOTH *scrambles around the apartment and finds the camera.* LINCOLN *quickly
puts on the getup, including 2 thin smears of white pancake makeup, more like war
paint than whiteface.)*

LINCOLN: They didnt fire me cause I wasnt no good. They fired me cause
they was cutting back. Me getting dismissed didnt have no reflection 140
on my performance. And I was a damn good Honest Abe considering.

BOOTH: Yeah. You look great man, really great. Fix yr hat. Get in thuh light.
Smile.

LINCOLN: Lincoln didnt never smile.

BOOTH: Sure he smiled.   145

LINCOLN: No he didnt, man, you seen thuh pictures of him. In all his pictures he was real serious.

BOOTH: You got a new job, yr having a good day, right?

LINCOLN: Yeah.

BOOTH: So smile.   150

LINCOLN: Snapshots gonna look pretty stupid with me—

(BOOTH *takes a picture.*)

BOOTH: Thisll look great in thuh album.

LINCOLN: Lets take one together, you and me.

BOOTH: No thanks. Save the film for the wedding.

LINCOLN: This wasnt a bad job. I just outgrew it. I could put in a word for   155
    you down there, maybe when business picks up again theyd hire you.

BOOTH: No thanks. That shit aint for me. I aint into pretending Im
    someone else all day.

LINCOLN: I was just sitting there in thuh getup. I wasnt pretending nothing.

BOOTH: What was going on in yr head?   160

LINCOLN: I would make up songs and shit.

BOOTH: And think about women.

LINCOLN: Sometimes.

BOOTH: Cookie.

LINCOLN: Sometimes.   165

BOOTH: And how she came over here one night looking for you.

LINCOLN: I was at Luckys.

BOOTH: She didnt know that.

LINCOLN: I was drinking.

BOOTH: All she knew was you couldnt get it up. You couldnt get it up with   170
    her so in her head you was tired of her and had gone out to screw
    somebody new and this time maybe werent never coming back.
    (*Rest.*)
    She had me pour her a drink or 2. I didnt want to. She wanted to get
    back at you by having some fun of her own and when I told her to go
    out and have it, she said she wanted to have her fun right here. With   175
    me. (Rest.)
    And then, just like that, she changed her mind.
    (*Rest.*)
    But she'd hooked me. That bad part of me that I fight down everyday.
    You beat yrs down and it stays there dead but mine keeps coming up for
    another round. And the bad part of me took her clothing off and car-   180
    ried her into thuh bed and had her, Link, yr Cookie. It wasnt just thuh
    bad part of me it was all of me, man, I had her. Yr damn wife. Right in
    that bed.

LINCOLN: I used to think about her all thuh time but I dont think about her
no more.   185
BOOTH: I told her if she dumped you I'd marry her but I changed my mind.
LINCOLN: I dont think about her no more.
BOOTH: You dont go back.
LINCOLN: Nope.
BOOTH: Cause you cant. No matter what you do you cant get back to being   190
who you was. Best you can do is just pretend to be yr old self.
LINCOLN: Yr outa yr mind.
BOOTH: Least Im still me!
LINCOLN: Least I work. You never did like to work. You better come up with
some kinda way to bring home the bacon or Gracell drop you like a   195
hot rock.
BOOTH: I got plans!
LINCOLN: Yeah, you gonna throw thuh cards, right?
BOOTH: Thats right!
LINCOLN: You a double left-handed motherfucker who dont stand a chance   200
in all get out out there throwing no cards.
BOOTH: You scared. You scared I got yr shit.
LINCOLN: You aint never gonna do nothing.
BOOTH: You scared you gonna throw and Ima kick yr ass—like yr boss kicked
yr ass like yr wife kicked yr ass—then Ima go out there and dothuh   205
cards like you do and Ima be thuh man and you aint gonna be shit.
(*Rest.*)
Ima set it up. And you gonna throw. Or are you scared?
LINCOLN: Im gone.
(LINCOLN *goes to leave.*)
BOOTH: Fuck that!
LINCOLN   210
BOOTH
LINCOLN: Damn. I didnt know it went so deep for you lil bro. **Set up the**
cards.
BOOTH: Thought you was gone.
LINCOLN: Set it up.   215
BOOTH: Ima kick yr ass.
LINCOLN: Set it up!
(BOOTH *hurriedly sets up the milk crates and cardboard top.* LINCOLN *throws the*
cards.)
LINCOLN: Lean in close and watch me now: who see thuh black card who see
thuh black card I see thuh black card black cards thuh winner pick thuh 220
black card thats thuh winner pick thuh red card thats thuh loser pick thuh
other red card thats thuh other loser pick thuh black card you pick thuh

winner. Who see thuh black card who see thuh black card? You pick thuh
red card you pick a loser you pick that red card you pick a loser you pick
thuh black card thuh deuce of spades you pick a winner who sees thuh   225
deuce of spades thuh one who sees it never fades watch me now as I throw
thuh cards. Red losers black winner follow thuh deuce of spades chase
thuh black deuce. Dark deuce will get you thuh win. 10 will get you 20, 20
will get you 40. One good pickll get you in 2 good picks and you gone win.
(Rest.)

    Ok, man, wheres thuh black deuce?   230

(BOOTH points to a card. LINCOLN flips it over. It is the deuce of spades.)

BOOTH: Who thuh man?!

(LINCOLN turns over the other 2 cards, looking at them confusedly.)

LINCOLN: Hhhhh.

BOOTH: Who thuh man, Link?! Huh? Who thuh man, Link?!?!

LINCOLN: You thuh man, man.

BOOTH: I got yr shit down.   235

LINCOLN: Right.

BOOTH: "Right"? All you saying is "right"?

    (Rest.)

    You was out on the street throwing. Just today. Werent you? You wasnt
    gonna tell me.

LINCOLN: Tell you what?   240

BOOTH: That you was out throwing.

LINCOLN: I was gonna tell you, sure. Cant go and leave my little bro out
    thuh loop, can I? Didnt say nothing cause I thought you heard. Did all
    right today but Im still rusty, I guess. But hey—yr getting good.

BOOTH: But I'll get out there on thuh street and still fuck up, wont I?   245

LINCOLN: You seem pretty good, bro.

BOOTH: You gotta do it for real, man.

LINCOLN: I am doing it for real. And yr getting good.

BOOTH: I dunno. It didnt feel real. Kinda felt—well it didnt feel real.

LINCOLN: We're missing the essential elements. The crowd, the street, thuh traffic   250
    sounds, all that.

BOOTH: We missing something else too, thuh thing thatll really make it real.

LINCOLN: Whassat, bro?

BOOTH: Thuh cash. Its just bullshit without thuh money. Put some money
    down on thuh table then itd be real, then youd do it for real, then I'd   255
    win it for real.

    (Rest.)

    And dont be looking all glum like that. I know you got money. A
    whole pocketful. Put it down.

LINCOLN

BOOTH 260

BOOTH: You scared of losing it to thuh man, chump? Put it down, less you
    think thuh kid who got two left hands is gonna give you uh left hook.
    Put it down, bro, put it down.

(LINCOLN *takes the roll of bills from his pocket and places it on the table.*)

BOOTH: How much you got there?

LINCOLN: 500 bucks. 265

BOOTH: Cool.

    (*Rest.*)

    Ready?

LINCOLN: Does it feel real?

BOOTH: Yeah. Clean slate. Take it from the top. "One good pickll get you in
    2 good picks and you gone win." 270

    (*Rest.*)

    Go head.

LINCOLN: Watch me now:

BOOTH: Woah, man, woah.

    (*Rest.*)

    You think Ima chump.

LINCOLN: No I dont. 275

BOOTH: You aint going full out.

LINCOLN: I was just getting started.

BOOTH: But when you got good and started you wasnt gonna go full out.
    You wasnt gonna go all out. You was gonna do thuh pussy shit, not
    thuh real shit. 280

LINCOLN: I put my money down. Money makes it real.

BOOTH: But not if I dont put no money down tuh match it.

LINCOLN: You dont got no money.

BOOTH: I got money!

LINCOLN: You aint worked in years. You dont got shit. 285

BOOTH: I got money.

LINCOLN: Whatcha been doing, skimming off my weekly paycheck and
    squirreling it away?

BOOTH: I got money.

    (*Rest.*)

(*They stand there sizing eachother up.* BOOTH *breaks away, going over to his hiding
place from which he gets an old nylon stocking with money in the toe, a knot holding
the money secure.*)

LINCOLN 290
BOOTH

BOOTH: You know she was putting her stuff in plastic bags? She was just put-
    ting her stuff in plastic bags not putting but shoving. She was shoving

her stuff in plastic bags and I was standing in thuh doorway watching
her and she was so busy shoving thuh shit she didnt see me. "I aint   295
made of money," thats what he always saying. The guy she had on the
side. I would catch them together sometimes. Thuh first time I cut
school I got tired of hanging out so I goes home—figured I could tell
Mom I was sick and cover my ass. Come in thuh house real slow cause
Im sick and moving slow and quiet. He had her bent over. They both   300
had all they clothes on like they was about to do something like go out
dancing cause they was dressed to thuh 9s but at thuh last minute his
pants had fallen down and her dress had flown up and theyd ended up
doing something else.
(Rest.)
They didnt see me come in, they didnt see me watching them, they didnt   305
see me going out. That was uh Thursday. Something told me tuh cut
school thuh next Thursday and sure enough—. He was her Thursday
man. Every Thursday. Yeah. And Thursday nights she was always all
cleaned up and fresh and smelling nice. Serving up dinner. And Pops
would grab her cause she was all bright and she would look at me, like   310
she didnt know that I knew but she was asking me not to tell nohow.
She was asking me to—oh who knows.
(Rest.)
She was talking with him one day, her sideman, her Thursday dude,
her backdoor man, she needed some money for something, thered been
some kind of problem some kind of mistake had been made some kind   315
of mistake that needed cleaning up and she was asking Mr. Thursday for
some money to take care of it. "I aint made of money," he says. He was
putting his foot down. And then there she was 2 months later not showing yet, maybe she'd got rid of it maybe she hadnt maybe she'd stuffed
it along with all her other things in them plastic bags while he waited   320
outside in thuh car with thuh motor running. She musta known I was
gonna walk in on her this time cause she had my payoff—my *inheritance*—
she had it all ready for me. 500 dollars in a nylon stocking. Huh.
(He places the stuffed nylon stocking on the table across from LINCOLNS *money roll.)*
BOOTH: Now its real.
LINCOLN: Dont put that down.   325
BOOTH: Throw thuh cards.
LINCOLN: I dont want to play.
BOOTH: Throw thuh fucking cards, man!!
LINCOLN *(Rest.)*: 2 red cards but only one black. Pick thuh black you pick
    thuh winner. All thuh cards are face down you point out thuh cards   330
    and then you move them around. Now watch me now, now watch me
    real close. Put thuh winning deuce down in the center put thuh loser

reds on either side then you just move thuh cards around. Move them
slow or move them fast, Links thuh king he gonna last.
(Rest.)
Wheres thuh deuce of spades?   335

(BOOTH chooses a card and chooses correctly.)

BOOTH: HA!
LINCOLN: One good pickll get you in 2 good picks and you gone win.
BOOTH: I know man I know.
LINCOLN: Im just doing thuh talk.
BOOTH: Throw thuh fucking cards!   340
(Lincoln throws the cards.)
LINCOLN: Lean in close and watch me now: who see thuh black card who
    see thuh black card I see thuh black card black cards thuh winner pick
    thuh black card thats thuh winner pick thuh red card thats thuh loser
    pick thuh other red card thats thuh other loser pick thuh black card
    you pick thuh winner. Watch me as I throw thuh cards. Here we go.   345
    (Rest.)
    Ima show you thuh cards: 2 red cards but only one spade. Dark winner
    in thuh center and thuh red losers on thuh sides. Pick uh red card
    you got a loser pick thuh other red card you got a loser pick thuh
    black card you got a winner. Watch me watch me watch me now.
    (Rest.)
    Who see thuh black card who see thuh black card? You pick thuh red   350
    card you pick a loser you pick that red card you pick a loser you pick
    thuh black card thuh deuce of spades you pick a winner who sees
    thuh deuce of spades thuh one who sees it never fades watch me now
    as I throw thuh cards. Red losers black winner follow thuh deuce of
    spades chase thuh black deuce. Dark deuce will get you thuh win.   355
    (Rest.)
    Ok, 3-Card, you know which cards thuh deuce of spades? This is for
    real now, man. You pick wrong Im in yr wad and I keep mines.
BOOTH: I pick right I got yr shit.
LINCOLN: Yeah.
BOOTH: Plus I beat you for real.   360
LINCOLN: Yeah.
    (Rest.)
    You think we're really brothers?
BOOTH: Huh?
LINCOLN: I know we *brothers*, but is we really brothers, you know, blood
    brothers or not, you and me, whatduhyathink?   365
BOOTH: I think we're brothers.

BOOTH
LINCOLN
BOOTH
LINCOLN   370
BOOTH
LINCOLN

LINCOLN: Go head man, wheres thuh deuce?

(In a flash BOOTH *points out a card.)*

LINCOLN: You sure?

BOOTH: Im sure!   375

LINCOLN: Yeah? Dont touch thuh cards, now.

BOOTH: Im sure.

(The 2 brothers lock eyes. LINCOLN *turns over the card that* BOOTH *selected and*
BOOTH, *in a desperate break of concentration, glances down to see that he has chosen
the wrong card.)*

LINCOLN: Deuce of hearts, bro. Im sorry. Thuh deuce of spades was this one.
   (Rest.)
   I guess all this is mines.

(He slides the money toward himself.)

LINCOLN: You were almost right. Better luck next time.   380
   (Rest.)
   Aint yr fault if yr eyes aint fast. And you cant help it if you got 2 left
   hands, right? Throwing cards aint thuh whole world. You got other
   shit going for you. You got Grace.

BOOTH: Right.

LINCOLN: Whassamatter?   385

BOOTH: Mm.

LINCOLN: Whatsup?

BOOTH: Nothing.

LINCOLN *(Rest.)*: It takes a certain kind of understanding to be able to play this
   game.   390
   (Rest.)
   I still got thuh moves, dont I?

BOOTH: Yeah you still got thuh moves.

*(*LINCOLN *cant help himself. He chuckles.)*

LINCOLN: I aint laughing at you, bro, Im just laughing. Shit there is so much
   to this game. This game is—there is just so much to it.

*(*LINCOLN, *still chuckling, flops down in the easy chair. He takes up the nylon
stocking and fiddles with the knot.)*

LINCOLN: Woah, she sure did tie this up tight, didnt she?   395

BOOTH: Yeah. I aint opened it since she gived it to me.

LINCOLN: Yr kidding. 500 and you aint never opened it? Shit. Sure is tied tight. She said heres 500 bucks and you didnt undo thuh knot to get a look at the cash? You aint needed to take a peek in all these years? Shit. I woulda opened it right away. Just a little peek.   400

BOOTH: I been saving it.

(Rest.)

Oh, dont open it, man.

LINCOLN: How come?

BOOTH: You won it man, you dont gotta go opening it.

LINCOLN: We gotta see whats in it.   405

BOOTH: We know whats in it. Dont open it.

LINCOLN: You are a chump, bro. There could be millions in here! There could be nothing! I'll open it.

BOOTH: Dont.

LINCOLN   410

BOOTH

(Rest.)

LINCOLN: Shit this knot aint coming out. I could cut it, but that would spoil the whole effect, wouldnt it? Shit. Sorry. I aint laughing at you Im just laughing. Theres so much about those cards. You think you can learn them just by watching and just by playing but there is more 415 to them cards than that. And—. Tell me something, Mr. 3-Card, she handed you this stocking and she said there was money in it and then she split and you say you didnt open it. Howd you know she was for real?

BOOTH: She was for real.   420

LINCOLN: How you know? She coulda been jiving you, bro. Jiving you that there really *was* money in this thing. Jiving you big time. Its like thuh cards. And ooooh you certainly was persistent. But you was in such a hurry to learn thuh last move that you didnt bother learning thuh first one. That was yr mistake. Cause its thuh first move that separates thuh 425 Player from thuh Played. And thuh first move is to know that there aint no winning. Taadaaa! It may look like you got a chance but the only time you pick right is when thuh man lets you. And when its thuh real deal, when its thuh real fucking deal, bro, and thuh moneys on thuh line, thats when thuh man wont want you picking right. He will 430 want you picking wrong so he will make you pick wrong. Wrong wrong wrong. Ooooh, you thought you was finally happening, didnt you? You thought yr ship had come in or some shit, huh? Thought you was uh Player. But I played you, bro.

BOOTH: Fuck you. Fuck you FUCK YOU *FUCK YOU*!!   435

LINCOLN: Whatever, man. Damn this knot is tough. Ima cut it.

(LINCOLN *reaches in his boot, pulling out a knife. He chuckles all the while.*)

LINCOLN: Im not laughing at you, bro, Im just laughing.

(BOOTH *chuckles with him.* LINCOLN *holds the knife high, ready to cut the stocking.*)

LINCOLN: Turn yr head. You may not wanna look.

(BOOTH *turns away slightly. They both continue laughing.* LINCOLN *brings the knife down to cut the stocking.*)

BOOTH: I popped her.

LINCOLN: Huh?   440

BOOTH: Grace. I popped her. Grace.

   (Rest.)

   Who thuh fuck she think she is doing me like she done? Telling me I
   dont got nothing going on. I showed her what I got going on. Popped
   her good. Twice. 3 times. Whatever.

   (Rest.)

   She aint dead.   445

   (Rest.)

   She werent wearing my ring I gived her. Said it was too small. Fuck
   that. Said it hurt her. Fuck that. Said she was into bigger things. Fuck
   that. Shes alive not to worry, she aint going out that easy, shes alive
   shes shes—.

LINCOLN: Dead. Shes—   450

BOOTH: Dead.

LINCOLN: Ima give you back yr stocking, man. Here, bro—

BOOTH: Only so long I can stand that little brother shit. Can only take it so
   long. Im telling you—

LINCOLN: Take it back, man—   455

BOOTH: That little bro shit had to go—

LINCOLN: Cool—

BOOTH: Like Booth went—

LINCOLN: Here, 3-Card—

BOOTH: That Booth shit is over. 3-Cards thuh man now—   460

LINCOLN: Ima give you yr stocking back, 3-Card—

BOOTH: Who thuh man now, huh? Who thuh man now?! Think you can
   fuck with me, motherfucker think again motherfucker think again!
   Think you can take me like Im just some chump some two lefthanded
   pussy dickbreath chump who you can take and then go laugh at. Aint   465
   laughing at me you was just laughing bunch uh bullshit and you know it.

LINCOLN: Here. Take it.

BOOTH: I aint gonna be needing it. Go on. You won it you open it.

LINCOLN: No thanks.

BOOTH: Open it open it open it open it. *OPEN IT!!!*   470

(*Rest.*)

Open it up, bro.

LINCOLN

BOOTH

(LINCOLN *brings the knife down to cut the stocking. In a flash,* BOOTH *grabs* LINCOLN *from behind. He pulls his gun and thrusts it into the left side of* LINCOLNS *neck. They stop there poised.*)

LINCOLN: Dont.

(BOOTH *shoots* LINCOLN. LINCOLN *slumps forward, falling out of his chair and onto the floor. He lies there dead.* BOOTH *paces back and forth, like a panther in a cage, holding his gun.*)

BOOTH: Think you can take my shit? My shit. That shit was mines. I kept   475
   it. Saved it. All this while. Through thick and through thin. Through
   fucking thick and through fucking thin, motherfucker. And you just
   gonna come up in here and mock my shit and call me two lefthanded
   talking bout how she coulda been jiving me then go steal from me? My
   inheritance. You stole my *inheritance*, man. That aint right. That aint   480
   right and you know it. You had yr own. And you blew it. You blew it,
   motherfucker! I saved mines and you blew yrs. Thinking you all that
   and blew yr shit. And I *saved* mines.

   (*Rest.*)

   You aint gonna be needing yr fucking money-roll no more, dead moth
   erfucker, so I will pocket it thank you.   485

   (*Rest.*)

   Watch me close watch me close now: Ima go out there and make a
   name for myself that dont have nothing to do with you. And 3-Cards
   gonna be in everybodys head and in everybodys mouth like Link was.

   (*Rest.*)

   Ima take back my inheritance too. It was mines anyhow. Even when
   you stole it from me it was still mines cause she gave it to me. She   490
   didnt give it to you. And I been saving it all this while

(*He bends to pick up the money-filled stocking. Then he just crumples. As he sits
   beside* LINCOLNS *body, the money-stocking falls away.* BOOTH *holds* LINCOLNS
   body, hugging him close. He sobs.)

BOOTH: AAAAAAAAAAAAAAAAAAAAH!

END OF PLAY

- Find two specific passages that illustrate the difference in the speech rhythms of Lincoln and Booth. How are these differences significant to our understanding of their characters?

- Much of the play centers around Booth as he tries to master the patter of the 3-card monte scam. How does this patter relate to the action at various points within the play?

- Why would Parks name the characters "Lincoln" and "Booth"? Collect details from the play to show the different ways in which these names are appropriate (or terribly inappropriate) to the play's action.

Experiencing Literature through Writing

1. Select a single work from this chapter (or any other). If you are looking at a work of fiction, limit your analysis to one or two paragraphs. Describe the rhythm within that selection. Explain how rhythm is significant to our understanding of the text. As you write, consider the following questions:

   a. What specific words in this passage help you describe the rhythm?
   b. How do the sounds or the length of the words relate to the plot?
   c. Is this rhythm subtle or is it obvious? In places where it is not obvious, explain why it is significant.

2. The contrast of innocence and experience that we see in this chapter is often reflected in subtle changes within the works. Using a pair of Blake poems or some other example where you see a similar effect, discuss the relation of this contrast between innocence and experience within the rhythm of the passages.

3. As you read these texts (or as you see a film), think about the relation between the rhythm of that work and the plot. What elements of the work convey the rhythm? How does that rhythm reflect what is happening in the work? Find a specific scene to use as the basis for your discussion.

7 Images

Can We Trade a Picture for a Thousand Words?

Whenever we set out to describe our experiences to others, we need to do more than recount actions. Life isn't bound merely by "what happens"; the distinct quality of sensory impressions lends substance, particularity, and emotion to events. Things we see, hear, feel, smell, or taste oftentimes serve as an index to our most important memories. Sometimes a physical sensation *is* the memory. Yet it's also true that in the course of any given stretch of time, we can be unconscious of this most elemental truth. We move so quickly through a day that we sometimes don't pause to notice details. It's a common experience, for example, to drive for miles over familiar roads and then think, "Did we already pass Fairview?"

Artists work to make sure we don't pass through Fairview or any other place along the way without observing closely. They register sensory data in ways that make us alert to the physical substance of our experience. In many modest ways we're artists of our own lives. Our vacation pictures, for example, are fascinating to us because they help us pause over details of what we've seen. And they likely trigger memories of a special meal (a local fish caught fresh), a smell (crisp ocean air at daybreak), a sound (gulls squawking over breaking waves), a touch (wet sand under bare feet). We edit our vacation pictures carefully so that we can more deeply absorb our experience and sensitize ourselves to possibilities that lie ahead in future trips. And we're likely to present our vacation pictures to others from a desire to help them share what we felt, not merely know what we did.

Our reading experience again is not so different from our life experience; the disciplined practice of paying attention to our senses yields much of value in life and art. The novelist Henry James advised that we all try to be someone "upon whom nothing is lost." James's standard may be too high, but all types of experience offer a richness of imagery that must be paused over, not merely "passed through." In this chapter, we'll consider how sensory images intensify literary and, in turn, life experience.

CREATING PICTURES WITH WORDS

It would be hard to overestimate the sheer volume of **visual images** in communication. Ironically, images of color and shape—of things seen—are so pervasive that they sometimes become almost invisible. A too common image may lose all force. A "red rose," a "blue sky" can descend to the emptiness of advertising clichés like "golden brown French fries." Finding ways to make common descriptors convey an image vividly becomes a challenge that writers sometimes address consciously. Note how William Carlos Williams leads into the following poem by directly telling us that what we see—what we really see—counts for something however mundane it may be.

William Carlos Williams (1883–1963)

The Red Wheelbarrow (1923)

so much depends
upon

a red wheel
barrow

glazed with rain   5
water

beside the white
chickens.

We're drawn to see the red wheelbarrow here partly because we recognize in the simplicity of these images how much and how often we don't see what is plainly before us. Williams's opening line suggests that the physical act of seeing can become a worthy theme. "So much depends" upon what is before us in the immediate moment. Czeslaw Milosz also asks us to see, absorb, and reflect upon common sights. In "Watering Can" he suggests that images ground us in a concrete reality and help us hold tight against what can be threatening, debilitating abstractions.

Czeslaw Milosz (1911–2004)

Watering Can (Czeslaw Milosz and Robert Hass, trans.; 1998)

Of a green color, standing in a shed alongside rakes and spades, it comes alive when it is filled with water from the pond, and an abundant shower pours from its nozzle, in an act, we feel it, of charity towards plants. It is not certain, however, that the watering can would have such a place in our memory, were it not for our training in noticing things. For, after all, we have been trained. Our painters do not often imitate the Dutch, who liked to paint still lifes, and yet photography contributes to our paying attention to detail and the cinema taught us that objects, once they appear on the screen, would participate in the actions of the characters and therefore should be noticed. There are also museums where canvases glorify not only human figures and landscapes but also a multitude of objects. The watering can has thus a good chance of occupying a sizable place in our imagination, and, who knows, perhaps precisely in this, in our clinging to distinctly delineated shapes, does our hope reside, of salvation from the turbulent waters of nothingness and chaos. ❖

Milosz suggests that extremely close attention to the physical world that sur-rounds us is a responsibility no artist can afford to shirk. But what is involved in the powerful production and use of visual images? Why do some images work and others fail to convey anything vivid or substantial? Context is a partial answer to these questions. Artists find ways to frame images so that we focus our attention on them. "A red wheelbarrow" or a "watering can" doesn't automati-cally make for poetry, but Williams and Milosz make us pay attention. Williams structures his poem in a way that moves us patiently from image to image: "so much depends" not only on the red wheelbarrow, but upon the linked clauses that constitute the poem's layered imagery. Milosz employs a common rhetori-cal strategy: after introducing his modest subject he grants that it may not seem of much significance. But he quickly turns from that concession to place the watering can in relation to all physical things that we've been trained to notice by painters, filmmakers, photographers, and museum curators.

Milosz's point about attending to detail gets us back to specific qualities of the individual image and leads to a yet fuller sense of how images work. It is worth thinking about how we see and communicate a sense of what we see. Digital photography has made us much more aware that a picture emerges from small units of shape and color, whether those units are specks of paint, pixels, or words. Those who sell us digital cameras have taught us that if we pay more to increase our camera's ability to record increasingly minute pixels, the clearer the resolution we can gain in larger and larger reproductions of our image.

This paradox—the smaller the area where we are able to focus, the more complete our view of a larger object—drives much of the literature that we read and should help us in our own writing.

These digital images illustrate the increasing clarity that comes with dense, numerous, and minute pixels.

Georges Seurat, Port-en-Bessin, *Entrance to the Harbor* (1888). Seurat was influenced by optical color theories that were current in the later nineteenth century. Upon very large canvases, he placed tiny brush strokes or points of color that would blend as they were seen from a distance.

Tiny details of shape, size, and color are the raw materials of powerfully realized experiences. In Alice Munro's "How I Met My Husband" (a story included in the anthology of readings for Chapter 3), the narrator remembers the simple pleasures of bathing in what is for her the grand home of her employers. Those pleasures are linked concretely to images of sight and touch:

> The basin and the tub and the toilet were all pink, and there were glass doors with flamingoes painted on them, to shut off the tub. The light had a rosy cast and the mat sank under your feet like snow, except that it was warm. The mirror was three-way. With the mirror all steamed up and the air like a perfume cloud, from things I was allowed to use, I stood up on the side of the tub and admired myself naked, from three directions.

The intensity of the narrator's pleasure in her weekly bath is so great that she doesn't want to indulge it too often. An overload of such impressions might risk "making it less wonderful."

Experiencing Literature through Imagery

We can, of course, question our dependence on visual images by considering how people may live intensely without them. In "The Courtesy of the Blind," Wislawa Szymborska recognizes how difficult—even problematic—it may sometimes be to communicate what we see in words. Szymborska reflects on the visual images she is accustomed to use to connect with readers and to connect readers to the world. She displays a growing awareness of breakdowns between herself and others. In front of an audience of blind readers, she realizes how much of her work depends upon strategies that may often be naïve or misguided.

Wislawa Szymborska (1923– 2012)

The Courtesy of the Blind (Clare Cavanagh and Stanislaw Baranczak, trans.; 2006)

A poet reads his lines to the blind.
He hadn't guessed that it would be so hard.
His voice trembles.
His hands shake.

He senses that every sentence
is put to the test of darkness.   5

He must muddle through alone,
without the colors or lights.

A treacherous endeavor
for his poems' stars,   10
dawn, rainbows, clouds, their neon lights, their moon,
for the fish so silvery thus far beneath the water,
and the hawk so high and quiet in the sky.

He reads—since it's too late to stop now—
about the boy in a yellow jacket on a green valley,   15
red roofs that can be counted in the valley,
the restless numbers on soccer players' shirts,
and the naked stranger standing in a half-shut door.

He would like to skip—although it can't be done—
all the saints on that cathedral ceiling,   20
the parting wave from a train,
the microscope lens, the ring casting a glow,
the movie screens, mirrors, the photo albums.

But great is the courtesy of the blind,
great is their forbearance, their largesse.   25

They listen, smile, and applaud.
One of them even comes up
with a book turned wrongside out
asking for an unseen autograph.

In this poem, Szymborska uses an image such as "all the saints on that cathedral ceiling" to show how this particular audience has challenged her entire method of communicating. She may have grown too sure that readers had seen something like this cathedral ceiling (or a "green valley" or a "parting wave"). Perhaps she feels she has become too dependent upon only one of her five senses. In any case, she suddenly doubts the power of all of the images that she has used as a poet. And yet, by invoking these images in this context, her sighted audience is (like the audience for Williams's "The Red Wheelbarrow") encouraged to value the gift of sight—to *choose* to see what sometimes passes unnoticed.

REGISTERING TASTE AND SMELL

It's generally understood that taste and smell powerfully connect us to memories and to specific feelings. In a famous passage from Marcel Proust's *Swann's Way*, the narrator catches a whiff of tea and madeleines (a type of French cookie) and with it reconnects to childhood. The smell acts as a trigger of sorts; it activates a part of the brain that holds not just a memory of past events but a feeling for their reality. Recent research in the physiology of the brain suggests that Proust was onto something. But capturing in words the sense of taste and smell is a notoriously difficult task. Certainly, much food and wine criticism struggles against the challenge. We simply don't have the well-tested vocabulary for smell and taste that we have for visual images. And although the senses of taste and smell recall memories vividly, we have a hard time evoking those senses through memory. Still, in the hands of a skilled writer, the lack of a standard vocabulary can become an opportunity. If images grounded in the senses of taste and smell are less than plentiful, they can also be perhaps fresher.

Character Miles Raymond (Paul Giamatti) from *Sideways* (2004) describes the taste of his wine: "A little citrus. Maybe some strawberry. Mmm. Passion fruit, mm, and, oh, there's just like the faintest soupçon of like, uh, asparagus, and there's a, just a flutter of, like a, like a nutty Edam cheese."

Experiencing Literature through Images

Salman Rushdie's account of his love for bread is a contemporary classic of sorts. As you read this reflection on the pleasures of eating and smelling bread, you won't need to think much of plot or character. Concentrate first on his descriptions—on the images he uses to convey his experience of bread. Rushdie was born in India, and as an author living in England, much of his writing describes his native culture to those in the West. In this short essay, we get the smells and tastes that help Rushdie describe what he sees as an essential difference between the cultures of the East and West. As you read, pay attention to the different modes of representation Rushdie employs. At the start, for instance, Rushdie lists the varieties of unleavened bread that he grew up with in Bombay. Even if we are unfamiliar with these breads, he emphasizes the poetic quality of the names and gives us some feeling for the quality of each of these breads that, of course, we cannot access literally through his prose. The "piping hot" phulka is followed by a series of breads that come to life as they are compared with one another in terms of their sweetness or luxury. As you move beyond the first paragraph, notice how comparison continues to function. *Luxury* may not be a term that we immediately associate with bread, but as soon as Rushdie uses that term, we work to make sense of it within the sensual realm. He describes an experience that most of his readers will not have had, so to present his particular situation he compares his observations to things that might be more familiar to others. As you read, keep track of the way in which Rushdie uses sensory details (comments on texture, temperature, taste) to help us feel the cultural experience he recounts.

Hulton-Deutsch Collection/Historical/Corbis

Nun with Bread

Salman Rushdie (1947–   )

On Leavened Bread (1996)

There was leavened bread in Bombay, but it was sorry fare: dry, crumbling, tasteless—unleavened bread's paler, unluckier relative. It wasn't "real." Real bread was the chapatti, or phulka, served piping hot; the tandoori nan, and its sweeter Frontier variant, the Peshawari nan; and, for luxury, the reshmi roti, the shirmal, the paratha. Compared with these aristocrats, the leavened white loaves of my childhood seemed to merit the description that Shaw's immortal dustman, Alfred Doolittle, dreamed up for people like himself: they were, in truth, "the undeserving poor."

My first inkling that there might be more to leavened bread than I knew came while I was visiting Karachi, Pakistan, where I learned that a hidden order of nuns, in a place known as the Monastery of the Angels, baked a mean loaf. To buy it, you had to get up at dawn—that is, a servant had to get up at dawn—and stand in line outside a small hatch in the monastery's wall. The nun's baking facilities were limited, the daily run was small, and this secret bakery's reputation was high. Only the early bird caught the loaf. The hatch would open, and a nun would hand the bread out to the waiting populace. Loaves were strictly rationed. No bulk buying was permitted. And the price, of course, was high. (All this I knew only by hearsay, for I never got up at such an unearthly hour to see for myself.)

The nun's bread—white, crusty, full of flavor—was a small revelation, but it was also, on account of its unusual provenance, eccentric. It came from beyond the frontiers of the everyday, a mystery trailing an anecdote behind it. It was almost—well, fictional. (Later, it became fictional, when I put the monastery in my novel "Midnight's Children.") Now, in the matter of bread such extraordinariness is not good. You want bread to be a part of daily life. You want it to be ordinary. You want it to be there. You don't want to get up in the middle of the night and wait by a hatch in a wall. So, while the Angels' bread was tasty, it felt like an aberration, a break in the natural order. It didn't really change my mind.

Then, aged thirteen-and-a-half, I flew to England. And suddenly there it was, in every shop window. The White Crusty, the Sliced and Unsliced. The Small Tin, the Large Tin, the Danish Bloomer. The abandoned, plentiful promiscuity of it. The soft pillowy mattressiness of it. The well-sprung bounciness of it between your teeth. Hard crust and soft centre: the sensuality of that perfect textural contrast. I was done for. In the whorehouses of the bakeries, I was serially, gluttonously, irredeemably unfaithful to all those chapatis-next-door waiting for me back home. East was East, but yeast was West.

This, remember, was long before British bread counters were enlivened by the European invasion, long before ciabatta and brioche; this was 1961. But the love affair that began then has never lost its intensity; the new exotic breads have served only to renew the excitement.

I should add that there was a second discovery, almost as thrilling; that is, water. The water back home was dangerous and had to be thoroughly boiled. To be able to drink water from the tap was a privilege indeed. I have never forgotten that when I first arrived in these immeasurably wealthy and powerful lands I found the first proofs of my good fortune in loaf and glass. Since that time, a regime of bread and water has never sounded like a hardship to me. (*The New Yorker*, December 23 and 30, 1996) ❖

By the time that Rushdie reaches the fourth paragraph and what he describes as his serial gluttonous unfaithfulness to his native breads, the essay has built to a climax. It is memorable and often cited, perhaps because of the dense fabric of sensory details Rushdie weaves. This is the sort of text that enters into our real conversations, leading us to talk about our own favorite breads and Indian restaurants and childhood food memories.

THE INTERACTION OF THE SENSES

Our senses operate together. A good dinner isn't merely something tasted. It's well presented to the eye. If there is music playing in the background, it's the right music for the meal. Each bite will have a texture as well as a taste and an aroma. Literary works often build on the dense interaction of the senses to fully realize a scene. Think of, for example, how a nineteenth-century novelist describing a London street scene might register sounds, smells, as well as sights in communicating a sense of busy urban life.

"Paradise Lost" is an epic poem in which John Milton reimagines the biblical story of Adam and Eve and their loss of Eden. In the brief excerpt that follows, Satan (here variously called the "Serpent" and the "Evil-one") emerges from the horrors of Hell to encounter the beautiful Eve in the glorious setting of Eden. Milton wants us to appreciate the sensory experience of one who has been cut off from pleasures the unfallen world offers. We are to know Satan as a character largely through what he sees, hears, and feels as well as through our knowledge of what sights, sounds, and textures he has been denied.

We have divided this selection into three parts. In the first, Milton presents a **simile** (a comparison that links two things with *like* or *as*) so that the reader might be able to appreciate what Satan might feel as he moves from Hell into Eden. An **epic simile** (such as the one in the passage) greatly elaborates one side of the comparison; note in the example that the initial "as" is followed by such a long description that we almost lose track of what comparison is being made. This particular epic simile starts off by describing a person who has come to the country from the city. Eventually we return to Satan; it is he who is *like* the stroller presented at such length. Here Milton uses the simile to humanize Satan; instead of making him unexplainable, Milton creates a Satan whose motivations seem familiarly human. The second section moves from the description of the city dweller who walks into the country for fresh air into the mind of Satan; this is how Milton imagines Satan viewing Eve; she embodies beauty in a beautiful world, and Satan's awe at this sight is intensified by its unfamiliarity. He has grown accustomed to the dismal surroundings of Hell. In the third section, Satan overcomes his momentary lapse into stunned appreciation of beauty and resumes his usual wicked character. Track the sensory details in this passage to determine which are in the simile (after the initial "as") and which appear after the colon that ends the simile. Also note how Milton invokes multiple senses (sight, smell, touch, sound).

John Milton (1608–1674)

from Paradise Lost (1667)

As one who long in populous city pent,
Where houses thick and sewers annoy the air,
Forth issuing on a summer's morn, to breathe
Among the pleasant villages and farms
Adjoined, from each thing met conceives delight;   5
The smell of grain, or tedded grass, or kine,
Or dairy, each rural sight, each rural sound;
If chance, with nymph-like step, fair virgin pass,
What pleasing seemed, for her now pleases more;
She most, and in her look sums all delight: 10

Such pleasure took the Serpent to behold
This flowery plat, the sweet recess of Eve
Thus early, thus alone: Her heavenly form
Angelick, but more soft, and feminine,
Her graceful innocence, her every   15
Of gesture, or least action, overawed
His malice, and with rapine sweet bereaved
His fierceness of the fierce intent it brought:
That space the Evil-one abstracted stood
From his own evil, and for the time remained   20
Stupidly good; of enmity disarmed,
Of guile, of hate, of envy, of revenge:

But the hot Hell that always in him burns,
Though in mid Heaven, soon ended his delight,

And tortures him now more, the more he sees   25
Of pleasure, not for him ordained: then soon
Fierce hate he recollects, and all his thoughts
Of mischief, gratulating, thus excites.

In bringing this particular scene to life, Milton's strategy for making real the horror of hell, the glory of Eden, the turpitude of Satan, and the beauty of Eve is to call up an image that is generally familiar, even mundane. In his simile, he borrows the common conceit that cities are like Hell—there are too many people, too much pollution, and bad sewers—and turns it around; to imagine Hell, we should imagine a city because that is sort of what Hell is like. Satan emerging from Hell is like anyone who leaves a city to visit the country and is delighted by everything simply because it is different and fresh. Instead of being some creature from a horror film, this Satan is so happy to be out of Hell that he is like a tourist sightseeing. This passage is packed full of detail: "The smell of grain, or tedded grass, or kine [cattle],/Or dairy." In reading this passage, we must decide how to translate this scene into our picture of the Satan character who is about to seduce Eve (and, by extension, all of humanity) into disobeying the will of God. The naïve city person whom Milton uses to represent Satan and who is delighted by sights, smells, and sounds of the country is a bit more sophisticated than he appears, and the sensory images that we get in this passage help us understand this character as one shaken out of his usual sense of self and yet able to return quickly to that self. After all, how long are city folk generally excited by the smell of cattle?

Satan's visit to Eden raises a question of large importance for artists of all kinds: What happens when the demands on our senses exceed our ability to process, discriminate, and savor? A rush of sensory data can be exhilarating as it is momentarily for Satan. When our senses, in effect, overload, we may be forced to take in the world differently and as a result may feel a sense of discovery or revelation. Of course, a rush of sights, sounds, textures, tastes, and smells can also prompt feelings of confusion and disorientation. The critic Pauline Kael maintained that film was an art form especially equipped to take advantage of the immediacy and multiplicity of sensory experience. In a dark theater, sitting before a giant screen, we're focused intently on complex and rapidly shifting sights and sounds. We don't have either the time or the opportunity to back off and think about what our senses take in at the very moment they are engaged so actively.

Although such qualities are often exploited to no purpose (do we need more explosions and car chases in "action films"?), Kael's observation helps us appreciate the sources of power that a good movie may access. Think, for example, of Martin Scorsese's lavish re-creation of mid-nineteenth-century urban life in *Gangs of New York* (2002) , or contrastingly Sophia Coppola's spare, precise, patient, and quietly rendered scenes of loneliness from the hotel bar in *Lost in*

Translation (2003). These scenes convey sensory qualities of human life at a given moment: the mud, noise, and movement of the street; the soft and unconnected background noise in the near-empty bar late at night.

Gangs of New York (2002)

Mario Tursi/Miramax/Dimension Films/The Kobal Collection/Picture Desk

Lost in Translation (2003)

Yoshio Sato/Focus Feature/The Kobal Collection/Picture Desk

Experiencing Literature through Images

Of course, movies have no exclusive right to sensory intensity. Nor do our senses necessarily disconnect from abstract thought or inevitably supplant thought. Richard Wilbur conveys a dense and moving fabric of sight and sound to convey the image of a fire truck careening along a street. The abrupt appearance of the noisy, red, and large truck initially leaves those watching with the raw experience of the truck in the moment it passes but without an opportunity to think about the noise and the vehicle that has interrupted their routine activity. In this case, however, the overloading of the senses occasions a philosophical exploration of the relationships among objects, actions, and thoughts.

Richard Wilbur (1921–)

A Fire-Truck (1961)

Right down the shocked street with a siren-blast
That sends all else skittering to the curb,
Redness, brass, ladders and hats hurl past,
  Blurring to sheer verb,

Shift at the corner into uproarious gear   5
And make it around the turn in a squall of traction,
The headlong bell maintaining sure and clear,
  Thought is degraded action!

Beautiful, heavy, unweary, loud, obvious thing!
I stand here purged of nuance, my mind a blank.   10
All I was brooding upon has taken wing,
  And I have you to thank.

As you howl beyond hearing I carry you into my mind,
Ladders and brass and all, there to admire
Your phoenix-red simplicity, enshrined   15
  In that not extinguished fire.

In the first two lines, Wilbur reproduces the impact of a fire truck by announcing its "siren-blast" but also by showing us the effect of this siren on the rest of the "shocked street" where everything is "skittering to the curb." Next, he gives four details that we are allowed to pick out of the blur of the passing truck: "redness, brass, ladders and hats." Each of the details is something that we might associate with a fire truck, and each of us could easily fill in at least half a dozen other details of fire trucks, but these four words are enough to sketch the image that Wilbur calls up here. As soon as the image is distinct, Wilbur blurs it as it "hurl[s] past," and his narrator changes the concrete image into something else. The nouns that he has just listed blur "to sheer verb," and the fire truck itself, which begins as the representative noun or the object that we are trying to see in this poem, becomes representative of action.

Wilbur starts with sensory impressions that obliterate intellectual abstractions; ultimately, though, he asks that we reflect on that process of obliteration. Nouns describe objects; verbs describe action, and Wilbur uses the fire truck image to examine the problem of thinking itself. In his formulation, action happens; and thought, in an effort to make sense of that blurred fire truck, "degrade[s] action." A "fire truck" may be a specific object, but our experience of fire trucks is greater than the things that we see as it rushes past. An integral aspect of our experience of the fire truck is its action: the speed as it roars by and the life-saving actions that it facilitates in emergencies. Therefore, as we think about the specific noun *fire truck* we are also thinking about a series of verbs as well as

> ## Making Connections
>
> In Chapter 12, we consider how images may become **symbols**; that is, an image may come to represent something other than the specific object that the author names. One might argue that the fire truck in Wilbur's poem or the bread in Rushdie's essay signifies something else. To make such an argument, it is important to show how the author uses specific details in such a way that justifies our interpretation. It is also important to remember that images don't need to mean something *else* to connect to powerful feelings.

the next list of adjectives: *beautiful, heavy, unweary, loud, obvious.* Each applies to the fire truck with its redness and hats, but, by taking us into thought, Wilbur has left the realm of sensory experience. The adjectives that apply so well to a fire truck inspire a certain meditation that has very little to do with what the narrator here has actually observed; we now begin to think about the nature of beauty, heaviness, weariness, obviousness, and the paradoxical "simplicity" of this fire truck that has inspired the narrator to set this scene and bring us along on the narrator's own inner journey.

As striking as these images are, they play upon a fairly familiar notion: the most intense sensations and subtlest thoughts sometimes achieve a kind of fusion. This conflation of senses is part of what made *American Beauty* (1999) such a moving film for many people. Early in the film, the main character Lester Burnham (Kevin Spacey) inhabits a home and office environment stripped of any visual distinction. As Lester grows progressively rebellious, colors, textures, feelings, and sounds press upon him.

Perhaps by the end of the film, just before his death, Lester could ask: have you ever felt a piece of music to be so beautiful that it hurt? Or perhaps even tasted that music? This cross association—one kind of sensory experience evoking the experience of another kind—is called **synesthesia**. Until recently, synesthesia was considered a purely fanciful or "poetic" notion; whereas it might be telling to say a color is "loud," surely no one ever really heard a color. In the past decade, however, advances in brain research have suggested that we can't be so confident in absolute distinctions. Neural activity controlling our sensory responses isn't always neatly compartmentalized in discrete parts of the brain. Some people—especially creative people—do see sounds or feel colors. Those of us not gifted in this way may still discover an inexplicable power or aptness in two senses registered in a single image.

THE CONFLATION OF THOUGHT AND SENSATIONS

The Japanese **haiku** form of poetry foregrounds its attention to images. Often the poem itself seems as though it is nothing more than one or two specific images with no attempt to explain how that image is significant. In the following poetic sequence, the poet Yosa Buson offers a series of these short observational poems based upon the four seasons of the year. The third part of the poem, "Autumn," is one of the shorter sections, and Buson begins by describing the experience of stepping on a comb—the comb of an absent (some translate "dead") wife. List the details in scenes that make up "Autumn." What senses does Buson describe? How are the varied feelings connected to the immediate sensual experience of stepping on the comb? What details don't seem part of that immediate experience? How are all details important to Buson's experience of this moment? In the whole sequence, how are details interesting beyond the poet's experience of them?

Yosa Buson (1716–1784)

from Hokku Poems in Four Seasons (Yuki Sawa and Edith M. Shiffert, trans.; 1780)

SPRING

The year's first poem done,
with smug self confidence—
a haikai poet.

Daylight longer!
A pheasant has fluttered down   5
onto the bridge.

Yearning for the Past

Lengthening days
Accumulate—farther off
the days of long ago!   10

Slowly passing days,
their echoings are heard
here in Kyoto.

The white elbow
of a priest who is dozing!   15
Dusk in spring.

Into a nobleman
a fox has changed himself—
early evening of spring.

The light of a candle   20
is transferred to another candle—
spring twilight.

A short nap, then
awakening—the spring
day darkened.   25

Who is it for,
the small bed pillow,
twilight in spring?

The big gateway's
massive doors—   30
spring twilight.

Hazy moonlight!
Someone is standing
among the pear trees.

Flowers of the pear—   35
reading a letter by moon light,
a woman.

Springtime rain!
Almost dark, and yet
today still lingers   40

Springtime rain!
Little shells on a small beach,
enough to moisten them.

SUMMER

In the quietness
of a lull between visitors,
the peony flower!

A peony fallen—
on top of one another,
two petals, three petals.

Early summer rain—   50
facing toward the big river,
houses, two of them.

At a Place Called Kaya in Tanba

A summer river
being crossed, how pleasing!   55
Sandals in my hands.

The mountain stonecutter's
chisel is being cooled
in the clear water!

Rainfall on the grasses   60
just after the festival cart
passed by.

To my eyes it is delightful—
the fan of my beloved,
completely white.   65

Hototogisu
over the Heian castle town
flying aslant

In evening wind—
water is slapping against   70
legs of a blue heron.

An old well!
Jumping at a mosquito, a fish's
sound of darkness.

Young bamboo!   75
At Hashimoto, the harlot,
is she still there or not?

45

After it has fallen
its image still stands—
the peony flower.   80

Ascending the Eastern Slope

Flowering Thorn—
the pathway by my home village
is like this!

Feeling melancholy   85
while climbing the hill,
flowering thorn.

AUTUMN

It goes into me—
the comb of my long gone wife
to step on it in the bedroom.   90

Compared to last year,
this has even more loneliness—
autumn evening.

Being alone
may also even be pleasant—   95
autumn dusk.

Moon in the sky's center,
shabbiness on the village street—
just passing through.

While feeling sad   100
a fishing line being blown
by the autumn wind.

WINTER

I shall go to bed—
New Year's Day is a matter
for tomorrow.   105

Camphor tree roots
silently becoming wet
in a winter shower.

A handsaw
sounding like poverty   110
at midnight in winter.

An old man's love.
while trying to forget it,
a winter rainfall.

In an old pond   115
a straw sandal half sunken—
wet snowfall!

Haiku poetry may be identified by its three-line stanza structure. Each three-line unit in Buson's poem can be read as its own independent poem (the stanza that opens "Autumn" is often reprinted alone). In such short poems, there is often a concentrated attention upon a single image with little explanatory material; we access feeling through the quality and intensity of the image and the associations it provokes. Look back over Buson's poem and notice how many of these three-line units are self-sufficient, yet consider how they work together (just as the seasonal sections work together) to amplify their individual ideas. In what ways does this collection of sensory images create, in the aggregate, a larger commentary? Why does the poet divide his images by seasons? Look, for instance, at the poet's comments about age within each separate season.

A Note to Student Writers: Using Specific Detail

Your writing about literature and film will be most incisive and most immediate when you center your discussion on specific details and when you describe how these details lead you to the larger argumentative context that you provide in your analysis. It is important, though, *not* to get lost in details. While in the early predraft writing stage you might want to make lengthy lists of various things you notice in a work (key words, recurring images, specific stylistic features, and so on), you'll certainly want to edit, order, and reduce that list as you write the paper. Good critical papers aren't defined by how many things they include; rather, they are characterized by how thoughtfully they select and explain what they include. It is the critic's job to convey some significant *aspect* of our experience of a text. You shouldn't try to "cover" everything so much as seek to register precisely and explain fully what is most relevant to your particular reading. Focus is important. For example, a paper on imagery in *Trifles* will likely wander in several directions without every quite getting anywhere. A paper on images of unfinished work in *Trifles* might lead to real insight.

MODELING CRITICAL ANALYSIS: T. S. ELIOT, THE LOVE SONG OF J. ALFRED PRUFROCK

T. S. Eliot's "The Love Song of J. Alfred Prufrock" echoes the conventions we noted earlier that Milton employs to describe Satan's visit to Eden. The city is assumed or presented as a poisonous place of lonely, tired people. It's a place of grit and bad smells. Milton uses escape from the city to intensify Satan's rapt appreciation of the Edenic countryside. Eliot's poem keeps us confined almost entirely in the city. Prufrock never escapes. You'll note that Eliot's imagery, like Milton's, is vivid and varied. At the start, he uses a simile: "the evening is spread out against the sky/Like a patient etherized upon a table." He also employs **personification** (that is, he lends human/animal characteristics to an inanimate thing) to express a lingering, languidly moving, dirty quality of the "yellow fog" that hangs about the streets. His narrator's self-description (the bald spot, the clothes) as well as his descriptions of others ("Arms that are braceleted and white and bare") offers precisely selected details that register a particular social class and the stifling qualities of that class. This complex and difficult poem has been so well and so widely appreciated largely because of Eliot's ability to make us see, feel, and taste details of place and person; his imagery lends a power to the poem even upon a first reading. Through striking images, Eliot helps us acquire a sense of place, character, and situation essential to our experience of the poem.

T. S. Eliot (1888–1965)

The Love Song of J. Alfred Prufrock (1917)

S'io credessi che mia risposta fosse
A persona che mai tornasse al mondo,
Questa fiamma staria senza più scosse.
Ma perciocchè giammai di questo fondo
Non tornó vivo alcun, s'i'odo il vero,
Senza tema d'infamia ti rispondo.

Let us go then, you and I,
When the evening is spread out against the sky
Like a patient etherized upon a table;
Let us go, through certain half-deserted streets,
The muttering retreats
Of restless nights in one-night cheap hotels
And sawdust restaurants with oyster-shells:
Streets that follow like a tedious argument

Of insidious intent
To lead you to an overwhelming question. . . .   10
Oh, do not ask, "What is it?"
Let us go and make our visit.

In the room the women come and go
Talking of Michelangelo.
The yellow fog that rubs its back upon the window-panes,   15
The yellow smoke that rubs its muzzle on the window-panes
Licked its tongue into the corners of the evening,
Lingered upon the pools that stand in drains,
Let fall upon its back the soot that falls from chimneys,
Slipped by the terrace, made a sudden leap,   20
And seeing that it was a soft October night,
Curled once about the house, and fell asleep.

And indeed there will be time
For the yellow smoke that slides along the street,
Rubbing its back upon the window-panes;   25
There will be time, there will be time
To prepare a face to meet the faces that you meet;
There will be time to murder and create,
And time for all the works and days of hands
That lift and drop a question on your plate;   30
Time for you and time for me,
And time yet for a hundred indecisions,
And for a hundred visions and revisions,
Before the taking of a toast and tea.

In the room the women come and go   35
Talking of Michelangelo.

And indeed there will be time
To wonder, "Do I dare?" and, "Do I dare?"
Time to turn back and descend the stair,
With a bald spot in the middle of my hair—   40
(They will say: "How his hair is growing thin!")
My morning coat, my collar mounting firmly to the chin,
My necktie rich and modest, but asserted by a simple pin—
(They will say: "But how his arms and legs are thin!")
Do I dare   45
Disturb the universe?
In a minute there is time
For decisions and revisions which a minute will reverse.

For I have known them all already, known them all—
Have known the evenings, mornings, afternoons,   50
I have measured out my life with coffee spoons;
I know the voices dying with a dying fall
Beneath the music from a farther room.
   So how should I presume?

And I have known the eyes already, known them all—   55
The eyes that fix you in a formulated phrase,
And when I am formulated, sprawling on a pin,
When I am pinned and wriggling on the wall,
Then how should I begin
To spit out all the butt-ends of my days and ways?   60
   And how should I presume?

And I have known the arms already, known them all—
Arms that are braceleted and white and bare
(But in the lamplight, downed with light brown hair!)
Is it perfume from a dress   65
That makes me so digress?
Arms that lie along a table, or wrap about a shawl.
   And should I then presume?
   And how should I begin?

                 *   *   *

Shall I say, I have gone at dusk through narrow streets   70
And watched the smoke that rises from the pipes
Of lonely men in shirt-sleeves, leaning out of windows? . . .

I should have been a pair of ragged claws
Scuttling across the floors of silent seas.

                 *   *   *

And the afternoon, the evening, sleeps so peacefully!   75
Smoothed by long fingers,
Asleep . . . tired . . . or it malingers,
Stretched on the floor, here beside you and me.
Should I, after tea and cakes and ices,
Have the strength to force the moment to its crisis?   80
But though I have wept and fasted, wept and prayed,
Though I have seen my head (grown slightly bald) brought in upon a platter,
I am no prophet—and here's no great matter;
I have seen the moment of my greatness flicker,

And I have seen the eternal Footman hold my coat, and snicker,   85
And in short, I was afraid.

And would it have been worth it, after all,
After the cups, the marmalade, the tea,
Among the porcelain, among some talk of you and me,
Would it have been worth while,   90
To have bitten off the matter with a smile,
To have squeezed the universe into a ball
To roll it toward some overwhelming question,
To say: "I am Lazarus, come from the dead,
Come back to tell you all, I shall tell you all"—   95
If one, settling a pillow by her head,
     Should say: "That is not what I meant at all.
     That is not it, at all."

And would it have been worth it, after all,
Would it have been worth while,   100
After the sunsets and the dooryards and the sprinkled streets,
After the novels, after the teacups, after the skirts that trail along the floor—
And this, and so much more?—
It is impossible to say just what I mean!
But as if a magic lantern threw the nerves in patterns on a screen: 105
Would it have been worth while
If one, settling a pillow or throwing off a shawl,
And turning toward the window, should say:
     "That is not it at all,
     That is not what I meant, at all."   110

*   *   *

No! I am not Prince Hamlet, nor was meant to be;
Am an attendant lord, one that will do
To swell a progress, start a scene or two,
Advise the prince; no doubt, an easy tool,
Deferential, glad to be of use,   115
Politic, cautious, and meticulous;
Full of high sentence, but a bit obtuse;
At times, indeed, almost ridiculous—
Almost, at times, the Fool.

I grow old . . . I grow old . . .   120
I shall wear the bottoms of my trousers rolled.

Shall I part my hair behind? Do I dare to eat a peach?
I shall wear white flannel trousers, and walk upon the beach.
I have heard the mermaids singing, each to each.

I do not think that they will sing to me. 125
I have seen them riding seaward on the waves,
Combing the white hair of the waves blown back
When the wind blows the water white and black.

We have lingered in the chambers of the sea
By sea-girls wreathed with seaweed red and brown 130
Till human voices wake us, and we drown.

Using Images to Focus Writing and Discussion

- Locate significant images within this work.
- Is there any single image that seems to be especially significant? What details in the text signal this prominence?
- What sense (or senses) does the author use to convey these images?
- How does the author introduce images in this work? Do they come from a particular point of view? Do they come all at once?
- What is the significance of these images to specific characters within the text? How is this significance related to our experience of the text?
- Is there any pattern to the sorts of images that are prominent here? For instance, are they generally associated with a single place or time in the text or are they scattered throughout various places and times?
- How do the images relate to the ideas presented in the text?

Anthology

SOAP OPERA

The Genre of the Soap Opera

Soap operas are dramas, typically broadcast on television or on the radio, with a series of characters. The story lines typically focus on the emotional relationships of the various characters. The drama is sometimes described as melodramatic because characters are placed in situations of peril or pain to appeal to the emotions of the audience. A feature of the genre is that its plots are open-ended; plots span multiple episodes, sometimes multiple seasons. Multiple plot lines generally run concurrently. The "soap" in the genre title refers to the soap companies that sponsored early broadcasts of soap operas, and a defining feature of the drama (valued by the sponsors of the shows) was that each episode tended to conclude without any resolution, only with the promise that the story would continue and that the viewer should tune in next time to follow the emotional exploits of the characters (and, in the meantime, to buy more soap).

A CRITIC WRITES ABOUT IMAGES

In reviewing a film, writers have a few goals. Usually, we expect a clear argument about whether or not we should see a particular film, but occasionally the issue is more about the importance of a kind of film. Attention to common themes, plots, or character types leads to points about the broader cultural or social significance of a genre. An assessment of any one film isn't really important in this kind of review

Joan Acocella takes the re-release of *Footloose* (1984) as an opportunity to review teen dance movies as a genre. Acocella aknowledges that sometimes the dancing in these movies is suggested more by skillful editing than by actual performance. And if the dancing is really good, the acting may be dreadful. In addition, the plots and dialog are predictable. Indeed, some of the melodramtic qualities of these films (what Acocella calls at one point "the Gipper effect") suggest a blending of the teen dance genre with standard soap opera fare. But Acocella doesn't make such observations in order to dismiss these films. She sees the formulaic elements as a means to get at very significant matters: the tensions between high culture and low as well as between the rich and the poor get played out with great energy and verve through dance. She also notes that the social conflicts embodied in the clash between dance styles becomes a means to represent racial tensions. Her affection for the genre is heartfelt. And she obviously hopes the most comfortable, most "grown-up," most educated of her readers will be open to the spirit that animates movies like *Saturday Night Fever* and *Flashdance*. Think of your own experience with such films and call to mind the most vivid scenes. On occasion, the vitality of dance will be linked with vivid images: a emblematic period dress or a car, for example.

Komura, the main character in Haruki Murakami's "UFO in Kushiro" seems dead to such vivid impressions common in dance films. This story reflects in a surprising way feelings generated by the catastrophic earthquake that struck Kobe, Japan, in 1995. The first images are filtered through a television set: Komura's wife sits fixated on her couch before the "crumbled banks and hospitals, whole blocks of stories in flames, severed rail lines and expressways." Curiously, images of the home itself are spare and generic. For the wife, and perhaps for us, the most striking images are secondhand. The relative blandness of the living space itself suggests that home is not simply the place one lives. It is a place one must build in the imagination and the spirit. It is a place one chooses to be as opposed to a place one merely is. But Komura doesn't understand that, at least not at first. As you read, consider what is involved in his journey *away* from home—what is lost and found.

Murakami's story, teen dance films, and other stories, poems, and plays in this chapter present varied emotionally evocative images: bowls of ice cream, cold sand, a dead canary. Many of these images are placed in the context of domestic strife, the stuff of much popular fiction and film. When critics call a work a "soap opera," they are generally disparaging, suggesting that the author has created scenes and characters to exploit their emotional predicaments. How can we distinguish between images with rich emotional resonance and those that are crudely manipulative? That can be a problem if the writer stays at a level of cliché. But artists find ways to make even the oldest feelings new. Poets often-times achieve power in focus—in precision. We hear about a shared intimacy; even though we are outside it, we get to eavesdrop on the Brownings and sense some particular quality of what they feel. We might hear of enduring love or of betrayed love, or love that somehow gets lost, as in Denise Levertov's poems on marriage and divorce. You'll find that most of the short love poems in the follow-ing collection aren't finally concerned with discovering a new story about love or a new angle on love. Our conversation about these poems turns to the poet's creativity in finding some powerfully original way to capture an emotion that is at some level familiar. Language becomes a way to refresh feelings that can easily grow stale. We read this poetry for the words and the images that the poet has chosen. The Howard and Wyatt sonnets illustrate this mode of reading. Line by line, each poet says the same thing, yet each uses different words. We read for the subtle shadings that these different words evoke. We arrive at two overlapping, yet distinct experiences of the texts.

The reading and especially the nonreading of domestic details runs through-out Susan Glaspell's *Trifles*. The county attorney asks the women to "keep an eye out for anything that might be of use to us." The women do exactly that, but it hardly matters to the men who are in charge of the official investigation. The men see nothing. They are not good detectives (and they wouldn't be good literary critics) because they assume important things must be big things. And they don't make imaginative connections. They aren't able to appreciate the emotional resonance of details like the unwashed pans under the sink or the dish towel left on the kitchen table. Glaspell writes these "signs of incompleted work" into her stage directions because she wants to communicate something of the quality of the home life lived by Minnie Foster. She wants us to see and appreciate particular images in the way Mrs. Hale and Mrs. Peters do.

REVIEW

Joan Acocella (1945–)

Happy Feet: The Pleasures of Teen Dance Movies

A remake of the 1984 teen dance movie "Footloose" hit theaters the Friday before last. I was there. Movies about young people doing new dances that grown-ups consider filthy and low-class have been around for years. (See "Rock Around the Clock," from 1956.) The form probably peaked in the late seventies and early eighties. "Saturday Night Fever," from 1977, is the jewel in the crown. "Grease" (1978) and "Fame" (1980) are also wonderful. They are not as deep and touching as "Saturday Night Fever," but in my experience, all teen dance movies have serious messages.

About the social hierarchy, for one thing. In most of these films, two dance styles, representing two different social classes, confront each other. As a rule, this means ballet versus some form of "street," the latter ranging from jazz dance (roughly the kind of thing you see on Broadway) to break-dancing. I don't have to say what socioeconomic tiers these styles stand for. In "Saturday Night Fever" and elsewhere, what attracts the boy to the girl is partly that she is a ballet student. That is, she has class. In "Step Up," from 2006, the title comes right out and says it. If Tyler, a foster child who spends his life break-dancing and stealing cars, can land Nora, who eats dinner in a formal dining room with clanking silverware, he will have a chance for a future as an upstanding citizen.

The divide may be racial as well as social. The subject of race is in front of our faces from beginning to end in "Hairspray," both the 1988 original and the 2007 remake. When the cast isn't dancing, they're picketing for integration. (The film is set in 1963, in East Baltimore.) Furthermore, this film, more than any other I know, acknowledges that rock 'n' roll music and dancing were a melding of black and white talents, and that the black preceded the white. In some films, the couple is mixed-race. In the very touching "Save the Last Dance," the boy (Sean Patrick Thomas) is black and the girl (Julia Stiles) is white. People stare at them on the bus. In one important film the main character is mixed-race. Jennifer Beals, the star of the hugely popular "Flashdance," had an African-American father. This is not acknowledged in the movie but I think it is there subliminally, and that its purpose is to symbolize what the moviemakers believe are the special powers of dance: that it promotes unity, defeats injustice. In the words of the trailer for "Step Up 3," "People dance because dance can change things. One move can bring people together."

To add to the liberal credentials of the teen dance movies, they are notably feminist, even the old ones. In "Footloose," the heroine, Ariel, however décolleté, beats the crap out of her old boyfriend. (He had it coming.) In the beginning of "Flashdance," Alex (Beals) is being pursued by her employer, Nick. If she were to bag him, this would greatly improve her circumstances. (She is a steelworker by day and an exotic dancer by night.) Indeed, she might get installed in his nice big house with mullioned-glass windows. But no, she pushes him away, telling him that she doesn't believe in dating the boss. These girls are brave.

And bravery is the main theme of the teen dance movie. Normally, the   5
courage is hard-won, as folklorists will tell you is traditionally the case with young heroes. Almost all the protagonists of these films face harsh circum-stances. They are poor. They have dead-end jobs, if they have jobs. Few of them have both a mother and a father at home, and even if they do, the parents usu-ally disapprove of dance. When we encounter the young protagonists, they are sinking in this mire, and the turning point of the movie, almost always, is the moment when someone gives them a lecture on having guts. "Don't you under-stand?" Nick says to Alex in "Flashdance." "When you give up your dream, you die." She wants to try out for the Pittsburgh Dance and Repertory Company, but she's afraid to audition, because she's never had a formal dance class.

The frightened teen-ager may also be subject to the Gipper effect. In "Save the Last Dance," Sara's mother died in a car wreck as she was rushing to get to Sara's audition at Juilliard. Sara then gives up ballet. The kids from poor fami-lies have it worse, of course. In "Step Up," Tyler is choreographing a dance with Nora for the showcase or the finals or whatever big test it is that almost invariably provides the climax of these movies. Then Tyler's best friend's little brother, Skinny—whom Tyler loved—is killed in a street shooting, and Tyler throws up his hands. He doesn't want to try any more. There follows the lecture on guts, which, touchingly, comes from Skinny's brother, who had previously told him that dancing was a sissy thing. No matter who delivers the lecture, it has its effect, and our hero or heroine, re-galvanized, goes on to glory. Importantly, though, he does not abandon his native dance style. Instead, he combines it with the other one. The vaunted fusion is achieved.

But most of what I've said about these dance movies is subtext, or pretext. The text is dance itself. This does not mean the choreography. The editing is usually so choppy that you can't see the choreography, if there is any. The goal is to excite—as with MTV, the model here—and also, in certain cases, to disguise the presence of body doubles. The stars of these movies are sometimes chosen for their looks and their "presence" rather than for their dancing abil-ity, the premier example being Beals in "Flashdance." (Most of her dancing, carefully lit, was done by a French powerhouse, Marine Jahan.) But from what I can tell, the hiring principle is usually the opposite. The main cast members are selected for dancing ability, which explains why their acting is often so bad.

But acting is not their assignment. They're there to dance. In none of these films is there anyone to rival Travolta as a soloist, but most of the big numbers are ensemble routines. The break dancing in "You Got Served," the stepping (a highly regimented group dance, with marvelous arm and hand jive, that is popular at black colleges in the South) in "Stomp the Yard": these group numbers will go down in history as a significant part of the late twentieth century's contribution to world culture. I hope, however, that attention will also be paid to the less pyrotechnic numbers: the Madison in "Hairspray"; the country line dance in "Footloose," both the old one and the new. In this line dance, it is a joy to see everyone's individuality—the heroine's vanity, the hero's vigor, his best friend's shyness—tempered by the group pattern, but still visible, just as people once imagined that every soul, after death, would join in the heavenly chorus but still be themselves. Ideally, that's how it feels to watch these ensemble routines, as if you were looking at the heavenly host. In what is surely the most famous dance in "Fame," the boys and girls pour out of New York's High School of the Performing Arts in a kind of explosion. They stop traffic; the police have to be called. This is accompanied by the title song. "Fame!" the kids yell. "I'm gonna live forever!" They won't live forever, but as, with their strong, pretty legs, they hop on top of the cars trying to get down the street, and sing about this hope, you love them just for that.

FICTION

Alice McDermott (1953–   )

Born in Brooklyn, New York, McDermott earned her BA from the State University of New York at Oswego and her MA from the University of New Hampshire. Her fourth novel, *Charming Billy* (1998), was the winner of the American Book Award and the National Book Award. Her novels have earned both critical acclaim—three have been finalists for the Pulitzer Prize—as well as a popular following. A film version of her second novel, *That Night* (1987), was released in 1992.

Enough (2000)

Begin, then, with the ice-cream dishes, carried from the dining room into the narrow kitchen on a Sunday night, the rest of the family still sitting contented around the lace-covered table, her father's cigarette smoke just beginning to drift into the air that was still rich from the smell of the roast, and the roasted potatoes, the turnips and carrots and green beans, the biscuits and the

Sunday-only perfume of her mother and sisters. Carried just two dishes at a time because this was the good set, cabbage roses with gold trim. Two bowls at a time, silver spoons inside, carried carefully and carefully placed on the drainboard beside the soapy water where the dinner plates were already soaking, her mother being a great believer in soaking, whether children or dishes or clothes, or souls. Let it soak; the stained blouse, the bruised knee, the sin—sending them into their rooms with a whole rosary to pray, on their knees, and a full hour in which to do it.

She was the youngest child, the third girl with three brothers, and since the boys were excused and the kitchen too small, their mother said, to hold a pair of sisters in it together, this final task, the clearing of the ice-cream dishes, was hers alone. Two at a time, she gathered the plates while the others sat, contented, limp, stupefied with food, while she herself felt her stomach straining against the now tight waist of her good dress, felt her legs grown heavy from all she had eaten. Sunday dinner was the only meal they had with their father, who worked two jobs to keep them all fed (that was the way it was put by mother and father both, without variance), and the bounty of the spread seemed to be their parents' defiant proof of the man's long week of labor. They always ate too much at Sunday dinner and they always had dessert. Pie on the first Sunday of the month, then cake, ice cream, stewed fruit—one Sunday after the other and always in that same rotation. Ice cream being the pinnacle for her, stewed fruit the depths from which she would have to rise, through pie (if mincemeat, hardly a step in the right direction, if blueberry, more encouraging), then cake—always yellow with eggs and dusted with powdered sugar—and then at last, again, ice cream, store-bought or homemade, it hardly made a difference to she who was told once a month that a lady takes a small spoonful, swallows it, and then takes another. She does *not* load the spoon up and then run the stuff in and out of her mouth, studying each time the shape her lips have made ("Look how cross-eyed she gets when she's gazing at it"). A lady doesn't want to show her tongue at the dinner table.

Carefully, she collected the bowls and carried them two by two into the narrow kitchen. She placed one on the drainboard and then lifted the spoon out of the other and, always, with a glance over her shoulder, licked the spoon, front and back, and then raised the delicate bowl to her chin and licked that, too, licked the cabbage roses and the pale spaces in between, long strokes of the tongue from gold-edged rim to gold-edged rim and then another tour around the middle. Place it down softly and pick up the next. The creamy dregs spotting her nose and her cheeks, vanilla or chocolate, peach or strawberry—strawberry the best because her brothers and a sister always left behind any big pieces of the fruit. Heel of her hand to the sticky tip of her nose (lick that, too) and then back into the dining room again for the next two bowls. Oh, it was good, as good as the whole heaping bowl that had been filled by her father at the head of the table, passed hand to hand by her sisters and brothers, and set before her.

Extrapolate, then, from the girlhood ritual (not to say, of course, that it ended with her girlhood) to what came to be known as her trouble with the couch. Trouble *on* the couch would have been more accurate, she understood later, when she had a sense of humor about these things that at the time had no humor in them at all. But such precision was the last thing her family would have sought, not in these matters. Her trouble with the couch, it was called. Mother walking into what should have been the empty apartment except that the boiler at the school had broken and the pastor had sent them all home and here she was with the boy from upstairs, side by side on the couch, her two cheeks flushed fever pink and her mouth a bleary, fullblown rose, and her mother would have her know (once the boy had slipped out the door) that she wasn't born yesterday and Glory Be to God fourteen years old was a fine age to be starting this nonsense and wasn't it a good thing that tomorrow was Saturday and the confessionals at church would be fully manned. She'd had a good soaking in recriminations all that evening and well into Saturday afternoon when she finished the rosary the priest himself had prescribed, the end coming only after she returned from the Communion rail on Sunday morning and her mother caught and held her eye. A stewed-fruit Sunday no doubt.

Her oldest sister found her next, on the couch with her high-school   5
sweetheart, midafternoon once again—their mother, widowed now, off work-
ing in an office—and the first four buttons of her dress undone, the lace bodice of her pale-pink slip all exposed. And then not a month or two later that same sister found her there with another boy, his head in her lap and his hand brushing up and down from her ankle to her knees.

Then there was that Saturday night during the war when her oldest brother, too drunk to go home to his new wife on the next block, let himself in and found her stretched out on the couch in the embrace of some mid-shipman who, it was clear, despite their quick rearranging of clothes, had his fingers tangled up in her garter. There were buttons undone that time, too, and yet again when she was spied on by the second sister, who never did marry herself but who had an eyeful, let me tell you—a marine, this time, his mouth, to put it delicately, where her corsage should have been and her own hands twisted into his hair as if to hold him there—which led to such a harangue about her trouble with the couch that, finally, even her old mother was moved to say that there was a war on, after all.

Later, her best girlfriend joked that maybe she would want to bring that couch along with her on her wedding night. And joked again, nine months to the week later, when her first son was born, that she didn't seem to need that old couch after all.

There were seven children born altogether, the first followed and each of
the others preceded by a miscarriage, so that there were thirteen pregnancies in
all, every loss mourned so ferociously that both her husband and her mother
advised, each time, not to try again, each birth celebrated with a christening
party that packed the small house—made smaller by the oversized floral couch
and high-backed chairs and elaborate lamps she had chosen—and spilled out
into the narrow yard and breezeway, where there would be dancing, if the
weather allowed. A phonograph placed behind the screen in the kitchen window and the records going all through the long afternoon, and on into the
evening. You'd see her there after the last guest had gone, the baby on her
shoulder and maybe another child on her hip, dancing to something slow
and reluctant and melancholy ("One for my baby, and one more for the
road"). Lipstick and face powder on the white christening gown that night,
as well as the scent of the party itself, cigarette smoke and perfume and the
cocktails on her breath.

She was a mother forever rubbing a licked finger to her children's
cheeks, scrubbing at the pink traces of her own kisses, forever swelling up
again with the next birth. Kids in her lap and her arms wrapped around
them even after their limbs had grown longer than her own. The boys, before
she knew it, lifting her off her feet when she took them in her arms.

She was forty-six when she gave birth to the last, and he was eighteen and   10
on a weekend home from college when he recognized, for the first time in
his life, what the sighs and the stirrings coming from his parents' bedroom
on that Saturday morning actually signified. (He did a quick calculation of
their ages, just to be sure he had it right and then thought, Still?, amazed
and a little daunted.) For the rest of the weekend, he imagined ways he
might rib them about it, although he couldn't bring himself to come out
with anything, knowing full well that even the most good-natured mention
of what went on behind their bedroom door could get him the back of his
father's hand—or, worse yet, cause a blush to rise from his own cheeks well
before he'd managed to raise any kind of glow in theirs.

And there was the Christmas, some years later, when one of them had
given their parents a nostalgic collection of forties music and, listening to
Bing Crosby sing in his slow, sleepy way, "Kiss me once and kiss me twice
(and kiss me once again)," hadn't their mother said, for all assembled to
hear, "If you don't turn this off, I'm going to have to find a place to be alone
with your father." And hadn't he and his siblings, every one of them well
versed by then in matters of love and sex, sat dumbfounded, calculating, no
doubt...seventy-one, seventy-two...still?

Shades of the trouble with the couch, she took her husband's hand in his
last days and unbuttoned her blouse and didn't seem to care a bit who saw her,

doctor or nurse, son or daughter or grandchild—or older sister who'd never married herself and couldn't help but say, out in the waiting room, "Now, really." She leaned forward, now and again, to whisper to him, even after he was well past hearing, her open lips brushing both the surgical tape that secured the respirator in his mouth and the stubbly gray beard of his cheek.

Growing plump in her widowhood, though she was the first to admit she'd never been what you would call thin, she travelled in busloads of retirees— mostly widows, although there was the occasional man or two—only missing a museum trip or a foliage tour or a luncheon (with a cocktail) at this or that historic site or country inn if a grandchild was in need of minding. What she could do best—her own daughters marvelled at it, who else would have the patience—was sit for hours and hours at a time with a colicky baby over her shoulder or a worn-out toddler on her knee and talk or sing. She told nonsense stories, more sound than substance, or sang every tune in her lifetime reper- toire, from Beatles songs to ancient hymns, hypnotizing the children somehow (her sons and daughters were sure of it) into sleep, or sometimes just a dazed contentedness, tucked under her arm or under her chin, seconds, minutes, then hours ticking by, the bars of summer or winter, late-afternoon or early- morning sunlight moving across them, across the length of a room, and neither of them, adult or child, seeming to mark the time gone by.

But take a look in your freezer after she's gone, the daughters reported to one another and to the better-liked sisters-in-law as well. Nearly a full gallon eaten—or all but a final spoonful so she didn't have to put the carton in the trash and give herself away. She's welcome to it, of course, but at her age it's a weight thing. She needs to watch her weight. It's the deceptiveness, too, don't you see. What does she eat when she's alone?

Alone, in an apartment now, ever since the night a stranger crept up   15 the breezeway, broke the kitchen window, and made off with her purse, the portable TV, and the boxed silver in the dining room which had been her mother's, she licked chocolate pudding from the back of a spoon, sherbet, gelato, sorbet, ice cream, of course. She scraped the sides of the carton, ran a finger around the rim.

On visits to her out-of-state children she'd get up in the night, stand by the light of the refrigerator, take a few tablespoons from the gallon, or a sin- gle icecream bar, but always end up going back for more. A daughter-in-law found her one morning, 2 A.M., with the last chocolate/vanilla ice-cream cup and a tiny wooden spoon—leftovers from the grandchild's birthday party she had made the trip specifically to attend—and gave her such a lecture, as she put it when she got home, that you'd think she'd been shooting heroin.

It was the weight that concerned them, said her children, conferring. They were afraid it was the weight that was keeping her these days from those senior trips she used to love, from the winter vacations in Florida she'd once looked forward to. Now that the grandchildren were grown out of the need for a sitter, she should be doing more of those things, not fewer. They solicited a talking-to for their mother from her doctor, who instead reminded them all that she was past eighty and healthy enough and free to do, or not do, what she liked.

They took to stopping by to see her, on lunch hours, or before going to the grocery store, keeping their car keys in their hands, and urging her to turn off the television, to plan something, to do something. Her grandchildren, driving cars now, asked her out to their kinds of places, treated her to frothy lattes topped with whipped cream that would repeat on her the rest of the afternoon and on into the evening, despite bicarbs and antacids, until she brought herself to tell them when they called, "Thank you, dear, but I'm quite content at home."

Peach, strawberry, and reliable vanilla. Rocky road and butter pecan and mint chocolate chip. Looking at ninety and still, still, the last thing she feels at the end of each day is that longing to wrap her legs around him, around someone. The pleasure of the taste, of loading up a spoon and finishing it bit by bit, and then taking another spoonful and another—one kind of pleasure, enhanced by stealth and guilt, when it is someone else's carton, someone else's home in the middle of the night, another kind when it's her own and she carries her bowl, in full light, to the couch before the television in the living room. Forbidden youthful passion and domestic married love, something like that, anyway, if you want to extrapolate. If you want to begin with the ice-cream dishes licked clean by a girl who is now the old woman past all usefulness, closing her eyes at the first taste. If you want to make a metaphor out of her lifelong cravings, something she is not inclined to do. Pleasure is pleasure. A remnant of strawberries, a young man's hands, a newborn in your arms, or your own child's changing face. Your lips to the familiar stubble of your husband's cheek. Your tongue to the last vein of fudge in the empty carton. Pleasure is pleasure. If you have an appetite for it, you'll find there's plenty. Plenty to satisfy you—lick the back of the spoon. Take another, and another. Plenty. Never enough.

■ The events depicted here are episodes from a life rather than a coherent plot—what ties them together? What is coherent about the character that McDermott has created through the senses that she experiences at these various moments in her life?

■ Find examples of each sense presented in this story. Are there connections among them? Is there any pattern to the presentation?

■ At the end of the story, she says, "Pleasure is pleasure." Is each of the scenes that she has described pleasurable? If not, how can we reconcile her final thoughts with any of the scenes that might be seen as less than experiences of pleasure?

Susan Minot (1956–   )

Susan Minot was born in Manchester, Massachusetts, a northern suburb of Boston. One of seven children, she attended Brown University and then returned home to help care for her father and sister after the death of her mother in a car accident. Several years later she enrolled in the MFA program at Columbia University; she published her first short stories while a student there. Minot's first novel, *Monkeys*, focuses on the way in which the loss of a mother affects a large family very much like her own. Her subsequent short story collection and novels have tended to focus on male–female relationships and on the very different ways in which men and women view those relationships.

Lust (1989)

Leo was from a long time ago, the first one I ever saw nude. In the spring before the Hellmans filled their pool, we'd go down there in the deep end, with baby oil, and like that. I met him the first month away at boarding school. He had a halo from the campus light behind him. I flipped.

Roger was fast. In his illegal car, we drove to the reservoir, the radio blaring, talking fast, fast, fast. He was always going for my zipper. He got kicked out sophomore year.

By the time the band got around to playing "Wild Horses," I had tasted Bruce's tongue. We were clicking in the shadows on the other side of the amplifier, out of Mrs. Donovan's line of vision. It tasted like salt, with my neck bent back, because we had been dancing so hard before.

Tim's line: "I'd like to see you in a bathing suit." I knew it was his line when he said the exact same thing to Annie Hines.

You'd go on walks to get off campus. It was raining like hell, my sweater   5
as sopped as a wet sheep. Tim pinned me to a tree, the woods light brown and dark brown, a white house half hidden with the lights already on. The water was as loud as a crowd hissing. He made certain comments about my forehead, about my cheeks.

We started off sitting at one end of the couch and then our feet were squished against the armrest and then he went over to turn off the TV and came back after he had taken off his shirt and then we slid onto the floor and he got up again to close the door, then came back to me, a body waiting on the rug.

You'd try to wipe off the table or to do the dishes and Willie would untuck your shirt and get his hands up under in front, standing behind you, making puffy noises in your ear.

He likes it when I wash my hair. He covers his face with it and if I start to say something, he goes, "Shush."

For a long time, I had Philip on the brain. The less they noticed you, the more you got them on the brain.

My parents had no idea. Parents never really know what's going on,   10
especially when you're away at school most of the time. If she met them, my mother might say, "Oliver seems nice" or "I like that one" without much of an opinion. If she didn't like them, "He's a funny fellow, isn't he?" or "Johnny's perfectly nice but a drink of water." My father was too shy to talk to them at all unless they played sports and he'd ask them about that.

The sand was almost cold underneath because the sun was long gone. Eben piled a mound over my feet, patting around my ankles, the ghostly surf rumbling behind him in the dark. He was the first person I ever knew who died, later that summer, in a car crash. I thought about it for a long time.

"Come here," he says on the porch.
I go over to the hammock and he takes my wrist with two fingers.
"What?"
He kisses my palm then directs my hand to his fly.   15

Songs went with whichever boy it was. "Sugar Magnolia" was Tim, with the line "Rolling in the rushes/down by the riverside." With "Darkness Darkness," I'd picture Philip with his long hair. Hearing "Under My Thumb" there'd be the smell of Jamie's suede jacket.

We hid in the listening rooms during study hall. With a record cover over the door's window, the teacher on duty couldn't look in. I came out flushed and heady and back at the dorm was surprised how red my lips were in the mirror.

One weekend at Simon's brother's, we stayed inside all day with the shades down, in bed, then went out to Store 24 to get some ice cream. He stood at the magazine rack and read through *MAD* while I got butterscotch sauce, craving something sweet.

I could do some things well. Some things I was good at, like math or painting or even sports, but the second a boy put his arm around me, I forgot about wanting to do anything else, which felt like a relief at first until it became like sinking into a muck.

It was different for a girl.   20

When we were little, the brothers next door tied up our ankles. They held the door of the goat house and wouldn't let us out till we showed them our underpants. Then they'd forget about being after us and when we played whiffle ball, I'd be just as good as they were.

Then it got to be different. Just because you have on a short skirt, they yell from the cars, slowing down for a while, and if you don't look, they screech off and call you a bitch.

"What's the matter with me?" they say, point-blank.

Or else, "Why won't you go out with me? I'm not asking you to get married," about to get mad.

Or it'd be, trying to be reasonable, in a regular voice, "Listen, I just   25 want to have a good time."

So I'd go because I couldn't think of something to say back that wouldn't be obvious, and if you go out with them, you sort of have to do something.

I sat between Mack and Eddie in the front seat of the pickup. They were having a fight about something. I've a feeling about me.

Certain nights you'd feel a certain surrender, maybe if you'd had wine. The surrender would be forgetting yourself and you'd put your nose to his neck and feel like a squirrel, safe, at rest, in a restful dream. But then you'd start to slip from that and the dark would come in and there'd be a cave. You make out the dim shape of the windows and feel yourself become a cave, filled absolutely with air, or with a sadness that wouldn't stop.

Teenage years. You know just what you're doing and don't see the things that start to get in the way.

Lots of boys, but never two at a time. One was plenty to keep you in a   30 state. You'd start to see a boy and something would rush over you like a fast storm cloud and you couldn't possibly think of anyone else. Boys took it differently. Their eyes perked up at any little number that walked by. You'd act like you weren't noticing.

The joke was that the school gave out the pill like aspirin. He didn't ask you anything. I was fifteen. We had a picture of him in assembly, holding up an IUD shaped like a T. Most girls were on the pill, if anything, because they couldn't handle a diaphragm. I kept the dial in my top drawer like my mother and thought of her each time I tipped out the yellow tablets in the morning before chapel.

If they were too shy, I'd be more so. Andrew was nervous. We stayed up with his family album, sharing a pack of Old Golds. Before it got light, we turned on the TV. A man was explaining how to plant seedlings. His mouth jerked to the side in a tic. Andrew thought it was a riot and kept imitating him. I laughed to be polite. When we finally dozed off, he dared to put his arm around me, but that was it.

You wait till they come to you. With half fright, half swagger, they stand one step down. They dare to touch the button on your coat then lose their nerve and quickly drop their hand so you—you'd do anything for them. You touch their cheek.

The girls sit around in the common room and talk about boys, smoking their heads off.

"What are you complaining about?" says Jill to me when we talk about   35
problems.

"Yeah," says Giddy. "You always have a boyfriend."

I look at them and think, As if.

I thought the worst thing anyone could call you was a cock-teaser. So, if you flirted, you had to be prepared to go through with it. Sleeping with someone was perfectly normal once you had done it. You didn't really worry about it. But there were other problems. The problems had to do with something else entirely.

Mack was during the hottest summer ever recorded. We were renting a house on an island with all sorts of other people. No one slept during the heat wave, walking around the house with nothing on which we were used to because of the nude beach. In the living room, Eddie lay on top of a coffee table to cool off. Mack and I, with the bedroom door open for air, sweated and sweated all night.

"I can't take this," he said at three A.M. "I'm going for a swim." He and   40
some guys down the hall went to the beach. The heat put me on edge. I sat on a cracked chest by the open window and smoked and smoked till I felt even worse, waiting for something—I guess for him to get back.

One was on a camping trip in Colorado. We zipped our sleeping bags together, the coyotes' hysterical chatter far away. Other couples murmured in other tents. Paul was up before sunrise, starting a fire for breakfast. He wasn't much of a talker in the daytime. At night, his hand leafed about in the hair at my neck.

There'd be times when you overdid it. You'd get carried away. All the next day, you'd be in a total fog, delirious, absent-minded, crossing the street and nearly getting run over.

The more girls a boy has, the better. He has a bright look, having reaped fruits, blooming. He stalks around, sure-shouldered, and you have the feeling he's got more in him, a fatter heart, more stories to tell. For a girl, with each boy it's as though a petal gets plucked each time.

Then you start to get tired. You begin to feel diluted, like watered-down stew.

Oliver came skiing with us. We lolled by the fire after everyone had gone 45
to bed. Each creak you'd think was someone coming downstairs. The silver
loop bracelet he gave me had been a present from his girlfriend before.

On vacations, we went skiing, or you'd go south if someone invited you.
Some people had apartments in New York that their families hardly ever used.
Or summer houses, or older sisters. We always managed to find someplace to go.

We made the plan at coffee hour. Simon snuck out and met me at Main
Gate after lights-out. We crept to the chapel and spent the night in the balcony.
He tasted like onions from a submarine sandwich.

The boys are one of two ways: either they can't sit still or they don't
move. In front of the TV, they won't budge. On weekends they play touch
football while we sit on the sidelines, picking blades of grass to chew on, and
watch. We're always watching them run around. We shiver in the stands,
knocking our boots together to keep our toes warm, and they whizz across
the ice, chopping their sticks around the puck. When they're in the rink,
they refuse to look at you, only eyeing each other beneath low helmets. You
cheer for them but they don't look up, even if it's a face-off when nothing's
happening, even if they're doing drills before any game has started at all.

Dancing under the pink tent, he bent down and whispered in my ear.
We slipped away to the lawn on the other side of the hedge. Much later, as
he was leaving the buffet with two plates of eggs and sausage, I saw the grass
stains on the knees of his white pants.

Tim's was shaped like a banana, with a graceful curve to it. They're 50
all different. Willie's like a bunch of walnuts when nothing was happening,
another's as thin as a thin hot dog. But it's like faces; you're never really surprised.

Still, you're not sure what to expect.

I look into his face and he looks back. I look into his eyes and they look
back at mine. Then they look down at my mouth so I look at his mouth, then
back to his eyes then, backing up, at his whole face. I think, Who? Who are
you? His head tilts to one side.
I say, "Who are you?"
"What do you mean?"
"Nothing." 55
I look at his eyes again, deeper. Can't tell who he is, what he thinks.
"What?" he says. I look at his mouth.
"I'm just wondering," I say and go wandering across his face. Study the
chin line. It's shaped like a persimmon.
"Who are you? What are you thinking?"

He says, "What the hell are you talking about?" 60

Then they get mad after, when you say enough is enough. After, when it's easier to explain that you don't want to. You wouldn't dream of saying that maybe you weren't really ready to in the first place.

Gentle Eddie. We waded into the sea, the waves round and plowing in, buffalo-headed, slapping our thighs. I put my arms around his freckled shoulders and he held me up, buoyed by the water, and rocked me like a sea shell.

I had no idea whose party it was, the apartment jam-packed, stepping over people in the hallway. The room with the music was practically empty, the bare floor, me in red shoes. This fellow slides onto one knee and takes me around the waist and we rock to jazzy tunes, with my toes pointing heavenward, and waltz and spin and dip to "Smoke Gets in Your Eyes" or "I'll Love You Just for Now." He puts his head to my chest, runs a sweeping hand down my inside thigh and we go loose-limbed and sultry and as smooth as silk and I stamp my red heels and he takes me into a swoon. I never saw him again after that but I thought, I could have loved that one.

You wonder how long you can keep it up. You begin to feel as if you're showing through, like a bathroom window that only lets in gray light, the kind you can't see out of.

They keep coming around. Johnny drives up at Easter vacation from 65
Baltimore and I let him in the kitchen with everyone sound asleep. He has friends waiting in the car.
"What are you crazy? It's pouring out there," I say.
"It's okay," he says. "They understand."
So he gets some long kisses from me, against the refrigerator, before he goes because I hate those girls who push away a boy's face as if she were made out of Ivory soap, as if she's that much greater than he is.

The note on my cubby told me to see the headmaster. I had no idea for what. He had received complaints about my amorous displays on the town green. It was Willie that spring. The headmaster told me he didn't care what I did but that Casey Academy had a reputation to uphold in the town. He lowered his glasses on his nose. "We've got twenty acres of woods on this campus," he said. "If you want to smooch with your boyfriend, there are twenty acres for you to do it out of the public eye. You read me?"

Everybody'd get weekend permissions for different places, then we'd 70
all go to someone's house whose parents were away. Usually there'd be more boys than girls. We raided the liquor closet and smoked pot at the kitchen table and you'd never know who would end up where, or with whom.

There were always disasters. Ceci got bombed and cracked her head open on the banister and needed stitches. Then there was the time Wendel Blair walked through the picture window at the Lowes' and got slashed to ribbons.

He scared me. In bed, I didn't dare look at him. I lay back with my eyes closed, luxuriating because he knew all sorts of expert angles, his hands never fumbling, going over my whole body, pressing the hair up and off the back of my head, giving an extra hip shove, as if to say *There*. I parted my eyes slightly, keeping the screen of my lashes low because it was too much to look at him, his mouth loose and pink and parted, his eyes looking through my forehead, or kneeling up, looking through my throat. I was ashamed but couldn't look him in the eye.

You wonder about things feeling a little off-kilter. You begin to feel like a piece of pounded veal.

At boarding school, everyone gets depressed. We go in and see the house-mother, Mrs. Gunther. She got married when she was eighteen. Mr. Gunther was her high school sweetheart, the only boyfriend she ever had.
"And you knew you wanted to marry him right off?" we ask her.
She smiles and says, "Yes."   75
"They always want something from you," says Jill, complaining about her boyfriend.
"Yeah," says Giddy. "You always feel like you have to deliver something."
"You do," says Mrs. Gunther. "Babies."

After sex, you curl up like a shrimp, something deep inside you ruined, slammed in a place that sickens at slamming, and slowly you fill up with an overwhelming sadness, an elusive gaping worry. You don't try to explain it, filled with the knowledge that it's nothing after all, everything filling up finally and absolutely with death. After the briskness of loving, loving stops. And you roll over with death stretched out alongside you like a feather boa, or a snake, light as air, and you...you don't even ask for anything or try to say something to him because it's obviously your own damn fault. You haven't been able to—to what? To open your heart. You open your legs but can't, or don't dare anymore, to open your heart.

It starts this way: 80
You stare into their eyes. They flash like all the stars are out. They look at you seriously, their eyes at a low burn and their hands no matter what starting off shy and with such a gentle touch that the only thing you can do is take that tenderness and let yourself be swept away. When, with one attentive finger they tuck the hair behind your ear, you—
You do everything they want.

Then comes after. After when they don't look at you. They scratch their balls, stare at the ceiling. Or if they do turn, their gaze is altogether changed. They are surprised. They turn casually to look at you, distracted, and get a mild distracted surprise. You're gone. Their blank look tells you that the girl they were fucking is not there anymore. You seem to have disappeared.

■ How does the narrator distinguish among her different encounters here and among specific encounters and comments about encounters in general? Compare the language that she uses in each instance. What language or images repeat in the different descriptions?

■ What constant identity links each of these together? Find specific examples that work to define this identity.

■ What does the narrator learn from her experiences? How does this knowledge contrast with the various instructions that she receives?

Haruki Murakami (1949–   )

Haruki Murakami was born in Kyoto, Japan, and now lives in Tokyo. His collection of stories *After the Quake* from which the following selection is taken reflects upon the emotional aftershocks of the 1995 Kobe earthquake. Murakami's works have won many literary prizes, both internationally and in Japan.

UFO in Kushiro (Jay Rubin, trans.; 2002)

Five straight days she spent in front of the television, staring at crumbled banks and hospitals, whole blocks of stores in flames, severed rail lines and expressways. She never said a word. Sunk deep in the cushions of the sofa, her mouth clamped shut, she wouldn't answer when Komura spoke to her. She wouldn't shake her head or nod. Komura could not be sure the sound of his voice was even getting through to her.

Komura's wife came from way up north in Yamagata and, as far as he knew, she had no friends or relatives who could have been hurt in Kobe. Yet she stayed rooted in front of the television from morning to night. In his presence, at least, she ate nothing and drank nothing and never went to the toilet. Aside from an occasional flick of the remote control to change the channel, she hardly moved a muscle.

Komura would make his own toast and coffee, and head off to work. When he came home in the evening, he'd fix himself a snack with whatever he found in the refrigerator and eat alone. She'd still be glaring at the late news when he dropped off to sleep. A stone wall of silence surrounded her. Komura gave up trying to break through.

When he came home from work that Sunday, the sixth day, his wife had disappeared.

Komura was a salesman at one of the oldest hi-fi-equipment specialty stores   5
in Tokyo's Akihabara "Electronics Town." He handled top-of-the-line stuff
and earned a sizeable commission whenever he made a sale. Most of his
clients were doctors, wealthy independent businessmen, and rich provin-
cials. He had been doing this for eight years and had a decent income right
from the start. The economy was healthy, real-estate prices were rising, and
Japan was overflowing with money. People's wallets were bursting with ten
thousand-yen bills, and everyone was dying to spend them. The most expensive items were the first to sell out.

Komura was tall and slim and a stylish dresser. He was good with people.
In his bachelor days he had dated a lot of women. But after getting married, at
twenty-six, he found that his desire for sexual adventures simply and mysteriously
vanished. He hadn't slept with any woman but his wife during the five years of
their marriage. Not that the opportunity had never presented itself, but he had
lost all interest in fleeting affairs and one-night stands. He much preferred to
come home early, have a relaxed meal with his wife, talk with her for a while
on the sofa, then go to bed and make love. This was everything he wanted.

Komura's friends and colleagues were puzzled by his marriage. Alongside
him with his clean, classic good looks, his wife could not have seemed more
ordinary. She was short with thick arms, and she had a dull, even stolid appearance. And it wasn't just physical: there was nothing attractive about her personality either. She rarely spoke and always wore a sullen expression.

Still, though he did not quite understand why, Komura always felt his
tension dissipate when he and his wife were together under one roof; it was
the only time he could truly relax. He slept well with her, undisturbed by the
strange dreams that had troubled him in the past. His erections were hard; his
sex life was warm. He no longer had to worry about death or venereal disease
or the vastness of the universe.

His wife, on the other hand, disliked Tokyo's crowds and longed for
Yamagata. She missed her parents and her two elder sisters, and she would
go home to see them whenever she felt the need. Her parents operated a successful inn, which kept them financially comfortable. Her father was crazy
about his youngest daughter and happily paid her round-trip fares. Several
times, Komura had come home from work to find his wife gone and a note
on the kitchen table telling him that she was visiting her parents for a while.
He never objected. He just waited for her to come back, and she always did,
after a week or ten days, in a good mood.

But the letter his wife left for him when she vanished five days after the earth-   10
quake was different: I am never coming back, she had written, then went on
to explain, simply but clearly, why she no longer wanted to live with him.

The problem is that you never give me anything, she wrote. Or, to put it more precisely, you have nothing inside you that you can give me. You are good and kind and handsome, but living with you is like living with a chunk of air. It's not entirely your fault, though. There are lots of women who will fall in love with you. But please don't call me. Just get rid of all the stuff I'm leaving behind.

In fact, she hadn't left much of anything behind. Her clothes, her shoes, her umbrella, her coffee mug, her hair dryer: all were gone. She must have packed them in boxes and shipped them out after he left for work that morning. The only things still in the house that could be called "her stuff" were the bike she used for shopping and a few books. The Beatles and Bill Evans CDs that Komura had been collecting since his bachelor days had also vanished.

The next day, he tried calling his wife's parents in Yamagata. His mother-in-law answered the phone and told him that his wife didn't want to talk to him. She sounded somewhat apologetic. She also told him that they would be sending him the necessary forms soon and that he should put his seal on them and send them back right away.

Komura answered that he might not be able to send them "right away." This was an important matter, and he wanted time to think it over.

"You can think it over all you want, but I know it won't change   15
anything," his mother-in-law said.

She was probably right, Komura told himself. No matter how much he thought or waited, things would never be the same. He was sure of that.

Shortly after he had sent the papers back with his seal stamped on them, Komura asked for a week's paid leave. His boss had a general idea of what had been happening, and February was a slow time of the year, so he let Komura go without a fuss. He seemed on the verge of saying something to Komura, but finally said nothing.

Sasaki, a colleague of Komura's, came over to him at lunch and said, "I hear you're taking time off. Are you planning to do something?"

"I don't know," Komura said. "What should I do?"

Sasaki was a bachelor, three years younger than Komura. He had a   20
delicate build and short hair, and he wore round, gold-rimmed glasses. A lot of people thought he talked too much and had a rather arrogant air, but he got along well enough with the easygoing Komura.

"What the hell, as long as you're taking the time off, why not make a nice trip out of it?"

"Not a bad idea," Komura said.

Wiping his glasses with his handkerchief, Sasaki peered at Komura as if looking for some kind of clue.

"Have you ever been to Hokkaido?" he asked.

"Never."   25

"Would you like to go?"

"Why do you ask?"

Sasaki narrowed his eyes and cleared his throat. "To tell you the truth, I've got a small package I'd like to send to Kushiro, and I'm hoping you'll take it there for me. You'd be doing me a big favor, and I'd be glad to pay for a round-trip ticket. I could cover your hotel in Kushiro, too."

"A small package?"

"Like this," Sasaki said, shaping a four-inch cube with his hands.   30
"Nothing heavy."

"Something to do with work?"

Sasaki shook his head. "Not at all," he said. "Strictly personal. I just don't want it to get knocked around, which is why I can't mail it. I'd like you to deliver it by hand, if possible. I really ought to do it myself, but I haven't got time to fly all the way to Hokkaido."

"Is it something important?"

His closed lips curling slightly, Sasaki nodded. "It's nothing fragile, and there are no 'hazardous materials.' There's no need to worry about it. They're not going to stop you when they X-ray it at the airport. I promise I'm not going to get you in trouble. And it weighs practically nothing. All I'm asking is that you take it along the way you'd take anything else. The only reason I'm not mailing it is I just don't feel like mailing it."

Hokkaido in February would be freezing cold, Komura knew, but cold   35
or hot it was all the same to him.

"So who do I give the package to?"

"My sister. My younger sister. She lives up there."

Komura decided to accept Sasaki's offer. He hadn't thought about how to spend his week off, and making plans now would have been too much trouble. Besides, he had no reason for not wanting to go to Hokkaido. Sasaki called the airline then and there, reserving a ticket to Kushiro. The flight would leave two days later, in the afternoon.

At work the next day, Sasaki handed Komura a box like the ones used for human ashes, only smaller, wrapped in manila paper. Judging from the feel, it was made of wood. As Sasaki had said, it weighed practically nothing. Broad strips of transparent tape went all around the package over the paper. Komura held it in his hands and studied it a few seconds. He gave it a little shake but he couldn't feel or hear anything moving inside.

"My sister will pick you up at the airport. And she'll be arranging a room   40
for you," Sasaki said. "All you have to do is stand outside the gate with the package in your hands where she can see it. Don't worry, the airport's not very big."

Komura left home with the box in his suitcase, wrapped in a thick under-shirt. The plane was far more crowded than he had expected. Why were all these people going from Tokyo to Kushiro in the middle of winter? he wondered.

The morning paper was full of earthquake reports. He read it from beginning to end on the plane. The number of dead was rising. Many areas were still
without water or electricity, and countless people had lost their homes. Each
article reported some new tragedy, but to Komura the details seemed oddly
lacking in depth. All sounds reached him as far-off, monotonous echos. The
only thing he could give any serious thought to was his wife as she retreated
ever farther into the distance.

Mechanically he ran his eyes over the earthquake reports, stopped now
and then to think about his wife, then went back to the paper. When he grew
tired of this, he closed his eyes and napped. And when he woke, he thought
about his wife again. Why had she followed the TV earthquake reports with
such intensity, from morning to night, without eating or sleeping? What could
she have seen in them?

Two young women wearing overcoats of similar design and color approached
Komura at the airport. One was fair-skinned and maybe five feet six, with short
hair. The area from her nose to her full upper lip was oddly extended in a way
that made Komura think of shorthaired ungulates. Her companion was more
like five feet one and would have been quite pretty if her nose hadn't been
so small. Her long hair fell straight to her shoulders. Her ears were exposed,
and there were two moles on her right earlobe which were emphasized by the
earrings she wore. Both women looked to be in their mid-twenties. They took
Komura to a cafè in the airport.

"I'm Keiko Sasaki," the taller woman said. "My brother told me how   45
helpful you've been to him. This is my friend Shimao."

"Nice to meet you," Komura said.

"Hi," Shimao said.

"My brother tells me your wife recently passed away," Keiko Sasaki said
with a respectful expression.

Komura waited a moment before answering, "No, she didn't die."

"I just talked to my brother the day before yesterday. I'm sure he said   50
quite clearly that you'd lost your wife."

"I did. She divorced me. But as far as I know she's alive and well."

"That's odd. I couldn't possibly have misheard something so important."
She gave him an injured look. Komura put a small amount of sugar in his
coffee and gave it a gentle stir before taking a sip. The liquid was thin, with no
taste to speak of, more sign than substance. What the hell am I doing here?
he wondered.

"Well, I guess I did mishear it. I can't imagine how else to explain the
mistake," Keiko Sasaki said, apparently satisfied now. She drew in a deep
breath and chewed her lower lip. "Please forgive me. I was very rude."

"Don't worry about it. Either way, she's gone."

Shimao said nothing while Komura and Keiko spoke, but she smiled   55
and kept her eyes on Komura. She seemed to like him. He could tell from
her expression and her subtle body language. A brief silence fell over the
three of them.

"Anyway, let me give you the important package I brought," Komura
said. He unzipped his suitcase and pulled the box out of the folds of the thick
ski undershirt he had wrapped it in. The thought struck him then: I was
supposed to be holding this when I got off the plane. That's how they were
going to recognize me. How did they know who I was?

Keiko Sasaki stretched her hands across the table, her expressionless eyes
fixed on the package. After testing its weight, she did as Komura had done
and gave it a few shakes by her ear. She flashed him a smile as if to signal that
everything was fine, and slipped the box into her oversize shoulder bag.

"I have to make a call," she said. "Do you mind if I excuse myself for a
moment?"

"Not at all," Komura said. "Feel free."

Keiko slung the bag over her shoulder and walked off toward a distant   60
phone booth. Komura studied the way she walked. The upper half of her body
was still, while everything from the hips down made large, smooth, mechanical movements. He had the strange impression that he was witnessing some
moment from the past, shoved with random suddenness into the present.

"Have you been to Hokkaido before?" Shimao asked.

Komura shook his head.

"Yeah, I know. It's a long way to come."

Komura nodded, then turned to survey his surroundings. "Funny," he
said, "sitting here like this, it doesn't feel as if I've come all that far."

"Because you flew. Those planes are too damn fast. Your mind can't   65
keep up with your body."

"You may be right."

"Did you want to make such a long trip?"

"I guess so," Komura said.

"Because your wife left?"

He nodded.   70

"No matter how far you travel, you can never get away from yourself,"
Shimao said.

Komura was staring at the sugar bowl on the table as she spoke, but then
he raised his eyes to hers.

"It's true," he said. "No matter how far you travel, you can never get
away from yourself. It's like your shadow. It follows you everywhere."

Shimao looked hard at Komura. "I'll bet you loved her, didn't you?"

Komura dodged the question. "You're a friend of Keiko Sasaki's?"   75

"Right. We do stuff together."

"What kind of stuff?"

Instead of answering him, Shimao asked, "Are you hungry?"

"I wonder," Komura said. "I feel kind of hungry and kind of not."

"Let's go and eat something warm, the three of us. It'll help you relax."   80

Shimao drove a small four-wheel-drive Subaru. It had to have way over a hundred thousand miles on it, judging from how battered it was. The rear bumper had a huge dent in it. Keiko Sasaki sat next to Shimao, and Komura had the cramped rear seat to himself. There was nothing particularly wrong with Shimao's driving, but the noise in back was terrible, and the suspension was nearly shot. The automatic transmission slammed into gear whenever it downshifted, and the heater blew hot and cold. Shutting his eyes, Komura felt as if he had been imprisoned in a washing machine.

No snow had been allowed to gather on the streets in Kushiro, but dirty, icy mounds stood at random intervals on both sides of the road. Dense clouds hung low and, although it was not yet sunset, everything was dark and desolate. The wind tore through the city in sharp squeals. There were no pedestrians. Even the traffic lights looked frozen.

"This is one part of Hokkaido that doesn't get much snow," Keiko Sasaki explained in a loud voice, glancing back at Komura. "We're on the coast and the wind is strong, so whatever piles up gets blown away. It's cold, though, *freezing* cold. Sometimes it feels like it's taking your ears off."

"You hear about drunks who freeze to death sleeping on the street," Shimao said.

"Do you get bears around here?" Komura asked.   85

Keiko giggled and turned to Shimao. "Bears, he says."

Shimao gave the same kind of giggle.

"I don't know much about Hokkaido," Komura said by way of explanation.

"I know a good story about bears," Keiko said. "Right, Shimao?"

"A *great* story!" Shimao said.   90

But their talk broke off at that point, and neither of them told the bear story. Komura didn't ask to hear it. Soon they reached their destination, a big noodle shop on the highway. They parked in the lot and went inside. Komura had a beer and a hot bowl of ramen noodles. The place was dirty and empty, and the chairs and tables were rickety, but the ramen was excellent, and when he had finished eating, Komura did, in fact, feel a little more relaxed.

"Tell me, Mr. Komura," Keiko Sasaki said, "do you have something you want to do in Hokkaido? My brother tells me you're going to spend a week here."

Komura thought about it for a moment, but couldn't come up with anything he wanted to do.

"How about a hot spring? Would you like a nice, long soak in a tub? I know a little country place not far from here."

"Not a bad idea," Komura said.   95

"I'm sure you'd like it. It's really nice. No bears or anything." The two women looked at each other and laughed again. "Do you mind if I ask you about your wife?" Keiko said.

"I don't mind."

"When did she leave?"

"Hmm...five days after the earthquake, so that's more than two weeks ago now."

"Did it have something to do with the earthquake?"   100

Komura shook his head. "Probably not. I don't think so."

"Still, I wonder if things like that aren't connected somehow," Shimao said with a tilt of the head.

"Yeah," Keiko said. "It's just that you can't see how."

"Right," Shimao said. "Stuff like that happens all the time."

"Stuff like what?" Komura asked.   105

"Like, say, what happened with somebody I know," Keiko said.

"You mean Mr. Saeki?" Shimao asked.

"Exactly," Keiko said. "There's this guy—Saeki. He lives in Kushiro. He's about forty. A hairstylist. His wife saw a UFO last year, in the autumn. She was driving on the edge of town all by herself in the middle of the night and she saw a huge UFO land in a field. *Whoosh!* Like in *Close Encounters.* A week later, she left home. They weren't having any domestic problems or anything. She just disappeared and never came back."

"Into thin air," Shimao said.

"And it was because of the UFO?" Komura asked.   110

"I don't know why," Keiko said. "She just walked out. No note or anything. She had two kids in elementary school, too. The whole week before she left, all she'd do was tell people about the UFO. You couldn't get her to stop. She'd go on and on about how big and beautiful it was."

She paused to let the story sink in.

"My wife left a note," Komura said. "And we don't have any kids."

"So your situation's a little better than Saeki's," Keiko said.

"Yeah. Kids make a big difference," Shimao said, nodding.   115

"Shimao's father left home when she was seven," Keiko explained with a frown. "Ran off with his wife's younger sister."

"All of a sudden. One day," Shimao said, smiling.

A silence settled over the group.

"Maybe Mr. Saeki's wife didn't run away but was captured by aliens from the UFO," Komura said to smooth things over.

"It's possible," Shimao said with a somber expression. "You hear   120
stories like that all the time."

"You mean like you're-walking-along-the-street-and-a-bear-eats-you kind of thing?" Keiko asked. The two women laughed again.

The three of them left the noodle shop and went to a nearby love hotel. It was on the edge of town, on a street where love hotels alternated with gravestone dealers. The hotel Shimao had chosen was an odd building, constructed to look like a European castle. A triangular red flag flew on its highest tower.

Keiko got the key at the front desk, and the three of them took the elevator to the room. The windows were tiny, compared with the absurdly big bed. Komura hung his down jacket on a hanger and went into the toilet. During the few minutes he was in there, the two women managed to run a bath, dim the lights, check the heat, turn on the television, examine the delivery menus from local restaurants, test the light switches at the head of the bed, and check the contents of the minibar.

"The owners are friends of mine," Keiko said. "I had them get their biggest room ready. It *is* a love hotel, but don't let that bother you. You're not bothered, are you?"

"Not at all," Komura said.   125

"I thought this would make a lot more sense than sticking you in a cramped little room in some cheap business hotel by the station."

"You may be right," Komura said.

"Why don't you take a bath? I filled the tub."

Komura did as he was told. The tub was huge. He felt uneasy soaking in it alone. The couples who came to this hotel probably took baths together.

When he emerged from the bathroom, Komura was surprised to find that   130
Keiko Sasaki had left. Shimao was still there, drinking beer and watching TV.

"Keiko went home," Shimao said. "She wanted me to apologize and tell you that she'll be back tomorrow morning. Do you mind if I stay here a little while and have a beer?"

"Fine," Komura said.

"You're sure it's no problem? Like, you want to be alone or you can't relax if somebody else is around or something?"

Komura insisted it was no problem. Drinking a beer and drying his hair with a towel, he watched TV with Shimao. It was a news special on the Kobe earthquake. The usual images appeared again and again: tilted buildings, buckled streets, old women weeping, confusion and aimless anger. When a commercial came on, Shimao used the remote to switch off the TV.

"Let's talk," she said, "as long as we're here."   135

"Fine," Komura said.

"Hmm, what should we talk about?"

"In the car, you and Keiko said something about a bear, remember? You said it was a great story."

"Oh yeah," she said, nodding. "The bear story."

"You want to tell it to me?"   140

"Sure, why not?"

Shimao got a fresh beer from the minibar and filled both their glasses.

"It's a little raunchy," she said. "You don't mind?"

Komura shook his head.

"I mean, some men don't like hearing a woman tell certain kinds of   145
stories."

"I'm not like that."

"It's something that actually happened to me, so it's a little embarrassing."

"I'd like to hear it if you're OK with it."

"I'm OK, if you're OK."

"I'm OK," Komura said.   150

"Three years ago—back around the time I entered junior college—I was dating this guy. He was a year older than me, a college student. He was the first guy I had sex with. One day the two of us were out hiking—in the mountains way up north."

She took a sip of beer.

"It was fall, and the hills were full of bears. That's the time of year when the bears are getting ready to hibernate, so they're out looking for food and they're really dangerous. Sometimes they attack people. They did an awful job on one hiker just three days before we went out. So somebody gave us a bell to carry—about the same size as a wind-bell. You're supposed to shake it when you walk so the bears know there are people around and won't come out. Bears don't attack people on purpose. I mean, they're pretty much vegetarians. They don't *have* to attack people. What happens is they suddenly bump into people in their territory and they get surprised or angry and they attack out of reflex. So if you walk along ringing your bell, they'll avoid you. Get it?"

"I get it."

"So that's what we were doing, walking along and ringing the bell. We   155
got to this place where there was nobody else around, and all of a sudden he said he wanted to...do it. I kind of liked the idea, too, so I said OK and we went into this bushy place off the trail where nobody could see us, and we spread out a piece of plastic. But I was afraid of the bears. I mean, think how awful it would be to have some bear attack you from behind and kill you when you're having sex! I would never want to die that way. Would you?"

Komura agreed that he would not want to die that way.

"So there we were, shaking the bell with one hand and having sex. Kept it up from start to finish. *Ding-a-ling! Ding-a-ling!*"

"Which one of you shook the bell?"

"We took turns. We'd trade off when our hands got tired. It was so weird, shaking this bell the whole time we were doing it! I think about it sometimes even now, when I'm having sex, and I start laughing."

Komura gave a little laugh, too.   160

Shimao clapped her hands. "Oh, that's wonderful," she said. "You *can* laugh after all!"

"Of course I can laugh," Komura said, but come to think of it, this was the first time he had laughed in quite a while. When was the last time?

"Do you mind if I take a bath, too?" Shimao asked.

"Fine," he said.

While she was bathing, Komura watched a variety show emceed by   165
some comedian with a loud voice. He didn't find it the least bit funny, but he couldn't tell whether that was the show's fault or his own. He drank a beer and opened a pack of nuts from the minibar, Shimao stayed in the bath for a very long time. Finally, she came out wearing nothing but a towel and sat on the edge of the bed. Dropping the towel, she slid in between the sheets like a cat and lay there looking straight at Komura.

"When was the last time you did it with your wife?" she asked.

"At the end of December, I think."

"And nothing since?"

"Nothing."

"Not with anybody?"   170

Komura closed his eyes and shook his head.

"You know what *I* think," Shimao said. "You need to lighten up and learn to enjoy life a little more. I mean, think about it tomorrow there could be an earthquake; you could be kidnapped by aliens; you could be eaten by a bear. Nobody knows what's going to happen."

"Nobody knows what's going to happen," Komura echoed.

"*Ding-a-ling,*" Shimao said.

After several failed attempts to have sex with Shimao, Komura gave up.   175
This had never happened to him before.

"You must have been thinking about your wife," Shimao said.

"Yup," Komura said, but in fact what he had been thinking about was the earthquake. Images of it had come to him one after another, as if in a slide show, flashing on the screen and fading away. Highways, flames, smoke, piles of rubble, cracks in streets. He couldn't break the chain of silent images.

Shimao pressed her ear against his naked chest.

"These things happen," she said.

"Uh-huh."   180

"You shouldn't let it bother you."

"I'll try not to," Komura said.

"Men always let it bother them, though."

Komura said nothing.

Shimao played with his nipple.   185

"You said your wife left a note, didn't you?"

"I did."

"What did it say?"

"That living with me was like living with a chunk of air."

"A chunk of air?" Shimao tilted her head back to look up at Komura.   190
"What does *that* mean?"

"That there's nothing inside me, I guess."

"Is it true?"

"Could be," Komura said. "I'm not sure, though. I may have nothing inside me, but what would *something* be?"

"Yeah, really, come to think of it. What *would* something be? My mother was crazy about salmon skin. She always used to wish there were a kind of salmon made of nothing but skin. So there may be some cases when it's *better* to have nothing inside. Don't you think?"

Komura tried to imagine what a salmon made of nothing but skin   195
would be like. But even supposing there were such a thing, wouldn't the skin itself be the *something* inside? Komura took a deep breath, raising and then lowering Shimao's head on his chest.

"I'll tell you this, though," Shimao said, "I don't know whether you've got nothing or something inside you, but I think you're terrific. I'll bet the world is full of women who would understand you and fall in love with you."

"It said that, too."

"What? Your wife's note?"

"Uh-huh."

"No kidding," Shimao said, lowering her head to Komura's chest   200
again. He felt her earring against his skin like a secret object.

"Come to think of it," Komura said, "what's the *something* inside that box I brought up here?"

"Is it bothering you?"

"It wasn't bothering me before. But now, I don't know, it's starting to."

"Since when?"

"Just now."   205

"All of a sudden?"

"Yeah, once I started thinking about it, all of a sudden."

"I wonder why it's started to bother you now, all of a sudden?"

Komura glared at the ceiling for a minute to think. "I wonder."

They listened to the moaning of the wind. The wind: it came from some-   210
place unknown to Komura, and it blew past to someplace unknown to him.

"I'll tell you why," Shimao said in a low voice. "It's because that box contains the *something* that was inside you. You didn't know that when you carried it here and gave it to Keiko with your own hands. Now, you'll never get it back."

Komura lifted himself from the mattress and looked down at the woman. Tiny nose, moles on the earlobe. In the room's deep silence, his heart beat with a loud, dry sound. His bones cracked as he leaned forward. For one split second, Komura realized that he was on the verge of committing an act of overwhelming violence.

"Just kidding," Shimao said when she saw the look on his face. "I said the first thing that popped into my head. It was a lousy joke. I'm sorry. Try not to let it bother you. I didn't mean to hurt you."

Komura forced himself to calm down and, after a glance around the room, sank his head into his pillow again. He closed his eyes and took a deep breath. The huge bed stretched out around him like a nocturnal sea. He heard the freezing wind. The fierce pounding of his heart shook his bones.

"Are you starting to feel a *little* as if you've come a long way?"   215
Shimao asked.

"Hmm. Now I feel as if I've come a very long way," Komura answered honestly.

Shimao traced a complicated design on Komura's chest with her fingertip, as if casting a magic spell.

"But really," she said, "you're just at the beginning." ❖

- Why does Komura leave home? What specific images lead us to understand his situation?
- Locate specific images within the foreground and background of each section of the story. Where do these images appear, and how do they help define the section of the story in which they appear?
- What significance can we ascribe to the box that Komura delivers?

POETRY

Anonymous

My Love in Her Attire (1602)

My Love in her attire doth show her wit,
It doth so well become her:
For every season she hath dressings fit,
For Winter, Spring, and Summer.
No beauty she doth miss   5
When all her robes are on;

But Beauty's self she is
When all her robes are gone.

■ Look at the words that are capitalized. How is this capitalization significant? How does it impact the meaning of the poem?

■ What is the difference between the two beauties that the poet describes in the final four lines?

Anonymous

Western Wind (ca. 1500)

Western wind, when wilt thou blow,
The small rain down can rain?
Christ, if my love were in my arms,
And I in my bed again!

■ What meaning might we find in the fact that the poet addresses "Western wind"?

■ How can we interpret the question that the poet asks in the first two lines? How is this question related to the desire that the poet expresses in the final two lines?

John Fletcher (1579–1625)

[Take, oh take those lips away] (1639)

Take, oh take those lips away,
That so sweetly were forsworn,
And those eyes, the break of day,
Lights that do mislead the morn:
But my kisses bring again,   5
Seals of love, but sealed in vain.
Hide, oh hide those hills of snow,
Which thy frozen bosom bears,
On whose tops the pinks that grow
Are yet of those that April wears.   10
But first set my poor heart free,
Bound in those icy chains by thee.

■ How is the opening command in this poem at odds with the poem's intent? What specific words help us see this contrast?

Henry Howard, Earl of Surrey (1517–1547)

[Love that doth reign and live within my thought] (1557)

Love that doth reign and live within my thought
And built his seat within my captive breast,
Clad in the arms wherein with me he fought,
Oft in my face he doth his banner rest.
But she that taught me love and suffer pain,   5
My doubtful hope and eke my hot desire
With shamefast look to shadow and refrain,
Her smiling grace converteth straight to ire.
And coward Love then to the heart apace
Taketh his flight, where he doth lurk and plain   10
His purpose lost, and dare not show his face.
For my lord's guilt thus faultless bide I pain;
Yet from my lord shall not my foot remove:
Sweet is the death that taketh end by love.

Thomas Wyatt (1503–1642)

[The long love that in my heart doth harbor] (1810)

The long love that in my heart doth harbor
And in mine heart doth keep his residence,
Into my face presseth with bold pretence
And therein campeth, spreading his banner.
She that me learneth to love and suffer   5
And will that my trust and lust's negligence
Be reined by reason, shame, and reverence,
With his hardiness taketh displeasure.
Wherewithal unto the heart's forest he fleeth,
Leaving his enterprise with pain and cry,   10
And there him hideth and not appeareth.
What may I do when my master feareth
But in the field with him to live and die?
For good is the life ending faithfully.

■ Compare Howard's poem to Wyatt's poem. How closely related are the two
    structures?

■ Find specific instances where their parallel lines express a similar idea in
different words. In what way does this slight difference lead to a difference
in the idea that the poem is expressing?

Galway Kinnell (1927–2014)

Shelley (2004)

When I was twenty the one true
free spirit I had heard of was Shelley,
Shelley, who wrote tracts advocating
atheism, free love, the emancipation
of women, the abolition of wealth and class,   5
and poems on the bliss of romantic love,
Shelley, who, I learned later, perhaps
almost too late, remarried Harriet,
then pregnant with their second child,
and a few months later ran off with Mary,   10
already pregnant herself, bringing
with them Mary's stepsister Claire,
who very likely also became his lover,
and in this malaise à trois, which Shelley
had imagined would be "a paradise of exiles,"   15
they lived, along with the spectre of Harriet,
who drowned herself in the Serpentine,
and of Mary's half sister Fanny,
who killed herself, maybe for unrequited
love of Shelley, and with the spirits   20
of adored but often neglected
children conceived incidentally
in the pursuit of Eros—Harriet's
Ianthe and Charles, denied to Shelley
and consigned to foster parents; Mary's   25
Clara, dead at one; her Willmouse,
Shelley's favorite, dead at three; Elena,
the baby in Naples, almost surely
Shelley's own, whom he "adopted"
and then left behind, dead at one and a half;   30
Allegra, Claire's daughter by Byron,

whom Byron sent off to the convent
at Bagnacavallo at four, dead at five—

and in those days, before I knew
any of this, I thought I followed Shelley,   35
who thought he was following radiant desire.

■ Look up a brief biography of Percy Shelley (a source such as Wikipedia is
appropriate for this exercise). Compare this poem to that biography and
discuss how the tone of the poem is different from that of the biography.

Robert Burns (1759–1796)

A Red, Red Rose (1794)

O, my Love's like a red, red rose,
That's newly sprung in June:
O my Love's like the melodie,
That's sweetly play'd in tune.

As fair art thou, my bonnie lass,   5
So deep in love am I;
And I will love thee still, my dear,
Till a' the seas gang dry.

Till a' the seas gang dry, my dear,
And the rocks melt wi' the sun;   10
And I will love thee still, my dear,
While the sands o' life shall run.

And fare-thee-weel, my only Love!
And fare-thee-weel, a while!
And I will come again, my Love,   15
Tho' 'twere ten thousand mile.

■ The poet writes his English in order to replicate the sounds of Scottish
speech. What impact does this dialect have on the tone of the poem?

■ How does the poetic structure of this poem contribute to a tone that is
distinct from that of the previous poem? How does this difference account
for our interpretation of the poem?

Sharon Olds (1942–   )

Topography (1987)

After we flew across the country we
got into bed, laid our bodies
delicately together, like maps laid
face to face, East to West, my
San Francisco against your New York, your   5
Fire Island against my Sonoma, my
New Orleans deep in your Texas, your Idaho
bright on my Great Lakes, my Kansas
burning against your Kansas your Kansas
burning against my Kansas, your Eastern   10
Standard Time pressing into my
Pacific Time, my Mountain Time
beating against your Central Time, your
sun rising swiftly from the right my
sun rising swiftly from the left your   15
moon rising slowly from the left my
moon rising slowly from the right until
all four bodies of the sky
burn above us, sealing us together,
all our cities twin cities,   20
all our states united, one
nation, indivisible, with liberty and justice for all

- How does the poet use enjambment throughout this poem?
- What are the specific juxtapositions that the poet makes in the poem?
  Explain how the two images together (such as San Francisco and New York)
  bring out specific aspects of the other.

Denise Levertov (1923–   )

The Ache of Marriage (1966)

The ache of marriage:

thigh and tongue, beloved,
are heavy with it,
it throbs in the teeth

We look for communion
and are turned away, beloved,
each and each

It is leviathan and we
in its belly
looking for joy, some joy   10
not to be known outside it

two by two in the ark of
the ache of it.

Denise Levertov (1923–   )

Divorcing (1975)

One garland
of flowers, leaves, thorns
was twined round our two necks.
Drawn tight, it could choke us,
yet we loved its scratchy grace,   5
our fragrant yoke.

We were Siamese twins.
Our blood's not sure
if it can circulate,
now we are cut apart.   10
Something in each of us is waiting
to see if we can survive,
severed.

■ In both poems, the poet sets out words (*communion, leviathan, ark, garland,*
and *Siamese twins*) as points of exploration. Compare the use of this strategy
in the two poems. Where do we see similar sentiments in the different poems?

Christopher Marlowe (1564–1593)

The Passionate Shepherd to His Love (ca. 1599)

Come live with me and be my love,
And we will all the pleasures prove
That valleys, groves, hills, and fields,
Woods, or steepy mountain yields.

And we will sit upon the rocks,   5
Seeing the shepherds feed their flocks
By shallow rivers, to whose falls
Melodious birds sing madrigals.

And I will make thee beds of roses
And a thousand fragrant posies,   10
A cap of flowers and a kirtle
Embroidered all with leaves of myrtle;

A gown made of the finest wool
Which from our pretty lambs we pull;
Fair-linèd slippers for the cold,   15
With buckles of the purest gold;

A belt of straw and ivy buds,
With coral clasps and amber studs.
And if these pleasures may thee move,
Come live with me and be my love.   20

The shepherds' swains shall dance and sing
For thy delight each May morning.
If these delights thy mind may move,
Then live with me and be my love.

Sir Walter Raleigh (1554–1619)

The Nymph's Reply to the Shepherd (1600)

If all the world and love were young,
And truth in every shepherd's tongue,
These pretty pleasures might me move
To live with thee and be thy love.

Time drives the flocks from field to fold,   5
When rivers rage and rocks grow cold;
And Philomel becometh dumb;
The rest complains of cares to come.

The flowers do fade, and wanton fields
To wayward winter reckoning yields: 10
A honey tongue, a heart of gall,
Is fancy's spring, but sorrow's fall.

Thy gowns, thy shoes, thy beds of roses,
Thy cap, thy kirtle, and thy posies
Soon break, soon wither, soon forgotten,   15
In folly ripe, in reason rotten.

Thy belt of straw and ivy buds,
Thy coral clasps and amber studs,
All these in me no means can move
To come to thee and be thy love.   20

But could youth last, and love still breed,
Had joys no date, nor age no need,
Then these delights my mind might move
To live with thee and be thy love.

■ How does Raleigh use Marlowe's words to change the point of view in
   "The Nymph's Reply to the Shepherd"?

■ How do the two poems, with their contrasting approach to nature and their
   pastoral setting, represent different approaches to love and to poetry itself?
   Begin by contrasting the tone and themes of the two poems.

Andrew Marvell (1621–1678)

To His Coy Mistress (1681)

Had we but world enough and time,
This coyness, lady, were no crime.
We would sit down and think which way
To walk, and pass our long love's day.
Thou by the Indian Ganges' side   5
Should'st rubies find; I by the tide
Of Humber would complain. I would
Love you ten years before the Flood,
And you should, if you please, refuse
Till the conversion of the Jews.   10
My vegetable love should grow
Vaster than empires, and more slow.
An hundred years should go to praise
Thine eyes, and on thy forehead gaze,
Two hundred to adore each breast,   15
But thirty thousand to the rest.

An age at least to every part,
And the last age should show your heart.
For, lady, you deserve this state,
Nor would I love at lower rate. 20
    But at my back I always hear
Time's wingèd chariot hurrying near,
And yonder all before us lie
Deserts of vast eternity.
Thy beauty shall no more be found, 25
Nor in thy marble vault shall sound
My echoing song; then worms shall try
That long preserved virginity,
And your quaint honor turn to dust,
And into ashes all my lust. 30
The grave's a fine and private place,
But none, I think, do there embrace.
    Now therefore, while the youthful hue
Sits on thy skin like morning dew
And while thy willing soul transpires 35
At every pore with instant fires,
Now let us sport us while we may;
And now, like amorous birds of prey,
Rather at once our time devour
Than languish in his slow-chapped power. 40
Let us roll all our strength and all
Our sweetness up into one ball
And tear our pleasures with rough strife
Thorough the iron gates of life.
Thus, though we cannot make our sun 45
Stand still, yet we will make him run.

- Look at the pace of this poem and at specific words that indicate the passage of time. How does the pace shift from the beginning to the end of the poem?

- How do images within the poem reflect this quickening pace?

Edna St. Vincent Millay (1892–1950)

What lips my lips have kissed (1923)

What lips my lips have kissed, and where, and why,
I have forgotten, and what arms have lain

Under my head till morning; but the rain
Is full of ghosts tonight, that tap and sigh
Upon the glass and listen for reply,   5
And in my heart there stirs a quiet pain
For unremembered lads that not again
Will turn to me at midnight with a cry.
Thus in the winter stands the lonely tree,
Nor knows what birds have vanished one by one,   10
Yet knows its boughs more silent than before:
I cannot say what loves have come and gone,
I only know that summer sang in me
A little while, that in me sings no more.

- What are the "ghosts" that the poet detects? How else does she describe
  them in the poem?
- Look at the line breaks throughout the poem. Where does the poet break
  up sentences in unexpected places? How do these breaks contribute to the
  impact of the poem?

Elizabeth Barrett Browning (1806–1861)

[How do I love thee? Let me count the ways.]

(1850)

How do I love thee? Let me count the ways.
I love thee to the depth and breadth and height
My soul can reach, when feeling out of sight
For the ends of Being and ideal Grace.
I love thee to the level of everyday's   5
Most quiet need, by sun and candle-light.
I love thee freely, as men strive for Right.
I love thee purely, as they turn from Praise.
I love thee with the passion put to use
In my old griefs, and with my childhood's faith.   10
I love thee with a love I seemed to lose
With my lost saints,—I love thee with the breath,
Smiles, tears, of all my life!—and, if God choose,
I shall but love thee better after death.

Elizabeth Barrett Browning (1806–1861)

[When our two souls stand up] (1897)

When our two souls stand up erect and strong,
Face to face, silent, drawing nigh and nigher,
Until the lengthening wings break into fire
At either curvèd point,—what bitter wrong
Can the earth do us, that we should not long   5
Be here contented? Think. In mounting higher,
The angels would press on us and aspire
To drop some golden orb of perfect song
Into our deep, dear silence. Let us stay
Rather on earth, Belovèd,—where the unfit   10
Contrarious moods of men recoil away
And isolate pure spirits, and permit
A place to stand and love in for a day,
With darkness and the death-hour rounding it.

- In both poems, look at the poetic structure. How does this structure contribute to the impact of the poem?

- How do the otherworldly images of "lost saints" and "pure spirits" contribute to the argument in these two poems? Describe how each poem reaches a different conclusion to that argument.

Robert Browning (1812–1886)

Meeting at Night (1845)

The gray sea and the long black land;
And the yellow half-moon large and low;
And the startled little waves that leap
In fiery ringlets from their sleep,
As I gain the cove with pushing prow,   5
And quench its speed i' the slushy sand.

Then a mile of warm sea-scented beach;
Three fields to cross till a farm appears;
A tap at the pane, the quick sharp scratch
And blue spurt of a lighted match,   10
And a voice less loud, thro' its joys and fears,
Than the two hearts beating each to each!

Robert Browning (1812–1886)

Parting at Morning (1845)

Round the cape of a sudden came the sea,
And the sun look'd over the mountain's rim:
And straight was a path of gold for him,
And the need of a world of men for me.

■ Narrate the action that the poet describes in these two poems. Identify the
specific verbs that the poet uses. How does the poet indicate action without
verbs?

DRAMA

Susan Glaspell (1882–1948)

Susan Glaspell was born in Davenport, Iowa. She earned her BA from Drake
University in Des Moines before beginning her writing career as a reporter for the
Des Moines Daily News and the *Des Moines Capital*. In addition to her work as a
journalist, she published short stories in women's magazines. After a tour of Europe
in 1910, Glaspell fell in love with George Cram Cook and began incorporating his
socialist ideas into her own writings. Her works began to feature strong female
characters who often undergo experiences of self-discovery. In 1915, Glaspell and
Cook founded the Provincetown Players, and the group produced many of Glaspell's
plays, including *Trifles* (1916), a story of a woman who murders her abusive
husband. Glaspell's career flourished during this time, and her play *Alison's House*
(1930) was awarded a Pulitzer Prize.

Trifles (1916)

CHARACTERS

GEORGE HENDERSON, *county attorney*
HENRY PETERS, *sheriff*
LEWIS HALE, *a neighboring farmer*
MRS. PETERS
MRS. HALE

SCENE. *The kitchen in the now abandoned farmhouse of John Wright, a gloomy kitchen,
and left without having been put in order—unwashed pans under the sink, a loaf of*

bread outside the bread-box, a dish-towel on the table—other signs of incompleted work. At the rear the outer door opens and the SHERIFF *comes in followed by the* COUNTY ATTORNEY *and* HALE. *The* SHERIFF *and* HALE *are men in middle life, the* COUNTY ATTORNEY *is a young man; all are much bundled up and go at once to the stove. They are followed by the two women—the* SHERIFF'S *wife first; she is a slight wiry woman, a thin nervous face.* MRS. HALE *is larger and would ordinarily be called more comfortable looking, but she is disturbed now and looks fearfully about as she enters. The women have come in slowly, and stand close together near the door.*

COUNTY ATTORNEY (*Rubbing his hands.*): This feels good. Come up to the fire, ladies.

MRS. PETERS (*After taking a step forward.*): I'm not—cold.

SHERIFF (*Unbuttoning his overcoat and stepping away from the stove as if to mark the beginning of official business.*): Now, Mr. Hale, before we move things about, you explain to Mr. Henderson just what you saw when you came here yesterday morning.

COUNTY ATTORNEY: By the way, has anything been moved? Are things just as you left them yesterday?

SHERIFF (*Looking about.*): It's just the same. When it dropped below zero last   5
night I thought I'd better send Frank out this morning to make a fire for us—no use getting pneumonia with a big case on, but I told him not to touch anything except the stove—and you know Frank.

COUNTY ATTORNEY: Somebody should have been left here yesterday.

SHERIFF: Oh—yesterday. When I had to send Frank to Morris Center for that man who went crazy—I want you to know I had my hands full yesterday. I knew you could get back from Omaha by today and as long as I went over everything here myself—

COUNTY ATTORNEY: Well, Mr. Hale, tell just what happened when you came here yesterday morning.

HALE: Harry and I had started to town with a load of potatoes. We came along the road from my place and as I got here I said, "I'm going to see if I can't get John Wright to go in with me on a party telephone." I spoke to Wright about it once before and he put me off, saying folks talked too much anyway, and all he asked was peace and quiet—I guess you know about how much he talked himself; but I thought maybe if I went to the house and talked about it before his wife, though I said to Harry that I didn't know as what his wife wanted made much difference to John—

COUNTY ATTORNEY: Let's talk about that later, Mr. Hale. I do want to talk   10
about that, but tell now just what happened when you got to the house.

HALE: I didn't hear or see anything; I knocked at the door, and still it was all quiet inside. I knew they must be up, it was past eight o'clock.

So I knocked again, and I thought I heard somebody say, "Come in."
I wasn't sure, I'm not sure yet, but I opened the door—this door (*indicating the door by which the two women are still standing*) and there in that rocker— (*pointing to it*) sat Mrs. Wright.

(*They all look at the rocker.*)

COUNTY ATTORNEY: What—was she doing?

HALE: She was rockin' back and forth. She had her apron in her hand and was kind of—pleating it.

COUNTY ATTORNEY: And how did she—look?

HALE: Well, she looked queer.   15

COUNTY ATTORNEY: How do you mean—queer?

HALE: Well, as if she didn't know what she was going to do next. And kind of done up.

COUNTY ATTORNEY: How did she seem to feel about your coming?

HALE: Why, I don't think she minded—one way or other. She didn't pay much attention. I said, "How do, Mrs. Wright, it's cold, ain't it?" And she said, "Is it?"—and went on kind of pleating at her apron. Well, I was surprised; she didn't ask me to come up to the stove, or to set down, but just sat there, not even looking at me, so I said, "I want to see John." And then she—laughed. I guess you would call it a laugh. I thought of Harry and the team outside, so I said a little sharp: "Can't I see John?" "No," she says, kind o' dull like. "Ain't he home?" says I. "Yes," says she, "he's home." "Then why can't I see him?" I asked her, out of patience. "'Cause he's dead," says she. "*Dead?*" says I. She just nodded her head, not getting a bit excited, but rockin' back and forth. "Why—where is he?" says I, not knowing what to say. She just pointed upstairs—like that (*himself pointing to the room above*). I got up, with the idea of going up there. I walked from there to here—then I says, "Why, what did he die of?" "He died of a rope round his neck," says she, and just went on pleatin' at her apron. Well, I went out and called Harry. I thought I might—need help. We went upstairs and there he was lyin'—

COUNTY ATTORNEY: I think I'd rather have you go into that upstairs, where   20
you can point it all out. Just go on now with the rest of the story.

HALE: Well, my first thought was to get that rope off. It looked . . . (*Stops, his face twitches*) . . . but Harry, he went up to him, and he said, "No, he's dead all right, and we'd better not touch anything." So we went back downstairs. She was still sitting that same way. "Has anybody been notified?" I asked. "No," says she, unconcerned. "Who did this, Mrs. Wright?" said Harry. He said it business-like—and she stopped pleatin' of her apron. "I don't know," she says. "You don't *know?*" says Harry. "No," says she. "Weren't you sleepin' in the bed with him?" says Harry. "Yes," says she, "but I was on the inside." "Somebody slipped a rope round his neck and strangled him and you didn't wake up?" says Harry. "I didn't wake up," she said after him. We must 'a looked as if we didn't see how that could be, for after a minute she said, "I sleep sound." Harry was going to ask her more questions but I said maybe we ought to let her tell her story first to the coroner, or the sheriff, so Harry went fast as he could to Rivers' place, where there's a telephone.

COUNTY ATTORNEY: And what did Mrs. Wright do when she knew that you had gone for the coroner?

HALE: She moved from that chair to this one over here (*Pointing to a small chair in the corner*) and just sat there with her hands held together and looking down. I got a feeling that I ought to make some conversation, so I said I had come in to see if John wanted to put in a telephone, and at that she started to laugh, and then she stopped and looked at me—scared. (*The* COUNTY ATTORNEY, *who has had his notebook out, makes a note.*) I dunno, maybe it wasn't scared. I wouldn't like to say it was. Soon Harry got back, and then Dr. Lloyd came, and you, Mr. Peters, and so I guess that's all I know that you don't.

COUNTY ATTORNEY (*Looking around.*): I guess we'll go upstairs first—and then out to the barn and around there. (*To the* SHERIFF.) You're convinced that there was nothing important here—nothing that would point to any motive.

SHERIFF: Nothing here but kitchen things. 25

(*The* COUNTY ATTORNEY, *after again looking around the kitchen, opens the door of a cupboard closet. He gets up on a chair and looks on a shelf. Pulls his hand away, sticky.*)

COUNTY ATTORNEY: Here's a nice mess.

(*The women draw nearer.*)

MRS. PETERS (*To the other woman.*): Oh, her fruit; it did freeze. (*To the* LAWYER.) She worried about that when it turned so cold. She said the fire'd go out and her jars would break.

SHERIFF: Well, can you beat the woman! Held for murder and worryin' about her preserves.

COUNTY ATTORNEY: I guess before we're through she may have something more serious than preserves to worry about.

HALE: Well, women are used to worrying over trifles. 30

(*The two women move a little closer together.*)

COUNTY ATTORNEY (*With the gallantry of a young politician.*): And yet, for all their worries, what would we do without the ladies? (*The women do not unbend. He goes to the sink, takes a dipperful of water from the pail and pouring it into a basin, washes his hands. Starts to wipe them on the roller-towel, turns it for a cleaner place.*) Dirty towels! (*Kicks his foot against the pans under the sink.*) Not much of a housekeeper, would you say, ladies?

MRS. HALE (*Stiffly.*): There's a great deal of work to be done on a farm.

COUNTY ATTORNEY: To be sure. And yet (*With a little bow to her.*) I know there are some Dickson county farmhouses which do not have such roller towels.

(*He gives it a pull to expose its full length again.*)

MRS. HALE: Those towels get dirty awful quick. Men's hands aren't always as clean as they might be.

COUNTY ATTORNEY: Ah, loyal to your sex, I see. But you and Mrs. Wright were neighbors. I suppose you were friends, too. 35

MRS. HALE (*Shaking her head.*): I've not seen much of her of late years. I've not been in this house—it's more than a year.

COUNTY ATTORNEY: And why was that? You didn't like her?

MRS. HALE: I liked her all well enough. Farmers' wives have their hands full, Mr. Henderson. And then—

COUNTY ATTORNEY: Yes—?

MRS. HALE (*Looking about.*): It never seemed a very cheerful place. 40

COUNTY ATTORNEY: No—it's not cheerful. I shouldn't say she had the homemaking instinct.

MRS. HALE: Well, I don't know as Wright had, either.

COUNTY ATTORNEY: You mean that they didn't get on very well?

MRS. HALE: No, I don't mean anything. But I don't think a place'd be any cheerfuller for John Wright's being in it.

COUNTY ATTORNEY: I'd like to talk more of that a little later. I want to get the lay of things upstairs now. 45

(*He goes to the left, where three steps lead to a stair door.*)

SHERIFF: I suppose anything Mrs. Peters does'll be all right. She was to take in some clothes for her, you know, and a few little things. We left in such a hurry yesterday.

COUNTY ATTORNEY: Yes, but I would like to see what you take, Mrs. Peters, and keep an eye out for anything that might be of use to us.

MRS. PETERS: Yes, Mr. Henderson.

(*The women listen to the men's steps on the stairs, then look about the kitchen.*)

MRS. HALE: I'd hate to have men coming into my kitchen, snooping around and criticising.

(*She arranges the pans under sink which the lawyer had shoved out of place.*)

MRS. PETERS: Of course it's no more than their duty. 50

MRS. HALE: Duty's all right, but I guess that deputy sheriff that came out to make the fire might have got a little of this on. (*Gives the roller towel a pull.*) Wish I'd thought of that sooner. Seems mean to talk about her for not having things slicked up when she had to come away in such a hurry.

MRS. PETERS (*Who has gone to a small table in the left rear corner of the room, and lifted one end of a towel that covers a pan.*): She had bread set.

(*Stands still.*)

MRS. HALE (*Eyes fixed on a loaf of bread beside the breadbox, which is on a low shelf at the other side of the room. Moves slowly toward it.*): She was going to put this in there. (*Picks up loaf, then abruptly drops it. In a manner of returning to familiar things.*) It' a shame about her fruit. I wonder if it's all gone. (*Gets up on the chair and looks.*) I think there's some here that's all right, Mrs. Peters. Yes—here; (*Holding it toward the window*) this is cherries, too. (*Looking again.*) I declare I believe that's the only one. (*Gets down, bottle in her hand. Goes to the sink and wipes it off on the outside.*) She'll feel awful bad after all her hard work in the hot weather. I remember the afternoon I put up my cherries last summer.

(*She puts the bottle on the big kitchen table, center of the room. With a sigh, is about to sit down in the rocking-chair. Before she is seated realizes what chair it is; with a slow look at it, steps back. The chair which she has touched rocks back and forth.*)

MRS. PETERS: Well, I must get those things from the front room closet. (*She goes to the door at the right, but after looking into the other room, steps back.*) You coming with me, Mrs. Hale? You could help me carry them.

(*They go in the other room; reappear,* MRS. PETERS *carrying a dress and skirt,* MRS. HALE *following with a pair of shoes.*)

MRS. PETERS: My, it's cold in there. 55

(*She puts the clothes on the big table, and hurries to the stove.*)

MRS. HALE (*Examining the skirt.*): Wright was close. I think maybe that's why she kept so much to herself. She didn't even belong to the Ladies Aid. I suppose she felt she couldn't do her part, and then you don't enjoy things when you feel shabby. She used to wear pretty clothes and be lively, when she was Minnie Foster, one of the town girls singing in the choir. But that—oh, that was thirty years ago. This all you was to take in?

MRS. PETERS: She said she wanted an apron. Funny thing to want, for there isn't much to get you dirty in jail, goodness knows. But I suppose just to make her feel more natural. She said they was in the top drawer in this cupboard. Yes, here. And then her little shawl that always hung behind the door. (*Opens stair door and looks.*) Yes, here it is.

(*Quickly shuts door leading upstairs.*)

MRS. HALE (*Abruptly moving toward her.*): Mrs. Peters?

MRS. PETERS: Yes, Mrs. Hale?

MRS. HALE: Do you think she did it? 60

MRS. PETERS (*In a frightened voice.*): Oh, I don't know.

MRS. HALE: Well, I don't think she did. Asking for an apron and her little shawl. Worrying about her fruit.

MRS. PETERS (*Starts to speak, glances up, where footsteps are heard in the room above. In a low voice.*): Mr. Peters says it looks bad for her. Mr. Henderson is awful sarcastic in a speech and he'll make fun of her sayin' she didn't wake up.

MRS. HALE: Well, I guess John Wright didn't wake when they was slipping that rope under his neck.

MRS. PETERS: No, it's strange. It must have been done awful crafty and still. 65 They say it was such a—funny way to kill a man, rigging it all up like that.

MRS. HALE: That's just what Mr. Hale said. There was a gun in the house. He says that's what he can't understand.

MRS. PETERS: Mr. Henderson said coming out that what was needed for the case was a motive; something to show anger, or—sudden feeling.

MRS. HALE (*Who is standing by the table.*): Well, I don't see any signs of anger around here. (*She puts her hand on the dish towel which lies on the table, stands looking down at table, one half of which is clean, the other half messy.*) It's wiped to here. (*Makes a move as if to finish work, then turns and looks at loaf of bread outside the breadbox. Drops towel. In that voice of coming back to familiar things.*) Wonder how they are finding things upstairs. I hope she had it a little more red-up up there. You know, it seems kind of sneaking. Locking her up in town and then coming out here and trying to get her own house to turn against her!

MRS. PETERS: But Mrs. Hale, the law is the law.

MRS. HALE: I s'pose 'tis. (*Unbuttoning her coat.*) Better loosen up your things, 70 Mrs. Peters. You won't feel them when you go out.

(MRS. PETERS *takes off her fur tippet, goes to hang it on hook at back of room, stands looking at the under part of the small corner table.*)

MRS. PETERS: She was piecing a quilt.

(*She brings the large sewing basket and they look at the bright pieces.*)

MRS. HALE: It's log cabin pattern. Pretty, isn't it? I wonder if she was goin' to quilt it or just knot it?

(*Footsteps have been heard coming down the stairs. The sheriff enters followed by* HALE *and the* COUNTY ATTORNEY.)

SHERIFF: They wonder if she was going to quilt it or just knot it!

(*The men laugh, the women look abashed.*)

COUNTY ATTORNEY (*Rubbing his hands over the stove.*): Frank's fire didn't do much up there, did it? Well, let's go out to the barn and get that cleared up.

(*The men go outside.*)

MRS. HALE (*Resentfully.*): I don't know as there's anything so strange, our takin' 75 up our time with little things while we're waiting for them to get the evidence. (*She sits down at the big table smoothing out a block with decision.*) I don't see as it's anything to laugh about.

MRS. PETERS (*Apologetically.*): Of course they've got awful important things on their minds.

(*Pulls up a chair and joins* MRS. HALE *at the table.*)

MRS. HALE (*Examining another block.*): Mrs. Peters, look at this one. Here, this is the one she was working on, and look at the sewing! All the rest of it has been so nice and even. And look at this! It's all over the place! Why, it looks as if she didn't know what she was about!

(*After she has said this they look at each other, then start to glance back at the door. After an instant* MRS. HALE *has pulled at a knot and ripped the sewing.*)

MRS. PETERS: Oh, what are you doing, Mrs. Hale?

MRS. HALE (*Mildly.*): Just pulling out a stitch or two that's not sewed very good. (*Threading a needle.*) Bad sewing always made me fidgety.

MRS. PETERS (*Nervously.*): I don't think we ought to touch things. 80

MRS. HALE: I'll just finish up this end. (*Suddenly stopping and leaning forward.*) Mrs. Peters?

MRS. PETERS: Yes, Mrs. Hale?

MRS. HALE: What do you suppose she was so nervous about?

MRS. PETERS: Oh—I don't know. I don't know as she was nervous. I sometimes sew awful queer when I'm just tired. (*Mrs. Hale starts to say something, looks at Mrs. Peters, then goes on sewing.*) Well I must get these things wrapped up. They may be through sooner than we think. (*Putting apron and other things together.*) I wonder where I can find a piece of paper, and string.

MRS. HALE: In that cupboard, maybe. 85

MRS. PETERS (*Looking in cupboard.*): Why, here's a bird-cage. (*Holds it up.*) Did she have a bird, Mrs. Hale?

MRS. HALE: Why, I don't know whether she did or not—I've not been here for so long. There was a man around last year selling canaries cheap, but I don't know as she took one; maybe she did. She used to sing real pretty herself.

MRS. PETERS (*Glancing around.*): Seems funny to think of a bird here. But she must have had one, or why would she have a cage? I wonder what happened to it.

MRS. HALE: I s'pose maybe the cat got it.

MRS. PETERS: No, she didn't have a cat. She's got that feeling some people 90 have about cats—being afraid of them. My cat got in her room and she was real upset and asked me to take it out.

MRS. HALE: My sister Bessie was like that. Queer, ain't it?

MRS. PETERS (*Examining the cage.*): Why, look at this door. It's broke. One hinge is pulled apart.

MRS. HALE (*Looking too.*): Looks as if someone must have been rough with it.

MRS. PETERS: Why, yes.

(*She brings the cage forward and puts it on the table.*)

MRS. HALE: I wish if they're going to find any evidence they'd be about it. 95 I don't like this place.

MRS. PETERS: But I'm awful glad you came with me, Mrs. Hale. It would be lonesome for me sitting here alone.

MRS. HALE: It would, wouldn't it? (*Dropping her sewing.*) But I tell you what I do wish, Mrs. Peters. I wish I had come over sometimes when she was here. I— (*Looking around the room.*) —wish I had.

MRS. PETERS: But of course you were awful busy, Mrs. Hale—your house and your children.

MRS. HALE: I could've come. I stayed away because it weren't cheerful—and that's why I ought to have come. I—I've never liked this place. Maybe because it's down in a hollow and you don't see the road. I dunno what it is, but it's a lonesome place and always was. I wish I had come over to see Minnie Foster sometimes. I can see now—
(*Shakes her head.*)

MRS. PETERS: Well, you mustn't reproach yourself, Mrs. Hale. Somehow we   100
just don't see how it is with other folks until—something comes up.

MRS. HALE: Not having children makes less work—but it makes a quiet house, and Wright out to work all day, and no company when he did come in. Did you know John Wright, Mrs. Peters?

MRS. PETERS: Not to know him; I've seen him in town. They say he was a good man.

MRS. HALE: Yes—good; he didn't drink, and kept his word as well as most, I guess, and paid his debts. But he was a hard man, Mrs. Peters. Just to pass the time of day with him— (*Shivers.*) Like a raw wind that gets to the bone. (*Pauses, her eye falling on the cage.*) I should think she would 'a wanted a bird. But what do you suppose went with it?

MRS. PETERS: I don't know, unless it got sick and died.
(*She reaches over and swings the broken door, swings it again, both women watch it.*)

MRS. HALE: You weren't raised round here, were you? (*Mrs. Peters shakes her*   105
head.) You didn't know—her?

MRS. PETERS: Not till they brought her yesterday.

MRS. HALE: She—come to think of it, she was kind of like a bird herself—real sweet and pretty, but kind of timid and—fluttery. How—she—did—change. (*Silence; then as if struck by a happy thought and relieved to get back to everyday things*.) Tell you what, Mrs. Peters, why don't you take the quilt in with you? It might take up her mind.

MRS. PETERS: Why, I think that's a real nice idea, Mrs. Hale. There couldn't possibly be any objection to it, could there? Now, just what would I take? I wonder if her patches are in here—and her things.
(*They look in the sewing basket.*)

MRS. HALE: Here's some red. I expect this has got sewing things in it. (*Brings out a fancy box.*) What a pretty box. Looks like something somebody would give you. Maybe her scissors are in here. (*Opens box. Suddenly puts her hand to her nose.*) Why— (*Mrs. Peters bends nearer, then turns her face away.*) There's something wrapped up in this piece of silk.

MRS. PETERS: Why, this isn't her scissors.   110

MRS. HALE (*Lifting the silk.*): Oh, Mrs. Peters—its—
(MRS. PETERS *bends closer.*)

MRS. PETERS: It's the bird.

MRS. HALE (*Jumping up.*): But, Mrs. Peters—look at it! Its neck! Look at its neck! It's all—other side *to*.

MRS. PETERS: Somebody—wrung—its—neck.

(*Their eyes meet. A look of growing comprehension, of horror. Steps are heard outside.*
MRS. HALE slips box under quilt pieces, and sinks into her chair. Enter SHERIFF
and COUNTY ATTORNEY. MRS. PETERS rises.)

COUNTY ATTORNEY (*As one turning from serious things to little pleasantries.*): Well,   115
ladies, have you decided whether she was going to quilt it or knot it?

MRS. PETERS: We think she was going to—knot it.

COUNTY ATTORNEY: Well, that's interesting, I'm sure. (*Seeing the birdcage.*)
Has the bird flown?

MRS. HALE (*Putting more quilt pieces over the box.*): We think the—cat got it.

COUNTY ATTORNEY (*Preoccupied.*): Is there a cat?

(MRS. HALE *glances in a quick covert way at* MRS. PETERS.)

MRS. PETERS: Well, not now. They're superstitious, you know. They leave.   120

COUNTY ATTORNEY (*To SHERIFF PETERS, continuing an interrupted conversation.*):
No sign at all of anyone having come from the outside. Their own rope.
Now let's go up again and go over it piece by piece. (*They start upstairs.*)
It would have to have been someone who knew just the—

(MRS. PETERS *sits down. The two women sit there not looking at one another, but as*
if peering into something and at the same time holding back. When they talk now
it is in the manner of feeling their way over strange ground, as if afraid of what they
are saying, but as if they can not help saying it.)

MRS. HALE: She liked the bird. She was going to bury it in that pretty box.

MRS. PETERS (*In a whisper.*): When I was a girl—my kitten—there was a boy took
a hatchet, and before my eyes—and before I could get there—(*Covers her*
face an instant.) If they hadn't held me back I would have—(*Catches herself,*
looks upstairs where steps are heard, falters weakly)—hurt him.

MRS. HALE (*With a slow look around her.*): I wonder how it would seem never
to have had any children around. (*Pause.*) No, Wright wouldn't like the
bird—a thing that sang. She used to sing. He killed that, too.

MRS. PETERS (*Moving uneasily.*): We don't know who killed the bird.   125

MRS. HALE: I knew John Wright.

MRS. PETERS: It was an awful thing was done in this house that night, Mrs. Hale.
Killing a man while he slept, slipping a rope around his neck that
choked the life out of him.

MRS. HALE: His neck. Choked the life out of him.

(*Her hand goes out and rests on the bird-cage.*)

MRS. PETERS (*With rising voice.*): We don't know who killed him. We don't *know.*

MRS. HALE (*Her own feeling not interrupted.*): If there'd been years and years   130
of nothing, then a bird to sing to you, it would be awful—still, after
the bird was still.

MRS. PETERS (*Something within her speaking.*): I know what stillness is. When we
homesteaded in Dakota, and my first baby died—after he was two years
old, and me with no other then—

MRS. HALE (*Moving.*): How soon do you suppose they'll be through, looking for the evidence?

MRS. PETERS: I know what stillness is. (*Pulling herself back.*) The law has got to punish crime, Mrs. Hale.

MRS. HALE (*Not as if answering that.*): I wish you'd seen Minnie Foster when she wore a white dress with blue ribbons and stood up there in the choir and sang. (*A look around the room.*) Oh, I wish I'd come over here once in a while! That was a crime! That was a crime! Who's going to punish that?

MRS. PETERS (*Looking upstairs.*): We mustn't—take on.   135

MRS. HALE: I might have known she needed help! I know how things can be—for women. I tell you, it's queer, Mrs. Peters. We live close together and we live far apart. We all go through the same things—it's all just a different kind of the same thing. (*Brushes her eyes, noticing the bottle of fruit, reaches out for it.*) If I was you I wouldn't tell her her fruit was gone. Tell her it ain't. Tell her it's all right. Take this in to prove it to her. She—she may never know whether it was broke or not.

MRS. PETERS (*Takes the bottle, looks about for something to wrap it in; takes petticoat from the clothes brought from the other room, very nervously begins winding this around the bottle. In a false voice.*): My, it's a good thing the men couldn't hear us. Wouldn't they just laugh! Getting all stirred up over a little thing like a—dead canary. As if that could have anything to do with—with—wouldn't they *laugh!*

(*The men are heard coming down stairs.*)

MRS. HALE (*Under her breath.*): Maybe they would—maybe they wouldn't.

COUNTY ATTORNEY: No, Peters, it's all perfectly clear except a reason for doing it. But you know juries when it comes to women. If there was some definite thing. Something to show—something to make a story about—a thing that would connect up with this strange way of doing it—

(*The women's eyes meet for an instant. Enter* HALE *from outer door.*)

HALE: Well, I've got the team around. Pretty cold out there.   140

COUNTY ATTORNEY: I'm going to stay here a while by myself. (*To the* SHERIFF.) You can send Frank out for me, can't you? I want to go over everything. I'm not satisfied that we can't do better.

SHERIFF: Do you want to see what Mrs. Peters is going to take in?

(*The* LAWYER *goes to the table, picks up the apron, laughs.*)

COUNTY ATTORNEY: Oh, I guess they're not very dangerous things the ladies have picked out. (*Moves a few things about, disturbing the quilt pieces which cover the box. Steps back.*) No, Mrs. Peters doesn't need supervising. For that matter, a sheriff's wife is married to the law. Ever think of it that way, Mrs. Peters?

MRS. PETERS: Not—just that way.

SHERIFF (*Chuckling.*): Married to the law. (*Moves toward the other room.*)   145
I just want you to come in here a minute, George. We ought to take a look at these windows.

COUNTY ATTORNEY (*Scoffingly.*): Oh, windows!

SHERIFF: We'll be right out, Mr. Hale.

(HALE *goes outside. The* SHERIFF *follows the* COUNTY ATTORNEY *into the other room. Then* MRS. HALE *rises, hands tight together, looking intensely at* MRS. PETERS, *whose eyes make a slow turn, finally meeting* MRS. HALE's. *A moment* MRS. HALE *holds her, then her own eyes point the way to where the box is concealed. Suddenly* MRS. PETERS *throws back quilt pieces and tries to put the box in the handbag she is carrying. It is too big. She opens box, starts to take bird out, cannot touch it, goes to pieces, stands there helpless. Sound of a knob turning in the other room. Mrs. Hale snatches the box and puts it in the pocket of her big coat. Enter* COUNTY ATTORNEY *and* SHERIFF.)

COUNTY ATTORNEY (*Facetiously.*): Well, Henry, at least we found out that she was not going to quilt it. She was going to—what is it you call it, ladies?

MRS. HALE (*Her hand against her pocket.*): We call it—knot it, Mr. Henderson.

(CURTAIN)

■ How do the women and men see details differently in this play? Give specific details and explain why this difference is significant to our understanding of the play.

■ How does the bird function as an image in this play? How is it presented in the script and how does it relate to any themes in the story?

Experiencing Literature through Writing

1. Select a single image from one of the works in this chapter (or any other). Explain how the author conveys this image and how it is significant within the work.
   a. What details work together to create this image? Talk about the use of any senses that contribute to the effect.
   b. What makes this image stand out among any others that might be in the same text?
   c. What is the significance of this particular image? Is this significance easy to see? Sometimes the more obscure significances are worth our attention.
2. Often we are most aware of our senses when we leave familiar surroundings. The reading selections talk about being "home and away." Discuss the ways in which a particular work uses a single image to signal the disjunction that comes from entering into an unfamiliar environment.
3. When we consider images, those images are often an aspect of our surroundings. Find a specific image in a text that you can discuss as separate from its setting. Explain why it is interesting to consider the image independently of its context.

8 Coherence

How Does the Work Hold Together?

In "real life," things are not neatly ordered. Anyone who has ever tried to organize a desk or a computer's desktop knows that maintaining order requires constant vigilance. Personal messages, advertisements, and interesting articles come to us in a random fashion. As receivers of these messages we must develop some strategy to keep the avalanche of information from becoming incoherent noise that prevents us from doing the work that information is supposed to be facilitating. On desktops, we create folders to help group similar items together. Some people design very simple and transparent organizational plans. Others set up elaborate structures of networked folders that have an internal logic that is so complex, no one outside of the organizer would ever recognize it. There must be method, though, in even the maddest systems.

In Nick Hornby's novel *High Fidelity* (1995), the main character, Rob Fleming, an avid thirty-something collector of vinyl records, deals with the emotional turmoil in his life by imposing order on something he can control. When his girlfriend leaves him, he turns to his record collection.

Nick Hornby (1957–)

from **High Fidelity** (1995)

Tuesday night I reorganize my record collection; I often do this at periods of emotional stress. There are some people who would find this a pretty dull way to spend an evening, but I'm not one of them. This is my life, and it's nice to be able to wade in, immerse your arms in it, touch it.

When Laura was here I had the records arranged alphabetically; before that I had them filed in chronological order, beginning with Robert Johnson, and ending with, I don't know, Wham!, or somebody African, or whatever else I was listening to when Laura and I met. Tonight, though, I fancy something different, so I try to remember the order I bought them in: that way I hope to write my own autobiography, without having to do anything like pick up a pen. I pull the records off the shelves, put them in piles all over the sitting room floor, look for *Revolver*, and go on from there; and when I've finished, I'm flushed with a sense of self, because this, after all, is who I am. I like being able to see how I got from Deep Purple to Howlin' Wolf in twenty-five moves; I am no longer pained by the memory of listening to "Sexual Healing" all the way through a period of enforced celibacy, or embarrassed by the reminder of forming a rock club at school, so that I and my fellow fifth-formers could get together and talk about Ziggy Stardust and *Tommy*.

But what I really like is the feeling of security I get from my new filing system; I have a couple of thousand records, and you have to be me—or, at the very least, a doctor of Flemingology—to know how to find any of them. If I want to play, say *Blue* by Joni Mitchell, I have to remember that I bought it for someone in the autumn of 1983, and thought better of giving it to her, for reasons I don't really want to go into. Well, you don't know any of that, so you're knackered, really aren't you? You'd have to ask me to dig it out for you, and for some reason I find this enormously comforting. ❖

Fleming's love of—or need for—order shows itself at other important times in his life. Later, as he considers dating someone new, he muses over the proper arrangement of a mixed tape:

I spent hours putting that cassette together. To me, making a tape is like writing a letter—there's a lot of erasing and rethinking and starting again, and I wanted it to be a good one, because . . . to be honest, because I hadn't met anyone as promising as Laura since I'd started the DJ-ing, and meeting promising women was partly what the DJ-ing was supposed to be about. A good compilation tape, like breaking up, is hard to do. You've got to kick off with a corker, to hold that attention (I started with "Got to Get You off My Mind," but then realized that she might not get any further than track one, side one if I delivered what she wanted straightaway, so I buried it in the middle of side two), and then you've got to up it a notch, or cool it a notch, and you can't have white music and black music together, unless the white music sounds like black music, and you can't have two tracks by the same artist side by side, unless you've done the whole thing in pairs, and . . . oh, there are loads of rules. ❖

Fleming's life is obviously less ordered than his record collection or his meticulously arranged song sets. Fleming is not alone in this novel in devising strategies to maintain order amid chaos; his friends also make lists that neatly arrange life. For our purposes, it's important to note that Hornby uses his characters' obsession with order as the structuring device in his novel; the list making and cataloging connect the various parts of the story and become a subject of scrutiny within the story. Hornby weaves together a dense fabric of systems people employ and prompts his reader to think of how—and how well—those systems function. Most chapters in his novel begin with a new list and some discussion of the standards used to generate that list: the best episode of *Cheers*, best A-side singles of all time, "my desert-island, all-time, top five most memorable split-ups, in chronological order." To the readers these lists are sometimes quite funny but also indicative of how hard it can sometimes be to assert control over the events of a life. They function to make the novel thematically coherent. They help us read and make sense of a lengthy narrative.

In this chapter, we'll examine a variety of strategies that writers and filmmakers employ to achieve a forceful, coherent work. We'll also call attention to ways that you, as a critical writer, can learn from these strategies.

DESIGN AND SHAPE

Every literary work or film employs some strategy for how the various pieces fit together. Sometimes the strategy is obvious at a glance. For instance, there is a tradition of creating a poem in the physical shape of the poem's subject; in other words, the lines of the poem illustrate their own subject matter. This is often called **concrete poetry**. Perhaps the most famous of these **concrete** or **shape poems** is George Herbert's "Easter Wings," which actually looks like two pairs of wings.

George Herbert (1593–1633)

Easter Wings (1633)

> Lord, Who createdst man in wealth and store,
>   Though foolishly he lost the same,
>   Decaying more and more,
>   Till he became
>   Most poore: 5
>
>   With Thee
>   O let me rise,
>   As larks, harmoniously,
>   And sing this day Thy victories:
> Then shall the fall further the flight in me.   10

> My tender age in sorrow did beginne;
> And still with sicknesses and shame
> Thou didst so punish sinne,
> That I became
> Most thinne.   15

> With Thee
> Let me combine,
> And feel this day Thy victorie;
> For, if I imp my wing on Thine,
> Affliction shall advance the flight in me.   20

Writing such a poem requires considerable craftsmanship. The poet must conceive of the poem's arrangement on the page as well as its theme and then find the words and the poetic structure necessary to carry out this plan. Herbert has managed to make the meaning of the lines themselves reflect the appearance of the poem. Where the lines reach their narrowest points, he describes a man who has constricted to become "most poore" and "most thinne." As the lines that follow expand, Herbert's idea of resurrection takes flight. Our awareness of the poem's shape helps us see the poem's ideas. It is no accident that the poem looks like wings, and, as soon as we see these wings, we can look for corresponding winglike ideas in the poem.

Thomas Hardy's "The Convergence of the Twain" displays a similar correspondence between shape and theme. His poem, written in response to the loss of the *Titanic,* suggests the shape of a ship and the shape of the iceberg in each stanza. Hardy challenges us to meditate on the tragic bringing together of the two. Perhaps the poem's design also forcefully weights each stanza downward; the last line of each rests heavily at the bottom.

Thomas Hardy (1840–1928)

The Convergence of the Twain (1912)
Lines on the Loss of the Titanic

1
In a solitude of the sea
Deep from human vanity,
And the Pride of Life that planned her, stilly couches she.

2
Steel chambers, late the pyres
Of her salamandrine fires,   5
Cold currents third, and turn to rhythmic tidal lyres.

3

Over the mirrors meant
To glass the opulent
The sea-worm crawls—grotesque, slimed, dumb, indifferent.

4

Jewels in joy designed   10
To ravish the sensuous mind
Lie lightless, all their sparkles bleared and black and blind.

5

Dim moon-eyed fishes near
Gaze at the gilded gear
And query: "What does this vaingloriousness down here?"   15

6

Well: while was fashioning
This creature of cleaving wing,
The Immanent Will that stirs and urges everything

7

Prepared a sinister mate
For her—so gaily great—   20
A Shape of Ice, for the time far and dissociate.

8

And as the smart ship grew
In stature, grace, and hue,
In shadowy silent distance grew the Iceberg too.

9

Alien they seemed to be: 25
No mortal eye could see
The intimate welding of their later history,

10

Or sign that they were bent
By paths coincident
On being anon twin halves of one august event,   30

11

Till the Spinner of the Years
Said "Now!" And each one hears,
And consummation comes, and jars two hemispheres.

Such play with form and content provides an excellent exercise for a poet. For a reader, the design provides a concrete representation of an abstract idea. The shape provides a clear idea about what focus the poet feels is important. If we have trouble reading poems like "Easter Wings" or "The Convergence of the Twain" we can consult the shape to test interpretations we develop as we read.

TRADITIONAL STRUCTURES

Just as our awareness of the shape of the previous poems helps us read those poems for complementary details and themes, an awareness of traditional literary structures will help us understand how works hold together. Extended narratives may build upon large units that help readers pause over and process complex actions. For example, a chapter in a novel (often both numbered and titled) offers readers a chance to break from the story and reflect back on what has unfolded, as well as project ahead to what may occur next. Short story writers may insert subtler graphic signals. A visual cue like extra white space between lines might mark a change of place, time, or point of view. William Faulkner divides his short story "A Rose for Emily" into five numbered parts. The division by five in this case underscores the development of the story from initial exposition (establishment of setting and character) through stages in Emily's life that lead to the ultimate revelation and resolution. Faulkner's five-part short story might remind us of the division of a full-length play into five acts. The acts in a play can serve multiple functions. They often help an audience appreciate the building and release of tension, but the acts also function to allow physical changes on the set.

Very short works, particularly short poems, often build upon highly specific and elaborate traditions. The **sonnet** is a fourteen-line poetic structure that has been a proving ground for poets for centuries. Fourteen lines are enough to convey and explore a single coherent in some detail, but much discipline is required. Each line must have the same number of syllables (ten), and the final word in each line must follow a specific rhyme scheme that underscores a clearly marked **stanzaic structure**; that is, the rhyme scheme groups lines in regular, definable verse paragraphs. As arbitrary as these defining characteristics might sound, the structure lends itself to a particular kind of tightly logical development and allows for some variation ("defining characteristics" are not "rules"). The sonnet form has proven to be, in the hands of expert poets, dynamic and forceful.

Still, we should approach sonnets with the main organizational types in mind. A consciousness of basic structuring principles will help us read and understand. The **Italian** or **Petrarchan sonnet** is divided into two parts: the **octave** (eight lines) and the **sestet** (six lines). The pattern of rhyme that distinguishes the octave defines two **quatrains** (stanzas of four lines each). The sestet may be marked by various rhyme schemes. The **English** or **Shakespearean sonnet** organizes itself quite differently. Instead of an octave/sestet (eight/six) division, the English sonnet breaks into three quatrains (each with a rhyme scheme of its own) and a **couplet** (a rhymed pair of lines); we have then a twelve (four, four, four)/two division (see p. 750).

The structural differences between these two principal sonnet forms should not obscure the rhetorical or argumentative logic they share—a logic that coheres each form. An Italian sonnet raises a problem, asks a question, or establishes a subject in the octave. An English sonnet does the same in the first twelve lines. The sonnet's opening section is often called the **complication**. In an Italian sonnet, the sestet responds to the problem, answers the question, or draws meaning from the subject established in the octave. The couplet in an English sonnet serves this same purpose. This second part of the sonnet's argumentative or rhetorical structure can be called the **resolution** (at least if the particular poem allows for such a confident word). The brief transition space that gives us pause just between the complication and resolution is called the **turn**. Understanding an Italian sonnet or an English sonnet involves understanding the movement from the problem to the response. The following models represent the common stanzaic structures and signal the underlying argumentative logic of the sonnet (the letters along the left margin represent how the end rhymes are patterned).

Poets have melded aspects of the two main forms and experimented boldly with many different patterns of rhyme. The Italian sonnet and the English sonnet should not be understood as unbending or exclusive forms, but as grids from which poets have worked. It's also useful to appreciate the different effects these principal forms lend themselves to. Because the Italian sonnet allows space for a rather full response to the complication, it tends to achieve a meditative feel. The English sonnet, on the other hand, will often achieve in the compression of the couplet the effect of surprise or even shock as it turns suddenly on the complication. The couplet will also more easily allow a witty, playfully punning resolution.

Experiencing Literature through Form

Although the sonnet has a well-defined form, close reading of some great sonnets quickly reveals that variety can be realized within the fourteen lines. Knowing the basic forms can be very helpful partly because variations upon a fixed form often signal something meaningful. Sometimes an author can underscore or redefine a message simply by breaking an established pattern (see Chapter 9). If a poem, for instance, has a steady rhyming pattern, we notice when the author breaks that pattern. Structural variations as well as structural consistency are part of a writer's resources. As you read the three sonnets that follow, identify patterns of rhyme and trace the argumentative logic those patterns imply. Also consider how in each case the sonnet form becomes part of the poem's meaning. In "Nuns Fret Not," William Wordsworth examines the constrictions of tradition and finds constriction liberating. In "I, Being Born

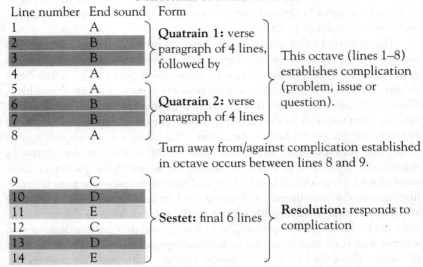

Petrarchan or Italian Sonnet

Line number	End sound	Form	
1	A	**Quatrain 1:** verse paragraph of 4 lines, followed by	This octave (lines 1–8) establishes complication (problem, issue or question).
2	B		
3	B		
4	A		
5	A	**Quatrain 2:** verse paragraph of 4 lines	
6	B		
7	B		
8	A		

Turn away from/against complication established in octave occurs between lines 8 and 9.

9	C	**Sestet:** final 6 lines	**Resolution:** responds to complication
10	D		
11	E		
12	C		
13	D		
14	E		

Shakespearean Sonnet

Line number	End sound	Form	
1	A	**Quatrain 1:** verse paragraph of 4 lines, followed by	Three quatrains establish the complication (problem, issue, or question).
2	B		
3	A		
4	B		
5	C	**Quatrain 2:** verse paragraph of 4 lines, followed by	Each quatrain typically represents a variation upon or elaboration of the complication.
6	D		
7	C		
8	D		
9	E	**Quatrain 3:** verse paragraph of 4 lines	These quatrains generally employ iambic pentameter and are sometimes called **heroic quatrains.**
10	F		
11	E		
12	F		

Turn away from/against complication established in quatrains occurs between lines 12 and 13.

13	G	**Couplet:** 2 lines rhymed	**Resolution:** responds to complication
14	G		

a Woman and Distressed," Edna St. Vincent Millay uses the sonnet to critique gender assumptions that sonnets by males have long perpetuated. Note in particular how in the octave the words grouped as A rhymes differ significantly from those of the B rhymes. That difference clarifies the problem or conflict Millay wants to establish. Finally, Robert Frost in "Design" uses the scale and tightness of his sonnet's construction to raise profound questions of scale and design in the universe.

William Wordsworth (1770–1850)

Nuns Fret Not (1807)

Nuns fret not at their convent's narrow room;
And hermits are contented with their cells;
And students with their pensive citadels;
Maids at the wheel, the weaver at his loom,
Sit blithe and happy; bees that soar for bloom,   5
High as the highest Peak of Furness-fells,
Will murmur by the hour in foxglove bells:
In truth the prison, unto which we doom
Ourselves, no prison is: and hence for me,
In sundry moods, 'twas pastime to be bound   10
Within the Sonnet's scanty plot of ground;
Pleased if some Souls (for such there needs must be)
Who have felt the weight of too much liberty,
Should find brief solace there, as I have found.

Edna St. Vincent Millay (1892–1950)

I, Being Born a Woman and Distressed (1932)

I, being born a woman and distressed
By all the needs and notions of my kind,
Am urged by your propinquity to find
Your person fair, and feel a certain zest
To feel your body's weight upon my breast: 5
So subtly is the fume of life designed,
To clarify the pulse and cloud the mind,
And leave me once again undone, possessed.
Think not for this, however, the poor treason
Of my stout blood against my staggering brain,   10

I shall remember you with love, or season
My scorn with pity,—let me make it plain:
I find this frenzy insufficient reason
For conversation when we meet again.

Robert Frost (1874–1963)

Design (1936)

I found a dimpled spider, fat and white,
On a white heal-all, holding up a moth
Like a white piece of rigid satin cloth—
Assorted characters of death and blight
Mixed ready to begin the morning right,   5
Like the ingredients of a witches' broth—
A snow-drop spider, a flower like a froth,
And dead wings carried like a paper kite.

What had that flower to do with being white,
The wayside blue and innocent heal-all?   10
What brought the kindred spider to that height,
Then steered the white moth thither in the night?
What but design of darkness to appall?—
If design govern in a thing so small.

Wordsworth explores the paradox of all structure. He asks, Does a confining structure have to be a prison? Is there some relief in "escaping" from the stress of living (and writing) in a world where one has "too much liberty"? Wordsworth suggests that there is. The sonnet form offers some comfort to the reader as well. We expect to hear rhymes at the end of each line, and they are there.

This regularity helps us read. Because we are not "surprised" by the form, we can direct our attention to the content of a sonnet. We know something of the convention that this particular poem is joining, so we can pay closer attention to the use of words and to the poet's skill at placing these words within a predetermined form. We can also compare this particular example of the form to other sonnets that we might have read.

> **Making Connections**
>
> Robert Pinsky's "Lines in Any Order" (Chapter 2) is a perplexing poem that adopts the form of the sonnet. Explain how thinking of this poem in terms of the sonnet's essential structure helps you make sense of the seeming randomness of the lines. Could you argue that there is a turn before the final two lines? That the final two lines reflect back on the chaos of the first ten lines?

The sonnet is the poetic form with perhaps the richest history, but it is hardly the only form. In French verse, the **sestina**, for example, consists of six sestets (six-line stanzas) and three final lines. In this form, the final words in each line of the first sestet are repeated as the final words of each line in each of the next five sestets, but the order changes in each sestet according to a specific pattern. As you can see just from this one obscure example, lists of rules regarding poetic forms as well as the names of the forms can quickly feel intimidating; sometimes the best approach is to simply attend closely to what a specific poem actually does. Look at each line of the poem. Look for rhyming patterns among the lines. Sometimes a poem will be written in **blank verse**, a verse form without rhyme but with consistent rhythms, generally iambic pentameter, in each of its lines.

We'll close this section with one more example of a poetic form, the **villanelle**. It's unlikely you will ever read enough villanelles to make memorizing rules of much value, so we'll concentrate on highlighting the form's defining characteristics and we'll use the most famous example, "Do Not Go Gentle into That Good Night" by Dylan Thomas. As you look for the pattern here, pay attention to rhyming words, to repetitions, and to the number and groupings of lines.

Dylan Thomas (1914–1953)

Do Not Go Gentle into That Good Night (1952)

Do not go gentle into that good night,
Old age should burn and rave at close of day;
Rage, rage against the dying of the light.

Though wise men at their end know dark is right,
Because their words had forked no lightning they   5
Do not go gentle into that good night,

Good men, the last wave by, crying how bright
Their frail deeds might have danced in a green bay,
Rage, rage against the dying of the light.

Wild men who caught and sang the sun in flight,   10
And learn, too late, they grieved it on its way,
Do not go gentle into that good night,

Grave men, near death, who see with blinding sight
Blind eyes could blaze like meteors and be gay,
Rage, rage against the dying of the light.   15

And you, my father, there on the sad height,
Curse, bless, me now with your fierce tears, I pray.
Do not go gentle into that good night,
Rage, rage against the dying of the light.

If you are interested in writing poetry, this form provides an excellent challenge. The rigorous form requires thirteen words with the first rhyming sound (A) and six words with the second rhyming sound (B). The poet must work quite dexterously with words to convey any idea within such a constricted form. A less than expert poet will expend all creative energy on merely fitting words into the scheme; a less than expert reader will simply identify the scheme. A really accomplished poet will discover in the structure a form that accommodates a particular expression; a really accomplished reader will appreciate that melding of form and content. Thomas has chosen to use a strategy of repetition to fit the structure, but this strategy does more than that. He alternates the line "Rage, rage against the dying of the light" with the line "Do not go gentle into that good night" at the end of each stanza. Each time we see the same line again, it has acquired new meaning so that the repetition amplifies the original meaning by adding to it. For instance, the third repetition of the "rage, rage" line takes on an added power because the other two lines speak of blindness. This loss of *sight* (the word that will rhyme with *light*) is an added incentive to "rage."

A Note to Student Writers: Complicating a Thesis

The argumentative logic that we've seen operating at the core of a sonnet is a highly compacted form of a common rhetorical ploy that critical writers often use. At the start of an essay, critical writers may establish an issue, a problem, a question. Then they turn to some striking assertion—a thesis—that responds to the issue/problem/question. The complication/turn/resolution that underlies sonnets is similar to the movement that characterizes introductory paragraphs in many critical essays. Consider the following example. Note how the writer quickly establishes a problem (special effects in movies are getting tiresome) and turns against the complication (however) to respond to the issue raised (special effects in this case are made meaningful).

In many action films, special effects overwhelms everything else. Lost amidst the crashes and explosions is any sense of character, coherence, or even purpose. Do we need movies to show us ever more buildings collapsing, cars colliding, planes falling? Why do we need to see such extravagant destruction and dramatic escapes? Do we care anymore? It seems that as special effects get more special, movies get more ordinary. Alfonso Cuaron's *Gravity* reminds us, however, that the dismal state of big budget action films can't be blamed altogether on an excess of technical wizardry. Cuaron manages to make the special effects in his film integral to feelings of helplessness and loneliness.

Cuaron creates illusions of scale and weightlessness that make Dr. Ryan Stone's (Sandra Bullock) struggles mean far more than struggles usually mean in "cliff-hanger" adventure films. Dr. Stone doesn't just fight for her life. She fights to salvage some sense that her life has meaning (or weight) amidst an enormous space in which people become very, very small.

COHERENCE WITHOUT TRADITIONAL OR FIXED STRUCTURE

Achieving coherence is not merely a matter of poetic shape or form. There is little that is traditional in the form of the following poem by Joe Kane, yet there is clearly some sense of structure—some way the whole poem holds together and achieves force.

Joe Kane (1952–   )

The Boy Who Nearly Won the Texaco Art Competition (2005)

he took a large sheet
of white paper and on this
he made the world an african world
of flat topped trees and dried grasses
and he painted an elephant in the middle   5
and a lion with a big mane and several giraffes
stood over the elephant and some small animals to fill
in the gaps he worked all day had a bath this was saturday

on sunday he put six jackals
in the world and a great big snake   10
and buzzards in the sky and tickbirds
on the elephants back he drew down blue
from the sky to make a river and got the elephants
legs all wet and smudged and one of the jackals got drowned
he put red flowers in the front of the picture and daffodils in the bottom   15
   corners
and his dog major chewing a bone and mrs murphys two cats tom and jerry
and milo the milkman with a cigarette in the corner of his mouth
and his merville dairy float pulled by his wonder horse trigger
that would walk when he said click click and the holy family

in the top right corner with the donkey and cow   20
and sheep and baby jesus and got the 40A bus
on monday morning in to abbey street to hand
it in and the man on the door said
thats a sure winner

This poem is held together by the momentum of the narrative. From the moment the boy "took a large sheet of white paper" to the time he hands it in, we follow his creative process as he adds figure after figure to the world that he is creating. Notice how each line grows longer than the line before it as his project develops. There is no punctuation, and this could make the poem confusing. But there is, nevertheless, a logic to the sentence structure. Lines 1–8 make up a continuous sentence linked by "and" after "and" as the boy populates the world on the paper. The account of creativity here, with this series of linked clauses, echoes the day-by-day story of creation as it is narrated in the first chapter of Genesis. This allusion is strengthened when the first sentence ends on line 8 with the bath that interrupts his art and reminds us that he is a young boy and "this was Saturday." On the second day of his work, the pieces of the picture begin to interact: "he drew down blue / from the sky to make a river" and smudge the elephants' legs. Then, at line 16, as the lines begin to shorten, the world of his life and the world of his picture begin to converge until unnamed "man on the door" pronounces "thats a sure winner." This progress, largely chronological, is a common structuring device. Kane narrates the seemingly random creative process that this boy goes through, and, as we think about the poem this way, we begin to realize how much structure Kane has added to render this otherwise anarchic process as a poem, simple in its profundity. Kane's poem reminds us that a simple truth about **free verse** is that "free" doesn't mean artless. The term merely indicates the poem employs no regular meter or rhyme scheme.

What Kane does in "The Boy Who Nearly Won the Texaco Art Competition" suggests one of the principle ways in which not only poems, but also stories, novels, plays, and films achieve coherence: Carefully managed **repetition** of a key element, image, or phrase can be extraordinarily valuable. In the case of this poem, the boy repeats the action of adding animals (and other features) to the paper world and the increasing specificity of his presentation. The word **motif** is used sometimes to refer to a recurring element in literature or film. In this sense of the word, a play or novel that opens with a fresh-faced young country boy's decision to move to the city employs a motif; the audience may expect a story of innocence lost because so many stories have opened with just this scene. The word *motif*, however, is used not only for something that recurs *across* numerous texts, but also applies to an image, word, or action that is repeated *within* a single text. A motif provides structure; it may signal a theme or sustain a mood. This chapter opened with a discussion of how Nick Hornby employs notions of cataloging as a cohering motif in his novel *High Fidelity*. In any lengthy work, there is a danger that the various parts will become disconnected. Novelists must certainly deal with that danger.[1]

Even the longest and most complex works may be grounded in a key image or phrase. For example, whiteness (as a blank, as a mystery, as both a kind of innocence and a kind of terrifying emptiness) dominates Herman Melville's *Moby Dick*. In *Macbeth*, Shakespeare employs the motif of ill-fitting clothes; Macbeth murders the king to become king, but he finds that his new robes are too big for him. The repeated play upon ill-fitting clothes helps us pull together the whole of the action thematically: a person cannot become something greater than he or she is. In Francis Ford Coppola's *Godfather* films, the offhand invocation of business ("just business"; "we're all businessmen here"; "smart business") in the context of the most brutal actions keeps readers alert to the suffering linked to our culture's competitive ethic of material success.

> **Making Connections**
>
> We can think back to Christopher Nolan's *Memento* in context of this discussion of coherence. We discussed that film in the first chapter to clarify how artists may ask us to reflect upon the meaning of plot as plot. But without a deliberate "playback" to a scene that just unfolded, without heavy repetition, an audience could easily become as confused as the main character. The main character's life is fragmented by his inability to remember from moment to moment, but our grasp of the film's meaning is strong. Nolan has figured out a way to help us understand a film that is largely about misunderstanding.

MODELING CRITICAL ANALYSIS: T. S. ELIOT, THE LOVE SONG OF J. ALFRED PRUFROCK

Especially difficult works of art may seem on the surface to be formless—to defy a reader's search for coherence. It's often true, however, that these difficult works employ a variety of devices to help the audience through. Consider again T. S. Eliot's "The Love Song of J. Alfred Prufrock" that we first introduced in our discussion of images (p. 685 in Chapter 7). Many readers find this poem, upon first reading, to be very confusing. Basic questions such as "Where are we?," "What is happening?," and "Who is involved?" become hard to answer. But if we stay alert, we'll find Eliot gives us considerable help.

---

1. **And so,** too, must critical writers attend to the dangers of disconnection. By referring back to Hornby here we're trying to underscore our concern for coherence, but we're also trying to build the chapter as a coherent whole. In this case, we're circling back in order to tie together.

We are guided through "The Love Song of J. Alfred Prufrock" by a single speaker, one who invites us on a walk through dinghy streets and allows us in on thoughts concerning aging, death, failure, cowardice, and so on. We are first centered on a collection of images that make us feel the city's inhospitable environment. It is soon clear that Prufrock is very much a part of the whole environment—of the evening spread against the sky "like a patient etherized upon a table," of the lonely city of narrow "half-deserted streets." In fact, Eliot echoes the clinical simile of the city midway through the poem when Prufrock thinks of himself as a mere specimen of others' study: "And when I am formulated, sprawling on a pin, / When I am pinned and wriggling on the wall." It's clear that the speaker is alien to the world he so timidly encounters. He is even disassociated from his own life.

Repetition functions powerfully to help us grasp the whole of a poem that seems to scorn transitions. We get a series of questions that aren't answered but that collectively make us feel the speaker's inability to take charge or to take risks ("Do I dare?"; "So how should I presume?"; "Then how should I begin"; Shall I part my hair behind?"). We also become aware of Prufrock's painfully self-conscious manner; a line like "They will say: 'How his hair is growing thin!'" prepares us for the fear he explicitly registers in line 85 as well as the fear he has that the grandest assertions may meet flat dismissal: "That is not what I meant at all." And consider the following stanza:

> In the room the women come and go
> Talking of Michelangelo.

This stanza appears twice. While these lines seem to come from nowhere, the repetition cues us in on their place in the whole. Prufrock is a man who hasn't found substance in life. He doesn't find relief from a cold and dreary city in social chat. His disconnection comes through profoundly in relation to women—women whose emptiness makes him intensely aware of his own hollow self. The airy nothingness of the repeated stanza plays out in other clearly painful sexual encounters. The women are mere "eyes" that "fix" him coolly in place or disembodied "arms" that do not caress. It can be of no surprise to us that he thinks it would have been better to be altogether removed from such an empty social life and from the burden of his own humanity: "I should have been a pair of ragged claws/Scuttling across the floors of silent seas."

Using Coherence to Focus Writing and Discussion

- What structuring devices appear in this work?
- How does the physical layout on the page signal this structure? Look first for line-level divisions. In poetry, see how long each line is. Is there some consistent pattern?

- Next, look for sectional divisions. What defines each of the sections? Are all sections of equal length?
- Can you label this structuring device with any of the terms that we have discussed?
- How does this structure help shape the impact of the work?

Anthology

PUZZLE STORY: A CRITIC WRITES ABOUT COHERENCE

Charlie Flora sees the "overtly non-linier episodic" structure of *Pulp Fiction* (1994) as the key to understanding Tarantino's achievements. To Flora, there is nothing arbitrary about the sequence of events that unfold in the film. In fact, she treats the assorted episodes as puzzle parts that, when moved around, clarify the rightness of the final arrangement Tarantino settles on. *Pulp Fiction* is, to her mind, not a **portmanteau film** (an anthology film composed of a series of short films tied together by a single idea or an interlocking character, event, or setting); *Pulp Fiction* has its own coherence. Flora finds this coherence in the spirit of the pop materials Tarantino invokes. That spirit, to her mind, allows figures of fiction—Vincent Vega in particular—to transcend time. Vincent's swaggering exit from the diner suggests he will live, even if he was killed in the middle of the movie.

This chapter asks you to look at the specific structures and stylistic strategies that shape the literary works we read. These structures and strategies are not arbitrary. Writers work to make every choice meaningful. Charles Chestnutt, Edith Wharton, and Kate Chopin put their protagonists in situations that demand choice. The characters ultimately act in ways that force them out of the rituals and routines they have been accustomed to operating within; we might say that they act "out of character." The patient establishing of character and social context is crucial to appreciating the weight of these final choices. As you read these stories, notice how carefully Chestnut, Wharton, and Chopin set up the crisis. We learn much about the main characters and about the world those characters inhabit. Each gains dignity from his or her willingness to take in the situation and to act from a personal sense of right. These stories have a clearly dramatic quality. We can describe them in structural terms much as we would describe a full-length play or film. At the most basic level, they build tension and then release tension.

REVIEW

Charlie Flora (1987–   )

What's Go'in On? Narrative Turns in *Pulp Fiction* (1994)

Unlike most critics, I didn't much like Quentin Tarantino's *Reservoir Dogs* (1992). Tarantino seemed to me a very smart guy who might never be a significant film-maker. Like *Reservoir Dogs*, Tarantino's second film *Pulp Fiction* is violent and profane; it's filled with fast and dense talk among characters (or should that be "characters") that exist in a universe of movies, television shows, pop songs, commercials, and cartoons. Like *Reservoir Dogs*, *Pulp Fiction* strikes me as not only stylized, but as *about* style. Finally, and most importantly, the plots of both films unfold in an overtly non-linier episodic fashion.

Against all my expectations, *Pulp Fiction* blew me away. I'm left asking: What might I have missed in the earlier film? What is it in the new film that works so wonderfully? I'll have to answer the first question some other time, after I've had a chance to see *Reservoir Dogs* again. For now, I'll say *Pulp Fiction* is the most exhilarating film I've seen in years. So I'm writing—on a deadline—in response to the second question.

Some might suggest the hint I need is underscored by the opening title card that foregrounds definitions of pulp. We're told, in a straightforward way, that everything to follow needs to be seen in terms of pop culture productions. The reference points are indeed many, varied, and specific. Tarantino embraces campy as well as classic movies, images from fashion's trendsetters, TV sitcoms, advertising jingles, top 50 radio songs, hard-boiled detective novels, and about everything else that's part of the mediated experience of post baby boom America. Reality, the argument goes, can be seen as another word for experience, and the experience of many white middle class young adults has been built in front of screens or around tables at fast food restaurants. But Tarantino's love for and command of his material has never been in question. And before seeing *Pulp Fiction*, I had thought of that love and command as impediments to his artistic, intellectual, and emotional growth.

So perhaps we should highlight "fiction" as much as "pulp." By doing that, we're brought to matters of structure. We have in this film a narrative puzzle to piece together. Tarantino has presented a simple (albeit eventful) genre story with all the familiar elements of betrayal, revenge, redemption, but he has done that in a very complicated and unfamiliar way. Why does he disregard conventional sequence? I believe there is something about the parts that when mixed in unexpected ways become a bigger whole.

Bear with me as I untangle and re-mix key pieces that make up *Pulp*   5
Fiction. The *story* Tarantino and his fellow screenwriter Roger Avary tell
starts some years before the main action with Captain Koons (Christoper
Walken) presenting a watch to a young boy named Butch. That story of
the gold watch picks up about 20 years later and ultimately encompasses
the story of two hit men, their boss, and his wife. At the very end of all the
action, the grown up Butch (Bruce Willis) rides off on a chopper with his
girlfriend after a more than harrowing day. But that's not how Tarantino's
film unfolds. The *film* starts and ends in a diner with a completely different set of characters. And one of the two characters walking with great style
and confidence out of that diner in the final scene, Vincent Vega (John
Travolta), had been killed unceremoniously rising from the toilet by Butch
in the middle of his story. To put it another way, the end of Butch's *story*
occurs in the middle of Tarantino's *film* while the end of Tarantino's film
comes in chronological time before the end of Butch's story.

We have here something more than a pretentiously artful scrambling
of time and sequence. Tarantino doesn't simply replicate what he loves in
pop fiction and film. Rather, he crystalizes and conveys the feeling of love
itself. The arrangement of the episodes in *Pulp Fiction* beautifully preserves
that feeling. Think of it this way: if Butch's story did end the film, we'd have
a redemption tale with the hero and his lover driving off to a better world
by the power of grace—the word painted on the chopper. We would have
left Vincent dead in the bathroom and hour before the closing credits and
would have nearly forgotten about his partner Jules' (Samuel L. Jackson)
quest for enlightenment. Anyone who watches *Pulp Fiction* though will see
Vincent and Jules as the principal spirits. By looping back to the middle
in making the end, Tarantino allows Vincent to live as an expression of an
absolutely un-killable cool self-possession. And we know too that Jules will
begin his quest anew every time he walks out a door. That's the way we want
it. That's the way we will remember it. The chopper it turns out is not the
only engine of grace that operates in *Pulp Fiction*.

FICTION

Edith Wharton (1862–1937)

Edith Wharton was born Edith Jones in New York City. Her family was relatively
wealthy but, due to declining economic fortunes, moved to Europe when she
was four years old. The following six years gave the future author a wide experience of travel and a grounding in European culture and languages. Though the

Jones family returned to the United States, Wharton never lost her fascination with Europe, and after her marriage to Edward Wharton she maintained an apartment in Paris, where she and her husband spent several months each year. Shortly after her divorce from Edward, she moved permanently to Europe. Wharton was one of the most prominent writers of her generation and produced important works of travel writing and fiction. In 1921, she was awarded the Pulitzer Prize for her best-known novel, *The Age of Innocence*.

Roman Fever (1934)

From the table at which they had been lunching two American ladies of ripe but well-cared-for middle age moved across the lofty terrace of the Roman restaurant and, leaning on its parapet, looked first at each other, and then down on the outspread glories of the Palatine and the Forum, with the same expression of vague but benevolent approval.

As they leaned there a girlish voice echoed up gaily from the stairs leading to the court below. "Well, come along, then," it cried, not to them but to an invisible companion, "and let's leave the young things to their knitting"; and a voice as fresh laughed back: "Oh, look here, Babs, not actually *knitting*—" "Well, I mean figuratively," rejoined the first. "After all, we haven't left our poor parents much else to do...." and at that point the turn of the stairs engulfed the dialogue.

The two ladies looked at each other again, this time with a tinge of smiling embarrassment, and the smaller and paler one shook her head and colored slightly.

"Barbara!" she murmured, sending an unheard rebuke after the mocking voice in the stairway.

The other lady, who was fuller, and higher in color, with a small determined nose supported by vigorous black eyebrows, gave a good-humored laugh. "That's what our daughters think of us!"

Her companion replied by a deprecating gesture. "Not of us individually. We must remember that. It's just the collective modern idea of Mothers. And you see—" Half-guiltily she drew from her handsomely mounted black handbag a twist of crimson silk run through by two fine knitting needles. "One never knows," she murmured. "The new system has certainly given us a good deal of time to kill; and sometimes I get tired just looking—even at this." Her gesture was now addressed to the stupendous scene at their feet.

The dark lady laughed again, and they both relapsed upon the view, contemplating it in silence, with a sort of diffused serenity which might have been borrowed from the spring effulgence of the Roman skies. The luncheon hour was long past, and the two had their end of the vast terrace to themselves. At its opposite extremity a few groups, detained by a lingering look at the outspread city, were gathering up guidebooks and fumbling for tips. The last of them scattered, and the two ladies were alone on the air-washed height.

"Well, I don't see why we shouldn't just stay here," said Mrs. Slade, the lady of the high color and energetic brows. Two derelict basket chairs stood near, and she pushed them into the angle of the parapet, and settled herself in one, her gaze upon the Palatine. "After all, it's still the most beautiful view in the world."

"It always will be, to me," assented her friend Mrs. Ansley, with so slight a stress on the "me" that Mrs. Slade, though she noticed it, wondered if it were not merely accidental, like the random underlinings of old-fashioned letter writers.

"Grace Ansley was always old-fashioned," she thought; and added aloud, with a retrospective smile: "It's a view we've both been familiar with for a good many years. When we first met here we were younger than our girls are now. You remember?"

"Oh, yes, I remember," murmured Mrs. Ansley, with the same undefinable stress. "There's that headwaiter wondering," she interpolated. She was evidently far less sure than her companion of herself and of her rights in the world.

"I'll cure him of wondering," said Mrs. Slade, stretching her hand toward a bag as discreetly opulent-looking as Mrs. Ansley's. Signing to the head-waiter, she explained that she and her friend were old lovers of Rome, and would like to spend the end of the afternoon looking down on the view—that is, if it did not disturb the service? The headwaiter, bowing over her gratuity, assured her that the ladies were most welcome, and would be still more so if they would condescend to remain for dinner. A full-moon night, they would remember. . . .

Mrs. Slade's black brows drew together, as though references to the moon were out of place and even unwelcome. But she smiled away her frown as the headwaiter retreated. "Well, why not? We might do worse. There's no know-ing, I suppose, when the girls will be back. Do you even know back from *where*? I don't!"

Mrs. Ansley again colored slightly. "I think those young Italian aviators we met at the Embassy invited them to fly to Tarquinia for tea. I suppose they'll want to wait and fly back by moonlight."

"Moonlight—moonlight! What a part it still plays. Do you suppose they're as sentimental as we were?"

"I've come to the conclusion that I don't in the least know what they are," said Mrs. Ansley. "And perhaps we didn't know much more about each other."

"No; perhaps we didn't."

Her friend gave her a shy glance. "I never should have supposed you were sentimental, Alida."

10

15

"Well, perhaps I wasn't." Mrs. Slade drew her lids together in retrospect; and for a few moments the two ladies, who had been intimate since childhood, reflected how little they knew each other. Each one, of course, had a label ready to attach to the other's name; Mrs. Delphin Slade, for instance, would have told herself, or anyone who asked her, that Mrs. Horace Ansley, twenty-five years ago, had been exquisitely lovely—no, you wouldn't believe it, would you? . . . though, of course, still charming, distinguished. . . . Well, as a girl she had been exquisite; far more beautiful than her daughter Barbara, though certainly Babs, according to the new standards at any rate, was more effective—had more *edge*, as they say. Funny where she got it, with those two nullities as parents. Yes; Horace Ansley was—well, just the duplicate of his wife. Museum specimens of old New York. Good-looking, irreproachable, exemplary. Mrs. Slade and Mrs. Ansley had lived opposite each other— actually as well as figuratively—for years. When the drawingroom curtains in No. 20 East 73rd Street were renewed, No. 23, across the way, was always aware of it. And of all the movings, buyings, travels, anniversaries, illnesses— the tame chronicle of an estimable pair. Little of it escaped Mrs. Slade. But she had grown bored with it by the time her husband made his big *coup* in Wall Street, and when they bought in upper Park Avenue had already begun to think: "I'd rather live opposite a speakeasy for a change; at least one might see it raided." The idea of seeing Grace raided was so amusing that (before the move) she launched it at a woman's lunch. It made a hit, and went the rounds—she sometimes wondered if it had crossed the street, and reached Mrs. Ansley. She hoped not, but didn't much mind. Those were the days when respectability was at a discount, and it did the irreproachable no harm to laugh at them a little.

A few years later, and not many months apart, both ladies lost their   20
husbands. There was an appropriate exchange of wreaths and condolences, and a brief renewal of intimacy in the half-shadow of their mourning; and now, after another interval, they had run across each other in Rome, at the same hotel, each of them the modest appendage of a salient daughter. The similarity of their lot had again drawn them together, lending itself to mild jokes, and the mutual confession that, if in old days it must have been tiring to "keep up" with daughters, it was now, at times, a little dull not to.

No doubt, Mrs. Slade reflected, she felt her unemployment more than poor Grace ever would. It was a big drop from being the wife of Delphin Slade to being his widow. She had always regarded herself (with a certain conjugal pride) as his equal in social gifts, as contributing her full share to the making of the exceptional couple they were: but the difference after his death was irremediable. As the wife of the famous corporation lawyer, always with an international case or two on hand, every day brought its exciting and unexpected obligation: the impromptu entertaining of eminent colleagues from abroad, the hurried dashes on legal business to London, Paris or Rome, where the entertaining was so handsomely reciprocated; the amusement of hearing in her wake: "What, that handsome woman with the good clothes and the eyes is Mrs. Slade—*the* Slade's wife? Really? Generally the wives of celebrities are such frumps."

Yes; being *the* Slade's widow was a dullish business after that. In living up to such a husband all her faculties had been engaged; now she had only her daughter to live up to, for the son who seemed to have inherited his father's gifts had died suddenly in boyhood. She had fought through that agony because her husband was there, to be helped and to help; now, after the father's death, the thought of the boy had become unbearable. There was nothing left but to mother her daughter; and dear Jenny was such a perfect daughter that she needed no excessive mothering. "Now with Babs Ansley I don't know that I *should* be so quiet," Mrs. Slade sometimes half-enviously reflected; but Jenny, who was younger than her brilliant friend, was that rare accident, an extremely pretty girl who somehow made youth and prettiness seem as safe as their absence. It was all perplexing—and to Mrs. Slade a little boring. She wished that Jenny would fall in love—with the wrong man, even; that she might have to be watched, out-maneuvered, rescued. And instead, it was Jenny who watched her mother, kept her out of drafts, made sure that she had taken her tonic. . . .

Mrs. Ansley was much less articulate than her friend, and her mental portrait of Mrs. Slade was slighter, and drawn with fainter touches. "Alida Slade's awfully brilliant; but not as brilliant as she thinks," would have summed it up; though she would have added, for the enlightenment of strangers, that Mrs. Slade had been an extremely dashing girl; much more so than her daughter, who was pretty, of course, and clever in a way, but had none of her mother's—well, "vividness," someone had once called it. Mrs. Ansley would take up current words like this, and cite them in quotation marks, as unheard-of audacities. No; Jenny was not like her mother. Sometimes Mrs. Ansley thought Alida Slade was disappointed; on the whole she had had a sad life. Full of failures and mistakes; Mrs. Ansley had always been rather sorry for her. . . .

So these two ladies visualized each other, each through the wrong end of her little telescope.

II.

For a long time they continued to sit side by side without speaking. It seemed as though, to both, there was a relief in laying down their somewhat futile activities in the presence of the vast Memento Mori which faced them. Mrs. Slade sat quite still, her eyes fixed on the golden slope of the Palace of the Caesars, and after a while Mrs. Ansley ceased to fidget with her bag, and she too sank into meditation. Like many intimate friends, the two ladies had never before had occasion to be silent together, and Mrs. Ansley was slightly embarrassed by what seemed, after so many years, a new stage in their intimacy, and one with which she did not yet know how to deal.

Suddenly the air was full of that deep clangor of bells which periodically covers Rome with a roof of silver. Mrs. Slade glanced at her wristwatch. "Five o'clock already," she said, as though surprised.

Mrs. Ansley suggested interrogatively: "There's bridge at the Embassy at five." For a long time Mrs. Slade did not answer. She appeared to be lost in contemplation, and Mrs. Ansley thought the remark had escaped her. But after a while she said, as if speaking out of a dream: "Bridge, did you say? Not unless you want to. . . . But I don't think I will, you know."

"Oh, no," Mrs. Ansley hastened to assure her. "I don't care to at all. It's so lovely here; and so full of old memories, as you say." She settled herself in her chair, and almost furtively drew forth her knitting. Mrs. Slade took sideway note of this activity, but her own beautifully cared for hands remained motionless on her knee.

"I was just thinking," she said slowly, "what different things Rome stands for to each generation of travelers. To our grandmothers, Roman fever; to our mothers, sentimental dangers—how we used to be guarded!—to our daughters, no more dangers than the middle of Main Street. They don't know it—but how much they're missing!" The long golden light was beginning to pale, and Mrs. Ansley lifted her knitting a little closer to her eyes. "Yes; how we were guarded!" 5

"I always used to think," Mrs. Slade continued, "that our mothers had a much more difficult job than our grandmothers. When Roman fever stalked the streets it must have been comparatively easy to gather in the girls at the danger hour; but when you and I were young, with such beauty calling us, and the spice of disobedience thrown in, and no worse risk than catching cold during the cool hour after sunset, the mothers used to be put to it to keep us in—didn't they?"

She turned again toward Mrs. Ansley, but the latter had reached a delicate point in her knitting. "One, two, three—slip two; yes, they must have been," she assented, without looking up. Mrs. Slade's eyes rested on her with a deepened attention. "She can knit—in the face of *this*! How like her. . . ."

Mrs. Slade leaned back, brooding, her eyes ranging from the ruins which faced her to the long green hollow of the Forum, the fading glow of the church fronts beyond it, and the outlying immensity of the Colosseum. Suddenly she thought: "It's all very well to say that our girls have done away with sentiment and moonlight. But if Babs Ansley isn't out to catch that young aviator—the one who's a Marchese—then I don't know anything. And Jenny has no chance beside her. I know that too. I wonder if that's why Grace Ansley likes the two girls to go everywhere together? My poor Jenny as a foil—!" Mrs. Slade gave a hardly audible laugh, and at the sound Mrs. Ansley dropped her knitting.

"Yes—?"

"I—oh, nothing. I was only thinking how your Babs carries everything   10 before her. That Campolieri boy is one of the best matches in Rome. Don't look so innocent, my dear—you know he is. And I was wondering, ever so respectfully, you understand . . . wondering how two such exemplary characters as you and Horace had managed to produce anything quite so dynamic." Mrs. Slade laughed again, with a touch of asperity.

Mrs. Ansley's hands lay inert across her needles. She looked straight out at the great accumulated wreckage of passion and splendor at her feet. But her small profile was almost expressionless. At length she said: "I think you overrate Babs, my dear."

Mrs. Slade's tone grew easier. "No; I don't. I appreciate her. And perhaps envy you. Oh, my girl's perfect; if I were a chronic invalid I'd—well, I think I'd rather be in Jenny's hands. There must be times . . . but there! I always wanted a brilliant daughter . . . and never quite understood why I got an angel instead."

Mrs. Ansley echoed her laugh in a faint murmur. "Babs is an angel too."

"Of course—of course! But she's got rainbow wings. Well, they're wandering by the sea with their young men; and here we sit . . . and it all brings back the past a little too acutely."

Mrs. Ansley had resumed her knitting. One might almost have imag-   15 ined (if one had known her less well, Mrs. Slade reflected) that, for her also, too many memories rose from the lengthening shadows of those august ruins. But no; she was simply absorbed in her work. What was there for her to worry about? She knew that Babs would almost certainly come back engaged to the extremely eligible Campolieri. "And she'll sell the New York house, and settle down near them in Rome, and never be in their way . . . she's much too tactful. But she'll have an excellent cook, and just the right people in for bridge and cocktails . . . and a perfectly peaceful old age among her grandchildren."

Mrs. Slade broke off this prophetic flight with a recoil of self-disgust. There was no one of whom she had less right to think unkindly than of Grace Ansley. Would she never cure herself of envying her? Perhaps she had begun too long ago.

She stood up and leaned against the parapet, filling her troubled eyes with the tranquilizing magic of the hour. But instead of tranquilizing her the sight seemed to increase her exasperation. Her gaze turned toward the Colosseum. Already its golden flank was drowned in purple shadow, and above it the sky curved crystal clear, without light or color. It was the moment when afternoon and evening hang balanced in mid-heaven.

Mrs. Slade turned back and laid her hand on her friend's arm. The gesture was so abrupt that Mrs. Ansley looked up, startled.

"The sun's set. You're not afraid, my dear?"

"Afraid—?"   20

"Of Roman fever or pneumonia? I remember how ill you were that winter. As a girl you had a very delicate throat, hadn't you?"

"Oh, we're all right up here. Down below, in the Forum, it does get deathly cold, all of a sudden . . . but not here."

"Ah, of course you know because you had to be so careful." Mrs. Slade turned back to the parapet. She thought: "I must make one more effort not to hate her." Aloud she said: "Whenever I look at the Forum from up here, I remember that story about a great-aunt of yours, wasn't she? A dreadfully wicked great-aunt?"

"Oh, yes; great-aunt Harriet. The one who was supposed to have sent her young sister out to the Forum after sunset to gather a nightblooming flower for her album. All our great-aunts and grandmothers used to have albums of dried flowers."

Mrs. Slade nodded. "But she really sent her because they were in love   25
with the same man—"

"Well, that was the family tradition. They said Aunt Harriet confessed it years afterward. At any rate, the poor little sister caught the fever and died. Mother used to frighten us with the story when we were children."

"And you frightened *me* with it, that winter when you and I were here as girls. The winter I was engaged to Delphin."

Mrs. Ansley gave a faint laugh. "Oh, did I? Really frightened you? I don't believe you're easily frightened."

"Not often; but I was then. I was easily frightened because I was too happy. I wonder if you know what that means?"

"I—yes . . ." Mrs. Ansley faltered.   30

"Well, I suppose that was why the story of your wicked aunt made such an impression on me. And I thought: 'There's no more Roman fever, but the Forum is deathly cold after sunset—especially after a hot day. And the Colosseum's even colder and damper.'"

"The Colosseum—?"

"Yes. It wasn't easy to get in, after the gates were locked for the night. Far from easy. Still, in those days it could be managed; it *was* managed, often. Lovers met there who couldn't meet elsewhere. You knew that?"

"I—I dare say. I don't remember."

"You don't remember? You don't remember going to visit some ruins   35
or other one evening, just after dark, and catching a bad chill? You were supposed to have gone to see the moon rise. People always said that expedition
was what caused your illness."

There was a moment's silence; then Mrs. Ansley rejoined: "Did they? It was all so long ago."

"Yes. And you got well again—so it didn't matter. But I suppose it struck your friends—the reason given for your illness, I mean—because everybody knew you were so prudent on account of your throat, and your mother took such care of you. . . . You *had* been out late sightseeing, hadn't you, that night?"

"Perhaps I had. The most prudent girls aren't always prudent. What made you think of it now?"

Mrs. Slade seemed to have no answer ready. But after a moment she broke out: "Because I simply can't bear it any longer—!"

Mrs. Ansley lifted her head quickly. Her eyes were wide and very pale.   40
"Can't bear what?"

"Why—your not knowing that I've always known why you went."

"Why I went—?"

"Yes. You think I'm bluffing, don't you? Well, you went to meet the man I was engaged to—and I can repeat every word of the letter that took you there."

While Mrs. Slade spoke Mrs. Ansley had risen unsteadily to her feet.   45
Her bag, her knitting and gloves, slid in a panic-stricken heap to the ground. She looked at Mrs. Slade as though she were looking at a ghost.

"No, no—don't," she faltered out.

"Why not? Listen, if you don't believe me. 'My one darling, things can't go on like this. I must see you alone. Come to the Colosseum immediately after dark tomorrow. There will be somebody to let you in. No one whom you need fear will suspect'—but perhaps you've forgotten what the letter said?"

Mrs. Ansley met the challenge with an unexpected composure. Steadying herself against the chair she looked at her friend, and replied: "No; I know it by heart too."

"And the signature? 'Only *your* D.S.' Was that it? I'm right, am I? That was the letter that took you out that evening after dark?"

Mrs. Ansley was still looking at her. It seemed to Mrs. Slade that a slow   50
struggle was going on behind the voluntarily controlled mask of her small quiet face. "I shouldn't have thought she had herself so well in hand," Mrs. Slade reflected, almost resentfully. But at this moment Mrs. Ansley spoke. "I don't know how you knew. I burnt that letter at once."

"Yes; you would, naturally—you're so prudent!" The sneer was open now. "And if you burnt the letter you're wondering how on earth I know what was in it. That's it, isn't it?"

Mrs. Slade waited, but Mrs. Ansley did not speak.

"Well, my dear, I know what was in that letter because I wrote it!"

"You wrote it?"

"Yes."   55

The two women stood for a minute staring at each other in the last golden light. Then Mrs. Ansley dropped back into her chair. "Oh," she murmured, and covered her face with her hands.

Mrs. Slade waited nervously for another word or movement. None came, and at length she broke out: "I horrify you."

Mrs. Ansley's hands dropped to her knee. The face they uncovered was streaked with tears. "I wasn't thinking of you. I was thinking—it was the only letter I ever had from him!"

"And I wrote it. Yes; I wrote it! But I was the girl he was engaged to. Did you happen to remember that?"

Mrs. Ansley's head drooped again. "I'm not trying to excuse myself . . . I 60 remembered. . . . "

"And still you went?"

"Still I went."

Mrs. Slade stood looking down on the small bowed figure at her side. The flame of her wrath had already sunk, and she wondered why she had ever thought there would be any satisfaction in inflicting so purposeless a wound on her friend. But she had to justify herself.

"You do understand? I'd found out—and I hated you, hated you. I knew you were in love with Delphin—and I was afraid; afraid of you, of your quiet ways, your sweetness . . . your . . . well, I wanted you out of the way, that's all. Just for a few weeks; just till I was sure of him. So in a blind fury I wrote that letter . . . I don't know why I'm telling you now."

"I suppose," said Mrs. Ansley slowly, "it's because you've always gone 65 on hating me."

"Perhaps. Or because I wanted to get the whole thing off my mind." She paused. "I'm glad you destroyed the letter. Of course I never thought you'd die."

Mrs. Ansley relapsed into silence, and Mrs. Slade, leaning above her, was conscious of a strange sense of isolation, of being cut off from the warm current of human communion. "You think me a monster!"

"I don't know. . . . It was the only letter I had, and you say he didn't write it?"

"Ah, how you care for him still!"

"I cared for that memory," said Mrs. Ansley. 70

Mrs. Slade continued to look down on her. She seemed physically reduced by the blow—as if, when she got up, the wind might scatter her like a puff of dust. Mrs. Slade's jealousy suddenly leapt up again at the sight. All these years the woman had been living on that letter. How she must have loved him, to treasure the mere memory of its ashes! The letter of the man her friend was engaged to. Wasn't it she who was the monster?

"You tried your best to get him away from me, didn't you? But you failed; and I kept him. That's all."

"Yes. That's all."

"I wish now I hadn't told you. I'd no idea you'd feel about it as you do; I thought you'd be amused. It all happened so long ago, as you say; and you must do me the justice to remember that I had no reason to think you'd ever taken it seriously. How could I, when you were married to Horace Ansley two months afterward? As soon as you could get out of bed your mother rushed you off to Florence and married you. People were rather surprised—they wondered at its being done so quickly; but I thought I knew. I had an idea you did it out of *pique*—to be able to say you'd got ahead of Delphin and me. Girls have such silly reasons for doing the most serious things. And your marrying so soon convinced me that you'd never really cared."

"Yes. I suppose it would," Mrs. Ansley assented.   75

The clear heaven overhead was emptied of all its gold. Dusk spread over it, abruptly darkening the Seven Hills. Here and there lights began to twinkle through the foliage at their feet. Steps were coming and going on the deserted terrace—waiters looking out of the doorway at the head of the stairs, then reappearing with trays and napkins and flasks of wine. Tables were moved, chairs straightened. A feeble string of electric lights flickered out. Some vases of faded flowers were carried away, and brought back replenished. A stout lady in a dust coat suddenly appeared, asking in broken Italian if anyone had seen the elastic band which held together her tattered Baedeker. She poked with her stick under the table at which she had lunched, the waiters assisting.

The corner where Mrs. Slade and Mrs. Ansley sat was still shadowy and deserted. For a long time neither of them spoke. At length Mrs. Slade began again: "I suppose I did it as a sort of joke—"

"A joke?"

"Well, girls are ferocious sometimes, you know. Girls in love especially. And I remember laughing to myself all that evening at the idea that you were waiting around there in the dark, dodging out of sight, listening for every sound, trying to get in—Of course I was upset when I heard you were so ill afterward."

Mrs. Ansley had not moved for a long time. But now she turned slowly   80 toward her companion. "But I didn't wait. He'd arranged everything. He was there. We were let in at once," she said.

Mrs. Slade sprang up from her leaning position. "Delphin there? They let you in?—Ah, now you're lying!" she burst out with violence.

Mrs. Ansley's voice grew clearer, and full of surprise. "But of course he was there. Naturally he came—"

"Came? How did he know he'd find you there? You must be raving!"

Mrs. Ansley hesitated, as though reflecting. "But I answered the letter. I told him I'd be there. So he came."

Mrs. Slade flung her hands up to her face. "Oh, God—you answered! I never thought of your answering. . . ." 85

"It's odd you never thought of it, if you wrote the letter."

"Yes. I was blind with rage."

Mrs. Ansley rose, and drew her fur scarf about her. "It is cold here. We'd better go . . . I'm sorry for you," she said, as she clasped the fur about her throat.

The unexpected words sent a pang through Mrs. Slade. "Yes; we'd better go." She gathered up her bag and cloak. "I don't know why you should be sorry for me," she muttered.

Mrs. Ansley stood looking away from her toward the dusky secret mass 90 of the Colosseum. "Well—because I didn't have to wait that night."

Mrs. Slade gave an unquiet laugh. "Yes; I was beaten there. But I oughtn't to begrudge it to you, I suppose. At the end of all these years. After all, I had everything; I had him for twenty-five years. And you had nothing but that one letter that he didn't write."

Mrs. Ansley was again silent. At length she turned toward the door of the terrace. She took a step, and turned back, facing her companion.

"I had Barbara," she said, and began to move ahead of Mrs. Slade toward the stairway.

- Characterize the relationship between Mrs. Slade and Mrs. Ansley. Who dominates the conversation that the two women have? How do the final words of the story change our understanding of what has come before?

- How does the current atmosphere relate to the historical atmosphere that the two women review? How do children appear within the narrative?

- Look carefully at the descriptions of the setting, including descriptions of the built environment as well as those of the light and weather. How do these descriptions relate to the development of the narrative?

Charles W. Chestnut (1858–1936)

Charles W. Chestnut was born in 1858 in Cleveland, Ohio, but his family moved to North Carolina after the end of the Civil War. Because his parents were both of mixed race, there was nothing typically African American about his own features. His opportunities were limited in the South, however, and after marrying he decided to relocate to the North, eventually settling in Ohio. While working for a

railroad and studying law, Chestnut also found time to begin writing, and in a relatively short time had established himself as a prominent writer of short stories. He
published several novels as well, all of them concentrating in one way or another
on the racial problem in the United States. These novels, including *House Behind
the Cedars* and *The Colonel's Dream,* were not financial successes, due in large
part to the discomfort white readers felt with Chestnut's subject matter. He is now
regarded as one of the pioneers of African American writing.

Wife of His Youth (1898)

I

Mr. Ryder was going to give a ball. There were several reasons why this was
an opportune time for such an event.

Mr. Ryder might aptly be called the dean of the Blue Veins. The
original Blue Veins were a little society of colored persons organized in
a certain Northern city shortly after the war. Its purpose was to establish
and maintain correct social standards among a people whose social condition presented almost unlimited room for improvement. By accident,
combined perhaps with some natural affinity, the society consisted of
individuals who were, generally speaking, more white than black. Some
envious outsider made the suggestion that no one was eligible for membership who was not white enough to show blue veins. The suggestion
was readily adopted by those who were not of the favored few, and since
that time the society, though possessing a longer and more pretentious
name, had been known far and wide as the "Blue Vein Society," and its
members as the "Blue Veins."

The Blue Veins did not allow that any such requirement existed for
admission to their circle, but, on the contrary, declared that character and
culture were the only things considered; and that if most of their members
were light-colored, it was because such persons, as a rule, had had better
opportunities to qualify themselves for membership. Opinions differed, too,
as to the usefulness of the society. There were those who had been known
to assail it violently as a glaring example of the very prejudice from which
the colored race had suffered most; and later, when such critics had succeeded in getting on the inside, they had been heard to maintain with zeal
and earnestness that the society was a life-boat, an anchor, a bulwark and a
shield,—a pillar of cloud by day and of fire by night, to guide their people
through the social wilderness. Another alleged prerequisite for Blue Vein
membership was that of free birth; and while there was really no such
requirement, it is doubtless true that very few of the members would have
been unable to meet it if there had been. If there were one or two of the

older members who had come up from the South and from slavery, their history presented enough romantic circumstances to rob their servile origin of its grosser aspects.

While there were no such tests of eligibility, it is true that the Blue Veins had their notions on these subjects, and that not all of them were equally liberal in regard to the things they collectively disclaimed. Mr. Ryder was one of the most conservative. Though he had not been among the founders of the society, but had come in some years later, his genius for social leadership was such that he had speedily become its recognized adviser and head, the custodian of its standards, and the preserver of its traditions. He shaped its social policy, was active in providing for its entertainment, and when the interest fell off, as it sometimes did, he fanned the embers until they burst again into a cheerful flame.

There were still other reasons for his popularity. While he was not 5 as white as some of the Blue Veins, his appearance was such as to confer distinction upon them. His features were of a refined type, his hair was almost straight; he was always neatly dressed; his manners were irreproachable, and his morals above suspicion. He had come to Groveland a young man, and obtaining employment in the office of a railroad company as messenger had in time worked himself up to the position of stationery clerk, having charge of the distribution of the office supplies for the whole company. Although the lack of early training had hindered the orderly development of a naturally fine mind, it had not prevented him from doing a great deal of reading or from forming decidedly literary tastes. Poetry was his passion. He could repeat whole pages of the great English poets; and if his pronunciation was sometimes faulty, his eye, his voice, his gestures, would respond to the changing sentiment with a precision that revealed a poetic soul, and disarm criticism. He was economical, and had saved money; he owned and occupied a very comfortable house on a respectable street. His residence was handsomely furnished, containing among other things a good library, especially rich in poetry, a piano, and some choice engravings. He generally shared his house with some young couple, who looked after his wants and were company for him; for Mr. Ryder was a single man. In the early days of his connection with the Blue Veins he had been regarded as quite a catch, and ladies and their mothers had maneuvred with much ingenuity to capture him. Not, however, until Mrs. Molly Dixon visited Groveland had any woman ever made him wish to change his condition to that of a married man.

Mrs. Dixon had come to Groveland from Washington in the spring, and before the summer was over she had won Mr. Ryder's heart. She possessed many attractive qualities. She was much younger than he; in fact, he was old enough to have been her father, though no one knew exactly how old he was. She was whiter than he, and better educated. She had moved in the best colored society of the country, at Washington, and had taught in the schools of that city. Such a superior person had been eagerly welcomed to the Blue Vein Society, and had taken a leading part in its activities. Mr. Ryder had at first been attracted by her charms of person, for she was very good looking and not over twenty-five; then by her refined manners and by the vivacity of her wit. Her husband had been a government clerk, and at his death had left a considerable life insurance. She was visiting friends in Groveland, and, finding the town and the people to her liking, had prolonged her stay indefinitely. She had not seemed displeased at Mr. Ryder's attentions, but on the contrary had given him every proper encouragement; indeed, a younger and less cautious man would long since have spoken. But he had made up his mind, and had only to determine the time when he would ask her to be his wife. He decided to give a ball in her honor, and at some time during the evening of the ball to offer her his heart and hand. He had no special fears about the outcome, but, with a little touch of romance, he wanted the surroundings to be in harmony with his own feelings when he should have received the answer he expected.

Mr. Ryder resolved that this ball should mark an epoch in the social history of Groveland. He knew, of course,—no one could know better,—the entertainments that had taken place in past years, and what must be done to surpass them. His ball must be worthy of the lady in whose honor it was to be given, and must, by the quality of its guests, set an example for the future. He had observed of late a growing liberality, almost a laxity, in social matters, even among members of his own set, and had several times been forced to meet in a social way persons whose complexions and callings in life were hardly up to the standard which he considered proper for the society to maintain. He had a theory of his own.

"I have no race prejudice," he would say, "but we people of mixed blood are ground between the upper and the nether millstone. Our fate lies between absorption by the white race and extinction in the black. The one doesn't want us yet, but may take us in time. The other would welcome us, but it would be for us a backward step. 'With malice towards none, with charity for all,' we must do the best we can for ourselves and those who are to follow us. Self-preservation is the first law of nature."

His ball would serve by its exclusiveness to counteract leveling tendencies, and his marriage with Mrs. Dixon would help to further the upward process of absorption he had been wishing and waiting for.

II

The ball was to take place on Friday night. The house had been put in order, the carpets covered with canvas, the halls and stairs decorated with palms and potted plants; and in the afternoon Mr. Ryder sat on his front porch, which the shade of a vine running up over a wire netting made a cool and pleasant lounging-place. He expected to respond to the toast "The Ladies," at the supper, and from a volume of Tennyson—his favorite poet—was fortifying himself with apt quotations. The volume was open at "A Dream of Fair Women." His eyes fell on these lines, and he read them aloud to judge better of their effect:—

> "At length I saw a lady within call.
> Stiller than chisell'd marble, standing there;
> A daughter of the gods, divinely tall, And most divinely fair."

He marked the verse, and turning the page read the stanza beginning,—

> O sweet pale Margaret,
> O rare pale Margaret.

He weighed the passage a moment, and decided that it would not do. Mrs. Dixon was the palest lady he expected at the ball, and she was of a rather ruddy complexion, and of lively disposition and buxom build. So he ran over the leaves until his eye rested on the description of Queen Guinevere:—

> She seem'd a part of joyous Spring:
> A gown of grass-green silk she wore,
> Buckled with golden clasps before;
> A light-green tuft of plumes she bore
> Closed in a golden ring.
> She look'd so lovely, as she sway'd
> The rein with dainty finger-tips,
> A man had given all other bliss,
> And all his worldly worth for this,
> To waste his whole heart in one kiss
> Upon her perfect lips.

As Mr. Ryder murmured these words audibly, with an appreciative thrill, he heard the latch of his gate click, and a light footfall sounding on the steps. He turned his head, and saw a woman standing before the door.

She was a little woman, not five feet tall, and proportioned to her   5
height. Although she stood erect, and looked around her with very bright and restless eyes, she seemed quite old; for her face was crossed and recrossed with a hundred wrinkles, and around the edges of her bonnet could be seen protruding here and there a tuft of short gray wool. She wore a blue calico gown of ancient cut, a little red shawl fastened around her shoulders with an old-fashioned brass brooch, and a large bonnet profusely

ornamented with faded red and yellow artificial flowers. And she was very black—so black that her toothless gums, revealed when she opened her mouth to speak, were not red, but blue. She looked like a bit of the old plantation life, summoned up from the past by the wave of a magician's wand, as the poet's fancy had called into being the gracious shapes of which Mr. Ryder had just been reading.

He rose from his chair and came over to where she stood.

"Good-afternoon, madam," he said.

"Good-evenin', suh," she answered, ducking suddenly with a quaint curtsy. Her voice was shrill and piping, but softened somewhat by age. "Is dis yere whar Mistuh Ryduh lib, suh?" she asked, looking around her doubtfully, and glancing into the open windows, through which some of the preparations for the evening were visible.

"Yes," he replied, with an air of kindly patronage, unconsciously flat-tered by her manner, "I am Mr. Ryder. Did you want to see me?"

"Yas, suh, ef I ain't 'sturbin' of you too much."   10

"Not at all. Have a seat over here behind the vine, where it is cool. What can I do for you?"

"'Scuse me, suh," she continued, when she had sat down on the edge of a chair, "'scuse me, suh, I's lookin' for my husban'. I heerd you wuz a big man an' had libbed heah a long time, an' I 'lowed you wouldn't min' ef I'd come roun' an' ax you ef you'd eber heerd of a merlatter man by de name er Sam Taylor 'quirin' roun' in de chu 'ches ermongs' de people fer his wife 'Liza Jane?"

Mr. Ryder seemed to think for a moment.

"There used to be many such cases right after the war," he said, "but it has been so long that I have forgotten them. There are very few now. But tell me your story, and it may refresh my memory."

She sat back farther in her chair so as to be more comfortable, and   15 folded her withered hands in her lap.

"My name's 'Liza," she began, "'Liza Jane. Wen I wuz young I us'ter b'long ter Marse Bob Smif, down in old Missourn. I wuz bawn down dere. W 'en I wuz a gal I wuz married ter a man named Jim. But Jim died, an' after dat I married a merlatter man named Sam Taylor. Sam wuz free-bawn, but his mammy and daddy died, an' de w'ite folks 'prenticed him ter my marster fer ter work fer 'im 'tel he wuz growed up. Sam worked in de fiel', an' I wuz de cook. One day Ma'y Ann, ole miss's maid, come rushin' out ter de kitchen, an' says she, 'Liza Jane, ole marse gwine sell yo' Sam down de ribber.'

"'Go way f 'm yere,' says I; 'my husban's free!'

"'Don' make no diff 'ence. I heerd ole marse tell ole miss he wuz gwine take yo ' Sam 'way wid 'im ter-morrow, fer he needed money, an' he knowed whar he could git a t 'ousan' dollars fer Sam an' no questions axed.'

"W 'en Sam come home f 'm de fiel' dat night, I tole him 'bout ole marse gwine steal 'im, an' Sam run erway. His time wuz mos' up, an' he swo' dat w'en he wuz twenty-one he would come back an' he'p me run erway, er else save up de money ter buy my freedom. An' I know he'd 'a' done it, fer he thought a heap er me, Sam did. But w'en he come back he didn' fin' me, fer I wuzn' dere. Ole marse had heerd dat I warned Sam, so he had me whip' an' sol' down de ribber.

"Den de wah broke out, an' w'en it wuz ober de cullud folks wuz scat-   20
tered. I went back ter de ole home; but Sam wuzn' dere, an' I couldn' l'arn nuffin' 'bout 'im. But I knowed he'd be'n dere to look fer me an' hadn' foun' me, an' had gone erway ter hunt fer me.

"I's be'n lookin' fer 'im eber sence," she added simply, as though twenty-five years were but a couple of weeks, "an' I knows he's be'n lookin' fer me. Fer he sot a heap er sto' by me, Sam did, an' I know he's be'n huntin' fer me all dese years,—'less'n he's be'n sick er sump'n, so he couldn' work, er out'n his head, so he couldn' 'member his promise. I went back down de ribber, fer I 'lowed he'd gone down dere lookin' fer me. I's be'n ter Noo Orleans, an' Atlanty, an' Charleston, an' Richmon'; an' w'en I'd be'n all ober de Souf I come ter de Norf. Fer I knows I'll fin' 'im some er dese days," she added softly, "er he'll fin' me, an' den we'll bofe be as happy in freedom as we wuz in de ole days befo' de wah." A smile stole over her withered countenance as she paused a moment, and her bright eyes softened into a far-away look.

This was the substance of the old woman's story. She had wandered a little here and there. Mr. Ryder was looking at her curiously when she finished.

"How have you lived all these years?" he asked.

"Cookin', suh. I's a good cook. Does you know anybody w'at needs a good cook, suh? I's stoppin' wid a cullud fam'ly roun' de corner yonder 'tel I kin git a place."

"Do you really expect to find your husband? He may be dead long ago."   25

She shook her head emphatically. "Oh no, he ain' dead. De signs an' de tokens tells me. I dremp three nights runnin' on 'y dis las' week dat I foun' him."

"He may have married another woman. Your slave marriage would not have prevented him, for you never lived with him after the war, and without that your marriage doesn't count."

"Wouldn' make no diff'ence wid Sam. He wouldn' marry no yuther 'ooman 'tel he foun' out 'bout me. I knows it," she added. "Sump'n 's be'n tellin' me all dese years dat I's gwine fin' Sam 'fo I dies."

"Perhaps he's outgrown you, and climbed up in the world where he wouldn't care to have you find him."

"No, indeed, suh," she replied, "Sam ain' dat kin' er man. He wuz good   30
ter me, Sam wuz, but he wuzn' much good ter nobody e 'se, fer he wuz one
er de triflin 'es' han's on de plantation. I 'spec's ter haf ter suppo't 'im w'en
I fin' 'im, fer he nebber would work 'less'n he had ter. But den he wuz free,
an' he didn' git no pay fer his work, an' I don' blame 'im much. Mebbe he's
done better sence he run erway, but I ain' 'spectin' much."

"You may have passed him on the street a hundred times during the
twenty-five years, and not have known him; time works great changes."

She smiled incredulously. "I'd know 'im 'mongs' a hund'ed men. Fer dey
wuzn' no yuther merlatter man like my man Sam, an' I couldn' be mistook.
I's toted his picture roun' wid me twenty-five years."

"May I see it?" asked Mr. Ryder. "It might help me to remember whether
I have seen the original."

As she drew a small parcel from her bosom, he saw that it was fastened
to a string that went around her neck. Removing several wrappers, she
brought to light an old-fashioned daguerreotype in a black case. He looked
long and intently at the portrait. It was faded with time, but the features were
still distinct, and it was easy to see what manner of man it had represented.

He closed the case, and with a slow movement handed it back to her.   35

"I don't know of any man in town who goes by that name," he said,
"nor have I heard of any one making such inquiries. But if you will leave
me your address, I will give the matter some attention, and if I find out
anything I will let you know."

She gave him the number of a house in the neighborhood, and went
away, after thanking him warmly.

He wrote down the address on the flyleaf of the volume of Tennyson,
and, when she had gone, rose to his feet and stood looking after her curiously. As she walked down the street with mincing step, he saw several
persons whom she passed turn and look back at her with a smile of kindly
amusement. When she had turned the corner, he went upstairs to his
bedroom, and stood for a long time before the mirror of his dressing-case,
gazing thoughtfully at the reflection of his own face.

III

At eight o'clock the ballroom was a blaze of light and the guests had begun
to assemble; for there was a literary programme and some routine business of the society to be gone through with before the dancing. A black
servant in evening dress waited at the door and directed the guests to the
dressing-rooms.

The occasion was long memorable among the colored people of the
city; not alone for the dress and display, but for the high average of intelligence and culture that distinguished the gathering as a whole. There were

a number of school-teachers, several young doctors, three or four lawyers, some professional singers, an editor, a lieutenant in the United States army spending his furlough in the city, and others in various polite callings; these were colored, though most of them would not have attracted even a casual glance because of any marked difference from white people. Most of the ladies were in evening costume, and dress coats and dancing-pumps were the rule among the men. A band of string music, stationed in an alcove behind a row of palms, played popular airs while the guests were gathering.

The dancing began at half past nine. At eleven o'clock supper was served. Mr. Ryder had left the ballroom some little time before the inter-mission, but reappeared at the supper-table. The spread was worthy of the occasion, and the guests did full justice to it. When the coffee had been served, the toastmaster, Mr. Solomon Sadler, rapped for order. He made a brief introductory speech, complimenting host and guests, and then presented in their order the toasts of the evening. They were responded to with a very fair display of after-dinner wit.

"The last toast," said the toast-master, when he reached the end of the list, "is one which must appeal to us all. There is no one of us of the sterner sex who is not at some time dependent upon woman,—in infancy for protection, in manhood for companionship, in old age for care and comforting. Our good host has been trying to live alone, but the fair faces I see around me to-night prove that he too is largely dependent upon the gentler sex for most that makes life worth living,—the society and love of friends,—and rumor is at fault if he does not soon yield entire subjection to one of them. Mr. Ryder will now respond to the toast,—The Ladies."

There was a pensive look in Mr. Ryder's eyes as he took the floor   5
and adjusted his eyeglasses. He began by speaking of woman as the gift of Heaven to man, and after some general observations on the relations of the sexes he said: "But perhaps the quality which most distinguishes woman is her fidelity and devotion to those she loves. History is full of examples, but has recorded none more striking than one which only to-day came under my notice."

He then related, simply but effectively, the story told by his visitor of the afternoon. He told it in the same soft dialect, which came readily to his lips, while the company listened attentively and sympathetically. For the story had awakened a responsive thrill in many hearts. There were some present who had seen, and others who had heard their fathers and grandfathers tell, the wrongs and sufferings of this past generation, and all of them still felt, in their darker moments, the shadow hanging over them. Mr. Ryder went on:—

"Such devotion and such confidence are rare even among women. There are many who would have searched a year, some who would have waited five years, a few who might have hoped ten years; but for twenty-five years this woman has retained her affection for and her faith in a man she has not seen or heard of in all that time.

"She came to me to-day in the hope that I might be able to help her find this long-lost husband. And when she was gone I gave my fancy rein, and imagined a case I will put to you.

"Suppose that this husband, soon after his escape, had learned that his wife had been sold away, and that such inquiries as he could make brought no information of her whereabouts. Suppose that he was young, and she much older than he; that he was light, and she was black; that their marriage was a slave marriage, and legally binding only if they chose to make it so after the war. Suppose, too, that he made his way to the North, as some of us have done, and there, where he had larger opportunities, had improved them, and had in the course of all these years grown to be as different from the ignorant boy who ran away from fear of slavery as the day is from the night. Suppose, even, that he had qualified himself, by industry, by thrift, and by study, to win the friendship and be considered worthy the society of such people as these I see around me to-night, gracing my board and filling my heart with gladness; for I am old enough to remember the day when such a gathering would not have been possible in this land. Suppose, too, that, as the years went by, this man's memory of the past grew more and more indistinct, until at last it was rarely, except in his dreams, that any image of this bygone period rose before his mind. And then suppose that accident should bring to his knowledge the fact that the wife of his youth, the wife he had left behind him,—not one who had walked by his side and kept pace with him in his upward struggle, but one upon whom advancing years and a laborious life had set their mark,—was alive and seeking him, but that he was absolutely safe from recognition or discovery, unless he chose to reveal himself. My friends, what would the man do? I will suppose that he was one who loved honor, and tried to deal justly with all men. I will even carry the case further, and suppose that perhaps he had set his heart upon another, whom he had hoped to call his own. What would he do, or rather what ought he to do, in such a crisis of a lifetime?

"It seemed to me that he might hesitate, and I imagined that I was 10 an old friend, a near friend, and that he had come to me for advice; and I argued the case with him. I tried to discuss it impartially. After we had looked upon the matter from every point of view, I said to him, in words that we all know:

'This above all: to thine own self be true,
And it must follow, as the night the day,
Thou canst not then be false to any man.'

"Then, finally, I put the question to him, 'Shall you acknowledge her?'

"And now, ladies and gentlemen, friends and companions, I ask you, what should he have done?"

There was something in Mr. Ryder's voice that stirred the hearts of those who sat around him. It suggested more than mere sympathy with an imaginary situation; it seemed rather in the nature of a personal appeal. It was observed, too, that his look rested more especially upon Mrs. Dixon, with a mingled expression of renunciation and inquiry.

She had listened, with parted lips and streaming eyes. She was the first to speak: "He should have acknowledged her."

"Yes," they all echoed, "he should have acknowledged her." 15

"My friends and companions," responded Mr. Ryder, "I thank you, one and all. It is the answer I expected, for I knew your hearts."

He turned and walked toward the closed door of an adjoining room, while every eye followed him in wondering curiosity. He came back in a moment, leading by the hand his visitor of the afternoon, who stood startled and trembling at the sudden plunge into this scene of brilliant gayety. She was neatly dressed in gray, and wore the white cap of an elderly woman.

"Ladies and gentlemen," he said, "this is the woman, and I am the man, whose story I have told you. Permit me to introduce to you the wife of my youth." ❖

- Locate and define the divisions within this story. How do they reflect the social divisions that the story describes?

- How does the form of the poetry that he reads constrain Mr. Ryder?

- How does the structure of the story impact our reading of the traditions and social structures that he describes?

- The central event of the ball allows Mr. Ryder to use a public moment to work out his private standards. How does the pressure of public opinion shape his actions and our response to those actions?

Kate Chopin (1851–1904)

Kate Chopin was born in St. Louis, Missouri, in 1851. As a young woman, she developed an interest in the arts that remained with her for the rest of her life, as well as a gift for storytelling. She married and had six children, but her husband died young of a fever. It was following this loss, and at the advice of her family physician, that Chopin began writing. She is best remembered today for those tales that were groundbreaking in their depictions of married life and sexuality, but it was precisely these elements that were problematic in her own day.

The discomfort some readers and editors felt with this aspect of her work came to a head with the publication of her second novel, *The Awakening*. While the indignation the book aroused effectively ended Chopin's career, it is now regarded by many as a masterpiece.

The Story of an Hour (1894)

Knowing that Mrs. Mallard was afflicted with a heart trouble, great care was taken to break to her as gently as possible the news of her husband's death.

It was her sister Josephine who told her, in broken sentences, veiled hints that revealed in half concealing. Her husband's friend Richards was there, too, near her. It was he who had been in the newspaper office when intelligence of the railroad disaster was received, with Brently Mallard's name leading the list of "killed." He had only taken the time to assure himself of its truth by a second telegram, and had hastened to forestall any less careful, less tender friend in bearing the sad message.

She did not hear the story as many women have heard the same, with a paralyzed inability to accept its significance. She wept at once, with sudden, wild abandonment, in her sister's arms. When the storm of grief had spent itself she went away to her room alone. She would have no one follow her.

There stood, facing the open window, a comfortable, roomy armchair. Into this she sank, pressed down by a physical exhaustion that haunted her body and seemed to reach into her soul.

She could see in the open square before her house the tops of trees   5
that were all aquiver with the new spring life. The delicious breath of rain was in the air. In the street below a peddler was crying his wares. The notes of a distant song which some one was singing reached her faintly, and countless sparrows were twittering in the eaves.

There were patches of blue sky showing here and there through the clouds that had met and piled one above the other in the west facing her window.

She sat with her head thrown back upon the cushion of the chair, quite motionless, except when a sob came up into her throat and shook her, as a child who has cried itself to sleep continues to sob in its dreams.

She was young, with a fair, calm face, whose lines bespoke repression and even a certain strength. But now there was a dull stare in her eyes, whose gaze was fixed away off yonder on one of those patches of blue sky. It was not a glance of reflection, but rather indicated a suspension of intelligent thought.

There was something coming to her and she was waiting for it, fearfully. What was it? She did not know; it was too subtle and elusive to name. But she felt it, creeping out of the sky, reaching toward her through the sounds, the scents, the color that filled the air.

Now her bosom rose and fell tumultuously. She was beginning to rec-   10
ognize this thing that was approaching to possess her, and she was striving
to beat it back with her will—as powerless as her two white slender hands
would have been.

When she abandoned herself a little whispered word escaped her
slightly parted lips. She said it over and over under her breath: "Free, free,
free!" The vacant stare and the look of terror that had followed it went
from her eyes. They stayed keen and bright. Her pulses beat fast, and the
coursing blood warmed and relaxed every inch of her body.

She did not stop to ask if it were not a monstrous joy that held her.
A clear and exalted perception enabled her to dismiss the suggestion as
trivial.

She knew that she would weep again when she saw the kind, tender
hands folded in death; the face that had never looked save with love upon
her, fixed and gray and dead. But she saw beyond that bitter moment a
long procession of years to come that would belong to her absolutely. And
she opened and spread her arms out to them in welcome.

There would be no one to live for during those coming years; she
would live for herself. There would be no powerful will bending her in
that blind persistence with which men and women believe they have a
right to impose a private will upon a fellow creature. A kind intention or a
cruel intention made the act seem no less a crime as she looked upon it in
that brief moment of illumination.

And yet she had loved him—sometimes. Often she had not. What did   15
it matter! What could love, the unsolved mystery, count for in face of this
possession of self-assertion which she suddenly recognized as the strongest
impulse of her being.

"Free! Body and soul free!" she kept whispering.

Josephine was kneeling before the closed door with her lips to the keyhole, imploring for admission. "Louise, open the door! I beg; open the
door—you will make yourself ill. What are you doing, Louise? For heaven's
sake open the door."

"Go away. I am not making myself ill." No; she was drinking in a very
elixir of life through that open window.

Her fancy was running riot along those days ahead of her. Spring
days, and summer days, and all sorts of days that would be her own. She
breathed a quick prayer that life might be long. It was only yesterday she
had thought with a shudder that life might be long.

She arose at length and opened the door to her sister's importunities.   20
There was a feverish triumph in her eyes, and she carried herself unwittingly
like a goddess of Victory. She clasped her sister's waist, and together they
descended the stairs. Richards stood waiting for them at the bottom.

Some one was opening the front door with a latchkey. It was Brently Mallard who entered, a little travel-stained, composedly carrying his grip-sack and umbrella. He had been far from the scene of the accident, and did not even know there had been one. He stood amazed at Josephine's piercing cry; at Richards' quick motion to screen him from the view of his wife.

But Richards was too late.

When the doctors came they said she had died of heart disease—of joy that kills.

- The story ends with a misinterpretation. How has the author prepared us to understand simultaneously how the doctors might arrive at this conclusion and how their conclusion is wrong?

- "There would be no one to live for during those coming years": How does this sentence contain the dual perspective that is repeatedly presented in this story?

- How do the physical descriptions offered in the story contribute to our understanding of Mrs. Mallard's condition?

Margaret Atwood (1939–)

The most prominent Canadian writer of her generation, Margaret Atwood was born in Ottawa. She began her literary career as a poet and then moved into other genres. Over the course of her career she has become an important cultural spokesperson, focusing in particular on feminist concerns. In addition to writing in almost every genre, she is a painter and illustrator. Atwood focuses often in her poetry on images of violence, and critics have commented on the impersonality of her early poetry, while noting the relative openness of her more recent work. It is not as a poet, however, that she is best known, but as the author of such best-selling novels as *The Handmaid's Tale*, which was made into a motion picture, and *Cat's Cradle*.

Happy Endings (1992)

John and Mary meet.

What happens next?

If you want a happy ending, try A.

A. John and Mary fall in love and get married. They both have worthwhile and remunerative jobs which they find stimulating and challenging. They buy a charming house. Real estate values go up. Eventually, when they can afford live-in help, they have two

children, to whom they are devoted. The children turn out well.
John and Mary have a stimulating and challenging sex life and
worthwhile friends. They go on fun vacations together. They retire.
They both have hobbies which they find stimulating and challenging. Eventually they die. This is the end of the story.

B. Mary falls in love with John but John doesn't fall in love with Mary.   5
He merely uses her body for selfish pleasure and ego gratification of
a tepid kind. He comes to her apartment twice a week and she cooks
him dinner, you'll notice that he doesn't even consider her worth
the price of a dinner out, and after he's eaten the dinner he fucks
her and after that he falls asleep, while she does the dishes so he
won't think she's untidy, having all those dirty dishes lying around,
and puts on fresh lipstick so she'll look good when he wakes up, but
when he wakes up he doesn't even notice, he puts on his socks and
his shorts and his pants and his shirt and his tie and his shoes, the
reverse order from the one in which he took them off. He doesn't
take off Mary's clothes, she takes them off herself, she acts as if she's
dying for it every time, not because she likes sex exactly, she doesn't,
but she wants John to think she does because if they do it often
enough surely he'll get used to her, he'll come to depend on her
and they will get married, but John goes out the door with hardly so
much as a good-night and three days later he turns up at six o'clock
and they do the whole thing over again.

Mary gets run-down. Crying is bad for your face, everyone
knows that and so does Mary but she can't stop. People at work
notice. Her friends tell her John is a rat, a pig, a dog, he isn't good
enough for her, but she can't believe it. Inside John, she thinks, is
another John, who is much nicer. This other John will emerge like
a butterfly from a cocoon, a Jack from a box, a pit from a prune, if
the first John is only squeezed enough.

One evening John complains about the food. He has never
complained about the food before. Mary is hurt.

Her friends tell her they've seen him in a restaurant with
another woman, whose name is Madge. It's not even Madge that
finally gets to Mary: it's the restaurant. John has never taken Mary
to a restaurant. Mary collects all the sleeping pills and aspirins she
can find, and takes them and a half a bottle of sherry. You can see
what kind of a woman she is by the fact that it's not even whiskey.
She leaves a note for John. She hopes he'll discover her and get her
to the hospital in time and repent and then they can get married,
but this fails to happen and she dies.

John marries Madge and everything continues as in A.

C. John, who is an older man, falls in love with Mary, and Mary,   10
    who is only twenty-two, feels sorry for him because he's worried
    about his hair falling out. She sleeps with him even though she's
    not in love with him. She met him at work. She's in love with
    someone called James, who is twenty-two also and not yet ready to
    settle down.

    John on the contrary settled down long ago: this is what
    is bothering him. John has a steady, respectable job and is get-
    ting ahead in his field, but Mary isn't impressed by him, she's
    impressed by James, who has a motorcycle and a fabulous record
    collection. But James is often away on his motorcycle, being free.
    Freedom isn't the same for girls, so in the meantime Mary spends
    Thursday evenings with John. Thursdays are the only days John
    can get away.

    John is married to a woman called Madge and they have
    two children, a charming house which they bought just before
    the real estate values went up, and hobbies which they find
    stimulating and challenging, when they have the time. John tells
    Mary how important she is to him, but of course he can't leave
    his wife because a commitment is a commitment. He goes on
    about this more than is necessary and Mary finds it boring, but
    older men can keep it up longer so on the whole she has a fairly
    good time.

    One day James breezes in on his motorcycle with some top-
    grade California hybrid and James and Mary get higher than you'd
    believe possible and they climb into bed. Everything becomes very
    underwater, but along comes John, who has a key to Mary's apart-
    ment. He finds them stoned and entwined. He's hardly in any
    position to be jealous, considering Madge, but nevertheless he's
    overcome with despair. Finally he's middle-aged, in two years he'll
    be bald as an egg and he can't stand it. He purchases a handgun,
    saying he needs it for target practice—this is the thin part of the
    plot, but it can be dealt with later—and shoots the two of them
    and himself.

    Madge, after a suitable period of mourning, marries an under-
    standing man called Fred and everything continues as in A, but
    under different names.

D. Fred and Madge have no problems. They get along exceptionally   15
    well and are good at working out any little difficulties that may arise.
    But their charming house is by the seashore and one day a giant tidal
    wave approaches. Real estate values go down. The rest of the story
    is about what caused the tidal wave and how they escape from it.

They do, though thousands drown, but Fred and Madge are virtuous and lucky. Finally on high ground they clasp each other, wet and dripping and grateful, and continue as in A.

E. Yes, but Fred has a bad heart. The rest of the story is about how kind and understanding they both are until Fred dies. Then Madge devotes herself to charity work until the end of A. If you like, it can be "Madge," "cancer," "guilty and confused," and "bird watching."

F. If you think this is all too bourgeois, make John a revolutionary and Mary a counterespionage agent and see how far that gets you. Remember, this is Canada. You'll still end up with A, though in between you may get a lustful brawling saga of passionate involvement, a chronicle of our times, sort of.

You'll have to face it, the endings are the same however you slice it. Don't be deluded by any other endings, they're all fake, either deliberately fake, with malicious intent to deceive, or just motivated by excessive optimism if not by downright sentimentality.

The only authentic ending is the one provided here:

John and Mary die. John and Mary die. John and Mary die. 20

So much for endings. Beginnings are always more fun. True connoisseurs, however, are known to favor the stretch in between, since it's the hardest to do anything with.

That's about all that can be said for plots, which anyway are just one thing after another, a what and a what and a what. Now try How and Why.

■ This short story makes us think about the genre of stories, especially the conventions of endings. How could we label each of the endings that the author gives here? Define the elements that characterize each of these genres.

■ What, if anything, happens in this story? Where do we see coherent action in spite of the sectional breaks?

■ How do the final three paragraphs fit into the rest of this story? To what extent do these remarks shape our understanding of the previous six sections? To what extent is it true that this is a story without "the stretch in between" the beginning and the ending?

POETRY

John Donne (1572–1631)

A Valediction Forbidding Mourning (1611)

As virtuous men pass mildly away,
　　And whisper to their souls to go,
While some of their sad friends do say,
　　The breath goes now, and some say, no:

So let us melt, and make no noise,　　　　　　　　　　　5
　　No tear-floods, nor sigh-tempests move;
'Twere profanation of our joys
　　To tell the laity our love.

Moving of th' earth brings harms and fears,
　　Men reckon what it did and meant,　　　　　　　　　10
But trepidation of the spheres,
　　Though greater far, is innocent.

Dull sublunary lovers' love
　　(Whose soul is sense) cannot admit
Absence, because it doth remove　　　　　　　　　　　15
　　Those things which elemented it.

But we by a love so much refined,
　　That ourselves know not what it is,
Inter-assurèd of the mind,
　　Care less, eyes, lips, and hands to miss.　　　　　　20

Our two souls therefore, which are one,
　　Though I must go, endure not yet
A breach, but an expansion,
　　Like gold to airy thinness beat.

If they be two, they are two so　　　　　　　　　　　25
　　As stiff twin compasses are two;
Thy soul the fixed foot, makes no show
　　To move, but doth, if th' other do.

And though it in the center sit,
    Yet when the other far doth roam,   30
It leans, and hearkens after it,
    And grows erect, as that comes home.

Such wilt thou be to me, who must
    Like th' other foot, obliquely run;
Thy firmness makes my circle just,   35
    And makes me end, where I begun.

- The "twin compasses" that the poet refers to are the tool that we use to draw circles rather than the tool that we use to find the direction north. Locate the specific details that he uses to make the analogy between the compasses and "our love."
- How does this image resolve the tension of the first half of the poem?

e. e. cummings (1894–1962)

in Just (1923)

in Just-
spring   when the world is mud-
luscious the little
lame balloonman

whistles far and wee   5

and eddieandbill come
running from marbles and
piracies and it's
spring

when the world is puddle-wonderful   10

the queer
old balloonman whistles
far and wee
and bettyandisbel come dancing

from hop-scotch and jump-rope and   15

it's
spring
and
   the

      goat-footed   20

balloonMan whistles
far
and
wee

- Find specific lines where the rhythm of the words helps establish meaning.
- Where does the poet use images to create meaning out of nonsense words? How do these neologisms work differently than a familiar word would in the same place?

Walt Whitman (1819–1892)

There Was a Child Went Forth (1855)

There was a child went forth every day,
And the first object he looked upon, that object he became,
And that object became part of him for the day or a certain part of the day,
Or for many years or stretching cycles of years.

The early lilacs became part of this child,   5
And grass and white and red morning-glories, and white and red clover,
   and the song of the phoebe-bird,
And the Third-month lambs and the sow's pink-faint litter, and the mare's
   foal and the cow's calf,

And the noisy brood of the barnyard or by the mire of the pond-side,
And the fish suspending themselves so curiously below there, and the
   beautiful curious liquid,
And the water-plants with their graceful flat heads, all became part of him.   10

The field-sprouts of Fourth-month and Fifth-month became part of him,
Winter-grain sprouts and those of the light-yellow corn, and the esculent
   roots of the garden,
And the apple-trees covered with blossoms and the fruit afterward, and
   wood-berries, and the commonest weeds by the road,

And the old drunkard staggering home from the outside of the tavern
    whence he had lately risen,
And the schoolmistress that passed on her way to the school,   15
And the friendly boys that passed, and the quarrelsome boys,
And the tidy and fresh-cheeked girls, and the barefoot negro boy and girl,
And all the changes of city and country wherever he went.

His own parents, he that had fathered him and she that had conceived him
    in her womb and birthed him,
They gave this child more of themselves than that,   20

They gave him afterward every day, they became part of him.
The mother at home quietly placing the dishes on the supper-table,
The mother with mild words, clean her cap and gown, a wholesome odor
    falling off her person and clothes as she walks by,
The father, strong, self-sufficient, manly, mean, angered, unjust,
The blow, the quick word, the tight bargain, the crafty lure,   25
The family usages, the language, the company, the furniture, the yearning
    and swelling heart,
Affection that will not be gainsayed, the sense of what is real, the thought if
    after all it should prove unreal,
The doubts of day-time and the doubts of night-time, the curious whether
    and how,
Whether that which appears so is so, or is it all flashes and specks?
Men and women crowding fast in the streets, if they are not flashes and   30
    specks what are they?
The streets themselves and the facades of houses, and goods in the windows,
Vehicles, teams, the heavy-planked wharves, the huge crossing at the ferries,
The village on the highland seen from afar at sunset, the river between,
Shadows, aureola and mist, the light falling on roofs and gables of white or
    brown two miles off,
The schooner near by sleepily dropping down the tide, the little boat   35
    slacktowed astern,
The hurrying tumbling waves, quick-broken crests, slapping,
The strata of colored clouds, the long bar of maroon-tint away solitary by
    itself, the spread of purity it lies motionless in,
The horizon's edge, the flying sea-crow, the fragrance of salt marsh and shore mud,
These became part of that child who went forth every day, and who now
    goes, and will always go forth every day.

■ How does the poet indicate how an object "became part of him for the day"?

■ What image of community emerges from the variety of objects that the child
    encounters in this poem?

DRAMA

Oscar Wilde (1854–1900)

Oscar Wilde was born in Dublin, Ireland, into a family that encouraged his interest in the arts. Wilde, from an early age, seemed to see himself as representing (in his writing, his dress, and his public presence) art and beauty; to his mind, the late Victorian world was very much in need of both. A precocious child, Wilde went on to establish himself as a poet before graduating from Oxford. His literary and public career was cut short when he was tried, convicted, and imprisoned on charges related to his homosexuality. The scandal ruined him, and he died in Paris in 1900. Of his many works, he is perhaps best known today for two plays, *The Importance of Being Ernest* and *Lady Windemere's Fan,* and his one novel, *The Picture of Dorian Gray.*

The Importance of Being Earnest (1895)

CHARACTERS

JOHN WORTHING, J.P.

ALGERNON MONCRIEFF

REV. CANON CHASUBLE, D.D.

MERRIMAN (*Butler*)

LANE (*Manservant*)

LADY BRACKNELL

HON. GWENDOLEN FAIRFAX

CECILY CARDEW

MISS PRISM (*Governess*)

THE SCENES OF THE PLAY

ACT   I. Algernon Moncrieff's Flat in Half-Moon Street, W.

ACT II. The Garden at the Manor House, Woolton.

ACT III. Drawing-Room of the Manor House, Woolton.

TIME: *The Present.*

PLACE: *London.*

ACT ONE

Morning-room in ALGERNON's *flat in Half-Moon Street. The room is luxuriously and artistically furnished. The sound of a piano is heard in the adjoining room.*

(LANE *is arranging afternoon tea on the table, and after the music has ceased,* ALGERNON *enters.*)

ALGERNON: Did you hear what I was playing, Lane?

LANE: I didn't think it polite to listen, sir.

ALGERNON: I'm sorry for that, for your sake. I don't play accurately—
anyone can play accurately—but I play with wonderful expression.
As far as the piano is concerned, sentiment is my forte. I keep   5
science for Life.

LANE: Yes, sir.

ALGERNON: And, speaking of the science of Life, have you got the
cucumber sandwiches cut for Lady Bracknell?

LANE: Yes, sir. (*Hands them on a salver.*)   10

ALGERNON: (*Inspects them, takes two, and sits down on the sofa.*) Oh! . . . by
the way, Lane, I see from your book that on Thursday night, when
Lord Shoreman and Mr. Worthing were dining with me, eight bottles
of champagne are entered as having been consumed.

LANE: Yes, sir; eight bottles and a pint.   15

ALGERNON: Why is it that at a bachelor's establishment the servants
invariably drink the champagne? I ask merely for information.

LANE: I attribute it to the superior quality of the wine, sir. I have often
observed that in married households the champagne is rarely of a
first-rate brand.   20

ALGERNON: Good Heavens! Is marriage so demoralizing as that?

LANE: I believe it *is* a very pleasant state, sir. I have had very little experience
of it myself up to the present. I have only been married once. That
was in consequence of a misunderstanding between myself and
a young woman.   25

ALGERNON: (*Languidly.*) I don't know that I am much interested in your
family life, Lane.

LANE: No, sir; it is not a very interesting subject. I never think of it myself.

ALGERNON: Very natural, I am sure. That will do, Lane, thank you.

LANE: Thank you, sir. (LANE *goes out.*)   30

ALGERNON: Lane's views on marriage seem somewhat lax. Really, if the
lower orders don't set us a good example, what on earth is the use
of them? They seem, as a class, to have absolutely no sense of moral
responsibility.

(*Enter* LANE.)

LANE: Mr. Ernest Worthing.   35

(*Enter* JACK. LANE *goes out.*)

ALGERNON: How are you, my dear Ernest? What brings you up to town?

JACK: Oh, pleasure, pleasure! What else should bring one anywhere?
Eating as usual, I see, Algy!

ALGERNON: (*Stiffly.*) I believe it is customary in good society to take
some slight refreshment at five o'clock. Where have you been since   40
last Thursday?

JACK: (*Sitting down on the sofa.*) In the country.

ALGERNON: What on earth do you do there?

JACK: (*Pulling off his gloves.*) When one is in town one amuses oneself. When one is in the country one amuses other people. It is excessively boring.   45

ALGERNON: And who are the people you amuse?

JACK: (*Airily.*) Oh, neighbours, neighbours.

ALGERNON: Got nice neighbours in your part of Shropshire?

JACK: Perfectly horrid! Never speak to one of them.   50

ALGERNON: How immensely you must amuse them! (*Goes over and takes sandwich.*) By the way, Shropshire is your county, is it not?

JACK: Eh? Shropshire? Yes, of course. Hallo! Why all these cups? Why cucumber sandwiches? Why such reckless extravagance in one so young? Who is coming to tea?   55

ALGERNON: Oh! merely Aunt Augusta and Gwendolen.

JACK: How perfectly delightful!

ALGERNON: Yes, that is all very well; but I am afraid Aunt Augusta won't quite approve of your being here.

JACK: May I ask why?   60

ALGERNON: My dear fellow, the way you flirt with Gwendolen is perfectly disgraceful. It is almost as bad as the way Gwendolen flirts with you.

JACK: I am in love with Gwendolen. I have come up to town expressly to propose to her.

ALGERNON: I thought you had come up for pleasure? . . . I call that business.   65

JACK: How utterly unromantic you are!

ALGERNON: I really don't see anything romantic in proposing. It is very romantic to be in love. But there is nothing romantic about a definite proposal. Why, one may be accepted. One usually is, I believe. Then the excitement is all over. The very essence of romance is uncertainty.   70
If ever I get married, I'll certainly try to forget the fact.

JACK: I have no doubt about that dear Algy. The Divorce Court was specially invented for people whose memories are so curiously constituted.

ALGERNON: Oh! there is no use speculating on that subject. Divorces are   75
made in Heaven—(JACK *puts out his hand to take a sandwich.* ALGERNON *at once interferes.*) Please don't touch the cucumber sandwiches. They are ordered specially for Aunt Augusta. (*Takes one and eats it.*)

JACK: Well, you have been eating them all the time.

ALGERNON: That is quite a different matter. She is my aunt. (*Takes plate   80
from below.*) Have some bread and butter. The bread and butter is for Gwendolen. Gwendolen is devoted to bread and butter.

JACK: (*Advancing to table and helping himself.*) And very good bread and butter it is, too.

ALGERNON: Well, my dear fellow, you need not eat as if you were going   85
to eat it all. You behave as if you were married to her already. You are
not married to her already, and I don't think you ever will be.

JACK: Why on earth do you say that?

ALGERNON: Well, in the first place girls never marry the men they flirt
with. Girls don't think it right.   90

JACK: Oh, that is nonsense!

ALGERNON: It isn't. It is a great truth. It accounts for the extraordinary
number of bachelors that one sees all over the place. In the second
place, I don't give my consent.

JACK: Your consent!   95

ALGERNON: My dear fellow, Gwendolen is my first cousin. And before
I allow you to marry her, you will have to clear up the whole question
of Cecily. (*Rings bell.*)

JACK: Cecily! What on earth do you mean? What do you mean, Algy,
by Cecily? I don't know anyone of the name of Cecily.   100

(*Enter* LANE.)

ALGERNON: Bring me that cigarette case Mr. Worthing left in the
smoking-room the last time he dined here.

LANE: Yes, sir. (LANE *goes out.*)

JACK: Do you mean to say you have had my cigarette case all this time?
I wish to goodness you had let me know. I have been writing   105
frantic letters to Scotland Yard about it. I was very nearly offering
a large reward.

ALGERNON: Well, I wish you would offer one. I happen to be more than
usually hard up.

JACK: There is no good offering a large reward now that the thing   110
is found.

(*Enter* LANE *with the cigarette case on a salver.* ALGERNON *takes it at once.*
LANE *goes out.*)

ALGERNON: I think that is rather mean of you, Ernest, I must say. (*Opens
case and examines it.*) However, it makes no matter, for, now that I look
at the inscription, I find that the thing isn't yours after all.

JACK: Of course it's mine. (*Moving to him.*) You have seen me with it a   115
hundred times, and you have no right whatsoever to read what is
written inside. It is a very ungentlemanly thing to read a private
cigarette case.

ALGERNON: Oh! it is absurd to have a hard-and-fast rule about what one
should read and what one shouldn't. More than half of modern culture   120
depends on what one shouldn't read.

JACK: I am quite aware of the fact, and I don't propose to discuss modern culture. It isn't the sort of thing one should talk of in private. I simply want my cigarette case back.

ALGERNON: Yes; but this isn't your cigarette case. This cigarette case is a 125 present from someone of the name of Cecily, and you said you didn't know anyone of that name.

JACK: Well, if you want to know, Cecily happens to be my aunt.

ALGERNON: Your aunt!

JACK: Yes. Charming old lady she is, too. Lives at Tunbridge Wells. Just 130 give it back to me, Algy.

ALGERNON: (*Retreating to back of sofa.*) But why does she call herself little Cecily if she is your aunt and lives at Tunbridge Wells? (*Reading.*) "From little Cecily with her fondest love."

JACK: (*Moving to sofa and kneeling upon it.*) My dear fellow, what on earth 135 is there in that? Some aunts are tall, some aunts are not tall. That is a matter that surely an aunt may be allowed to decide for herself. You seem to think that every aunt should be exactly like your aunt! That is absurd! For Heaven's sake give me back my cigarette case. (*Follows* ALGERNON *round the room.*) 140

ALGERNON: Yes. But why does your aunt call you her uncle? "From little Cecily, with her fondest love to her dear Uncle Jack." There is no objection, I admit, to an aunt being a small aunt, but why an aunt, no matter what her size may be, should call her own nephew her uncle, I can't quite make out. Besides, your name isn't Jack at all; it is Ernest. 145

JACK: It isn't Ernest; it's Jack.

ALGERNON: You have always told me it was Ernest. I have introduced you to everyone as Ernest. You answer to the name of Ernest. You look as if your name was Ernest. You are the most earnest looking person I ever saw in my life. It is perfectly absurd your saying that your name 150 isn't Ernest. It's on your cards. Here is one of them. (*Taking it from case.*) "Mr. Ernest Worthing, B 4, The Albany." I'll keep this as a proof your name is Ernest if ever you attempt to deny it to me, or to Gwendolen, or to anyone else. (*Puts the card in his pocket.*)

JACK: Well, my name is Ernest in town and Jack in the country, and the 155 cigarette case was given to me in the country.

ALGERNON: Yes, but that does not account for the fact that your small Aunt Cecily, who lives at Tunbridge Wells, calls you her dear uncle. Come, old boy, you had much better have the thing out at once.

JACK: My dear Algy, you talk exactly as if you were a dentist. It is very 160 vulgar to talk like a dentist when one isn't a dentist. It produces a false impression.

ALGERNON: Well, that is exactly what dentists always do. Now, go on!
Tell me the whole thing. I may mention that I have always suspected
you of being a confirmed and secret Bunburyist; and I am quite sure   165
of it now.

JACK: Bunburyist? What on earth do you mean by a Bunburyist?

ALGERNON: I'll reveal to you the meaning of that incomparable expression
as soon as you are kind enough to inform me why you are Ernest in
town and Jack in the country.   170

JACK: Well, produce my cigarette case first.

ALGERNON: Here it is. (*Hands cigarette case.*) Now produce your explanation,
and pray make it improbable. (*Sits on sofa.*)

JACK: My dear fellow, there is nothing improbable about my explanation
at all. In fact it's perfectly ordinary. Old Mr. Thomas Cardew, who   175
adopted me when I was a little boy, made me in his will guardian to
his grand-daughter, Miss Cecily Cardew. Cecily, who addresses me as
her uncle from motives of respect that you could not possibly appreciate,
lives at my place in the country under the charge of her admirable
governess, Miss Prism.   180

ALGERNON: Where is that place in the country, by the way?

JACK: That is nothing to you, dear boy. You are not going to be invited. . . .
I may tell you candidly that the place is not in Shropshire.

ALGERNON: I suspected that, my dear fellow! I have Bunburyed all over
Shropshire on two separate occasions. Now, go on. Why are you Ernest   185
in town and Jack in the country?

JACK: My dear Algy, I don't know whether you will be able to understand
my real motives. You are hardly serious enough. When one is placed in
the position of guardian, one has to adopt a very high moral tone on all
subjects. It's one's duty to do so. And as a high moral tone can hardly   190
be said to conduce very much to either one's health or one's happiness,
in order to get up to town I have always pretended to have a younger
brother of the name of Ernest, who lives in the Albany, and gets into
the most dreadful scrapes. That, my dear Algy, is the whole truth pure
and simple.   195

ALGERNON: The truth is rarely pure and never simple. Modern life would
be very tedious if it were either, and modern literature a complete
impossibility!

JACK: That wouldn't be at all a bad thing.

ALGERNON: Literary criticism is not your forte, my dear fellow. Don't try   200
it. You should leave that to people who haven't been at a University.
They do it so well in the daily papers. What you really are is a Bunburyist. I was quite right in saying you were a Bunburyist. You are one
of the most advanced Bunburyists I know.

JACK: What on earth do you mean?   205

ALGERNON: You have invented a very useful younger brother called Ernest,
in order that you may be able to come up to town as often as you like.
I have invented an invaluable permanent invalid called Bunbury,
in order that I may be able to go down into the country whenever
I choose. Bunbury is perfectly invaluable. If it wasn't for Bunbury's   210
extraordinary bad health, for instance, I wouldn't be able to dine with
you at Willis's to-night, for I have been really engaged to Aunt Augusta
for more than a week.

JACK: I haven't asked you to dine with me anywhere tonight.

ALGERNON: I know. You are absolutely careless about sending out   215
invitations. It is very foolish of you. Nothing annoys people so much
as not receiving invitations.

JACK: You had much better dine with your Aunt Augusta.

ALGERNON: I haven't the smallest intention of doing anything of the
kind. To begin with, I dined there on Monday, and once a week is   220
quite enough to dine with one's own relatives. In the second place,
whenever I do dine there I am always treated as a member of the
family, and sent down with either no woman at all, or two. In the
third place, I know perfectly well whom she will place me next to,
to-night. She will place me next Mary Farquhar, who always flirts   225
with her own husband across the dinner-table. That is not very
pleasant. Indeed, it is not even decent . . . and that sort of thing is
enormously on the increase. The amount of women in London who
flirt with their own husbands is perfectly scandalous. It looks so
bad. It is simply washing one's clean linen in public. Besides, now   230
that I know you to be a confirmed Bunburyist I naturally want to
talk to you about Bunburying. I want to tell you the rules.

JACK: I'm not a Bunburyist at all. If Gwendolen accepts me, I am going
to kill my brother, indeed I think I'll kill him in any case. Cecily is a
little too much interested in him. It is rather a bore. So I am going   235
to get rid of Ernest. And I strongly advise you to do the same with
Mr. . . . with your invalid friend who has the absurd name.

ALGERNON: Nothing will induce me to part with Bunbury, and if you
ever get married, which seems to be extremely problematic, you will
be very glad to know Bunbury. A man who marries without knowing   240
Bunbury has a very tedious time of it.

JACK: That is nonsense. If I marry a charming girl like Gwendolen, and she
is the only girl I ever saw in my life that I would marry, I certainly won't
want to know Bunbury.

ALGERNON: Then your wife will. You don't seem to realize, that in   245
married life three is company and two is none.

JACK: (*Sententiously.*) That, my dear young friend, is the theory that the corrupt French Drama has been propounding for the last fifty years.

ALGERNON: Yes; and that the happy English home has proved in half the time.   250

JACK: For heaven's sake, don't try to be cynical. It's perfectly easy to be cynical.

ALGERNON: My dear fellow, it isn't easy to be anything now-a-days. There's such a lot of beastly competition about. (*The sound of an electric bell is heard.*) Ah! that must be Aunt Augusta. Only relatives, or creditors, ever   255 ring in that Wagnerian manner. Now, if I get her out of the way for ten minutes, so that you can have an opportunity for proposing to Gwendolen, may I dine with you to-night at Willis's?

JACK: I suppose so if you want to.

ALGERNON: Yes, but you must be serious about it. I hate people who are not   260 serious about meals. It is so shallow of them.

(*Enter* LANE.)

LANE: Lady Bracknell and Miss Fairfax. (ALGERNON *goes forward to meet them. Enter* LADY BRACKNELL *and* GWENDOLEN.)

LADY BRACKNELL: Good afternoon, dear Algernon, I hope you are behaving very well.   265

ALGERNON: I'm feeling very well, Aunt Augusta.

LADY BRACKNELL: That's not quite the same thing. In fact the two things rarely go together. (*Sees* JACK *and bows to him with icy coldness.*)

ALGERNON: (*To* GWENDOLEN.) Dear me, you are smart!

GWENDOLEN: I am always smart! Aren't I, Mr. Worthing?   270

JACK: You're quite perfect, Miss Fairfax.

GWENDOLEN: Oh! I hope I am not that. It would leave no room for developments, and I intend to develop in *many directions.* (GWENDOLEN *and* JACK *sit down together in the corner.*)

LADY BRACKNELL: I'm sorry if we are a little late, Algernon, but I was   275 obliged to call on dear Lady Harbury. I hadn't been there since her poor husband's death. I never saw a woman so altered; she looks quite twenty years younger. And now I'll have a cup of tea, and one of those nice cucumber sandwiches you promised me.

ALGERNON: Certainly, Aunt Augusta. (*Goes over to tea-table.*)   280

LADY BRACKNELL: Won't you come and sit here, Gwendolen?

GWENDOLEN: Thanks, mamma, I'm quite comfortable where I am.

ALGERNON: (*Picking up empty plate in horror.*) Good heavens! Lane! Why are there no cucumber sandwiches? I ordered them specially.

LANE: (*Gravely.*) There were no cucumbers in the market this morning,   285 sir. I went down twice.

ALGERNON: No cucumbers!

LANE: No, sir. Not even for ready money.

ALGERNON: That will do, Lane, thank you.

LANE: Thank you sir. (*Goes out.*)   290

ALGERNON: I am greatly distressed, Aunt Augusta, about there being no cucumbers, not even for ready money.

LADY BRACKNELL: It really makes no matter, Algernon. I had some crumpets with Lady Harbury, who seems to me to be living entirely for pleasure now.   295

ALGERNON: I hear her hair has turned quite gold from grief.

LADY BRACKNELL: It certainly has changed its colour. From what cause I, of course, cannot say. (ALGERNON *crosses and hands tea.*) Thank you. I've quite a treat for you to-night, Algernon. I am going to send you down with Mary Farquhar. She is such a nice woman, and so attentive to   300
her husband. It's delightful to watch them.

ALGERNON: I am afraid, Aunt Augusta, I shall have to give up the pleasure of dining with you to-night after all.

LADY BRACKNELL: (*Frowning.*) I hope not, Algernon. It would put my table completely out. Your uncle would have to dine upstairs. Fortunately he   305
is accustomed to that.

ALGERNON: It is a great bore, and, I need hardly say, a terrible disappointment to me, but the fact is I have just had a telegram to say that my poor friend Bunbury is very ill again. (*Exchanges glances with* JACK.) They seem to think I should be with him.   310

LADY BRACKNELL: It is very strange. This Mr. Bunbury seems to suffer from curiously bad health.

ALGERNON: Yes; poor Bunbury is a dreadful invalid.

LADY BRACKNELL: Well, I must say, Algernon, that I think it is high time that Mr. Bunbury made up his mind whether he was going to live or   315
to die. This shilly-shallying with the question is absurd. Nor do I in any way approve of the modern sympathy with invalids. I consider it morbid. Illness of any kind is hardly a thing to be encouraged in others. Health is the primary duty of life. I am always telling that to your poor uncle, but he never seems to take much notice . . . as far   320
as any improvement in his ailments goes. I should be much obliged if you would ask Mr. Bunbury, from me, to be kind enough not to have a relapse on Saturday, for I rely on you to arrange my music for me. It is my last reception and one wants something that will encourage conversation, particularly at the end of the season when   325
everyone has practically said whatever they had to say, which, in most cases, was probably not much.

ALGERNON: I'll speak to Bunbury, Aunt Augusta, if he is still conscious, and I think I can promise you he'll be all right by Saturday. You see, if one plays good music, people don't listen, and if one plays bad music   330

people don't talk. But I'll run over the programme I've drawn out, if
you will kindly come into the next room for a moment.

LADY BRACKNELL: Thank you, Algernon. It is very thoughtful of you.
(*Rising, and following* ALGERNON.) I'm sure the programme will be
delightful, after a few expurgations. French songs I cannot possibly   335
allow. People always seem to think that they are improper, and either
look shocked, which is vulgar, or laugh, which is worse. But German
sounds a thoroughly respectable language, and indeed, I believe is so.
Gwendolen, you will accompany me.

GWENDOLEN: Certainly, mamma. (LADY BRACKNELL *and* ALGERNON *go into*   340
the music-room, GWENDOLEN *remains behind.*)

JACK: Charming day it has been, Miss Fairfax.

GWENDOLEN: Pray don't talk to me about the weather, Mr. Worthing.
Whenever people talk to me about the weather, I always feel quite
certain that they mean something else. And that makes me   345
so nervous.

JACK: I do mean something else.

GWENDOLEN: I thought so. In fact, I am never wrong.

JACK: And I would like to be allowed to take advantage of Lady Bracknell's
temporary absence . . .   350

GWENDOLEN: I would certainly advise you to do so. Mamma has a way of
coming back suddenly into a room that I have often had to speak to
her about.

JACK: (*Nervously.*) Miss Fairfax, ever since I met you I have admired you
more than any girl . . . I have ever met since . . . I met you.   355

GWENDOLEN: Yes, I am quite aware of the fact. And I often wish that in
public, at any rate, you had been more demonstrative. For me you
have always had an irresistible fascination. Even before I met you
I was far from indifferent to you. (JACK *looks at her in amazement.*) We
live, as I hope you know, Mr. Worthing, in an age of ideals. The fact is   360
constantly mentioned in the more expensive monthly magazines, and
has reached the provincial pulpits I am told: and my ideal has always
been to love some one of the name of Ernest. There is something in
that name that inspires absolute confidence. The moment Algernon
first mentioned to me that he had a friend called Ernest, I knew I was   365
destined to love you.

JACK: You really love me, Gwendolen?

GWENDOLEN: Passionately!

JACK: Darling! You don't know how happy you've made me.

GWENDOLEN: My own Ernest!   370

JACK: But you don't really mean to say that you couldn't love me if my
name wasn't Ernest?

GWENDOLEN: But your name is Ernest.

JACK: Yes, I know it is. But supposing it was something else? Do you
mean to say you couldn't love me then?   375

GWENDOLEN: (*Glibly.*) Ah! that is clearly a metaphysical speculation, and
like most metaphysical speculations has very little reference at all to
the actual facts of real life, as we know them.

JACK: Personally, darling, to speak quite candidly, I don't much care
about the name of Ernest . . . I don't think that name suits me at all.   380

GWENDOLEN: It suits you perfectly. It is a divine name. It has a music of
its own. It produces vibrations.

JACK: Well, really, Gwendolen, I must say that I think there are lots of
other much nicer names. I think, Jack, for instance, a charming name.

GWENDOLEN: Jack? . . . No, there is very little music in the name Jack, if any   385
at all, indeed. It does not thrill. It produces absolutely no vibration. . . .
I have known several Jacks, and they all, without exception, were more
than usually plain. Besides, Jack is a notorious domesticity for John!
And I pity any woman who is married to a man called John. She would   390
probably never be allowed to know the entrancing pleasure of a single
moment's solitude. The only really safe name is Ernest.

JACK: Gwendolen, I must get christened at once—I mean we must get married at once. There is no time to be lost.

GWENDOLEN: Married, Mr. Worthing?   395

JACK: (*Astounded.*) Well . . . surely. You know that I love you, and you led me
to believe, Miss Fairfax, that you were not absolutely indifferent to me.

GWENDOLEN: I adore you. But you haven't proposed to me yet. Nothing
has been said at all about marriage. The subject has not even been
touched on.   400

JACK: Well . . . may I propose to you now?

GWENDOLEN: I think it would be an admirable opportunity. And to spare
you any possible disappointment, Mr. Worthing, I think it only fair
to tell you quite frankly beforehand that I am fully determined to
accept you.

JACK: Gwendolen!   405

GWENDOLEN: Yes, Mr. Worthing, what have you got to say to me?

JACK: You know what I have got to say to you.

GWENDOLEN: Yes, but you don't say it.

JACK: Gwendolen, will you marry me? (*Goes on his knees.*)

GWENDOLEN: Of course I will, darling. How long you have been about it!   410
I am afraid you have had very little experience in how to propose.

JACK: My own one, I have never loved anyone in the world but you.

GWENDOLEN: Yes, but men often propose for practice. I know my brother
Gerald does. All my girl-friends tell me so. What wonderfully blue eyes

you have, Ernest! They are quite, quite blue. I hope you will always look   415
at me just like that, especially when there are other people present.

(*Enter* LADY BRACKNELL.)

LADY BRACKNELL: Mr. Worthing! Rise, sir, from this semirecumbent posture.
It is most indecorous.

GWENDOLEN: Mamma! (*He tries to rise; she restrains him.*) I must beg you to
retire. This is no place for you. Besides, Mr. Worthing has not quite   420
finished yet.

LADY BRACKNELL: Finished what, may I ask?

GWENDOLEN: I am engaged to Mr. Worthing, mamma.

(*They rise together.*)

LADY BRACKNELL: Pardon me, you are not engaged to anyone. When you
do become engaged to some one, I, or your father, should his health   425
permit him, will inform you of the fact. An engagement should come
on a young girl as a surprise, pleasant or unpleasant, as the case may
be. It is hardly a matter that she could be allowed to arrange for
herself. . . . And now I have a few questions to put to you, Mr. Worthing.
While I am making these inquiries, you, Gwendolen, will wait for me   430
below in the carriage.

GWENDOLEN: (*Reproachfully.*) Mamma!

LADY BRACKNELL: In the carriage, Gwendolen! (GWENDOLEN *goes to the door.
She and* JACK *blow kisses to each other behind* LADY BRACKNELL's *back.* LADY
BRACKNELL *looks vaguely about as if she could not understand what the noise*   435
was. Finally turns round.) Gwendolen, the carriage!

GWENDOLEN: Yes, mamma. (*Goes out, looking back at* JACK.)

LADY BRACKNELL: (*Sitting down.*) You can take a seat, Mr. Worthing. (*Looks
in her pocket for note-book and pencil.*)

JACK: Thank you, Lady Bracknell, I prefer standing.   440

LADY BRACKNELL: (*Pencil and note-book in hand.*) I feel bound to tell you that you
are not down on my list of eligible young men, although I have the same
list as the dear Duchess of Bolton has. We work together, in fact. However,
I am quite ready to enter your name, should your answers be what a really
affectionate mother requires. Do you smoke?   445

JACK: Well, yes, I must admit I smoke.

LADY BRACKNELL: I am glad to hear it. A man should always have an
occupation of some kind. There are far too many idle men in London
as it is. How old are you?

JACK: Twenty-nine.   450

LADY BRACKNELL: A very good age to be married at. I have always been of opinion that a man who desires to get married should know either everything or nothing. Which do you know?

JACK: (*After some hesitation.*) I know nothing, Lady Bracknell.

LADY BRACKNELL: I am pleased to hear it. I do not approve of anything that   455
tampers with natural ignorance. Ignorance is like a delicate exotic fruit; touch it and the bloom is gone. The whole theory of modern education is radically unsound. Fortunately in England, at any rate, education produces no effect whatsoever. If it did, it would prove a serious danger to the upper classes, and probably lead to acts of violence in Grosvenor   460
Square. What is your income?

JACK: Between seven and eight thousand a year.

LADY BRACKNELL: (*Makes a note in her book.*) In land, or in investments?

JACK: In investments, chiefly.

LADY BRACKNELL: That is satisfactory. What between the duties expected of   465
one during one's life-time, and the duties exacted from one after one's death, land has ceased to be either a profit or a pleasure. It gives one position, and prevents one from keeping it up. That's all that can be said about land.

JACK: I have a country house with some land, of course, attached to it,   470
about fifteen hundred acres, I believe; but I don't depend on that for my real income. In fact, as far as I can make out, the poachers are the only people who make anything out of it.

LADY BRACKNELL: A country house! How many bedrooms? Well, that point can be cleared up afterwards. You have a town house, I hope?   475
A girl with a simple, unspoiled nature, like Gwendolen, could hardly be expected to reside in the country.

JACK: Well, I own a house in Belgrave Square, but it is let by the year to Lady Bloxham. Of course, I can get it back whenever I like, at six months' notice.   480

LADY BRACKNELL: Lady Bloxham? I don't know her.

JACK: Oh, she goes about very little. She is a lady considerably advanced in years.

LADY BRACKNELL: Ah, now-a-days that is no guarantee of respectability of character. What number in Belgrave Square?   485

JACK: 149.

LADY BRACKNELL: (*Shaking her head.*) The unfashionable side. I thought there was something. However, that could easily be altered.

JACK: Do you mean the fashion, or the side?

LADY BRACKNELL: (*Sternly.*) Both, if necessary, I presume. What are   490
your politics?

JACK: Well, I am afraid I really have none. I am a Liberal Unionist.

LADY BRACKNELL: Oh, they count as Tories. They dine with us. Or comes in
the evening, at any rate. Now to minor matters. Are your parents living?

JACK: I have lost both my parents.

LADY BRACKNELL: Both? . . . That seems like carelessness. Who was   495
your father? He was evidently a man of some wealth. Was he born
in what the Radical papers call the purple of commerce, or did he
rise from the ranks of the aristocracy?

JACK: I am afraid I really don't know. The fact is, Lady Bracknell, I said I had
lost my parents. It would be nearer the truth to say that my parents seem to   500
have lost me . . . I don't actually know who I am by birth. I was . . . well,
I was found.

LADY BRACKNELL: Found!

JACK: The late Mr. Thomas Cardew, an old gentleman of a very charitable
and kindly disposition, found me, and gave me the name of Worthing,   505
because he happened to have a first-class ticket for Worthing in his
pocket at the time. Worthing is a place in Sussex. It is a seaside resort.

LADY BRACKNELL: Where did the charitable gentleman who had a first-class
ticket for this seaside resort find you?

JACK: (*Gravely.*) In a hand-bag.   510

LADY BRACKNELL: A hand-bag?

JACK: (*Very seriously.*) Yes, Lady Bracknell. I was in a hand-bag—a somewhat large, black leather hand-bag, with handles to it—an ordinary
hand-bag in fact.

LADY BRACKNELL: In what locality did Mr. James, or Thomas, Cardew   515
come across this ordinary hand-bag?

JACK: In the cloak-room at Victoria Station. It was given to him in
mistake for his own.

LADY BRACKNELL: The cloak-room at Victoria Station?

JACK: Yes. The Brighton line.   520

LADY BRACKNELL: The line is immaterial. Mr. Worthing, I confess I feel
somewhat bewildered by what you have just told me. To be born, or at
any rate bred, in a hand-bag, whether it had handles or not, seems to
me to display a contempt for the ordinary decencies of family life that
remind one of the worst excesses of the French Revolution. And   525
I presume you know what that unfortunate movement led to? As for the
particular locality in which the hand-bag was found, a cloak-room at a
railway station might serve to conceal a social indiscretion—has probably,
indeed, been used for the purpose before now—but it could hardly be
regarded as an assured basis for a recognized position in good society.   530

JACK: May I ask you then what you would advise me to do? I need
hardly say I would do anything in the world to ensure Gwendolen's
happiness.

LADY BRACKNELL: I would strongly advise you, Mr. Worthing, to try and
acquire some relations as soon as possible, and to make a definite effort   535
to produce at any rate one parent, of either sex, before the season is
quite over.

JACK: Well, I don't see how I could possibly manage to do that. I can
produce the hand-bag at any moment. It is in my dressing-room at
home. I really think that should satisfy you, Lady Bracknell.   540

LADY BRACKNELL: Me, sir! What has it to do with me? You can hardly
imagine that I and Lord Bracknell would dream of allowing our only
daughter—a girl brought up with the utmost care—to marry into a
cloak-room, and form an alliance with a parcel? Good morning,
Mr. Worthing! (LADY BRACKNELL *sweeps out in majestic indignation.*)   545

JACK: Good morning! (ALGERNON, *from the other room, strikes up the Wedding
March.* JACK *looks perfectly furious, and goes to the door.*) For goodness'
sake don't play that ghastly tune, Algy! How idiotic you are! (*The music
stops, and* ALGERNON *enters cheerily.*)

ALGERNON: Didn't it go off all right, old boy? You don't mean to say   550
Gwendolen refused you? I know it is a way she has. She is always
refusing people. I think it is most ill-natured of her.

JACK: Oh, Gwendolen is as right as a trivet. As far as she is concerned,
we are engaged. Her mother is perfectly unbearable. Never met such a
Gorgon . . . I don't really know what a Gorgon is like, but I am quite   555
sure that Lady Bracknell is one. In any case, she is a monster, without
being a myth, which is rather unfair. . . . I beg your pardon, Algy, I suppose
I shouldn't talk about your own aunt in that way before you.

ALGERNON: My dear boy, I love hearing my relations abused. It is the only
thing that makes me put up with them at all. Relations are simply a   560
tedious pack of people, who haven't got the remotest knowledge of
how to live, nor the smallest instinct about when to die.

JACK: Oh, that is nonsense!

ALGERNON: It isn't!

JACK: Well, I won't argue about the matter. You always want to argue   565
about things.

ALGERNON: That is exactly what things were originally made for.

JACK: Upon my word, if I thought that, I'd shoot myself . . . (*A pause.*)
You don't think there is any chance of Gwendolen becoming like her
mother in about a hundred and fifty years, do you, Algy?   570

ALGERNON: All women become like their mothers. That is their tragedy.
No man does. That's his.

JACK: Is that clever?

ALGERNON: It is perfectly phrased! and quite as true as any observation in
civilized life should be.   575

JACK: I am sick to death of cleverness. Everybody is clever now-a-days.
You can't go anywhere without meeting clever people. The thing has
become an absolute public nuisance. I wish to goodness we had a few
fools left.

ALGERNON: We have.   580

JACK: I should extremely like to meet them. What do they talk about?

ALGERNON: The fools? Oh! about the clever people, of course.

JACK: What fools!

ALGERNON: By the way, did you tell Gwendolen the truth about your being
Ernest in town, and Jack in the country?   585

JACK: (*In a very patronising manner.*) My dear fellow, the truth isn't quite the
sort of thing one tells to a nice, sweet, refined girl. What extraordinary
ideas you have about the way to behave to a woman!

ALGERNON: The only way to behave to a woman is to make love to her, if she
is pretty, and to someone else if she is plain.   590

JACK: Oh, that is nonsense.

ALGERNON: What about your brother? What about the profligate Ernest?

JACK: Oh, before the end of the week I shall have got rid of him. I'll say
he died in Paris of apoplexy. Lots of people die of apoplexy, quite
suddenly, don't they?   595

ALGERNON: Yes, but it's hereditary, my dear fellow. It's a sort of thing that
runs in families. You had much better say a severe chill.

JACK: You are sure a severe chill isn't hereditary, or anything of that kind?

ALGERNON: Of course it isn't!

JACK: Very well, then. My poor brother Ernest is carried off suddenly in   600
Paris, by a severe chill. That gets rid of him.

ALGERNON: But I thought you said that . . . Miss Cardew was a little
too interested in your poor brother Ernest? Won't she feel his loss
a good deal?

JACK: Oh, that is all right. Cecily is not a silly, romantic girl, I am glad   605
to say. She has got a capital appetite, goes for long walks, and pays no
attention at all to her lessons.

ALGERNON: I would rather like to see Cecily.

JACK: I will take very good care you never do. She is excessively pretty,
and she is only just eighteen.   610

ALGERNON: Have you told Gwendolen yet that you have an excessively
pretty ward who is only just eighteen?

JACK: Oh! one doesn't blurt these things out to people. Cecily and Gwendolen
are perfectly certain to be extremely great friends. I'll bet you anything
you like that half an hour after they have met, they will be calling each   615
other sister.

ALGERNON: Women only do that when they have called each other a
    lot of other things first. Now, my dear boy, if we want to get a good
    table at Willis's, we really must go and dress. Do you know it is
    nearly seven?   620

JACK: (*Irritably.*) Oh! it always is nearly seven.

ALGERNON: Well, I'm hungry.

JACK: I never knew you when you weren't. . . .

ALGERNON: What shall we do after dinner? Go to a theatre?

JACK: Oh, no! I loathe listening.   625

ALGERNON: Well, let us go to the Club?

JACK: Oh, no! I hate talking.

ALGERNON: Well, we might trot round to the Empire at ten?

JACK: Oh, no! can't bear looking at things. It is so silly.

ALGERNON: Well, what shall we do?   630

JACK: Nothing!

ALGERNON: It is awfully hard work doing nothing. However, I don't mind
    hard work where there is no definite object of any kind.

(*Enter* LANE.)

LANE: Miss Fairfax.

(*Enter* GWENDOLEN. LANE *goes out.*)

ALGERNON: Gwendolen, upon my word!   635

GWENDOLEN: Algy, kindly turn your back. I have something very
    particular to say to Mr. Worthing.

ALGERNON: Really, Gwendolen, I don't think I can allow this at all.

GWENDOLEN: Algy, you always adopt a strictly immoral attitude towards
    life. You are not quite old enough to do that. (ALGERNON *retires to*   640
    the fireplace.)

JACK: My own darling!

GWENDOLEN: Ernest, we may never be married. From the expression on
    mamma's face I fear we never shall. Few parents now-a-days pay any
    regard to what their children say to them. The old-fashioned respect   645
    for the young is fast dying out. Whatever influence I ever had over
    mamma, I lost at the age of three. But although she may prevent us
    from becoming man and wife, and I may marry someone else, and
    marry often, nothing that she can possibly do can alter my eternal
    devotion to you.   650

JACK: Dear Gwendolen.

GWENDOLEN: The story of your romantic origin, as related to me by
    mamma, with unpleasing comments, has naturally stirred the

deeper fibers of my nature. Your Christian name has an irresistible
fascination. The simplicity of your character makes you exquisitely   655
incomprehensible to me. Your town address at the Albany I have.
What is your address in the country?

JACK: The Manor House, Woolton, Hertfordshire. (ALGERNON, *who has
been carefully listening, smiles to himself, and writes the address on his shirt-
cuff. Then picks up the Railway Guide.*)   660

GWENDOLEN: There is a good postal service, I suppose? It may be
necessary to do something desperate. That, of course, will require
serious consideration. I will communicate with you daily.

JACK: My own one!   665

GWENDOLEN: How long do you remain in town?

JACK: Till Monday.

GWENDOLEN: Good! Algy, you may turn round now.

ALGERNON: Thanks, I've turned round already.

GWENDOLEN: You may also ring the bell.   670

JACK: You will let me see you to your carriage, my own darling?

GWENDOLEN: Certainly.

JACK: (*To* LANE, *who now enters.*) I will see Miss Fairfax out.

LANE: Yes, sir. (JACK *and* GWENDOLEN *go off.* LANE *presents several letters on a
salver to* ALGERNON. *It is to be surmised that they are bills, as* ALGERNON,   675
after looking at the envelopes, tears them up.)

ALGERNON: A glass of sherry, Lane.

LANE: Yes, sir.

ALGERNON: To-morrow, Lane, I'm going Bunburying.

LANE: Yes, sir.   680

ALGERNON: I shall probably not be back till Monday. You can put up my
dress clothes, my smoking jacket, and all the Bunbury suits . . .

LANE: Yes, sir. (*Handing sherry.*)

ALGERNON: I hope to-morrow will be a fine day, Lane.

LANE: It never is, sir.   685

ALGERNON: Lane, you're a perfect pessimist.

LANE: I do my best to give satisfaction, sir.

(*Enter* JACK. LANE *goes off.*)

JACK: There's a sensible, intellectual girl! the only girl I ever cared for in
my life. (ALGERNON *is laughing immoderately.*) What on earth are you so
amused at?   690

ALGERNON: Oh, I'm a little anxious about poor Bunbury, that's all.

JACK: If you don't take care, your friend Bunbury will get you into a
serious scrape some day.

ALGERNON: I love scrapes. They are the only things that are never serious.

JACK: Oh, that's nonsense, Algy. You never talk anything but nonsense.   695
ALGERNON: Nobody ever does. (JACK *looks indignantly at him, and leaves the room.* ALGERNON *lights a cigarette, reads his shirt-cuff and smiles.*)

ACT TWO

Garden at the Manor House. A flight of gray stone steps leads up to the house. The garden, an old-fashioned one, full of roses. Time of year, July. Basket chairs, and a table covered with books, are set under a large yew tree.

(MISS PRISM *discovered seated at the table.* CECILY *is at the back watering flowers.*)

MISS PRISM: (*Calling.*) Cecily, Cecily! Surely such a utilitarian occupation as the watering of flowers is rather Moulton's duty than yours? Especially at a moment when intellectual pleasures await you. Your German grammar is on the table. Pray open it at page fifteen. We will repeat yesterday's lesson.   5
CECILY: (*Coming over very slowly.*) But I don't like German. It isn't at all a becoming language. I know perfectly well that I look quite plain after my German lesson.
MISS PRISM: Child, you know how anxious your guardian is that you should improve yourself in every way. He laid particular stress on your   10
German, as he was leaving for town yesterday. Indeed, he always lays stress on your German when he is leaving for town.
CECILY: Dear Uncle Jack is so very serious! Sometimes he is so serious that I think he cannot be quite well.
MISS PRISM: (*Drawing herself up.*) Your guardian enjoys the best of health,   15
and his gravity of demeanour is especially to be commended in one so comparatively young as he is. I know no one who has a higher sense of duty and responsibility.
CECILY: I suppose that is why he often looks a little bored when we three are together.   20
MISS PRISM: Cecily! I am surprised at you. Mr. Worthing has many troubles in his life. Idle merriment and triviality would be out of place in his conversation. You must remember his constant anxiety about that unfortunate young man, his brother.
CECILY: I wish Uncle Jack would allow that unfortunate young man,   25
his brother, to come down here sometimes. We might have a good influence over him, Miss Prism. I am sure you certainly would. You know German, and geology, and things of that kind influence a man very much. (CECILY *begins to write in her diary.*)
MISS PRISM: (*Shaking her head.*) I do not think that even I could produce any   30
effect on a character that, according to his own brother's admission, is

irretrievably weak and vacillating. Indeed, I am not sure that I would desire to reclaim him. I am not in favour of this modern mania for turning bad people into good people at a moment's notice. As a man sows so let him reap. You must put away your diary, Cecily. I really 35
don't see why you should keep a diary at all.

CECILY: I keep a diary in order to enter the wonderful secrets of my life. If I didn't write them down I should probably forget all about them.

MISS PRISM: Memory, my dear Cecily, is the diary that we all carry about with us. 40

CECILY: Yes, but it usually chronicles the things that have never happened, and couldn't possibly have happened. I believe that Memory is responsible for nearly all the three-volume novels that Mudie sends us.

MISS PRISM: Do not speak slightingly of the three-volume novel, Cecily. I wrote one myself in earlier days. 45

CECILY: Did you really, Miss Prism? How wonderfully clever you are! I hope it did not end happily? I don't like novels that end happily. They depress me so much.

MISS PRISM: The good ended happily, and the bad unhappily. That is what Fiction means. 50

CECILY: I suppose so. But it seems very unfair. And was your novel ever published?

MISS PRISM: Alas! no. The manuscript unfortunately was abandoned. I use the word in the sense of lost or mislaid. To your work, child, these speculations are profitless. 55

CECILY: (*Smiling.*) But I see dear Dr. Chasuble coming up through the garden.

MISS PRISM: (*Rising and advancing.*) Dr. Chasuble! This is indeed a pleasure.

(*Enter* CANON CHASUBLE.)

CHASUBLE: And how are we this morning? Miss Prism, you are, I trust, well?

CECILY: Miss Prism has just been complaining of a slight headache. 60
I think it would do her so much good to have a short stroll with you in the park, Dr. Chasuble.

MISS PRISM: Cecily, I have not mentioned anything about a headache.

CECILY: No, dear Miss Prism, I know that, but I felt instinctively that you had a headache. Indeed I was thinking about that, and not 65
about my German lesson, when the Rector came in.

CHASUBLE: I hope, Cecily, you are not inattentive.

CECILY: Oh, I am afraid I am.

CHASUBLE: That is strange. Were I fortunate enough to be Miss Prism's pupil, I would hang upon her lips. (MISS PRISM *glares.*) I spoke 70
metaphorically.—My metaphor was drawn from bees. Ahem!
Mr. Worthing, I suppose, has not returned from town yet?

MISS PRISM: We do not expect him till Monday afternoon.

CHASUBLE: Ah yes, he usually likes to spend his Sunday in London. He
is not one of those whose sole aim is enjoyment, as, by all accounts,   75
that unfortunate young man, his brother, seems to be. But I must not
disturb Egeria and her pupil any longer.

MISS PRISM: Egeria? My name is Lætitia, Doctor.

CHASUBLE: (*Bowing.*) A classical allusion merely, drawn from the Pagan
authors. I shall see you both no doubt at Evensong.   80

MISS PRISM: I think, dear Doctor, I will have a stroll with you. I find
I have a headache after all, and a walk might do it good.

CHASUBLE: With pleasure, Miss Prism, with pleasure. We might go as far
as the schools and back.

MISS PRISM: That would be delightful. Cecily, you will read your Political   85
Economy in my absence. The chapter on the Fall of the Rupee
you may omit. It is somewhat too sensational. Even these metallic
problems have their melodramatic side.

(*Goes down the garden with* DR. CHASUBLE.)

CECILY: (*Picks up books and throws them back on table.*) Horrid Political
Economy! Horrid Geography! Horrid, horrid German!   90

(*Enter* MERRIMAN *with a card on a salver.*)

MERRIMAN: Mr. Ernest Worthing has just driven over from the station.
He has brought his luggage with him.

CECILY: (*Takes the card and reads it.*) "Mr. Ernest Worthing, B 4 The
Albany, W." Uncle Jack's brother! Did you tell him Mr. Worthing
was in town?   95

MERRIMAN: Yes, Miss. He seemed very much disappointed. I mentioned
that you and Miss Prism were in the garden. He said he was anxious to
speak to you privately for a moment.

CECILY: Ask Mr. Ernest Worthing to come here. I suppose you had better
talk to the housekeeper about a room for him.   100

MERRIMAN: Yes, Miss.

(MERRIMAN *goes off.*)

CECILY: I have never met any really wicked person before. I feel rather
frightened. I am so afraid he will look just like everyone else.

(*Enter* ALGERNON, *very gay and debonair.*)

He does!

ALGERNON: (*Raising his hat.*) You are my little cousin Cecily, I'm sure.   105

CECILY: You are under some strange mistake. I am not little. In fact, I am
more than usually tall for my age. (ALGERNON *is rather taken aback.*) But

I am your cousin Cecily. You, I see from your card, are Uncle Jack's
brother, my cousin Ernest, my wicked cousin Ernest.

ALGERNON: Oh! I am not really wicked at all, cousin Cecily. You mustn't   110
think that I am wicked.

CECILY: If you are not, then you have certainly been deceiving us all in a
very inexcusable manner. I hope you have not been leading a double life,
pretending to be wicked and being really good all the time. That would
be hypocrisy.   115

ALGERNON: (*Looks at her in amazement.*) Oh! of course I have been rather
reckless.

CECILY: I am glad to hear it.

ALGERNON: In fact, now you mention the subject, I have been very bad in
my own small way.   120

CECILY: I don't think you should be so proud of that, though I am sure it
must have been very pleasant.

ALGERNON: It is much pleasanter being here with you.

CECILY: I can't understand how you are here at all. Uncle Jack won't be
back till Monday afternoon.   125

ALGERNON: That is a great disappointment. I am obliged to go up by the
first train on Monday morning. I have a business appointment that
I am anxious . . . to miss.

CECILY: Couldn't you miss it anywhere but in London?

ALGERNON: No; the appointment is in London.   130

CECILY: Well, I know, of course, how important it is not to keep a business
engagement, if one wants to retain any sense of the beauty of life,
but still I think you had better wait till Uncle Jack arrives. I know he
wants to speak to you about your emigrating.

ALGERNON: About my what?   135

CECILY: Your emigrating. He has gone up to buy your outfit.

ALGERNON: I certainly wouldn't let Jack buy my outfit. He has no taste in
neckties at all.

CECILY: I don't think you will require neckties. Uncle Jack is sending you
to Australia.   140

ALGERNON: Australia! I'd sooner die.

CECILY: Well, he said at dinner on Wednesday night, that you would have
to choose between this world, the next world, and Australia.

ALGERNON: Oh, well! The accounts I have received of Australia and the
next world, are not particularly encouraging. This world is good   145
enough for me, cousin Cecily.

CECILY: Yes, but are you good enough for it?

ALGERNON: I'm afraid I'm not that. That is why I want you to reform
me. You might make that your mission, if you don't mind, cousin
Cecily.   150

CECILY: I'm afraid I've not time, this afternoon.

ALGERNON: Well, would you mind my reforming myself this afternoon?

CECILY: That is rather Quixotic of you. But I think you should try.

ALGERNON: I will. I feel better already.

CECILY: You are looking a little worse.   155

ALGERNON: That is because I am hungry.

CECILY: How thoughtless of me. I should have remembered that when one is going to lead an entirely new life, one requires regular and wholesome meals. Won't you come in?

ALGERNON: Thank you. Might I have a button-hole first? I never have any   160
appetite unless I have a button-hole first.

CECILY: A Maréchal Niel? (*Picks up scissors.*)

ALGERNON: No, I'd sooner have a pink rose.

CECILY: Why? (*Cuts a flower.*)

ALGERNON: Because you are like a pink rose, cousin Cecily.   165

CECILY: I don't think it can be right for you to talk to me like that. Miss Prism never says such things to me.

ALGERNON: Then Miss Prism is a short-sighted old lady. (CECILY *puts the rose in his button-hole.*) You are the prettiest girl I ever saw.

CECILY: Miss Prism says that all good looks are a snare.   170

ALGERNON: They are a snare that every sensible man would like to be caught in.

CECILY: Oh! I don't think I would care to catch a sensible man. I shouldn't know what to talk to him about.

(*They pass into the house.* MISS PRISM *and* DR. CHASUBLE *return.*)

MISS PRISM: You are too much alone, dear Dr. Chasuble. You should get   175
married. A misanthrope I can understand—a womanthrope, never!

CHASUBLE: (*With a scholar's shudder.*) Believe me, I do not deserve so neologistic a phrase. The precept as well as the practice of the Primitive Church was distinctly against matrimony.

MISS PRISM: (*Sententiously.*) That is obviously the reason why the   180
Primitive Church has not lasted up to the present day. And you do not seem to realize, dear Doctor, that by persistently remaining single, a man converts himself into a permanent public temptation. Men should be careful; this very celibacy leads weaker vessels astray.

CHASUBLE: But is a man not equally attractive when married?   185

MISS PRISM: No married man is ever attractive except to his wife.

CHASUBLE: And often, I've been told, not even to her.

MISS PRISM: That depends on the intellectual sympathies of the woman. Maturity can always be depended on. Ripeness can be trusted. Young women are green. (DR. CHASUBLE *starts.*) I spoke horticulturally. My   190
metaphor was drawn from fruits. But where is Cecily?

CHASUBLE: Perhaps she followed us to the schools.

(*Enter* JACK *slowly from the back of the garden. He is dressed in the deepest mourning, with crepe hatband and black gloves.*)

MISS PRISM: Mr. Worthing!

CHASUBLE: Mr. Worthing?

MISS PRISM: This is indeed a surprise. We did not look for you till   195
Monday afternoon.

JACK: (*Shakes* MISS PRISM's *hand in a tragic manner.*) I have returned sooner
than I expected. Dr. Chasuble, I hope you are well?

CHASUBLE: Dear Mr. Worthing, I trust this garb of woe does not betoken
some terrible calamity?   200

JACK: My brother.

MISS PRISM: More shameful debts and extravagance?

CHASUBLE: Still leading his life of pleasure?

JACK: (*Shaking his head.*) Dead!

CHASUBLE: Your brother Ernest dead?   205

JACK: Quite dead.

MISS PRISM: What a lesson for him! I trust he will profit by it.

CHASUBLE: Mr. Worthing, I offer you my sincere condolence. You have
at least the consolation of knowing that you were always the most
generous and forgiving of brothers.   210

JACK: Poor Ernest! He had many faults, but it is a sad, sad blow.

CHASUBLE: Very sad indeed. Were you with him at the end?

JACK: No. He died abroad; in Paris, in fact. I had a telegram last night
from the manager of the Grand Hotel.

CHASUBLE: Was the cause of death mentioned?   215

JACK: A severe chill, it seems.

MISS PRISM: As a man sows, so shall he reap.

CHASUBLE: (*Raising his hand.*) Charity, dear Miss Prism, charity! None of
us are perfect. I myself am peculiarly susceptible to draughts. Will the
interment take place here?   220

JACK: No. He seems to have expressed a desire to be buried in Paris.

CHASUBLE: In Paris! (*Shakes his head.*) I fear that hardly points to any
very serious state of mind at the last. You would no doubt wish me
to make some slight allusion to this tragic domestic affliction next
Sunday. (JACK *presses his hand convulsively.*) My sermon on the meaning   225
of the manna in the wilderness can be adapted to almost any occasion,
joyful, or, as in the present case, distressing. (*All sigh.*) I have preached
it at harvest celebrations, christenings, confirmations, on days of
humiliation and festal days. The last time I delivered it was in the

Cathedral, as a charity sermon on behalf of the Society for the Preven-   230
tion of Discontentment among the Upper Orders. The Bishop, who
was present, was much struck by some of the analogies I drew.

JACK: Ah, that reminds me, you mentioned christenings I think,
Dr. Chasuble? I suppose you know how to christen all right?
(DR. CHASUBLE *looks astounded.*) I mean, of course, you are continually   235
christening, aren't you?

MISS PRISM: It is, I regret to say, one of the Rector's most constant duties
in this parish. I have often spoken to the poorer classes on the subject. But they don't seem to know what thrift is.

CHASUBLE: But is there any particular infant in whom you are interested,   240
Mr. Worthing? Your brother was, I believe, unmarried, was he not?

JACK: Oh, yes.

MISS PRISM: (*Bitterly.*) People who live entirely for pleasure usually are.

JACK: But it is not for any child, dear Doctor. I am very fond of children.
No! the fact is, I would like to be christened myself, this afternoon, if   245
you have nothing better to do.

CHASUBLE: But surely, Mr. Worthing, you have been christened already?

JACK: I don't remember anything about it.

CHASUBLE: But have you any grave doubts on the subject?

JACK: I certainly intend to have. Of course, I don't know if the thing   250
would bother you in any way, or if you think I am a little too old now.

CHASUBLE: Not at all. The sprinkling, and, indeed, the immersion of
adults is a perfectly canonical practice.

JACK: Immersion!

CHASUBLE: You need have no apprehensions. Sprinkling is all that is   255
necessary, or indeed I think advisable. Our weather is so changeable.
At what hour would you wish the ceremony performed?

JACK: Oh, I might trot around about five if that would suit you.

CHASUBLE: Perfectly, perfectly! In fact I have two similar ceremonies to
perform at that time. A case of twins that occurred recently in one of   260
the outlying cottages on your own estate. Poor Jenkins the carter, a
most hard-working man.

JACK: Oh! I don't see much fun in being christened along with other
babies. It would be childish. Would half-past five do?

CHASUBLE: Admirably! Admirably! (*Takes out watch.*) And now, dear   265
Mr. Worthing, I will not intrude any longer into a house of sorrow.
I would merely beg you not to be too much bowed down by grief. What
seem to us bitter trials at the moment are often blessings in disguise.

MISS PRISM: This seems to me a blessing of an extremely obvious kind.

(*Enter* CECILY *from the house.*)

CECILY: Uncle Jack! Oh, I am pleased to see you back. But what horrid   270
clothes you have on! Do go and change them.

MISS PRISM: Cecily!

CHASUBLE: My child! my child! (CECILY *goes towards* JACK; *he kisses her brow
in a melancholy manner.*)

CECILY: What is the matter, Uncle Jack? Do look happy! You look as if you   275
had a toothache and I have such a surprise for you. Who do you think is
in the dining-room? Your brother!

JACK: Who?

CECILY: Your brother Ernest. He arrived about half an hour ago.

JACK: What nonsense! I haven't got a brother.   280

CECILY: Oh, don't say that. However badly he may have behaved to you
in the past he is still your brother. You couldn't be so heartless as to
disown him. I'll tell him to come out. And you will shake hands with
him, won't you, Uncle Jack. (*Runs back into the house.*)

CHASUBLE: These are very joyful tidings.   285

MISS PRISM: After we had all been resigned to his loss, his sudden return
seems to me peculiarly distressing.

JACK: My brother is in the dining-room? I don't know what it all means.
I think it is perfectly absurd.

(*Enter* ALGERNON *and* CECILY *hand in hand. They come slowly up to* JACK.)

JACK: Good heavens! (*Motions* ALGERNON *away.*)   290

ALGERNON: Brother John, I have come down from town to tell you that
I am very sorry for all the trouble I have given you, and that I intend
to lead a better life in the future. (JACK *glares at him and does not take
his hand.*)

CECILY: Uncle Jack, you are not going to refuse your own brother's hand?   295

JACK: Nothing will induce me to take his hand. I think his coming down
here disgraceful. He knows perfectly well why.

CECILY: Uncle Jack, do be nice. There is some good in every-one. Ernest
has just been telling me about his poor invalid friend, Mr. Bunbury,
whom he goes to visit so often. And surely there must be much good   300
in one who is kind to an invalid, and leaves the pleasures of London
to sit by a bed of pain.

JACK: Oh, he has been talking about Bunbury, has he?

CECILY: Yes, he has told me all about poor Mr. Bunbury, and his terrible
state of health.   305

JACK: Bunbury! Well, I won't have him talk to you about Bunbury or
about anything else. It is enough to drive one perfectly frantic.

ALGERNON: Of course I admit that the faults were all on my side. But I
must say that I think that Brother John's coldness to me is peculiarly

painful. I expected a more enthusiastic welcome, especially considering   310
it is the first time I have come here.

CECILY: Uncle Jack, if you don't shake hands with Ernest I will never
forgive you.

JACK: Never forgive me?

CECILY: Never, never, never!   315

JACK: Well, this is the last time I shall ever do it. (*Shakes hands with*
ALGERNON *and glares.*)

CHASUBLE: It's pleasant, is it not, to see so perfect a reconciliation? I think
we might leave the two brothers together.

MISS PRISM: Cecily, you will come with us.   320

CECILY: Certainly, Miss Prism. My little task of reconciliation is over.

CHASUBLE: You have done a beautiful action to-day, dear child.

MISS PRISM: We must not be premature in our judgments.

CECILY: I feel very happy. (*They all go off.*)

JACK: You young scoundrel, Algy, you must get out of this place as soon   325
as possible. I don't allow any Bunburying here.

(*Enter* MERRIMAN.)

MERRIMAN: I have put Mr. Ernest's things in the room next to yours, sir.
I suppose that is all right?

JACK: What?

MERRIMAN: Mr. Ernest's luggage, sir. I have unpacked it and put it in the   330
room next to your own.

JACK: His luggage?

MERRIMAN: Yes, sir. Three portmanteaus, a dressing-case, two hat-boxes,
and a large luncheon-basket.

ALGERNON: I am afraid I can't stay more than a week this time.   335

JACK: Merriman, order the dog-cart at once. Mr. Ernest has been suddenly
called back to town.

MERRIMAN: Yes, sir. (*Goes back into the house.*)

ALGERNON: What a fearful liar you are, Jack. I have not been called back
to town at all.   340

JACK: Yes, you have.

ALGERNON: I haven't heard anyone call me.

JACK: Your duty as a gentleman calls you back.

ALGERNON: My duty as a gentleman has never interfered with my
pleasures in the smallest degree.   345

JACK: I can quite understand that.

ALGERNON: Well, Cecily is a darling.

JACK: You are not to talk of Miss Cardew like that. I don't like it.

ALGERNON: Well, I don't like your clothes. You look perfectly ridiculous
in them. Why on earth don't you go up and change? It is perfectly   350
childish to be in deep mourning for a man who is actually staying for
a whole week with you in your house as a guest. I call it grotesque.

JACK: You are certainly not staying with me for a whole week as a guest or
anything else. You have got to leave . . . by the four-five train.

ALGERNON: I certainly won't leave you so long as you are in mourning.   355
It would be most unfriendly. If I were in mourning you would stay
with me, I suppose. I should think it very unkind if you didn't.

JACK: Well, will you go if I change my clothes?

ALGERNON: Yes, if you are not too long. I never saw anybody take so long
to dress, and with such little result.   360

JACK: Well, at any rate, that is better than being always over-dressed as
you are.

ALGERNON: If I am occasionally a little over-dressed, I make up for it by
being always immensely over-educated.

JACK: Your vanity is ridiculous, your conduct an outrage, and your   365
presence in my garden utterly absurd. However, you have got to catch
the four-five, and I hope you will have a pleasant journey back to town.
This Bunburying, as you call it, has not been a great success for you.
(*Goes into the house.*)

ALGERNON: I think it has been a great success. I'm in love with Cecily,   370
and that is everything. (*Enter* CECILY *at the back of the garden. She picks
up the can and begins to water the flowers.*) But I must see her before I go,
and make arrangements for another Bunbury. Ah, there she is.

CECILY: Oh, I merely came back to water the roses. I thought you were
with Uncle Jack.   375

ALGERNON: He's gone to order the dog-cart for me.

CECILY: Oh, is he going to take you for a nice drive?

ALGERNON: He's going to send me away.

CECILY: Then have we got to part?

ALGERNON: I am afraid so. It's a very painful parting.   380

CECILY: It is always painful to part from people whom one has known for
a very brief space of time. The absence of old friends one can endure
with equanimity. But even a momentary separation from anyone to
whom one has just been introduced is almost unbearable.

ALGERNON: Thank you.   385

(*Enter* MERRIMAN.)

MERRIMAN: The dog-cart is at the door, sir. (ALGERNON *looks appealingly
at* CECILY.)

CECILY: It can wait, Merriman . . . for . . . five minutes.

MERRIMAN: Yes, miss.

(*Exit* MERRIMAN.)

ALGERNON: I hope, Cecily, I shall not offend you if I state quite frankly and   390
openly that you seem to me to be in every way the visible personification
of absolute perfection.

CECILY: I think your frankness does you great credit, Ernest. If you will
allow me I will copy your remarks into my diary. (*Goes over to table and
begins writing in diary.*)   395

ALGERNON: Do you really keep a diary? I'd give any thing to look at it.
May I?

CECILY: Oh, no. (*Puts her hand over it.*) You see, it is simply a very young
girl's record of her own thoughts and impressions, and consequently
meant for publication. When it appears in volume form I hope you   400
will order a copy. But pray, Ernest, don't stop. I delight in taking
down from dictation. I have reached "absolute perfection." You can
go on. I am quite ready for more.

ALGERNON: (*Somewhat taken aback.*) Ahem! Ahem!

CECILY: Oh, don't cough, Ernest. When one is dictating one should   405
speak fluently and not cough. Besides, I don't know how to spell a
cough. (*Writes as* ALGERNON *speaks.*)

ALGERNON: (*Speaking very rapidly.*) Cecily, ever since I first looked upon
your wonderful and incomparable beauty, I have dared to love you
wildly, passionately, devotedly, hopelessly.   410

CECILY: I don't think that you should tell me that you love me wildly,
passionately, devotedly, hopelessly. Hopelessly doesn't seem to make
much sense, does it?

ALGERNON: Cecily!

(*Enter* MERRIMAN.)

MERRIMAN: The dog-cart is waiting, sir.   415

ALGERNON: Tell it to come round next week, at the same hour.

MERRIMAN: (*Looks at* CECILY, *who makes no sign.*) Yes, sir.

(MERRIMAN *retires.*)

CECILY: Uncle Jack would be very much annoyed if he knew you were
staying on till next week, at the same hour.

ALGERNON: Oh, I don't care about Jack. I don't care for anybody in   420
the whole world but you. I love you, Cecily. You will marry me,
won't you?

CECILY: You silly you! Of course. Why, we have been engaged for the last
three months.

ALGERNON: For the last three months?   425

CECILY: Yes, it will be exactly three months on Thursday.

ALGERNON: But how did we become engaged?

CECILY: Well, ever since dear Uncle Jack first confessed to us that he
    had a younger brother who was very wicked and bad, you of course
    have formed the chief topic of conversation between myself and   430
    Miss Prism. And of course a man who is much talked about is always
    very attractive. One feels there must be something in him after all.
    I daresay it was foolish of me, but I fell in love with you, Ernest.

ALGERNON: Darling! And when was the engagement actually settled?

CECILY: On the 14th of February last. Worn out by your entire ignorance of   435
    my existence, I determined to end the matter one way or the other, and
    after a long struggle with myself I accepted you under this dear old tree
    here. The next day I bought this little ring in your name, and this is the
    little bangle with the true lovers' knot I promised you always to wear.

ALGERNON: Did I give you this? It's very pretty, isn't it?   440

CECILY: Yes, you've wonderfully good taste, Ernest. It's the excuse I've
    always given for your leading such a bad life. And this is the box
    in which I keep all your dear letters. (*Kneels at table, opens box, and
    produces letters tied up with blue ribbon.*)

ALGERNON: My letters! But my own sweet Cecily, I have never written you   445
    any letters.

CECILY: You need hardly remind me of that, Ernest. I remember only too
    well that I was forced to write your letters for you. I wrote always three
    times a week, and sometimes oftener.

ALGERNON: Oh, do let me read them, Cecily?   450

CECILY: Oh, I couldn't possibly. They would make you far too conceited.
    (*Replaces box.*) The three you wrote me after I had broken off the
    engagement are so beautiful, and so badly spelled, that even now I can
    hardly read them without crying a little.

ALGERNON: But was our engagement ever broken off?   455

CECILY: Of course it was. On the 22nd of last March. You can see the entry
    if you like. (*Shows diary.*) "Today I broke off my engagement with Ernest.
    I feel it is better to do so. The weather still continues charming."

ALGERNON: But why on earth did you break it off? What had I done?   460
    I had done nothing at all. Cecily, I am very much hurt indeed to hear
    you broke it off. Particularly when the weather was so charming.

CECILY: It would hardly have been a really serious engagement if it
    hadn't been broken off at least once. But I forgave you before the
    week was out.   465

ALGERNON: (*Crossing to her, and kneeling.*) What a perfect angel you
    are, Cecily.

CECILY: You dear romantic boy. (*He kisses her, she puts her fingers through his hair.*) I hope your hair curls naturally, does it?

ALGERNON: Yes, darling, with a little help from others.   470

CECILY: I am so glad.

ALGERNON: You'll never break off our engagement again, Cecily?

CECILY: I don't think I could break it off now that I have actually met you. Besides, of course, that is the question of your name.

ALGERNON: Yes, of course. (*Nervously.*)   475

CECILY: You must not laugh at me, darling, but it had always been a girl-ish dream of mine to love some one whose name was Ernest. (ALGER-NON *rises,* CECILY *also.*) There is something in that name that seems to inspire absolute confidence. I pity any poor married woman whose husband is not called Ernest.   480

ALGERNON: But, my dear child, do you mean to say you could not love me if I had some other name?

CECILY: But what name?

ALGERNON: Oh, any name you like—Algernon, for instance. . . .

CECILY: But I don't like the name of Algernon.   485

ALGERNON: Well, my own dear, sweet, loving little darling, I really can't see why you should object to the name of Algernon. It is not at all a bad name. In fact, it is rather an aristocratic name. Half of the chaps who get into the Bankruptcy Court are called Algernon. But seriously, Cecily . . . (*Moving to her.*) . . . if my name was Algy, couldn't you love me?   490

CECILY: I might respect you, Ernest, I might admire your character, but I fear that I should not be able to give you my undivided attention.

ALGERNON: Ahem! Cecily! (*Picking up hat.*) Your Rector here is, I suppose, thoroughly experienced in the practice of all the rites and ceremonials of the church?   495

CECILY: Oh, yes. Dr. Chasuble is a most learned man. He has never written a single book, so you can imagine how much he knows.

ALGERNON: I must see him at once on a most important christening—I mean on most important business.

CECILY: Oh!   500

ALGERNON: I sha'n't be away more than half an hour.

CECILY: Considering that we have been engaged since February the 14th, and that I only met you to-day for the first time, I think it is rather hard that you should leave me for so long a period as half an hour. Couldn't you make it twenty minutes?   505

ALGERNON: I'll be back in no time. (*Kisses her and rushes down the garden.*)

CECILY: What an impetuous boy he is. I like his hair so much. I must enter his proposal in my diary.

(*Enter* MERRIMAN.)

MERRIMAN: A Miss Fairfax has just called to see Mr. Worthing. On very
important business, Miss Fairfax states.   510

CECILY: Isn't Mr. Worthing in his library?

MERRIMAN: Mr. Worthing went over in the direction of the Rectory some
time ago.

CECILY: Pray ask the lady to come out here; Mr. Worthing is sure to be
back soon. And you can bring tea.   515

MERRIMAN: Yes, miss.

(Goes out.)

CECILY: Miss Fairfax! I suppose one of the many good elderly women who
are associated with Uncle Jack in some of his philanthropic work in
London. I don't quite like women who are interested in philanthropic
work. I think it is so forward of them.   520

(Enter MERRIMAN.*)*

MERRIMAN: Miss Fairfax.

(Enter GWENDOLEN. *Exit* MERRIMAN.*)*

CECILY: *(Advancing to meet her.)* Pray let me introduce myself to you.
My name is Cecily Cardew.

GWENDOLEN: Cecily Cardew? *(Moving to her and shaking hands.)* What a very
sweet name! Something tells me that we are going to be great friends.   525
I like you already more than I can say. My first impressions of people are
never wrong.

CECILY: How nice of you to like me so much after we have known each
other such a comparatively short time. Pray sit down.

GWENDOLEN: *(Still standing up.)* I may call you Cecily, may I not?   530

CECILY: With pleasure!

GWENDOLEN: And you will always call me Gwendolen, won't you?

CECILY: If you wish.

GWENDOLEN: Then that is all quite settled, is it not?

CECILY: I hope so. *(A pause. They both sit down together.)*   535

GWENDOLEN: Perhaps this might be a favorable opportunity for my
mentioning who I am. My father is Lord Bracknell. You have never
heard of papa, I suppose?

CECILY: I don't think so.

GWENDOLEN: Outside the family circle, papa, I am glad to say, is entirely   540
unknown. I think that is quite as it should be. The home seems to me
to be the proper sphere for the man. And certainly once a man begins
to neglect his domestic duties he becomes painfully effeminate, does
he not? And I don't like that. It makes men so very attractive. Cecily,

mamma, whose views on education are remarkably strict, has brought   545
me up to be extremely short-sighted; it is part of her system; so do you
mind my looking at you through my glasses?

CECILY: Oh, not at all, Gwendolen. I am very fond of being looked at.

GWENDOLEN: (*After examining* CECILY *carefully through a lorgnette.*) You are
here on a short visit, I suppose.   550

CECILY: Oh, no, I live here.

GWENDOLEN: (*Severely.*) Really? Your mother, no doubt, or some female
relative of advanced years, resides here also?

CECILY: Oh, no. I have no mother, nor, in fact, any relations.

GWENDOLEN: Indeed?   555

CECILY: My dear guardian, with the assistance of Miss Prism, has the
arduous task of looking after me.

GWENDOLEN: Your guardian?

CECILY: Yes, I am Mr. Worthing's ward.

GWENDOLEN: Oh! It is strange he never mentioned to me that he had a   560
ward. How secretive of him! He grows more interesting hourly. I am
not sure, however, that the news inspires me with feelings of unmixed
delight. (*Rising and going to her.*) I am very fond of you, Cecily; I have
liked you ever since I met you. But I am bound to state that now that
I know that you are Mr. Worthing's ward, I cannot help expressing a   565
wish you were—well, just a little older than you seem to be—and not
quite so very alluring in appearance. In fact, if I may speak candidly—

CECILY: Pray do! I think that whenever one has anything unpleasant to
say, one should always be quite candid.

GWENDOLEN: Well, to speak with perfect candour, Cecily, I wish that you   570
were fully forty-two, and more than usually plain for your age. Ernest
has a strong upright nature. He is the very soul of truth and honour.
Disloyalty would be as impossible to him as deception. But even men
of the noblest possible moral character are extremely susceptible
to the influence of the physical charms of others. Modern, no less   575
than Ancient History, supplies us with many most painful examples
of what I refer to. If it were not so, indeed, History would be quite
unreadable.

CECILY: I beg your pardon, Gwendolen, did you say Ernest?

GWENDOLEN: Yes.   580

CECILY: Oh, but it is not Mr. Ernest Worthing who is my guardian. It is
his brother—his elder brother.

GWENDOLEN: (*Sitting down again.*) Ernest never mentioned to me that he
had a brother.

CECILY: I am sorry to say they have not been on good terms for a   585
long time.

GWENDOLEN: Ah! that accounts for it. And now that I think of it I have never heard any man mention his brother. The subject seems distasteful to most men. Cecily, you have lifted a load from my mind. I was growing almost anxious. It would have been terrible if any cloud had come across 590 a friendship like ours, would it not? Of course you are quite, quite sure that it is not Mr. Ernest Worthing who is your guardian?

CECILY: Quite sure. (*A pause.*) In fact, I am going to be his.

GWENDOLEN: (*Enquiringly.*) I beg your pardon?

CECILY: (*Rather shy and confidingly.*) Dearest Gwendolen, there is no reason 595 why I should make a secret of it to you. Our little county newspaper is sure to chronicle the fact next week. Mr. Ernest Worthing and I are engaged to be married.

GWENDOLEN: (*Quite politely, rising.*) My darling Cecily, I think there must be some slight error. Mr. Ernest Worthing is engaged to me. The 600 announcement will appear in the *Morning Post* on Saturday at the latest.

CECILY: (*Very politely, rising.*) I am afraid you must be under some misconception. Ernest proposed to me exactly ten minutes ago. (*Shows diary.*)

GWENDOLEN: (*Examines diary through her lorgnette carefully.*) It is certainly very curious, for he asked me to be his wife yesterday afternoon at 605 5:30. If you would care to verify the incident, pray do so. (*Produces diary of her own.*) I never travel without my diary. One should always have something sensational to read in the train. I am so sorry, dear Cecily, if it is any disappointment to you, but I am afraid *I* have the prior claim. 610

CECILY: It would distress me more than I can tell you, dear Gwendolen, if it caused you any mental or physical anguish, but I feel bound to point out that since Ernest proposed to you he clearly has changed his mind.

GWENDOLEN: (*Meditatively.*) If the poor fellow has been entrapped into 615 any foolish promise I shall consider it my duty to rescue him at once, and with a firm hand.

CECILY: (*Thoughtfully and sadly.*) Whatever unfortunate entanglement my dear boy may have got into, I will never reproach him with it after we are married. 620

GWENDOLEN: Do you allude to me, Miss Cardew, as an entanglement? You are presumptuous. On an occasion of this kind it becomes more than a moral duty to speak one's mind. It becomes a pleasure.

CECILY: Do you suggest, Miss Fairfax, that I entrapped Ernest into an engagement? How dare you? This is no time for wearing the shallow 625 mask of manners. When I see a spade I call it a spade.

GWENDOLEN: (*Satirically.*) I am glad to say that I have never seen a spade. It is obvious that our social spheres have been widely different.

(*Enter* MERRIMAN, *followed by the footman. He carries a salver, tablecloth, and plate-stand.* CECILY *is about to retort. The presence of the servants exercises a restraining influence, under which both girls chafe.*)

MERRIMAN: Shall I lay tea here as usual, miss?

CECILY: (*Sternly, in a calm voice.*) Yes, as usual. (MERRIMAN *begins to clear and lay*   630
cloth. *A long pause.* CECILY *and* GWENDOLEN *glare at each other.*)

GWENDOLEN: Are there many interesting walks in the vicinity, Miss Cardew?

CECILY: Oh, yes, a great many. From the top of one of the hills quite close
one can see five counties.

GWENDOLEN: Five counties! I don't think I should like that. I hate crowds.   635

CECILY: (*Sweetly.*) I suppose that is why you live in town? (GWENDOLEN *bites
her lip, and beats her foot nervously with her parasol.*)

GWENDOLEN: (*Looking around.*) Quite a well-kept garden this is,
Miss Cardew.

CECILY: So glad you like it, Miss Fairfax.   640

GWENDOLEN: I had no idea there were any flowers in the country.

CECILY: Oh, flowers are as common here, Miss Fairfax, as people are
in London.

GWENDOLEN: Personally I cannot understand how anybody manages to
exist in the country, if anybody who is anybody does. The country   645
always bores me to death.

CECILY: Ah! This is what the newspapers call agricultural depression, is
it not? I believe the aristocracy are suffering very much from it just at
present. It is almost an epidemic amongst them, I have been told. May
I offer you some tea, Miss Fairfax?   650

GWENDOLEN: (*With elaborate politeness.*) Thank you. (*Aside.*) Detestable girl!
But I require tea!

CECILY: (*Sweetly.*) Sugar?

GWENDOLEN: (*Superciliously.*) No, thank you. Sugar is not fashionable any
more. (CECILY *looks angrily at her, takes up the tongs and puts four lumps of*   655
sugar into the cup.)

CECILY: (*Severely.*) Cake or bread and butter?

GWENDOLEN: (*In a bored manner.*) Bread and butter, please. Cake is rarely
seen at the best houses nowadays.

CECILY: (*Cuts a very large slice of cake, and puts it on the tray.*) Hand that to   660
Miss Fairfax. (MERRIMAN *does so, and goes out with footman.* GWENDOLEN
*drinks the tea and makes a grimace. Puts down cup at once, reaches out
her hand to the bread and butter, looks at it, and finds it is cake. Rises
in indignation.*)

GWENDOLEN: You have filled my tea with lumps of sugar, and though   665
I asked most distinctly for bread and butter, you have given me cake.

I am known for the gentleness of my disposition, and the extraordinary sweetness of my nature, but I warn you, Miss Cardew, you may go too far.

CECILY: (*Rising.*) To save my poor, innocent, trusting boy from the machina- 670
tions of any other girl there are no lengths to which I would not go.

GWENDOLEN: From the moment I saw you I distrusted you. I felt that you were false and deceitful. I am never deceived in such matters. My first impressions of people are invariably right.

CECILY: It seems to me, Miss Fairfax, that I am trespassing on your valuable 675
time. No doubt you have many other calls of a similar character to make in the neighbourhood.

(*Enter* JACK.)

GWENDOLEN: (*Catching sight of him.*) Ernest! My own Ernest!

JACK: Gwendolen! Darling! (*Offers to kiss her.*)

GWENDOLEN: (*Drawing back.*) A moment! May I ask if you are engaged to be 680
married to this young lady? (*Points to* CECILY.)

JACK: (*Laughing.*) To dear little Cecily! Of course not! What could have put such an idea into your pretty little head?

GWENDOLEN: Thank you. You may. (*Offers her cheek.*)

CECILY: (*Very sweetly.*) I knew there must be some misunderstanding, Miss 685
Fairfax. The gentleman whose arm is at present around your waist is my dear guardian, Mr. John Worthing.

GWENDOLEN: I beg your pardon?

CECILY: This is Uncle Jack.

GWENDOLEN: (*Receding.*) Jack! Oh! 690

(*Enter* ALGERNON.)

CECILY: Here is Ernest.

ALGERNON: (*Goes straight over to* CECILY *without noticing anyone else.*) My own love! (*Offers to kiss her.*)

CECILY: (*Drawing back.*) A moment, Ernest! May I ask you—are you 695
engaged to be married to this young lady?

ALGERNON: (*Looking round.*) To what young lady? Good heavens! Gwendolen!

CECILY: Yes, to good heavens, Gwendolen, I mean to Gwendolen.

ALGERNON: (*Laughing.*) Of course not! What could have put such an idea into your pretty little head? 700

CECILY: Thank you. (*Presenting her cheek to be kissed.*) You may. (ALGERNON *kisses her.*)

GWENDOLEN: I felt there was some slight error, Miss Cardew. The gentleman who is now embracing you is my cousin, Mr. Algernon Moncrieff.

CECILY: (*Breaking away from* ALGERNON.) Algernon Moncrieff! Oh! (*The two*   705
girls *move towards each other and put their arms round each other's waists as*
if for protection.)

CECILY: Are you called Algernon?

ALGERNON: I cannot deny it.

CECILY: Oh!   710

GWENDOLEN: Is your name really John?

JACK: (*Standing rather proudly.*) I could deny it if I liked. I could deny
anything if I liked. But my name certainly is John. It has been John
for years.

CECILY: (*To* GWENDOLEN.) A gross deception has been practiced on both   715
of us.

GWENDOLEN: My poor wounded Cecily!

CECILY: My sweet, wronged Gwendolen!

GWENDOLEN: (*Slowing and seriously.*) You will call me sister, will you not?
(*They embrace.* JACK *and* ALGERNON *groan and walk up and down.*)   720

CECILY: (*Rather brightly.*) There is just one question I would like to be
allowed to ask my guardian.

GWENDOLEN: An admirable idea! Mr. Worthing, there is just one
question I would like to be permitted to put to you. Where is your
brother Ernest? We are both engaged to be married to your brother   725
Ernest, so it is a matter of some importance to us to know where
your brother Ernest is at present.

JACK: (*Slowly and hesitatingly.*) Gwendolen—Cecily—it is very painful for me
to be forced to speak the truth. It is the first time in my life that I have
ever been reduced to such a painful position, and I am really quite   730
inexperienced in doing anything of the kind. However I will tell you
quite frankly that I have no brother Ernest. I have no brother at all.
I never had a brother in my life, and I certainly have not the smallest
intention of ever having one in the future.

CECILY: (*Surprised.*) No brother at all?   735

JACK: (*Cheerily.*) None!

GWENDOLEN: (*Severely.*) Had you never a brother of any kind?

JACK: (*Pleasantly.*) Never. Not even of any kind.

GWENDOLEN: I am afraid it is quite clear, Cecily, that neither of us is
engaged to be married to anyone.   740

CECILY: It is not a very pleasant position for a young girl suddenly to find
herself in. Is it?

GWENDOLEN: Let us go into the house. They will hardly venture to come
after us there.

CECILY: No, men are so cowardly, aren't they? (*They retire into the house*   745
with scornful looks.)

JACK: This ghastly state of things is what you call Bunburying, I suppose?

ALGERNON: Yes, and a perfectly wonderful Bunbury it is. The most wonderful
Bunbury I have ever had in my life.

JACK: Well, you've no right whatsoever to Bunbury here. 750

ALGERNON: That is absurd. One has a right to Bunbury anywhere one
chooses. Every serious Bunburyist knows that.

JACK: Serious Bunburyist! Good heavens!

ALGERNON: Well, one must be serious about something, if one wants to
have any amusement in life. I happen to be serious about Bunburying. 755
What on earth you are serious about I haven't got the remotest idea.
About everything, I should fancy. You have such an absolutely trivial
nature.

JACK: Well, the only small satisfaction I have in the whole of this
wretched business is that your friend Bunbury is quite exploded. You 760
won't be able to run down to the country quite so often as you used
to do, dear Algy. And a very good thing, too.

ALGERNON: Your brother is a little off colour, isn't he, dear Jack? You
won't be able to disappear to London quite so frequently as your
wicked custom was. And not a bad thing, either. 765

JACK: As for your conduct towards Miss Cardew, I must say that your
taking in a sweet, simple, innocent girl like that is quite inexcusable.
To say nothing of the fact that she is my ward.

ALGERNON: I can see no possible defence at all for your deceiving a
brilliant, clever, thoroughly experienced young lady like Miss Fairfax. 770
To say nothing of the fact that she is my cousin.

JACK: I wanted to be engaged to Gwendolen, that is all. I love her.

ALGERNON: Well, I simply wanted to be engaged to Cecily. I adore her.

JACK: There is certainly no chance of your marrying Miss Cardew.

ALGERNON: I don't think there is much likelihood, Jack, of you and 775
Miss Fairfax being united.

JACK: Well, that is no business of yours.

ALGERNON: If it was my business, I wouldn't talk about it. (*Begins to eat
muffins.*) It is very vulgar to talk about one's business. Only people
like stock-brokers do that, and then merely at dinner parties. 780

JACK: How you can sit there, calmly eating muffins, when we are in this
horrible trouble, I can't make out. You seem to me to be perfectly
heartless.

ALGERNON: Well, I can't eat muffins in an agitated manner. The butter
would probably get on my cuffs. One should always eat muffins quite 785
calmly. It is the only way to eat them.

JACK: I say it's perfectly heartless your eating muffins at all, under the
circumstances.

ALGERNON: When I am in trouble, eating is the only thing that consoles
me. Indeed, when I am in really great trouble, as anyone who knows 790
me intimately will tell you, I refuse everything except food and drink.
At the present moment I am eating muffins because I am unhappy.
Besides, I am particularly fond of muffins. (*Rising.*)

JACK: (*Rising.*) Well, that is no reason why you should eat them all in that
greedy way. (*Takes muffin from* ALGERNON.) 795

ALGERNON: (*Offering tea-cake.*) I wish you would have tea-cake instead.
I don't like tea-cake.

JACK: Good heavens! I suppose a man may eat his own muffins in
his own garden.

ALGERNON: But you have just said it was perfectly heartless to eat 800
muffins.

JACK: I said it was perfectly heartless of you, under the circumstances.
That is a very different thing.

ALGERNON: That may be. But the muffins are the same. (*He seizes the
muffin dish from* JACK.) 805

JACK: Algy, I wish to goodness you would go.

ALGERNON: You can't possibly ask me to go without having some dinner.
It's absurd. I never go without my dinner. No one ever does, except
vegetarians and people like that. Besides I have just made arrangements with Dr. Chasuble to be christened at a quarter to six under 810
the name of Ernest.

JACK: My dear fellow, the sooner you give up that nonsense the better.
I made arrangements this morning with Dr. Chasuble to be christened
myself at 5:30, and I naturally will take the name of Ernest. Gwendolen
would wish it. We can't both be christened Ernest. It's absurd. 815
Besides, I have a perfect right to be christened if I like. There is no
evidence at all that I ever have been christened by any-body. I should
think it extremely probable I never was, and so does Dr. Chasuble. It
is entirely different in your case. You have been christened already.

ALGERNON: Yes, but I have not been christened for years. 820

JACK: Yes, but you have been christened. That is the important thing.

ALGERNON: Quite so. So I know my constitution can stand it. If you are
not quite sure about your ever having been christened, I must say I
think it rather dangerous your venturing on it now. It might make you
very unwell. You can hardly have forgotten that someone very closely 825
connected with you was very nearly carried off this week in Paris by a
severe chill.

JACK: Yes, but you said yourself that a severe chill was not hereditary.

ALGERNON: It usedn't to be, I know—but I daresay it is now. Science is
always making wonderful improvements in things. 830

JACK: (*Picking up the muffin-dish.*) Oh, that is nonsense; you are always talking nonsense.

ALGERNON: Jack, you are at the muffins again! I wish you wouldn't. There are only two left. (*Takes them.*) I told you I was particularly fond of muffins. 835

JACK: But I hate tea-cake.

ALGERNON: Why on earth then do you allow tea-cake to be served up for your guests? What ideas you have of hospitality!

JACK: Algernon! I have already told you to go. I don't want you here. Why don't you go? 840

ALGERNON: I haven't quite finished my tea yet, and there is still one muffin left. (JACK *groans, and sinks into a chair.* ALGERNON *still continues eating.*)

ACT THREE

Morning-room at the Manor House. GWENDOLEN *and* CECILY *are at the window, looking out into the garden.*

GWENDOLEN: The fact that they did not follow us at once into the house, as anyone else would have done, seems to me to show that they have some sense of shame left.

CECILY: They have been eating muffins. That looks like repentance.

GWENDOLEN: (*After a pause.*) They don't seem to notice us at all. Couldn't 5 you cough?

GWENDOLEN: They're looking at us. What effrontery!

CECILY: They're approaching. That's very forward of them.

GWENDOLEN: Let us preserve a dignified silence.

CECILY: Certainly. It's the only thing to do now. 10

(*Enter* JACK, *followed by* ALGERNON. *They whistle some dreadful popular air from a British opera.*)

GWENDOLEN: This dignified silence seems to produce an unpleasant effect.

CECILY: A most distasteful one.

GWENDOLEN: But we will not be the first to speak.

CECILY: Certainly not.

GWENDOLEN: Mr. Worthing, I have something very particular to ask you. 15 Much depends on your reply.

CECILY: Gwendolen, your common sense is invaluable. Mr. Moncrieff, kindly answer me the following question. Why did you pretend to be my guardian's brother?

ALGERNON: In order that I might have an opportunity of meeting you. 20

CECILY: (*To* GWENDOLEN.) That certainly seems a satisfactory explanation, does it not?

GWENDOLEN: Yes, dear, if you can believe him.

CECILY: I don't. But that does not affect the wonderful beauty of his answer. 25

GWENDOLEN: True. In matters of grave importance, style, not sincerity, is the vital thing. Mr. Worthing, what explanation can you offer to me for pretending to have a brother? Was it in order that you might have an opportunity of coming up to town to see me as often as possible?

JACK: Can you doubt it, Miss Fairfax? 30

GWENDOLEN: I have the gravest doubts upon the subject. But I intend to crush them. This is not the moment for German skepticism. (*Moving to* CECILY.) Their explanations appear to be quite satisfactory, especially Mr. Worthing's. That seems to me to have the stamp of truth upon it.

CECILY: I am more than content with what Mr. Moncrieff said. His voice alone inspires one with absolute credulity. 35

GWENDOLEN: Then you think we should forgive them?

CECILY: Yes. I mean no.

GWENDOLEN: True! I had forgotten. There are principles at stake that one cannot surrender. Which of us should tell them? The task is not a pleasant one. 40

CECILY: Could we not both speak at the same time?

GWENDOLEN: An excellent idea! I nearly always speak at the same time as other people. Will you take the time from me?

CECILY: Certainly. (GWENDOLEN *beats time with uplifted finger.*) 45

GWENDOLEN *and* CECILY: (*Speaking together.*) Your Christian names are still an insuperable barrier. That is all!

JACK *and* ALGERNON: (*Speaking together.*) Our Christian names! Is that all? But we are going to be christened this afternoon.

GWENDOLEN: (*To* JACK.) For my sake you are prepared to do this terrible thing? 50

JACK: I am.

CECILY: (*To* ALGERNON.) To please me you are ready to face this fearful ordeal?

ALGERNON: I am! 55

GWENDOLEN: How absurd to talk of the equality of the sexes! Where questions of self-sacrifice are concerned, men are infinitely beyond us.

JACK: We are. (*Clasps hands with* ALGERNON.)

CECILY: They have moments of physical courage of which we women know absolutely nothing. 60

GWENDOLEN: (*To* JACK.) Darling!

ALGERNON: (*To* CECILY.) Darling! (*They fall into each other's arms.*)

(Enter MERRIMAN. *When he enters he coughs loudly, seeing the situation.)*

MERRIMAN: Ahem! Ahem! Lady Bracknell!

JACK: Good heavens!

(Enter LADY BRACKNELL. *The couples separate in alarm. Exit* MERRIMAN.)

LADY BRACKNELL: Gwendolen! What does this mean?   65

GWENDOLEN: Merely that I am engaged to be married to Mr. Worthing, Mamma.

LADY BRACKNELL: Come here. Sit down. Sit down immediately. Hesitation of any kind is a sign of mental decay in the young, of physical weakness in the old. *(Turns to* JACK.) Apprised, sir, of my daughter's sudden flight   70
by her trusty maid, whose confidence I purchased by means of a small coin, I followed her at once by a luggage train. Her unhappy father is, I am glad to say, under the impression that she is attending a more than usually lengthy lecture by the University Extension Scheme on the Influence of a Permanent Income on Thought. I do not propose to   75
undeceive him. Indeed I have never undeceived him on any question. I would consider it wrong. But of course, you will clearly understand that all communication between yourself and my daughter must cease immediately from this moment. On this point, as indeed on all points, I am firm.   80

JACK: I am engaged to be married to Gwendolen, Lady Bracknell!

LADY BRACKNELL: You are nothing of the kind, sir. And now, as regards Algernon! . . . Algernon!

ALGERNON: Yes, Aunt Augusta.

LADY BRACKNELL: May I ask if it is in this house that your invalid friend   85
Mr. Bunbury resides?

ALGERNON: *(Stammering.)* Oh, no! Bunbury doesn't live here. Bunbury is somewhere else at present. In fact, Bunbury is dead.

LADY BRACKNELL: Dead! When did Mr. Bunbury die? His death must have been extremely sudden.   90

ALGERNON: *(Airily.)* Oh, I killed Bunbury this afternoon. I mean poor Bunbury died this afternoon.

LADY BRACKNELL: What did he die of?

ALGERNON: Bunbury? Oh, he was quite exploded.

LADY BRACKNELL: Exploded! Was he the victim of a revolutionary outrage?   95
I was not aware that Mr. Bunbury was interested in social legislation. If so, he is well punished for his morbidity.

ALGERNON: My dear Aunt Augusta, I mean he was found out! The doctors found out that Bunbury could not live, that is what I mean—so Bunbury died.   100

LADY BRACKNELL: He seems to have had great confidence in the opinion of his physicians. I am glad, however, that he made up his mind at the last to some definite course of action, and acted under proper medical advice. And now that we have finally got rid of this Mr. Bunbury, may I ask, Mr. Worthing, who is that young person whose hand my   105
nephew Algernon is now holding in what seems to me a peculiarly unnecessary manner?

JACK: That lady is Miss Cecily Cardew, my ward. (LADY BRACKNELL *bows coldly to* CECILY.)

ALGERNON: I am engaged to be married to Cecily, Aunt Augusta.   110

LADY BRACKNELL: I beg your pardon?

CECILY: Mr. Moncrieff and I are engaged to be married, lady Bracknell.

LADY BRACKNELL: (*With a shiver, crossing to the sofa and sitting down.*) I do not know whether there is anything peculiarly exciting in the air of this particular part of Hertfordshire, but the number of engagements   115
that go on seems to me considerably above the proper average that statistics have laid down for our guidance. I think some preliminary enquiry on my part would not be out of place. Mr. Worthing, is Miss Cardew at all connected with any of the larger railway stations in London? I merely desire information. Until yesterday I had no idea   120
that there were any families or persons whose origin was a Terminus. (JACK *looks perfectly furious, but restrains himself.*)

JACK: (*In a clear, cold voice.*) Miss Cardew is the granddaughter of the late Mr. Thomas Cardew of 149, Belgrave Square, S.W.; Gervase Park, Dorking, Surrey; and the Sporran, Fifeshire, N.B.   125

LADY BRACKNELL: That sounds not unsatisfactory. Three addresses always inspire confidence, even in tradesmen. But what proof have I of their authenticity?

JACK: I have carefully preserved the Court Guide of the period. They are open to your inspection, Lady Bracknell.   130

LADY BRACKNELL: (*Grimly.*) I have known strange errors in that publication.

JACK: Miss Cardew's family solicitors are Messrs. Markby, Markby, and Markby.

LADY BRACKNELL: Markby, Markby, and Markby? A firm of the very highest position in their profession. Indeed I am told that one of   135
the Mr. Markbys is occasionally to be seen at dinner parties. So far I am satisfied.

JACK: (*Very irritably.*) How extremely kind of you, Lady Bracknell! I have also in my possession, you will be pleased to hear, certificates of Miss Cardew's birth, baptism, whooping cough, registration, vaccination, confirmation,   140
and the measles; both the German and the English variety.

LADY BRACKNELL: Ah! A life crowded with incident, I see; though perhaps
somewhat too exciting for a young girl. I am not myself in favour of
premature experiences. (*Rises, looks at her watch.*) Gwendolen! the time
approaches for our departure. We have not a moment to lose. As a   145
matter of form, Mr. Worthing, I had better ask you if Miss Cardew
has any little fortune?

JACK: Oh, about a hundred and thirty thousand pounds in the Funds.
That is all. Good-bye, Lady Bracknell. So pleased to have seen you.

LADY BRACKNELL: (*Sitting down again.*) A moment, Mr. Worthing. A hundred   150
and thirty thousand pounds! And in the Funds! Miss Cardew seems to
me a most attractive young lady, now that I look at her. Few girls of the
present day have any really solid qualities, any of the qualities that last,
and improve with time. We live, I regret to say, in an age of surfaces.
(*To* CECILY.) Come over here, dear. (CECILY *goes across.*) Pretty child! your   155
dress is sadly simple, and your hair seems almost as Nature might have
left it. But we can soon alter all that. A thoroughly experienced French
maid produces a really marvelous result in a very brief space of time.
I remember recommending one to young Lady Lancing, and after three
months her own husband did not know her.   160

JACK: (*Aside.*) And after six months nobody knew her.

LADY BRACKNELL: (*Glares at* JACK *for a few moments. Then bends, with a
practised smile, to* CECILY.) Kindly turn round, sweet child. (CECILY *turns
completely round.*) No, the side view is what I want. (CECILY *presents her
profile.*) Yes, quite as I expected. There are distinct social possibilities   165
in your profile. The two weak points in our age are its want of principle
and its want of profile. The chin a little higher, dear. Style largely
depends on the way the chin is worn. They are worn very high, just
at present. Algernon!

ALGERNON: Yes, Aunt Augusta!   170

LADY BRACKNELL: There are distinct social possibilities in Miss Cardew's
profile.

ALGERNON: Cecily is the sweetest, dearest, prettiest girl in the whole
world. And I don't care twopence about social possibilities.

LADY BRACKNELL: Never speak disrespectfully of society, Algernon. Only   175
people who can't get into it do that. (*To* CECILY.) Dear child, of course
you know that Algernon has nothing but his debts to depend upon.
But I do not approve of mercenary marriages. When I married Lord
Bracknell I had no fortune of any kind. But I never dreamed for a
moment of allowing that to stand in my way. Well, I suppose I must   180
give my consent.

ALGERNON: Thank you, Aunt Augusta.

LADY BRACKNELL: Cecily, you may kiss me!

CECILY: (*Kisses her.*) Thank you, Lady Bracknell.

LADY BRACKNELL: You may also address me as Aunt Augusta for the 185
future.

CECILY: Thank you, Aunt Augusta.

LADY BRACKNELL: The marriage, I think, had better take place quite soon.

ALGERNON: Thank you, Aunt Augusta.

CECILY: Thank you, Aunt Augusta. 190

LADY BRACKNELL: To speak frankly, I am not in favour of long engagements. They give people the opportunity of finding out each other's
character before marriage, which I think is never advisable.

JACK: I beg your pardon for interrupting you, Lady Bracknell, but this
engagement is quite out of the question. I am Miss Cardew's guardian, 195
and she cannot marry without my consent until she comes of age.
That consent I absolutely decline to give.

LADY BRACKNELL: Upon what grounds, may I ask? Algernon is an
extremely, I may almost say an ostentatiously, eligible young man. He
has nothing, but he looks everything. What more can one desire? 200

JACK: It pains me very much to have to speak frankly to you, Lady Bracknell,
about your nephew, but the fact is that I do not approve at all of his
moral character. I suspect him of being untruthful. (ALGERNON *and*
CECILY *look at him in indignant amazement.*)

LADY BRACKNELL: Untruthful! My nephew Algernon? Impossible! He is 205
an Oxonian.

JACK: I fear there can be no possible doubt about the matter. This afternoon,
during my temporary absence in London on an important question
of romance, he obtained admission to my house by means of the false
pretence of being my brother. Under an assumed name he drank, I've just 210
been informed by my butler, an entire pint bottle of my Perrier-Jouet, Brut,
'89; a wine I was specially reserving for myself. Continuing his disgraceful
deception, he succeeded in the course of the afternoon in alienating the
affections of my only ward. He subsequently stayed to tea, and devoured
every single muffin. And what makes his conduct all the more heartless 215
is, that he was perfectly well aware from the first that I have no brother,
that I never had a brother, and that I don't intend to have a brother,
not even of any kind. I distinctly told him so myself yesterday afternoon.

LADY BRACKNELL: Ahem! Mr. Worthing, after careful consideration I have
decided entirely to overlook my nephew's conduct to you. 220

JACK: That is very generous of you, Lady Bracknell. My own decision,
however, is unalterable. I decline to give my consent.

LADY BRACKNELL: (*To* CECILY.) Come here, sweet child. (CECILY *goes over.*)
How old are you, dear?

CECILY: Well, I am really only eighteen, but I always admit to twenty   225
when I go to evening parties.

LADY BRACKNELL: You are perfectly right in making some slight alteration.
Indeed, no woman should ever be quite accurate about her age. It looks
so calculating . . . (*In meditative manner.*) Eighteen, but admitting to
twenty at evening parties. Well, it will not be very long before you are of   230
age and free from the restraints of tutelage. So I don't think your guardian's
consent is, after all, a matter of any importance.

JACK: Pray excuse me, Lady Bracknell, for interrupting you again, but it
is only fair to tell you that according to the terms of her grandfather's
will Miss Cardew does not come legally of age till she is thirty-five.   235

LADY BRACKNELL: That does not seem to me to be a grave objection.
Thirty-five is a very attractive age. London society is full of women of
the very highest birth who have, of their own free choice, remained
thirty-five for years. Lady Dumbleton is an instance in point. To my
own knowledge she has been thirty-five ever since she arrived at the age   240
of forty, which was many years ago now. I see no reason why our dear
Cecily should not be even still more attractive at the age you mention
than she is at present. There will be a large accumulation of property.

CECILY: Algy, could you wait for me till I was thirty-five?

ALGERNON: Of course I could, Cecily. You know I could.   245

CECILY: Yes, I felt it instinctively, but I couldn't wait all that time. I hate
waiting even five minutes for anybody. It always makes me rather
cross. I am not punctual myself, I know, but I do like punctuality in
others, and waiting, even to be married, is quite out of the question.

ALGERNON: Then what is to be done, Cecily?   250

CECILY: I don't know, Mr. Moncrieff.

LADY BRACKNELL: My dear Mr. Worthing, as Miss Cardew states positively
that she cannot wait till she is thirty-five—a remark which I am bound
to say seems to me to show a somewhat impatient nature—I would beg
of you to reconsider your decision.   255

JACK: But my dear Lady Bracknell, the matter is entirely in your own
hands. The moment you consent to my marriage with Gwendolen,
I will most gladly allow your nephew to form an alliance with my ward.

LADY BRACKNELL: (*Rising and drawing herself up.*) You must be quite aware that
what you propose is out of the question.   260

JACK: Then a passionate celibacy is all that any of us can look forward to.

LADY BRACKNELL: That is not the destiny I propose for Gwendolen.
Algernon, of course, can choose for himself. (*Pulls out her watch.*)
Come, dear, (GWENDOLEN *rises.*) we have already missed five,
if not six, trains. To miss any more might expose us to comment   265
on the platform.

(*Enter* DR. CHASUBLE.)

CHASUBLE: Everything is quite ready for the christenings.

LADY BRACKNELL: The christenings, sir! Is not that somewhat premature?

CHASUBLE: (*Looking rather puzzled, and pointing to* JACK *and* ALGERNON.) Both these gentlemen have expressed a desire for immediate baptism.

LADY BRACKNELL: At their age? The idea is grotesque and irreligious!   270
Algernon, I forbid you to be baptized. I will not hear of such excesses.
Lord Bracknell would be highly displeased if he learned that that was
the way in which you wasted your time and money.

CHASUBLE: Am I to understand then that there are to be no christenings
at all this afternoon?   275

JACK: I don't think that, as things are now, it would be of much practical
value to either of us, Dr. Chasuble.

CHASUBLE: I am grieved to hear such sentiments from you, Mr. Worthing.
They savour of the heretical views of the Anabaptists, views that I have
completely refuted in four of my unpublished sermons. However, as   280
your present mood seems to be one peculiarly secular, I will return
to the church at once. Indeed, I have just been informed by the
pewopener that for the last hour and a half Miss Prism has been
waiting for me in the vestry.

LADY BRACKNELL: (*Starting.*) Miss Prism! Did I hear you mention a   285
Miss Prism?

CHASUBLE: Yes, Lady Bracknell. I am on my way to join her.

LADY BRACKNELL: Pray allow me to detain you for a moment. This matter
may prove to be one of vital importance to Lord Bracknell and myself.
Is this Miss Prism a female of repellent aspect, remotely connected   290
with education?

CHASUBLE: (*Somewhat indignantly.*) She is the most cultivated of ladies, and
the very picture of respectability.

LADY BRACKNELL: It is obviously the same person. May I ask what position
she holds in your household?   295

CHASUBLE: (*Severely.*) I am a celibate, madam.

JACK: (*Interposing.*) Miss Prism, Lady Bracknell, has been for the last three
years Miss Cardew's esteemed governess and valued companion.

LADY BRACKNELL: In spite of what I hear of her, I must see her at once.
Let her be sent for.   300

CHASUBLE: (*Looking off.*) She approaches; she is nigh.

(*Enter* MISS PRISM *hurriedly.*)

MISS PRISM: I was told you expected me in the vestry, dear Canon. I have
been waiting for you there for an hour and three-quarters. (*Catches*

sight of LADY BRACKNELL, *who has fixed her with a stony glare.* MISS PRISM   305
grows pale and quails. She looks anxiously round as if desirous to escape.)

LADY BRACKNELL: (*In a severe, judicial voice.*) Prism! (MISS PRISM *bows her
head in shame.*) Come here, Prism! (MISS PRISM *approaches in a humble
manner.*) Prism! Where is that baby? (*General consternation. The Canon
starts back in horror.* ALGERNON *and* JACK *pretend to be anxious to shield
CECILY and* GWENDOLEN *from hearing the details of a terrible public scandal.*)   310
Twenty-eight years ago, Prism, you left Lord Bracknell's house,
Number 104, Upper Grosvenor Street, in charge of a perambulator
that contained a baby, of the male sex. You never returned. A few
weeks later, through the elaborate investigations of the Metropolitan
police, the perambulator was discovered at midnight, standing by   315
itself in a remote corner of Bayswater. It contained the manuscript of
a three-volume novel of more than usually revolting sentimentality.
(MISS PRISM *starts in involuntary indignation.*) But the baby was not there!
(*Everyone looks at* MISS PRISM.) Prism, where is that baby? (*A pause.*)

MISS PRISM: Lady Bracknell, I admit with shame that I do not know. I only   320
wish I did. The plain facts of the case are these. On the morning of the
day you mention, a day that is forever branded on my memory, I prepared
as usual to take the baby out in its perambulator. I had also with me a
somewhat old but capacious hand-bag in which I had intended to place
the manuscript of a work of fiction that I had written during my few   325
unoccupied hours. In a moment of mental abstraction, for which I never
can forgive myself, I deposited the manuscript in the bassinette, and placed
the baby in the hand-bag.

JACK: (*Who has been listening attentively.*) But where did you deposit the
hand-bag?   330

MISS PRISM: Do not ask me, Mr. Worthing.

JACK: Miss Prism, this is a matter of no small importance to me. I insist on
knowing where you deposited the hand-bag that contained that infant.

MISS PRISM: I left it in the cloak-room of one of the larger railway stations
in London.   335

JACK: What railway station?

MISS PRISM: (*Quite crushed.*) Victoria. The Brighton line. (*Sinks into a chair.*)

JACK: I must retire to my room for a moment. Gwendolen, wait here for me.

GWENDOLEN: If you are not too long, I will wait here for you all my life.

(*Exit* JACK *in great excitement.*)

CHASUBLE: What do you think this means, Lady Bracknell?   340

LADY BRACKNELL: I dare not even suspect, Dr. Chasuble. I need hardly
tell you that in families of high position strange coincidences are not
supposed to occur. They are hardly considered the thing. (*Noises heard
overhead as if someone was throwing trunks about. Everybody looks up.*)

CECILY: Uncle Jack seems strangely agitated.   345

CHASUBLE: Your guardian has a very emotional nature.

LADY BRACKNELL: This noise is extremely unpleasant. It sounds as if he was having an argument. I dislike arguments of any kind. They are always vulgar, and often convincing.

CHASUBLE: (*Looking up.*) It has stopped now. (*The noise is redoubled.*)   350

LADY BRACKNELL: I wish he would arrive at some conclusion.

GWENDOLEN: The suspense is terrible. I hope it will last.

(*Enter* JACK *with a hand-bag of black leather in his hand.*)

JACK: (*Rushing over to* MISS PRISM.) Is this the hand-bag, Miss Prism? Examine it carefully before you speak. The happiness of more than one life depends on your answer.   355

MISS PRISM: (*Calmly.*) It seems to be mine. Yes, here is the injury it received through the upsetting of a Gower Street omnibus in younger and happier days. Here is the stain on the lining caused by the explosion of a temperance beverage, an incident that occurred at Leamington. And here, on the lock, are my initials. I had forgotten that in an extravagant   360 mood I had had them placed there. The bag is undoubtedly mine. I am delighted to have it so unexpectedly restored to me. It has been a great inconvenience being without it all these years.

JACK: (*In a pathetic voice.*) Miss Prism, more is restored to you than this hand-bag. I was the baby you placed in it.   365

MISS PRISM: (*Amazed.*) You?

JACK: (*Embracing her.*) Yes . . . mother!

MISS PRISM: (*Recoiling in indignant astonishment.*) Mr. Worthing! I am unmarried!

JACK: Unmarried! I do not deny that is a serious blow. But after all, who   370 has the right to cast a stone against one who has suffered? Cannot repentance wipe out an act of folly? Why should there be one law for men and another for women? Mother, I forgive you. (*Tries to embrace her again.*)

MISS PRISM: (*Still more indignant.*) Mr. Worthing, there is some error.   375 (*Pointing to* LADY BRACKNELL.) There is the lady who can tell you who you really are.

JACK: (*After a pause.*) Lady Bracknell, I hate to seem inquisitive, but would you kindly inform me who I am?

LADY BRACKNELL: I am afraid that the news I have to give you will   380 not altogether please you. You are the son of my poor sister, Mrs. Moncrieff, and consequently Algernon's elder brother.

JACK: Algy's elder brother! Then I have a brother after all. I knew I had a brother! I always said I had a brother! Cecily,—how could you have ever doubted that I had a brother? (*Seizes hold of* ALGERNON.) Dr. Chasuble,   385 my unfortunate brother. Miss Prism, my unfortunate brother. Gwendolen, my unfortunate brother. Algy, you young scoundrel, you will have to treat me with more respect in the future. You have never behaved to me like a brother in all your life.

ALGERNON: Well, not till to-day, old boy, I admit. I did my best, however,   390
though I was out of practice. (*Shakes hands.*)

GWENDOLEN: (*To* JACK.) My own! But what own are you? What is your
Christian name, now that you have become someone else?

JACK: Good heavens! . . . I had quite forgotten that point. Your decision on
the subject of my name is irrevocable, I suppose?   395

GWENDOLEN: I never change, except in my affections.

CECILY: What a noble nature you have, Gwendolen!

JACK: Then the question had better be cleared up at once. Aunt Augusta,
a moment. At the time when Miss Prism left me in the hand-bag, had
I been christened already?   400

LADY BRACKNELL: Every luxury that money could buy, including christening,
had been lavished on you by your fond and doting parents.

JACK: Then I was christened! That is settled. Now, what name was
I given? Let me know the worst.

LADY BRACKNELL: Being the eldest son you were naturally christened after   405
your father.

JACK: (*Irritably.*) Yes, but what was my father's Christian name?

LADY BRACKNELL: (*Meditatively.*) I cannot at the present moment recall
what the General's Christian name was. But I have no doubt he had
one. He was eccentric, I admit. But only in later years. And that was   410
the result of the Indian climate, and marriage, and indigestion, and
other things of that kind.

JACK: Algy! Can't you recollect what our father's Christian name was?

ALGERNON: My dear boy, we were never even on speaking terms. He died
before I was a year old.   415

JACK: His name would appear in the Army Lists of the period, I suppose,
Aunt Augusta?

LADY BRACKNELL: The General was essentially a man of peace, except in
his domestic life. But I have no doubt his name would appear in any
military directory.   420

JACK: The Army Lists of the last forty years are here. These delightful
records should have been my constant study. (*Rushes to bookcase and
tears the books out.*) M. Generals . . . Mallam, Maxbohm, Magley,
what ghastly names they have—Markby, Migsby, Mobbs, Moncrieff!
Lieutenant 1840, Captain, Lieutenant-Colonel, Colonel, General   425
1869, Christian names, Ernest John. (*Puts book very quietly down and*

speaks quite calmly.) I always told you, Gwendolen, my name was Ernest didn't I? Well, it is Ernest after all, I mean it naturally is Ernest.

LADY BRACKNELL: Yes, I remember the General was called Ernest. I knew I had some particular reason for disliking the name.   430

GWENDOLEN: Ernest! My own Ernest! I felt from the first that you could have no other name!

JACK: Gwendolen, it is a terrible thing for a man to find out suddenly that all his life he has been speaking nothing but the truth. Can you forgive me?   435

GWENDOLEN: I can. For I feel sure that you are sure to change.

JACK: My own one!

CHASUBLE: (*To* MISS PRISM.) Lætitia! (*Embraces her.*)

MISS PRISM: (*Enthusiastically.*) Frederick! At last!

ALGERNON: Cecily! (*Embraces her.*) At last!   440

JACK: Gwendolen! (*Embraces her.*) At last!

LADY BRACKNELL: My nephew, you seem to be displaying signs of triviality.

JACK: On the contrary, Aunt Augusta, I've now realized for the first time in my life the vital Importance of Being Earnest.   445

- Oscar Wilde didn't think of art as "natural." Nor did he seek the illusion of natural or "realistic." Rather, he celebrated the craft that went into creating a kind of perfection not possible in everyday life. To put it another way, Wilde didn't see "artifice" as a pejorative word. Describe the structural contrivances of *The Importance of Being Earnest.* Then, reflect upon the pleasures of Wilde's brand of perfection. What is gained or lost by the polish he applies to his play?

- Wilde's play addresses a very particular culture and time. A twenty-first-century American audience won't likely pick up on the loaded notions of the word/name *earnest,* for example, without some knowledge of literary and social history. Yet *The Importance of Being Earnest* remains a dependable standard for theater groups throughout the United States. What about the play other than individual witty lines accounts for this enduring popularity?

Experiencing Literature through Writing

1. Select a single work from this chapter (or any other chapter). Look for structural elements that hold the work together, and explain how these structuring devices influence our understanding of the work.

    a. What are the components of each element? For instance, you may say that every line in a poem has *x* number of syllables.

    b. What pattern emerges among these elements?

    c. Is there any part of the work that violates the pattern you have found? How can you explain this departure?

2. The characters presented in this chapter generally behave consistently, but other characters in their stories might think that the behavior they are observing is a break from previously established patterns. To see the coherence, we need some sort of an outside perspective. Using one or more of the selected works, discuss the extent to which the outsider in the work disrupts the routine that structures the lives of the people whom the work is observing.

3. Looking for structures can be fairly formulaic. A work either is or is not a sonnet. Every work in this book has some sort of structure that we can label. A number of those structures come out of efforts to escape other structures. Find a work that seems to be resisting traditional structural labels, and explore how that structural effort contributes to the final impact of that work.

9 Interruption

Where Did That Come From?
Why Is This Here?

The previous chapter details literary structures and conventions that create a sense of coherence within a crafted text. One of the great attractions of...Cut the transition. Let's move on to the subject of this chapter: interruption.

Although we do as much as we can to separate our lives into distinct, coherent units (and books into tidy chapters), those divisions inevitably disintegrate. Other people tend not to respect the careful structures that we build for ourselves. Perhaps the most ubiquitous interruptions in our current culture are the cell phone ringtones that blast out of someone else's purse or pocket during class or at some quiet moment in the middle of a movie. These interruptions break the trance that the undisturbed moment held. But in some respects they are more normal than the perfect silence they violate: how much time in any given week do we spend quietly sitting in a lecture hall or movie theater? Interruptions compel us to be aware of how unusual settled composure is. In this respect, interruption and coherence are closely related. Without order, an interruption is insignificant. Without interruption, we'd hardly appreciate order. In this chapter, we'll look at specific interruptions and interruptive techniques that writers use to create an impact or suggest a theme.

INTERRUPTING THE FICTIONAL FRAME

The technique of interruption sometimes allows an author to signal a self-conscious attitude toward narrative. The popular children's film *The Princess Bride* (Rob Reiner, 1987) begins with a grandfather (Peter Falk) reading a story to his grandson. As the story (in the book) begins, the movie leaves the child's bedroom and follows the "fictional" story. At points, the grandfather's voice interrupts the narrative of the fantasy "book" world, and the film returns to the child's bedroom until we plunge again into the world of the book. The abrupt shifts remind us of the fragile nature of the imaginary world we are entering. The grandson resists entering the book world at the outset of the film, but, as the story goes on, he doesn't want anything to interrupt the story. By watching this child, we see something of our own role as an audience. We choose to embrace the fiction of this story just as the skeptical grandson does. The gap between reading a story and being in the story allows the director to play a bit more than usual with the conventions of the fantasy world. There is a sense that the film is allowed to laugh at these conventions even as it employs them. Calling dangerous and fearful creatures "Rodents of Unusual Size," for instance, has a certain literariness; it is a bookish name that might not sound right without the interrupting frame that shows us that this is a story that is coming out of a book.

There is a long and distinguished history of strategic breaks in fictional narratives. In *Oedipus Rex*, Sophocles employs a **chorus** to interrupt, interpret, and even take part in the play's action. This group of voices begins and ends scenes in the play. They analyze Oedipus's actions. They act like a community in response to this king. They ask him questions; they announce the arrival of characters

© 20th Century Fox/The Kobal Collection

Mel Smith, Andre the Giant, and Mandy Patinkin in the fantasy world of the fairy tale.

Fred Savage and Peter Falk in the "real world" where Falk reads the fairy tale to his grandson.

on stage; they react to the developments within the play. We can think of the chorus as the first audience for what occurs on stage; in that capacity, they help shape our (the second audience's) reactions. If the chorus were to be removed, we would be without an important interpretive guide. If the choral lines were given to specific characters (or even new characters) within the play, we would be forced to assess different questions of perspective. How did she know that? Why did he tell us that? Of course, some choral lines might seem simply inappropriate coming from the mouth of an actual character. The chorus provides an interruption that guides our response without undermining our investment in the reality of the main action. *The Princess Bride* lets us see two worlds simultaneously; how does the use of the chorus in *Oedipus Rex* achieve a similar effect?

Experiencing Literature through Interruption

In dramatic presentations, characters may actually intrude into the action and change our consciousness of the action. When a character stands apart from the action, faces the audience, and delivers a **soliloquy**, we expect to learn something about the character that we might not learn from the action alone. For instance, Shakespeare's Juliet tells us about both her love for Romeo and her awareness of the family barriers to that love: "a rose by any other name would smell as sweet." When he gets the widow of the king he has just murdered to agree to marry him, Shakespeare's deformed Richard III lets us know that he is as amazed at his success as we are: "Was ever woman in this manner woo'd?" In the case of Juliet, we simply hear the character speaking her private thoughts aloud, but, in some performances (see for example, Ian McKellen's performance in the 1995 film), Richard's character speaks directly to us; he acknowledges that the audience exists—has he exited his fictional world, or have we entered it? This sort of interruption gives the illusion that a different consciousness is available to understand the events that are being narrated, that there is a strand of thought and conversation about these events other than the single strand that the main narrative recounts.

In Shakespeare's *The Taming of the Shrew*, the main action of the play concerns Petruchio who "tames" (modern audiences might say that he abuses into submission) the independent Kate when he marries her against her will. But the first action of the play is not the main action; in the first two scenes, drunken Christopher Sly is tricked into believing that he is actually a lord and that the play we are about to watch is being performed for him. So (like *The Princess Bride*) the main narrative is a play within a play, and we watch not just the play that we are watching but also the characters within those first scenes who are watching this play. Depending upon how this frame is staged, it is not uncommon for these characters to interrupt the play, either just by being there and distracting us now and then or more actively by reacting to what is happening on the larger stage in front of them. How does this additional fictional layer impact our understanding of the play? At the end of the play, the tamed Kate rebukes her sister for failing to listen to her own husband. Some modern productions use the framing story to undercut the apparently misogynistic message of the play, to suggest, through the interruptions of the frame, that the final speech "place your hands beneath your husband's foot" is not sincerely met because it is part of the fantasy that is being performed for the drunken Sly.

Making Connections

Interruptions like the ones we've just discussed raise questions of perspective—specifically, of reliability or the lack of reliability. The interruption of another audience gives us a presence from outside the story that can comment upon, judge, or add to the main action. But do we necessarily trust that audience over the story? And if we do, why should we? Do you think a single character seems a stronger, surer guide than a chorus? Or do you find it easier to trust the chorus? What do you look for to indicate how much you should trust the "outside" voice? What might indicate that these additional characters outside the main narrative are no more the author's voice than any other part of the text?

STRUCTURAL INTERRUPTIONS

In the previous examples, a primary effect of the interruption has been to enhance the audience's awareness of its own role within the action. The chorus, for example, models an audience that is more involved in the action than any actual audience. Interruption, though, can do more than create audience awareness. It can draw our attention to important moments. For example, read the following poem by William Butler Yeats.

William Butler Yeats (1865–1939)

The Folly of Being Comforted (1902)

One that is ever kind said yesterday:
"Your well-belovèd's hair has threads of grey,
And little shadows come about her eyes;
Time can but make it easier to be wise
Though now it seems impossible, and so   5
All that you need is patience."
                                            Heart cries, "No,
I have not a crumb of comfort, not a grain.
Time can but make her beauty over again:
Because of that great nobleness of hers   10
The fire that stirs about her, when she stirs,
Burns but more clearly. O she had not these ways
When all the wild Summer was in her gaze."
O heart! O heart! if she'd but turn her head,
You'd know the folly of being comforted.   15

You don't even need to read the words to notice that line 7 looks different from the rest of the poem; it is markedly shorter than any of the others. When we look closely at the poetic structure of the poem, we see that this line should be part of line 6; "no" rhymes with "so" and the poem is made up of a series of rhyming couplets. But this break reflects a real break within the action the poem recounts. The first part of the poem is an offer of comfort, but here at line 7, the poet rejects that comfort. The comforting thought is interrupted, just as the line is interrupted, with Heart's cry. There is a certain passionate violence to this interruption. The broken line shows us that Heart has lost patience listening to the kind words. The break in the pattern of the poem illustrates the passion of the heart that refuses all rational words of comfort.

   Look for a similar division within Mary Oliver's "Bone Poem." The poem begins with a focus on the "litter" from owl meals as it "sinks into the wet leaves" (line 4). At line 5, the poem begins to change as "time sits with her slow spoon." Within the next three lines (5–8), we move forward through "light years" until the poet speaks of a singular "we"; from this distance, distinct beings are reduced to the primal substances that make up all living things.

Mary Oliver (1935–   )

Bone Poem (1979)

The litter under the tree
Where the owl eats—shrapnel

Of rat bones, gull debris—
Sinks into the wet leaves

Where time sits with her slow spoon,   5
Where *we* becomes singular, and a quickening

From light years away
Saves and maintains. O holy

Protein, o hallowed lime,
O precious clay!   10

Tossed under the tree
The cracked bones

Of the owl's most recent feast
Lean like shipwreck, starting

The long fall back to the center—   15
The seepage, the flowing,

The equity: sooner or later
In the shimmering leaves

The rat will learn to fly, the owl
Will be devoured.   20

The interruption occurs in the middle of line 8. One sentence ends, and, suddenly, "O holy" crowds into the line. The exclamation continues for two more lines (9–10) ("O holy / Protein, o hallowed lime, / O precious clay!") proclaiming the substances that are the essence of this more distant point of view.

After this outburst, the poem returns to the specific debris from "the owl's most recent feast" as these bones start their "long fall back to the center" (line 15) and to their elemental nature. Here the interruption is a central outburst, almost a big bang after which the poem returns to the form, subject, and philosophical musings that it had before the interruption.

Experiencing Film through Interruption

Interruptions often cause us, as the audience of the work, to reexamine our relation to the work that we are viewing. Think about the following example.

Many performing arts venues want to quiet the electronic noises that interrupt too many performances. One strategy has been to create a loud ringtone just as the show is about to get underway. This fake interruption (followed by an announcement about turning off all phones) makes people in the audience uncomfortable. First, we are ready to glare at the offender. Then, we realize that we have been drawn into a fiction. This ringtone is not real, but our own real phone has the potential to be just as disruptive. As audience members, we participate in the performance, even if our part in the performance is simply our silence. In fact, this created "interruption" illustrates an aspect of the complex relation that we have to fiction itself. Where people tend to ignore an announcement they have heard many times before (such as the emergency information that flight attendants recite before a plane takes off), they react to this fictional interruption differently. They are prompted to think about the way they relate to the fiction.

Film has been particularly adept at playing with the relations between the fictional world on the screen and the world outside that screen—between reel life and real life. Which of these worlds is the interruption? Are we challenged to question what we take as real by such films as Woody Allen's *The Purple Rose of Cairo*? In that 1984 film a movie hero steps out of the screen and into the life of a lonely woman watching the picture. That break leads us (like the woman, we are moviegoers) to reflect on our desire to stay in the fictional world that is on the screen. Gary Ross's *Pleasantville* (1998) reverses the ploy; two contemporary characters are thrust into a 1950s black-and-white TV world. This abrupt interruption of a contemporary suburban family drama eventually leads us to rethink our problems as well as our nostalgia for a "better time" that we like to believe really existed. Films can also break our narrative expectations and thereby make us more sensitive to those expectations. At the end of *Monty Python and the Holy Grail* (1975), Arthur and his knights are preparing to storm a castle when modern-day police storm the field, arrest Arthur, and knock the film out of the camera, abruptly ending the film. This is not a realistic film, but the jarring end makes us realize how much we expect even a rather outrageous portrayal of medieval England to maintain that fiction throughout.

JUXTAPOSITION

Juxtaposition is the rhetorical technique of putting two (or more) things next to each other; the resulting contrast or similarity makes us see both objects differently than we saw them when each stood by itself. A simple exercise in juxtaposition uses two colored fabrics. When two colors are placed next to each other, the juxtaposition will bring out qualities in both colors that are not evident when the colors sit separately. For instance, it might be difficult to determine whether a particular fabric is black or navy blue. By setting the fabric in question next to a fabric that you know to be black, it becomes easier to judge. Neither color has changed, but slight differences become apparent with the comparison. In works of art, juxtapositions are often more strongly marked; radical contrasts break or interrupt our customary ways of interpreting the world. The pairing of objects that initially appear unrelated forces us to search for connections amid obvious differences.

Juxtaposition is especially effective in photography. Margaret Bourke-White's photograph of a bread line of real people (African Americans) standing in front of a fictional white family in the propaganda poster delivers a clear message. The contrast between the real and the imaginary here is stark. The seriousness

Margaret Bourke-White's photograph "World's Highest Standard of Living"

Margaret Bourke-White/Masters/Time Life Pictures/Getty Images of the people standing in line makes a mockery of the claim on the billboard. The jubilant white family enjoying a comfortable life above seems to bear no real relation to the American lives being led by the people in line below. "There's no way like the American way" takes on a different meaning from the billboard's intent because of Bourke-White's juxtaposition. In the photograph, we see an irony of race and class in American society. The sign insists that the country has the "World's Highest Standard of Living," but the real people in this scene have no access to the material goods that the family in the poster behind them are celebrating.

Making Connections

Irony can be considered a strategy of interruption because it works by introducing the unexpected. In general, irony arises from a gap between expectation and actuality, intention and realization, appearance and truth. Because irony depends upon suggestion rather than explicit statement, it requires that a viewer or reader be alert to small signals. It is by nature complex and subject to subtle shading and **ambiguity** (uncertainty or multiplicity of meaning, suggestive qualities of expression, contradictory implications). Critics often specify distinct types of irony. **Dramatic irony** refers to a gap between what a character knows and what an audience understands; a character who doesn't appreciate the significance of the words he or she speaks conveys a dramatic irony. The audience is, in effect, alerted to meanings that the author wants to communicate from outside the character's consciousness. A character that deliberately plays upon the difference between words and meaning expresses **verbal irony**; such a character might deliberately understate a problem to emphasize its gravity, or overstate a problem to highlight its triviality. Bourke-White's photograph illustrates what is often called **contextual** or **situational irony**—an irony that arises from coincidence or circumstances.

As we use this photograph to illustrate the idea of juxtaposition, it is important to acknowledge that there is no necessary relation between the particular people standing in line and the billboard that happens to be behind them. As soon as we look at Bourke-White's composition here, the convergence of real people and propaganda takes on meaning. **Synchronicity** refers to events that coincide in time and appear to be related but have no discoverable causal connection. In this instance, the people and the poster illustrate tensions within American society more clearly than any extended exploration of race and class in our culture. This moment that Bourke-White has captured symbolizes larger social problems. We should notice the sophistication necessary to read the ironic juxtaposition that appears here. Unless we are aware of the discrepancy between white and black culture and unless we can read the markers of wealth and poverty, we cannot appreciate the synchronicity that Bourke-White has captured. When we compared our two fabrics to discover which one was blue we had a particular standard that we were trying to test; the comparison was useful because we knew what we were looking for. When we come to this photograph, we bring a set of cultural standards that help us see the meanings that Bourke-White presents.

Experiencing Literature through Juxtaposition

In "Tattoo," Ted Kooser uses juxtaposition to examine the tattoo that he sees on a man's arm at a yard sale. But instead of describing just the tattoo, Kooser describes the context in which he sees that mark. Thus, he reads the tattoo as a signal of an identity that seems out of place in the mundane domestic world of a yard sale.

Ted Kooser (1939–)

Tattoo (2005)

What once was meant to be a statement—
a dripping dagger held in the fist
of a shuddering heart—is now just a bruise
on a bony old shoulder, the spot
where vanity once punched him hard   5
     and the ache lingered on. He looks like
someone you had to reckon with,
strong as a stallion, fast and ornery,
but on this chilly morning, as he walks
between the tables at a yard sale   10
     with the sleeves of his tight black T-shirt
rolled up to show us who he was,
he is only another old man, picking up
broken tools and putting them back,
his heart gone soft and blue with stories.   15

Compare the scene that Kooser presents here with Bourke-White's photograph. In the photograph, we see a scene that captures disturbing inequities within American culture. What does Kooser capture in the tattoo that he sees at this yard sale? Think, too, about the process of conveying this juxtaposition. Bourke-White has just the image. What commentary does Kooser add to the image that he sees? Look at the specific words and phrases that he uses so that we will see the juxtaposition as he sees it.

MONTAGE

In elementary school, you may have been asked to do a collage—that is, you were to paste a collection of images onto a single sheet of paper. The images might at first glance seem altogether random, but randomness wasn't the point of the assignment. The idea was to have you create an effect or underscore a theme through juxtaposed images. **Montage** (echoing a French verb "to assemble") extends this notion to narrative and is a useful word in the study of both film and literature.

In film criticism, montage refers to a style of editing that uses sudden juxtapositions of images, surprising cuts, and radical shifts in perspective. This technique differs greatly from what has been called the "classic Hollywood" or "invisible" style of editing—a style that seeks to achieve naturalistic effects. The montage style is essentially interruptive; it shakes viewers from a settled attention to narrative and character and forces them to experience film as film. It deliberately breaks the illusion we often seek in films of observing actions as they actually happen.

Literary critics have borrowed the word *montage* to describe dramatic juxtapositions of images or scenes or even narrative voices. A novelist might, for example, break a narrative to insert actual advertising jingles, headlines, even news stories from the historical time of the narrative in order to contextualize the fictional action. A fictional or dramatic montage might also be constructed from a collection of short stories/skits or character sketches—almost snapshots of life. If you've read Sandra Cisneros's *The House on Mango Street*, you've experienced a well-assembled montage. A poet might give us a series of images, as does Wallace Stevens in "Thirteen Ways of Looking at a Blackbird" and not require us to connect the images thematically. Stevens had, for example, written that his famous poem aimed at communicating a series of "sensations."

Experiencing Film through Juxtaposition

Juxtaposition is an especially effective tool for satire in film. Some of the most effective material that Jon Stewart presents in his *Daily Show* on Comedy Central, for instance, consists of a simple formula: a video clip of a politician making one statement at one time to one audience and the same politician at another time in another venue making another statement that is completely at odds with the first. Showing the two clips consecutively is enough to make an argument. Filmmaker Michael Moore is a master of this strategy, a gift that has earned him both an Oscar and harsh criticism. In his first film, the documentary *Roger and Me* (1989), Moore argues that corporations have a responsibility to the communities in which they work and not just to their shareholders. This film traces the actions of General Motors in Flint,

Michigan, where the company had recently shut down manufacturing plants and moved production to countries where labor was cheaper. Films and dramatic productions can, of course, add sound as yet another element into the mix: what we see clashes with what we hear. In the devastating final scene, Moore shows General Motors chair Roger Smith, the "Roger" of the film's title, delivering a banal Christmas address to GM workers, talking about compassion, and quoting Charles Dickens as "an expert on Christmas," while a choir sings in the background. Moore cuts away from the film footage of the speech to show the family of a laid-off GM worker in Flint being evicted from its home on Christmas Eve. On the soundtrack, Smith continues to drone on about caring for others while we watch the eviction officer setting the family's Christmas tree and presents out by the curb. As Moore has edited this scene, Smith's words seem empty, self-serving, and hypocritical. By juxtaposing the bland unreality of Smith's speech and the harsh suffering of the evicted family, Moore uses the scene as the culmination of the argument he is making in his film that Smith, who serves as a symbol of corporate America, is responsible for both the content of this speech and for the corporate actions that impact American workers. The images and words set in such marked contrast make Moore's argument.

In this context, the juxtaposition echoes the work of Bourke-White. Because editing is so apparent in Moore's work, some critics argue that his "documentary" distorts the truth. His editorial techniques, they claim, create a fictional version of reality that suits his political purpose. Try to use the same critique to challenge Bourke-White's image. This photograph suggests that the people standing in line have some actual relation to the poster. Are they deliberately contradicting its image? Is the poster there to mock them? Is the single image more or less manipulative than film? However we respond to such questions, it is clear that we are responding to a crafted work of art.

A Note to Student Writers: Making Comparisons Relevant

Observing juxtaposition as an effective strategy in these crafted texts can help us in our own writing. A common writing assignment will ask students to "compare and contrast" two subjects (books, characters, settings, poems, films, etc.). This technique casts a wide net in the hope that students might find something of value in the comparisons. By juxtaposing, we gain a clearer sense of the issues/elements under analysis. The technique, however, brings with it potential problems.

All writers must be careful to measure and evaluate the demands any form of interruption makes on a reader. In Ted Kooser's "Tattoo," juxtaposition is used to imply or suggest a thought or feeling. Kooser never tells us that the man at the yard sale was foolish to get a tattoo in his earlier life or that the man has now settled down into some sort of domesticity or that his former ferociousness has faded. It is up to us to draw conclusions from the juxtaposition of the yard sale scene and the tattoo's image. The suggestive power of the poem is part of its beauty. An analytical paper that stays at the level of suggestion and implication won't likely be read so favorably. Critical papers usually need to be more explicit about the purpose and the point of the comparison. In a similar way, an abrupt turn in a poem, story, play, or movie might serve as an effective interruption. It might jar us into paying attention or shake us out of our standard way of seeing things. But a strong interruption in a critical essay might be taken as incoherence, or just plain sloppiness. Writers must understand that readers don't come to every text with the same set of expectations and demands.

Compare/contrast assignments are challenging largely because they require you to bring together what might seem unlike things. The very nature of the task carries a risk of confusing the reader (what does A have to do with B?; does a discussion of B merely interrupt the discussion of A?). In writing a compare/contrast paper, you are required to bring together ideas whether or not an author has done that for you already. In this sort of paper, the comparison is entirely yours. You must, therefore, justify your approach. It's not enough in a compare/contrast paper to simply note similarities and differences and trust the reader to make sense of how everything adds up. You need to think about how the process of setting two texts alongside each other allows you to see something you might otherwise miss.

As a writer, it is helpful to imagine a nagging voice at your ear, constantly asking, "So what?" about everything that you write down. Your answer to that question is the beginning of your analysis. It is this answer that will structure the paper. Until you answer that question, you have made only observations about the materials you are studying. And after you answer that question the first time, you should continue to ask it of every point of comparison or contrast. The more insistent you can be in challenging your own material, the more effective your analysis will be.

There is yet another lesson about compare/contrast papers to be learned from Michael Moore's film: an organizational lesson. Moore keeps the policies of Roger Smith parallel to the poverty in Flint, Michigan. His attempts to talk with Roger Smith are part of the discussions that he carries on with the unemployed people of Flint. When he talks with the managers at GM, he talks about the responsibility of the corporation to the workers it employs and to the surrounding community. He does not devote half the film to poverty and then switch to a discussion of GM policies. The two strands of the discussion are consistently integrated. By the time we reach the climactic final scenes in the film, Moore has prepared us as viewers to see the connections between Smith's words and the agent who is evicting the family. Whether or not we agree with Moore's argument, we can see that it is a powerful rhetorical strategy and one that you can adopt for your own purposes.

MODELING CRITICAL ANALYSIS:
T. S. ELIOT, THE LOVE SONG OF J. ALFRED PRUFROCK

As we return to Eliot's "Prufrock" (see Chapters 7 and 8), we see how much this poem is marked by interruptions of various sorts. The stanzas are irregular. There are rhymed couplets that might be described as a chorus ("In the room the women come and go / Talking of Michelangelo"). Stanzas are divided sometimes with simply a blank line (see for instance, the division between lines 12 and 13), other times there are sectional markers dividing them (between lines 69 and 70, 74 and 75, 110 and 111). Within the stanzas, ellipses (lines 10, 72, 77, and 120), dashes (lines 83, 95, 102, and 103), and parentheses (lines 41, 44, and 64) interrupt the narrative. Often, it seems the speaker is interrupted before he can complete an idea. In this poem the sheer volume of the interruption is staggering, It is useful to go through and to mark each interruption, but, in our analysis, we will concentrate on just a few and explain why we find those particular interruptions significant to our growing understanding of this complex poem.

The poem begins with a command "Let us go" and throughout the first stanza we see that command three times (lines 1, 4, and 12). The narrator describes the scenes where he means to be going, but, by line 10 we feel the tension between that impulse to move forward and the voice that signals inertia. The interruption at line 10 is a series of four dots. The poem's first sentence has finally ended, and the three dots indicate a pause. At the end of this sentence, the narrator compares the streets he describes to a form of intellectual inquiry ("like a tedious argument / Of insidious intent / To lead you to an overwhelming question"). As the speaker interrupts his rambling simile about "half-deserted streets," we begin to see the irony within this voice: in spite of the "let us go" that begins the sentence, this tendency to lapse into intense scrutiny is precisely what keeps the speaker from going anywhere. We hear that conflict in line 11, a line that interrupts the abstraction of the "overwhelming question" by getting back to the desire to go: "Oh, do not ask, "What is it? / Let us go and make our visit." Suddenly, we have two sentences in two lines. There are no images to wade through here. This rhymed couplet reacts against the wandering construction of the first ten lines of the poem. This interruption sounds like a different voice than the voice that offers elaborate descriptions, not of any destination, but of the circuitous route that they must take as they go. So the interruption here gets us out of the first stanza as it shows us that there are opposing impulses leading us through the poem.

Lines 13 and 14 offer another interruption: "In the room the women come and go / Talking of Michelangelo." We are suddenly off the street. These women and their room appear out of nowhere. What can we do with these two lines? As we noted in the Chapter 8 on coherence it's helpful to note that they are repeated in lines 35 and 36. When a song has a chorus, a soloist might sing the verse and invite the audience to join in at the chorus. The chorus is usually short and simple enough that everyone can join in at the appropriate moment. In a song it functions to anchor us rhythmically, emotionally, and thematically. But what does Michelangelo have to do with Prufrock's visit? This chorus suggests that the talk about Michelangelo may be rather empty even as it is intimidating to someone who is not part of the women's social circle. The women belong to a place where Prufrock might like to be, but a place he cannot quite bring himself to go. The lines function to interrupt and disconcert Prufrock—the confident chorus in contrast to his tentative indecision. At the same time, they lend some coherence to the poetic form. The repeated interruption offers something familiar within a poem that appears at first to be nothing but interruptions. And as we mentioned at the start of the chapter, if there were no structure, there would be nothing to interrupt.

Using Interruption to Focus Writing and Discussion

- An interruption suggests that there should be some established order to interrupt. What is that order? How is it established in this particular work?

- Is there some interruption of the stasis within the text? For instance, is action interrupted by inaction; inaction interrupted by action; action interrupted by another action; a thought interrupted by action; a thought interrupted by another thought? Is there some interruption of the movement of the text itself? For instance, does a poem suddenly stop rhyming or is the rhythm thrown off; does a narrator become incoherent; does the style of the section change? Is there something that is simply surprising and difficult to account for? What is the interruption?

- Identify the moment that the interruption occurs in the text. Try to isolate the moment as specifically as possible. Is there a single sentence, phrase, or word that embodies the interruption?

- How is this word (or series of words) somehow different from the words around it? What makes it stand out? Is there some graphic method of representing the difference? What does the author do to announce this interruption? What makes us notice this interruption?

- What are we supposed to do with the interruption? Does the author give us any clues? Does the author offer any analysis of the moment? If so, describe how the author tells us that interruption is important. Why is this interruption interesting?

- Is there a return to the original order that was interrupted? Or is there some new order? Or has all order been lost? Or has the text simply gone on to something else? Is there some pattern of interruptions?

- Why is this interruption interesting? As we look at an increasing numbers of different interruptions, we begin to see patterns in their significance. How does this specific interruption fit into the patterns of interruptions that we have studied within this chapter?

- What is the purpose of the interruptions? What happens in the text that could not happen without the interruption?
- Locate specific juxtapositions that the interruptions in the text make available to us.
  - What two images, ideas, characters, or situations have been paired in this particular text?
  - How is it that the audience gains access to each image?
  - How does one add meaning to the other?
  - In what ways do the two images work differently?
  - How does the author compel the audience to look at the two together?
- How does the comparison of the world of the text before and after the interruption offer insight into the routine that has been interrupted? How much of this insight is available to characters within the text and how much is available to those of us who are reading the text?

Anthology

ESPIONAGE: A CRITIC WRITES ABOUT INTERRUPTION

David Denby remarks that the main character of the Jason Bourne movies—*The Bourne Identity* (2002), *The Bourne Supremacy* (2004), and *The Bourne Ultimatum* (2007) hurtles through the film like an object. Denby claims he has always been a purist about action scenes: fight scenes, for example, should show whole bodies in motion and not convey human movement through editing tricks. But the choreographed action of these films works for Denby. Paul Greengrass, the director of the final two, manages to both make us feel the the rush and danger the hunted Bourne feels, but also keeps us aware from the outside of what is happening. The physical intensity of some of the scenes can be seen as interrupting moments of Bourne's tense quiet, And in turn that intensity can also be dialed back to make us reflect on the consequences of actions. It's largely these shifts in momentum, these cinematic interruptions, that make the Bourne series special for Denby, for ultimately through the film's rhythm's we feel the finally our bodies in synch with the hero. Note how Denby's own review closes with a kind of interruption. After generally praising the film, he looks ahead to the future of the franchise and offers satiric suggestions for possible titles still to use.

Matt Damon as Jason Bourne

Characteristics of the Espionage Genre

The general scenario of the espionage genre is that countries cannot trust each other. Their public conversations directly contradict their real thoughts about one another. In the action of espionage, we delight in watching the spies as they seek to infiltrate the secret spaces of the opponent. A key convention of this genre is the importance of disguise. Characters are not who they seem to be, and even the characters whose point of view we share, are generally in disguise or trying to hide their identities. In this genre, a character's safety is directly related to his or her ability to maintain some fictional identity. The *Bourne films* vary this formula in that their central character does not know his own identity. He finds himself with all of the accoutrements of a professional spy—false passports, foreign currency, and an ability to see imminent trouble and respond with deadly force—but he doesn't know how he obtained these conventions of the genre.

Laura Riding's brief poem "The Map of Places" questions assurances. People make maps (and plans, and dreams), but the spirit of exploration depends upon a deeply felt sense that we have no maps to guide us with certainty. Maps of places, Riding notes at the outset, are subject to change. The paper they are printed on tears. There is somehow another level of reality that exists securely whether it is charted or not. That insight is interrupted and the second stanza turns abruptly to a distinct sense of a modern condition: "now" we seem to have things covered—firmly fixed. But Riding leaves us with a sense that this condition is a debilitating illusion. Jason Bourne's experience may be extreme, but some mystery seems essential to our humanity.

The readings in this cluster move us to consider how we frame (contain, order, represent) both physical and emotional space. Yet they (like Riding) interrupt the effort. The frame of reference gets broken and we're back to the sense that life must remain exploratory. Perhaps Joseph Conrad's "The Secret Sharer" would seem an exception. After all, his young captain learns to take charge decisively, to assert control within his sphere of action. But he is quite self-conscious about this process of maturation; he comes to impose an understanding on his situation. He creates through his choices a sense of self that will serve him well in a career at sea. He is, in a profound way, a self-made man. And all the strenuous self-reflection is prompted by a sudden interruption in routine. The captain's hiding of his secret sharer makes maintaining composure difficult. If a life and a career were not at stake, one could narrate the hiding, the narrow escapes, and the awkward contrivances (think of how confused the poor steward is by the captain's seemingly capricious orders) as a bit of slapstick comedy.

Jorge Luis Borges might be considered a master of interruptive strategies. "The Garden of Forking Paths" is interrupted even before it gets started. We're made immediately alert to issues relating to the construction of narratives. Borges opens his story with what seems a scholarly note that abruptly introduces the fragment to follow. Here the announcement of "missing pages" serves to remind us of what we don't know—or what stories can and cannot tell us. The fragment itself contains references to other bits of fragmentary information that must be put together—mapped out—in order to be read. This story takes us on many turns through its own garden of forking paths. As you move through, think of how Borges has made you aware of the reader/seeker role you take every time you engage with a constructed work of art.

Coleridge's "The Rime of the Ancient Mariner" also starts with an interruption; the ancient mariner calls aside the guest who is trying to go into a wedding. Throughout the poem we hear bits of the wedding that the guest is missing, and at the end of the poem, this guest who thought that he would be participating in a celebration "went like one that hath been stunn'd . . . A sadder and a wiser man."

Shakespeare's *Much Ado about Nothing* is a play in which the characters are very much aware of the mechanics of theater. In an early scene, the characters wear masks, and after a conversation with Beatrice, Benedict (who knew that he was talking to Beatrice) wonders if Beatrice knew that she was talking to Benedict. Her words take on one meaning if she is talking directly to him and another if she believes that she is talking to someone else; he needs to know what she knew in order to interpret her words. This is a play in which characters spy on one another. They stage conversations for others to "overhear." Our understanding of the action depends upon our knowledge of who knows what about the other characters. Throughout the play, observing action is not enough; we watch characters watching one another, and each of these frames gives meaning to the action.

REVIEW

David Denby (1943–   )

War Wounds (2007)

Matt Damon, at least in the "Bourne" series, looks like a bullet. He has short hair, no stubble to speak of, and a blunt nose. In violent scenes, his eyes go dead, and he has a strong, compact body, which he hurls through the frame, ricocheting off walls, windows, cars, and fences. In person, Damon is thoughtful and friendly, with a ready smile, and he has shown an increasing range as an actor. Sociable and fast-talking in "The Departed," he was glum and all but immobile in "The Good Shepherd." As the C.I.A. assassin Jason Bourne, however, Damon is a smooth and deadly object. His directors in the series—Doug Liman in "The Bourne Identity" and Paul Greengrass in "The Bourne Supremacy" and now "The Bourne Ultimatum"—have kept him almost continuously in motion, racing down streets and along corridors, leaping across rooftops. Bourne is intimate with many cities—Berlin, London, Paris, Madrid—and, incapable of hesitation, he runs without a stumble though their mazelike neighborhoods, markets, and railroad stations. No office or hotel-room door remains impenetrable; no safe remains locked. Robert Ludlum created the character—in his 1980 novel, "The Bourne Identity"—as a black-ops assassin whose brain had been wiped clean before he was programmed to kill. The writers who adapted Bourne for the screen (Tony Gilroy has been a constant, along with various collaborators) took over Ludlum's notion for the character while dropping his literary sludge; they enhanced Bourne's locomotive skills, and gave him a soul.

This Jason Bourne is so anguished by his crimes that he develops amnesia, but he gradually remembers the bad things he has done, and is haunted by them.

Having participated in illegal operations, Bourne is a menace to the C.I.A., which has no further use for him and would like to be rid of him. The basic setup of all three movies is that the agency tracks his movements with banks of computers and surveillance equipment under the control of powerful people barking intel gibberish at one another, while Bourne tries to evade them and also the various goons, some working for the C.I.A., some not, who are trying to kill him. Eventually, he gets himself in a position to survey the surveyors and hunt the hunters. He has them under his control. But all he wants to do is reclaim himself from his induced oblivion. Summing up the first two films, Manohla Dargis (then at the Los Angeles *Times*) said that the drama of "Identity" was existential (Who am I?), and the drama of "Supremacy" was moral (What did I do?). I would say that the drama of "Ultimatum" is redemptive: How can I escape what I am? The creators of the black-ops program are shown to have used such techniques as hooding and waterboarding to break down and remake Bourne's personality, and he wants to find them. Commenting acidly on current interrogation techniques, the filmmakers suggest that such games were played with Americans as well as with outsiders. This may be a fiction, but it's a sinister thought. In the end, Bourne reaches the sadist who trained him—played by Albert Finney, whose voice is now so gravelly you could walk on it.

The material is formulaic, but, of all the current action franchises, this one is the most enjoyable. Cut off from the C.I.A. and from himself, Bourne has nothing to draw on but tradecraft and instinct. As Damon plays him—silent, wary—Bourne thinks with his body. He seems to have sensors attached to his limbs and his head, and he reacts instantly to threats. I used to be a purist about action sequences, demanding that bodies in combat be seen in full frame and without too much cutting. A few directors are still capable of that kind of classicism (Wolfgang Petersen in "Troy," David Cronenberg in "A History of Violence"), but Paul Greengrass, who also made the superb "United 93," shoots scenes in tiny fragments, and when he does it I see the point—the gain in speed and power is extraordinary. The camera trembles and shakes and hurtles in "Ultimatum," as if we were trapped inside the moving Bourne, and yet, on the fly, we see what we need to see. Gathering the fragments, Greengrass keeps some of the chase scenes going for ten minutes at a time. You come out of the movie both excited and soothed, as if your body had been worked on by felt-covered drumsticks.

I doubt that Bourne will cease his wandering any time soon. Ludlum, having turned out the three "Bourne"s (among many other volumes), died in 2001, so the writer Eric Van Lustbader, none of whose books have ever been made into a movie, unselfishly stepped forward and committed a few extra "Bourne"s to keep the ball rolling. One of these productions, with the curious title "Robert Ludlum's The Bourne Betrayal," was published only a couple of months ago. I salute Lustbader's entrepreneurial energy, but why should he be the only one allowed to get in on the act? I haven't yet made a deal with the Ludlum estate, but I suggest the following titles: "The Bourne Topography" (Bourne prevents the C.I.A. from taking over the Kyzyl Kum Desert in Uzbekistan); "The Bourne Infarction" (Bourne causes a systemic breakdown at C.I.A. headquarters in Langley); and, my most ambitious idea, "The Bourne Arpeggio," in which Bourne, now a violist, prevents the assassination of a Russian dissenter at the reopening of Alice Tully Hall.

FICTION

Jorge Luis Borges (1899–1986)

Jorge Luis Borges was born in Buenos Aires, Argentina. Because his paternal grandmother was English, Borges was fluent in both English and Spanish from an early age. His frail health prevented him from having what might be considered a normal childhood, but he compensated by spending much of his time reading in his father's well-stocked library. These childhood preoccupations with language and learning are also central themes in the mature Borges's poetry and fiction. Borges's fiction has received the most international acclaim, in part because of the relatively larger audience for fiction and because it loses less in translation than does poetry, but he was also one of the preeminent modern poets in Spanish. Particularly influential are Borges's many meta-fictions, short stories in which the boundaries between art and life, reality and fantasy, writer and work, are blurred or eliminated.

The Garden of Forking Paths (1941)

Translated by Andrew Hurley

For Victoria Ocampo

On page 242 of *The History of the World War*, Liddell Hart tells us that an Allied offensive against the Serre-Montauban line (to be mounted by thirteen British divisions backed by one thousand four hundred artillery pieces) had been planned for July 24, 1916, but had to be put off until the morning of the twenty-ninth. Torrential rains (notes Capt. Liddell Hart) were the cause of that delay—a delay that entailed no great consequences, as it turns out.

The statement which follows—dictated, reread, and signed by Dr. Yu Tsun, former professor of English in the *Hochschule* at Tsingtao—throws unexpected light on the case. The two first pages of the statement are missing.

. . . and I hung up the receiver. Immediately afterward, I recognised the voice that had answered in German. It was that of Capt. Richard Madden. Madden's presence in Viktor Runeberg's flat meant the end of our efforts and (though this seemed to me quite secondary, or *should have seemed*) our lives as well. It meant that Runeberg had been arrested, or murdered.[1] Before the sun set on that day, I would face the same fate. Madden was implacable—or rather, he was obliged to be implacable. An Irishman at the orders of the English, a man accused of a certain lack of zealousness, perhaps even treason, how could he fail to embrace and give thanks for this miraculous favour—the discovery, capture, perhaps death, of two agents of the German Empire? I went upstairs to my room; absurdly, I locked the door, and then I threw myself, on my back, onto my narrow iron bed. Outside the window were the usual rooftops and the overcast six o'clock sun. I found it incredible that this day, lacking all omens and premonitions, should be the day of my implacable death. Despite my deceased father, despite my having been a child in a symmetrical garden in Hai Feng—was I, now, about to die? Then I reflected that all things happen to *oneself*, and happen precisely, precisely *now*. Century follows century, yet events occur only *in the present*; countless men in the air, on the land and sea, yet everything that truly happens, happens *to me*. . . . The almost unbearable memory of Madden's horsey face demolished those mental ramblings. In the midst of my hatred and my terror (now I don't mind talking about terror—now that I have foiled Richard Madden, now that my neck hungers for the rope), it occurred to me that that brawling and undoubtedly happy warrior did not suspect that I possessed the Secret—the name of the exact location of the new British artillery park on the Ancre. A bird furrowed the grey sky, and I blindly translated it into an aeroplane, and that aeroplane into many (in the French sky), annihilating the artillery park with vertical bombs. If only my throat, before a bullet crushed it, could cry out that name so that it might be heard in Germany. . . . But my human voice was so terribly inadequate. How was I to make it reach the Leader's ear—the ear of that sick and hateful man who knew nothing of Runeberg and me save that we were in Staffordshire, and who was vainly awaiting word from us in his arid office in Berlin, poring infinitely through the newspapers? . . . *I must flee*, I said aloud. I sat up noiselessly, in needless but perfect silence, as though Madden were already just outside my door. Something—perhaps the mere show of proving that my resources were non-existent—made me go through my pockets. I found what I knew I would find: the American watch, the nickel-plated chain and quadrangular coin, the key ring with the compromising and useless keys to Runeberg's flat, the note-book, a letter I resolved to destroy at once (and never did), the false passport,

---

1 An hypothesis both hateful and odd. The Prussian spy Hans Rabener, alias Viktor Runeberg, attacked with drawn automatic the bearer of the warrant for his arrest, Captain Richard Madden. The latter, in self-defense, inflicted the wound which brought about Runeberg's death. (Editor's note.)

one crown, two shillings, and a few odd pence, the red-and-blue pencil, the handkerchief, the revolver with its single bullet. Absurdly, I picked it up and hefted it, to give myself courage. I vaguely reflected that a pistol shot can be heard at a considerable distance. In ten minutes, my plan was ripe. The telephone book gave me the name of the only person able to communicate the information: he lived in a suburb of Fenton, less than a half hour away by train.

I am a coward. I can say that, now that I have carried out a plan whose dangerousness and daring no man will deny. I know that it was a terrible thing to do. I did not do it for Germany. What do I care for a barbaric country that has forced me to the ignominy of spying? Furthermore, I know of a man of England—a modest man—who in my view is no less a genius than Goethe. I spoke with him for no more than an hour, but for one hour he was Goethe. . . . No—I did it because I sensed that the Leader looked down on the people of my race—the countless ancestors whose blood flows through my veins. I wanted to prove to him that a yellow man could save his armies. And I had to escape from Madden. His hands, his voice, could beat upon my door at any moment. I silently dressed, said good-bye to myself in the mirror, made my way downstairs, looked up and down the quiet street, and set off. The train station was not far from my flat, but I thought it better to take a cab. I argued that I ran less chance of being recognised that way; the fact is, I felt I was visible and vulnerable—infinitely vulnerable—in the deserted street. I recall that I told the driver to stop a little ways from the main entrance to the station. I got down from the cab with willed and almost painful slowness. I would be going to the village of Ashgrove, but I bought a ticket for a station farther down the line. The train was to leave at eight-fifty, scant minutes away. I had to hurry; the next train would not be until nine-thirty. There was almost no one on the platform. I walked through the cars; I recall a few workmen, a woman dressed in mourning weeds, a young man fervently reading Tracitus' *Annals*, and a cheerful-looking wounded soldier. The train pulled out at last. A man I recognised ran, vainly, out to the end of the platform; it was Capt. Richard Madden. Shattered, trembling, I huddled on the other end of the seat, far from the feared window.

From that shattered state I passed into a state of almost abject cheerfulness. 5 I told myself that my duel had begun, and that in dodging my adversary's thrust—even by forty minutes, even thanks to the slightest smile from fate—the first round had gone to me. I argued that this small win prefigured total victory. I argued that the win was not really even so without the precious hour that the trains had given me, I'd be in gaol, or dead. I argued (no less sophistically) that my cowardly cheerfulness proved that I was a man capable of following this adventure through to its successful end. From that weakness I drew strength that was never to abandon me. I foresee that mankind will resign itself more and more fully every day to more and more horrendous undertakings; soon there will be nothing but warriors and brigands. I give them this piece of advice: *He who is to perform a horrendous act should imagine to himself that it is already done, should impose upon himself a future as irrevocable as the past.* That is what I did, while my eyes—the eyes of a man already dead—registered the flow of that day perhaps to be my last, and the spreading of the night. The train ran sweetly, gently, through woods of ash trees. It stopped virtually in the middle of the countryside. No one called out the name of the station. "Ashgrove?" I asked some boys on the platform. "Ashgrove," they said, nodding. I got off the train.

A lamp illuminated the platform, but the boys' faces remained within the area of shadow. "Are you going to Dr. Stephen Albert's house?" one queried. Without waiting for an answer, another of them said: "The house is far way, but you'll not get lost if you follow that road there to the left, and turn left at every crossing." I tossed them a coin (my last), went down some stone steps, and started down the solitary road. It ran ever so slightly downhill and was of elemental dirt. Branches tangled overhead, and the low round moon seemed to walk along beside me.

For one instant, I feared that Richard Madden had somehow seen through my desperate plan, but I soon realized that that was impossible. The boy's advice to turn always to the left reminded me that that was the common way of discovering the central lawn of a certain type of maze. I am something of a *connoisseur* of mazes: not for nothing am I the great-grandson of that Ts'ui Pen who was governor of Yunan province and who renounced all temporal power in order to write a novel containing more characters than the *Hung Lu Meng* and construct a labyrinth in which all men would lose their way. Ts'ui Pen devoted thirteen years to those disparate labours, but the hand of a foreigner murdered him and his novel made no sense and no one ever found the labyrinth. It was under English trees that I meditated on that lost labyrinth: I pictured it perfect and inviolate on the secret summit of a mountain; I pictured its outlines blurred by rice paddies, or underwater; I pictured it as infinite—a labyrinth not of octagonal pavillions and paths that turn back upon themselves, but of rivers and provinces and kingdoms. . . . I imagined a labyrinth of labyrinths, a maze of mazes, a twisting, turning, ever-widening labyrinth that contained both past and future and somehow implied the stars. Absorbed in those illusory imaginings, I forgot that I was a pursued man; I felt myself, for an indefinite while, the abstract perceiver of the world. The vague, living countryside, the moon, the remains of the day did their work in me; so did the gently downward road, which forestalled all possibility of weariness. The evening was near, yet infinite.

The road dropped and forked as it cut through the now-formless meadows. A keen and vaguely syllabic song, blurred by leaves and distance, came and went on the gentle gusts of breeze. I was struck by the thought that a man may be the enemy of other men, the enemy of other men's other moments, yet not be the enemy of a country—of fireflies, words, gardens, watercourses, zephyrs. It was amidst such thoughts that I came to a high rusty gate. Through the iron bars I made out a drive lined with poplars, and a gazebo of some kind. Suddenly, I realised two things—the first trivial, the second almost incredible: the music I had heard was coming from that gazebo, or pavillion, and the music was Chinese. That was why unconsciously I had fully given myself over to it. I do not recall whether there was a bell or whether I had to clap my hands to make my arrival known.

The sputtering of the music continued, but from the rear of the intimate house, a lantern was making its way toward me—a lantern cross-hatched and sometimes blotted out altogether by the trees, a paper lantern the shape of a drum and the colour of the moon. It was carried by a tall man. I could not see his face because the light blinded me. He opened the gate and slowly spoke to me in my own language.

"I see that the compassionate Hsi P'eng has undertaken to remedy my   10 solitude. You will no doubt wish to see the garden?"

I recognised the name of one of our consuls, but I could only disconcertedly repeat, "The garden?"

'The garden of forking paths."

Something stirred in my memory, and I spoke with incomprehensible assurance.

"The garden of my ancestor Ts'ui Pen."

"Your ancestor? Your illustrious ancestor? Please—come in."   15

The dew-drenched path meandered like the paths of my childhood. We came to a library of Western and Oriental books. I recognised, bound in yellow silk, several handwritten volumes of the Lost Encyclopedia compiled by the third emperor of the Luminous Dynasty but never printed. The disk on the gramophone revolved near a bronze phoenix. I also recall a vase of *famille* rose and another, earlier by several hundred years, of that blue colour our artificers copied from the potters of ancient Persia. . . .

Stephen Albert, with a smile, regarded me. He was, as I have said, quite tall, with sharp features, grey eyes, and a grey beard. There was something priestlike about him, somehow, but something sailorlike as well; later he told me he had been a missionary in Tientsin "before aspiring to be a Sinologist."

We sat down, I on a long low divan, he with his back to the window and a tall circular clock. I figured that my pursuer, Richard Madden, could not possibly arrive for at least an hour. My irrevocable decision could wait.

"An amazing life, Ts'ui Pen's," Stephen Albert said. "Governor of the province in which he had been born, a man learned in astronomy, astrology, renowned poet and calligrapher—he abandoned it all in order to compose a book and a labyrinth. He renounced the pleasures of oppression, justice, the populous marriage bed, banquets, and even erudition in order to sequester himself for thirteen years in the Pavillion of Limpid Solitude. Upon his death, his heirs found nothing but chaotic manuscripts. The family, as you perhaps are aware, were about to deliver them to the fire, but his counsellor—a Taoist or Buddhist monk—insisted upon publishing them."

"To this day," I replied, "we who are descended from Ts'ui Pen execrate   20 that monk. It was senseless to publish those manuscripts. The book is a contradictory jumble of irresolute drafts. I once examined it myself; in the third chapter the hero dies, yet in the fourth he is alive again. As for Ts'ui Pen's other labor, his Labyrinth. . . ."

"Here is the Labyrinth," Albert said, gesturing towards a tall lacquered writing cabinet.

"An ivory labyrinth!" I exclaimed. "A very small sort of labyrinth . . . "

"A labyrinth of symbols," he corrected me. "An invisible labyrinth of time. I, an English barbarian, have somehow been chosen to unveil the diaphanous mystery. Now, more than a hundred years after the fact, the precise details are irrecoverable, but it is not difficult to surmise what happened. Ts'ui Pen must at one point have remarked, 'I shall retire to write a book,' and at another point, 'I shall retire to construct a labyrinth.' Everyone pictured two projects; it occurred to no one that book and labyrinth were one and the same. The Pavillion of Limpid Solitude was erected in the centre of a garden that was, perhaps, most intricately laid out; that fact might well have suggested a physical labyrinth. Ts'ui Pen died; no one in all the wide lands that had been his could find the labyrinth. The novel's confusion—confusedness, I mean, of course—suggested to me that it was that labyrinth. Two circumstances lent me the final solution of the problem—one, the curious legend that Ts'ui Pen had intended to construct a labyrinth which was truly infinite, and two, a fragment of a letter I discovered."

Albert stood. His back was turned to me for several moments; he opened a drawer in the black-and-gold writing cabinet. He turned back with a paper that had once been crimson but was now pink and delicate and rectangular. It was written in Ts'ui Pen's renowned calligraphy. Eagerly yet uncomprehendingly I read the words that a man of my own lineage had written with painstaking brushstrokes: *I leave to several futures (not to all) my garden of forking paths.* I wordlessly handed the paper back to Albert. He continued:

"Before unearthing this letter, I had wondered how a book could be in-   25 finite. The only way I could surmise was that it be a cyclical, or circular, volume, a volume whose last page would be identical to the first, so that one might go on indefinitely. I also recalled that night at the centre of the *1001 Nights*, when the queen Scheherazade (through some magical distractedness on the part of the copyist) begins to retell, verbatim, the story of the 1001 Nights, with the risk of returning once again to the night on which she is telling it—and so on, *ad infinitum*. I also pictured to myself a platonic, hereditary sort of work, passed down from father to son, in which each new individual would add a chapter or with reverent care correct his elders' pages. These imaginings amused and distracted me, but none of them seemed to correspond even remotely to Ts'ui Pen's contradictory chapters. As I was floundering about in the mire of these perplexities, I was sent from Oxford the document you have just examined. I paused, as you may well imagine, at the sentence 'I leave to several futures (not to all) my garden of forking paths.' Almost instantly, I saw it—the garden of forking paths was the chaotic novel; the phrase 'several futures (not all)' suggested to me the image of a forking in *time*, rather than in space. A full rereading of the book confirmed my theory. In all fictions, each time a man meets diverse alternatives, he chooses one and eliminates the others; in the work of the virtually impossible-to-disentangle Ts'ui Pen, the character chooses—simultaneously—all of them. *He creates*, thereby, 'several futures,' several *times*, which themselves proliferate and fork. That is the explanation for the novel's contradictions. Fang, let us say, has a secret; a stranger knocks at his door; Fang decides to kill him. Naturally, there are various possible outcomes—Fang can kill the intruder, the intruder can kill Fang, they can both live, they can both be killed, and so on. In Ts'ui Pen's novel, *all* the outcomes in fact occur; each is the starting point for further bifurcations. Once in a while, the paths of that labyrinth converge: for example, you come to this house, but in one of the possible pasts you are my enemy, in another my friend. If you can bear my incorrigible pronunciation, we shall read a few pages."

His face, in the vivid circle of the lamp, was undoubtedly that of an old man, though with something indomitable and even immortal about it. He read with slow precision two versions of a single epic chapter. In the first, an army marches off to battle through a mountain wilderness; the horror of the rocks and darkness inspires in them a disdain for life, and they go on to an easy victory. In the second, the same army passes through a palace in which a ball is being held; the brilliant battle seems to them a continuation of the *fête*, and they win it easily.

I listened with honourable veneration to those ancient fictions, which were themselves perhaps not as remarkable as the fact that a man of my blood had invented them and a man of a distant empire was restoring them to me on an island in the West in the course of a desperate mission. I recall the final words, repeated in each version like some secret commandment: "Thus the heroes fought, their admirable hearts calm, their swords violent, they themselves resigned to killing and to dying."

From that moment on, I felt all about me and within my obscure body an invisible, intangible pullulation—not that of the divergent, parallel, and finally coalescing armies, but an agitation more inaccessible, more inward than that, yet one those armies somehow prefigured. Albert went on:

"I do not believe that your venerable ancestor played at idle variations. I cannot think it probable that he would sacrifice thirteen years to the infinite performance of a rhetorical exercise. In your country, the novel is a subordinate genre; at that time it was a genre beneath contempt. Ts'ui Pen was a novelist of genius, but he was also a man of letters, and surely would not have considered himself a mere novelist. The testimony of his contemporaries proclaims his metaphysical, mystical leanings—and his life is their fullest confirmation. Philosophical debate consumes a good part of his novel. I know that of all problems, none disturbed him, none gnawed at him like the unfathomable problem of time. How strange, then, that that problem should be the only one that does not figure in the pages of his *Garden*. He never even uses the word. How do you explain that wilful omission?"

I proposed several solutions—all unsatisfactory. We discussed them;   30 finally, Stephen Albert said:

"In a riddle whose answer is chess, what is the only word that must not be used?"

I thought for a moment.

"The word 'chess,'" I replied.

"Exactly," Albert said. "*The Garden of Forking Paths* is a huge riddle, or parable, whose subject is time; that secret purpose forbids Ts'ui Pen the merest mention of its name. To *always* omit one word, to employ awkward metaphors and obvious circumlocutions, is perhaps the most emphatic way of calling attention to that word. It is, at any rate, the tortuous path chosen by the devious Ts'ui Pen at each and every one of the turnings of his inexhaustible novel. I have compared hundreds of manuscripts, I have corrected the errors introduced through the negligence of copyists, I have reached a hypothesis for the plan of that chaos, I have reestablished, or believe I've reestablished, its fundamental order—I have translated the entire work; and I know that not once does the word 'time' appear. The explanation is obvious: *The Garden of Forking Paths* is an incomplete, but not false, image of the universe as conceived by Ts'ui Pen. Unlike Newton and Schopenhauer, your ancestor did not believe in a uniform and absolute time; he believed in an infinite series of times, a growing, dizzying web of divergent, convergent, and parallel times. That fabric of times that approach one another, fork, are snipped off, or are simply unknown for centuries, contains *all* possibilities. In most of those times, we do not exist; in some, you exist but I do not; in others, I do and you do not; in others still, we both do. In this one, which the favouring hand of chance has dealt me, you have come to my home; in another, when you come through my garden you find me dead; in another, I say these same words, but I am an error, a ghost."

'In all," I said, not without a tremble, "I am grateful for, and I venerate,   35 your re-creation of the garden of Ts'ui Pen."

"Not in all," he whispered with a smile. "Time forks, perpetually, into countless futures. In one of them, I am your enemy."

I felt again that pullulation I have mentioned. I sensed that the dew-drenched garden that surrounded the house was saturated, infinitely, with invisible persons. Those persons were Albert and myself—secret, busily at work, multiform—in other dimensions of time. I raised my eyes and the gossamer nightmare faded. In the yellow-and-black garden there was but a single man—but that man was as mighty as a statue, and that man was coming down the path, and he was Capt. Richard Madden.

"The future is with us," I replied, "but I am your friend. May I look at the letter again?"

Albert rose once again. He stood tall as he opened the drawer of the tall writing cabinet; he turned his back to me for a moment. I had cocked the revolver. With utmost care, I fired. Albert fell without a groan, without a sound, on the instant. I swear that he died instantly—one clap of thunder.

The rest is unreal, insignificant. Madden burst into the room and arrested   40 me. I have been sentenced to hang. I have most abhorrently triumphed: I have communicated to Berlin the secret name of the city to be attacked. Yesterday it was bombed—I read about it in the same newspapers that posed to all of England the enigma of the murder of the eminent Sinologist Stephen Albert by a stranger, Yu Tsun. The leader solved the riddle. He knew that my problem was how to report (over the deafening noise of the war) the name of the city named Albert, and that the only way I could find was murdering a person of that name. He does not know (no one can know) my endless contrition, and my weariness.

- Locate the various ways in which this story is interrupted, beginning by noticing that we begin on "page 242" of a particular history and "The first two pages of the statement [that we are about to read] are missing." How can we recover any coherent narrative from these interruptions?

- What are the different labyrinths that the narrator encounters in the story? How can a book be a labyrinth?

- How does the espionage story here relate to the solution that the narrator discovers of "The Garden of Forking Paths"?

Joseph Conrad (1857–1942)

Joseph Conrad was born in Russian-occupied Poland. He became a sailor for the British Merchant Service, and it was this career that led him to become a British citizen. Life as a sailor was difficult, but it provided him with much of the raw material he was to refine and develop in his literary production. Though he struggled as a writer at first, Conrad eventually achieved both commercial and critical success. His best-known work, *Heart of Darkness*, which draws upon the author's own experiences in central Africa, focuses on the ways in which European colonists are tormented and perverted by their own drives to dominate and exploit. His work as a whole is remarkable for the attention it brings to both societal structures and to the working of the individual mind under stress.

The Secret Sharer (1910)

On my right hand there were lines of fishing stakes resembling a mysterious system of half-submerged bamboo fences, incomprehensible in its division of the domain of tropical fishes, and crazy of aspect as if abandoned forever by some nomad tribe of fishermen now gone to the other end of the ocean; for there was no sign of human habitation as far as the eye could reach. To the left a group of barren islets, suggesting ruins of stone walls, towers, and block-houses, had its foundations set in a blue sea that itself looked solid, so still and stable did it lie below my feet; even the track of light from the westering sun shone smoothly, without that animated glitter which tells of an imperceptible ripple. And when I turned my head to take a parting glance at the tug which had just left us anchored outside the bar, I saw the straight line of the flat shore joined to the stable sea, edge to edge, with a perfect and unmarked closeness, in one leveled floor half brown, half blue under the enormous dome of the sky. Corresponding in their insignificance to the islets of the sea, two small clumps of trees, one on each side of the only fault in the impeccable joint, marked the mouth of the river Meinam we had just left on the first preparatory stage of our homeward journey; and, far back on the inland level, a larger and loftier mass, the grove surrounding the great Paknam pagoda, was the only thing on which the eye could rest from the vain task of exploring the monotonous sweep of the horizon. Here and there gleams as of a few scattered pieces of silver marked the windings of the great river; and on the nearest of them, just within the bar, the tug steaming right into the land became lost to my sight, hull and funnel and masts, as though the impassive earth had swallowed her up without an effort, without a tremor. My eye followed the light cloud of her smoke, now here, now there, above the plain, according to the devious curves of the stream, but always fainter and farther away, till I lost it at last behind the miter-shaped hill of the great pagoda. And then I was left alone with my ship, anchored at the head of the Gulf of Siam. She floated at the starting point of a long journey, very still in an immense stillness, the shadows of her spars flung far to the eastward by the setting sun. At that moment I was alone on her decks. There was not a sound in her—and around us nothing moved, nothing lived, not a canoe on the water, not a bird in the air, not a cloud in the sky. In this breathless pause at the threshold of a long passage we seemed to be measuring our fitness for a long and arduous enterprise, the appointed task of both our existences to be carried out, far from all human eyes, with only sky and sea for spectators and for judges.

There must have been some glare in the air to interfere with one's sight, because it was only just before the sun left us that my roaming eyes made out beyond the highest ridges of the principal islet of the group something which did away with the solemnity of perfect solitude. The tide of darkness flowed on swiftly; and with tropical suddenness a swarm of stars came out above the shadowy earth, while I lingered yet, my hand resting lightly on my ship's rail as if on the shoulder of a trusted friend. But, with all that multitude of celestial bodies staring down at one, the comfort of quiet communion with her was gone for good. And there were also disturbing sounds by this time—voices, footsteps forward; the steward flitted along the main-deck, a busily ministering spirit; a hand bell tinkled urgently under the poop deck. . . .

I found my two officers waiting for me near the supper table, in the lighted cuddy. We sat down at once, and as I helped the chief mate, I said:

"Are you aware that there is a ship anchored inside the islands? I saw her mastheads above the ridge as the sun went down."

He raised sharply his simple face, overcharged by a terrible growth of   5
whisker, and emitted his usual ejaculations: "Bless my soul, sir! You don't say so!"

My second mate was a round-cheeked, silent young man, grave beyond his years, I thought; but as our eyes happened to meet I detected a slight quiver on his lips. I looked down at once. It was not my part to encourage sneering on board my ship. It must be said, too, that I knew very little of my officers. In consequence of certain events of no particular significance, except to myself, I had been appointed to the command only a fortnight before. Neither did I know much of the hands forward. All these people had been together for eighteen months or so, and my position was that of the only stranger on board. I mention this because it has some bearing on what is to follow. But what I felt most was my being a stranger to the ship; and if all the truth must be told, I was somewhat of a stranger to myself. The youngest man on board (barring the second mate), and untried as yet by a position of the fullest responsibility, I was willing to take the adequacy of the others for granted. They had simply to be equal to their tasks; but I wondered how far I should turn out faithful to that ideal conception of one's own personality every man sets up for himself secretly.

Meantime the chief mate, with an almost visible effect of collaboration on the part of his round eyes and frightful whiskers, was trying to evolve a theory of the anchored ship. His dominant trait was to take all things into earnest consideration. He was of a painstaking turn of mind. As he used to say, he "liked to account to himself" for practically everything that came in his way, down to a miserable scorpion he had found in his cabin a week before. The why and the wherefore of that scorpion—how it got on board and came to select his room rather than the pantry (which was a dark place and more what a scorpion would be partial to), and how on earth it managed to drown itself in the inkwell of his writing desk—had exercised him infinitely. The ship within the islands was much more easily accounted for; and just as we were about to rise from table he made his pronouncement. She was, he doubted not, a ship from home lately arrived. Probably she drew too much water to cross the bar except at the top of spring tides. Therefore she went into that natural harbor to wait for a few days in preference to remaining in an open roadstead.

"That's so," confirmed the second mate, suddenly, in his slightly hoarse voice. "She draws over twenty feet. She's the Liverpool ship Sephora with a cargo of coal. Hundred and twenty-three days from Cardiff."

We looked at him in surprise.

"The tugboat skipper told me when he came on board for your letters,   10 sir," explained the young man. "He expects to take her up the river the day after tomorrow."

After thus overwhelming us with the extent of his information he slipped out of the cabin. The mate observed regretfully that he "could not account for that young fellow's whims." What prevented him telling us all about it at once, he wanted to know.

I detained him as he was making a move. For the last two days the crew had had plenty of hard work, and the night before they had very little sleep. I felt painfully that I—a stranger—was doing something unusual when I directed him to let all hands turn in without setting an anchor watch. I proposed to keep on deck myself till one o'clock or thereabouts. I would get the second mate to relieve me at that hour.

"He will turn out the cook and the steward at four," I concluded, "and then give you a call. Of course at the slightest sign of any sort of wind we'll have the hands up and make a start at once."

He concealed his astonishment. "Very well, sir." Outside the cuddy he put his head in the second mate's door to inform him of my unheard-of caprice to take a five hours' anchor watch on myself. I heard the other raise his voice incredulously——"What? The Captain himself?" Then a few more murmurs, a door closed, then another. A few moments later I went on deck.

My strangeness, which had made me sleepless, had prompted that   15 unconventional arrangement, as if I had expected in those solitary hours of the night to get on terms with the ship of which I knew nothing, manned by men of whom I knew very little more. Fast alongside a wharf, littered like any ship in port with a tangle of unrelated things, invaded by unrelated shore people, I had hardly seen her yet properly. Now, as she lay cleared for sea, the stretch of her main-deck seemed to me very fine under the stars. Very fine, very roomy for her size, and very inviting. I descended the poop and paced the waist, my mind picturing to myself the coming passage through the Malay Archipelago, down the Indian Ocean, and up the Atlantic. All its phases were familiar enough to me, every characteristic, all the alternatives which were likely to face me on the high seas—everything! . . . except the novel responsibility of command. But I took heart from the reasonable thought that the ship was like other ships, the men like other men, and that the sea was not likely to keep any special surprises expressly for my discomfiture.

Arrived at that comforting conclusion, I bethought myself of a cigar and went below to get it. All was still down there. Everybody at the after end of the ship was sleeping profoundly. I came out again on the quarterdeck, agreeably at ease in my sleeping suit on that warm breathless night, barefooted, a glowing cigar in my teeth, and, going forward, I was met by the profound silence of the fore end of the ship. Only as I passed the door of the forecastle, I heard a deep, quiet, trustful sigh of some sleeper inside. And suddenly I rejoiced in the great security of the sea as compared with the unrest of the land, in my choice of that untempted life presenting no disquieting problems, invested with an elementary moral beauty by the absolute straightforwardness of its appeal and by the singleness of its purpose.

The riding light in the forerigging burned with a clear, untroubled, as if symbolic, flame, confident and bright in the mysterious shades of the night. Passing on my way aft along the other side of the ship, I observed that the rope side ladder, put over, no doubt, for the master of the tug when he came to fetch away our letters, had not been hauled in as it should have been. I became annoyed at this, for exactitude in some small matters is the very soul of discipline. Then I reflected that I had myself peremptorily dismissed my officers from duty, and by my own act had prevented the anchor watch being formally set and things properly attended to. I asked myself whether it was wise ever to interfere with the established routine of duties even from the kindest of motives. My action might have made me appear eccentric. Goodness only knew how that absurdly whiskered mate would "account" for my conduct, and what the whole ship thought of that informality of their new captain. I was vexed with myself.

Not from compunction certainly, but, as it were mechanically, I proceeded to get the ladder in myself. Now a side ladder of that sort is a light affair and comes in easily, yet my vigorous tug, which should have brought it flying on board, merely recoiled upon my body in a totally unexpected jerk. What the devil!. . . I was so astounded by the immovableness of that ladder that I remained stockstill, trying to account for it to myself like that imbecile mate of mine. In the end, of course, I put my head over the rail.

The side of the ship made an opaque belt of shadow on the darkling glassy shimmer of the sea. But I saw at once something elongated and pale floating very close to the ladder. Before I could form a guess a faint flash of phosphorescent light, which seemed to issue suddenly from the naked body of a man, flickered in the sleeping water with the elusive, silent play of summer lightning in a night sky. With a gasp I saw revealed to my stare a pair of feet, the long legs, a broad livid back immersed right up to the neck in a greenish cadaverous glow. One hand, awash, clutched the bottom rung of the ladder. He was complete but for the head. A headless corpse! The cigar dropped out of my gaping mouth with a tiny plop and a short hiss quite audible in the absolute stillness of all things under heaven. At that I suppose he raised up his face, a dimly pale oval in the shadow of the ship's side. But even then I could only barely make out down there the shape of his black-haired head. However, it was enough for the horrid, frost-bound sensation which had gripped me about the chest to pass off. The moment of vain exclamations was past, too. I only climbed on the spare spar and leaned over the rail as far as I could, to bring my eyes nearer to that mystery floating alongside.

As he hung by the ladder, like a resting swimmer, the sea lightning   20
played about his limbs at every stir; and he appeared in it ghastly, silvery, fishlike. He remained as mute as a fish, too. He made no motion to get out of the water, either. It was inconceivable that he should not attempt to come on board, and strangely troubling to suspect that perhaps he did not want to. And my first words were prompted by just that troubled incertitude.

"What's the matter?" I asked in my ordinary tone, speaking down to the face upturned exactly under mine.

"Cramp," it answered, no louder. Then slightly anxious, "I say, no need to call anyone."

"I was not going to," I said.

"Are you alone on deck?"

"Yes."   25

I had somehow the impression that he was on the point of letting go the ladder to swim away beyond my ken—mysterious as he came. But, for the moment, this being appearing as if he had risen from the bottom of the sea (it was certainly the nearest land to the ship) wanted only to know the time. I told him. And he, down there, tentatively:

"I suppose your captain's turned in?"

"I am sure he isn't," I said.

He seemed to struggle with himself, for I heard something like the low, bitter murmur of doubt. "What's the good?" His next words came out with a hesitating effort.

"Look here, my man. Could you call him out quietly?"   30

I thought the time had come to declare myself.

"I am the captain."

I heard a "By Jove!" whispered at the level of the water. The phosphorescence flashed in the swirl of the water all about his limbs, his other hand seized the ladder.

"My name's Leggatt."

The voice was calm and resolute. A good voice. The self-possession of   35
that man had somehow induced a corresponding state in myself. It was very quietly that I remarked:

"You must be a good swimmer."

"Yes. I've been in the water practically since nine o'clock. The question for me now is whether I am to let go this ladder and go on swimming till I sink from exhaustion, or—to come on board here."

I felt this was no mere formula of desperate speech, but a real alternative in the view of a strong soul. I should have gathered from this that he was young; indeed, it is only the young who are ever confronted by such clear issues. But at the time it was pure intuition on my part. A mysterious communication was established already between us two—in the face of that silent, darkened tropical sea. I was young, too; young enough to make no comment. The man in the water began suddenly to climb up the ladder, and I hastened away from the rail to fetch some clothes.

Before entering the cabin I stood still, listening in the lobby at the foot of the stairs. A faint snore came through the closed door of the chief mate's room. The second mate's door was on the hook, but the darkness in there was absolutely soundless. He, too, was young and could sleep like a stone. Remained the steward, but he was not likely to wake up before he was called. I got a sleeping suit out of my room and, coming back on deck, saw the naked man from the sea sitting on the main hatch, glimmering white in the darkness, his elbows on his knees and his head in his hands. In a moment he had concealed his damp body in a sleeping suit of the same graystripe pattern as the one I was wearing and followed me like my double on the poop. Together we moved right aft, barefooted, silent.

"What is it?" I asked in a deadened voice, taking the lighted lamp   40
out of the binnacle, and raising it to his face.

"An ugly business."

He had rather regular features; a good mouth; light eyes under somewhat heavy, dark eyebrows; a smooth, square forehead; no growth on his cheeks; a small, brown mustache, and a well-shaped, round chin. His expression was concentrated, meditative, under the inspecting light of the lamp I held up to his face; such as a man thinking hard in solitude might wear. My sleeping suit was just right for his size. A well-knit young fellow of twenty-five at most. He caught his lower lip with the edge of white, even teeth.

"Yes," I said, replacing the lamp in the binnacle. The warm, heavy tropical night closed upon his head again.

"There's a ship over there," he murmured.

"Yes, I know. The Sephora. Did you know of us?"   45

"Hadn't the slightest idea. I am the mate of her——" He paused and corrected himself. "I should say I *was*."

"Aha! Something wrong?"

"Yes. Very wrong indeed. I've killed a man."

"What do you mean? Just now?"

"No, on the passage. Weeks ago. Thirty-nine south. When I say a   50
man—"

"Fit of temper," I suggested, confidently.

The shadowy, dark head, like mine, seemed to nod imperceptibly above
the ghostly gray of my sleeping suit. It was, in the night, as though I had been
faced by my own reflection in the depths of a somber and immense mirror.

"A pretty thing to have to own up to for a Conway boy," murmured my
double, distinctly.

"You're a Conway boy?"

"I am," he said, as if startled. Then, slowly . . ."Perhaps you too——"   55

It was so; but being a couple of years older I had left before he joined.
After a quick interchange of dates a silence fell; and I thought suddenly of
my absurd mate with his terrific whiskers and the "Bless my soul—you don't
say so" type of intellect. My double gave me an inkling of his thoughts by saying: "My father's a parson in Norfolk. Do you see me before a judge and jury
on that charge? For myself I can't see the necessity. There are fellows that an
angel from heaven——And I am not that. He was one of those creatures that
are just simmering all the time with a silly sort of wickedness. Miserable devils
that have no business to live at all. He wouldn't do his duty and wouldn't let
anybody else do theirs. But what's the good of talking! You know well enough
the sort of ill-conditioned snarling cur——"

He appealed to me as if our experiences had been as identical as our
clothes. And I knew well enough the pestiferous danger of such a character
where there are no means of legal repression. And I knew well enough also
that my double there was no homicidal ruffian. I did not think of asking him
for details, and he told me the story roughly in brusque, disconnected sentences. I needed no more. I saw it all going on as though I were myself inside
that other sleeping suit.

"It happened while we were setting a reefed foresail, at dusk. Reefed foresail! You understand the sort of weather. The only sail we had left to keep the
ship running; so you may guess what it had been like for days. Anxious sort of
job, that. He gave me some of his cursed insolence at the sheet. I tell you I was
overdone with this terrific weather that seemed to have no end to it. Terrific,
I tell you—and a deep ship. I believe the fellow himself was half crazed with
funk. It was no time for gentlemanly reproof, so I turned round and felled him
like an ox. He up and at me. We closed just as an awful sea made for the ship.
All hands saw it coming and took to the rigging, but I had him by the throat,
and went on shaking him like a rat, the men above us yelling, 'Look out! look
out!' Then a crash as if the sky had fallen on my head. They say that for over
ten minutes hardly anything was to be seen of the ship—just the three masts
and a bit of the forecastle head and of the poop all awash driving along in a
smother of foam. It was a miracle that they found us, jammed together behind

the forebitts. It's clear that I meant business, because I was holding him by the throat still when they picked us up. He was black in the face. It was too much for them. It seems they rushed us aft together, gripped as we were, screaming 'Murder!' like a lot of lunatics, and broke into the cuddy. And the ship running for her life, touch and go all the time, any minute her last in a sea fit to turn your hair gray only a-looking at it. I understand that the skipper, too, started raving like the rest of them. The man had been deprived of sleep for more than a week, and to have this sprung on him at the height of a furious gale nearly drove him out of his mind. I wonder they didn't fling me overboard after getting the carcass of their precious shipmate out of my fingers. They had rather a job to separate us, I've been told. A sufficiently fierce story to make an old judge and a respectable jury sit up a bit. The first thing I heard when I came to myself was the maddening howling of that endless gale, and on that the voice of the old man. He was hanging on to my bunk, staring into my face out of his sou'wester.

" 'Mr. Leggatt, you have killed a man. You can act no longer as chief mate of this ship.' "

His care to subdue his voice made it sound monotonous. He rested a   60
hand on the end of the skylight to steady himself with, and all that time did not stir a limb, so far as I could see. "Nice little tale for a quiet tea party," he concluded in the same tone.

One of my hands, too, rested on the end of the skylight; neither did I stir a limb, so far as I knew. We stood less than a foot from each other. It occurred to me that if old "Bless my soul—you don't say so" were to put his head up the companion and catch sight of us, he would think he was seeing double, or imagine himself come upon a scene of weird witchcraft; the strange captain having a quiet confabulation by the wheel with his own gray ghost. I became very much concerned to prevent anything of the sort. I heard the other's soothing undertone.

"My father's a parson in Norfolk," it said. Evidently he had forgotten he had told me this important fact before. Truly a nice little tale.

"You had better slip down into my stateroom now," I said, moving off stealthily. My double followed my movements; our bare feet made no sound; I let him in, closed the door with care, and, after giving a call to the second mate, returned on deck for my relief.

"Not much sign of any wind yet," I remarked when he approached.

"No, sir. Not much," he assented, sleepily, in his hoarse voice, with just   65
enough deference, no more, and barely suppressing a yawn.

"Well, that's all you have to look out for. You have got your orders."

"Yes, sir."

I paced a turn or two on the poop and saw him take up his position face forward with his elbow in the ratlines of the mizzen rigging before

I went below. The mate's faint snoring was still going on peacefully. The cuddy lamp was burning over the table on which stood a vase with flowers, a polite attention from the ship's provision merchant—the last flowers we should see for the next three months at the very least. Two bunches of bananas hung from the beam symmetrically, one on each side of the rudder casing. Everything was as before in the ship—except that two of her captain's sleeping suits were simultaneously in use, one motionless in the cuddy, the other keeping very still in the captain's stateroom.

It must be explained here that my cabin had the form of the capital letter L, the door being within the angle and opening into the short part of the letter. A couch was to the left, the bed place to the right; my writing desk and the chronometers' table faced the door. But anyone opening it, unless he stepped right inside, had no view of what I call the long (or vertical) part of the letter. It contained some lockers surmounted by a bookcase; and a few clothes, a thick jacket or two, caps, oilskin coat, and such like, hung on hooks. There was at the bottom of that part a door opening into my bathroom, which could be entered also directly from the saloon. But that way was never used.

The mysterious arrival had discovered the advantage of this particular   70
shape. Entering my room, lighted strongly by a big bulkhead lamp swung on gimbals above my writing desk, I did not see him anywhere till he stepped out quietly from behind the coats hung in the recessed part.

"I heard somebody moving about, and went in there at once," he whispered.

I, too, spoke under my breath.

"Nobody is likely to come in here without knocking and getting permission."

He nodded. His face was thin and the sunburn faded, as though he had been ill. And no wonder. He had been, I heard presently, kept under arrest in his cabin for nearly seven weeks. But there was nothing sickly in his eyes or in his expression. He was not a bit like me, really; yet, as we stood leaning over my bed place, whispering side by side, with our dark heads together and our backs to the door, anybody bold enough to open it stealthily would have been treated to the uncanny sight of a double captain busy talking in whispers with his other self.

"But all this doesn't tell me how you came to hang on to our side   75
ladder," I inquired, in the hardly audible murmurs we used, after he had told me something more of the proceedings on board the Sephora once the bad weather was over.

"When we sighted Java Head I had had time to think all those matters out several times over. I had six weeks of doing nothing else, and with only an hour or so every evening for a tramp on the quarter-deck."

He whispered, his arms folded on the side of my bed place, staring through the open port. And I could imagine perfectly the manner of this thinking out—a stubborn if not a steadfast operation; something of which I should have been perfectly incapable.

"I reckoned it would be dark before we closed with the land," he continued, so low that I had to strain my hearing near as we were to each other, shoulder touching shoulder almost. "So I asked to speak to the old man. He always seemed very sick when he came to see me—as if he could not look me in the face. You know, that foresail saved the ship. She was too deep to have run long under bare poles. And it was I that managed to set it for him. Anyway, he came. When I had him in my cabin—he stood by the door looking at me as if I had the halter round my neck already—I asked him right away to leave my cabin door unlocked at night while the ship was going through Sunda Straits. There would be the Java coast within two or three miles, off Angier Point. I wanted nothing more. I've had a prize for swimming my second year in the Conway."

"I can believe it," I breathed out.

"God only knows why they locked me in every night. To see some of their faces you'd have thought they were afraid I'd go about at night strangling people. Am I a murdering brute? Do I look it? By Jove! If I had been he wouldn't have trusted himself like that into my room. You'll say I might have chucked him aside and bolted out, there and then—it was dark already. Well, no. And for the same reason I wouldn't think of trying to smash the door. There would have been a rush to stop me at the noise, and I did not mean to get into a confounded scrimmage. Somebody else might have got killed—for I would not have broken out only to get chucked back, and I did not want any more of that work. He refused, looking more sick than ever. He was afraid of the men, and also of that old second mate of his who had been sailing with him for years—a gray-headed old humbug; and his steward, too, had been with him devil knows how long—seventeen years or more—a dogmatic sort of loafer who hated me like poison, just because I was the chief mate. No chief mate ever made more than one voyage in the Sephora, you know. Those two old chaps ran the ship. Devil only knows what the skipper wasn't afraid of (all his nerve went to pieces altogether in that hellish spell of bad weather we had)—of what the law would do to him—of his wife, perhaps. Oh, yes! she's on board. Though I don't think she would have meddled. She would have been only too glad to have me out of the ship in any way. The 'brand of Cain' business, don't you see. That's all right. I was ready enough to go off wandering on the face of the earth—and that was price enough to pay for an Abel of that sort. Anyhow, he wouldn't listen to me. 'This thing must take its course. I represent the law here.' He was shaking like a leaf. 'So you won't?' 'No!' 'Then I hope you will be able to sleep on that,' I said, and turned my back on him. 'I wonder that you can,' cries he, and locks the door.

80

"Well after that, I couldn't. Not very well. That was three weeks ago. We have had a slow passage through the Java Sea; drifted about Carimata for ten days. When we anchored here they thought, I suppose, it was all right. The nearest land (and that's five miles) is the ship's destination; the consul would soon set about catching me; and there would have been no object in bolting to these islets there. I don't suppose there's a drop of water on them. I don't know how it was, but tonight that steward, after bringing me my supper, went out to let me eat it, and left the door unlocked. And I ate it—all there was, too. After I had finished I strolled out on the quarterdeck. I don't know that I meant to do anything. A breath of fresh air was all I wanted, I believe. Then a sudden temptation came over me. I kicked off my slippers and was in the water before I had made up my mind fairly. Somebody heard the splash and they raised an awful hullabaloo. 'He's gone! Lower the boats! He's committed suicide! No, he's swimming.' Certainly I was swimming. It's not so easy for a swimmer like me to commit suicide by drowning. I landed on the nearest islet before the boat left the ship's side. I heard them pulling about in the dark, hailing, and so on, but after a bit they gave up. Everything quieted down and the anchorage became still as death. I sat down on a stone and began to think. I felt certain they would start searching for me at daylight. There was no place to hide on those stony things—and if there had been, what would have been the good? But now I was clear of that ship, I was not going back. So after a while I took off all my clothes, tied them up in a bundle with a stone inside, and dropped them in the deep water on the outer side of that islet. That was suicide enough for me. Let them think what they liked, but I didn't mean to drown myself. I meant to swim till I sank—but that's not the same thing. I struck out for another of these little islands, and it was from that one that I first saw your riding light. Something to swim for. I went on easily, and on the way I came upon a flat rock a foot or two above water. In the daytime, I dare say, you might make it out with a glass from your poop. I scrambled up on it and rested myself for a bit. Then I made another start. That last spell must have been over a mile."

His whisper was getting fainter and fainter, and all the time he stared straight out through the porthole, in which there was not even a star to be seen. I had not interrupted him. There was something that made comment impossible in his narrative, or perhaps in himself; a sort of feeling, a quality, which I can't find a name for. And when he ceased, all I found was a futile whisper: "So you swam for our light?"

"Yes—straight for it. It was something to swim for. I couldn't see any stars low down because the coast was in the way, and I couldn't see the land, either. The water was like glass. One might have been swimming in a confounded thousand-feet deep cistern with no place for scrambling out anywhere; but what I didn't like was the notion of swimming round and round like a crazed bullock before I gave out; and as I didn't mean to go back . . . No. Do you see me being hauled back, stark naked, off one of these little islands by the scruff of the neck and fighting like a wild beast? Somebody would have got killed for certain, and I did not want any of that. So I went on. Then your ladder——"

"Why didn't you hail the ship?" I asked, a little louder.

He touched my shoulder lightly. Lazy footsteps came right over our heads and stopped. The second mate had crossed from the other side of the poop and might have been hanging over the rail for all we knew. 85

"He couldn't hear us talking—could he?" My double breathed into my very ear, anxiously.

His anxiety was an answer, a sufficient answer, to the question I had put to him. An answer containing all the difficulty of that situation. I closed the porthole quietly, to make sure. A louder word might have been overheard.

"Who's that?" he whispered then.

"My second mate. But I don't know much more of the fellow than you do."

And I told him a little about myself. I had been appointed to take charge while I least expected anything of the sort, not quite a fortnight ago. 90 I didn't know either the ship or the people. Hadn't had the time in port to look about me or size anybody up. And as to the crew, all they knew was that I was appointed to take the ship home. For the rest, I was almost as much of a stranger on board as himself, I said. And at the moment I felt it most acutely. I felt that it would take very little to make me a suspect person in the eyes of the ship's company.

He had turned about meantime; and we, the two strangers in the ship, faced each other in identical attitudes.

"Your ladder——" he murmured, after a silence. "Who'd have thought of finding a ladder hanging over at night in a ship anchored out here! I felt just then a very unpleasant faintness. After the life I've been leading for nine weeks, anybody would have got out of condition. I wasn't capable of swimming round as far as your rudder chains. And, lo and behold! there was a ladder to get hold of. After I gripped it I said to myself, 'What's the good?' When I saw a man's head looking over I thought I would swim away presently and leave him shouting—in whatever language it was. I didn't mind being looked at. I—I liked it. And then you speaking to me so quietly—as if you had expected me—made me hold on a little longer. It had been a confounded lonely time—I don't mean while swimming. I was glad to talk a little to somebody that didn't belong to the Sephora. As to asking for the captain, that was a mere impulse. It could have been no use, with all the ship knowing about me and the other people pretty certain to be round here in the morning. I don't know—I wanted to be seen, to talk with somebody, before I went on. I don't know what I would have said. . . . 'Fine night, isn't it?' or something of the sort."

"Do you think they will be round here presently?" I asked with some incredulity.

"Quite likely," he said, faintly.

He looked extremely haggard all of a sudden. His head rolled on his   95
shoulders.

"H'm. We shall see then. Meantime get into that bed," I whispered. "Want help? There."

It was a rather high bed place with a set of drawers underneath. This amazing swimmer really needed the lift I gave him by seizing his leg. He tumbled in, rolled over on his back, and flung one arm across his eyes. And then, with his face nearly hidden, he must have looked exactly as I used to look in that bed. I gazed upon my other self for a while before drawing across carefully the two green serge curtains which ran on a brass rod. I thought for a moment of pinning them together for greater safety, but I sat down on the couch, and once there I felt unwilling to rise and hunt for a pin. I would do it in a moment. I was extremely tired, in a peculiarly intimate way, by the strain of stealthiness, by the effort of whispering and the general secrecy of this excitement. It was three o'clock by now and I had been on my feet since nine, but I was not sleepy; I could not have gone to sleep. I sat there, fagged out, looking at the curtains, trying to clear my mind of the confused sensation of being in two places at once, and greatly bothered by an exasperating knocking in my head. It was a relief to discover suddenly that it was not in my head at all, but on the outside of the door. Before I could collect myself the words "Come in" were out of my mouth, and the steward entered with a tray, bringing in my morning coffee. I had slept, after all, and I was so frightened that I shouted, "This way! I am here, steward," as though he had been miles away. He put down the tray on the table next the couch and only then said, very quietly, "I can see you are here, sir." I felt him give me a keen look, but I dared not meet his eyes just then. He must have wondered why I had drawn the curtains of my bed before going to sleep on the couch. He went out, hooking the door open as usual.

I heard the crew washing decks above me. I knew I would have been told at once if there had been any wind. Calm, I thought, and I was doubly vexed. Indeed, I felt dual more than ever. The steward reappeared suddenly in the doorway. I jumped up from the couch so quickly that he gave a start.

"What do you want here?"

"Close your port, sir—they are washing decks."   100

"It is closed," I said, reddening.

"Very well, sir." But he did not move from the doorway and returned my stare in an extraordinary, equivocal manner for a time. Then his eyes wavered, all his expression changed, and in a voice unusually gentle, almost coaxingly:

"May I come in to take the empty cup away, sir?"

"Of course!" I turned my back on him while he popped in and out. Then I unhooked and closed the door and even pushed the bolt. This sort of thing could not go on very long. The cabin was as hot as an oven, too. I took a peep at my double, and discovered that he had not moved, his arm was still over his eyes; but his chest heaved; his hair was wet; his chin glistened with perspiration. I reached over him and opened the port.

"I must show myself on deck," I reflected.   105

Of course, theoretically, I could do what I liked, with no one to say nay to me within the whole circle of the horizon; but to lock my cabin door and take the key away I did not dare. Directly I put my head out of the companion I saw the group of my two officers, the second mate barefooted, the chief mate in long India-rubber boots, near the break of the poop, and the steward halfway down the poop ladder talking to them eagerly. He happened to catch sight of me and dived, the second ran down on the main-deck shouting some order or other, and the chief mate came to meet me, touching his cap.

There was a sort of curiosity in his eye that I did not like. I don't know whether the steward had told them that I was "queer" only, or downright drunk, but I know the man meant to have a good look at me. I watched him coming with a smile which, as he got into point-blank range, took effect and froze his very whiskers. I did not give him time to open his lips.

"Square the yards by lifts and braces before the hands go to breakfast."

It was the first particular order I had given on board that ship; and I stayed on deck to see it executed, too. I had felt the need of asserting myself without loss of time. That sneering young cub got taken down a peg or two on that occasion, and I also seized the opportunity of having a good look at the face of every foremast man as they filed past me to go to the after braces. At breakfast time, eating nothing myself, I presided with such frigid dignity that the two mates were only too glad to escape from the cabin as soon as decency permitted; and all the time the dual working of my mind distracted me almost to the point of insanity. I was constantly watching myself, my secret self, as dependent on my actions as my own personality, sleeping in that bed, behind that door which faced me as I sat at the head of the table. It was very much like being mad, only it was worse because one was aware of it.

I had to shake him for a solid minute, but when at last he opened his   110 eyes it was in the full possession of his senses, with an inquiring look.

"All's well so far," I whispered. "Now you must vanish into the bathroom."

He did so, as noiseless as a ghost, and then I rang for the steward, and facing him boldly, directed him to tidy up my stateroom while I was having my bath—"and be quick about it." As my tone admitted of no excuses, he said, "Yes, sir," and ran off to fetch his dustpan and brushes. I took a bath and did most of my dressing, splashing, and whistling softly for the steward's edification, while the secret sharer of my life stood drawn up bolt upright in that little space, his face looking very sunken in daylight, his eyelids lowered under the stern, dark line of his eyebrows drawn together by a slight frown.

When I left him there to go back to my room the steward was finishing dusting. I sent for the mate and engaged him in some insignificant conversation. It was, as it were, trifling with the terrific character of his whiskers; but my object was to give him an opportunity for a good look at my cabin. And then I could at last shut, with a clear conscience, the door of my stateroom and get my double back into the recessed part. There was nothing else for it. He had to sit still on a small folding stool, half smothered by the heavy coats hanging there. We listened to the steward going into the bathroom out of the saloon, filling the water bottles there, scrubbing the bath, setting things to rights, whisk, bang, clatter—out again into the saloon—turn the key—click. Such was my scheme for keeping my second self invisible. Nothing better could be contrived under the circumstances. And there we sat; I at my writing desk ready to appear busy with some papers, he behind me out of sight of the door. It would not have been prudent to talk in daytime; and I could not have stood the excitement of that queer sense of whispering to myself. Now and then, glancing over my shoulder, I saw him far back there, sitting rigidly on the low stool, his bare feet close together, his arms folded, his head hanging on his breast—and perfectly still. Anybody would have taken him for me.

I was fascinated by it myself. Every moment I had to glance over my shoulder. I was looking at him when a voice outside the door said:

"Beg pardon, sir."   115

"Well! . . . " I kept my eyes on him, and so when the voice outside the door announced, "There's a ship's boat coming our way, sir," I saw him give a start—the first movement he had made for hours. But he did not raise his bowed head.

"All right. Get the ladder over."

I hesitated. Should I whisper something to him? But what? His immobility seemed to have been never disturbed. What could I tell him he did not know already? . . . Finally I went on deck.

II

The skipper of the Sephora had a thin red whisker all round his face, and the sort of complexion that goes with hair of that color; also the particular, rather smeary shade of blue in the eyes. He was not exactly a showy figure; his shoulders were high, his stature but middling—one leg slightly more bandy than the other. He shook hands, looking vaguely around. A spiritless tenacity was his main characteristic, I judged. I behaved with a politeness which seemed to disconcert him. Perhaps he was shy. He mumbled to me as if he were ashamed of what he was saying; gave his name (it was something like Archbold—but at

this distance of years I hardly am sure), his ship's name, and a few other particulars of that sort, in the manner of a criminal making a reluctant and doleful
confession. He had had terrible weather on the passage out—terrible—terrible—
wife aboard, too.

By this time we were seated in the cabin and the steward brought in a
tray with a bottle and glasses. "Thanks! No." Never took liquor. Would have
some water, though. He drank two tumblerfuls. Terrible thirsty work. Ever
since daylight had been exploring the islands round his ship.

"What was that for—fun?" I asked, with an appearance of polite interest.

"No!" He sighed. "Painful duty."

As he persisted in his mumbling and I wanted my double to hear every   5
word, I hit upon the notion of informing him that I regretted to say I was
hard of hearing.

"Such a young man, too!" he nodded, keeping his smeary blue, unintel-
ligent eyes fastened upon me. "What was the cause of it—some disease?" he
inquired, without the least sympathy and as if he thought that, if so, I'd got
no more than I deserved.

"Yes; disease," I admitted in a cheerful tone which seemed to shock
him. But my point was gained, because he had to raise his voice to give me
his tale. It is not worth while to record his version. It was just over two months
since all this had happened, and he had thought so much about it that he
seemed completely muddled as to its bearings, but still immensely impressed.

"What would you think of such a thing happening on board your own ship?
I've had the Sephora for these fifteen years. I am a well-known shipmaster."

He was densely distressed—and perhaps I should have sympathized with
him if I had been able to detach my mental vision from the unsuspected
sharer of my cabin as though he were my second self. There he was on the
other side of the bulkhead, four or five feet from us, no more, as we sat in the
saloon. I looked politely at Captain Archbold (if that was his name), but it
was the other I saw, in a gray sleeping suit, seated on a low stool, his bare feet
close together, his arms folded, and every word said between us falling into
the ears of his dark head bowed on his chest.

"I have been at sea now, man and boy, for seven-and-thirty years, and   10
I've never heard of such a thing happening in an English ship. And that it
should be my ship. Wife on board, too."

I was hardly listening to him.

"Don't you think," I said, "that the heavy sea which, you told me,
came aboard just then might have killed the man? I have seen the sheer
weight of a sea kill a man very neatly, by simply breaking his neck."

"Good God!" he uttered, impressively, fixing his smeary blue eyes on
me. "The sea! No man killed by the sea ever looked like that." He seemed
positively scandalized at my suggestion. And as I gazed at him certainly not

prepared for anything original on his part, he advanced his head close to mine and thrust his tongue out at me so suddenly that I couldn't help starting back.

After scoring over my calmness in this graphic way he nodded wisely. If I had seen the sight, he assured me, I would never forget it as long as I lived. The weather was too bad to give the corpse a proper sea burial. So next day at dawn they took it up on the poop, covering its face with a bit of bunting; he read a short prayer, and then, just as it was, in its oilskins and long boots, they launched it amongst those mountainous seas that seemed ready every moment to swallow up the ship herself and the terrified lives on board of her.

"That reefed foresail saved you," I threw in. 15

"Under God—it did," he exclaimed fervently. "It was by a special mercy, I firmly believe, that it stood some of those hurricane squalls."

"It was the setting of that sail which——" I began.

"God's own hand in it," he interrupted me. "Nothing less could have done it. I don't mind telling you that I hardly dared give the order. It seemed impossible that we could touch anything without losing it, and then our last hope would have been gone."

The terror of that gale was on him yet. I let him go on for a bit, then said, casually—as if returning to a minor subject:

"You were very anxious to give up your mate to the shore people, 20 I believe?"

He was. To the law. His obscure tenacity on that point had in it something incomprehensible and a little awful; something, as it were, mystical, quite apart from his anxiety that he should not be suspected of "countenancing any doings of that sort." Seven-and-thirty virtuous years at sea, of which over twenty of immaculate command, and the last fifteen in the Sephora, seemed to have laid him under some pitiless obligation.

"And you know," he went on, groping shame-facedly amongst his feelings, "I did not engage that young fellow. His people had some interest with my owners. I was in a way forced to take him on. He looked very smart, very gentlemanly, and all that. But do you know—I never liked him, somehow. I am a plain man. You see, he wasn't exactly the sort for the chief mate of a ship like the Sephora."

I had become so connected in thoughts and impressions with the secret sharer of my cabin that I felt as if I, personally, were being given to understand that I, too, was not the sort that would have done for the chief mate of a ship like the Sephora. I had no doubt of it in my mind.

"Not at all the style of man. You understand," he insisted, superfluously, looking hard at me.

I smiled urbanely. He seemed at a loss for a while. 25

"I suppose I must report a suicide."

"Beg pardon?"

"Suicide! That's what I'll have to write to my owners directly I get in."

"Unless you manage to recover him before tomorrow," I assented, dispassionately. . . . "I mean, alive."

He mumbled something which I really did not catch, and I turned my ear to him in a puzzled manner. He fairly bawled: 30

"The land—I say, the mainland is at least seven miles off my anchorage."

"About that."

My lack of excitement, of curiosity, of surprise, of any sort of pronounced interest, began to arouse his distrust. But except for the felicitous pretense of deafness I had not tried to pretend anything. I had felt utterly incapable of playing the part of ignorance properly, and therefore was afraid to try. It is also certain that he had brought some ready-made suspicions with him, and that he viewed my politeness as a strange and unnatural phenomenon. And yet how else could I have received him? Not heartily! That was impossible for psychological reasons, which I need not state here. My only object was to keep off his inquiries. Surlily? Yes, but surliness might have provoked a point-blank question. From its novelty to him and from its nature, punctilious courtesy was the manner best calculated to restrain the man. But there was the danger of his breaking through my defense bluntly. I could not, I think, have met him by a direct lie, also for psychological (not moral) reasons. If he had only known how afraid I was of his putting my feeling of identity with the other to the test! But, strangely enough—(I thought of it only afterwards)—I believe that he was not a little disconcerted by the reverse side of that weird situation, by something in me that reminded him of the man he was seeking—suggested a mysterious similitude to the young fellow he had distrusted and disliked from the first.

However that might have been, the silence was not very prolonged. He took another oblique step.

"I reckon I had no more than a two-mile pull to your ship. Not a bit more."   35

"And quite enough, too, in this awful heat," I said.

Another pause full of mistrust followed. Necessity, they say, is mother of invention, but fear, too, is not barren of ingenious suggestions. And I was afraid he would ask me point-blank for news of my other self.

"Nice little saloon, isn't it?" I remarked, as if noticing for the first time the way his eyes roamed from one closed door to the other. "And very well fitted out, too. Here, for instance," I continued, reaching over the back of my seat negligently and flinging the door open, "is my bathroom."

He made an eager movement, but hardly gave it a glance. I got up, shut the door of the bathroom, and invited him to have a look round, as if I were very proud of my accommodation. He had to rise and be shown round, but he went through the business without any raptures whatever.

"And now we'll have a look at my stateroom," I declared, in a voice as   40
loud as I dared to make it, crossing the cabin to the starboard side with purposely heavy steps.

He followed me in and gazed around. My intelligent double had
vanished. I played my part.

"Very convenient—isn't it?"

"Very nice. Very comf . . . " He didn't finish and went out brusquely as
if to escape from some unrighteous wiles of mine. But it was not to be. I had
been too frightened not to feel vengeful; I felt I had him on the run, and I
meant to keep him on the run. My polite insistence must have had something
menacing in it, because he gave in suddenly. And I did not let him off a single item; mate's room, pantry, storerooms, the very sail locker which was also
under the poop—he had to look into them all. When at last I showed him
out on the quarter-deck he drew a long, spiritless sigh, and mumbled dismally
that he must really be going back to his ship now. I desired my mate, who had
joined us, to see to the captain's boat.

The man of whiskers gave a blast on the whistle which he used to wear
hanging round his neck, and yelled, "Sephora's away!" My double down there
in my cabin must have heard, and certainly could not feel more relieved than
I. Four fellows came running out from somewhere forward and went over the
side, while my own men, appearing on deck too, lined the rail. I escorted my
visitor to the gangway ceremoniously, and nearly overdid it. He was a tenacious
beast. On the very ladder he lingered, and in that unique, guiltily conscientious manner of sticking to the point:

"I say . . . you . . . you don't think that—"   45

I covered his voice loudly:

"Certainly not. . . . I am delighted. Good-by."

I had an idea of what he meant to say, and just saved myself by the privilege of defective hearing. He was too shaken generally to insist, but my mate,
close witness of that parting, looked mystified and his face took on a thoughtful cast. As I did not want to appear as if I wished to avoid all communication
with my officers, he had the opportunity to address me.

"Seems a very nice man. His boat's crew told our chaps a very extraordinary story, if what I am told by the steward is true. I suppose you had it from
the captain, sir?"

"Yes. I had a story from the captain."   50

"A very horrible affair—isn't it, sir?"

"It is."

"Beats all these tales we hear about murders in Yankee ships."

"I don't think it beats them. I don't think it resembles them in the least."

"Bless my soul—you don't say so! But of course I've no acquaintance   55
whatever with American ships, not I, so I couldn't go against your knowledge.

It's horrible enough for me. . . . But the queerest part is that those fellows seemed to have some idea the man was hidden aboard here. They had really. Did you ever hear of such a thing?"

"Preposterous—isn't it?"

We were walking to and fro athwart the quarter-deck. No one of the crew forward could be seen (the day was Sunday), and the mate pursued:

"There was some little dispute about it. Our chaps took offense. 'As if we would harbor a thing like that,' they said. 'Wouldn't you like to look for him in our coal-hole?' Quite a tiff. But they made it up in the end. I suppose he did drown himself. Don't you, sir?"

"I don't suppose anything."

"You have no doubt in the matter, sir?"   60

"None whatever."

I left him suddenly. I felt I was producing a bad impression, but with my double down there it was most trying to be on deck. And it was almost as trying to be below. Altogether a nerve-trying situation. But on the whole I felt less torn in two when I was with him. There was no one in the whole ship whom I dared take into my confidence. Since the hands had got to know his story, it would have been impossible to pass him off for anyone else, and an accidental discovery was to be dreaded now more than ever. . . .

The steward being engaged in laying the table for dinner, we could talk only with our eyes when I first went down. Later in the afternoon we had a cautious try at whispering. The Sunday quietness of the ship was against us; the stillness of air and water around her was against us; the elements, the men were against us—everything was against us in our secret partnership; time itself—for this could not go on forever. The very trust in Providence was, I suppose, denied to his guilt. Shall I confess that this thought cast me down very much? And as to the chapter of accidents which counts for so much in the book of success, I could only hope that it was closed. For what favorable accident could be expected?

"Did you hear everything?" were my first words as soon as we took up our position side by side, leaning over my bed place.

He had. And the proof of it was his earnest whisper, "The man told   65
you he hardly dared to give the order."

I understood the reference to be to that saving foresail.

"Yes. He was afraid of it being lost in the setting."

"I assure you he never gave the order. He may think he did, but he never gave it. He stood there with me on the break of the poop after the main topsail blew away, and whimpered about our last hope—positively whimpered about it and nothing else—and the night coming on! To hear one's skipper go on like that in such weather was enough to drive any fellow out of his mind. It worked me up into a sort of desperation. I just took it into my own hands and went away from him, boiling, and——But what's the use telling you? *You* know! . . . Do you think that if I had not been pretty fierce with them I should have got the men to do anything? Not I! The bo's'n perhaps? Perhaps! It wasn't a heavy sea— it was a sea gone mad! I suppose the end of the world will be something like that; and a man may have the heart to see it coming once and be done with it— but to have to face it day after day——I don't blame anybody. I was precious little better than the rest. Only—I was an officer of that old coal wagon, anyhow——"

"I quite understand," I conveyed that sincere assurance into his ear. He was out of breath with whispering; I could hear him pant slightly. It was all very simple. The same strung-up force which had given twenty-four men a chance, at least, for their lives, had, in a sort of recoil, crushed an unworthy mutinous existence.

But I had no leisure to weigh the merits of the matter—footsteps in the 70 saloon, a heavy knock. "There's enough wind to get under way with, sir." Here was the call of a new claim upon my thoughts and even upon my feelings.

"Turn the hands up," I cried through the door. "I'll be on deck directly."

I was going out to make the acquaintance of my ship. Before I left the cabin our eyes met—the eyes of the only two strangers on board. I pointed to the recessed part where the little campstool awaited him and laid my finger on my lips. He made a gesture—somewhat vague—a little mysterious, accompanied by a faint smile, as if of regret.

This is not the place to enlarge upon the sensations of a man who feels for the first time a ship move under his feet to his own independent word. In my case they were not unalloyed. I was not wholly alone with my command; for there was that stranger in my cabin. Or rather, I was not completely and wholly with her. Part of me was absent. That mental feeling of being in two places at once affected me physically as if the mood of secrecy had penetrated my very soul. Before an hour had elapsed since the ship had begun to move, having occasion to ask the mate (he stood by my side) to take a compass bearing of the pagoda, I caught myself reaching up to his ear in whispers. I say I caught myself, but enough had escaped to startle the man. I can't describe it otherwise than by saying that he shied. A grave, preoccupied manner, as though he were in possession of some perplexing intelligence, did not leave him henceforth. A little later I moved away from the rail to look at the compass with such a stealthy gait that the helmsman noticed it—and I could not help noticing the unusual roundness of his eyes. These are trifling instances, though it's to no commander's advantage to be suspected of ludicrous eccentricities. But I was also more seriously affected. There are to a seaman certain words, gestures, that should in given conditions come as naturally, as instinctively as the winking of a menaced eye. A certain order should spring on to his lips without thinking; a certain sign should get itself made, so to speak, without reflection. But all unconscious alertness had abandoned me. I had to make an effort of will to recall myself back (from the cabin) to the conditions of the moment. I felt that I was appearing an irresolute commander to those people who were watching me more or less critically.

And, besides, there were the scares. On the second day out, for instance, coming off the deck in the afternoon (I had straw slippers on my bare feet) I stopped at the open pantry door and spoke to the steward. He was doing something there with his back to me. At the sound of my voice he nearly jumped out of his skin, as the saying is, and incidentally broke a cup.

"What on earth's the matter with you?" I asked, astonished.   75

He was extremely confused. "Beg your pardon, sir. I made sure you were in your cabin."

"You see I wasn't."

"No, sir. I could have sworn I had heard you moving in there not a mo- ment ago. It's most extraordinary . . . very sorry, sir."

I passed on with an inward shudder. I was so identified with my secret double that I did not even mention the fact in those scanty, fearful whispers we exchanged. I suppose he had made some slight noise of some kind or other. It would have been miraculous if he hadn't at one time or another. And yet, haggard as he appeared, he looked always perfectly self-controlled, more than calm—almost invulnerable. On my suggestion he remained almost entirely in the bathroom, which, upon the whole, was the safest place. There could be really no shadow of an excuse for anyone ever wanting to go in there, once the steward had done with it. It was a very tiny place. Sometimes he reclined on the floor, his legs bent, his head sustained on one elbow. At others I would find him on the campstool, sitting in his gray sleeping suit and with his cropped dark hair like a patient, unmoved convict. At night I would smuggle him into my bed place, and we would whisper together, with the regular footfalls of the officer of the watch passing and repassing over our heads. It was an infinitely miserable time. It was lucky that some tins of fine preserves were stowed in a locker in my stateroom; hard bread I could always get hold of; and so he lived on stewed chicken, PATE DE FOIE GRAS, asparagus, cooked oysters, sardines—on all sorts of abominable sham delicacies out of tins. My early-morning coffee he always drank; and it was all I dared do for him in that respect.

Every day there was the horrible maneuvering to go through so that my   80
room and then the bathroom should be done in the usual way. I came to hate the sight of the steward, to abhor the voice of that harmless man. I felt that it was he who would bring on the disaster of discovery. It hung like a sword over our heads.

The fourth day out, I think (we were then working down the east side of the Gulf of Siam, tack for tack, in light winds and smooth water)—the fourth day, I say, of this miserable juggling with the unavoidable, as we sat at our evening meal, that man, whose slightest movement I dreaded, after putting down the dishes ran up on deck busily. This could not be dangerous. Presently he came down again; and then it appeared that he had remembered a coat of mine which I had thrown over a rail to dry after having been wetted in a shower which had passed over the ship in the afternoon. Sitting stolidly at the head of the table I became terrified at the sight of the garment on his arm. Of course he made for my door. There was no time to lose.

"Steward," I thundered. My nerves were so shaken that I could not govern my voice and conceal my agitation. This was the sort of thing that made my terrifically whiskered mate tap his forehead with his forefinger. I had detected him using that gesture while talking on deck with a confidential air to the carpenter. It was too far to hear a word, but I had no doubt that this pantomime could only refer to the strange new captain.

"Yes, sir," the pale-faced steward turned resignedly to me. It was this maddening course of being shouted at, checked without rhyme or reason, arbitrarily chased out of my cabin, suddenly called into it, sent flying out of his pantry on incomprehensible errands, that accounted for the growing wretchedness of his expression.

"Where are you going with that coat?"

"To your room, sir."   85

"Is there another shower coming?"

"I'm sure I don't know, sir. Shall I go up again and see, sir?"

"No! never mind."

My object was attained, as of course my other self in there would have heard everything that passed. During this interlude my two officers never raised their eyes off their respective plates; but the lip of that confounded cub, the second mate, quivered visibly.

I expected the steward to hook my coat on and come out at once. He   90 was very slow about it; but I dominated my nervousness sufficiently not to shout after him. Suddenly I became aware (it could be heard plainly enough) that the fellow for some reason or other was opening the door of the bathroom. It was the end. The place was literally not big enough to swing a cat in. My voice died in my throat and I went stony all over. I expected to hear a yell of surprise and terror, and made a movement, but had not the strength to get on my legs. Everything remained still. Had my second self taken the poor wretch by the throat? I don't know what I could have done next moment if I had not seen the steward come out of my room, close the door, and then stand quietly by the sideboard.

"Saved," I thought. "But, no! Lost! Gone! He was gone!"

I laid my knife and fork down and leaned back in my chair. My head swam. After a while, when sufficiently recovered to speak in a steady voice, I instructed my mate to put the ship round at eight o'clock himself.

"I won't come on deck," I went on. "I think I'll turn in, and unless the wind shifts I don't want to be disturbed before midnight. I feel a bit seedy."

"You did look middling bad a little while ago," the chief mate remarked without showing any great concern.

They both went out, and I stared at the steward clearing the table. 95 There was nothing to be read on that wretched man's face. But why did he avoid my eyes, I asked myself. Then I thought I should like to hear the sound of his voice.

"Steward!"

"Sir!" Startled as usual.

"Where did you hang up that coat?"

"In the bathroom, sir." The usual anxious tone. "It's not quite dry yet, sir."

For some time longer I sat in the cuddy. Had my double vanished as 100 he had come? But of his coming there was an explanation, whereas his disappearance would be inexplicable. . . . I went slowly into my dark room, shut the door, lighted the lamp, and for a time dared not turn round. When at last I did I saw him standing bolt-upright in the narrow recessed part. It would not be true to say I had a shock, but an irresistible doubt of his bodily existence flitted through my mind. Can it be, I asked myself, that he is not visible to other eyes than mine? It was like being haunted. Motionless, with a grave face, he raised his hands slightly at me in a gesture which meant clearly, "Heavens! What a narrow escape!" Narrow indeed. I think I had come creeping quietly as near insanity as any man who has not actually gone over the border. That gesture restrained me, so to speak.

The mate with the terrific whiskers was now putting the ship on the other tack. In the moment of profound silence which follows upon the hands going to their stations I heard on the poop his raised voice: "Hard alee!" and the distant shout of the order repeated on the main-deck. The sails, in that light breeze, made but a faint fluttering noise. It ceased. The ship was coming round slowly: I held my breath in the renewed stillness of expectation; one wouldn't have thought that there was a single living soul on her decks. A sudden brisk shout, "Mainsail haul!" broke the spell, and in the noisy cries and rush overhead of the men running away with the main brace we two, down in my cabin, came together in our usual position by the bed place.

He did not wait for my question. "I heard him fumbling here and just managed to squat myself down in the bath," he whispered to me. "The fellow only opened the door and put his arm in to hang the coat up. All the same——"

"I never thought of that," I whispered back, even more appalled than before at the closeness of the shave, and marveling at that something unyielding in his character which was carrying him through so finely. There was no agitation in his whisper. Whoever was being driven distracted, it was not he.

He was sane. And the proof of his sanity was continued when he took up the whispering again.

"It would never do for me to come to life again."

It was something that a ghost might have said. But what he was allud-   105
ing to was his old captain's reluctant admission of the theory of suicide. It would obviously serve his turn—if I had understood at all the view which seemed to govern the unalterable purpose of his action.

"You must maroon me as soon as ever you can get amongst these islands off the Cambodge shore," he went on.

"Maroon you! We are not living in a boy's adventure tale," I protested. His scornful whispering took me up.

"We aren't indeed! There's nothing of a boy's tale in this. But there's nothing else for it. I want no more. You don't suppose I am afraid of what can be done to me? Prison or gallows or whatever they may please. But you don't see me coming back to explain such things to an old fellow in a wig and twelve respectable tradesmen, do you? What can they know whether I am guilty or not—or of WHAT I am guilty, either? That's my affair. What does the Bible say? 'Driven off the face of the earth.' Very well, I am off the face of the earth now. As I came at night so I shall go."

"Impossible!" I murmured. "You can't."

"Can't?. . . Not naked like a soul on the Day of Judgment. I shall freeze   110
on to this sleeping suit. The Last Day is not yet—and . . . you have understood thoroughly. Didn't you?"

I felt suddenly ashamed of myself. I may say truly that I understood—and my hesitation in letting that man swim away from my ship's side had been a mere sham sentiment, a sort of cowardice.

"It can't be done now till next night," I breathed out. "The ship is on the off-shore tack and the wind may fail us."

"As long as I know that you understand," he whispered. "But of course you do. It's a great satisfaction to have got somebody to understand. You seem to have been there on purpose." And in the same whisper, as if we two whenever we talked had to say things to each other which were not fit for the world to hear, he added, "It's very wonderful."

We remained side by side talking in our secret way—but sometimes silent or just exchanging a whispered word or two at long intervals. And as usual he stared through the port. A breath of wind came now and again into our faces. The ship might have been moored in dock, so gently and on an even keel she slipped through the water, that did not murmur even at our passage, shadowy and silent like a phantom sea.

At midnight I went on deck, and to my mate's great surprise put the   115
ship round on the other tack. His terrible whiskers flitted round me in silent criticism. I certainly should not have done it if it had been only a question of

get- ting out of that sleepy gulf as quickly as possible. I believe he told the second mate, who relieved him, that it was a great want of judgment. The other
only yawned. That intolerable cub shuffled about so sleepily and lolled against
the rails in such a slack, improper fashion that I came down on him sharply.

"Aren't you properly awake yet?"

"Yes, sir! I am awake."

"Well, then, be good enough to hold yourself as if you were. And keep
a lookout. If there's any current we'll be closing with some islands before
daylight."

The east side of the gulf is fringed with islands, some solitary, others
in groups. On the blue background of the high coast they seem to float on
silvery patches of calm water, arid and gray, or dark green and rounded like
clumps of evergreen bushes, with the larger ones, a mile or two long, showing the outlines of ridges, ribs of gray rock under the dark mantle of matted
leafage. Unknown to trade, to travel, almost to geography, the manner of
life they harbor is an unsolved secret. There must be villages—settlements of
fishermen at least—on the largest of them, and some communication with the
world is probably kept up by native craft. But all that forenoon, as we headed
for them, fanned along by the faintest of breezes, I saw no sign of man or
canoe in the field of the telescope I kept on pointing at the scattered group.

At noon I gave no orders for a change of course, and the mate's whiskers   120
became much concerned and seemed to be offering themselves unduly to my
notice. At last I said:

"I am going to stand right in. Quite in—as far as I can take her."

The stare of extreme surprise imparted an air of ferocity also to his eyes,
and he looked truly terrific for a moment.

"We're not doing well in the middle of the gulf," I continued, casually.
"I am going to look for the land breezes tonight."

"Bless my soul! Do you mean, sir, in the dark amongst the lot of all them
islands and reefs and shoals?"

"Well—if there are any regular land breezes at all on this coast one   125
must get close inshore to find them, mustn't one?"

"Bless my soul!" he exclaimed again under his breath. All that afternoon
he wore a dreamy, contemplative appearance which in him was a mark of perplexity. After dinner I went into my stateroom as if I meant to take some rest.
There we two bent our dark heads over a half-unrolled chart lying on my bed.

"There," I said. "It's got to be Koh-ring. I've been looking at it ever
since sunrise. It has got two hills and a low point. It must be inhabited. And
on the coast opposite there is what looks like the mouth of a biggish river—
with some towns, no doubt, not far up. It's the best chance for you that I
can see."

"Anything. Koh-ring let it be."

He looked thoughtfully at the chart as if surveying chances and distances from a lofty height—and following with his eyes his own figure wandering on the blank land of Cochin-China, and then passing off that piece of paper clean out of sight into uncharted regions. And it was as if the ship had two captains to plan her course for her. I had been so worried and restless running up and down that I had not had the patience to dress that day. I had remained in my sleeping suit, with straw slippers and a soft floppy hat. The closeness of the heat in the gulf had been most oppressive, and the crew were used to seeing me wandering in that airy attire.

"She will clear the south point as she heads now," I whispered into his   130 ear. "Goodness only knows when, though, but certainly after dark. I'll edge her in to half a mile, as far as I may be able to judge in the dark—"

"Be careful," he murmured, warningly—and I realized suddenly that all my future, the only future for which I was fit, would perhaps go irretrievably to pieces in any mishap to my first command.

I could not stop a moment longer in the room. I motioned him to get out of sight and made my way on the poop. That unplayful cub had the watch. I walked up and down for a while thinking things out, then beckoned him over.

"Send a couple of hands to open the two quarter-deck ports," I said, mildly.

He actually had the impudence, or else so forgot himself in his wonder at such an incomprehensible order, as to repeat:

"Open the quarter-deck ports! What for, sir?"   135

"The only reason you need concern yourself about is because I tell you to do so. Have them open wide and fastened properly."

He reddened and went off, but I believe made some jeering remark to the carpenter as to the sensible practice of ventilating a ship's quarter-deck. I know he popped into the mate's cabin to impart the fact to him because the whiskers came on deck, as it were by chance, and stole glances at me from below—for signs of lunacy or drunkenness, I suppose.

A little before supper, feeling more restless than ever, I rejoined, for a moment, my second self. And to find him sitting so quietly was surprising, like something against nature, inhuman.

I developed my plan in a hurried whisper.

"I shall stand in as close as I dare and then put her round. I will pres-   140 ently find means to smuggle you out of here into the sail locker, which communicates with the lobby. But there is an opening, a sort of square for hauling the sails out, which gives straight on the quarter-deck and which is never closed in fine weather, so as to give air to the sails. When the ship's way is deadened in stays and all the hands are aft at the main braces you will have a clear road to slip out and get overboard through the open quarterdeck port. I've had them both fastened up. Use a rope's end to lower yourself into the water so as to avoid a splash—you know. It could be heard and cause some beastly complication."

He kept silent for a while, then whispered, "I understand."

"I won't be there to see you go," I began with an effort. "The rest . . . I only hope I have understood, too."

"You have. From first to last"—and for the first time there seemed to be a faltering, something strained in his whisper. He caught hold of my arm, but the ringing of the supper bell made me start. He didn't though; he only released his grip.

After supper I didn't come below again till well past eight o'clock. The faint, steady breeze was loaded with dew; and the wet, darkened sails held all there was of propelling power in it. The night, clear and starry, sparkled darkly, and the opaque, lightless patches shifting slowly against the low stars were the drifting islets. On the port bow there was a big one more distant and shadowily imposing by the great space of sky it eclipsed.

On opening the door I had a back view of my very own self looking at   145 a chart. He had come out of the recess and was standing near the table.

"Quite dark enough," I whispered.

He stepped back and leaned against my bed with a level, quiet glance. I sat on the couch. We had nothing to say to each other. Over our heads the officer of the watch moved here and there. Then I heard him move quickly. I knew what that meant. He was making for the companion; and presently his voice was outside my door.

"We are drawing in pretty fast, sir. Land looks rather close."

"Very well," I answered. "I am coming on deck directly."

I waited till he was gone out of the cuddy, then rose. My double moved 150 too. The time had come to exchange our last whispers, for neither of us was ever to hear each other's natural voice.

"Look here!" I opened a drawer and took out three sovereigns. "Take this anyhow. I've got six and I'd give you the lot, only I must keep a little money to buy some fruit and vegetables for the crew from native boats as we go through Sunda Straits."

He shook his head.

"Take it," I urged him, whispering desperately. "No one can tell what—"

He smiled and slapped meaningly the only pocket of the sleeping jacket. It was not safe, certainly. But I produced a large old silk handkerchief of mine, and tying the three pieces of gold in a corner, pressed it on him. He was touched, I supposed, because he took it at last and tied it quickly round his waist under the jacket, on his bare skin.

Our eyes met; several seconds elapsed, till, our glances still mingled, I   155 extended my hand and turned the lamp out. Then I passed through the cuddy, leaving the door of my room wide open. . . . "Steward!"

He was still lingering in the pantry in the greatness of his zeal, giving a rub-up to a plated cruet stand the last thing before going to bed. Being careful not to wake up the mate, whose room was opposite, I spoke in an undertone.

He looked round anxiously. "Sir!"

"Can you get me a little hot water from the galley?"

"I am afraid, sir, the galley fire's been out for some time now."

"Go and see."   160

He flew up the stairs.

"Now," I whispered, loudly, into the saloon—too loudly, perhaps, but I was afraid I couldn't make a sound. He was by my side in an instant—the double captain slipped past the stairs—through a tiny dark passage . . . a sliding door. We were in the sail locker, scrambling on our knees over the sails. A sudden thought struck me. I saw myself wandering barefooted, bareheaded, the sun beating on my dark poll. I snatched off my floppy hat and tried hurriedly in the dark to ram it on my other self. He dodged and fended off silently. I wonder what he thought had come to me before he understood and suddenly desisted. Our hands met gropingly, lingered united in a steady, motionless clasp for a second. . . . No word was breathed by either of us when they separated.

I was standing quietly by the pantry door when the steward returned.

"Sorry, sir. Kettle barely warm. Shall I light the spirit lamp?"

"Never mind."   165

I came out on deck slowly. It was now a matter of conscience to shave the land as close as possible—for now he must go overboard whenever the ship was put in stays. Must! There could be no going back for him. After a moment I walked over to leeward and my heart flew into my mouth at the nearness of the land on the bow. Under any other circumstances I would not have held on a minute longer. The second mate had followed me anxiously.

I looked on till I felt I could command my voice.

"She will weather," I said then in a quiet tone.

"Are you going to try that, sir?" he stammered out incredulously.

I took no notice of him and raised my tone just enough to be heard by   170
the helmsman.

"Keep her good full."

"Good full, sir."

The wind fanned my cheek, the sails slept, the world was silent. The strain of watching the dark loom of the land grow bigger and denser was too much for me. I had shut my eyes—because the ship must go closer. She must! The stillness was intolerable. Were we standing still?

When I opened my eyes the second view started my heart with a thump. The black southern hill of Koh-ring seemed to hang right over the ship like a towering fragment of everlasting night. On that enormous mass of blackness there was not a gleam to be seen, not a sound to be heard. It was gliding irresistibly towards us and yet seemed already within reach of the hand. I saw the vague figures of the watch grouped in the waist, gazing in awed silence.

"Are you going on, sir?" inquired an unsteady voice at my elbow.   175
I ignored it. I had to go on.

"Keep her full. Don't check her way. That won't do now," I said
warningly.

"I can't see the sails very well," the helmsman answered me, in strange,
quavering tones.

Was she close enough? Already she was, I won't say in the shadow of the
land, but in the very blackness of it, already swallowed up as it were, gone too
close to be recalled, gone from me altogether.

"Give the mate a call," I said to the young man who stood at my elbow as
still as death. "And turn all hands up."

My tone had a borrowed loudness reverberated from the height of the   180
land. Several voices cried out together: "We are all on deck, sir."

Then stillness again, with the great shadow gliding closer, towering
higher, without a light, without a sound. Such a hush had fallen on the ship
that she might have been a bark of the dead floating in slowly under the
very gate of Erebus.

"My God! Where are we?"

It was the mate moaning at my elbow. He was thunderstruck, and as it
were deprived of the moral support of his whiskers. He clapped his hands
and absolutely cried out, "Lost!"

"Be quiet," I said, sternly.

He lowered his tone, but I saw the shadowy gesture of his despair.   185
"What are we doing here?"

"Looking for the land wind."

He made as if to tear his hair, and addressed me recklessly.

"She will never get out. You have done it, sir. I knew it'd end in something like this. She will never weather, and you are too close now to stay.
She'll drift ashore before she's round. O my God!"

I caught his arm as he was raising it to batter his poor devoted head,
and shook it violently.

"She's ashore already," he wailed, trying to tear himself away.   190

"Is she? . . . Keep good full there!"

"Good full, sir," cried the helmsman in a frightened, thin, childlike
voice.

I hadn't let go the mate's arm and went on shaking it. "Ready about,
do you hear? You go forward"—shake—"and stop there"—shake—"and hold
your noise"—shake—"and see these head-sheets properly overhauled"— shake,
shake—shake.

And all the time I dared not look towards the land lest my heart
should fail me. I released my grip at last and he ran forward as if fleeing
for dear life.

I wondered what my double there in the sail locker thought of this 195
commotion. He was able to hear everything—and perhaps he was able to
understand why, on my conscience, it had to be thus close—no less. My first
order "Hard alee!" re-echoed ominously under the towering shadow of Koh-
ring as if I had shouted in a mountain gorge. And then I watched the land
intently. In that smooth water and light wind it was impossible to feel the
ship coming-to. No! I could not feel her. And my second self was making
now ready to ship out and lower himself overboard. Perhaps he was gone
already. . . ?

The great black mass brooding over our very mastheads began to pivot
away from the ship's side silently. And now I forgot the secret stranger ready to
depart, and remembered only that I was a total stranger to the ship. I did not
know her. Would she do it? How was she to be handled?

I swung the mainyard and waited helplessly. She was perhaps
stopped, and her very fate hung in the balance, with the black mass of
Koh-ring like the gate of the everlasting night towering over her taffrail.
What would she do now? Had she way on her yet? I stepped to the side
swiftly, and on the shadowy water I could see nothing except a faint phosphorescent flash revealing the glassy smoothness of the sleeping surface. It
was impossible to tell—and I had not learned yet the feel of my ship. Was
she moving? What I needed was something easily seen, a piece of paper,
which I could throw overboard and watch. I had nothing on me. To run
down for it I didn't dare. There was no time. All at once my strained,
yearning stare distinguished a white object floating within a yard of the
ship's side. White on the black water. A phosphorescent flash passed under
it. What was that thing? . . . I recognized my own floppy hat. It must have
fallen off his head . . . and he didn't bother. Now I had what I wanted—the
saving mark for my eyes. But I hardly thought of my other self, now gone
from the ship, to be hidden forever from all friendly faces, to be a fugitive
and a vagabond on the earth, with no brand of the curse on his sane forehead to stay a slaying hand . . . too proud to explain.

And I watched the hat—the expression of my sudden pity for his mere
flesh. It had been meant to save his homeless head from the dangers of the
sun. And now—behold—it was saving the ship, by serving me for a mark to help
out the ignorance of my strangeness. Ha! It was drifting forward, warning me
just in time that the ship had gathered sternaway.

"Shift the helm," I said in a low voice to the seaman standing still like
a statue.

The man's eyes glistened wildly in the binnacle light as he jumped 200
round to the other side and spun round the wheel.

I walked to the break of the poop. On the over-shadowed deck all
hands stood by the forebraces waiting for my order. The stars ahead seemed

to be gliding from right to left. And all was so still in the world that I heard the quiet remark, "She's round," passed in a tone of intense relief between two seamen.

"Let go and haul."

The foreyards ran round with a great noise, amidst cheery cries. And now the frightful whiskers made themselves heard giving various orders. Already the ship was drawing ahead. And I was alone with her. Nothing! no one in the world should stand now between us, throwing a shadow on the way of silent knowledge and mute affection, the perfect communion of a seaman with his first command.

Walking to the taffrail, I was in time to make out, on the very edge of a darkness thrown by a towering black mass like the very gateway of Erebus— yes, I was in time to catch an evanescent glimpse of my white hat left behind to mark the spot where the secret sharer of my cabin and of my thoughts, as though he were my second self, had lowered himself into the water to take his punishment: a free man, a proud swimmer striking out for a new destiny.

- The story begins with a series of interruptions. List the interruptions that the narrator describes and explain how each of these help us understand some established order that has been broken as this story begins.

- How does his juxtaposition with Leggatt help the narrator explore and establish his own position on the ship? Look at specific connections that the two establish. How is the narrator more closely connected to Leggatt than he is to the captain of the other ship?

- Discuss the function of the hat at the end of the story. How does the narrator describe the help that it offers him? Why is it significant that an item he gave to help Leggatt ends up helping the narrator?

Jennifer Egan (1962–   )

Jennifer Egan's *A Visit from the Goon Squad* (2010) won the Pulitzer Prize for Fiction. Because this work does not fit into the conventional form of a novel, Madison Smartt Bell (in a *New York Times* review) calls her "refreshingly unclassifiable." This book, for instance, is made up of a series of short stories, each of which might stand on its own, but most of the stories are related to a couple of central characters who are involved in the music business. She experiments with form: One of the sections is structured as a PowerPoint presentation, but her characters are highly realistic. Egan grew up in San Francisco, and majored in English at the University of Pennsylvania. "Black Box" was originally published as a series of tweets over nine days beginning May 25, 2012.

Black Box (2012)

1

People rarely look the way you expect them to, even when you've seen pictures.

The first thirty seconds in a person's presence are the most important.

If you're having trouble perceiving and projecting, focus on projecting.

Necessary ingredients for a successful projection: giggles; bare legs; shyness.

The goal is to be both irresistible and invisible.

When you succeed, a certain sharpness will go out of his eyes.

2

Some powerful men actually call their beauties "Beauty."

Counter to reputation, there is a deep camaraderie among beauties.

If your Designated Mate is widely feared, the beauties at the house party where you've gone undercover to meet him will be especially kind.

Kindness feels good, even when it's based on a false notion of your identity and purpose.

3

Posing as a beauty means not reading what you would like to read on a rocky shore in the South of France.

Sunlight on bare skin can be as nourishing as food.

Even a powerful man will be briefly self-conscious when he first disrobes to his bathing suit.

It is technically impossible for a man to look better in a Speedo than in swim trunks.

If you love someone with dark skin, white skin looks drained of something vital.

4

When you know that a person is violent and ruthless, you will see violent ruthlessness in such basic things as his swim stroke.

"What are you doing?" from your Designated Mate amid choppy waves after he has followed you into the sea may or may not betray suspicion.

Your reply—"Swimming"—may or may not be perceived as sarcasm.

"Shall we swim together toward those rocks?" may or may not be a question.

"All that way?" will, if spoken correctly, sound ingenuous.

We'll have privacy there" may sound unexpectedly ominous.

5

A hundred feet of blue-black Mediterranean will allow you ample time to deliver a strong self-lecture.

At such moments, it may be useful to explicitly recall your training:

"You will be infiltrating the lives of criminals.

"You will be in constant danger.

"Some of you will not survive, but those who do will be heroes.

"A few of you will save lives and even change the course of history.

"We ask of you an impossible combination of traits: ironclad scruples and a willingness to violate them;

"An abiding love for your country and a willingness to consort with individuals who are working actively to destroy it;

"The instincts and intuition of experts, and the blank records and true freshness of ingénues.

"You will each perform this service only once, after which you will return to your lives.

"We cannot promise that your lives will be exactly the same when you go back to them."

6

Eagerness and pliability can be expressed even in the way you climb from the sea onto chalky yellow rocks.

"You're a very fast swimmer," uttered by a man who is still submerged, may not be intended as praise.

Giggling is sometimes better than answering.

"You are a lovely girl" may be meant straightforwardly.

Ditto "I want to fuck you now."

"Well? What do you think about that?" suggests a preference for direct verbal responses over giggling.

"I like it" must be uttered with enough gusto to compensate for a lack of declarative color.

"You don't sound sure" indicates insufficient gusto.

"I'm *not* sure" is acceptable only when followed, coyly, with "You'll have to convince me."

Throwing back your head and closing your eyes allows you to give the appearance of sexual readiness while concealing revulsion.

7

Being alone with a violent and ruthless man, surrounded by water, can make the shore seem very far away.

You may feel solidarity, at such a time, with the beauties just visible there in their bright bikinis.

You may appreciate, at such a time, why you aren't being paid for this work.

Your voluntary service is the highest form of patriotism.

Remind yourself that you aren't being paid when he climbs out of the water and lumbers toward you.

Remind yourself that you aren't being paid when he leads you behind a boulder and pulls you onto his lap.

The Dissociation Technique is like a parachute—you must pull the cord at the correct time.

Too soon, and you may hinder your ability to function at a crucial moment;

Too late, and you will be lodged too deeply inside the action to wriggle free.

You will be tempted to pull the cord when he surrounds you with arms whose bulky strength reminds you, fleetingly, of your husband's.

You will be tempted to pull it when you feel him start to move against you from below.

You will be tempted to pull it when his smell envelops you: metallic, like a warm hand clutching pennies.

The directive "Relax" suggests that your discomfort is palpable.

"No one can see us" suggests that your discomfort has been understood as fear of physical exposure.

"Relax, relax," uttered in rhythmic, throaty tones, suggests that your discomfort is not unwelcome.

8

Begin the Dissociation Technique only when physical violation is imminent.

Close your eyes and slowly count backward from ten.

With each number, imagine yourself rising out of your body and moving one step farther away from it.

By eight, you should be hovering just outside your skin.

By five, you should be floating a foot or two above your body, feeling only vague anxiety over what is about to happen to it.

By three, you should feel fully detached from your physical self.

By two, your body should be able to act and react without your participation.

By one, your mind should drift so free that you lose track of what is happening below.

White clouds spin and curl.

A blue sky is as depthless as the sea.

The sound of waves against rocks existed millennia before there were creatures who could hear it.

Spurs and gashes of stone narrate a violence that the earth itself has long forgotten.

Your mind will rejoin your body when it is safe to do so.

9

Return to your body carefully, as if you were reëntering your home after a hurricane.

Resist the impulse to reconstruct what has just happened.

Focus instead on gauging your Designated Mate's reaction to the new intimacy between you.

In some men, intimacy will prompt a more callous, indifferent attitude.

In others, intimacy may awaken problematic curiosity about you.

"Where did you learn to swim like that?," uttered lazily, while supine, with two fingers in your hair, indicates curiosity.

Tell the truth without precision.

"I grew up near a lake" is both true and vague.

"Where was the lake?" conveys dissatisfaction with your vagueness.

"Columbia County, New York" suggests precision while avoiding it.

"Manhattan?" betrays unfamiliarity with the geography of New York State.

Never contradict your Designated Mate.

"Where did you grow up?," asked of a man who has just asked you the same thing, is known as "mirroring."

Mirror your Designated Mate's attitudes, interests, desires, and tastes.

Your goal is to become part of his atmosphere: a source of comfort and ease.

Only then will he drop his guard when you are near.

Only then will he have significant conversations within your earshot.

Only then will he leave his possessions in a porous and unattended state.

Only then can you begin to gather information systematically.

10

"Come. Let's go back," uttered brusquely, suggests that your Designated Mate has no more wish to talk about himself than you do.

Avoid the temptation to analyze his moods and whims.

Salt water has a cleansing effect.

11

You will see knowledge of your new intimacy with your Designated Mate in the eyes of every beauty on shore.

"We saved lunch for you" may or may not be an allusion to the reason for your absence.

Cold fish is unappealing, even when served in a good lemon sauce.

Be friendly to other beauties, but not solicitous.

When you are in conversation with a beauty, it is essential that you be perceived as no more or less than she is.

Be truthful about every aspect of your life except marriage (if any).

If married, say that you and your spouse have divorced, to give an impression of unfettered freedom.

"Oh, that's sad!" suggests that the beauty you're chatting with would like to marry.

12

If your Designated Mate abruptly veers toward the villa, follow him.

Taking his hand and smiling congenially can create a sense of low-key accompaniment

An abstracted smile in return, as if he'd forgotten who you are, may be a sign of pressing concerns.

The concerns of your Designated Mate are your concerns.

The room assigned to a powerful man will be more lavish than the one you slept in while awaiting his arrival.

Never look for hidden cameras: the fact that you're looking will give you away.

Determine whether your Designated Mate seeks physical intimacy; if not, feign the wish for a nap.

Your pretense of sleep will allow him to feel that he is alone.

Curling up under bedclothes, even those belonging to an enemy subject, may be soothing.

You're more likely to hear his handset vibrate if your eyes are closed.

13

A door sliding open signals his wish to take the call on the balcony.

Your Designated Mate's important conversations will take place outdoors.

If you are within earshot of his conversation, record it.

Since beauties carry neither pocketbooks nor timepieces, you cannot credibly transport recording devices.

A microphone has been implanted just beyond the first turn of your right ear canal.

Activate the microphone by pressing the triangle of cartilage across your ear opening.

You will hear a faint whine as recording begins.

In extreme quiet, or to a person whose head is adjacent to yours, this whine may be audible.

Should the whine be detected, swat your ear as if to deflect a mosquito, hitting the on/off cartilage to deactivate the mike.

You need not identify or comprehend the language your subject is using.

Your job is proximity; if you are near your Designated Mate, recording his private speech, you are succeeding.

Profanity sounds the same in every language.

An angry subject will guard his words less carefully.

14

If your subject is angry, you may leave your camouflage position and move as close to him as possible to improve recording quality.

You may feel afraid as you do this.

Your pounding heartbeat will not be recorded.

If your Designated Mate is standing on a balcony, hover in the doorway just behind him.

If he pivots and discovers you, pretend that you were on the verge of approaching him.

Anger usually trumps suspicion.

If your subject brushes past you and storms out of the room, slamming the door, you have eluded detection.

15

If your Designated Mate leaves your company a second time, don't follow him again.

Deactivate your ear mike and resume your "nap."

A moment of repose may be a good time to reassure your loved ones.

Nuanced communication is too easily monitored by the enemy.

Your Subcutaneous Pulse System issues pings so generic that detection would reveal neither source nor intent.

A button is embedded behind the inside ligament of your right knee (if right-handed).

Depress twice to indicate to loved ones that you are well and thinking of them.

You may send this signal only once each day.

A continuous depression of the button indicates an emergency.

You will debate, each day, the best time to send your signal.

You will reflect on the fact that your husband, coming from a culture of tribal allegiance, understands and applauds your patriotism.

You will reflect on the enclosed and joyful life that the two of you have shared since graduate school.

You will reflect on the fact that America is your husband's chosen country, and that he loves it.

You will reflect on the fact that your husband's rise to prominence would have been unimaginable in any other nation.

You will reflect on your joint conviction that your service had to be undertaken before you had children.

You will reflect on the fact that you are thirty-three, and have spent your professional life fomenting musical trends.

You will reflect on the fact that you must return home the same person you were when you left.

You will reflect on the fact that you've been guaranteed you will not be the same person.

You will reflect on the fact that you had stopped being that person even before leaving.

You will reflect on the fact that too much reflection is pointless.

You will reflect on the fact that these "instructions" are becoming less and less instructive.

Your Field Instructions, stored in a chip beneath your hairline, will serve as both a mission log and a guide for others undertaking this work.

Pressing your left thumb (if right-handed) against your left middle fingertip begins recording.

For clearest results, mentally speak the thought, as if talking to yourself.

Always filter your observations and experience through the lens of their didactic value.

Your training is ongoing; you must learn from each step you take.

When your mission is complete, you may view the results of the download before adding your Field Instructions to your mission file.

Where stray or personal thoughts have intruded, you may delete them.

16

Pretend sleep can lead to actual sleep. Sleep is restorative in almost every circumstance.

The sound of showering likely indicates the return of your Designated Mate.

As a beauty, you will be expected to return to your room and change clothes often; a fresh appearance at mealtimes is essential.

The goal is to be a lovely, innocuous, evolving surprise.

A crisp white sundress against tanned skin is widely viewed as attractive.

Avoid overbright colors; they are attention-seeking and hinder camouflage.

White is not, technically speaking, a bright color.

White is, nevertheless, bright.

Gold spike-heeled sandals may compromise your ability to run or jump, but they look good on tanned feet.

Thirty-three is still young enough to register as "young."

Registering as "young" is especially welcome to those who may not register as "young" much longer.

If your Designated Mate leads you to dinner with an arm at your waist, assume that your attire change was successful.

17

When men begin serious talk, beauties are left to themselves.

"How long have you been divorced?" suggests the wish to resume a prior conversation.

"A few months," when untrue, should be uttered without eye contact.

"What was he like, your husband?" may be answered honestly.

"From Africa. Kenya" will satisfy your wish to talk about your husband.

"Black?," with eyebrows raised, may indicate racism.

"Yes. Black," in measured tones, should deliver a gentle reprimand.

"How black?" suggests that it did not.

"Very black" is somewhat less gentle, especially when accompanied by a pointed stare.

"Nice" hints at personal experience.

"Yes. It is nice" contradicts ones alleged divorce. "Was nice" is a reasonable correction.

"But not nice enough?," with laughter, indicates friendly intimacy. Especially when followed by "Or too nice!"

18

House-party hosts are universally eager to make guests eat.

For most beauties, the lure of food is a hazard; as a beauty of limited tenure, you may eat what you want.

Squab can be consumed by ripping the bird apart with your hands and sucking the meat from the bones.

A stunned expression reveals that your host expected the use of utensils.

A host who caters to violent guests will understand implicitly the need for discretion.

The adjacency of your host's chair to your own may presage a confidence.

If your job is to appear simpleminded, a confidence may mean that you have failed.

Everyone should brush his teeth before dinner.

Turning your ear toward your host's mouth will prevent you from having to smell the breath coming from it.

Ears must be kept clean at all times.

If your host warns you that your Designated Mate may pose an immediate danger to you, assume that your Designated Mate has left the room.

19

Going to the rest room is the most efficient means of self-jettisoning.

Never betray urgency, not even in an empty hallway.

If you have no idea in which direction your Designated Mate has gone, hold still.

If you find yourself hovering beside a pair of glass doors, you may open them and step outside.

Nights in the South of France are a strange, dark, piercing blue.

A bright moon can astonish, no matter how many times you have seen it.

If you were a child who loved the moon, looking at the moon will forever remind you of childhood.

Fatherless girls may invest the moon with a certain paternal promise.

Everyone has a father.

A vague story like "Your father died before you were born" may satisfy a curious child for an unlikely number of years.

The truth of your paternity, discovered in adulthood, will make the lie seem retroactively ludicrous.

Publicists occasionally have flings with their movie-star clients.

Discovering that you are a movie star's daughter is not necessarily a comfort.

It is especially not a comfort when the star in question has seven other children from three different marriages.

Discovering that you are a movie star's daughter may prompt you to watch upward of sixty movies, dating from the beginning of his career.

You may think, watching said movies, You don't know about me, but I am here.

You may think, watching said movies. I'm invisible to you, but I am here.

A sudden reconfiguration of your past can change the fit and feel of your adulthood.

It may cleave you, irreparably, from the mother whose single goal has been your happiness.

If your husband has transformed greatly in his own life, he will understand your transformation.

Avoid excessive self-reflection; your job is to look out, not in.

20

"There you are," whispered from behind by your Designated Mate, suggests that he has been looking for you.

Holding still can sometimes prove more effective than actively searching.

"Come," uttered softly, may communicate a renewed wish for intimate contact.

The moon's calm face can make you feel, in advance, that you are understood and forgiven.

The sea is audible against the rocks well before you see it.

Even at night, the Mediterranean is more blue than black.

If you wish to avoid physical intimacy, the sight of a speedboat will bring relief, despite the myriad new problems it presents.

If no words are exchanged between your Designated Mate and the speedboat's captain, their meeting was likely prearranged.

A man known for his cruelty may still show great care in guiding his beauty into a rocking speedboat.

He may interpret her hesitation to board as a fear of falling in.

Resist the impulse to ask where you are going.

Try, when anxious, to summon up a goofy giggle.

Locate your Personal Calming Source and use it.

If your Personal Calming Source is the moon, be grateful that it is dark and that the moon is especially bright.

Reflect on the many reasons you can't yet die:

You need to see your husband.

You need to have children.

You need to tell the movie star that he has an eighth child, and that she is a hero.

21

The moon may appear to move, but really it is you who are moving.

At high velocity, a speedboat slams along the tops of waves.

Fear and excitement are sometimes indistinguishable.

When the captain of a boat adjusts his course in response to commands from your Designated Mate, he may not know where he is taking you.

If your Designated Mate keeps looking up, he's probably using the stars for navigation.

The Mediterranean is vast enough to have once seemed infinite.

A beauty should require no more context than the presence of her Designated Mate.

A beauty must appear to enjoy any journey he initiates.

Simulate said enjoyment by putting an affectionate arm around him and nestling your head close to his.

A beauty whose head is aligned with her Designated Mate's can share in his navigation and thus calculate the route.

At night, far from shore, stars pulse with a strength that is impossible to conceive of in the proximity of light.

Your whereabouts will never be a mystery; you will be visible at all times as a dot of light on the screens of those watching over you.

You are one of hundreds, each a potential hero.

Technology has afforded ordinary people a chance to glow in the cosmos of human achievement.

Your lack of espionage and language training is what makes your record clean and neutral.

You are an ordinary person undertaking an extraordinary task.

You need not be remarkable for your credentials or skill sets, only for your bravery and equilibrium.

Knowing that you are one of hundreds shouldn't feel belittling.

In the new heroism, the goal is to merge with something larger than yourself.

In the new heroism, the goal is to throw off generations of self-involvement.

In the new heroism, the goal is to renounce the American fixation with being seen and recognized.

In the new heroism, the goal is to dig beneath your shiny persona.

You'll be surprised by what lies under it: a rich, deep crawl space of possibilities.

Some liken this discovery to a dream in which a familiar home acquires new wings and rooms.

The power of individual magnetism is nothing against the power of combined selfless effort.

You may accomplish astonishing personal feats, but citizen agents rarely seek individual credit.

They liken the need for personal glory to cigarette addiction: a habit that feels life-sustaining even as it kills you.

Childish attention-seeking is usually satisfied at the expense of real power.

An enemy of the state could not have connived a better way to declaw and distract us.

Now our notorious narcissism is our camouflage.

22

After a juddering ride of several hours, you may not notice at first that the boat is approaching a shore.

A single lighted structure stands out strongly on a deserted coastline.

Silence after a roaring motor is a sound of its own.

The speedboat's immediate departure signals that you won't be making a return trip anytime soon.

Knowing your latitude and longitude is not the same as knowing where you are.

A new remote and unfamiliar place can make the prior remote and unfamiliar place seem like home.

Imagining yourself as a dot of light on a screen is oddly reassuring.

Because your husband is a visionary in the realm of national security, he occasionally has access to that screen.

If it calms you to imagine your husband tracking your dot of light, then imagine it.

Do not, however, close your eyes while ascending a rocky path in darkness.

At Latitude X, Longitude Y, the flora is dry and crumbles under your feet.

A voice overhead suggests that your arrival was expected and observed.

An empty shore is not necessarily unpatrolled.

The best patrols are imperceptible.

23

A formal handshake between your new host and your Designated Mate implies that this is their first meeting.

A formal handshake followed by a complex and stylized hand gesture implies a shared allegiance.

So does the immediate use of a language you don't recognize.

In certain rich, powerful men, physical slightness will seem a source of strength.

The failure of your new host to acknowledge you may indicate that women do not register in his field of vision.

Being invisible means that you won't be closely watched.

Your job is to be forgotten yet still present.

A white, sparkling villa amid so much scrabbly darkness will appear miragelike.

A man to whom women are invisible may still have many beauties in his domain.

These neglected beauties will vie for his scant attention.

Among neglected beauties, there is often an alpha beauty who assumes leadership.

As you enter the house, her cool scrutiny will ripple through the other beauties and surround you.

The sensation will remind you of going as a child with your mother to visit families with two parents and multiple children.

At first, the knot of unfamiliar kids would seem impenetrable.

You would wish, keenly, that you had a sibling who could be your ally.

Feeling at the mercy of those around you prompted a seismic internal response.

The will to dominate was deeper than yourself.

You were never childish, even as a child.

Your unchildishness is something your husband has always loved in you.

Once the new children were under your control, it was crushing to leave their midst.

24

A small table and chairs carved into a spindly clifftop promontory are doubtless designed for private conversation.

If your Designated Mate brings you with him to this place, it may mean that he feels less than perfectly at ease with your new host.

When your new host dismisses his own alpha beauty, important business may be under way.

An alpha beauty will not tolerate her own exclusion if another beauty is included.

If your new host makes a motion of dismissal at you, look to your Designated Mate.

Take orders from no one but your Designated Mate.

If your Designated Mate keeps an arm around you in the face of your new host's dismissal, you have become the object of a power play.

If your new host moves close to your face and speaks directly into it, he is likely testing your ignorance of his language.

If your Designated Mate stiffens beside you, your new host's words are probably offensive.

When you become an object of contention, try to neutralize the conflict.

A giggle and a look of incomprehension are a beauty's most reliable tools.

If the men relax into their chairs, neutralization has been successful.

Your new host has insulted you and, by extension, your Designated Mate.

Your Designated Mate has prevailed in his claim that you're too harmless to bother sending away.

Congratulate yourself on preserving your adjacency and activate your ear mike.

25

In the presence of business conversation, project an utter lack of interest or curiosity.

Notice where you are at all times.

On a high, narrow promontory at Latitude X, Longitude Y, the ocean and heavens shimmer in all directions.

There will be moments in your mission, perhaps very few, when you'll sense the imminence of critical information.

It may come in the form of a rush of joy.

This joy may arise from your discovery that the moon, hard and radiant, is still aloft.

It may arise from the knowledge that, when your task is complete, you will return to the husband you adore.

It may arise from the extremity of the natural beauty around you, and the recognition that you are alive in this moment.

It may arise from your knowledge that you have accomplished every goal you've set for yourself since childhood.

It may arise from the knowledge that at long last you've found a goal worthy of your considerable energies.

It may arise from the knowledge that, by accomplishing this goal, you'll have helped to perpetuate American life as you know it.

A wave of joy can make it difficult to sit still.

Beware of internal states—positive or negative—that obscure what is happening around you.

When two subjects begin making sketches, concrete planning may have commenced.

The camera implanted in your left eye is operated by pressing your left tear duct.

In poor light, a flash may be activated by pressing the outside tip of your left eyebrow.

When using the flash, always cover your non-camera eye to shield it from temporary blindness occasioned by the flash.

Never deploy flash photography in the presence of other people.

26

Springing from your seat with a gasp and peering toward the house will focus the attention of others in that direction.

Having heard something inaudible to others puts you in an immediate position of authority.

"What? What did you hear?," uttered close to your face by your Designated Mate, means that your diversion was successful.

Wait until their eagerness to know verges on anger, evidenced by the shaking of your shoulders.

Then tell them, faintly, "I heard screaming."

Men with a history of violence live in fear of retribution.

Your new host will be the first to depart in the direction of alleged screaming.

Your Designated Mate's glance toward the dock, far below, may reveal that his interests are not fully aligned with your new host's.

His attention to his handset may portend that your diversion has run amok, undermining the transaction you meant to capture.

Among the violent, there is always a plan for escape.

27

It is reasonable to hope that a back-lit screen will distract its user from a camera flash at some slight distance.

Move close to the sketches you wish to photograph, allowing them to fill your field of vision.

Hold very still.

A flash is far more dramatic in total darkness.

An epithet in another language, followed by "What the fuck was that?," means you overestimated your Designated Mate's handset absorption.

A bright, throbbing total blindness means that you neglected to cover your non-camera eye.

Distance yourself from agency in the flash by crying out, truthfully, "I can't see!"

It is hard to safely navigate a clifftop promontory at high speed while blind.

It is hard to defer said navigation when your Designated Mate is forcefully yanking your hand.

A distant buzz presages an approaching speedboat.

Cooler air and a downward slope indicate that you are now below the cliff's edge.

Trying to negotiate a crumbling wooded path in a state of blindness (and heels) will soon lead to tripping and collapsing.

Receding downhill footfalls indicate that you've overtaxed your limited value to your Designated Mate.

A sense of helpless disorientation may prevent you from doing much more than sitting there in the dirt.

28

Variegation in the textures around you is a first sign that your temporary blindness has begun to fade.

Temporary blindness sharpens one's appreciation for not being blind.

In the aftermath of blindness, the accretion of objects around you may have an almost sensual quality.

A boat departing at high speed will send a vibration trembling up through the soil.

The knowledge that you are alone, without your Designated Mate, will settle upon you slowly and coldly.

Each new phase of aloneness reveals that you were previously less alone than you thought.

This more profound isolation may register, at first, as paralysis.

If it soothes you to lie back in the dirt, then lie back.

The moon shines everywhere.

The moon can seem as expressive as a face.

Human beings are fiercely, primordially resilient.

In uneasy times, draw on the resilience you carry inside you.

Recall that the mythical feats you loved to read about as a child are puny beside the accomplishments of human beings on earth.

29

The presence of another person can be sensed, even when not directly perceived.

The discovery of another person at close range, when you thought you were alone, may occasion fear.

Leaping from a supine into a standing posture will induce a head rush.

"I see you. Come out" must be uttered calmly, from the Readiness Position.

If you show fear, make sure that it isn't the fear you actually feel.

When you've expected a man, the appearance of a woman may be shocking.

Despite all that you know and are, you may experience that shock as a relief.

"Why are you here?," uttered by your new host's alpha beauty, is likely hostile.

Respond to abstract questions on the most literal level: "He left without me."

"Bastard," muttered bitterly, suggests familiarity with the phenomenon of being left behind.

Sympathy from an unexpected source can prompt a swell of emotion.

Measure the potential liability of shedding tears before you let them fall.

The perfumed arm of a beauty may pour strength and hope directly into your skin.

30

A lavish clifftop villa may look even more miragelike on a second approach.

Sustaining an atmosphere of luxury in a remote place requires an enormous amount of money.

So does coördinated violence.

Your job is to follow money to its source.

A powerful man whose associate has fled the premises after a false alarm is unlikely to be cheerful.

The reappearance of the vanished associate's stranded beauty will likely startle him.

Astonishment is satisfying to witness on any face.

"Where the fuck did he go?" is remarkably easy to decipher, even in a language you don't recognize.

A shrug is comprehensible to everyone.

An alpha beauty's complete indifference to the consternation of her mate may mean that he's easily moved to consternation.

It may also mean that he's not her mate.

As a beauty, you will sometimes be expected to change hands.

Generally, you will pass from the hands of a less powerful man to those of a more powerful man.

Greater proximity to the source of money and control is progress.

Your job is identical regardless of whose hands you are in.

If your vulnerability and helplessness have drawn the interest of an enemy subject, accentuate them.

Scraped and dirty legs may accentuate your vulnerability to the point of disgust.

They might get you a hot shower, though.

31

Homes of the violent rich have excellent first-aid cabinets.

If, after tending to your scrapes, you are shown to a bathing area with a stone- encrusted waterfall, assume you won't be alone for long.

The fact that a man has ignored and then insulted you does not mean that he won't want to fuck you.

Slim, powerful men often move with catlike swiftness.

Begin your countdown early—as he lowers himself into the tub.

By the time he seizes your arm, you should be at five.

By the time your forehead is jammed against a rock, you should perceive your body only vaguely, from above.

32

If you feel, on returning to your body, that much time has passed, don't dwell on how much.

If your limbs are sore and your forehead scraped and raw, don't dwell on why.

When you emerge from a warm, churning bath where you've spent an indeterminate period of time, expect to feel shaky and weak.

Remind yourself that you are receiving no payment, in currency or kind, for this or any act you have engaged in.

These acts are forms of sacrifice.

An abundance of diaphanous bathrobes suggests that the occupants of this bathroom are often female.

A soiled and tattered white sundress can seem oddly precious when it's all you have.

Keep with you the things that matter—you won't come back for them later.

The stationing of a male attendant outside the bathroom means that you haven't been forgotten.

If he shows you to a tiny room containing a very large bed, your utility to your new host may not have been exhausted.

A tray containing a meat pie, grapes, and a pitcher of water suggests that visits such as yours are routine.

At times, you may wish to avoid the moon.

At times, the moon may appear like a surveillance device, tracking your movements.

The ability to sleep in stressful conditions is essential to this work.

Sleep whenever you can safely do so.

33

Your abrupt awakening may feel like a reaction to a sound.

In moments of extreme solitude, you may believe you've heard your name.

We reassure ourselves by summoning, in our dreams, those we love and miss.

Having awakened to find them absent, we may be left with a sense of having spoken with them.

Even the most secure houses achieve, in deep night, a state of relative unconsciousness.

A beauty in a diaphanous lavender bathrobe can go anywhere, as long as she appears to be delivering herself to someone.

34

A universal principle of home construction makes it possible to guess which door will lead to the master bedroom.

Linen closets, with doors closed, can resemble master bedrooms.

So can bathrooms.

Bare feet are virtually soundless on a stone floor.

Even a slim, catlike man may snore.

When trespassing in a sleeping man's bedroom, go straight to his bed, as if you were seeking him out.

An alpha beauty who has appeared to have no tie to your new host may turn out to be his intimate, after all.

Their sleeping entanglement may contradict everything you have witnessed between them.

A small crib near the bed may indicate the presence of a baby.

Avoid indulging your own amazement; it wastes time.

Master bedrooms in lavish homes often divide into "his" and "hers" areas.

A beauty's closet is unmistakable, like a quiver of bright arrows.

The closet of a slight, catlike man will usually be compact.

Having penetrated a man's personal space, immediately seek out his Sweet Spot.

The Sweet Spot is where he empties his pockets at the end of the day and stores the essentials he needs to begin the next.

The Sweet Spot of a secretive, cat-like man will most often be inside a cupboard or a drawer.

When you find it, consider using a Data Surge to capture the contents of his handset.

A Data Surge must be deployed with extreme caution, and only if you feel confident of an exceptional yield.

The quantity of information captured will require an enormous amount of manpower to tease apart.

Its transmission will register on any monitoring device.

We can guarantee its effectiveness only once.

35

Reach between your right fourth and pinky toes (if right-handed) and remove the Data Plug from your Universal Port.

Attached to the plug is a cable with a connection pin at one end for insertion into the handset's data port.

Sit on the floor, away from sharp surfaces, and brace your back against a wall.

A red ribbon has been tucked inside your Universal Port; enclose this in one of your palms.

Spread apart your toes and gently reinsert the plug, now fused to your subject's handset into your Universal Port.

You will feel the surge as the data flood your body.

The surge may contain feeling, memory, heat, cold, longing, pain, even joy.

Although the data are alien, the memories dislodged will be your own:

Peeling an orange for your husband in bed on a Sunday, sunlight splashing the sheets;

The smoky earthen smell of the fur of your childhood cat;

The flavor of the peppermints your mother kept for you inside her desk.

The impact of a Data Surge may prompt unconsciousness or short-term memory loss.

The purpose of the red ribbon is to orient you; if you awaken to find yourself clutching one, look to your foot.

When your body is quiet, unplug the handset and return it to its original location.

36

A Data Surge leaves a ringing in your ears that may obscure the sound of another person's arrival.

A face that brought you relief once may trigger relief a second time.

When an alpha beauty accosts you at high volume in an unfamiliar language, it may mean she's too sleepy to remember who you are.

It may also mean she's calling someone else.

Beauty status will not excuse, for another beauty, your appearance where you are not supposed to be.

Should you be perceived as an enemy, prepare to defend yourself at the first sign of physical encroachment.

Your new host lunging at you, shouting, "What the fuck are you doing?," constitutes physical encroachment.

Thrust your elbow upward into the tender socket underneath his jaw, sending him backward onto the floor.

The wails of a newborn will lure its mother away from almost anything, including the physical travails of her mate.

A man disabled by an elbow blow will have little reaction to infant cries.

37

At the revelation of martial-arts expertise, a man who has perceived you as merely a beauty will recalculate your identity and purpose.

Watch his eyes: he'll be measuring the distance to his nearest firearm.

An immediate exit is advisable.

A slim, catlike man may well rebound before a hasty exit can be made.

Obstructing the path of a violent man to his firearm will nearly always result in another encroachment.

Kicking him in the foreneck, even barefoot, will temporarily occlude his windpipe.

The alpha beauty of a violent man will know where his firearm is kept, and how to use it.

A woman holding a gun and a baby no longer qualifies as a beauty.

No beauty is really a beauty.

Disabling a gun holder is likely to hurt the baby she is holding, too.

When self-preservation requires that you harm the innocent, we can provide no more than guidelines.

As Americans, we value human rights above all else and cannot sanction their violation.

When someone threatens *our* human rights, however, a wider leeway becomes necessary.

Follow your instincts while bearing in mind that we must, and will, hew to our principles.

A woman holding a thrashing baby in one arm may have trouble aiming a firearm with the other.

Bullets do actually whistle in an enclosed space.

If a person has shot at you and missed, incapacitate her before she can fire again.

We are most reluctant to hurt those who remind us of ourselves.

38

A lag time exists between getting shot and knowing that you have been shot.

Assuming there is no artery involvement, wounds to the upper limbs are preferable.

Bony, tendony body parts bleed less, but are harder to reconstruct if shattered.

The right shoulder is a bony, tendony part.

When shots have been fired in a powerful man's home, you have minutes, if not seconds, before the arrival of security.

Your physical person is our Black Box; without it, we have no record of what has happened on your mission.

It is imperative that you remove yourself from enemy possession.

When you find yourself cornered and outnumbered, you may unleash, as a last resort, your Primal Roar.

The Primal Roar is the human equivalent of an explosion, a sound that combines screaming, shrieking, and howling.

The Roar must be accompanied by facial contortions and frenetic body movement, suggesting a feral, unhinged state.

The Primal Roar must transform you from a beauty into a monster.

The goal is to horrify your opponent, the way trusted figures, turned evil, are horrifying in movies and in nightmares.

Deploy your camera flash repeatedly while Roaring.

When approached by a howling, spasmodic, flashing monster, most women holding newborns will step aside.

Discontinue Roaring the instant you're free from immediate danger.

Those stampeding to the aid of a powerful man will barely notice a dishevelled beauty they pass in a hallway.

If you're lucky, this will buy you time to flee his house.

Resume your beauty role while running: smooth your hair and cover your bleeding wound with the sundress scrunched in your pocket.

The fact that you can't hear alarms doesn't mean you haven't set them off.

39

After violence in a closed room, cool night air will have a clarifying effect.

Get to the bottom of a hill any way you can, including sliding and rolling.

In residences of the violent rich, there will be at least one guard at each port of egress.

In deep night, if you are extremely lucky (and quiet), that guard will be asleep.

Assume, as well as you can, the air of a beauty larkishly gambolling.

If running barefoot onto a dock transports you back to your childhood, pain may be making you hallucinate.

Lying with girlfriends on a still-warm dock in upstate New York, watching shooting stars, is a sensation you remember after many years.

Hindsight creates the illusion that your life has led you inevitably to the present moment.

It's easier to believe in a foregone conclusion than to accept that our lives are governed by chance.

Showing up for a robotics course by accident, because of a classroom mixup, is chance.

Finding an empty seat beside a boy with very dark skin and beautiful hands is chance.

When someone has become essential to you, you will marvel that you could have lain on a warm dock and not have known him yet.

Expect reimmersion in your old life to be difficult.

Experience leaves a mark, regardless of the reasons and principles behind it.

What our citizen agents most often require is simply for time to pass.

Our counsellors are available around the clock for the first two weeks of your reimmersion and during business hours thereafter.

We ask that you allow our Therapeutic Agents, rather than those in the general population, to address your needs.

Secrecy is the basis of what we do, and we require your extreme discretion.

40

Even preternatural swimming strength cannot propel you across a blue-black sea.

Staring with yearning ferocity from the end of a dock cannot propel you across a blue-black sea.

When your body has been granted exceptional powers, it is jarring to encounter a gulf between your desires and your abilities.

For millennia, engineers have empowered human beings to accomplish mythical feats.

Your husband is an engineer.

Children raised among wild animals learn to detect irregular movements in their landscape.

That particular awareness, coupled with scientific genius, has made your husband a national-security hero.

Intimacy with another human can allow you to scrutinize your surroundings as he would.

Along a rocky, moonlit shore, the irregular movement is the one that is lurching in time with the water beneath an overhang of brush.

A speedboat has most likely been hidden by your new host as a means of emergency escape.

The key will be inside it.

41

Slither between branches and board the boat; untie it and lower its motor into the water.

Be grateful for the lakes in upstate New York where you learned to pilot motorboats.

Fluff up your hair with your functional arm and essay a wide, carefree smile.

A smile is like a shield; it freezes your face into a mask of muscle that you can hide behind.

A smile is like a door that is both open and closed.

Turn the key and gun the motor once before aiming into the blue-black sea and jamming the accelerator.

Wave and giggle loudly at the stunned, sleepy guard.

Steer in a zigzag motion until you are out of gunshot range.

42

The exultation of escape will be followed almost immediately by a crushing onslaught of pain.

The house, its occupants, even the gunshots will seem like phantoms beside this clanging immediacy.

If the pain makes thought impossible, concentrate solely on navigation.

Only in specific Geographic Hotspots can we intervene.

While navigating toward a Hotspot, indicate an emergency by pressing the button behind your knee for sixty continuous seconds.

You must remain conscious.

If it helps, imagine yourself in the arms of your husband.

If it helps, imagine yourself in your apartment, where his grandfather's hunting knife is displayed inside a Plexiglas box.

If it helps, imagine harvesting the small tomatoes you grow on your fire escape in summer.

If it helps, imagine that the contents of the Data Surge will help thwart an attack in which thousands of American lives would have been lost.

Even without enhancements, you can pilot a boat in a semi-conscious state.

Human beings are superhuman.

Let the moon and the stars direct you.

43

When you reach the approximate location of a Hotspot, cut the engine.

You will be in total darkness, in total silence.

If you wish, you may lie down at the bottom of the boat.

The fact that you feel like you're dying doesn't mean that you will die.

Remember that, should you die, your body will yield a crucial trove of information.

Remember that, should you die, your Field Instructions will provide a record of your mission and lessons for those who follow.

Remember that, should you die, you will have triumphed merely by delivering your physical person into our hands.

The boat's movement on the sea will remind you of a cradle.

You'll recall your mother rocking you in her arms when you were a baby.

You'll recall that she has always loved you fiercely and entirely.

You'll discover that you have forgiven her.

You'll understand that she concealed your paternity out of faith that her own inexhaustible love would be enough.

The wish to tell your mother that you forgive her is yet another reason you must make it home alive.

You will not be able to wait, but you will have to wait.

We can't tell you in advance what direction relief will come from.

We can only reassure you that we have never yet failed to recover a citizen agent, dead or alive, who managed to reach a Hotspot.

44

Hotspots are not hot.

Even a warm night turns frigid at the bottom of a wet boat.

The stars are always there, scattered and blinking.

Looking up at the sky from below can feel like floating, suspended, and looking down.

The universe will seem to hang beneath you in its milky glittering mystery.

Only when you notice a woman like yourself, crumpled and bleeding at the bottom of a boat, will you realize what has happened.

You've deployed the Dissociation Technique without meaning to.

There is no harm in this.

Released from pain, you can waft free in the night sky.

Released from pain, you can enact the fantasy of flying that you nurtured as a child.

Keep your body in view at all times; if your mind loses track of your body, it may be hard—even impossible—to reunite the two.

As you waft free in the night sky, you may notice a steady rhythmic churning in the gusting wind.

Helicopter noise is inherently menacing.

A helicopter without lights is like a mixture of bat, bird, and monstrous insect.

Resist the urge to flee this apparition; it has come to save you.

45

Know that in returning to your body you are consenting to be racked, once again, by physical pain.

Know that in returning to your body you are consenting to undertake a jarring reimmersion into an altered life.

Some citizen agents have chosen not to return.

They have left their bodies behind, and now they shimmer sublimely in the heavens.

In the new heroism, the goal is to transcend individual life, with its petty pains and loves, in favor of the dazzling collective.

You may picture the pulsing stars as the heroic spirits of former agent beauties.

You may imagine Heaven as a vast screen crowded with their dots of light.

46

If you wish to return to your body, it is essential that you reach it before the helicopter does.

If it helps, count backward.

By eight, you should be close enough to see your bare and dirty feet.

By five, you should be close enough to see the bloody dress wrapped around your shoulder.

By three, you should be close enough to see the dimples you were praised for as a child.

By two, you should hear the shallow bleating of your breath.

47

Having returned to your body, witness the chopper's slow, throbbing descent.

It may appear to be the instrument of a purely mechanical realm.

It may look as if it had come to wipe you out.

It may be hard to believe that there are human beings inside it.

You won't know for sure until you see them crouching above you, their faces taut with hope, ready to jump.

- This story is presented as an apparently disjointed series of mental notes, so it may be appropriate to locate some traditional elements within this unconventional format.
  - Character: What evidence do we have that these notes come from a coherent character?
  - Plot: What specific action takes place in this narrative?
  - Setting: Where does this action take place?
  - Point of view: How does this character present action? How does this particular point of view both obscure and reveal particular aspects of the narrative's action?
- The entire story is fragmented, but there are moments that are clearly interruptions; for instance, in section 43: "You'll recall your mother rocking you in her arms when you were a baby." How is this interruption appropriate at this point in the narrative?

Raymond Carver (1938–1988)

Raymond Carver was born in Clatskanie, Oregon. Carver grew up among loggers, mechanics, waitresses, and factory workers, and he memorialized these people in his fiction. After high school, Carver earned an AB degree from Humboldt State College (now California State University) in 1963 and an MFA from the University of Iowa in 1966. Carver used fiction and poetry to portray the lives of average Americans, and his works often explore themes of love, dissolving relationships, and financial and emotional hardships. His stories are often bleak and ambiguous, and his characters must find comfort and satisfaction in life's everyday occurrences. Carver's honors included the 1970 National Endowment for the Arts Discovery Award for Poetry, a 1977 National Book Award nomination for *Will You Please Be Quiet, Please?*, and Pulitzer Prize nominations for Cathedral (1985) and *Where I'm Calling From: New and Selected Stories* (1988).

Cathedral (1983)

This blind man, an old friend of my wife's, he was on his way to spend the night. His wife had died. So he was visiting the dead wife's relatives in Connecticut. He called my wife from his in-laws'. Arrangements were made. He would come by train, a five-hour trip, and my wife would meet him at the station. She hadn't seen him since she worked for him one summer in Seattle ten years ago. But she and the blind man had kept in touch. They made tapes and mailed them back and forth. I wasn't enthusiastic about his visit. He was no one I knew. And his being blind bothered me. My idea of blindness came from the movies. In the movies, the blind moved slowly and never laughed. Sometimes they were led by seeing eye dogs. A blind man in my house was not something I looked forward to.

That summer in Seattle she had needed a job. She didn't have any money. The man she was going to marry at the end of the summer was in officers' training school. He didn't have any money, either. But she was in love with the guy, and he was in love with her, etc. She'd seen something in the paper: HELP WANTED— Reading to Blind Man, and a telephone number. She phoned and went over, was hired on the spot. She'd worked with this blind man all summer. She read stuff to him, case studies, reports, that sort of thing. She helped him organize his little office in the county social-service department. They'd become good friends, my wife and the blind man. How do I know these things? She told me. And she told me something else. On her last day in the office, the blind man asked if he could touch her face. She agreed to this. She told me he touched his fingers to every part of her face, her nose—even her neck! She never forgot it. She even tried to write a poem about it. She was always trying to write a poem. She wrote a poem or two every year, usually after something really important had happened to her.

When we first started going out together, she showed me the poem. In the poem, she recalled his fingers and the way they had moved around over her face. In the poem, she talked about what she had felt at the time, about what went through her mind when the blind man touched her nose and lips. I can remember I didn't think much of the poem. Of course, I didn't tell her that. Maybe I just don't understand poetry. I admit it's not the first thing I reach for when I pick up something to read.

Anyway, this man who'd first enjoyed her favors, the officer-to-be, he'd been her childhood sweetheart. So okay. I'm saying that at the end of the summer she let the blind man run his hands over her face, said goodbye to him, married her childhood etc., who was now a commissioned officer, and she moved away from Seattle. But they'd kept in touch, she and the blind man. She made the first contact after a year or so. She called him up one night from an Air Force base in Alabama. She wanted to talk. They talked. He asked her to send a tape and tell him about her life. She did this. She sent the tape. On the tape, she told the blind man about her husband and about their life together in the military. She told the blind man she loved her husband but she didn't like it where they lived and she didn't like it that he was part of the military-industrial thing. She told the blind man she'd written a poem and he was in it. She told him that she was writing a poem about what it was like to be an Air Force officer's wife. The poem wasn't finished yet. She was still writing it. The blind man made a tape. He sent her the tape. She made a tape. This went on for years. My wife's officer was posted to one base and then another. She sent tapes from Moody AFB, McGuire, McConnell, and finally Travis, near Sacramento, where one night she got to feeling lonely and cut off from people she kept losing in that moving-around life. She got to feeling she couldn't go it another step. She went in and swallowed all the pills and capsules in the medicine chest and washed them down with a bottle of gin. Then she got into a hot bath and passed out.

But instead of dying, she got sick. She threw up. Her officer—why should he have a name? he was the childhood sweetheart, and what more does he want?—came home from somewhere, found her, and called the ambulance. In time, she put it all on a tape and sent the tape to the blind man. Over the years, she put all kinds of stuff on tapes and sent the tapes off lickety-split. Next to writing a poem every year, I think it was her chief means of recreation. On one tape, she told the blind man she'd decided to live away from her officer for a time. On another tape, she told him about her divorce. She and I began going out, and of course she told her blind man about it. She told him everything, or so it seemed to me. Once she asked me if I'd like to hear the latest tape from the blind man. This was a year ago. I was on the tape, she said. So I said okay, I'd listen to it. I got us drinks and we settled down in the living room. We made ready to listen. First she inserted the tape into the player and adjusted a couple of dials. Then she pushed a lever. The tape squeaked and someone began to talk in this loud voice. She lowered the volume. After a few minutes of harmless chitchat, I heard my own name in the mouth of this stranger, this blind man I didn't even know! And then this: "From all you've said about him, I can only conclude—" But we were interrupted, a knock at the door, something, and we didn't ever get back to the tape. Maybe it was just as well. I'd heard all I wanted to.

Now this same blind man was coming to sleep in my house.

"Maybe I could take him bowling," I said to my wife. She was at the draining board doing scalloped potatoes. She put down the knife she was using and turned around.

"If you love me," she said, "you can do this for me. If you don't love me, okay. But if you had a friend, any friend, and the friend came to visit, I'd make him feel comfortable." She wiped her hands with the dish towel.

"I don't have any blind friends," I said.

"You don't have *any* friends," she said. "Period. Besides," she said, "god-damn it, his wife's just died! Don't you understand that? The man's lost his wife!"

I didn't answer. She'd told me a little about the blind man's wife. Her name was Beulah. Beulah! That's a name for a colored woman.

"Was his wife a Negro?" I asked.

"Are you crazy?" my wife said. "Have you just flipped or something?" She picked up a potato. I saw it hit the floor, then roll under the stove.

"What's wrong with you?" she said. "Are you drunk?"

"I'm just asking," I said.

Right then my wife filled me in with more detail than I cared to know. I made a drink and sat at the kitchen table to listen. Pieces of the story began to fall into place.

Beulah had gone to work for the blind man the summer after my wife had stopped working for him. Pretty soon Beulah and the blind man had themselves a church wedding. It was a little wedding—who'd want to go to such a wedding in the first place?—just the two of them, plus the minister and the minister's wife. But it was a church wedding just the same. It was what Beulah had wanted, he'd said. But even then Beulah must have been carrying the cancer in her glands. After they had been inseparable for eight years—my wife's word, *inseparable*—Beulah's health went into a rapid decline. She died in a Seattle hospital room, the blind man sitting beside the bed and holding on to her hand. They'd married, lived and worked together, slept together—had sex, sure—and then the blind man had to bury her. All this without his having ever seen what the goddamned woman looked like. It was beyond my understanding. Hearing this, I felt sorry for the blind man for a little bit. And then I found myself thinking what a pitiful life this woman must have led. Imagine a woman who could never see herself as she was seen in the eyes of her loved one. A woman who could go on day after day and never receive the smallest compliment from her beloved. A woman whose husband could never read the expression on her face, be it misery or something better. Someone who could wear makeup or not—what difference to him? She could, if she wanted, wear green eye-shadow around one eye, a straight pin in her nostril, yellow slacks, and purple shoes, no matter. And then to slip off into death, the blind man's hand on her hand, his blind eyes streaming tears—I'm imagining now—her last thought maybe this: that he never even knew what she looked like, and she on an express to the grave. Robert was left with a small insurance policy and a half of a twenty-peso Mexican coin. The other half of the coin went into the box with her. Pathetic.

So when the time rolled around, my wife went to the depot to pick him up. With nothing to do but wait—sure, I blamed him for that—I was having a drink and watching the TV when I heard the car pull into the drive. I got up from the sofa with my drink and went to the window to have a look.

I saw my wife laughing as she parked the car. I saw her get out of the car and shut the door. She was still wearing a smile. Just amazing. She went around to the other side of the car to where the blind man was already starting to get out. This blind man, feature this, he was wearing a full beard! A beard on a blind man! Too much, I say. The blind man reached into the backseat and dragged out a suitcase. My wife took his arm, shut the car door, and, talking all the way, moved him down the drive and then up the steps to the front porch. I turned off the TV. I finished my drink, rinsed the glass, dried my hands. Then I went to the door.

My wife said, "I want you to meet Robert. Robert, this is my husband. I've told you all about him." She was beaming. She had this blind man by his coat sleeve.

The blind man let go of his suitcase and up came his hand.   20

I took it. He squeezed hard, held my hand, and then he let it go.

"I feel like we've already met," he boomed.

"Likewise," I said. I didn't know what else to say. Then I said, "Welcome. I've heard a lot about you." We began to move then, a little group, from the porch into the living room, my wife guiding him by the arm. The blind man was carrying his suitcase in his other hand. My wife said things like, "To your left here, Robert. That's right. Now watch it, there's a chair. That's it. Sit down right here. This is the sofa. We just bought this sofa two weeks ago."

I started to say something about the old sofa. I'd liked that old sofa. But I didn't say anything. Then I wanted to say something else, small-talk, about the scenic ride along the Hudson. How going *to* New York, you should sit on the right-hand side of the train, and coming *from* New York, the left-hand side.

"Did you have a good train ride?" I said. "Which side of the train did   25
you sit on, by the way?"

"What a question, which side!" my wife said. "What's it matter which
side?" she said.

"I just asked," I said.

"Right side," the blind man said. "I hadn't been on a train in nearly forty
years. Not since I was a kid. With my folks. That's been a long time. I'd nearly
forgotten the sensation. I have winter in my beard now," he said. "So I've been
told, anyway. Do I look distinguished, my dear?" the blind man said to my wife.

"You look distinguished, Robert," she said. "Robert," she said. "Robert,
it's just so good to see you."

My wife finally took her eyes off the blind man and looked at me. I had   30
the feeling she didn't like what she saw. I shrugged.

I've never met, or personally known, anyone who was blind. This blind
man was late forties, a heavy-set, balding man with stooped shoulders, as if he
carried a great weight there. He wore brown slacks, brown shoes, a light brown
shirt, a tie, a sports coat. Spiffy. He also had this full beard. But he didn't use
a cane and he didn't wear dark glasses. I'd always thought dark glasses were a
must for the blind. Fact was, I wished he had a pair. At first glance, his eyes
looked like anyone else's eyes. But if you looked close, there was something
different about them. Too much white in the iris, for one thing, and the pupils
seemed to move around in the sockets without his knowing it or being able to
stop it. Creepy. As I stared at his face, I saw the left pupil turn in toward his
nose while the other made an effort to keep in one place. But it was only an
effort, for that eye was on the roam without his knowing it or wanting it to be.

I said, "Let me get you a drink. What's your pleasure? We have a little of everything. It's one of our pastimes."

"Bub, I'm a Scotch man myself," he said fast enough in this big voice.

"Right," I said. Bub! "Sure you are. I knew it."

He let his fingers touch his suitcase, which was sitting alongside the   35
sofa. He was taking his bearings. I didn't blame him for that.

"I'll move that up to your room," my wife said.

"No, that's fine," the blind man said loudly. "It can go up when I go
up."

"A little water with the Scotch?" I said.

"Very little," he said.

"I knew it," I said.   40

He said, "Just a tad. The Irish actor, Barry Fitzgerald? I'm like that fellow. When I drink water, Fitzgerald said, I drink water. When I drink
whiskey, I drink whiskey." My wife laughed. The blind man brought his hand
up under his beard. He lifted his beard slowly and let it drop.

I did the drinks, three big glasses of Scotch with a splash of water in each. Then we made ourselves comfortable and talked about Robert's travels. First the long flight from the West Coast to Connecticut, we covered that. Then from Connecticut up here by train. We had another drink concerning that leg of the trip.

I remembered having read somewhere that the blind didn't smoke because, as speculation had it, they couldn't see the smoke they exhaled. I thought I knew that much and that much only about blind people. But this blind man smoked his cigarette down to the nubbin and then lit another one. This blind man filled his ashtray and my wife emptied it.

When we sat down at the table for dinner, we had another drink. My wife heaped Robert's plate with cube steak, scalloped potatoes, green beans. I buttered him up two slices of bread. I said, "Here's bread and butter for you." I swallowed some of my drink. "Now let us pray," I said, and the blind man lowered his head. My wife looked at me, her mouth agape. "Pray the phone won't ring and the food doesn't get cold," I said.

We dug in. We ate everything there was to eat on the table. We ate like 45 there was no tomorrow. We didn't talk. We ate. We scarfed. We grazed that table. We were into serious eating. The blind man had right away located his foods, he knew just where everything was on his plate. I watched with admiration as he used his knife and fork on the meat. He'd cut two pieces of meat, fork the meat into his mouth, and then go all out for the scalloped potatoes, the beans next, and then he'd tear off a hunk of buttered bread and eat that. He'd follow this up with a big drink of milk. It didn't seem to bother him to use his fingers once in a while, either.

We finished everything, including half a strawberry pie. For a few moments, we sat as if stunned. Sweat beaded on our faces. Finally, we got up from the table and left the dirty plates. We didn't look back. We took ourselves into the living room and sank into our places again. Robert and my wife sat on the sofa. I took the big chair. We had us two or three more drinks while they talked about the major things that had come to pass for them in the past ten years. For the most part, I just listened. Now and then I joined in. I didn't want him to think I'd left the room, and I didn't want her to think I was feeling left out. They talked of things that had happened to them—to them!—these past ten years. I waited in vain to hear my name on my wife's sweet lips: "And then my dear husband came into my life"— something like that. But I heard nothing of the sort. More talk of Robert. Robert had done a little of everything, it seemed, a regular blind jack-of-all-trades. But most recently he and his wife had had an Amway distributorship, from which, I gathered, they'd earned their living, such as it was. The blind man was also a ham radio operator. He talked in his loud voice about conversations he'd had with fellow operators in Guam, in the Philippines, in Alaska, and even in Tahiti. He said he'd have a lot of friends there if he ever wanted to go visit those places. From time to time, he'd turn his blind face toward me, put his hand under his beard, ask me something. How long had I been in my present position? (Three years.) Did I like my work? (I didn't.) Was I going to stay with it? (What were the options?) Finally, when I thought he was beginning to run down, I got up and turned on the TV.

My wife looked at me with irritation. She was heading toward a boil. Then she looked at the blind man and said, "Robert, do you have a TV?"

The blind man said, "My dear, I have two TVs. I have a color set and a black-and-white thing, an old relic. It's funny, but if I turn the TV on, and I'm always turning it on, I turn on the color set. It's funny, don't you think?"

I didn't know what to say to that. I had absolutely nothing to say to that. No opinion. So I watched the news program and tried to listen to what the announcer was saying.

"This is a color TV," the blind man said. "Don't ask me how, but I can   50 tell."

"We traded up a while ago," I said.

The blind man had another taste of his drink. He lifted his beard, sniffed it, and let it fall. He leaned forward on the sofa. He positioned his ashtray on the coffee table, then put the lighter to his cigarette. He leaned back on the sofa and crossed his legs at the ankles.

My wife covered her mouth, and then she yawned. She stretched. She said, "I think I'll go upstairs and put on my robe. I think I'll change into something else. Robert, you make yourself comfortable," she said.

"I'm comfortable," the blind man said.

"I want you to feel comfortable in this house," she said.   55

"I am comfortable," the blind man said.

After she'd left the room, he and I listened to the weather report and then to the sports roundup. By that time, she'd been gone so long I didn't know if she was going to come back. I thought she might have gone to bed. I wished she'd come back downstairs. I didn't want to be left alone with a blind man. I asked him if he wanted another drink, and he said sure. Then I asked if he wanted to smoke some dope with me. I said I'd just rolled a number. I hadn't, but I planned to do so in about two shakes.

"I'll try some with you," he said.

"Damn right," I said. "That's the stuff."

I got our drinks and sat down on the sofa with him. Then I rolled   60 us two fat numbers. I lit one and passed it. I brought it to his fingers. He took it and inhaled.

"Hold it as long as you can," I said. I could tell he didn't know the first thing.

My wife came back downstairs wearing her pink robe and her pink slippers.

"What do I smell?" she said.

"We thought we'd have us some cannabis," I said.

My wife gave me a savage look. Then she looked at the blind man and 65 said, "Robert, I didn't know you smoked."

He said, "I do now, my dear. There's a first time for everything. But I don't feel anything yet."

"This stuff is pretty mellow," I said. "This stuff is mild. It's dope you can reason with," I said. "It doesn't mess you up."

"Not much it doesn't, bub," he said, and laughed.

My wife sat on the sofa between the blind man and me. I passed her the number. She took it and toked and then passed it back to me. "Which way is this going?" she said. Then she said, "I shouldn't be smoking this. I can hardly keep my eyes open as it is. That dinner did me in. I shouldn't have eaten so much."

"It was the strawberry pie," the blind man said. "That's what did it," he 70 said, and he laughed his big laugh. Then he shook his head.

"There's more strawberry pie," I said.

"Do you want some more, Robert?" my wife said.

"Maybe in a little while," he said.

We gave our attention to the TV. My wife yawned again. She said, "Your bed is made up when you feel like going to bed, Robert. I know you must have had a long day. When you're ready to go to bed, say so." She pulled his arm. "Robert?"

He came to and said, "I've had a real nice time. This beats tapes, 75 doesn't it?"

I said, "Coming at you," and I put the number between his fingers. He inhaled, held the smoke, and then let it go. It was like he'd been doing it since he was nine years old.

"Thanks, bub," he said. "But I think this is all for me. I think I'm beginning to feel it," he said. He held the burning roach out for my wife.

"Same here," she said. "Ditto. Me, too." She took the roach and passed it to me. "I may just sit here for a while between you two guys with my eyes closed. But don't let me bother you, okay? Either one of you. If it bothers you, say so. Otherwise, I may just sit here with my eyes closed until you're ready to go to bed," she said. "Your bed's made up, Robert, when you're ready. It's right next to our room at the top of the stairs. We'll show you up when you're ready. You wake me up now, you guys, if I fall asleep." She said that and then she closed her eyes and went to sleep.

The news program ended. I got up and changed the channel. I sat back down on the sofa. I wished my wife hadn't pooped out. Her head lay across the back of the sofa, her mouth open. She'd turned so that her robe slipped away from her legs, exposing a juicy thigh. I reached to draw her robe back over her, and it was then that I glanced at the blind man. What the hell! I flipped the robe open again.

"You say when you want some strawberry pie," I said.   80

"I will," he said.

I said, "Are you tired? Do you want me to take you up to your bed? Are you ready to hit the hay?"

"Not yet," he said. "No, I'll stay up with you, bub. If that's all right. I'll stay up until you're ready to turn in. We haven't had a chance to talk. Know what I mean? I feel like me and her monopolized the evening." He lifted his beard and he let it fall. He picked up his cigarettes and his lighter.

"That's all right," I said. Then I said, "I'm glad for the company."

And I guess I was. Every night I smoked dope and stayed up as long   85
as I could before I fell asleep. My wife and I hardly ever went to bed at the same time. When I did go to sleep, I had these dreams. Sometimes I'd wake up from one of them, my heart going crazy.

Something about the church and the Middle Ages was on the TV. Not your run-of-the-mill TV fare. I wanted to watch something else. I turned to the other channels. But there was nothing on them, either. So I turned back to the first channel and apologized.

"Bub, it's all right," the blind man said. "It's fine with me. Whatever you want to watch is okay. I'm always learning something. Learning never ends. It won't hurt me to learn something tonight. I got ears," he said.

We didn't say anything for a time. He was leaning forward with his head turned at me, his right ear aimed in the direction of the set. Very disconcerting. Now and then his eyelids drooped and then they snapped open again. Now and then he put his fingers into his beard and tugged, like he was thinking about something he was hearing on the television.

On the screen, a group of men wearing cowls was being set upon and tormented by men dressed in skeleton costumes and men dressed as devils. The men dressed as devils wore devil masks, horns, and long tails. This pageant was part of a procession. The Englishman who was narrating the thing said it took place in Spain once a year. I tried to explain to the blind man what was happening.

"Skeletons," he said. "I know about skeletons," he said, and nodded.   90

The TV showed this one cathedral. Then there was a long, slow look at another one. Finally, the picture switched to the famous one in Paris, with its flying buttresses and its spires reaching up to the clouds. The camera pulled away to show the whole of the cathedral rising above the skyline.

There were times when the Englishman who was telling the thing would shut up, would simply let the camera move around the cathedrals. Or else the camera would tour the countryside, men in fields walking behind oxen. I waited as long as I could. Then I felt I had to say something. I said, "They're showing the outside of this cathedral now. Gargoyles. Little statues carved to look like monsters. Now I guess they're in Italy. Yeah, they're in Italy. There's paintings on the walls of this one church."

"Are those fresco paintings, bub?" he asked, and he sipped from his drink.

I reached for my glass. But it was empty. I tried to remember what I could remember. "You're asking me are those frescoes?" I said. "That's a good question. I don't know."

The camera moved to a cathedral outside Lisbon. The differences in   95
the Portuguese cathedral compared with the French and Italian were not that great. But they were there. Mostly the interior stuff. Then something occurred to me, and I said, "Something has occurred to me. Do you have any idea what a cathedral is? What they look like, that is? Do you follow me? If somebody says cathedral to you, do you have any notion what they're talking about? Do you know the difference between that and a Baptist church, say?"

He let the smoke dribble from his mouth. "I know they took hundreds of workers fifty or a hundred years to build," he said. "I just heard the man say that, of course. I know generations of the same families worked on a cathedral. I heard him say that, too. The men who began their life's work on them, they never lived to see the completion of their work. In that wise, bub, they're no different from the rest of us, right?" He laughed. Then his eyelids drooped again. His head nodded. He seemed to be snoozing. Maybe he was imagining himself in Portugal. The TV was showing another cathedral now. This one was in Germany. The Englishman's voice droned on. "Cathedrals," the blind man said. He sat up and rolled his head back and forth. "If you want the truth, bub, that's about all I know. What I just said. What I heard him say. But maybe you could describe one to me? I wish you'd do it. I'd like that. If you want to know, I really don't have a good idea."

I stared hard at the shot of the cathedral on the TV. How could I even begin to describe it? But say my life depended on it. Say my life was being threatened by an insane guy who said I had to do it or else.

I stared some more at the cathedral before the picture flipped off into the countryside. There was no use. I turned to the blind man and said, "To begin with, they're very tall." I was looking around the room for clues. "They reach way up. Up and up. Toward the sky. They're so big, some of them, they have to have these supports. To help hold them up, so to speak. These supports are called buttresses. They remind me of viaducts, for some reason. But maybe you don't know viaducts, either? Sometimes the cathedrals have devils and such carved into the front. Sometimes lords and ladies. Don't ask me why this is," I said.

He was nodding. The whole upper part of his body seemed to be moving back and forth.

"I'm not doing so good, am I?" I said.   100

He stopped nodding and leaned forward on the edge of the sofa. As he listened to me, he was running his fingers through his beard. I wasn't getting through to him, I could see that. But he waited for me to go on just the same. He nodded, like he was trying to encourage me. I tried to think what else to say. "They're really big," I said. "They're massive. They're built of stone. Marble, too, sometimes. In those olden days, when they built cathedrals, men wanted to be close to God. In those olden days, God was an important part of everyone's life. You could tell this from their cathedral-building. I'm sorry," I said, "but it looks like that's the best I can do for you. I'm just no good at it."

"That's all right, bub," the blind man said. "Hey, listen. I hope you don't mind my asking you. Can I ask you something? Let me ask you a simple question, yes or no. I'm just curious and there's no offense. You're my host. But let me ask if you are in any way religious? You don't mind my asking?"

I shook my head. He couldn't see that, though. A wink is the same as a nod to a blind man. "I guess I don't believe in it. In anything. Sometimes it's hard. You know what I'm saying?"

"Sure, I do," he said.

"Right," I said.   105

The Englishman was still holding forth. My wife sighed in her sleep. She drew a long breath and went on with her sleeping.

"You'll have to forgive me," I said. "But I can't tell you what a cathedral looks like. It just isn't in me to do it. I can't do any more than I've done."

The blind man sat very still, his head down, as he listened to me.

I said, "The truth is, cathedrals don't mean anything special to me. Nothing. Cathedrals. They're something to look at on late-night TV. That's all they are." It was then that the blind man cleared his throat. He brought something up. He took a handkerchief from his back pocket. Then he said, "I get it, bub. It's okay. It happens. Don't worry about it," he said. "Hey, listen to me. Will you do me a favor? I got an idea. Why don't you find us some heavy paper? And a pen. We'll do something. We'll draw one together. Get us a pen and some heavy paper. Go on, bub, get the stuff," he said.

So I went upstairs. My legs felt like they didn't have any strength in   110
them. They felt like they did after I'd done some running. In my wife's room, I looked around. I found some ballpoints in a little basket on her table. And then I tried to think where to look for the kind of paper he was talking about.

Downstairs, in the kitchen, I found a shopping bag with onion skins in the bottom of the bag. I emptied the bag and shook it. I brought it into the living room and sat down with it near his legs. I moved some things, smoothed the wrinkles from the bag, spread it out on the coffee table.

The blind man got down from the sofa and sat next to me on the carpet.

He ran his fingers over the paper. He went up and down the sides of the paper. The edges, even the edges. He fingered the corners.

"All right," he said. "All right, let's do her."

He found my hand, the hand with the pen. He closed his hand over   115
my hand. "Go ahead, bub, draw," he said. "Draw. You'll see. I'll follow along with you. It'll be okay. Just begin now like I'm telling you. You'll see. Draw," the blind man said.

So I began. First I drew a box that looked like a house. It could have been the house I lived in. Then I put a roof on it. At either end of the roof, I drew spires. Crazy.

"Swell," he said. "Terrific. You're doing fine," he said. "Never thought anything like this could happen in your lifetime, did you, bub? Well, it's a strange life, we all know that. Go on now. Keep it up."

I put in windows with arches. I drew flying buttresses. I hung great doors. I couldn't stop. The TV station went off the air. I put down the pen and closed and opened my fingers. The blind man felt around over the paper. He moved the tips of his fingers over the paper, all over what I had drawn, and he nodded.

"Doing fine," the blind man said.

I took up the pen again, and he found my hand. I kept at it. I'm no   120
artist. But I kept drawing just the same.

My wife opened up her eyes and gazed at us. She sat up on the sofa, her robe hanging open. She said, "What are you doing? Tell me, I want to know."

I didn't answer her.

The blind man said, "We're drawing a cathedral. Me and him are working on it. Press hard," he said to me. "That's right. That's good," he said. "Sure. You got it, bub, I can tell. You didn't think you could. But you can, can't you? You're cooking with gas now. You know what I'm saying? We're going to really have us something here in a minute. How's the old arm?" he said. "Put some people in there now. What's a cathedral without people?"

My wife said, "What's going on? Robert, what are you doing? What's going on?"

"It's all right," he said to her. "Close your eyes now," the blind man   125
said to me.

I did it. I closed them just like he said.

"Are they closed?" he said. "Don't fudge."

"They're closed," I said.

"Keep them that way," he said. He said, "Don't stop now. Draw."

So we kept on with it. His fingers rode my fingers as my hand went   130
over the paper. It was like nothing else in my life up to now.

Then he said, "I think that's it. I think you got it," he said. "Take a look. What do you think?"

But I had my eyes closed. I thought I'd keep them that way for a little
longer. I thought it was something I ought to do.

"Well?" he said. "Are you looking?"

My eyes were still closed. I was in my house. I knew that. But I didn't
feel like I was inside anything.

"It's really something," I said.   135

- What events interrupt each of the scenes? Where does each of these
  interruptions originate? How does each of these interruptions lead to an
  exploration of the issues that the narrator is thinking about?

- Trace references to blindness throughout the story. If we think about the
  story in terms of mapping and exploration, what exploration takes place?
  What sort of map do we have by the end of the story?

- How does the final scene, where the narrator is drawing with Robert,
  resolve some of the questions that the narrator has been pondering throughout the story?

POETRY

Samuel Taylor Coleridge (1772–1834)

The Rime of the Ancient Mariner (1798, revised 1817)[2]

PART I

An ancient Mariner meeteth
three gallants bidden to a
wedding feast, and detaineth
one.

It is an ancient Mariner,
And he stoppeth one of three.
"By thy long beard and glittering eye,
Now wherefore stopp'st thou me?

The Bridegroom's doors are opened wide,   5
And I am next of kin;
The guests are met, the feast is set:
May'st hear the merry din."

The Wedding-Guest is spell-
bound by the eye of the old
seafaring man, and constrained
to hear his tale.

He holds him with his skinny hand,
"There was a ship," quoth he.   10
"Hold off! unhand me, grey-beard loon!"
Eftsoons his hand dropt he.

---

2 The marginal glosses were added to the poem by Coleridge in the revised edition of 1817.

He holds him with his glittering eye—
The Wedding-Guest stood still,
And listens like a three years' child: 15
The Mariner hath his will.
The Wedding-Guest sat on a stone:
He cannot choose but hear;
And thus spake on that ancient man,
The bright-eyed Mariner.   20

"The ship was cheer'd, the harbour clear'd,
Merrily did we drop
Below the kirk, below the hill,
Below the lighthouse top.

The Mariner tells how the ship
sailed southward with a good
wind and fair weather, till it
reached the Line.

The Sun came up upon the left,   25
Out of the sea came he!
And he shone bright, and on the right
Went down into the sea.

Higher and higher every day,
Till over the mast at noon—"   30
The Wedding-Guest here beat his breast,
For he heard the loud bassoon.

The Wedding-Guest heareth the bridal
music; but the Mariner continueth
his tale.

The bride hath paced into the hall,
Red as a rose is she;
Nodding their heads before her goes   35
The merry minstrelsy.

The Wedding-Guest he beat his breast,
Yet he cannot choose but hear;
And thus spake on that ancient man,
The bright-eyed Mariner.   40

The ship driven by a storm
toward the South Pole.

"And now the Storm-blast came, and he
Was tyrannous and strong:
He struck with his o'ertaking wings,
And chased us south along.

With sloping masts and dipping prow,   45
As who pursued with yell and blow
Still treads the shadow of his foe,
And forward bends his head,
The ship drove fast, loud roar'd the blast,
The southward aye we fled.   50

And now there came both mist and snow,
And it grew wondrous cold:
And ice, mast-high, came floating by,
As green as emerald.

The land of ice, and of
fearful sounds, where no
living thing was to be seen.

And through the drifts the snowy clifts   55
Did send a dismal sheen:
Nor shapes of men nor beasts we ken—
The ice was all between.

The ice was here, the ice was there,
The ice was all around: 60
It crack'd and growl'd, and roar'd and howl'd,
Like noises in a swound!

Till a great sea-bird, called the
Albatross, came through the snow-fog,
and was received with great joy and
hospitality.

At length did cross an Albatross,
Through the fog it came;
As if it had been a Christian soul,   65
We hail'd it in God's name.

It ate the food it ne'er had eat,
And round and round it flew.
The ice did split with a thunder-fit;
The helmsman steer'd us through!   70

And lo! the Albatross proveth a bird of
good omen, and followeth the ship as
it returned northward through fog and
floating ice.

And a good south wind sprung up behind;
The Albatross did follow,
And every day, for food or play,
Came to the mariners' hollo!

In mist or cloud, on mast or shroud,   75
It perch'd for vespers nine;
Whiles all the night, through fog-smoke white,
Glimmer'd the white moonshine."

The ancient Mariner inhospitably kil-
leth the pious bird of good omen.

"God save thee, ancient Mariner!
From the fiends, that plague thee thus!—   80
Why look'st thou so?"—"With my crossbow
I shot the Albatross."

PART II
"The Sun now rose upon the right:
Out of the sea came he,
Still hid in mist, and on the left   85
Went down into the sea.

And the good south wind still blew behind,
But no sweet bird did follow,
Nor any day for food or play
Came to the mariners' hollo!   90

His shipmates cry out against the
ancient Mariner for killing the bird of
good luck.

And I had done an hellish thing,
And it would work 'em woe:
For all averr'd, I had kill'd the bird
That made the breeze to blow.
Ah wretch! said they, the bird to slay,   95
That made the breeze to blow!

But when the fog cleared off, they
justify the same, and thus make themselves accomplices in the crime.

Nor dim nor red, like God's own head,
The glorious Sun uprist:
Then all averr'd, I had kill'd the bird
That brought the fog an mist.   100
'Twas right, said they, such birds to slay,
That bring the fog and mist.

The fair breeze continues; the ship
enters the Pacific Ocean, and sails
northward, even till it reaches the
Line.

The fair breeze blew, the white foam flew,
The furrow follow'd free;
We were the first that ever burst   105
Into that silent sea.

The ship hath been suddenly
becalmed.

Down dropt the breeze, the sails dropt down,
'Twas sad as sad could be;
And we did speak only to break
The silence of the sea!   110

All in a hot and copper sky,
The bloody Sun, at noon,
Right up above the mast did stand,
No bigger than the Moon.

Day after day, day after day,   115
We stuck, nor breath nor motion;
As idle as a painted ship
Upon a painted ocean.

Water, water, everywhere,
And all the boards did shrink;   120
Water, water, everywhere,
Nor any drop to drink.

And the Albatross begins to
be avenged.

The very deep did rot: O Christ!
That ever this should be!

Yea, slimy things did crawl with legs   125
Upon the slimy sea.

About, about, in reel and rout
The death-fires danced at night;
The water, like a witch's oils,
Burnt green, and blue, and white.   130

A Spirit had followed them; one
of the invisible inhabitants of this
planet, neither departed souls nor
angels; concerning whom the learned
Jew, Josephus, and the Platonic
Constantinopolitan, Michael Psellus,
may be consulted. They are very
numerous, and there is no climate or
element without one or more.

And some in dreams assurèd were
Of the Spirit that plagued us so;
Nine fathom deep he had followed us
From the land of mist and snow.

And every tongue, through utter drought, 135
Was wither'd at the root;
We could not speak, no more than if
We had been choked with soot.

The shipmates, in their sore distress,
would fain throw the whole guilt on the
ancient Mariner: in sign whereof they
hang the dead sea-bird round his neck.

Ah! well a-day! what evil looks
Had I from old and young!   140
Instead of the cross, the Albatross
About my neck was hung."

PART III

The ancient Mariner beholdeth a sign
in the element afar off.

"There passed a weary time. Each throat
Was parch'd, and glazed each eye.
A weary time! a weary time!   145
How glazed each weary eye!
When looking westward, I beheld
A something in the sky.

At first it seem'd a little speck,
And then it seem'd a mist;   150
It moved and moved, and took at last
A certain shape, I wist.

A speck, a mist, a shape, I wist!
And still it near'd and near'd:
As if it dodged a water-sprite,   155
It plunged, and tack'd, and veer'd.

At its nearer approach, it seemeth him
to be a ship; and at a dear ransom he
freeth his speech from the bonds of
thirst.

With throats unslaked, with black lips baked,
We could nor laugh nor wail;
Through utter drought all dumb we stood!
I bit my arm, I suck'd the blood!   160
And cried, A sail! a sail!

With throats unslaked, with black lips baked,
Agape they heard me call:

A flash of joy;

Gramercy! they for joy did grin,
And all at once their breath drew in, 165
As they were drinking all.

And horror follows. For can it be
a ship that comes onward without
wind or tide?

See! see! (I cried) she tacks no more!
Hither to work us weal—
Without a breeze, without a tide,
She steadies with upright keel! 170

The western wave was all aflame,
The day was wellnigh done!
Almost upon the western wave
Rested the broad, bright Sun;
When that strange shape drove suddenly 175
Betwixt us and the Sun.

It seemeth him but the skeleton of
a ship.

And straight the Sun was fleck'd with bars
(Heaven's Mother send us grace!),
As if through a dungeon-grate he peer'd
With broad and burning face. 180

Alas! (thought I, and my heart beat loud)
How fast she nears and nears!
Are those her sails that glance in the Sun,
Like restless gossameres?

And its ribs are seen as bars on the
face of the setting Sun. The Spectre-
Woman and her Death-mate, and
no other on board the skeleton ship.
Like vessel, like crew!

Are those her ribs through which the Sun 185
Did peer, as through a grate?
And is that Woman all her crew?
Is that a Death? and are there two?
Is Death that Woman's mate?

Her lips were red, her looks were free, 190
Her locks were yellow as gold:
Her skin was as white as leprosy,
The Nightmare Life-in-Death was she,
Who thicks man's blood with cold.

Death and Life-in-Death have diced
for the ship's crew, and she (the
latter) winneth the ancient
Mariner.

The naked hulk alongside came, 195
And the twain were casting dice;
'The game is done! I've won! I've won!'
Quoth she, and whistles thrice.

No twilight within the courts of the Sun.	The Sun's rim dips; the stars rush out:
	At one stride comes the dark; 200
	With far-heard whisper, o'er the sea,
	Off shot the spectre-bark.

We listen'd and look'd sideways up!
Fear at my heart, as at a cup,
My life-blood seem'd to sip!   205
The stars were dim, and thick the night,
The steersman's face by his lamp gleam'd white;
From the sails the dew did drip—

At the rising of the Moon,

Till clomb above the eastern bar
The hornèd Moon, with one bright star   210
Within the nether tip.

One after another,

One after one, by the star-dogg'd Moon,
Too quick for groan or sigh,
Each turn'd his face with a ghastly pang,
And cursed me with his eye.   215

His shipmates drop down dead.

Four times fifty living men
(And I heard nor sigh nor groan),
With heavy thump, a lifeless lump,
They dropp'd down one by one.

But Life-in-Death begins her work on the ancient Mariner.

The souls did from their bodies fly—   220
They fled to bliss or woe!
And every soul, it pass'd me by
Like the whizz of my crossbow!"

PART IV

The Wedding-Guest feareth that a spirit is talking to him;

"I fear thee, ancient Mariner!
I fear thy skinny hand!   225
And thou art long, and lank, and brown,
As is the ribb'd sea-sand.

But the ancient Mariner assureth him of his bodily life, and proceedeth to relate his horrible penance.

I fear thee and thy glittering eye,
And thy skinny hand so brown."—
"Fear not, fear not, thou Wedding-Guest! 230
This body dropt not down.

Alone, alone, all, all alone,
Alone on a wide, wide sea!
And never a saint took pity on
My soul in agony.   235

He despiseth the creatures of the calm,

The many men, so beautiful!
And they all dead did lie:
And a thousand thousand slimy things
Lived on; and so did I.

And envieth that they should live, and so many lie dead.

I look'd upon the rotting sea,   240
And drew my eyes away;
I look'd upon the rotting deck,
And there the dead men lay.

I look'd to heaven, and tried to pray;
But or ever a prayer had gusht,   245
A wicked whisper came, and made
My heart as dry as dust.

I closed my lids, and kept them close,
And the balls like pulses beat;
For the sky and the sea,   250
    and the sea and the sky,
Lay like a load on my weary eye,
And the dead were at my feet.

But the curse liveth for him in the eye of the dead men.

The cold sweat melted from their limbs,
Nor rot nor reek did they:
The look with which they look'd on me   255
Had never pass'd away.

An orphan's curse would drag to hell
A spirit from on high;
But oh! more horrible than that
Is the curse in a dead man's eye!   260
Seven days, seven nights, I saw that curse,
And yet I could not die.

In his loneliness and fixedness he yearneth towards the journeying Moon, and the stars that still sojourn, yet still move onward; and everywhere the blue sky belongs to them, and is their appointed rest and their native country and their own natural homes, which they enter unannounced, as lords that are certainly expected, and yet there is a silent joy at their arrival.

The moving Moon went up the sky,
And nowhere did abide;
Softly she was going up,   265
And a star or two beside—

Her beams bemock'd the sultry main,
Like April hoar-frost spread;
But where the ship's huge shadow lay,
The charmèd water burnt alway   270
A still and awful red.

By the light of the Moon he beholdeth God's creatures of the great calm.

Beyond the shadow of the ship,
I watch'd the water-snakes:
They moved in tracks of shining white,
And when they rear'd, the elfish light   275
Fell off in hoary flakes.

Within the shadow of the ship
I watch'd their rich attire:
Blue, glossy green, and velvet black,
They coil'd and swam; and every track   280
Was a flash of golden fire.

Their beauty and their happiness.

He blesseth them in his heart.

The spell begins to break.

O happy living things! no tongue
Their beauty might declare:
A spring of love gush'd from my heart,
And I bless'd them unaware: 285

The selfsame moment I could pray;
And from my neck so free
The Albatross fell off, and sank
Like lead into the sea."

PART V

"O sleep! it is a gentle thing,
Beloved from pole to pole!   290
To Mary Queen the praise be given!
She sent the gentle sleep from Heaven,
That slid into my soul.

By grace of the holy Mother, the ancient Mariner is refreshed with rain.

The silly buckets on the deck,   295
That had so long remain'd,
I dreamt that they were fill'd with dew;
And when I awoke, it rain'd.

My lips were wet, my throat was cold,
My garments all were dank;   300
Sure I had drunken in my dreams,
And still my body drank.

I moved, and could not feel my limbs:
I was so light—almost
I thought that I had died in sleep,   305
And was a blessèd ghost.

He heareth sounds and seeth
strange sights and commotions in
the sky and the element.

And soon I heard a roaring wind:
It did not come anear;
But with its sound it shook the sails,
That were so thin and sere.   310

The upper air burst into life;
And a hundred fire-flags sheen;
To and fro they were hurried about!
And to and fro, and in and out,
The wan stars danced between.   315

And the coming wind did roar more loud,
And the sails did sigh like sedge;
And the rain pour'd down from
        one black cloud;
The Moon was at its edge.

The thick black cloud was cleft, and still   320
The Moon was at its side;
Like waters shot from some high crag,
The lightning fell with never a jag,
A river steep and wide.

The bodies of the ship's crew are
inspirited, and the ship moves on;

The loud wind never reach'd the ship,   325
Yet now the ship moved on!
Beneath the lightning and the Moon
The dead men gave a groan.

They groan'd, they stirr'd, they all uprose,
Nor spake, nor moved their eyes;   330
It had been strange, even in a dream,
To have seen those dead men rise.

The helmsman steer'd, the ship moved on;
Yet never a breeze up-blew;
The mariners all 'gan work the ropes,   335
Where they were wont to do;
They raised their limbs like lifeless tools—
We were a ghastly crew.

The body of my brother's son
Stood by me, knee to knee: 340
The body and I pull'd at one rope,
But he said naught to me."

But not by the souls of the men, nor by demons of earth or middle air, but by a blessed troop of angelic spirits, sent down by the invocation of the guardian saint.

"I fear thee, ancient Mariner!"
"Be calm, thou Wedding-Guest:
'Twas not those souls that fled in pain,   345
Which to their corses came again,
But a troop of spirits blest:

For when it dawn'd—they dropp'd their arms,
And cluster'd round the mast;
Sweet sounds rose slowly through   350
     their mouths,
And from their bodies pass'd.

Around, around, flew each sweet sound,
Then darted to the Sun;
Slowly the sounds came back again,
Now mix'd, now one by one.   355

Sometimes a-dropping from the sky
I heard the skylark sing;
Sometimes all little birds that are,
How they seem'd to fill the sea and air
With their sweet jargoning!   360
And now 'twas like all instruments,
Now like a lonely flute;
And now it is an angel's song,
That makes the Heavens be mute.

It ceased; yet still the sails made on   365
A pleasant noise till noon,
A noise like of a hidden brook
In the leafy month of June,
That to the sleeping woods all night
Singeth a quiet tune.   370

Till noon we quietly sail'd on,
Yet never a breeze did breathe:
Slowly and smoothly went the ship,
Moved onward from beneath.

The lonesome Spirit from the South Pole carries on the ship as far as the Line, in obedience to the angelic troop, but still requireth vengeance.

Under the keel nine fathom deep,   375
From the land of mist and snow,
The Spirit slid: and it was he
That made the ship to go.
The sails at noon left off their tune,
And the ship stood still also.   380

The Sun, right up above the mast,
Had fix'd her to the ocean:
But in a minute she 'gan stir,
With a short uneasy motion—
Backwards and forwards half her length   385
With a short uneasy motion.

Then like a pawing horse let go,
She made a sudden bound:
It flung the blood into my head,
And I fell down in a swound.   390

How long in that same fit I lay,
I have not to declare;
But ere my living life return'd,
I heard, and in my soul discern'd
Two voices in the air.   395

'Is it he?' quoth one, 'is this the man?
By Him who died on cross,
With his cruel bow he laid full low
The harmless Albatross.

The Spirit who bideth by himself   400
In the land of mist and snow,
He loved the bird that loved the man
Who shot him with his bow.'

The other was a softer voice,
As soft as honey-dew: 405
Quoth he, 'The man hath penance done,
And penance more will do.' "

The Polar Spirit's fellow-demons, the invisible inhabitants of the element, take part in his wrong; and two of them relate, one to the other, that penance long and heavy for the ancient Mariner hath been accorded to the Polar Spirit, who returneth southward.

PART VI

First Voice: " 'But tell me, tell me! speak again,
Thy soft response renewing—
What makes that ship drive on so fast?   410
What is the Ocean doing?'

Second Voice: 'Still as a slave before his lord,
The Ocean hath no blast;
His great bright eye most silently
Up to the Moon is cast—   415

The Mariner hath been cast into a trance; for the angelic power causeth the vessel to drive northward faster than human life could endure.

If he may know which way to go;
For she guides him smooth or grim.
See, brother, see! now graciously
She looketh down on him.'

First Voice: 'But why drives on that ship so fast,   420
Without or wave or wind?'
Second Voice: 'The air is cut away before,
And closes from behind.

Fly, brother, fly! more high, more high!
Or we shall be belated: 425
For slow and slow that ship will go,
When the Mariner's trance is abated.'

The supernatural motion is retarded; the Mariner awakes, and his penance begins anew.

I woke, and we were sailing on
As in a gentle weather:
'Twas night, calm night, the Moon was high;   430
The dead men stood together.
All stood together on the deck,
For a charnel-dungeon fitter:
All fix'd on me their stony eyes,
That in the Moon did glitter.   435

The curse is finally expiated.

The pang, the curse, with which they died,
Had never pass'd away:
I could not draw my eyes from theirs,
Nor turn them up to pray.

And now this spell was snapt: once more   440
I viewed the ocean green,
And look'd far forth, yet little saw
Of what had else been seen—

Like one that on a lonesome road
Doth walk in fear and dread,   445
And having once turn'd round, walks on,
And turns no more his head;
Because he knows a frightful fiend
Doth close behind him tread.

But soon there breathed a wind on me,   450
Nor sound nor motion made:
Its path was not upon the sea,
In ripple or in shade.

It raised my hair, it fann'd my cheek
Like a meadow-gale of spring—   455
It mingled strangely with my fears,
Yet it felt like a welcoming.

Swiftly, swiftly flew the ship,
Yet she sail'd softly too:
Sweetly, sweetly blew the breeze—   460
On me alone it blew.

And the ancient Mariner beholdeth his native country.

O dream of joy! is this indeed
The lighthouse top I see?
Is this the hill? is this the kirk?
Is this mine own countree?   465

We drifted o'er the harbour-bar,
And I with sobs did pray—
O let me be awake, my God!
Or let me sleep alway.

The harbour-bay was clear as glass,   470
So smoothly it was strewn!
And on the bay the moonlight lay,
And the shadow of the Moon.

The rock shone bright, the kirk no less
That stands above the rock: 475
The moonlight steep'd in silentness
The steady weathercock.

The angelic spirits leave the
dead bodies,

And the bay was white with silent light
Till rising from the same,
Full many shapes, that shadows were,   480
In crimson colours came.

And appear in their own
forms of light.

A little distance from the prow
Those crimson shadows were:
I turn'd my eyes upon the deck—
O Christ! what saw I there!   485

Each corse lay flat, lifeless and flat,
And, by the holy rood!
A man all light, a seraph-man,
On every corse there stood.

This seraph-band, each waved his hand: 490
It was a heavenly sight!
They stood as signals to the land,
Each one a lovely light;

This seraph-band, each waved his hand,
No voice did they impart—   495
No voice; but O, the silence sank
Like music on my heart.

But soon I heard the dash of oars,
I heard the Pilot's cheer;
My head was turn'd perforce away,   500
And I saw a boat appear.

The Pilot and the Pilot's boy,
I heard them coming fast:
Dear Lord in Heaven! it was a joy
The dead men could not blast.   505

I saw a third—I heard his voice:
It is the Hermit good!
He singeth loud his godly hymns
That he makes in the wood.
He'll shrieve my soul, he'll wash away   510
The Albatross's blood."

PART VII

The Hermit of the Wood

"This Hermit good lives in that wood
Which slopes down to the sea.
How loudly his sweet voice he rears!
He loves to talk with marineres   515
That come from a far countree.

He kneels at morn, and noon, and eve—
He hath a cushion plump:
It is the moss that wholly hides
The rotted old oak-stump.   520

The skiff-boat near'd: I heard them talk,
'Why, this is strange, I trow!
Where are those lights so many and fair,
That signal made but now?'

Approacheth the ship with
wonder.

'Strange, by my faith!' the Hermit said—   525
'And they answer'd not our cheer!
The planks looked warp'd! and see those sails,
How thin they are and sere!
I never saw aught like to them,
Unless perchance it were   530

Brown skeletons of leaves that lag
My forest-brook along;
When the ivy-tod is heavy with snow,
And the owlet whoops to the wolf below,
That eats the she-wolf's young.'   535

'Dear Lord! it hath a fiendish look—
(The Pilot made reply)
I am a-fear'd'—'Push on, push on!'
Said the Hermit cheerily.

The boat came closer to the ship,   540
But I nor spake nor stirr'd;
The boat came close beneath the ship,
And straight a sound was heard.

The ship suddenly sinketh.

Under the water it rumbled on,
Still louder and more dread: 545
It reach'd the ship, it split the bay;
The ship went down like lead.

The ancient Mariner is
saved in the Pilot's boat.

Stunn'd by that loud and dreadful sound,
Which sky and ocean smote,
Like one that hath been seven days drown'd   550
My body lay afloat;
But swift as dreams, myself I found
Within the Pilot's boat.

Upon the whirl, where sank the ship,
The boat spun round and round;   555
And all was still, save that the hill
Was telling of the sound.

I moved my lips—the Pilot shriek'd
And fell down in a fit;

The holy Hermit raised his eyes,   560
And pray'd where he did sit.

I took the oars: the Pilot's boy,
Who now doth **crazy go**,
Laugh'd loud and long, and all the while
His eyes went to and fro.   565
'Ha! ha!' quoth he, 'full plain I see
The Devil knows how to row.'

And now, all in my own countree,
I stood on the firm land!
The Hermit stepp'd forth from the boat,   570
And scarcely he could stand.

The ancient Mariner
earnestly entreateth the
Hermit to shrieve him;
and the penance of life
falls on him.

'O shrieve me, shrieve me, holy man!'
The Hermit cross'd his brow.
'Say quick,' quoth he, 'I bid thee say—
What manner of man art thou?'   575

Forthwith this frame of mine was wrench'd
With a woful agony,
Which forced me to begin my tale;
And then it left me free.

And ever and anon
throughout his future life
an agony constraineth
him to travel from land
to land;

Since then, at an uncertain hour,   580
That agony returns:
And till my ghastly tale is told,
This heart within me burns.

I pass, like night, from land to land;
I have strange power of speech;   585
That moment that his face I see,
I know the man that must hear me:
To him my tale I teach.

What loud uproar bursts from that door!
The wedding-guests are there: 590
But in the garden-bower the bride
And bride-maids singing are:
And hark the little vesper bell,
Which biddeth me to prayer!

O Wedding-Guest! this soul hath been   595
Alone on a wide, wide sea:

So lonely 'twas, that God Himself
Scarce seemèd there to be.

O sweeter than the marriage-feast,
'Tis sweeter far to me,   600
To walk together to the kirk
With a goodly company!—

To walk together to the kirk,
And all together pray,
While each to his great Father bends,   605
Old men, and babes, and loving friends,
And youths and maidens gay!

And to teach, by his own
example, love and rever-
ence to all things that God
made and loveth.

Farewell, farewell! but this I tell
To thee, thou Wedding-Guest!
He prayeth well, who loveth well   610
Both man and bird and beast.

He prayeth best, who loveth best
All things both great and small;
For the dear God who loveth us,
He made and loveth all."   615

The Mariner, whose eye is bright,
Whose beard with age is hoar,
Is gone: and now the Wedding-Guest
Turn'd from the bridegroom's door.

He went like one that hath been stunn'd,   620
And is of sense forlorn:
A sadder and a wiser man
He rose the morrow morn.

- The poem establishes a number of clear patterns that the poet uses throughout, including rhyme, stanzas, and sections. Identify these structural devices.

- How does the poem depend upon interruptions to move the plot forward?
  Look also at the way in which the poet's own explanation of the poem in the
  margins interrupts our reading. How does such interruption also help us as
  readers by breaking up the poem's rhythm?

Emily Dickinson (1830–1886)

[The Brain—is wider than the Sky—] (ca. 1862)

The Brain—is wider than the Sky—
For—put them side by side—
The one the other will contain
With ease—and you—beside—

The Brain is deeper than the sea— 5
For—hold them—Blue to Blue—
The one the other will absorb—
As Sponges—Buckets—do—

The Brain is just the weight of God—
For—Heft them—Pound for Pound— 10
And they will differ—if they do—
As Syllable from Sound—

Emily Dickinson (1830–1886)

[I never saw a Moor—] (ca. 1865)

I never saw a Moor—
I never saw the Sea—
Yet know I how the Heather looks
And what a Billow be.
I never spoke with God 5
Nor visited in Heaven—
Yet certain am I of the spot
As if the Checks were given—

Emily Dickinson (1830–1886)

[Tell all the Truth but tell it slant—] (ca. 1868)

Tell all the Truth but tell it slant—
Success in Circuit lies
Too bright for our infirm Delight
The Truth's superb surprise

As Lightning to the Children eased 5
With explanation kind
The Truth must dazzle gradually
Or every man be blind—

Emily Dickinson (1830–1886)

[To make a prairie it takes a clover and one bee] (ca. 1861)

To make a prairie it takes a clover and one bee,
One clover, and a bee,
And revery.
The revery alone will do,
If bees are few.   5

■ How does attention to a single geographic feature lead to a larger meditation in each of these poems?

■ Every one of these poems uses dashes. How do these dashes function both
to interrupt the flow of the poem and to contribute to the meaning?

Laura Riding (1901–1968)

The Map of Places (1927)

The map of places passes.
The reality of paper tears.
Land and water where they are
Are only where they were
When words read *here* and *here*   5
Before ships happened there.

Now on naked names feet stand,
No geographies in the hand.
And paper reads anciently,
And ships at sea   10
Turn round and round.
All is known, all is found.
Death meets death everywhere.
Holes in maps look through to nowhere.

■ Explain the distinction that the poet makes between "When words read
here and here / Before ships happened there."

■ What is the difference that the second stanza describes? What does it
mean that "Holes in maps look through to nowhere"?

DRAMA

William Shakespeare (1564–1616)

William Shakespeare, the most renowned poet in the English language, and argu-ably in any language, was born in Stratford-upon-Avon, England. Although the exact date of Shakespeare's birth is unknown, it is thought to have been on or around April 23. Shakespearean biography is complicated by the fact that there exists rela-tively little hard information about the author's life. We know for certain that he married Anne Hathaway in 1582 and that the couple's first child, Susanna, was born in 1583. In 1585, the couple had twins, a daughter, Judith, and a son, Hamnet, who died at the age of eleven in 1596. A man of many talents, Shakespeare was active not only as a playwright and actor but also, as part owner of the Globe Theatre, a businessman. He earned a substantial income through his various activi-ties and was able to purchase a large house and much land in Stratford, where he retired several years before his death on April 23, 1616. Shakespeare wrote lyric and narrative poetry in addition to his verse dramas. His best-known lyric poems are the Sonnets, widely regarded as containing some of the finest love poetry in the language. His narrative poems include *Venus and Adonis* and *The Rape of Lucrece*. It is as a playwright, though, that William Shakespeare is best remembered.

Much Ado about Nothing (1598)

CHARACTERS

DON PEDRO, *Prince of Arragon*
DON JOHN, *his bastard brother*
CLAUDIO, *young lord of Florence*
BENEDICK, *young lord of Padua*
LEONATO, *Governer of Messina*
ANTONIO, *brother of Leonato*
BALTHASAR, *servant to Don Pedro*
BORACHIO, *follower of Don John*
CONRADE, *follower of Don John*
DOGBERRY, *a constable*
VERGES, *a headborough*
FRIAR FRANCIS
A SEXTON
A BOY
HERO, *daughter of Leonato*
BEATRICE, *niece of Leonato*
MARGARET, *gentlewoman to Hero*
URSULA, *gentlewoman to Hero*
MESSENGERS, WATCH, *and* ATTENDANTS

ACT I

Scene 1

SCENE: *Before* LEONATO's *house.*

(*Enter* LEONATO, HERO, *and* BEATRICE, *with a* MESSENGER.)

LEONATO: I learn in this letter that Don Peter of Aragon comes this night to Messina.

MESSENGER: He is very near by this. He was not three leagues off when I left him.

LEONATO: How many gentlemen have you lost in this action? 5

MESSENGER: But few of any sort, and none of name.

LEONATO: A victory is twice itself when the achiever brings home full numbers. I find here that Don Peter hath bestowed much honor on a young Florentine called Claudio.

MESSENGER: Much deserved on his part and equally remembered by Don 10 Pedro. He hath borne himself beyond the promise of his age, doing, in the figure of a lamb, the feats of a lion. He hath indeed better bettered expectation than you must expect of me to tell you how.

LEONATO: He hath an uncle here in Messina will be very much glad of it.

MESSENGER: I have already delivered him letters, and there appears much 15 joy in him, even so much that joy could not show itself modest enough without a badge of bitterness.

LEONATO: Did he break out into tears?

MESSENGER: In great measure.

LEONATO: A kind overflow of kindness. There are no faces truer than 20 those that are so washed. How much better is it to weep at joy than to joy at weeping!

BEATRICE: I pray you, is Signior Mountanto returned from the wars or no?

MESSENGER: I know none of that name, lady. There was none such in the army of any sort. 25

LEONATO: What is he that you ask for, niece?

HERO: My cousin means Signior Benedick of Padua.

MESSENGER: O, he's returned; and as pleasant as ever he was.

BEATRICE: He set up his bills here in Messina and challenged Cupid at the flight, and my uncle's Fool, reading the challenge, subscribed for 30 Cupid, and challenged him at the bird-bolt. I pray you, how many hath he killed and eaten in these wars? But how many hath he killed? For indeed I promised to eat all of his killing.

LEONATO: Faith, niece, you tax Signior Benedick too much, but he'll be meet with you, I doubt it not. 35

MESSENGER: He hath done good service, lady, in these wars.

BEATRICE: You had musty victual, and he hath holp to eat it. He is a very
valiant trencherman; he hath an excellent stomach.

MESSENGER: And a good soldier too, lady.

BEATRICE: And a good soldier to a lady, but what is he to a lord?   40

MESSENGER: A lord to a lord, a man to a man, stuffed with all honorable
virtues.

BEATRICE: It is so, indeed. He is no less than a stuffed man, but for the
stuffing—well, we are all mortal.

LEONATO: You must not, sir, mistake my niece. There is a kind of   45
merry war betwixt Signior Benedick and her. They never meet but
there's a skirmish of wit between them.

BEATRICE: Alas! he gets nothing by that. In our last conflict four of his
five wits went halting off, and now is the whole man governed with
one, so that if he have wit enough to keep himself warm, let him   50
bear it for a difference between himself and his horse, for it is all the
wealth that he hath left, to be known a reasonable creature. Who is
his companion now? He hath every month a new sworn brother.

MESSENGER: Is't possible?   55

BEATRICE: Very easily possible. He wears his faith but as the fashion of his
hat; it ever changes with the next block.

MESSENGER: I see, lady, the gentleman is not in your books.

BEATRICE: No. An he were, I would burn my study. But, I pray you, who is
his companion? Is there no young squarer now that will make a voyage   60
with him to the devil?

MESSENGER: He is most in the company of the right noble Claudio.

BEATRICE: O Lord, he will hang upon him like a disease! He is sooner
caught than the pestilence, and the taker runs presently mad. God
help the noble Claudio! If he have caught the Benedick, it will cost   65
him a thousand pound ere he be cured.

MESSENGER: I will hold friends with you, lady.

BEATRICE: Do, good friend.

LEONATO: You will never run mad, niece.

BEATRICE: No, not till a hot January.   70

MESSENGER: Don Pedro is approached.

(*Enter* DON PEDRO, DON JOHN, CLAUDIO, BENEDICK, *and* BALTHASAR.)

DON PEDRO: Good Signior Leonato, you are come to meet your trouble?
The fashion of the world is to avoid cost, and you encounter it.

LEONATO: Never came trouble to my house in the likeness of your Grace,
for trouble being gone, comfort should remain, but when you depart   75
from me, sorrow abides and happiness takes his leave.

DON PEDRO: You embrace your charge too willingly. I think this is your
daughter.

LEONATO: Her mother hath many times told me so.

BENEDICK: Were you in doubt, sir, that you asked her?   80

LEONATO: Signior Benedick, no, for then were you a child.

DON PEDRO: You have it full, Benedick. We may guess by this what you are, being a man. Truly, the lady fathers herself.—Be happy, lady; for you are like an honorable father.

BENEDICK: If Signior Leonato be her father, she would not have his   85
head on her shoulders for all Messina, as like him as she is.

BEATRICE: I wonder that you will still be talking, Signior Benedick: nobody marks you.

BENEDICK: What, my dear Lady Disdain! Are you yet living?

BEATRICE: Is it possible disdain should die while she hath such meet   90
food to feed it as Signior Benedick? Courtesy itself must convert to disdain, if you come in her presence.

BENEDICK: Then is courtesy a turncoat. But it is certain I am loved of all ladies, only you excepted; and I would I could find in my heart that I had not a hard heart, for truly I love none.   95

BEATRICE: A dear happiness to women. They would else have been troubled with a pernicious suitor. I thank God and my cold blood I am of your humour for that. I had rather hear my dog bark at a crow than a man swear he loves me.

BENEDICK: God keep your Ladyship still in that mind, so some   100
gentleman or other shall 'scape a predestinate scratched face.

BEATRICE: Scratching could not make it worse, an 'twere such a face as yours were.

BENEDICK: Well, you are a rare parrot-teacher.

BEATRICE: A bird of my tongue is better than a beast of yours.   105

BENEDICK: I would my horse had the speed of your tongue, and so good a continuer. But keep your way, o' God's name, I have done.

BEATRICE: You always end with a jade's trick. I know you of old.

DON PEDRO: That is the sum of all, Leonato. Signior Claudio and Signior Benedick, my dear friend Leonato hath invited you all. I tell him   110
we shall stay here at the least a month; and he heartily prays some occasion may detain us longer. I dare swear he is no hypocrite, but prays from his heart.

LEONATO: If you swear, my lord, you shall not be forsworn.

(*To* DON JOHN.)

Let me bid you welcome, my lord, being reconciled to the Prince your brother, I owe you all duty.   115

DON JOHN: I thank you. I am not of many words, but I thank you.

LEONATO: Please it your grace lead on?

DON PEDRO: Your hand, Leonato. We will go together.

(*Exeunt all except* BENEDICK *and* CLAUDIO.)

CLAUDIO: Benedick, didst thou note the daughter of Signior Leonato?

BENEDICK: I noted her not; but I looked on her.   120

CLAUDIO: Is she not a modest young lady?

BENEDICK: Do you question me, as an honest man should do, for my
    simple true judgment? Or would you have me speak after my custom,
    as being a professed tyrant to their sex?

CLAUDIO: No, I pray thee, speak in sober judgment.   125

BENEDICK: Why, i' faith, methinks she's too low for a high praise, too
    brown for a fair praise and too little for a great praise. Only this com-
    mendation I can afford her, that were she other than she is, she were
    unhandsome, and being no other but as she is, I do not like her.

CLAUDIO: Thou thinkest I am in sport. I pray thee tell me truly how thou   130
    likest her.

BENEDICK: Would you buy her that you inquire after her?

CLAUDIO: Can the world buy such a jewel?

BENEDICK: Yea, and a case to put it into. But speak you this with a
    sad brow? Or do you play the flouting jack, to tell us Cupid is a
    good harefinder and Vulcan a rare carpenter? Come, in what   135
    key shall a man take you, to go in the song?

CLAUDIO: In mine eye she is the sweetest lady that ever I looked on.

BENEDICK: I can see yet without spectacles and I see no such matter.
    There's her cousin, an she were not possessed with a fury, exceeds
    her as much in beauty as the first of May doth the last of December.   140
    But I hope you have no intent to turn husband, have you?

CLAUDIO: I would scarce trust myself, though I had sworn the contrary, if
    Hero would be my wife.

BENEDICK: Is't come to this? In faith, hath not the world one man but he   145
    will wear his cap with suspicion? Shall I never see a bachelor of
    threescore again? Go to, i' faith, an thou wilt needs thrust thy neck
    into a yoke, wear the print of it and sigh away Sundays. Look Don
    Pedro is returned to seek you.

(*Re-enter* DON PEDRO.)

DON PEDRO: What secret hath held you here, that you followed not to   150
    Leonato's?

BENEDICK: I would your grace would constrain me to tell.

DON PEDRO: I charge thee on thy allegiance.

BENEDICK: You hear, Count Claudio, I can be secret as a dumb man,
    I would have you think so, but on my allegiance—mark you this,   155
    on my allegiance—he is in love. With who? Now that is your Grace's
    part. Mark how short his answer is: With Hero, Leonato's short daughter.

CLAUDIO: If this were so, so were it uttered.

BENEDICK: Like the old tale, my lord: "It is not so, nor 'twas not so, but, indeed, God forbid it should be so."   160

CLAUDIO: If my passion change not shortly, God forbid it should be otherwise.

DON PEDRO: Amen, if you love her, for the lady is very well worthy.

CLAUDIO: You speak this to fetch me in, my lord.

DON PEDRO: By my troth, I speak my thought.

CLAUDIO: And, in faith, my lord, I spoke mine.   165

BENEDICK: And, by my two faiths and troths, my lord, I spoke mine.

CLAUDIO: That I love her, I feel.

DON PEDRO: That she is worthy, I know.

BENEDICK: That I neither feel how she should be loved nor know how she should be worthy is the opinion that fire cannot melt out of me.   170
I will die in it at the stake.

DON PEDRO: Thou wast ever an obstinate heretic in the despite of beauty.

CLAUDIO: And never could maintain his part but in the force of his will.

BENEDICK: That a woman conceived me, I thank her; that she brought me up, I likewise give her most humble thanks. But that I will have a   175
recheat winded in my forehead or hang my bugle in an invisible baldrick, all women shall pardon me. Because I will not do them the wrong to mistrust any, I will do myself the right to trust none.
And the fine is, for the which I may go the finer, I will live a bachelor.

DON PEDRO: I shall see thee, ere I die, look pale with love.   180

BENEDICK: With anger, with sickness, or with hunger, my lord, not with love: prove that ever I lose more blood with love than I will get again with drinking, pick out mine eyes with a ballad-maker's pen and hang me up at the door of a brothel-house for the sign of blind Cupid.

DON PEDRO: Well, if ever thou dost fall from this faith, thou wilt prove a   185
notable argument.

BENEDICK: If I do, hang me in a bottle like a cat and shoot at me; and he that hits me, let him be clapped on the shoulder, and called Adam.

DON PEDRO: Well, as time shall try. In time the savage bull doth bear the yoke.

BENEDICK: The savage bull may, but if ever the sensible Benedick bear   190
it, pluck off the bull's horns and set them in my forehead, and let me be vilely painted, and in such great letters as they write "Here is good horse to hire" let them signify under my sign "Here you may see Benedick the married man."

CLAUDIO: If this should ever happen, thou wouldst be horn-mad.   195

DON PEDRO: Nay, if Cupid have not spent all his quiver in Venice, thou wilt quake for this shortly.

BENEDICK: I look for an earthquake too, then.

DON PEDRO: Well, you temporize with the hours. In the meantime, good
  Signior Benedick, repair to Leonato's. Commend me to him and tell   200
  him. I will not fail him at supper; for indeed he hath made great
  preparation.
BENEDICK: I have almost matter enough in me for such an
  embassage, and so I commit you—
CLAUDIO: To the tuition of God: From my house, if I had it—
DON PEDRO: The sixth of July: Your loving friend, Benedick.   205
BENEDICK: Nay, mock not, mock not. The body of your discourse is some-
  time guarded with fragments, and the guards are but slightly basted
  on neither. Ere you flout old ends any further, examine your con-
  science. And so I leave you.
(Exit.)
CLAUDIO: My liege, your highness now may do me good.   210
DON PEDRO: My love is thine to teach. Teach it but how,
  And thou shalt see how apt it is to learn
  Any hard lesson that may do thee good.
CLAUDIO: Hath Leonato any son, my lord?
DON PEDRO: No child but Hero; she's his only heir.   215
  Dost thou affect her, Claudio?
CLAUDIO: O, my lord,
  When you went onward on this ended action,
  I look'd upon her with a soldier's eye,
  That liked, but had a rougher task in hand
  Than to drive liking to the name of love.   220
  But now I am return'd and that war thoughts
  Have left their places vacant, in their rooms
  Come thronging soft and delicate desires,
  All prompting me how fair young Hero is,
  Saying I liked her ere I went to wars.   225
DON PEDRO: Thou wilt be like a lover presently
  And tire the hearer with a book of words.
  If thou dost love fair Hero, cherish it,
  And I will break with her and with her father,
  And thou shalt have her. Was't not to this end   230
  That thou began'st to twist so fine a story?
CLAUDIO: How sweetly you do minister to love,
  That know love's grief by his complexion!
  But lest my liking might too sudden seem,
  I would have salved it with a longer treatise.   235
DON PEDRO: What need the bridge much broader than the flood?
  The fairest grant is the necessity.

Look, what will serve is fit. 'Tis once, thou lovest,
And I will fit thee with the remedy.
I know we shall have revelling tonight. 240
I will assume thy part in some disguise
And tell fair Hero I am Claudio,
And in her bosom I'll unclasp my heart
And take her hearing prisoner with the force
And strong encounter of my amorous tale. 245
Then after to her father will I break,
And the conclusion is, she shall be thine.
In practise let us put it presently.

(Exeunt.)

Scene 2

SCENE: *A room in* LEONATO's *house.*

(Enter LEONATO *and* ANTONIO, *meeting.)*

LEONATO: How now, brother, where is my cousin, your son? Hath he
provided this music?

ANTONIO: He is very busy about it. But, brother, I can tell you strange
news that you yet dreamt not of.

LEONATO: Are they good? 5

ANTONIO: As the event stamps them, but they have a good cover; they
show well outward. The Prince and Count Claudio, walking in a
thick-pleached alley in mine orchard, were thus much overheard by a
man of mine: the Prince discovered to Claudio that he loved my niece
your daughter and meant to acknowledge it this night in a dance, and 10
if he found her accordant, he meant to take the present time by the
top and instantly break with you of it.

LEONATO: Hath the fellow any wit that told you this?

ANTONIO: A good sharp fellow. I will send for him, and question him
yourself.

LEONATO: No, no, we will hold it as a dream till it appear itself. But 15
I will acquaint my daughter withal, that she may be the better
prepared for an answer, if peradventure this be true. Go you and
tell her of it.

(Enter Attendants.)

Cousins, you know what you have to do.—O, I cry you mercy, friend.
Go you with me and I will use your skill.—Good cousin, have a care this
busy time.

(Exeunt.)

Scene 3

SCENE: *The same.*

(*Enter* DON JOHN *and* CONRADE.)

CONRADE: What the goodyear, my lord, why are you thus out of measure
    sad?

DON JOHN: There is no measure in the occasion that breeds. Therefore
    the sadness is without limit.

CONRADE: You should hear reason.

DON JOHN: And when I have heard it, what blessing brings it?   5

CONRADE: If not a present remedy, at least a patient sufferance.

DON JOHN: I wonder that thou, being, as thou sayest thou art, born
    under Saturn, goest about to apply a moral medicine to a mortifying
    mischief. I cannot hide what I am. I must be sad when I have cause,
    and smile at no man's jests; eat when I have stomach, and wait for no   10
    man's leisure; sleep when I am drowsy, and tend on no man's busi-
    ness; laugh when I am merry, and claw no man in his humor.

CONRADE: Yea, but you must not make the full show of this till you may
    do it without controlment. You have of late stood out against your
    brother, and he hath ta'en you newly into his grace, where it is   15
    impossible you should take true root but by the fair weather that you make
    yourself. It is needful that you frame the season for your own harvest.

DON JOHN: I had rather be a canker in a hedge than a rose in his grace,
    and it better fits my blood to be disdained of all than to fashion a
    carriage to rob love from any. In this, though I cannot be said to be a   20
    flattering honest man, it must not be denied but I am a plain-dealing
    villain. I am trusted with a muzzle and enfranchised with a clog; there-
    fore I have decreed not to sing in my cage. If I had my mouth, I would
    bite; if I had my liberty, I would do my liking. In the meantime, let
    me be that I am and seek not to alter me.   25

CONRADE: Can you make no use of your discontent?

DON JOHN: I make all use of it, for I use it only. Who comes here?
    (*Enter* BORACHIO.) What news, Borachio?

BORACHIO: I came yonder from a great supper: the Prince your brother is
    royally entertained by Leonato, and I can give you intelligence of an   30
    intended marriage.

DON JOHN: Will it serve for any model to build mischief on? What is he for a
    fool that betroths himself to unquietness?

BORACHIO: Marry, it is your brother's right hand.

DON JOHN: Who, the most exquisite Claudio?   35

BORACHIO: Even he.

DON JOHN: A proper squire. And who, and who? Which way looks he?

BORACHIO: Marry, on Hero, the daughter and heir of Leonato.

DON JOHN: A very forward March chick! How came you to this?

BORACHIO: Being entertained for a perfumer, as I was smoking a musty   40
room, comes me the Prince and Claudio, hand in hand, in sad conference. I whipped me behind the arras, and there heard it agreed upon
that the Prince should woo Hero for himself, and having obtained
her, give her to Count Claudio.

DON JOHN: Come, come, let us thither. This may prove food to my   45
displeasure. That young start-up hath all the glory of my overthrow. If I
can cross him any way, I bless myself every way. You are both sure, and
will assist me?

CONRADE: To the death, my lord.

DON JOHN: Let us to the great supper. Their cheer is the greater that I am
subdued. Would the cook were o' my mind! Shall we go prove what's   50
to be done?

BORACHIO: We'll wait upon your Lordship.

(*Exeunt.*)

ACT II

Scene 1

SCENE: *A hall in* LEONATO's *house.*

(*Enter* LEONATO, ANTONIO, HERO, BEATRICE, *and others.*)

LEONATO: Was not Count John here at supper?

ANTONIO: I saw him not.

BEATRICE: How tartly that gentleman looks! I never can see him but I am
heartburned an hour after.

HERO: He is of a very melancholy disposition.   5

BEATRICE: He were an excellent man that were made just in the midway
between him and Benedick. The one is too like an image and says
nothing, and the other too like my lady's eldest son, evermore tattling.

LEONATO: Then half Signior Benedick's tongue in Count John's mouth,
and half Count John's melancholy in Signior Benedick's face—   10

BEATRICE: With a good leg and a good foot, uncle, and money enough in
his purse, such a man would win any woman in the world, if he could
get her good-will.

LEONATO: By my troth, niece, thou wilt never get thee a husband, if thou
be so shrewd of thy tongue.   15

ANTONIO: In faith, she's too curst.

BEATRICE: Too curst is more than curst. I shall lessen God's sending that
way, for it is said "God sends a curst cow short horns," but to a cow
too curst he sends none.

LEONATO: So, by being too curst, God will send you no horns.   20

BEATRICE: Just, if he send me no husband, for the which blessing I am at him
upon my knees every morning and evening. Lord, I could not endure a
husband with a beard on his face. I had rather lie in the woolen!

LEONATO: You may light on a husband that hath no beard.

BEATRICE: What should I do with him? Dress him in my apparel and
make him my waiting gentlewoman? He that hath a beard is more   25
than a youth, and he that hath no beard is less than a man; and he
that is more than a youth is not for me, and he that is less than a
man, I am not for him. Therefore, I will even take sixpence in earnest
of the bearherd, and lead his apes into hell.   30

LEONATO: Well then, go you into hell?

BEATRICE: No, but to the gate; and there will the devil meet me like an
old cuckold with horns on his head, and say "Get you to heaven,
Beatrice, get you to heaven; here's no place for you maids." So deliver
I up my apes and away to Saint Peter for the heavens, he shows me   35
where the bachelors sit, and there live we as merry as the day is long.

ANTONIO (*To* HERO.):   Well, niece, I trust you will be ruled by your father.

BEATRICE: Yes, faith, it is my cousin's duty to make curtsy and say "Father,
as it please you." But yet for all that, cousin, let him be a handsome
fellow, or else make another curtsy and say "Father, as it please me." 40

LEONATO: Well, niece, I hope to see you one day fitted with a husband.

BEATRICE: Not till God make men of some other metal than earth.
Would it not grieve a woman to be overmastered with a pierce of valiant dust? To make an account of her life to a clod of wayward marl?
No, uncle, I'll none. Adam's sons are my brethren, and, truly I hold it   45
a sin to match in my kindred.

LEONATO: Daughter, remember what I told you. If the Prince do solicit
you in that kind, you know your answer.

BEATRICE: The fault will be in the music, cousin, if you be not wooed in
good time. If the Prince be too important, tell him there is measure in   50
everything, and so dance out the answer. For hear me, Hero, wooing,
wedding, and repenting is as a Scotch jig, a measure, and a cinquepace. The first suit is hot and hasty, like a Scotch jig, and full as
fantastical; the wedding, mannerly modest as a measure, full of state
and ancientry; and then comes repentance, and with his bad legs falls   55
into the cinquepace faster and faster till he sink into his grave.

LEONATO: Cousin, you apprehend passing shrewdly.

BEATRICE: I have a good eye, uncle; I can see a church by daylight.

LEONATO: The revellers are entering, brother: make good room.
    (*All put on their masks.*)

(*Enter* DON PEDRO, CLAUDIO, BENEDICK, BALTHASAR, DON JOHN, BORACHIO,
MARGARET, URSULA *and others, masked.*)

DON PEDRO: Lady, will you walk a bout with your friend?   60

HERO: So you walk softly, and look sweetly, and say nothing, I am yours
for the walk especially when I walk away.

DON PEDRO: With me in your company?

HERO: I may say so when I please.

DON PEDRO: And when please you to say so?   65

HERO: When I like your favor, for God defend the lute should be like the case.

DON PEDRO: My visor is Philemon's roof; within the house is Jove.

HERO: Why, then, your visor should be thatched.

DON PEDRO: Speak low if you speak love.

(Drawing her aside.)

BALTHASAR: Well, I would you did like me.   70

MARGARET: So would not I, for your own sake, for I have many ill qualities.

BALTHASAR: Which is one?

MARGARET: I say my prayers aloud.

BALTHASAR: I love you the better; the hearers may cry, "Amen."   75

MARGARET: God match me with a good dancer!

BALTHASAR: Amen.

MARGARET: And God keep him out of my sight when the dance is done. Answer, clerk.

BALTHASAR: No more words. The clerk is answered.   80

URSULA: I know you well enough. You are Signior Antonio.

ANTONIO: At a word, I am not.

URSULA: I know you by the waggling of your head.

ANTONIO: To tell you true, I counterfeit him.

URSULA: You could never do him so ill-well unless you were the very man.   85
Here's his dry hand up and down. You are he, you are he.

ANTONIO: At a word, I am not.

URSULA: Come, come, do you think I do not know you by your excellent wit? Can virtue hide itself? Go to, mum, you are he. Graces will appear, and there's an end.   90

BEATRICE: Will you not tell me who told you so?

BENEDICK: No, you shall pardon me.

BEATRICE: Nor will you not tell me who you are?

BENEDICK: Not now.

BEATRICE: That I was disdainful, and that I had my good wit out of   95
The Hundred Merry Tales! Well, this was Signior Benedick that said so.

BENEDICK: What's he?

BEATRICE: I am sure you know him well enough.

BENEDICK: Not I, believe me.

BEATRICE: Did he never make you laugh?

BENEDICK: I pray you, what is he?   100

BEATRICE: Why, he is the Prince's jester: a very dull fool; only his gift is in devising impossible slanders. None but libertines delight in him,

and the commendation is not in his wit, but in his villany, for he both
pleases men and angers them, and then they laugh at him and beat   105
him. I am sure he is in the fleet. I would he had boarded me.

BENEDICK: When I know the gentleman, I'll tell him what you say.

BEATRICE: Do, do. He'll but break a comparison or two on me, which, per
adventure not marked or not laughed at, strikes him into melancholy,
and then there's a partridge wing saved, for the fool will eat no supper   110
that night. (*Music.*) We must follow the leaders.

BENEDICK: In every good thing.

BEATRICE: Nay, if they lead to any ill, I will leave them at the next turning.

(*Dance. Then exeunt all except* DON JOHN, BORACHIO, *and* CLAUDIO.)

DON JOHN: Sure my brother is amorous on Hero, and hath withdrawn her
father to break with him about it. The ladies follow her and but one   115
visor remains.

BORACHIO: And that is Claudio. I know him by his bearing.

DON JOHN: Are not you Signior Benedick?

CLAUDIO: You know me well. I am he.

DON JOHN: Signior, you are very near my brother in his love. He is   120
enamoured on Hero. I pray you, dissuade him from her. She is no equal
for his birth. You may do the part of an honest man in it.

CLAUDIO: How know you he loves her?

DON JOHN: I heard him swear his affection.

BORACHIO: So did I too, and he swore he would marry her tonight.   125

DON JOHN: Come, let us to the banquet.

(*Exeunt* DON JOHN *and* BORACHIO.)

CLAUDIO: Thus answer I in the name of Benedick,
But hear these ill news with the ears of Claudio.
'Tis certain so, the Prince wooes for himself.
Friendship is constant in all other things   130
Save in the office and affairs of love.
Therefore all hearts in love use their own tongues.
Let every eye negotiate for itself
And trust no agent; for beauty is a witch
Against whose charms faith melteth into blood.   135
This is an accident of hourly proof,
Which I mistrusted not. Farewell therefore, Hero!

(*Re-enter* BENEDICK.)

BENEDICK: Count Claudio?

CLAUDIO: Yea, the same.

BENEDICK: Come, will you go with me?   140

CLAUDIO: Whither?

BENEDICK: Even to the next willow, about your own business, county.
   What fashion will you wear the garland of? About your neck, like an
   usurer's chain? Or under your arm like a lieutenant's scarf? You must
   wear it one way, for the Prince hath got your Hero.   145

CLAUDIO: I wish him joy of her.

BENEDICK: Why, that's spoken like an honest drover: so they sell bullocks.
   But did you think the Prince would have served you thus?

CLAUDIO: I pray you, leave me.

BENEDICK: Ho, now you strike like the blind man. 'Twas the boy that stole   150
   your meat, and you'll beat the post.

CLAUDIO: If it will not be, I'll leave you.

(Exit.)

BENEDICK: Alas, poor hurt fowl, now will he creep into sedges. But that
   my Lady Beatrice should know me, and not know me! The Prince's
   fool! Ha, it may be I go under that title because I am merry. Yea, but   155
   so I am apt to do myself wrong. I am not so reputed! It is the base,
   though bitter, disposition of Beatrice that puts the world into her
   person and so gives me out. Well, I'll be revenged as I may.

(Re-enter DON PEDRO.*)*

DON PEDRO: Now, signior, where's the Count? Did you see him?

BENEDICK: Troth, my lord, I have played the part of Lady Fame. I found   160
   him here as melancholy as a lodge in a warren. I told him, and I think I
   told him true, that your Grace had got the good will of this young lady,
   and I offered him my company to a willow tree, either to make him a
   garland, as being forsaken, or to bind him up a rod, as being worthy to
   be whipped.   165

DON PEDRO: To be whipped? What's his fault?

BENEDICK: The flat transgression of a schoolboy who, being overjoyed with
   finding a bird's nest, shows it his companion, and he steals it.

DON PEDRO: Wilt thou make a trust a transgression? The transgression is in
   the stealer.

BENEDICK: Yet it had not been amiss the rod had been made, and the   170
   garland too, for the garland he might have worn himself, and the rod he
   might have bestowed on you, who, as I take it, have stolen his bird's nest.

DON PEDRO: I will but teach them to sing and restore them to the owner.

BENEDICK: If their singing answer your saying, by my faith, you say honestly.

DON PEDRO: The Lady Beatrice hath a quarrel to you. The gentleman that   175
   danced with her told her she is much wronged by you.

BENEDICK: O, she misused me past the endurance of a block! An oak
   but with one green leaf on it would have answered her. My very visor
   began to assume life and scold with her. She told me, not thinking I
   had been myself, that I was the Prince's jester, that I was duller than a   180
   great thaw, huddling jest upon jest with such impossible conveyance

upon me that I stood like a man at a mark, with a whole army shooting at me. She speaks poniards, and every word stabs. If her breath
were as terrible as her terminations, there were no living near her; she
would infect to the North Star. I would not marry her though she were   185
endowed with all that Adam had left him before he transgressed. She
would have made Hercules have turned spit, yea, and have cleft his
club to make the fire, too. Come, talk not of her. You shall find her
the infernal Ate in good apparel. I would to God some scholar would
conjure her, for certainly, while she is here, a man may live as quiet in hell   190
as in a sanctuary, and people sin upon purpose, because they would go
thither. So, indeed, all disquiet, horror, and perturbation follows her.
DON PEDRO: Look, here she comes.

(*Enter* CLAUDIO, BEATRICE, HERO, *and* LEONATO.)

BENEDICK: Will your Grace command me any service to the world's end?
I will go on the slightest errand now to the Antipodes that you can   195
devise to send me on. I will fetch you a toothpicker now from the
furthest inch of Asia, bring you the length of Prester John's foot, fetch
you a hair off the great Cham's beard, do you any embassage to the
Pigmies, rather than hold three words' conference with this harpy.
You have no employment for me?
DON PEDRO: None, but to desire your good company.   200
BENEDICK: O God, sir, here's a dish I love not! I cannot endure my Lady
Tongue.

(*Exit.*)

DON PEDRO: Come, lady, come, you have lost the heart of Signior Benedick.
BEATRICE: Indeed, my lord, he lent it me awhile, and I gave him use for it,
a double heart for his single one. Marry, once before he won it of me   205
with false dice. Therefore your Grace may well say I have lost it.
DON PEDRO: You have put him down, lady, you have put him down.
BEATRICE: So I would not he should do me, my lord, lest I should prove
the mother of fools. I have brought Count Claudio, whom you sent   210
me to seek.
DON PEDRO: Why, how now, count, wherefore are you sad?
CLAUDIO: Not sad, my lord.
DON PEDRO: How then, sick?
CLAUDIO: Neither, my lord.
BEATRICE: The Count is neither sad, nor sick, nor merry, nor well;   215
but civil count, civil as an orange, and something of that jealous
complexion.
DON PEDRO: I' faith, lady, I think your blazon to be true, though, I'll be
sworn, if he be so, his conceit is false.—Here, Claudio, I have wooed in
thy name, and fair Hero is won. I have broke with her father and his
goodwill obtained. Name the day of marriage, and God give thee joy.   220

LEONATO: Count, take of me my daughter, and with her my fortunes. His Grace hath made the match, and an grace say "Amen" to it.

BEATRICE: Speak, count, 'tis your cue.

CLAUDIO: Silence is the perfectest herald of joy. I were but little happy if I could say how much.—Lady, as you are mine, I am yours. I give away 225 myself for you and dote upon the exchange.

BEATRICE: Speak, cousin; or, if you cannot, stop his mouth with a kiss and let not him speak neither.

DON PEDRO: In faith, lady, you have a merry heart.

BEATRICE: Yea, my lord. I thank it, poor fool, it keeps on the windy side 230 of care. My cousin tells him in his ear that he is in her heart.

CLAUDIO: And so she doth, cousin.

BEATRICE: Good Lord for alliance! Thus goes every one to the world but I, and I am sunburnt. I may sit in a corner and cry "Heigh-ho for a husband!" 235

DON PEDRO: Lady Beatrice, I will get you one.

BEATRICE: I would rather have one of your father's getting. Hath your Grace ne'er a brother like you? Your father got excellent husbands, if a maid could come by them.

DON PEDRO: Will you have me, lady? 240

BEATRICE: No, my lord, unless I might have another for working days? Your Grace is too costly to wear every day. But I beseech your Grace pardon me. I was born to speak all mirth and no matter.

DON PEDRO: Your silence most offends me, and to be merry best becomes you, for, out o' question you were born in a merry hour. 245

BEATRICE: No, sure, my lord, my mother cried, but then there was a star danced, and under that was I born.—Cousins, God give you joy!

LEONATO: Niece, will you look to those things I told you of?

BEATRICE: I cry you mercy, uncle.—By your Grace's pardon.

(*Exit.*)

DON PEDRO: By my troth, a pleasant-spirited lady. 250

LEONATO: There's little of the melancholy element in her, my lord. She is never sad but when she sleeps, and not ever sad then, for I have heard my daughter say she hath often dreamt of unhappiness and waked herself with laughing.

DON PEDRO: She cannot endure to hear tell of a husband. 255

LEONATO: O, by no means. She mocks all her wooers out of suit.

DON PEDRO: She were an excellent wife for Benedict.

LEONATO: O Lord, my lord, if they were but a week married, they would talk themselves mad.

DON PEDRO: County Claudio, when mean you to go to church? 260

CLAUDIO: Tomorrow, my lord. Time goes on crutches till love have all his rites.

LEONATO: Not till Monday, my dear son, which is hence a just sevennight, and a time too brief, too, to have all things answer my mind.

DON PEDRO: Come, you shake the head at so long a breathing, but, I   265
warrant thee, Claudio, the time shall not go dully by us. I will in the
interim undertake one of Hercules' labors, which is, to bring Signior
Benedick and the Lady Beatrice into a mountain of affection, th' one
with th' other. I would fain have it a match, and I doubt not but to
fashion it, if you three will but minister such assistance as I shall give   270
you direction.

LEONATO: My lord, I am for you, though it cost me ten nights' watchings.

CLAUDIO: And I, my lord.

DON PEDRO: And you too, gentle Hero?

HERO: I will do any modest office, my lord, to help my cousin to a good husband.   275

DON PEDRO: And Benedick is not the unhopefullest husband that I know.
Thus far can I praise him: he is of a noble strain, of approved valour, and
confirmed honesty. I will teach you how to humor your cousin
that she shall fall in love with Benedick.—And I, with your two helps,
will so practise on Benedick that, in despite of his quick wit and his queasy   280
stomach, he shall fall in love with Beatrice. If we can do this, Cupid
is no longer an archer; his glory shall be ours, for we are the only love
gods. Go in with me, and I will tell you my drift.

(*Exeunt.*)

Scene 2

SCENE: *The same.*

(*Enter* DON JOHN *and* BORACHIO.)

DON JOHN: It is so. The Count Claudio shall marry the daughter of
Leonato.

BORACHIO: Yea, my lord, but I can cross it.

DON JOHN: Any bar, any cross, any impediment will be med'cinable to
me. I am sick in displeasure to him, and whatsoever comes athwart
his affection ranges evenly with mine. How canst thou cross this   5
marriage?

BORACHIO: Not honestly, my lord, but so covertly that no dishonesty shall
appear in me.

DON JOHN: Show me briefly how.

BORACHIO: I think I told your Lordship a year since, how much I am in
the favor of Margaret, the waiting gentlewoman to Hero.   10

DON JOHN: I remember.

BORACHIO: I can, at any unseasonable instant of the night, appoint her to
look out at her lady's chamber window.

DON JOHN: What life is in that to be the death of this marriage?

BORACHIO: The poison of that lies in you to temper. Go you to the Prince   15
your brother; spare not to tell him that he hath wronged his honor in
marrying the renowned Claudio, whose estimation do you mightily
hold up, to a contaminated stale, such a one as Hero.

DON JOHN: What proof shall I make of that?

BORACHIO: Proof enough to misuse the Prince, to vex Claudio, to undo   20
Hero, and kill Leonato. Look you for any other issue?

DON JOHN: Only to despite them I will endeavour any thing.

BORACHIO: Go then; find me a meet hour to draw Don Pedro and the
Count Claudio alone. Tell them that you know that Hero loves me;
intend a kind of zeal both to the Prince and Claudio, as in love of   25
your brother's honor, who hath made this match, and his friend's
reputation, who is thus like to be cozened with the semblance of a
maid, that you have discovered thus. They will scarcely believe this
without trial. Offer them instances, which shall bear no less likelihood than to see me at her chamber window, hear me call Margaret   30
"Hero," hear Margaret term me "Claudio," and bring them to see this
the very night before the intended wedding, for in the meantime I
will so fashion the matter that Hero shall be absent, and there shall
appear such seeming truth of Hero's disloyalty that jealousy shall be
called assurance and all the preparation overthrown.   35

DON JOHN: Grow this to what adverse issue it can, I will put it in practise.
Be cunning in the working this, and thy fee is a thousand ducats.

BORACHIO: Be you constant in the accusation, and my cunning shall not
shame me.

DON JOHN: I will presently go learn their day of marriage.   40
(*Exeunt.*)

Scene 3

SCENE: LEONATO's *orchard.*

(*Enter* BENEDICK.)

BENEDICK: Boy!

(*Enter* BOY.)

BOY: Signior?

BENEDICK: In my chamber window lies a book. Bring it hither to me in
the orchard.

BOY: I am here already, sir.   5

BENEDICK: I know that; but I would have thee hence and here again. (*Exit*
BOY.) I do much wonder that one man, seeing how much another man
is a fool when he dedicates his behaviors to love, will, after he hath

laughed at such shallow follies in others, become the argument of his
own scorn by falling in love—and such a man is Claudio. I have known   10
when there was no music with him but the drum and the fife, and
now had he rather hear the tabor and the pipe; I have known when
he would have walked ten mile a-foot to see a good armour, and now
will he lie ten nights awake carving the fashion of a new doublet. He
was wont to speak plain and to the purpose, like an honest man and   15
a soldier; and now is he turned orthography; his words are a very
fantastical banquet, just so many strange dishes. May I be so converted and see with these eyes? I cannot tell; I think not. I will not be
sworn but love may transform me to an oyster, but I'll take my oath
on it, till he have made an oyster of me, he shall never make me such   20
a fool. One woman is fair, yet I am well; another is wise, yet I am well;
another virtuous, yet I am well; but till all graces be in one woman,
one woman shall not come in my grace. Rich she shall be, that's
certain; wise, or I'll none; virtuous, or I'll never cheapen her; fair, or
I'll never look on her; mild, or come not near me; noble, or not I for   25
an angel; of good discourse, an excellent musician, and her hair shall
be of what colour it please God. Ha! The Prince and Monsieur Love! I
will hide me in the arbor.

(Withdraws.)

(Enter DON PEDRO, CLAUDIO, *and* LEONATO.)

DON PEDRO: Come, shall we hear this music?

CLAUDIO: Yea, my good lord. How still the evening is,
As hushed on purpose to grace harmony!   30

DON PEDRO: See you where Benedick hath hid himself?

CLAUDIO: O, very well, my lord. The music ended,
We'll fit the kid-fox with a pennyworth.

(Enter BALTHASAR *with Music.)*

DON PEDRO: Come, Balthasar, we'll hear that song again.

BALTHASAR: O, good my lord, tax not so bad a voice   35
To slander music any more than once.

DON PEDRO: It is the witness still of excellency
To put a strange face on his own perfection.
I pray thee, sing, and let me woo no more.

BALTHASAR: Because you talk of wooing, I will sing,   40
Since many a wooer doth commence his suit
To her he thinks not worthy, yet he woos,
Yet will he swear he loves.

DON PEDRO: Now, pray thee, come;
Or, if thou wilt hold longer argument,
Do it in notes.   45

BALTHASAR: Note this before my notes:
There's not a note of mine that's worth the noting.

DON PEDRO: Why, these are very crotchets that he speaks!
Note notes, forsooth, and noting.

(Air.)

BENEDICK: Now, divine air! Now is his soul ravished! Is it not strange that
sheeps' guts should hale souls out of men's bodies? Well, a horn for   50
my money, when all's done.

(The Song.)

BALTHASAR: Sigh no more, ladies, sigh no more,
Men were deceivers ever,
One foot in sea and one on shore,
To one thing constant never: 55
Then sigh not so, but let them go,
And be you blithe and bonny,
Converting all your sounds of woe
Into Hey nonny, nonny.

Sing no more ditties, sing no mo,   60
Of dumps so dull and heavy.
The fraud of men was ever so,
Since summer first was leavy.
Then sigh not so, but let them go,
And be you blithe and bonny,   65
Converting all sounds of woe
Into Hey, nonny nonny.

DON PEDRO: By my troth, a good song.

BALTHASAR: And an ill singer, my lord.

DON PEDRO: Ha, no, no, faith, thou sing'st well enough for a shift.   70

BENEDICK: An he had been a dog that should have howled thus, they
would have hanged him. And I pray God his bad voice bode no
mischief. I had as lief have heard the night raven, come what plague
could have come after it.

DON PEDRO: Yea, marry, dost thou hear, Balthasar? I pray thee get us some   75
excellent music, for tomorrow night we would have it at the Lady
Hero's chamberwindow.

BALTHASAR: The best I can, my lord.

DON PEDRO: Do so. Farewell.

(Exit BALTHASAR.*)*

Come hither, Leonato. What was it you told me of today, that your niece   80
Beatrice was in love with Signior Benedick?

CLAUDIO: O, ay. Stalk on, stalk on; the fowl sits.—I did never think that
lady would have loved any man.

LEONATO: No, nor I neither; but most wonderful that she should so dote
    on Signior Benedick, whom she hath in all outward behaviors seemed   85
    ever to abhor.

BENEDICK: Is't possible? Sits the wind in that corner?

LEONATO: By my troth, my lord, I cannot tell what to think of it but
    that she loves him with an enraged affection, it is past the infinite of
    thought.

DON PEDRO: May be she doth but counterfeit.   90

CLAUDIO: Faith, like enough.

LEONATO: O God! Counterfeit? There was never counterfeit of passion
    came so near the life of passion as she discovers it.

DON PEDRO: Why, what effects of passion shows she?

CLAUDIO: Bait the hook well; this fish will bite.   95

LEONATO: What effects, my lord? She will sit you—you heard my daughter
    tell you how.

CLAUDIO: She did indeed.

DON PEDRO: How, how pray you? You amaze me. I would have I thought   100
    her spirit had been invincible against all assaults of affection.

LEONATO: I would have sworn it had, my lord, especially against Benedick.

BENEDICK: I should think this a gull but that the white-bearded fellow speaks
    it. Knavery cannot, sure, hide himself in such reverence.

CLAUDIO: He hath ta'en th' infection. Hold it up.   105

DON PEDRO: Hath she made her affection known to Benedick?

LEONATO: No, and swears she never will. That's her torment.

CLAUDIO: 'Tis true, indeed, so your daughter says. "Shall I," says she, "that
    have so oft encountered him with scorn, write to him that I love him?"

LEONATO: This says she now when she is beginning to write to him, for   110
    she'll be up twenty times a night, and there will she sit in her smock till
    she have writ a sheet of paper. My daughter tells us all.

CLAUDIO: Now you talk of a sheet of paper, I remember a pretty jest your
    daughter told us of.

LEONATO: O, when she had writ it and was reading it over, she found   115
    "Benedick" and "Beatrice" between the sheet?

CLAUDIO: That.

LEONATO: O, she tore the letter into a thousand halfpence, railed at
    herself that she should be so immodest to write to one that she
    knew would flout her. "I measure him," says she, "by my own spirit,   120
    for I should flout him, if he writ to me, yea, though I love him, I should."

CLAUDIO: Then down upon her knees she falls, weeps, sobs, beats her
    heart, tears her hair, prays, curses: "O sweet Benedick, God give
    me patience!"

LEONATO: She doth indeed, my daughter says so, and the ecstasy hath so   125
    much overborne her that my daughter is sometime afeared she will do a
    desperate outrage to herself. It is very true.

DON PEDRO: It were good that Benedick knew of it by some other, if she
will not discover it.

CLAUDIO: To what end? He would make but a sport of it and torment the   130
poor lady worse.

DON PEDRO: An he should, it were an alms to hang him. She's an excellent sweet lady, and, out of all suspicion, she is virtuous.

CLAUDIO: And she is exceeding wise.

DON PEDRO: In everything but in loving Benedick.   135

LEONATO: O, my lord, wisdom and blood combating in so tender a body,
we have ten proofs to one that blood hath the victory. I am sorry for
her, as I have just cause, being her uncle and her guardian.

DON PEDRO: I would she had bestowed this dotage on me. I would have
daffed all other respects and made her half myself. I pray you, tell   140
Benedick of it, and hear what he will say.

LEONATO: Were it good, think you?

CLAUDIO: Hero thinks surely she will die, for she says she will die, if he
love her not, and she will die ere she make her love known, and she
will die if he woo her, rather than she will bate one breath of her   145
accustomed crossness.

DON PEDRO: She doth well. If she should make tender of her love, 'tis very
possible he'll scorn it, for the man, as you know all, hath a contempt-
ible spirit.

CLAUDIO: He is a very proper man.   150

DON PEDRO: He hath indeed a good outward happiness.

CLAUDIO: Before God, and in my mind, very wise.

DON PEDRO: He doth indeed show some sparks that are like wit.

CLAUDIO: And I take him to be valiant.

DON PEDRO: As Hector, I assure you, and in the managing of quarrels you   155
may say he is wise, for either he avoids them with great discretion, or
undertakes them with a most Christianlike fear.

LEONATO: If he do fear God, he must necessarily keep peace. If he break the
peace, he ought to enter into a quarrel with fear and trembling.

DON PEDRO: And so will he do, for the man doth fear God, howsoever   160
it seems not in him by some large jests he will make. Well, I am sorry for
your niece. Shall we go seek Benedick and tell him of her love?

CLAUDIO: Never tell him, my lord, let her wear it out with good counsel.

LEONATO: Nay, that's impossible; she may wear her heart out first.   165

DON PEDRO: Well, we will hear further of it by your daughter. Let it cool the
while. I love Benedick well, and I could wish he would modestly examine
himself to see how much he is unworthy so good a lady.

LEONATO: My lord, will you walk? Dinner is ready.

CLAUDIO: If he do not dote on her upon this, I will never trust my expectation.   170

DON PEDRO: Let there be the same net spread for her, and that must your
daughter and her gentlewomen carry. The sport will be when they hold
one an opinion of another's dotage, and no such matter. That's the
scene that I would see, which will be merely a dumb show. Let us send
her to call him in to dinner.   175

(*Exeunt* DON PEDRO, CLAUDIO, *and* LEONATO.)

BENEDICK (*Coming forward.*):   This can be no trick. The conference was sadly
borne; they have the truth of this from Hero; they seem to pity the
lady. It seems her affections have their full bent. Love me? Why, it
must be requited! I hear how I am censured. They say I will bear
myself proudly if I perceive the love come from her. They say too   180
that she will rather die than give any sign of affection. I did never
think to marry. I must not seem proud. Happy are they that hear
their detractions and can put them to mending. They say the lady
is fair; 'tis a truth, I can bear them witness. And virtuous; 'tis so,
I cannot reprove it. And wise, but for loving me; by my troth, it is no   185
addition to her wit, nor no great argument of her folly, for I will be
horribly in love with her! I may chance have some odd quirks and
remnants of wit broken on me because I have railed so long against
marriage, but doth not the appetite alter? A man loves the meat in his
youth that he cannot endure in his age. Shall quips and sentences and   190
these paper bullets of the brain awe a man from the career of his
humour? No! The world must be peopled. When I said I would die
a bachelor, I did not think I should live till I were married. Here comes
Beatrice. By this day, she's a fair lady. I do spy some marks of love in her.

(*Enter* BEATRICE.)

BEATRICE: Against my will, I am sent to bid you come in to dinner.   195

BENEDICK: Fair Beatrice, I thank you for your pains.

BEATRICE: I took no more pains for those thanks than you take pains to thank
me. If it had been painful, I would not have come.

BENEDICK: You take pleasure then in the message?

BEATRICE: Yea, just so much as you may take upon a knife's point and   200
choke a daw withal. You have no stomach, signior. Fare you well.

(*Exit.*)

BENEDICK: Ha! "Against my will I am sent to bid you come in to dinner."
There's a double meaning in that. "I took no more pains for those
thanks than you took pains to thank me." That's as much as to say
"Any pains that I take for you is as easy as thanks." If I do not take   205
pity of her, I am a villain; if I do not love her, I am a Jew. I will go
get her picture.

(*Exit.*)

ACT III

Scene 1

SCENE: LEONATO's *garden.*

(Enter HERO, MARGARET, *and* URSULA.*)*

HERO: Good Margaret, run thee to the parlor.
    There shalt thou find my cousin Beatrice
    Proposing with the Prince and Claudio:
    Whisper her ear and tell her I and Ursula
    Walk in the orchard, and our whole discourse   5
    Is all of her. Say that thou overheardst us,
    And bid her steal into the pleached bower
    Where honeysuckles ripened by the sun
    Forbid the sun to enter, like favourites
    Made proud by princes, that advance their pride   10
    Against that power that bred it. There will she hide her
    To listen our purpose. This is thy office.
    Bear thee well in it, and leave us alone.

MARGARET: I'll make her come, I warrant you, presently.

(Exit.)

HERO: Now, Ursula, when Beatrice doth come,   15
    As we do trace this alley up and down,
    Our talk must only be of Benedick.
    When I do name him, let it be thy part
    To praise him more than ever man did merit.
    My talk to thee must be how Benedick   20
    Is sick in love with Beatrice. Of this matter
    Is little Cupid's crafty arrow made,
    That only wounds by hearsay. Now begin,
    For look where Beatrice like a lapwing runs
    Close by the ground, to hear our conference.   25

(Enter BEATRICE, *behind.)*

URSULA: The pleasant'st angling is to see the fish
    Cut with her golden oars the silver stream
    And greedily devour the treacherous bait.
    So angle we for Beatrice; who even now
    Is couched in the woodbine coverture.   30
    Fear you not my part of the dialogue.

HERO: Then go we near her, that her ear lose nothing
    Of the false sweet bait that we lay for it.—
    (Approaching the bower.) No, truly, Ursula, she is too disdainful.
    I know her spirits are as coy and wild   35

As haggerds of the rock.

URSULA: But are you sure
That Benedick loves Beatrice so entirely?

HERO: So says the Prince and my new-trothed lord.

URSULA: And did they bid you tell her of it, madam?

HERO: They did entreat me to acquaint her of it,   40
But I persuaded them, if they loved Benedick,
To wish him wrestle with affection
And never to let Beatrice know of it.

URSULA: Why did you so? Doth not the gentleman
Deserve as full as fortunate a bed   45
As ever Beatrice shall couch upon?

HERO: O god of love! I know he doth deserve
As much as may be yielded to a man,
But Nature never framed a woman's heart
Of prouder stuff than that of Beatrice.   50
Disdain and scorn ride sparkling in her eyes,
Misprising what they look on, and her wit
Values itself so highly that to her
All matter else seems weak. She cannot love,
Nor take no shape nor project of affection,   55
She is so self-endeared.

URSULA: Sure, I think so,
And therefore certainly it were not good
She knew his love, lest she make sport at it.

HERO: Why, you speak truth. I never yet saw man,   60
How wise, how noble, young, how rarely featured,
But she would spell him backward. If fair-faced,
She would swear the gentleman should be her sister;
If black, why, Nature, drawing of an antic,
Made a foul blot; if tall, a lance ill-headed;   65
If low, an agate very vilely cut;
If speaking, why, a vane blown with all winds;
If silent, why, a block moved with none.
So turns she every man the wrong side out,
And never gives to truth and virtue that   70
Which simpleness and merit purchaseth.

URSULA: Sure, sure, such carping is not commendable.

HERO: No, not to be so odd and from all fashions
As Beatrice is cannot be commendable.
But who dare tell her so? If I should speak,   75
She would mock me into air; O, she would laugh me

Out of myself, press me to death with wit.
Therefore let Benedick, like covered fire,
Consume away in sighs, waste inwardly.
It were a better death than die with mocks,   80
Which is as bad as die with tickling.
URSULA: Yet tell her of it. Hear what she will say.
HERO: No, rather I will go to Benedick
And counsel him to fight against his passion;
And truly I'll devise some honest slanders   85
To stain my cousin with. One doth not know
How much an ill word may empoison liking.
URSULA: O, do not do your cousin such a wrong!
She cannot be so much without true judgment,
Having so swift and excellent a wit   90
As she is prized to have, as to refuse
So rare a gentleman as Signior Benedick.
HERO: He is the only man of Italy,
Always excepted my dear Claudio.
URSULA: I pray you be not angry with me, madam,   95
Speaking my fancy: Signior Benedick,
For shape, for bearing, argument, and valour,
Goes foremost in report through Italy.
HERO: Indeed, he hath an excellent good name.
URSULA: His excellence did earn it ere he had it.   100
When are you married, madam?
HERO: Why, every day, tomorrow. Come, go in:
I'll show thee some attires and have thy counsel
Which is the best to furnish me tomorrow.
URSULA: She's limed, I warrant you. We have caught her, madam.   105
HERO: If it proves so, then loving goes by haps;
Some Cupid kills with arrows, some with traps.
(*Exeunt* HERO *and* URSULA.)
BEATRICE (*Coming forward.*):
What fire is in mine ears? Can this be true?
   Stand I condemned for pride and scorn so much?
Contempt, farewell, and maiden pride, adieu!   110
   No glory lives behind the back of such.
And, Benedick, love on; I will requite thee,
   Taming my wild heart to thy loving hand.
If thou dost love, my kindness shall incite thee
   To bind our loves up in a holy band.   115
For others say thou dost deserve, and I
Believe it better than reportingly.

(*Exit.*)

Scene 2

SCENE: *A room in* LEONATO's *house*

(*Enter* DON PEDRO, CLAUDIO, BENEDICK, *and* LEONATO.)

DON PEDRO: I do but stay till your marriage be consummate, and then go
I toward Aragon.

CLAUDIO: I'll bring you thither, my lord, if you'll vouchsafe me.

DON PEDRO: Nay, that would be as great a soil in the new gloss of your
marriage as to show a child his new coat and forbid him to wear it. I   5
will only be bold with Benedick for his company, for from the crown
of his head to the sole of his foot he is all mirth. He hath twice or
thrice cut Cupid's bowstring and the little hangman dare not shoot at
him. He hath a heart as sound as a bell, and his tongue is the clapper,
for what his heart thinks, his tongue speaks.   10

BENEDICK: Gallants, I am not as I have been.

LEONATO: So say I. Methinks you are sadder.

CLAUDIO: I hope he be in love.

DON PEDRO: Hang him, truant! There's no true drop of blood in him
to be truly touched with love. If he be sad, he wants money.   15

BENEDICK: I have the toothache.

DON PEDRO: Draw it.

BENEDICK: Hang it!

CLAUDIO: You must hang it first, and draw it afterwards.

DON PEDRO: What, sigh for the toothache?   20

LEONATO: Where is but a humor or a worm.

BENEDICK: Well, everyone can master a grief but he that has it.

CLAUDIO: Yet say I, he is in love.

DON PEDRO: There is no appearance of fancy in him, unless it be a fancy
that he hath to strange disguises, as to be a Dutchman today, a   25
Frenchman tomorrow, or in the shape of two countries at once, as a
German from the waist downward, all slops, and a Spaniard from
the hip upward, no doublet. Unless he have a fancy to this foolery,
as it appears he hath, he is no fool for fancy, as you would have
it appear he is.   30

CLAUDIO: If he be not in love with some woman, there is no believing old
signs. He brushes his hat o' mornings. What should that bode?

DON PEDRO: Hath any man seen him at the barber's?

CLAUDIO: No, but the barber's man hath been seen with him, and the old
ornament of his cheek hath already stuffed tennis balls.   35

LEONATO: Indeed, he looks younger than he did, by the loss of a beard.

DON PEDRO: Nay, a' rubs himself with civet. Can you smell him out by that?

CLAUDIO: That's as much as to say, the sweet youth's in love.

DON PEDRO: The greatest note of it is his melancholy.

CLAUDIO: And when was he wont to wash his face?

DON PEDRO: Yea, or to paint himself? For the which I hear what they say of him. 40

CLAUDIO: Nay, but his jesting spirit, which is now crept into a lute string and now governed by stops—

DON PEDRO: Indeed, that tells a heavy tale for him. Conclude, conclude he is in love. 45

CLAUDIO: Nay, but I know who loves him.

DON PEDRO: That would I know too. I warrant, one that knows him not.

CLAUDIO: Yes, and his ill conditions; and, in despite of all, dies for him.

DON PEDRO: She shall be buried with her face upwards.

BENEDICK: Yet is this no charm for the toothache.—Old signior, walk aside 50
with me. I have studied eight or nine wise words to speak to you,
which these hobby-horses must not hear.

(*Exeunt* BENEDICK *and* LEONATO.)

DON PEDRO: For my life, to break with him about Beatrice!

CLAUDIO: 'Tis even so. Hero and Margaret have by this played their parts
with Beatrice, and then the two bears will not bite one another when 55
they meet.

(*Enter* DON JOHN.)

DON JOHN: My lord and brother, God save you.

DON PEDRO: Good e'en, brother.

DON JOHN: If your leisure served, I would speak with you.

DON PEDRO: In private? 60

DON JOHN: If it please you. Yet Count Claudio may hear, for what I would
speak of concerns him.

DON PEDRO: What's the matter?

DON JOHN (*To* CLAUDIO.): Means your lordship to be married tomorrow?

DON PEDRO: You know he does. 65

DON JOHN: I know not that, when he knows what I know.

CLAUDIO: If there be any impediment, I pray you discover it.

DON JOHN: You may think I love you not. Let that appear hereafter, and
aim better at me by that I now will manifest. For my brother, I think
he holds you well, and in dearness of heart hath holp to effect your 70
ensuing marriage—surely suit ill spent and labour ill bestowed.

DON PEDRO: Why, what's the matter?

DON JOHN: I came hither to tell you; and, circumstances shortened, for she
has been too long a talking of, the lady is disloyal.

CLAUDIO: Who, Hero?   75

DON PEDRO: Even she: Leonato's Hero, your Hero, every man's Hero.

CLAUDIO: Disloyal?

DON JOHN: The word is too good to paint out her wickedness. I could
say she were worse. Think you of a worse title, and I will fit her to it.
Wonder not till further warrant. Go but with me tonight, you shall see   80
her chamber window entered, even the night before her wedding day.
If you love her then, tomorrow wed her. But it would better fit your
honor to change your mind.

CLAUDIO: May this be so?

DON PEDRO: I will not think it.   85

DON JOHN: If you dare not trust that you see, confess not that you know. If
you will follow me, I will show you enough, and when you have seen
more and heard more, proceed accordingly.

CLAUDIO: If I see any thing tonight why I should not marry her tomorrow
in the congregation, where I should wed, there will I shame her.   90

DON PEDRO: And as I wooed for thee to obtain her, I will join with thee to
disgrace her.

DON JOHN: I will disparage her no farther till you are my witnesses. Bear it
coldly but till midnight, and let the issue show itself.

DON PEDRO: O day untowardly turned!   95

CLAUDIO: O mischief strangely thwarting!

DON JOHN: O plague right well prevented! So will you say when you have
seen THE sequel.

(Exeunt.)

Scene 3

SCENE: A *street.*

(Enter DOGBERRY *and* VERGES *with the* WATCH.*)*

DOGBERRY: Are you good men and true?

VERGES: Yea, or else it were pity but they should suffer salvation, body and
soul.

DOGBERRY: Nay, that were a punishment too good for them if they should
have any allegiance in them, being chosen for the Prince's watch.   5

VERGES: Well, give them their charge, neighbor Dogberry.

DOGBERRY: First, who think you the most desartless man to be constable?

FIRST WATCHMAN: Hugh Otecake, sir, or George Seacole, for they can write
and read.

DOGBERRY: Come hither, neighbour Seacole. God hath blessed you with   10
a good name. To be a well-favoured man is the gift of fortune, but to
write and read comes by nature.

FIRST WATCHMAN: Both which, master constable—

DOGBERRY: You have. I knew it would be your answer. Well, for your
favor, sir, why, give God thanks, and make no boast of it, and for your   15
writing and reading, let that appear when there is no need of such
vanity. You are thought here to be the most senseless and fit man for
the constable of the watch; therefore bear you the lantern. This is
your charge: you shall comprehend all vagrom men; you are to bid any
man stand, in the Prince's name.   20

SECOND WATCHMAN: How if he will not stand?

DOGBERRY: Why, then, take no note of him, but let him go, and presently
call the rest of the watch together and thank God you are rid of a
knave.

VERGES: If he will not stand when he is bidden, he is none of the Prince's
subjects.   25

DOGBERRY: True, and they are to meddle with none but the Prince's subjects.—You shall also make no noise in the streets; for, for the watch to
babble and to talk is most tolerable and not to be endured.

WATCHMAN: We will rather sleep than talk. We know what belongs to a
watch.   30

DOGBERRY: Why, you speak like an ancient and most quiet watchman, for
I cannot see how sleeping should offend; only have a care that your
bills be not stolen. Well, you are to call at all the alehouses and bid
those that are drunk get them to bed.

WATCHMAN: How if they will not?   35

DOGBERRY: Why then, let them alone till they are sober. If they make you
not then the better answer, you may say they are not the men you took
them for.

WATCHMAN: Well, sir.

DOGBERRY: If you meet a thief, you may suspect him, by virtue of your   40
office, to be no true man, and, for such kind of men, the less you
meddle or make with them, why the more is for your honesty.

WATCHMAN: If we know him to be a thief, shall we not lay hands on him?

DOGBERRY: Truly, by your office, you may, but I think they that touch pitch
will be defiled: the most peaceable way for you, if you do take a thief, is   45
to let him show himself what he is and steal out of your company.

VERGES: You have been always called a merciful man, partner.

DOGBERRY: Truly, I would not hang a dog by my will, much more a man
who hath any honesty in him.

VERGES: If you hear a child cry in the night, you must call to the nurse and   50
bid her still it.

WATCHMAN: How if the nurse be asleep and will not hear us?

DOGBERRY: Why, then, depart in peace, and let the child wake her with crying, for the ewe that will not hear her lamb when it baas will never answer a calf when he bleats.   55

VERGES: 'Tis very true.

DOGBERRY: This is the end of the charge. You, constable, are to present the Prince's own person. If you meet the Prince in the night, you may stay him.

VERGES: Nay, by'r lady, that I think he cannot.

DOGBERRY: Five shillings to one on't, with any man that knows the stat- 60
utes, he may stay him—marry, not without the Prince be willing, for indeed the watch ought to offend no man, and it is an offence to stay a man against his will.

VERGES: By'r lady, I think it be so.

DOGBERRY: Ha, ah ha!—Well, masters, goodnight. An there be any matter 65
of weight chances, call up me. Keep your fellows' counsels and your own, and goodnight. Come, neighbor.

WATCHMAN: Well, masters, we hear our charge. Let us go sit here upon the church bench till two, and then all to bed.

DOGBERRY: One word more, honest neighbors. I pray you watch about 70
Signior Leonato's door, for the wedding being there tomorrow, there is a great coil tonight. Adieu, be vigitant, I beseech you.

(*Exeunt* DOGBERRY *and* VERGES.)

(*Enter* BORACHIO *and* CONRADE.)

BORACHIO: What, Conrade!

WATCHMAN (*Aside*.): Peace, stir not.

BORACHIO: Conrade, I say!   75

CONRADE: Here, man; I am at thy elbow.

BORACHIO: Mass, and my elbow itched, I thought there would a scab follow.

CONRADE: I will owe thee an answer for that. And now forward with thy tale.

BORACHIO: Stand thee close, then, under this pent-house, for it drizzles rain, and I will, like a true drunkard, utter all to thee.   80

WATCHMAN (*Aside*.): Some treason, masters. Yet stand close.

BORACHIO: Therefore know, I have earned of Don John a thousand ducats.

CONRADE: Is it possible that any villany should be so dear?

BORACHIO: Thou shouldst rather ask if it were possible any villany should be so rich. For when rich villains have need of poor ones, poor ones 85
may make what price they will.

CONRADE: I wonder at it.

BORACHIO: That shows thou art unconfirmed. Thou knowest that the fashion of a doublet, or a hat, or a cloak, is nothing to a man.

CONRADE: Yes, it is apparel.   90

BORACHIO: I mean the fashion.

CONRADE: Yes, the fashion is the fashion.

BORACHIO: Tush, I may as well say the fool's the fool. But seest thou not what a deformed thief this fashion is?

WATCHMAN *(Aside.)*:   I know that Deformed. He has been a vile thief this   95
seven year. He goes up and down like a gentleman. I remember his name.

BORACHIO: Didst thou not hear somebody?

CONRADE: No, 'twas the vane on the house.

BORACHIO: Seest thou not, I say, what a deformed thief this fashion is, how giddily he turns about all the hot bloods between fourteen and   100
five-and-thirty, sometimes fashioning them like Pharaoh's soldiers in the reechy painting, sometimes like god Bel's priests in the old church window, sometimes like the shaven Hercules in the smirched worm-eaten tapestry, where his codpiece seems as massy as his club?

CONRADE: All this I see, and I see that the fashion wears out more apparel   105
than the man. But art not thou thyself giddy with the fashion too, that thou hast shifted out of thy tale into telling me of the fashion?

BORACHIO: Not so, neither. But know that I have tonight wooed Margaret, the Lady Hero's gentlewoman, by the name of Hero. She leans me out at her mistress' chamber window, bids me a thousand times   110
good night. I tell this tale vilely. I should first tell thee how the Prince, Claudio and my master, planted and placed and possessed by my master Don John, saw afar off in the orchard this amiable encounter.

CONRADE: And thought they Margaret was Hero?

BORACHIO: Two of them did, the Prince and Claudio, but the devil my   115
master knew she was Margaret; and partly by his oaths, which first possessed them, partly by the dark night, which did deceive them, but chiefly by my villany, which did confirm any slander that Don John had made, away went Claudio enraged, swore he would meet her as he was appointed, next morning at the temple, and there, before the   120
whole congregation, shame her with what he saw o'er night and send her home again without a husband.

FIRST WATCHMAN: We charge you, in the Prince's name, stand!

SECOND WATCHMAN: Call up the right Master Constable. We have here recovered the most dangerous piece of lechery that ever was known in   125
the commonwealth.

FIRST WATCHMAN: And one Deformed is one of them. I know him; he wears a lock.

CONRADE: Masters, masters—

SECOND WATCHMAN: You'll be made bring Deformed forth, I warrant you.

CONRADE: Masters, never speak, we charge you let us obey you to go with us.   130

BORACHIO: We are like to prove a goodly commodity, being taken up of these men's bills.

CONRADE: A commodity in question, I warrant you.—Come, we'll obey you. (*Exeunt.*)

Scene 4

SCENE: HERO's *apartment*.

(*Enter* HERO, MARGARET, *and* URSULA.)

HERO: Good Ursula, wake my cousin Beatrice and desire her to rise.

URSULA: I will, lady.

HERO: And bid her come hither.

URSULA: Well.
(*Exit.*)

MARGARET: Troth, I think your other rabato were better.   5

HERO: No, pray thee, good Meg, I'll wear this.

MARGARET: By my troth, 's not so good, and I warrant your cousin will say so.

HERO: My cousin's a fool, and thou art another. I'll wear none but this.

MARGARET: I like the new tire within excellently, if the hair were a thought browner; and your gown's a most rare fashion, i' faith. I saw   10
the Duchess of Milan's gown that they praise so.

HERO: O, that exceeds, they say.

MARGARET: By my troth, 's but a night-gown in respect of yours—cloth o' gold, and cuts, and laced with silver, set with pearls, down sleeves, side sleeves, and skirts round underborne with a bluish tinsel. But for   15
a fine, quaint, graceful, and excellent fashion, yours is worth ten on 't.

HERO: God give me joy to wear it, for my heart is exceeding heavy.

MARGARET: 'Twill be heavier soon by the weight of a man.

HERO: Fie upon thee! Art not ashamed?

MARGARET: Of what, lady? Of speaking honorably? Is not marriage   20
honorable in a beggar? Is not your lord honorable without marriage? I think you would have me say "Saving your reverence, a husband." An bad thinking do not wrest true speaking, I'll offend nobody. Is there any harm in "the heavier for a husband"? None, I think, and it be the   25
right husband and the right wife. Otherwise 'tis light, and not heavy. Ask my Lady Beatrice else. Here she comes.

(*Enter* BEATRICE.)

HERO: Good morrow, coz.

BEATRICE: Good morrow, sweet Hero.

HERO: Why, how now? Do you speak in the sick tune?

BEATRICE: I am out of all other tune, methinks.   30

MARGARET: Clap's into "Light o' love." That goes without a burden. Do you sing it, and I'll dance it.

BEATRICE: Ye light o' love, with your heels! Then, if your husband have stables enough, you'll see he shall lack no barns.

MARGARET: O, illegitimate construction! I scorn that with my heels.   35

BEATRICE: 'Tis almost five o'clock, cousin. 'Tis time you were ready. By my troth, I am exceeding ill. Heigh-ho!

MARGARET: For a hawk, a horse, or a husband?

BEATRICE: For the letter that begins them all, H.

MARGARET: Well, and you be not turned Turk, there's no more sailing by   40
the star.

BEATRICE: What means the fool, trow?

MARGARET: Nothing, I; but God send every one their heart's desire.

HERO: These gloves the Count sent me, they are an excellent perfume.

BEATRICE: I am stuffed, cousin. I cannot smell.   45

MARGARET: A maid, and stuffed! There's goodly catching of cold.

BEATRICE: O, God help me, God help me! How long have you professed apprehension?

MARGARET: Even since you left it. Doth not my wit become me rarely?

BEATRICE: It is not seen enough; you should wear it in your cap. By my   50
troth, I am sick.

MARGARET: Get you some of this distilled *carduus benedictus*, and lay it to your heart. It is the only thing for a qualm.

HERO: There thou prick'st her with a thistle.

BEATRICE: *Benedictus!* why *benedictus?* You have some moral in this *benedictus.*   55

MARGARET: Moral? No, by my troth, I have no moral meaning; I meant plain holy thistle. You may think perchance that I think you are in love. Nay, by'r Lady, I am not such a fool to think what I list, nor I list not to think what I can, nor indeed I cannot think, if I would think my heart out of thinking, that you are in love or that you will be in   60 love or that you can be in love. Yet Benedick was such another, and now is he become a man. He swore he would never marry, and yet now, in despite of his heart, he eats his meat without grudging. And how you may be converted I know not, but methinks you look with your eyes as other women do.

BEATRICE: What pace is this that thy tongue keeps?   65

MARGARET: Not a false gallop.

(Re-enter URSULA.)

URSULA: Madam, withdraw: the Prince, the Count, Signior Benedick, Don John, and all the gallants of the town are come to fetch you to church.

HERO: Help to dress me, good coz, good Meg, good Ursula.

(*Exeunt.*)

Scene 5

SCENE: *Another room in* LEONATO's *house.*

(*Enter* LEONATO, *with* DOGBERRY *and* VERGES.)

LEONATO: What would you with me, honest neighbor?

DOGBERRY: Marry, sir, I would have some confidence with you that
      decerns you nearly.

LEONATO: Brief, I pray you, for you see it is a busy time with me.

DOGBERRY: Marry, this it is, sir.   5

VERGES: Yes, in truth it is, sir.

LEONATO: What is it, my good friends?

DOGBERRY: Goodman Verges, sir, speaks a little off the matter: an old
      man, sir, and his wits are not so blunt as, God help, I would desire
      they were, but, in faith, honest as the skin between his brows.   10

VERGES: Yes, I thank God I am as honest as any man living that is an old
      man and no honester than I.

DOGBERRY: Comparisons are odorous: *palabras*, neighbor Verges.

LEONATO: Neighbors, you are tedious.

DOGBERRY: It pleases your Worship to say so, but we are the poor duke's   15
      officers. But truly, for mine own part, if I were as tedious as a king, I
      could find it in my heart to bestow it all of your Worship.

LEONATO: All thy tediousness on me, ah?

DOGBERRY: Yea, an 'twere a thousand pound more than 'tis, for I hear
      as good exclamation on your Worship as of any man in the city, and   20
      though I be but a poor man, I am glad to hear it.

VERGES: And so am I.

LEONATO: I would fain know what you have to say.

VERGES: Marry, sir, our watch tonight, excepting your Worship's pres-
      ence, ha' ta'en a couple of as arrant knaves as any in Messina.   25

DOGBERRY: A good old man, sir. He will be talking. As they say, "When
      the age is in, the wit is out." God help us, it is a world to see!—Well
      said, i' faith, neighbor Verges.—Well, God's a good man. An two men
      ride of a horse, one must ride behind. An honest soul, i' faith, sir, by
      my troth he is, as ever broke bread, but God is to be worshipped, all   30
      men are not alike, alas, good neighbor!

LEONATO: Indeed, neighbor, he comes too short of you.

DOGBERRY: Gifts that God gives.

LEONATO: I must leave you.

DOGBERRY: One word, sir. Our watch, sir, have indeed comprehended   35
      two auspicious persons, and we would have them this morning exam-
      ined before your Worship.

LEONATO: Take their examination yourself and bring it me. I am now in
great haste, as it may appear unto you.

DOGBERRY: It shall be suffigance.   40

LEONATO: Drink some wine ere you go. Fare you well.

(*Enter a* MESSENGER.)

MESSENGER: My lord, they stay for you to give your daughter to her husband.

LEONATO: I'll wait upon them. I am ready.

(*Exeunt* LEONATO *and* MESSENGER.)

DOGBERRY: Go, good partner, go, get you to Francis Seacole. Bid him bring
his pen and inkhorn to the jail. We are now to examination these men.   45

VERGES: And we must do it wisely.

DOGBERRY: We will spare for no wit, I warrant you. Here's that shall drive
some of them to a noncome. Only get the learned writer to set down
our excommunication and meet me at the jail.   50

(*Exeunt.*)

ACT IV

Scene 1

SCENE: A *church.*

(*Enter* DON PEDRO, DON JOHN, LEONATO, FRIAR FRANCIS, CLAUDIO, BENEDICK,
HERO, BEATRICE, *and Attendants.*)

LEONATO: Come, Friar Francis, be brief, only to the plain form of marriage, and you shall recount their particular duties afterwards.

FRIAR FRANCIS: You come hither, my lord, to marry this lady?

CLAUDIO: No.

LEONATO: To be married to her.—Friar, you come to marry her.   5

FRIAR FRANCIS: Lady, you come hither to be married to this count?

HERO: I do.

FRIAR FRANCIS: If either of you know any inward impediment why you
should not be conjoined, charge you, on your souls, to utter it.

CLAUDIO: Know you any, Hero?   10

HERO: None, my lord.

FRIAR FRANCIS: Know you any, count?

LEONATO: I dare make his answer, none.

CLAUDIO: O, what men dare do! What men may do! What men daily do,
not knowing what they do!   15

BENEDICK: How now, interjections? Why, then, some be of laughing, as,
ah, ha, he!

CLAUDIO: Stand thee by, friar.—Father, by your leave,
Will you with free and unconstrained soul
Give me this maid, your daughter?

LEONATO: As freely, son, as God did give her me.   20
CLAUDIO: And what have I to give you back, whose worth
   May counterpoise this rich and precious gift?
DON PEDRO: Nothing, unless you render her again.
CLAUDIO: Sweet prince, you learn me noble thankfulness.—
   There, Leonato, take her back again.   25
   Give not this rotten orange to your friend.
   She's but the sign and semblance of her honor.
   Behold how like a maid she blushes here!
   O, what authority and show of truth
   Can cunning sin cover itself withal!   30
   Comes not that blood as modest evidence
   To witness simple virtue? Would you not swear,
   All you that see her, that she were a maid,
   By these exterior shows? But she is none.
   She knows the heat of a luxurious bed.   35
   Her blush is guiltiness, not modesty.
LEONATO: What do you mean, my lord?
CLAUDIO: Not to be married,
   Not to knit my soul to an approved wanton.
LEONATO: Dear my lord, if you, in your own proof   40
   Have vanquished the resistance of her youth,
   And made defeat of her virginity—
CLAUDIO: I know what you would say: if I have known her,
   You will say she did embrace me as a husband,
   And so extenuate the 'forehand sin.   45
   No, Leonato,
   I never tempted her with word too large,
   But, as a brother to his sister, showed
   Bashful sincerity and comely love.
HERO: And seemed I ever otherwise to you?   50
CLAUDIO: Out on thee, seeming! I will write against it.
   You seem to me as Dian in her orb,
   As chaste as is the bud ere it be blown.
   But you are more intemperate in your blood
   Than Venus, or those pampered animals   55
   That rage in savage sensuality.
HERO: Is my lord well that he doth speak so wide?
LEONATO: Sweet prince, why speak not you?
DON PEDRO: What should I speak?
   I stand dishonoured that have gone about   60
   To link my dear friend to a common stale.

LEONATO: Are these things spoken, or do I but dream?

DON JOHN: Sir, they are spoken, and these things are true.

BENEDICK: This looks not like a nuptial.

HERO: True! O God!   65

CLAUDIO: Leonato, stand I here?
Is this the Prince? Is this the Prince's brother?
Is this face Hero's? Are our eyes our own?

LEONATO: All this is so, but what of this, my lord?

CLAUDIO: Let me but move one question to your daughter;   70
And, by that fatherly and kindly power
That you have in her, bid her answer truly.

LEONATO: I charge thee do so, as thou art my child.

HERO: O, God defend me, how am I beset!—
What kind of catechising call you this?   75

CLAUDIO: To make you answer truly to your name.

HERO: Is it not Hero? Who can blot that name
With any just reproach?

CLAUDIO: Marry, that can Hero!
Hero itself can blot out Hero's virtue.   80
What man was he talked with you yesternight
Out at your window betwixt twelve and one?
Now, if you are a maid, answer to this.

HERO: I talked with no man at that hour, my lord.

DON PEDRO: Why, then are you no maiden.—Leonato,   85
I am sorry you must hear. Upon mine honor,
Myself, my brother, and this grieved count
Did see her, hear her, at that hour last night
Talk with a ruffian at her chamber window
Who hath indeed, most like a liberal villain,   90
Confessed the vile encounters they have had
A thousand times in secret.

DON JOHN: Fie, fie, they are not to be named, my lord,
Not to be spoke of!
There is not chastity enough in language,
Without offence, to utter them.—Thus, pretty lady,   95
I am sorry for thy much misgovernment.

CLAUDIO: O Hero, what a Hero hadst thou been
If half thy outward graces had been placed
About thy thoughts and counsels of thy heart!
But fare thee well, most foul, most fair. Farewell,   100
Thou pure impiety and impious purity.
For thee I'll lock up all the gates of love

And on my eyelids shall conjecture hang,
To turn all beauty into thoughts of harm,
And never shall it more be gracious.   105
LEONATO: Hath no man's dagger here a point for me?
(HERO *swoons.*)
BEATRICE: Why, how now, cousin, wherefore sink you down?
DON JOHN: Come, let us go. These things, come thus to light, Smother
  her spirits up.
(*Exeunt* DON PEDRO, DON JOHN, *and* CLAUDIO.)
BENEDICK: How doth the lady?
BEATRICE: Dead, I think.—Help, uncle!—   110
  Hero, why, Hero! Uncle! Signior Benedick! Friar!
LEONATO: O Fate, take not away thy heavy hand!
  Death is the fairest cover for her shame
  That may be wished for.
BEATRICE: How now, cousin Hero?   115
FRIAR FRANCIS: Have comfort, lady.
LEONATO: Dost thou look up?
FRIAR FRANCIS: Yea, wherefore should she not?
LEONATO: Wherefore! Why, doth not every earthly thing
  Cry shame upon her? Could she here deny   120
  The story that is printed in her blood?—
  Do not live, Hero; do not ope thine eyes,
  For, did I think thou wouldst not quickly die,
  Thought I thy spirits were stronger than thy shames,
  Myself would, on the rearward of reproaches,   125
  Strike at thy life. Grieved I I had but one?
  Chid I for that at frugal Nature's frame?
  O, one too much by thee! Why had I one?
  Why ever wast thou lovely in my eyes?
  Why had I not with charitable hand   130
  Took up a beggar's issue at my gates,
  Who smirched thus and mired with infamy,
  I might have said "No part of it is mine;
  This shame derives itself from unknown loins"?
  But mine, and mine I loved, and mine I praised,   135
  And mine that I was proud on, mine so much
  That I myself was to myself not mine,
  Valuing of her—why she, O, she is fall'n
  Into a pit of ink, that the wide sea
  Hath drops too few to wash her clean again,   140
  And salt too little which may season give
  To her foul tainted flesh!

BENEDICK: Sir, sir, be patient.
    For my part, I am so attired in wonder
    I know not what to say.   145
BEATRICE: O, on my soul, my cousin is belied!
BENEDICK: Lady, were you her bedfellow last night?
BEATRICE: No, truly not; although, until last night
    I have this twelvemonth been her bedfellow.
LEONATO: Confirmed, confirmed! O, that is stronger made   150
    Which was before barred up with ribs of iron!
    Would the two princes lie and Claudio lie,
    Who loved her so that, speaking of her foulness,
    Washed it with tears? Hence from her. Let her die!
FRIAR FRANCIS: Hear me a little,   155
    For I have only been silent so long,
    And given way unto this course of fortune,
    By noting of the lady. I have marked
    A thousand blushing apparitions
    To start into her face, a thousand innocent shames   160
    In angel whiteness beat away those blushes,
    And in her eye there hath appeared a fire
    To burn the errors that these princes hold
    Against her maiden truth. Call me a fool,
    Trust not my reading nor my observations,   165
    Which with experimental seal doth warrant
    The tenor of my book; trust not my age,
    My reverence, calling, nor divinity,
    If this sweet lady lie not guiltless here
    Under some biting error.   170
LEONATO: Friar, it cannot be.
    Thou seest that all the grace that she hath left
    Is that she will not add to her damnation
    A sin of perjury. She not denies it.
    Why seek'st thou then to cover with excuse   175
    That which appears in proper nakedness?
FRIAR FRANCIS: Lady, what man is he you are accused of?
HERO: They know that do accuse me. I know none:
    If I know more of any man alive
    Than that which maiden modesty doth warrant,   180
    Let all my sins lack mercy!—O my father,
    Prove you that any man with me conversed
    At hours unmeet, or that I yesternight
    Maintained the change of words with any creature,
    Refuse me, hate me, torture me to death!   185

FRIAR FRANCIS: There is some strange misprision in the princes.
BENEDICK: Two of them have the very bent of honour,
    And if their wisdoms be misled in this,
    The practice of it lives in John the Bastard,
    Whose spirits toil in frame of villainies.   190
LEONATO: I know not. If they speak but truth of her,
    These hands shall tear her. If they wrong her honor,
    The proudest of them shall well hear of it.
    Time hath not yet so dried this blood of mine,
    Nor age so eat up my invention,   195
    Nor fortune made such havoc of my means,
    Nor my bad life reft me so much of friends,
    But they shall find, awaked in such a kind,
    Both strength of limb and policy of mind,
    Ability in means and choice of friends,
    To quit me of them throughly.   200
FRIAR FRANCIS: Pause awhile,
    And let my counsel sway you in this case.
    Your daughter here the princes left for dead.
    Let her awhile be secretly kept in,
    And publish it that she is dead indeed.   205
    Maintain a mourning ostentation,
    And on your family's old monument
    Hang mournful epitaphs and do all rites
    That appertain unto a burial.
LEONATO: What shall become of this? What will this do?   210
FRIAR FRANCIS: Marry, this well carried shall on her behalf
    Change slander to remorse. That is some good.
    But not for that dream I on this strange course,
    But on this travail look for greater birth.
    She, dying, as it must so be maintained,   215
    Upon the instant that she was accused,
    Shall be lamented, pitied, and excused
    Of every hearer. For it so falls out
    That what we have we prize not to the worth   220
    Whiles we enjoy it, but being lacked and lost,
    Why, then we rack the value, then we find
    The virtue that possession would not show us
    Whiles it was ours. So will it fare with Claudio.
    When he shall hear she died upon his words,   225
    Th' idea of her life shall sweetly creep
    Into his study of imagination,

And every lovely organ of her life
Shall come appareled in more precious habit,
More moving, delicate, and full of life, 230
Into the eye and prospect of his soul,
Than when she lived indeed. Then shall he mourn,
If ever love had interest in his liver,
And wish he had not so accused her,
No, though he thought his accusation true. 235
Let this be so, and doubt not but success
Will fashion the event in better shape
Than I can lay it down in likelihood.
But if all aim but this be leveled false,
The supposition of the lady's death 240
Will quench the wonder of her infamy.
And if it sort not well, you may conceal her,
As best befits her wounded reputation,
In some reclusive and religious life,
Out of all eyes, tongues, minds, and injuries. 245

BENEDICK: Signior Leonato, let the Friar advise you.
And though you know my inwardness and love
Is very much unto the Prince and Claudio,
Yet, by mine honor, I will deal in this
As secretly and justly as your soul 250
Should with your body.

LEONATO: Being that I flow in grief,
The smallest twine may lead me.

FRIAR FRANCIS: 'Tis well consented. Presently away,
For to strange sores strangely they strain the cure.— 255
Come, lady, die to live: this wedding day
Perhaps is but prolonged. Have patience and endure

(*Exeunt all but* BENEDICK *and* BEATRICE.)

BENEDICK: Lady Beatrice, have you wept all this while?

BEATRICE: Yea, and I will weep a while longer.   260

BENEDICK: I will not desire that.

BEATRICE: You have no reason. I do it freely.

BENEDICK: Surely I do believe your fair cousin is wronged.

BEATRICE: Ah, how much might the man deserve of me that would right her!

BENEDICK: Is there any way to show such friendship?   265

BEATRICE: A very even way, but no such friend.

BENEDICK: May a man do it?

BEATRICE: It is a man's office, but not yours.

BENEDICK: I do love nothing in the world so well as you. Is not that strange?

BEATRICE: As strange as the thing I know not. It were as possible for me   270
to say I loved nothing so well as you, but believe me not, and yet I lie
not, I confess nothing, nor I deny nothing. I am sorry for my cousin.

BENEDICK: By my sword, Beatrice, thou lovest me!

BEATRICE: Do not swear and eat it.

BENEDICK: I will swear by it that you love me, and I will make him eat it   275
that says I love not you.

BEATRICE: Will you not eat your word?

BENEDICK: With no sauce that can be devised to it. I protest I love thee.

BEATRICE: Why, then, God forgive me!

BENEDICK: What offence, sweet Beatrice?   280

BEATRICE: You have stayed me in a happy hour: I was about to protest I
loved you.

BENEDICK: And do it with all thy heart.

BEATRICE: I love you with so much of my heart that none is left to protest.

BENEDICK: Come, bid me do any thing for thee.   285

BEATRICE: Kill Claudio.

BENEDICK: Ha! Not for the wide world.

BEATRICE: You kill me to deny it. Farewell.

BENEDICK: Tarry, sweet Beatrice.

BEATRICE: I am gone, though I am here. There is no love in you. Nay,   290
I pray you, let me go.

BENEDICK: Beatrice—

BEATRICE: In faith, I will go.

BENEDICK: We'll be friends first.

BEATRICE: You dare easier be friends with me than fight with mine enemy.   295

BENEDICK: Is Claudio thine enemy?

BEATRICE: Is he not approved in the height a villain, that hath slandered,
scorned, dishonored my kinswoman? O, that I were a man! What,
bear her in hand until they come to take hands, and then, with public
accusation, uncovered slander, unmitigated rancour—O God, that I   300
were a man! I would eat his heart in the marketplace.

BENEDICK: Hear me, Beatrice—

BEATRICE: Talk with a man out at a window! A proper saying.

BENEDICK: Nay, but Beatrice—

BEATRICE: Sweet Hero, she is wronged, she is slandered, she is undone.   305

BENEDICK: Beat—

BEATRICE: Princes and counties! Surely a princely testimony, a goodly
count, Count Comfect, a sweet gallant, surely! O, that I were a man
for his sake! Or that I had any friend would be a man for my sake!
But manhood is melted into courtesies, valor into compliment, and   310
men are only turned into tongue, and trim ones, too. He is now as

valiant as Hercules that only tells a lie and swears it. I cannot be a
man with wishing; therefore I will die a woman with grieving.

BENEDICK: Tarry, good Beatrice. By this hand, I love thee.

BEATRICE: Use it for my love some other way than swearing by it. 315

BENEDICK: Think you in your soul the Count Claudio hath wronged Hero?

BEATRICE: Yea, as sure as I have a thought or a soul.

BENEDICK: Enough, I am engaged. I will challenge him. I will kiss your
hand, and so I leave you. By this hand, Claudio shall render me a
dear account. As you hear of me, so think of me. Go, comfort your 320
cousin. I must say she is dead, and so farewell.

(*Exeunt.*)

Scene 2

SCENE: A *prison.*

(*Enter* DOGBERRY, VERGES, *and* SEXTON, *in gowns; and the* WATCH, *with* CONRADE
and BORACHIO.)

DOGBERRY: Is our whole dissembly appeared?

VERGES: O, a stool and a cushion for the Sexton.

SEXTON: Which be the malefactors?

DOGBERRY: Marry, that am I, and my partner.

VERGES: Nay, that's certain, we have the exhibition to examine. 5

SEXTON: But which are the offenders that are to be examined? Let them
come before Master Constable.

DOGBERRY: Yea, marry, let them come before me. What is your name,
friend?

BORACHIO: Borachio.

DOGBERRY: Pray, write down "Borachio."—Yours, sirrah? 10

CONRADE: I am a gentleman, sir, and my name is Conrade.

DOGBERRY: Write down, "Master Gentleman Conrade."— Masters, do
you serve God?

CONRADE & BORACHIO: Yea, sir, we hope.

DOGBERRY: Write down that they hope they serve God; and write God 15
first, for God defend but God should go before such villains!—Masters,
it is proved already that you are little better than false knaves, and it
will go near to be thought so shortly. How answer you for yourselves?

CONRADE: Marry, sir, we say we are none.

DOGBERRY: A marvellous witty fellow, I assure you, but I will go about 20
with him.—Come you hither, sirrah; a word in your ear. Sir, I say to
you, it is thought you are false knaves.

BORACHIO: Sir, I say to you we are none.

DOGBERRY: Well, stand aside.—'Fore God, they are both in a tale. Have
you writ down that they are none? 25

SEXTON: Master constable, you go not the way to examine. You must call
forth the watch that are their accusers.

DOGBERRY: Yea, marry, that's the eftest way.—Let the watch come forth.
Masters, I charge you, in the Prince's name, accuse these men.

FIRST WATCHMAN: This man said, sir, that Don John, the Prince's brother,   30
was a villain.

DOGBERRY: Write down Prince John a villain. Why, this is flat perjury, to
call a prince's brother villain!

BORACHIO: Master constable—

DOGBERRY: Pray thee, fellow, peace: I do not like thy look, I promise thee.   35

SEXTON: What heard you him say else?

SECOND WATCHMAN: Marry, that he had received a thousand ducats of Don
John for accusing the Lady Hero wrongfully.

DOGBERRY: Flat burglary as ever was committed.

VERGES: Yea, by Mass, that it is.   40

SEXTON: What else, fellow?

FIRST WATCHMAN: And that Count Claudio did mean, upon his words, to
disgrace Hero before the whole assembly, and not marry her.

DOGBERRY: O, villain! Thou wilt be condemned into everlasting redemption for this.   45

SEXTON: What else?

WATCHMAN: This is all.

SEXTON: And this is more, masters, than you can deny. Prince John is this
morning secretly stolen away. Hero was in this manner accused, in
this very manner refused, and upon the grief of this suddenly died.—   50
Master constable, let these men be bound and brought to Leonato's: I
will go before and show him their examination.

(*Exit.*)

DOGBERRY: Come, let them be opinioned.

VERGES: Let them be in the hands—

CONRADE: Off, coxcomb!   55

DOGBERRY: God's my life, where's the Sexton? Let him write down the
Prince's officer "coxcomb." Come, bind them.—Thou naughty varlet!

CONRADE: Away! You are an ass, you are an ass!

DOGBERRY: Dost thou not suspect my place? Dost thou not suspect my
years? O, that he were here to write me down an ass! But masters,   60
remember that I am an ass, though it be not written down, yet forget
not that I am an ass.—No, thou villain, thou art full of piety, as shall
be proved upon thee by good witness. I am a wise fellow and, which is
more, an officer, and, which is more, a householder and, which is
more, as pretty a piece of flesh as any is in Messina, and one that   65
knows the law, go to, and a rich fellow enough, go to, and a fellow

that hath had losses, and one that hath two gowns and every thing
handsome about him.—Bring him away.—O, that I had been writ
down an ass!

(*Exeunt.*)

ACT V

Scene 1

SCENE: *Before* LEONATO'*s house.*

(*Enter* LEONATO *and* ANTONIO.)

ANTONIO: If you go on thus, you will kill yourself,
    And 'tis not wisdom thus to second grief
    Against yourself.

LEONATO: I pray thee, cease thy counsel,
    Which falls into mine ears as profitless   5
    As water in a sieve. Give not me counsel,
    Not let no comforter delight mine ear
    But such a one whose wrongs do suit with mine.
    Bring me a father that so loved his child,
    Whose joy of her is overwhelmed like mine,   10
    And bid him speak of patience.
    Measure his woe the length and breadth of mine,
    And let it answer every strain for strain,
    As thus for thus, and such a grief for such,
    In every lineament, branch, shape, and form.   15
    If such a one will smile and stroke his beard,
    Bid sorrow wag, cry "hem" when he should groan,
    Patch grief with proverbs, make misfortune drunk
    With candle-wasters, bring him yet to me,
    And I of him will gather patience.   20
    But there is no such man. For, brother, men
    Can counsel and speak comfort to that grief
    Which they themselves not feel, but tasting it,
    Their counsel turns to passion, which before
    Would give preceptial med'cine to rage,   25
    Fetter strong madness in a silken thread,
    Charm ache with air and agony with words.
    No, no, 'tis all men's office to speak patience
    To those that wring under the load of sorrow,
    But no man's virtue nor sufficiency   30
    To be so moral when he shall endure

The like himself. Therefore give me no counsel.
My griefs cry louder than advertisement.

ANTONIO: Therein do men from children nothing differ.

LEONATO: I pray thee, peace. I will be flesh and blood,   35
For there was never yet philosopher
That could endure the toothache patiently,
However they have writ the style of gods
And made a push at chance and sufferance.

ANTONIO: Yet bend not all the harm upon yourself.   40
Make those that do offend you suffer too.

LEONATO: There thou speak'st reason. Nay, I will do so.
My soul doth tell me Hero is belied,
And that shall Claudio know; so shall the Prince
And all of them that thus dishonor her.   45

ANTONIO: Here comes the Prince and Claudio hastily.

(*Enter* DON PEDRO *and* CLAUDIO.)

DON PEDRO: Good e'en, good e'en.

CLAUDIO: Good day to both of you.

LEONATO: Hear you, my lords—

DON PEDRO: We have some haste, Leonato.   50

LEONATO: Some haste, my lord! Well, fare you well, my lord.
Are you so hasty now? Well, all is one.

DON PEDRO: Nay, do not quarrel with us, good old man.

ANTONIO: If he could right himself with quarreling,
Some of us would lie low.   55

CLAUDIO: Who wrongs him?

LEONATO: Marry, thou dost wrong me, thou dissembler, thou.
Nay, never lay thy hand upon thy sword.
I fear thee not.

CLAUDIO: Marry, beshrew my hand   60
If it should give your age such cause of fear.
In faith, my hand meant nothing to my sword.

LEONATO: Tush, tush, man, never fleer and jest at me.
I speak not like a dotard nor a fool,
As under privilege of age to brag   65
What I have done being young, or what would do
Were I not old. Know, Claudio, to thy head,
Thou hast so wronged mine innocent child and me
That I am forced to lay my reverence by,
And, with grey hairs and bruise of many days   70
Do challenge thee to trial of a man.
I say thou hast belied mine innocent child.

Thy slander hath gone through and through her heart,
And she lies buried with her ancestors,
O, in a tomb where never scandal slept, 75
Save this of hers, framed by thy villainy.

CLAUDIO: My villainy?

LEONATO: Thine, Claudio, thine, I say.

DON PEDRO: You say not right, old man.

LEONATO: My lord, my lord, 80
I'll prove it on his body if he dare,
Despite his nice fence and his active practice,
His May of youth and bloom of lustihood.

CLAUDIO: Away! I will not have to do with you.

LEONATO: Canst thou so daff me? Thou hast killed my child. 85
If thou kill'st me, boy, thou shalt kill a man.

ANTONIO: He shall kill two of us, and men indeed,
But that's no matter. Let him kill one first.
Win me and wear me! Let him answer me.—
Come, follow me, boy. Come, sir boy, come, follow me. 90
Sir boy, I'll whip you from your foining fence,
Nay, as I am a gentleman, I will.

LEONATO: Brother—

ANTONIO: Content yourself. God knows I loved my niece,
And she is dead, slandered to death by villains 95
That dare as well answer a man indeed
As I dare take a serpent by the tongue.—
Boys, apes, braggarts, jacks, milksops!

LEONATO: Brother Antony—

ANTONIO: Hold you content. What, man! I know them, yea, 100
And what they weigh, even to the utmost scruple—
Scrambling, outfacing, fashionmonging boys,
That lie and cog and flout, deprave and slander,
Go anticly show outward hideousness,
And speak off half a dozen dang'rous words 105
How they might hurt their enemies, if they durst,
And this is all.

LEONATO: But, brother Antony—

ANTONIO: Come, 'tis no matter.
Do not you meddle. Let me deal in this. 110

DON PEDRO: Gentlemen both, we will not wake your patience.
My heart is sorry for your daughter's death,
But, on my honor, she was charged with nothing
But what was true and very full of proof.

LEONATO: My lord, my lord—   115
DON PEDRO: I will not hear you.
LEONATO: No? Come, brother; away! I will be heard.
ANTONIO: And shall, or some of us will smart for it.
(*Exeunt* LEONATO *and* ANTONIO.)
DON PEDRO: See, see, here comes the man we went to seek.
(*Enter* BENEDICK.)
CLAUDIO: Now, signior, what news?   120
BENEDICK: Good day, my lord.
DON PEDRO: Welcome, signior. You are almost come to part almost a fray.
CLAUDIO: We had like to have had our two noses snapped off with two old
    men without teeth.
DON PEDRO: Leonato and his brother. What think'st thou? Had we   125
    fought, I doubt we should have been too young for them.
BENEDICK: In a false quarrel there is no true valor. I came to seek you both.
CLAUDIO: We have been up and down to seek thee, for we are high-proof
    melancholy and would fain have it beaten away. Wilt thou use thy wit?
BENEDICK: It is in my scabbard. Shall I draw it?   130
DON PEDRO: Dost thou wear thy wit by thy side?
CLAUDIO: Never any did so, though very many have been beside their wit.
    I will bid thee draw, as we do the minstrels: draw to pleasure us.
DON PEDRO: As I am an honest man, he looks pale.—Art thou sick, or
    angry?   135
CLAUDIO: What, courage, man! What though care killed a cat? Thou hast
    mettle enough in thee to kill care.
BENEDICK: Sir, I shall meet your wit in the career, and you charge it
    against me. I pray you choose another subject.
CLAUDIO: Nay, then, give him another staff. This last was broke 'cross.   140
DON PEDRO: By this light, he changes more and more. I think he be angry
    indeed
CLAUDIO: If he be, he knows how to turn his girdle.
BENEDICK: Shall I speak a word in your ear?
CLAUDIO: God bless me from a challenge!   145
BENEDICK (*Aside to* CLAUDIO.): You are villain. I jest not. I will make it good
    how you dare, with what you dare, and when you dare. Do me right,
    or I will protest your cowardice. You have killed a sweet lady, and her
    death shall fall heavy on you. Let me hear from you.
CLAUDIO: Well, I will meet you, so I may have good cheer.   150
DON PEDRO: What, a feast, a feast?
CLAUDIO: I' faith, I thank him. He hath bid me to a calf's head and a
    capon, the which if I do not carve most curiously, say my knife's
    naught. Shall I not find a woodcock too?

BENEDICK: Sir, your wit ambles well; it goes easily.   155

DON PEDRO: I'll tell thee how Beatrice praised thy wit the other day. I said,
thou hadst a fine wit: "True," said she, "a fine little one." "No,"
said I, "a great wit:" "Right," says she, "a great gross one." "Nay,"
said I, "a good wit:" "Just," said she, "it hurts nobody." "Nay," said I,
"the gentleman is wise:" "Certain," said she, "a wise gentleman."   160
"Nay," said I, "he hath the tongues:" "That I believe," said she, "for he
swore a thing to me on Monday night, which he forswore on Tuesday
morning; there's a double tongue; there's two tongues." Thus did she
an hour together transshape thy particular virtues. Yet at last she con
cluded with a sigh, thou wast the properest man in Italy.   165

CLAUDIO: For the which she wept heartily and said she cared not.

DON PEDRO: Yea, that she did. But yet for all that, an if she did not hate
him deadly, she would love him dearly. The old man's daughter told
us all.

CLAUDIO: All, all. And, moreover, God saw him when he was hid in the   170
garden.

DON PEDRO: But when shall we set the savage bull's horns on the sensible
Benedick's head?

CLAUDIO: Yea, and text underneath: "Here dwells Benedick the married man"?

BENEDICK: Fare you well, boy. You know my mind. I will leave you now to   175
your gossip-like humor. You break jests as braggarts do their blades,
which God be thanked, hurt not.—My lord, for your many courtesies
I thank you. I must discontinue your company. Your brother the
Bastard is fled from Messina: you have among you killed a sweet and
innocent lady. For my Lord Lackbeard there, he and I shall meet, and   180
till then peace be with him.

(*Exit.*)

DON PEDRO: He is in earnest.

CLAUDIO: In most profound earnest; and, I'll warrant you, for the love of
Beatrice

DON PEDRO: And hath challenged thee?   185

CLAUDIO: Most sincerely.

DON PEDRO: What a pretty thing man is when he goes in his doublet and
hose and leaves off his wit!

CLAUDIO: He is then a giant to an ape; but then is an ape a doctor to such
a man.   190

DON PEDRO: But, soft you, let me be. Pluck up, my heart, and be sad. Did
he not say my brother was fled?

(*Enter* DOGBERRY, VERGES, *and the* WATCH, *with* CONRADE *and* BORACHIO.)

DOGBERRY: Come you, sir. If justice cannot tame you, she shall ne'er
weigh more reasons in her balance. Nay, an you be a cursing hypocrite
once, you must be looked to.   195

DON PEDRO: How now, two of my brother's men bound! Borachio one!

CLAUDIO: Hearken after their offence, my lord.

DON PEDRO: Officers, what offence have these men done?

DOGBERRY: Marry, sir, they have committed false report; moreover, they
have spoken untruths; secondarily, they are slanders; sixth and lastly,   200
they have belied a lady; thirdly, they have verified unjust things; and,
to conclude, they are lying knaves.

DON PEDRO: First, I ask thee what they have done; thirdly, I ask thee
what's their offence; sixth and lastly, why they are committed; and, to
conclude, what you lay to their charge.   205

CLAUDIO: Rightly reasoned, and in his own division; and, by my troth,
there's one meaning well suited.

DON PEDRO: Who have you offended, masters, that you are thus bound to
your answer? This learned constable is too cunning to be understood.
What's your offense?   210

BORACHIO: Sweet prince, let me go no farther to mine answer. Do you
hear me, and let this count kill me. I have deceived even your very
eyes. What your wisdoms could not discover, these shallow fools have
brought to light, who in the night overheard me confessing to this
man how Don John your brother incensed me to slander the Lady   215
Hero, how you were brought into the orchard and saw me court
Margaret in Hero's garments, how you disgraced her when you should
marry her. My villainy they have upon record, which I had rather seal
with my death than repeat over to my shame. The lady is dead upon
mine and my master's false accusation. And, briefly, I desire nothing   220
but the reward of a villain.

DON PEDRO: Runs not this speech like iron through your blood?

CLAUDIO: I have drunk poison whiles he uttered it.

DON PEDRO: But did my brother set thee on to this?

BORACHIO: Yea, and paid me richly for the practice of it.   225

DON PEDRO: He is composed and framed of treachery,
And fled he is upon this villainy.

CLAUDIO: Sweet Hero, now thy image doth appear
In the rare semblance that I loved it first.

DOGBERRY: Come, bring away the plaintiffs. By this time our sexton hath   230
reformed Signior Leonato of the matter. And, masters, do not forget
to specify, when time and place shall serve, that I am an ass.

VERGES: Here, here comes master Signior Leonato, and the Sexton too.

(*Reenter* LEONATO *and* ANTONIO, *with the* SEXTON.)

LEONATO: Which is the villain? Let me see his eyes,
That, when I note another man like him,   235
I may avoid him. Which of these is he?

BORACHIO: If you would know your wronger, look on me.

LEONATO: Art thou the slave that with thy breath hast killed
 Mine innocent child?

BORACHIO: Yea, even I alone.   240

LEONATO: No, not so, villain; thou beliest thyself:
 Here stand a pair of honourable men—
 A third is fled—that had a hand in it.—
 I thank you, princes, for my daughter's death.
 Record it with your high and worthy deeds.   245
 'Twas bravely done, if you bethink you of it.

CLAUDIO: I know not how to pray your patience,
 Yet I must speak. Choose your revenge yourself.
 Impose me to what penance your invention
 Can lay upon my sin. Yet sinned I not   250
 But in mistaking.

DON PEDRO: By my soul, nor I,
 And yet, to satisfy this good old man
 I would bend under any heavy weight
 That he'll enjoin me to.   255

LEONATO: I cannot bid you bid my daughter live—
 That were impossible—but, I pray you both,
 Possess the people in Messina here
 How innocent she died. And if your love
 Can labor ought in sad invention,   260
 Hang her an epitaph upon her tomb
 And sing it to her bones. Sing it tonight.
 Tomorrow morning come you to my house,
 And since you could not be my son-in-law,
 Be yet my nephew. My brother hath a daughter,   265
 Almost the copy of my child that's dead,
 And she alone is heir to both of us.
 Give her the right you should have giv'n her cousin,
 And so dies my revenge.

CLAUDIO: O, noble sir!   270
 Your over-kindness doth wring tears from me.
 I do embrace your offer and dispose
 For henceforth of poor Claudio.

LEONATO: Tomorrow then I will expect your coming.
 Tonight I take my leave. This naughty man   275
 Shall face to face be brought to Margaret,
 Who I believe was packed in all this wrong,
 Hired to it by your brother.

BORACHIO: No, by my soul, she was not,
   Nor knew not what she did when she spoke to me,   280
   But always hath been just and virtuous
   In anything that I do know by her.

DOGBERRY: Moreover, sir, which indeed is not under white and black,
   this plaintiff here, the offender, did call me ass. I beseech you, let it be
   remembered in his punishment. And also the watch heard them talk   285
   of one Deformed. They say he wears a key in his ear and a lock hanging by it and borrows money in God's name, the which he hath used
   so long and never paid that now men grow hardhearted and will lend
   nothing for God's sake. Pray you, examine him upon that point.

LEONATO: I thank thee for thy care and honest pains.

DOGBERRY: Your Worship speaks like a most thankful and reverend
   youth, and I praise God for you.   280

LEONATO: There's for thy pains.

DOGBERRY: God save the foundation.

LEONATO: Go, I discharge thee of thy prisoner, and I thank thee.

DOGBERRY: I leave an arrant knave with your Worship; which I beseech
   your Worship to correct yourself, for the example of others. God keep   285
   your Worship! I wish your Worship well. God restore you to health.
   I humbly give you leave to depart, and if a merry meeting may be
   wished, God prohibit it!—Come, neighbor.

(*Exeunt* DOGBERRY *and* VERGES.)

LEONATO: Until tomorrow morning, lords, farewell.

ANTONIO: Farewell, my lords. We look for you tomorrow.   290

DON PEDRO: We will not fail.

CLAUDIO: Tonight I'll mourn with Hero.

LEONATO (*To the Watch.*):
   Bring you these fellows on.—We'll talk with Margaret, How her acquaintance grew with this lewd fellow.   295

(*Exeunt, severally.*)

Scene 2

SCENE: LEONATO's *garden.*

(*Enter* BENEDICK *and* MARGARET, *meeting.*)

BENEDICK: Pray thee, sweet Mistress Margaret, deserve well at my hands
   by helping me to the speech of Beatrice.

MARGARET: Will you then write me a sonnet in praise of my beauty?

BENEDICK: In so high a style, Margaret, that no man living shall come
   over it, for in most comely truth, thou deservest it.   5

MARGARET: To have no man come over me? Why, shall I always keep below stairs?

BENEDICK: Thy wit is as quick as the greyhound's mouth; it catches.

MARGARET: And yours as blunt as the fencer's foils, which hit, but hurt
not.

BENEDICK: A most manly wit, Margaret; it will not hurt a woman. And so,   10
I pray thee, call Beatrice: I give thee the bucklers.

MARGARET: Give us the swords; we have bucklers of our own.

BENEDICK: If you use them, Margaret, you must put in the pikes with a vice,
and they are dangerous weapons for maids.

MARGARET: Well, I will call Beatrice to you, who I think hath legs.   15

BENEDICK: And therefore will come.

(*Exit* MARGARET.)

(*Sings.*)

> The god of love
> That sits above,
> And knows me, and knows me,
> How pitiful I deserve—   20

I mean in singing. But in loving, Leander the good swimmer, Troilus
the first employer of panders, and a whole bookful of these quondam
carpetmongers, whose names yet run smoothly in the even road of
a blank verse, why, they were never so truly turnedover and over as
my poor self in love. Marry, I cannot show it in rhyme; I have tried: 25
I can find out no rhyme to "lady" but "baby,"—an innocent rhyme;
for "scorn," "horn,"—a hard rhyme; for "school," "fool,"—a babbling
rhyme; very ominous endings. No, I was not born under a rhyming
planet, nor I cannot woo in festival terms. (*Enter* BEATRICE.)
Sweet Beatrice, wouldst thou come when I called thee?   30

BEATRICE: Yea, signior, and depart when you bid me.

BENEDICK: O, stay but till then!

BEATRICE: "Then" is spoken; fare you well now. And yet, ere I go, let
me go with that I came, which is, with knowing what hath passed
between you and Claudio.   35

BENEDICK: Only foul words; and thereupon I will kiss thee.

BEATRICE: Foul words is but foul wind, and foul wind is but foul breath,
and foul breath is noisome. Therefore I will depart unkissed.

BENEDICK: Thou hast frighted the word out of his right sense, so forcible
is thy wit. But I must tell thee plainly, Claudio undergoes my chal-   40
lenge, and either I must shortly hear from him, or I will subscribe
him a coward. And I pray thee now, tell me for which of my bad parts
didst thou first fall in love with me?

BEATRICE: For them all together, which maintained so politic a state of
evil that they will not admit any good part to intermingle with them.   45
But for which of my good parts did you first suffer love for me?

BENEDICK: Suffer love! A good epithet! I do suffer love indeed, for I love
thee against my will.

BEATRICE: In spite of your heart, I think. Alas, poor heart, if you spite it
for my sake, I will spite it for yours, for I will never love that which my   50
friend hates.

BENEDICK: Thou and I are too wise to woo peaceably.

BEATRICE: It appears not in this confession. There's not one wise man
among twenty that will praise himself.

BENEDICK: An old, an old instance, Beatrice, that lived in the lime of   55
good neighbours. If a man do not erect in this age his own tomb ere
he dies, he shall live no longer in monument than the bell rings and
the widow weeps.

BEATRICE: And how long is that, think you?

BENEDICK: Question: why, an hour in clamour and a quarter in rheum.   60
Therefore is it most expedient for the wise, if Don Worm, his conscience, find no impediment to the contrary, to be the trumpet of his
own virtues, as I am to myself. So much for praising myself, who, I
myself will bear witness, is praiseworthy. And now tell me, how doth
your cousin?   65

BEATRICE: Very ill.

BENEDICK: And how do you?

BEATRICE: Very ill, too.

BENEDICK: Serve God, love me, and mend. There will I leave you too, for
here comes one in haste.   70

(*Enter* URSULA.)

URSULA: Madam, you must come to your uncle. Yonder's old coil at
home. It is proved my Lady Hero hath been falsely accused, the Prince
and Claudio mightily abused, and Don John is the author of all, who
is fed and gone. Will you come presently?

BEATRICE: Will you go hear this news, signior?   75

BENEDICK: I will live in thy heart, die in thy lap, and be buried in thy
eyes—and, moreover, I will go with thee to thy uncle's.

(*Exeunt.*)

Scene 3

SCENE: *A church.*

(*Enter* DON PEDRO, CLAUDIO, *and three or four with tapers.*)

CLAUDIO: Is this the monument of Leonato?

LORD: It is, my lord.

CLAUDIO (*Reading out of a scroll.*):

    Done to death by slanderous tongues
    Was the Hero that here lies.
    Death, in guerdon of her wrongs,   5

      Gives her fame which never dies.
      So the life that died with shame
      Lives in death with glorious fame.
   Hang thou there upon the tomb
   Praising her when I am dumb.   10
   Now, music, sound, and sing your solemn hymn.
(*Song.*)
      Pardon, goddess of the night,
      Those that slew thy virgin knight,
      For the which, with songs of woe,
      Round about her tomb they go,   15
      Midnight, assist our moan.
      Help us to sigh and groan,
      Heavily, heavily.
      Graves, yawn and yield your dead,
      Till death be uttered,   20
      Heavily, heavily.
CLAUDIO: Now, unto thy bones, goodnight.
   Yearly will I do this rite.
DON PEDRO: Good morrow, masters. Put your torches out.
   The wolves have preyed; and look, the gentle day   25
   Before the wheels of Phoebus, round about
   Dapples the drowsy east with spots of gray.
   Thanks to you all, and leave us. Fare you well.
CLAUDIO: Good morrow, masters. Each his several way.
DON PEDRO: Come, let us hence, and put on other weeds,   30
   And then to Leonato's we will go.
CLAUDIO: And Hymen now with luckier issue speed's
   Than this for whom we rendered up this woe.
(*Exeunt.*)

Scene 4
SCENE: *A room in* LEONATO's *house.*

(*Enter* LEONATO, ANTONIO, BENEDICK, BEATRICE, MARGARET, URSULA, FRIAR FRANCIS,
    and HERO.)
FRIAR FRANCIS: Did I not tell you she was innocent?
LEONATO: So are the Prince and Claudio, who accused her
   Upon the error that you heard debated.
   But Margaret was in some fault for this,
   Although against her will, as it appears   5
   In the true course of all the question.
ANTONIO: Well, I am glad that all things sort so well.

BENEDICK: And so am I, being else by faith enforced
     To call young Claudio to a reckoning for it.
LEONATO: Well, daughter, and you gentlewomen all,   10
     withdraw into a chamber by yourselves,
     And when I send for you, come hither masked.
(Exeunt Ladies.)
     The Prince and Claudio promised by this hour
     To visit me.—You know your office, brother.
     You must be father to your brother's daughter,   15
     And give her to young Claudio.
ANTONIO: Which I will do with confirmed countenance.
BENEDICK: Friar, I must entreat your pains, I think.
FRIAR FRANCIS: To do what, signior?
BENEDICK: To bind me, or undo me, one of them.—   20
     Signior Leonato, truth it is, good signior,
     Your niece regards me with an eye of favor.
LEONATO: That eye my daughter lent her: 'tis most true.
BENEDICK: And I do with an eye of love requite her.
LEONATO: The sight whereof I think you had from me,   25
     From Claudio and the Prince. But what's your will?
BENEDICK: Your answer, sir, is enigmatical.
     But, for my will, my will is your goodwill
     May stand with ours, this day to be conjoined
     In the state of honorable marriage—   30
     In which, good friar, I shall desire your help.
LEONATO: My heart is with your liking.
FRIAR FRANCIS: And my help.
     Here comes the Prince and Claudio.
(Enter DON PEDRO *and* CLAUDIO, *and two or three others.)*
DON PEDRO: Good morrow to this fair assembly.
LEONATO: Good morrow, prince; good morrow, Claudio.   35
     We here attend you. Are you yet determined
     Today to marry with my brother's daughter?
CLAUDIO: I'll hold my mind were she an Ethiope.
LEONATO: Call her forth, brother. Here's the Friar ready.
(Exit ANTONIO.)
DON PEDRO: Good morrow, Benedick. Why, what's the matter   40
     That you have such a February face,
     So full of frost, of storm and cloudiness?
CLAUDIO: I think he thinks upon the savage bull.
     Tush, fear not, man. We'll tip thy horns with gold,
     And all Europa shall rejoice at thee,   45

As once Europa did at lusty Jove
When he would play the noble beast in love.
BENEDICK: Bull Jove, sir, had an amiable low,
And some such strange bull leapt your father's cow
And got a calf in that same noble feat   50
Much like to you, for you have just his bleat.
CLAUDIO: For this I owe you. Here comes other reck'nings.
(Re-enter ANTONIO, *with the Ladies masked.)*
Which is the lady I must seize upon?
ANTONIO: This same is she, and I do give you her.
CLAUDIO: Why, then, she's mine.—Sweet, let me see your face.   55
LEONATO: No, that you shall not, till you take her hand
Before this friar and swear to marry her.
CLAUDIO: Give me your hand before this holy friar.
I am your husband, if you like of me.
HERO: And when I lived, I was your other wife,   60
(Unmasking.)
And when you loved, you were my other husband.
CLAUDIO: Another Hero!
HERO: Nothing certainer.
One Hero died defiled, but I do live,
And surely as I live, I am a maid.
DON PEDRO: The former Hero! Hero that is dead!   65
LEONATO: She died, my lord, but whiles her slander lived.
FRIAR FRANCIS: All this amazement can I qualify,
When after that the holy rites are ended,
I'll tell you largely of fair Hero's death.
Meantime let wonder seem familiar,   70
And to the chapel let us presently.
BENEDICK: Soft and fair, friar.—Which is Beatrice?
BEATRICE *(Unmasking.):*   I answer to that name. What is your will?
BENEDICK: Do not you love me?
BEATRICE: Why no, no more than reason.
BENEDICK: Why then, your uncle and the Prince and Claudio   75
Have been deceived. They swore you did.
BEATRICE: Do not you love me?
BENEDICK: Troth, no no more than reason.
BEATRICE: Why, then my cousin Margaret and Ursula
Are much deceived, for they did swear you did.
BENEDICK: They swore that you were almost sick for me.   80
BEATRICE: They swore that you were well-nigh dead for me.
BENEDICK: 'Tis no such matter. Then you do not love me?
BEATRICE: No, truly, but in friendly recompense.

LEONATO: Come, cousin, I am sure you love the gentleman.

CLAUDIO: And I'll be sworn upon't that he loves her,   85
For here's a paper written in his hand,
A halting sonnet of his own pure brain,
Fashion'd to Beatrice.

HERO: And here's another,
Writ in my cousin's hand, stol'n from her pocket,
Containing her affection unto Benedick.   90

BENEDICK: A miracle! Here's our own hands against our hearts. Come, I
will have thee, but by this light, I take thee for pity.

BEATRICE: I would not deny you, but, by this good day, I yield upon great
persuasion, and partly to save your life, for I was told you were in a
consumption.   95

BENEDICK: Peace! I will stop your mouth.
(Kissing her.)

DON PEDRO: How dost thou, Benedick, the married man?

BENEDICK: I'll tell thee what, prince: a college of wit-crackers cannot
flout me out of my humor. Dost thou think I care for a satire or an
epigram? No. If a man will be beaten with brains, he shall wear noth-   100
ing handsome about him. In brief, since I do purpose to marry, I will
think nothing to any purpose that the world can say against it, and
therefore never flout at me for what I have said against it. For man is
a giddy thing, and this is my conclusion.—For thy part, Claudio, I did
think to have beaten thee, but in that thou art like to be my kinsman,   105
live unbruised, and love my cousin.

CLAUDIO: I had well hoped thou wouldst have denied Beatrice, that
I might have cudgelled thee out of thy single life, to make thee a
double-dealer, which out of question thou wilt be, if my cousin do not
look exceedingly narrowly to thee.   110

BENEDICK: Come, come, we are friends: let's have a dance ere we are
married, that we may lighten our own hearts and our wives' heels.

LEONATO: We'll have dancing afterward.

BENEDICK: First, of my word! Therefore play, music.—Prince, thou art sad.
Get thee a wife, get thee a wife. There is no staff more reverend than   115
one tipped with horn.
(Enter a MESSENGER.*)*

MESSENGER: My lord, your brother John is ta'en in flight,
And brought with armed men back to Messina.

BENEDICK: Think not on him till tomorrow: I'll devise thee brave punish-
ments for him.—Strike up, pipers!   120
(Dance.)
(Exeunt.)

■ Find the scenes in this play where point of view has an impact on the plot. Look at instances where characters misunderstand what they see or hear or where they misreport what they have witnessed. In each instance, establish whose point of view moves the plot forward (for instance, Dogberry reports X; therefore, Don Pedro does Y), and explain why that particular point of view proves problematic.

■ If not for a few "chance" turns of events, this play could easily have been a tragedy. The misunderstandings here are, by themselves, no more comic than the misunderstandings that result in Romeo's and Juliet's suicides in another play by the same author. Where, if ever, does this play shift from this tragic potential to comedy? What issues are not resolved by the end of the play?

■ Look at the central couples in this play: Beatrice and Benedick, Hero and Claudio. In what ways is one couple more complex than the other? To what extent is one couple more important to the action of the play than the other?

Experiencing Literature through Writing

1. Locate a specific interruption within the text. Give details to indicate how it is apparent that this is an interruption.
   a. What is it that has been interrupted? Is it the structure of the text? Is it some event within the text? Is it some idea within the text?
   b. What is the nature of the interruption? Is there any other similar moment within the text? How is this moment different from others within the text?
   c. What is the impact of the interruption? How does the text change after the interruption? How much of this change is obvious to characters within the text? How much is an impact upon those who are reading the text?
   d. Why is the interruption significant? How does attention to this interruption offer either some avenue to interpret the text or insight into the ways in which this text functions?
2. This collection of works shares a common concern with the idea of "framing, mapping, and exploration." As you think about the works in the collection, discuss the sorts of exploration that the text presents. What tools do the texts offer for their explorations? How does the idea of creating a map of some exterior space allow introspection?
3. Filmic juxtaposition sets images (and scenes) next to one another to create a powerful emotional impact. Find a specific instance in one work where the author creates a set of juxtaposed images to create such an impact. Explain how the author sets up this impact and constructs the text to control our reaction in some specific way.

10 Tone

Did I Hear That Right?

A tone is simply a sound—a sound that by duration, pitch, or volume achieves a certain quality. The tones we notice most contrast sharply with what we usually hear: "When my mother uses that tone, all trouble stops" or "Don't use that tone with me young man." When we talk about tone, we talk about the way that a person delivers a message rather than just the message itself. This delivery includes the quality of voice as well as the choice of words; it tells us about the deliverer's attitude toward the message, and it has an impact upon how we hear the message.

The visual arts also use the quality of tone to describe the impact that an artist creates. The blinking light on the photocopy machine tells us that the machine is low on toner, the pigment used to create the range of black and gray that makes up the images on our page. In black-and-white photography, the photographer might replace the black with the rich brown of sepia to give the print an older appearance. Attention to such toning elements does not change the document that we are photocopying or the scene in the photograph, but it has a marked impact upon the printed images that we see. The photocopy may look quite light whereas the original photograph looks like it came from another time. The tone determines how we receive these visual images just as a tone of voice influences our understanding of the words that we hear.

HEARING RIGHT

Hearing right can make all the difference. The same words delivered with a different tone of voice can have very different meanings. Consider the following poem:

Margaret Atwood (1939–)

You Fit Into Me (1971)

You fit into me
like a hook into an eye
A fish hook
An open eye

The first words make the poem seem like a love poem. Working through the simile, we imagine the hook and eye that are used as clothing fasteners, but the last two lines shock us out of this reading with the violent image of a fish hook piercing an eyeball. That change in the final lines suggests a severe bitterness about the relation between the narrator and the "you" in the poem. It is no mistake that we read the first lines as almost loving, yet we must abruptly rethink that immediate response. We realize in the final lines that what we read as a shift in tone is really a shift in our understanding of that tone. The narrator has been bitter throughout the poem; we simply do not realize it until we get to the third line.

We usually pick up on conversational signals instantly, but when words are written down it is sometimes difficult to "hear" clearly. How can you tell that someone is being reverent rather than ironic? One clue is our knowledge of that person. The same sort of knowledge is useful when we read though it can be more challenging to come by. We learn about certain authors, so we know what to expect from them. This knowledge often makes us better readers. As you get to know authors, your ability to hear their tone improves. But in the previous poem, Atwood might be taking advantage of what a reader doesn't know about her attitudes toward the difficult complexity of relationships. **Irony** requires us to hold up two possible meanings simultaneously—the narrator could be expressing a great love or could be expressing great revulsion—and to pick one of those readings. Setting up the first interpretation by playing to our investment in the idea of romantic love makes the second (real) interpretation so much more stinging and darkly humorous. Atwood presses toward **sarcasm**—an extreme and aggressive form of **verbal irony** in which the thing *said* and the thing *meant* stand in stark opposition. When we discuss tone in a text, we generally refer to complex forms of expression that do not announce their attentions clearly. A **sincere** tone, for instance, may accurately describe a particular work, but would rarely generate much discussion. Sincerity may be taken as the other extreme of sarcasm, for a sincere expression matches word and meaning. When we talk about tone, we usually refer to the distortions that influence how we hear words and how we learn to interpret those words.

What if you haven't ever read an author before? How can you hear the tone of someone whose work is new to you? Remember that, even in conversation, you are aware of the context in which something has been said. A commonplace saying like "have a nice day" could be either sarcastic or sincere, but it is unlikely we would have trouble in most cases hearing the difference. When someone says that this is the best time they have ever had, you have clues surrounding you about whether or not that person seems to be having a good time. Is the person enthusiastic? Do things really appear to be going well? Those clues help you figure out what meaning to take from the words.

Experiencing Literature through Tone

Dorothy Parker, whom you should never trust to deliver a toneless poem, uses the conventions of love poetry to talk about the "perfect rose" that she has received.

Dorothy Parker (1893–1967)

One Perfect Rose (1926)

A single flower he sent me, since we met.
   All tenderly his messenger he chose;
Deep-hearted, pure, with scented dew still wet—
   One perfect rose.

I knew the language of the floweret;   5
   "My fragile leaves," it said, "his heart enclose."
Love long has taken for his amulet
   One perfect rose.

Why is it no one ever sent me yet
   One perfect limousine, do you suppose?   10
Ah no, it's always just my luck to get
   One perfect rose.

Look closely at her word choice here to show how she suggests the tone of conventional love poetry in her first two stanzas. Which word changes the tone of this entire poem? How does this shift change the meaning of all of the lines that have come before it? By the end of the poem, we're ready to go back and read everything differently. Like Atwood, Parker turns against the conventions of romantic love. But her turn doesn't communicate quite the same painful edginess.

Next, look at another of Parker's poems. What common ideas do you associate with the title "Thought for a Sunshiny Morning"?

Dorothy Parker (1893–1967)

Thought for a Sunshiny Morning (1936)

It costs me never a stab nor squirm
To tread by chance upon a worm.
"Aha, my little dear," I say,
"Your clan will pay me back one day."

Notice that having read another poem by Parker does not spoil this second poem. In fact, our experience with the two poems helps us form a preliminary feeling for Parker's distinctive voice. We do have some idea of the sort of thing that we might expect, but here the tone begins with a title that contrasts sharply with the subject of death. The simple rhyme scheme and rhythmic pattern also contribute to the almost cheerful fatalism of Parker's poetic voice. With these two examples, how might you begin to define Parker's tone?

The tone in John Donne's poem "The Flea" is altogether different, but understanding the tone remains an essential key to unlocking the poem. Donne also holds up multiple meanings; he dismisses serious issues of virtue by asking whether a flea has stolen his lover's virginity by sucking first his blood and then hers. Even as Donne delights in turning the metaphor inside out, he hardly seems to be mocking virtue or his beloved. We might say he maintains a playfully sincere tone in this poem.

John Donne (1572–1631)

The Flea (1633)

Mark but this flea, and mark in this,
How little that which thou deniest me is;
It suck'd me first, and now sucks thee,
And in this flea our two bloods mingled be.
Thou know'st that this cannot be said   5

A sin, nor shame, nor loss of maidenhead;
   Yet this enjoys before it woo,
   And pamper'd swells with one blood made of two;
   And this, alas! is more than we would do.

O stay, three lives in one flea spare,   10
Where we almost, yea, more than married are.
This flea is you and I, and this
Our marriage bed, and marriage temple is.
Though parents grudge, and you, we're met,
And cloister'd in these living walls of jet.   15
   Though use make you apt to kill me,
   Let not to that self-murder added be,
   And sacrilege, three sins in killing three.

Cruel and sudden, hast thou since
Purpled thy nail in blood of innocence?   20
Wherein could this flea guilty be,
Except in that drop which it suck'd from thee?
Yet thou triumph'st, and say'st that thou
Find'st not thyself nor me the weaker now.
   'Tis true; then learn how false fears be;   25
   Just so much honour, when thou yield'st to me,
   Will waste, as this flea's death took life from thee.

As we make our way through this poem, Donne's language of virtue constantly must compete with the fact that his subject is really the flea that she kills. Her nail "Purpled" in the "blood of innocence" gives the event an inappropriately lofty language. Until we realize that his single goal here is to break down her virtue, this language may make the poem itself appear much loftier than it is. Donne wants the flea, now dead even though it had swallowed her blood, to symbolize the meaninglessness of conventions that enforce virginity.

MIXING AND BALANCING OPPOSING TONES

Ted Kooser writes a poem in which he captures the idiosyncratic tone of a person who might be anyone's "Aunt Belle" remarking on a terrible tragedy. The name of the person gives us a sense of the chattiness and random connections that often accompany such relations where there are shared memories and understandings that help maintain a sense of family. As you read this "letter," note how the tone shifts abruptly as a core story haltingly unfolds. In what ways is this uneven tone appropriate? What details from Aunt Belle's correspondence define this tone for you? Is this poem ultimately about a tragic event or about a character? Perhaps it is about a specific character's response to tragedy.

Ted Kooser (1939–   )

A Letter from Aunt Belle (2004)

You couldn't have heard about it there—
I'll send the clippings later on.

The afternoon that the neighbors' stove exploded—
how it reminded me of.... Sarah's garden wedding!
Do you remember? It was beautiful.   5

As I was watering those slips
I promised you—the violets—
there was an awful thud, and Samson's wall
puffed up and blew the windows out.
It turned some pictures in the living room,   10
and that lovely vase you children gave to me
Christmas of '56 fell down, but I can glue it.

That Franklin boy you knew in school—
the one who got that girl in trouble—
ran in the Samson's house, but she was dead;   15
the blast collapsed her lungs, poor thing.
She always made me think of you,
but on the stretcher with her hair pinned up
and one old sandal off, she looked as old
as poor old me.   20
               I have to go—
I've baked a little coffee cake
for Mr. Samson and the boys.

The violet slips are ready—
               Write.

Identify the clues here that help you recognize the tone of this letter: the questions, the promises of future correspondence, the references to an old neighbor, the assumption of authority over the reader, the neighborliness, the chattiness, the gossipy delivery of the tragic news. All of these details teach us to know the character who is writing and help us interpret her words.

Notice how this tone nearly hides the most significant news the letter has to communicate. Buried inside the offer of violet slips and memories of Sarah's garden wedding is the death of a wife and mother. But the chatty delivery of this news doesn't lessen the poem's impact. It actually deepens our sense of the speaker; it helps us know her better than she knows herself. Aunt Belle may revert to conversational niceties, but she is struck by this death: "she looked as old / as poor old me." And she does what she can to alleviate the grief of "Mr. Samson and the boys." The poem offers a full account of her old-fashioned neighborliness: she gossips, but she also feels a responsibility to those who live around her.

Experiencing Literature through Tone

Like all considerations of tone, humor requires some understanding of the context in which the performance occurs. Much humor involves an upsetting of traditional, recognizable, and well-understood structures. To recognize that a structure has been upset, one must be fairly familiar with the original. To appreciate irreverence, one needs some experience with reverence. In some ways, irreverence may be the more complex attitude, at least in terms of interpretation. In the following passage from *Mules and Men*, Zora Neale Hurston sets us down in the middle of a conversation about the nature of religious controversy in a small town. The main character, Charlie, creates a story that conflates several familiar stories from the New Testament. To appreciate Charlie's story (and to laugh with the others around this particular table), one has to know the originals. The religious teachings of Jesus sometimes depend upon a clear literalness; other times he speaks metaphorically. When Jesus says to Peter, "Upon this rock, I will build my church," it is generally understood that he is playing with the derivation of Peter's name—he will build a church upon the bedrock, the faith that Peter (*petra*, rock) has professed. In other biblical incidents, the Christian tradition emphasizes the literalness of Jesus's miraculous work—he was able to feed thousands of people with only five loaves of bread, and he turned water into wine. This particular story finds its humor by having Charlie take everything literally.

Zora Neale Hurston (1891–1960)

"Peter's Rock" from Mules and Men (1935)

As the prayer ended the bell of Macedonia, the Baptist church, began to ring.
"Prayer meetin' night at Macedony," George Thomas said.

"It's too bad that it must be two churches in Eatonville," I commented. "De town's too little. Everybody ought to go to one."

"It's too bad, Zora, and you know better. Fack is, "de Christian churches nowhere don't stick together," this from Charlie.

Everybody agreed that this was true. So Charlie went on. "Look at   5 all de kind of denominations we got. But de people can't help dat cause de church wasn't built on no solid foundation to start wid."

"Oh yes, it twas!" Johnnie Mae disputed him. "It was built on solid rock. Didn't Jesus say 'On dis rock Ah build my church?' "

"Yeah," chimed in Antie Hoyt. And de song says "On christ solid rock I stand and 'Rock of Ages.'"

Charlie was calm and patient. "Yeah, he built it on a rock, but it wasn't solid. It was a pieced-up rock and that's how come de church split up now. Here's de very way it was:

Christ was walkin' long one day wid all his disciples and he said, "We're goin' for a walk today. Everybody pick up a rock and come along." So everybody got their selves a nice big rock 'ceptin' Peter. He was lazy so he picked up a li'l bit of a pebble and dropped it in his side pocket and come along.

Well, they walked all day long and de other 'leven disciples changed   10 them rocks from one arm to de other but they kept on totin' 'em. Long towards sundown they come 'long by de Sea of Galilee and Jesus tole 'em, "Well, le's fish awhile. Cast in yo' nets right here." They done like he tole 'em and caught a great big mess of fish. Then they cooked 'em and Christ said, "Now, all y'all bring up yo' rocks." So they all brought they rocks and Christ turned 'em into bread and they all had a plenty to eat wid they fish exceptin' Peter. He couldn't hardly make a moufful offa de li'l bread he had and he didn't like dat a bit.

Two or three days after dat Christ went out doors and looked up at de sky and says, "Well, we're goin' for an other walk today. Everybody git yo'self a rock and come along."

They all picked up a rock apiece and was ready to go. All but Peter. He went and tore down half a mountain. It was so big he couldn't move it wid his hands. He had to take a pinch-bar to move it. All day long Christ walked and talked to his disciples and Peter sweated and strained wid dat rock of his'n.

Way long in de evenin' Christ went up under a great big ole tree and set down and called all of his disciples around 'im and said, "Now everybody bring up yo' rocks."

So everybody brought theirs but Peter. Peter was about mile down de road punchin' dat half a mountain he was bringin'. So Christ waited till he got dere. He looked at de rocks dat de other 'leven disciples had, den he seen dis great big mountain dat Peter had and so he got up and walked over to it and put one foot up on it and said, "Why Peter, dis is a fine rock you got here! It's a noble rock! And Peter, on dis rock Ab'm gointer build my church."

Peter says, "Naw you ain't neither. You won't build no church house   15
on dis rock. You gointer turn dis rock into bread."

Christ knowed dat Peter meant dat thing so he turnt de hillside into bread and dat mountain is de bread he fed de 5,000 wid. Den he took dem 'leven other rocks and glued 'em together and built his church on it.

And that's how come de Christian churches is split up into so many different kinds cause it's built on pieced-up rock.

The humorous tone of Hurston's story is also created out of the informal retelling of what are taken as sacred texts. Such mixing of **colloquial** (spoken) with con- sciously literary (written) styles is a common way to refresh or chal- lenge language that has grown distant in its formality. Charlie may not have a strong command of the King James Bible (an early- seventeenth-century translation that has been called "the noblest monument of English prose"), but he cannot be accused of being a passive reader. We might ask, How does Hurston want us to see Charlie? Do we come away from this comic dialogue with a sense of his foolishness or an appreciation for his wit?

> **Making Connections**
>
> Consider how the tonal clash between different kinds of language and representation function in other works you've read or films you've seen. Shakespeare, for example, famously mixes the formal and the informal, the "high" and the "low." What specific instances in *Much Ado about Nothing* (Chapter 9) strike you as especially meaningful? Or, to take another dramatic example, think about *Topdog/Underdog* by Suzan-Lori Parks (Chapter 6). In that play, one character enacts in a cheap boardwalk show a major event in U.S. history that has been recounted solemnly in standard textbooks. Does Parks use the tone of one against that of the other to comment on the attitude we usually take toward the national tragedy of President Lincoln's assassination? Does she seek to make us rethink the kind of importance we typically grant it?

IRONY AND INTROSPECTION

There is something appealing about the fact that opposites can coexist. Peter and his disjointed united church present an explanation of one such coexistence. In the following poem, William Carlos Williams suggests the terror posed by a crowd: the individual details are beautiful, but the mass moves "without thought."

William Carlos Williams (1883–1963)

At the Ball Game (1923)

The crowd at the ball game
is moved uniformly

by a spirit of uselessness
which delights them—

all the exciting detail   5
of the chase

and the escape, the error
the flash of genius—

all to no end save beauty
the eternal—   10

So in detail they, the crowd,
are beautiful

for this
to be warned against

saluted and defied—   15
It is alive, venomous

it smiles grimly
its words cut—

The flashy female with her
mother, gets it—   20

The Jew gets it straight—it
is deadly, terrifying—

It is the Inquisition, the
Revolution

It is beauty itself   25
that lives

day by day in them
idly—

This is
the power of their faces   30

It is summer, it is the solstice
the crowd is

cheering, the crowd is laughing
in detail

permanently, seriously   35
without thought

The crowd at the ball game moves together, applauding and cheering the fine details of the chase, but to anyone who becomes the subject of a crowd's attention, this harmless fascination in the game becomes ominous. They may be laughing mindlessly at details, but when such a group laughs mindlessly at specific people ("the flashly female," "the Jew"), their amusement is deadly and terrifying. This irony is based on perceptions, on the different points of view; the crowd at the ball game seems to be harmless, but the attitudes that characterize this crowd (uselessness, idleness, mindlessness, appreciation of beauty) also characterize the most disturbing mass movements. We perceive the crowd completely differently. Suddenly, what we may have heard as communal recreation (idle cheering) sounds repressive and brutal.

> ## Making Connections
>
> Williams's poem requires that we know something of history. If we have no knowledge of the Spanish Inquisition or the *Communist Manifesto* (with its call to revolution), we will not fully appreciate the dramatic range of tones his poem encompasses. In Chapter 14 we address the art of allusion—that is, enriching a work of art by referencing other works of art. The strategy is a common one and is not limited to references to "high" culture. The deliberate mixing of very different types of materials often contributes to a comic or satiric tone. Think, for example, of almost any episode of *The Simpsons*. Within 30 minutes an alert viewer is likely to note allusions to other cartoons, to films, to classic literature, to television commercials, and so on.

Often tonal shifts signal ironic gaps between the passionate beliefs of a character and the quite different judgments of the narrator or author. In Chinua Achebe's "Dead Men's Path," for instance, Michael Obi's conviction that the old needs to be replaced by the modern must be assessed in light of the quiet assurance of the narrative (and of the village priest) that old ways must be respected. As you read, note how the story sets up Obi, and note the specific instances in the narrative where Obi's confident convictions seem foolish rather than insightful.

Chinua Achebe (1930–2013)

Dead Men's Path (1972)

Michael Obi's hopes were fulfilled much earlier than he had expected. He was appointed headmaster of Ndume Central School in January 1949. It had always been an unprogressive school, so the Mission authorities decided to send a young and energetic man to run it. Obi accepted this responsibility with enthusiasm. He had many wonderful ideas and this was an opportunity to put them into practice. He had sound secondary school education which designated him a "pivotal teacher" in the official records and set him apart from the other headmasters in the mission field. He was outspoken in his condemnation of the narrow views of these older and often less-educated ones.

"We shall make a good job of it, shan't we?" he asked his young wife when they first heard the joyful news of his promotion.

"We shall do our best," she replied. "We shall have such beautiful gardens and everything will be just modern and delightful ..." In their two years of married life she had become completely infected by his passion for "modern methods" and his denigration of "these old and superannuated people in the teaching field who would be better employed as traders in the Onitsha market." She began to see herself already as the admired wife of the young headmaster, the queen of the school.

The wives of the other teachers would envy her position. She would set the fashion in everything.... Then, suddenly, it occurred to her that there might not be other wives. Wavering between hope and fear, she asked her husband, looking anxiously at him.

"All our colleagues are young and unmarried," he said with enthusiasm which for once she did not share. "Which is a good thing," he continued. 5

"Why?"

"Why? They will give all their time and energy to the school."

Nancy was downcast. For a few minutes she became skeptical about the new school; but it was only for a few minutes. Her little personal misfortune could not blind her to her husband's happy prospects. She looked at him as he sat folded up in a chair. He was stoop-shouldered and looked frail. But he sometimes surprised people with sudden bursts of physical energy. In his present posture, however, all his bodily strength seemed to have retired behind his deepset eyes, giving them an extraordinary power of penetration. He was only twenty-six, but looked thirty or more. On the whole, he was not unhandsome.

"A penny for your thoughts, Mike," said Nancy after a while, imitating the woman's magazine she read.

"I was thinking what a grand opportunity we've got at last to show   10
these people how a school should be run." Ndume School was backward in every sense of the word. Mr. Obi put his whole life into the
work, and his wife hers too. He had two aims. A high standard of teaching was insisted upon, and the school compound was to be turned into
a place of beauty. Nancy's dreamgardens came to life with the coming
of the rains, and blossomed. Beautiful hibiscus and allamanda hedges
in brilliant red and yellow marked out the carefully tended school compound from the rank neighborhood bushes.

One evening as Obi was admiring his work he was scandalized to see an
old woman from the village hobble right across the compound, through a mari-
gold flower-bed and the hedges. On going up there he found faint signs of an
almost disused path from the village across the school compound to the bush
on the other side.

"It amazes me," said Obi to one of his teachers who had been three years
in the school, "that you people allowed the villagers to make use of this footpath. It is simply incredible." He shook his head.

"The path," said the teacher apologetically, "appears to be very important
to them. Although it is hardly used, it connects the village shrine with their
place of burial."

"And what has that got to do with the school"? asked the headmaster.

"Well, I don't know," replied the other with a shrug of the shoulders.   15
"But I remember there was a big row some time ago when we attempted to
close it."

"That was some time ago. But it will not be used now," said Obi as he
walked away. "What will the Government Education Officer think of this
when he comes to inspect the school next week? The villagers might, for all I
know, decide to use the schoolroom for a pagan ritual during the inspection."

Heavy sticks were planted closely across the path at the two places where
it entered and left the school premises. These were further strengthened with
barbed wire.

Three days later the village priest of Ani called on the headmaster. He was an
old man and walked with a slight stoop. He carried a stout walking-stick which
he usually tapped on the floor, by way of emphasis, each time he made a new
point in his argument.

"I have heard," he said after the usual exchange of cordialities, "that our
ancestral footpath has recently been closed...."

"Yes," replied Mr. Obi. "We cannot allow people to make a highway   20
of our school compound."

"Look here, my son," said the priest bringing down his walking-stick,
"this path was here before you were born and before your father was born.

The whole life of this village depends on it. Our dead relatives depart by it and our ancestors visit us by it. But most important, it is the path of children coming in to be born..."

Mr. Obi listened with a satisfied smile on his face.

"The whole purpose of our school," he said finally, "is to eradicate just such beliefs as that. Dead men do not require footpaths. The whole idea is just fantastic. Our duty is to teach your children to laugh at such ideas."

"What you say may be true," replied the priest, "but we follow the practices of our fathers. If you re-open the path we shall have nothing to quarrel about. What I always say is: let the hawk perch and let the eagle perch." He rose to go.

"I am sorry," said the young headmaster. "But the school compound   25 cannot be a thoroughfare. It is against our regulations. I would suggest your constructing another path, skirting our premises. We can even get our boys to help in building it. I don't suppose the ancestors will find the little detour too burdensome."

"I have no more words to say," said the old priest, already outside.

Two days later a young woman in the village died in childbed. A diviner was immediately consulted and he prescribed heavy sacrifices to propitiate ancestors insulted by the fence.

Obi woke up next morning among the ruins of his work. The beautiful hedges were torn up not just near the path but right round the school, the flowers trampled to death and one of the school buildings pulled down.... That day, the white Supervisor came to inspect the school and wrote a nasty report on the state of the premises but more seriously about the "tribal-war situation developing between the school and the village, arising in part from the misguided zeal of the new headmaster."

Authors often want us to understand more than their characters can grasp of a situation. In this sense, we sometimes need to hear things differently, pick up different tones, than do key characters. This gap between a character's understanding and our own is called **dramatic irony**. When Achebe's narrator speaks of Obi, for instance, the narrator and the reader see the irony while Obi does not. Williams's crowd cannot see how it terrorizes. When Hurston presents the story of Peter's rock, the critique is of a church that the speakers participate in. The same technique, though, applies well to **introspection**—a personal willingness to take in and reflect upon ideas that may seem to conflict, but at some level make sense together. We have a **paradox** when some truth is embodied in what on the surface seems a contradiction. Czeslaw Milosz's poem "If There Is No God" contemplates the responsibilities that come with a godless universe. How would such a "fact" change the nature of existence?

Czeslaw Milosz (1911–2004)

If There Is No God

Trans. from Polish by the author and Robert Haas; 2004

> If there is no God,
> Not everything is permitted to man.
> He is still his brother's keeper
> And he is not permitted to sadden his brother
> By saying there is no God.

Milosz suggests that the religious responsibilities of the atheist would actually increase if there were no God. Recognizing paradox often seems to result from introspection and to result in an introspective tone. How is Milosz's tone here different from the religious inquiry in "Peter's Rock" or the tender affection that Kooser offers in "A Letter from Aunt Belle"? Do you feel that Milosz speaks more directly through his speaker? Is the effect more sincere and less ironic?

A Note to Student Writers: Signaling Your Own Understanding of Tonal Shifts

When you write critically about a literary text or film, it's important that you be very clear about signaling your own understanding of tonal shifts or of ironic gaps between author and character. Your reader, of course, will understand that a character, a speaker, and an author may possess distinct voices, but if you do not keep the distinctions clear, your *own* understanding may be called into question. Therefore, build into your text explicit explanations. For example, there is an enormous difference between the following two summary remarks regarding a paragraph (the eleventh) from "Dead Men's Path":

1. Mr. Obi is assigned to work in a school stuck in a primitive past. He brings a very high educational standard as well as a love of beauty to the backward village.
2. Mr. Obi can only view the school as backward and in great need of rigourous teaching. He also wants to transform the school compound into a place that meets his preconceived ideal of beauty.

The first summary registers Mr. Obi's thoughts without suggesting that any other thoughts might be important in the story. It doesn't suggest a coming transition to any other perspective. In short, it fails to catch distinctive qualities of tone in Achebe's story.

The second makes it clear that words such as *backward, rigorous, transform,* and *beautiful* convey meanings within the value system of Mr. Obi. It will allow the writer to move easily between distinctly different perspectives (those of the narrator and the village chief). It prepares us to "hear" a different tone than Mr. Obi himself can appreciate.

MODELING CRITICAL ANALYSIS: JOEL COEN AND ETHAN COEN, O BROTHER, WHERE ART THOU?

On its surface, O *Brother, Where Art Thou?* (2000) might appear to offer an accurate re-creation of Depression-era Mississippi. Every image from the film, especially the tin of Dapper Dan pomade, looks as though it came directly out of that era, and the soundtrack transformed obscure folk music from the time and region into a popular album. This movie serves as a useful example in the discussion of tone because, in spite of its careful re-creation of historical detail, the audience does not judge the film as it might judge a historical epic. If a film purports to present a true story, we expect it to be faithful to that story; we will challenge such a film when it chooses to depart into fiction. But the opening sequence here sets a tone for the film that frees us from a narrow demand for historical accuracy. A chain gang in striped prison garb opens the film singing and keeping time with their picks and hammers. The film next shifts to three prisoners, chained together, escaping from the gang. Hampered by their chains, they trip over one another as a traditional version of the folk classic "Big Rock Candy Mountain" plays above them. The music and the carefully choreographed movement of the characters tilt the film more toward the comic rather than historic mode.

The episodic story stars George Clooney as Ulysses Everett McGill, a hero with a powerful "gift of gab" and an extraordinary attention to his slicked-back hair through all of his adventures. His convoluted language, with its slight grammatical slips, period idioms ("You two are just dumber than a bag of hammers"), and foolishly pretentious vocabulary are hardly what we expect to hear in an argument between escaped prisoners:

> Pete, the personal rancor reflected in that remark I don't intend to dignify with comment. But I would like to address your general attitude of hopeless negativism. Consider the lilies of the goddamn field or.... hell! Take at look at Delmar here as your paradigm of hope.

McGill's tireless analytical bent displays a limited self-consciousness that straddles the past in the historical character he inhabits and our present. For instance, he claims that he deserves to be the leader of the group because unlike his fellow travelers he has a "capacity for abstract thought." He is a walking encyclopedia of information completely useless to someone in his particular circumstances. In answer to a question about the physical description of the devil, he answers, "Well, there are all manner of lesser imps and demons, Pete, but the great Satan hisself is red and scaly with a bifurcated tail, and he carries a hay fork." This out-of-place encyclopedic knowledge can help us hear a tone in a film that announces in the opening credits that it is "based upon The Odyssey by Homer."

Bibb County chain gang in Georgia, 1937.

AP Images/Corbis

O Brother, Where Art Thou? (2000)

Touchs Tone/Universal/The Kobal Collection/Picture Desk

Like McGill, the film itself offers choice tidbits of knowledge that seem randomly delivered. Some links to the *Odyssey* are clear enough: John Goodman plays a one-eyed Bible salesman who resembles a Cyclops; three women Sirens doing laundry and singing a lullaby lure the travelers from their journey. Other connections to Homer's epic are far more obscure, but the often wild mixture of parts is what constitutes the tone of the whole. There is something serious about this comedy. *Oh Brother, Where Art Thou?* juxtaposes shots that borrow images from the socially conscious photography of Walker Evans or Dorothea Lange with slapstick comedy. In what ways does the still from *O Brother, Where Art Thou?* differ from the 1937 photo of shackled convicts returning to the Bibb County jail after a day of work? What details help you identify the tone in the film still?

The film offers a rather subtle reading of the *Odyssey*, but in their publicity for the movie, the Coen brothers claim that they never read the original. This self-deprecation makes them seem like students who write book reports for class without doing the reading and disguises through the disarmingly dim characters of Ulysses and his companions a thorough knowledge of the epic as well as a detailed rendering of American history, American cinema, and American music. *Oh Brother, Where Art Thou?* ultimately comments on weighty matters of race, class, progress, and religion. From the early scenes, the Coen brothers establish a tone that guides us to insights none of their characters could ever realize. To put it another way, we hear what the characters say, but understand that Ethan and Joel Coen want to say a good deal more to us.

Using Tone to Focus Writing and Discussion

In every literary work we should be able to find some consistent tone. To define that tone, use the following questions:

- How does the author set the tone? Is there some lens that teaches us, as readers, how to read what follows? Remember that tone can come out of many of the other literary elements that we have discussed, including setting, character, point of view, and rhythm.

- Does the author reveal the tone immediately? Or does the piece depend upon our discovery of that tone later in the work?

- What is the prevailing effect in this work? Is the tone light or dark? Earnest or mocking? Straightforward or sarcastic? Outraged or enraptured? These are only a few possibilities, but they offer a good starting point for our definition of the tone that we find within any specific work.

- Is there a specific character who speaks or a specific occasion that might give us some clue about the mood of this particular work?

- What role does the tone play in this particular work? Is the tone transparent—is it something that we don't really notice as we read—or is the tone visible? Is it integral to the story?

- Does the tone change over the course of the text? For instance, there might be two different characters who approach a scene differently. The contrast between their tones might be an important barometer into meaning within the work.

- How can a discussion of tone benefit our analysis of this particular work? For instance, contrasts in tone can serve as a topic of discussion, and it may also be fruitful to discuss works that share particular tonal elements.

Anthology

NOIR: A CRITIC WRITES ABOUT TONE

In his discussion of film-noir classics, Richard Brody attends to tonal signals that characterize the genre. While he offers very brief summaries of four films, the qualities that make those films worth seeing aren't those of narrative or character. Matters of style are what make the films resonant. To Brody's mind, "these bitter-toned, highly stylized, low-budget movies" managed to record more about uncomfortable social and psychological traumas than most high-end films of the same period. Brody's critical vocabulary registers those tonal qualities: *Drive a Crooked Road* (1954) is "sunlit, doom-laden." *My Name Is Julia Ross* (1945) is a "terrifyingly claustrophobic drama" that manages to convey much about the horror of World War II without being about the war at all. And with *The Reckless Moment* (1949), the director Max Ophuls manages to lend a small-town blackmail story "an exquisite dignity." As you read Brody, think of films you've seen where tonal qualities become crucial to theme and effect.

Characteristics of Noir

In their 1955 *A Panorama of American Film Noir*, Raymond Borde and Etienne Chaumeton listed five attributes that typically describe film noir: strange, erotic, ambivalent, cruel, and oneiric (dreamlike). Any single film may not exhibit each of these qualities equally, but it is the noir style, often black and white, with strong shadows in which dim lighting mirrors the moral ambiguity of the narrative.

Traditionally, noir is associated with urban environments. Typical characters are deeply flawed, for instance, a private eye with no official connection to law enforcement who may be difficult to differentiate from the criminal he is chasing or a femme fatale whose charms lure men into dangerous situations.

Tone in any genre can be hard to read because often there seems a built-in tension between what we usually think of as opposing feelings. *O Brother, Where Art Thou?* sets the tone for our discussion of the often delicate balance between laughter and tears. The film addresses in a consistently comic vein weighty and even tragic matters. The Coen brothers depict a largely rural community contemplating the impact of industrialization, a region beset by racial tension, a political system subject to systematic abuse. All, of course, ends happily and there are many laughs along the way through the journey of Ulysses, but the action involves racial injustice, abysmal poverty, political corruption, and two barely thwarted lynchings. The tension between laughter and tears is evident throughout. If we cannot "hear" right, we'll dismiss the film as a confused mess. If we tune in, we'll appreciate how *Oh Brother, Where Art Thou?* challenges and complicates simple formulations about a region—indeed about a nation's history and culture in relation to that region.

Flannery O'Connor's "A Good Man Is Hard to Find" poises us uncomfortably between a man who accepts no limits and becomes a monster and an old woman who accepts severe limits and becomes a caricature of her society's essentially shallow propriety. The resulting dynamic results in what is for O'Connor a characteristically shocking insight. We are not left with a tidy sense of "good," although we are led to concur that a good man is indeed hard to find. As you read this and other works in this cluster, attend to what happens when one presses toward or crosses a boundary. What meaning do we draw from the experience? What value or violation has taken shape in the work of art?

Billy Collins takes as an inspiration Art Blakey's jazz rendition of a simple children's song. What Blakey does in Collins's mind is draw out as obvious something we typically overlook. The playful repetition of the song, the tone of excited merriment, covers up a sad story of those poor, blind, frightened, and finally tailless mice. Blakey and then Collins after him prompt us to bring tone into a closer relation to action. In so doing, they make us wonder what other instances of avoidance we habitually practice—what other false notes we hit.

REVIEW

Richard Brody (1958–   )

Mothers and Lovers (2014)

Women onscreen in two series of film-noir classics, at Film Forum and MOMA.

THE FILM NOIR REMAINS the most enduring old-Hollywood genre, as confirmed by a pair of simultaneous retrospectives, "Femmes Noirs," at Film Forum, and "Lady in the Dark: Crime Films from Columbia Pictures, 1932–1957," at the Museum of Modern Art. The physical and emotional violence of these bitter-toned, highly stylized, low-budget movies exposed lurid fantasies and social traumas that went unmentioned in the studios' more prestigious productions. Almost all of these films were directed by men, so it's no surprise that, as the titles of the series indicate, many are centered on women—women in trouble or women who are trouble.

MOMAS program is distinguished by such rare movies as the director Richard Quine's sunlit, doom-laden **"Drive a Crooked Road,"** from 1954. Quine dramatizes the stereotypical male gaze with derisive scenes of four brawny auto mechanics slobbering and hooting as women walk past their shop-window. But their shy, slight, and plainspoken co-worker (Mickey Rooney), who shuns such displays, is the one who gets snared in the criminal schemes of a seductress (Dianne Foster). Here, the carnal leer, despite its simian repugnance, suggests a fitness for the battle of the sexes, to which the sensitive romantic shows up unarmed.

The sacred vows of motherhood are debased in several of the best films in MOMA'S series, including **"My Name Is Julia Ross,"** a terrifyingly claustrophobic drama by the audacious stylist Joseph H. Lewis, from 1945. Nina Foch stars in the title role, as an American woman alone and adrift in London, who is hired as a private secretary by an elderly dowager, Mrs. Hughes (Dame May Whitty). The job turns out to be part of Mrs. Hughes's plot to cover up her son's murder of his wife; she holds Julia captive in a rural mansion and attempts to brainwash her and efface her identity. The story runs on a local version of the dictator's big lie. Without a word about war, Lewis, showing bars and gates, a striped dress, and the credulous regard of well-meaning neighbors, conjures visions of the concentration camps, which went largely unnoticed during wartime and came to light just before the start of filming.

The grand ironist Max Ophuls gave a similar story of furious maternal devotion a bittersweet tinge in **"The Reckless Moment,"** from 1949 (also at MOMA). A headstrong teen-age girl in a California seaside town accidentally kills her caddish boyfriend. Her mother (Joan Bennett) tries to cover it up, but is blackmailed by a suave grifter (James Mason), who ends up falling in love with her. With his elegantly gliding and soaring images, Ophuls lends an exquisite dignity to unfulfilled longing and criminal passion alike.

The Film Forum series includes **"Angel Face"** (1952), in which Otto   5
Preminger, a rationalistic master of hidden madness, stages a conflict between two feminine tropes, the evil stepmother and the predatory vixen, and a male one, the freelancer with a roving eye. A writer (Herbert Marshall) who was widowed during the London Blitz lives in California with his second wife (Barbara O'Neil), a wealthy woman who clashes with him and his viperish daughter, Diane (Jean Simmons). The sexually swaggering Frank (Robert Mitchum), an ambulance driver whose irrepressible lust is his point of vulnerability, is called to the house, where he falls under Diane's spell and gets pulled into her plot to kill her stepmother. Preminger, who studied law, builds tragic results from the evenhanded workings of the judicial system.

FICTION

Flannery O'Connor (1925–1964)

Flannery O'Connor was born in Savannah, Georgia. When she was sixteen, her father died of disseminated lupus, the disease that would later claim her own life. She received her AB in 1945 from Women's College of Georgia (now Georgia College) and her MFA from the State University of Iowa in 1947. At the age of twenty-five she suffered her first attack of lupus, and from then on she lived with her mother. O'Connor died when she was thirty-nine years old. O'Connor is widely regarded as one of the preeminent fiction writers of the twentieth century. Though often violent, her works are essentially religious, in that they express her Catholic vision of the world as a fallen place in need of redemption. Among her works are the novels *Wise Blood* (1952) and *The Violent Bear It Away* (1960) and the story collections *A Good Man Is Hard to Find* (1955) and *Everything That Rises Must Converge* (1965).

A Good Man Is Hard to Find (1953)

The dragon is by the side of the road, watching those who pass. Beware lest he devour you. We go to the Father of Souls, but it is necessary to pass by the dragon.

—St. Cyril of Jerusalem

The grandmother didn't want to go to Florida. She wanted to visit some of her connections in east Tennessee and she was seizing at every chance to change Bailey's mind. Bailey was the son she lived with, her only boy. He was sitting on the edge of his chair at the table, bent over the orange sports section of the Journal. "Now look here, Bailey," she said, "see here, read this," and she stood with one hand on her thin hip and the other rattling the newspaper at his bald head. "Here this fellow that calls himself The Misfit is aloose from the Federal Pen and headed toward Florida and you read here what it says he did to these people. Just you read it. I wouldn't take my children in any direction with a criminal like that aloose in it. I couldn't answer to my conscience if I did."

Bailey didn't look up from his reading so she wheeled around then and faced the children's mother, a young woman in slacks, whose face was as broad and innocent as a cabbage and was tied around with a green headkerchief that had two points on the top like a rabbit's ears. She was sitting on the sofa, feeding the baby his apricots out of a jar. "The children have been to Florida before," the old lady said. "You all ought to take them somewhere else for a change so they would see different parts of the world and be broad. They never have been to east Tennessee."

The children's mother didn't seem to hear her but the eight-year-old boy, John Wesley, a stocky child with glasses, said, "If you don't want to go to Florida, why dontcha stay at home?" He and the little girl, June Star, were reading the funny papers on the floor.

"She wouldn't stay at home to be queen for a day," June Star said without raising her yellow head.

"Yes and what would you do if this fellow, The Misfit, caught you?" the grandmother asked.   5

"I'd smack his face," John Wesley said.

"She wouldn't stay at home for a million bucks," June Star said. "Afraid she'd miss something. She has to go everywhere we go."

"All right, Miss," the grandmother said. "Just remember that the next time you want me to curl your hair."

June Star said her hair was naturally curly.

The next morning the grandmother was the first one in the car, ready to go. She had her big black valise that looked like the head of a hippopotamus in one corner, and underneath it she was hiding a basket with Pitty Sing, the cat, in it. She didn't intend for the cat to be left alone in the house for three days because he would miss her too much and she was afraid he might brush against one of the gas burners and accidentally asphyxiate himself. Her son, Bailey, didn't like to arrive at a motel with a cat.   10

She sat in the middle of the back seat with John Wesley and June Star on either side of her. Bailey and the children's mother and the baby sat in front and they left Atlanta at eight forty-five with the mileage on the car at 55890.

The grandmother wrote this down because she thought it would be interesting to say how many miles they had been when they got back. It took them twenty minutes to reach the outskirts of the city.

The old lady settled herself comfortably, removing her white cotton gloves and putting them up with her purse on the shelf in front of the back window. The children's mother still had on slacks and still had her head tied up in a green kerchief, but the grandmother had on a navy blue straw sailor hat with a bunch of white violets on the brim and a navy blue dress with a small white dot in the print. Her collars and cuffs were white organdy trimmed with lace and at her neck she had pinned a purple spray of cloth violets containing a sachet. In case of an accident, anyone seeing her dead on the highway would know at once that she was a lady.

She said she thought it was going to be a good day for driving, neither too hot nor too cold, and she cautioned Bailey that the speed limit was fifty-five miles an hour and that the patrolmen hid themselves behind billboards and small clumps of trees and sped out after you before you had a chance to slow down. She pointed out interesting details of the scenery: Stone Mountain; the blue granite that in some places came up to both sides of the highway; the brilliant red clay banks slightly streaked with purple; and the various crops that made rows of green lace-work on the ground. The trees were full of silver-white sunlight and the meanest of them sparkled. The children were reading comic magazines and their mother had gone back to sleep.

"Let's go through Georgia fast so we won't have to look at it much," John Wesley said.

"If I were a little boy," said the grandmother, "I wouldn't talk about my native state that way. Tennessee has the mountains and Georgia has the hills."   15

"Tennessee is just a hillbilly dumping ground," John Wesley said, "and Georgia is a lousy state too."

"You said it," June Star said.

"In my time," said the grandmother, folding her thin veined fingers, "children were more respectful of their native states and their parents and everything else. People did right then. Oh look at the cute little pickaninny!" she said and pointed to a Negro child standing in the door of a shack. "Wouldn't that make a picture, now?" she asked and they all turned and looked at the little Negro out of the back window. He waved.

"He didn't have any britches on," June Star said.

"He probably didn't have any," the grandmother explained. "Little niggers in the country don't have things like we do. If I could paint, I'd paint that picture," she said.   20

The children exchanged comic books.

The grandmother offered to hold the baby and the children's mother passed him over the front seat to her. She set him on her knee and bounced him and told him about the things they were passing. She rolled her eyes and screwed up her mouth and stuck her leathery thin face into his smooth bland one. Occasionally he gave her a faraway smile. They passed a large cotton field with five or six graves fenced in the middle of it, like a small island. "Look at the graveyard!" the grandmother said, pointing it out. "That was the old family burying ground. That belonged to the plantation."

"Where's the plantation?" John Wesley asked.

"Gone With the Wind," said the grandmother. "Ha. Ha."

When the children finished all the comic books they had brought,   25 they opened the lunch and ate it. The grandmother ate a peanut butter sandwich and an olive and would not let the children throw the box and the paper napkins out the window. When there was nothing else to do they played a game by choosing a cloud and making the other two guess what shape it suggested. John Wesley took one the shape of a cow and June Star guessed a cow and John Wesley said, no, an automobile, and June Star said he didn't play fair, and they began to slap each other over the grandmother.

The grandmother said she would tell them a story if they would keep quiet. When she told a story, she rolled her eyes and waved her head and was very dramatic. She said once when she was a maiden lady she had been courted by a Mr. Edgar Atkins Teagarden from Jasper, Georgia. She said he was a very good-looking man and a gentleman and that he brought her a watermelon every Saturday afternoon with his initials cut in it, E. A. T. Well, one Saturday, she said, Mr. Teagarden brought the watermelon and there was nobody at home and he left it on the front porch and returned in his buggy to Jasper, but she never got the watermelon, she said, because a nigger boy ate it when he saw the initials, E.A.T.! This story tickled John Wesley's funny bone and he giggled and giggled but June Star didn't think it was any good. She said she wouldn't marry a man that just brought her a watermelon on Saturday. The grandmother said she would have done well to marry Mr. Teagarden because he was a gentleman and had bought Coca-Cola stock when it first came out and that he had died only a few years ago, a very wealthy man.

They stopped at The Tower for barbecued sandwiches. The Tower was a part stucco and part wood filling station and dance hall set in a clearing outside of Timothy. A fat man named Red Sammy Butts ran it and there were signs stuck here and there on the building and for miles up and down the highway saying, TRY RED SAMMY'S FAMOUS BARBECUE. NONE LIKE FAMOUS RED SAMMY'S! RED SAM! THE FAT BOY WITH THE HAPPY LAUGH. A VETERAN! RED SAMMY'S YOUR MAN!

Red Sammy was lying on the bare ground outside The Tower with his head under a truck while a gray monkey about a foot high, chained to a small chinaberry tree, chattered nearby. The monkey sprang back into the tree and got on the highest limb as soon as he saw the children jump out of the car and run toward him.

Inside, The Tower was a long dark room with a counter at one end and tables at the other and dancing space in the middle. They all sat down at a board table next to the nickelodeon and Red Sam's wife, a tall burnt-brown woman with hair and eyes lighter than her skin, came and took their order. The children's mother put a dime in the machine and played "The Tennessee Waltz," and the grandmother said that tune always made her want to dance. She asked Bailey if he would like to dance but he only glared at her. He didn't have a naturally sunny disposition like she did and trips made him nervous. The grandmother's brown eyes were very bright. She swayed her head from side to side and pretended she was dancing in her chair. June Star said play something she could tap to so the children's mother put in another dime and played a fast number and June Star stepped out onto the dance floor and did her tap routine.

"Ain't she cute?" Red Sam's wife said, leaning over the counter. 30
"Would you like to come be my little girl?"

"No I certainly wouldn't," June Star said. "I wouldn't live in a broken down place like this for a million bucks!" and she ran back to the table.

"Ain't she cute?" the woman repeated, stretching her mouth politely.

"Aren't you ashamed?" hissed the grandmother.

Red Sam came in and told his wife to quit lounging on the counter 35
and hurry up with these people's order. His khaki trousers reached just to his hip bones and his stomach hung over them like a sack of meal swaying under his shirt. He came over and sat down at a table nearby and let out a combination sigh and yodel. "You can't win," he said. "You can't win," and he wiped his sweating red face off with a gray handkerchief. "These days you don't know who to trust," he said. "Ain't that the truth?"

"People are certainly not nice like they used to be," said the grandmother.

"Two fellers come in here last week," Red Sammy said, "driving a Chrysler. It was a old beat-up car but it was a good one and these boys looked all right to me. Said they worked at the mill and you know I let them fellers charge the gas they bought? Now why did I do that?"

"Because you're a good man!" the grandmother said at once.

"Yes'm, I suppose so," Red Sam said as if he were struck with this answer. His wife brought the orders, carrying the five plates all at once without a tray, two in each hand and one balanced on her arm. "It isn't a soul in this green world of God's that you can trust," she said. "And I don't count nobody out of that, not nobody," she repeated, looking at Red Sammy.

"Did you read about that criminal, The Misfit, that's escaped?" asked 40
the grandmother.

"I wouldn't be a bit surprised if he didn't attact this place right here," said the woman. "If he hears about it being here, I wouldn't be none surprised to see him. If he hears it's two cent in the cash register, I wouldn't be a tall surprised if he . . . ."

"That'll do," Red Sam said. "Go bring these people their Co'-Colas," and the woman went off to get the rest of the order.

"A good man is hard to find," Red Sammy said. "Everything is getting terrible. I remember the day you could go off and leave your screen door unlatched. Not no more."

He and the grandmother discussed better times. The old lady said that in her opinion Europe was entirely to blame for the way things were now. She said the way Europe acted you would think we were made of money and Red Sam said it was no use talking about it, she was exactly right. The children ran outside into the white sunlight and looked at the monkey in the lacy chinaberry tree. He was busy catching fleas on himself and biting each one carefully between his teeth as if it were a delicacy.

They drove off again into the hot afternoon. The grandmother took   45 cat naps and woke up every few minutes with her own snoring. Outside of Toombsboro she woke up and recalled an old plantation that she had visited in this neighborhood once when she was a young lady. She said the house had six white columns across the front and that there was an avenue of oaks leading up to it and two little wooden trellis arbors on either side in front where you sat down with your suitor after a stroll in the garden. She recalled exactly which road to turn off to get to it. She knew that Bailey would not be willing to lose any time looking at an old house, but the more she talked about it, the more she wanted to see it once again and find out if the little twin arbors were still standing. "There was a secret panel in this house," she said craftily, not telling the truth but wishing that she were, "and the story went that all the family silver was hidden in it when Sherman came through but it was never found . . . ."

"Hey!" John Wesley said. "Let's go see it! We'll find it! We'll poke all the woodwork and find it! Who lives there? Where do you turn off at? Hey Pop, can't we turn off there?"

"We never have seen a house with a secret panel!" June Star shrieked.

"Let's go to the house with the secret panel! Hey Pop, can't we go see the house with the secret panel!"

"It's not far from here, I know," the grandmother said. "It won't take over twenty minutes."

Bailey was looking straight ahead. His jaw was as rigid as a horseshoe.   50
"No," he said.

The children began to yell and scream that they wanted to see the house with the secret panel. John Wesley kicked the back of the front seat and June Star hung over her mother's shoulder and whined desperately into her ear that they never had any fun even on their vacation, that they could never do what THEY wanted to do. The baby began to scream and John Wesley kicked the back of the seat so hard that his father could feel the blows in his kidney.

"All right!" he shouted and drew the car to a stop at the side of the road. "Will you all shut up? Will you all just shut up for one second? If you don't shut up, we won't go anywhere."

"It would be very educational for them," the grandmother murmured.

"All right," Bailey said, "but get this: this is the only time we're going   55
to stop for anything like this. This is the one and only time."

"The dirt road that you have to turn down is about a mile back," the grandmother directed. "I marked it when we passed."

"A dirt road," Bailey groaned.

After they had turned around and were headed toward the dirt road, the grandmother recalled other points about the house, the beautiful glass over the front doorway and the candle-lamp in the hall. John Wesley said that the secret panel was probably in the fireplace.

"You can't go inside this house," Bailey said. "You don't know who lives there."

"While you all talk to the people in front, I'll run around behind and   60
get in a window," John Wesley suggested.

"We'll all stay in the car," his mother said.

They turned onto the dirt road and the car raced roughly along in a swirl of pink dust. The grandmother recalled the times when there were no paved roads and thirty miles was a day's journey. The dirt road was hilly and there were sudden washes in it and sharp curves on dangerous embankments. All at once they would be on a hill, looking down over the blue tops of trees for miles around, then the next minute, they would be in a red depression with the dust-coated trees looking down on them.

"This place had better turn up in a minute," Bailey said, "or I'm going to turn around."

The road looked as if no one had traveled on it for months.

"It's not much farther," the grandmother said and just as she said it,   65
a horrible thought came to her. The thought was so embarrassing that she turned red in the face and her eyes dilated and her feet jumped up, upsetting her valise in the corner. The instant the valise moved, the newspaper top she had over the basket under it rose with a snarl and Pitty Sing, the cat, sprang onto Bailey's shoulder.

The children were thrown to the floor and their mother, clutching the baby, was thrown out the door onto the ground; the old lady was thrown into the front seat. The car turned over once and landed right-side-up in a gulch off the side of the road. Bailey remained in the driver's seat with the cat—graystriped with a broad white face and an orange nose—clinging to his neck like a caterpillar.

As soon as the children saw they could move their arms and legs, they scrambled out of the car, shouting, "We've had an ACCIDENT!" The grandmother was curled up under the dashboard, hoping she was injured so that Bailey's wrath would not come down on her all at once. The horrible thought she had before the accident was that the house she had remembered so vividly was not in Georgia but in Tennessee.

Bailey removed the cat from his neck with both hands and flung it out the window against the side of a pine tree. Then he got out of the car and started looking for the children's mother. She was sitting against the side of the red gutted ditch, holding the screaming baby, but she only had a cut down her face and a broken shoulder. "We've had an ACCIDENT!" the children screamed in a frenzy of delight.

"But nobody's killed," June Star said with disappointment as the grandmother limped out of the car, her hat still pinned to her head but the broken front brim standing up at a jaunty angle and the violet spray hanging off the side. They all sat down in the ditch, except the children, to recover from the shock. They were all shaking.

"Maybe a car will come along," said the children's mother hoarsely.   70

"I believe I have injured an organ," said the grandmother, pressing her side, but no one answered her. Bailey's teeth were clattering. He had on a yellow sport shirt with bright blue parrots designed in it and his face was as yellow as the shirt. The grandmother decided that she would not mention that the house was in Tennessee.

The road was about ten feet above and they could see only the tops of the trees on the other side of it. Behind the ditch they were sitting in there were more woods, tall and dark and deep. In a few minutes they saw a car some distance away on top of a hill, coming slowly as if the occupants were watching them. The grandmother stood up and waved both arms dramatically to attract their attention. The car continued to come on slowly, disappeared around a bend and appeared again, moving even slower, on top of the hill they had gone over. It was a big black battered hearse-like automobile. There were three men in it.

It came to a stop just over them and for some minutes, the driver looked down with a steady expressionless gaze to where they were sitting, and didn't speak. Then he turned his head and muttered something to the other two and they got out. One was a fat boy in black trousers and a red sweat shirt with a silver stallion embossed on the front of it. He moved around on the right side of them and stood staring, his mouth partly open in a kind of loose grin. The other had on khaki pants and a blue striped coat and a gray hat pulled down very low, hiding most of his face. He came around slowly on the left side. Neither spoke.

The driver got out of the car and stood by the side of it, looking down at them. He was an older man than the other two. His hair was just beginning to gray and he wore silver-rimmed spectacles that gave him a scholarly look. He had a long creased face and didn't have on any shirt or undershirt. He had on blue jeans that were too tight for him and was holding a black hat and a gun. The two boys also had guns.

"We've had an ACCIDENT!" the children screamed.   75

The grandmother had the peculiar feeling that the bespectacled man was someone she knew. His face was as familiar to her as if she had known him all her life but she could not recall who he was. He moved away from the car and began to come down the embankment, placing his feet carefully so that he wouldn't slip. He had on tan and white shoes and no socks, and his ankles were red and thin. "Good afternoon," he said. "I see you all had you a little spill."

"We turned over twice!" said the grandmother.

"Oncet," he corrected. "We seen it happen. Try their car and see will it run, Hiram," he said quietly to the boy with the gray hat.

"What you got that gun for?" John Wesley asked. "Whatcha gonna do with that gun?"

"Lady," the man said to the children's mother, "would you mind   80 calling them children to sit down by you? Children make me nervous. I want all you all to sit down right together there where you're at."

"What are you telling US what to do for?" June Star asked,

Behind them the line of woods gaped like a dark open mouth. "Come here," said their mother.

"Look here now," Bailey said suddenly, "we're in a predicament! We're in . . . ."

The grandmother shrieked. She scrambled to her feet and stood staring. "You're The Misfit!" she said. "I recognized you at once!"

"Yes'm," the man said, smiling slightly as if he were pleased in spite   85 of himself to be known, "but it would have been better for all of you, lady, if you hadn't of reckernized me."

Bailey turned his head sharply and said something to his mother that shocked even the children. The old lady began to cry and The Misfit reddened.

"Lady," he said, "don't you get upset. Sometimes a man says things he don't mean. I don't reckon he meant to talk to you thataway."

"You wouldn't shoot a lady, would you?" the grandmother said and removed a clean handkerchief from her cuff and began to slap at her eyes with it.

The Misfit pointed the toe of his shoe into the ground and made a little hole and then covered it up again. "I would hate to have to," he said.

"Listen," the grandmother almost screamed, "I know you're a good   90 man. You don't look a bit like you have common blood. I know you must come from nice people!"

"Yes mam," he said, "finest people in the world." When he smiled he showed a row of strong white teeth. "God never made a finer woman than my mother and my daddy's heart was pure gold," he said. The boy with the red sweat shirt had come around behind them and was standing with his gun at his hip. The Misfit squatted down on the ground. "Watch them children, Bobby Lee," he said. "You know they make me nervous." He looked at the six of them huddled together in front of him and he seemed to be embarrassed as if he couldn't think of anything to say. "Ain't a cloud in the sky," he remarked, looking up at it. "Don't see no sun but don't see no cloud neither."

"Yes, it's a beautiful day," said the grandmother. "Listen," she said, "you shouldn't call yourself The Misfit because I know you're a good man at heart. I can just look at you and tell."

"Hush!" Bailey yelled. "Hush! Everybody shut up and let me handle this!" He was squatting in the position of a runner about to sprint forward but he didn't move.

"I pre-chate that, lady," The Misfit said and drew a little circle in the ground with the butt of his gun.

"It'll take a half a hour to fix this here car," Hiram called, looking   95
over the raised hood of it.

"Well, first you and Bobby Lee get him and that little boy to step over yonder with you," The Misfit said, pointing to Bailey and John Wesley. "The boys want to ast you something," he said to Bailey. "Would you mind stepping back in them woods there with them?"

"Listen," Bailey began, "we're in a terrible predicament! Nobody realizes what this is," and his voice cracked. His eyes were as blue and intense as the parrots in his shirt and he remained perfectly still.

The grandmother reached up to adjust her hat brim as if she were going to the woods with him but it came off in her hand. She stood staring at it and after a second she let it fall to the ground. Hiram pulled Bailey up by the arm as if he were assisting an old man. John Wesley caught hold of his father's hand and Bobby Lee followed. They went off toward the woods and just as they reached the dark edge, Bailey turned and supporting himself against a gray naked pine trunk, he shouted, "I'll be back in a minute, Mamma, wait on me!"

"Come back this instant!" his mother shrilled but they all disappeared into the woods.

"Bailey Boy!" the grandmother called in a tragic voice but she found   100
she was looking at The Misfit squatting on the ground in front of her. "I just know you're a good man," she said desperately. "You're not a bit common!"

"Nome, I ain't a good man," The Misfit said after a second as if he had considered her statement carefully, "but I ain't the worst in the world neither. My daddy said I was a different breed of dog from my brothers and sisters. 'You know,' Daddy said, 'it's some that can live their whole life out without asking about it and it's others has to know why it is, and this boy is one of the latters. He's going to be into everything!'" He put on his black hat and looked up suddenly and then away deep into the woods as if he were embarrassed again.

"I'm sorry I don't have on a shirt before you ladies," he said, hunching his shoulders slightly. "We buried our clothes that we had on when we escaped and we're just making do until we can get better. We borrowed these from some folks we met," he explained.

"That's perfectly all right," the grandmother said. "Maybe Bailey has an extra shirt in his suitcase."

"I'll look and see terrectly," The Misfit said.

"Where are they taking him?" the children's mother screamed.

"Daddy was a card himself," The Misfit said. "You couldn't put any- 105 thing over on him. He never got in trouble with the Authorities though. Just had the knack of handling them."

"You could be honest too if you'd only try," said the grandmother. "Think how wonderful it would be to settle down and live a comfortable life and not have to think about somebody chasing you all the time."

The Misfit kept scratching in the ground with the butt of his gun as if he were thinking about it. "Yes'm, somebody is always after you," he murmured.

The grandmother noticed how thin his shoulder blades were just behind his hat because she was standing up looking down on him. "Do you ever pray?" she asked.

He shook his head. All she saw was the black hat wiggle between his shoulder blades. "Nome," he said.

There was a pistol shot from the woods, followed closely by another. Then 110 silence. The old lady's head jerked around. She could hear the wind move through the tree tops like a long satisfied insuck of breath. "Bailey Boy!" she called.

"I was a gospel singer for a while," The Misfit said. "I been most everything. Been in the arm service, both land and sea, at home and abroad, been twict married, been an undertaker, been with the railroads, plowed Mother Earth, been in a tornado, seen a man burnt alive oncet," and he looked up at the children's mother and the little girl who were sitting close together, their faces white and their eyes glassy; "I even seen a woman flogged," he said.

"Pray, pray," the grandmother began, "pray, pray . . . ."

"I never was a bad boy that I remember of," The Misfit said in an almost dreamy voice, "but somewheres along the line I done something wrong and got sent to the penitentiary. I was buried alive," and he looked up and held her attention to him by a steady stare.

"That's when you should have started to pray," she said. "What did you do to get sent to the penitentiary that first time?"

"Turn to the right, it was a wall," The Misfit said, looking up again at 115 the cloudless sky. "Turn to the left, it was a wall. Look up it was a ceiling, look down it was a floor. I forget what I done, lady. I set there and set there, trying to remember what it was I done and I ain't recalled it to this day. Oncet in a while, I would think it was coming to me, but it never come."

"Maybe they put you in by mistake," the old lady said vaguely.

"Nome," he said. "It wasn't no mistake. They had the papers on me."

"You must have stolen something," she said.

The Misfit sneered slightly. "Nobody had nothing I wanted," he said. "It was a head-doctor at the penitentiary said what I had done was kill my daddy but I known that for a lie. My daddy died in nineteen ought nineteen of the epidemic flu and I never had a thing to do with it. He was buried in the Mount Hopewell Baptist churchyard and you can see for yourself."

"If you would pray," the old lady said, "Jesus would help you."   120

"That's right," The Misfit said.

"Well then, why don't you pray?" she asked trembling with delight suddenly.

"I don't want no hep," he said. "I'm doing all right by myself."

Bobby Lee and Hiram came ambling back from the woods. Bobby Lee was dragging a yellow shirt with bright blue parrots in it.

"Throw me that shirt, Bobby Lee," The Misfit said. The shirt came fly-   125
ing at him and landed on his shoulder and he put it on. The grandmother couldn't name what the shirt reminded her of. "No, lady," The Misfit said while he was buttoning it up, "I found out the crime don't matter. You can do one thing or you can do another, kill a man or take a tire off his car, because sooner or later you're going to forget what it was you done and just be punished for it."

The children's mother had begun to make heaving noises as if she couldn't get her breath. "Lady," he asked, "would you and that little girl like to step off yonder with Bobby Lee and Hiram and join your husband?"

"Yes, thank you," the mother said faintly. Her left arm dangled help-lessly and she was holding the baby, who had gone to sleep, in the other.

"Hep that lady up, Hiram," The Misfit said as she struggled to climb out of the ditch, "and Bobby Lee, you hold onto that little girl's hand."

"I don't want to hold hands with him," June Star said. "He reminds me of a pig."

The fat boy blushed and laughed and caught her by the arm and   130
pulled her off into the woods after Hiram and her mother.

Alone with The Misfit, the grandmother found that she had lost her voice. There was not a cloud in the sky nor any sun. There was nothing around her but woods. She wanted to tell him that he must pray. She opened and closed her mouth several times before anything came out. Finally she found herself saying, "Jesus, Jesus," meaning Jesus will help you, but the way she was saying it, it sounded as if she might he cursing.

"Yes'm," The Misfit said as if he agreed. "Jesus thown everything off bal-ance. It was the same case with Him as with me except He hadn't committed any crime and they could prove I had committed one because they had the papers on me. Of course," he said, "they never shown me my papers. That's why I sign myself now. I said long ago, you get your signature and sign everything you do and keep a copy of it. Then you'll know what you done and you can hold up the crime to the punishment and see do they match and in the end you'll have something to prove you ain't been treated right. I call myself The Misfit," he said, "because I can't make what all I done wrong fit what all I gone through in punishment."

There was a piercing scream from the woods, followed closely by a pis- tol report. "Does it seem right to you, lady, that one is punished a heap and another ain't punished at all?"

"Jesus!" the old lady cried. "You've got good blood! I know you wouldn't shoot a lady! I know you come from nice people! Pray! Jesus, you ought not to shoot a lady. I'll give you all the money I've got!"

"Lady," The Misfit said, looking beyond her far into the woods, "there   135 never was a body that give the undertaker a tip."

There were two more pistol reports and the grandmother raised her head like a parched old turkey hen crying for water and called, "Bailey Boy, Bailey Boy!" as if her heart would break.

"Jesus was the only One that ever raised the dead," The Misfit continued, "and He shouldn't have done it. He thown everything off balance. If He did what He said, then it's nothing for you to do but thow away everything and follow Him, and if He didn't, then it's nothing for you to do but enjoy the few minutes you got left the best way you can—by killing somebody or burning down his house or doing some other meanness to him. No pleasure but meanness," he said and his voice had become almost a snarl.

"Maybe He didn't raise the dead," the old lady mumbled, not knowing what she was saying and feeling so dizzy that she sank down in the ditch with her legs twisted under her.

"I wasn't there so I can't say He didn't," The Misfit said. "I wisht I had of been there," he said, hitting the ground with his fist. "It ain't right I wasn't there because if I had of been there I would of known. Listen lady," he said in a high voice, "if I had of been there I would of known and I wouldn't be like I am now." His voice seemed about to crack and the grandmother's head cleared for an instant. She saw the man's face twisted close to her own as if he were going to cry and she murmured, "Why you're one of my babies. You're one of my own children!" She reached out and touched him on the shoulder. The Misfit sprang back as if a snake had bitten him and shot her three times through the chest. Then he put his gun down on the ground and took off his glasses and began to clean them.

Hiram and Bobby Lee returned from the woods and stood over the   140 ditch, looking down at the grandmother who half sat and half lay in a puddle of blood with her legs crossed under her like a child's and her face smiling up at the cloudless sky.

Without his glasses, The Misfit's eyes were red-rimmed and pale and defenseless-looking. "Take her off and thow her where you thown the others," he said, picking up the cat that was rubbing itself against his leg.

"She was a talker, wasn't she?" Bobby Lee said, sliding down the ditch with a yodel.

"She would of been a good woman," The Misfit said, "if it had been somebody there to shoot her every minute of her life."

"Some fun!" Bobby Lee said.

"Shut up, Bobby Lee," The Misfit said. "It's no real pleasure in life."   145

- Identify details that seem to be irrelevant to the story. What purpose do they serve in the narrative?
- Identify places later in the story where specific earlier details gain a new meaning.
- Whose point of view do we get throughout this story?
- In what ways does O'Connor make each character unsympathetic?
- How do the various characters relate to one another?
- How does the assertion "She would of been a good woman" help us identify a theme in this story?

Joyce Carol Oates (1938–   )

Joyce Carol Oates was born in Lockport, New York, in 1938. She began writing as a child, and submitted a novel to a publisher when she was only fifteen. She earned her BA from Syracuse University and her MA from the University of Wisconsin, then embarked on a career as a writer. Although she is best known for her fiction, Oates has also written essays, plays, and poetry, and she has dealt with a wide variety of subjects, from race relations to boxing. She has been a prolific writer, producing an average of two books per year, and a respected one, winning the National Book Award and several O. Henry Awards.

Where Are You Going, Where Have You Been? (1970)

For Bob Dylan

Her name was Connie. She was fifteen and she had a quick nervous giggling habit of craning her neck to glance into mirrors, or checking other people's faces to make sure her own was all right. Her mother, who noticed everything and knew everything and who hadn't much reason any longer to look at her own face, always scolded Connie about it. "Stop gawking at yourself, who are you? You think you're so pretty?" she would say. Connie would raise her eyebrows at these familiar complaints and look right through her mother, into a shadowy vision of herself as she was right at that moment: she knew she was pretty and that was everything. Her mother had been pretty once too, if you could believe those old snapshots in the album, but now her looks were gone and that was why she was always after Connie.

"Why don't you keep your room clean like your sister? How've you got your hair fixed—what the hell stinks? Hair spray? You don't see your sister using that junk."

Her sister June was twenty-four and still lived at home. She was a secretary in the high school Connie attended, and if that wasn't bad enough—with her in the same building—she was so plain and chunky and steady that Connie had to hear her praised all the time by her mother and her mother's sisters. June did this, June did that, she saved money and helped clean the house and cooked and Connie couldn't do a thing, her mind was all filled with trashy daydreams. Their father was away at work most of the time and when he came home he wanted supper and he read the newspaper at supper and after supper he went to bed. He didn't bother talking much to them, but around his bent head Connie's mother kept picking at her until Connie wished her mother was dead and she herself was dead and it was all over. "She makes me want to throw up sometimes," she complained to her friends. She had a high, breathless, amused voice which made everything she said sound a little forced, whether it was sincere or not.

There was one good thing: June went places with girl friends of hers, girls who were just as plain and steady as she, and so when Connie wanted to do that her mother had no objections. The father of Connie's best girl friend drove the girls the three miles to town and left them off at a shopping plaza, so that they could walk through the stores or go to a movie, and when he came to pick them up again at eleven he never bothered to ask what they had done.

They must have been familiar sights, walking around that shopping   5
plaza in their shorts and flat ballerina slippers that always scuffed the sidewalk, with charm bracelets jingling on their thin wrists; they would lean together to whisper and laugh secretly if someone passed by who amused or interested them. Connie had long dark blond hair that drew anyone's eye to it, and she wore part of it pulled up on her head and puffed out and the rest of it she let fall down her back. She wore a pull-over jersey blouse that looked one way when she was at home and another way when she was away from home. Everything about her had two sides to it, one for home and one for anywhere that was not home: her walk that could be childlike and bobbing, or languid enough to make anyone think she was hearing music in her head, her mouth which was pale and smirking most of the

time, but bright and pink on these evenings out, her laugh which was cynical and drawling at home—"Ha, ha, very funny"—but high-pitched and nervous anywhere else like the jingling of the charms on her bracelet.

Sometimes they did go shopping or to a movie, but sometimes they went across the highway, ducking fast across the busy road, to a drive-in restaurant where older kids hung out. The restaurant was shaped like a big bottle, though squatter than a real bottle, and on its cap was a revolving figure of a grinning boy who held a hamburger aloft. One night in midsummer they ran across, breathless with daring, and right away someone leaned out a car window and invited them over, but it was just a boy from high school they didn't like. It made them feel good to be able to ignore him. They went up through the maze of parked and cruising cars to the bright-lit, fly-infested restaurant, their faces pleased and expectant as if they were entering a sacred building that loomed out of the night to give them what haven and what blessing they yearned for. They sat at the counter and crossed their legs at the ankles, their thin shoulders rigid with excitement, and listened to the music that made everything so good: the music was always in the background like music at a church service, it was something to depend upon.

A boy named Eddie came in to talk with them. He sat backwards on his stool, turning himself jerkily around in semi-circles and then stopping and turning again, and after a while he asked Connie if she would like something to eat. She said she did and so she tapped her friend's arm on her way out—her friend pulled her face up into a brave droll look—and Connie said she would meet her at eleven, across the way. "I just hate to leave her like that," Connie said earnestly, but the boy said that she wouldn't be alone for long. So they went out to his car and on the way Connie couldn't help but let her eyes wander over the windshields and faces all around her, her face gleaming with a joy that had nothing to do with Eddie or even this place; it might have been the music. She drew her shoulders up and sucked in her breath with the pure pleasure of being alive, and just at that moment she happened to glance at a face just a few feet from hers. It was a boy with shaggy black hair, in a convertible jalopy painted gold. He stared at her and then his lips widened into a grin. Connie slit her eyes at him and turned away, but she couldn't help glancing back and there he was still watching her. He wagged a finger and laughed and said, "Gonna get you, baby," and Connie turned away again without Eddie noticing anything.

She spent three hours with him, at the restaurant where they ate hamburgers and drank Cokes in wax cups that were always sweating, and then down an alley a mile or so away, and when he left her off at five to eleven only the movie house was still open at the plaza. Her girl friend was there, talking with a boy. When Connie came up the two girls smiled at each other and Connie said, "How was the movie?" and the girl said, "You should know." They rode off

with the girl's father, sleepy and pleased, and Connie couldn't help but look
at the darkened shopping plaza with its big empty parking lot and its signs that
were faded and ghostly now, and over at the drive-in restaurant where cars were
still circling tirelessly. She couldn't hear the music at this distance.

Next morning June asked her how the movie was and Connie said, "So-so."

She and that girl and occasionally another girl went out several times a   10
week that way, and the rest of the time Connie spent around the house—it
was summer vacation—getting in her mother's way and thinking, dreaming, about the boys she met. But all the boys fell back and dissolved into a
single face that was not even a face, but an idea, a feeling, mixed up with
the urgent insistent pounding of the music and the humid night air of July.
Connie's mother kept dragging her back to the daylight by finding things
for her to do or saying, suddenly, "What's this about the Pettinger girl?"

And Connie would say nervously, "Oh, her. That dope." She always drew
thick clear lines between herself and such girls, and her mother was simple and
kindly enough to believe her. Her mother was so simple, Connie thought, that
it was maybe cruel to fool her so much. Her mother went scuffling around the
house in old bedroom slippers and complained over the telephone to one sister about the other, then the other called up and the two of them complained
about the third one. If June's name was mentioned her mother's tone was
approving, and if Connie's name was mentioned it was disapproving. This did
not really mean she disliked Connie and actually Connie thought that her
mother preferred her to June because she was prettier, but the two of them
kept up a pretense of exasperation, a sense that they were tugging and struggling over something of little value to either of them. Sometimes, over coffee,
they were almost friends, but something would come up—some vexation that
was like a fly buzzing suddenly around their heads—and their faces went hard
with contempt.

One Sunday Connie got up at eleven—none of them bothered with
church—and washed her hair so that it could dry all day long, in the sun. Her
parents and sister were going to a barbecue at an aunt's house and Connie said
no, she wasn't interested, rolling her eyes to let her mother know just what she
thought of it. "Stay home alone then," her mother said sharply. Connie sat out
back in a lawn chair and watched them drive away, her father quiet and bald,
hunched around so that he could back the car out, her mother with a look that
was still angry and not at all softened through the windshield, and in the back
seat poor old June all dressed up as if she didn't know what a barbecue was,
with all the running yelling kids and the flies. Connie sat with her eyes closed
in the sun, dreaming and dazed with the warmth about her as if this were a
kind of love, the caresses of love, and her mind slipped over onto thoughts of
the boy she had been with the night before and how nice he had been, how
sweet it always was, not the way someone like June would suppose but sweet,

gentle, the way it was in movies and promised in songs; and when she opened her eyes she hardly knew where she was, the back yard ran off into weeds and a fence-line of trees and behind it the sky was perfectly blue and still. The asbestos "ranch house" that was now three years old startled her—it looked small. She shook her head as if to get awake.

It was too hot. She went inside the house and turned on the radio to drown out the quiet. She sat on the edge of her bed, barefoot, and listened for an hour and a half to a program called XYZ Sunday Jamboree, record after record of hard, fast, shrieking songs she sang along with, interspersed by exclamations from "Bobby King": "An' look here you girls at Napoleon's—Son and Charley want you to pay real close attention to this song coming up!"

And Connie paid close attention herself, bathed in a glow of slowpulsed joy that seemed to rise mysteriously out of the music itself and lay languidly about the airless little room, breathed in and breathed out with each gentle rise and fall of her chest.

After a while she heard a car coming up the drive. She sat up at once,   15
startled because it couldn't be her father so soon. The gravel kept crunching all the way in from the road—the driveway was long—and Connie ran to the window. It was a car she didn't know. It was an open jalopy, painted a bright gold that caught the sunlight opaquely. Her heart began to pound and her fingers snatched at her hair, checking it, and she whispered "Christ. Christ," wondering how bad she looked. The car came to a stop at the side door and the horn sounded four short taps as if this were a signal Connie knew.

She went into the kitchen and approached the door slowly, then hung out the screen door, her bare toes curling down off the step. There were two boys in the car and now she recognized the driver: he had shaggy, shabby black hair that looked crazy as a wig and he was grinning at her.

"I ain't late, am I?" he said.

"Who the hell do you think you are?" Connie said.

"Toldja I'd be out, didn't I?"

"I don't even know who you are."   20

She spoke sullenly, careful to show no interest or pleasure, and he spoke in a fast, bright monotone. Connie looked past him to the other boy, taking her time. He had fair brown hair, with a lock that fell onto his forehead. His sideburns gave him a fierce, embarrassed look, but so far he hadn't even bothered to glance at her. Both boys wore sunglasses. The driver's glasses were metallic and mirrored everything in miniature.

"You wanta come for a ride?" he said.

Connie smirked and let her hair fall loose over one shoulder.

"Don'tcha like my car? New paint job," he said. "Hey."

"What?"   25

"You're cute."

She pretended to fidget, chasing flies away from the door.

"Don'tcha believe me, or what?" he said.

"Look, I don't even know who you are," Connie said in disgust.

"Hey, Ellie's got a radio, see. Mine's broke down." He lifted his friend's   30
arm and showed her the little transistor the boy was holding, and now
Connie began to hear the music. It was the same program that was playing
inside the house.

"Bobby King?" she said.

"I listen to him all the time. I think he's great."

"He's kind of great," Connie said reluctantly.

"Listen, that guy's great. He knows where the action is."

Connie blushed a little, because the glasses made it impossible for her to   35
see just what this boy was looking at. She couldn't decide if she liked him or
if he was just a jerk, and so she dawdled in the doorway and wouldn't come
down or go back inside. She said, "What's all that stuff painted on your car?"

"Can'tcha read it?" He opened the door very carefully, as if he was afraid
it might fall off. He slid out just as carefully, planting his feet firmly on the
ground, the tiny metallic world in his glasses slowing down like gelatine hardening and in the midst of it Connie's bright green blouse. "This here is my name,
to begin with," he said. ARNOLD FRIEND was written in tarlike black letters
on the side, with a drawing of a round grinning face that reminded Connie of
a pumpkin, execpt it wore sunglasses. "I wanta introduce myself, I'm Arnold
Friend and that's my real name and I'm gonna be your friend, honey, and inside
the car's Ellie Oscar, he's kinda shy." Ellie brought his transistor radio up to his
shoulder and balanced it there. "Now these numbers are a secret code, honey,"
Arnold Friend explained. He read off the numbers 33, 19, 17 and raised his
eyebrows at her to see what she thought of that, but she didn't think much of it.
The left rear fender had been smashed and around it was written, on the gleaming gold background, DONE BY CRAZY WOMAN DRIVER. Connie had to
laugh at that. Arnold Friend was pleased at her laughter and looked up at her.
"Around the other side's a lot more—you wanta come and see them?"

"No."

"Why not?"

"Why should I?"

"Don'tcha wanta see what's on the car? Don'tcha wanta go for a ride?"   40

"I don't know."

"Why not?"

"I got things to do."

"Like what?"

"Things."   45

He laughed as if she had said something funny. He slapped his thighs. He
was standing in a strange way, leaning back against the car as if he were balancing himself. He wasn't tall, only an inch or so taller than she would be if she

came down to him. Connie liked the way he was dressed, which was the way all of them dressed: tight faded jeans stuffed into black, scuffed boots, a belt that pulled his waist in and showed how lean he was, and a white pull-over shirt that was a little soiled and showed the hard small muscles of his arms and shoulders. He looked as if he probably did hard work, lifting and carrying things. Even his neck looked muscular. And his face was a familiar face, some-how: the jaw and chin and cheeks slightly darkened, because he hadn't shaved for a day or two, and the nose long and hawk-like, sniffing as if she were a treat he was going to gobble up and it was all a joke.

"Connie, you ain't telling the truth. This is your day set aside for a ride with me and you know it," he said, still laughing. The way he straightened and recovered from his fit of laughing showed that it had been all fake.

"How do you know what my name is?" she said suspiciously.

"It's Connie."

"Maybe and maybe not." 50

"I know my Connie," he said, wagging his finger. Now she remembered him even better, back at the restaurant, and her cheeks warmed at the thought of how she sucked in her breath just at the moment she passed him—how she must have looked to him. And he had remembered her. "Ellie and I come out here especially for you," he said. "Ellie can sit in back. How about it?"

"Where?"

"Where what?"

"Where're we going?"

He looked at her. He took off the sunglasses and she saw how pale the 55 skin around his eyes was, like holes that were not in shadow but instead in light. His eyes were chips of broken glass that catch the light in an amiable way. He smiled. It was as if the idea of going for a ride somewhere, to some place, was a new idea to him.

"Just for a ride, Connie sweetheart."

"I never said my name was Connie," she said.

"But I know what it is. I know your name and all about you, lots of things," Arnold Friend said. He had not moved yet but stood still leaning back against the side of his jalopy. "I took a special interest in you, such a pretty girl, and found out all about you like I know your parents and sister are gone some-wheres and I know where and how long they're going to be gone, and I know who you were with last night, and your best girl friend's name is Betty. Right?"

He spoke in a simple lilting voice, exactly as if he were reciting the words to a song. His smile assured her that everything was fine. In the car Ellie turned up the volume on his radio and did not bother to look around at them.

"Ellie can sit in the back seat," Arnold Friend said. He indicated his 60 friend with a casual jerk of his chin, as if Ellie did not count and she should not bother with him.

"How'd you find out all that stuff?" Connie said.

"Listen: Betty Schultz and Tony Fitch and Jimmy Pettinger and Nancy Pettinger," he said, in a chant. "Raymond Stanley and Bob Hutter—"

"Do you know all those kids?"

"I know everybody."

"Look, you're kidding. You're not from around here." 65

"Sure."

"But—how come we never saw you before?"

"Sure you saw me before," he said. He looked down at his boots, as if he were a little offended. "You just don't remember."

"I guess I'd remember you," Connie said.

"Yeah?" He looked up at this, beaming. He was pleased. He began 70 to mark time with the music from Ellie's radio, tapping his fists lightly together. Connie looked away from his smile to the car, which was painted so bright it almost hurt her eyes to look at it. She looked at that name, ARNOLD FRIEND. And up at the front fender was an expression that was familiar—MAN THE FLYING SAUCERS. It was an expression kids had used the year before, but didn't use this year. She looked at it for a while as if the words meant something to her that she did not yet know.

"What're you thinking about? Huh?" Arnold Friend demanded. "Not worried about your hair blowing around in the car, are you?"

"No."

"Think I maybe can't drive good?"

"How do I know?"

"You're a hard girl to handle. How come?" he said. "Don't you know 75 I'm your friend? Didn't you see me put my sign in the air when you walked by?"

"What sign?"

"My sign." And he drew an X in the air, leaning out toward her. They were maybe ten feet apart. After his hand fell back to his side the X was still in the air, almost visible. Connie let the screen door close and stood perfectly still inside it, listening to the music from her radio and the boy's blend together. She stared at Arnold Friend. He stood there so stiffly relaxed, pretending to be relaxed, with one hand idly on the door handle as if he were keeping himself up that way and had no intention of ever moving again. She recognized most things about him, the tight jeans that showed his thighs and buttocks and the greasy leather boots and the tight shirt, and even that slippery friendly smile of his, that sleepy dreamy smile that all the boys used to get across ideas they didn't want to put into words. She recognized all this and also the singsong way he talked, slightly mocking, kidding, but serious and a little melancholy, and she recognized the way he tapped one fist against the other in homage to the perpetual music behind him. But all these things did not come together.

She said suddenly, "Hey, how old are you?"

His smile faded. She could see then that he wasn't a kid, he was much older—thirty, maybe more. At this knowledge her heart began to pound faster.

"That's a crazy thing to ask, Can'tcha see I'm your own age?"   80

"Like hell you are."

"Or maybe a coupla years older, I'm eighteen."

"Eighteen?" she said doubtfully.

He grinned to reassure her and lines appeared at the corners of his mouth. His teeth were big and white. He grinned so broadly his eyes became slits and she saw how thick the lashes were, thick and black as if painted with a black tarlike material. Then he seemed to become embarrassed, abruptly, and looked over his shoulder at Ellie. "Him, he's crazy," he said. "Ain't he a riot, he's a nut, a real character." Ellie was still listening to the music. His sunglasses told nothing about what he was thinking. He wore a bright orange shirt unbuttoned halfway to show his chest, which was a pale, bluish chest and not muscular like Arnold Friend's. His shirt collar was turned up all around and the very tips of the collar pointed out past his chin as if they were protecting him. He was pressing the transistor radio up against his ear and sat there in a kind of daze, right in the sun.

"He's kinda strange," Connie said.   85

"Hey, she says you're kinda strange! Kinda strange!" Arnold Friend cried. He pounded on the car to get Ellie's attention. Ellie turned for the first time and Connie saw with shock that he wasn't a kid either—he had a fair, hairless face, cheeks reddened slightly as if the veins grew too close to the surface of his skin, the face of a forty-year-old baby. Connie felt a wave of dizziness rise in her at this sight and she stared at him as if waiting for something to change the shock of the moment, make it all right again. Ellie's lips kept shaping words, mumbling along with the words blasting in his ear.

"Maybe you two better go away," Connie said faintly.

"What? How come?" Arnold Friend cried. "We come out here to take you for a ride. It's Sunday." He had the voice of the man on the radio now. It was same voice, Connie thought. "Don'tcha know it's Sunday all day and honey, no matter who you were with last night today you're with Arnold Friend and don't you forget it!—Maybe you better step out here," he said, and this last was in a different voice. It was a little flatter, as if the heat was finally getting to him.

"No. I got things to do."

"Hey."   90

"You two better leave."

"We ain't leaving until you come with us."

"Like hell I am—"

"Connie, don't fool around with me. I mean, I mean, don't fool *around*," he said, shaking his head. He laughed incredulously. He placed his sunglasses on top of his head, carefully, as if he were indeed wearing a wig, and brought the stems down behind his ears. Connie stared at him, another wave of dizziness and fear rising in her so that for a moment he wasn't even in focus but was just a blur, standing there against his gold car, and she had the idea that he had driven up the driveway all right but had come from nowhere before that and belonged nowhere and that everything about him and even about the music that was so familiar to her was only half real.

"If my father comes and sees you—" 95

"He ain't coming. He's at a barbecue."

"How do you know that?"

"Aunt Tillie's. Right now they're—uh—they're drinking. Sitting around," he said vaguely, squinting as if he were staring all the way to town and over to Aunt Tillie's backyard. Then the vision seemed to get clear and he nodded energetically. "Yeah. Sitting around. There's your sister in a blue dress, huh? And high heels, the poor sad bitch—nothing like you sweetheart! And your mother's helping some fat woman with the corn, they're cleaning the corn—husking the corn—"

"What fat woman?" Connie cried. "How do I know what fat woman. I 100 don't know every goddam fat woman in the world!" Arnold Friend laughed.

"Oh, that's Mrs. Hornby.... Who invited her?" Connie said. She felt a little light-headed. Her breath was coming quickly.

"She's too fat. I don't like them fat. I like them the way you are, honey," he said, smiling sleepily at her. They stared at each other for a while, through the screen door. He said softly, "Now what you're going to do is this: you're going to come out that door. You're going to sit up front with me and Ellie's going to sit in the back, the hell with Ellie, right? This isn't Ellie's date. You're my date. I'm your lover, honey."

"What? You're crazy—"

"Yes, I'm your lover. You don't know what that is but you will," he said. "I know that too. I know all about you. But look: it's real nice and you couldn't ask for nobody better than me, or more polite. I always keep my word. I'll tell you how it is, I'm always nice at first, the first time. I'll hold you so tight you won't think you have to try to get away or pretend anything because you'll know you can't. And I'll come inside you where it's all secret and you'll give in to me and you'll love me—"

"Shut up! You're crazy!" Connie said. She backed away from the door. 105 She put her hands against her ears as if she'd heard something terrible, something not meant for her. "People don't talk like that, you're crazy," she muttered. Her heart was almost too big now for her chest and its pumping made sweat break out all over her. She looked out to see Arnold Friend pause and then take a step toward the porch lurching. He almost fell. But, like a clever drunken man, he managed to catch his balance. He wobbled in his high boots and grabbed hold of one of the porch posts.

"Honey?" he said. "You still listening?"

"Get the hell out of here!"

"Be nice, honey. Listen."

"I'm going to call the police—"

He wobbled again and out of the side of his mouth came a fast spat   110
curse, an aside not meant for her to hear. But even this "Christ!" sounded
forced. Then he began to smile again. She watched this smile come, awkward as if he were smiling from inside a mask. His whole face was a mask,
she thought wildly, tanned down onto his throat but then running out as
if he had plastered makeup on his face but had forgotten about his throat.

"Honey—? Listen, here's how it is. I always tell the truth and I promise you
this: I ain't coming in that house after you."

"You better not! I'm going to call the police if you—if you don't—"

"Honey," he said, talking right through her voice, "honey, I'm not coming
in there but you are coming out here. You know why?"

She was panting. The kitchen looked like a place she had never seen
before, some room she had run inside but which wasn't good enough, wasn't
going to help her. The kitchen window had never had a curtain, after three
years, and there were dishes in the sink for her to do—probably—and if you ran
your hand across the table you'd probably feel something sticky there.

"You listening, honey? Hey?"   115

"—going to call the police—"

"Soon as you touch the phone I don't need to keep my promise and can
come inside. You won't want that."

She rushed forward and tried to lock the door. Her fingers were shaking. "But why lock it," Arnold Friend said gently, talking right into her face.
"It's just a screen door. It's just nothing." One of his boots was at a strange
angle, as if his foot wasn't in it. It pointed out to the left, bent at the ankle. "I
mean, anybody can break through a screen door and glass and wood and iron
or anything else if he needs to, anybody at all and specially Arnold Friend. If
the place got lit up with a fire honey you'd come running out into my arms,
right into my arms and safe at home—like you knew I was your lover and'd
stopped fooling around. I don't mind a nice shy girl but I don't like no fooling
around." Part of those words were spoken with a slight rhythmic lilt, and Connie somehow recognized them—the echo of a song from last year, about a girl
rushing into her boy friend's arms and coming home again—

Connie stood barefoot on the linoleum floor, staring at him. "What do
you want?" she whispered.

"I want you," he said.   120

"What?"

"Seen you that night and thought, that's the one, yes sir. I never needed to
look any more."

"But my father's coming back. He's coming to get me. I had to wash my hair first—" She spoke in a dry, rapid voice, hardly raising it for him to hear. "No, your daddy is not coming and yes, you had to wash your hair and you washed it for me. It's nice and shining and all for me, I thank you, sweetheart," he said with a mock bow, but again he almost lost his balance. He had to bend and adjust his boots. Evidently his feet did not go all the way down; the boots must have been stuffed with something so that he would seem taller. Connie stared out at him and behind him Ellie in the car, who seemed to be looking off toward Connie's right, into nothing. This Ellie said, pulling the words out of the air one after another as if he were just discovering them, "You want me to pull out the phone?"

"Shut your mouth and keep it shut," Arnold Friend said, his face red   125
from bending over or maybe from embarrassment because Connie had seen his boots. "This ain't none of your business."

"What—what are you doing? What do you want?" Connie said. "If I call the police they'll get you, they'll arrest you—"

"Promise was not to come in unless you touch that phone, and I'll keep that promise," he said. He resumed his erect position and tried to force his shoulders back. He sounded like a hero in a movie, declaring something important. He spoke too loudly and it was as if he were speaking to someone behind Connie. "I ain't made plans for coming in that house where I don't belong but just for you to come out to me, the way you should. Don't you know who I am?"

"You're crazy," she whispered. She backed away from the door but did not want to go into another part of the house, as if this would give him permission to come through the door. "What do you....You're crazy, you...."

"Huh? What're you saying, honey?"

Her eyes darted everywhere in the kitchen. She could not remember   130
what it was, this room.

"This is how it is, honey: you come out and we'll drive away, have a nice ride. But if you don't come out we're gonna wait till your people come home and then they're all going to get it."

"You want that telephone pulled out?" Ellie said. He held the radio away from his ear and grimaced, as if without the radio the air was too much for him.

"I toldja shut up, Ellie," Arnold Friend said, "you're deaf, get a hearing aid, right? Fix yourself up. This little girl's no trouble and's gonna be nice to me, so Ellie keep to yourself, this ain't your date—right? Don't hem in on me. Don't hog. Don't crush. Don't bird dog. Don't trail me," he said in a rapid meaningless voice, as if he were running through all the expressions he'd learned but was no longer sure which one of them was in style, then rushing on to new ones, making them up with his eyes closed, "Don't crawl under my fence, don't squeeze in my chipmunk hole, don't sniff my glue, suck my popsicle, keep your own greasy fingers on yourself!" He shaded his eyes and peered in at Connie, who was backed against the kitchen table. "Don't mind him honey he's just a creep. He's a dope. Right? I'm the boy for you and like I said you come out here nice like a lady and give me your hand, and nobody else gets hurt, I mean, your nice old bald-headed daddy and your mummy and your sister in her high heels. Because listen: why bring them in this?"

"Leave me alone," Connie whispered.

"Hey, you know that old woman down the road, the one with the   135 chickens and stuff—you know her?"

"She's dead!"

"Dead? What? You know her?" Arnold Friend said.

"She's dead—"

"Don't you like her?"

"She's dead—she's—she isn't here any more—"   140

"But don't you like her, I mean, you got something against her? Some grudge or something?" Then his voice dipped as if he were conscious of a rudeness. He touched the sunglasses perched on top of his head as if to make sure they were still there. "Now you be a good girl."

"What are you going to do?"

"Just two things, or maybe three," Arnold Friend said. "But I promise it won't last long and you'll like me that way you get to like people you're close to. You will. It's all over for you here, so come on out. You don't want your people in any trouble, do you?"

She turned and bumped against a chair or something, hurting her leg, but she ran into the back room and picked up the telephone. Something roared in her ear, a tiny roaring, and she was so sick with fear that she could do nothing but listen to it—the telephone was clammy and very heavy and her fingers groped down to the dial but were too weak to touch it. She began to scream into the phone, into the roaring. She cried out, she cried for her mother, she felt her breath start jerking back and forth in her lungs as if it were something Arnold Friend were stabbing her with again and again with no tenderness. A noisy sorrowful wailing rose all about her and she was locked inside it the way she was locked inside the house.

After a while she could hear again. She was sitting on the floor with   145 her wet back against the wall.

Arnold Friend was saying from the door, "That's a good girl. Put the phone back."

She kicked the phone away from her.

"No, honey. Pick it up. Put it back right."

She picked it up and put it back. The dial tone stopped.

"That's a good girl. Now you come outside."   150

She was hollow with what had been fear, but what was now just an emptiness. All that screaming had blasted it out of her. She sat, one leg cramped under her, and deep inside her brain was something like a pinpoint of light that kept going and would not let her relax. She thought, I'm not going to see my mother again. She thought, I'm not going to sleep in my bed again. Her bright green blouse was all wet.

Arnold Friend said, in a gentle-loud voice that was like a stage voice, "The place where you came from ain't there any more, and where you had in mind to go is cancelled out. This place you are now—inside your daddy's house—is nothing but a cardboard box I can knock down any time. You know that and always did know it. You hear me?"

She thought, I have got to think. I have to know what to do.

"We'll go out to a nice field, out in the country here where it smells so nice and it's sunny," Arnold Friend said. "I'll have my arms around you so you won't need to try to get away and I'll show you what love is like, what it does. The hell with this house! It looks solid all right," he said. He ran a fingernail down the screen and the noise did not make Connie shiver, as it would have the day before. "Now put your hand on your heart, honey. Feel that? That feels solid too but we know better, be nice to me, be sweet like you can because what else is there for a girl like you but to be sweet and pretty and give in?—and get away before her people come back?"

She felt her pounding heart. Her hand seemed to enclose it. She   155
thought for the first time in her life that it was nothing that was hers, that belonged to her, but just a pounding, living thing inside this body that wasn't really hers either.

"You don't want them to get hurt," Arnold Friend went on. "Now get up, honey. Get up all by yourself."

She stood.

"Now turn this way. That's right. Come over here to me—Ellie, put that away, didn't I tell you? You dope. You miserable creepy dope," Arnold Friend said. His words were not angry but only part of an incantation. The incantation was kindly. "Now come out through the kitchen to me honey and let's see a smile, try it, you're a brave sweet little girl and now they're eating corn and hotdogs cooked to bursting over an outdoor fire, and they don't know one thing about you and never did and honey you're better than them because not a one of them would have done this for you."

Connie felt the linoleum under her feet; it was cool. She brushed her hair back out of her eyes. Arnold Friend let go of the post tentatively and opened his arms for her, his elbows pointing in toward each other and his wrists limp, to show that this was an embarrassed embrace and a little mocking, he didn't want to make her self-conscious.

She put out her hand against the screen. She watched herself push   160
the door slowly open as if she were safe back somewhere in the other door-way, watching this body and this head of long hair moving out into the sunlight where Arnold Friend waited.

"My sweet little blue-eyed girl," he said, in a half-sung sigh that had noth-ing to do with her brown eyes but was taken up just the same by the vast sunlit reaches of the land behind him and on all sides of him, so much land that Connie had never seen before and did not recognize except to know that she was going to it.

- What details convey the character of Arnold Friend? How does this particular character echo and develop the evil characters that we have seen in such places as *Doctor Faustus* (Chapter 1) and "Young Goodman Brown" (Chapter 11)?

- When Arnold Friend claims that "these numbers are a secret code," he cites 33, 19, 17. If you look in the Bible at Judges 19:17, you will find a story that anticipates the title, plot, and structure of this story. How does such an influence shape our reading of this text?

- Oates dedicates this story to Bob Dylan and recounts how she was listening to his song "It's All Over Now, Baby Blue." Track down an audio recording of this song. How do any elements (including the structure) of this story reflect specific lines or specific feelings evoked by the song?

- In the mid-1960s in Tucson, Arizona, Charles Schmid, a five-foot-three, twenty-three-year-old who stuffed three or four inches of rags and cans into his boots to make himself look taller, was arrested for the murder of three teenage girls whom he picked up at Johnie's Drive-in. The similarities to the short story go on. How is it possible to analyze this story as an independent work of literature when so many of its components come from other sources?

POETRY

Billy Collins (1941–)

I Chop Some Parsley While Listening to Art Blakey's Version of "Three Blind Mice" (1998)

And I start wondering how they came to be blind.
If it was congenital, they could be brothers and sister,
and I think of the poor mother
brooding over her sightless young triplets.

Or was it a common accident, all three caught   5
in a searing explosion, a firework perhaps?
If not,
if each came to his or her blindness separately,

how did they ever manage to find one another?
Would it not be difficult for a blind mouse   10
to locate even one fellow mouse with vision
let alone two other blind ones?

And how, in their tiny darkness,
could they possibly have run after a farmer's wife
or anyone else's wife for that matter?   15
Not to mention why.

Just so she could cut off their tails
with a carving knife, is the cynic's answer,
but the thought of them without eyes
and now without tails to trail through the moist grass   20

or slip around the corner of a baseboard
has the cynic who always lounges within me
up off his couch and at the window
trying to hide the rising softness that he feels.

By now I am on to dicing an onion   25
which might account for the wet stinging
in my own eyes, though Freddie Hubbard's
mournful trumpet on "Blue Moon,"

which happens to be the next cut,
cannot be said to be making matters any better.

■ Art Blakey is a jazz drummer, and the poem refers to a specific jazz album
  in which "Blue Moon" is the song directly after "Three Blind Mice." How
  important is this information to your understanding of the poem?

■ Which questions that the poet asks about the familiar Mother Goose story
  seem like reasonable questions? How do these questions make us think
  about the nursery rhyme differently? How are they at odds with the tone of
  the nursery rhyme?

Ted Kooser (1939–   )

A Hairnet with Stars (1980)

I ate at the counter.
The waitress was wearing
a hairnet with stars,

pale blue stars
over the white clouds   5
of her hair, a woman
still lovely at sixty
or older, full breasted
and proud, her hands
strong and sensual,   10
smoothing the apron
over her belly.
I sighed and she turned
to me smiling.
"Mustard?" she asked.   15

- How are stars significant to this poem?
- How is the question "Mustard?" an intrusion into the world that the poem is describing and the tone that the poet presents here?

Yusef Komunyakaa (1947–   )

A Break from the Bush (1988)

The South China Sea
drives in another herd.
The volleyball's a punching bag:
Clem's already lost a tooth
& Johnny's left eye is swollen shut.   5
Frozen airlifted steaks burn
on a wire grill, & miles away
machine guns can be heard.
Pretending we're somewhere else,
we play harder.   10
Lee Otis, the point man,
high on Buddha grass,
buries himself up to his neck
in sand. "Can you see me now?
In this spot they gonna build   15
a Hilton. Invest in Paradise.
Bang, bozos! You're dead."
Frenchie's cassette player
unravels Hendrix's "Purple Haze."
Snake, 17, from Daytona,   20

sits at the water's edge,
the ash on his cigarette
pointing to the ground
like a crooked finger. CJ,
who in three days will trip   25
a fragmentation mine,
runs after the ball
into the whitecaps,
laughing.

- The scene here describes American soldiers in Vietnam. What details help
  us recognize them as Americans during this particular conflict?

- Look at the details in this poem that indicate that the soldiers are conscious
  of their own soldiering. What do they say about their own situation? What
  is their opinion of the war that they are fighting?

Experiencing Literature through Writing

1. Identify a prevailing attitude in the work that you are discussing. How
   does the recognition of this tone help us recognize interesting aspects of
   this text?

   a. What details reveal this attitude to you?

   b. Is this attitude connected to a single character or to multiple
      characters?

   c. Does the author share the same attitude as the characters in the text?

2. The selections included here present situations in which a character
   might either laugh or cry. Understanding the tone of the work often
   informs us about how we should react. Looking closely at a particular
   work in this selection, identify the words within that work that provide
   a breaking point. Explain how that specific passage tells us which way to
   take the work; how do we know from that selection whether we should
   laugh or cry?

3. Using a specific work from this chapter (or another), discuss the role of
   tone in developing coherence within the work. How is tone a structuring
   device that the author uses to hold the work together? Show how particular details throughout the work reinforce the tone (or shift the tone).

11 Word Choice

Why This Word and Not Another?

If you have ever stood in front of a display of greeting cards around Valentine's Day, you have faced the difficulty of translating true sentiment into language. When you walk into that card shop, you are motivated by the desire to express a real emotion to a person you care about. But as you look through all of the cards for sale, you discover that you are standing with other customers who are all buying the same cards to express the same emotions to their own significant others. You might feel frustrated at this point because as clever as any single card might be, it fails to capture a sincere, powerful, and individual emotion. If you sit down and try to write your own poetry, you may feel a similar futility: all the variations of "Roses are red, violets are blue" have already been written by someone else, and original and inspiring verses of your own are elusive.

In this chapter, we ask you, as a reader, to consider how authors make words count, how they communicate distinct emotions and ideas with words that may seem common in other contexts. Remember that every word you read is the result of a choice. The author has decided to use this specific word instead of any other that has a similar meaning. By following authors through some of their choices (and the context within which the choices are made), we can see how attention to language can lead us to the sort of critical analysis that we have been describing throughout this book. We will also look at two important language resources—the dictionary and the thesaurus—and suggest ways in which these tools can deepen our conversations about the literature we read.

PRECISION AND PLAYFULNESS

Desiderius Erasmus, a sixteenth-century humanist whose many interests included developing methods for instruction in language and writing, recommended that writers have at their disposal a plentiful supply of words. In his colloquy on copiousness (abundance), *De Duplici Copia Verborum et Rerum* (1512), he encourages writers to invent different ways of saying the same thing. Such an exercise stimulates a writer's creativity; also, as his examples show, each variation creates a slightly different meaning. Erasmus chose to begin with the banal phrase "Your letter pleased me very much"; he then wrote 150 variations. Before you read any further, try this exercise yourself. Generate at least five different variations of Erasmus's core sentence. Then examine this selection of Erasmus's variations, translated from his original Latin. The first examples are largely technical:

> **Replace the original words with synonyms.**
> Your epistle gladdened me wonderfully.
> **Change the sentence construction.**
> It is impossible to say how gladdened I was by your writing.
> **Change the verbs.**
> I got incredible pleasure from your letter.
> Your writing brought me no mean joy.
> Your writing filled me with joy.
> Your letter moved me with singular pleasure.
> **Using the verb "to be," focus on modifying the pleasure.**
> Your letter was in many ways most pleasing to me.
> Your letter was as pleasurable as could be.
> Your letter was an unspeakable pleasure to us.
> Your letter was an incredible happiness.
> **Use a negative construction.**
> Nothing in my life more pleasing than your letter has befallen me.
> I never took so much pleasure in anything as in your very lovely letter.
> **Put into the form of a question.**
> What in life could have been more pleasing than your letter?

If we stay in the simple mode of reading for meaning, Erasmus's sentences quickly grow monotonous. But if we read to appreciate subtle differences in tone, we can appreciate his artistry. It is especially useful to read aloud to capture the glorious absurdity of the exercise, especially as Erasmus moves on to literary tropes and his mundane phrase begins to take on literary airs and resemble the very worst poetry:

> The banquet of your writing refreshed us with most delightful dishes.
> Your kind epistle far surpassed all carob and Attic honey and sugar, nectar, and ambrosia of the gods.

> As long as the boar loves the mountain ridges, as long as fish love the stream, I will recall the sweetness of your letter.
>
> What clover is to bees, what willow boughs are to goats, what honey is to the bear, your letter is to me.
>
> No luxuries titillate the palate more agreeably than what you wrote titillates my mind.

These effusions are but a sampling of the examples that Erasmus offers, but they are enough to show that as much as these sentences reproduce the initial thought, the later sentences are certainly not the same as the first. The basic idea may be the same, but the specific method of expression greatly changes the nature of that expression. In these final examples, Erasmus is writing poetically about a situation that simply does not deserve the poetic treatment that he gives it. No sober writer would use any of these expressions to thank a correspondent for a letter, but the exercise demonstrates the author's facility with words as well as the author's judgment about which words are most appropriate for a given situation.

In fact, Erasmus wrote about this systematic approach to invention to instruct students to develop their writing skills. The technique was widely used in English schools in the sixteenth century, so it is likely that Shakespeare, for instance, would have encountered this sort of school exercise in his youth. Erasmus's exercise aims to make writers conscious of word choice or **diction**. It raises an interesting question for writers of literature: Does a work of art require special diction, **poetic diction**? In the eighteenth century, some poets perhaps too well trained by exercises like the previous one maintained that the language of poetry was *necessarily not* the language of common life. At its most extreme, this led to what seem now some comic choices: a school of fish could, for example, become a "finny tribe" or a flock of sheep a "fleecy tribe." Wordsworth, Coleridge, and other poets of the early nineteenth century insisted that absolute distinctions between poetic language and the language of everyday use were unnecessary. And while we now allow literary artists a wide range of words to choose from, no one will ever settle on a simple standard for appropriate diction. Writers must always contend with questions of what is the best word for a particular situation: the best word may or may not be a common one.

A consciousness of levels of formality is certainly essential. A **colloquial** expression may register a speaker's everyday conversation and help us relate to that speaker. But a deliberate move to literary language might be necessary to emphasize an emotional or thematic shift. The quality of specific choices can never be divorced from context. For example, a **euphemism** (a deliberately indirect mode of expression) could be comic ("afflicted by vapors" instead of *suffering from gas*); dignified (a "passing" instead of a *death*); or morally problematic ("collateral damage" in place of *civilians killed*).

Experiencing Film and Literature through Diction

The film *Moulin Rouge* (Baz Luhrmann, 2001) explores the problem of living in a world where various forms of cultural production have already anticipated all emotions any of us could ever feel. As is true of most works we discuss, this film could fit in just about any section of this book. The story is set in a stylized version of late-nineteenth-century Paris and borrows many narrative elements from popular opera, even from ancient mythology. The sets create a fictional version of the cityscape that is indebted to a tradition of artistic representations of Paris at least as much as it is inspired by actual Parisian settings. The rich texture of the entire film, especially the gaudy colors and elaborate sets, allude to an entire history of movie musicals, perhaps the least realistic of film types, as characters express their emotions with staged outbursts of song. The film particularly salutes India's Bollywood films, world cinema's most vibrant musicals.

But the problems raised by word choice itself are especially prominent in *Moulin Rouge*'s musical numbers; characters sing familiar late-twentieth-century pop music with all the familiar words in nineteenth-century settings. For instance, the "original" song "Elephant Love Medley" weaves a musical conversation out of pop hits from the last half century. The young poet Christian (Ewan McGregor) believes that his emotions are truly original, and he seeks to find a language to voice these emotions. But whenever he bursts into song, we hear words that we already know. To tell the kindhearted prostitute Satine (Nichole Kidman) that he loves her, he begins with a sentence that has become clichéd through decades of abuse as, among other things, a song title and a movie title: "Love is a many splendored thing." Then he begins his potpourri of musical quotations with Joe Cocker and Jennifer Warnes's "Love lifts us up where we belong." He quotes the Beatles, "All you need is love." Throughout the medley, Satine counters his quotation from idealist love songs with her own from more cynical songs about the same subject.

This medley and the film as a whole undercut Christian's youthful enthusiasm by showing us that his "unique" artistic output, as well as his personal emotion, falls into a long tradition. He might feel something that is new to him, but when he tries to express that new feeling he has to depend on words that have been used over and over again by others before him. So the director/writer Luhrmann manages to have us both share in Christian's enthusiasm for his love and reflect upon the language all of us to register and communicate love. We can enjoy the humor in the fact that Christian is a fictional character in fin-de-siècle (end-of-the-century) Paris producing this derivative poetry long before the actual songs that he is quoting ever were written.

Baz Luhrmann (1962–   )

Moulin Rouge "Elephant Love Medley" Lyrics (2001)

CHRISTIAN: Love is a many splendored thing
     Love lifts us up where we belong
     All you need is love
SATINE: Please don't start that again
CHRISTIAN: All you need is love
SATINE: A girl has got to eat
CHRISTIAN: All you need is love
SATINE: She'll end up on the street
CHRISTIAN: All you need is love
SATINE: Love is just a game
CHRISTIAN: I was made for loving you baby
     You were made for loving me
SATINE: The only way of loving me baby
     Is to pay a lovely fee
CHRISTIAN: Just one night
     Give me just one night
SATINE: There's no way
     'Cause you can't pay
CHRISTIAN: In the name of love
     One night in the name of love
SATINE: You crazy fool
     I won't give in to you
CHRISTIAN: Don't leave me this way
     I can't survive without your sweet love
     Oh baby don't leave me this way
SATINE: You think that people would have enough of silly love songs
CHRISTIAN: I look around me and I see it isn't so, oh no
SATINE: Some people wanna fill the world with silly love songs
CHRISTIAN: Well what's wrong with that
     I'd like to know
     Cause here I go again
CHRISTIAN: Love lifts us up where we belong
     Where the eagles fly
     On a mountain high
SATINE: Love makes us act like we are fools
     Throw our lives away
     For one happy day

CHRISTIAN: We can be heroes
    Just for one day
SATINE: You, you will be mean
CHRISTIAN: No I won't
SATINE: And I, I'll drink all the time
CHRISTIAN: We should be lovers
SATINE: We can't do that
CHRISTIAN: We should be lovers
    And that's a fact
SATINE: No nothing would keep us together
CHRISTIAN: We could steal time
CHRISTIAN *& Satine:* Just for one day
    We can be heroes
    Forever and ever
    We can be heroes
    Forever and ever
    We can be heroes
CHRISTIAN: Just because I, and I will always love you
SATINE: I only can't help
CHRISTIAN *&* SATINE: Loving You
SATINE: How wonderful life is now
CHRISTIAN *and* SATINE: You're in the world

Moulin Rouge (2001)

Luhrmann has done something remarkable in this patched-together song. While all of his word choices are culled from about thirteen familiar late twentieth-century pop songs, they feel altogether original in this rousing musical number. The words aren't different if we think of them only as words, but in the setting Luhrmann has created we hear them as fresh and alive. We're convinced that Christian does indeed love Satine even though we know his passion (from a larger perspective) is hardly as unique as he thinks it is.

Variation upon a common theme—the challenge of making distinctive and individual feelings that are universal—is a central concern also in Shakespeare's sonnet sequence. In the brief selection that follows, you'll note considerable thematic overlap from poem to poem. But the sequence doesn't get stalled; each poem offers a distinct experience for the reader.

> ## Making Connections
>
> The Making Connections features in this book act as interruptions of the main text throughout. But at some level, the intent is to connect (connect to ideas in other chapters, to experiences you may have beyond the classroom, to the writing process). Here, we interrupt to suggest that before you read these poems, you should recall the specific elements of the **sonnet** form that we discussed in Chapter 8. Take note of structural features, track, the rhyme, and sum up the argument (the complication and the resolution). Notice how Shakespeare sets up a general principle in the first four lines (quatrain). The next two quatrains apply this general principle to the specific instance that he is describing. And the final couplet offers a conclusion and a way for the young man addressed in the sonnet to rectify the "problem" that the poem has just described.

William Shakespeare (1564–1616)

Sonnet 1 (1609)

From fairest creatures we desire increase,
That thereby beauty's rose might never die,
But as the riper should by time decease,
His tender heir might bear his memory:
But thou, contracted to thine own bright eyes,   5
Feed'st thy light's flame with self-substantial fuel,
Making a famine where abundance lies,
Thyself thy foe, to thy sweet self too cruel.
Thou that art now the world's fresh ornament
And only herald to the gaudy spring,   10
Within thine own bud buriest thy content
And, tender churl, makest waste in niggarding.
   Pity the world, or else this glutton be,
    To eat the world's due, by the grave and thee.

The poet admires the beauty he sees in the young man he addresses and argues that this youth has a responsibility to procreate. But this simple message is less interesting than the strategies that the poet uses to make his argument; Shakespeare surprises us with the word choices that he makes. In the first quatrain (lines 1–4), the poet speaks of a general desire for immortality, yet he never uses that word. We desire the "fairest creatures," he says, to "increase" (line 1). Notably, he avoids any of the words that we might think to use in summarizing this poem: reproduction, procreation, fatherhood, children, or any other simple variation of that idea. Instead, he talks about a "tender heir" (line 4) of "beauty's rose" (line 2) that "might bear his memory" (line 4), implying that when we see beauty (in something like a rose), we wish that that beauty might endure. In the second quatrain (lines 5–8), the poet shifts to a condemnation of the youth: "thou, contracted to thine own bright eyes" (line 5). Instead of sharing his beauty, this subject is self-absorbed, and the poet claims that this inward tendency defies the natural order and creates "a famine where abundance lies" (line 7). What is this famine? It seems a lack of beauty in the world, exacerbated by the knowledge that, without an heir, the young man's beauty will vanish. The final lines of the poem emphasize this waste. The youth should be "herald to the gaudy spring" (line 10). He should be father to a whole field, but instead remains a solitary flower. As a flower, the poet tells him "[thou] buriest thy content" within "thine own bud" (line 11) instead of sharing with the passing wildlife, thereby preventing the propagation of other flowers. The act of propagation, as it is depicted in these lines, appears quite passive. By the end of this third quatrain (lines 9–12), the young man is denigrated as a "churl" who paradoxically "makest waste in niggarding" (line 12). How can saving (or hoarding) be a wasteful activity? In the final couplet (lines 13–14), "beauty's rose" has become a "glutton" (line 13) consuming the "world's due" (line 14), killing off potential fields of flowers through his selfishness and knowing that he must eventually die. As is often the case in the sonnet form, the final couplet affects our reading of the previous twelve lines. The **hyperbole** in these final lines (the deliberate exaggeration or overstatement) marks a stark contrast to the apparent restraint at the beginning. Through the poet's choice of words and images, feelings escalate through the sonnet as the narrator becomes more aggressive in pursuit of connections to the flower image.

Let's go back to our initial summary of the poem: "The poet admires the beauty he sees in the young man he addresses and argues that this youth has a responsibility to procreate." Although this summary may accurately recount the general subject of the poem, it fails to capture the poem's impact because the poem is not a generalization, it is a series of precise words. Yes, the poem is a plea for this young man to sow his seed, but until we look closely at the words that the poet uses to make this plea, we cannot see the images, the twists of meaning, the logical games that the poet plays; in short, we have not begun any analysis.

Of course, this process should go beyond what we present here. What can we say about the tone of this particular narrative? As we look at more sonnets, do we develop some sense of a consistent character narrating these individual units? How do differences between similar sonnets alter our readings?

Now, compare your findings from the first sonnet to this second sonnet in Shakespeare's sequence. How different is your summary of this sonnet from that of the first? Does Shakespeare use the same pattern here? Where are the differences? Does his use of clothing as an image (instead of harvests) change the nature of the case that he makes? How directly are the elements of clothing related to his demand? How does this image develop throughout the sonnet?

Sonnet 2 (1609)

When forty winters shall beseige thy brow,
And dig deep trenches in thy beauty's field,
Thy youth's proud livery, so gazed on now,
Will be a tatter'd weed, of small worth held:
Then being ask'd where all thy beauty lies,   5
Where all the treasure of thy lusty days,
To say, within thine own deep-sunken eyes,
Were an all-eating shame and thriftless praise.
How much more praise deserved thy beauty's use,
If thou couldst answer "This fair child of mine   10
Shall sum my count and make my old excuse,"
Proving his beauty by succession thine!
    This were to be new made when thou art old,
    And see thy blood warm when thou feel'st it cold.

As you move through the following sonnets, you will find that reading for a simple summary is no longer necessary. Shakespeare's first twenty sonnets form a sequence that is rather similar to the Erasmian exercise in copiousness. Instead of reading for their general meaning—as they all convey essentially the same message—you should be reading for the specific words Shakespeare uses to conjure ideas and images about love. Look for any words or combinations of words that are repeated among the sonnets. As you read, try to group the sonnets into categories that highlight distinguishing features that you find. Look for the juxtaposition of words that might not seem to fit together—for instance, can "Nature" really have such attributes as "thriftiness"? Bear in mind Shakespeare's presence in the poems: He does like to play with puns upon his own name; he is a writer who has some interest in promoting his particular profession. The sonnets serve the poet as a forum for showing off his rhetorical skills. His cleverness is evident in his ingenious variations of the repeated message.

Sonnet 3 (1609)

Look in thy glass, and tell the face thou viewest
Now is the time that face should form another;
Whose fresh repair if now thou not renewest,
Thou dost beguile the world, unbless some mother.
For where is she so fair whose unear'd womb   5
Disdains the tillage of thy husbandry?
Or who is he so fond will be the tomb
Of his self-love, to stop posterity?
Thou art thy mother's glass, and she in thee
Calls back the lovely April of her prime: 10
So thou through windows of thine age shall see
Despite of wrinkles this thy golden time.
    But if thou live, remember'd not to be,
      Die single, and thine image dies with thee.

Sonnet 9 (1609)

Is it for fear to wet a widow's eye
That thou consum'st thyself in single life?
Ah! if thou issueless shalt hap to die,
The world will wail thee, like a makeless wife;
The world will be thy widow and still weep   5
That thou no form of thee hast left behind,
When every private widow well may keep
By children's eyes her husband's shape in mind.
Look, what an unthrift in the world doth spend
Shifts but his place, for still the world enjoys it;   10
But beauty's waste hath in the world an end,
And kept unus'd, the user so destroys it.
    No love toward others in that bosom sits
      That on himself such murd'rous shame commits.

Sonnet 18 (1609)

Shall I compare thee to a summer's day?
Thou art more lovely and more temperate:
Rough winds do shake the darling buds of May,
And summer's lease hath all too short a date:
Sometime too hot the eye of heaven shines,   5
And often is his gold complexion dimm'd;

And every fair from fair sometime declines,
By chance or nature's changing course untrimm'd;
But thy eternal summer shall not fade
Nor lose possession of that fair thou owest;   10
Nor shall Death brag thou wander'st in his shade,
When in eternal lines to time thou growest:
So long as men can breathe or eyes can see,
So long lives this and this gives life to thee.

As you read these sonnets in sequence, you may recognize sonnets that you have read before. Sonnet 18, for example, is often the first sonnet that students read when they read Shakespearean sonnets. How does reading a familiar sonnet in the context of the other sonnets lend it additional meaning? Does the sonnet itself seem different when it appears here with the others?

A Note to Student Writers: On Paraphrase

To summarize is to convey in your own words an essential idea from a source. To paraphrase is to *restate* in a fairly detailed way the original source. Anytime we paraphrase, we are making choices about the words that we use. However closely we attend to the piece we paraphrase, we inevitably change it in our restatement. As we saw earlier in Erasmus's exercise, subtle changes emerge with each variation we choose. Often, the difference is not immediately apparent, but if we paraphrase our own paraphrase, we will begin to see how specific words in different combinations create different meanings. Look back at one of Shakespeare's sonnets and write three distinct paraphrases of it. By generating multiple paraphrases of the poem, you should begin to clarify your own understanding of that poem. At the same time, you will also realize that a poem cannot be reduced to any paraphrase.

DEFINITION AND USAGE

Shakespeare's talent for variation shouldn't lead us to think that variation in and of itself is a virtue. To grant ourselves a wider vocabulary we can turn to a thesaurus, but the choices it offers aren't necessarily helpful. As we begin to look through the entries under love, for instance, we will find a list like this:

> fondness, liking, inclination, desire, regard, admiration, affection, tenderness, heart, attachment, yearning, gallantry, passion, flame, devotion, infatuation, adoration, idolatry, benevolence

None of these words precisely replaces the word love. Some of them won't do at all for expressing the particular kind of love we want to communicate. But to an inexpert user, the thesaurus might give the false impression that it is appropriate to substitute any one of these words for another. The results of such a misunderstanding can be amusing or bewildering. A bad choice makes it instantly clear: subtleties matter. The poet Billy Collins suggests that we find unnatural groupings in a thesaurus. As you read, follow the images Collins creates to describe the project of clustering synonyms.

Billy Collins (1941–   )

Thesaurus (1995)

It could be the name of a prehistoric beast
that roamed the Paleozoic earth, rising up
on its hind legs to show off its large vocabulary,
or some lover in a myth who is metamorphosed into a book.

It means treasury, but it is just a place   5
where words congregate with their relatives,
a big park where hundreds of family reunions
are always being held,
house, home, abode, dwelling, lodgings, and *digs,*
all sharing the same picnic basket and thermos;   10
hairy, hirsute, woolly, furry, fleecy, and *shaggy*
all running a sack race or throwing horseshoes,
inert, static, motionless, fixed and *immobile*
standing and kneeling in rows for a group photograph.

Here father is next to sire and brother close   15
to sibling, separated only by fine shades of meaning.
And every group has its odd cousin, the one
who traveled the farthest to be here:
astereognosis, polydipsia, or some eleven
syllable, unpronounceable substitute for the word *tool.*   20
Even their own relatives have to squint at their name tags.

I can see my own copy up on a high shelf.
I rarely open it, because I know there is no
such thing as a synonym and because I get nervous
around people who always assemble with their own kind,   25
forming clubs and nailing signs to closed front doors
while others huddle alone in the dark streets.

I would rather see words out on their own, away
from their families and the warehouse of Roget,
wandering the world where they sometimes fall   30
in love with a completely different word.
Surely, you have seen pairs of them standing forever
next to each other on the same line inside a poem,
a small chapel where weddings like these,
between perfect strangers, can take place.   35

Collins appreciates the "warehouse" that Roget has created in the thesaurus, but
it is a tool that he keeps high on a shelf, he tells us. Collins learns more when
he finds words that appear in unexpected and perhaps unusual pairings. As
Collins demonstrates, a synonym never really means the *same* thing as another
word. Each word has its own meaning; as similar as it may be to another, it is
not identical.

The thesaurus tries to generalize; it gives us groupings of words that have
approximately the same meaning. The dictionary, on the other hand, makes
distinctions among words. While a dictionary's definitions generally begin with
synonyms, the best dictionaries then clarify and justify these definitions with
examples or elaboration. The *Oxford English Dictionary*, for example, will list a
series of quotations using the specified word and show how that word has been
used differently at different times. Such a project shows that deriving a precise
definition for an abstract term can be a difficult process. Here are only a few
excerpts from the *OED* definitions of *love* that begin to show how words can
never be pinned down:

1. That disposition or state of feeling with regard to a person which
   (arising from recognition of attractive qualities, from instincts of
   natural relationship, or from sympathy) manifests itself in solicitude for
   the welfare of the object, and usually also in delight in his or her presence and desire for his or her approval; warm affection, attachment.
   Const. *of, for, to, towards*.

2. In religious use, applied in an eminent sense to the paternal benevolence
   and affection of God towards His children, to the affectionate devotion
   due to God from His creatures, and to the affection of one created being
   to another so far as it is prompted by the sense of their common relationship to God. (Cf. CHARITY 1.) Theologians distinguish the *love
   of complacency*, which implies approval of qualities in the object, and
   the *love of benevolence*, which is bestowed irrespective of the character
   of the object.

3. Strong predilection, liking or fondness *for*, or devotion *to* (something).
   Const. *of, for, to* (arch.), *unto. to give, bear love to*: to be devoted or addicted to.

4. That feeling of attachment which is based upon difference of sex; the affection which subsists between lover and sweetheart and is the normal basis of marriage. *for love* (*in love*): by reason of love (often placed in opposition to pecuniary considerations); also in weakened sense; *love at first sight*: the action or state of falling in love with someone whom one has never previously seen; *love's young dream*: the relationship of young lovers; the object of someone's love, a man regarded as the perfect lover.

Perusing the entries for a specific word, comparing the entries in different dictionaries, and thinking about the relation between definitions and specific uses of a word can serve as the subject of extended discussions. The complete entry on *love* from the *OED* is a record of a scholarly conversation about the meaning of this very familiar word; the editors assemble a collection of specific instances in which the word *love* has been used to show how definitions evolve over time.

The entry on love from the *OED* (only a small part of which we have included here) aims to register far more than the literal meaning of the word—its **denotation**. Such a definition would be impossibly narrow. Note how much of what is quoted here concerns a wide range of associations suggested by the word. A grasp of a word's **connotations** (what it suggests beyond the most literal level) is essential to our understanding. Oftentimes it's useful to use a dictionary to look up a word that you already know, for the dictionary may help you catch shadings that could easily be missed. In the same way, a thesaurus is not just a tool to find a different word, but a means to reflect upon a widened range of possible associations.

Experiencing Literature through Word Choice

Our understanding of words, our own use of language comes not from our knowledge of words in isolation but from our familiarity with their use. In the following poem, Robert Sward enacts a frustration to express what he feels as true in the face of an overbearing tradition of words and the conventions of poetry. His wife in this poem complains that the words that he writes are a different enterprise than "attending to me." To some extent, she is right. The need to choose the precise words turns attention from her to, as the title notes, the dictionary. Yet, although the impersonal definitions in the dictionary make the words that the poet uses mechanical, his own acknowledgment of this challenge helps reclaim those words. He admits to his words' shortcomings, but embraces them as his best and only tools. As he plays with words at the end of the poem, he makes them his own and makes them (one would imagine) meaningful to Gloria.

Robert Sward (1933–   )

For Gloria on Her 60th Birthday, or Looking for Love in Merriam-Webster (1991)

"Beautiful, splendid, magnificent,
delightful, charming, appealing,"
     says the dictionary.
And that's how I start… But I hear her say,
"Make it less glorious and more Gloria."   5

Imperious, composed, skeptical, serene,
lustrous, irreverent,
she's marked by glory, she attracts glory
"Glory," I say, "Glory, Glory."
"Is there a hallelujah in there?"   10
she asks, when I read her lines one and two.
"Not yet," I say, looking up from my books.
She protests, "Writing a poem isn't the same

"As *really* attending to me." "But it's for
your birthday," I say. Pouting,   15
playfully cross, "That's the price you pay
when your love's a poet."

She has chestnut-colored hair,
old fashioned Clara Bow lips,
moist brown eyes…   20
                    arms outstretched, head thrown back
she glides toward me and into her seventh decade.

Her name means "to adore,"
"to rejoice, to be jubilant,
to magnify and honor as in worship, to give or ascribe glory—"
     my love, O Gloria, I do, I do.   25

The literate self-consciousness that we see in this poem differs from the more common *Moulin Rouge* dilemma of borrowing the words of others to express our own feelings. We pick out the words that we believe have come closest to what we think; perhaps these words even shape our thoughts.

CRITICALLY REFLECTING ON WORDS

Writers sometimes refine their sense of "right words" but noting what makes for imprecise or ineffective choices. Words deliberately chosen for their wrongness makes for a satiric game. In the annual Bulwer-Lytton contest, writers take a perverse pleasure competing to compose the worst opening line for an imaginary novel. The contest often favors entries that rely upon overly melodramatic diction. But before we present samples of those entries, we'll insert a brief observation on bad writing from *The Turkey City Lexicon*. These phrases come from a science fiction writers' workshop where writers gather, reading one another's work, seeking to improve their own writing through mutually constructive criticism. What follows are common problems identified so that they can be avoided.

Lewis Shiner (1950–)

from The Turkey City Lexicon: A Primer for Science Fiction Workshops (1990)

Gingerbread: Useless ornament in prose, such as fancy sesquipedalian Latinate words where short clear English ones will do. Novice authors sometimes use "gingerbread" in the hope of disguising faults and conveying an air of refinement. (Attr. Damon Knight)

Not Simultaneous: The mis-use of the present participle is a common structural sentence-fault for beginning writers. "Putting his key in the door, he leapt up the stairs and got his revolver out of the bureau." Alas, our hero couldn't do this even if his arms were forty feet long. This fault shades into "Ing Disease," the tendency to pepper sentences with words ending in "-ing," a grammatical construction which tends to confuse the proper sequence of events. (Attr. Damon Knight)

Pushbutton Words: Words used to evoke a cheap emotional response without engaging the intellect or the critical faculties. Commonly found in story titles, they include such bits of bogus lyricism as "star," "dance," "dream," "song," "tears" and "poet," clichés calculated to render the SF audience misty-eyed and tender-hearted.

Roget's Disease: The ludicrous overuse of far-fetched adjectives, piled into a festering, fungal, tenebrous, troglodytic, ichorous, leprous, synonymic heap. (Attr. John W. Campbell)

With descriptions from the lexicon in mind, look at the following prize-winning examples of overwrought, hyperventilated prose (often called "purple prose") from the Bulwer-Lytton Contest. Explain why judges might deem each entry as worth a prize for badness. Which insights from the *Turkey City Lexicon* best apply to each?

Bulwer-Lytton Contest Winners

On reflection, Angela perceived that her relationship with Tom had always been rocky, not quite a roller-coaster ride but more like when the toilet-paper roll gets a little squashed so it hangs crooked and every time you pull some off you can hear the rest going bumpity-bumpity in its holder until you go nuts and push it back into shape, a degree of annoyance that Angela had now almost attained.

—Rephah Berg, Oakland, CA (2002)

Sultry it was and humid, but no whisper of air caused the plump, laden spears of golden grain to nod their burdened heads as they unheedingly awaited the cyclic rape of their gleaming treasure, while overhead the burning orb of luminescence ascended its ever-upward path toward a sweltering celestial apex, for although it is not in Kansas that our story takes place, it looks godawful like it.

—Judy Frazier, Lathrop, Missouri (1991)

The bone-chilling scream split the warm summer night in two, the first half being before the scream when it was fairly balmy and calm and pleasant for those who hadn't heard the scream at all, but not calm or balmy or even very nice for those who did hear the scream, discounting the little period of time during the actual scream itself when your ears might have been hearing it but your brain wasn't reacting yet to let you know.

—Patricia E. Presutti, Lewiston, New York (1986)

Dolores breezed along the surface of her life like a flat stone forever skipping across smooth water, rippling reality sporadically but oblivious to it consistently, until she finally lost momentum, sank, and due to an overdose of fluoride as a child which caused her to lie forever on the floor of her life as useless as an appendix and as lonely as a five-hundred-pound barbell in a steroid-free fitness center.

—Linda Vernon, Newark, California (1990)

Now at the penultimate point of the current chapter in the tome you, dear reader, currently peruse, it's time to turn attention to a film that has much to add to our discussion of diction.

MODELING CRITICAL ANALYSIS: JOEL COEN AND ETHAN COEN, O BROTHER, WHERE ART THOU?

When Ulysses Everett McGill finally first sees his "Penelope"—the wife Penny (Holly Hunter) he has sought to return to—the meeting hardly begins well. Penny has told her seven children (all girls) that their father was run over by a train, a more respectable end she thinks than the reality (Ulysses is a convicted con artist and petty thief who was serving hard time on the chain gang before his escape). Penny has grown tired of waiting for Ulysses and has agreed to marry Vernon T. Waldrip (Ray McKinnon); indeed the marriage is set for the next day. The Coen brothers set up the romantic struggle in broadly comic terms. Vernon T. Waldrip, as the name might suggest, is hardly a dashing adventurer. He is, however, a man with "prospects"; indeed, he is (as we hear from Penny and the older children) "bona-fide." These descriptors aptly capture the whole of Vernon's limited attractions. There is no romance in the relationship between Penny and Vernon, but Vernon offers stability and a kind of social legitimacy that Ulysses has failed to provide.

The initial contest between the men is contained by words of law and possession, not the sorts of words that suggest caring or passion. Ulysses says that as the "paterfamilias" he is "put in a difficult position vis-à-vis my progeny." *Paterfamilias* is a latin word for "father" or "master of the house." In Roman society, the term had specific legal meaning: it designated an independent man in charge of a family's holdings. Ulysses's use of *vis-à-vis* (literally, "face-to-face" but suggesting here "in relation to") continues the dispute in comically legalistic terms. In this context, the words *husband*, *wife*, and *fiancé* are about social arrangements. Even the word *daddy* gets swallowed up in matters of legal status: Ulysses might be "Daddy" today, but "Uncle Vernon" will be "Daddy" tomorrow if the marriage comes off as planned. Ulysses will then be no longer a "husband," and will be "just a drifter, a no-good drifter."

But there are real emotions barely covered by the silly, Latinate, and inappropriate language of law and property. The Coen brothers make sure we know that Ulysses Everett McGill feels passionately for his Penny. That passion shows partly in the desperate way he attacks her: "you lying, unconstant succubus." The "unconstant" may be less than correct (*inconstant* is the word he wants), and "succubus" is typical of his verbal overreaching. But the words do suggest anger and the hurt that generates anger. More significantly, in the middle of all the foolish talk (and silly diction), Ulysses has a line that lends real dignity to his quest: "I've traveled many a weary mile to be back with my wife." The plainness of this statement and apt fit between the character's education, his situation, and his dreams reminds us that something is at stake in this comic odyssey. Here, the simple language stands out because so much of the surrounding language is not simple.

The Coen brothers shift the level of their hero's diction to help us hear what lies behind all the fancy expressions. Such moves from a high to a low register (or the other way around) are often used to lend power to words that might, in other contexts, be overlooked.

Using Word Choice to Focus Writing and Discussion

- To examine a selection's word choice, begin by summarizing. As you put the ideas into your own words, which of the author's words seem unusual or are words that you would not have chosen? For instance, are there words here that seem archaic?

- Are there any cases in which the author uses a word in such a way that is different from the conventional definition of the word? When you think about word choice, it is useful to keep a dictionary at hand. There are often multiple definitions of words. Check to see whether an author is using an older or less common definition of a word.

- If there are different characters in the text, do they choose their words differently? Point to specific examples of such differences. Can you tell from their words which character is speaking?

- How do specific words in the passage convey a tone or attitude about the subject matter? Often, attention to words will help us make our arguments about other elements in the text.

- How are words placed next to one another? Find specific instances where the combination of words makes us notice the words.

- Does the author break grammatical conventions? If so, what is the impact of this break?

Anthology

HISTORICAL FICTION: A CRITIC WRITES ABOUT WORD CHOICE IN HISTORICAL FICTION

Nancy Franklin begins her review of the television series *Deadwood* by summarizing characteristics of the western genre. It's not a genre she felt offered much to a current generation of artists, but she finds that David Milch (the series' creator) makes things vibrant, real, and relevant. Part of the success, Franklin notes, arises from the carefully researched and fully realized look of the production. And she gives much credit to a talented cast. But language too is crucial. Franklin notes how the dialogue presses boundaries; it's both "ornate and profane." The stylized and brutal qualities of language that characterize every episode are, to Franklin's mind, essential to Milch's achievement. Through language he registers subtle differences among characters. And he's aware of how the most brutal language can be juxtaposed against the most conventionally comforting language. All in all, the dialogue works with all aspects of the production.

This idea of using language to help create a particular time and place (a particular setting) is central to the project of *Deadwood*. In the selected works, note how the language of the piece (while it may accomplish many different tasks) sets it into a particular time. In some cases this placement may be due to the time it was written, but even in some of the older pieces, the authors have used language in a way that makes it seem antique, even to them. In other instances, authors create a contrast between the words that they use in different sections of a work to emphasize different settings. In still others, they have worked to deliver a language that feels of the moment—to what extent does this "current" language hold up when we read it now?

Characteristics of Historical Fiction

Historical fiction draws upon actual historical records to tell a story. It sets its fictional story within the frame of a specific historical moment. The resulting story combines the fictional with the actual. Generally, the author attempts to capture the manners and social conditions of the historical period and gives careful attention to details that locate the story within a particular time period (e.g., fashion, technology, or speech).

Each of the selections here engages in some aspect of real history that has been incorporated into the creative texts that you are reading. The authors of these works generally have conducted research in order to understand the specific historical moment that they present in their story or poem. They often incorporate the primary texts of history (letters, journals, newspaper articles) into their fictional account.

For instance, "Gojira, King of the Monsters" tells the story of real Japanese special effects director Eiji Tsuburaya (1901-1970), who was one of the co-creators of the Godzilla movies. The accounts of the film production are accurate. Jim Shepard based his narrative on extensive research about Tsuburaya and the mechanics of making the film, and he has blended this material with research that he has done about Tsuburaya's personal life in order to create a story with a narrative arch. Emma Donoghue's "Man and Boy" is told in the voice of Matthew Scott, the real nineteenth-century keeper of Jumbo the elephant (1860-1885) at the London Zoological Gardens. She has assembled this fictionalized voice from various sources from the period including Scott's autobiography, *Jumbo's Keeper* (1885). "Young Goodman Brown" by Nathaniel Hawthorne, uses seventeenth-century Salem, Massachusetts, as the setting for its story of a fictional resident of the community. In this case, the characters are not drawn from life, but the language, the costumes, and the religious concerns of the story fit the setting. Whether this story (or any work of historical fiction) presents an accurate picture of the period that it portrays is another question entirely.

REVIEW

Nancy Franklin (1956–   )

Dead On: David Milch Explores the Dakota Territory (2006)

It has been many years since Westerns were essentially black-and-white, cut-and-dried stories of good versus evil: morality tales with lots of horses and guns and one of everything else—a sheriff, an outlaw, an embattled hero, a town drunk, a whore with a heart of gold, a honky-tonk piano, and a schoolteacher from Illinois, who found out shortly after arriving in town that, for worse and for better, there was more to life than book learnin'. Indians were, for the most part, the obstacle that had to be overcome—although sometimes there was a "good one." Although Westerns have evolved, the conventions are still often glaring, making even Westerns that have gray, shadowy moral areas a tough sell to some people. There's just too much dust, leather, whinnying, shooting, and mud—too much *brown*—and not enough talking, understanding, humor, and complexity. The trappings of Westerns make them seem fake and message-y, even as they strain to be realistic. David Milch's "Deadwood," which begins its third season on HBO on Sunday, is the exception to the rule; in what I'd assumed was very poor soil, he's produced a gorgeously living thing.

"Deadwood" is set, of course, in Deadwood, in the Dakota Territory. It begins in 1876, when the settlement was just a few buildings in the crease between two hills, lining the sides of a muddy street, there to meet the needs of the men who flocked to the Black Hills after gold was discovered in the area. The settlement is so small that your eye can take in the whole town at a glance; in a sense, viewers have the same perspective as Al Swearengen (Ian McShane), the saloonkeeper and power broker of the camp, who conducts much of his business from his second-story quarters, above the bar, but often goes out on his balcony to observe the goings on in town below. Over the first two seasons, we have watched Deadwood grow—the real Deadwood went from being a cluster of prospectors to a roiling community in less than a year. In the show, the cemetery expands; bigger, louder equipment is brought in to get at the gold deep underground; more prostitutes are shipped in. Seeing America being built in this way, we see what it is made of. Men are constantly digging, hauling, and hammering, and the desire, hard work, and risk that it took to create this place are always front and center. "Deadwood" takes you past the familiar cardboard cutouts of Wild Bill Hickok, Calamity Jane, and "the Old West," and acquaints you with the real forces and peoples that converged to form our country.

Milch, who co-created "NYPD Blue," with Steven Bochco, has a deep understanding of tortured souls and a gift for depicting the ways in which people are torn apart and come together. You never feel as though he were imposing a contemporary outlook onto the past in order to make his drama more "relatable"; instead, he shows how the past still lives in us. It's obvious that serious research went into "Deadwood," but, as Milch says, he learned as much as he could and then threw out most of what he knew when he began writing the show. "Deadwood" draws on history without being slavishly beholden to the facts; it smells and sounds right, and every aspect of the luxuriant production contributes to that sense: tile costumes and sets seem to have perfectly calibrated levels of wear and tear. There are at least a dozen sensational performances, among them Keith Carradine as Hickok; Dayton Callie as his sidekick, Charlie Utter; Robin Weigert as Calamity Jane; Jeffrey Jones as the nosy newspaper publisher A. W. Merrick; Paula Malcomson as Trixie, a prostitute with higher aspirations; and Geri Jewell as Jewel, Swearengen's crippled maid. Ian McShane's Swearengen is a murderer, a monster, a clever beast you cannot help being drawn to; he wears a pin-striped suit over long johns, which emphasizes his hugely thick neck and his large head—he's an unstoppable wall of man coming at you, episode after episode (except when he is pitiably felled, temporarily, by a kidney stone). But you don't really notice the casting per se, because you're too engrossed in the characters, listening to what they say, and trying to get inside their heads and hearts.

"Deadwood" has ten or so writers and nearly as many directors, but there is a unity to the dialogue (Milch is one of the executive producers). It is ornate and profane—far beyond, on both counts, anything that's ever been on television. But you never feel that tile show's creators have injected the swearing gratuitously. It even has different colors, depending on who's doing it—when Calamity Jane is trying to comfort a little girl whose family has just been hacked to death, by singing "Row, Row, Row Your Boat" to her with Charlie Utter, there's something touching about the way she yells "God damn it!" when he screws up the timing. What I find more brutal than the language is seeing freshly dead bodies fed to the pigs, or people not stopping to help Jewel when she falls in the street. (In the scene, a horse walks by in the foreground, its large, all-seeing eye rebuking human cruelty.) People just go about their business, and their business is making money.

But even making money the Deadwood way is small potatoes compared to the interests that start descending on the town when the stakes get big—one of whom is George Hearst (Gerald McRaney), the father of William Randolph   5

Hearst, whose arrival signals the beginning of strong-arm capitalism. It remains to be seen whether, in season three, Swearengen and his cohorts will adapt to the new ways. What we surely won't see is Deadwood evolving into what it is today—a tourist trap. "Deadwood" has not been renewed for a fourth season, though there is a slim chance that it will return. Milch is now working on another pilot for HBO, called "John from Cincinnati," which he has described as "surf noir." Sounds iffy, but so did a show about a mafioso who goes to a psychiatrist. ❖

FICTION

Jim Shepard (1956–   )

Jim Shepard teaches creative writing and film at Williams College. He earned a BA at Trinity College and an MFA from Brown University. Shepard often uses extensive historical research as the basis for his fictional stories, and the collection, in which this story appears, *You Think That's Bad*, included an extensive bibliography. In his review of this collection, Art Winslow describes Shepard's attention to historical detail: "Shepard's use of relatively accurate biographical fact is bent to his own dramatic needs. Unlike memoirs that skew the truth, this is fiction that uses truth to warp into its own staged, often memoir-like reality."

Gojira, King of the Monsters (2011)

Once again he weathered an afternoon of unease and little progress. He'd forgotten that today was the Star Festival, one of his wife's favorites, and was beginning to wonder at which he was more adept: hurting Masano inadvertently or intentionally. He'd settled into the backseat that morning and spread onto his lap his section of the production board, glued on heavy stock and color coded, when the driver had reminded him about the festival. The driver had noticed the paper cows and kimonos Masano had hung in their potted bamboo out front. They had to have been there when Tsuburaya had come home the night before.

The driver at that point had already turned onto the main street and Tsuburaya had considered asking to be returned to his home, but then had finally said, "Oh, keep going." Immediately he'd understood how that compounded his offense. He imagined himself telling Masano, "I forgot. And when I remembered, I kept going anyway."

She had signed the first love note she'd ever sent to him "Shokujo," the name of the Weaver Princess Star, the central figure of festival. It had been a reference to the extent to which their discipline for work had suffered in the face of their feelings. According to the legend, the princess had fallen in love with a cow herder; and as a reward for their diligence and industry, the king allowed them to marry, but their lovemaking had become for them such a delirium that she had neglected her weaving, and the herder had allowed his cows to stray, so in his exasperation the king had forced them to remain on opposite sides of the Milky Way, to approach each other only once a year. Every July Masano had celebrated the festival, in recent years more and more often with only Akira, their youngest child. The previous July, while Tsuburaya had looked on, she had shown Akira through his toy telescope how on this night and this night alone the Weaver Princess Star and the Herdboy Star were allowed to meet on the banks of the river of heaven. Tsuburaya had watched as if she were having this conversation with her son in order to have it with him. And if it rained? Akira had asked. If it rained, his mother told him, the two stars had to wait an additional year.

He was falling behind everywhere: in his wife's affections and his work's responsibilities. But in the case of her latter, whether he put in fourteen- or sixteen-hour days, each evening left his production team with still more to accomplish, with principal photography set to commence one way or the other on August first.

He told his staff whenever they protested that there was no sense in   5 blaming Tanaka, since he hadn't misled anyone. "Well, then he's the first producer who hasn't," one of his assistants grumbled. But it was true, Tsuhuraya reminded them: at the meeting at which Tsuburaya had agreed to come aboard, Tanaka had begun by saying, "The good news is: do you want to make this movie with me, or not? The bad news is, we won't have enough time."

Tanaka had a huge hit with *Eagles of the Pacific* a year earlier, in 1953, but only bad luck since. Two projects collapsed when rights he'd thought were in hand turned out to be too expensive, and the most recent production had been all set to go until the Indonesian government panicked in the face of all the anti-Japanese protests and canceled the cast and crew's visas. Tanaka said he spent the flight back from Jakarta bathed in his own sweat. Toho, poised to regain its market leadership, had seen its hottest young producer allow its biggest project of the year to blow up in his face. He'd telephoned from the Jakarta airport to ask Mori, the executive production manager, how soon he'd need to come up with a replacement for that spot in the production slate, and Mori had answered that he'd better have one by the time he landed. He spent the flight peering miserably out his window at the endless ocean and found his mind wandering to *Lucky Dragon No. 5*. He claimed he'd been so animated when his big idea hit him that the woman beside him had been startled out of her sleep.

In March the Americans had detonated a fifteen-megaton hydrogen weapon over Bikini atoll in the central Pacific, and *Lucky Dragon No. 5* was one of those little trawlers out for tuna that found itself inside the test zone.

They'd been where they were supposed to be but the detonation was twice as large as predicted. They reported seeing the sun rise in the west and then being covered by a powdery white ash for the hour that it took them to retrieve their net. Back in port it was determined that all twenty-three crew members and their entire haul had been heavily contaminated. And it turned out that the radioactive tuna had entered the Japanese market from other trawlers before the contamination was discovered, and the result was months of nuclear fear and anti-American hostility. Tabloids had called it the Americans' third atomic attack on Japan.

The year before Tsuburaya had forced Tanaka to go to see his beloved *King Kong*, which had just earned four times as much in its worldwide rerelease as it had originally, and Tanaka had also been impressed by the global numbers for Warner Bros.' *The Beast from 20,000 Fathoms*, the story of a dinosaur thawed from its hibernation by American nuclear testing in Baffin Bay.

The United States government estimated that 856 ships in the Japanese fishing fleet had been exposed to radiation, and that more than five hundred tons of fish had to be destroyed, and offered a settlement for the survivors that the Japanese government declined to accept. And Tanaka recounted that it struck him as he looked out over the Pacific below that the stories could be combined; and the rest of the flight he scribbled on the back of a folder that his seatmate had lent him the outline of a story in which a prehistoric creature was awakened by an H-bomb test in the Pacific and then went on to destroy Tokyo.

When Tsuburaya finally returned home for dinner on the night of the Star   10
Festival, Masano served soba noodles and mashed fish. While he ate, she was sober and quiet. He mentioned again by way of conversation a cough that wouldn't go away and she prepared for him without comment what she called her broth of the seven plants, which included shepherd's purse, chickweed, parsley, cottonweed, and radish. She sat with him while he drank it and, once he finished, told him he should smoke less.

For months his project was known at Toho only as Project G, for giant, but lately the staff had taken to calling it *Gojira*, a fusion of the word for gorilla, because of the monster's agility, and the one for whale, because of its size. Tanaka and Honda, the director, liked that as much as anything else anyone had come up with.

Upon leaving the following morning Tsuburaya noticed the telescope in the entryway and remembered to ask how the starviewing had gone. Masano asked how he thought it could have gone, given that it had rained.

The rest of the morning was spent laboring through an interview with the *Weekly Asahi*. The reporter, a young man with goggle-sized glasses, seemed to prize his own skepticism and asked each of his questions as if jabbing a tied dog with a stick. Did Eiji Tsuburaya, the Master of Miniatures and head of

Toho's Special Arts Department, *feel* the burden of his responsibility for the Visual effects on which Toho's new flagship production would either float or sink? Tsuburaya assured him that he did. Was it true there was a nuclear subtext to the story? Tsuburaya admitted that there was. And would Mr. Tsuburaya be willing to favor the *Weekly Asahi's* readers with an exclusive first glimpse of the movie's monster? Mr. Tsuburaya would not.

Eiji Tsuburaya was born in the village of Sukagawa, two hundred and twenty kilometers north of Tokyo in the Fukushima prefecture, and his grandmother and uncle told him every day of his childhood that he'd been delivered on a date propitious for creativity. His parents were Nichiren-sect Buddhists and as members of the rural gentry had been granted exclusive license to operate the local general-goods store, which remained the main clearinghouse, in that region, for sake, soy, and miso. His mother died when she was nineteen and he was three. In both of the photographs of her which remained, she appeared birdlike and consumptive and tilted him toward the camera much as a school-girl might display an examination on which had been scrawled a failing grade. In both she seemed to regard the photographer with a kind of pensive anxiety.

With his father subsequently forever at the store, he was raised by his   15
grandmother Natsu and his uncle Ichiro. He and Ichiro were so close in age that his uncle seemed more like an older brother, and so people stopped using Tsuburaya's given name, which meant first son, and started calling him Eiji, or second son.

When he was nine Ichiro took him to see Tokugawa and Hino at the Yoyogi Parade Grounds. Captains in the Imperial Army, they were aviation pioneers who'd made the first successful powered flights in Japan. He spent the next four years teaching himself how to build model airplanes out of wood, especially Tokugawa's Henry Farman biplane. He'd wake each morning at four and light his lamp and work until he had to leave for school and then, when classes were dismissed, he'd rush home and pick up where he'd left off. Once he'd achieved the verisimilitude he sought, he began increasing the scale until he was working on aircraft so large their wingspans no longer fit into his room. His father disapproved, but Tsuburaya believed he was building something that would fly him away and around the world. The bigger models ended up causing enough of a stir with the neighbors that the local newspaper did a feature about him entitled "The Child Craftsman." And throughout his career Tsuburaya was teased about the fact that the first time he saw a motion picture, he found him-self more fascinated with the projector than with what was going on onscreen.

Akira was their third child and second son, born much later than the other two. Their daughter, Miyako, had died in her sleep two years after her birth. She'd had a small fever and called out in the night to Masano, who told her that she would be fine and then fell back asleep after everything had quieted.

For three months afterwards Masano could not be induced to leave the house. Neither her family nor her friends had any effect. She came around only mechanically at first to the notion that they still had a son to raise, and Hajime, who was two years older, cried himself to sleep each night in terror and helplessness while his mother gently stroked his head.

Tsuburaya was then a camera operator and kept himself busy with his production schedule and with brainstorming apparatuses that would improve his work. He'd patented and sold the Auto Snap, a pedal-operated shutter cable that freed the hands for other tasks, and had also experimented so successfully with smoke pots for in-camera effects that he'd become known around the industry as Smoke Tsuburaya. When he came home, though, such news had to be left at the front door.

Hajime had finally regained his mother's attention by telling her he was   20
collecting stones for the roadside Jizo image. According to the legend, the souls of all dead children went to the underground river where a she-devil got them to pile stones on the bank by assuring them that if they made their piles high enough they could climb to paradise, but then she perpetually knocked over their work. Jizo, a roadside deity, comforted them, and every stone placed in the lap of one of his statues was supposed to shorten their task. Each morning before school, then, Hajime and Masano would add one or two stones to the nearest statue's pile.

In this way, his wife had pulled herself along, moment by moment. She enjoyed it if her husband sat quietly beside her. She submitted to his ministrations but declined to touch him. She seemed to appreciate being put to bed at night.

That was the year *King Kong* came to Japan. Tsuburaya had seen *The Lost World* some years earlier, but this was staggering: Willis O'Brien had with his little figures and suitcase jungles transformed RKO Radio Pictures from whatever it had been before into a world power. Tsuburaya wrote him with questions but never discovered if his letters had gotten through. He saw the film six times. He took Hajime, who was so terrified that they had to leave in the middle. Without a response from O'Brien, his only recourse was to use his connections to obtain a 35mm print and break down its effects himself, frame by frame. One evening he brought Masano in from where she was sitting and situated her next to him beside the projector. The following evening he let her remain where she was.

A week after the Star Festival, Tsuburaya was beginning dinner at his desk when Honda telephoned with news of yet another logistical catastrophe, then caught himself in the middle of his narrative and said, "Oh, but today you have to be home: It's the Obon." And he was right: of all the days of the year, this was not the one to come home late. If the Star Festival for Masano was all about how exhilarated they'd once been as lovers, the Obon was the principal commemoration of her lost little girl. She had reminded Tsuburaya once, at the beginning of the week, and then had not mentioned it again. She'd be celebrating for the full three days, and on the first night she intended that as a family they would light the paper lantern and hang it on the grave to invite their daughter's spirit to come forth and visit their home. On the table for the dead her meal would already be set out, with tiny portions featuring her favorite dishes. Akira, as always, had been given charge of arranging the display.

Hajime, now nineteen, was invited, but had yet to indicate whether he would appear. Masano had requested it when they'd last seen him, on a school holiday, and he'd answered that he'd see what he could do. He then pointed out that he'd finished his technical training, and asked his father whether he might work with him as assistant camera operator on the miniatures team.

Tsuburaya discussed what that would involve, and Masano interrupted   25
to ask if they could return to the subject of their daughter and Hajime's sister. Then Hajime said he would make every effort, and his mother told him he should see that he did.

That night she informed Tsuburaya that she considered their son's request a bad idea, at least for the time being; that he should stay in school; that he didn't need additional training in how to ignore his family. Tsuburaya felt the need to defend his profession.

"Well, at least promise you'll do nothing without consulting me," she finally requested.

"Who Toho hires is none of your concern," he reminded her.

"What you do with our son is my concern," she answered. And neither of them pursued the matter after that.

When Mori and Honda first approached him, he'd been thrilled at the   30
prospect after all of those years of finally being able to work on the kind of stop-motion effects he had so admired in *King Kong*. But when Mori asked him to write up a projected preproduction and shooting schedule for his unit, even after every shortcut he could conceive, he was forced to report that to do the job right he would need a little less than seven years. On the phone he could hear Mori repeating what he'd said to the others in his office, and there was a general hilarity in the background. When Mori returned to the line he was still chuckling. He said he could give Tsuburaya two months for preproduction and another two for shooting.

That left Tsuburaya's department with few options other than what they knew best: miniature building. Which was what everyone expected of him anyway.

His big break had come when Toho was urged by the government during the war to pour nearly all of its resources into *The War at Sea*, the epic charged with the task of persuading the public that the new war with the

Americans was one the Japanese could win. Using photographs supplied by the navy, his unit had re-created Pearl Harbor on a six-acre outdoor set on Toho's backlot, and had done so with such persuasive detail that the footage of the attack on Battleship Row was confiscated by U.S. occupation officials after the war because they'd taken it to be real. The movie returned the highest grosses ever recorded in Japan, tripled his budgets and staff, and ensured that anyone in the country with a special-effects problem would seek out the celebrated Tsuburaya.

So if on this new project O'Brien's solutions were denied to them, it meant only that they had to approach the situation in a new way. This didn't dishearten them, since they already understood that whenever fixed rules were applied to a problem, only parts of it might be perceived. They operated on the principle that you weren't ready for a task until you admitted it was beyond you.

He came up with the idea of an entire 1/25 scale miniature set of the capital, detailed inside as well as out in order to be convincing when trampled. Breakaway walls would reveal entire floors with all of their furnishings when the monster sheared away the outside surfaces. Various aspects of the city's infrastructure, such as mailboxes or street lamps, would be rendered in wax and melted by huge offscreen heat lamps to simulate the monster's radioactive breath. Small and precisely calibrated pyrotechnic charges would be installed to reproduce the explosive destruction as fuel and automobile gas tanks ignited.

And 1/25 scale would allow a monster of the proper size to be generated   35
by simply putting a man in a suit.

The simplicity of the plan held enormous appeal. He'd always been drawn to the handmade approach, and of course the studio appreciated the relative lack of expense. Something made from nothing was how he liked to put it.

Mori and Honda loved the budget and feared the plan. A man in a suit? Tsuburaya only shrugged at their unease. They either trusted him or they didn't. Proof was stronger than argument.

The day after the logistical catastrophe, Honda called to report that he'd handled it without Tsuburaya's help. Honda was probably Tsuburaya's closest friend, though at that suggestion Masano once responded that she would love to see Honda's face when someone told him as much. Honda was forever sporting an American's rumpled little fishing hat and was fond of walking great distances. He and Tanaka met when hiking the Diamond Mountains in Korea in the early thirties. Mori and Tanaka had both thought Honda would be the perfect director for this new project since he'd had so little trouble with all the visual effects in *Eagles of the Pacific*, and had worked so well with Tsuburaya. Having been a longtime assistant to Kurosawa, he was experienced in dealing with lunatic perfectionists. "Or, in other words, Tsuburaya," Mori had said at their first full staff meeting.

They also liked that Honda had no patience for storylines that dawdled. They'd handed a first attempt at the script to the mystery writer Kayama and what he'd produced was far too tame, involving a nondescript dolphinlike creature that attacked only fishing boats and only to feed its insatiable hunger. Most of the story had involved the poor thing swimming this way and that in search of food.

Honda had clear-cut Kayama's script, demanding something terrible 40 enough to evoke both the fire raids on Tokyo and the bombing of Hiroshima and Nagasaki. He'd served three tours of duty as an infantryman, had been a prisoner of war in China, been repatriated near Hiroshima, and then had wandered the devastation three months after the surrender.

He thought much like Tsuburaya did: that the director, like a department head, had to include in his leadership the responsibility to protect the artisans under his umbrella. And, of course, to recruit those artisans. And where were they to be found? They had to have the right sensibility toward beauty, sufficient technical training and scientific knowledge, and a strong will, passion, and creative talent.

Honda claimed he drew his belief in himself from the soil of his life experience. His mother had also died when he was small, and his father soon afterward. He'd been left unable to attend school and had taught himself to read while carrying firewood for his neighbors. He knew that encountering the unfamiliar might involve many errors before a solution was found, and he had an intuition that seemed to draw on an extraordinary visual resourcefulness. When he loved something, he'd exclaim, "Oh, this is spring water!" Again like Tsuburaya, he knew that the craftsman worked with and for his world, but ultimately went his own way, not seeking praise. When *Eagles of the Pacific* premiered, Honda was on a little lake, fishing. Because the objects themselves were one's best signature.

As a young man, Tsuburaya had been struck by how different the Japanese hand was from the big, untrained hands of the other races. Masano had a calligrapher's hands, long-fingered and tapering, and he'd been seduced by their dexterity and sensitivity when watching her set out her simple gifts for him in the hospital. The daughter of a Kyoto engineering magnate, she was fond of movie stars and thanks to her father's influence, was touring the studio when the camera crane Tsuburaya had invented collapsed and he crashed to the floor in front of her. The shattered lens shield had slightly cut her forehead but even so she cradled his face and neck while his assistants came running. She later claimed he'd reached up to touch her injury, but he had no memory of that. On the same afternoon she'd appeared in his hospital room, bearing her gifts, and remaining behind after everyone else had left. They'd married a year later, when she was nineteen.

Their courtship had mostly taken the form of long-distance love notes, in which Tsuburaya found a courage of expression based on longing and the safety of isolation. *All of us,* he wrote later: *when we make a little progress, we're captivated by our cleverness.*

Their feelings were an act of faith, just as the sublimity of an artisan's   45
pot was a gift and not a calculation. They gave themselves over to those feelings the way lips kissed the thickness of a tea bowl's rim.

They honeymooned in the old Okinawa, which was now gone. Its capital had been a dream city, its narrow streets mossy and hushed, over which
dark leaves threw down their shade. Eaves on the ancient red-tiled roofs
featured heraldic animals fired from clay.

But lately it seemed to him that their minds were bound by obsessions
that deprived them of freedom. They each put in longer days, he in his
innovations and his wife in her grieving. All the rituals that had solidified
their happiness now reflected back its opposite. In Masano's photo albums
of her loss, baby girls on their thirty-third day were taken to the shrine
in thanksgiving by their grandmothers, who prayed for their welfare. As
always, the tinier the tot, the more brilliantly it was dressed. Some photographs of these celebrations were prominently displayed on the family altar.
Or, in the event of the child's death, on the grave.

Tsuburaya's experience was that one who was gone was forgotten, day
by day. As his grandmother put it, "Destiny's in heaven, and rice dumplings
are on the shelf."

But Masano knew spilt water never returned to the tray. And if she forgot,
she said, Tsuburaya reminded her by going on with his life. She said that in the
face of her unhappiness, he was like a blind man peeping through a fence.

"I'm sorry for my myopia," he told her after the Obon had concluded,   50
and after she'd followed some late-night tenderness with despair. He once
again had come home nearly at dawn and she'd risen to meet him, backing
him across the room with her beautiful hands.

"I suppose its like that old saying that the lighthouse doesn't shine on
its own base," she'd remarked some hours later, while each still smelled of
the other's touch.

Before getting fired, Kayama suggested that the comic-book artist Abe should
design the creature. Abe had been the illustrator for *Kenya Boy,* a series about
an orphaned Japanese boy who was lost in Africa and continually had to fight
off prehistoric monsters. Why Africa was overrun with prehistoric monsters
was never explained. Abe produced a month's worth of designs, each of which
was less useful than the previous one. He was finally let go when he put forward
a proposal that featured a giant frog's body and a head shaped like a mushroom
cloud. With no time to hire another designer, Honda and Tsuburaya decided
to simply hybridize a dinosaur of their own conception. Various illustrations
were pulled from libraries and children's books and mixed and matched on the

drafting table. Of course it would have a tyrannosaur's head, but an Iguanodon's body seemed an easier fit for a stuntman's requirements, in terms of operating the suit. And Honda added a stegosaur's back plates along the spine to ensure their creature would appear distinct from any recorded species.

During the clay-rendering stage they had his staff experiment with scaly, warty, and alligator skin before settling on the last. And with that decided, one whole unit was turned over to the suit's construction.

The first version was framed in cloth-covered wire, over which rubber that had been melted in a steel drum was applied in layers. The result was immobile and weighed three hundred and fifty-five pounds. In the next attempt, the cloth itself was painted with the base coat, so only two layers of rubber were necessary, but the result was still a staggeringly heavy two hundred and twenty pounds. But after a month of further futility, they had to concede that rubber applied any less thickly would crack at the joints, so the second version would have to do.

To minimize the length of time the poor stuntman would have to   55
spend in the thing, another suit was produced and cut into two sections for shots requiring only part of the monster, waist-up or waist-down. For screen tests of the latter, Nakajima, the stuntman, galumphed around in his heavy suspenders like someone wearing clown pants or waders, his great rubber feet crushing the rough models they'd arranged around the stage.

They chose Nakajima not only for his height and physical conditioning but also for his dogged determination. To prepare for his role, he'd taken a projector home with him and worn out Tsuburaya's print of *King Kong*, and he told anyone who would listen that he'd spent two full weeks of evenings observing bears at the Ueno Zoo.

Another unit had successfully produced a smaller-scale, hand-operated puppet of the head that could spray a stream of mist from its jaws, for close-ups of the creature's radioactive breath.

"So is your monster ready to go?" Masano asked the night before shooting was set to commence, out of the dark, when Tsuburaya had thought she was asleep.

"I think he is, yes," Tsuburaya answered, surprising even himself.

One of the first recitations that he remembered from primary school   60
involved the five terrors, in ascending order: "earthquake, storm, flood, fire, father." It surprised no one that "father" was judged the most dangerous. As preoccupied as their fathers were, when it came to their sons they still found time for disappointment and punishment. And waiting to see that disappointment coalesce on his father's face, during those rare occasions in which Tsuburaya spent time with him: those were some of his unhappiest memories.

His academic performance was always adequate but his father was particularly unhappy about his refusal to moderate the time he devoted after school to airplane building, and in the event of a harsh report on this from his grandmother, his father gave him the option of having his most recent model-building efforts reduced to kindling or having his hand burned. Like many before him, his father believed in the deterrent effect of burning rolled wormwood fibers on the clenched fist of a misbehaving boy. Once lit, the fibers lifted off from their own convection currents after a moment or two, but even so always left behind a white scar.

Afterwards his father treated the burn himself, with a cooling paste, and talked about the lessons his own father had taught him. He always began with the maxim that with either good acts or bad, the dust thus amassed would make a mountain. He had other favorites as well. When addressing elders or the opposite sex, the mouth was the entrance to calamity. Hard work in school had its usefulness, because what seemed stupid now might prove useful later. We should love our children with a stick. And it was always better not to say than to say.

His father reminded him that in the old days a child like Tsuburaya would be made to swallow a small salamander alive as a cure for nervous weakness. One rainy morning in a park, when his father thought he'd been too peevish, he held one up to Tsuburaya's mouth and said that a childhood classmate of his had reported he could feel it moving about his stomach for some minutes afterward.

Yet Tsuburaya also remembered him taking them on the hottest days for shaved ice with grape, strawberry, or lemon syrup, the syrup never getting down as far as the red beans at the base of the paper cone. He remembered a delivery in a downpour in which they sat in their wagon watching farmers in a field in the distance, in their raincoats woven from rushes looking like so many porcupines while they squatted to rest. He remembered insect festivals in the evenings when the autumn grasses bloomed and the singing insects they'd gathered in their tiny cages were, at an agreed-upon stroke, all freed, and how they waited—himself, his grandmother, Ichiro, and his father—for that moment when the cicadas would get their bearings, puzzle out their freedom, and let loose their rejoicing in song.

For the first day of principal photography, the visual-effects team was divided into its three units, one for location photography to shoot the plates for the process and composite shots, one for the lab work, and one for the miniatures. Tsuburaya called Hajime that morning to let him know that he could join the unit. Hajime was so excited, he claimed, that he ran all the way to the studio when the streetcar was late.

"Why didn't you take a cab?" Honda asked once he arrived. "You're sweating on our work," he added, when Hajime only grinned for an answer.

Tsuburaya told him that he had three minutes to get the film casings loaded, and the boy disappeared to cool himself off as best he could at the sinks in the washroom before returning with his hair askew and in a borrowed shirt.

It turned out that before they'd even gotten through a half a day, another stuntman, Tezuka, was needed to spell Nakajima, so exhausting was the part. The suit was stifling in the August heat even without the studio lights, but with them it was a roasting pan. Added to that were the fumes from the burning kerosene rags intended to simulate Tokyo's fires. Under the searing lights Nakajima was barely able to breathe or see, and could only spend a maximum of fifteen minutes in the suit before being too overcome to continue. Each time he stepped out of it, the supporting technicians drained the leg as if pouring water out of a boot. One measured a cup and a half of sweat from each leg.

The second half of the first day's schedule involved the destruction of the National Diet. Tezuka fainted and broke his jaw on the top of the parliament building as he fell, so they were back to Nakajima again. While awaiting his recovery, they repaired the damage to the building.

Upon Nakajima's return, everything went off in one shot. While he   70
maneuvered his way down the row of buildings, crew members at Tsuburaya's signal heaved on the cable that ran up through a pulley in the rafters and worked the tail. When it crashed into the side of the National Diet, another technician detonated the pyrotechnics and plastic and wooden parts rained down on everyone in the studio. Honda said it looked even better through the eyepiece than they might have hoped. And they all felt at once exultation and disquiet. While the men extinguishing the fires sprayed everything down, the fastenings were undone and the top part of the creature was peeled from poor Nakajima's head and shoulders. While he was given some water it hung before him like a sack.

Tanaka came by to see the last part of the shot and reported that Mori had taken to calling what they were doing "suitmation."

"How'd the boy work out?" he asked Honda, half-teasing.

"I haven't heard any complaints," Honda told him in response. And Hajime pretended to be too absorbed in sealing the rush canisters to have heard what they said.

Masano was asleep when Tsuburaya was finally dropped off after the first day of shooting, and asleep when he left the next morning. Toward the end of the second day, an assistant informed him during a break that she'd telephoned to let him know that Hajime would be joining them for dinner that night.

His son was lugging film cans to the processing wagon while Tsuburaya   75
read the note. "You're dining with us tonight?" he called to him.

"That's what I'm told," Hajima answered.

They rode home together. It was still bright out and the dining table was flooded with a quiet white light from the paper windows. Masano collected Imari porcelain and had set out for the occasion her most prized bowls and cups.

Seeming even more grim than usual, she asked how their days had been. Tsuburaya told her his had gone well. Hajime smiled like a guest in someone else's home, and Akira seemed beside himself with joy at his brother's unexpected presence, though even he seemed to register the tension. For appetizers there were a number of variations on raw radishes, Hajime's favorite, including some involving three kinds of flavored salts. Masano had begun believing more and more fiercely in the purifying usefulness of salt.

There was a silence while they ate, except for Akira smacking his lips. When they finished, Masano cleared the table and served, for dessert, more radishes, pickled and sugared. She asked if they had anything to tell her.

"Do you have anything to tell your mother?" Tsuburaya asked the 80 older boy.

Hajime seemed to give it some knit-browed thought. "It's nice to see you?" he finally offered.

She sat back with her arms folded and watched them exchange looks. "I've tried to give our son some direction; a little instruction," she finally remarked. "But you know what that's like. It's like praying into a horse's ear."

"I've taken Hajime on as my camera assistant," Tsuburaya to her.

"Yes, I thought that might be the situation," she answered, and even Akira acknowledged the extent of her anger by hunching his shoulders. "The Personnel Department called, needing informtion," she added.

He'd provided their oldest son with a job, and a good one. Tsuburaya 85 reminded her. That seemed cause for celebration, and not complaint.

"As you say, I have no cause for complaint," Masano told him. But something in her shoulders once she'd turned away left him so dismayed that he found he no longer had the heart to argue. They sat facing each other like mirror images of defeat.

"Thank you for this excellent meal," Hajime told her.

"Thank you for coming," Masano answered. Tsuburaya put his hand atop hers, at the table, and she let him leave it there.

But she didn't speak to him again until later that night, when he threw off his covers in the heat. She said then that as a young woman she'd felt anxious about seeming awkward when she tried to express herself. And that until she'd met him, she'd feared it had something to do with being too self-centered. And that their letters—their feelings—had helped her understand that something else was possible.

"Remember how thrilled we'd be when we saw my name in the credits?" 90 Tsuburaya asked her.

"I read some of those letters today," she told him. In the dark he couldn't see her face. "They're such strange things. So full of connection."

"Hajime can work for Toho and remain a loving son," he told her.

"I need to sleep now," she explained, after a pause. And after another pause, she did.

He departed earlier than usual for the studio the next day, and at his driver's horn-blowing, he raised his head from his work to find his car in a great migration of bicycles ridden by delivery boys, bakery boys, and messenger boys, some of them negotiating astonishing loads: glaziers' boys balancing great panes of glass, soba boys shouldering pyramids of boxed soups, peddlers' boys with pickle barrels, all weaving along at high speed. When a toddler in a tram window reached out to touch one, the cyclist veered away down a side street.

Honda greeted him that morning with Ifukube's score, which he played 95 for everyone on the upright piano. No surprises there. Ifukube had spent the war composing nationalist marches, and what he'd presented to Honda was a mishmash of some of his favorites. Apparently he hadn't even looked at the rushes. "Close your eyes and you're back on the home front," Tanaka called acidly from the hallway while Honda was playing it.

That afternoon two full sequences were filmed. After Honda approved the second, he asked if Tsuburaya had come up with anything to conceal the wires for the attacking jets. Tsuburaya showed him on the Moviola the little test he'd conducted, and Honda was stupefied and overjoyed: what had Tsuburaya done? Where had the wires gone? Tsuburaya explained that he'd hung and flown the models upside down, then had inverted the image. The wires were still there, but no one noticed them *below* the aircraft instead of above. Honda wanted to call some others in and make a fuss about it, but Tsuburaya reminded him that if time and budget were the main walls around the moviemaker, it was his job to help punch through them. "So we can get on to other things," Honda agreed. And Tsuburaya could imagine Masano's response, had she heard.

Early in the war they'd brought Hajime to see the rare birds and animals that had been added to the Ueno Zoo after the conquests in the south. Tsuburaya remembered the days being perpetually sunny. Hajime had also loved the rooftop pool of the Matsuzakaya department store, where shoppers were treated to mock battles between electrically controlled models of the Japanese and Allied fleets while the store's customer service manager talked about the need for consumer restraint. Plaques bearing the phrase "Honor Home" were in the windows of every house that had a father or son off at the war, and Masano had joked to her friends that only her husband's age had held him back, and that national mobilization was never a problem if all that was asked of men was that they cast off parents, wives, or children before going off to war.

But by that point he was already working in the Special Arts Department at Toho. The ten major studios had been forced to consolidate into just three, all making mostly war films in order to promote national policy and strengthen the country's resolve. The rooftop display had given him the idea for the miniatures photography for Toho s first drama about the China war, *Navy Bomber Squadron*. And the climactic battle sequence had gone off so well that he'd then been given responsibility for the scene in which the Chinese primary school, once destroyed, turned out to have been a secret armaments depot. Those sequences had resulted in his first screen credit for visual effects, though the sight of the bombed Chinese school seemed to cripple Masano's enjoyment at the premiere.

Had they ever been closer, though? The ongoing national emergency had seemed to revive her sense of all that she still had to lose, and nearly every night her face found his in their bed once they had extinguished the light. Every family was urged to start the day at the same hour with radio calisthenics, and during the first six months after Pearl Harbor there were nothing but victories to report, so the radio made for good listening. Hajime found it hilarious to watch his parents huff and sweat. More and more disappeared from public life to exist only in private, the way before the war the censors had edited out of foreign films all instances of socialism or kissing.

Accounts of each battle were concluded with a rendition of Ifukube's Naval 100 March. But then as the war turned, announcements of this or that territory's strategic importance were reversed, and its loss apparently meant nothing, whereas its capture had been wildly celebrated the year before. Hajime spent even longer hours in school undergoing mandatory vocational and military training. And Masano was further saddened at the eradication of neighborhood birds by the heavy guns of an artillery training division billeted nearby.

Tsuburaya told her one night that it was just like Japan to go to war with the nation upon whom she was most dependent for the raw materials essential to prosecuting that war. Modern warfare began in the mine and continued in the factory feeding on coal and steel and oil, and ninety percent of the oil Japan consumed before the war was imported, nearly all of it from the United States. She seemed to find this point even more painful than he did.

They were told that Leyte was the battle that would determine the fate of the nation. Once Leyte was lost, it turned out that Luzon was the key. After Luzon, Iwo Jima. After Iwo Jima, Okinawa, "Well, apparently the mountain moves Masano answered, a little bitterly, when he remarked to her about it. She was especially demoralized by a newspaper account of the destruction of Okinawa's capital, and the printed photo of their narrow and hushed streets from all those years ago shelled into rubble.

By then there were no pleasures. Food was miserable, lovemaking was impossible, there was no time even for reading, and they constantly feared that even at his age Hajime would be called up. Dinners were rice bran, fried in a pan, which looked like custard but made Hajime cry when he ate it. Movie production had come to a halt due to a lack of nitrate for film stock. Workers at Toho were serving as labor volunteers in the countryside, helping farmers and returning each night with a few sweet potatoes for their work.

And then came the raids. Hajime demanded to be taken to a public exhibition of a B-29 in Hibiya Park, where the bomber had been reconstructed from the parts of various downed aircraft and was displayed alongside one of Japan's latest interceptors. The fighter looked like a peanut beside a dinner plate. Such was the Americans' nonchalance by that point that they dropped leaflets the day before detailing where and when they would strike. Aloft, these leaflets resembled a small, fleecy cloud, but as they fluttered down they dispersed over the city.

The fire raid on March ninth centered on the area hit by the 1923 earth- 105 quake, the trauma that had separated him forever from his father. The one on the tenth extended the destruction. The next morning they returned to acres of ruin where their homes had been. Block after block was burned flat, with lonely telephone poles erect at odd angles like grave markers, leaving only ash and brick and the occasional low shell of a concrete building. Where the deso- lation wasn't complete, the neighborhood associations were still holding air- defense drills and doing their best to resettle those bombed out of their homes.

The only topic of conversation by then was food, or the failure of the rationing system. Everyone spent their days foraging. They were told to col- lect acorns for flour because they had the same nutritive value as rice. They ate weeds and boiled licorice greens and bracken ferns. And then they heard that as the result of an attack by a very small number of B-29's, the city of Hiroshima had been considerably damaged. And that the Emperor would be addressing the nation by radio for the first time in history.

When Tsuburaya mentioned by way of offering encouragement that they'd completed the first month of shooting, Masano said in response, "You take as much time as you need to. Whatever your lack of interest, our routine is going to continue as it has."

He was taken aback. She'd caught him struggling into his rain shell and preoccupied with the problem of the high-tension wires the monster was to destroy on his way into Tokyo. She was at their kitchen table working on a gourd that was supposed to afford the sparrows some protection from rats. The gourd would hang from a nail under the eave outside their front door.

This wasn't how things would always be, he assured her. Soon the shooting and even postproduction would be over.

"I'll continue to maintain your household and raise our child, whatever 110 happens between us," she told him.

"What does that mean, 'whatever happens between us'?" he asked. He was shaken, the notion of yet more separation like a fear of the dark.

"Akira's very proud of you," she answered. "And his brother. Do you know what he said to me before he left for school? He said he understood why neither of you liked him."

"Do I need to stay home?" Tsuburaya asked her, and set down his work satchel. "Do we need to talk about this now?"

"He's nine years old and he sounded like me," she said.

He unbuckled his rain shell in contrition, pained at her attempt to   115
keep her composure. "I'll talk to him this evening," he told her. "Hajime
will talk to him as well."

"It's one thing if it's just myself," she said. "But I can't watch this happen
to him, too."

"I'll go see him now," he said. He had his driver wait outside Akira's
school, but the boy's classroom was empty when he finally found it. The
instructor in an adjacent room said he thought the class might have gone off on
a nature walk.

When Tsuburaya was twenty-two, his father took the train to Tokyo for business and left his grandmother and Ichiro in charge of the store. The idea
seemed to be that he might partner up with a larger distribution chain. But
he might also have been trying to exert some influence on his son.

Tsuburaya had by that point given up his dreams of aviation, and after
serving in the Imperial Infantry had returned to the store, uncertain of his
future. Before his call-up, a chance encounter had led to his training as a cam-
eraman for Edamasa, the famous director, whom he'd worked for until his
conscription notice had arrived. Back at home, he stocked shelves and took
inventory. His father claimed his son's choices were his own, but his grandmother hectored him to give up dreaming about movies and airplanes and
to give some thought to his family and especially his father and uncle, who
shouldered the burden of the family business alone.

But when he heard from Edamasa again, the pull was too strong, and   120
when he was sent out to buy rice one morning, he left a note stating he
wouldn't return until he'd succeeded in the motion-picture business or died
trying. When he telephoned from Tokyo a week later to let them know he
was safe and settled into a place where they could reach him, Ichiro came to
the phone but his father and grandmother did not. Ichiro said his mother
still hadn't recovered from the effrontery of the note.

So he was surprised to receive his father's invitation to lunch. They
arranged it for the day of his father's arrival, but that morning the truck had
broken down on some location shooting for which Tsuburaya had volunteered in the hills and he found himself stranded out of town.

The day his truck broke down and his father arrived at the capital was
September 1, 1923, and a few minutes before noon his father was still expecting him for lunch when the Great Kanto Earthquake brought the Imperial
Hotel's chandelier down onto the table before him. He said he'd just lifted his
water glass away from his place setting when it was as if a giant had stamped
it flat. He stood up with his pant leg open at the knee like a haversack. Something in the shattered and telescoping table had lashed open his lower thigh.

The moment before, he'd been peering over at the lunch room's little indoor pond, where dull carp drowsed in the tepid water. Then there was a rumbling and the first shock, a vertical jolt. At the second jolt, the chandelier came down, and the floor began to pitch and rock so that the heavy parquet snapped and ricocheted like fireworks, and after he'd stood he was unable to run and got thrown onto his side. From there he saw the office concern across the street collapse into a dust cloud so intense that it was as if the hotel windows had been permanently chalked with yellow.

Out on a side street, he managed to tie his tattered pant leg around for his thigh, casting around for his son, and with every jolt the hotel and an adjacent bank flexed like buggy whips and cracks appeared along their walls, from which window casings and marble avalanched into the street. He said that with each shock it was as if the earth had been pulled out from under him. Where was Eiji? Where was his son? He ran, searching, as the concussions changed to undulations. And then it appeared to be over, though every few minutes the aftershocks were sufficient to knock him to his knees.

He found himself in a little park, panting. Sparrows under a stand of 125 orange trees seemed somehow to have been grounded, hopping about, for all the freneticism of their wings achieving only a few feet of altitude before fluttering back into the dirt. He was weeping, he realized, in fear for his son. Should he go back? All avenues in that direction had been blocked by massive slides of debris.

All of this he'd related to Ichiro the last time Tsuburaya saw him. Only the oval of his face had been spared the salve and the bandages. Tsuburaya had wondered if the doctors had applied the same cooling paste his father had used on his burns. He said hello to his father, who then directed him and his grandmother to wait outside the ward. His grandmother went off to berate the overworked medical teams from the Relief Bureau, but he held his ear to the open door.

"Keep him away from me," his father said, and Tsuburaya couldn't fully register what he'd just heard. His father went on to tell his uncle that within a minute the city had been cut off from everything, the water and gas mains ruptured, the telegraph and telephone wires down. The trolley rails where he crossed them had sprung upward after snapping. He'd called for Eiji and in response heard cries in all directions. And then he noticed the rice-cracker shop already on fire, the smoke rising into the still, hot air. There seemed to be no one present, no one making an effort to put out the flames.

Later Tsuburaya thought that he'd probably heard more of his father's voice that day than he had for the previous five years. He was crying for his father's pain and because of his banishment from the room. Every so often Ichiro asked if the pain was very bad and never received an answer. When his grandmother returned, she whispered something and tried to pull Tsuburaya away from the door, but he tore his elbow away with such ferocity that she never tried again. *You should go back into that room*, he told himself. Instead he stood where he was and listened.

Everything had been destroyed and the gas mains shattered just as lunch fires were being lit in hibachis and stoves all over Tokyo, in hotels and lunch counters and apartments and factory work stations from Ota to Arakawa. All of those braziers scattered their coals onto tatami mats on crooked old streets and alleys just wide enough to provide sufficient drafts. His father saw firemen—their water mains now dry—trying to use nearby moats and canals. He said those not trying to pull the trapped from the rubble did their best to put out the fires, but there were too many of them, and almost no water. Then the wind picked up.

Because there was no single point of origin neither was there a single   130 advancing front of fire, and no one knew where to go or what was safe. Everyone who could headed to the river, and along its banks the mobs were increasingly herded toward the bridges, where they were crushed or tipped over the side until the bridges themselves caught fire. His father struggled toward anyone who resembled his son until he was knocked into the water by a handcart, and there he stayed alive by keeping submerged until oil from ruptured storage tanks ignited upstream, the fire cascading at him along the surface. He scrambled out just ahead of its arrival.

Beside the Yasuda Gardens he pitched himself into a broad, bare lot that had been the site of the Army Clothing Depot, where uniforms were stored for shipment. Its size and location along the river promised more safety—across its twelve acres there was very little to burn—and thousands poured into it all through the afternoon, as everywhere else became more and more of a conflagration. They came singly and in groups, some pulling carts piled with outlandish goods, and found places for themselves. Patients from nearby hospitals were carried in on stretchers. Everyone was polite, settling down shoulder-to-shoulder to wait. They watched the fire surrounding them burn. The crush was so pronounced that he gave up the notion of hunting the crowd for his son.

Someone behind him complained that he'd forgotten his chess set. The bitter taste of smoke in the air intensified. He wished he'd had some lunch.

And then, across the river, starbursts of spark and flame seemed to be climbing the columns of smoke high into the clouds. He asked the man beside him for the time, and the man told him it was a little after four. The wind was intensifying, and from the west they could hear the sound of a huge airplane flying low across the river. Was it a rescue mission? It was flying toward them, but in that direction the sky was enveloped in black. And then he saw it wasn't the sky but a column so wide it seemed to cover the horizon, and that it was spinning and shot through with fire. Debris crossed its face and reappeared again. By then they could hear nothing else.

It seemed to detonate everything on the other side of the river before it came across. It swept away the barges. It blew apart the School of Industry. It drew river water forty feet up into the funnel before it sheared off as steam. By the time it hit the Clothing Depot it sounded like gargantuan waterfalls crashing together.

Two policemen agape on a refugee's cart were blown away. Tsuburaya's 135 father was knocked down and blasted along the ground until his hand caught onto something. A teenaged girl on fire flew by over his head. Human beings all around him were sucked into the air like sparks. He shut his eyes against the wind and heat. A tree was wrenched from the ground, roots and all, before him, and he crawled into the loose earth and was able to breathe. Some ruptured water mains there had created a bog, and he tunneled into the mud.

When he revived, the backs of his hands had been burned to the bone. Everyone was gone. The skin atop his head was gone. His ears were gone. Something beside him he couldn't recognize was still squirming.

At their store that evening, two hundred and twenty kilometers away. Tsuburaya's grandmother reported that the columns of smoke and cloud carried upward by the convection currents made everyone wonder if a new volcano had been born. An intense red glow spread across the southern horizon.

His father said he remembered only fitful things afterward. Someone carried him somewhere eventually. An army cart in one of the burned-out areas stopped to pass out cupfuls of water to refugees. A riderless horse stood in the road too badly burned to move. Bodies looked like black rucksacks except for the occasional raised leg or hand. He remembered a shirt like his son's under a cascade of lumbers. A functioning well with a long queue beside it. He died soon after he mentioned the well, describing the water he so enjoyed from it.

In the years following his death Tsuburaya talked to historians and scientists and survivors. The historians informed him that over four thousand acres of Tokyo had burned, ten times the acreage of the Great Fire of London's, and that a hundred thousand people had perished, a hundred times the number consumed in the Americans' San Francisco fire. The scientists informed him that the updraft that produced the columns his grandmother witnessed had caused a gigantic vacuum near the ground and the surrounding air had swept in to fill it before being drawn upwards itself, resulting in a furnace four thousand acres wide and an updraft that generated tornadoes as it pulled the fire up into it: fire tornadoes. And the survivors told him stories like the ones his father had related. Though of course once Masano and Tsuburaya had endured the fire raids at the end of the war, he no longer needed to turn to others for that sort of understanding. "Smoke Tsuburaya," she'd said to herself one night as they'd hurried down the steps to a shelter. He'd had less trouble than others negotiating a safe route through the fires, since he knew from his father's experience which way to go.

"Do you think he knew I was listening?" he'd asked his uncle on the   140
morning his family had returned home from his father's deathbed. He'd
shamed himself by weeping so much on the train that his grandmother had
finally taken a seat opposite him.

"I don't think he gave it any thought," Ichiro answered.

At the sound bay, everyone was very excited about the roar Ifukube had come
up with. Tsuburaya had charged him with the task of creating for the monster's
cry something melancholy and ear-splitting—"Try producing *that* combination," Ifukube had complained when given the instructions—and he'd spent
two weeks sorting through recordings of wild animals before he'd finally given
up and settled on drawing a heavy work glove across the strings of a contrabass
and manipulating the sound in an echo chamber. The result was hair-raising.
The entire production team was beside itself with happiness. He had also over-
laid a recording of a taiko drum with an electronically altered mine detonation
to produce the monster's footfalls.

Halfway through the shooting Honda told Tsuburaya that he was using many
more close-ups of the monster's face than he'd thought he would, because its
dilemma was becoming more real to him. Man had created war and the Bomb
and now nature was going to exact its revenge, with tormented Gojira its way
of making radiation visible. That's why he'd insisted that its skin be thick and
furrowed like the keloid scars of the atomic survivors.

Tanaka was uneasy, in fact, with how often the movie referenced the war.
And he worried that the long shots of the burned-out city would recall for
everyone the newspaper images of Hiroshima and Nagasaki.

In the rushes of the final scenes, Honda noted how sad Gojira looked   145
when he turned from the camera.

"That's the way I made the mask," Tsuburaya reminded him.

"No," Honda said. "The face itself is changing through the context of
what we've seen him go through. By the time the movie ends he's like a hero
whose departure we regret. The paradox of fearsomeness and longing is what
the whole thing's about."

"I wouldn't know about that," Tsuburaya told him.

"It's like part of *us* leaving," Honda said. "That's what makes it so hard.
The monster the child knows best is the monster he feels himself to be." After
Tsuburaya didn't respond, he added, "That's why I love those shots of the city
after the monster's gone. All that emptiness, like a no-man's land in which eloquence and silence are joined. If you don't have both, the dread evaporates."

That was true, Tsuburaya conceded. He volunteered that he was par-   150
ticularly proud of the shots of the harbor at night before the creature's erup-
tion from the sea: all along the waterfront, silence. Silence like thunder.

Akira was turned to the wall in his sleep when Tsuburaya got home. One foot hung over the pallet, exposing an impossibly thin ankle. He left for the boy a little maquette that the team had used to model Gojira's head, standing it on the floor next to his mat.

Masano had apparently taken to mounting amulets throughout the house where their influence was desired, against pestilence at the doorway or against storms on the ceiling. The house was dark and still. Tsuburaya went through some old production notes at his desk. Atop one of the shot lists he found some gingko leaves and a note from Akira. His instructor at school had told him they kept the bookworms away.

"I'm a bad father," Tsuburaya told Honda before his unit got started the next morning. His friend seemed unfazed by the news, so he added, "A bad husband, too."

"Supposedly the cat forgets in three days the kindnesses of three years," Honda answered.

They shot the scene of the creature crashing through the rail yards at   155 Shinagawa. The suit's rubber feet were continually turn up by even the thin-nest steel of the model rails, and shot after shot after shot proved unsatisfac-tory. Some of their work was as repetitive as a carpenter's hammering. But the house still had to be built.

Tsuburaya repaired the feet himself with cotton swabs and a glue pot and a fine brush while Nakajima drank tea and enjoyed the break. Handcraftsmanship justified itself as an expression of intimacy with the world. Honda made jokes about the number of people standing around on salary, but Tsuburaya reminded him that the potter accepted long hours at the kiln with his body and soul.

"That's good to know," Honda responded. "But in the meantime, nobody gets to eat."

Mori mounted a publicity blitz four full weeks before the release, including an eleven-installment radio serial, and by the premiere their monster's face glowered down from every bus and tramway stop, and a nearly full-sized Gojira balloon swayed and bowed in the wind over an automobile dealership in the Ginza district.

It worked: *Gojira* recorded the best opening-day ticket sales in Tokyo's history and had a better first week than Kurosawa's *Seven Samurai*. "It's like a dream!" Akira shrieked at the showing his family attended, and Masano watched the destruction in respectful silence. Some of the older audience members left the theater in tears.

Mori had already begun to arrange the sequel. Since *Gojira* ended with   160 the scientist's warning that if the world continued with nuclear weapons there would someday appear another such monster, the sequel would involve two: Gojira and his bitter enemy, yet to be designed. One possibility for the latter appeared to Tsuburaya in a dream the night after the premiere, a gigantic tussock moth rendered with enough scientific accuracy that its face and mouth part were horrific. In the dream it was obsessed with two magical little girls. Tsuburaya even glimpsed the teaser line. "The Mightiest Monster in All Creation—Ravishing a Universe for Love."

American investors had already won the auction for *Gojira's* international rights and decided to add new footage involving an American reporter trapped in Tokyo during the rampage, in order to give Western audiences someone for whom to care. They announced they were also going to tone down the nuclear references. They retitled it *Godzilla*, and added the subtitle *King of the Monsters*.

A month after the premiere, Tsuburaya walked home alone late one December night, bundled against the cold. In the fishmonger's shop the dried bonito looked like whetstones in the window. He stopped at a sushi stall for some boiled rice with vinegar.

The boy who served him had a bamboo crest motif on his coat and he asked why Tsuburaya was smiling. Tsuburaya nearly told him that in all of his work he'd always been looking for the patterns that were an object's essence, and that on the boy's coat the bamboo was an emblem of the living bamboo there inside it. The best patterns became the nation's communal property, like that bamboo or England's lion. Or his monster.

The boy suddenly asked why he was weeping. He said he was weeping for all that he'd been granted, and for everything he'd thrown away, then thanked the boy for his concern.

In his toast at the dinner following the premiere, Honda had noted that   165
Tsuburaya's success was centered around his talent for developing a team and uncaging each member's skills. He joked that Tsuburaya led by example and cajoling and intimidation, that for him nothing was ever perfect and no one was ever finished, and he got a laugh by concluding that a day with Tsuburaya was like four with Kurosawa, in terms of consigning someone ever more irrevocably to misery.

For Tsuburaya on nights like that December night, a long walk meant an even later arrival. In his father's childhood, after sunset, villages were dark and quiet and cold. A gong might call worshippers to the candlelit temple. A dog might bark. Otherwise what one saw and heard was up to the moonlight and wind.

Masano hadn't spoken to him about the movie, though she had told Hajime that by the end she'd been moved by how profoundly it had affected the other patrons her age. That December night, the moment Tsuburaya finally arrived at home, Hajime announced he was leaving to work on a picture in Malaysia. Masano stopped serving from her platter and looked at her husband as though all had been fine before he'd come in. "There he is with his warm smile," she finally said to Hajime. "Orchestrating his catastrophes."

"This wasn't his idea; it was mine," Hajime answered.

Akira stood up from the table and ran from the room, distraught at his brother's announcement.

"We'll be sorry to see you go," Tsuburaya told his son. 170

"The only thing you're sorry about is a production delay," Masano told him, and Tsuburaya remembered that crows supposedly couldn't feel the sun's heat because they'd already been scorched black.

She went off to see to Akira, and Hajime finished his meal in silence. Tsuburaya retired to his study and noted that the nowhere in which he chose to dwell was the abode of perfect focus. He was like the blind old teacher who never knew to stop lecturing when the breeze blew out the light.

He told Hajime this story at the station the next day while they waited for the train. That he had difficulty keeping his son's attention made him as sad as the departure. Hajime finally said that he'd rarely heard Tsuburaya talk so much before. The train pulled in, and they were silent while the arriving passengers streamed off. They might both have been imagining Akira, back in his room alone.

Your brother's going to be very sad to see you go," Tsuburaya finally said.

This seemed to irk Hajime. "When did I become the villain?" he asked. 175

"No one's calling you a villain," Tsuburaya told him.

Hajime handed his bag up to the porter. "You know who you've always reminded me of?" he asked. "Prince Konoye. The two of you, actually." Then he climbed the steps to the car.

Tsuburaya was too surprised to respond. He did manage to ask Hajime if he had enough money, but the porter's departure call distracted them both and the train pulled out. Once it gathered some momentum Hajime waved, once, before his car passed out of sight around the curve with surprising speed.

Tsuburaya was left on the platform, where he remained after the other well-wishers had left. The wind swept a seed pod of some sort onto his foot.

Konoye had been Prime Minister before the attack on Pearl Harbor. 180 He'd always understood what war with America would mean but with each new step toward destruction had lacked the will to insist that the nation do what was right. The joke about him had been that he was so perpetually unsure of his intentions he sometimes got lost en route to the toilet.

Tsuburaya and Masano had talked about Konoye more than once, especially after his death. She'd been very upset about it, in fact. He had poisoned himself before his arrest by the Americans, leaving behind in his room only his family seal and a book, the newspapers had reported. In the book, written by the Englishman Oscar Wilde, Konoye had underlined a single passage, as if he'd hoped to make his amends in pencil: *Nobody great or small can be ruined except by his own hand, and terrible as was what the world did to me, even more terrible still was what I did to myself.*

■ Compare the descriptions of filming to the descriptions of the director's relationships with his wife, his father, and his son. How are they different? Where do they overlap? What specific scenes from his life appear in the films that he makes?

Emma Donoghue (1969–   )

Born in Ireland, Emma Donoghue earned a degree from University College Dublin and a PhD in English from Cambridge University. She now lives in Canada. Her first novel *Stir Fry* (1994) won the 1997 American Library Association's Gay, Lesbian and Bisexual Book Award for Literature. *Slammerkin* (2000) won the Ferro-Grumley Award for Lesbian Fiction. Her novel *Room* (2010) was a finalist for the Man Booker Prize. Her most recent novel, *Frog Music* (2014), is a work of historical fiction based on the life of a murdered nineteenth century frog catcher. The following story comes from the collection *Astray* (2012).

Man and Boy (2012)

Off your tuck this morning, aren't you? That's not like you. It's the chill, perhaps. These March winds come straight from the Urals, up the Thames, or so they say. No, that's not your favorite Horse Guards playing, can't fool you; you never like it when they change the band. Fancy a bun? You'll feel the better for a good breakfast. Come along, have a couple of buns. . . . Please yourself, then.

Maybe later, after your bath.

I had some unpleasantness with the superintendent this morning. Yes, over you, my boy, need you ask? He's applied to the trustees for permission to buy a gun.

Calm down, no one's going to shoot you, or my name's not Matthew Scott. But let it be a warning. I don't mean to lay blame, but this is what comes of tantrums. (*Demented rampages*, the superintendent calls them.) Look at this old patched wall here; who was it that stove it in? To err is human and all that, but it don't excuse such an exhibition. You only went and hurt yourself, and you're still not the better for that abscess.

Anyway, the superintendent has an iddy-fix that you're a danger to the   5
kiddies, now you're a man, as it were. Oh, you know and I know that's all my eye, you dote on the smalls. You don't care for confinement, that's all, and who can blame you? I can always settle you with a little wander round the Gardens to meet your friends. But the superintendent says, "What if you're off the premises, Scott, when the musth next comes on Jumbo? No other keeper here can handle him; every time I assign you an assistant, the creature terrorizes the fellow and sends him packing. It's a most irregular state of affairs, not to mention the pungency, and stains, and. . . well, engorgement. That member's wife almost fainted when she caught sight!"

I pointed out you could hardly help that.

"Besides, bull Africans are known for killing their keepers," he lectured me. "In one of his furies, he could swat you down with his little tail, then crush you with his skull."

"Not this elephant," I said, "nor this keeper."

Then he went off on a gory story about a crazed elephant he saw gunned down in the Strand when he was knee-high, 152 bullets it took, the superintendent's never been the same since. Well, that explains a lot about him.

I assure you, my boy, I stood up for you. I looked the old man in the   10
watery eye and said, "We all have our off days. But Jumbo's a cleanly, hard-working fellow, as a rule. I have never felt afraid of him for one moment in the seventeen years he's been in my care."

He muttered something impertinent about that proving my arrogance rather than your safety. "I believe it's gone to your head, Scott."

"What has, Superintendent?"

"Jumbo's fame. You fancy yourself the cock of the walk."

I drew myself up. "If I enjoy a certain position in this establishment, if I was awarded a medal back in 'sixty-six, that is due to having bred, nursed, and reared more exotic animals and birds than any other living man."

He pursed his lips. "Not to mention the fortune you pocket from those   15
tuppenny rides—"

The nerve! "Aren't I the one who helps the kiddies up the ladder, and leads Jumbo round the Gardens, and makes sure they don't topple off?" (By rights the cash should be half yours, lad, but what use would it be to you? You like to mouth the coins with your trunk and slip them into my pocket.)

The superintendent plucked at his beard. "Be that as it may, it's inequitable; bad for morale. You're all charm when it earns you tips, Scott, but flagrantly rude to your superiors in this Society, and as for your fellow keepers, they're nervous of saying a word to you these days."

That crew of ignorami!

"I have plenty of conversation," I told him, "but I save it for those as appreciate it."

"They call you a tyrant."   20

Well, I laughed. After all, I'm the fifteenth child of seventeen, no silver spoons in my infant mouth, a humble son of toil who's made good in a precarious profession, and I need apologize to nobody. We don't mind the piddling tiddlers of this world, do we, boy? We just avert our gaze.

*   *   *

There's a crate sitting outside on the grass this morning. Pitch-pine planking, girded with iron, on a kind of trolley with wheels. Gives me a funny feeling. It's twelve feet high, as near as I can guess; that's just half a foot more than you. Nobody's said a word to me about it. Best to mind my own business, I suppose. This place—there's too much gossip and interference already.

It'll be time to stretch a leg soon, boy. The kiddies will be lined up outside in their dozens. They missed you yesterday, when it was raining. Here, kneel down and we'll get your howdah on. Yes, yes, I'll remember to put a double fold of blanket under the corner where it was rubbing. Aren't your toenails looking pearly after that scrub I gave them?

There's two men out there by the crate now, setting up some kind of ramp. I don't like the looks of this at all. If this is what I think it is, it's too blooming much—

I'm off to the superintendent's office, none of this *Please make an*   25
appointment. Here's a sack of oats to be getting on with. Oh, don't take on, hush your bellowing, I'll be back before you miss me.

Well, Jumbo, I could bloody spit! pardon my French, but there are moments in a man's life on this miserable earth—

And to think, the superintendent didn't give me so much as a word of warning. Just fancy, after all these years of working at the Society together—after the perils he and I have run, sawing off that rhinoceros's deformed horn and whatnot—it makes me shudder, the perfidiousness of it. "I'll thank you," says I, "to tell me what's afoot in the matter of my elephant."

"Yours, Scott?" says he with a curl of the lip.

"Figure of speech," says I. "As keeper here thirty-one years, man and boy, I take a natural interest in all property of the Society."

He was all stuff and bluster, I'd got him on the wrong foot. "Since you   30
inquire," says he, "I must inform you that Jumbo is now the property of another party."

Didn't I stare! "Which other party?"

His beard began to tremble. "Mr. P. T. Barnum."

"The Yankee showman?"

He couldn't deny it. Then wasn't there a row, not half. My dear boy, I can hardly get the words out, but he's only been and gone and sold you to the circus!

It's a shocking smirch on the good name of the London Zoological   35
Society, that's what I say. Such sneaking, double-dealing treachery behind closed doors. In the best interests of the British public, my hat! Two thousand pounds, that's the price the superintendent put on you, though it's not as if they need the funds, and who's the chief draw but the Children's Pal, the Beloved Pachydermic Behemoth, as the papers call you? Why, you may be the most magnificent elephant the world has ever seen, due to falling so fortuitously young into my hands as a crusty little stray, to be nursed back from the edge of the grave and fed up proper. And who's to say how long your poor tribe will last, with ivory so fashionable? The special friend of our dear queen as

well as generations of young Britons born and unborn, and yet the Society has flogged you off like horse meat, and all because of a few whiffs and tantrums!

Oh, Jumbo. You might just settle down now. Your feelings do you credit and all that, but there's no good in such displays. You must be a brave boy. You've got through worse before, haven't you? When the traders gunned down your whole kin in front of you—

Hush now, my mouth, I shouldn't bring up painful recollections. Going into exile in America can't be half as bad, that's all I mean. Worse things happen. Come to think of it, if I hadn't rescued you from that wretched Jardin des Plantes, you'd have got eaten by hungry Frogs during the Siege of Seventy-one! So best to put a brave face on.

I just hope you don't get seasick. I reminded the superintendent you'd need two hundred pounds of hay a day on the voyage to New York, not to speak of sweet biscuits, potatoes, loaves, figs, and onions, your favorite. . . . You'll be joining the Greatest Show on Earth, I suppose that has a sort of ring to it, if a vulgar one. (The superintendent claims travel may calm your rages, or if it doesn't, then such a huge circus will have "facilities for seclusion," though I don't like the sound of that, not half.) No tricks to learn, I made sure of that much: you'll be announced as "The Most Enormous Land Animal in Captivity" and walk round the ring, that's all. I was worried you'd have to tramp across the whole United Stares, but you'll tour in your own comfy railway carriage, fancy that! The old millionaire's got twenty other elephants, but you'll be the king. Oh, and rats, I told him to pass on word that you're tormented by the sight of a rat ever since they ate half your feet when you were a nipper.

Of course you'll miss England, and giving the kiddies rides, that's only to be expected. And doing headstands in the Pool, wandering down the Parrot Walk, the Carnivora Terrace, all the old sights. You'll find those American winters a trial in your spirits, I shouldn't wonder. And I expect once in a while you'll spare a thought for your old pa—

When you came to London, a filthy baby no taller than me, you used   40
to wake streaming at night and sucking your trunk for comfort, and I'd give you a cuddle and you'd start to leak behind the ears. . . .

Pardon me, boy, I'm overcome.

Today's the evil day, Jumbo, I believe you know it. You're all a-shiver, and your trunk hovers in front of my face as if to take me in. It's like some tree turned hairy snake, puffing warm wet air on me. There, there. Have a bit of gingerbread. Let me give your leg a good hard pat. Will I blow into your trunk, give your tongue a last little rub?

Come along, bad form to keep anyone waiting, I suppose, even a jumped-up Yankee animal handler like this "Elephant Bill" Newman. (Oh, those little watery eyes of yours, lashes like a ballet dancer—I can hardly look you in the face.) That's a boy; down this passage to the left; I know it's not the usual way, but a change is as good as a rest, don't they say? This way, now. Up the little ramp and into the crate you go. Plenty of room in there, if you put your head down. Go on.

Ah, now, let's have no nonsense. Into your crate this minute. What good will it do to plunge and bellow? No, stop it, don't lie down, up, boy, up. Bad boy Jumbo!

You're all right, don't take on so. You're back in your quarters for the moment; it's getting dark out. Such a to-do! They're only chains. I know you dislike the weight of them, but they're temporary. No, I can't take them off tonight or this Elephant Bill will raise a stink. He says we must try you again first thing tomorrow. The chains are for securing you inside the crate, till the crane hoists you on board the steamer. No, calm down, boy. Enough of that roaring. Drink your scotch. Oi! Pick up my bowler and give it back. Thank you. 45

The Yankee, Elephant Bill, has some cheek. He began by informing me that Barnum's agents tried to secure the captured King of the Zulus for exhibition, and then the cottage where Shakespeare was born; you're only their third choice of British treasures. Well, I bristled, you can imagine.

When you wouldn't walk into the crate no matter how we urged and pushed, even after he took the whip to your poor saggy posterior—when I'd led you round the corner and tried again half a dozen times—he rolled his eyes, said it was clear as day you'd been spoiled.

"Spoiled?" I repeated.

"Made half pet, half human," says the American, "by all these treats and pattings and chit-chat. Is it true what the other fellows say, Scott, that you share a bottle of whiskey with the beast every night, and caterwaul like sweethearts, curled up together in his stall?"

Well, I didn't want to dignify that kind of impertinence with a reply. But then I thought of how you whine like a naughty child if I don't come back from the pub by bedtime, and a dreadful thought occurred to me. "Elephants are family-minded creatures, you must know that much," I told him. "I hope you don't mean to leave Jumbo alone at night? He only sleeps two or three hours, on and off; he'll need company when he wakes." 50

A snort from the Yank. "I don't bed down with nobody but human females."

Which shows the coarseness of the man.

Settle down, Jumbo, it's only three in the morning. No, I can't sleep neither. I haven't had a decent kip since that blooming crate arrived. Don't those new violet-bottomed mandrills make an awful racket?

Over seven thousand visitors counted at the turnstile today. All because of you, Jumbo. Your sale's been in the papers; you'd hardly credit what a fuss it's making. Heartbroken letters from kiddies, denunciations of the trustees, offers to raise a subscription to ransom you back. It's said the Prince of Wales has voiced his objections, and Mr. Ruskin, and some Fellows of the Society are going to court to prove the sale illegal!

I wish you could read some of the letters you're getting every day now,   55 from grown-ups as well as kiddies. Money enclosed, and gingerbread, not to mention cigars. (I ate the couple of dozen oysters, as I knew you wouldn't fancy them.) A bun stuck with pins; that's some sot's idea of a joke. And look at this huge floral wreath for you to wear, with a banner that says A TROPHY OF TRIUMPH OVER THE AMERICAN SLAVERS. I've had letters myself, some offering me bribes to "do something to prevent this," others calling me a Judas. If they only knew the mortifications of my position!

Oh, dear, I did think today's attempt would have gone better. It was my own idea that since you'd taken against the very sight of the crate, it should be removed from view. I told this Elephant Bill I'd lead you through the streets, the full six miles, and surely by the time you reached the docks, you'd be glad to go into your crate for a rest.

But you saw right through me, didn't you, artful dodger? No, no tongue massage for you tonight, Badness! You somehow knew this wasn't an ordinary stroll. Not an inch beyond the gates of the Gardens but you dropped to your knees. Playing to the crowd, rather, I thought, and how they whooped at the sight of you on all fours like some plucky martyr for the British cause. The public's gone berserk over your *sit-down strike*, you wouldn't believe the papers.

I almost lost my temper with you today at the gates, boy, when you wouldn't get up for me, and yet I couldn't help but feel a sort of pride to see you put up such a good fight.

That Yank is a nasty piece of work. When I pointed out that it might prove impossible to force you onto that ship, he muttered about putting you on low rations to damp your spirit, or even bull hooks to the ears and hot irons.

"I'll have you know, we don't stand for that kind of barbarism in this   60 country," I told him, and he grinned and said the English were more squeamish about beating their animals than their children. He showed me a gun he carries and drawled something about getting you to New York dead or alive.

The lout was just trying to put the wind up me, of course. Primitive tactics. "Jumbo won't be of much use to your employer if he's in the former state," says I coldly.

Elephant Bill shrugged, and said he didn't know about that, Barnum could always stuff your hide and tour it as "The Conquered Briton."

That left me speechless.

Will we take a stroll round the Gardens this morning before the gates open? Over eighteen thousand visitors yesterday, and as many expected today, to catch what might be a last glimpse of you. Such queues for the rides! We could charge a guinea apiece if we chose, not that we would.

Let's you and me go and take a look at your crate. It's nothing to be afraid   65
of, idiot boy; only a big box. Look, some fresh writing since yesterday: *Jumbo
don't go,* that's kind. More flowers. Dollies, books, even. See that woman on
her knees outside the gates? A lunatic, but the civil kind. She's handing out
leaflets and praying for divine intervention to stop your departure.

But the thing is, lad, you're going to have to go sooner or later. You know
that, don't you? There comes a time in every man's life when he must knuckle
down and do the necessary. The judge has ruled your sale was legal. Barnum's
told the *Daily Telegraph* he won't reconsider, not for a hundred thousand
pounds. So the cruel fact is that our days together are numbered. Why not step
on into your crate now, this very minute, get the wrench of parting over, since
it must come to that in the end? Quick, now, as a favor to your sorrowful pa?
Argh! Be that way, then; suit yourself, but don't blame me if the Yank comes at
you with hooks and irons.

It's like trying to move a mountain, sometimes. Am I your master or your
servant, that's what I want to know? It's a queer business.

That superintendent! To think I used to be amused by his little ways, almost fond of
the old gent. Well, a colder fish I never met. Sits there in his dusty top hat and frock
coat flecked with hippopotami's whatsits, tells me he's giving me a little holiday.

"A holiday?" I was taken aback, as you can imagine. I haven't taken a day
off in years, you'd never stand for it.

He fixes me with his yellowing eyes and tells me that my temporary   70
removal will allow Mr. Newman to accustom himself to the elephant's habits
and tastes before departure.

"You know Jumbo's tastes already," I protest. "He can't stand that Yank.
And if the fellow dares to try cruel measures, word will get out and you'll have
the police down on you like a shot, spark off riots, I shouldn't wonder."

Which sends the superintendent off on a rant about how I've been con-
spicuously unwilling to get you into that create.

"Oh. I like that," says I. "I've only loaded the unfortunate creature with
shackles, pushed and roared to drive all six and a half tons of him into that
blooming trap, so how is it my fault if he won't go?"

He fixes me with a stare. "Mr. Newman informs me that you must be
engaging in sabotage, by giving the elephant secret signals. I have suspected as
much on previous occasions, when I sent you perfectly competent assistants
and Jumbo ran amok and knocked them down like ninepins."

"Secret signals?" I repeat, flabbergasted.   75

"All I know is that your hold over that beast is uncanny," says the superintendent between his teeth.

Uncanny? What's uncanny about it? Nothing more natural than that
you'd have a certain regard for your pa, after he's seen to all your little wants

day and night for the last seventeen years. Why does the lamb love Mary so, and all that rot.

Well, boy, at that moment I hear a little click in my head. It's like at the halls when a scene flies up and another one descends. I suddenly say—prepare yourself, lad—I say, "Then why don't you send a telegraph to this Barnum and tell him to take me too?"

The superintendent blinks.

"I'm offering my services as Jumbo's keeper," says I, "as long as his 80 terms are liberal."

"What makes you imagine Mr. Barnum would hire such a stubborn devil as you, Scott?"

That threw me, but only for a second. "Because he must be a stubborn devil himself to have paid two thousand pounds for an elephant he can't get onto the ship."

A long stare, and the superintendent says, "I knew I was right. You have been thwarting me all along, using covert devices to keep Jumbo in the zoo."

I smirked, letting him believe it. Covert devices, my eye! To the impure, all things are impure. "Just you send that telegraph," I told him, "and you'll be soon rid of both of us."

Now, now, boy, let me explain. Doesn't it strike you that we've had enough 85 of England? Whoa! No chucking your filth on the walls, that's a low habit. Hear me out. I know what a patriotic heart you've got—specially considering you come from the French Sudan, not our Empire at all—but how have you been repaid? Yes, the plain people dote on you, but it strikes me that you've grown out of these cramped quarters. If the Society's condemned you to transportation for smashing a few walls and shocking a few members' wives, why, then—let's up stakes and be off to pastures new, I say. You're not twenty-one yet, and I'm not fifty. We're self-made prodigies, come up from nothing and now headline news. We can make a fresh start in the land of the free and home of the brave. We'll be ten times as famous, and won't England feel the loss of us, won't Victoria weep!

I expect the superintendent will call me in right after lunch, the wonders of modern telegraphy being what they are. (Whatever Barnum offers me, I'll accept it. The Society can kiss my you-know-exactly-what-I-mean.) I'll come straight back here and lead you out to the crate. Now, whatever you do, Jumbo, don't make a liar of me. I don't have any secret signals or hidden powers; all I can think to do is to walk into the crate first, and turn, and open my arms and call you. Trust me, dearest boy, and I'll see you safe across the ocean, and stay by your side for better for worse, and take a father's and mother's care of you till the end. Are you with me?

■ Who are the characters in this text? How are they identified? How does the narrator's language confuse or explain your identification of these characters?

- What outside information do you need to know to understand this story? What does the narrator mean when he says "Yankee"? Who is P. T. Barnum?
- How does the author's note at the end of the text influence your interpretation of the story?

Nathaniel Hawthorne (1804–1864)

Nathaniel Hawthorne was born in Salem, Massachusetts. His childhood was marred by the tragic death of his father, and Hawthorne, his mother, and his siblings moved to Maine to reside with relatives. Hawthorne attended Bowdoin College in Maine and graduated in 1825. After graduation, Hawthorne returned to Salem, where he spent twelve years as a literary apprentice. In 1836, he moved to Boston, where he and his sister began writing children's books. He continued to publish short stories but took various jobs, including weigher and surveyor, to support himself. After marrying in 1842, Hawthorne moved to Concord, where he associated with the transcendentalists Henry David Thoreau, Ralph Waldo Emerson, and Louisa May Alcott; after only three years, the Hawthorne family returned to Salem. In 1850, he published the now classic novel *The Scarlet Letter*. Like most of his previous writings, Hawthorne's second novel explored the themes of sin, guilt, and forgiveness through the use of symbolism.

Young Goodman Brown (1835)

Young Goodman Brown came forth at sunset into the street at Salem village; but put his head back, after crossing the threshold, to exchange a parting kiss with his young wife. And Faith, as the wife was aptly named, thrust her own pretty head into the street, letting the wind play with the pink ribbons of her cap while she called to Goodman Brown.

"Dearest heart," whispered she, softly and rather sadly, when her lips were close to his ear, "prithee put off your journey until sunrise and sleep in your own bed tonight. A lone woman is troubled with such dreams and such thoughts that she's afeared of herself sometimes. Pray tarry with me this night, dear husband, of all nights in the year."

"My love and my Faith," replied young Goodman Brown, "of all nights in the year, this one night must I tarry away from thee. My journey, as thou callest it, forth and back again, must needs be done 'twixt now and sunrise. What, my sweet, pretty wife, dost thou doubt me already, and we but three months married?"

"Then God bless you!" said Faith, with the pink ribbons; "and may you find all well when you come back."

"Amen!" cried Goodman Brown, "Say thy prayers, dear Faith, and go   5
to bed at dusk, and no harm will come to thee."

So they parted; and the young man pursued his way until, being about to turn the corner by the meeting-house, he looked back and saw the head of Faith still peeping after him with a melancholy air, in spite of her pink ribbons.

"Poor little Faith!" thought he, for his heart smote him. "What a wretch am I to leave her on such an errand! She talks of dreams, too. Methought as she spoke there was trouble in her face, as if a dream had warned her what work is to be done tonight. But no, no; 't would kill her to think it. Well, she's a blessed angel on earth; and after this one night I'll cling to her skirts and follow her to heaven."

With this excellent resolve for the future, Goodman Brown felt himself justified in making more haste on his present evil purpose. He had taken a dreary road, darkened by all the gloomiest trees of the forest, which barely stood aside to let the narrow path creep through, and closed immediately behind. It was all as lonely as could be; and there is this peculiarity in such a solitude, that the traveler knows not who may be concealed by the innumerable trunks and the thick boughs overhead; so that with lonely footsteps he may yet be passing through an unseen multitude.

"There may be a devilish Indian behind every tree," said Goodman Brown to himself; and he glanced fearfully behind him as he added, "What if the devil himself should be at my very elbow!"

His head being turned back, he passed a crook of the road, and, look-   10
ing forward again, beheld the figure of a man, in grave and decent attire, seated at the foot of an old tree. He arose at Goodman Brown's approach and walked onward side by side with him.

"You are late, Goodman Brown," said he. "The clock of the Old South was striking as I came through Boston, and that is full fifteen minutes agone."

"Faith kept me back a while," replied the young man, with a tremor in his voice, caused by the sudden appearance of his companion, though not wholly unexpected.

It was now deep dusk in the forest, and deepest in that part of it where these two were journeying. As nearly as could be discerned, the second traveler was about fifty years old, apparently in the same rank of life as Goodman Brown, and bearing a considerable resemblance to him, though perhaps more in expression than features. Still they might have been taken for father and son. And yet, though the elder person was as simply clad as the younger, and as simple in manner too, he had an indescribable air of one who knew the world, and who would not have felt abashed at the governor's dinner table or in King William's court, were it possible that his affairs should call him thither. But the only thing about him that could be fixed upon as remarkable was his staff, which bore the likeness of a great black snake, so curiously wrought that it might almost be seen to twist and wriggle itself like a living serpent. This, of course, must have been an ocular deception, assisted by the uncertain light.

"Come, Goodman Brown," cried his fellow-traveler, "this is a dull pace for the beginning of a journey. Take my staff, if you are so soon weary."

"Friend," said the other, exchanging his slow pace for a full stop, "hav- 15 ing kept covenant by meeting thee here, it is my purpose now to return whence I came. I have scruples touching the matter thou wot'st of."

"Sayest thou so?" replied he of the serpent, smiling apart. "Let us walk on, nevertheless, reasoning as we go; and if I convince thee not thou shalt turn back. We are but a little way in the forest yet."

"Too far! too far!" exclaimed the goodman, unconsciously resuming his walk. "My father never went into the woods on such an errand, nor his father before him. We have been a race of honest men and good Christians since the days of the martyrs; and shall I be the first of the name of Brown that ever took this path and kept"—

"Such company, thou wouldst say," observed the elder person, interpreting his pause. "Well said, Goodman Brown! I have been as well acquainted with your family as with ever a one among the Puritans; and that's no trifle to say. I helped your grandfather, the constable, when he lashed the Quaker woman so smartly through the streets of Salem; and it was I that brought your father a pitch-pine knot, kindled at my own hearth, to set fire to an Indian village, in King Philip's war. They were my good friends, both; and many a pleasant walk have we had along this path, and returned merrily after midnight. I would fain be friends with you for their sake."

"If it be as thou sayest," replied Goodman Brown, "I marvel they never spoke of these matters; or, verily, I marvel not, seeing that the least rumor of the sort would have driven them from New England. We are a people of prayer, and good works to boot, and abide no such wickedness."

"Wickedness or not," said the traveler with the twisted staff, "I have a very 20 general acquaintance here in New England. The deacons of many a church have drunk the communion wine with me; the selectmen of divers towns make me their chairman; and a majority of the Great and General Court are firm supporters of my interest. The governor and I, too—But these are state secrets."

"Can this be so?" cried Goodman Brown, with a stare of amazement at his undisturbed companion. "Howbeit, I have nothing to do with the governor and council; they have their own ways, and are no rule for a simple husband-man like me. But, were I to go on with thee, how should I meet the eye of that good old man, our minister, at Salem village? Oh, his voice would make me tremble both Sabbath day and lecture day."

Thus far the elder traveler had listened with due gravity; but now burst into a fit of irrepressible mirth, shaking himself so violently that his snakelike staff actually seemed to wriggle in sympathy.

"Ha! ha! ha!" shouted he again and again; then composing himself, "Well, go on, Goodman Brown, go on; but, prithee, don't kill me with laughing."

"Well, then, to end the matter at once," said Goodman Brown, considerably nettled, "there is my wife, Faith. It would break her dear little heart; and I'd rather break my own."

"Nay, if that be the case," answered the other, "e'en go thy ways,   25
Goodman Brown. I would not for twenty old women like the one hobbling before us that Faith should come to any harm."

As he spoke he pointed his staff at a female figure on the path, in whom Goodman Brown recognized a very pious and exemplary dame, who had taught him his catechism in youth, and was still his moral and spiritual adviser, jointly with the minister and Deacon Gookin.

"A marvel, truly that Goody Cloyse should be so far in the wilderness at nightfall," said he. "But with your leave, friend, I shall take a cut through the woods until we have left this Christian woman behind. Being a stranger to you, she might ask whom I was consorting with and whither I was going."

"Be it so," said his fellow-traveler. "Betake you to the woods, and let me keep the path."

Accordingly the young man turned aside, but took care to watch his companion, who advanced softly along the road until he had come within a staff's length of the old dame. She, meanwhile, was making the best of her way, with singular speed for so aged a woman, and mumbling some indistinct words—a prayer, doubtless—as she went. The traveler put forth his staff and touched her withered neck with what seemed the serpent's tail.

"The devil!" screamed the pious old lady.   30

"Then Goody Cloyse knows her old friend?" observed the traveler, confronting her and leaning on his writhing stick.

"Ah, forsooth, and is it your worship indeed?" cried the good dame. "Yea, truly is it, and in the very image of my old gossip, Goodman Brown, the grandfather of the silly fellow that now is. But—would your worship believe it?—my broomstick hath strangely disappeared, stolen, as I suspect, by that unhanged witch, Goody Cory, and that, too, when I was all anointed with the juice of smallage, and cinquefoil, and wolfsbane"—

"Mingled with fine wheat and the fat of a newborn babe," said the shape of old Goodman Brown.

"Ah, your worship knows the recipe," cried the old lady, cackling aloud. "So, as I was saying, being all ready for the meeting, and no horse to ride on, I made up my mind to foot it; for they tell me there is a nice young man to be taken into communion tonight. But now your good worship will lend me your arm, and we shall be there in a twinkling."

"That can hardly be," answered her friend. "I may not spare you my   35
arm, Goody Cloyse; but here is my staff, if you will."

So saying, he threw it down at her feet, where, perhaps, it assumed life, being one of the rods which its owner had formerly lent to the Egyptian magi.

Of this fact, however, Goodman Brown could not take cognizance. He had cast up his eyes in astonishment, and, looking down again, beheld neither Goody Cloyse nor the serpentine staff, but his fellow-traveler alone, who waited for him as calmly as if nothing had happened.

"That old woman taught me my catechism," said the young man; and there was a world of meaning in this simple comment.

They continued to walk onward, while the elder traveler exhorted his companion to make good speed and persevere in the path, discoursing so aptly that his arguments seemed rather to spring up in the bosom of his auditor than to be suggested by himself. As they went, he plucked a branch of maple to serve for a walking stick, and began to strip it of the twigs and little boughs, which were wet with evening dew. The moment his fingers touched them they became strangely withered and dried up as with a week's sunshine. Thus the pair proceeded, at a good free pace, until suddenly, in a gloomy hollow of the road, Goodman Brown sat himself down on the stump of a tree and refused to go any farther.

"Friend," he said, stubbornly, "my mind is made up. Not another step will I budge on this errand. What if a wretched old woman do choose to go to the devil when I thought she was going to heaven: is that any reason why I should quit my dear Faith and go after her?"

"You will think better of this by and by," said his acquaintance, com-   40 posedly. "Sit here and rest yourself a while; and when you feel like moving again, there is my staff to help you along."

Without more words, he threw his companion the maple stick, and was as speedily out of sight as if he had vanished into the deepening gloom. The young man sat a few moments by the roadside, applauding himself greatly, and thinking with how clear a conscience he should meet the minister in his morning walk, nor shrink from the eye of good old Deacon Gookin. And what calm sleep would be his that very night, which was to have been spent so wickedly, but so purely and sweetly now, in the arms of Faith! Amidst these pleasant and praiseworthy meditations, Goodman Brown heard the tramp of horses along the road, and deemed it advisable to conceal himself within the verge of the forest, conscious of the guilty purpose that had brought him thither, though now so happily turned from it.

On came the hoof tramps and the voices of the riders, two grave old voices, conversing soberly as they drew near. These mingled sounds appeared to pass along the road, within a few yards of the young man's hiding-place; but, owing doubtless to the depth of the gloom at that particular spot, neither the travelers nor their steeds were visible. Though their figures brushed the small boughs by the wayside, it could not be seen that they intercepted, even for a moment, the faint gleam from the strip of bright sky athwart which they must have passed. Goodman Brown alternately crouched and stood on tiptoe,

pulling aside the branches and thrusting forth his head as far as he durst without discerning so much as a shadow. It vexed him the more, because he could
have sworn, were such a thing possible, that he recognized the voices of the
minister and Deacon Gookin, jogging along quietly, as they were wont to do,
when bound to some ordination or ecclesiastical council. While yet within
hearing, one of the riders stopped to pluck a switch,

"Of the two, reverend sir," said the voice like the deacon's, "I had rather
miss an ordination dinner than tonight's meeting. They tell me that some of
our community are to be here from Falmouth and beyond, and others from
Connecticut and Rhode Island, besides several of the Indian powwows, who,
after their fashion, know almost as much deviltry as the best of us. Moreover,
there is a goodly young woman to be taken into communion."

"Mighty well, Deacon Gookin!" replied the solemn old tones of the
minister. "Spur up, or we shall be late. Nothing can be done, you know, until
I get on the ground."

The hoofs clattered again; and the voices, talking so strangely in the   45
empty air, passed on through the forest, where no church had ever been
gathered or solitary Christian prayed. Whither, then, could these holy
men be journeying so deep into the heathen wilderness? Young Goodman
Brown caught hold of a tree for support, being ready to sink down on the
ground, faint and overburdened with the heavy sickness of his heart. He
looked up to the sky, doubting whether there really was a heaven above
him. Yet there was the blue arch, and the stars brightening in it.

"With heaven above and Faith below, I will yet stand firm against the
devil!" cried Goodman Brown.

While he still gazed upward into the deep arch of the firmament and had
lifted his hands to pray, a cloud, though no wind was stirring, hurried across
the zenith and hid the brightening stars. The blue sky was still visible, except
directly overhead, where this black mass of cloud was sweeping swiftly northward. Aloft in the air, as if from the depths of the cloud, came a confused and
doubtful sound of voices. Once the listener fancied that he could distinguish
the accents of townspeople of his own, men and women, both pious and
ungodly, many of whom he had met at the communion table, and had seen
others rioting at the tavern. The next moment, so indistinct were the sounds,
he doubted whether he had heard aught but the murmur of the old forest,
whispering without a wind. Then came a stronger swell of those familiar tones,
heard daily in the sunshine at Salem village, but never until now from a cloud
of night. There was one voice, of a young woman, uttering lamentations, yet
with an uncertain sorrow, and entreating for some favor, which, perhaps, it
would grieve her to obtain; and all the unseen multitude, both saints and
sinners, seemed to encourage her onward.

"Faith!" shouted Goodman Brown, in a voice of agony and desperation; and the echoes of the forest mocked him, crying, "Faith! Faith!" as if bewildered wretches were seeking her all through the wilderness.

The cry of grief, rage, and terror was yet piercing the night, when the unhappy husband held his breath for a response. There was a scream, drowned immediately in a louder murmur of voices, fading into far-off laughter, as the dark cloud swept away, leaving the clear and silent sky above Goodman Brown. But something fluttered lightly down through the air and caught on the branch of a tree. The young man seized it, and beheld a pink ribbon.

"My Faith is gone!" cried he after one stupefied moment. "There is no good on earth; and sin is but a name. Come, devil; for to thee is this world given." 50

And, maddened with despair, so that he laughed loud and long, did Goodman Brown grasp his staff and set forth again, at such a rate that he seemed to fly along the forest path rather than to walk or run. The road grew wilder and drearier and more faintly traced, and vanished at length, leaving him in the heart of the dark wilderness, still rushing onward with the instinct that guides mortal man to evil. The whole forest was peopled with frightful sounds—the creaking of the trees, the howling of wild beasts, and the yell of Indians; while sometimes the wind tolled like a distant church bell, and sometimes gave a broad roar around the traveler, as if all Nature were laughing him to scorn. But he was himself the chief horror of the scene, and shrank not from its other horrors.

"Ha! ha! ha!" roared Goodman Brown when the wind laughed at him. "Let us hear which will laugh loudest. Think not to frighten me with your deviltry. Come witch, come wizard, come Indian powwow, come devil himself, and here comes Goodman Brown. You may as well fear him as he fear you."

In truth, all through the haunted forest there could be nothing more frightful than the figure of Goodman Brown. On he flew among the black pines, brandishing his staff with frenzied gestures, now giving vent to an inspiration of horrid blasphemy, and now shouting forth such laughter as set all the echoes of the forest laughing like demons around him. The fiend in his own shape is less hideous than when he rages in the breast of man. Thus sped the demoniac on his course, until, quivering among the trees, he saw a red light before him, as when the felled trunks and branches of a clearing have been set on fire, and throw up their lurid blaze against the sky, at the hour of midnight. He paused, in a lull of the tempest that had driven him onward, and heard the swell of what seemed a hymn, rolling solemnly from a distance with the weight of many voices. He knew the tune; it was a familiar one in the choir of the village meeting-house. The verse died heavily away, and was lengthened by a chorus, not of human voices, but of all the sounds of the benighted wilderness pealing in awful harmony together. Goodman Brown cried out, and his cry was lost to his own ear by its unison with the cry of the desert.

In the interval of silence he stole forward until the light glared full upon his eyes. At one extremity of an open space, hemmed in by the dark wall of the forest, arose a rock, bearing some rude, natural resemblance either to an altar or a pulpit, and surrounded by four blazing pines, their tops aflame, their stems untouched, like candles at an evening meeting. The mass of foliage that had overgrown the summit of the rock was all on fire, blazing high into the night and fitfully illuminating the whole field. Each pendent twig and leafy festoon was in a blaze. As the red light arose and fell, a numerous congregation alternately shone forth, then disappeared in shadow, and again grew, as it were, out of the darkness, peopling the heart of the solitary woods at once.

"A grave and dark-clad company," quoth Goodman Brown.   55

In truth they were such. Among them, quivering to and fro between gloom and splendor, appeared faces that would be seen next day at the council board of the province, and others which, Sabbath after Sabbath, looked devoutly heavenward, and benignantly over the crowded pews, from the holiest pulpits in the land. Some affirm that the lady of the governor was there. At least there were high dames well known to her, and wives of honored husbands, and widows, a great multitude, and ancient maidens, all of excellent repute, and fair young girls, who trembled lest their mothers should espy them. Either the sudden gleams of light flashing over the obscure field bedazzled Goodman Brown, or he recognized a score of the church members of Salem village famous for their especial sanctity. Good old Deacon Gookin had arrived, and waited at the skirts of that venerable saint, his revered pastor. But, irreverently consorting with these grave, reputable, and pious people, these elders of the church, these chaste dames and dewy virgins, there were men of dissolute lives and women of spotted fame, wretches given over to all mean and filthy vice, and suspected even of horrid crimes. It was strange to see that the good shrank not from the wicked, nor were the sinners abashed by the saints. Scattered also among their pale-faced enemies were the Indian priests, or powwows, who had often scared their native forest with more hideous incantations than any known to English witchcraft.

"But where is Faith?" thought Goodman Brown; and, as hope came into his heart, he trembled.

Another verse of the hymn arose, a slow and mournful strain, such as the pious love, but joined to words which expressed all that our nature can conceive of sin, and darkly hinted at far more. Unfathomable to mere mortals is the lore of fiends. Verse after verse was sung; and still the chorus of the desert swelled between like the deepest tone of a mighty organ; and with the final peal of that dreadful anthem there came a sound, as if the roaring wind, the rushing streams, the howling beasts, and every other voice of the unconcerted wilderness were mingling and according with the voice of guilty man in homage to the prince of all. The four blazing pines threw up a loftier flame, and obscurely discovered shapes and visages of horror on the smoke wreaths above the impious assembly. At the same moment the fire on the rock shot redly forth and formed a glowing arch above its base, where now appeared a figure. With reverence be it spoken, the figure bore no slight similitude, both in garb and manner, to some grave divine of the New England churches.

"Bring forth the converts!" cried a voice that echoed through the field and rolled into the forest.

At the word, Goodman Brown stepped forth from the shadow of the 60 trees and approached the congregation, with whom he felt a loathful brotherhood by the sympathy of all that was wicked in his heart. He could have wellnigh sworn that the shape of his own dead father beckoned him to advance, looking downward from a smoke wreath, while a woman, with dim features of despair, threw out her hand to warn him back. Was it his mother? But he had no power to retreat one step, nor to resist, even in thought, when the minister and good old Deacon Gookin seized his arms and led him to the blazing rock. Thither came also the slender form of a veiled female, led between Goody Cloyse, that pious teacher of the catechism, and Martha Carrier, who had received the devil's promise to be queen of hell. A rampant hag was she. And there stood the proselytes beneath the canopy of fire.

"Welcome, my children," said the dark figure, "to the communion of your race. Ye have found thus young your nature and your destiny. My children, look behind you!"

They turned; and flashing forth, as it were, in a sheet of flame, the fiend worshipers were seen; the smile of welcome gleamed darkly on every visage.

"There," resumed the sable form, "are all whom ye have reverenced from youth. Ye deemed them holier than yourselves and shrank from your own sin, contrasting it with their lives of righteousness and prayerful aspirations heavenward. Yet here are they all in my worshiping assembly. This night it shall be granted you to know their secret deeds: how hoary-bearded elders of the church have whispered wanton words to the young maids of their households; how many a woman, eager for widows' weeds, has given her husband a drink at bedtime and let him sleep his last sleep in her bosom; how beardless youths have made haste to inherit their fathers' wealth; and how fair damsels—blush not, sweet ones—have dug little graves in the garden, and bidden me, the sole guest, to an infant's funeral. By the sympathy of your human hearts for sin ye shall scent out all the places—whether in church, bedchamber, street, field, or forest—where crime has been committed, and shall exult to behold the whole earth one stain of guilt, one mighty blood spot. Far more than this. It shall be yours to penetrate, in every bosom, the deep mystery of sin, the fountain of all wicked arts, and which inexhaustibly supplies more evil impulses than human power—than my power at its utmost—can make manifest in deeds. And now, my children, look upon each other."

They did so; and, by the blaze of the hell-kindled torches, the wretched man beheld his Faith, and the wife her husband, trembling before that unhallowed altar.

"Lo, there ye stand, my children," said the figure, in a deep and solemn   65
tone, almost sad with its despairing awfulness, as if his once angelic nature could yet mourn for our miserable race, "Depending upon one another's hearts, ye had still hoped that virtue were not all a dream. Now are ye undeceived. Evil is the nature of mankind. Evil must be your only happiness. Welcome again, my children, to the communion of your race."

"Welcome," repeated the fiend worshipers; in one cry of despair and triumph.

And there they stood, the only pair, as it seemed, who were yet hesitating on the verge of wickedness in this dark world. A basin was hollowed, naturally, in the rock. Did it contain water, reddened by the lurid light? or was it blood? or, perchance, a liquid flame? Herein did the shape of evil dip his hand and prepare to lay the mark of baptism upon their foreheads, that they might be partakers of the mystery of sin, more conscious of the secret guilt of others, both in deed and thought, than they could now be of their own. The husband cast one look at his pale wife, and Faith at him. What polluted wretches would the next glance show them to each other, shuddering alike at what they disclosed and what they saw!

"Faith! Faith!" cried the husband, "look up to heaven, and resist the wicked one."

Whether Faith obeyed he knew not. Hardly had he spoken when he found himself amid calm night and solitude, listening to a roar of the wind which died heavily away through the forest. He staggered against the rock, and felt it chill and damp; while a hanging twig, that had been all on fire, besprinkled his cheek with the coldest dew.

The next morning young Goodman Brown came slowly into the street   70
of Salem village, staring around him like a bewildered man. The good old minister was taking a walk along the graveyard to get an appetite for breakfast and meditate his sermon, and bestowed a blessing, as he passed, on Goodman Brown. He shrank from the venerable saint as if to avoid an anathema. Old Deacon Gookin was at domestic worship, and the holy words of his prayer were heard through the open window. "What God doth the wizard pray to?" quoth Goodman Brown. Goody Cloyse, that excellent

old Christian, stood in the early sunshine at her own lattice, catechizing a little girl who had brought her a pint of morning's milk. Goodman Brown snatched away the child as from the grasp of the fiend himself. Turning the corner by the meeting-house, he spied the head of Faith, with the pink ribbons, gazing anxiously forth, and bursting into such joy at sight of him that she skipped along the street and almost kissed her husband before the whole village. But Goodman Brown looked sternly and sadly into her face, and passed on without a greeting.

Had Goodman Brown fallen asleep in the forest and only dreamed a wild dream of a witch-meeting?

Be it so if you will; but, alas! it was a dream of evil omen for young Goodman Brown. A stern, a sad, a darkly meditative, a distrustful, if not a desperate man did he become from the night of that fearful dream. On the Sabbath day, when the congregation were singing a holy psalm, he could not listen because an anthem of sin rushed loudly upon his ear and drowned all the blessed strain. When the minister spoke from the pulpit with power and fervid eloquence, and, with his hand on the open Bible, of the sacred truths of our religion, and of saintlike lives and triumphant deaths, and of future bliss or misery unutterable, then did Goodman Brown turn pale, dreading lest the roof should thunder down upon the gray blasphemer and his hearers. Often, awaking suddenly at midnight, he shrank from the bosom of Faith; and at morning or eventide, when the family knelt down at prayer, he scowled and muttered to himself, and gazed sternly at his wife, and turned away. And when he had lived long, and was borne to his grave a hoary corpse, followed by Faith, an aged woman, and children and grandchildren, a goodly procession, besides neighbors not a few, they carved no hopeful verse upon his tombstone, for his dying hour was gloom.

- How is Young Goodman Brown's wife presented? What does she say? Where does she appear in the story?

- Why does Goodman Brown go out into the woods? Where does he present his reasons for this trip?

- Look carefully at the details Hawthorne presents about Brown's guide. What words does he use? Why might these details give insight into Brown's character?

- What does Brown see in the woods? How is this scene described? Whose perspective is this?

- What happens once Brown comes home? Look at the specific words used to describe how his experience influences the rest of his life.

POETRY

Phillis Wheatley (1753–1784)

On Being Brought from Africa to America (1773)

Twas mercy brought me from my Pagan land,
Taught my benighted soul to understand
That there's a God, that there's a Saviour too:
Once I redemption neither sought nor knew.
Some view our sable race with scornful eye,   5
"Their colour is a diabolic die."
Remember, Christians, Negros, black as Cain,
May be refin'd and join th'angelic train.

- How does the title of the poem help us interpret specific words within the poem?
- Because we are reading this poem more than two centuries after it was written, how might our interpretation of the author's conversion differ from the sentiments that she expresses here?

Allen Ginsberg (1926–1997)

Supermarket in California (1956)

What thoughts I have of you tonight, Walt Whitman, for I walked down the
   sidestreets under the trees with a headache self-conscious looking at the full
   moon.
In my hungry fatigue, and shopping for images, I went into the neon fruit supermarket, dreaming of your enumerations!
What peaches and what penumbras! Whole families shopping at night! Aisles
   full of husbands! Wives in the avocados, babies in the tomatoes—and you,
   Garcia Lorca, what were you doing down by the watermelons?

I saw you, Walt Whitman, childless, lonely old grubber, poking among the meats
   in the refrigerator and eyeing the grocery boys.
I heard you asking questions of each: Who killed the pork chops? What   5
   price bananas? Are you my Angel?
I wandered in and out of the brilliant stacks of cans following you, and followed
   in my imagination by the store detective.

We strode down the open corridors together in our solitary fancy tasting arti-
chokes, possessing every frozen delicacy, and never passing the cashier.

Where are we going, Walt Whitman? The doors close in an hour. Which way
does your beard point tonight?

(I touch your book and dream of our odyssey in the supermarket and feel
absurd.)

Will we walk all night through solitary streets? The trees add shade to shade,   10
lights out in the houses, we'll both be lonely.

Will we stroll dreaming of the lost America of love past blue automobiles in
driveways, home to our silent cottage?

Ah, dear father, graybeard, lonely old courage-teacher, what America did you
have when Charon quit poling his ferry and you got out on a smoking
bank and stood watching the boat disappear on the black waters of Lethe?

Berkeley 1955

■ How does the phrase"shopping for Images" explain the poet's problem in
this poem?

■ How might the world that the poet describes here be different from the
one that Whitman, who got out of Charon's ferry in 1892, described in his
poetry? How do these differences influence the poet's sense of what are
appropriate images for American poetry?

James Tate (1943–   )

Shiloh (2003)

On Monday, Miss Francis told her sixth-grade class that she was getting married soon. The class was very happy for her, and they asked her lots of questions about her wedding plans. They never once mentioned the Civil War.
On Tuesday, she came in late wiping tears from her eyes, and told them there
was going to be no wedding. The class let out a collective sigh. They tried
to console her throughout the hour. No one mentioned Appomattox. On
Wednesday, she surprised them all by announcing that the wedding would,
indeed, take place, and that it was going to be bigger and fancier than originally planned. The class cheered and applauded. They wanted to know all the
details. She drew a picture of her gown on the blackboard. She told them all
about the food and the music. Little Rory sat in the back of the class listening,
but what he saw was Pickett's charge up the ridge at Gettysburg, the mayhem
and slaughter, the horse shot and collapsing, a total of 51,000 dead. And four

months later, Lincoln's great speech at the cemetery, 267 words, given in four minutes. Rory knew the speech by heart, and was saying it to himself, barely able to hold back tears, when Rebecca Crothers had the impertinency to ask Miss Francis if she was a virgin. "Long ago and far away," Miss Francis replied. Rory pictured her camped beside the battlefield, nervously waiting for her man, who would never return.

- "Shiloh" was the site of a significant 1862 battle in the Civil War. Why is the poem called "Shiloh"?

- How does the poem contrast Rory's view with that of Miss Francis and the rest of the class? Note where he appears in the poem and how his point of view differs from that of other students.

Meghan O'Rourke (1976–   )

The Window at Arles (2008)

Even the moon set him going, with its blank stare;
even the walls of the café, which seemed to tilt
and sway as he watched them, green with absinthe.
"It is a wonderful thing to draw a human being."
All night, Van Gogh painted, and then scraped paint from the easel;   5
The stiff sound of palette knife on canvas,
scratching, made him think of a hungry animal.
Women came and posed.
"It is a wonderful thing to paint a human being, something
that lives," he told Theo; "it is confoundedly difficult,   10
but after all it is splendid."
When the money for models ran out,
he bought plaster casts of hands and hung them
from the crossbeams of his room,
and woke to the sound of their knocking in the wind.   15

*

One night Van Gogh sat in a chair, staring.
Brush in one hand, milk saucer in the other.
The tea was weak. Nothing came. In the morning,
one of his models brought bread and cheese
and made him eat. That afternoon,   20

he broke the plaster casts, banging hand into hand
until he stood in a storm of dust, coughing.

*

When he worked he felt a scratch at his calf,
a scarlet wound a whoop of blood. He was hungry;
even his eyes were hungry.   25
All he saw was red: red snow, red legs of women
in the village rues, red pinwheels of hay.
"It is a wonderful thing
to hurt a human being, something
that lives. It is confoundedly difficult, but after all it is splendid."   30

*

Beyond the window, a cave opened
in the trees and led into emptiness,
a yellow you couldn't quite see an end to.
Van Gogh walked into it,
and his body began to shake. It was a color-riot.   35
He could hear, somewhere, a dog
thumping its tail in the dark.
"How splendid yellow is!" he said.

*

Color was electricity, it turned you blind
if you got hold of it.   40
It turned you blind if something could
got hold of you and blistered.
Walls falling toward you.
When you turn color into a weapon,
something gets left over: 45
a charred body
What you must do is take the plaster
and turn it to praise
as light turns grass in the evening
into fear gone blind into the hunt.   50

■ Vincent Van Gough (1853–1890) spent two of his last years (1888–1889) in
  Arles where he hoped to found a utopian artists' colony. It was in Arles that
  he famously severed his own ear. O'Rourke's Van Gogh not only sees but
  feels colors. How do the poet's words make us both see and feel from the
  painter's perspective?

Chidiock Tichborne (1558–1586)

Elegy Written with His Own Hand in the Tower before His Execution (1586)

My prime of youth is but a frost of cares,
My feast of joy is but a dish of pain,
My crop of corn is but a field of tares,
And all my good is but vain hope of gain;
The day is past, and yet I saw no sun,   5
And now I live, and now my life is done.

My tale was heard and yet it was not told,
My fruit is fallen and yet my leaves are green,
My youth is spent and yet I am not old,
I saw the world and yet I was not seen;   10
My thread is cut and yet it is not spun,
And now I live, and now my life is done.

I sought my death and found it in my womb,
I looked for life and saw it was a shade,
I trod the earth and knew it was my tomb,   15
And now I die, and now I was but made;
My glass is full, and now my glass is run,
And now I live, and now my life is done.

- The entire poem is constructed of apparent paradoxes. How does the poem itself reconcile them?

- Chidiock Tichborne was a practicing Roman Catholic at a time when the religion had become outlawed in England. His offense was conspiring to murder Queen Elizabeth. This poem was written to his wife. How does this contextual information add to a reading of the poem?

Gwendolyn Brooks (1917–2000)

De Witt Williams on His Way to Lincoln Cemetery (1987)

He was born in Alabama.
He was bred in Illinois.

He was nothing but a
Plain black boy.

Swing low swing low sweet sweet chariot.   5
Nothing but a plain black boy.

Drive him past the Pool Hall.
Drive him past the Show.
Blind within his casket,
But maybe he will know.   10

Down through Forty-seventh Street:
Underneath the L,
And—Northwest Corner, Prairie,
That he loved so well.

Don't forget the Dance Halls—   15
Warwick and Savoy,
Where he picked his women, where
He drank his liquid joy.

Born in Alabama.
Bred in Illinois.   20
He was nothing but a
Plain black boy.

Swing low swing low sweet sweet chariot.
Nothing but a plain black boy

- How do the images and the narrative in this poem function in ways similar
  to what we have read in "When Lilacs Last in the Dooryard Bloom'd"?
- The repeated line "Swing low swing low sweet sweet chariot" comes from a
  well-known African American spiritual. The next line of the hymn is "coming for
  to carry me home." How does the poet rework that line throughout the poem?

David Shumate (1950–   )

High Water Mark (2004)

It's hard to believe, but at one point the water rose to this level. No one had
seen anything like it. People on rooftops. Cows and coffins floating through
the streets. Prisoners carrying invalids from their rooms. The barkeeper consoling the preacher. A coon hound who showed up a month later forty miles

downstream. And all that mud it left behind. You never forget times like those. They become part of who you are. You describe them to your grandchildren. But they think it's just another tale in which animals talk and people live forever. I know it's not the kind of thing you ought to say... But I wouldn't mind seeing another good flood before I die. It's been dry for decades. Next time I think I'll just let go and drift downstream and see where I end up.

- Describe the kind or level of Shumate's diction. How does word choice create a sense of character?

- How might thinking of "High Water Mark" in terms of the rhetorical structure of a sonnet help you appreciate the turn from description to reflection evident in the final lines?

Experiencing Literature through Writing

1. Looking closely at a specific word, choose a word or a grouping of words that seems to be significant within this particular presentation. In your discussion, explain what it is about this language choice that makes this particular work distinctive.

    a. How does this word usage adhere to or depart from conventional usage? Use a dictionary to help here.
    b. How does this word usage set a style for the rest of this particular text?
    c. How is this word usage significant to our understanding of the larger text?

2. Using one or more works in this chapter (or works in another chapter), explore the tension between an author's attempt to convey some original emotion and the impact of certain words that convention dictates should be used when discussing that emotion. In this exploration, think about the constraints that language places upon the attempt to create a life out of words.

12 Symbolism

How Do I Know When an Event or an Image Is Supposed to Stand for Something Else?

Whether we know it or not, we're all readers of signs. When we see a red light at an intersection, we know we should stop. That much is easy. Literature and film also employ some easy-to-read signs. In monster movies from the 1950s and early 1960s, the monster would die in the final scene and the closing credits would announce "The End" and a question mark would emerge from the darkened screen.

Every person in the theater knew that the terrifying creature that had lurked beneath the dark waters of the lake didn't actually die as the characters in the

The Blob (1958)

film thought. All in the audience realized that "The End . . .?" meant "sort of the end": leave the theater, but take your scary feelings home with you because the monster is still "out there." Although this sign prompts a bit more open interpretation than a road sign does, it still severely limits likely responses. In both literature and life, we are trained to read and interpret the most common signs in particular ways by experience. The simplest signs express a remarkably narrow range of meanings.

What happens, though, when one thing suggests possible meanings without being specific about any particular single meaning? How can we read and interpret a sign when we are not taught by established custom exactly how to read it? Or when the function of the sign is *not* to communicate a specific, limited meaning (a prohibition, an order, a direction)? What happens when a sign provokes conflicting responses? At some point we need a new word. We need to move from sign to **symbol**. In the broadest sense, all words are symbols in that words stand for something else; the word *tree* isn't an actual tree. For purposes of literary analysis, it's useful to define *symbol* as something (an object, a word, an image) that is used to suggest a range of associations, ideas, or feelings. Symbols prompt reflection and inquiry; they don't usually point us to a highly defined action or message. Symbols force us to grapple with meanings that are suggestive, resonant, and subtly nuanced. This can lead to uncomfortable territory for some readers. One of the most frustrating experiences many people have with complex literary works and films arises from the sense that one thing means something else, yet that "something else" cannot easily be identified, captured, or named. To a person who wants things clear-cut, a discussion of symbols can seem like an imposition: a "reading into" a text rather than a reading of a text.

But we cannot dismiss the power of symbols because we sometimes find them hard to read. And we need not be helpless before them. Writers don't want symbols to obscure meaning. They want to use symbols to reach new meaning. Our efforts to understand and articulate how symbols emerge and take on meaning can be profoundly rewarding. In this chapter, we'll consider how we can be cut loose from explicit and easily identified directions and still develop grounded, persuasive readings.

FIGURATIVE LANGUAGE

Figurative language is broadly defined as any language that is used in ways that deviate from standard significance, order, or meaning. Such language may lend freshness or strength to expression. It may also extend or complicate the meaning of a word or expression. Figurative language, then, moves us from signs to symbols.

Figurative language is often divided into two types. A **rhetorical figure** uses a word or words in an unusual context or sequence, but does not radically change the customary meaning of the word or words. For example, an **apostrophe** refers to the speaker's direct address to an absent person or to some abstract idea or spirit; although we don't usually speak to someone or something that is not physically present, the words themselves may be familiar. Of greater importance for our purposes is the second type of figurative language. A **trope** (sometimes called a **figure of thought**) differs from a rhetorical figure in that it moves us to a changed or significantly extended meaning of a word or words. **Personification** is an example of a trope; to personify is to cast an abstract concept or inanimate material as a living thing endowed with human qualities. Before Dwayne Johnson became a movie star, he was a wrestler named "The Rock." He chose that stage name to personify qualities of strength, indestructibility, hardness. When he first turned to movies (and was still "The Rock") that name came to take on broader meanings depending on the roles he played (solidity, steadiness, and so on). As he sought other roles (in light comedies, for example) he chose to become again simply Dwayne Johnson—a name that didn't tie him to a specific character or genre type.

Similes and metaphors are also tropes. A **simile** explicitly associates (through words *like* or *as*) an abstraction with a concrete image. For example, "love is like a red rose." Such comparisons direct our interpretation, but similes can provoke complex responses to likenesses: "Love, like a red rose, is beautiful in bloom—full, richly layered, deeply fragrant. But rosebushes do have thorns. Red roses in particular wither quickly." The simile initiates not just a simple thought, but a cluster of thoughts. A **metaphor** presses the interpretive possibilities further still. In a metaphor, the explicit connection (*like* or *as*) is dropped: "Love is not merely like a red rose, it *is* a red rose." A simile, then, invites comparison; it calls attention to sometimes surprising likenesses and asks that we test out or seek the meaning prompted by the aligned parts. A metaphor, in contrast, presses toward some elemental correspondence that may create new meaning. Metaphors are more suggestive (less directive) than similes.

We should note that the root of the word *trope* is from the Greek "to turn," or "a turning." Tropes use words to *turn* someone from conventional understanding; they test the elasticity of language. This "turning" is different from arbitrarily redefining a word. If we were all to invent our own definitions for words, language would fail. We depend upon some common understanding to communicate. An effectively employed trope will use the old or the familiar as an interpretive lead. We go forward from what we know. What we're suggesting here is that readers don't "hunt" for symbols as an archeologist hunts for evidence of a buried civilization. To find symbols, don't dig randomly for what is covered. Start by paying close attention to the common signals a text provides on the surface.

Experiencing Film through Symbolism

An early scene in David O. Russell's *American Hustle* (2013) shows Irving Rosenfeld (Christian Bale), an expert scam artist, laboriously doing his hair. Irving glues patches of fake hair beneath long strands of his own hair that he combs over to hide his baldness. The result is neither convincing nor attractive. It's an obvious, comically inept cover up. We could enjoy the scene simply for what it establishes about the main character: Irving seems equal parts brazen confidence and deep insecurity. And the bad comb-over also contributes to the sense of time and place that Russell so carefully builds. Yet we can think of Irving's hair as symbolic or even argue that we are prompted to think of it as symbolic.

Well before we get into the labyrinth of deceit that constitutes the whole plot, we see the central character laboriously attending to his hair. It's a fairly long scene and in terms of the story, it's altogether unnecessary. But as the film unfolds, Irving's comb-over becomes an apt expression of theme. Irving succeeds as a scam artist because he knows belief depends more on desire than truth. Because desperate people are highly motivated to believe in something that aligns with their needs, Irving doesn't need to present much of substance to prospective clients or victims. A few simple props like an office and an attractive associate (Sydney Prosser, played by Amy Adams) help, but Irving closes deals because he has the discipline to let others credit the illusions he merely hints at. As he says, people will see what they want to see. Knowing this simple truth gives Irving great power. And yet, it doesn't mean he is somehow beyond that truth. His comb-over might suggest that at some level, Irving has his own desires that translate into not seeing. Maybe he even thinks his hair looks pretty good.

Bradley Cooper (left) and Christian Bale in *American Hustle* (2013)

Annapurna Productions/Photos 12/Alamy

We're also prompted to consider bad hair as a symbol by other scenes in the film. Remember, symbols become symbols in context of the fabric of the whole. Irving is not the only scammer to have bad hair. Nor is the opening scene the only one that focuses on the labor of doing one's hair. About midway through the film we see Richie DiMaso (Bradley Cooper) working on his perm. Again, the scene has no plot function., but it does **foreground** (that is, draw attention to) hairstyles. The fact that Richie is an FBI agent provides another layer to consider, for his hair along with his role blurs moral lines between the felons and those who pursue them: All are playing games, but none are what they seem. It would be hard not to notice the hairstyles in this film, but without the scenes before the mirrors, we might not press beyond the simple fact of bad hair. To encourage us to reflect further, Sydney calls attention to Richie's hair, too. She says it doesn't fool anybody, but that it's a good look on him.

RECOGNIZING SYMBOLS

As we've noted, there isn't anything inherently symbolic about a bad comb-over, nor is there any specific meaning necessarily attached to any particular symbol. But Russell treats Irving's hair in a way that makes us think of the obvious things we refuse to see. Moreover, he makes us think about why we refuse to see as well as about the benefits and problems that go along with delusions. He seeks to say something essential about American dreams and desires. He tells us that passion for success or for escaping failure can blur judgment, muddle truth, or encourage blindness. And he suggests something about what constitutes success or failure in our culture. Some critics have described *American Hustle* as a fun but ultimately shallow period film. But perhaps they aren't thinking hard enough about how symbols are used and what they can suggest to us now. To sum up, we need to always consider how the surrounding material supports a symbolic (rather than a strictly literal) interpretation. The chart on the following page contains images with apples in various contexts. Consider how the apple's use in each image supports a different symbolic reading.

Now, think for a moment of an orange, a fruit whose symbolic use is less common than the apple's. What comes to mind? First responses are likely to be to the thing itself: color, weight, shape, smell, and taste. We think in terms of concrete images. And as we pointed out in Chapter 7, we don't always need or want to go beyond those images. Gary Soto's "Oranges" concretely registers physical characteristics of the fruit; there are real pleasures communicated by his grounded description. Still, you will likely come to think of the oranges as symbols. How does Soto persuade us to move from one kind of understanding to

What does an apple symbolize?

© Bettmann/Corbis

Churchman's Cigarettes

Gravity

© Blue Lantern Studio/CORBIS

© Bettmann/Corbis

©Royalty-Free/Corbis

another? Compare his first mention of a cold twelve-year-old, "weighted down/ With two oranges" (lines 3–4) with his glorious "I peeled my orange" (line 51) at the end of the poem. He mentions "orange" only three times, yet our sense of how we interpret oranges changes considerably. What has happened to give the orange symbolic meaning?

Gary Soto (1952–   )

Oranges (1995)

The first time I walked
With a girl, I was twelve,
Cold, and weighted down
With two oranges in my jacket.
December. Frost cracking   5
Beneath my steps, my breath
Before me, then gone,
As I walked toward
Her house, the one whose
Porch light burned yellow   10
Night and day, in any weather.
A dog barked at me, until
She came out pulling
At her gloves, face bright
With rouge. I smiled,   15
Touched her shoulder, and led
Her down the street, across
A used car lot and a line
Of newly planted trees,
Until we were breathing   20
Before a drugstore. We
Entered, the tiny bell
Bringing a saleslady
Down a narrow aisle of goods.
I turned to the candies   25
Tiered like bleachers,
And asked what she wanted—
Light in her eyes, a smile
Starting at the corners
Of her mouth. I fingered   30
A nickel in my pocket,

And when she lifted a chocolate
That cost a dime,
I didn't say anything.
I took the nickel from   35
My pocket, then an orange,
And set them quietly on
The counter. When I looked up,
The lady's eyes met mine,
And held them, knowing   40
Very well what it was all
About.

Outside,
A few cars hissing past,
Fog hanging like old   45
Coats between the trees.
I took my girl's hand
In mine for two blocks,
Then released it to let
Her unwrap the chocolate.   50
I peeled my orange
That was so bright against
The gray of December
That, from some distance,
Someone might have thought   55
I was making a fire in my hands.

By the time Soto gives us his most precise physical description of the orange
(near the end of the poem), the orange has grown symbolically rich. His
desire to impress this girl is so intense that he has persuaded the woman
behind the counter in the drugstore to enter into his world. She has accepted
his orange as sufficient payment for the candy bar that the girl wants; the
saleswoman understands that he has only half as much money as he needs
to buy this candy bar and that to admit his poverty here will destroy him. He
persuades the woman to abandon the conventional sign—one candy bar is
equivalent to one dime—and to accept his substitution of an orange for the
missing nickel. This story describes the triumph of the poet's act of symbolism. He presents his symbol powerfully enough that someone outside his
consciousness agrees to accept that symbol. In the final scene he revels in his
triumph, consuming an orange that means so much more than it meant at
the beginning of the poem.

ALLEGORY AND SYMBOL

Allegory builds from a symbolic system; it develops a parallel between the concrete and the abstract that is generally sustained throughout a narrative. In allegory, we observe two levels of meaning that play out in a consistent manner as actions unfold. The Red Cross Knight in Edmund Spenser's *Faerie Queene* meets a variety of challenges, but he remains always on a quest for truth. Every narrated encounter teaches us something about the difficulties goodness faces in a fallen world. The fabric of the whole work helps us interpret each action; our reading is conditioned by the entire created structure. We've suggested that symbols generally encourage readers to reflect upon meaning that is luminous, multiple, and abstract. Allegory, in contrast, directs readers to a level of meaning that is relatively defined, uniform, and instructional.

LEARNING THROUGH LIKENESS

We sometimes forget that the literary experience can be socially and morally instructive. Works driven by an explicit morally instructive purpose are called **didactic works**. One of the clearest examples of a transparently didactic allegorical tale is Gertrude Crampton's *Tootle* (1945), a children's picture book that remains in print and tells the story of a little train who must learn that it is wrong to go off the tracks. When Tootle wanders out into a delightful meadow, his teacher Bill conspires with the inhabitants of Lower Trainswitch to make him think that life off the established track is filled with red flags. After experiencing much frustration with the red flags planted in the meadow, Tootle submits to discipline; he has learned that the greatest freedom involves staying where he belongs: on the tracks. Bill and the townspeople have successfully made their point.

Allegories constructed to force us down a single line can quickly grow tiresome. Fortunately, allegories need not be so controlling. If we get down to the core simile of *Tootle*, we have something like the following: Social conventions are like railroad tracks. Left at that elemental level, we can play more freely with the comparison than Crampton might wish. Social customs and rules may, like tracks, keep us moving toward something. These tracks (when we stay on them properly) help us avoid collisions with others. Tracks allow us to move faster. But we can also be "stuck" on the tracks. We can be "railroaded." We may complain of someone who has a "one-track mind." And tracks are fixed whereas customs and rules are varied, changeable, and open. Tracks are something we are either on or off. People may engage with customs and rules actively—even playfully. A simile such as "social conventions are like railroad tracks" might lead us to think from many different perspectives. An allegory could well be built on such a simile that would extend or complicate the possibilities—not just shut them down.

A Note to Student Writers: Using Analogies in Arguments

A simile involves a comparison between what might seem to be unlike things; a simile leaves the reader to tease out the meaning or effect. An **analogy** also involves a comparison. With an analogy, though, the comparison depends upon likeness and is intended to serve a point—to build a logically forceful argument. Students are often warned not to build arguments from perceived similarities: "Don't argue from analogy" or "That's a false analogy." Although it is certainly true that you're not likely to successfully sustain an argument based on likeness throughout an entire paper, it is possible to illustrate a point or develop part of an argument through a carefully thought-out analogy. For instance, Oliver Wendell Holmes, while chief justice of the Supreme Court, argued that the right to free speech must be limited when the speech in question is like someone shouting "FIRE" in a crowded theater.

Because many writers have, along with Holmes, used analogy effectively in analytical and argumentative essays, it seems plain wrong to require students to avoid analogies altogether. But it's not wrong to warn students to construct (or evaluate) an analogy with care. When you use (or read) an analogy, consider the following: First, are the two things that are put together really similar? Second, is the similarity *relevant* to the point made? Third, is there some difference between the two things that undermines the point? Use these questions to test a specific application of Holmes's analogy.

Experiencing Literature through Allegory

Crampton's train is part of a tradition of stories in which the actors are not human; Tootle is a personification of an unruly child. This train acts exactly like a child, but the story (and the pictures) are engaging precisely because a train is *not* a child: we see a familiar world altered. Even children who don't want to accept Crampton's lesson might smile at the thought of a train sitting in a school room. In this sort of story, anthropomorphic animals often present models of appropriate and inappropriate human behavior. The most famous may be the many ingenious animals that Aesop created to personify human dilemmas.

Aesop (620–564 BCE)

The Crow and the Pitcher (ca. 300 BCE)

A Thirsty Crow found a Pitcher with some water in it, but so little was there that, try as she might, she could not reach it with her beak, and it seemed as though she would die of thirst within sight of the remedy. At last she hit upon a clever plan. She began dropping pebbles into the Pitcher, and with

Walter Crane, *Illustration for Aesop's "The Crow and the Pitcher"*

each pebble the water rose a little higher until at last it reached the brim, and the knowing bird was enabled to quench her thirst.

    Moral: *Necessity is the mother of invention.* ❖

In Aesop's **fable**, the crow is hardly developed as a character. It is important that she be a crow primarily so that she cannot have hands to pick up the pitcher. Her only attributes in this short paragraph are her ingenuity and her thirst. In illustrations of this tale, the crow looks like a crow. Unlike the story of Tootle, the fable of the crow and the pitcher seems like it could be true. The pithy moral conjoined to the image of the crow using pebbles to quench her thirst has a remarkable staying power.

    Part of that power arises from the fit between concrete images and intangible qualities. Aesop helps us picture necessity, invention, and resourcefulness (all qualities difficult to describe). The thirsty crow stands for all forms of necessity; the pebble trick signifies all forms of invention. Readers take it from there. We're not bound by the moral to limit "necessity" to thirst. As soon as we understand the situation of the crow, we see how this instance could be illustrated by many other similar situations (even though few seem to be able to do it as economically as Aesop's tale). His fable is very clear, yet it's not restrictive.

EMBODYING TIMELESS QUALITIES

Most of us recognize the blindfolded figure of Justice holding a set of scales in one hand and a sword in the other. We have learned that the blindfold helps her be impartial so that she will weigh the two sides in a dispute evenhandedly without bias, and her sword will render that verdict. When she makes her decision, the figure suggests, her verdict will be fair and will help contribute to the civility of our society. We are familiar with the image largely because it has been repeated in various forms at courthouses throughout the country.

The allegorical figure of Fortune may be a bit less familiar, but the explanation of the objects in the image is clear enough. The female Fortune holds a cornucopia representing the bounty that she offers, but she sits upon a bubble (easily burst) to indicate the fleeting nature of her gifts. The man with her is Chance, whose lottery tickets offer little more than the dream of owning that cornucopia.

©The J. Paul Getty Museum, Los Angeles

Dosso Dossi, *Allegory of Fortune* (ca. 1530)

© Bettmann/CORBIS

Engraving of Statue of Justice holding a sword and scales

These images deal with qualities we often consider universal or timeless. Justice is not thought of as a construction of a particular culture; we typically assume it's a transcendent value that all must seek. Chance is a condition that operates far above any individual level. If we doubt the eternal quality of such notions, the figures of Justice and Fortune may start to look a bit tacky and outdated. The poet Billy Collins observes that the contemporary literary scene is largely devoid of allegorical figures. As he introduces each figure, he calls up familiar images from a tradition in which these figures played much more prominent roles. He then observes that it is only the plainest things—bare of any explicit meaning—that we choose to invoke.

Billy Collins (1941–)

The Death of Allegory (1999)

I am wondering what become of all those tall abstractions
that used to pose, robed and statuesque, in paintings
and parade about on the pages of the Renaissance
displaying their capital letters like license plates.

Truth cantering on a powerful horse,   5
Chastity, eyes downcast, fluttering with veils.
Each one was marble come to life, a thought in a coat,
Courtesy bowing with one hand always extended,

Villainy sharpening an instrument behind a wall,
Reason with her crown and Constancy alert behind a helm,   10
They are all retired now, consigned to a Florida for tropes.
Justice is there standing by an open refrigerator.

Valor lies in bed listening to the rain.
Even Death has nothing to do but mend his cloak and hood,
and all their props are locked away in a warehouse,   15
hourglasses, globes, blindfolds and shackles.

Even if you called them back, there are no places left
for them to go, no Garden of Mirth or Bower of Bliss.
The Valley of Forgiveness is lined with condominiums
and chainsaws are howling in the Forest of Despair.   20

Here on the table near the window is a vase of peonies
and next to it black binoculars and a money clip,

exactly the kind of thing we now prefer,
objects that sit quietly on a line in lower case,

themselves and nothing more, a wheelbarrow,   25
an empty mailbox, a razor blade resting in a glass ashtray.
As for the others, the great ideas on horseback
and the long-haired virtues in embroidered gowns,

it looks as though they have traveled down
that road you see on the final page of storybooks,   30
the one that winds up a green hillside and disappears
into an unseen valley where everyone must be fast asleep.

Collins speaks longingly of a time when artists engaged with big ideas, and compares that to a current time when allegorical figures are much less meaningful, when artists concentrate on the details of everyday life. The ideas that have replaced such "tall abstractions" as Truth and Chastity are the "lowercase objects" that populate this poem. Although it seems true that contemporary artists resist grand generalities and abstractions, Collins's observation says much about allegory in any age. Our inclination to use allegory, even in the older times that Collins celebrates, begins with the sense that big ideas are a thing of the past. The statue that adorns the Department of Justice was not a product of ancient Greece or Rome, but was made deliberately to invoke those times. Its form suggests the links between the modern courthouse and classical civilization. The statue depicts an ancient ideal of justice and gives us more faith in the system than we might gain from a statue of a modern lawyer. Allegory has long exploited this sense of an idealized past. When Edmund Spenser wrote the *Faerie Queene* in 1596, he constructed a deliberately artificial and antique language in which to present his allegories. Just as the statue of Justice hearkens to an earlier iconography, Spenser, like many of the artists in the Renaissance, gave his own work an appearance of being older than it really was to lend seriousness to his project. So even in the sixteenth century Spenser's allegory seemed like a literary style from the past.

> **Making Connections**
>
> Reread Milosz's "Watering Can" and Williams's "The Red Wheelbarrow" (Chapter 7) in light of Billy Collins's remarks on the decline of allegory. Explore the differences among the ideas presented by these three poets. How does Collins's lament about the decline of allegory relate to Milosz and Williams and their insistence on things? How would you defend Milosz and Williams against a charge that they diminish poetry's grand potential?

Experiencing Film through Allegory

In Book VII of *The Republic*, Plato uses the image of a dark cave as an instructional device so that the students of Socrates (the primary speaker in Plato's dialogues) can understand his distinction between the physical, observable world and some greater reality unavailable to ordinary human perception. Prisoners in a cave who are able to see only shadows cast from a light outside mistake those shadows for the substantial reality behind them. For these prisoners, the shadows are the truth. Escape from the cave, Socrates explains, wouldn't be immediately liberating, for the newly free prisoners would not be equipped to see clearly or interpret accurately. Pain and confusion precede achieving a vision of the real and the true. Yet once that vision is achieved, the prisoner will never want to return to the shadows or accept old illusions. Plato spells out the elements of the allegory; he seeks to present the lesson as a timeless truth.

Scene from *The Matrix* with Keanu Reeves and Carrie-Anne Moss

© Ronald Siemoneit/Sygma/Corbis

In the film *The Matrix* (1999), Andy and Larry Wachowski create a film version of Plato's allegory. By turning the allegory into action, the Wachowskis must test the limits of the scenario that Plato has created. An advantage of pushing beyond the static quality of Plato's allegorical world is that further development reveals problems that Glaucon had not noted. In moving from

Plato's largely descriptive "story" into the plot of a mainstream movie, the tension that emerges occurs between those bound to shadows and those who have seen the light. Plato describes the difficulty of convincing prisoners with limited life experience that there was anything that they might want to escape. The screenwriters, though, begin to ask questions that the original allegory does not ask or does not attempt to answer. For instance, why are these people being held prisoner? What sort of an evil force would be responsible for such cruelty? How could anyone ever escape from this enslavement? Would escape be desirable if the real world that remains turned out to be dreary and hard?

The Matrix's plot concerns the difficulty of conveying the message of the light to the prisoners. Neo (Keanu Reeves) must battle against these prison keepers as well as against his own perception of which world is reality. The life that he has experienced before his awakening is, like the cave, merely a shadow that has been presented to him by the machines to keep him in captivity. In opening up Plato's allegory, though, the Wachowski brothers also stumble upon ironies they seem unable to solve (or perhaps do not even recognize). For example, it is often not noticed amid all the expertly choreographed action that Neo kills the sorts of people he is supposed to be liberating. The guards and police officers gunned down in the final scene are shadows projected by the prison keepers, but these shadows are connected to the mental activity of real people wired into the matrix by the masters. Their death in the projected world leads to their physical death in the world not seen. So are these unconscious victims mere collateral damage? Are we to assume that some shadows are more equal than others? Does Neo (or anyone else in his group) stop to think of the difference between the puppets/humans and the puppet masters/machines? Sometimes allegory becomes most interesting when it breaks down and allows the reader/viewer to participate strongly in the creation of meaning.

MODELING CRITICAL ANALYSIS: JOÃO GUIMARÃES ROSA, THE THIRD BANK OF THE RIVER

"The Third Bank of the River" by João Guimarães Rosa defies easy interpretation. If we think of it as a realistic story, it becomes confusing. The general tone seems fairly straightforward and there is nothing startling in the first few paragraphs, but the story's action quickly grows impossible. This father leaves his family and lives silently for many years on a little boat just beyond the old home. How could he survive? The narrator tells us that he has been taking him food, but that hardly seems a satisfactory answer. No one could live for long on such a boat subject to the elements in complete silence. We can't answer many other simple questions about this story: Why doesn't someone go bring the father in? Why doesn't the father ever seem delirious? How is it that the family grows accustomed to such a strange situation? The fact that we cannot easily respond to these questions suggests that they are the wrong kinds of questions. Guimarães Rosa may well be writing about something very real, but this is not a realistic story. We are, then, prompted to think in terms of symbols—to consider how each part along the way means or suggests something. This prompting isn't license to make Guimarães Rosa's tale mean anything we want it to mean, but it does presume we can't stop with the concrete elements of the tale.

Some have read this story as about a process of grieving or of separation. The son may stand in for all children who lose parents or even more broadly all children who need to grow into their own selves separate from parents. The father's "going out" on the river may be an abandonment that is both essential and inevitable. Perhaps we're to consider how a son registers the death of a father, how he contends with the loss or tries to deny the full meaning of the loss. The river in Guimarães Rosa's story can suggest a widely resonate and textured set of meanings. We may think of how the experience of death unfolds for those left behind and consider how Guimarães Rosa projects feelings of loneliness (as a feeling or as a necessary fact of human existence?). If the correspondences between characters and ideas can be seen as consistently woven through the whole tale, we're in the realm of allegory.

João Guimarães Rosa (1908–1967)

The Third Bank of the River (1967)

Translated by William L. Grossman

My father was a dutiful, orderly, straightforward man. And according to several reliable people of whom I inquired, he had had these qualities since adolescence or even childhood. By my own recollection, he was neither jollier nor more melancholy than the other men we knew. Maybe a little quieter. It was Mother, not Father, who ruled the house. She scolded us daily—my sister, my brother, and me. But it happened one day that Father ordered a boat.

He was very serious about it. It was to be made specially for him, of mimosa wood. It was to be sturdy enough to last twenty or thirty years and just large enough for one person. Mother carried on plenty about it. Was her husband going to become a fisherman all of a sudden? Or a hunter? Father said nothing. Our house was less than a mile from the river, which around there was deep, quiet, and so wide you couldn't see across it.

I can never forget the day the rowboat was delivered. Father showed no joy or other emotion. He just put on his hat as he always did and said good-by to us. He took along no food or bundle of any sort. We expected Mother to rant and rave, but she didn't. She looked very pale and bit her lip, but all she said was: "If you go away, stay away. Don't ever come back!"

Father made no reply. He looked gently at me and motioned me to walk along with him. I feared Mother's wrath, yet I eagerly obeyed. We headed toward the river together. I felt bold and exhilarated, so much so that I said: "Father, will you take me with you in your boat?"

He just looked at me, gave me his blessing, and by a gesture, told me   5
to go back. I made as if to do so but, when his back was turned, I ducked behind some bushes to watch him. Father got into the boat and rowed away. Its shadow slid across the water like a crocodile, long and quiet.

Father did not come back. Nor did he go anywhere, really. He just rowed and floated across and around, out there in the river. Everyone was appalled. What had never happened, what could not possibly happen, was happening. Our relatives, neighbors, and friends came over to discuss the phenomenon.

Mother was ashamed. She said little and conducted herself with great composure. As a consequence, almost everyone thought (though no one said it) that Father had gone insane. A few, however, suggested that Father might be fulfilling a promise he had made to God or to a saint, or that he might have some horrible disease, maybe leprosy, and that he left for the sake of the family, at the same time wishing to remain fairly near them.

Travelers along the river and people living near the bank on one side or the other reported that Father never put foot on land, by day or night. He just moved about on the river, solitary, aimless, like a derelict. Mother and our relatives agreed that the food which he had doubtless hidden in the boat would soon give out and that then he would either leave the river and travel off somewhere (which would be at least a little more respectable) or he would repent and come home.

How far from the truth they were! Father had a secret source of provisions: me. Every day I stole food and brought it to him. The first night after he left, we all lit fires on the shore and prayed and called to him. I was deeply distressed and felt a need to do something more. The following day I went down to the river with a loaf of corn bread, a bunch of bananas, and some bricks of raw brown sugar. I waited impatiently a long, long hour. Then I saw the boat, far off, alone, gliding almost imperceptibly on the smoothness of the river. Father was sitting in the bottom of the boat. He saw me but he did not row toward me or make any gesture. I showed him the food and then I placed it in a hollow rock on the river bank; it was safe there from animals, rain, and dew. I did this day after day, on and on and on. Later I learned, to my surprise, that Mother knew what I was doing and left food around where I could easily steal it. She had a lot of feelings she didn't show.

Mother sent for her brother to come and help on the farm and in 10
business matters. She had the schoolteacher come and tutor us children at
home because of the time we had lost. One day, at her request, the priest put
on his vestments, went down to the shore, and tried to exorcise the devils
that had got into my father. He shouted that Father had a duty to cease his
unholy obstinacy. Another day she arranged to have two soldiers come and
try to frighten him. All to no avail. My father went by in the distance, sometimes so far away he could barely be seen. He never replied to anyone and
no one ever got close to him. When some newspapermen came in a launch
to take his picture, Father headed his boat to the other side of the river and
into the marshes, which he knew like the palm of his hand but in which
other people quickly got lost. There in his private maze, which extended for
miles, with heavy foliage overhead and rushes on all sides, he was safe.

We had to get accustomed to the idea of Father's being out on the river.
We had to but we couldn't, we never could. I think I was the only one who
understood to some degree what our father wanted and what he did not
want. The thing I could not understand at all was how he stood the hardship. Day and night, in sun and rain, in heat and in the terrible midyear
cold spells, with his old hat on his head and very little other clothing, week
after week, month after month, year after year, unheedful of the waste and
emptiness in which his life was slipping by. He never set foot on earth or
grass, on isle or mainland shore. No doubt he sometimes tied up the boat at
a secret place, perhaps at the tip of some island, to get a little sleep. He never
lit a fire or even struck a match and he had no flashlight. He took only a
small part of the food that I left in the hollow rock—not enough, it seemed
to me, for survival. What could his state of health have been? How about the
continual drain on his energy, pulling and pushing the oars to control the
boat? And how did he survive the annual floods, when the river rose and
swept along with it all sorts of dangerous objects—branches of trees, dead
bodies of animals—that might suddenly crash against his little boat?

He never talked to a living soul. And we never talked about him. We
just thought. No, we could never put our father out of mind. If for a short
time we seemed to, it was just a lull from which we would be sharply awakened by the realization of his frightening situation.

My sister got married, but Mother didn't want a wedding party. It
would have been a sad affair, for we thought of him every time we ate
some especially tasty food. Just as we thought of him in our cozy beds on a
cold, stormy night—out there, alone and unprotected, trying to bail out the
boat with only his hands and a gourd. Now and then someone would say
that I was getting to look more and more like my father. But I knew that
by then his hair and beard must have been shaggy and his nails long. I pictured him thin and sickly, black with hair and sunburn, and almost naked
despite the articles of clothing I occasionally left for him.

He didn't seem to care about us at all. But I felt affection and respect for him, and, whenever they praised me because I had done something good, I said: "My father taught me to act that way."

It wasn't exactly accurate but it was a truthful sort of lie. As I said, Father didn't seem to care about us. But then why did he stay around there? Why didn't he go up the river or down the river, beyond the possibility of seeing us or being seen by us? He alone knew the answer.

15

My sister had a baby boy. She insisted on showing Father his grandson. One beautiful day we all went down to the riverbank, my sister in her white wedding dress, and she lifted the baby high. Her husband held a parasol above them. We shouted to Father and waited. He did not appear. My sister cried; we all cried in each other's arms.

My sister and her husband moved far away. My brother went to live in a city. Times changed, with their usual imperceptible rapidity. Mother finally moved too; she was old and went to live with her daughter. I remained behind, a leftover. I could never think of marrying. I just stayed there with the impedimenta of my life. Father, wandering alone and forlorn on the river, needed me. I knew he needed me, although he never even told me why he was doing it. When I put the question to people bluntly and insistently, all they told me was that they heard that Father had explained it to the man who made the boat. But now this man was dead and nobody knew or remembered anything. There was just some foolish talk, when the rains were especially severe and persistent, that my father was wise like Noah and had the boat built in anticipation of a new flood; I dimly remember people saying this. In any case, I would not condemn my father for what he was doing. My hair was beginning to turn gray.

I have only sad things to say. What bad had I done, what was my great guilt? My father always away and his absence always with me. And the river, always the river, perpetually renewing itself. The river, always. I was beginning to suffer from old age, in which life is just a sort of lingering. I had attacks of illness and of anxiety. I had a nagging rheumatism. And he? Why, why was he doing it? He must have been suffering terribly. He was so old. One day, in his failing strength, he might let the boat capsize; or he might let the current carry it downstream, on and on, until it plunged over the waterfall to the boiling turmoil below. It pressed upon my heart. He was out there and I was forever robbed of my peace. I am guilty of I know not what, and my pain is an open wound inside me. Perhaps I would know—if things were different. I began to guess what was wrong.

Out with it! Had I gone crazy? No, in our house that word was never spoken, never through all the years. No one called anybody crazy, for nobody is crazy. Or maybe everybody. All I did was go there and wave a handkerchief so he would be more likely to see me. I was in complete command of myself. I waited. Finally he appeared in the distance, there, then over there, a vague

shape sitting in the back of the boat. I called to him several times. And I said
what I was so eager to say, to state formally and under oath. I said it as loud
as I could:

"Father, you have been out there long enough. You are old. . . . Come   20
back, you don't have to do it anymore. . . . Come back and I'll go instead.
Right now, if you want. Any time. I'll get into the boat. I'll take your place."

And when I had said this my heart beat more firmly.

He heard me. He stood up. He maneuvered with his oars and headed
the boat toward me. He had accepted my offer. And suddenly I trembled,
down deep. For he had raised his arm and waved—the first time in so
many, so many years. And I couldn't . . . In terror, my hair on end, I ran,
I fled madly. For he seemed to come from another world. And I'm begging
forgiveness, begging, begging.

I experienced the dreadful sense of cold that comes from deadly fear,
and I became ill. Nobody ever saw or heard about him again. Am I a man,
after such a failure? I am what never should have been. I am what must be
silent. I know it is too late. I must stay in the deserts and unmarked plains
of my life, and I fear I shall shorten it. But when death comes I want them
to take me and put me in a little boat in this perpetual water between the
long shores; and I, down the river, lost in the river, inside the river . . .
the river . . . ❖

What happens if we try to read this story as an allegory? It's worth noticing that
the father is "very serious" about the boat. It is made to carry one person and
one person only. When it is delivered, the father shows no emotion. He simply
says "good-by" to the family and heads off to the river. The son wants to go with
him, but the father sends him back and moves off silently, alone. Is it possible
that Guimarães Rosa's story allegorizes death and the process of grief? If we
think in such terms, we may be prepared to answer new questions: How is it that
the father doesn't "come back" or "go anywhere"? How can he be so present and
so absent? The boat carries only one because only one dies; others left behind
must deal with the death. The father is no longer a physical presence in the life
of his family, but his death has not ended a relationship that transcends the
physical. The son, in particular, struggles with his own identity in the father's
absence. He works hard to keep the father alive in memory.

Such a reading begins to open possibilities, but it doesn't suddenly snap everything into place. It seems that Guimarães Rosa's story has allegorical elements
but never sustains a clear and consistent parallel between the concrete and the
abstract. We're invited to consider alternative readings. Perhaps rather than
death, Guimarães Rosa's allegory concerns more generally disconnection and
loneliness in families. Or perhaps the emphasis needs to shift to the narrator, to
the son. How do we read this story if we think of it as the struggles of a young
man to grow up? Is separation from the father a crucial part of that maturation?

Has the narrator been unable to accept the distance his father has established in their relationship? Understanding how allegory works helps us enter the world of this story and respond to it powerfully.

Using Symbolism and Allegory to Focus Writing and Discussion

- What makes you think that this object or image is a symbol?
- What clues does the author give us that we should look at this object symbolically?
- How can we justify the meaning that we ascribe to this symbol?
- What alternate meanings might this symbol have? Does it make sense to entertain these alternate meanings simultaneously? Why might it be appropriate to abandon these alternate meanings?
- What nuances does this particular symbol give to the meaning that we identify here? What does the author gain by using a symbol rather than stating the idea directly?
- For whom does this symbol have meaning? Is it necessary to be part of some particular group or to have some specific experience for this symbol to have significance?
- How does our attention to this detail as a symbol enhance our understanding of the text?
- If you have reason to think that the whole work can be read allegorically, set up a table to explain the significance of specific characters within the work. To develop this chart, identify the character by name, the idea that this character represents, and your justification (from the text itself) that allows you to make this connection.
- What is the advantage of reading the text allegorically?
- Why is it useful for the author to approach this particular subject indirectly?

Anthology

GOTHIC ROMANCE: A CRITIC WRITES ABOUT SYMBOLISM

Richard Brody's discussion of the significance of *Mean Girls* (2004), illustrates the point we have been making throughout this chapter: that any discussion of symbolism must begin with a careful consideration of various elements at play in the object being studied, in this case its source material and its audience.

In *Mean Girls*, fictional teenagers populate a fictional high school. At the level of character and setting, these high school students may be seen as typical of high school students anywhere, but as Brody demonstrates, this film is a bit more interesting. Each fictional character is based upon a set of attributes that Rosalind Wiseman identified in interviews with real teenagers for her nonfiction book *Queen Bees and Wannabes*. Scenes in the film are based on actual situations described in the book and brought to life by the writing of Tina Fey and by the skill of the young actors. In his analysis, Brody describes how these fictional characters, their fictional high school and their invented dialogue symbolize the high school experience (with "the pitch-perfect parsing of social syndromes"). For his daughters, the film has even greater resonance. The lines that they cite to one another call up their family's shared enjoyment of the film, and Brody suggests that this presentation of the high school experience has actually shaped the teen-age experiences of his daughters who had seen and were conversant in the film's details long before they entered high school.

The Genre of Gothic Romance

The form of the Gothic romance was shaped in the late eighteenth and early nineteenth centuries. These novels typically featured a young female character in some sort of mysterious circumstances. The setting is generally dark and vaguely medieval, often featuring an old manor house or the ruins of a castle as well as some element of the supernatural and fascination with the dead. These background elements are often highly symbolic and tend to be interpreted as reflecting the state of the main character.

Two of the selections in this chapter are twenty-first-century versions of the Gothic romance: Karen Russell's "Haunting Olivia," and Moira Buffini's "A Vampire Story." In each of the works, innocent young protagonists inhabit a borderland between a familiar world and a mysterious, supernatural world. In each we ask how real those supernatural forces are—are they merely the imagination of the characters? That which is presented as possibly supernatural also has historical dimensions. Throughout Gothic fiction, a fascination with spirits and with the dead might also be described as an interest in recovering history. How reliable are their accounts of their world and their experience? In Russell's story and Buffini's play, we find images that we could interpret as symbolic, and we must ask whether or not our will to interpret these symbols is any more reliable than the characters' narrative of their own experiences. Is it useful to think that these characters stand for some abstract ideas? Does this symbolic reading allow us to account for all of the details that we find interesting within each text?

The poems in this cluster find many symbols to explore profound moments akin to those that Hann has described in Hitchcock. Some of the symbols are fairly traditional. The sea in Matthew Arnold's "Dover Beach" is something to look upon and describe. But it sets up an ever-widening set of thoughts on time, suffering, and faith. And tides do change. Arnold finds that the "Sea of Faith," once full upon the shore, has drawn back. Without the fullness of that faith, the speaker feels compelled to seek comfort in the love of an individual. Any wider sense of human interaction seems dangerous and threatening. In "The Wild Swans at Coole," William Butler Yeats adopts a somewhat less obvious symbol to communicate a related mood. He watches the "nine-and-fifty swans" that swim upon the waters of a lake within the grounds of Coole Park, a country estate of a friend whom Yeats often visited. The swans are wild and beautiful. They represent for Yeats something of the place they inhabit, but also of an entire social world that he loves. The precarious state of that world is registered through the unpredictability of the swans' movement. Will they someday be gone? Will this world survive? Note in this poem how the word *still* helps reinforce symbolic qualities of the swans. *Still* can mean "placid" or "quiet" (for example, "in the still of the night"). It can also suggest continuity over time ("do you still feel that way?"). The swans at Coole Park encompass both senses of that word. By such repetition, Yeats helps us grasp the force of his central symbol.

REVIEW

Richard Brody (1958–   )

Why "Mean Girls" Is a Classic (2014)

When I mentioned to my daughters that it's the tenth anniversary of the release of "Mean Girls," it was no news to them: the firstborn, now twenty-one, is wearing her "You can't sit with us" T-shirt, and her sister, sixteen, is dressed in pink (it's Wednesday). They knew the movie by heart long before they knew from high school. To the catchphrases that were common coin at home, from "Singin' in the Rain," "Marnie," "The Gang's All Here," "The Little Mermaid," "Mary Poppins," and "Legally Blonde," there was added a torrent of word vomit:

> "Four for Glenn Coco! You go, Glenn Coco! None for Gretchen Wieners."
> "You can't just ask people why they're white."
> "You *will* get chlamydia and die."
> "It's like I have ESPN or something."   5
> "Brutus is just as cute as Caesar, right?"
> "I'm the *cool* mom."
> And, of course, the inevitable "I can't help it if I've got a heavy flow and
>   a wide-set vagina." And "Well, this has been sufficiently awkward."

Reading these lines to oneself does little, but reading them after seeing the movie brings them back with the inflections and the distinctive voices of the superb actors who deliver them—including Tina Fey, who's also the screenwriter— and give them an imposing, three-dimensional authority, like mobile language- sculptures. The cast of eccentric presences includes the rising stars Rachel McAdams and Amanda Seyfried, as well as the resonant free radical Lizzy Caplan, who's still awaiting her much-deserved big moment, but "Mean Girls" is held together by the extraordinarily energetic normalcy of Lindsay Lohan.

Part of the appeal of the movie is its faux naïveté. It's a first-person story   10 that's filled with the interior monologue of a smart and perceptive middle- class suburban girl who's distinguished from her classmates by the fact of never having had classmates. She was raised in Africa and home-schooled by her zoologist parents; through her eyes, the unexceptional appears strange and novel. It's a simple and clever conceit, but one that depends on an anchoring star who is, in effect, the Jamesian central consciousness.

That's where Lohan's art is most decisively revealed, and it's why she's perfectly, irreplaceably, cast in "Mean Girls." The power to seem active while doing nothing is the crucial trait of classic-era movie stars; it's the defining aspect of what it means to be loved by the camera. What's called charisma is nothing but the sense of a complex inner life that comes through in the time- sliver of a photograph and that, in the extended stillness of the movie image, rises with a silent wild music of conflicting dreams and desires. It's the part of acting that can't be learned and can't be trained, and Lohan—perhaps more than any actor of her generation—has it. Fey's construction of the story provides the discerning perspective, and Lohan brings that perspective to life.

The sense of discernment also comes from the movie's roots in actual observation: it's based on a nonfiction book, "Queen Bees and Wannabes," by the youth organizer Rosalind Wiseman, and the movie is filled with situ- ations that she describes, which arose in her interviews with teenagers. But, on repeated viewings (and in our home the viewings seem countless), the pitch-perfect parsing of social syndromes betray a peculiarly hermetic sense of class.

Money-awareness is lively in children and in teens. My daughters and their friends have had, since early childhood, a discerning eye for real-estate com- forts and inconveniences to rival that of brokers, and differences in purchas- ing power are inseparable from differences in style. I went to a suburban high school in a generally prosperous suburb, but friendships cut perceptibly across economic lines (which, however, didn't vanish but were uneasily negotiated). In "Mean Girls," there's no such issue. Tellingly, the only struggle with money is the one faced by Tina Fey's character, Ms. Norbury, the newly divorced math teacher who moonlights as a bartender. (There is, however, a hint of a vestige of an abandoned plot line, in the goth girl Janis Ian's after-school shopping-mall job, which suggests a fault line in the backstory of her broken friendship with the queen bee Regina George.)

By coincidence, when I turned on TV the other night to watch a DVD, I caught a few minutes of another modern high-school classic from 2004, one of our family favorites: "Napoleon Dynamite." It and that highlighted, in a random instant, what's missing from "Mean Girls." There, the director Jared Hess, working with a script that he co-wrote with his wife, Jerusha, filmed in their home town of Preston, Idaho, and made its distinctive cultural history—its Mormon heritage—the unexpressed but discernible core around which the story is elaborated, and made its characters' money matters central to the movie as well.

Hess also has other sorts of tone-deafness, starting with the movie's   15
embarrassing racial stereotyping, which reflects the very insularity that the movie runs on even as it expresses the desire to break out of that insularity while remaining within the community. In other words, even the movie's defects arise from a conflict that's built into the filmmakers' vision.

"Mean Girls" is certainly, deservedly, a classic, but it's a classic along the lines of "Casablanca," renowned for its performances and for its dialogue, for a seemingly wondrous synergy of all involved. But there are other movies from the same period—whether "To Have and Have Not" or "The Best Years of Our Lives" or "A Letter to Three Wives"—that offer those enduring enticements, too, along with a unified and rarefied directorial inspiration that focuses them brightly and hotly into a world view.

High-school life in an upper-middle-class urban suburb (in "Mean Girls," it's Evanston, Illinois) is still awaiting its directorial aesthetic, and it's likely to arise from a filmmaker who goes home. I'm waiting for Judd Apatow—already a director with an aesthetic sense of his own—to make his growing-up-on-Long-Island movie; I suspect that it would be a cinematic liberation.

FICTION

Karen Russell (1981–   )

Born in Florida, Karen Russell's first novel, *Swamplandia!* (2011), is set in a run-down amusement park in the Florida Everglades. It was a finalist for the Pulitzer Prize for Fiction. She received a MacAuthur Fellowship, commonly referred to as a "genius grant," in 2013 and is currently writer-in-residence at Bard College. She has also published two collections of short stories, *St. Lucy's Home for Girls Raised by Wolves* (2006) and *Vampires in the Lemon Grove* (2013).

Haunting Olivia (2005)

My brother Wallow has been kicking around Gannon's Boat Graveyard for more than an hour, too embarrassed to admit that he doesn't see any ghosts. Instead, he slaps at the ocean with jilted fury. Curse words come piping out of his snorkel. He keeps pausing to readjust the diabolical goggles.

The diabolical goggles were designed for little girls. They are pink, with a floral snorkel attached to the side. They have scratchproof lenses and an adjustable band. Wallow says that we are going to use them to find our dead sister, Olivia.

My brother and I have been making midnight scavenging trips to Gannon's all summer. It's a watery junk yard, a place where people pay to abandon their old boats. Gannon, the grizzled, tattooed undertaker, tows wrecked ships into his marina. Battered sailboats and listing skiffs, yachts with stupid names—Knot at Work and Sail-la-Vie—the paint peeling from their puns. They sink beneath the water in slow increments, covered with rot and barnacles. Their masts jut out at weird angles. The marina is an open, easy grave to rob. We ride our bikes along the rock wall, coasting quietly past Gannon's tin shack, and hop off at the derelict pier. Then we creep down to the ladder, jump onto the nearest boat, and loot.

It's dubious booty. We mostly find stuff with no resale value: soggy flares and UHF radios, a one-eyed cat yowling on a dinghy. But the goggles are a first. We found them floating in a live-bait tank, deep in the cabin of La Calavera, a swamped Largo schooner. We'd pushed our way through a small hole in the prow. Inside, the cabin was rank and flooded. There was no bait living in that tank, just the goggles and a foamy liquid the color of root beer. I dared Wallow to put the goggles on and stick his head in it. I didn't actually expect him to find anything; I just wanted to laugh at Wallow in the pink goggles, bobbing for diseases. But when he surfaced, tearing at the goggles, he told me that he'd seen the orange, unholy light of a fish ghost. Several, in fact—a school of ghoulish mullet.

"They looked just like regular baitfish, bro," Wallow said. "Only deader." I told my brother that I was familiar with the definition of a ghost. Not that I believed a word of it, you understand.

Now Wallow is trying the goggles out in the marina, to see if his vision extends beyond the tank. I'm dangling my legs over the edge of the pier, half-expecting something to grab me and pull me under. "Wallow! You see anything phantasmic yet?"

"Nothing," he bubbles morosely through the snorkel. "I can't see a thing."

I'm not surprised. The water in the boat basin is a cloudy mess. But I'm impressed by Wallow's one-armed doggy paddle.

5

Wallow shouldn't be swimming at all. Last Thursday, he slipped on one of the banana peels that Granana leaves around the house. I know. I didn't think it could happen outside of cartoons, either. Now his right arm is in a plaster cast, and in order to enter the water he has to hold it above his head. It looks like he's riding an aquatic unicycle. That buoyancy—it's unexpected. On land, Wallow's a loutish kid. He bulldozes whatever gets in his path: baby strollers, widowers, me.

For brothers, Wallow and I look nothing alike. I've got Dad's blond hair   10 and blue eyes, his embraceably lanky physique. Olivia was equally Heartland, apple cheeks and unnervingly white teeth. Not Wallow. He's got this dental affliction which gives him a tusky, warthog grin. He wears his hair in a greased pompadour and has a thick pelt of back hair. There's no accounting for it. Dad jokes that our mom must have had dalliances with a Minotaur.

Wallow is not Wallow's real name, of course. His real name is Waldo Swallow. Just like I'm Timothy Sparrow and Olivia was—is—Olivia Lark. Our parents used to be bird enthusiasts. That's how they met: Dad spotted my mother on a bird-watching tour of the swamp, her beauty magnified by his 10x binoculars. Dad says that by the time he lowered them the spoonbills he'd been trying to see had scattered, and he was in love. When Wallow and I were very young, they used to take us on their creepy bird excursions, kayaking down island canals, spying on blue herons and coots. These days, they're not enthusiastic about much, feathered or otherwise. They leave us with Granana for months at a time.

Shortly after Olivia's death, my parents started travelling regularly in the Third World. No children allowed. Granana lives on the other side of the island. She's eighty-four, I'm twelve, and Wallow's fourteen, so it's a little ambiguous as to who's babysitting whom. This particular summer, our parents are in São Paulo. They send us postcards of bullet-pocked favelas and flaming hillocks of trash. "glad you're not here! xoxo, the 'rents.'" I guess the idea is that all the misery makes their marital problems seem petty and inconsequential.

"Hey!" Wallow is directly below me, clutching the rails of the ladder. "Move over."

He climbs up and heaves his big body onto the pier. Defeat puddles all around him. Behind the diabolical goggles, his eyes narrow into slits.

"Did you see them?"   15

Wallow just grunts. "Here." He wrestles the lady-goggles off his face and thrusts them at me. "I can't swim with this cast, and these bitches are too small for my skull. You try them."

I sigh and strip off my pajamas, bobbling before him. The elastic band of the goggles bites into the back of my head. Somehow, wearing them makes me feel even more naked. My penis is curling up in the salt air like a small pink snail. Wallow points and laughs.

"Sure you don't want to try again?" I ask him. From the edge of the pier, the ocean looks dark and unfamiliar, like the liquid shadow of something truly awful. "Try again, Wallow. Maybe it's just taking a while for your eyes to adjust—"

Wallow holds a finger to his lips. He points behind me. Boats are creaking in the wind, waves slap against the pilings, and then I hear it, too, the distinct thunk of boots on wood. Someone is walking down the pier. We can see the tip of a lit cigarette, suspended in the dark. We hear a man's gargly cough.

"Looking for buried treasure, boys?" Gannon laughs. He keeps walking 20
toward us. "You know, the court still considers it trespassing, be it land or sea." Then he recognizes Wallow. He lets out the low, mournful whistle that all the grownups on the island use to identify us now.

"Oh, son. Don't tell me you're out here looking for—"

"My dead sister?" Wallow asks with terrifying cheer. "Good guess!"

"You're not going to find her in my marina, boys."

In the dark, Gannon is a huge stencil of a man, wisps of smoke curling from his nostrils. There is a long, pulsing silence, during which Wallow stares at him, squaring his jaw. Then Gannon shrugs. He stubs out his cigarette and shuffles back toward the shore.

"All right, bro," Wallow says. "It's go time." He takes my elbow and 25
gentles me down the planks with such tenderness that I am suddenly very afraid. But there's no sense making the plunge slow and unbearable. I take a running leap down the pier—

"Ayyyyiii!"

—and launch over the water. It's my favorite moment: I'm one toe away from flight and my body takes over. The choice is made, but the consequence is still just an inky shimmer beneath me. I'm rushing to meet my own reflection—gah!

Then comes the less beautiful moment when I'm up to my eyeballs in tar water, and the goggles fill with stinging brine. And, for what seems like a very long time, I can't see anything at all, dead or alive.

When my vision starts to clear, I see a milky, melting light moving swiftly above the ocean floor. Drowned moonbeams, I think at first. Only there is no moon tonight.

Olivia disappeared on a new-moon night. It was exactly two years, or twenty- 30
four new moons, ago. Wallow says that means that tonight is Olivia's unbirth-day, the anniversary of her death. It's weird: our grief is cyclical, synched with the lunar cycles. It accordions out as the moon slivers away. On new-moon nights, it rises with the tide.

Even before we lost my sis, I used to get uneasy when the moon was gone. That corner of the sky, as black as an empty safe. Whatever happened to Olivia, I hope she at least had the orange residue of sunset to see by. I can't stand to think of her out here alone after nightfall.

The last time we saw Olivia was at twilight. We'd spent all day crab sledding down the beach. It's the closest thing we island kids have to a winter sport. You climb into the upended exoskeleton of a giant crab, then you go yeehaw slaloming down the powdery dunes. The faster you go, the more sand whizzes around you, a fine spray on either side of your crab sled. By the time you hit the water, you're covered in it, grit in your teeth and your eyelids, along the line of your scalp.

Herb makes the crab sleds—he guts the crabs and blowtorches off the eyestalks and paints little racer stripes along the side. Then he rents them down at Pier 2, for two dollars an hour, twelve dollars for a full day. The three of us had been racing down the beach all afternoon. We were sunburned, and hungry, and loused up with sea bugs. Wallow had stepped on a sea urchin and broken his fall on more urchins. I wanted Jiffy Pop and aloe vera. Wallow wanted prescription painkillers and porno. We voted to head over to Granana's beach cottage, because she has Demerol and an illegal cable box.

Olivia threw a fit. "But we still have half an hour on the sled rental!" A gleam came into her eyes, that transparent little-kid craftiness. "You guys don't have to come with me, you know."

Legally, we did. According to official Herb's Crab Sledding policy, under-twelves must be accompanied by a guardian—a rule that Herb has really cracked down on since Olivia's death. But neither Wallow nor I felt like chaperoning. And Olivia was eight and a half, which rounds up to twelve. "Stick to the perimeter of the island," Wallow told her. "And get that crab sled back before sundown. Any late fees are coming out of your allowance."

"Yeah, yeah," she assured us, clambering into the sled. The sun was already low in the sky. "I'm just going out one last time."

We helped Olivia drag the sled up the white dunes. She sat Indian style in the center of the shell, humming tunelessly. Then we gave her a final push that sent her racing down the slopes. We watched as she flew out over the rock crags and into the foamy water. By the time we'd gathered our towels and turned to go, Olivia was just a speck on the horizon. Neither of us noticed how quickly the tide was going out.

Most people think that tides are caused by the moon alone, but that is not the case. Once a month, the sun and the moon are both on the same side of the globe. Then the Atlantic kowtows to their conglomerate gravity. It's the earth playing tug-of-war with the sky.

On new-moon nights, the sky is winning. The spring tide swells exceptionally high. The spring tide has teeth. It can pull a boat much farther than your average quarter-moon neap tide. When they finally found Olivia's crab sled, it was halfway to Cuba, and empty.

"What do you see, bro?" "Oh, not much." I cough. I peer back under the   40
surface of the water. There's an aurora borealis exploding inches from my
submerged face. "Probably just plankton."

When I come up to clear the goggles, I can barely see Wallow. He is
silhouetted against the lone orange lamp, watching me from the pier. Water
seeps out of my nose, my ears. It weeps down the corners of the lenses. I
push the goggles up and rub my eyes with my fists, which just makes things
worse. I kick to stay afloat, the snorkel digging into my cheek, and wave at
my brother. Wallow doesn't wave back.

I don't want to tell Wallow, but I have no idea what I just saw, although
I'm sure there must be some ugly explanation for it. I tell myself that it
was just cyanobacteria, or lustrous pollutants from the Bimini glue factory.
Either way, I don't want to double-check. I shiver in the water, letting the
salt dry on my shoulders, listening to the echo of my breath in the snorkel.
I fantasize about towels. But Wallow is still watching me, his face a blank
oval. I tug at the goggles and stick my head under for a second look.

Immediately, I bite down on the mouthpiece of the snorkel to stop
myself from screaming. The goggles: they work. And every inch of the ocean
is haunted. There are ghost fish swimming all around me. My hands pass
right through their flat bodies. Phantom crabs shake their phantom claws
at me from behind a sunken anchor. Octopuses cartwheel by, leaving an
effulgent red trail. A school of minnows swims right through my belly button. Dead, I think. They are all dead.

"Um, Wallow?" I gasp, spitting out the snorkel. "I don't think I can do this."
"Sure you can."   45

Squat, boulder-shouldered, Wallow is standing over the ladder, guarding
it like a gargoyle. There's nowhere for me to go but back under the water.

Getting used to aquatic ghosts is like adjusting to the temperature of
the ocean. After the initial shock gives way, your body numbs. It takes a few
more close encounters with the lambent fish before my pulse quiets down.
Once I realize that the ghost fish can't hurt me, I relax into something I'd
call delight if I weren't supposed to be feeling bereaved.

I spend the next two hours pretending to look for Olivia. I shadow the
spirit manatees, their backs scored with keloid stars from motorboat propel-
lers. I somersault through stingrays. Bonefish flicker around me like mute
banshees. I figure out how to braid the furry blue light of dead coral reef
through my fingertips. I've started to enjoy myself, and I've nearly succeeded
in exorcising Olivia from my thoughts, when a bunch of ghost shrimp mate-
rialize in front of my goggles, like a photo rinsed in a developing tray. The
shrimp twist into a glowing alphabet, some curling, some flattening, touching
tails to antennae in smoky contortions. Then they loop together to form
words, as if drawn by some invisible hand: "g-l-o-ww-o-r-m g-r-o-t-t-o."

We thought the Glowworm Grotto was just more of Olivia's make-believe. Olivia was a cartographer of imaginary places. She'd crayon elaborate maps of invisible castles and sunken cities. When the Glowworm Grotto is part of a portfolio that includes Mr. Waffle Cone, it's hard to take it seriously.

I loved Olivia. But that doesn't mean I didn't recognize that she was   50
one weird little kid. She used to suffer these intense bouts of homesickness in her own bedroom. When she was very small, she would wake up tearing at her bedspread and shrieking, "I wanna go home! I wanna go home!"— which was distressing to all of us, of course, because she *was* home.

That said, I wouldn't be surprised to learn that Olivia was an adoptee from some other planet. She used to change into Wallow's rubbery yellow flippers on the bus, then waddle around the school halls like some disoriented mallard. She played "house" by getting the broom and sweeping the neon corpses of dead jellyfish off the beach. Her eyes were a stripey cerulean, inhumanly bright. Dad used to tell Olivia that a merman artisan had made them, out of bits of sea glass from Atlantis.

Wallow saved all of her drawings. The one labelled "glowerm groto" is a sketch of a dusky red cave, with a little stick-Olivia swimming into the entrance. Another drawing shows the roof of the cave. It looks like a swirly firmament of stars, dalmatianed with yellow dots.

"That's what you see when you're floating on your back," Olivia told us, rubbing the gray crayon down to its nub. "The Glowworm Grotto looks just like the night sky."

"That's nice," we said, exchanging glances. Neither Wallow nor I knew of any caves along the island shore. I figured it must be another Olivia utopia, a no-place. Wallow thought it was Olivia's oddball interpretation of Gannon's Boat Graveyard.

"Maybe that rusty boat hangar looked like the entrance to a cave to   55
her," he'd said. Maybe. If you were eight, and nearsighted, and nostalgic for places that you'd never been.

But, if the Glowworm Grotto actually exists, that changes everything. Olivia's ghost could be there now, twitching her nose with rabbity indignation— "But I left you a map!" Wondering what took us so long to find her.

When I surface, the stars have vanished. The clouds are turning red around their edges. I can hear Wallow snoring on the pier. I pull my naked body up and flop onto the warm planks, feeling salt-shucked and newborn. When I spit the snorkel out of my mouth, the unfiltered air tastes acrid and foreign. The Glowworm Grotto. I wish I didn't have to tell Wallow. I wish we'd never found the stupid goggles. There are certain things that I don't want to see.

When we get back to Granana's, her cottage is shuttered and dark. Fat raindrops, the icicles of the Tropics, hang from the eaves. We can hear her

watching "Evangelical Bingo" in the next room. "Revelation 20:13!" she
hoots. "Bingo!"

Our breakfast is on the table: banana pancakes, with a side of banana
pudding. The kitchen is sticky with brown peels and syrup. Granana no
longer has any teeth. For the past two decades, she has subsisted almost
entirely on bananas, banana-based dishes, and other foods that you can
gum. This means that her farts smell funny, and her calf muscles frequently
give out. It means that Wallow and I eat out a lot during the summer.

Wallow finds Olivia's old drawings of the Glowworm Grotto. We   60
spread them out on the table, next to a Crab Shack menu with a cartoon
map of the island. Wallow is busy highlighting the jagged shoreline, circling
places that might harbor a cave, when Granana shuffles into the kitchen.
"What's all this?" She peers over my shoulder. "Christ," she says. "Still
mooning over that old business?"

Granana doesn't understand what the big deal is. She didn't cry at
Olivia's funeral, and I doubt she even remembers Olivia's name. Granana
lost, like, ninety-two million kids in childbirth. All of her brothers died
in the war. She survived the Depression by stealing radish bulbs from her
neighbors' garden, and fishing the elms for pigeons. Dad likes to say this
in a grave voice, as if it explained her jaundiced pitilessness: "Boys. Your
grandmother ate pigeons."

"Wasn't much for drawing, was she?" Granana says. She taps at stick-
Olivia. "Wasn't much for swimming, either."

Wallow visibly stiffens. For a second, I'm worried that he's going to
slug Granana in her wattled neck. Then she raises her drawn-on eyebrows.
"Would you look at that—the nudey cave. Your grandfather used to take
me skinny-dipping there."

Wallow and I do an autonomic, full-body shudder. I get a sudden mental image of two shelled walnuts floating in a glass.

"You mean you recognize this place, Granana?"   65

"No thanks to this chicken scratch!" She points to an orange dot in the
corner of the picture, so small that I hadn't even noticed it. "But look where
she drew the sunset. Use your noggins. Must be one of them coves on the
western side of the island. I don't remember exactly where."

"What about the stars on the roof?"

Granana snorts. "Worm shit!"

"Huh?"

"Worm shit," she repeats. "You never heard of glowworms, Mr. Straight-A   70
Science Guy? Their shit glows in the dark. All them coves are covered with it."

We never recovered Olivia's body. Two days after she went missing, Tropical
Storm Vita brought wind and chaos and interrupted broadcasts, and

the search was called off. Too dangerous, the Coast Guard lieutenant said. He was a fat, earnest man, with tiny black eyes set like watermelon seeds in his pink face.

"When wind opposes sea," he said in a portentous singsong, "the waves build fast."

"Thank you, Billy Shakespeare," my father growled under his breath. For some reason, this hit Dad the hardest—harder than Olivia's death itself, I think. The fact that we had nothing to bury.

It's possible that Olivia washed up on a bone-white Cojimar beach, or got tangled in some Caribbean fisherman's net. It's probable that her lungs filled up with buckets of tarry black water and she sank. But I don't like to think about that. It's easier to imagine her turning into an angelfish and swimming away, or being bodily assumed into the clouds.

Most likely, Dad says, a freak wave knocked her overboard. Then the current yanked the sled away faster than she could swim. In my night terrors, I watch the sea turn into a great, gloved hand that rises out of the ocean to snatch her. I told Wallow this once, hoping to stir up some fraternal empathy. Instead, Wallow sneered at me. 75

"Are you serious? That's what you have nightmares about, bro? Some lame-ass Mickey Mouse glove that comes out of the sea?" His lip curled up, but there was envy in his voice, too. "I just see my own hands, you know? Pushing her down that hill."

The following evening, Wallow and I head over to Herb's Crab Sledding Rentals. Herb smokes on his porch in his yellowed boxers and a threadbare Santa hat, rain or shine. Back when we were regular sledders, Wallow always used to razz Herb about his getup.

"Ho ho ho," Herb says reflexively. "Merry Christmas. Sleigh bells ring, are ya listening." He gives a halfhearted shake to a sock full of quarters. "Hang on, nauticats. Can't sled without informed consent."

Thanks to the Olivia Bill, new island legislation requires all island children to take a fourteen-hour Sea Safety! course before they can sled. They have to wear helmets and life preservers, and sign multiple waivers. Herb is dangling the permission form in front of our faces. Wallow accepts it with a genial "Thanks, Herb!" Then he crushes it in his good fist.

"Now wait a sec . . ." Herb scratches his ear. "I, ah, I didn't recognize you boys. I'm sorry, but you know I can't rent to you. Anyhow, it'll be dark soon, and neither one of you is certified." 80

Wallow walks over to one of the sleds and, unhelmeted, unjacketed, shoves it into the water. The half shell bobs there, one of the sturdier two-seaters, a boiled-red color. He picks up a pair of oars, so that we can row against the riptides. He glares at Herb.

"We are going to take the sled out tonight, and tomorrow night, and every night until our parents get back. We are going to keep taking it out until we find Olivia." He pauses. "And we are going to pay you three hundred and seventy-six dollars in cash." Coincidentally, this is the exact dollar amount of Granana's Social Security check.

Herb doesn't say a word. He takes the wad of cash, runs a moistened finger through it, and stuffs it under his Santa hat. He waits until we are both in the sled before he opens his mouth.

"Boys," he says. "You have that crab sled back here before dawn. Otherwise, I'm calling the Coast Guard."

Every night, we go a little farther. Out here, you can see dozens of shooting   85
stars, whole galactic herds of them, winking out into cheery oblivion. They make me think of lemmings, flinging themselves over an astral cliff.

We are working our way around the island, with Gannon's Boat Graveyard as our ground zero. I swim parallel to the beach, and Wallow follows along in the crab sled, marking up the shoreline that we've covered on our map. "X" marks all the places where Olivia is not. It's slow going. I'm not a strong swimmer, and I have to paddle back to Wallow every fifteen minutes.

"And just what are we going to do when we find her?" I want to know. It's the third night of our search. We are halfway around the island, on the sandbar near the twinkling lights of the Bowl-a-Bed Hotel. Wallow's face is momentarily illuminated by the cycloptic gaze of the lighthouse. It arcs out over the water, a thin scythe of light that serves only to make the rest of the ocean look scarier. "What exactly are we going to do with her, Wallow?"

This question has been weighing on my mind more and more heavily of late. Because let's just say, for argument's sake, that there is a Glowworm Grotto, and that Olivia's ghost haunts it. Then what? Do we genie-in-a-bottle her? Keep her company on weekends? I envision eternal Saturday nights spent treading cold water in a cave, crooning lullabies to the husk of Olivia, and shudder.

"What do you mean?" Wallow says, frowning. "We'll rescue her. We'll preserve her, uh, you know, her memory."

"And how exactly do you propose we do that?"   90

"I don't know, bro!" Wallow furrows his brow, flustered. You can tell he hasn't thought much beyond finding Olivia. "We'll—we'll put her in an aquarium."

"An aquarium?" Now it's my turn to be derisive. "And then what? Are you going to get her a kiddie pool?"

It seems to me that nobody's asking the hard questions here. For example, what if ghost-Olivia doesn't have eyes anymore? Or a nose? What if an eel has taken up residence inside her skull, and every time it lights up it sends this unholy electricity radiating through her sockets?

Wallow fixes me with a baleful stare. "Are you pussying out, bro? She's your sister, for Christ's sake. You telling me you're afraid of your own kid sister? Don't worry about what we're going to do with her, bro. We have to find her first."

I say nothing. But I keep thinking: It's been two years. What if all the   95
Olivia-ness has already seeped out of her and evaporated into the violet welter of clouds? Evaporated, and rained down, and evaporated, and rained down. Olivia slicking over all the rivers and trees and dirty cities in the world. So that now there is only silt, and our stupid, salt-diluted longing. And nothing left of our sister to find.

On the fourth night of our search, I see a churning clump of ghost children. They are drifting straight for me, all kelped together, an eyeless panic of legs and feet and hair. I kick for the surface, heart hammering.

"Wallow!" I scream, hurling myself at the crab sled. "I just saw—I just— I'm not doing this anymore, bro, I am *not*. You can go stick your face in dead kids for a change. Let Olivia come find us."

"Calm it down." Wallow pokes at the ocean with his oar. "It's only trash." He fishes out a nasty mass of diapers and chicken gristle and whiskery red seaweed, all threaded around the plastic rings of a six-pack. "See?"

I sit huddled in the corner of the sled, staring dully at the blank surface of the water. I know what I saw.

The goggles are starting to feel less like a superpower and more like a divine   100
punishment, one of those particularly inventive cruelties that you read about in Greek mythology. Every now and then, I think about how much simpler and more pleasant things would be if the goggles conferred a dif- ferent kind of vision. Like if I could read messages written in squid ink, or laser through the Brazilian girls' tankinis. But then Wallow interrupts these thoughts by dunking me under the water. Repeatedly.

"Keep looking," he snarls, water dripping off his face.

On the fifth night of our search, I see a plesiosaur. It is a megawatt behemoth, bronze and blue-white, streaking across the sea floor like a torpid comet. Watching it, I get this primordial déjà vu, like I'm watching a dream return to my body. It wings toward me with a slow, avian grace. Its long neck is arced in an S-shaped curve; its lizard body is the size of Granana's carport. Each of its ghost flippers pinwheels colored light. I try to swim out of its path, but the thing's too big to avoid. That Leviathan fin, it shivers right through me. It's a light in my belly, cold and familiar. And I flash back to a snippet from school, a line from a poem or a science book, I can't remember which:

There are certain prehistoric things that swim beyond extinction.

I wake up from one of those naps which leach the strength from your bones to a lightning storm. I must have fallen asleep in the crab sled. Otherworldly light goes roiling through an eerie blue froth of clouds.

Wallow is standing at the prow of the sled. Each flash of lightning 105 limns his bared teeth, the hollows of his eyes. It's as if somebody up there were taking an X-ray of grief, again and again.

"I just want to tell her that I'm sorry," Wallow says softly. He doesn't know that I'm awake. He's talking to himself, or maybe to the ocean. There's not a trace of fear in his voice. And it's clear then that Wallow is a better brother than I could ever hope to be.

We have rowed almost all the way around the island. In a quarter of an hour, we'll be back at Gannon's Boat Graveyard. Thank merciful Christ. Our parents are coming back tomorrow, and I can go back to playing video games and feeling dry and blameless.

Then the lighthouse beacon sweeps out again. It bounces off an outcropping of rocks that we didn't notice on our first expedition. White sequins of light pop along the water.

"Did you see that? That's it!" Wallow says excitedly. "That's gotta be it!"

"Oh. Excellent." 110

We paddle the rest of the way out in silence. I row the crab sled like a condemned man. The current keeps pushing us back, but we make a quiet kind of progress. I keep praying that the crags will turn out to be low, heaped clouds, or else a seamless mass of stone. Instead, you can tell that they are pocked with dozens of holes. For a second, I'm relieved—nobody, not even string-beany Olivia, could swim into such narrow openings. Wallow's eyes dart around wildly.

"There has to be an entrance," he mutters. "Look!"

Sure enough, there is a muted glow coming from the far end of a salteaten overhang, like light from under a door.

"No way can I fit through there," I gasp, knowing immediately that I can. And that the crab sled can't, of course. Which means I'll be going in to meet her alone.

What if the light, I am thinking, is Olivia? 115

"It's just worms, bro," Wallow says, as if reading my mind. But there's this inscrutable sadness on his face. His muddy eyes swallow up the light and give nothing back.

I look over my shoulder. We're less than half a mile out from shore, could skip a stone to the mangrove islets; and yet the land draws back like a fat swimmer's chimera, impossibly far away.

"Ready?" He grabs at the scruff of my neck and pushes me toward the water. "Set?"

"No!" Staring at the unlit spaces in the crags, I am choked with horror. I fumble the goggles off my face. "Do your own detective work!" I dangle the goggles over the edge of the sled. "I quit."

Wallow lunges forward and pins me against the side of the boat. He tries   120
to spatula me overboard with his one good arm, but I limbo under his cast.

"Don't do it, Timothy," he cautions, but it is too late.

"This is what I think of your diabolical goggles!" I howl. I hoist the goggles over my head and, with all the force in my puny arms, hurl them to the floor of the crab sled.

This proves to be pretty anticlimactic. Naturally, the goggles remain intact. There's not even a hairline fracture. Stupid scratchproof lenses.

The worst part is that Wallow just watches me impassively, his cast held aloft in the air, as if he were patiently waiting to ask the universe a question. He nudges the goggles toward me with his foot.

"You finished?"   125

"Wally!" I blubber, a last-ditch plea. "This is crazy. What if something happens to me in there and you can't come in after me? Let's go back."

"What?" Wallow barks, disgusted. "And leave Olivia here for dead? Is that what you want?"

"Bingo!" That is exactly what I want. Maybe Granana is slightly off target when it comes to the Food Pyramid, but she has the right idea about death. I want my parents to stop sailing around taking pictures of Sudanese leper colonies. I want Wallow to row back to shore and sleep through the night. I want everybody in the goddam family to leave Olivia here for dead.

But there's my brother. Struggling with his own repugnance, like an entomologist who has just discovered a loathsome new species of beetle. "What did you say?"

"I said I'll go," I mumble, not meeting his eyes. I position myself on the   130
edge of the boat. "I'll go." So that's what it comes down to, then. I'd rather drown in Olivia's ghost than have him look at me that way.

To enter the grotto, you have to slide in on your back, like a letter through a mail slot. Something scrapes my coccyx bone on the way in. There's a polar chill in the water tonight. No outside light can wiggle its way inside.

But, sure enough, phosphorescent dots spangle the domed roof of the grotto. It's like a radiant checkerboard of shit. You can't impose any mental pictures on it—it's too uniform. It defies the mind's desire to constellate randomness. The Glowworm Grotto is nothing like the night sky. The stars here are all equally bright and evenly spaced, like a better-ordered cosmos.

"Olivia?"

The grotto smells like salt and blood and bat shit. Shadows web the walls. I try and fail to touch the bottom.

"Oliviaaa?"   135

Her name echoes around the cave. After a while, there is only rippled water again, and the gonged absence of sound. Ten more minutes, I think.

I could splash around here for ten more minutes and be done with this. I could take off the goggles, even. I could leave without ever looking below the surface of the water, and Wallow would never know.

"Oli–"

I take a deep breath, and dive.

Below me, tiny fish are rising out of golden cylinders of coral. It looks like an undersea calliope, piping a song that you can see instead of hear. One of the fish swims right up and taps against my scratchproof lenses. It's just a regular blue fish, solid and alive. It taps and taps, oblivious of the thick glass. My eyes cross, trying to keep it in focus.

The fish swims off to the beat of some subaqueous music. Everything   140 down here is dancing–the worms' green light and the undulant walls and the leopard-spotted polyps. Everything. And following this fish is like trying to work backward from the dance to the song. I can't hear it, though; I can't remember a single note of it. It fills me with a hitching sort of sadness.

I trail the fish at an embarrassed distance, feeling warm-blooded and ridiculous in my rubbery flippers, marooned in this clumsy body. Like I'm an impostor, an imperfect monster.

I look for my sister, but it's hopeless. The goggles are all fogged up. Every fish burns lantern- bright, and I can't tell the living from the dead. It's all just blurry light, light smeared like some celestial fingerprint all over the rocks and the reef and the sunken garbage. Olivia could be everywhere.

■ If a traditional Gothic romance was set in some grand-old building in a remote section of England, what equivalent does Russell give us here? How do the old boats and the boatyard reflect in any way the main characters in this story?

■ What is the medium through which the narrator seeks to find his sister? How does he function as a sort of everyman within this story?

■ How does the conclusion of this story sustain or refute the symbolism that you have found throughout the narrative?

Bram Stoker (1847–1912)

Bram Stoker graduated with honors in mathematics from Trinity College, Dublin where as president of the Philosophical Society, he recommended Oscar Wilde as a new member. Several years later, he married Florence Balcombe, who had also been courted by Wilde. For nearly thirty years, Stoker served as the business manager of the highly successful Lyceum Theatre in London and mingled with notable figures in the arts (James MacNeil Whistler and Arthur Conan Doyle) and on American tours was twice invited to the White House (William McKinley and Theodore Roosevelt). His is most famous for his 1897 novel *Dracula*, based on his research of European folklore and mythology about vampires. Although he traveled extensively, he never visited Eastern Europe, the setting for a good part of the novel. The short story, "Dracula's Guest" was published in 1914 (after Stoker's death) by his widow.

Dracula's Guest (1892)

PREFACE

A few months before the lamented death of my husband—I might say even as the shadow of death was over him—he planned three series of short stories for publication, and the present volume is one of them. To his original list of stories in this book, I have added an hitherto unpublished episode from Dracula. It was originally excised owing to the length of the book, and may prove of interest to the many readers of what is considered my husband's most remarkable work. The other stories have already been published in English and American periodicals. Had my husband lived longer, he might have seen fit to revise this work, which is mainly from the earlier years of his strenuous life. But, as fate has entrusted to me the issuing of it, I consider it fitting and proper to let it go forth practically as it was left by him.

FLORENCE BRAM STOKER

When we started for our drive the sun was shining brightly on Munich, and the air was full of the joyousness of early summer. Just as we were about to depart, Herr Delbrueck (the maitre d'hotel of the Quatre Saisons, where I was staying) came down, bareheaded, to the carriage and, after wishing me a pleasant drive, said to the coachman, still holding his hand on the handle of the carriage door:

"Remember you are back by nightfall. The sky looks bright but there is a shiver in the north wind that says there may be a sudden storm. But I am sure you will not be late." Here he smiled, and added, "for you know what night it is."

Johann answered with an emphatic, "Ja, mein Herr," and, touching his hat, drove off quickly. When we had cleared the town, I said, after signalling to him to stop:

"Tell me, Johann, what is tonight?"

He crossed himself, as he answered laconically: "Walpurgis nacht."   5

Then he took out his watch, a great, old-fashioned German silver thing as big as a turnip, and looked at it, with his eyebrows gathered together and a little impatient shrug of his shoulders. I realised that this was his way of respectfully protesting against the unnecessary delay, and sank back in the carriage, merely motioning him to proceed. He started off rapidly, as if to make up for lost time. Every now and then the horses seemed to throw up their heads and sniffed the air suspiciously. On such occasions I often looked round in alarm. The road was pretty bleak, for we were traversing a sort of high, wind-swept plateau. As we drove, I saw a road that looked but little used, and which seemed to dip through a little, winding valley. It looked so inviting that, even at the risk of offending him, I called Johann to stop—and when he had pulled up, I told him I would like to drive down that road. He made all sorts of excuses, and frequently crossed himself as he spoke. This somewhat piqued my curiosity, so I asked him various questions. He answered fencingly, and repeatedly looked at his watch in protest. Finally I said:

"Well, Johann, I want to go down this road. I shall not ask you to come unless you like; but tell me why you do not like to go, that is all I ask." For answer he seemed to throw himself off the box, so quickly did he reach the ground. Then he stretched out his hands appealingly to me, and implored me not to go. There was just enough of English mixed with the German for me to understand the drift of his talk. He seemed always just about to tell me something—the very idea of which evidently frightened him; but each time he pulled himself up, saying, as he crossed himself: "Walpurgis-Nacht!"

I tried to argue with him, but it was difficult to argue with a man when I did not know his language. The advantage certainly rested with him, for although he began to speak in English, of a very crude and broken kind, he always got excited and broke into his native tongue—and every time he did so, he looked at his watch. Then the horses became restless and sniffed the air. At this he grew very pale, and, looking around in a frightened way, he suddenly jumped forward, took them by the bridles and led them on some twenty feet. I followed, and asked why he had done this. For answer he crossed himself, pointed to the spot we had left and drew his carriage in the direction of the other road, indicating a cross, and said, first in German, then in English: "Buried him—him what killed themselves."

I remembered the old custom of burying suicides at cross-roads: "Ah! I see, a suicide. How interesting!" But for the life of me I could not make out why the horses were frightened.

Whilst we were talking, we heard a sort of sound between a yelp and a bark. It was far away; but the horses got very restless, and it took Johann all his time to quiet them. He was pale, and said, "It sounds like a wolf—but yet there are no wolves here now."

"No?" I said, questioning him; "isn't it long since the wolves were so near the city?"   10

"Long, long," he answered, "in the spring and summer; but with the snow the wolves have been here not so long."

Whilst he was petting the horses and trying to quiet them, dark clouds drifted rapidly across the sky. The sunshine passed away, and a breath of cold wind seemed to drift past us. It was only a breath, however, and more in the nature of a warning than a fact, for the sun came out brightly again. Johann looked under his lifted hand at the horizon and said:

"The storm of snow, he comes before long time." Then he looked at his watch again, and, straightway holding his reins firmly—for the horses were still pawing the ground restlessly and shaking their heads—he climbed to his box as though the time had come for proceeding on our journey.

I felt a little obstinate and did not at once get into the carriage.

"Tell me," I said, "about this place where the road leads," and I pointed   15 down.

Again he crossed himself and mumbled a prayer, before he answered, "It is unholy."

"What is unholy?" I enquired.

"The village."

"Then there is a village?"

"No, no. No one lives there hundreds of years." My curiosity was   20 piqued, "But you said there was a village."

"There was."

"Where is it now?"

Whereupon he burst out into a long story in German and English, so mixed up that I could not quite understand exactly what he said, but roughly I gathered that long ago, hundreds of years, men had died there and been buried in their graves; and sounds were heard under the clay, and when the graves were opened, men and women were found rosy with life, and their mouths red with blood. And so, in haste to save their lives (aye, and their souls!—and here he crossed himself) those who were left fled away to other places, where the living lived, and the dead were dead and not—not something. He was evidently afraid to speak the last words. As he proceeded with his narration, he grew more and more excited. It seemed as if his imagination had got hold of him, and he ended in a perfect paroxysm of fear—white-faced, perspiring, trembling and looking round him, as if expecting that some dreadful presence would manifest itself there in the bright sunshine on the open plain. Finally, in an agony of desperation, he cried:

"Walpurgis nacht!" and pointed to the carriage for me to get in. All my English blood rose at this, and, standing back, I said:

"You are afraid, Johann—you are afraid. Go home; I shall return alone;   25 the walk will do me good." The carriage door was open. I took from the seat my oak walking-stick—which I always carry on my holiday excursions—and closed the door, pointing back to Munich, and said, "Go home, Johann—Walpurgis-nacht doesn't concern Englishmen."

The horses were now more restive than ever, and Johann was trying to hold them in, while excitedly imploring me not to do anything so foolish.

I pitied the poor fellow, he was deeply in earnest; but all the same I could not help laughing. His English was quite gone now. In his anxiety he had forgotten that his only means of making me understand was to talk my language, so he jabbered away in his native German. It began to be a little tedious. After giving the direction, "Home!" I turned to go down the cross-road into the valley.

With a despairing gesture, Johann turned his horses towards Munich. I leaned on my stick and looked after him. He went slowly along the road for a while: then there came over the crest of the hill a man tall and thin. I could see so much in the distance. When he drew near the horses, they began to jump and kick about, then to scream with terror. Johann could not hold them in; they bolted down the road, running away madly. I watched them out of sight, then looked for the stranger, but I found that he, too, was gone.

With a light heart I turned down the side road through the deepening valley to which Johann had objected. There was not the slightest reason, that I could see, for his objection; and I daresay I tramped for a couple of hours without thinking of time or distance, and certainly without seeing a person or a house. So far as the place was concerned, it was desolation itself. But I did not notice this particularly till, on turning a bend in the road, I came upon a scattered fringe of wood; then I recognised that I had been impressed unconsciously by the desolation of the region through which I had passed.

I sat down to rest myself, and began to look around. It struck me that it was considerably colder than it had been at the commencement of my walk—a sort of sighing sound seemed to be around me, with, now and then, high overhead, a sort of muffled roar. Looking upwards I noticed that great thick clouds were drifting rapidly across the sky from North to South at a great height. There were signs of coming storm in some lofty stratum of the air. I was a little chilly, and, thinking that it was the sitting still after the exercise of walking, I resumed my journey.

The ground I passed over was now much more picturesque. There 30 were no striking objects that the eye might single out; but in all there was a charm of beauty. I took little heed of time and it was only when the deepening twilight forced itself upon me that I began to think of how I should find my way home. The brightness of the day had gone. The air was cold, and the drifting of clouds high overhead was more marked. They were accompanied by a sort of far-away rushing sound, through which seemed to come at intervals that mysterious cry which the driver had said came from a wolf. For a while I hesitated. I had said I would see the deserted village, so on I went, and presently came on a wide stretch of open country, shut in by hills all around. Their sides were covered with trees which spread down to the plain, dotting, in clumps, the gentler slopes and hollows which showed here and there. I followed with my eye the winding of the road, and saw that it curved close to one of the densest of these clumps and was lost behind it.

As I looked there came a cold shiver in the air, and the snow began to fall. I thought of the miles and miles of bleak country I had passed, and then hurried on to seek the shelter of the wood in front. Darker and darker grew the sky, and faster and heavier fell the snow, till the earth before and around me was a glistening white carpet the further edge of which was lost in misty vagueness. The road was here but crude, and when on the level its boundaries were not so marked, as when it passed through the cuttings; and in a little while I found that I must have strayed from it, for I missed underfoot the hard surface, and my feet sank deeper in the grass and moss. Then the wind grew stronger and blew with ever increasing force, till I was fain to run before it. The air became icy-cold, and in spite of my exercise I began to suffer. The snow was now falling so thickly and whirling around me in such rapid eddies that I could hardly keep my eyes open. Every now and then the heavens were torn asunder by vivid lightning, and in the flashes I could see ahead of me a great mass of trees, chiefly yew and cypress all heavily coated with snow.

I was soon amongst the shelter of the trees, and there, in comparative silence, I could hear the rush of the wind high overhead. Presently the blackness of the storm had become merged in the darkness of the night. By-and-by the storm seemed to be passing away: it now only came in fierce puffs or blasts. At such moments the weird sound of the wolf appeared to be echoed by many similar sounds around me.

Now and again, through the black mass of drifting cloud, came a straggling ray of moonlight, which lit up the expanse, and showed me that I was at the edge of a dense mass of cypress and yew trees. As the snow had ceased to fall, I walked out from the shelter and began to investigate more closely. It appeared to me that, amongst so many old foundations as I had passed, there might be still standing a house in which, though in ruins, I could find some sort of shelter for a while. As I skirted the edge of the copse, I found that a low wall encircled it, and following this I presently found an opening. Here the cypresses formed an alley leading up to a square mass of some kind of building. Just as I caught sight of this, however, the drifting clouds obscured the moon, and I passed up the path in darkness. The wind must have grown colder, for I felt myself shiver as I walked; but there was hope of shelter, and I groped my way blindly on.

I stopped, for there was a sudden stillness. The storm had passed; and, perhaps in sympathy with nature's silence, my heart seemed to cease to beat. But this was only momentarily; for suddenly the moonlight broke through the clouds, showing me that I was in a graveyard, and that the square object before me was a great massive tomb of marble, as white as the snow that lay on and all around it. With the moonlight there came a fierce sigh of the storm, which appeared to resume its course with a long, low howl, as of many dogs or wolves. I was awed and shocked, and felt the cold perceptibly grow upon me till it seemed to grip me by the heart. Then while the flood

of moonlight still fell on the marble tomb, the storm gave further evidence
of renewing, as though it was returning on its track. Impelled by some sort
of fascination, I approached the sepulchre to see what it was, and why such
a thing stood alone in such a place. I walked around it, and read, over the
Doric door, in German:

COUNTESS DOLINGEN OF GRATZ
IN STYRIA
SOUGHT AND FOUND DEATH
1801

On the top of the tomb, seemingly driven through the solid marble—for   35
the structure was composed of a few vast blocks of stone—was a great iron
spike or stake. On going to the back I saw, graven in great Russian letters:

"The dead travel fast."

There was something so weird and uncanny about the whole thing
that it gave me a turn and made me feel quite faint. I began to wish, for
the first time, that I had taken Johann's advice. Here a thought struck me,
which came under almost mysterious circumstances and with a terrible
shock. This was Walpurgis Night!

Walpurgis Night, when, according to the belief of millions of people, the
devil was abroad—when the graves were opened and the dead came forth and
walked. When all evil things of earth and air and water held revel. This very
place the driver had specially shunned. This was the depopulated village of
centuries ago. This was where the suicide lay; and this was the place where
I was alone—unmanned, shivering with cold in a shroud of snow with a wild
storm gathering again upon me! It took all my philosophy, all the religion
I had been taught, all my courage, not to collapse in a paroxysm of fright.

And now a perfect tornado burst upon me. The ground shook as though
thousands of horses thundered across it; and this time the storm bore on its
icy wings, not snow, but great hailstones which drove with such violence that
they might have come from the thongs of Balearic slingers—hailstones that
beat down leaf and branch and made the shelter of the cypresses of no more
avail than though their stems were standing-corn. At the first I had rushed
to the nearest tree; but I was soon fain to leave it and seek the only spot that
seemed to afford refuge, the deep Doric doorway of the marble tomb. There,
crouching against the massive bronze door, I gained a certain amount of protection from the beating of the hailstones, for now they only drove against me
as they ricocheted from the ground and the side of the marble.

As I leaned against the door, it moved slightly and opened inwards. The
shelter of even a tomb was welcome in that pitiless tempest, and I was about

to enter it when there came a flash of forked-lightning that lit up the whole expanse of the heavens. In the instant, as I am a living man, I saw, as my eyes were turned into the darkness of the tomb, a beautiful woman, with rounded cheeks and red lips, seemingly sleeping on a bier. As the thunder broke overhead, I was grasped as by the hand of a giant and hurled out into the storm. The whole thing was so sudden that, before I could realise the shock, moral as well as physical, I found the hailstones beating me down. At the same time I had a strange, dominating feeling that I was not alone. I looked towards the tomb. Just then there came another blinding flash, which seemed to strike the iron stake that surmounted the tomb and to pour through to the earth, blasting and crumbling the marble, as in a burst of flame. The dead woman rose for a moment of agony, while she was lapped in the flame, and her bitter scream of pain was drowned in the thundercrash. The last thing I heard was this mingling of dreadful sound, as again I was seized in the giant-grasp and dragged away, while the hailstones beat on me, and the air around seemed reverberant with the howling of wolves. The last sight that I remembered was a vague, white, moving mass, as if all the graves around me had sent out the phantoms of their sheeted-dead, and that they were closing in on me through the white cloudiness of the driving hail.

* * * * *

Gradually there came a sort of vague beginning of consciousness; then a sense   40
of weariness that was dreadful. For a time I remembered nothing; but slowly my senses returned. My feet seemed positively racked with pain, yet I could not move them. They seemed to be numbed. There was an icy feeling at the back of my neck and all down my spine, and my ears, like my feet, were dead, yet in torment; but there was in my breast a sense of warmth which was, by comparison, delicious. It was as a nightmare—a physical nightmare, if one may use such an expression; for some heavy weight on my chest made it difficult for me to breathe.

This period of semi-lethargy seemed to remain a long time, and as it faded away I must have slept or swooned. Then came a sort of loathing, like the first stage of sea-sickness, and a wild desire to be free from something—I knew not what. A vast stillness enveloped me, as though all the world were asleep or dead—only broken by the low panting as of some animal close to me. I felt a warm rasping at my throat, then came a consciousness of the awful truth, which chilled me to the heart and sent the blood surging up through my brain. Some great animal was lying on me and now licking my throat. I feared to stir, for some instinct of prudence bade me lie still; but the brute seemed to realise that there was now some change in me, for it raised its head. Through my eyelashes I saw above me the two great flaming eyes of a gigantic wolf. Its sharp white teeth gleamed in the gaping red mouth, and I could feel its hot breath fierce and acrid upon me.

For another spell of time I remembered no more. Then I became conscious of a low growl, followed by a yelp, renewed again and again. Then, seemingly very far away, I heard a "Holloa! holloa!" as of many voices calling in unison. Cautiously I raised my head and looked in the direction whence the sound came; but the cemetery blocked my view. The wolf still continued to yelp in a strange way, and a red glare began to move round the grove of cypresses, as though following the sound. As the voices drew closer, the wolf yelped faster and louder. I feared to make either sound or motion. Nearer came the red glow, over the white pall which stretched into the darkness around me. Then all at once from beyond the trees there came at a trot a troop of horsemen bearing torches. The wolf rose from my breast and made for the cemetery. I saw one of the horsemen (soldiers by their caps and their long military cloaks) raise his carbine and take aim. A companion knocked up his arm, and I heard the ball whizz over my head. He had evidently taken my body for that of the wolf. Another sighted the animal as it slunk away, and a shot followed. Then, at a gallop, the troop rode forward—some towards me, others following the wolf as it disappeared amongst the snow-clad cypresses.

As they drew nearer I tried to move, but was powerless, although I could see and hear all that went on around me. Two or three of the soldiers jumped from their horses and knelt beside me. One of them raised my head, and placed his hand over my heart.

"Good news, comrades!" he cried. "His heart still beats!"

Then some brandy was poured down my throat; it put vigour into me, 45 and I was able to open my eyes fully and look around. Lights and shadows were moving among the trees, and I heard men call to one another. They drew together, uttering frightened exclamations; and the lights flashed as the others came pouring out of the cemetery pell-mell, like men possessed. When the further ones came close to us, those who were around me asked them eagerly:

"Well, have you found him?"

The reply rang out hurriedly:

"No! no! Come away quick—quick! This is no place to stay, and on this of all nights!"

"What was it?" was the question, asked in all manner of keys. The answer came variously and all indefinitely as though the men were moved by some common impulse to speak, yet were restrained by some common fear from giving their thoughts.

"It—it—indeed!" gibbered one, whose wits had plainly given out for the 50 moment.

"A wolf—and yet not a wolf!" another put in shudderingly.

"No use trying for him without the sacred bullet," a third remarked in a more ordinary manner.

"Serve us right for coming out on this night! Truly we have earned our thousand marks!" were the ejaculations of a fourth.

"There was blood on the broken marble," another said after a pause—"the lightning never brought that there. And for him—is he safe? Look at his throat! See, comrades, the wolf has been lying on him and keeping his blood warm."

The officer looked at my throat and replied: 55

"He is all right; the skin is not pierced. What does it all mean? We should never have found him but for the yelping of the wolf."

"What became of it?" asked the man who was holding up my head, and who seemed the least panic-stricken of the party, for his hands were steady and without tremor. On his sleeve was the chevron of a petty officer.

"It went to its home," answered the man, whose long face was pallid, and who actually shook with terror as he glanced around him fearfully. "There are graves enough there in which it may lie. Come, comrades—come quickly! Let us leave this cursed spot."

The officer raised me to a sitting posture, as he uttered a word of command; then several men placed me upon a horse. He sprang to the saddle behind me, took me in his arms, gave the word to advance; and, turning our faces away from the cypresses, we rode away in swift, military order.

As yet my tongue refused its office, and I was perforce silent. I must have   60
fallen asleep; for the next thing I remembered was finding myself standing up, supported by a soldier on each side of me. It was almost broad daylight, and to the north a red streak of sunlight was reflected, like a path of blood, over the waste of snow. The officer was telling the men to say nothing of what they had seen, except that they found an English stranger, guarded by a large dog.

"Dog! that was no dog," cut in the man who had exhibited such fear. "I think I know a wolf when I see one."

The young officer answered calmly: "I said a dog."

"Dog!" reiterated the other ironically. It was evident that his courage was rising with the sun; and, pointing to me, he said, "Look at his throat. Is that the work of a dog, master?"

Instinctively I raised my hand to my throat, and as I touched it I cried out in pain. The men crowded round to look, some stooping down from their saddles; and again there came the calm voice of the young officer:

"A dog, as I said. If aught else were said we should only be laughed at."   65

I was then mounted behind a trooper, and we rode on into the suburbs of Munich. Here we came across a stray carriage, into which I was lifted, and it was driven off to the Quatre Saisons—the young officer accompanying me, whilst a trooper followed with his horse, and the others rode off to their barracks.

When we arrived, Herr Delbrueck rushed so quickly down the steps to meet me, that it was apparent he had been watching within. Taking me by both hands he solicitously led me in. The officer saluted me and was turning to withdraw, when I recognised his purpose, and insisted that he should come to my rooms. Over a glass of wine I warmly thanked him and his brave comrades for saving me. He replied simply that he was more than glad, and that Herr Delbrueck had at the first taken steps to make all the searching party pleased; at which ambiguous utterance the maitre d'hotel smiled, while the officer pleaded duty and withdrew.

"But Herr Delbrueck," I enquired, "how and why was it that the soldiers searched for me?"

He shrugged his shoulders, as if in depreciation of his own deed, as he replied:

"I was so fortunate as to obtain leave from the commander of the regi-   70
ment in which I served, to ask for volunteers."

"But how did you know I was lost?" I asked.

"The driver came hither with the remains of his carriage, which had been upset when the horses ran away."

"But surely you would not send a search-party of soldiers merely on this account?"

"Oh, no!" he answered; "but even before the coachman arrived, I had this telegram from the Boyar whose guest you are," and he took from his pocket a telegram which he handed to me, and I read:

Bistritz

Be careful of my guest—his safety is most precious to me. Should aught   75
happen to him, or if he be missed, spare nothing to find him and ensure his safety. He is English and therefore adventurous. There are often dangers from snow and wolves and night. Lose not a moment if you suspect harm to him. I answer your zeal with my fortune.—*Dracula*.

As I held the telegram in my hand, the room seemed to whirl around me; and, if the attentive maitre d'hotel had not caught me, I think I should have fallen. There was something so strange in all this, something so weird and impossible to imagine, that there grew on me a sense of my being in some way the sport of opposite forces—the mere vague idea of which seemed in a way to paralyse me. I was certainly under some form of mysterious protection. From a distant country had come, in the very nick of time, a message that took me out of the danger of the snow-sleep and the jaws of the wolf.

■ This short story is sometimes thought to have been a rejected draft of a first chapter of Stoker's novel *Dracula*. Note instances where the main character/narrator presents his own curiosity and suspicions. How does he resolve the various questions that he raises?

- What mysteries remain unresolved at the end of the story? How might those mysteries press us to think of symbolic readings?
- What details in this story are familiar within the genre of the vampire tale?

POETRY

Matthew Arnold (1822–1888)

Dover Beach (1867)

The sea is calm tonight.
The tide is full, the moon lies fair
Upon the straits;—on the French coast the light
Gleams and is gone; the cliffs of England stand,
Glimmering and vast, out in the tranquil bay.   5
Come to the window, sweet is the night-air!
Only, from the long line of spray
Where the sea meets the moon-blanched land,
Listen! you hear the grating roar
Of pebbles which the waves draw back, and fling,   10
At their return, up the high strand,
Begin, and cease, and then again begin,
With tremulous cadence slow, and bring
The eternal note of sadness in.

Sophocles long ago   15
Heard it on the Aegean, and it brought
Into his mind the turbid ebb and flow
Of human misery; we
Find also in the sound a thought,
Hearing it by this distant northern sea.   20

The Sea of Faith
Was once, too, at the full, and round earth's shore
Lay like the folds of a bright girdle furled.
But now I only hear
Its melancholy, long, withdrawing roar,   25
Retreating, to the breath
Of the night-wind, down the vast edges drear
And naked shingles of the world.

Ah, love, let us be true
To one another! for the world, which seems   30
To lie before us like a land of dreams,
So various, so beautiful, so new,
Hath really neither joy, nor love, nor light,
Nor certitude, nor peace, nor help for pain;
And we are here as on a darkling plain   35
Swept with confused alarms of struggle and flight,
Where ignorant armies clash by night.

■ How can we reconcile the poet's claim that the world "Hath really neither
joy, nor love, nor light" with the earlier suggestion that the waves carry
"The eternal note of sadness"? Why does the poet simultaneously find
meaning in the natural world (reading the world as a symbol) and acknowledge that that meaning is not really there?

Jimmy Santiago Baca (1952–   )

Green Chile (1989)

I prefer red chile over my eggs
and potatoes for breakfast.
Red chile *ristras* decorate my door,
dry on my roof, and hang from eaves.
They lend open-air vegetable stands   5
historical grandeur, and gently swing
with an air of festive welcome.
I can hear them talking in the wind,
haggard, yellowing, crisp, rasping
tongues of old men, licking the breeze.   10
            But grandmother loves green chile.
When I visit her,
she holds the green chile pepper
in her wrinkled hands.
Ah, voluptuous, masculine,   15
an air of authority and youth simmers
from its swan-neck stem, tapering to a flowery
collar, fermenting resinous spice.
A well-dressed gentleman at the door
my grandmother takes sensuously in her hand,   20

rubbing its firm glossed sides,
caressing the oily rubbery serpent,
with mouth-watering fulfillment,
fondling its curves with gentle fingers.
Its bearing magnificent and taut   25
as flanks of a tiger in mid-leap,

she thrusts her blade into
and cuts it open, with lust
on her hot mouth, sweating over the stove,
bandanna round her forehead,   30
mysterious passion on her face
and she serves me green chile con carne
between soft warm leaves of corn tortillas,
with beans and rice—her sacrifice
to her little prince.   35
I slurp from my plate
with last bit of tortilla, my mouth burns
and I hiss and drink a tall glass of cold water.

All over New Mexico, sunburned men and women
drive rickety trucks stuffed with gunny-sacks   40
of green chile, from Belen, Veguita, Willard, Estancia,
San Antonio y Socorro, from fields
to roadside stands, you see them roasting green chile
in screen-sided homemade barrels, and for a dollar a bag,
we relive this old, beautiful ritual again and again.   45

■ What form does the green chile take when the poet's grandmother begins
to work with it? How is this form important to the ritual that the poet
describes? How does the ritual extend beyond the poet's family?

e. e. cummings (1894–1962)

[anyone lived in a pretty how town] (1940)

anyone lived in a pretty how town
(with up so floating many bells down)
spring summer autumn winter
he sang his didn't he danced his did.

Women and men (both little and small)   5
cared for anyone not at all
they sowed their isn't they reaped their same
sun moon stars rain

children guessed (but only a few
and down they forgot as up they grew   10
autumn winter spring summer)
that noone loved him more by more

when by now and tree by leaf
she laughed his joy she cried his grief
bird by snow and stir by still   15
anyone's any was all to her

someones married their everyones
laughed their cryings and did their dance
(sleep wake hope and then) they
said their nevers they slept their dream   20

stars rain sun moon
(and only the snow can begin to explain
how children are apt to forget to remember
with up so floating many bells down)

one day anyone died i guess   25
(and noone stooped to kiss his face)
busy folk buried them side by side
little by little and was by was

all by all and deep by deep
and more by more they dream their sleep   30
noone and anyone earth by april
wish by spirit and if by yes.

Women and men (both dong and ding)
summer autumn winter spring
reaped their sowing and went their came   35
sun moon stars rain

■ How does the poet use the pronouns "anyone" and "noone" symbolically?
   How does each word refer simultaneously to an individual and to a collective experience?

■ What are possible meanings of the line "(and noone stooped to kiss his face)"?

Emily Dickinson (1830–1886)

[The Soul selects her own Society—] (ca. 1862)

The Soul selects her own Society—
Then—shuts the Door—
To her divine Majority—
Present no more—

Unmoved—she notes the Chariots—pausing—   5
At her low Gate—
Unmoved—an Emperor be kneeling
Upon her Mat—

I've known her—from an ample nation—
Choose One—   10
Then—close the Valves of her attention—
Like Stone—

■ Explain the significance of the kneeling Emperor and "Valves of her
   attention" closed "Like Stone." How does the poem connect these
   two images?

Peter Meinke (1932–)

Sunday at the Apple Market (1977)

Apple-smell everywhere!
Haralson   McIntosh   Fireside   Rome
old ciderpresses weathering in the shed
old ladders tilting at empty branches
boxes and bins of apples by the cartload   5
yellow and green and red
piled crazy in the storehouse barn
miraculous profusion, the crowd
around the testing table laughing rolling
the cool applechunks in their mouths   10
dogs barking at children in the appletrees
couples holding hands, so many people
out in the country carrying bushels
and baskets and bags and boxes of apples
to their cars, the smell of apples   15

making us for one Sunday afternoon free
and happy as people must have been meant to be.

- How do the images fit together into a coherent scene? How does that setting convey a particular tone?
- Look at the various photos of apples on pages 1152 and 1153. Which image (if any) fits with this poem? Explain your answer.

William Butler Yeats (1865–1939)

The Wild Swans at Coole (1919)

The trees are in their autumn beauty,
The woodland paths are dry,
Under the October twilight the water
Mirrors a still sky;
Upon the brimming water among the stones   5
Are nine and fifty swans.

The nineteenth Autumn has come upon me
Since I first made my count;
I saw, before I had well finished,
All suddenly mount   10
And scatter wheeling in great broken rings
Upon their clamorous wings.

I have looked upon those brilliant creatures,
And now my heart is sore.
All's changed since I, hearing at twilight,   15
The first time on this shore,
The bell-beat of their wings above my head,
Trod with a lighter tread.

Unwearied still, lover by lover,
They paddle in the cold,   20
Companionable streams or climb the air;
Their hearts have not grown old;
Passion or conquest, wander where they will,
Attend upon them still.

But now they drift on the still water   25
Mysterious, beautiful;

Among what rushes will they build,
By what lake's edge or pool
Delight men's eyes, when I awake some day
To find they have flown away?   30

- How do the swans make the poet's heart sore?
- What is symbolized by their flying away?
- What is the relation between the swans and the human community?

DRAMA

Moira Buffini (1965–   )

Moira Buffini was born in Carlisle, in the north of England, and studied English and Drama at London University. She has written numerous plays that have been staged throughout the United Kingdom. She is also a screenwriter, and wrote the screenplay for *Tamara Drewe* (2010) from Posy Simmon's novel of the same name. In 2011, she wrote an adaptation of *Jane Eyre* for BBC Films. Buffini adapted "A Vampire Story" (2008) into the screenplay that she wrote for *Byzantium* (2013), a film directed by Neil Jordan.

A Vampire Story (2008)

CHARACTERS

ELLA: *aged sixteen, present day*
ELEANOR: *aged sixteen, nineteenth century*
CLAIRE: *aged twenty-one, present day*
CLARA: *aged twenty-one nineteenth century*
FRANK BRIGGS MOON: *schoolboys, present day*
DEBIT POINT: *schoolgirls, present day*
MINT: *a drama teacher*
FILLET: *a food technology teacher*
MARIANNE: *a child prostitute*
RUTHVEN: *a gambler*
DARVELL: *a stranger*
TINA: *Frank's mother*
GEOFF: *Frank's father*

LETTY AND HARRIET: *schoolgirls, nineteenth century*
BETTINA: *a maidservant*

Mint and Fillet can be played
by male or female actors

Setting

A town, somewhere in Britain.
Present day

SCENE ONE

Eleanor is sixteen. She is dressed in a costume of 1822. She is on stage almost all the time. There is a small writing desk where she occasionally sits and writes, although her focus should always be on the action.

ELEANOR: People will always believe the most fabulous tale you can tell. It's the one that they secretly long for. It must be unprovable, impossible, fantastical. To believe it then becomes an act of faith. An act of faith.

Scene One. A Train.

Ella and Claire are dressed in modern-day clothes. Ella is sixteen, Claire, twenty-one. Claire is very fashionably and stylishly attired. Ella dresses as if the whole concept of fashion is confusing and alien to her.

CLAIRE: Guess what your name is
ELLA: I can't
CLAIRE: Go on
ELLA: Just tell me
CLAIRE: You'll never guess   5
ELLA: Don't make me
CLAIRE: It's fun
ELLA: No
CLAIRE: Come on, it's interesting
ELLA: No   10
CLAIRE: I'll give you a clue. My name's Claire
ELLA: Claire what?
CLAIRE: Wythenshawe
ELLA: Claire Wythenshawe
CLAIRE: And you're my little sister, Eleanor   15
ELLA: Oh

CLAIRE: Isn't that great? I thought you'd be pleased with that
ELLA: Eleanor Wythenshawe
CLAIRE: That's right. And I'm Claire
ELLA: You found two sisters called Eleanor and Claire?   20
CLAIRE: Fancy that
ELLA: What happened to them?
CLAIRE: Killed in a car crash. Identities there for the taking
ELLA: What about their parents?
CLAIRE: They only had a dad. And I'm afraid he recently died   25
ELLA: How?

> *Claire blandly shrugs.*

Don't you feel anything?
CLAIRE: Like what?
ELLA: For them
CLAIRE: I feel glad we got away. You didn't think we would, did you?   30
ELLA: One day, we won't

> *Pause.*

So where are we going, Claire?
CLAIRE: A lovely small town
ELLA: I told you; no more small towns
CLAIRE: They're the best places   35
ELLA: They're a nightmare
CLAIRE: We're going to a lovely British small town surrounded
          by beautiful countryside
ELLA: I'll be sick
CLAIRE: No you won't   40
ELLA: I'll go mad
CLAIRE: You always say that
ELLA: I'll kill myself
CLAIRE: You could try
ELLA: I could kill you   45
CLAIRE: Then you'd be all alone. I love these small towns, Ella.
          The people are lovely
ELLA: So gullible
CLAIRE: I've rented us a nice little flat and I'll get a job in a bar or something
ELLA: You're a very sad person   50
CLAIRE: I thought you had doubts as to whether I was a person at all.
          (*She looks out of the window.*) Look at those lovely little gardens. The way
          the sun dapples the patios. They've planted magnolias in the multiplex

car park—and the bins—they're rainforest green. It's going to be good for
us here, I can feel it   55

ELLA: You said that about the last place

CLAIRE: That town we just left? I've already forgotten it

ELLA: So what am I going to do in this dump?

CLAIRE: There are two schools—

ELLA: Not school again!   60

CLAIRE: What else can I do with you? You refuse to grow up; you won't
behave like an adult—

ELLA: I feel ancient

CLAIRE: Well, the effect is utterly teenage. You don't know how lucky
you are; all that knowledge you've got, all that education. One day,   65
Ella, you'll put it together and calculate the most important thing.
How to survive

ELLA: Fine. School, then

CLAIRE: Don't do English Literature again. It makes you depressed.
What about Computing?   70

ELLA: Done it

CLAIRE: Music, then

ELLA: No thanks

CLAIRE: Art

ELLA: Done it   75

CLAIRE: Or that subject where you make benches

ELLA: That is not a subject

CLAIRE: Can you do Espionage at A Level?

ELLA: No

CLAIRE: What about Cooking?   80

ELLA: You mean Food Technology?

CLAIRE: About time you learnt to cook

ELLA: What's the point?

CLAIRE: Ella, you don't have to eat all the stuff. Do it for me

ELLA: Food Technology   85

CLAIRE: And what else is there? A nice, light subject, You could do
with a laugh. I know—

ELLA: I won't do it

CLAIRE: What's wrong with you?

ELLA: You can't make me   90

CLAIRE: I haven't even said / what it is yet

ELLA: I know what you're going to say. And how can I do that? It's all
about laying yourself open to vicious attack, exposing your soul,
performing like a flea in a / flea circus

CLAIRE: Oh, come on. What subject can be so terrible?   95

SCENE TWO

ELEANOR: Scene Two

FRANK: A-Level Drama

Frank has sensitive eyes and a nervous demeanour. Mint is full of fervour and frustration. Mint's students, Briggs, Point, Debit and Moon, have perfected an air of cultivated boredom. They look as if they haven't had any fresh air in years. They look in fact, like detached, fashionable, effortlessly nonchalant vampires.

MINT: So, same old spoilt rebels and fashion victims as last year. Not allowed to swear with disappointment or I would. Briggs

BRIGGS: Mint   5

MINT: I'm gutted to see you; I thought you'd be shovelling fries for the rest of your life. And Debit

DEBIT: Hello, Mint

MINT: You actually passed an exam?

DEBIT: Might have   10

MINT: So there's a brain somewhere under all that hair spray

DEBIT: It's mousse

MINT: Well, let's see how long you last

POINT: No, Mint, why don't we see how long you last?

MINT: We're off to a great start already. Now, I'm more than delighted   15
to see that we have some new blood. What are your names?

ELLA: Eleanor Wythenshawe

MINT: And?

FRANK: Frank Adam Stein

MINT: OK, Ella and—one name will do—Frank. I'm going to throw you in   20
at the deep end. What's the first rule of making drama? Come on! First
rule of making drama?

DEBIT: Just say "Yes"

MINT: Thank you, Debit. "Yes". Yes to an idea, yes to each other, yes to
the energy, to the communal experience, yes to the mighty, universal   25
"Yes". That's what we aspire to in this class, isn't it?

MOON: No

MINT: So. The hot seat. Frank—let's start with you

FRANK: What?

Mint takes Frank to a seat apart from the group.

MINT: We're going to put you on the hot seat   30

FRANK: What for? Why?

BRIGGS: To scald your arse

MINT: The hot seat, guys, is a place of discovery, OK? Now we usually use it when we're "in character," but I'm going to do something we've never tried before. I'm an instinctive teacher and my instincts are 35 saying, "Go, Mint, go." So I'm going to throw away the code of good practice and hot seat you as yourself

MOON: That's psychological torture, Mint

MINT: It's going to be fun, OK?

MOON: You could leave him permanently scarred 40

MINT: Frank, the rest of the group will ask you questions

MOON: You're infringing his human rights

MINT: And your only job is to be truthful

MOON: These are torture chamber conditions

MINT: It's a simple question and answer exercise. Are you being tortured, 45 Frank?

FRANK: Um

MINT: Now, think about everything that has brought you to this moment in time. People, when I clap my hands we're going to begin—so have your questions for Frank ready 50

Frank is full of dread. Mint claps.

MOON: Do you feel that in doing this, Mint is infringing your human rights?

FRANK: Um

BRIGGS: What's your name?

FRANK: I've already said it

BRIGGS: I didn't listen 55

FRANK: Frank

BRIGGS: Frank what?

FRANK: Stein

BRIGGS: What's that short for?

FRANK: Franklin 60

MOON: Your name's Franklinstein?

BRIGGS: *(laughing)* Are you lying?

FRANK: My dad thought it was funny too. In fact, it was his last big joke before his sense of humour calcified and had to be removed

POINT: Are you a monster? 65

FRANK: Probably

BRIGGS: Are you a wanker?

MINT: Briggs!

DEBIT: What school were you at before, Franklin?

FRANK: I'm home-educated 70

DEBIT: What?

FRANK: My mum and dad have been teaching me at home

BRIGGS: How long for?

FRANK: Since I was a foetus

MOON: You've never been to school? 75

FRANK: No

POINT: Why not?

FRANK: You'll have to ask my parents that really

POINT: No thanks

FRANK: Perhaps they were worried that I might grow up normal if I went 80
to school so they decided to concentrate all their efforts on turning me
into a freak

POINT: Why?

FRANK: Well, they're freaks, so I expect they just wanted me to fit in

MINT: Frank, I can understand your defensiveness, but just try to 85
be open. Say yes

FRANK: Well, to be fair on my mum and dad—that's Tina and Geoff—I
think they had high hopes. They wanted me to fulfil my potential

POINT: What potential is that, Franklin?

FRANK: Tina and Geoff thought that if I learnt everything there is to know 90
by the age of sixteen I might turn out to be a leader of men or a genius
or something but I eventually had to point out the flaw in their plan
and say, "Tina and Geoff, if you don't let me go to school and talk to
some other people, I'll end up in a nut house before I'm twenty," and
to drive home my point I painted my bedroom black and drowned 95
Tina's pot plants so, given that I've got four "A"s at A Level already,
they decided to let me come. They see it as a bit of a gap year, I think

MOON: Did you say you were a genius?

FRANK: No, I'm a great disappointment

BRIGGS: Are you gay? 100

MINT: Question not allowed

MOON: Is God a man or a woman?

FRANK: Pardon?

MINT: I think he means are you religious?

MOON: No, is God a man or a woman? 105

FRANK: Um, if there was a deity or creator I'd say it would be unlikely
to have recognisable genitalia

DEBIT: That's rude

FRANK: God probably transcends gender. The deity is probably asexual
or even polysexual 110

POINT: Is that what you are, Frank?

FRANK: It may even be formless, dare I say it, non-existent and therefore
imaginable in any form

DEBIT: I think you're shy about sex

FRANK: Is that a question?   115
DEBIT: That's cute. You got any diseases?
MINT: Not allowed
DEBIT: Have you got a girlfriend, Frank?
FRANK: No
BRIGGS: Have you got any friends at all? .   120
FRANK: Yes, no, well, it depends what you mean by friends. If you mean
        actual living people who like me, then no
DEBIT: That's a bit sad, isn't it?
FRANK: I used to have an imaginary friend, but he moved out. He was
        great; really funny; much more daring than me. He used to subvert   125
        Geoff's quizzes and put lighted matches in the bin, but in the end
        he had to go
MOON: Why?
FRANK: It turned out he was hiding pornography under the bed and
        Tina found it. She had a massive row with him. He came in to tell me 130
        he was leaving and I haven't seen him since
ELLA: Do you miss him?
FRANK: Yes
DEBIT: So what d'you do for fun, Frank?
FRANK: Fun?   135
MOON: Apart from the pornography
FRANK: That wasn't mine; it was imaginary
MINT: One last question: what made you choose Drama, Frank?
FRANK: Um, my parents think it's a totally useless subject so it seemed
        like the obvious choice   140
MINT: OK. Well done. Respect. Round of applause

Only Mint and Ella clap.

BRIGGS: Frank
FRANK: Yes?
BRIGGS: I love you

Frank flinches as if he's about to be hit.

MINT: Eleanor, we're going to do something different with you, OK?   145
        We're going to play "Lifegame." Are you ready?
ELLA: No
MINT: Learn to say yes. OK, you barbarians, get off your chairs. Eleanor,
        I'm going to be "in role" as the interviewer. (To *the rest of the group.*)
        And from what I glean in the interview, you lot are going to act out   150
        episodes in Ella's life
POINT: Bore me to death

MINT: Someone's already beaten me to it, Point. Move these chairs

  Ella and Frank move their chairs.

ELLA: That was brave
FRANK: No, it wasn't   155
ELLA: I've never told the truth about myself
FRANK: Why not?
ELLA: Because no one would believe it
MINT: I said move your chairs

  The others move their chairs.

FRANK: I would   160

  Ella looks at him. Eleanor joins her. Remains close by.

MINT: Right. Welcome to "Lifegame." Today we have as our special
  guest Eleanor Wythenshawe
MOON: *(without enthusiasm)*   Yo
MINT: And we're going to be recreating, before her very own eyes, episodes
  from her true-life story. Eleanor, let's take a journey back to your early   165
  childhood. Can you share with us one of your earliest memories?
ELEANOR: Yes
ELLA: I'm at Miss Skullpepper's school. It's a rainy night. I'm about six years
  old and I'm in bed with two of my friends
POINT: What sort of a school was this?   170
ELLA: It was a private orphanage. We all had benefactors who paid our
  fees. Most of us didn't know who they were. It's hard to describe really;
  such places don't exist any more
MINT: When was this?
ELEANOR/ELLA: Must have been 1812   175
MINT: Eleanor, I think I can feel some improvising going on here, which,
  in a different exercise would be totally cool but as this game's about the
  Real You, just stick to the truth for now, OK?
ELLA: I have a clear memory of celebrating the rout of Napoleon in Russia,
  that's why I'm so sure it was 1812. It was night   180
BRIGGS: What were you doing in bed with two girls?
ELLA: Space was short and in winter the house was so cold
BRIGGS: Were you naked?
ELLA: No
DEBIT: What were your friends called?   185
ELLA: Harriet and Leticia
MINT: OK, in the spirit of saying yes, we're going to go along with
  Ella's impro

ELLA: It's not an impro—it's a memory

MINT: Point, you play Eleanor, Debit, you play Harriet, and Briggs,   190
you're Leticia

BRIGGS: No way

MINT: I beg your pardon?

BRIGGS: I'm not playing a girl

MINT: Get over it, or get out. You're three in a bed   195

BRIGGS: Tell me about my character

ELLA: Leticia was very shy and sweet

BRIGGS: Was she buff?

ELLA: Pardon?

BRIGGS: Cos I'm not playing a dog   200

ELLA: She was dark and slight. I thought her beautiful. Her mother had
died on her way home from the Gold Coast, after giving birth to her
child of shame

BRIGGS: Her what?

ELLA: Leticia was a child of shame. We all were. Harriet was the daughter   205
of a tea merchant. Her mother was a whore, like mine

DEBIT: Did you just say my mother was a whore?

MINT: Eleanor, this certainly shows you've done some very interesting
reading

MOON: If this was 1812, why haven't you decomposed?   210

ELEANOR/ELLA: I freely confess that I have stayed alive for all these years
by drinking human blood

This causes a sensation; from shock to laughter.

MOON: Yuk

POINT: Oh my God

BRIGGS: That's disgusting   215

DEBIT: You fucking weirdo

MINT: Language

POINT: That is so freaked out

MOON: Are you saying you're a vampire?

ELLA: Yes   220

MINT: Eleanor, you know sometimes, when we've gone through a trau-
matic event, maybe bereavement or parental divorce, we retreat into
fantasy to try to make sense of it all. Now, I don't think that's wrong.
You've found a sympathetic ear here / OK?

DEBIT: No she hasn't   225

POINT: Is this supposed to be a drama lesson? Because it's like stepping
into someone's nervous breakdown, Mint

MINT: Let's have a tableau
MOON: A tableau of what?
MINT: Of Eleanor's story. She's at school, in bed with her friends,   230
Leticia and Harriet
MOON: What about me?
MINT: You're the bed

> *They form a tableau. Point, as a vampire, is trying to suck Briggs's blood. Briggs swoons, girlishly. Debit does Munch's "Scream". Moon attention-seeks as the bed.*

MINT: Eleanor, is that how it was?
ELLA: No. We were six years old. They were asleep   235
MINT: You two—you're asleep. You're six years old
BRIGGS: What is the point of being asleep? Are we supposed to learn something, being asleep?
MINT: I ask myself that question every time you enter this Studio
POINT: We've spent enough time on this freakish shit   240
MINT: Language! Eleanor, you've got a great imagination—and that's a vital tool for making effective theatre. Now, I don't want to finish yet, OK? I don't want you to walk out of here feeling that you've failed
ELLA: I won't
MINT: I want you to leave this studio with your head held high, OK?   245
ELLA: I will
MINT: Let's fast-forward to the present, to the twenty-first century here and now, and find out about the real Eleanor
DEBIT: How many people have you drunk?
BRIGGS: Do you suck anything else apart from blood?   250
MINT: Who do you live with, Eleanor?
ELLA: Claire
FRANK: Who's Claire?
ELLA: She's my legal guardian
DEBIT: What about your mum and dad?   255
ELLA: My father was a sperm. I never knew him
MINT: And your mum?
ELEANOR/ELLA: My mother is a vampire
POINT: She is a mental emergency, Mint
MINT: OK, thank you, Eleanor. One final question: what made   260
you choose Drama?

> *Ella giggles at their consternation.*

ELLA: My hilarious sense of fun

SCENE THREE

FILLET: Scene Three

MOON: Food Technology

FILLET: And so, we begin our exploration with the humble root vegetable.
They grow and thrive in the darkness, down in the rich heart of our
mother earth. Gastronauts, have your peelers at the ready. Today, we're   5
going to discover the science of mash

> *The students start peeling their root vegetables. Ella is working next
> to Frank.*

FRANK: One thing's puzzling me; it's daylight

ELLA: Yes

FRANK: So if you were a vampire you'd be a little pile of dust. And I'm
surprised you haven't cringed away from me shrieking by now   10

ELLA: Why's that?

FRANK: Because Tina made me garlic sandwiches for lunch

ELLA: True vampires live and move in society just like everyone else

FRANK: You haven't even got pointy teeth

ELLA: We don't die in daylight. We're not scared of garlic. We can use   15
our teeth but we find it more effective to let the blood with a knife

FRANK: You don't look like someone who's committed countless
motiveless killings

ELLA: I do have a motive—my own survival

FILLET: Make sure every blemish is removed. We need perfect specimens   20

FRANK: Eleanor, if you really were a vampire, why would you tell us?

ELLA: I've carried the secret for so long. When I told it I thought—I don't
know—the walls would come crashing down. I might have known that
no one would believe me. It was a mistake. No one usually notices me
and now I've put myself in their sights   25

FILLET: As we boil, we are going to observe the physico-chemical alterations
of cell-wall constituents. What is the behaviour of the vegetable during
cooking? Does it scream with pain?

FRANK: Well, if it cheers you up, I don't think I made any friends either.
I don't know how to be in groups. I bring out the worst in people.   30
They can probably sense that there's something not quite right
about me

FILLET: Let us meditate on the fate of the potato

ELLA: What's not right about you, Frank?

FRANK: I see the world too clearly   35

ELLA: Do you?

FILLET: This humble tuber will lead us to ponder the morals of the
food chain

FRANK: It's all in fragments but I see everything all the time, splintered, fractured, all of creation, the beauty, the horror, the madness, the   40
inescapable ride towards destruction
ELLA: Yes
FRANK: The, the machinations of far-off power, the monsters of—
ELLA: Yes
FRANK: The terrible and ridiculous monsters of—   45
ELLA: Monsters of what?
FRANK: Sorry. Monsters of my own making. My own thoughts
ELLA: That's not what you were going to say
FRANK: No. Some days I think we're so monstrous that we'll destroy
this earth, that's all   50
ELLA: You think humanity is monstrous?
FRANK: I don't know. Just asleep, maybe. Otherwise they'd do something
ELLA: They're happy, Frank; that's what it is. They appear asleep because
they're happy
FRANK: How can you be happy in a world like this?   55
FILLET: The subject of food on this planet is like a door, a metaphysical
door opening between worlds: the scientific, the political, the environmental, the culinary and yes, the spiritual. Gastronauts, today, by
peeling and boiling this potato, you will be taking your first step into a
bigger universe   60
FRANK: So, where d'you keep your coffin, anyway?

Ella smiles.

ELLA: No one ever got around to burying me

Frank smiles.

FRANK: They're giving me an appointment to see the school shrink
ELLA: Me too

Eleanor comes forward.

ELEANOR: 1812. I am six years old. At night, I sleep in a bed with two other   65
abandoned girls. They are my friends, Letty and Harriet.

Clara enters. Claire enters.

One night, I wake up in the dark to see a lovely woman in a shining dress
sitting on our bed. She is staring at me, as if I am something precious.
"Who are you?" I say
CLARA/CLAIRE: I'm your mother   70
ELEANOR: She replies, and I am glad because my mother is dead and now
I know she is an angel

SCENE FOUR

CLARA: Scene Four

Clara exits.

CLAIRE: Happy Hour

Claire's bar. A spectacle in which the whole company except Ella and Eleanor can take part.

Friday night happy hour. The bar staff are busy, the dance floor already crowded. Socialising, hedonism, drink; male behaviours and female behaviours. The spectacle is full of energy and charge. People are already dancing. Moon plays the fool, Briggs shows off his wares, Point plays hard to get and Debit is drunk.

Claire watches from behind the bar, pulling a pint in slow motion, her serenity a counterpoint to all the movement—as if time is standing still for her. She focuses on Briggs, taking note of everything he does. Point tries to attract Briggs's attention. But Briggs has seen Claire staring at him—and now he's staring back. Point becomes angry. She yells:

POINT: Let's go

BRIGGS: I can't

POINT: Why not? 5

BRIGGS: I'm staring at her

Point looks at Claire and back to Briggs. Briggs ignores her.

POINT: Loser. Boy band loser

Point throws her drink at him. She exits. Briggs tries to wipe the alcopop off his face. Claire holds out a napkin. As Briggs takes it, the bar falls silent and all the movement continues in slow motion—as if Briggs has joined Claire in her pocket of time.

CLAIRE: What's your name?

BRIGGS: Dave Briggs

CLAIRE: Well, Dave Briggs, I'm Claire Wythenshawe 10

BRIGGS: Wythenshawe? Shit—have you got a sister?

CLAIRE: Might have

BRIGGS: What's her name?

CLAIRE: Eleanor

BRIGGS: I don't believe it 15

CLAIRE: D'you know her?

BRIGGS: She is something else, isn't she?

CLAIRE: Is she?
BRIGGS: Well, you know; she's a bit—
CLAIRE: Bit what?   20
BRIGGS: Well, not meaning to disrespect your family, but she's a
          fucking mentalist
CLAIRE: Oh
BRIGGS: I'm not knocking her but—
CLAIRE: Yeah, she's a strange one   25
BRIGGS: What a looper. I can't believe she's got a sister like you
CLAIRE: How d'you know her then, Dave? You at school with her?
BRIGGS: We both do Drama. Man, she is so crap. I mean, I know she's
          your sister and everything but you should see her trying to act. It is like
          watching a door trying to walk. Honestly, what a freakoid   30
CLAIRE: Well, that's strange because Eleanor's only in Year Twelve
BRIGGS: Yeah?
CLAIRE: So, you're in here underage drinking, aren't you, Dave?
BRIGGS: No
CLAIRE: I rake a very dim view of that   35
BRIGGS: How dim?

> Briggs has one of his hands spread out on the bar. Claire leans for-
> ward, digging her elbow into the back of it. It brings her very close
> to him. The action in the bar has been going slower and slower. It
> now freezes.

CLAIRE: I could lose my job for serving you
BRIGGS: I'm eighteen
CLAIRE: Show me some ID
BRIGGS: I haven't got any. I never get asked cos I look so mature   40
CLAIRE: Get out
BRIGGS: You see, you're saying that, but then you've got your elbow
          digging into the back of my hand so I can't actually move and so I'm
          getting mixed messages, you know? You smell lovely. What did you say
          your name was again?   45
CLAIRE: Claire
BRIGGS: Claire, I know there's an age difference between us, but—
CLAIRE: You going to give me some bullshit, Dave?
BRIGGS: Yeah, I was going to try
CLAIRE: About how you could prove you were all grown up by giving me   50
          the shag of a lifetime?
BRIGGS: I was going to put it nicer than that
CLAIRE: Shall we cut to the chase?
BRIGGS: Are you chasing me, Claire?

CLAIRE: I'm always in pursuit of pleasure, Dave. I like to live in the   55
moment, in the eternal second of present time

> *Claire clicks her fingers. The bar suddenly empties. Briggs and Claire are alone.*

D'you get me?
BRIGGS: Yeah
CLAIRE: It's what I exist for. The present that I seek is random and indis
criminate and when I find it, there is no guilt or consequence. Just   60
gratification and a moment of bliss
BRIGGS: Wow
CLAIRE: Do you consent?
BRIGGS: To what?
CLAIRE: To be my next pleasure   65
BRIGGS: I think that's the best offer I've ever had
CLAIRE: Is that a yes, then?
BRIGGS: You don't mess about, do you?
CLAIRE: Never

> *Clara takes the tray of drinks from Claire.*

CLARA: Scene Five   70

SCENE FIVE

Ella is sitting at a small desk.

ELEANOR: Coursework
ELLA: Write a short scene incorporating some of Brecht's techniques of
alienation. Subject matter: a secret

> *Ella starts to write. Characters enter and position themselves as she speaks.*

A smoky, opulent room. Bodies lie drunkenly scattered in slumber. Ruthven,
a gambler and Darvell—   5
ELEANOR: It is him
ELLA: —are at a card table. They are deep in their game. Clara Webb serves
them with drinks.

> *Ruthven and Darvell are at a card table. Clara serves them with drinks.*

Clara, to us—
CLARA: This game of cards has been going on for the last five hours   10
ELLA: Ruthven—
RUTHVEN: *(to Darvell)* I'll see your hundred and add two
ELLA: Darvell—

DARVELL: As you wish, My Lord

ELLA: Darvell puts the last of his money on the table   15

> *Darvell puts the last of his money on the table. Marianne, little more*
> *than a child, is cradling a drunk.*

MARIANNE: *(to us)* You're in a house of ill-repute. That's to say a brothel.
That's to say a whorehouse, a fleshpot, full of sluts, trollops, tarts,
strumpets, whores / and men

ELEANOR: And men

> *Ella writes, concentrating deeply.*

MARIANNE: You're lucky to be here—and so am I for that matter because   20
it's one of London's finest. It is run by a woman called / Clara Webb

ELEANOR: Clara Webb

MARIANNE: That's her. She survived her brutal childhood to become, at the
age of just twenty-one, London's pushiest and most ambitious whore

CLARA: Have you given that man what he's paid for?   25

MARIANNE: I don't think he's capable, really

CLARA: Chuck him out on the street and see to someone else

MARIANNE: Clara Webb is a hard-faced slag if ever there was one, but she
pays alright. She won't let them beat us and there's always a doctor on
call for our clap. What more could a prostitute ask for? It's 1816, after   30
all—our life expectancy's only twenty

ELLA: Marianne exits, dragging the unconscious lord

MARIANNE: What do I say next?

ELLA: Nothing

MARIANNE: Is this it? Is this the whole of my part?   35

ELLA: Yes

MARIANNE: But I'm an interesting character

ELLA: This story is not about you

> *Marianne exits, dragging the unconscious lord.*

CLARA: My business turns over two thousand a year, all of it tax free.
I plough a lot back in, providing the gentlemen with the very finest   40
service in these decadent surroundings. The profits I make, I secrete
in a trust for my daughter

> *Ruthven has put more money on the table.*

RUTHVEN: So what are you to do, sir? Where do we go from here?

CLARA: My daughter is the only thing in the world I love. When the mid
wife put her on my chest it was like a revelation. I had never known what   45

love was until I felt her thundering heartbeat and smelt her tiny, blood-
ied head. Everything I have done since then has been for her

DARVELL: You'll need to accept a credit note. I've no more cash on me,
My Lord

RUTHVEN: You're mistaking me for an idiot   50

DARVELL: Then what will you accept?

RUTHVEN: Admit defeat. To go on is past reason

CLARA: My daughter's at a little school, where she'll learn how to marry
and have a safe life. She's been told that her mother is dead. And the
fiction will soon be true. In my profession we don't last long; even us   55
clever ones. My lungs are rotting by inches—and I'm so angry about it
I am spitting blood

DARVELL: I have something far more valuable than cash. Perhaps we
should play for that

RUTHVEN: What is it?   60

DARVELL: I have a secret

RUTHVEN: Don't waste my time

DARVELL: I am offering you Time. I possess the knowledge of a place where
one can find life everlasting

RUTHVEN: I'm insulted   65

DARVELL: Lord Ruthven, I can give you immortality. Where is the insult in
that? I have seen it

> *Clara remains in the shadows, watching, fascinated.*

RUTHVEN: Immortality?

DARVELL: You could move through time without aging, young forever

RUTHVEN: How?   70

DARVELL: I was travelling through Asia Minor—

RUTHVEN: When?

DARVELL: Last spring. I was with an old friend of mine. We were
nearing Byzantium—

RUTHVEN: Constantinople, surely?   75

DARVELL: —Byzantium, when he caught a fever and fell gravely ill

RUTHVEN: What friend? His name, please

ELLA/DARVELL: I have sworn never to reveal his name

RUTHVEN: Then your story is full of holes

DARVELL: We were up in the mountains when his fever heightened and   80
I knew that he would be dead before I could get him down. We came
upon a high, deserted cemetery overshadowed by an ancient ruin, a
temple with a half-blasted statue—of Artemis the huntress. In the heat
of the day, the birds circling above, I laid him down to die

RUTHVEN: Your powers of fiction are most compelling, Sir   85

At some point during the next speech, Ella stops writing. She looks up, as if she is seeing what Darvell describes. Some of the sleepers begin to wake and listen.

DARVELL: He begged me for water. I got it and when I returned, I saw on a rock nearby a great bird with a serpent writhing in its beak

ELLA/DARVELL: It was looking at me.

DARVELL: I shouted a curse. The bird tossed the serpent into the air and devoured it. Then it spread its great wings and flew with slow grace   90
over the graves

Ella and Eleanor spread their arms as if they are wings.

I gave my friend water. Upon his neck was a mark, red and angry—like the two-pronged bite of a snake. "A miracle," he whispered. With the last of his strength he made me swear to tell no one of his death—an oath that I am breaking now—and he said that in a month's time, when the moon rose—   95

RUTHVEN: *(laughing)* What a fabulous tale. This is too fantastic!

Darvell stands.

DARVELL: You don't deserve my secret. The thought of bestowing that priceless gift on you—you'd waste it

Darvell looks straight at Clara.

I'd do better offering it to this girl. It'd be a fine thing, don't you think, to have an immortal whore? She could reap vengeance on mankind for ever more   100

All of the sleepers are now awake, listening.

RUTHVEN: What happened to your friend?

DARVELL: My friend died

RUTHVEN: He whispered the secret and died—perfect

DARVELL: I held him until he was cold as the rock he lay on

RUTHVEN: And then what?   105

DARVELL: I dug his grave. The bird watched as I worked, perched on the broken goddess, a hunched silhouette. In the shadows, it seemed to have a human shape. I buried him and then ran, stumbled through the night. At first light I saw the coast and found a town. I lay in a fever for a month, hallucinating terrors. I sent letters to Byzantium, requesting aid   110

RUTHVEN: Constantinople, surely—

DARVELL: And then, the evening that my boat was due to sail, I saw him—my friend—walking down by the harbour. At first I thought it was an apparition, but he approached and gripped my arm. A strange light was in his eyes, a cold burning as if everything he looked upon was a source   115
of wonder

RUTHVEN: A cold burning; very nice
DARVELL: He shook me by the hand and thanked me for my care of him.
     He was freezing
RUTHVEN: I don't believe a word   120
DARVELL: That's because you have no faith. But you're longing for it to be
     true. My secret for your fortune. I will tell you all: the location of the
     cemetery, the significance of the bird and what befell my friend
RUTHVEN: Where is he now?
DARVELL: Do we play?   125
RUTHVEN: We play
CLARA: I hardly dared breathe, hoping that the stranger would—

     Frank has entered. He stands just behind Ella.

FRANK: Hi

     Ella startles. The characters in her scene freeze.

Ella, sorry, did I scare you?
ELLA: No   130
FRANK: What are you doing?
ELLA: Drama coursework
FRANK: Oh, how's it going?
ELLA: Fine. I'll put it away

     She closes her book. Eleanor clicks her fingers. The characters in the
     scene disappear—except Clara.

FRANK: Mine's crap. I don't know what the hell he's talking about   135
ELLA: Who?
FRANK: Brecht. I mean, what's alienation anyway? Will you go out with me?
ELLA: What?
FRANK: Don't say yes. Forget I asked. I've just come from my session with
     the shrink   140
ELLA: Oh
FRANK: Yes, he wants to refer me
ELLA: To whom?
FRANK: More shrinks. Have you seen him yet?
ELLA: No   145
FRANK: Don't tell the truth, will you? It's a bad mistake
ELLA: Thank you
FRANK: I've been watching a lot of vampire films
ELLA: What for?
FRANK: Oh, you know, thought I'd try and get to know you better. They   150
     say some great stuff. I mean, once you get past the cape era you start

wondering what they're a metaphor for; you know, it might be Aids, heroin, anorexia, it might be the whole spiralling chaos of western society; not knowing the difference between good and evil—I mean not even being able to define the terms. And they're sexy and heartbroken and   155 mostly Californian and they keep coming out with fantastic clichés like, "It's easier to succumb to the darkness within than to fight the darkness without," and you get the feeling that if it wasn't for their nihilistic disregard for human life, they'd be the nearest thing we've got these days to gods   160

ELLA: Could you say that again?

FRANK: They used to be there just to terrify, as if the forces they represented had to be crushed by the righteous, but we don't want to crush them now. They fascinate us. Perhaps we are all becoming vampires. I mean, the way we devour everything. *(Pause.)* Can you see your reflec-   165 tion in a mirror, by the way?

ELLA: Not properly, no

FRANK: That must be disturbing

ELLA: It was at first. I'm used to it now

FRANK: I love your psychosis, Ella. It's epic. It's amazing   170

ELLA: You don't listen

FRANK: I'm having a party. It's not really a party. I'm only inviting you. But it's my birthday. Will you come?

ELLA: Yes

FRANK: Great   175

ELLA: I love the way you speak

FRANK: Do you?

ELLA: You're so human

CLARA: The great thing about being a whore is that no one remembers you're there. I could have been furniture that night   180

ELEANOR/CLARA: The stranger lost

CLARA: He forfeited his secret—and it fell right into my eavesdropping ear. Lord Ruthven soon departed for the East. I said that if he took me with him, he would get my constant service, free. By the time we reached Byzantium, my lungs were seeping blood. I prayed that I would live to   185 see my daughter grow

SCENE SIX

ELEANOR: Scene Six

GEOFF: Franklin's Party

TINA: Every year, since Franklin was five, he's had a geography quiz on his birthday

Tina is offering Ella a plate piled high with Jammie Dodgers.

GEOFF: Which African nation was known until recently as Zaire?   5

Tina makes a buzzing sound.

Tina
TINA: The Congo
GEOFF: I'm sorry, it's the Democratic Republic of Congo
TINA: Silly me
GEOFF: What phenomenon produces opposite weather conditions   10
    to El Niño?
TINA: Don't you like Jammie Dodgers, Eleanor?
ELLA: No thank you

Tina picks up another plate. Frank makes a buzzing sound.

GEOFF: Franklin
FRANK: La Niña   15
GEOFF: Ten points. Name two languages of Eritrea
TINA: These are luncheon-meat wrap-arounds. I made them myself
ELLA: No thank you
GEOFF: Come on, languages of Eritrea
TINA: Oh!   20

Tina makes a buzzing sound.

GEOFF: Tina
TINA: Tigrinyan and Arabic
GEOFF: Correct. One step closer to those chockies, Tina
TINA: How exciting

Tina exits with her plates.

GEOFF: If I was looking at a Sprite, where would I be?   25

Frank sighs. He buzzes.

Franklin
FRANK: You'd be in the middle of a lightning storm above the clouds
GEOFF: Ten points. Name the debris deposited by a receding glacier
ELLA: Terminal moraine
GEOFF: I'm sorry; strictly speaking it's just moraine   30
ELLA: Oh
FRANK: Will you give her the points?
GEOFF: I was looking for the generic term

Tina enters with a plate piled high with tinned peach halves.

FRANK: Give her the points, Geoff

GEOFF: Besides, I can't give her the points because she didn't buzz. You've   35
got to buzz, Eleanor

TINA: *(to Ella)* Do you like tinned peach halves? Franklin only gets them as
a very special treat

FRANK: Dad, will you please give Ella the points?

TINA: Have a peach half   40

ELLA: No thank you

GEOFF: I'm the / quizmaster

FRANK: You're totally unfair

ELLA: It doesn't matter

FRANK: Yes / it does   45

GEOFF: I can't award points unless they've been properly won according
to the rules

TINA: Go on, Eleanor—they're yummy

ELLA: No

TINA: What's wrong with them?   50

GEOFF: Name three different / kinds of—

FRANK: Right, I'm not playing

GEOFF: Franklin, I've bought these chocolates specially and I've spent
time and effort compiling a question list. We do a geography quiz
every year and we do it because you like it   55

FRANK: But I'm seventeen—

GEOFF: And I've taken that into account with my choice of questions.
Now pull yourself together and name three different kinds of
igneous rock

FRANK: I've had enough   60

TINA: Pumice

FRANK: I don't want to play

GEOFF: Buzz, Tina, buzz

Tina makes a buzzing sound.

Tina

FRANK: Shut up   65

TINA: Pumice, soapstone and—

FRANK: Shut up now, or I'll swear

GEOFF: How dare you

FRANK: I don't want to do a geography quiz. I don't want peach halves.
I don't want you or Tina at my party   70

TINA: Franklin, how could you say that?

GEOFF: You are so ungrateful. We did everything right

FRANK: Oh not / this again

GEOFF: We devoted ourselves to you. We could have had careers, holidays,
    fulfilling adult lives, but no. We exhausted ourselves ensuring your   75
    development. You had a reading age of twelve by the time you were
    six years old and one day you'll appreciate what that meant

FRANK: It meant I was alone, always

ELLA: Let's go for a walk in the car park, Frank. The magnolias are
    coming into bloom   80

FRANK: Yes

ELLA: And the bins are rainforest green

Frank takes Ella's hand.

FRANK: Eleanor's a vampire

TINA: Are you?

ELLA: Yes   85

FRANK: She's been alive for over two hundred years

TINA: Have you?

ELLA: Yes

TINA: I thought there was something about you, some whiff of depression

FRANK: Let's go   90

TINA: I know what it is. You're an anorexic

ELLA: No

TINA: I've got no patience with anorexics. I think you're rude and freakish.
    What's wrong with food?

FRANK: Come on   95

ELLA: I'm coming

GEOFF: Wherever you're going, young lady, whatever weird, starvation-
    induced visions you might be having, don't pull our son down
    with you

TINA: She won't even eat peaches, Franklin. She is embracing death.   100
    Keep away from her

SCENE SEVEN

FRANK: Scene Seven

CLAIRE: Car Park

ELLA: Embracing death?

FRANK: They won an award for designing this car park. I'm not surprised;
    if it wasn't for the cars you'd think you were in nirvana   5

ELLA: I'm not embracing death

FRANK: That was my best party yet

ELLA: I feel alive. I feel like I'm burning all the time. I feel raw with it

FRANK: Yes

ELLA: Something's going to happen. I can feel it coming; some   10
terrible change

FRANK: What if it's not terrible? What if it's good? What if it's amazing?

Frank tries to kiss her. Ella breaks away.

ELLA: I have to go

FRANK: Where?

ELLA: Back to Claire   15

FRANK: I'll come with you

ELLA: You can't

FRANK: Why not?

ELLA: Claire won't like you

FRANK: Doesn't matter   20

ELLA: You won't like her

FRANK: Why not?

ELLA: Because she'll tell you lies. Claire will try and tell you that I'm only
sixteen. She'll try to tell you that our mother died three years ago of
cancer. She'll try to tell you that they couldn't trace our useless sperm of   25
a father so they put me in a care home, Claire will tell you I got raped
there. She came and found me all withdrawn and suicidal. She'll tell you
how she fought for me, rescued me, breathed her life force into me. Since
then, she has been my mother. She'll tell you that we go from town to
town avoiding social workers and police, and that she sticks at low-paid   30
jobs because they give her opportunity to steal. She'll tell you how her
magpie heart is satisfied by simple, little pleasures. She'll say she lives each
moment to the full—and so she does. My sister-mother is ruthless Frank,
and so am I

FRANK: You're not ruthless—   35

Claire enters, laden with bags from fashion stores.

ELLA: Why don't you believe me? I keep telling you the truth

CLAIRE: So who's this, then?

They startle.

FRANK: Hi

ELLA: This is Frank. He's my friend

CLAIRE: Your *what?*   40

FRANK: Are you Claire? Great to meet you. I hear you're really good at
shoplifting and identity theft

CLAIRE: *(to Ella)* They've called me into your school. Why would that be?

ELLA: I expect it's because someone tried to put a stake through my heart

CLAIRE: Come indoors. Now. *(Referring to Frank.)* And send that home   45

She exits.

ELLA: You'd better go
FRANK: Why?
ELLA: She doesn't like you
FRANK: So what?
ELEANOR/ELLA: I don't want to hurt you   50
FRANK: I wouldn't care if you did
ELLA: Scene Eight
FRANK: Kiss me
ELLA: Scene Eight
FRANK: That's what vampires do, isn't it?   55
CLAIRE: Scene Eight

SCENE EIGHT

ELEANOR: Costume Cupboard
CLAIRE: You can call me Claire
MINT: Thank you so much for coming, Claire
CLAIRE: This is a nice classroom
MINT: It's a drama studio   5
CLAIRE: Lovely and dark. What's this over here?
MINT: The costume cupboard
CLAIRE: Oh I like dressing up, don't you?

Claire picks up Marianne's costumes. Eleanor is watching from the shadows.

MINT: Claire
CLAIRE: These are just like the real thing   10
MINT: How long have you had sole care of Eleanor?
CLAIRE: Since I was legally able. When our mother died three years ago,
    Ella was put in a care home. I got her out as soon as I could and she's
    been with me ever since
MINT: That's a great responsibility for someone so young   15
CLAIRE: There were monsters in that care home. I couldn't have left her
MINT: Well—respect
CLAIRE: Sorry, what's your name again?
MINT: The kids like to call me Mint
CLAIRE: You've got very nice hands, Mint   20
MINT: Thank you
CLAIRE: Can't help noticing. Elegant fingers
MINT: I'm sorry I had to call you in
CLAIRE: What's she been up to, Mint?

MINT: It's hard to know where to start. Because usually she's fine at school.   25
Usually, I'm not bothered

MINT: As part of their coursework the kids have to write a short scene

> *Eleanor clicks her fingers. Ruthven enters. He is looking for some-*
> *thing. He is not aware of Mint and Claire.*

MINT: Some kids just do little monologues, but Eleanor's written the best
part of a play—which is great/ don't get me wrong—

CLAIRE: A play? Isn't she clever?   30

MINT: The reason I've asked you to come in is the subject matter. Eleanor
is quite convinced that she's a vampire

> *Clara enters. She watches Ruthven, unaware of Claire and Mint.*

CLAIRE: I'm sorry?

MINT: Yes, and not only that; she thinks you're a vampire too

CLAIRE: What?   35

MINT: She says that you're not really her sister at all. She says you're
her mother

CLAIRE: A vampire mother?

RUTHVEN: *(to Clara)* What are you looking at?

CLARA: Nothing, My Lord   40

MINT: She says you were a nineteeth-century hooker

CLAIRE: She never did

MINT: And you became a vampire when she was just six years old—youth
everlasting

CLAIRE: Unbelievable   45

RUTHVEN: *(to Clara)* Are you laughing at me?

CLARA: I wouldn't dare

MINT: It's a really amazing story. I'm giving her an "A". She's got you
following some lord to a ruined cemetery near Constantinople

CLAIRE: Istanbul, surely   50

MINT: Lord Ruthven, she calls him. It's a name ripped off from an early
vampire story. You're dying of consumption, looking for the secret of
eternal life

RUTHVEN: I've searched every rock and stone in this godforsaken ruin and
no revelation has come. He lied to me. The secret is not here   55

CLARA: You don't see it, do you?

> *Clara is laughing. She is physically frail.*

RUTHVEN: Why are you laughing? What did he tell you? Where is it?

> *Clara shakes her head. Ruthven grabs her, furious.*

You know how to get it, don't you? You'd better tell me, or by God you'll
   regret it
MINT: He becomes totally incensed   60
RUTHVEN: If you make a fool of me, I swear I'll kill you
MINT: And he strikes you—very violent, quite disturbing, actually. In your
   weakened state, he kills you

> *Clara is dying—but smiling, triumphantly.*

CLARA: Eternal life will only come to those prepared to die
RUTHVEN: Then die   65
MINT: He lobs you into a tomb and leaves you. By the next full moon,
   he's preparing to sail for home and you find yourself reborn
CLAIRE: Wow

> *Ruthven has picked up Marianne's costume. He embraces it, as if
> it is a girl.*

MINT: You wake with a terrible thirst and set out to find Lord Ruthven.
   He's in a hotel room with a little girl he's paid to entertain him   70
CLARA: My Lord
RUTHVEN: Clara

> *Clara touches him. Ruthven is terrified.*

You're cold
CLARA: I'm burning
MINT: You realise that the worst fate for him would be to die slowly of all 75
   the sexually transmitted diseases he's picked up over the years

> *Clara takes Marianne's dress from Ruthven.*

CLARA: Your own corruption will kill you. You'll never be immortal—but
   this girl will
MINT: And you kill and drink his innocent prostitute right in front of him.
   Just to show him how powerful you are   80
CLAIRE: I'd never do that. No way. I'd never kill an innocent—
MINT: Eleanor says you're indiscriminate
CLAIRE: She must hate me
MINT: You show no mercy
CLAIRE: Mint, I'm stunned   85
MINT: Can we come out of the cupboard, please?

> *Eleanor clicks her fingers. Clara and Ruthven exit.*

CLAIRE: How could she write about me like that?

MINT: The trouble is, her vampire delusion is so carefully maintained and
so convincing that the rest of the group has completely rejected her. It
doesn't help that one of them recently disappeared—a kid called Dave   90
Briggs. Ran away from home, we think

CLAIRE: Dave what?

MINT: Briggs. D'you know him?

CLAIRE: Never come across him

MINT: Eleanor had taken an active dislike to him and now the others are   95
accusing her of macabre and outlandish crimes

> *Elsewhere. Point, Moon and Debit enter. They are wheeling a trolley
> on which Ella is tied, Hannibal Lecter-style. She has a sock shoved
> in her mouth.*

DEBIT: What have you done with him?

POINT: Where's Dave, you freak?

> *Point is brandishing a wooden stake. Ella tries to speak.*

DEBIT: Don't lie to us, you bloodsucking bitch—where's he gone?

POINT: He'd never disappear like that   100

MOON: He was too boring

POINT: And we were in love

DEBIT: So tell us where he is before we put a stake through your heart

> *Ella is furiously trying to make herself understood.*

MOON: If you took the sock out of her mouth she might talk. Otherwise
it's just mindless torture and I'm a member of Amnesty, OK, so I'm   105
a bit uncomfortable with this

POINT: *(pulling out the sock)* Where's Briggs?

ELLA: You have no idea how hard I'm fighting not to use my powers,
not to tear through these bonds and make a bloodbath of your flesh.
You have no idea how much self-control and godlike compassion   110
I am exercising

DEBIT: That is so pathetic

POINT: What did you do to Briggs?

ELLA: Nothing

POINT: He was beautiful   115

ELLA: He was an idiot—just the kind of moron I'd love to have killed,
but I didn't

POINT: Where is he?

MOON: There's a very real possibility that he just ran away. You know how
much he wanted to be interesting   120

POINT: He'd never have gone without me. We had dreams. We were going
    to live in a van and write songs about meaningful sex

ELLA: I wish I had claimed him as prey, I wish I'd gorged on his every last
    corpuscle—but I didn't

POINT: Something terrible has happened to him   125

ELLA: I'd have done humanity a service in culling him, but I didn't

DEBIT: You're going to pick us off one by one, aren't you?

POINT: Unless we finish you first—mutant

DEBIT: Stake her

POINT: Watch her age two hundred years. She'll decompose before   130
    our eyes

DEBIT: Her scream will rip out her throat

    Point raises the wooden stake.

MOON: I'm freaking out! I'm freaking out! I don't know what to do!
    We need a teacher

    Moon hurriedly wheels Ella off.

DEBIT: Bring her back here, Moon   135

POINT: I want violence! Violence!

    Point and Debit exit after Moon.

MINT: We found her outside the staff room, still tied to the trolley. There
    was a wooden stake shoved down her cardy

CLAIRE: I've tried so hard to be a mum to her—and a sister

MINT: I'm sure you've done everything you could   140

CLAIRE: She's my whole life, Mint

MINT: I've been speaking to the head teacher and to her counsellor.
    He's keen to refer her to psychiatric services

CLAIRE: You're not sending her to shrinks. They'd split us up

MINT: Maybe a short stay in a residential—   145

CLAIRE: NO WAY

MINT: Look, we're very sympathetic, but we can't ignore her problems.
    Eleanor needs more help than this school can currently offer

CLAIRE: Mint, if they took her away from me—my heart would break;
    right here   150

    Claire has taken Mint's hand and put it on her heart.

MINT: What are you doing? Let go of my hand please, Claire

    Claire moves closer.

CLAIRE: You want to help me, Mint; you know you do. Look at me

MINT: Claire, I made a decision a long time ago that relationships, feelings, human interaction; these things would only happen in the theatre for me—because real emotion doesn't come near the wild spectacle of the   155
stage. I live for creating drama. I've made it my life

CLAIRE: You must be so alone

MINT: No, anything can come out of this darkness, any character, any marvellous scene. I've been happy to wear down my health in the service of theatre   160

CLAIRE: You're so devoted

MINT: Yes—and the pinnacle of my achievement is A Level Drama. It sustains me every year. Claire, the worst thing about all of this, about your sister's breakdown, Briggs disappearing, the traumatising bullying, the very worst thing—   165

CLAIRE: What is it?

MINT: —the group won't work together. They are saying "No". Please try to understand

CLAIRE: I'll try

MINT: If I don't get Eleanor out of my class, they'll get a bad mark in their   170
practical. They might even get "D"s

Claire looks at Mint in utter disbelief. She moves closer.

CLAIRE: My heart bleeds for you. It really does

SCENE NINE

Eleanor is sitting at Ella's desk. Ruthven is behind her.

ELEANOR: Scene Nine

RUTHVEN: Education

Eleanor writes.

ELEANOR: Third of January 1822. Beloved diary, I love your clean white pages. They're like sheets in which my lonely thoughts can lie. Today I am sixteen   5

Ella enters. She is wearing a modern, pink nightdress.

ELLA: Sixteen

Eleanor rises. Ella sits in her place and starts writing.

ELLA/ELEANOR: Perhaps I will prick my finger on a spinning wheel and die

ELLA: Leticia and Harriet enter. Bettina, a maidservant, follows

Letty and Harriet enter. Bettina, a maidservant, follows.

LETTY: Eleanor?

HARRIET: There's a gentleman to see you— 10
LETTY: A gentleman in our school
ELEANOR: A gentleman?
HARRIET: He said
RUTHVEN: I'm here for Miss Webb
LETTY: For you, for you 15
BETTINA: *(taking Ruthven's coat)* I got to take his coat, and as he gave it
   to me he said
RUTHVEN: Thank you, child
BETTINA: And his hand brushed against my wrist, like a feather and, oh,
   it was like lightning, miniature lightning rushing up my arm 20
ELEANOR: Who is he?
ELLA: Lord Ruthven
HARRIET/LETTY: Lord Ruthven
BETTINA: Him
ELEANOR: But I don't know him. I've never heard of him 25
BETTINA: Mrs Skullpepper led him into the library. She asked him the
   purpose of his visit. He said—
ELLA/RUTHVEN: I have news of her mother
BETTINA: Mrs Skullpepper tried to question him, but he sent her away
RUTHVEN: My time is precious 30
HARRIET: He wants to see you alone
LETTY: Alone
HARRIET/LETTY: We're so jealous
ELEANOR: He has news of my mother?
BETTINA: He touched me right there 35
ELLA/ELEANOR: My mother is dead
LETTY: Look at his jacket
HARRIET: The best tailoring—just the best
BETTINA: Smell it
HARRIET: Oh, you can't! 40
BETTINA: Late nights
LETTY: Tobacco, some kind of faint scent
HARRIET: Don't! He'll be able to tell
LETTY: It smells of male
BETTINA: Did you see his boots? 45
HARRIET: Spattered with mud from his manly life
ELEANOR: My mother is dead. Why is he here?
HARRIET: It must be something dreadfully important
BETTINA: His expression
LETTY: It was grave, Ella 50
BETTINA: Dark and brooding

HARRIET: As if he's prey to some cureless inquietetude of mind
ELEANOR: Some what?
HARRIET: Inquietetude. He looks dangerous
ELEANOR: All men look dangerous when you're us. We've never seen   55
    any men
LETTY: He looks somehow blighted, too
BETTINA: Like a poor, wounded beast
HARRIET: Full of dark mystery
ELEANOR: Oh, stop it   60
BETTINA: When he touched me, it was lightning I felt. I'll never, never
    be the same again

    Bettina, Harriet and Letty exit. Eleanor approaches Ruthven.

ELEANOR: My Lord? I am Eleanor Webb

    She curtsies.

RUTHVEN: Eleanor Webb. Look at you. I know your mother
ELEANOR: My mother is dead, My Lord   65
RUTHVEN: Nonsense. I've been searching for her this past decade—ever
    since she stole my secret—and last week I found her. She is living not
    two miles from here and doing what she does best
ELEANOR: My Lord?
RUTHVEN: Keeping a brothel, a kennel, a dungheap, a whorehouse—do   70
    you understand me, child? Your mother sells human flesh
ELEANOR: *(to Ella)* Stop writing
ELLA: No
ELEANOR: Stop now
ELLA/RUTHVEN: And she preys on her customers like a carrion crow—picks   75
    them off one by one
ELEANOR: You know how it ends; please stop
ELLA: I don't understand you. My mother is dead
ELEANOR: *(to Ruthven)* I don't understand you. My mother is dead
RUTHVEN: Is that what they've told you?   80
ELEANOR: *(to Ella)* Don't make me go on!
RUTHVEN: My dear, they have nourished you on lies
ELLA/ELEANOR: What do you mean?
RUTHVEN: I'll be brief with you, Miss Webb. Your mother stole a secret
    from me and I'm here to steal something from her   85

    Ruthven takes hold of Eleanor.

ELEANOR: Let me go

RUTHVEN: Imagine my delight when I discovered you existed. Her precious, treasured daughter, the jewel she's hidden away for all these years

ELLA/ELEANOR: My mother is dead

RUTHVEN: Your mother believes that the pact of blood she made with the   90
gods and monsters makes her invincible. But I will cause her pain. I will
make her rage—as I raged when she stole my secret

ELEANOR: *(to Ella)* Don't let him touch me

RUTHVEN: I am dying, Miss Webb. I could have lived for ever but I'll soon
be dead. Your mother robbed me of life and I will rob you. You will   95
share my disease

ELEANOR: Mother—

RUTHVEN: A terrible disease for an innocent to catch. For there is only one
way to catch it, Miss Webb

ELEANOR: Mother—   100

RUTHVEN: And when I have finished with you—

> *Ella and Eleanor close their eyes and put their hands over their ears.*
> *The action freezes. Claire enters.*

CLAIRE: What are you doing? Ella

> *Claire takes Ella's hands from her ears.*

I've just been to see your teacher. Why are you telling people that we're
vampires?

ELLA: Leave me alone

CLAIRE: They will cart you away to the nuthouse   105

ELLA: Get out

CLAIRE: Why are you like this?

ELLA: YOU MADE ME LIKE THIS

> *Claire grabs Ella's script.*

CLAIRE: You are condemning yourself. They will section you. And once
they write "personality disorder" on your notes they will throw away   110
the key. I am fed up trying to save you

ELLA: Suppose I don't want to be saved?

CLAIRE: Is this your play?

ELLA: Yes

CLAIRE: How dare you   115

> *Claire reads the scene.*

RUTHVEN: Eleanor Webb. I know your mother

ELEANOR: My mother is dead

RUTHVEN: A dungheap. Carrion crow

ELEANOR: I don't understand
RUTHVEN: Nourished on lies   120
ELEANOR: My mother is dead
RUTHVEN: A secret
ELEANOR: Let me go
RUTHVEN: Disease
ELEANOR: Mother   125
RUTHVEN: Terrible for an innocent
ELEANOR: Mother
RUTHVEN: And when I have finished with you

> *Claire stops reading.*

CLAIRE: Very clever. What comes next?
ELLA: I can't write it   130
CLAIRE: A rape scene without a rape?

> *She drops the script.*

Why are you calling him Ruthven?

> *Ella doesn't respond. Claire exits. Ruthven releases Eleanor.*

RUTHVEN: Welcome to the adult world. Welcome, Miss Webb. Welcome
to a slow death. Welcome, you whore

> *He throws a coin at her.*

Give my regards to your mother   135

> *Ruthven exits. Ella goes to Eleanor. They cling to each other.*

ELLA: Eleanor, he didn't kill you
ELEANOR: I'm still dying
ELLA: He didn't kill you
ELEANOR: I'm dying
ELLA: Why have you let him win?   140

> *Eleanor fights her way out of Ella's arms. She exits. Ella is shocked
> that she has gone. Claire returns with a suitcase.*

CLAIRE: Right. Get packing

> *She starts putting Ella's things in the case.*

ELLA: What are you doing?
CLAIRE: We have to go
ELLA: Why?
CLAIRE: Because you've been telling people we're vampires!   145

ELLA: *(suspiciously)* What have you done, Mother?

CLAIRE: Don't call me that. I'm your sister

ELLA: What have you done?

CLAIRE: Nothing

ELLA: Then I'm not leaving   150

CLAIRE: We have to

ELLA: Why?

CLAIRE: Because you're right. This place is killing you. You're going small-town crazy. We'll go to London, wherever you like—

ELLA: I want to stay here   155

CLAIRE: Why?

ELLA: The magnolias are blooming. The bins are rainforest green

CLAIRE: When did you last eat?

ELLA: What's that got to do with anything?

CLAIRE: When did you last feed yourself? *(Pause.)* You're so unique,   160
Ella, you're so amazing. When are you going to start living? Look at you, you're starving

SCENE TEN

POINT: Scene Ten

FILLET: The Beast

> *The students of A Level Food Technology gather themselves. Ella is ill, withdrawn.*

In order to do my proper duty to you as a teacher of Food Technology—

FRANK: Eleanor

FILLET: —I have been trying to teach you about every edible thing on this   5
planet. We've gone into the Earth and returned bearing fruits

FRANK: I'm leaving Tina and Geoff. Come to London with me. We'll find somewhere to live, even if it's a protest tent on Westminster Green

ELLA: I can't

FRANK: Yes, you can   10

FILLET: We've spent many weeks delving into the vegetable. And now we must encounter the beast

FRANK: We can get crap jobs and at nights we'll lie there

FILLET: A new heading. Meat

FRANK: Trying to find stars in the light pollution, thinking up ways to   15
attack the consumerist system

FILLET: Franklin Stein! This lesson may bring you learning that will affect the rest of your life. I want you young people to leave my class secure in the knowledge that if society broke down and all the supermarkets

closed, you could walk into a field, butcher an animal and prepare   20
enough food to feed a village for a week

DEBIT: *(to Point)* Have you heard about Mint?

POINT: What?

FILLET: I'm harking back to a purer time, when we didn't consume meat
from factory abattoirs, vacuum-sealed in plastic; I'm harking back to   25
a time when we stroked and petted every beast we ate

DEBIT: Found this morning; dead as a doornail in the costume cupboard

POINT: No! Poor Mint

FILLET: If we killed it, we'd respect it

DEBIT: They're trying to tell us it was a stroke   30

POINT: No

FILLET: I am going to teach you to respect the beast. And one day, when
order breaks down into violence and chaos and starving hordes are
roaming the land, you will be the one who can hold up your cleaver
and say, "I did A Level Food Technology. I can save humanity!" So   35
today, adults of tomorrow, we shall begin our study of the beast by
investigating its life force. We are going to make blood pudding

Moon faints. Fillet arranges the ingredients.

FILLET: Onions finely chopped, a kilo of diced pork fat, two metres of
intestine, a litre of double cream, oatmeal, barley, salt, mace

*Fillet lifts a bowl filled with pig's blood onto the table. Ella stares at
it longingly.*

And here is our pig's blood. Pig's blood is identical to human blood by ninety-   40
eight per cent. Isn't that a strange fact? We are only two per cent different
from a pig. Mint is dead. Mint, my comrade, your teacher, has fallen. We
shall have a minute's silence at the end of the lesson but for now, contem-
plate this: GOD, WHY DID YOU MAKE US ONLY TWO PER CENT
DIFFERENT FROM A PIG? Forgive me. I'm wreckage this morning. I   45
loved Mint. Mint was an innocent. You get gallons of blood from each
mature beast, but here I have just two litres

FRANK: Eleanor—

Ella has walked up to the desk as if in a trance.

FILLET: Now, the pudding sticks better if the blood is warm. Get back to
your seat. Get back, I said. What are you doing?   50

ELLA: Forgive me

Ella lifts the bowl. She puts it to her lips.

Starving

The class erupts into screams. Pandemonium, as Ella drinks the blood.

POINT: It's her!
DEBIT: Her!
POINT: She killed Briggs   55
DEBIT: She killed Mint
DEBIT/POINT: Vampire!

A cacophony of screaming. Frank is watching, aghast. Blackout.

SCENE ELEVEN

CLARA: Scene Eleven

In the darkness:

ELEANOR: Deathbed
CLARA: Eleanor
ELEANOR: Who's there?

Clara strikes a light. She is sitting on the end of Eleanor's bed. Eleanor is wearing Ella's pink nightdress.

Who are you?   5
CLARA: My name is Clara Webb
ELEANOR: I've seen you before. When I was a child
CLARA: You're right
ELEANOR: You are an angel
CLARA: I used to climb in through your window and watch you while   10
    you slept
ELEANOR: My mother
CLARA: My girl
ELEANOR: I'm dying
CLARA: There's no need to die. I'll take you away with me   15
ELEANOR: A man was here
CLARA: I'll teach you how to live
ELEANOR: He has killed me
CLARA: You shall not die
ELEANOR: Mother   20
CLARA: I'll never leave you. Never leave you again

Clara gently bares Eleanor's neck. She blows out the light.

SCENE TWELVE

CLAIRE: Scene Twelve
DARVELL: Immortal
ELLA: Let me out of here! Let me out!

FILLET: You stay in that drama studio, down there in the darkness where
          you belong. My lab looks like carnage; apocalyptic. I'm not letting you   5
          out until they're here
ELLA: Who?
FILLET: The mental health-care professionals, those in authority, those
          with absolute power
ELLA: You've got no right to keep me   10
FILLET: Mint had files on you. Mint knew something was wrong
ELLA: What files? I demand to see them
FILLET: Mint was trying to help you, and look what you did
ELLA: I've done nothing

> *Ella looks down at her bloodsoaked clothes. She cries. Elsewhere,*
> *Claire is robbing a till.*

FRANK: Claire   15
CLAIRE: Who's asking?
FRANK: I'm Frank, your sister's friend
CLAIRE: Her what?
FRANK: You've got to come. They've contained her—locked her in the
          drama studio   20
CLAIRE: What's she done?
FRANK: She drank blood
CLAIRE: You're lying. You're sick for saying that
FRANK: She needs to get away. I want to take her to London with me
CLAIRE: You what?   25
FRANK: I'm running away from my parents
CLAIRE: How teen and cute
FRANK: I want to take Ella with me
CLAIRE: You're just her type, I must say. Earnest, clueless, about as sexy as a
          pair of sandals. But I know what's best for Eleanor. We're leaving now.   30
          And no one at that shit-heap school will ever hear of us again

> *Claire slams the till and makes to go.*

FRANK: Maybe that's why she did it
CLAIRE: Did what?
FRANK: Drank the blood—an act of protest
CLAIRE: Against what?   35
FRANK: You. Eleanor's written a story where she's spent two hundred years
          with you. So that must be what it feels like
CLAIRE: Ella couldn't survive without me
FRANK: I think it's the other way round. I think you rely on her for
          everything. You don't let anyone near her, do you? You're worse than   40
          my parents

CLAIRE: If it wasn't for me she'd be dead
FRANK: Personally, I think you're slowly killing her
CLAIRE: Are you in love with her, little Frank?
FRANK: Do you know anything about Mint's death?   45
CLAIRE: I beg your pardon?
FRANK: When we met you in the car park you were on your way to meet
    him. And next morning he was dead. And Briggs. Point saw you
    talking to him the night he went away
CLAIRE: You're playing a very dangerous game, little Frank   50

    Frank makes his fingers into a crucifix.

FRANK: Are you threatening me?
CLAIRE: I'm just giving you a warning. I am by nature indiscriminate.
    I learnt to be promiscuous when I was still a child. But with Ella,
    it's all about love
FRANK: What do you mean?   55
CLAIRE: It's tragic really. It's like the saying with her: "Each man kills
    the thing he loves"
FRANK: Ella's not a man
CLAIRE: When she's finished with you, you'll be left hanging like a cheap
    suit on a washing line. We use people up. That's what we do. We're   60
    survivors

    The drama studio. Ella has dressed up in a costume from the costume
    cupboard.
    Eleanor enters, wearing Ella's pink nightgown.

ELEANOR: People will always believe the most fabulous tale you can tell.
    The fabulous tale is the one that they long for. It must be unprovable,
    impossible, fantastical. To believe it then becomes an act of faith
ELLA: An act of faith. Every prisoner should have the means to write. It   65
    says so in the Geneva dramatic convention. I demand a pen and paper
ELEANOR: Enter Darvell. He is dressed as a Doctor of Psychiatry

    Darvell enters. He is dressed as a Doctor of Psychiatry.

DARVELL: Eleanor? My name is Darvell
ELLA: What do you want?
DARVELL: I'm a doctor   70
ELLA: What kind of doctor?
DARVELL: The kind who seeks to heal
ELLA: Do I know you?
DARVELL: I'd like to help you, Eleanor
ELLA: May I have a pen and paper?   75

DARVELL: In due time, you shall have everything you want

ELLA: I need to finish my story

DARVELL: Of course you do

ELLA: It's about a girl. She meets a boy. He's a genius, but every bit as
friendless as she. The girl has been alone for a long time. The boy   80
tries to bring her back to life. But her past is gone; the present
hurts; she has no future. She is the beetle who crawled into amber

DARVELL: What do you mean?

ELLA: I cannot die, though I know I am dead. I am hungry all the time
but I cannot eat. My desires are destructive. I live off others. I am   85
alone. I am a vampire. / Do you believe me?

ELEANOR: Do you believe me? Am I mad?

DARVELL: I don't know what madness is. There is only pain and our
ability to bear it. Sometimes, when the pain is too great, the mind
can no longer withstand it, and it breaks   90

ELLA: When we devour, it's because it's our nature

DARVELL: But our natures are able to change. Change can be painful.
It can feel like a mortal blow

ELLA: It hurts

DARVELL: All pain can be relieved   95

ELLA: I feel immortal, sir, but not alive

     Eleanor clicks her fingers. Claire and Frank enter.

CLAIRE: She's sixteen. She's a sixteen-year-old kid. You can't legally section
her—she's too young

DARVELL: In order to help her, I need to take her away

FRANK: Ella, he's from a secure institution. Don't go with him. There's   100
nothing wrong with you

CLAIRE: *(to Frank)* Listen, you tank-topped desperado, you've got no
right to be here and nothing to say. This situation is none of your
business

FRANK: Yes, it is   105

CLAIRE: I'm her legal guardian. She's mine

DARVELL: Eleanor is free to come with me

CLAIRE: Ella, he thinks he's God in a white coat

ELLA: Mother—

CLARA: My girl   110

CLAIRE: I'm not your mother. Don't leave me

CLARA: Please

CLAIRE/CLARA: I got nothing else

ELLA: *(turning to him)* Frank—

FRANK: I want nothing from you   115

DARVELL: You're under my protection now
ELLA: Frank—
FRANK: Run. This way. Quick
ELLA: No—through here

> *Eleanor clicks her fingers. The action freezes, as if Frank and Ella are alone in a pocket of time.*

FRANK: This isn't the exit   120
ELLA: I know
FRANK: Where are we?
ELLA: The costume cupboard. Lock the door

> *Clara, Claire and Darvell exit.*

FRANK: We're trapped, Ella. Why didn't you run for the exit?
ELLA: I love it in here. You can be anything you like   125
FRANK: Come to London with me
ELLA: We'll protest
FRANK: Yes
ELLA: Against what?
FRANK: Ella, unless we act, unless we stop devouring everything, unless   130
          we try to understand what it means to be human, in two hundred,
          a hundred, in fifty years' time . . . we'll be nothing. We must protest
          even if we're inarticulate, even if our only word is "No". There's so
          much to do. Don't hide away in your pain
ELLA: I love the way you speak   135

> *Frank tries to kiss her. She stops him.*

I'm writing a story, Frank. It's a vampire story
FRANK: I know. But it's just a story. It isn't real. You're real
ELLA: Frank
ELEANOR: *(writing)* Frank, you can't have a vampire story
ELLA: You can't have a vampire story   140
ELEANOR: Unless
ELLA: Unless there are vampires in it
ELEANOR: I'm sorry
ELLA: I'm so sorry
FRANK: Don't be sorry   145

> *Frank and Ella kiss. A beautiful kiss, straight from a Gothic tale. As the kiss goes on, Ella gently bares Frank's neck. Eleanor watches them.*

SCENE THIRTEEN

DARVELL: Scene Thirteen
ELEANOR: Byzantium

Morning light. Birdsong.

DARVELL: Good morning, Eleanor
ELEANOR I've finished my story, Doctor
DARVELL: Well done   5
ELEANOR: I worked all night. Right though the darkness
DARVELL: That's very good. I look forward to it. You have a wonderful flair
ELEANOR: Thank you
DARVELL: Now, you've been alone in here long enough. It's time to come
  down. Your sister is coming to visit   10
ELEANOR: My mother?
DARVELL: Your sister. Did you forget?

Eleanor turns away.

Perhaps you'll try and eat a bit of something for her today

Eleanor nods.

That's very good. Now, what would you like to wear? Eleanor, will you choose
  some clothes?   15
ELEANOR: I'd like to wear my costume, please

The End.

- Buffini claims that vampires are the most sympathetic of the monsters we have created. Does that sentiment appear in this play?
- How do the characters exhibit qualities that are appropriate to vampires? How are these images conveyed to the people they associate with?
- Are Clara and Eleanor vampires?

Experiencing Literature through Writing

1. Locate a single symbol within a specific work. Describe how attention to this symbol is appropriate and lends insight into the larger work.
   a. How can you justify your claim that this particular detail is symbolic? Explain how this detail relates to other specific details within the text.
   b. Are there strong alternative readings of this symbol? What would be the implications of this alternative?
   c. How is attention to this symbol important to the text as a whole?

2. Identify the allegorical elements within a particular text. As you make your claim that this text functions allegorically, you must justify your argument that it is appropriate to find allegory in the text.

   a. What signals has the author given to justify an allegorical reading?
   b. How does the surface narrative lend itself to allegorical interpretations?
   c. What tensions do you find between the surface narrative and the allegorical reading?
   d. How does this allegory allow an approach to a social, political, or cultural issue that might not be possible with a less subtle approach?

3. Some of the readings in this chapter are grouped under the broad category of Gothic romance. The idea of truth with a capital *T* signals an ideal that we assume is impossible to achieve. Allegory here is useful because the enterprise itself is fantastic. Discuss the element of the fantastic as it appears in one (or more) of these works. What details give the work a fantastic feel? How do these elements support (or undermine) the allegorical or didactic elements of the work?

4. The inclination to find a clear meaning or message in a text sometimes blinds us to other significant aspects of that text. In this discussion, argue against the impulse to make these texts allegorical. Explain how a reading of the surface narrative allows an interesting insight into this text that an allegorical reading might ignore.

13 Context

What Factors Outside the Text Influence Our Experience of the Text? What Do We Really Need to Know?

It's often claimed that great art transcends the specific context within which it is produced: great works are timeless. That common assertion seems credible enough when we think of Greek drama, or *Othello*, or *Don Quixote*. But as durable as such masterpieces have proven to be, it seems far too simple to cite abstract "universals" like *anger*, *love*, *jealousy*, and *idealism* as the source of our continued appreciation. It's more accurate to say that great art prompts fresh, varied, powerful, new, and concrete experiences of fundamental human concerns. A play like *Othello* hasn't so much transcended our time as it has *absorbed* our time and remained powerful. Issues of race, for example, can't ultimately mean the same thing for twenty-first-century Americans that they meant for the Elizabethan audience. That gap between then and now contributes to literature's power to make us bigger—to enlarge our sense of who we are and of the world that surrounds us.

Good reading involves sustaining a healthy tension. On one hand, we don't want to disregard a text's origins. We want to understand the history and culture the author was a part of. Yet on the other hand we cannot—and should not—avoid experiencing art in terms of who we are now. We cannot avoid bringing new knowledge to old texts. In this chapter, we'll consider how our contemporary situation affects our experience of art as well as how knowledge of a work's historical context can deepen that experience.

HOW DOES NEW KNOWLEDGE INFLUENCE OUR EXPERIENCE OF OLD TEXTS?

In writing about the action that takes place in a literary text, it's customary to use the present tense. Shakespeare wrote *Othello* early in the seventeenth century, but Othello *kills* Desdemona every time we read the play. This is a small stylistic convention, but it's a convention that suggests something important. *A literary text comes alive as we experience it; the action is always present.* Othello the play and Othello the character aren't frozen in place by the words on the page. If we keep this in mind, we can understand how it is that our *Othello* isn't necessarily the same *Othello* that someone in Victorian England might have experienced. And, of course, texts Victorians produced aren't necessarily read today as they were when they first appeared.

Over a century and a half ago, Alfred, Lord Tennyson read a newspaper account of a confused and disastrous cavalry charge of British soldiers in the Crimean War. He was inspired to commemorate that event. Tennyson's poetic intent was to valorize his country's military men. They served, followed orders, and died valiantly in a cause. Tennyson's key themes were loyalty, courage, discipline, and patriotism. He wrote from a conviction of his country's goodness and the legitimacy of its imperialistic endeavors. The poem was a great success in some ways, exactly the sort of poem a poet laureate (the official poet of the state) was expected to produce. Since its appearance, many a school child both in Great Britain and in the United States has stood before a class and dutifully recited "The Charge of the Light Brigade." Despite the poem's popularity, there has always been a ripple of uneasiness among some readers about the tone of unqualified military zeal it endorses. The actual light brigade, after all, charged forward to death on botched orders in service of a dubious cause. That ripple grew to waves in England after the First World War and in the United States during the Vietnam War. Tennyson's poem today hardly works as a lofty tribute; we're more likely to respond to themes of waste, futility, and patriotic vanity—themes that Tennyson himself didn't intend to strike.

Alfred, Lord Tennyson (1809–1892)

The Charge of the Light Brigade (1854)

1

Half a league, half a league,
Half a league onward,
All in the valley of Death

Rode the six hundred.
"Forward the Light Brigade!   5
Charge for the guns!" he said.
Into the valley of Death
Rode the six hundred.

                    2
"Forward, the Light Brigade!"
Was there a man dismayed?   10
Not though the soldier knew
   Someone had blundered.
Theirs not to make reply,
Theirs not to reason why,
Theirs but to do and die.   15
Into the valley of Death
   Rode the six hundred.

                    3
Cannon to right of them,
Cannon to left of them,
Cannon in front of them   20
   Volleyed and thundered;
Stormed at with shot and shell,
Boldly they rode and well,
Into the jaws of Death,
Into the mouth of hell   25
   Rode the six hundred.

                    4
Flashed all their sabers bare,
Flashed as they turned in air
Sab'ring the gunners there,
Charging an army, while   30
   All the world wondered.
Plunged in the battery smoke
Right through the line they broke;
Cossack and Russian
Reeled from the saber stroke   35
   Shattered and sundered.
Then they rode back, but not,
   Not the six hundred.

5

Cannon to right of them,
Cannon to left of them,
Cannon behind them
   Volleyed and thundered;
Stormed at with shot and shell,
While horse and hero fell.
They that had fought so well
Came through the jaws of Death,
Back from the mouth of hell,
All that was left of them,
   Left of six hundred.

40

45

6

When can their glory fade?
O the wild charge they made!
   All the world wondered.
Honor the charge they made!
Honor the Light Brigade,
   Noble six hundred!

50

55

Tennyson invokes a number of abstractions he could expect to be taken as "universals": nobility, bravery, self-sacrifice, and honor. He writes with a confident assumption that those abstractions will long endure: "All the world" is caught in rapt admiration of the brigade's martial virtues. The closing stanza asks the question ("When can their glory fade?") that implies an answer: not for a long, long time, not for as long as we honor courage and steadfast loyalty to a cause.

Tennyson could not envision the human costs of the First World War, nor could he be expected to imagine wars in Vietnam or Iraq from the perspective of a U.S. citizen. But these wars are part of our political, moral, and historical identity. Lines like "Theirs not to reason why, / Theirs but to do and die" strike most of us as disturbing and even dangerous. It's worth noting that we commonly misquote these lines in a way that diminishes the discomfort they have come to produce. One may hear the phrase repeated as "theirs but to do *or* die." It may seem a small matter, but *or* serves to soften Tennyson's point and perhaps helps sustain his romantic notions of war. If we charge forward boldly enough, we may die but we may instead accomplish something and still live (do and *not* die). Tennyson, writing in 1856, seemed so secure in his ideals of duty that a perfect willingness to "do *and* die" only underscored for him the nobility of the act.

Perhaps the quickest way to imagine a modern counterpoint to Tennyson's vision is to recall any one of several notable American films about the war in Vietnam. For example, Francis Ford Coppola's *Apocalypse Now* (1979) depicts

Apocalypse Now (1979)

commitment to the cause as a kind of insanity, or perhaps even more accurately Coppola depicts zealous military commitment as a cause of insanity. *Apocalypse Now* is based on Joseph Conrad's novel of the effects of imperialism in the Congo at the end of the nineteenth century. Both *Heart of Darkness* and *Apocalypse Now* strip away the sorts of abstract notions that Tennyson calls on for inspira-

> **Making Connections**
>
> Varied elements of any work of art will work together to achieve an effect. How does the rhythm and pace of "Charge of the Light Brigade" complement the theme? How do the rhymes work to mark Tennyson's perspective on the event? Does Tennyson's technical command make the poem compelling, or does it merely exaggerate themes many modern readers find problematic (see Chapter 6)?

tion. Coppola uses the grand sweep of the film screen to suggest the enormity of destruction, cruelty, and death. He undercuts rather than invokes patriotic themes.

HOW IS KNOWLEDGE "OUTSIDE" THE TEXT HELPFUL?

Some poems manage to generalize on matters of the human condition in ways that hold up, or promise to hold up, very well. As much as we warn you against easy notions of "universals," we don't want to dismiss what has long been a

©Zoetrope/United Artists/The Kobal Collection

motivating belief in the enduring power of art. Czeslaw Milosz, in "A Song on the End of the World," relies upon simple images to invoke a sense of the universal. In Milosz's poem, nature provides a constant: bees approach the flower, porpoises jump, sparrows play. Human activity runs a familiar course: fishermen mend nets, women walk in fields, a drunkard "grows sleepy." While Milosz employs concrete images of nature and everyday life, in the body of the poem he has deliberately avoided the sorts of specifics that allow us to "locate" the action in any narrow way; we are not tied to any particular time and place.

Czeslaw Milosz (1911–2004)

A Song on the End of the World (1944)

On the day the world ends
A bee circles a clover,
A fisherman mends a glimmering net.
Happy porpoises jump in the sea,
By the rainspout young sparrows are playing   5
And the snake is gold-skinned as it should always be.

On the day the world ends
Women walk through the fields under the umbrellas,
A drunkard grows sleepy at the edge of a lawn,
Vegetable peddlers shout in the street   10
And a yellow-sailed boat comes nearer the island,
The voice of a violin lasts in the air
And leads into a starry night.

And those who expected lightning and thunder
Are disappointed.   15
And those who expected signs and archangels' trumps
Do not believe it is happening now.
As long as the sun and the moon are above,
As long as the bumblebee visits a rose,
As long as rosy infants are born   20
No one believes it is happening now.
Only a white-haired old man, who would be a prophet
Yet is not a prophet, for he's much too busy,
Repeats while he binds his tomatoes:
There will be no other end of the world,   25
There will be no other end of the world.

Warsaw, 1944

Now ask yourself, what is the last line of this poem? One answer seems obvious: "There will be no other end of the world." But another possible answer lies just below that line: "*Warsaw, 1944.*" Milosz included that identifying place and date in the text of the poem as it appears in his collected poems. If taken as part of the poem, it stands as a resonant and dramatic close that influences how we absorb the lines that precede it. Poland was sacrificed to the Germans by the rest of the world in hopes that Hitler's ambitions would find a limit. Those ambitions knew no limits, and the cost to Poland, particularly Polish Jews, was staggering. By 1944, the disaster had unfolded for all to see who were willing to look and not flinch. Only the most deliberately resistant could refuse to acknowledge the end of the world that was "happening."

Milosz has achieved in this poem a balanced tension that he seeks in so many of his poems: The desire to find something real and eternal is set against a recognition of the most profound dishonesty or disconnection; the need to identify what it means to be human is placed in the context of a brutal, inhuman history. He wants us to engage the universal and the particular, the abstract and the concrete. If we don't know anything of Milosz's life, of the history he has experienced—if we erase "*Warsaw, 1944*" from the end of his poem, we still have a beautiful poem. But with that historical marker, we're prompted to think not only of Poland's tragic history, but also of how the poem applies to the various large-scale traumas that have unfolded within our own history. We can add new particulars to give the abstractions life. The best readers will respond with curiosity about Milosz's closing signal and a willingness to follow it by learning more of the author, his poetry, and the history he grapples with. Those readers will also consider how Milosz speaks from this rich context to our condition now.

Experiencing Literature in Context

The following biographical sketch of Milosz touches only lightly on major events of a long and full life, but even the barest knowledge of such events will influence responses to Milosz's poetry.

CZESLAW MILOSZ BIOGRAPHY

Czeslaw Milosz (1911–2004) was born in Wilno, Lithuania, which was then controlled by czarist Russia. At the outbreak of World War I, his father was drafted as a engineer by the czar's army, and the family spent the war years traveling throughout Russia and Siberia. After the Russian Revolution in 1917, the family returned to the village of his birth. Milosz published his first poems in 1930, the year after he graduated from high school.

In 1935, he began to work for Polish Radio. During the first days of World War II, he was sent to the front as a radio operator. In January 1940, he returned to Wilno and was caught there when Soviet tanks entered the city. In July, he escaped across Soviet lines into Poland and spent most of the war in Nazi-occupied Warsaw working for underground presses.

After the war, Milosz came to the United States as a diplomat for the new government of the People's Republic of Poland. In 1950, he was transferred to Paris where he requested and was granted asylum the following year. He spent the next decade writing in Paris. Among the most famous of his works during this period is *The Captive Mind* (1953), in which Milosz writes about "the vulnerability of the twentieth-century mind to seduction by sociopolitical doctrines and its readiness to accept totalitarian terror for the sake of a hypothetical future." In 1960, he accepted a post at the University of California, Berkeley. He was awarded the Nobel Prize in Literature in 1981. That year, he returned to Poland for the first time since his exile in 1951 and met with solidarity leader Lech Walesa. Shortly thereafter, Polish presses published Milosz's poetry, making it possible for Poles to read their celebrated national poet for the first time. Milosz's wife, Janka, died in 1986 after a ten-year battle with Alzheimer's disease. His second wife, Carol, died in 2002.

Now as you read the next Milosz poem, you are prepared in subtle yet profound ways to experience more in the act of reading. His reflection in "Christopher Robin" on much-loved characters from a famous children's book, for example, can hardly be seen as mere playfulness once we know something of what Milosz had lived through.

Czeslaw Milosz (1911–2004)

Christopher Robin (1998)

In April of 1996, the international press carried the news of the death, at age seventy-five, of Christopher Robin Milne, immortalized as Christopher Robin in the book,
Winnie-the-Pooh, by his father, A. A. Milne.

I must think suddenly of matters too difficult for a bear of little brain. I have never asked myself what lies beyond the place where we live, I and Rabbit, Piglet and Eeyore, with our friend Christopher Robin. That is, we continued to live here, and nothing changed, and I just ate my little something. Only Christopher Robin left for a moment.

Owl says that immediately beyond our garden Time begins, and that it is an awfully deep well. If you fall in it, you go down and down, very quickly, and no one knows what happens to you next. I was a bit worried about Christopher Robin falling in, but he came back and then I asked him about the well. "Old Bear," he answered. "I was in it and I was falling and I wore trousers down to the ground, I had a gray beard, then I died. It was probably just a dream, it was quite unreal. The only real thing was you, old bear, and our shared fun. Now I won't go anywhere, even if I'm called for an afternoon snack."

What do you make of Christopher Robin's remark to Pooh that falling   5
into "Time" is "quite unreal"? Is Milosz suggesting that "real" life is full of delusions? Could he be commenting instead (or in addition) on how strenuously some people escape living actively and responsibly? Do you think the world of "Time" is real for Milosz?

DO WE NEED TO KNOW *EVERYTHING* IN ORDER TO UNDERSTAND?

Poems like "The Charge of the Light Brigade," "A Song on the End of the World," and "Christopher Robin" help us consider questions about what knowledge we need to bring to texts as well as what knowledge we unavoidably bring to texts. These poems also help us respond to a problem some people have with reading serious literature or seeing ambitious plays and films: serious works (the complaint goes) demand "too much" knowledge. We believe that it's a rare text that asks "too much" of a reader. The charge of "too much" builds on a mistaken and unrealistic notion of "understanding." Understanding or not understanding is rarely an either–or proposition. In reading or viewing a challenging text, it's common that we gain some understanding as we read or view it, and seek more as we write, reread, and "re-see" it. It's also normal to *not* understand some things at the same time we respond powerfully to others. Dismissing the task as too hard from the outset presumes that reading is something we do in a straight line and that when we get to the end of the line our reading is over; once the pages are turned we're *done*. This misleading notion of reading presumes that the only good reading is a "complete" reading. But denying the centrality of process cuts us off from the chance to discover what the text may offer. It forces us to think of one final understanding that we must get to validate our effort. It dismisses the renewed and deepened pleasure one can experience in successive readings. It also prevents us from acquiring the "knowledge" that we sometimes complain we don't possess. So what we don't know about European history shouldn't stop us from reading Milosz and coming to a valuable understanding of his work; and reading Milosz will help us learn a great deal about European history.

It might seem odd to move from Milosz's poem to a one-liner in a Woody Allen story, but jokes illustrate nicely how one can sometimes "understand"

©Warner Bros/First National/The Kobal Collection

"Just don't get ontological, not now. I couldn't bear it if you were ontological with me."

quite a bit without "knowing" much. In "Mr. Big," a comic detective piece, Allen presents a scene in which a glamorous woman clings to a tough, "hard-boiled" detective named Kaiser Lupowitz and pleads, "Just don't get ontological, not now. I couldn't bear it if you were ontological with me." Even with the minimal context we've supplied, it's possible you find the line funny. We can use it as a caption for the photograph from *The Maltese Falcon* (1941) to mimic the joke's working dynamic.

If the photograph has absolutely no resonance for you (you've *never* seen Bogart play a detective, *never* read Raymond Chandler or Dashiell Hammet, *never* read or seen other works of this type), the line will fall flat. Although some slight knowledge is absolutely necessary, extensive knowledge really isn't required to "get" the joke. You need to know only enough to sense, for example, that most tough guys in detective stories aren't named "Kaiser Lupowitz." More important, you need to know enough to recognize that the word *ontological* doesn't fit the character type of the speaker. You don't even need to know what *ontological* means as long as you recognize that the word doesn't sound tough, sexy, or colloquial. So we can have one kind of understanding (the word *sounds* funny) without another kind of understanding (the definition of the word). In this case, the former kind of understanding is far more important than the latter. By the way, *ontological* pertains to a philosophical theory of reality that presumes universal and essential characteristics of all existence. Knowing that, we think, doesn't make the joke much funnier.

We're not suggesting that knowing things isn't important, but we are claiming that

- We often *do* know more than we realize.
- We don't need to know *everything* to *understand many things* very well.
- We acquire new knowledge by encountering things we don't know.

Experiencing Art in Context

Look carefully at the painting *Young Man at His Window*. The painting evokes in most people a sense of loneliness. The young man, back turned to us, stands by himself in a room and looks out on almost empty streets. Everything darkens from the window inward; the young man seems boxed in. The railing and the window frame separate the young man from the world outside. That outside world also seems contained. The large buildings across from his room close in the street on all sides. Only a small bit of sky shows at the top of the picture. The city is all around, and yet people

Man at the Window. 1875 (oil on canvas), Caillebotte, Gustave (1848-94)/Private Collection/The Bridgeman Art Library

Gustave Caillebotte, *Young Man at His Window* (1875)

are almost entirely absent. Only one woman is visible on the streets below the young man's window, and she is a distant figure. The young man seems tired, disconnected, and alone.

This interpretation may be argued from the painting itself. What is within the frame can inspire a thoughtful response—a valuable level of understanding. But we don't need to stop at that level. Caillebotte was not only a painter, he was also a collector and a scholar. He knew Caspar David Friedrich's "Wanderer above the Sea of Fog" (see Chapter 4, p. 391) very well. Friedrich's painting spoke to the Byronic spirit of his day. That is, it captured a feeling for the powerful man depicted by the Romantic poet Byron who sought to move beyond the limits set by society. It placed a grand figure on a mountaintop aggressively confronting the vastness of nature itself. One could argue that Caillebotte echoes Friedrich's painting. He has his figure stand—like the wanderer—with his back to us as he looks over the world before him. But Caillebotte's figure strikes a less-confident pose. A visible shrug seems much different than the posture of the one who has just strode to the top of a mountain. The city, not nature, spreads out in front of Caillebotte's young man. In fact, nature has nearly been squeezed out of the picture. If we see Caillebotte's painting as a conscious revision of (and commentary on) Friedrich's well-known work, our response to "Young Man at His Window" will become more richly textured, although not necessarily more correct or even necessarily different in the main points. The theme of "loneliness" now might be seen more sharply as a condition of urban life. Caillebotte may well be commenting on a broad-scale cultural change: As an earlier generation "conquered" nature, the new generation has become progressively disconnected from life as it deals with the consequences of that conquering. There's no space for Caillebotte's young man to move, no opportunities for a heroic gesture.

> ## Making Connections
>
> Artists who choose to deal with historically distant subjects may find ways to build the necessary context into their work. In "Shelley," for example, the contemporary poet Galway Kinnell provides information that allows readers who may know nothing of the title subject to understand the essential point he wants to make (see Chapter 7). The poem is for the most part a brief and wrenching summary of key events in Shelley's domestic life (suicides of lovers, deaths of children). That summary is framed by two different perspectives: one of youthful idolatry and the other of painful disengagement. Kinnell includes a great deal of fairly short space that allows readers to understand his poem without having read previously about Shelley's life. To what extent does reading Kinnell's poem prompt you to learn more? Do you think it likely that reading a more sympathetic biography would influence your experience of Kinnell's "Shelley"?

WHAT IF SUBSTANTIAL OUTSIDE KNOWLEDGE IS ESSENTIAL?

What happens to a literary text that gets heavily caught up in historical particulars? Can an audience's shifting interests and changed knowledge base make a great work into an irrelevant or hopelessly opaque work? These are questions that we need to consider even if we can't finally answer them. Some texts do require us to work, and it's reasonable that we ask if the effort is worth it. Herman Melville's "The House-Top," like Milosz's "A Song on the End of the World," makes a date important to the reading of the poem. Melville provides the date up front with a subheading that fleshes out the setting (on a "house-top" at night). But for most readers, the date marks nothing specific that easily comes to mind. And the setting hardly helps upon first reading. Our guess is that you'll find it impossible to get a grip on the following poem without some background from outside the text that lies outside most readers' knowledge base. Still, we'll present the poem here without preparation. Read it to the end, even though you'll likely feel lost. Then return to the poem once you've read the background information we provide.

Herman Melville (1819–1891)

The House-Top (1866)

A Night Piece.
(July, 1863)

No sleep. The sultriness pervades the air
And binds the brain—a dense oppression,
As tawny tigers feel in matter shades,
Vexing their blood and making apt for ravage.
Beneath the stars the roofy desert spreads   5
Vacant as Libya. All is hushed near by.
Yet fitfully from the far breaks a mixed surf
Of muffled sound, the Atheist roar of riot.
Yonder, where parching Sirius set in drought,
Balefully glares red Arson—there—and there.   10
The Town is taken by its rats—ship-rats
And rats of the wharves. All civil charms
And priestly spells which late held hearts in awe—
Fear-bound, subjected to a better sway
Than sway of self; these like a dream dissolve,   15

And man rebounds whole aeons back in nature.
Hail to the low dull rumble, dull and dead,
And ponderous drag that shakes the wall.
Wise Draco comes, deep in the midnight roll
Of black artillery; he comes, though late;   20
In code corroborating Calvin's creed
And cynic tyrannies of honest kings;
He comes, nor parlies; and the Town, redeemed,
Gives thanks devout; nor, being thankful, heeds
The grimy slur on the Republic's faith implied,   25
Which holds that Man is naturally good,
And—more—is Nature's Roman, never to be scourged.

In "The House-Top," Melville is casting a very specific event in broad philosophical and theological terms. He's placing a contemporary situation in relation to
distant historical periods to universalize the poem; he raises fundamental questions about law, power, and human nature. The problem is that almost all readers today are at a loss to get either the specific or the general as it plays out in
this poem. Melville was a voracious reader, and the knowledge he draws on can
be baffling—even off-putting. To make things more difficult still, the event that
inspired him to write is not one that gets much space in most general history
textbooks. Is this poem, then, dead as a piece of literature? If not, what must we
do to rescue it or, as a scholar might say, preserve it as literature?

The questions we've asked are the sorts of questions you'll ultimately have
to answer for yourself, but we think that "The House-Top" is absolutely worth
the demands it makes, that even the slightest historical gloss makes the poem
not only accessible but urgently alive. July 1863 is the date of the draft riots that
occurred in the city of New York. Hundreds of young men (mostly poor young
men because the wealthy could choose to buy their way out of the draft) rebelled
at the prospect of forced service in the union cause. These men blamed the city's
blacks for their situation. If it were not for the North's abhorrence of slavery,
there would be no civil war. At least that was the feeling of the moment. The
angry crowds moved through the city at night and turned much of their frenzied
energy on those they blamed. They burned a black church and a black orphanage: people suffered, people died. Melville, who lived in New York, was appalled.
For him, the fact of slavery made the Civil War a moral necessity for the North.
That citizens would attack helpless people in defiance of that cause was a profound mark of human depravity. The rioters, then, are the "rats" that have taken
the town. The personified "red Arson" glares from flames seen, and the "Atheist
roar" can be heard from the house-top. The town is overtaken by an evil that is
no longer controlled by "civil charms" (laws) or "priestly spells" (religious beliefs)
that had earlier worked effectively through the power of fear.

This endorsement of fear as a means to control helps us understand the darkness of Melville's vision and the depth of his anger. Laws and beliefs at least forced people to obey something outside their own selfish nature (the "sway of self"). Draco, the harsh lawgiver, marches to reassert order, but Melville's Draco is not the severe and cruel figure of common understanding; he is "wise," for he understands Calvin's insight: humans are by nature bad. The town's citizens are "redeemed," but that word must be seen as loaded with irony. They are thankful for being saved from themselves, yet they do not acknowledge the underlying (and unpleasant) message (the "grimy slur") about their foolish belief in the natural goodness of humankind. A Roman citizen was not subject to the punishment of whipping; Americans, Melville suggests, like to think of themselves as Nature's Roman citizens. But in fact, they deserved, needed, and received a whipping from authorities who came to reclaim the city.

If this summary replaces the poem, then the poem is indeed dead. But we'd suggest you take the information and read the poem several times. Melville's images, his word choice, his allusions, his close engagement with a powerful moment in his own history, and his willingness to imagine what that moment means in larger terms operate together to create a powerful and unsettling vision of society and law. Our summary informs, but it doesn't encourage, the kind of experience available in a work of art. And though the context we've supplied may seem substantial, it is not hard to acquire. Professional scholars will often provide useful glosses that accompany modern editions of older works. And standard reference books along with useful websites allow us to quickly access information about names we don't recognize, events we hadn't learned in class, ideas we hadn't encountered in our earlier reading.

A Note to Student Writers: Using Electronic Sources for Research

The birth of the World Wide Web has changed strategies for doing background research, but it's important to understand the limits of the web. Although you can find much useful information online, an enormous amount of irrelevant, erroneous, and distracting information waits there too. Wikipedia has become a favorite online source for many college students; it's fun to enter space where everyone can pitch in on a favorite subject. But fun is also a source of trouble; Wikipedia's openness allows few checks on the quality or accuracy of the entries. And a Google search of "Draco" yields over 34,000 entries; far more of those address Draco Malfoy, the villain in the Harry Potter series, than the Roman man of law Melville alludes to. "Wise Draco" gets us quickly to the poem itself, but that is no help. "Cynic" yields over a million hits. "Calvin's creed" leads to discussions of Calvinism (a promising start), but a closer look reveals that the first discussion in the list of possibilities comes from a very specific political interest group. Of course, by the time you are reading this note, any search you undertake will differ because the content on the Web is constantly changing. And you certainly can and should learn to become an astute online researcher. But along the way, you'll face the same sorts of traps and bad leads we've just described. The problems won't keep you from the Web, of course, but they should remind you of the importance of careful assessment and good judgment in any research endeavor.

One source a student of literature should know about is the *Oxford English Dictionary* (commonly referred to as the *OED*). As we discussed in Chapter 11, the *OED* provides not just definitions, but histories of words. At the simplest level, it helps us through the confusion over words that may arise with change: "berries" can be "rude" in Milton's work because "rude" in the seventeenth century could mean "unripe." But the *OED* can provoke us to explore fundamental interpretive matters. Hamlet's charge to Ophelia, "get thee to a nunnery," seems straightforward enough, but the *OED* tells us that "nunnery" in Shakespeare's day could also refer to a house of prostitution. Does Shakespeare want us to set the two meanings in opposition? Does he want us to understand Hamlet's command as cruelly sarcastic? What might we learn from the *OED* about Melville's use of the "cynic" to modify the "tyrannies" that are expressed by "honest kings"?

As you might imagine, the *OED* in print is a huge multivolume work. Your library, however, will have the *OED* in electronic form. This makes it possible to quickly cross-reference words. It also allows you to search the *OED* for quotations (every entry has examples of a word's use over time). For anyone who studies texts from the first half of the twentieth century or before, the *OED* is invaluable. Obviously, if you are concerned only with the contemporary meaning and usage of a word, consult one of the many current dictionaries now available.

Specialized handbooks, encyclopedias, dictionaries, and "companions" provide brief, informative discussions of plots, authors, characters, critical terms, and aesthetic movements. One accessible and very useful series that offers much biographical, textual, and historical background is published by the Oxford University Press and is available online: *The Oxford Companion to English Literature, The Oxford Companion to American Literature, The Oxford Companion to the Theatre, The Oxford Companion to Film* (and to *Art,* to the *Bible,* and so on). There are also substantial and sophisticated online reference works that provide much information helpful to critical writers who desire a broad grasp of intellectual context: *The Stanford Encyclopedia of Philosophy* and *A Dictionary of the History of Ideas* are valuable for students of literature and film.

The range, variety, and accessibility of such works make even poems as densely packed as Melville's "The House-Top" quite approachable. So we hope that you read ambitiously and without fear of what you don't know; we also hope that you'll read with confidence about what you do know and what you can learn.

MODELING CRITICAL ANALYSIS: JOÃO GUIMARÃES ROSA, THE THIRD BANK OF THE RIVER

In the last chapter, we considered how João Guimarães Rosa's "The Third Bank of the River" provokes allegorical or symbolic readings. The title itself demands that we move beyond the limits of a realistic story. What would a "third bank of a river" be, after all? We might try to imagine a sharp bend in a river that makes from some perspectives a sort of third bank, but such a literal approach would surely seem strained. Given the story we read, it seems clear that Rosa asks us to consider some new dimension to what we ordinarily consider the real. So far, we have taken on the challenge without addressing any matters of Guimarães Rosa's life or language.

It's likely that you haven't read Guimarães Rosa before. He is greatly admired and the author of a novel many critics consider to be one of the great works of the twentieth century, *Grande Sertão: Veredes* (*The Devil to Pay in the Backlands*). But Guimarães Rosa writes in Portuguese, not a language as widely translated for English readers as, say, Spanish or French. Some of his books are also quite demanding—even for those who are native speakers of Portuguese. Fortunately, "The Third Bank of the River" doesn't require any special context for a deeply rewarding reading in English. But that hardly means that context is irrelevant. Consider how any of the following background might help you return to "The Third Bank of the River" with an openness to new interpretive possibilities.

Guimarães Rosa has been considered by some a regional writer; to the extent that that is true, his region is Minas Gerais—a state in Brazil's interior notable for its mining and its agriculture. He was trained and practiced as a medical doctor in Minas. Some of his stories catch the flavor of local idioms and legends he may have heard from patients. But *regionalist* is far too narrow a word to describe his ambition or achievement. Guimarães Rosa possessed a lifelong fascination with languages; he spoke six well and read several other languages. He was a diplomat (stationed for some years in Colombia), and he was an avid reader of world literatures. His stories are not tied to regional traditions either in subject matter or in technique.

In 1958, at the age of fifty, Guimarães Rosa suffered a life-threatening heart attack. The collection in which "The Third Bank of the River" appeared came out four years later. It was titled *Primeiros Estórias*. These were not "first stories" in the usual sense, but they were the first stories Guimarães Rosa wrote and published after the heart attack. The stories in this collection, according to one critic, involve a profound change that "implies the crossing of a threshold." In this respect, "The Third Bank of the River" seems typical—even central. In fact, the English translation of *Primeiros Estórias* is titled "*The Third Bank of the River and Other Stories*." And in an index to the first edition of the stories, Guimarães Rosa signaled themes of change, transition, and transcendence in what we might call a set of hieroglyphics for every story. The hieroglyphic line for "The Third Bank of the River" ends with a symbol of infinity. The entire line appears as follows:

VI − A TERCEIRA MARGEM DO RIO ....

Does knowledge of Guimarães Rosa's medical training, his heart attack, the general themes of the stories in the collection that followed that heart attack, the title of the collection in which the story first appeared, and the hieroglyph pictured contribute to your understanding of "The Third Bank of the River"? Does any of this contextual material enrich or change your reading? Does it merely reinforce an original impression? How is this knowledge relevant or irrelevant to your reading experience?

Using Context to Focus Writing and Discussion

- What outside knowledge do you have in addition to the knowledge the text itself offers? How is any piece of this information relevant to the text that you are reading? For instance, we might know when the author lived. If the author wrote a work of fiction set in some historical event that the author experienced, how would that knowledge influence our reading of the fictional text? If the author wrote a work of fiction set in a different time, how would our knowledge of the author's life help us read this work of fiction?

- What specific connections can you draw between the literary work and its context? Why are these connections interesting? (Just finding connections isn't enough to make them interesting.)

- How does your understanding of the text change as you learn historical or biographical facts that relate to its production?

- How influential is the context in guiding your reading of the text? For instance, were you aware of or asking questions about the author's life and times as you were reading the text?

- How does the work change as we read it in different contexts? For instance, how do you read a poem that was written to raise spirits about a war that is long over?

- Make a list of abstract words that appear in more than one text in the cluster (like *courage*, *hero*, *great*). Explain how these words take on different meanings depending upon the context the writer supplies or assumes.

- How are readers encouraged to generalize—or discouraged from generalizing—the meaning of a particular work? In other words, how closely are we tied to the specific war or battle that is the subject of the work? Is there any work in which the specific historical circumstances are unimportant?

- Which works demand the most contextual knowledge? Are any unreadable without substantial background information? What kinds of information do you need to achieve understanding? Conversely, what kinds of information seem nonessential to your understanding?

Anthology

WAR FILM: A CRITIC WRITES ABOUT CONTEXT

When David Denby reviews the 2009 film *The Hurt Locker,* notice how much attention he gives to the context in which this film appears, specifically about the "mixed emotions of frustration and repugnance" with which an audience approaches any film about war, but especially a film about the war in Iraq, which had been going on for nearly a decade when this film came out. Denby begins by citing the fact that many films had been made about that war but that audiences were apparently not interested in seeing them. As he discusses the film, Denby examines a number of different contexts in which this particular work appears. First, there is the context of the Iraq War, but he is primarily interested in film audience reactions to depictions of that war. Next, there is the genre of war films—this film "narrows the war to the existential confrontation of man and deadly threat" by focusing on the soldiers who defuse explosive devices and thus does not fit precisely into the genre. Then there is the context of Kathryn

First Light Productions/Kingsgatefilms/The Kobal Collection/Picture Desk

The Hurt Locker (2009)

Bigelow's career: she is a female director who has been successful at making films in genres that one might think of as primarily male. Denby gives particular attention to her depiction of violence. Here he argues that her editing style presents a "tight and coherent" violence that is more realistic than what he finds in most action films. By setting the work in these multiple contexts, Denby ultimately calls *The Hurt Locker* "a small classic of tension, bravery, and fear, which will be studied twenty years from now when people want to understand something of what happened to American soldiers in Iraq."

Characteristics of War Film and Literature

Works about war often explore stark contrasts: the contrast between war and peace, between civilization and savagery, between bravery and brutality, between moments of quiet and serenity and moments of chaos and violence, between the life of a soldier and that of a civilian. Within these contrasts, authors explore questions about the nature of civilization itself. War films often refer to two different contexts simultaneously: the film is historical in that it addresses events that happened at a specific time in history, and the film itself occurs within its own historical context. So a film about the historical events of World War II may also comment on current events in Iraq or Afghanistan. Some will present the war with great attention to historical detail—how was the Civil War battle fought? What was it like to be a sailor on a German submarine? In other instances, a war might appear as a marker of a historical period. The drama of *Downton Abbey*, for instance, explores the social upheavals caused by World War I. Another aspect of the genre is that people who participated in war as soldiers, officers, prisoners, nurses, protesters, or in various other capacities may be the authors of these creative works about war. Their participation gives the creative presentation a certain authority.

Language and War: Considering Context in Analysis

War inevitably forces us to measure abstractions against human lives. Tennyson's notions of loyalty and bravery haven't, for most readers, measured up very well to the specific action he commemorates in "The Charge of the Light Brigade." Still, the notions aren't discarded: Every person who considers the subject of war is left to measure again: What is the value? What are the prospects? What is the likely cost?

The First World War (1914–1918) lent those questions—in the wake of an unfolding disaster—great urgency. The scale and speed of the devastation forced an entire generation of writers to question the words that justified or valorized the event. In a review article ("The Big One," *The New Yorker*, August 23, 2004), Adam Gopnik writes powerfully of the raw facts: "The scale and suddenness of the killing that began that summer still has the power to amaze us. The war began on August 4th. By August 29th, there were two hundred and sixty thousand French dead." And of course, this was only the first month in what was to be a long fight. The fierce trench warfare along the Western Front came to symbolize for many the brutal futility of the whole endeavor. Again, Gopnik: "On one day during the Battle of the Somme, in the summer of 1916, more than fifty thousand British troops died walking directly into German fire, without advancing the front by a single foot. In fact, the entire front, which cost the lives of more than three million human beings, moved scarcely five miles in three years." It's no wonder that the rhythmic pounding of Tennyson's charge struck post World War I writers as obscenely upbeat.

Many of the works in this cluster are poised around the First World War. The poems by Sir Henry Newbolt and Edgar Guest served to support the war effort in the most confident tones. The poems of Wilfred Owen, Siegfried Sassoon, and e. e. cummings as well as much of Hemingway's early fiction take on an especially hard edge in response. These works weren't only opposing the war; they were contesting a whole way of speaking about war. They were trying to offer a picture and feeling of immediate experience that would blow away any inspiring abstractions. It's important in reading this material to keep in mind the facts that Gopnik provides and the language Newbolt and Guest employ. Context, both historical and literary, is essential to a full reading of these postwar works.

Other works in this cluster address other wars, but similar themes recur. In every case we need to learn what we can of the occasion for the text and at the same time consider how our own history is relevant to reading. The tension between old and new, between ideal and real, between abstract and concrete plays out in Melville's "A Utilitarian View of the Monitor's Fight." The *Monitor* was an ironclad warship in the Union navy. It battled the Confederacy's ironclad, the *Merrimac*, in 1862. This battle signaled for Melville a profound change in the nature of warfare. There could be no pretense to pomp or romantic heroism in such a mechanized struggle. "Warriors" in this poem become mere "operatives." Units of energy, "caloric," are calculated in the management of the battle; the quality of passion, the *heroic*, can't be so measured. Yet the battle was intense and the demands on the men greater than those exacted by earlier wars. Melville seems to register a faint regret that something ennobling has been lost while at the same time recognizes that that loss is appropriate. The harsh mechanization of war ultimately helps reveal war's truer nature. To see war clearly for what it is, is to see that war is less grand than peace.

Siegfried Sassoon's "Repression of War Experience" and Hemingway's "Soldier's Home" both remind us that wars don't end simply because the fighting stops. Those who battle accrue memories and feelings that cannot be simply set aside. Tim O'Brien's "The Things They Carried" provides a densely textured record of war experience. He, along with Anne Sexton, suggests that the feelings behind a notion such as courage are more complicated than Tennyson ever suggested. So complicated, in fact, that war's effects can be understood only by those who have fought.

REVIEW

David Denby (1943–   )

Anxiety Tests (2009)

The Iraq war has been dramatized on film many times, and those films have been ignored just as many times by theatre audiences. But Kathryn Bigelow's "The Hurt Locker" is the most skillful and emotionally involving picture yet made about the conflict. The film, from a script by Mark Boal, has a new subject: the heroism of the men who defuse improvised explosive devices, sloppily made but lethal bombs planted under a bag or a pile of garbage or just beneath the dirt of a Baghdad street. Bigelow stages one prolonged and sinister shoot-out in the desert, but the movie couldn't be called a combat film, nor is it political, except by implication—a mutual distrust between American occupiers and Iraqi citizens is there in every scene. The specialized nature of the subject is part of what makes it so powerful, and perhaps American audiences worn out by the mixed emotions of frustration and repugnance inspired by the war can enjoy this film without ambivalence or guilt. "The Hurt Locker" narrows the war to the existential confrontation of man and deadly threat.

Over and over, Staff Sergeant William James (Jeremy Renner), following a tip-off, walks to a bomb site in a heavy protective suit and tries to figure out how to pull apart clumsily tangled wires and flimsy triggering devices. We've seen James's predecessor die on the job: a man watching him from a nearby store detonated a bomb with a cell phone. As James goes in, slowly, under a hot sun, treading like a spaceman through trash-filled streets, people gather in doorways or look out windows. Which of them is hostile, which friendly, which merely curious? The two other members of James's team, the frightened young Eldridge (Brian Geraghty) and the wary, experienced Sanborn (Anthony Mackie), cover James, screaming at anyone who moves. The two men feel entirely vulnerable; they both admire and detest James, who pulls them into situations they would rather leave to someone else.

In the past, Kathryn Bigelow, now fifty-seven, has outdone the macho movie boys at their own game. In her "Blue Steel" (1989), as Jamie Lee Curtis, playing a cop, geared up for a day's work, Bigelow focussed on her revolver, her leather holster, and her shoes, in gleaming closeup. The sequence hovered somewhere between fetish and parody. Bigelow went into the ocean with Patrick Swayze and Keanu Reeves in the surfer-crime movie "Point Break" (1991), and brought off scenes of languorously slo-mo destruction in the cultish sci-fi crime movie "Strange Days" (1995). By the mid-nineties, I had her figured as a violence junkie with a strong tendency to stylize everything into stunning images that didn't always mean much. As a filmmaker, Bigelow is still obsessed with violence, but she's become a master at staging it. In "The Hurt Locker," there are no wasted shots or merely beautiful images. As Eldridge and Sanborn jerk their guns this way and that at a bomb scene, Bigelow, working with the great cinematographer Barry Ackroyd, jerks the camera around, too. She wants us to be there, to feel the danger, the mystery.

This kind of immediacy is commonplace in action filmmaking, but, unlike so many directors today, who jam together crashes, explosions, and people sailing through the air in nonsensical montages of fantasy movement, Bigelow keeps the space tight and coherent. No matter how many times she cuts away, you know exactly where James is in relation to a bomb—whether he's in the kill zone or far enough away to be safe. (You can't break up the integrity of space when space is the subject of your movie.) And Bigelow prolongs the moment, stretching out our anxiety almost to the point at which it becomes pain. "The Hurt Locker" is quite a feat: in this period of antic fragmentation, Bigelow has restored the wholeness of time and space as essentials for action. Occasionally, a plaintive reader writes me a note after I've panned some violent fantasy movie and says something like "Some of us *like* explosions. Ease up." Well, I like *these* explosions, because I believe in them. Realism has its thrills, too.

The insistence on plainness, the absence of stylization, carries over to   5
the performances as well. Jeremy Renner has played the serial killer Jeffrey Dahmer and many minor roles in action movies. He has a round face, with a beautiful smile that he mostly keeps hidden, and a strong but unglamorous body. Bigelow's idea in casting him, I think, was to make her star a competent but physically ordinary American serviceman whose greatest gifts are within. William James, it turns out, is implacably heroic. He never steps away from danger. You might say that he's drawn to it and needs it, but he never makes a fuss about what he's doing. His charisma consists of having no obvious charisma except phenomenal concentration and guts. And since he knows, handling bombs, when to be cautious and when not to be, he can be hair-raisingly casual, tossing aside a disabled device as if it were an empty juice carton. At one point, he shucks his headset, too, and Sanborn, who needs to stay in touch with what James is doing, is so enraged that he slugs him. In the nineteen-fifties, Aldo Ray played men like William James—war lovers, completely at home on the battlefield but hapless in the normal relations of life.

(When James and his partners relax and get drunk, the only way they can show their affection is to punch one another in the stomach.) But Ray's military men were unreachable, stone-cold killers, while James has strong emotions, which he keeps pent up.

Bigelow and Mark Boal (the journalist who developed the real-life material that served as the basis of Paul Haggis's "In the Valley of Elah") don't always let us know exactly what's going on. As the soldiers swing into action, the filmmakers want a sense of strangeness and disorientation, a craziness that's on the verge of taking over the moment. As James is walking toward a bomb, an Iraqi drives into the scene in a taxi and won't obey commands to go back. What is he up to? Another man, strapped with explosives, changes his mind about suicide and tearfully begs James to rescue him. Is he a lure? The anguish of uncertainty is part of the men's daily life, and James himself, so sure in his odd profession, gets into a serious mixup over a friendly Iraqi boy who he thinks has been murdered by insurgents. Suddenly, he loses his bearings and charges around Baghdad like a madman. "The Hurt Locker" is a small classic of tension, bravery, and fear, which will be studied twenty years from now when people want to understand something of what happened to American soldiers in Iraq. If there are moviegoers who are exhausted by the current fashion for relentless fantasy violence, this is the convincingly blunt and forceful movie for them.

FICTION

Ernest Hemingway (1899–1961)

Ernest Hemingway was born in Oak Park, Illinois. His novels and short stories have become staples of American literature courses today, but Hemingway also experienced great popular and critical acclaim during his lifetime. His fantastic hunting and sporting adventures not only served as material for his writings but also were avidly followed by the media. Similarly, his service as an ambulance driver in Italy during World War I and his work as a war correspondent in Europe and Asia during the Greco-Turkish War, the Spanish Civil War, and World War II influenced his literature while simultaneously placing him in the public limelight. The "Hemingway Hero" is typically a strong, self-sufficient, quiet male character less afraid of physical death than a listless earthly existence. Hemingway's seventh novel, *The Old Man and the Sea*, was awarded the 1953 Pulitzer Prize, and in 1954 he received the Nobel Prize in literature. Despite his great success, Hemingway suffered emotionally and committed suicide in 1961.

Soldier's Home (1925)

Krebs went to the war from a Methodist college in Kansas. There is a picture which shows him among his fraternity brothers, all of them wearing exactly the same height and style collar. He enlisted in the Marines in 1917 and did not return to the United States until the second division returned from the Rhine in the summer of 1919.

There is a picture which shows him on the Rhine with two German girls and another corporal. Krebs and the corporal look too big for their uniforms. The German girls are not beautiful. The Rhine does not show in the picture.

By the time Krebs returned to his home town in Oklahoma the greeting of heroes was over. He came back much too late. The men from the town who had been drafted had all been welcomed elaborately on their return. There had been a great deal of hysteria. Now the reaction had set in. People seemed to think it was rather ridiculous for Krebs to be getting back so late, years after the war was over.

At first Krebs, who had been at Belleau Wood, Soissons, the Champagne, St. Mihiel, and in the Argonne did not want to talk about the war at all. Later he felt the need to talk but no one wanted to hear about it. His town had heard too many atrocity stories to be thrilled by actualities. Krebs found that to be listened to at all he had to lie, and after he had done this twice he, too, had a reaction against the war and against talking about it. A distaste for everything that had happened to him in the war set in because of the lies he had told. All of the times that had been able to make him feel cool and clear inside himself when he thought of them; the times so long back when he had done the one thing, the only thing for a man to do, easily and naturally, when he might have done something else, now lost their cool, valuable quality and then were lost themselves.

His lies were quite unimportant lies and consisted in attributing to himself things other men had seen, done, or heard of, and stating as facts certain apocryphal incidents familiar to all soldiers. Even his lies were not sensational at the pool room. His acquaintances, who had heard detailed accounts of German women found chained to machine guns in the Argonne forest and who could not comprehend, or were barred by their patriotism from interest in, any German machine gunners who were not chained, were not thrilled by his stories.

Krebs acquired the nausea in regard to experience that is the result of untruth or exaggeration, and when he occasionally met another man who had really been a soldier and they talked a few minutes in the dressing room at a dance he fell into the easy pose of the old soldier among other soldiers: that he had been badly, sickeningly frightened all the time. In this way he lost everything.

During this time, it was late summer, he was sleeping late in bed, getting up to walk down town to the library to get a book, eating lunch at home, reading on the front porch until he became bored, and then walking down through the town to spend the hottest hours of the day in the cool dark of the pool room. He loved to play pool.

In the evening he practiced on his clarinet, strolled down town, read, and went to bed. He was still a hero to his two young sisters. His mother would have given him breakfast in bed if he had wanted it. She often came in when he was in bed and asked him to tell her about the war, but her attention always wandered. His father was noncommittal.

Before Krebs went away to the war he had never been allowed to drive the family motor car. His father was in the real estate business and always wanted the car to be at his command when he required it to take clients out into the country to show them a piece of farm property. The car always stood outside the First National Bank building where his father had an office on the second floor. Now, after the war, it was still the same car.

Nothing was changed in the town except that the young girls had   10
grown up. But they lived in such a complicated world of already defined alliances and shifting feuds that Krebs did not feel the energy or the courage to break into it. He liked to look at them, though. There were so many goodlooking young girls. Most of them had their hair cut short. When he went away only little girls wore their hair like that or girls that were fast. They all wore sweaters and shirt waists with round Dutch collars. It was a pattern. He liked to look at them from the front porch as they walked on the other side of the street. He liked to watch them walking under the shade of the trees. He liked the round Dutch collars above their sweaters. He liked their silk stockings and flat shoes. He liked their bobbed hair and the way they walked.

When he was in town their appeal to him was not very strong. He did not like them when he saw them in the Greek's ice cream parlor. He did not want them themselves really. They were too complicated. There was something else. Vaguely he wanted a girl but he did not want to have to work to get her. He would have liked to have a girl but he did not want to have to spend a long time getting her. He did not want to get into the intrigue and the politics. He did not want to have to do any courting. He did not want to tell any more lies. It wasn't worth it.

He did not want any consequences. He did not want any consequences ever again. He wanted to live along without consequences. Besides he did not really need a girl. The army had taught him that. It was all right to pose as though you had to have a girl. Nearly everybody did that. But it wasn't true. You did not need a girl. That was the funny thing. First a fellow boasted how girls mean nothing to him, that he never thought of them, that they could not touch him. Then a fellow boasted that he could not get along without girls, that he had to have them all the time, that he could not go to sleep without them.

That was all a lie. It was all a lie both ways. You did not need a girl unless you thought about them. He learned that in the army. Then sooner or later you always got one. When you were really ripe for a girl you always got one. You did not have to think about it. Sooner or later it would come. He had learned that in the army.

Now he would have liked a girl if she had come to him and not wanted to talk. But here at home it was all too complicated. He knew he could never get through it all again. It was not worth the trouble. That was the thing about French girls and German girls. There was not all this talking. You couldn't talk much and you did not need to talk. It was simple and you were friends. He thought about France and then he began to think about Germany. On the whole he had liked Germany better. He did not want to leave Germany. He did not want to come home. Still, he had come home. He sat on the front porch.

He liked the girls that were walking along the other side of the street.   15
He liked the look of them much better than the French girls or the German girls. But the world they were in was not the world he was in. He would like to have one of them. But it was not worth it. They were such a nice pattern. He liked the pattern. It was exciting. But he would not go through all the talking. He did not want one badly enough. He liked to look at them all, though. It was not worth it. Not now when things were getting good again.

He sat there on the porch reading a book on the war. It was a history and he was reading about all the engagements he had been in. It was the most interesting reading he had ever done. He wished there were more maps. He looked forward with a good feeling to reading all the really good histories when they would come out with good detail maps. Now he was really learning about the war. He had been a good soldier. That made a difference.

One morning after he had been home about a month his mother came into his bedroom and sat on the bed. She smoothed her apron.

"I had a talk with your father last night, Harold," she said, "and he is willing for you to take the car out in the evenings."

"Yeah?" said Krebs, who was not fully awake. "Take the car out? Yeah?"

"Yes. Your father has felt for some time that you should be able to   20
take the car out in the evenings whenever you wished but we only talked it over last night."

"I'll bet you made him," Krebs said.

"No. It was your father's suggestion that we talk the matter over."

"Yeah. I'll bet you made him," Krebs sat up in bed.

"Will you come down to breakfast, Harold?" his mother said.

"As soon as I get my clothes on," Krebs said.   25

His mother went out of the room and he could hear her frying something downstairs while he washed, shaved, and dressed to go down into the dining-room for breakfast. While he was eating breakfast his sister brought in the mail.

"Well, Hare," she said. "You old sleepyhead. What do you ever get up for?"

Krebs looked at her. He liked her. She was his best sister.

"Have you got the paper?" he asked.

She handed him the Kansas City Star and he shucked off its brown   30
wrapper and opened it to the sporting page. He folded the Star open and propped it against the water pitcher with his cereal dish to steady it, so he could read while he ate.

"Harold," his mother stood in the kitchen doorway, "Harold, please don't muss up the paper. Your father can't read his Star if it's been mussed."

"I won't muss it," Krebs said.

His sister sat down at the table and watched him while he read.

"We're playing indoor over at school this afternoon," she said. "I'm going to pitch."

"Good," said Krebs. "How's the old wing?"   35

"I can pitch better than lots of the boys. I tell them all you taught me. The other girls aren't much good."

"Yeah?" said Krebs.

"I tell them all you're my beau. Aren't you my beau, Hare?"

"You bet."

"Couldn't your brother really be your beau just because he's your   40
brother?"

"I don't know."

"Sure you know. Couldn't you be my beau, Hare, if I was old enough and if you wanted to?"

"Sure. You're my girl now."

"Am I really your girl?"

"Sure."   45

"Do you love me?"

"Uh, huh."

"Will you love me always?"

"Sure."

"Will you come over and watch me play indoor?"   50

"Maybe."

"Aw, Hare, you don't love me. If you loved me, you'd want to come over and watch me play indoor."

Krebs's mother came into the dining-room from the kitchen. She carried a plate with two fried eggs and some crisp bacon on it and a plate of buckwheat cakes.

"You run along, Helen," she said. "I want to talk to Harold."

She put the eggs and bacon down in front of him and brought in a   55
jug of maple syrup for the buckwheat cakes. Then she sat down across the
table from Krebs.

"I wish you'd put down the paper a minute, Harold," she said.

Krebs took down the paper and folded it.

"Have you decided what you are going to do yet, Harold?" his mother said,
taking off her glasses.

"No," said Krebs.

"Don't you think it's about time?" His mother did not say this in a   60
mean way. She seemed worried.

"I hadn't thought about it," Krebs said.

"God has some work for everyone to do," his mother said. "There can be
no idle hands in His Kingdom."

"I'm not in His Kingdom," Krebs said.

"We are all of us in His Kingdom."

Krebs felt embarrassed and resentful as always.   65

"I've worried about you so much, Harold," his mother went on. "I know
the temptations you must have been exposed to. I know how weak men are. I
know what your own dear grandfather, my own father, told us about the Civil
War and I have prayed for you. I pray for you all day long, Harold."

Krebs looked at the bacon fat hardening on his plate.

"Your father is worried, too," his mother went on. "He thinks you have
lost your ambition, that you haven't got a definite aim in life. Charley Simmons, who is just your age, has a good job and is going to be married. The
boys are all settling down; they're all determined to get somewhere; you can see
that boys like Charley Simmons are on their way to being really a credit to the
community."

Krebs said nothing.

"Don't look that way, Harold," his mother said. "You know we love   70
you and I want to tell you for your own good how matters stand. Your
father does not want to hamper your freedom. He thinks you should be
allowed to drive the car. If you want to take some of the nice girls out riding with you, we are only too pleased. We want you to enjoy yourself. But
you are going to have to settle down to work, Harold. Your father doesn't
care what you start in at. All work is honorable as he says. But you've got
to make a start at something. He asked me to speak to you this morning
and then you can stop in and see him at his office."

"Is that all?" Krebs said.

"Yes. Don't you love your mother, dear boy?"

"No," Krebs said. His mother looked at him across the table. Her eyes
were shiny. She started crying.

"I don't love anybody," Krebs said.   75

It wasn't any good. He couldn't tell her, he couldn't make her see it. It was silly to have said it. He had only hurt her. He went over and took hold of her arm. She was crying with her head in her hands.

"I didn't mean it," he said. "I was just angry at something. I didn't mean I didn't love you."

His mother went on crying. Krebs put his arm on her shoulder.

"Can't you believe me, mother?"

His mother shook her head.   80

"Please, please, mother. Please believe me."

"All right," his mother said chokily. She looked up at him. "I believe you, Harold."

Krebs kissed her hair. She put her face up to him.

"I'm your mother," she said. "I held you next to my heart when you were a tiny baby."

Krebs felt sick and vaguely nauseated.   85

"I know, Mummy," he said. "I'll try and be a good boy for you."

"Would you kneel and pray with me, Harold?" his mother asked. They knelt down beside the dining-room table and Krebs's mother prayed.

"Now, you pray, Harold," she said.

"I can't," Krebs said.   90

"Try, Harold."

"I can't."

"Do you want me to pray for you?"

"Yes."

So his mother prayed for him and then they stood up and Krebs   95
kissed his mother and went out of the house. He had tried so to keep his life from being complicated. Still, none of it had touched him. He had felt sorry for his mother and she had made him lie. He would go to Kansas City and get a job and she would feel all right about it. There would be one more scene maybe before he got away. He would not go down to his father's office. He would miss that one. He wanted his life to go smoothly. It had just gotten going that way. Well, that was all over now, anyway. He would go over to the schoolyard and watch Helen play indoor baseball.

- Discuss the significance of specific details that the story presents about World War I.

- At the end of the sixth paragraph the narrator tells us, "In this way he lost everything." What details illustrate what Krebs has lost and how he has lost it?

■ How does the internal experience of Krebs that we see in the beginning of
   the story relate to the conversation that we hear in the second half? How is
   this contrast significant?

Tim O'Brien (1946–   )

Tim O'Brien was born in Worthington, Minnesota. In 1968, after he earned his
degree in political science, summa cum laude, at McAlester College in St. Paul, he
was drafted into the army during the Vietnam War. Though he had been an active
protester of the war and considered escaping to Canada, he feared losing connection with his family and home and agreed to join the Fifth Battalion, Forty-sixth
Infantry, for a year and a half. After gaining a Purple Heart for his service, he began
studying for his PhD in government at Harvard University while practicing his technical skills as a writer for the *Washington Post*. In 1978, he published *Going after
Cacciato*, a combination of real and invented events from his life, which earned
the National Book Award. After this publication, several of his stories appeared in
magazines and were soon adapted into the highly successful book *The Things They
Carried* (1990).

The Things They Carried (1990)

First Lieutenant Jimmy Cross carried letters from a girl named Martha, a junior at Mount Sebastian College in New Jersey. They were not love letters, but
Lieutenant Cross was hoping, so he kept them folded in plastic at the bottom
of his rucksack. In the late afternoon, after a day's march, he would dig his
foxhole, wash his hands under a canteen, unwrap the letters, hold them with
the tips of his fingers, and spend the last hour of light pretending. He would
imagine romantic camping trips into the White Mountains in New Hampshire.
He would sometimes taste the envelope flaps, knowing her tongue had been
there. More than anything, he wanted Martha to love him as he loved her, but
the letters were mostly chatty, elusive on the matter of love. She was a virgin,
he was almost sure. She was an English major at Mount Sebastian, and she
wrote beautifully about her professors and roommates and midterm exams,
about her respect for Chaucer and her great affection for Virginia Woolf.
She often quoted lines of poetry; she never mentioned the war, except to say,
Jimmy, take care of yourself. The letters weighed ten ounces. They were signed
"Love, Martha," but Lieutenant Cross understood that "Love" was only a way
of signing and did not mean what he sometimes pretended it meant. At dusk,
he would carefully return the letters to his rucksack. Slowly, a bit distracted, he
would get up and move among his men, checking the perimeter, then at full
dark he would return to his hole and watch the night and wonder if Martha
was a virgin.

The things they carried were largely determined by necessity. Among the necessities or near necessities were P-38 can openers, pocket knives, heat tabs, wrist watches, dog tags, mosquito repellent, chewing gum, candy, cigarettes, salt tablets, packets of Kool-Aid, lighters, matches, sewing kits, Military Payment Certificates, C rations, and two or three canteens of water. Together, these items weighed between fifteen and twenty pounds, depending upon a man's habits or rate of metabolism. Henry Dobbins, who was a big man, carried extra rations; he was especially fond of canned peaches in heavy syrup over pound cake. Dave Jensen, who practiced field hygiene, carried a toothbrush, dental floss, and several hotel-size bars of soap he'd stolen on R&R in Sydney, Australia. Ted Lavender, who was scared, carried tranquilizers until he was shot in the head outside the village of Than Khe in mid-April. By necessity, and because it was SOP°, they all carried steel helmets that weighed five pounds including the liner and camouflage cover. They carried the standard fatigue jackets and trousers. Very few carried underwear. On their feet they carried jungle boots—2.1 pounds—and Dave Jensen carried three pairs of socks and a can of Dr. Scholl's foot powder as a precaution against trench foot. Until he was shot, Ted Lavender carried six or seven ounces of premium dope, which for him was a necessity. Mitchell Sanders, the RTO°, carried condoms. Norman Bowker carried a diary. Rat Kiley carried comic books. Kiowa, a devout Baptist, carried an illustrated New Testament that had been presented to him by his father, who taught Sunday school in Oklahoma City, Oklahoma. As a hedge against bad times, however, Kiowa also carried his grandmother's distrust of the white man, his grandfather's old hunting hatchet. Necessity dictated. Because the land was mined and booby-trapped, it was SOP for each man to carry a steel-centered, nylon-covered flak jacket, which weighed 6.7 pounds, but which on hot days seemed much heavier. Because you could die so quickly, each man carried at least one large compress bandage, usually in the helmet band for easy access. Because the nights were cold, and because the monsoons were wet, each carried a green plastic poncho that could be used as a raincoat or ground sheet or makeshift tent. With its quilted liner, the poncho weighed almost two pounds, but it was worth every ounce. In April, for instance, when Ted Lavender was shot, they used his poncho to wrap him up, then to carry him across the paddy, then to lift him into the chopper that took him away.

They were called legs or grunts.

To carry something was to "hump" it, as when Lieutenant Jimmy Cross humped his love for Martha up the hills and through the swamps. In its intransitive form, "to hump" meant "to walk," or "to march," but it implied burdens far beyond the intransitive.

°**SOP:** Standard operating procedure. °**RTO:** Radio telephone operator

Almost everyone humped photographs. In his wallet, Lieutenant Cross   5
carried two photographs of Martha. The first was a Kodachrome snapshot
signed "Love," though he knew better. She stood against a brick wall. Her
eyes were gray and neutral, her lips slightly open as she stared straight-on
at the camera. At night, sometimes, Lieutenant Cross wondered who had
taken the picture, because he knew she had boyfriends, because he loved
her so much, and because he could see the shadow of the picture taker
spreading out against the brick wall. The second photograph had been
clipped from the 1968 Mount Sebastian yearbook. It was an action shot—
women's volleyball—and Martha was bent horizontal to the floor, reaching,
the palms of her hands in sharp focus, the tongue taut, the expression
frank and competitive. There was no visible sweat. She wore white gym
shorts. Her legs, he thought, were almost certainly the legs of a virgin,
dry and without hair, the left knee cocked and carrying her entire weight,
which was just over one hundred pounds. Lieutenant Cross remembered
touching that left knee. A dark theater, he remembered, and the movie was
Bonnie and Clyde, and Martha wore a tweed skirt, and during the final
scene, when he touched her knee, she turned and looked at him in a sad,
sober way that made him pull his hand back, but he would always remember the feel of the tweed skirt and the knee beneath it and the sound of the
gunfire that killed Bonnie and Clyde, how embarrassing it was, how slow
and oppressive. He remembered kissing her good night at the dorm door.
Right then, he thought, he should've done something brave. He should've
carried her up the stairs to her room and tied her to the bed and touched
that left knee all night long. He should've risked it. Whenever he looked at
the photographs, he thought of new things he should've done.

What they carried was partly a function of rank, partly of field specialty.

As a first lieutenant and platoon leader, Jimmy Cross carried a compass,
maps, code books, binoculars, and a .45-caliber pistol that weighed 2.9 pounds
fully loaded. He carried a strobe light and the responsibility for the lives of
his men.

As an RTO, Mitchell Sanders carried the PRC-25 radio, a killer, twenty-six
pounds with its battery.

As a medic, Rat Kiley carried a canvas satchel filled with morphine and
plasma and malaria tablets and surgical tape and comic books and all the
things a medic must carry, including M&M's for especially bad wounds, for a
total weight of nearly twenty pounds.

As a big man, therefore a machine gunner, Henry Dobbins carried   10
the M-60, which weighed twenty-three pounds unloaded, but which was
almost always loaded. In addition, Dobbins carried between ten and fifteen
pounds of ammunition draped in belts across his chest and shoulders.

As PFCs or Spec 4s, most of them were common grunts and carried the standard M-16 gas-operated assault rifle. The weapon weighed 7.5 pounds unloaded, 8.2 pounds with its full twenty-round magazine. Depending on numerous factors, such as topography and psychology, the riflemen carried anywhere from twelve to twenty magazines, usually in cloth bandoliers, adding on another 8.4 pounds at minimum, fourteen pounds at maximum. When it was available, they also carried M-16 maintenance gear—rods and steel brushes and swabs and tubes of LSA oil—all of which weighed about a pound. Among the grunts, some carried the M-79 grenade launcher, 5.9 pounds unloaded, a reasonably light weapon except for the ammunition, which was heavy. A single round weighed ten ounces. The typical load was twenty-five rounds. But Ted Lavender, who was scared, carried thirty-four rounds when he was shot and killed outside Than Khe, and he went down under an exceptional burden, more than twenty pounds of ammunition, plus the flak jacket and helmet and rations and water and toilet paper and tranquilizers and all the rest, plus the unweighed fear. He was dead weight. There was no twitching or flopping. Kiowa, who saw it happen, said it was like watching a rock fall, or a big sandbag or something—just boom, then down—not like the movies where the dead guy rolls around and does fancy spins and goes ass over teakettle—not like that, Kiowa said, the poor bastard just flat-fuck fell. Boom. Down. Nothing else. It was a bright morning in mid-April. Lieutenant Cross felt the pain. He blamed himself. They stripped off Lavender's canteens and ammo, all the heavy things, and Rat Kiley said the obvious, the guy's dead, and Mitchell Sanders used his radio to report one U.S. KIA° and to request a chopper. Then they wrapped Lavender in his poncho. They carried him out to a dry paddy, established security, and sat smoking the dead man's dope until the chopper came. Lieutenant Cross kept to himself. He pictured Martha's smooth young face, thinking he loved her more than anything, more than his men, and now Ted Lavender was dead because he loved her so much and could not stop thinking about her. When the dust-off arrived, they carried Lavender aboard. Afterward they burned Than Khe. They marched until dusk, then dug their holes, and that night Kiowa kept explaining how you had to be there, how fast it was, how the poor guy just dropped like so much concrete. Boom-down, he said. Like cement.

In addition to the three standard weapons—the M-60, M-16, and M-79—they carried whatever presented itself, or whatever seemed appropriate as a means of killing or staying alive. They carried catch-as-catchcan. At various times, in various situations, they carried M-14s and CAR-15s and Swedish Ks and grease guns and captured AK-47s and Chi-Coms and RPGs and Simonov carbines and black-market Uzis and .38-caliber Smith & Wesson handguns

°**KIA:** Killed in Action

and 66 mm LAWs and shotguns and silencers and blackjacks and bayonets and C-4 plastic explosives. Lee Strunk carried a slingshot; a weapon of last resort, he called it. Mitchell Sanders carried brass knuckles. Kiowa carried his grandfather's feathered hatchet. Every third or fourth man carried a Claymore antipersonnel mine—3.5 pounds with its firing device. They all carried fragmentation grenades— fourteen ounces each. They all carried at least one M-18 colored smoke grenade—twenty-four ounces. Some carried CS or tear-gas grenades. Some carried white-phosphorus grenades. They carried all they could bear, and then some, including a silent awe for the terrible power of the things they carried.

In the first week of April, before Lavender died, Lieutenant Jimmy Cross received a good-luck charm from Martha. It was a simple pebble, an ounce at most. Smooth to the touch, it was a milky-white color with flecks of orange and violet, oval-shaped, like a miniature egg. In the accompanying letter, Martha wrote that she had found the pebble on the Jersey shoreline, precisely where the land touched water at high tide, where things came together but also separated. It was this separate-but-together quality, she wrote, that had inspired her to pick up the pebble and to carry it in her breast pocket for several days, where it seemed weightless, and then to send it through the mail, by air, as a token of her truest feelings for him. Lieutenant Cross found this romantic. But he wondered what her truest feelings were, exactly, and what she meant by separate-but-together. He wondered how the tides and waves had come into play on that afternoon along the Jersey shoreline when Martha saw the pebble and bent down to rescue it from geology. He imagined bare feet. Martha was a poet, with the poet's sensibilities, and her feet would be brown and bare, the toenails unpainted, the eyes chilly and somber like the ocean in March, and though it was painful, he wondered who had been with her that afternoon. He imagined a pair of shadows moving along the strip of sand where things came together but also separated. It was phantom jealousy, he knew, but he couldn't help himself. He loved her so much. On the march, through the hot days of early April, he carried the pebble in his mouth, turning it with his tongue, tasting sea salts and moisture. His mind wandered. He had difficulty keeping his attention on the war. On occasion he would yell at his men to spread out the column, to keep their eyes open, but then he would slip away into daydreams, just pretending, walking barefoot along the Jersey shore, with Martha, carrying nothing. He would feel himself rising. Sun and waves and gentle winds, all love and lightness.

What they carried varied by mission.

When a mission took them to the mountains, they carried mosquito   15
netting, machetes, canvas tarps, and extra bug juice.

If a mission seemed especially hazardous, or if it involved a place they knew to be bad, they carried everything they could. In certain heavily mined

AOs°, where the land was dense with Toe Poppers and Bouncing Betties, they took turns humping a twenty-eight-pound mine detector. With its headphones and big sensing plate, the equipment was a stress on the lower back and shoulders, awkward to handle, often useless because of the shrapnel in the earth, but they carried it anyway, partly for safety, partly for the illusion of safety.

On ambush, or other night missions, they carried peculiar little odds and ends. Kiowa always took along his New Testament and a pair of moccasins for silence. Dave Jensen carried night-sight vitamins high in carotin. Lee Strunk carried his slingshot; ammo, he claimed, would never be a problem. Rat Kiley carried brandy and M&M's. Until he was shot, Ted Lavender carried the starlight scope, which weighed 6.3 pounds with its aluminum carrying case. Henry Dobbins carried his girlfriend's panty-hose wrapped around his neck as a comforter. They all carried ghosts. When dark came, they would move out single file across the meadows and paddies to their ambush coordinates, where they would quietly set up the Claymores and lie down and spend the night waiting.

Other missions were more complicated and required special equipment. In mid-April, it was their mission to search out and destroy the elaborate tunnel complexes in the Than Khe area south of Chu Lai. To blow the tunnels, they carried one-pound blocks of pentrite high explosives, four blocks to a man, sixty-eight pounds in all. They carried wiring, detonators, and battery-powered clackers. Dave Jensen carried earplugs. Most often, before blowing the tunnels, they were ordered by higher command to search them, which was considered bad news, but by and large they just shrugged and carried out orders. Because he was a big man, Henry Dobbins was excused from tunnel duty. The others would draw numbers. Before Lavender died there were seventeen men in the platoon, and whoever drew the number seventeen would strip off his gear and crawl in head first with a flashlight and Lieutenant Cross's .45-caliber pistol. The rest of them would fan out as security. They would sit down or kneel, not facing the hole, listening to the ground beneath them, imagining cobwebs and ghosts, whatever was down there—the tunnel walls squeezing in—how the flashlight seemed impossibly heavy in the hand and how it was tunnel vision in the very strictest sense, compression in all ways, even time, and how you had to wiggle in—ass and elbows—a swallowed-up feeling—and how you found yourself worrying about odd things—will your flashlight go dead? Do rats carry rabies? If you screamed, how far would the sound carry? Would your buddies hear it? Would they have the courage to drag you out? In some respects, though not many, the waiting was worse than the tunnel itself. Imagination was a killer.

On April 16, when Lee Strunk drew the number seventeen, he laughed and muttered something and went down quickly. The morning

---

°**AOs:** Areas of operation

was hot and very still. Not good, Kiowa said. He looked at the tunnel opening, then out across a dry paddy toward the village of Than Khe. Nothing moved. No clouds or birds or people. As they waited, the men smoked and drank Kool-Aid, not talking much, feeling sympathy for Lee Strunk but also feeling the luck of the draw. You win some, you lose some, said Mitchell Sanders, and sometimes you settle for a rain check. It was a tired line and no one laughed.

Henry Dobbins ate a tropical chocolate bar. Ted Lavender popped a   20
tranquilizer and went off to pee.

After five minutes, Lieutenant Jimmy Cross moved to the tunnel, leaned down, and examined the darkness. Trouble, he thought—a cave-in maybe. And then suddenly, without willing it, he was thinking about Martha. The stresses and fractures, the quick collapse, the two of them buried alive under all that weight. Dense, crushing love. Kneeling, watching the hole, he tried to concentrate on Lee Strunk and the war, all the dangers, but his love was too much for him, he felt paralyzed, he wanted to sleep inside her lungs and breathe her blood and be smothered. He wanted her to be a virgin and not a virgin, all at once. He wanted to know her. Intimate secrets—why poetry? Why so sad? Why that grayness in her eyes? Why so alone? Not lonely, just alone—riding her bike across campus or sitting off by herself in the cafeteria. Even dancing, she danced alone—and it was the aloneness that filled him with love. He remembered telling her that one evening. How she nodded and looked away. And how, later, when he kissed her, she received the kiss without returning it, her eyes wide open, not afraid, not a virgin's eyes, just flat and uninvolved.

Lieutenant Cross gazed at the tunnel. But he was not there. He was buried with Martha under the white sand at the Jersey shore. They were pressed together, and the pebble in his mouth was her tongue. He was smiling. Vaguely, he was aware of how quiet the day was, the sullen paddies, yet he could not bring himself to worry about matters of security. He was beyond that. He was just a kid at war, in love. He was twenty-two years old. He couldn't help it.

A few moments later Lee Strunk crawled out of the tunnel. He came up grinning, filthy but alive. Lieutenant Cross nodded and closed his eyes while the others clapped Strunk on the back and made jokes about rising from the dead. Worms, Rat Kiley said. Right out of the grave. Fuckin' zombie.

The men laughed. They all felt great relief.

Spook City, said Mitchell Sanders.   25

Lee Strunk made a funny ghost sound, a kind of moaning, yet very happy, and right then, when Strunk made that high happy moaning sound, when he went Ahhooooo, right then Ted Lavender was shot in the head on his way back from peeing. He lay with his mouth open. The teeth were broken. There was a swollen black bruise under his left eye. The cheekbone was gone. Oh shit, Rat

Kiley said, the guy's dead. The guy's dead, he kept saying, which seemed pro-found—the guy's dead. I mean really.

The things they carried were determined to some extent by superstition. Lieutenant Cross carried his good-luck pebble. Dave Jensen carried a rabbit's foot. Norman Bowker, otherwise a very gentle person, carried a thumb that had been presented to him as a gift by Mitchell Sanders. The thumb was dark brown, rubbery to the touch, and weighed four ounces at most. It had been cut from a VC° corpse, a boy of fifteen or sixteen. They'd found him at the bottom of an irrigation ditch, badly burned, flies in his mouth and eyes. The boy wore black shorts and sandals. At the time of his death he had been carrying a pouch of rice, a rifle, and three magazines of ammunition.

You want my opinion, Mitchell Sanders said, there's a definite moral here.

He put his hand on the dead boy's wrist. He was quiet for a time, as if counting a pulse, then he patted the stomach, almost affectionately, and used Kiowa's hunting hatchet to remove the thumb.

Henry Dobbins asked what the moral was.   30

Moral?

You know. Moral.

Sanders wrapped the thumb in toilet paper and handed it across to Norman Bowker. There was no blood. Smiling, he kicked the boy's head, watched the flies scatter, and said, It's like with that old TV show—Paladin. Have gun, will travel.

Henry Dobbins thought about it.

Yeah, well, he finally said. I don't see no moral.   35

There it *is*, man.

Fuck off.

They carried USO stationery and pencils and pens. They carried Sterno, safety pins, trip flares, signal flares, spools of wire, razor blades, chewing tobacco, lib-erated joss sticks and statuettes of the smiling Buddha, candles, grease pencils, *The Stars and Stripes*, fingernail clippers, Psy Ops leaflets°, bush hats, bolos, and much more. Twice a week, when the resupply choppers came in, they carried hot chow in green Mermite cans and large canvas bags filled with iced beer and soda pop. They carried plastic water containers, each with a two-gallon capac-ity. Mitchell Sanders carried a set of starched tiger fatigues for special occa-sions. Henry Dobbins carried Black Flag insecticide. Dave Jensen carried empty sandbags that could be filled at night for added protection. Lee Strunk carried tanning lotion. Some things they carried in common. Taking turns, they car-ried the big PRC77 scrambler radio, which weighed thirty pounds with its

---

°**VC:** Viet Cong °**Psy Ops leaflets:** Psychological Operations leaflets, propaganda

battery. They shared the weight of memory. They took up what others could no longer bear. Often, they carried each other, the wounded or weak. They carried infections. They carried chess sets, basketballs, Vietnamese-English dictionaries, insignia of rank, Bronze Stars and Purple Hearts, plastic cards imprinted with the Code of Conduct. They carried diseases, among them malaria and dysentery. They carried lice and ringworm and leeches and paddy algae and various rots and molds. They carried the land itself—Vietnam, the place, the soil—a powdery orange-red dust that covered their boots and fatigues and faces. They carried the sky. The whole atmosphere, they carried it, the humidity, the monsoons, the stink of fungus and decay, all of it, they carried gravity. They moved like mules. By daylight they took sniper fire, at night they were mortared, but it was not battle, it was just the endless march, village to village, without purpose, nothing won or lost. They marched for the sake of the march. They plodded along slowly, dumbly, leaning forward against the heat, unthinking, all blood and bone, simple grunts, soldiering with their legs, toiling up the hills and down into the paddies and across the rivers and up again and down, just humping, one step and then the next and then another, but no volition, no will, because it was automatic, it was anatomy, and the war was entirely a matter of posture and carriage, the hump was everything, a kind of inertia, a kind of emptiness, a dullness of desire and intellect and conscience and hope and human sensibility. Their principles were in their feet. Their calculations were biological. They had no sense of strategy or mission. They searched the villages without knowing what to look for, not caring, kicking over jars of rice, frisking children and old men, blowing tunnels, sometimes setting fires and sometimes not, then forming up and moving on to the next village, then other villages, where it would always be the same. They carried their own lives. The pressures were enormous. In the heat of early afternoon, they would remove their helmets and flak jackets, walking bare, which was dangerous but which helped ease the strain. They would often discard things along the route of march. Purely for comfort, they would throw away rations, blow their Claymores and grenades, no matter, because by nightfall the resupply choppers would arrive with more of the same, then a day or two later still more, fresh watermelons and crates of ammunition and sunglasses and woolen sweaters—the resources were stunning—sparklers for the Fourth of July, colored eggs for Easter. It was the great American war chest—the fruits of science, the smokestacks, the canneries, the arsenals at Hartford, the Minnesota forests, the machine shops, the vast fields of corn and wheat—they carried like freight trains; they carried it on their backs and shoulders—and for all the ambiguities of Vietnam, all the mysteries and unknowns, there was at least the single abiding certainty that they would never be at a loss for things to carry.

   After the chopper took Lavender away, Lieutenant Jimmy Cross led his men into the village of Than Khe. They burned everything. They shot chickens and dogs, they trashed the village well, they called in artillery and watched the wreckage, then they marched for several hours through the hot afternoon, and then at dusk, while Kiowa explained how Lavender died, Lieutenant Cross found himself trembling.

He tried not to cry. With his entrenching tool, which weighed five   40
pounds, he began digging a hole in the earth.

He felt shame. He hated himself. He had loved Martha more than his men, and as a consequence Lavender was now dead, and this was something he would have to carry like a stone in his stomach for the rest of the war.

All he could do was dig. He used his entrenching tool like an ax, slashing, feeling both love and hate, and then later, when it was full dark, he sat at the bottom of his foxhole and wept. It went on for a long while. In part, he was grieving for Ted Lavender, but mostly it was for Martha, and for himself, because she belonged to another world, which was not quite real, and because she was a junior at Mount Sebastian College in New Jersey, a poet and a virgin and uninvolved, and because he realized she did not love him and never would.

Like cement, Kiowa whispered in the dark. I swear to God—boom-down. Not a word.

I've heard this, said Norman Bowker.

A pisser, you know? Still zipping himself up. Zapped while zipping.   45

All right, fine. That's enough.

Yeah, but you had to see it, the guy just—

I *heard*, man. Cement. So why not shut the fuck *up*?

Kiowa shook his head sadly and glanced over at the hole where Lieutenant Jimmy Cross sat watching the night. The air was thick and wet. A warm, dense fog had settled over the paddies and there was the stillness that precedes rain.

After a time Kiowa sighed.   50

One thing for sure, he said. The Lieutenant's in some deep hurt. I mean that crying jag—the way he was carrying on—it wasn't fake or anything, it was real heavy-duty hurt. The man cares.

Sure, Norman Bowker said.

Say what you want, the man does care.

We all got problems.

Not Lavender.   55

No, I guess not, Bowker said. Do me a favor, though.

Shut up?

That's a smart Indian. Shut up.

Shrugging, Kiowa pulled off his boots. He wanted to say more, just to lighten up his sleep, but instead he opened his New Testament and arranged it beneath his head as a pillow. The fog made things seem hollow and unattached. He tried not to think about Ted Lavender, but then he was thinking how fast it was, no drama, down and dead, and how it was hard to feel anything except surprise. It seemed un-Christian. He wished he could find some great sadness, or even anger, but the emotion wasn't there and he couldn't make it happen. Mostly he felt pleased to be alive. He liked the smell of the New Testament under his cheek, the leather and ink and paper and glue, whatever the chemicals were. He liked hearing the sounds of night. Even his fatigue, it felt fine, the stiff muscles and the prickly awareness of his own body, a floating feeling. He enjoyed not being dead. Lying there, Kiowa admired Lieutenant Jimmy Cross's capacity for grief. He wanted to share the man's pain, he wanted to care as Jimmy Cross cared. And yet when he closed his eyes, all he could think was Boom-down, and all he could feel was the pleasure of having his boots off and the fog curling in around him and the damp soil and the Bible smells and the plush comfort of night.

After a moment Norman Bowker sat up in the dark.   60

What the hell, he said. You want to talk, *talk*. Tell it to me.

Forget it.

No, man, go on. One thing I hate, it's a silent Indian.

For the most part they carried themselves with poise, a kind of dignity. Now and then, however, there were times of panic, when they squealed or wanted to squeal but couldn't, when they twitched and made moaning sounds and covered their heads and said Dear Jesus and flopped around on the earth and fired their weapons blindly and cringed and sobbed and begged for the noise to stop and went wild and made stupid promises to themselves and to God and to their mothers and fathers, hoping not to die. In different ways, it happened to all of them. Afterward, when the firing ended, they would blink and peek up. They would touch their bodies, feeling shame, then quickly hiding it. They would force themselves to stand. As if in slow motion, frame by frame, the world would take on the old logic—absolute silence, then the wind, then sunlight, then voices. It was the burden of being alive. Awkwardly, the men would reassemble themselves, first in private, then in groups, becoming soldiers again. They would repair the leaks in their eyes. They would check for casualties, call in dust-offs, light cigarettes, try to smile, clear their throats and spit and begin cleaning their weapons. After a time someone would shake his head and say, No lie, I almost shit my pants, and someone else would laugh, which meant it was bad, yes, but the guy had obviously not shit his pants, it wasn't that bad, and in any case nobody would ever do such a thing and then go ahead and talk about it. They would squint into the dense, oppressive sunlight. For a few moments, perhaps, they would fall silent, lighting a joint and tracking its passage from man to man, inhaling, holding in the humiliation. Scary stuff, one of them might say. But then someone else would grin or flick his eyebrows and say, Roger-dodger, almost cut me a new asshole, *almost*.

There were numerous such poses. Some carried themselves with a sort   65
of istful resignation, others with pride or stiff soldierly discipline or good
humor or macho zeal. They were afraid of dying but they were even more
afraid to show it.

They found jokes to tell.

They used a hard vocabulary to contain the terrible softness. *Greased,*
they'd say. *Offed, lit up°, zapped while zipping°.* It wasn't cruelty, just stage presence. They were actors and the war came at them in 3-D. When someone died,
it wasn't quite dying, because in a curious way it seemed scripted, and because
they had their lines mostly memorized, irony mixed with tragedy, and because
they called it by other names, as if to encyst and destroy the reality of death
itself. They kicked corpses. They cut off thumbs. They talked grunt lingo. They
told stories about Ted Lavender's supply of tranquilizers, how the poor guy
didn't feel a thing, how incredibly tranquil he was.

There's a moral here, said Mitchell Sanders.

They were waiting for Lavender's chopper, smoking the dead man's   70
dope. The moral's pretty obvious, Sanders said, and winked. Stay away
from drugs. No joke, they'll ruin your day every time.

Cute, said Henry Dobbins.

Mind-blower, get it? Talk about wiggy—nothing left, just blood and brains.

They made themselves laugh.

There it is, they'd say, over and over, as if the repetition itself were an act
of poise, a balance between crazy and almost crazy, knowing without going.
There it is, which meant be cool, let it ride, because oh yeah, man, you can't
change what can't be changed, there it is, there it absolutely and positively and
fucking well *is.*

They were tough.   75

They carried all the emotional baggage of men who might die. Grief, terror,
love, longing—these were intangibles, but the intangibles had their own mass
and specific gravity, they had tangible weight. They carried shameful memories.
They carried the common secret of cowardice barely restrained, the instinct to
run or freeze or hide, and in many respects this was the heaviest burden of all,
for it could never be put down, it required perfect balance and perfect posture.
They carried their reputations. They carried the soldier's greatest fear, which
was the fear of blushing. Men killed, and died, because they were embarrassed
not to. It was what had brought them to the war in the first place, nothing
positive, no dreams of glory or honor, just to avoid the blush of dishonor. They
died so as not to die of embarrassment. They crawled into tunnels and walked
point and advanced under fire. Each morning, despite the unknowns, they
made their legs move. They endured. They kept humping. They did not submit

---

°**Offed, lit up:** Killed. °**zapped while zipping:** Killed while urinating

to the obvious alternative, which was simply to close the eyes and fall. So easy, really. Go limp and tumble to the ground and let the muscles unwind and not speak and not budge until your buddies picked you up and lifted you into the chopper that would roar and dip its nose and carry you off to the world. A mere matter of falling, yet no one ever fell. It was not courage, exactly; the object was not valor. Rather, they were too frightened to be cowards.

By and large they carried these things inside, maintaining the masks of composure. They sneered at sick call. They spoke bitterly about guys who had found release by shooting off their own toes or fingers. Pussies, they'd say. Candyasses. It was fierce, mocking talk, with only a trace of envy or awe, but even so, the image played itself out behind their eyes.

They imagined the muzzle against flesh. They imagined the quick, sweet pain, then the evacuation to Japan, then a hospital with warm beds and cute geisha nurses.

They dreamed of freedom birds.

At night, on guard, staring into the dark, they were carried away by jumbo jets. They felt the rush of takeoff. *Gone!* they yelled. And then velocity, wings and engines, a smiling stewardess—but it was more than a plane, it was a real bird, a big sleek silver bird with feathers and talons and high screeching. They were flying. The weights fell off, there was nothing to bear. They laughed and held on tight, feeling the cold slap of wind and altitude, soaring, thinking *It's over, I'm gone!*—they were naked, they were light and free—it was all lightness, bright and fast and buoyant, light as light, a helium buzz in the brain, a giddy bubbling in the lungs as they were taken up over the clouds and the war, beyond duty, beyond gravity and mortification and global entanglements—*Sin loi!* they yelled, *I'm sorry, motherfuckers, but I'm out of it, I'm goofed, I'm on a space cruise, I'm gone!*—and it was a restful, disencumbered sensation, just riding the light waves, sailing that big silver freedom bird over the mountains and oceans, over America, over the farms and great sleeping cities and cemeteries and highways and the golden arches of McDonald's. It was flight, a kind of fleeing, a kind of falling, falling thing weighed exactly nothing. *Gone!* they screamed, *I'm sorry but I'm gone!* And so at night, not quite dreaming, they gave themselves over to lightness, they were carried, they were purely borne.

On the morning after Ted Lavender died, First Lieutenant Jimmy Cross crouched at the bottom of his foxhole and burned Martha's letters. Then he burned the two photographs. There was a steady rain falling, which made it difficult, but he used heat tabs and Sterno to build a small fire, screening it with his body, holding the photographs over the tight blue flame with the tips of his fingers.

He realized it was only a gesture. Stupid, he thought. Sentimental, too, but mostly just stupid.

Lavender was dead. You couldn't burn the blame.

Besides, the letters were in his head. And even now, without photographs, Lieutenant Cross could see Martha playing volleyball in her white gym shorts and yellow T-shirt. He could see her moving in the rain.

When the fire died out, Lieutenant Cross pulled his poncho over his   85 shoulders and ate breakfast from a can.

There was no great mystery, he decided.

In those burned letters Martha had never mentioned the war, except to say, Jimmy, take care of yourself. She wasn't involved. She signed the letters "Love," but it wasn't love, and all the fine lines and technicalities did not matter.

The morning came up wet and blurry. Everything seemed part of everything else, the fog and Martha and the deepening rain.

It was a war, after all.

Half smiling, Lieutenant Jimmy Cross took out his maps. He shook   90 his head hard, as if to clear it, then bent forward and began planning the day's march. In ten minutes, or maybe twenty, he would rouse the men and they would pack up and head west, where the maps showed the country to be green and inviting. They would do what they had always done. The rain might add some weight, but otherwise it would be one more day layered upon all the other days.

He was realistic about it. There was that new hardness in his stomach.

No more fantasies, he told himself.

Henceforth, when he thought about Martha, it would be only to think that she belonged elsewhere. He would shut down the daydreams. This was not Mount Sebastian, it was another world, where there were no pretty poems or midterm exams, a place where men died because of carelessness and gross stupidity. Kiowa was right. Boom-down, and you were dead, never partly dead.

Briefly, in the rain, Lieutenant Cross saw Martha's gray eyes gazing back at him.

He understood.   95

It was very sad, he thought. The things men carried inside. The things men did or felt they had to do.

He almost nodded at her, but didn't.

Instead he went back to his maps. He was now determined to perform his duties firmly and without negligence. It wouldn't help Lavender, he knew that, but from this point on he would comport himself as a soldier. He would dispose of his good-luck pebble. Swallow it, maybe, or use Lee Strunk's slingshot, or just drop it along the trail. On the march he would impose strict field discipline. He would be careful to send out flank security, to prevent straggling or bunching up, to keep his troops moving at the proper pace and at the proper interval. He

would insist on clean weapons. He would confiscate the remainder of Lave.
dope. Later in the day, perhaps, he would call the men together and speak to
them plainly. He would accept the blame for what had happened to Ted Lavender. He would be a man about it. He would look them in the eyes, keeping his
chin level, and he would issue the new SOPs in a calm, impersonal tone of voice,
an officer's voice, leaving no room for argument or discussion. Commencing
immediately, he'd tell them, they would no longer abandon equipment along
the route of march. They would police up their acts. They would get their shit
together, and keep it together, and maintain it neatly and in good working order.

He would not tolerate laxity. He would show strength, distancing   100
himself. Among the men there would be grumbling, of course, and maybe
worse, because their days would seem longer and their loads heavier, but
Lieutenant Cross reminded himself that his obligation was not to be loved
but to lead. He would dispense with love; it was not now a factor. And
if anyone quarreled or complained, he would simply tighten his lips and
arrange his shoulders in the correct command posture. He might give a
curt little nod. Or he might not. He might just shrug and say Carry on,
then they would saddle up and form into a column and move out toward
the villages west of Than Khe.

- Explain how the narrator uses specific objects to reveal details about the
  experience of war. How does the narrative emerge from these details?
  Trace the details that lead us to understand that Ted Lavender died and the
  circumstances of his death. How is perspective important to our understanding of this event?

POETRY

Herman Melville (1819–1891)

A Utilitarian View of the Monitor's Fight (1866)

Plain be the phrase, yet apt the verse,
    More ponderous than nimble;
For since grimed War here laid aside
His painted pomp, 'twould ill befit
        Overmuch to ply   5
    The rhyme's barbaric symbol.

Hail to victory without the gaud
   Of glory; zeal that needs no fans
Of banners; plain mechanic power
Plied cogently in War now placed—   10
      Where War belongs—
   Among the trades and artisans.

Yet this was battle, and intense—
   Beyond the strife of fleets heroic;
Deadlier, closer, calm 'mid storm;   15
No passion; all went on by crank.
      Pivot, and screw,
   And calculations of caloric.

Needless to dwell; the story's known.
   The ringing of those plates on plates   20
Still ringeth round the world—
The clangor of the blacksmiths' fray.
      The anvil-din
   Resounds this message from the Fates:

War shall yet be, and to the end;   25
   But war-paint shows the streaks of weather;
War yet shall be, but the warriors
Are now but operatives; War's made
      Less grand than Peace,
   And a singe runs through lace and feather.   30

- The poem describes the Civil War confrontation between the *Monitor* and the *Merrimac,* two ironclad fighting ships. The novelty of a confrontation between these war machines inspired much discussion about the changing nature of war.

- How does the poet suggest that the nature of "grimed War" has changed? How do these ships signify this change? What remains the same?

e. e. cummings (1894–1962)

[i sing of Olaf glad and big] (1931)

i sing of Olaf glad and big
whose warmest heart recoiled at war:
a conscientious object-or

his wellbelovéd colonel(trig
westpointer most succinctly bred)   5
took erring Olaf soon in hand;
but—though an host of overjoyed
noncoms(first knocking on the head
him)do through icy waters roll
that helplessness which others stroke   10
with brushes recently employed
anent this muddy toiletbowl,
while kindred intellects evoke
allegiance per blunt instruments—
Olaf(being to all intents   15
a corpse and wanting any rag
upon what God unto him gave)
responds,without getting annoyed
"I will not kiss your fucking flag"

straightway the silver bird looked grave   20
(departing hurriedly to shave)

but—though all kinds of officers
(a yearning nation's blueeyed pride)
their passive prey did kick and curse
until for wear their clarion   25
voices and boots were much the worse,
and egged the firstclassprivates on
his rectum wickedly to tease
by means of skilfully applied
bayonets roasted hot with heat—   30
Olaf(upon what were once knees)
does almost ceaselessly repeat
"there is some shit I will not eat"

our president,being of which
assertions duly notified   35
threw the yellowsonofabitch
into a dungeon where he died

Christ(of His mercy infinite)
i pray to see;and Olaf,too

preponderatingly because   40
unless statistics lie he was
more brave than me:more blond than you.

- Who becomes the enemy in this poem? What details in the poem make their actions seem reprehensible?
- What heroic qualities does Olaf demonstrate?

Richard Eberhart (1904–2005)

The Fury of Aerial Bombardment (1945)

You would think the fury of aerial bombardment
Would rouse God to relent; the infinite spaces
Are still silent. He looks on shock-pried faces.
History, even, does not know what is meant.

You would feel that after so many centuries   5
God would give man to repent; yet he can kill
As Cain could, but with multitudinous will,
No farther advanced than in his ancient furies.

Was man made stupid to see his own stupidity?
Is God by definition indifferent, beyond us all?   10
Is the eternal truth man's fighting soul
Wherein the Beast ravens in its own avidity?

Of Van Wettering I speak, and Averill,
Names on a list, whose faces I do not recall
But they are gone to early death, who late in school   15
Distinguished the belt feed lever from the belt holding pawl.

- The "belt feed lever" and the "belt holding pawl" are parts of a machine gun. How does this poem describe the mechanical efficiency of modern warfare?
- How is this particular meditation distinct from Melville's comments (p. 1216) on a similar theme?

Edgar A. Guest (1881–1959)

The Things That Make a Soldier Great (1918)

The things that make a soldier great
and send him out to die,

To face the flaming cannon's mouth
nor ever question why,
Are lilacs by a little porch,   5
the row of tulips red,
The peonies and pansies, too,
the old petunia bed,
The grass plot where his children play,
the roses on the wall: 10
'Tis these that make a soldier great.
He's fighting for them all.

'Tis not the pomp and pride of kings
that make a soldier brave;
'Tis not allegiance to the flag   15
that over him may wave;
For soldiers never fight so well
on land or on the foam
As when behind the cause they see
the little place called home.   20
Endanger but that humble street
whereon his children run,
You make a soldier of the man
who never bore a gun.

What is it through the battle smoke   25
the valiant soldier sees?
The little garden far away,
the budding apple trees,
The little patch of ground back there,
the children at their play,   30
Perhaps a tiny mound behind
the simple church of gray.
The golden thread of courage
isn't linked to castle dome
But to the spot, where'er it be—   35
the humblest spot called home.

And now the lilacs bud again
and all is lovely there
And homesick soldiers far away
know spring is in the air;   40
The tulips come to bloom again,

the grass once more is green,
And every man can see the spot
where all his joys have been.
He sees his children smile at him,
he hears the bugle call,   45
And only death can stop him now—
he's fighting for them all.

■ Mark the ways in which this poem presents the dilemma of war in a
different light than the previous poems.

Sir Henry Newbolt (1862–1938)

Vitai Lampada (1897)

There's a breathless hush in the Close to-night—
Ten to make and the match to win—
A bumping pitch and a blinding light,
An hour to play and the last man in.
And it's not for the sake of a ribboned coat,   5
Or the selfish hope of a season's fame,
But his Captain's hand on his shoulder smote
"Play up! play up! and play the game!"

The sand of the desert is sodden red,—
Red with the wreck of a square that broke;—   10
The Gatling's jammed and the colonel dead,
And the regiment blind with dust and smoke.
The river of death has brimmed his banks,
And England's far, and Honour a name,
But the voice of schoolboy rallies the ranks,   15
"Play up! play up! and play the game!"

This is the word that year by year
While in her place the School is set
Every one of her sons must hear,
And none that hears it dare forget.   20
This they all with a joyful mind
Bear through life like a torch in flame,
And falling fling to the host behind—
"Play up! play up! and play the game!"

- How are the contexts for the cries "Play up!" different? Why is it appropriate to juxtapose them here?
- What is the impact of this repeated refrain? How does this poem fit among the other poems that are gathered here?

Wilfred Owen (1893–1918)

Anthem for Doomed Youth (1917)

What passing-bells for these who die as cattle?
Only the monstrous anger of the guns.
Only the stuttering rifles' rapid rattle
Can patter out their hasty orisons.
No mockeries now for them; no prayers nor bells,   5
Nor any voice of mourning save the choirs,—
The shrill, demented choirs of wailing shells;
And bugles calling for them from sad shires.
What candles may be held to speed them all?
Not in the hands of boys, but in their eyes   10
Shall shine the holy glimmers of good-byes.
The pallor of girls' brows shall be their pall;
Their flowers the tenderness of patient minds,
And each slow dusk of drawing-down of blinds.

Wilfred Owen (1893–1918)

Dulce et Decorum Est (1920)

Bent double, like old beggars under sacks,
Knock-kneed, coughing like hags, we cursed through sludge,
Till on the haunting flares we turned our backs,
And towards our distant rest began to trudge.
Men marched asleep. Many had lost their boots,   5
But limped on, blood-shod. All went lame, all blind;
Drunk with fatigue; deaf even to the hoots
Of gas-shells dropping softly behind.

Gas! GAS! Quick, boys!—An ecstasy of fumbling,
Fitting the clumsy helmets just in time,   10

But someone still was yelling out and stumbling
And flound'ring like a man in fire or lime.—
Dim through the misty panes and thick green light,
As under a green sea, I saw him drowning.
In all my dreams before my helpless sight   15
He plunges at me, guttering, choking, drowning.
If in some smothering dreams, you too could pace
Behind the wagon that we flung him in,
And watch the white eyes writhing in his face,
His hanging face, like a devil's sick of sin,   20
If you could hear, at every jolt, the blood
Come gargling from the froth-corrupted lungs
Bitter as the cud
Of vile, incurable sores on innocent tongues,—
My friend, you would not tell with such high zest   25
To children ardent for some desperate glory,
The old lie: *Dulce et decorum est*
Pro patria mori.

- Owen died as a soldier in World War I. How does this context add to the impact of the poem that calls the old Latin phrase "Sweet and honorable it is to die for one's country" a lie?

- What impact does the poet achieve by adopting a Latin phrase or "Anthem" for the titles of his poems? How do Owen's poems build upon the tradition that we see in Newbolt's poem?

Carl Sandburg (1878–1967)

Grass (1918)

Pile the bodies high at Austerlitz and Waterloo.
Shovel them under and let me work—
                    I am the grass; I cover all.

And pile them high at Gettysburg
And pile them high at Ypres and Verdun.   5
Shovel them under and let me work.
Two years, ten years, and passengers ask the conductor:
                  What place is this?
                  Where are we now?

> I am the grass.   10
> Let me work.

- What is the work that the grass is doing?
- What is the significance of the questions that the passengers ask the conductor?

Siegfried Sassoon (1886–1967)

The Rear-Guard (1918)

(Hindenburg Line, April 1917)

Groping along the tunnel, step by step,
He winked his prying torch with patching glare
From side to side, and sniffed the unwholesome air.

Tins, boxes, bottles, shapes too vague to know;
A mirror smashed, the mattress from a bed;   5
And he, exploring fifty feet below
The rosy gloom of battle overhead.

Tripping, he grabbed the wall; saw some one lie
Humped at his feet, half-hidden by a rug,
And stooped to give the sleeper's arm a tug.   10
"I'm looking for headquarters." No reply.
"God blast your neck!" (For days he'd had no sleep.)

"Get up and guide me through this stinking place."
Savage, he kicked a soft, unanswering heap,
And flashed his beam across the livid face   15
Terribly glaring up, whose eyes yet wore
Agony dying hard ten days before;
And fists of fingers clutched a blackening wound.

Alone he staggered on until he found
Dawn's ghost that filtered down a shafted stair   20
To the dazed, muttering creatures underground
Who hear the boom of shells in muffled sound.
At last, with sweat of horror in his hair,
He climbed through darkness to the twilight air,
Unloading hell behind him step by step.   25

Siegfried Sassoon (1886–1967)

Repression of War Experience (1918)

Now light the candles; one; two; there's a moth;
What silly beggars they are to blunder in
And scorch their wings with glory, liquid flame—
No, no, not that,—it's bad to think of war,
When thoughts you've gagged all day come back to scare you;   5
And it's been proved that soldiers don't go mad
Unless they lose control of ugly thoughts
That drive them out to jabber among the trees.

Now light your pipe; look, what a steady hand.
Draw a deep breath; stop thinking; count fifteen,   10
And you're as right as rain ...
                    Why won't it rain? ...
I wish there'd be a thunder-storm to-night,
With bucketsful of water to sluice the dark,
And make the roses hang their dripping heads.
Books; what a jolly company they are,   15
Standing so quiet and patient on their shelves,
Dressed in dim brown, and black, and white, and green,
And every kind of colour. Which will you read?
Come on; O *do* read something; they're so wise.
I tell you all the wisdom of the world   20
Is waiting for you on those shelves; and yet
You sit and gnaw your nails, and let your pipe out,
And listen to the silence: on the ceiling
There's one big, dizzy moth that bumps and flutters;
And in the breathless air outside the house   25
The garden waits for something that delays.
There must be crowds of ghosts among the trees,—
Not people killed in battle,—they're in France,—
Slow, natural deaths,—old men with ugly souls,
Who wore their bodies out with nasty sins.   30

* * *

You're quiet and peaceful, summering safe at home;
You'd never think there was a bloody war on! ...
O yes, you would ... why, you can hear the guns.
Hark! Thud, thud, thud,—quite soft ... they never cease—
Those whispering guns—O Christ, I want to go out   35

And screech at them to stop—I'm going crazy;
I'm going stark, staring mad because of the guns.

■ These two poems describe the experience of war from the perspective
of the soldier. How does the "Repression of War Experience" change the
context from that in "The Rear-Guard"? In this new context, what must the
protagonist fight? Compare the images that the poet uses to evoke horror in
the first poem to those that appear in the second.

Anne Sexton (1928–1974)

Courage (1975)

It is in the small things we see it.
The child's first step,
as awesome as an earthquake.
The first time you rode a bike,
wallowing up the sidewalk.   5
The first spanking when your heart
went on a journey all alone.
When they called you crybaby
or poor or fatty or crazy
and made you into an alien,   10
you drank their acid
and concealed it.

Later,
if you faced the death of bombs and bullets
you did not do it with a banner,   15
you did it with only a hat to
cover your heart.
You did not fondle the weakness inside you
though it was there.
Your courage was a small coal   20
that you kept swallowing.
If your buddy saved you
and died himself in so doing,
then his courage was not courage,
it was love; love as simple as shaving soap.   25

Later,
if you have endured a great despair,
then you did it alone,
getting a transfusion from the fire,

picking the scabs off your heart,   30
then wringing it out like a sock.
Next, my kinsman, you powdered your sorrow,
you gave it a back rub
and then you covered it with a blanket
and after it had slept a while   35
it woke to the wings of the roses
and was transformed.

Later,
when you face old age and its natural conclusion
your courage will still be shown in the little ways,   40
each spring will be a sword you'll sharpen,
those you love will live in a fever of love,
and you'll bargain with the calendar
and at the last moment
when death opens the back door   45
you'll put on your carpet slippers
and stride out.

- How do the four different contexts present different interpretations of the word *courage*? What do they each have in common? Is any one of the types of courage more courageous than the others? Explain how the poem supports your claim.

- In the second stanza, the soldier's "buddy" demonstrates love rather than courage. Who makes this distinction?

DRAMA

Václav Havel (1936–2011)

Václav Havel was born in Prague to a family that was involved in the culture and politics of Czechoslovakia before World War II. He served an apprenticeship as a chemical laboratory assistant and was denied admission into any university with a humanities program because his family's political heritage was a liability under the communist government. Havel turned to playwriting, and his absurdist dramas, with their critique of communist power, gained him an international reputation although his plays were banned in his own country after 1968. His political activity resulted in several prison terms, the longest of which lasted from 1979 to 1983. His best known and most influential essay is *The Power of the Powerless* in which he shows that under communism the citizens are compelled to accept a social order in which they "live within a lie." When the "Velvet Revolution" ended communist control of the country in 1989, Havel was elected to serve as president, and when the Czech Republic was formed in 1993, he was elected to be its first president. After serving as president, he continued to write plays, publishing *Leaving* in 2007. The play is based on Shakespeare's *King Lear* and on Chekhov's *The Cherry Orchard*.

Temptation (1985)

Translated by Marie Winn

For Zdenek Urbanek

CHARACTERS

DR. HENRY FOUSTKA, *scientist*
FISTULA, *a retired cripple*
DIRECTOR
VILMA, *a scientist*
DEPUTY DIRECTOR
MARKETA, *a secretary*
DR. LIBUSHE LORENCOVA, *a scientist*
DR. VILEM KOTRLY, *a scientist*
DR. ALOIS NEUWIRTH, *a scientist*
MRS. HOUBOVA, *Foustka's landlady*
DANCER
PETRUSHKA
SECRET MESSENGER
LOVER (*male*)
LOVER (*female*)

SCENES

The Institute
Foustka's apartment
The garden of the Institute
Vilma's apartment
The Institute
Intermission
Foustka's apartment
The Institute
Vilma's apartment
Foustka's apartment
The garden of the Institute

NOTE: *Before the curtain rises, during the pauses between scenes, and during the intermission, a particular piece of rock music of the "cosmic" or "astral" type may be heard. It is important that the pauses between scenes be as short as possible; consequently, the scene changes—in spite of various scenic requirements due to the alternating stage settings—should be carried out as swiftly as possible.*

Scene 1

One of the rooms of the scientific Institute where FOUSTKA *is employed. It is something between a business office, a doctor's office, a library, a club room, and a lobby. There are three doors, one at the rear, one at the front left, one at the front right. At the right rear is a bench, a small table, and two chairs; against the rear wall is a bookcase, a narrow couch covered with oilcloth, and a white cabinet with glass windows containing various exhibits, such as embryos, models of human organs, cult objects of primitive tribes, etc. At the left is a desk with a typewriter and various papers on it, behind it is an office chair, and against the wall is a file cabinet; in the middle of the room hangs a large chandelier. There might be some additional equipment around, such as a sun lamp, a sink, or an exercise apparatus against the wall (specifically, a rypstol, a Swedish ladderlike gymnastic apparatus). The furnishings of the room are not an indication of any specific areas of interest or even of any particular personality but correspond, rather, to the indeterminate mission of the entire Institute. The combination of objects of various sorts and of various designs emphasizes the timeless anonymity of a space in which things have been brought together more by chance than for any definite purpose. As the curtain rises,* LORENCOVA, KOTRLY, *and* NEUWIRTH *are onstage.* LORENCOVA, *wearing a white doctor's coat, is seated at the desk, with a mirror propped up against the typewriter, where she is powdering her nose.* KOTRLY, *wearing a white coat, is sprawled out on the bench reading a newspaper.* NEUWIRTH, *dressed in everyday clothing, is standing in the rear by the bookcase, his back to the audience, looking at a book. There is a short pause.*

LORENCOVA (*calling*): Marketa . . .
MARKETA (*wearing an office smock, enters through the door at left*):   Yes, Doctor?
LORENCOVA: Would you please make me a cup of coffee?
MARKETA: Certainly.
KOTRLY (*without glancing up*):   One for me too, please.   5
NEUWIRTH (*without turning around*):   And me.
MARKETA: Will that be three, then?
LORENCOVA: Right.

(MARKETA *exits through the left door. A short pause, after which* FOUSTKA *enters quickly through the rear door, a bit out of breath. He is wearing black trousers and a black sweater and carries a briefcase.*)

FOUSTKA: Hi.
KOTRLY (*putting aside the newspaper*):   Hello, Henry.   10
NEUWIRTH (*puts aside the book and turns around*):   Hi.

(LORENCOVA *tucks the compact away in the pocket of her jacket and crosses the stage to the bench where* KOTRLY *is sitting, obviously making way at the desk for* FOUSTKA. *He sets his briefcase on it and hastily takes out some papers. The others watch him with interest.*)

FOUSTKA: Were they here yet?

KOTRLY: Not yet.

LORENCOVA: What's with Vilma?

FOUSTKA: She just ran across the street for some oranges.   15

(MARKETA *enters through the left door with three cups of coffee on a small tray. She puts two down on the table in front of* LORENCOVA *and* KOTRLY, *the third she hands to* NEUWIRTH, *who is standing in the rear, leaning against the bookcase.*)

LORENCOVA: Thank you.

FOUSTKA: Marketa . . .

MARKETA (*stops*):   Yes, Doctor?

FOUSTKA: I'm sorry, but could you possibly make one more cup for me?

MARKETA: Certainly.   20

FOUSTKA: Thanks a lot.

(MARKETA *exits through the left door.* LORENCOVA, KOTRLY, *and* NEUWIRTH *stir their coffees, at the same time watching* FOUSTKA, *who has seated himself at the desk and is straightening out various papers and files. Finally* KOTRLY *interrupts the rather long and somewhat tense silence.*)

KOTRLY (*to* FOUSTKA):   So, what?

FOUSTKA: What, what?

KOTRLY: How's it going?

FOUSTKA: How's what going?   25

(LORENCOVA, KOTRLY, *and* NEUWIRTH *exchange glances and smile. A short pause.*)

LORENCOVA: Why, your private studies.

FOUSTKA: I don't know what studies you're talking about.

(LORENCOVA, KOTRLY, *and* NEUWIRTH *exchange glances and smile. A short pause.*)

NEUWIRTH: Come on, Henry, even the birds and bees in the trees are buzzing about it!

FOUSTKA: I'm not interested in what the birds and bees in the trees are   30
buzzing about, and I have no other scholarly pursuits besides those
directly concerned with my work at our Institute.

KOTRLY: You don't trust us, do you? I don't blame you. In certain situations caution is definitely in order.

NEUWIRTH: Especially if a person is playing both ends against the middle.   35

FOUSTKA (*quickly looks over at* NEUWIRTH):   What do you mean by that?

(NEUWIRTH *moves his outstretched finger meaningfully around the room, pointing finally to the door at right, by which he means to indicate the powers that run the Institute, after which he points up and down, by which he means to indicate the power of heaven and hell.*)

You've all got overactive imaginations! Is the office party on tonight?
LORENCOVA: Of course.

(*The* DEPUTY DIRECTOR, *in everyday clothes, and* PETRUSHKA, *in a white coat, enter through the right door. They are holding hands, and will continue to hold hands during the entire play. This means that* PETRUSHKA, *who doesn't speak a word during the entire play, usually follows the* DEPUTY DIRECTOR. *He, however, doesn't pay her any special attention, creating the impression, therefore, that he is dragging her around with him as some sort of prop or mascot.* LORENCOVA, KOTRLY, *and* FOUSTKA *stand up.*)

KOTRLY: Good morning, Sir.
DEPUTY: Hello there, my friends! And please sit down. You know that   40
neither I nor the director like to stand on ceremony here.

(LORENCOVA, KOTRLY, *and* FOUSTKA *sit down again. A short pause.*)

So what's new. Did you all get a good night's sleep? Do you have any
problems? I don't see Vilma here.
FOUSTKA: She called to say that her bus broke down. But apparently she managed to get a taxi and ought to be here very soon.   45

(*Short pause.*)

DEPUTY: Well, are you looking forward to the party? I hope you're all
coming.
KOTRLY: I'm definitely coming.
LORENCOVA: We're all coming.
DEPUTY: Wonderful! I personally consider our office parties to be a mar-   50
velous thing—mainly for their collectively psychotherapeutic effect. Just
think how quickly and easily those interpersonal problems that crop up
among us from time to time are resolved in that informal atmosphere!
And that's entirely due to the fact that as individuals we loosen up
there somehow, while as a community we somehow tighten up. Isn't   55
that the truth?
KOTRLY: That's precisely the way I feel about it.
DEPUTY: Apart from the fact that it would be an outright sin not to use
such a beautiful garden at least once in a while! (*Pause.*) I came a little
early on purpose . . .   60
NEUWIRTH: Did something happen?
DEPUTY: The director will tell you himself. Let me just ask you to be sensible, to try to understand him, and to try not to make his already rather
difficult situation even more difficult unnecessarily. After all, we know
we can't knock down walls with our heads, can we—why, then, should   65
we complicate life for others and for our own selves! I think we can be

glad we have the kind of director we have, so that by helping him we'll actually be helping our own selves. We should all bear in mind that essentially he's working for a good cause, that even he is not his own master, and that therefore we have no other alternative than to exercise   70
at least that minimal amount of self-control necessary to make sure that neither he, our Institute, nor, consequently, any of us has any unnecessary problems. Actually there's nothing unusual about any of this. After all, a certain amount of inner discipline is required of everyone everywhere in today's world! I believe that you understand what I'm   75
saying and that you won't expect me to tell you more than I can and have already told you. We're adults, after all, aren't we?

KOTRLY: Yes.

DEPUTY: So there you are! Have you received the soap allotment yet?

FOUSTKA: I'm going to distribute it today.   80

DEPUTY: Splendid!

(*The* DIRECTOR, *wearing a white coat, enters through the right door.* LORENCOVA, KOTRLY, *and* FOUSTKA *stand up immediately.*)

KOTRLY: Good morning, Sir.

DIRECTOR: Hello there, my friends! And please sit down. You know that I don't like to stand on ceremony here!

DEPUTY: That's precisely what I was telling our colleagues here just a   85
second ago, Sir!

(LORENCOVA, KOTRLY, *and* FOUSTKA *sit down again. The* DIRECTOR *looks intently at those present for a while, then steps up to* FOUSTKA *and holds out his hand.* FOUSTKA, *surprised, rises.*)

DIRECTOR (*to* FOUSTKA): Did you get a good night's sleep?

FOUSTKA: Yes, thank you.

DIRECTOR: Do you have any problems?

FOUSTKA: Not really . . .   90

(*The* DIRECTOR *presses Foustka's elbow in a friendly way and turns to the others.* FOUSTKA *sits down again.*)

DIRECTOR: Where's Vilma?

DEPUTY: She called to say that her bus broke down. But apparently she managed to get a taxi and ought to be here very soon.

(MARKETA *enters through the left door with a cup of coffee. She hands it to* FOUSTKA.)

FOUSTKA: Thank you.

MARKETA: Don't mention it. (*Exits through the left door.*)   95

DIRECTOR: Well, are you looking forward to our party?

KOTRLY: Very much, Sir.

DEPUTY: Friends, I have some very good news for you on that subject: our director has promised to drop in for a moment tonight.

LORENCOVA: Just for a moment? 100

DIRECTOR: That will depend on the circumstances. (*To* FOUSTKA:) I hope you're coming.

FOUSTKA: Of course, Sir.

DIRECTOR: Look, colleagues, there's no sense in my dragging this out unnecessarily—we've all got enough work of our own. So, to get to the 105 point: as you probably know by now, there have been an increasing number of complaints lately that our Institute is not fulfilling its mission in a way that responds to the present situation . . .

NEUWIRTH: What situation?

DIRECTOR: Let's not beat around the bush, my friend! Aren't you forget- 110 ting that we're supposed to be the first to hear about certain things and also the first to react to them? Isn't that what we're paid for! But that's not the problem. We're simply beginning to feel more and more pressure to start taking the offensive, meaning that through our widely publicized, popularized, pedagogical, cultural, scholarly, 115 and individually therapeutic scientific work we must finally start confronting—

DEPUTY: In the spirit of scientific inquiry, of course . . .

DIRECTOR: Doesn't that go without saying?

DEPUTY: Excuse me, Sir, but there does exist, unfortunately, a certain 120 science that is not based on the spirit of scientific inquiry.

DIRECTOR: That, in my opinion, is not a science! Where was I?

KOTRLY: You were saying that somehow we're supposed to finally start confronting . . .

DIRECTOR: Certain rather isolated but nonetheless alarming manifestations 125 of those irrational attitudes cropping up primarily among a particular segment of the younger generation, and originating in an incorrect . . .

(*The* SECRET MESSENGER *enters through the right door, steps up to the* DIRECTOR, *and whispers at length into his ear. The* DIRECTOR *nods his head gravely as he whispers. After a long while the* MESSENGER *concludes. The* DIRECTOR *nods one more time. The* MESSENGER *exits through the right door. A short pause.*)

Where was I?

KOTRLY: You were saying that those irrational attitudes we're supposed to confront originate in an incorrect . . . 130

DIRECTOR: Understanding of the systemic complexity of natural phenomena and the historical dynamic of civilizational processes out of which

certain incomplete aspects are extracted, only to be interpreted either
in the spirit of pseudoscientific theory . . .

DEPUTY: We know for a fact that a number of illegal typescripts by C. G.   135
Jung are circulating among the youth . . .

DIRECTOR: . . . or in the spirit of an entire spectrum of mystical prejudices,
superstitions, obscure doctrines, and practices disseminated by certain
charlatans, psychopaths, and intelligent people . . .

(VILMA, *out of breath, rushes in through the rear door, holding a bag of oranges.*)

VILMA: Please excuse me, Sir—I'm so sorry—but can you imagine that the   140
bus I was riding—

DIRECTOR: I know about it, sit down . . .

(VILMA *sits on the oilcloth-covered couch, waves at* FOUSTKA, *and tries to communicate something to him via gestures and mime.*)

Look, colleagues, there's no sense in my dragging this out unnecessarily—we've all got enough work of our own. I've acquainted you with
the basic facts of the situation, and our consequent duties, so now   145
everything depends entirely on you. I would only like to ask you to be
sensible, to try to understand me, and to try not to make my already
rather difficult situation even more difficult unnecessarily. It's all for
a good cause, after all! Aren't we living in a modern day and age, for
heaven's sake?   150

KOTRLY: We are.

DIRECTOR: So there you are! Have you received the soap allotment yet?

FOUSTKA: I'm going to distribute it today.

(*The* DIRECTOR *steps up to* FOUSTKA; FOUSTKA *stands up. The* DIRECTOR *places his
hand on his shoulder and gravely looks at him for a short while.*)

DIRECTOR (*gently*):   I'm counting on you, Henry.

FOUSTKA: For the soap?   155

DIRECTOR: The soap and everything else!

The curtain falls.

Scene 2

*Foustka's apartment. It is a smallish bachelor quarters with one door at the right
rear. The walls are covered with bookshelves, which are filled with a great quantity of
books. At the left is a window, in front of which is a desk covered with many papers
and more books. Behind it is a chair. At the right is a low sofa. Beside it is a large
globe. A star chart is hanging somewhere on the bookshelves. As the curtain rises,
FOUSTKA, in a dressing gown, is kneeling in the middle of the room with four burning*

candles on the floor around him. He holds a fifth one in his left hand and a piece of chalk in his right hand, with which he draws a circle around himself and the four candles. A large old volume lies opened on the floor beside him. The room is dimly lit. When FOUSTKA *completes his circle he glances at the book and studies something in it for a while. Then he shakes his head and mumbles something. At that moment someone knocks at the door.* FOUSTKA *is startled and jumps to his feet.*

FOUSTKA (*calling out*):   Just a minute!

(FOUSTKA *quickly turns on the light, blows out the candles, hastily puts them away somewhere behind his desk, puts away the volume, looks around, then with his foot tries to erase the chalk circle he had drawn on the floor.*)

    (*calling:*) Who is it?
HOUBOVA (*offstage*):   It's me, Professor.
FOUSTKA (*calling*):   Come in, Mrs. Houbova.
HOUBOVA (*entering*):   Boy, it's really smoky in here. You ought to air the   5
    place out.
FOUSTKA: I will, right away. Did something happen?
HOUBOVA: You have a visitor.
FOUSTKA: Me? Who?
HOUBOVA: I don't know. He didn't introduce himself.   10
FOUSTKA: So it's someone you don't know.
HOUBOVA: He hasn't been here before—at least I've never seen him.
FOUSTKA: What does he look like?
HOUBOVA: Well—how can I put it—a little seedy—and mainly, well . . .
FOUSTKA: What?   15
HOUBOVA: It's embarrassing . . .
FOUSTKA: Just say it, Mrs. Houbova!
HOUBOVA: Well, he simply . . . smells . . .
FOUSTKA: Really? But how?
HOUBOVA: It's hard to describe . . . sort of like Limburger cheese . . .   20
FOUSTKA: My word! Well, never mind, show him in.

(HOUBOVA *exits, leaving the door ajar.*)

HOUBOVA (*offstage*):   This way, please.

(FISTULA *enters. He is a smallish person, almost a dwarf, limping, and giving off a distinctly unsavory impression. He holds a paper bag containing his slippers.* HOUBOVA *casts a final glance after him, shrugs at* FOUSTKA, *and exits, closing the door behind her.* FISTULA *is grinning stupidly.* FOUSTKA *looks at him with surprise. A pause.*)

FOUSTKA: Good evening.

FISTULA: Greetings. (*Pause. Looks around him with interest.*) What a cozy place
you have here, just as I'd imagined it. Good books—a rare globe—every-   25
thing somehow as it ought to be—the balances don't lie.

FOUSTKA: I don't know what balances you're talking about. But first of all
I don't even know who I'm speaking to . . .

FISTULA: All in good time. May I sit down?

FOUSTKA: Please.   30

(FISTULA *sits on the couch. Takes off his shoes, removes the slippers from the paper
bag, puts them on, puts the shoes into the bag, and then places it on the sofa beside
him. A pause.*)

FISTULA: I assume that I don't have to ask you not to mention my visit to
anyone, for your sake as well as mine.

FOUSTKA: Why shouldn't I mention it?

FISTULA: You'll see why soon enough. My name is Fistula. Where I'm
employed is of no importance, and in any event I don't even have a   35
permanent position, nor do I need to have one, since I'm a cripple
with a pension. (*Grins stupidly as if he has made a joke.*)

FOUSTKA: I'd guess that you work in a safety-match factory.

FISTULA (*chuckles, then suddenly grows serious*):   That comes from a certain
unidentified fungus of the foot. It makes me quite miserable and I do   40
what I can for it, even though there's not much I can do.

(FOUSTKA *sits on the corner of the desk and looks at* FISTULA. *In his look we sense a
mixture of curiosity, mistrust, and revulsion. A longer pause.*)

Aren't you going to ask me what I want or why I've come?

FOUSTKA: I'm ever hopeful that you'll tell me that yourself.

FISTULA: That, of course, would be quite possible, but I had a particular
reason for not doing it until now.   45

FOUSTKA: What was it?

FISTULA: I was interested to see whether you'd figure it out for yourself.

FOUSTKA (*irately*):   How could I figure it out when I've never seen you before
in my life! In any case, I have neither the time nor the inclination to
play guessing games with you. Unlike you, I happen to have a job and   50
I'm leaving in a few minutes . . .

FISTULA: For the office party, right? But you've got heaps of time for that!

FOUSTKA: How do you know that I'm going to the office party?

FISTULA: And before my arrival you weren't exactly behaving like someone
in a hurry either . . .   55

FOUSTKA: You don't know a thing about what I was doing before your arrival.

FISTULA: I beg your pardon, but I certainly know better than you do what I
know and what I don't know, and how I know what I know!

(FISTULA *grins stupidly. A longer pause. Then* FOUSTKA *stands up, crosses to the other side of his desk, and turns gravely to* FISTULA.)

FOUSTKA: Look, Mister . . .   60
FISTULA: Fistula.
FOUSTKA: Look, Mister Fistula, I'm asking you plainly and simply, in all seriousness, and I'm expecting a plain and simple, serious answer from you: What do you want?

(*A short pause.*)

FISTULA: Does the name Marbuel say anything to you? Or Loradiel? Or   65
Lafiel?

(FOUSTKA *gives a start, quickly regains his control, gives a long shocked look at* FISTULA.)

FOUSTKA (*exclaiming*):   Out!
FISTULA: Excuse me?
FOUSTKA: I said: Out!
FISTULA: What do you mean—out?   70
FOUSTKA: Leave my apartment immediately and never set foot in it again!

(FISTULA *rubs his hands contentedly.*)

Did you hear me?
FISTULA: I heard you clearly and I'm delighted by this reaction of yours because it absolutely confirms that I've come to the right place.
FOUSTKA: What do you mean?   75
FISTULA: Your fright, don't you see, makes it perfectly clear that you're fully aware of the importance of my contacts, which you wouldn't be if you hadn't been interested in the aforementioned powers earlier.
FOUSTKA: Those names don't mean a thing to me, I haven't the faintest idea of what you're talking about; moreover, the suddenness of my   80
demand that you leave merely reflected the suddenness with which I became fed up with you. My disgust coming at the same time that you pronounced those names was a complete coincidence! And now, having given you this explanation, I can only repeat what I said before, but this time without any fear that you might mistake my meaning: Leave my   85
apartment immediately and never set foot in it again!
FISTULA: Your first request for me to leave—that I'll naturally grant, though probably not quite immediately. Your second request I will not grant, for which you will be very grateful to me later on.
FOUSTKA: You missed my meaning. Those weren't two independent   90
requests, in fact they weren't requests at all. It was a demand—a single and indivisible one at that!

FISTULA: I'll make a note of it. But I'd also like to point something out:
the haste with which you slipped in an additional motivation for
your demand, together with the interesting fact that even though you   95
claimed to be fed up with me, you considered it important enough to
slip in this additional motivation even at the risk of delaying my longed-
for departure—that haste together with that interesting fact are proof
to me of one single thing: that your original fear of me as a middle-
man for certain contacts has now been superseded by a fear of me as   100
a potential informer. Let me assure you, however, that I was counting
on this phase as well. In fact had it not set in I would have felt quite
uneasy. I would have considered it peculiar and would have wondered
myself whether in fact *you* weren't an informer yourself. But now let
me get down to business. There's obviously no way I can prove to you   105
that I'm not an informer; even if I were to conjure up Ariel himself
at this moment it still wouldn't eliminate the possibility of my being
an informer. Therefore, you have only three choices. First, to consider
me an informer and to continue to insist on my immediate departure.
Second, not to consider me an informer and to trust me. Third, not to   110
make up your mind for the time being as to whether I'm an informer
or not, but to adopt a waiting attitude, meaning on the one hand not
to kick me out immediately and on the other hand not to say anything
in front of me that might eventually be used against you if I actually
were an informer. I'd like to recommend the third alternative.   115

(FOUSTKA *paces the room deep in thought; finally he sits down at his desk and looks*
over at FISTULA.)

FOUSTKA: Very well, I'll accept that, but I'd like to point out that there's
obviously no need for me to control or restrict my speech in any way
because there's absolutely nothing I could possibly think, much less say,
that might possibly be used against me.

FISTULA (*exclaiming*):   Marvelous! (*Claps his hands with pleasure.*) You delight   120
me! If I were an informer I'd have to admit that you avoided the first
trap beautifully! Your declaration is clear evidence of your absolutely
solid caution, intelligence, and quick wit, qualities that I eagerly welcome, since they give me hope that I'll be able to depend on you and
that we'll be able to work together well.   125

(*Pause.*)

FOUSTKA: Listen, Mister . . .
FISTULA: Fistula.
FOUSTKA: Listen, Mister Fistula, I'd like to tell you two things. First of all,
your talk is a bit redundant for my taste. You really ought to get to the

point of what brought you here more quickly. You've said virtually   130
nothing, even though I asked you ages ago for a serious, direct, and
concise answer to the question of what you actually want. And secondly, it surprises me greatly to hear that we're supposed to be working
together on something. That requires two people, after all . . .

FISTULA: Your answer had eighty-six words. Considering its semantic value   135
that isn't exactly a small number, and if I were you I wouldn't reproach
anybody too severely for redundancy.

FOUSTKA: Bullshit is infectious, as we know.

FISTULA: I hope that as time goes by you'll adopt some of my more important skills as well.   140

FOUSTKA: You actually want to teach me something?

FISTULA: Not only to teach . . .

FOUSTKA: What else, for God's sake?

FISTULA (*crying out*):   Leave him out of this!

FOUSTKA: Well, what else are you planning to do with me?   145

FISTULA (*smiling*):   To initiate you . . .

(FOUSTKA *stands up abruptly and bangs his fist on the table.*)

FOUSTKA (*shouting*):   That's enough! I'm a scientist with a scientific outlook
on life, holding down a responsible job at one of our foremost scientific
establishments! If anyone were to speak in my presence in a way that's
obviously intended to spread superstition, I'd be forced to proceed in   150
accordance with my scientific conscience!

(*For a moment* FISTULA *stares stupidly at* FOUSTKA, *then he suddenly begins to laugh
wildly and dance around the room. Just as suddenly he falls silent, comes to a stop,
stoops to the ground, and with his finger slowly traces the circle that* FOUSTKA *had
drawn there earlier, after which he jumps up and begins to laugh wildly again. Then
he goes over to the desk, seizes one of the hidden candlesticks, waves it in the air and,
still laughing, places it on the desk.* FOUSTKA *watches him, goggle-eyed. Then suddenly,* FISTULA *becomes serious again, returns to the couch, and sits down.*)

FISTULA (*matter-of-factly*):   I know your views well, Doctor Foustka. I know
how much you love your work at the Institute, and I apologize for my
foolish joke. Anyhow, it's high time for me to cut out all this preliminary joking around. As your director emphasized again this morning,   155
one of your Institute's tasks is to fight against certain manifestations of
irrational mysticism that keep cropping up here and there as a sort of
obscurely preserved residue of the prescientific thinking of primitive
tribes and the Dark Ages of history. As a scientist you know perfectly
well that the more thoroughly you're armed with knowledge about   160
what you're supposed to be fighting against, that much more effective

your fight will be. You have at your disposal quite a decent collection of occult literature—almost all the basics are here, from Agrippa and Nostradamus to Eliphas Levy and Papus—nevertheless, theory isn't everything, and I can't believe that you've never felt the need to acquaint   165
yourself with the practice of black magic directly. I come to you as a sorcerer with several hundred successful magical and theurgical evocations under his belt who is ready and willing to acquaint you with certain aspects of this practice in order to give you a base for your scientific studies. And in case you're asking yourself why in the world a sorcerer   170
should want to join a battle against witchcraft, I can even give you a convincing reply to that: I seem to be in a tricky situation in which I might come to a bad end without cover of some sort. I am therefore offering you my own self for study, and I ask nothing in return besides your vouching for me, if the need arises, that I turned myself over to   175
the disposition of science, and that therefore it would be unfair to hold me responsible for the propagation of something which, in reality, I was helping to fight against.

(FISTULA *looks gravely at* FOUSTKA; FOUSTKA *reflects.*)

FOUSTKA (*quietly*):   I have a suggestion.
FISTULA: I'm listening.   180
FOUSTKA: To expedite our communications I'm going to pretend that I'm not endowed with a scientific outlook and that I'm interested in certain things purely out of curiosity.
FISTULA: I accept your suggestion!

(FISTULA *steps up to* FOUSTKA *and offers him his hand;* FOUSTKA *hesitates a moment, then gives his hand to* FISTULA, *who clasps it.* FOUSTKA *instantly pulls his hand away in alarm.*)

FOUSTKA (*crying out*):   Ow! (*Gasps with pain, rubs his hand and waves it in the*   185
air.) Man, your temperature must be fifty below zero.
FISTULA (*laughing*):   Not quite.

(FOUSTKA *finally recovers and resumes his seat at his desk.* FISTULA *also sits down, folds his hands in his lap, and stares with theatrically doglike resignation at* FOUSTKA. *A long pause.*)

FOUSTKA: So?

(*A long pause.*)

What's going on?

(*A long pause.*)

What's wrong with you. Have you lost your tongue all of a sudden?   190

FISTULA: I'm waiting.

FOUSTKA: For what?

FISTULA: For your command.

FOUSTKA: I don't understand: What command?

FISTULA: What better way for me to acquaint you with my work than for   195
you to assign me certain tasks whose fulfillment you can verify for yourself and whose fulfillment matters to you for some reason?

FOUSTKA: Aha, I see. And what kind of tasks—roughly—should they be?

FISTULA: That's for you to say!

FOUSTKA: All right—but still and all—it's hard to think of anything under   200
the circumstances . . .

FISTULA: Don't worry, I'll help you out. I think I have an idea for an
innocent little beginning of sorts. If I'm not mistaken, there's a certain
young lady you admire.

FOUSTKA: I don't know what you're talking about.   205

FISTULA: Doctor Foustka, after everything we've said here, you really must
admit that I might occasionally know somebody's little secret.

FOUSTKA: If you're talking about the secretary of our Institute, I'm not
denying that she's a pretty girl, but that doesn't necessarily mean . . .

FISTULA: What if tonight at the office party—quite unexpectedly and of   210
course quite briefly—she were to fall in love with you? How about that?

(FOUSTKA *paces nervously for a short while, and then turns abruptly to* FISTULA.)

FOUSTKA: Please leave!

FISTULA: Me? Why?

FOUSTKA: I repeat—go away!

FISTULA: Are you beginning that again? I thought we'd reached an   215
agreement.

FOUSTKA: You've insulted me.

FISTULA: How? In what way?

FOUSTKA: I'm not so badly off as to need magic for help in my love life!
I'm neither a weakling incapable of manfully facing the facts when he   220
doesn't manage to win by his own efforts, nor a cad who would carry
out experiments on innocent and completely unsuspecting young girls
for his own sensual pleasure. Do you take me for some sort of Blue-
beard or what, Fistula?

FISTULA: Which of us knows what we really are! But that's not the issue   225
now. If my well-intentioned, innocent, and quite spur-of-the-moment
little idea touched a raw nerve for some reason, I naturally apologize
and withdraw it!

FOUSTKA: And I didn't even mention my main objection: I'm involved
in a serious relationship, and I'm faithful to my girl friend.   230

FISTULA: Just as faithful as she is to you?

FOUSTKA (*startled*): What do you mean by that?

FISTULA: Forget it.

FOUSTKA: Wait a minute, I'm not going to let you get away with making
dirty insinuations like that! I'm not interested in gossip, and I don't   235
like impudence!

FISTULA: I'm sorry I said anything. If you've decided to be blind, that's your
business.

(FISTULA *removes his shoes from the paper bag and slowly begins to change footgear.*
FOUSTKA *watches him uneasily. A pause.*)

FOUSTKA: You're leaving? (*Pause.*) I guess I blew up a little.

(*Pause.* FISTULA *has changed into his shoes, places his slippers in the bag, stands up,
and slowly walks towards the door.*)

So what's going to happen?   240

FISTULA (*stops and turns around*): With what?

FOUSTKA: Well, with our agreement.

FISTULA: What about it?

FOUSTKA: Is it on?

FISTULA: That depends entirely on you. (*He grins.*)   245

The curtain falls.

Scene 3

*The garden of the Institute. It is night, and the garden is illuminated by Chinese lan-
terns strung along wires attached to trees. In the middle of the stage is a small bower.
Beyond it in the background is a space serving as a dance floor. In the front at the
left is a garden bench; at the right is an outdoor table with a variety of bottles and
glasses on it. All around are trees and bushes; these, together with the darkness, make
it hard to see the dancing in the background as well as the various movements of figures in the garden. Only the action in the foreground is always clearly visible. As the
curtain rises, the music grows softer and its character changes; faintly audible now as
if from a great distance are strains of popular dance music that will continue for the
entire scene. The male and female LOVERS are in the bower; they will remain there
for the entire scene, gently embracing, caressing each other, kissing, and whispering
into each other's ears, oblivious to the various goings-on around them. The DEPUTY
with PETRUSHKA, and KOTRLY with LORENCOVA, are dancing as couples on the dance
floor, while VILMA and the DIRECTOR are also there, each swaying separately to the
music. FOUSTKA is standing at the table, pouring drinks into two glasses. MARKETA
is sitting on the bench. Everyone is wearing evening clothes; the women wear long
gowns. As the scene begins, FOUSTKA is explaining something to MARKETA, who is*

listening intently. As he is speaking FOUSTKA *finishes pouring the drinks and slowly crosses over with them towards* MARKETA.

FOUSTKA: We must realize that out of an infinity of possible speeds, the expanding universe chose precisely the one that would allow the universe itself to come into being as we know it, that is, having sufficient time and other requirements needed for the formation of solid bodies so that life would be able to begin on them—at least on one of them!   5
Isn't that a remarkable coincidence!

MARKETA: That's really amazing!

(FOUSTKA *comes up to* MARKETA, *hands her a glass, sits down beside her, and both take a drink.*)

FOUSTKA: So there you are, and if you probe a bit further you'll discover that you owe your very existence to so unbelievable a multitude of similarly unbelievable coincidences that it exceeds the bounds of all   10
probability. All those things can't exist just for themselves, can they? Don't they conceal some deeper design of existence, of the world, and of nature willing you to be you, and me to be me, willing life, simply, to exist, and at its very height, as we understand it for now, the human soul, capable of fathoming it all! Or could it be, perhaps, that   15
the cosmos directly intended that one fine day it would see itself thus through our eyes and ask itself thus through our lips the very questions we're asking ourselves here and now?

MARKETA: Yes, yes, that's exactly the way I see it!

(VILMA, *who has in the interim left the dance floor, now appears at the table and pours herself a drink.*)

VILMA: Are you enjoying yourselves?   20

FOUSTKA: Marketa and I are doing a bit of philosophizing.

VILMA: Well, I seem to be in the way here. (VILMA *disappears with her glass, and after a while she can again be seen dancing alone in the background. A pause.*)

FOUSTKA: And here's another thing. Modern biology has known for a long   25
time that while the laws of survival and mutations and the like explain all sorts of things, they don't begin to explain the main thing: why does life actually exist in the first place, and above all why does it exist in that infinitely bright-colored multiplicity of its often quite self-serving   30
manifestations, which almost seem to be here only because existence wants to demonstrate its own power through them? But to demonstrate to whom? To itself? Have you ever wondered about that?

MARKETA: To tell you the truth, no, not in this way . . . but from now on
I'll probably think about it all the time. You know how to say things
so nicely.   35

(NEUWIRTH *emerges from somewhere at the right. He steps up to the bench and bows
to* MARKETA.)

NEUWIRTH: May I have the honor?
MARKETA (*in confusion*):   Yes . . . of course.

(*She throws* FOUSTKA *a pleading, unhappy glance, and then rises.*)

FOUSTKA: You'll come back again, won't you?
MARKETA: Of course! Everything was so very interesting.

(NEUWIRTH *offers his arm to* MARKETA *and disappears with her. After a while they
can be seen in the background dancing.* FOUSTKA *sips his drink, deep in thought.
Shortly thereafter the* DIRECTOR, *who has in the interim left the dance floor, emerges
from behind a bush at left, just in back of the bench.*)

DIRECTOR: A pleasant evening, isn't it?   40

(FOUSTKA *is a bit startled, and then quickly stands up.*)

FOUSTKA: Yes. We're in luck with the weather.
DIRECTOR: Please sit down. May I join you for a moment?
FOUSTKA: Of course.

(*They both sit down on the bench. An awkward pause. Then the* DIRECTOR *casually
takes* FOUSTKA's *hand and peers into his eyes.*)

DIRECTOR: Henry . . .
FOUSTKA: Yes?   45
DIRECTOR: What do you actually think of me?
FOUSTKA: I? Well . . . how shall I say it . . . I think that everyone in our
Institute is glad that you're the one in charge . . .
DIRECTOR: You don't understand. I'm interested in what you yourself think
of me—as a person—or, to be more precise, what you feel about me . . .   50
FOUSTKA: I respect you . . .
DIRECTOR: Is that all?
FOUSTKA: Well . . . how shall I say it . . . it's hard to . . . well, it's . . .

(*At that moment the* DEPUTY, *with* PETRUSHKA, *who have in the interim left the
dance floor, appear at the right, holding hands. When the* DIRECTOR *sees them he
drops* FOUSTKA's *hand.* FOUSTKA *is obviously relieved.*)

DEPUTY: here you are, Sir! We've been looking high and low for you.

DIRECTOR: Did something happen? 55

(*Making the most of the situation,* FOUSTKA *quietly stands up and quickly disappears.*)

DEPUTY: Nothing in particular. It's only that Petrushka here has a request to make of you, but she's just a little bashful about coming out with it . . .

DIRECTOR: What request?

DEPUTY: Whether she couldn't have a dance with you. 60

DIRECTOR: I don't know how to lead, and I'd only step all over her skirt. Really, there are so many better dancers here . . .

DEPUTY: In that case would you at least accept our invitation to come to the pool where our colleague Kotrly has constructed an adorable underwater light show. 65

(*The* DIRECTOR *peevishly gets to his feet and goes off somewhere to the right with the* DEPUTY *and* PETRUSHKA. *Just then* KOTRLY *and* LORENCOVA, *who have in the interim left the dance floor, appear at the left. They go to the table.*)

KOTRLY: Have you seen my underwater light show yet?

LORENCOVA: You're doing it stupidly, Willy.

KOTRLY: What am I doing stupidly?

(*They go up to the table and* KOTRLY *pours out two drinks and hands one to* LORENCOVA. *They sip their drinks.*)

LORENCOVA: You're being such an ass-kisser that even those two idiots will get sick of you. You'll end up a total joke and everybody will turn 70
against you.

KOTRLY: Maybe I'm doing it stupidly, but it's still a lot better than pretending not to be interested, and all the while telling them everything!

LORENCOVA: Are you referring to Neuwirth?

KOTRLY: Who, for instance, was the first to begin talking about Foustka's 75
interest in black magic? If they get wind of it, it'll be Neuwirth's doing!

LORENCOVA: But we all gossiped about it! You're being unfair to him and your only excuse is that you're jealous . . .

KOTRLY: It's just like you to stick up for him!

LORENCOVA: Are you beginning that again? 80

KOTRLY: Libby, give me your word of honor that you never had a thing with him!

LORENCOVA: Word of honor! Come on, let's dance!

(KOTRLY *and* LORENCOVA *put down their glasses on the table and exit somewhere off to the right. After a while they can be seen in the background, dancing. Meanwhile*

NEUWIRTH *and* MARKETA *enter from the left.* MARKETA *sits down on the bench.*
NEUWIRTH *hangs around nearby.* FOUSTKA *emerges from the bushes directly behind
the bench and sits down next to* MARKETA. *An awkward pause.*)

NEUWIRTH: Oh dear, I seem to be in the way here.

(NEUWIRTH *vanishes. After a while he can be seen in the background, dancing
with* LORENCOVA; *he has evidently cut in on* KOTRLY. *Meanwhile the* DEPUTY *and*
PETRUSHKA *have appeared on the dance floor as well, dancing together, as well as the*
DIRECTOR, *dancing alone again. A short pause.*)

MARKETA: Tell me more! Every word you say opens my eyes. I don't under-   85
stand how I could have been so blind, so superficial . . .

FOUSTKA: I'll begin, if you don't mind, by taking a new tack. Has it ever
occurred to you that we wouldn't be able to understand even the
simplest moral action that doesn't serve some practical purpose? In
fact, it would have to seem quite absurd to us if we didn't recognize   90
that hidden somewhere in its deepest depths is the presumption of
something higher, some sort of absolute, omniscient, and infinitely
fair judge or moral authority through which and within which all our
activities are somehow mysteriously appraised and validated and by
means of which each one of us is constantly in touch with eternity?   95

MARKETA: Yes, yes, that's exactly how I've felt about it all my life! I just
wasn't able to see it, let alone say it so beautifully.

FOUSTKA: So there you are! What's even more tragic is that modern man
has repressed everything that might allow him somehow to transcend
himself, and he ridicules the very idea that something above him   100
might even exist and that his life and the world might have a higher
meaning of some sort! He has crowned himself as the highest authority, so he can then observe with horror how the world is going to the
dogs under that authority!

MARKETA: How clear and simple it is! I admire the way you're able to   105
think about everything so . . . so, well, in your own way somehow,
differently from the way most people usually talk about it, and how
deeply you feel all those things! I don't think I'll ever forget this evening! I have a feeling that I'm becoming a new person every minute
I'm with you. Please forgive me for saying it so openly, but it's as if   110
something were radiating from inside of you that—I don't understand
how I could have walked by you so indifferently before—it's simply that
I've never felt anything like this before . . .

(KOTRLY *emerges from somewhere at the right, goes up to the bench, and bows to*
MARKETA.)

KOTRLY: May I have the honor?

MARKETA: I'm sorry, but I . . .   115

KOTRLY: Come on, Marketa, we haven't had a single dance together!

(MARKETA *looks unhappily at* FOUSTKA, *who just shrugs his shoulders helplessly;* MARKETA *stands up.*)

MARKETA (*to* FOUSTKA):   You'll wait here, won't you?

FOUSTKA: Of course I'll wait.

(KOTRLY *offers an arm to* MARKETA *and disappears with her. After a while they may be seen in the background, dancing.* FOUSTKA *sips his drink, deep in though. After a short while the* DIRECTOR, *who has in the interim left the dance floor, emerges from behind a bush directly in back of the bench.*)

DIRECTOR: Alone again?

(FOUSTKA *is a bit startled, then quickly stands up.*)

Sit down, Henry.   120

(FOUSTKA *sits again. The* DIRECTOR *sits down beside him. A short pause.*)

Do you smell that wonderful fragrance? Acacias . . . nasturtiums . . .

FOUSTKA: I don't know very much about fragrances.

(*An awkward pause. Then the* DIRECTOR *again casually takes Foustka's hand and gazes closely into his eyes.*)

DIRECTOR: Henry . . .

FOUSTKA: Yes?

DIRECTOR: Would you like to be my deputy?   125

FOUSTKA: Me?

DIRECTOR: I could arrange it.

FOUSTKA: But you already have a deputy.

DIRECTOR: If you only knew what a pain in the ass he gives me!

(*Just then the* SECRET MESSENGER *enters, goes up to the* DIRECTOR, *leans over, and whispers at length into his ear. The* DIRECTOR *gravely nods his head. After a longer time the* MESSENGER *concludes. The* DIRECTOR *nods one more time. The* MESSENGER *exits to the right. The* DIRECTOR, *who had not dropped Foustka's hand during the whispering, turns again to* FOUSTKA *and gazes closely into his eyes for a longer time.*)

Henry.   130

FOUSTKA: Yes?

DIRECTOR: Wouldn't you like to stop over at my place for a little while after the party? Or if you don't want to stay to the end, we could both slip away without anyone noticing. I've got some homemade cherry liqueur.

I could show you my collection of miniatures, we could chat in peace   135
and quiet, and if we happened to go on too long and you didn't feel
like going home that late, you could easily spend the night at my place!
You know that I live all alone, and what's more, it's only a hop and a
skip from our Institute, so you'd have it that much easier in the morning—what do you say?   140

FOUSTKA: I'm very honored by your invitation, Sir, but I'm afraid I've
already promised that I'd go to . . .

DIRECTOR: To Vilma's?

(FOUSTKA *nods. The* DIRECTOR *gazes closely into his eyes for another moment, then,*
all at once, drops his hand briskly, stands up abruptly, crosses over to the table,
pours himself a drink, and quickly drains it. FOUSTKA *remains seated on the bench,*
embarrassed. Then the DEPUTY, *with* PETRUSHKA, *who have in the interim left the*
dance floor, emerge from the left, holding hands.)

DEPUTY: Here you are! We've been looking all over . . .

DIRECTOR: Did something happen?   145

DEPUTY: Nothing in particular. Me and Petrushka here, we just wanted to
ask you if you had any plans after the party. We'd consider it quite an
honor if you'd accept our invitation to come over for a little nightcap
before bedtime. You could even spend the night at our house—if you
wanted to, of course . . .   150

DIRECTOR: I'm tired and I have to go home. Goodbye.

(*The* DIRECTOR *exits quickly to the right. The* DEPUTY *looks after him in confusion,*
then, somewhat crestfallen, disappears with PETRUSHKA *to the left. After a while they*
may be seen in the background, dancing. Just then NEUWIRTH *and* LORENCOVA, *who*
have in the interim left the dance floor, appear near the table at the right.)

NEUWIRTH: I've seen a lot of things in my day, but an educated person sucking up to his idiot bosses with ridiculous stunts like those light bulbs
in the pool—that really takes the cake! (*He pours two drinks, hands one to*
LORENCOVA: *they both sip.*)   155

LORENCOVA: Sucking up with the light bulbs is still a lot better than pretending not to be interested and all the while telling them everything!

NEUWIRTH: It's just like you to stick up for him!

LORENCOVA: Are you beginning that again?

NEUWIRTH: Libby, give me your word of honor that you never had a thing   160
with him!

LORENCOVA: Word of honor! Come on, let's dance!

(NEUWIRTH *and* LORENCOVA *put their glasses down on the table and exit somewhere*
to the left. After a while they can be seen in the background, dancing. Meanwhile

KOTRLY *and* MARKETA *enter from the right.* MARKETA *sits down on the bench next to* FOUSTKA. KOTRLY *hangs around nearby. An awkward pause.*)

KOTRLY: Oh dear, I seem to be in the way here.

(KOTRLY *vanishes. After a while he can be seen in the background, dancing with* LORENCOVA. *He has evidently cut in on* NEUWIRTH.)

FOUSTKA: When a person casts God from his heart, he opens a door for
the devil. When you think about the increasingly stupid willfulness of   165
the powerful and the increasingly stupid submission of the powerless,
and the awful destruction committed in today's world in the name of
science—and after all we *are* its somewhat grotesque standard-bearers—
isn't all that truly the work of the devil? We know that the devil is
a master of disguises, and what more ingenious disguise could one   170
imagine than the one offered him by the godlessness of modern times?
Why, he must find the most promising base of operations in those very
places where people have stopped believing in him! Please forgive me
for speaking so openly, Marketa, but I can't keep it stifled inside me
any longer! And who else can I confide in besides you?   175

(MARKETA *throws her glass into the bushes and grasps Foustka's hand emotionally.*)

MARKETA (*exclaiming*):   I love you!
FOUSTKA: No!
MARKETA: Yes, I'll love you forever!
FOUSTKA: Oh, you poor creature! I'd be your ruin!
MARKETA: I'd rather be ruined with you and live the truth than be without   180
you and live a lie!

(MARKETA *embraces* FOUSTKA *and begins to kiss him passionately. Just then* VILMA, *who has in the interim left the dance floor, appears at the table. For a moment she observes the embracing couple.*)

VILMA (*icily*):   Are you enjoying yourselves?

(FOUSTKA *and* MARKETA *immediately pull apart and look at* VILMA *in a state of shock.*)

The curtain falls.

Scene 4

Vilma's apartment. It is a cozy boudoir, furnished with antiques. There is a door at the rear. At the left is a large bed with a canopy. At the right are two small armchairs, a large Venetian mirror, and a vanity table with a large collection of perfumes on it. Scattered about the room are various female odds and ends and trinkets. The only thing folded neatly is Foustka's evening outfit next to the bed. The colors are all feminine, predominantly pink and purple. As the curtain rises, FOUSTKA *is sitting in his undershorts at the edge of the bed, and* VILMA, *in a lacy slip, is sitting at the vanity table combing her hair, facing the mirror with her back to* FOUSTKA. *A short pause.*

FOUSTKA: When was he here last?

VILMA: Who?

FOUSTKA: Stop asking stupid questions!

VILMA: You mean that dancer? About a week ago.

FOUSTKA: Did you let him in?   5

VILMA: He just brought me some violets. I told him I had no time, that I was hurrying to meet you.

FOUSTKA: I asked you whether you let him in.

VILMA: I don't remember anymore . . . maybe he came in for a moment.

FOUSTKA: So you kissed him!   10

VILMA: I kissed him on the cheek to thank him for the violets, that's all.

FOUSTKA: Vilma, don't treat me like a fool, for goodness sake! I just bet you could buy him off with a mere kiss on the cheek once you let him in! Surely he tried to dance with you at the very least.

VILMA: Henry, drop it, for goodness sake! Can't you talk about anything   15
more interesting?

FOUSTKA: Did he try or not?

VILMA: All right, he did, if you really must know! But I won't tell you another thing! I simply refuse to keep talking to you on this level, because it's embarrassing, undignified, insulting, and ridiculous! You   20
know very well that I love you, and that no dancer could possibly be a threat to you, so stop tormenting yourself with this endless cross-examination! I don't keep pumping you for details either—and I'd have far more reason to do so!

FOUSTKA: So you refuse to tell? Well in that case everything is quite clear.   25

VILMA: But I've told you a hundred times that I don't go out of my way to see him, I don't care for him, I don't dance with him, so what else am I supposed to do, damn it!

FOUSTKA: He hangs around you, he flatters you, he wants to dance with you all the time—and you enjoy it! If you didn't enjoy it, you'd have   30
gotten rid of him long ago.

VILMA: I won't deny that I enjoy it—any woman would enjoy it. His persistence is touching, and so is the very fact that he never gives up, even though he knows perfectly well that he doesn't have a chance. Would you, for instance, be capable of driving here at night from God knows   35
where for no other reason than to bring me some violets, even though you knew the situation was hopeless?

FOUSTKA: He's persistent because you deliberately dash his hopes in a way
that keeps them alive and you deliberately reject him in a way that
makes him long for you more and more! If you really slammed the door   40
on his hopes he'd never show up here again. But you wouldn't do that,
because it amuses you to play cat and mouse with him. You're a whore!

VILMA: You've decided to insult me?

FOUSTKA: How long did you dance together?

VILMA: Enough, Henry, you're beginning to be disgusting! I've always   45
known that you're eccentric, but I really never suspected that you're
capable of being this nasty! What's suddenly brought on this patho-
logical jealousy of yours? This insensitivity, tactlessness, maliciousness,
vengefulness? At least if you had any objective reason for it . . .

FOUSTKA: So you're planning to keep whoring around?   50

VILMA: You have no right to talk to me like that! You kept pawing at that
girl all evening, everybody's embarrassed, I wander around like an
idiot—people feel sorry for me all over the place—and now you have the
nerve to reproach me! Me! You do as you damn well please, I just have
to suffer in silence, and finally you make a scene here on account of   55
some crazy dancer! Do you see how absurd it is? Do you realize how terribly unfair it is? Do you have the faintest idea of how selfish and cruel
you are?

FOUSTKA: In the first place, I was certainly not pawing anyone and I'd like
you to please refrain from using words like that, especially when you're   60
referring to pure creatures like Marketa. In the second place, we're not
discussing me, but you, so kindly stop changing the subject. Sometimes
I get a feeling that there's some monstrous plan hidden behind all this.
First, you'll resurrect feelings within me that I'd assumed were dead
long ago, and then once you've deprived me thus of my well-known   65
objectivity, you'll begin to tighten a web of deceit around my heart,
lightly at first, but then ever more painfully, an especially treacherous one because it is composed of a multitude of delicate threads of
dancerly pseudoinnocence! But I won't let myself be tortured on this
rack any longer! I'll do something either to myself—or to him—or to   70
you—or to all of us!

(VILMA *puts down her comb, begins to clap her hands, and walks towards* FOUSTKA
with a smile. FOUSTKA *also begins to smile, stands up, and walks towards* VILMA.)

VILMA: You keep getting better and better!

FOUSTKA: You weren't bad yourself.

(FOUSTKA *and* VILMA *gently embrace, kiss, and then slowly get into bed together. They
settle down together comfortably, lean back against the pillows, and cover their legs*

with a blanket. FOUSTKA *lights a cigarette for himself and for* VILMA. VILMA *finally ends a long pause by speaking.*)

VILMA: Henry.

FOUSTKA: Hmm . . .   75

VILMA: Isn't it beginning to get on your nerves just a bit?

FOUSTKA: What?

VILMA: You know, that I keep making you play these games.

FOUSTKA: It did bother me for quite a long time.

VILMA: And now?   80

FOUSTKA: Now just the opposite—it's beginning to scare me.

VILMA: To scare you? Why?

FOUSTKA: I have a feeling that I'm beginning to get into it too much.

VILMA (*exclaiming*):   Henry! Don't tell me you're really beginning to get
   jealous! Now that's fantastic! Never in my wildest dreams did I hope it   85
   would succeed like this! I had become resigned to the idea that you'd
   never feel any jealousy other than the make-believe kind.

FOUSTKA: I'm sorry, but I can't share your delight.

VILMA: I don't understand what you're afraid of!

FOUSTKA: My own self!   90

VILMA: Come on!

FOUSTKA: Don't underestimate it, Vilma. Something's happening to me. I
   suddenly feel capable of doing all sorts of things that have always been
   alien to me. It's as if something dark inside of me were suddenly beginning to flow out of its hiding place and into the open.   95

VILMA: What an alarmist you are! You're beginning to feel a little healthy
   jealousy and that throws you into a complete panic! There's nothing
   wrong with you. Maybe you're just a little upset because your situation
   at the Institute came to a head this evening with that unfortunate incident with the director. That's obviously on your mind, and it's working 100
   away at your unconscious, looking for some way out, even though you
   won't admit it. That's why you're beginning to see bogeymen all over
   the place.

FOUSTKA: If only it were that simple.

(*Pause.*)

VILMA: Do you think he'll destroy you?   105

FOUSTKA: He'll certainly try. The question is whether he has enough power
   to do it.

VILMA: But he's got all the power he wants—all the power there is, actually—
   at least as far as we're concerned.

FOUSTKA: There are other kinds of power besides the kind he dispenses.   110

(VILMA, *horrified, jumps up and kneels on the pillow opposite* FOUSTKA.)

VILMA: Do you mean that seriously?

FOUSTKA: Hmm . . .

VILMA: Now you're scaring me! Promise me you won't dabble in that sort of thing!

FOUSTKA: And what if I won't promise? 115

VILMA: The minute you mentioned that cripple I knew there'd be hell to pay! He's addled your brains! You'd actually go so far as to get involved with him?

FOUSTKA: Why not?

VILMA: This is horrible! 120

FOUSTKA: At least you see that I wasn't just kidding around before.

(*Just then the doorbell rings.* VILMA *cries out in horror and quickly huddles up under the blankets.* FOUSTKA *smiles, calmly gets out of bed, and dressed just as he is—that is, in his undershorts—goes to the door and quickly opens it. There stands the dancer holding a bunch of violets behind his back.*)

DANCER: Good evening. Is Vilma home?

FOUSTKA: Why?

DANCER (*points to the flowers*): I just wanted to give her a little something.

FOUSTKA (*calling to the bed*): Wilma, you have a visitor. 125

(VILMA *climbs out of bed, is a bit confused, can't quickly find anything to cover up with, and therefore goes to the door dressed only in her slip.* FOUSTKA *steps to the side, but does not go away.*)

VILMA (*to the dancer, with embarrassment*): Is that you?

DANCER: I'm sorry to disturb you at this hour—we were on tour—I just wanted to give you—here.

(*The* DANCER *hands* VILMA *the violets,* VILMA *takes them and sniffs them.*)

VILMA: Thank you.

DANCER: Well, I'll be going again. I apologize again for disturbing you. 130

VILMA: Bye-bye.

(*The* DANCER *exits.* VILMA *closes the door, smiles uncertainly at* FOUSTKA, *puts down the violets somewhere, steps up to him, embraces him, and gently kisses his forehead, lips, and cheek.* FOUSTKA *stands motionless and looks coldly in front of him.*)

I love you.

(FOUSTKA *doesn't move a hair.* VILMA *continues to kiss him. Then, suddenly,* FOUSTKA *slaps her brutally in the face.* VILMA *falls to the ground.* FOUSTKA *kicks her.*)

The curtain falls.

Scene 5

The same room at the Institute as in Scene 1. As the curtain rises, nobody is onstage, but very soon VILMA *and* FOUSTKA *enter through the rear door.* FOUSTKA *is wearing the same evening clothes he wore at the party the previous day.* VILMA *is wearing a white coat. She has a black eye. They both seem happy.*

VILMA: We can't be the first!

FOUSTKA: Have you noticed that you come to work on time only when I stay over at your place?

VILMA: You're exaggerating.

*(*FOUSTKA *sits down at the desk and begins to sort out some papers.* VILMA *sits down on the oilcloth couch.)*

(Calling.) Marketa.   5

*(*MARKETA, *wearing an office smock, enters through the left door. When she sees* FOUSTKA *she stops abruptly and lowers her eyes.)*

Would you please make us two cups of coffee? A bit stronger, if possible.

MARKETA: Yes, of course.

*(*MARKETA *goes a bit nervously towards the left door, stealthily glancing over at* FOUSTKA, *who looks up from his papers and smiles at her jovially.)*

FOUSTKA: Well, did you get a good night's sleep?

MARKETA *(stuttering)*:   Thank you—yes—actually no. There were so many   10
thoughts racing through my head. *(*MARKETA, *in some confusion, exits through the left door.)*

VILMA: I think you turned that poor little thing's head last night.

FOUSTKA: Oh, she'll get over it.

(Pause.)

VILMA: Henry.   15

FOUSTKA: Yes, darling!

VILMA: It hasn't been that good in a long time, has it?

FOUSTKA: Hmm . . .

*(*LORENCOVA *in a dress,* KOTRLY *also in civilian clothes, and* NEUWIRTH *in a white coat enter through the rear door.)*

KOTRLY: You're here already?

VILMA: Hard to believe, isn't it?   20

*(*LORENCOVA *and* KOTRLY *sit down at their places on the bench;* NEUWIRTH *leans against the bookcase.)*

LORENCOVA (*looks at* VILMA's *face*):   My God, what's that?

VILMA: Oh you know, deathless passion.

(MARKETA *enters through the left door with two cups of coffee on a tray. She hands one to* VILMA, *and sets down the other with somewhat trembling hands in front of* FOUSTKA.)

FOUSTKA: Thanks.

LORENCOVA: Some for us too, Marketa.

MARKETA: Yes, Doctor Lorencova.   25

(MARKETA *exits quickly through the left door. The* DEPUTY, *in a white coat, and* PETRUSHKA, *in a dress, enter through the right door. They are holding hands. Everyone stands.*)

KOTRLY: Good morning, Sir.

DEPUTY: Hello there, my friends! I see we've got perfect attendance here today—that's fantastic—today of all days I would have least expected it. (*Everyone sits down again.*) I think that yesterday was a real success. You all deserve thanks for that. But I must express special appreciation to   30
our colleague Kotrly here for his underwater light effects.

KOTRLY: Please don't mention it.

DEPUTY: Well, my friends, there's no point in beating around the bush any longer.

NEUWIRTH: Did something happen?   35

DEPUTY: The director will tell you himself. At this time I just want to implore you all to understand that certain things have to be the way they are, to meet us halfway as we meet you halfway, and, mainly, to keep a cool head, a glowing heart, and clean hands at this crucial point in time. In short, there are times when people either come through   40
with flying colors, and then they have nothing to fear, or they don't come through, and then they have only themselves to blame for the unnecessary troubles they create as a result. But you're educated people, after all—I don't have to spell it all out for you. Who'll volunteer for garden cleanup?   45

KOTRLY: I might as well, after all I have to go there anyhow to terminate the light bulbs.

DEPUTY: Splendid!

(*The* DIRECTOR, *in civilian clothes, enters through the right door. Everyone stands again.*)

KOTRLY: Good morning, Sir.

DIRECTOR: Hello there, my friends! I see we've got perfect attendance here   50
today—that's fantastic—today of all days I would have least expected it and today of all days it's especially important.

DEPUTY: That's precisely what I was telling our colleagues just a second ago, Sir.

(*Everyone sits again. The* DIRECTOR *looks intently at those present for a moment and then steps up to* KOTRLY *and shakes his hand.* KOTRLY *stands up, surprised.*)

DIRECTOR: Did you get a good night's sleep?   55
KOTRLY: Yes, thank you.
DIRECTOR: Do you have any problems?
KOTRLY: Not really.

(*The* DIRECTOR *presses* KOTRLY's *elbow in a friendly way and turns again to the others.* KOTRLY *sits again.*)

DIRECTOR: There's no point in beating around the bush, friends . . .
NEUWIRTH: Did something happen?   60
DIRECTOR: As we know, our Institute is a kind of lighthouse of truthful knowledge. I'd even go so far as to say it's something of a faithful watchdog over the scientific core of science itself—it's something like the avant-garde of progress. Therefore one might simplify it thus: We think it today, they'll live it tomorrow!   65
DEPUTY: I've already reminded our colleagues, Sir, of the responsibility that our mission involves.
DIRECTOR: But here's why I'm saying all this: a serious thing has happened . . .

(*Just then the* SECRET MESSENGER *enters through the right door, steps up to the* DIRECTOR, *and whispers at length into his ear. The* DIRECTOR *gravely nods his head. After a long while the* MESSENGER *concludes. The* DIRECTOR *nods one more time and continues speaking. The* MESSENGER *exits through the right door.*)

But here's why I'm saying all this: a serious thing has happened . . .   70

(*Just then* MARKETA *enters through the left door carrying a tray with three cups of coffee on it. She places two on the table in front of* LORENCOVA *and* KOTRLY *and hands the third to* NEUWIRTH. *Then she heads back towards the left door.*)

But here's why I'm saying all this: a serious thing has happened . . .

(MARKETA *stops in her tracks, glances at the* DIRECTOR *and at* FOUSTKA, *then she quietly goes up to the left door and eavesdrops.*)

NEUWIRTH Did something happen?
DEPUTY (*to* NEUWIRTH):   Please stop interrupting the director! Didn't you hear him say that he's about to tell you . . .
DIRECTOR: A serious thing has happened: a virus has lodged itself where   75
one would have least expected it, yet in the very place it can do the

worst damage—that is, in the very center of antiviral battle—indeed, if I'm to stick with this metaphor, right in the central antibiotic warehouse!

(*Everyone looks at each other anxiously.* VILMA *and* FOUSTKA *exchange a glance that reveals they know there's trouble ahead.* FOUSTKA *nervously gropes for a cigarette and lights up.*)

KOTRLY: Are you saying, Sir, that right here, among us, there's someone . . .   80
DIRECTOR: Yes, with deep sorrow, bitterness, and shame I must say precisely that. We have a scientific worker here at this Institute—let me emphasize the word *scientific*—who has long and of course secretly, which only confirms his two-faced nature, been involved with various so-called occult disciplines, from astrology through alchemy all the way to black   85
magic and theurgy, in order to probe those murky waters for a would-be hidden wealth of an allegedly higher—that is prescientific—kind of learning.
KOTRLY: You mean he believes in spirits?
DIRECTOR: Not only that, but he is actually attempting to move from theory   90
to practice! We have ascertained that he has established contact—
LORENCOVA: With spirits?
DEPUTY: He'd have a bit of trouble doing that, wouldn't he, Sir?
DIRECTOR: That's enough! Please don't joke about things that leave a black mark on the work of our Institute, things that are a direct assault   95
on its reputation and therefore a low blow to us all, and especially to me as the one responsible for all of its scientific credibility. It is a grave and sad matter, my friends, and it's up to all of us to come to grips with it honorably! Where was I?
DEPUTY: You were discussing those contacts . . .   100
DIRECTOR: Ah yes. Well, then, we have learned that not long ago he established direct contact with a certain element from that no-man's-land of pseudoscience, common criminality, and moral turpitude, who is suspect not only because he spreads superstition and deludes the credulous by means of various tricks, but who actually dabbles in Satanism,   105
black magic, and other such poisonous practices. That's the fact of the matter, and now I'd like to open this up for discussion. Does anyone have any questions?

(*An oppressive pause.*)

KOTRLY (*quietly*):   Might I ask the name of this colleague?
DIRECTOR (*to the* DEPUTY):   Say it!   110
DEPUTY: I can hardly utter the words, but name him I must. We're talking about Doctor Foustka, here.

(An *oppressive pause.*)

DIRECTOR: Who else wishes to speak?
MARKETA (*timidly*):   I do.
FOUSTKA (*quietly to* MARKETA):   Please, I beg of you, stay out of this!   115
DIRECTOR: This concerns us all. Even the secretary here deserves a chance
   to speak her mind.
MARKETA: Please excuse me, Sir. I'm not a scientist and I don't know
   how to express myself too well, but that simply can't be true! Doctor
   Foustka is a wise and honorable man—I know he is—he worries about   120
   questions that we really all should be worrying about—he thinks for
   himself—he tries to get to the bottom of the deepest questions—the
   source of morality—of universal order—and all those other things—and
   those contacts you mentioned—I simply don't believe it! Surely these
   are all wicked lies spread by bad people who want to harm him.   125

(*A deathly silence falls over the room.* FOUSTKA *is obviously in despair over Marketa's
outburst. After a while the* DIRECTOR *turns matter-of-factly to the* DEPUTY.)

DIRECTOR (*to the* DEPUTY):   As soon as we're finished, please arrange for her
   immediate dismissal! Now of all times our Institute truly can't allow
   itself the luxury of employing a secretary who accuses the administra-
   tion of lying!
DEPUTY: I'll take care of it, Sir.   130
DIRECTOR (*to* MARKETA):   You may go get your things together.
FOUSTKA (*in a muffled voice to* MARKETA):   You've gone mad—to ruin your life
   so foolishly like this—why, you won't get a job anywhere!
MARKETA: I want to suffer with you!
FOUSTKA: Excuse me, Sir, but wouldn't it be more sensible to have her hos-   135
   pitalized? It's perfectly obvious that she doesn't know what she's saying.
DIRECTOR: Psychiatry, Doctor Foustka, is not a garbage dump for girls
   you've used and thrown away.
MARKETA: Henry, are you renouncing me? And everything you told me last
   night, are you renouncing that too?   140
FOUSTKA (*speaking furiously through clenched teeth*):   For God's sake, keep
   quiet!

(MARKETA *bursts into tears and runs out the left door. An awkward pause.*)

VILMA (*quietly to* FOUSTKA):   If she does something rash it'll be your fault!
FOUSTKA (*quietly to* VILMA):   And then you'll be satisfied, won't you?
VILMA (*quietly*):   Don't start that again.   145
FOUSTKA: I'm the one who started? Right?

DIRECTOR: Stop that! I'll ask at a higher level whether one of the local
    housing projects couldn't take her on as a cleaning lady.
LORENCOVA: I think that would be a very fortunate, humane, and sensible
    solution.   150
DIRECTOR (*to* FOUSTKA):   Do you want to take advantage of your right to
    respond to the charges against you?

(FOUSTKA *stands up slowly and leans against the desk as if it were a speaker's
podium.*)

FOUSTKA: Gentlemen, colleagues! I have complete faith in the objectivity
    and conscientiousness with which my case will be considered and I
    presume that at the right moment I will be given the opportunity to   155
    make an extensive explanation, and that certain circumstances with
    which I will acquaint you on that occasion will help prove my com-
    plete innocence. For the time being, therefore, I will confine myself
    to expressing the hope that the proceedings in this case—in keeping
    with our scientific approach to reality and our scientific morality—will   160
    be impartially and fully directed towards one goal alone: to discover
    the truth. This will further not only my own interests nor only the
    interests of science as such which this Institute is entrusted to guard
    and cultivate, but the interests of each of you as well. A different course
    of action, you see, might easily make my case merely the first link of a   165
    long chain of injustices the end of which I hardly dare contemplate.
    Thank you for your attention!

(FOUSTKA *sits down. An awkward pause. Everyone is slightly uneasy, albeit each for
different reasons.*)

DIRECTOR: We're living in a modern day and age, and nobody here has
    any intention of staging any kind of witch-hunt. That would merely
    resurrect the same ancient ignorance and fanaticism against which we   170
    are battling, but in a new guise. Let the manner in which our colleague
    Foustka's case is resolved become an inspirational model of a truly
    scientific approach to the facts! The truth must prevail, come what may!

(*A short pause.*)

    Who volunteered for garden clean-up?
KOTRLY: I did, Sir.   175

(*The* DIRECTOR *steps up to* KOTRLY. KOTRLY *stands up; the* DIRECTOR *places a hand
on his shoulder and looks gravely into his eyes for a while.*)

DIRECTOR (*tenderly*):   I'm glad you took the job, Vilem. I'll come to help you.

(MARKETA *enters through the left door, wearing a dress and carrying a small suitcase in her hand. Her face is tear-stained; she crosses the room as if sleepwalking and leaves through the rear door. Just as she closes it behind her, the chandelier crashes to the floor. It doesn't hit anyone but shatters into pieces on the floor.*)

The curtain falls.

Intermission

Scene 6

Foustka's apartment again. As the curtain rises, FISTULA *is alone on stage. He is sitting at the desk, going through the papers lying on it. He is wearing slippers, and the paper bag with his shoes in it is lying on the desk among the papers. After a while* FOUSTKA *enters, still in evening clothes. When he spots* FISTULA *he gives a start and cries out.*

FOUSTKA: What are you doing here?

FISTULA: I'm waiting for you.

FOUSTKA: How did you get in?

FISTULA: Not through the chimney, if that's what you're wondering. Through the door, which Mrs. Houbova kindly opened for me before she went out shopping, because I explained to her how urgently you needed to speak to me and how hard it would be for me to wait for you outside, what with my lame foot.   5

FOUSTKA: So you tricked her—how like you!

FISTULA: You don't believe that I'm a cripple?   10

FOUSTKA: My having to urgently speak to you is an out-and-out lie. Quite the contrary, after everything that happened I'd hoped I'd never see you again.

FISTULA: Quite the contrary, it's precisely *because* of what happened that our meeting has become many times more urgent.   15

FOUSTKA: And how dare you go through my papers!

FISTULA: Well, I had to do something to while away the time, didn't I?

FOUSTKA: And what about those shoes?

FISTULA: You make such a fuss about everything! (FISTULA *begins to grin stupidly, then he takes his bag, goes to the sofa, sits down, and places the bag beside him.*) Won't you sit down?   20

(FOUSTKA, *irritated, crosses to his desk, sits, and glares at* FISTULA.)

So what do you say to our success?

FOUSTKA: What success?

FISTULA: I never expected it to work so easily and so quickly. You're truly a gifted student.   25

FOUSTKA: I don't know what you're talking about!

FISTULA: You know perfectly well! We had agreed to do an innocent little
experiment first, hadn't we? And that turned out to surpass our fondest
expectations, don't you agree?

FOUSTKA: If you're referring to the fact that that unfortunate child devel-   30
oped a bit of a crush on me, then I'd like to say just two things. First,
there was no magic involved, especially not yours; the only reason it
happened was because it was the first time—

FISTULA: By pure chance—

FOUSTKA: That I actually had an opportunity to have a real talk with that   35
young woman and because I happened to be—

FISTULA: By pure chance—

FOUSTKA: In pretty good form last night, so that my thoughts charmed her.
Well, and as things seem to work with young girls, soon her interest was
transferred—   40

FISTULA: By pure chance—

FOUSTKA: From what was being explained to the one who was explaining.
I don't see anything about it that goes beyond the bounds of the ordinary. Second of all, seeing what happened to that poor child as a result
of our conversation, my conscience is filled with heavy reproaches that   45
it happened at all, even though I certainly never knew, and had no way
of knowing, that our talk would such consequences . . .

(FISTULA *begins to chortle and merrily slaps his thigh.*)

What's so funny about that?

FISTULA (*becomes serious*):   My dear Doctor Foustka! Everybody knows that
you don't believe in pure chance or coincidence. Don't you wonder   50
how it happened that a person like you who could hardly stutter a
request for a cup of coffee from that young woman until that moment
suddenly found himself endowed with such impressive eloquence
combined with the courage to express thoughts that are more than
dangerous to express on the premises of your Institute? And doesn't   55
it surprise you that it happened at just the very moment we had
dreamed up our little idea? Honestly, aren't you a bit amazed at how
your thoughts suddenly broke down that young woman's defenses—as
if someone had waved a magic wand and allowed her to fall madly and
indelibly in love in no time at all.   60

FOUSTKA: We all have moments in our lives when we seem to outdo
ourselves.

FISTULA: That's just what I'm talking about!

FOUSTKA: I don't understand what you mean.

FISTULA: You didn't really expect Jeviel, the spirit of love, to arrive at our   65
office party dressed in evening clothes all ready to fix everything up for
you as if he were some sort of matchmaker? How else do you imagine
he could do it than by means of your own self? He simply incorporated
himself into you! Or rather, he simply awakened and liberated certain
things that had always been dormant inside of you! Or to be even   70
more precise, it was actually you yourself who decided to drop the reins
restraining certain of your inner powers, and you yourself, therefore,
who filled in for him, so to speak, or who fulfilled his intentions and
thus won the day in his image, bearing his name!

FOUSTKA: There you are!   75

FISTULA: Of course a person isn't a static system of some sort—why you as a
scientist must know that better than I. If a little seed is to sprout it must
first be planted by someone.

FOUSTKA: If it's true that you and your . . .

FISTULA: Jeviel.   80

FOUSTKA: If you and your Jeviel are really responsible for planting this
unfortunate seed, then I curse you from the bottom of my heart! You're
a devil and I don't want to have anything to do with you.

FISTULA: You're missing the point again! If the devil exists, then above all
he exists within our own selves!   85

FOUSTKA: Then you, needless to say, must be his favorite residence!

FISTULA: You overestimate my value at least as much as you overestimated
your own just a second ago. Think of it this way: I'm only a catalyst
who helps his fellow creatures awaken or accelerate things that have
long existed within themselves even without his help. My help, you see,   90
merely enables them to discover their own courage to experience and
enjoy something thrilling in life and consequently to become more fulfilled themselves! We only live once; why then should we spend those
precious few decades that have been allotted to us stifling under the
cover of some sort of philistine scruples? Do you know why you called   95
me a devil? In order to shift your own responsibility—purely out of fear
of your own scruples and of that thing within you that breaks them
down—to a place outside of your own ego, in this case onto me, and
by means of this "transference" as you scientists call it, or "projection,"
to ease your conscience! You hoped to fool your own scruples by using   100
this kind of maneuver, and by assigning me that insulting name you
hoped you'd actually even please them. But think of it this way, Doctor
Foustka: I—a certain cripple, Fistula—wouldn't be able to move you an
inch if you hadn't secretly dreamed about moving in that direction
yourself long ago! Our little experiment had no other purpose than to   105
clarify these little trivialities for you.

FOUSTKA: And what about your assurance that it was innocent? That was a
      dirty trick!

FISTULA: Wrong again! You're still only deceiving your own self! After all,
      you could have talked to the girl about the beauties of the scientific   110
      worldview and the worldwide significance of your Institute and she
      would have avoided any danger. But even after you did it the other
      way, you didn't have to abandon her so selfishly when things began to
      seem hopeless! But that's not the point now. There's one thing I've got
      to hand you, with my deepest compliments, especially since you're a   115
      beginner: your disguise—that classic tool of Jeviel's—in the pious habit
      of an ecstatic seeker after that one (*points his finger skyward*) as the true
      source of meaning of all creation and of all moral imperatives—that was
      truly brilliant! Congratulations!

FOUSTKA (*angrily*):   What disguise? I was only saying what I believed!   120

FISTULA: My dear friend . . .

FOUSTKA: I'm not your friend!

FISTULA: My dear Sir, the truth isn't merely what we believe, after all, but
      also why and to whom and under what circumstances we say it!

(FOUSTKA *stares vacantly at* FISTULA *for a moment, then sadly nods his head, paces
back and forth across the room a few times, and sits down again. After a while he
begins to speak.*)

FOUSTKA (*quietly*):   It's not altogether clear to me how they did it, but they   125
      sniffed out my contacts with you somehow, for which I'll most likely
      be fired from the Institute, punished as an example, publicly disgraced,
      and probably deprived of my livelihood and everything else. But cer-
      tainly all this is merely superficial and immaterial, at least as far as I'm
      personally concerned. I see the true significance of what is in store   130
      for me as something else. It will be a deserved punishment for the
      unforgivable irresponsibility with which I behaved; for losing my moral
      vigilance and giving in to temptation, while under the poisonous influ-
      ence of unjustified, malicious, and totally self-centered jealousy. I was
      trying to kill two birds with one stone and, in this way, hoping to win   135
      over one person and at the same time to wound another. I was truly
      blinded by something diabolical within me, and therefore I'm grateful
      to you for enabling me to have this experience, no matter how or why
      you did it. You simultaneously awakened both that temptation and that
      mean-spirited jealousy in me, and thus you made it possible for me to   140
      come to understand my own self better, especially my darkest sides. But
      that's not all. Your explanation has helped illuminate the true source
      of my doubt, which really does lie nowhere else but in my own self.

Therefore I have no regrets about our meeting, if one can use that word
to describe the way you forced yourself on me. It was an important   145
lesson, and your dark designs have helped me discover a new inner
light. I'm telling you this because it's my hope that we'll never see each
other again, since I'm hoping that you'll leave this place immediately.

(A *long pause.* FISTULA *slowly takes his shoes out of the bag, looks at them thought-*
fully for a while, sniffs them, then finally places them on the ground in front of him
and turns with a smile to FOUSTKA.)

FISTULA: Each of us is master of his own fate! I really wanted to mention
something else, but now I'm not sure whether it wouldn't be better   150
to wait for a time when you'll be in more of a—please pardon the
expression—hot spot and, therefore, more receptive.
FOUSTKA: What did you want to mention?
FISTULA: I know that mechanism of thought rotation which you just
demonstrated as well as I know these shoes of mine! We sorcerers   155
call it the Smichovsky Compensation Syndrome.
FOUSTKA: What's that?
FISTULA: When a novice first manages to break through the armor of his
old defenses and opens himself up to the immense horizons of his
hidden potential, after a little while something like a hangover sets in   160
and he sinks into an almost masochistic state of self-accusation and
self-punishment. Psychologically this emotional reaction is quite under-
standable: in an effort to mollify his betrayed scruples, almost as an
afterthought, the novice mentally transforms the action through which
he betrayed them into some sort of purifying lesson which he had to   165
learn in order to become better. He makes of it, in short, a sort of small
dance floor on which to perform ritual celebrations of his principles. It
usually doesn't last long, and when he comes to his senses he recognizes
what we, of course, knew from the start, but what we couldn't rally
explain to him: that is, the grotesque discrepancy between the dubious   170
values in whose name he called down the most frightful punishment
on himself, and the fundamental, existential significance of the experience that he is trying to atone for by means of this punishment.

(FOUSTKA *jumps up and angrily smashes the table.*)

FOUSTKA: That's it—now I've really had enough! If you think that all your
high-flown oratory can get me tangled up in some new pseudoadven-   175
ture, you're very much mistaken!
FISTULA: It's you who are very much mistaken if you think you aren't
already tangled up . . .

FOUSTKA (*crying out*):   Get out!

FISTULA: I'd just like to warn you that when you get back in touch with   180
reality and suddenly feel the need for a consultation, I won't necessarily
be available. But that's your business, after all . . .

FOUSTKA: Please—go away! I want to be alone with my Smichovsky
Compensation Syndrome!

(FISTULA *slowly takes his shoes in his hands, all the while shaking his head in disbelief. Then, suddenly, he slams the shoes down on the floor, jumps up, and begins to
wildly smack himself on the forehead.*)

FISTULA: I can hardly believe it! Because he dared to philosophize for   185
a few minutes with another woman, his mistress throws a fit and
denounces him for associating with a sorcerer.

FOUSTKA: What? That's a dirty lie!

FISTULA: And for that he'd be willing to give up his earnings, his scientific
future, and maybe everything he owns without a fight! I've seen a lot   190
of things, but this is a first! Smichovsky himself would have had his
mind blown by this one!

FOUSTKA: I don't believe she'd stoop that low! After all those golden hours
of sheer happiness we've had together!

FISTULA: Ah, what do you know about a woman's heart? Maybe the very   195
memory of those hours provides the key to what she did! (FISTULA *calms
down, sits down, slowly takes off his slippers, sniffs them, then carefully puts
them away in his bag and begins to put on his shoes. A long pause.*)

FOUSTKA (*quietly*):   And what, in your opinion, could I still do?

FISTULA: Let's not get into that.   200

FOUSTKA: Come on, tell me.

FISTULA: As you've probably realized, I don't give concrete advice and
I don't make arrangements for anybody. At most I occasionally
inspire . . . (*His shoes on, he grabs his bag with the slippers and heads for
the door.*)   205

FOUSTKA (*screaming out*):   Say it straight out, damn it!

(FISTULA *stops, stands completely still for a moment, and then turns to* FOUSTKA.)

FISTULA: It would be enough if you mobilized, in the name of a good
cause, at least one thousandth of the cunning that your director mobi-
lizes from morning till night in the name of a bad one!

(FISTULA *begins to grin stupidly.* FOUSTKA *stares at him with amazement.*)

The curtain falls.

Scene 7

The same room of the Institute in which Scenes 1 and 5 take place. Instead of the chandelier, a light bulb is suspended from an electrical wire. As the curtain rises, LORENCOVA, KOTRLY, *and* NEUWIRTH *are onstage.* LORENCOVA, *wearing a white coat, is sitting at the desk, a compact propped up against the typewriter, powdering her nose.* KOTRLY, *wearing a white coat, is sprawled out on the bench, reading the newspaper.* NEUWIRTH, *in civilian clothes, is standing at the rear by the bookcase, his back to the audience, examining a book. A short pause.*

LORENCOVA: What are we going to do about the coffee?
KOTRLY (*without looking up*):   Why don't you make it?
LORENCOVA: Why don't you?

(FOUSTKA, *wearing a black sweater and black pants, quickly enters through the rear door, a briefcase in his hand, slightly out of breath.*)

FOUSTKA: Hi.
NEUWIRTH (*without turning around*):   Hi.   5

(*No one reacts to Foustka's entrance; all continue doing what they were doing before.* FOUSTKA *sets his briefcase down on the desk and begins to take out various papers.*)

FOUSTKA: Were they here yet?
NEUWIRTH (*without turning around*):   Not yet.

(*When* FOUSTKA *sees that* LORENCOVA *is not going to free the desk for him he crosses over to the bench where* KOTRLY *is sitting and sits down next to him. A pause.*)

LORENCOVA: Poor Marketa.

(FOUSTKA *looks up.*)

KOTRLY (*without looking up*):   What's with her?
LORENCOVA: She tried to slit her wrists.   10

(FOUSTKA *stands up, shaken.*)

KOTRLY (*without turning around*):   So it's true after all?
NEUWIRTH (*without turning around*):   They say she's in the psychiatric ward.
LORENCOVA: Poor thing.

(FOUSTKA *sits down again. The* DEPUTY, *in everyday clothes, and* PETRUSHKA, *in a white coat, enter through the right door, holding hands.* LORENCOVA *shoves the compact into her coat pocket.* KOTRLY *folds his newspaper.* NEUWIRTH *puts aside the book, and turns around.* LORENCOVA, KOTRLY, *and* FOUSTKA *stand up.*)

KOTRLY: Good morning, Sir.

DEPUTY: Hello there, my friends! And please sit down.   15

(LORENCOVA, KOTRLY, *and* FOUSTKA *sit down again. A short pause.*)

    I don't see Vilma here.

FOUSTKA: She's at the dentist.

(*Short pause.*)

DEPUTY: As you well know, the task we're facing today is not an easy one.
Nobody here—as our director said so nicely—has any intention of
staging a witch-hunt. The truth must prevail, come what may. But for   20
that very reason we must remind ourselves that looking for the truth
means looking for the whole, unadulterated truth. That is to say that
the truth isn't only something that can be demonstrated in one way
or another, it is also the purpose for which the demonstrated thing is
used or for which it may be misused, and who boasts about it and why,   25
and in what context it finds itself. As scientists we know well that by
tearing a certain fact out of its context we can not only completely shift
or change its meaning, but we can stand it right on its head and thus
make a lie out of the truth or vice versa. In short, then, we shouldn't
allow the living background of the acts with which we are going to   30
concern ourselves to disappear from our field of vision, nor the conclusions which we will draw about them. I hope I don't have to elaborate
any further—we aren't little children, damn it! Or are we?

KOTRLY: We aren't.

DEPUTY: So there you are! Who's feeding the carrier pigeons today?   35

NEUWIRTH: I am.

DEPUTY: Splendid!

(*The* DIRECTOR, *wearing a white coat, enters through the right door.* LORENCOVA,
KOTRLY, *and* FOUSTKA *rise immediately.*)

KOTRLY: Hi.

DIRECTOR: Hello there, my friends! And please sit down.

(LORENCOVA, KOTRLY, *and* FOUSTKA *sit down. A short pause.*)

    I don't see Vilma.   40

DEPUTY: I didn't see her either when I came. She's apparently at the
dentist.

(*The* DIRECTOR *approaches* KOTRLY *and holds out his hand.* KOTRLY *rises.*)

DIRECTOR (*to* KOTRLY):   Did you get a good night's sleep?

KOTRLY: Very good, thank you.

(*The* DIRECTOR *presses* KOTRLY's *elbow in a friendly manner and turns to the others.* KOTRLY *sits down.*)

DIRECTOR: As you well know, the task we're facing today is not an easy one.   45
DEPUTY: That's precisely what I was telling our colleagues just a second
    ago, Sir!
DIRECTOR: We all know the issue, so we can skip the preliminaries . . .

(VILMA, *out of breath, and carrying a large paper box in her hand, rushes in through the rear door.*)

VILMA: Please excuse me, Sir, I'm very sorry . . . I had an appointment at
    the dentist this morning, and can you imagine, I—   50
DIRECTOR: I know about it, sit down.

(VILMA *sits on the oilcloth couch, places the box at her feet, communicates something through gestures to* FOUSTKA, *and then shows that she is crossing her fingers for him.* LORENCOVA *leans over to her.*)

LORENCOVA (*quietly*):   What's this?
VILMA (*quietly*):   A toaster from the repair shop.
LORENCOVA (*quietly*):   I thought it was a new hat.
VILMA (*quietly*):   No.   55
DIRECTOR: Where was I?
KOTRLY: You were saying that we can skip the preliminaries . . .
DIRECTOR: Ah yes. So we can skip the preliminaries and get right to the
    subject. Doctor Foustka, if you would kindly . . .

(*The* DIRECTOR *motions to* FOUSTKA *to come to the front.* FOUSTKA *rises, crosses to the middle of the room, and stands in the place where the* DIRECTOR *has indicated.*)

    There, that's good. Shall we begin?   60
FOUSTKA: Certainly.
DIRECTOR: Well, then, could you tell us, my friend, whether it's true that
    for some time now . . .

(*At that moment the* SECRET MESSENGER *enters through the right door, steps up to the* DIRECTOR, *and whispers something at length in his ear. The* DIRECTOR *gravely nods his head. After a longer while the* SECRET MESSENGER *concludes. The* DIRECTOR *nods his head one last time. The* SECRET MESSENGER *exits through the right door.*)

    Where was I?
KOTRLY: You were asking him whether it's true that for some time now . . .   65
DIRECTOR: Ah yes. Well, then, could you tell us, Sir, whether it's true that
    for some time now you've been engaged in the study of what's known
    as occult literature?

FOUSTKA: It's true.

DIRECTOR: For how long? 70

FOUSTKA: I don't know exactly . . .

DIRECTOR: A round number will do. A half a year? A year?

FOUSTKA: Something like that.

DIRECTOR: How many such books, in your estimation, did you read in that period? 75

FOUSTKA: I didn't count them.

DIRECTOR: A round number will do. Five? Thirty? Fifty?

FOUSTKA: Maybe fifty.

DIRECTOR: To whom did you lend them out?

FOUSTKA: No one. 80

DIRECTOR: Now, now, Sir, you aren't going to tell us that nobody borrowed such desirable and rare books from you, books impossible to come by these days! Your friends obviously had to see them at your place.

FOUSTKA: I don't invite friends over to my place, and I never lend books.

DIRECTOR: Very well, then. And now please concentrate—this is an impor- 85
tant question: what led you to these studies? Why, actually, did you begin a systematic investigation of these things?

FOUSTKA: I'd been uneasy for a long time about our young people's mount-
ing interest in everything that has anything to do with the so-called supernatural. As a result of this uneasiness of mine I gradually decided 90
to write a brochure in which I would try to demonstrate, by means of mysticism itself, how incongruous that conglomeration of twisted fragments from various cultural circles is, and how strikingly inconsist-
ent these various idealistic and mystical theories of the past are with contemporary scientific knowledge. At the same time I especially chose 95
mysticism as the subject for my critical attention rather than any other because of the uncritical interest it is enjoying today. My project, of course, required—

DIRECTOR (*interrupting*):   None of us doubted, Sir, that you would answer that question precisely as you did. But in the meanwhile, none of us 100
knows how you intend to explain the shocking fact that you allegedly practiced black magic yourself.

FOUSTKA: I didn't really practice it much; mostly I just spread the word that I did.

DIRECTOR: Why? 105

FOUSTKA: Because that was the only way to build trust among people as mistrustful as today's sorcerers are.

DIRECTOR: So you craved their trust? Interesting, interesting! How far did you get in achieving it?

FOUSTKA: So far I've been only modestly successful, my success taking the   110
form of a certain source who visited me two times, about whom you
have been informed.

DIRECTOR: Did that source tell you why it sought you out?

FOUSTKA: Apparently it knew about my interest in the practice of black
magic and was willing to initiate me into it.   115

DIRECTOR: Did you agree to that?

FOUSTKA: Not expressly, but at the same time I didn't expressly refuse.
We're in a state of so-called mutual discussion.

DIRECTOR: What does it want in return?

FOUSTKA: For me to testify that it put itself at the disposal of science, if   120
the need arises.

DEPUTY: Do you hear that, Sir! What a cunning bunch they are!

DIRECTOR: It seems to me, Foustka, that it's high time to ask our pivotal
question: how do you explain the fact that on the one hand you claim
to have a scientific viewpoint, and consequently must know that black   125
magic is sheer charlatanism, while on the other hand you're trying to
gain the trust of sorcerers, and when one of them actually seeks you
out, not only do you *not* kick him out and laugh in his face, but on the
contrary, you make plans to collaborate with him, and indeed, even
to cover up for him? You'll surely find it hard to explain these murky   130
contacts and activities by invoking scientific-critical interests.

FOUSTKA: It may seem foolish to you, but I simply felt from the very first
that my efforts to help those seduced by charlatans and my intentions to fight effectively against such seducers must not be confined
to mere theoretical-propagandistic work. I was and am to this day   135
convinced that it wouldn't be honest to keep my hands entirely clear
of living reality in an effort to keep them clean, as it were, and to lull
my conscience with illusions about God knows what great practical
results coming out of my theoretical struggle. I simply felt that if you
start something you're obliged to finish it, and that it is my civic duty   140
to put my theoretical knowledge in the service of the practical struggle,
which means concretely searching for the hotbed of those activities, and
then uncovering and convicting the perpetrators. Why, we're constantly
boasting about our battle against fakery, mysticism, and superstition,
but if we had to point a finger at even a single disseminator of these   145
poisons, we couldn't do it! But not just us—it's almost unbelievable how
little success anybody has had in infiltrating those areas, and thanks to
that, how little is known about them! Small wonder, then, that they're
spreading so rampantly. That's why I decided to win the confidence of
those circles, infiltrate them, and there, in the field, to gather evidence   150

of their guilt! Which of course I couldn't do without pretending to have at least partial belief in their spirits, initiations, evocations, magical spells, incubi, and succubi and all that other rubbish. I'd probably even be forced to swear oaths of silence or provide eventual cover-ups. In short, I decided to enlist as an inconspicuous and possibly solitary   155
soldier in this silent war, as one might call it, because I arrived at the conclusion that my expertise put me under a direct obligation to do so. We're dealing, you see, with a sphere in which, unfortunately, a so-called broad perspective is still considered valuable, if not an actual prerequisite for any participation in its life.   160

(*A long pause. Everyone present is stunned, each looks in confusion at the others, then finally all looks come to center on the* DIRECTOR.)

DIRECTOR: So that you actually . . . I see . . . I see . . . (*Pause.*) Well, in fact, it wouldn't be such a bad thing if our Institute could pull off a truly concrete victory like that! Our colleague Foustka is right about one thing, brochures have never won wars.
DEPUTY (*to* FOUSTKA):   You would therefore be willing, if I understand you   165
correctly, to provide us with notes about each of your encounters, whether with that source of yours or with any others.
FOUSTKA: Of course! That's exactly why I'm doing it!
DEPUTY: That wouldn't be such a bad thing, as our director has already pointed out. But just one thing isn't clear to me: why did we have to   170
hear about your praiseworthy initiative only now, after certain unfair— as it turns out—accusations have been leveled against you? Why didn't you yourself keep us informed right from the start about your decision and your first steps?
FOUSTKA: I see now that it was a mistake. But I looked at it in a completely   175
different way. As a researcher who is inexperienced in hands-on field-work, I unconsciously compared my role to the situation of an independent scientific worker, who doesn't keep a running account of each of his professional moves either. I thought that it would be sufficient— just as it is in theoretical work—to write a report about my work only at   180
the point where there is really something to report about, that is, when I actually had something concretely relevant and useful in hand. It absolutely never crossed my mind that some chance information about my activities from someone uninformed about their purpose might in some way shake the confidence that I had hitherto enjoyed here.   185
DIRECTOR: You really can't be surprised at that, Foustka. Your decision, however noble-minded, is unfortunately so unusual, and, truth to tell,

so totally unexpected from you of all people, that logically our first
conclusions were more likely to be on the negative side.

DEPUTY: You really can't be surprised at that, Dr. Foustka.   190

DIRECTOR: Never mind—let's come to some sort of conclusion, then.
You've convinced me that this was all a sheer misunderstanding, and
I'm glad that everything was cleared up so quickly. Needless to say,
I think highly of your brave decision and I can assure you that this
work of yours will be prized all the more for it, especially once you   195
get in the habit of keeping thorough records of it and simultaneously
keeping us informed. Does anyone have anything further to add? (*An
awkward pause.*) Nobody does? In that case, the time has come for a
small surprise: tomorrow's get-together at the Institute garden will be
a costume party!   200

LORENCOVA: Bravo!

KOTRLY: A great idea!

DEPUTY: Oh, yes! I like it a lot too.

LORENCOVA: And what theme will it have?

DIRECTOR: Isn't it obvious? A witches' Sabbath!   205

(*A wave of commotion runs through the room.*)

A gathering of devils, witches, sorcerers, and magicians. Classy, what?
Originally I only saw it as an attempt to liven up the office party tradition with a certain parodistic element. It seemed to me that if at night
we made fun of the very thing we have to fight against so seriously
and soberly during the day, we could—in the spirit of modern group-   210
costume therapy—enhance our relationship to our own work. Simply
by treating the problem with frivolity for a few moments we would
emphasize its permanent unfrivolity, by making light of it we would
emphasize its gravity, by stepping away from it we would get closer to
it. Now, however, thanks to a timely coincidence, I think we can see it   215
in yet another way: as a playful tribute to the work of our colleague
Foustka here, who not only needs to find a disguise, in the metaphori-
cal sense of the word, but also may face the unenviable task of finding
a literal disguise soon—on that occasion when he decides to infiltrate
some actual black mass or other! (*Polite laughter.*) Ah well, let's all look 220
at it—at least in part—as a sort of jolly little ending to the serious transaction we just concluded! Who's feeding the carrier pigeons today?

NEUWIRTH: I am.

DIRECTOR: Splendid! (*To* KOTRLY.) Vilem, don't forget!

The curtain falls.

Scene 8

Vilma's apartment again. As the curtain rises, FOUSTKA, *wearing undershorts, is sitting on the bed, and* VILMA, *wearing a slip, is combing her hair at the mirror—the situation is the same as at the beginning of Scene 4.*

FOUSTKA: I just bet you could buy him off with a mere kiss on the cheek, once he was in the house! Surely he tried to dance with you at the very least!

VILMA: Henry, drop it, for goodness sake! I don't keep pumping you for details either—and I'd have far more reason to do so!   5

(A short pause. Then FOUSTKA *gets up and begins to walk back and forth, deep in thought.* VILMA *stops combing her hair and looks at him in surprise.)*

What's wrong?

FOUSTKA: What should be wrong?

VILMA: You began so well.

FOUSTKA: Somehow I'm not in the mood for it today.

VILMA: Does it arouse you too much?   10

FOUSTKA: It's not that.

VILMA: So what happened?

FOUSTKA: You know very well.

VILMA: I don't!

FOUSTKA: You really don't know? And who denounced me to the director   15
about the sorcerer coming to see me, you don't know that either?

*(*VILMA *freezes, then throws down the comb, jumps up excitedly, and looks at* FOUSTKA *with astonishment.)*

VILMA: For God's sake, Henry, you don't think that—

FOUSTKA: Nobody else at the Institute knew about it!

VILMA: Are you crazy? Why would I do it, for goodness sake? If you're going
to insult me with the thought that I could denounce anybody at all   20
to that imbecile, how can you imagine that I'd go and denounce *you?*
Why, that would be as bad as denouncing my own self! You know how
much I want you to be happy, and how I'm constantly worrying about
you! How could I possibly want to destroy you all of a sudden? And
my own self at the same time—our relationship—our life together—our   25
make-believe jealousy games—our love—so marvelously confirmed by
those flashes of true jealousy that you've begun to show in recent days,
our memories of all those golden hours of sheer happiness we've had
together—why, it would be pure madness!

FOUSTKA: What if it were precisely the memory of those golden hours that   30
provided the key to such an act? What do I know about a woman's

heart? Maybe you wanted to get even with me over Marketa—or maybe it was just fear of that cripple and an effort to save me from what you thought were his clutches in this way.

(VILMA *runs to the bed, throws herself face down on the pillows, and begins to sob desperately.* FOUSTKA *doesn't know what to do. He looks at* VILMA *helplessly for a while, then sits down beside her cautiously and begins to stroke her hair.*)

    Come on, Vilma.   35

(*Pause.* VILMA *sobs.*)

    I didn't mean it that way.

(*Pause.* VILMA *sobs.*)

    I was just kidding.

(*Pause.* VILMA *sobs.*)

    I just wanted to try a new game.

(*Pause.* VILMA *suddenly sits up briskly, dries her eyes with a handkerchief, and snuffles her nose to clear it. When she feels herself sufficiently calm and strong she speaks coldly.*)

VILMA: Go away!

(FOUSTKA *tries to stroke her; she pushes him away and cries out.*)

    Don't touch me—just go!   40
FOUSTKA: Vilma! I didn't say anything all that terrible! How many times did you want me to tell you far more terrible things!
VILMA: That was different. Are you even aware of what you just did? Why, you actually accused me of being a stool pigeon. I'm asking you to get dressed, to leave, and never to try to repair what you just destroyed so 45 brutally!
FOUSTKA: Are you serious?
VILMA: At least we'll have it over with. It would have happened sooner or later in any case!
FOUSTKA: Because of that dancer?   50
VILMA: No.
FOUSTKA: Why, then?
VILMA: I'm beginning to lose my respect for you.
FOUSTKA: This is the first I've heard of it.
VILMA: It doesn't take long to happen, you know. I actually realized it 55 only today, when I saw the way you saved your neck at the Institute. Offering the director to inform for him, and so shamelessly, in front of

everybody! And now, to top it all off, you, a voluntary and self-declared
stool pigeon, dare to accuse me, innocent and devoted me, of informing—and what's more, of informing on you! Do you see how absurd it   60
is? What's happened to you? What's gotten into you? Are you actually
the same person anymore? Maybe you really *are* possessed by some
devil! That fellow addled your brains. God knows what stuff he told
you. God knows what spell he cast on you.

(FOUSTKA *gets up and begins to walk back and forth across the room in agitation.*)

FOUSTKA: For your information he doesn't cast spells, he only helps people   65
understand their own selves better and face all the bad things dormant
inside them! Furthermore, about my being a stool pigeon, as you put
it, not only was that the only way I could save myself, it also the
only way I could help him as well! If they believe that I'm controlling
him, they'll leave him alone. And the third thing, my suspecting that   70
they found out about him from you—I simply couldn't hide it from
you. What would that have done to our relationship! You might have
said something unintentionally—in front of someone you trusted by
mistake—or somebody could have accidentally overheard you . . .
VILMA: I never said anything intentionally or not, and what bothers me   75
about your suspicions is not your speaking up about them, or even that
you spoke up so crudely, which you're now belatedly trying to make up
for, but that they occurred to you at all! If you're capable of thinking
something like that about me for even a split second, then there's really
no point in our staying together.   80

(*Pause.* FOUSTKA *sits down dejectedly in the armchair and stares dully into space.*)

FOUSTKA: I was a fool to say anything to you. I always spoil everything so
stupidly. What am I going to do without you? I can't stand myself.
VILMA: And now you're even feeling sorry for yourself!
FOUSTKA: Do you remember what we said to each other that time under
the elms at the riverbank?   85
VILMA: Don't drag those elms into this, it won't do you any good. You've
hurt me too much to talk your way out of it by manipulating our
memories of the past. And besides, I asked you to do something . . .
FOUSTKA: You mean that I should leave?
VILMA: Exactly!   90
FOUSTKA: You're expecting the dancer, aren't you?
VILMA: I'm not expecting anyone, I simply want to be alone!

(*A short pause. Then* FOUSTKA *suddenly jumps up, runs over to* VILMA, *knocks her
down roughly on the bed, and grabs her wildly by the neck.*)

FOUSTKA (*in a dark voice*):   You're lying, you whore!
VILMA (*crying out in terror*):   Help!

(FOUSTKA *begins to strangle* VILMA. *Just then the doorbell rings.* FOUSTKA *drops* VILMA *immediately, jumps away from her in confusion, stands there for a moment helplessly, then slowly heads for the armchair and lowers himself into it heavily.* VILMA *stands up, quickly straightens herself up a bit, goes to the door, and opens it. There stands the* DANCER, *holding a bunch of violets behind his back.*)

DANCER: Excuse me for disturbing you so late, I only wanted to bring you   95
these. (*The* DANCER *hands* VILMA *the violets.*)
VILMA: Thanks! Come in, please, and stay a while . . .

(*The* DANCER *looks at* VILMA *in surprise, and then at* FOUSTKA *collapsed in the armchair staring absently into space. An awkward pause.*)

He's not feeling well, you see—I'm a little worried.
DANCER: Some sort of heart trouble?
VILMA: Probably.   100
DANCER: So in the meanwhile we could dance a little bit, what do you say?
Maybe it would distract him.

The curtain falls.

Scene 9

Foustka's apartment again. As the curtain rises, FOUSTKA *is alone onstage. Dressed in a dressing gown, he is pacing back and forth, deep in thought. After a long while someone knocks at the door.* FOUSTKA *stops in his tracks, hesitates for a moment, and then calls.*

FOUSTKA: Who is it?
HOUBOVA (*offstage*):   It's me, Doctor Foustka.
FOUSTKA (*calling*):   Come in, Mrs. Houbova.
HOUBOVA (*entering*):   You've got a visitor.
FOUSTKA: I do! Who?   5
HOUBOVA: Well, it's him again . . . you know . . . the one that . . .
FOUSTKA: That smells?
HOUBOVA: Yes.
FOUSTKA: Show him in.

(*A short pause;* HOUBOVA *stands uncertainly.*)

What's the matter?   10
HOUBOVA: Doctor Foustka . . .
FOUSTKA: Did something happen?

HOUBOVA: I'm just a stupid woman. I know it's not my place to give you
   advice about anything.

FOUSTKA: What's on your mind?   15

HOUBOVA: I'm sorry, but if I were in your place I wouldn't trust that fellow!
   I can't really explain it—I don't even know what business he has with
   you—I just have a sort of strange feeling about him.

FOUSTKA: Last time you let him in yourself!

HOUBOVA: Because I was scared of him.   20

FOUSTKA: I'll admit he looks disreputable, but basically he's harmless. Or,
   to be more precise, he's too insignificant to do any serious damage.

HOUBOVA: Do you have to associate with people like him? You?

FOUSTKA: Mrs. Houbova, I'm a grown-up and I know what I'm doing,
   after all!   25

HOUBOVA: But I'm so worried about you! Don't you see, I remember you as
   a three-year-old. I don't have children of my own . . .

FOUSTKA: Of course, that's fine, I'm really grateful for your concern. I
   understand and I appreciate it, but I think that in this case it's really
   unnecessary. Show him in and don't worry about it anymore.   30

(HOUBOVA *exits, leaving the door ajar.*)

HOUBOVA (*offstage*):   This way, Mister.

(FISTULA *enters, carrying his bag in his hand.* HOUBOVA *takes one last look after
him into the room, shakes her head anxiously, and closes the door.* FISTULA, *grinning
stupidly, rushes directly to the sofa, sits down, takes off his shoes, takes his slippers
out of the bag and puts them on, puts the shoes into the bag, which he then places on
the sofa beside him. He looks up at* FOUSTKA *and begins to grin.*)

FISTULA: So, what?

FOUSTKA: What, what?

FISTULA: I'm waiting for you to begin your usual song and dance.

FOUSTKA: What song and dance?   35

FISTULA: That I should leave immediately and so on.

(FOUSTKA *walks around the room, deep in thought, then sits at his desk.*)

FOUSTKA: Listen! In the first place, I've come to understand that it's
   impossible simply to get rid of you and therefore it makes no sense to
   waste time trying to do something that's doomed to failure in advance.
   In the second place, without making too much of your inspirational   40
   influence, as you call it, I've come to the conclusion that time spent
   with you doesn't have to be a complete waste after all. If I have to be a
   subject for you, why, then, shouldn't you be a subject for me in turn?
   Or isn't that how your original proposal went: that you offer me an

inside look at your practices, for which I, in exchange, guarantee you a   45
certain cover? I've decided to accept your proposal.

FISTULA: I knew you'd work yourself up to it, which was one of the reasons
for my persistence. I'm glad that my persistence is finally rewarded. But
not to be too humble about it, again: I don't attribute your decision
to my persistence alone, but also to the obvious accomplishments our   50
collaboration has achieved . . .

FOUSTKA: What accomplishments are you referring to now?

FISTULA: Not only that you kept your job at the Institute, but that you
actually even improved your position there. Meanwhile, it gives me
great joy to state that in this particular case you even managed to avoid   55
Smichovsky's Compensatory Syndrome, which is a sign of real progress.

FOUSTKA: If you're trying to suggest that I lost all my moral values and gave
in to whatever it is that you're trying to awaken inside of me, then you
are very much mistaken. I'm still the same person. I'm just cooler and
more in control as a result of my recent experiences, which allows me   60
to know at all times just how far and in which direction—however new
it might be for me—I am able to go, without the risk of letting myself in
for something that I might bitterly regret later on.

(FISTULA *grows slightly uneasy, fidgets a bit, looks around.*)

What's the matter with you?

FISTULA: Oh nothing, nothing.   65

FOUSTKA: You look like you're afraid, which is a condition I don't recognize in you and which would especially surprise me after the explicit
promise of cover I just gave you.

(FISTULA *takes off his slippers and rubs the soles of his feet with both hands, sighing
all the while.*)

Does it hurt?

FISTULA: It's nothing, it'll go away. (*After a while he puts on his slippers again.*   70
Then he suddenly begins to cackle.)

FOUSTKA: What's so funny now?

FISTULA: May I be completely frank?

FOUSTKA: Suit yourself.

FISTULA: You are!   75

FOUSTKA: What? You find me funny? What nerve!

(FISTULA *grows serious and stares at the ground. After a while he suddenly glances up*
at FOUSTKA.)

FISTULA: Look here, Doctor Foustka. The fact that you saved your neck by
means of a little dirty work is quite all right. Why, Hajaha and I—

FOUSTKA: Who?

FISTULA: Hajaha, the spirit of politics—we were pointing you in that very   80
direction! What's not quite all right is that in the process you forgot the
rules of the game!

FOUSTKA: What rules? What game? What the devil are you talking about?

FISTULA: Don't you suppose that our work together has rules of its own
too? Break down your own scruples as much as you want—as you know,   85
I always welcome that sort of thing on principle. But to double-cross
the very one who is leading you along this thrilling and, I might even
say, revolutionary path—that, you really shouldn't do! Even a revolution
has its laws! Last time you called me a devil. Imagine for a moment that
I really were one! How do you suppose I'd react to your amateurish   90
attempt to deceive me?

FOUSTKA: But I'm not trying to deceive you.

FISTULA: Look, without actually making any explicit promises, we certainly
reached a sort of unspoken agreement not to talk about our work
together with anyone, much less make reports on it to hostile and   95
threatening authorities. One might even go so far as to say that we had
begun—naturally with some caution—to trust each other. If you failed
to understand the inner meaning of our agreement and you decided to
thumb your nose at it, that was your first serious mistake. You've done
enough reading, after all, to know that there are certain limits—even in 100
my sphere—that you can't overstep; in fact, precisely here, with so much
at stake, the commandment against overstepping them is especially
severe. Don't you understand that if we're capable of playing around
with the whole world, it is only and entirely because we depend on contacts that we're absolutely forbidden to play around with? To deceive a 105
liar is fine, to deceive a truth teller is still allowable, but to deceive the
very instrument that gives us the strength to deceive and that allows us
in advance to deceive with impunity—that, you truly cannot expect to
get away with! That one (*points skyward*), overwhelms Man with a multitude of unkeepable commandments, and therefore there's nothing 110
left for him but to forgive occasionally. The others, on the other hand,
liberate Man from all those unkeepable commandments, and therefore,
understandably, they are totally rid of the need, opportunity, and,
finally, even the capacity to forgive. But even if that weren't so, they
wouldn't be able to forgive the betrayal of the very agreement releasing 115
all that boundless freedom. Why, such forgiveness would make their
entire world collapse! But really, might not the obligation to be faithful
to the authority which gives us that sort of freedom actually be the only
guarantee of freedom from all obligation? Do you see what I mean?

(FOUSTKA, *who has been growing increasingly nervous during Fistula's speech, stands up and begins to pace about the room. A long pause.* FISTULA *watches him carefully. Then* FOUSTKA *suddenly comes to a stop at his desk, leans against it as if against a speaker's podium, and turns to* FISTULA.)

FOUSTKA: I see what you mean perfectly well, but I'm afraid you don't see   120
what *I* mean!

FISTULA: Is that so?

FOUSTKA: You can look at the promise you're obviously referring to as an
attempt to betray you only because you don't know why I made it and
was able to make it with a clear conscience!   125

FISTULA: You made it in order to save your neck.

FOUSTKA: Of course, but what good would it be if the price were betrayal!
I'm not that stupid! The only reason that I was able to make the promise was because I was determined right from the start not only *not* to
keep it, but at the same time to cleverly use the position it gained for   130
me—naturally in close consultation with you—for our purposes and to
our advantage. In other words, to gain control over their information,
while flooding them with our own disinformation; to erase the real
tracks, while keeping them busy with false ones; to use their own organization to rescue those of us who are threatened, while drowning those   135
who threaten us. And with all this, to serve our cause by being our own
man hidden in the heart of the enemy, indeed, in the very heart of the
enemy's division specifically designed to fight against us! I'm surprised
and disappointed that you didn't understand and appreciate my plan
immediately.   140

(FOUSTKA *sits.* FISTULA *leaps up and begins to cackle and jump around the room wildly. Then he suddenly stops and quite matter-of-factly turns to* FOUSTKA.)

FISTULA: Even if you just invented this conceit, I'll still accept it, if only to
give you one last chance. Actually it *is* possible to forgive, and to give
people a chance to make amends, even in our realm. If I claimed the
opposite a little while ago, it was only to scare you into coming out
with precisely the sort of unambiguous offer as the one you just made,   145
thereby allowing you to save yourself at the very edge of the abyss. But
obviously, and luckily for you, I'm really not the devil. He would never
have let you get away with the betrayal that I just let you get away with,
never!

(FOUSTKA *is visibly relieved, can't hide it, goes to* FISTULA *and embraces him.* FISTULA *jumps aside, his teeth begin to chatter, and he begins to quickly rub his arms.*)

Man, you must be a hundred below zero! 150
FOUSTKA (*laughing*): Not quite.

The curtain falls.

Scene 10

The Institute garden once again. Except that the bench is now on the right and the table with drinks now on the left, everything is exactly the same as it was in Scene 3, including the lighting. As the curtain rises, the music becomes quiet and changes in style just as at the beginning of Scene 3. This time, too, it will provide a background for the entire scene unless otherwise indicated. The two LOVERS *and* FOUSTKA *are onstage. The* LOVERS *dance together in the background, where they will continue to dance without interruption for almost the entire scene, leaving their bower empty for now.* FOUSTKA *is sitting on the bench, deep in thought. All three are wearing costumes that suit the "magic" theme of the party.* FOUSTKA *is wearing the traditional theatrical costume for Faust. All characters appearing in this scene are dressed or in some cases painted in this same spirit. Some of the best-known and most common motifs traditionally used in the theater for "hellish" or "witchlike" themes should make an appearance in this scene; for instance, the colors red and black should predominate, as well as a profusion of pendants and amulets of various sorts, wildly tangled women's wigs, devils' tails, hoofs, and chains, etc. A long pause. Then, from the right,* LORENCOVA *emerges with a broom under her arm. She crosses the stage towards the table, where she pours herself a drink. Pause.*

FOUSTKA: Do you happen to know if the director is here yet?
LORENCOVA: No I don't.

(*Pause.* LORENCOVA *finishes her drink, puts the glass down, and vanishes to the left. After a while she can be seen in the background, dancing alone with her broom. Pause. Then the* DEPUTY *enters from the left.*)

DEPUTY: Have you seen Petrushka?
FOUSTKA: She hasn't been here.

(*The* DEPUTY *shakes his head uncomprehendingly and vanishes to the right. After a while he may be seen in the background, swaying alone to the dance music.* FOUSTKA *gets up and goes to the table, where he pours himself a drink. The* DIRECTOR *and* KOTRLY, *holding hands, enter from the right. Unless otherwise noted, they will be holding hands for the whole scene. The* DIRECTOR, *in a particularly conspicuous devil costume, has horns on his head. The* DIRECTOR *and* KOTRLY *pay no attention to* FOUSTKA *and stop in the middle of the stage.* FOUSTKA, *at the table, watches them.*)

DIRECTOR (*to* KOTRLY): Where will you actually put it? Around here? 5
KOTRLY: I thought I'd put it in the bower.

DIRECTOR: All right. That would be better for safety reasons too.
KOTRLY: I'll light it in the gardener's shed, then I'll secretly bring it here—it
takes a few minutes to warm up. I'll set it down in the bower, and a
little while later you'll see . . . (DIRECTOR *and* KOTRLY *head towards the left.*)   10
FOUSTKA: Excuse me, Sir . . .

(*The* DIRECTOR *and* KOTRLY *stop.*)

DIRECTOR: Yes, Foustka?
FOUSTKA: I wonder if you have a minute or two?
DIRECTOR: I'm sorry, Foustka, but certainly not now.

(*The* DIRECTOR *and* KOTRLY *disappear to the left. After a while they may be seen
in the background, dancing together.* FOUSTKA, *holding his glass, crosses back to the
bench, deep in thought, and sits down. The music grows noticeably louder, some well-
known tango may be heard, for instance, "Tango Milonga."* VILMA *and the* DANCER
*rush onstage from the left and begin to do some complicated tango figures together.
These are choreographed mainly by the* DANCER, *obviously a professional, who continues to glide about the stage elaborately and skillfully with* VILMA. FOUSTKA *stares at
them in astonishment. After a while the tango comes to a climax and* VILMA *and the*
DANCER *do a closing figure. The music grows softer and changes its character. Out
of breath but happy,* VILMA *and the* DANCER *are holding hands and smiling at each
other.*)

FOUSTKA: Are you enjoying yourselves?   15
VILMA: As you can see.

(*The* DEPUTY, *who has in the interim left the dance floor, enters from the left.*)

DEPUTY: Have you seen Petrushka?
VILMA: She hasn't been here.

(*The* DEPUTY *shakes his head impatiently and vanishes to the right. After a while he
may be seen in the background, swaying alone to the dance music.* VILMA *seizes the*
DANCER *by the hand and leads him away. They both disappear to the left. After a
while they may be seen in the background, dancing.* FOUSTKA *stands up, crosses to
the table, and pours himself a drink. The* DIRECTOR *and* KOTRLY, *who have in the
interim disappeared from the dance floor, enter from the right, holding hands. They
pay no attention to* FOUSTKA *but stop in the middle of the stage.* FOUSTKA, *at the
table, watches them.*)

KOTRLY (*to the* DIRECTOR):   How will I know when it's the right time for it?
DIRECTOR: You'll figure it out somehow, or else I'll give you a signal. I'm   20
worried about something else.
KOTRLY: What?
DIRECTOR: Can you really guarantee that nothing will go wrong?

KOTRLY: What should go wrong?

DIRECTOR: Well, somebody might suffocate—or something might catch 25
fire . . .

KOTRLY: Don't worry.

(*The* DIRECTOR *and* KOTRLY *head towards the left.*)

FOUSTKA: Excuse me, Sir . . .

DIRECTOR: Yes, Foustka?

FOUSTKA: I realize that you have a lot of other things on your mind just 30
now, but I won't keep you long, and I'm certain that the thing I want
to talk to you about will interest you.

DIRECTOR: I'm sorry, but now it's really impossible . . .

(*Just then the* SECRET MESSENGER *enters from the right, goes up to the* DIRECTOR,
leans over, and whispers in his ear at length. The DIRECTOR *nods his head. While the*
MESSENGER *is whispering,* LORENCOVA, *who has in the interim left the dance floor,
enters from the right holding her broom in her hand. She remains standing near the
bench and gazes at the* MESSENGER. *After a long while the* MESSENGER *concludes. The*
DIRECTOR *nods one last time, at which point he disappears to the left with* KOTRLY.
After a while they may be seen in the background, dancing together. The MESSENGER
heads towards the right, just opposite LORENCOVA. *She is smiling at him. He stops
directly in front of her. For a moment both of them stare at each other intently, then
the* MESSENGER, *without taking his eyes off her, takes her broom from her hand, places
it on the ground meaningfully, and commences to embrace* LORENCOVA. *She embraces
him in return. For a moment they gaze meltingly into each other's eyes, then they begin
to kiss. When they move apart after a while, they disappear together to the right, arms
around each other's waists. After a while they may be seen in the background, dancing.*
FOUSTKA, *glass in hand and deep in thought, crosses the stage to the bench and sits
down. Suddenly, he becomes attentive and listens. Offstage a girl's voice may be heard,
singing the melody of the music that is just playing, Ophelia's song from Hamlet.*)

MARKETA (*singing offstage*):
And will 'a not come again?   35
And will 'a not come again?
No, no, he is dead,
Go to thy death bed,

(MARKETA *emerges at left. She is barefoot, her hair is loose and flowing; on her head
is a wreath made of wild flowers. She is wearing a white nightgown with the word
"psychiatry" stamped at the bottom in large letters. She approaches* FOUSTKA *slowly,
singing. He rises, aghast.*)

He never will come again.
His beard was as white as snow   40

All flaxen was his poll
He is gone, he is gone,
And we cast away moan.
God 'a' mercy on his soul!

FOUSTKA (*crying out*):   Marketa!   45

MARKETA: Oh where is that handsome Prince of Denmark?

(FOUSTKA, *horrified, walks backward in front of* MARKETA, *she walks behind him, they slowly circle the stage.*)

FOUSTKA: What are you doing here, for God's sake? Did you run away?

MARKETA: Tell him, please, when you see him, that all those things can't exist just for themselves, but that they must conceal some deeper design of existence, of the world, and of nature willing you . . .   50

FOUSTKA: Marketa, don't you recognize me? It's Henry . . .

MARKETA: Or could it be, perhaps, that the cosmos directly intended that one fine day it would see itself thus through our eyes and ask itself thus through our lips the very questions we're asking ourselves here and now?   55

FOUSTKA: You ought to go back—they'll help you—everything will be all right again—you'll see . . .

MARKETA (*singing*):
How should I your true love know
From another one?   60
By his cockle hat and staff,
And his sandal shoon.

(MARKETA *vanishes to the right. Offstage the sound of her singing can still be heard, gradually fading away.* FOUSTKA, *upset, crosses over to the table, quickly pours himself a drink, downs it in one gulp, and pours himself another. The* DIRECTOR *and* KOTRLY, *who have in the interim left the dance floor, appear at the right, holding hands. They pay no attention to* FOUSTKA *but are absorbed in their conversation.*)

DIRECTOR: Surely he tried to dance with you at the very least . . .

KOTRLY: Please stop it! Can't you talk about anything more interesting?

DIRECTOR: Did he try or not?   65

KOTRLY: All right, he did, if you really must know, then he did! But I won't tell you another thing.

(*The* DIRECTOR *and* KOTRLY *slowly cross the stage and head for the exit at left.*)

FOUSTKA: Excuse me, Sir . . .

(*The* DIRECTOR *and* KOTRLY *stop.*)

DIRECTOR: What do you want, Foustka?

(*Just then a cry of pain is heard from behind the bench.*)

NEUWIRTH (*offstage*):   Ow!   70

(*The* DIRECTOR, KOTRLY, *and* FOUSTKA *look towards the bench with surprise. Out of the bushes emerges* NEUWIRTH, *holding his ear, obviously wounded. He is groaning.*)

KOTRLY: What in the world happened to you, Louie?
NEUWIRTH: Oh, nothing.
DIRECTOR: Is something the matter with your ear?

(NEUWIRTH *nods.*)

KOTRLY: Did something bite you?

(NEUWIRTH *nods, and with his head indicates the bushes from which he had just emerged and out of which now emerges an embarrassed* PETRUSHKA. *She is nervously straightening her hair and her costume. The* DIRECTOR *and* KOTRLY *grin and exchange knowing looks.* NEUWIRTH, *groaning and holding his ear, drags himself off to the right and disappears.* PETRUSHKA *timidly crosses the stage to the table and with shaking hands pours herself a small drink, which she swiftly drinks. The* DIRECTOR *and* KOTRLY *try to leave.*)

FOUSTKA: Excuse me, Sir . . .   75
DIRECTOR: What do you want, Foustka?

(*Just then the* DEPUTY *enters from the left. At first he doesn't see* PETRUSHKA, *who is hidden by* FOUSTKA.)

DEPUTY: Have you seen Petrushka?

(PETRUSHKA *goes up to the* DEPUTY, *smiles at him, and takes his hand; from this moment on they will hold hands as before.*)

Where were you, sweetie pie?

(PETRUSHKA *whispers something to the* DEPUTY, *he listens carefully, finally he nods in satisfaction. The* DIRECTOR *and* KOTRLY *try to leave.*)

FOUSTKA: Excuse me, Sir . . .
DIRECTOR: What do you want, Foustka?   80
FOUSTKA: I realize that you have a lot of other things on your mind right now, but on the other hand . . . having learned my lesson by what happened before . . . I wouldn't want to neglect anything . . . You see, I have some new findings . . . I've even written them down on a piece of paper . . .   85

(FOUSTKA *beings to search, obviously looking for the paper. The* DIRECTOR *and the* DEPUTY *exchange knowing glances and then take a few steps forward, the one leading* KOTRLY *by the hand, the other,* PETRUSHKA, *and move to the center of the stage, where all four automatically form a sort of semicircle around* FOUSTKA. *A short pause.*)

DIRECTOR: Don't bother.

(FOUSTKA *looks at the* DIRECTOR *in surprise, then looks around at the others. A short, suspenseful pause.*)

FOUSTKA: I thought I . . .

(*Again, a suspenseful pause, which is finally interrupted by the* DIRECTOR.)

DIRECTOR (*sharply*):   I'm not interested in what you thought, I'm not
    interested in your piece of paper, I'm not interested in you. The
    comedy, my dear Sir, is ended!   90
FOUSTKA: I don't understand—what comedy?
DIRECTOR: You greatly overestimated yourself and you greatly underesti-
    mated us, taking us for bigger idiots than we are.
DEPUTY: You still don't understand?
FOUSTKA: No.   95
DIRECTOR: Very well, then, I'll give it to you straight. We knew all along
    what you thought of us, we knew you were merely pretending to be
    loyal while hiding your real interests and ideas from us. But in spite
    of that we decided to give you a last chance. And so while seeming to
    believe that cock-and-bull story about your intention to work for us   100
    out in the field, we were curious to see how you would behave after
    having had your lesson and your supposed narrow escape, wondering
    whether you might not come to your senses after all. But instead, you
    took the hand we offered you and spat on it in a despicable way, thus
    definitively sealing your own fate.   105
FOUSTKA: That's not true!
DIRECTOR: You know perfectly well that it is!
FOUSTKA: Then prove it!
DIRECTOR (*to the* DEPUTY):   Shall we oblige him?
DEPUTY: I'm in favor of it.   110

(*The* DIRECTOR *sharply whistles on his fingers. From the bower, where he had apparently been hidden for the entire scene,* FISTULA *leaps out.* FOUSTKA *is alarmed to see
him.* FISTULA *quickly limps over to the* DIRECTOR.)

FISTULA: Did you call, Boss?
DIRECTOR: What did he tell you when you were at his house yesterday?
FISTULA: That he would pretend to be working as an informer for you, but
    in reality he, together with those you are fighting against, would use
    all their power to damage your information service. He literally said   115
    that he would be our—meaning their—man hidden in the heart of the
    enemy . . .
FOUSTKA (*screaming*):   He's lying!
DIRECTOR: What did you say? Would you repeat that?

FOUSTKA: I said he's lying.   120

DIRECTOR: Man, you really have some nerve! How dare you accuse my close
and faithful friend of many years and one of our best external agents of
lying! Fistula never lies to us!

DEPUTY: That's precisely what I wanted to say, Sir! Fistula never lies to us!

(LORENCOVA *and the* SECRET MESSENGER *appear from the left, while at the same
time the* LOVERS *appear from the right, all of whom have, in the interim, left the
dance floor. Both pairs are holding hands. They join the others in such a way that
the semicircle in the center of which* FOUSTKA *is standing unobtrusively widens at
both sides in order to incorporate them.*)

FOUSTKA: So Fistula was an informer after all, and you planted him on   125
me to test me! What an imbecile I was not to throw him out right
away! Vilma, I apologize to you for my absurd suspicions that made
me lose you! Mrs. Houbova, I apologize to you—of course you knew
the truth right away.

DIRECTOR: Who's he talking to?   130

FISTULA: His landlady, Boss.

DIRECTOR: Naturally you're not the only person in the world I'm interested
in. I test everybody—you'd be surprised how long it sometimes takes,
compared to your trivial case—for me to get at the truth, in one way or
another!   135

FOUSTKA (*to* FISTULA):   So I fell for your line after all!

FISTULA: I beg your pardon, Doctor Foustka. (*To the* DIRECTOR) Is he still a
doctor?

DIRECTOR: Who gives a shit?

FISTULA: I beg your pardon, Doctor Foustka, but there you go again,   140
oversimplifying! Didn't I make it clear all along, by dropping hints and
even spelling it out, that you had a number of alternatives, and that
you alone were the master of your fate! You weren't a victim of my line,
but of your own; or rather, of your pride, which made you think that
you'd be able to play both ends against the middle and still get away   145
with it! Or have you forgotten how carefully I explained to you that if a
person doesn't want to come to a bad end, he must respect some form
of authority, it almost doesn't matter which, and that even a revolution has its own laws? I don't see how I could have made things more
obvious than that! My conscience is clear, I did what I could. Why, I   150
couldn't have fulfilled my mission more correctly! The fact that you
didn't understand anything, well, I'm afraid that's your tough luck.

DIRECTOR: Fistula is right, as ever. You cannot serve two masters at once
and deceive them both at the same time! You cannot take from everyone and give nothing in return! You simply must take a side!   155

DEPUTY: That's precisely what I just wanted to say, Sir! You simply must take a side!

(*The music grows noticeably louder. The tango that played earlier is heard again. At the same moment* VILMA *runs onstage from the left and the* DANCER *from the right, having in the interim left the dance floor. They run through the group of people to the center of the stage, where they fall into each other's arms and commence to do another complicated tango figure, during which the* DANCER *does a "dip" almost to the ground with* VILMA. *The music suddenly grows quiet, and* VILMA *and the* DANCER, *holding hands just as all the other couples in the room are doing, quietly join the semicircle.*)

FOUSTKA: It's paradoxical, but now that I've definitively lost and my knowledge serves no purpose to me, I'm finally beginning to understand it all! Fistula is right: I was an arrogant madman who thought he could   160
exploit the devil without signing away his soul to him! But as everyone knows, one can't deceive the devil!

(NEUWIRTH, *with a large bandage on his ear, enters from the right, just as* MARKETA *runs in from the left. When she sees* NEUWIRTH *she calls out to him.*)

MARKETA: Papa!

(MARKETA *runs up to* NEUWIRTH *and seizes his hand. He is a little embarrassed. And even they reluctantly become part of the semicircle.*)

FISTULA: Wait a minute, now! Hold it! I never said that there is such a thing as a devil, not even while I was engaged in that provocation.   165
FOUSTKA: But I'm saying it! And he's actually here among us!
FISTULA: Are you referring to me?
FOUSTKA: You're just a subordinate little fiend!
DIRECTOR: I know your opinions, Foustka, and therefore I understand this metaphor of yours as well. Through me, you want to accuse modern   170
science of being the true source of all evil. Isn't that right?
FOUSTKA: No, it isn't! Through you, I want to accuse the pride of that intolerant, all-powerful, and self-serving power that uses the sciences merely as a handy weapon for shooting down anything that threatens, it, that is, anything that doesn't derive its authority from this power or   175
that is related to an authority deriving its powers elsewhere.
DIRECTOR: That's the legacy you wish to leave this world, Foustka?
FOUSTKA: Yes!
DIRECTOR: I find it a little banal. In countries without censorship every halfway clever little hack journalist churns out stuff like that these days!   180
But a legacy is a legacy, so in spite of what you think of me, I'll give you an example of how tolerant I am by overlooking my reservations and applauding your last testament!

(*The* DIRECTOR *begins to clap lightly, and all the others gradually join in. At the same time the music grows louder—it is hard, wild, and aggressive rock music, a variation of the music heard before the performance and during the pauses. The clapping soon becomes rhythmic, in time with the music, which grows ever louder, slowly becoming almost deafening. Everyone onstage, with the exception of* FOUSTKA, *gradually begins to move suggestively in time with the music. At first, while clapping, they begin to wriggle gently, swaying and shaking to the music. Then this movement slowly changes into dancing. At first they each dance alone, then in couples, and finally all together. The dance is ever wilder, until it becomes a crazy, orgiastic masked ball or witches' Sabbath.* FOUSTKA *does not participate but wanders around in confusion, weaving in and out among the dancers, who variously bump into him, so that he completely loses his sense of direction and is unable to escape, though he would clearly like to.* KOTRLY, *who slipped away from the witches' Sabbath earlier, now returns, carrying a bowl with flames playing at the surface. He twists in and out among the dancers with it, trying to get to the bower, where he finally succeeds in putting the bowl down. However, on the way there he also manages to ignite* FOUSTKA's *cape, so that a new chaotic element is added to the witches' Sabbath in the person of the burning* FOUSTKA, *who now, completely panicked, races around the stage. Shortly thereafter everyone is surrounded by a thick cloud of smoke streaming in from the bower where* KOTRLY *has placed his bowl. The music blasts away. Nothing can be seen onstage. Smoke penetrates the audience. Then the music suddenly stops, the house lights go on, the smoke fades, and it becomes evident that at some point during all this the curtain has fallen. After a very brief silence, music comes on again, now at a bearable level of loudness—the most banal commercial music possible. If the smoke—or the play itself—hasn't caused the audience to flee, and if there are still a few left in the audience who might even want to applaud, let the first to take a bow and thank the audience be a fireman in full uniform with a helmet on his head and a fire extinguisher in his hand.*)

- Havel's personal story mirrors the history of his country. Before World War II, his father was an influential entrepreneur and Havel's maternal grandfather was an important journalist. Because of his family's prominence and its opposition to the communists, Havel himself was not allowed to pursue an education in the humanities at any state university. His plays were often critical of the communist government. This particular play takes aim at the morally corrosive nature of the bureaucracy by adapting the Faust legend to a twentieth-century setting. In order to read this play in light of its historical context, look into the history of Czechoslovakia—how is that history reflected in the fictional world of this play? Look at Havel's essay *The Power of the Powerless*—how is the argument that he constructs in that essay evident in the drama that you have just read? What specific characters in the play embody arguments that Havel makes in that essay?

- Compare Havel's presentation of the Faust myth to Marlowe's *Doctor Faustus* (Chapter 1). How has Havel altered the characters of Mephistopholes and

Faustus? What are the effects of these changes? Much of Marlowe's play concerns the fate and ownership of the human soul—how does Havel adapt that issue to his modern situation?

Experiencing Literature through Writing

1. Pick one specific work from the anthology here (or from one of the other chapters). Determine what contextual information is available to you. In this book, for instance, we give you the year in which the work was written, and we supply you with biographical information about the author.

   a. Once you have collected this information, how does it help you read this specific text? You will probably need some more contextual knowledge. For instance, in this chapter the works are related by the general theme of war. It is important to know what war, if any, was going on at the time the work was written. It would also be useful to have some basic details about that particular war—When was it fought? What were the results? What was at issue in the war? Who was impacted?

   b. Which of the issues that you know about this war (or event) are evident in this particular text? How can you demonstrate that they are important to the text?

   c. Remember that the text might also supply you with contextual information. What do you learn about this war from the text? How reliable is this information?

   d. Which details in the text take on added significance when you think about this particular context?

2. Consider context as you compare two texts within this chapter's anthology. How does one particular text take on added meaning in relation to some other text that meets one of the following criteria:

   a. It was written at the same time.

   b. It deals with the same historical moment but was written at a different time.

   c. It deals with the same theme but was written within a different context.

   As you compare the texts, point to specific details that seem similar in at least some way. How does the context in which the texts were written relate to these details? How do the different contexts help you explain some significant aspects of these details?

3. In Anne Sexton's poem "Courage," the poet offers an alternative to the common definition of courage in the context of war. Look at another work in this anthology and explain how its attention to language, specifically language in relation to war, presents both an unusual use of common words and a clearer understanding of the war experience that the text is describing.

14 Allusions

How Does a Text Build on or Depend upon Other Texts?

In personal conversations, we talk in passing about some event or person with only a reference to a name or a quick description of some part of the event. "Remember the story about your Uncle Sylvester who spent a fortune on modern gold mining equipment, spent years sifting through silt on the bank of some mountain stream, and came back with a pile of worthless rocks." This brief reference works on the assumption that those participating in the conversation are familiar with the events in question and interpret them similarly. We might shorten the reference considerably. For instance, as a warning to someone about to set off on some ill-conceived adventure: "Remember Uncle Vesty." Instead of retelling the story, we just refer to a story that we have told (probably many times) before. The longer people are together and the more experiences they share, the less they need to engage in the complexities of linguistic exchange. They develop a shorthand of brief phrases—code words, if you will—looks, and signs that convey meanings available only to those who have shared the same experiences. And these words and phrases need not be reductive. The smallest remark can trigger layered memories that convey emotions, beliefs, and values. Writers develop their own shorthand to thicken the texture of their works. They know their readers come to any new piece with some previous literary experience. They may invoke that experience through a brief reference to a passage or scene from another work—through an **allusion**.

CREATING COMMUNITY

An old joke tells of prisoners who had been together in the same cell block for many years. A new convict assigned to the cell block found their conversation bewildering. "Fifty-three" called a large bald fellow, and the rest burst out into riotous laughter. An ancient sailor with a blurred blue anchor tattooed on his arm hollered, "One hundred twenty-six!" Again the rest of the block dissolved in laughs. When he had a chance, the newcomer spoke privately with a white-haired old-timer. The old man explained that they had one joke book in the cell block. No one knew anymore where it came from, but the jokes in it never failed. The men in this cell had been telling them to one another for decades, yet each joke still struck all of them as much as it had the first time they had heard it. Over the years, they came to know the book so well, they didn't have to deliver the entire joke anymore. A guy would read the first line, and everyone would start laughing; no one needed to make it to the punch line. Now, they had reached the point that they just read out page numbers as their evening's entertainment. Emboldened, the new convict studied the ragged book. After about a week of listening evening after evening to hear the numbers called and the laughter in response, the new guy hollered out "Twenty-seven!" All the laughter stopped. The old-timer turned to him, "Some guys can just tell them better than others."

Within this joke, we see two important aspects of allusion. First, an allusion is brief. Instead of retelling an entire story, the speaker relies on the common knowledge of the audience to convey a complex idea that otherwise would have taken a long narrative or full explanation to provide. Second, an allusion may depend on, create, or limit a sense of community. Within the cell block, a long-established community defines its membership by a person's knowledge and command of a special language. Access to this community isn't easy. The new convict, for example, lacks the common experience that allows him to join. He studies the book but perhaps needs to observe and internalize the small gestures that will allow him both to hear and tell "jokes" in the cell block. Or perhaps he must be a recognized figure in the community in order to use their private language.

This power of allusion to exclude as well as include might make us wary of highly allusive works. Allusions do sometimes seem like a way for authors to show off, especially to any of us who feel kept outside the conversation that is going on. We might ask why an author needs to display knowledge, especially if the story can do without it. But mere display is rarely the point or the purpose of an allusion. When an author alludes to another work, that author is invoking some quality of the work to enrich the new text. The allusion isn't something merely to recognize; it is something to absorb and appreciate as an integral part of a whole.

Consider, for example, the famous opening sentence of J. D. Salinger's *The Catcher in the Rye*: "If you really want to hear about it, the first thing you'll probably want to know is where I was born, and what my lousy childhood was like, and how my parents were occupied and all before they had me, and all that David Copperfield kind of crap, but I don't feel like going into it, if you want to know the truth." The allusion here is to Charles Dickens's massive autobiographical novel; the first chapter is titled "I am Born." By having Holden refer so dismissively to this classic, Salinger achieves a good deal. We know immediately that the narrator doesn't accept conventional judgments. He's not interested in what other people consider "classic." He has his own opinions to register. We also understand that Holden's story will be a focused one. He's not working on a broad canvas as Dickens did. And if he is not to start where Dickens started, it's likely he won't end where Dickens ended (happily for David—with marriage, children, and professional success). The allusion catches a kind of attitude or tone that helps establish Holden's character.

As we read further in *The Catcher in the Rye*, the allusion to *David Copperfield* makes still more sense. We learn that Holden has been kicked out of Pencey Prep, his elite boarding school. He is failing four of his five courses, mostly because he finds those courses boring and irrelevant. For Holden, Pencey Prep is all about a sterile process of socialization. It's about attitude and gesture with no substance. Pencey people read Dickens because they are supposed to read Dickens; any real engagement with novels (or with history, or with any subject) won't happen in Pencey Prep courses. We can also imagine that the success David Copperfield wins in Dickens's novel would bother Holden because he sees success as built on dishonesty. When his history teacher Mr. Spencer echoes a common bit of wisdom about life as a game, Holden thinks to himself: "Game, my ass. Some game. If you get on the side where all the hot-shots are, then it's a game, all right—I'll admit that. But if you get on the other side, where there aren't any hot-shots, then what's a game about it? Nothing. No game." The kind of Victorian earnestness that Dickens affirms in *David Copperfield* has become for

Making Connections

Salinger's allusion to *David Copperfield* also works because of the place that novel had in the curriculum of college and college prep classes at the time *The Catcher in the Rye* was set and written (late 1940s and early 1950s). Salinger needed to invoke a book that was often assigned (not the same as often read) in a certain sort of class at a certain sort of school. He is alluding to the book not only for its content, but for its status as a cultural commodity. If you were to recast Salinger's novel in the context of a current college prep course, it's likely you'd pick a different book—a book you feel is assigned today out of habit. As we note in Chapter 15, standards of quality or relevance do change over time. What might be a good substitute for *David Copperfield* if you were to revise that first sentence for a reader today?

Holden a thoroughgoing "phoniness" that he cannot tolerate. Salinger's allusion defines a community of outsiders who will follow Holden through the narrative.

Experiencing Literature through Allusions

In "My Weariness of Epic Proportions," the poet Charles Simic's first sentence assumes that his reader knows Achilles. Classical mythology has been included in Western education for centuries; authors frequently use allusions to the most famous, widely read works of a given culture (like Homer, Shakespeare, Dante, Cervantes) without any explanation. But Simic's opening allusion doesn't assume we must all accept the classics for what they have often been taken to represent. Homer celebrates the exploits of Achilles and sets up most of the warriors who died in the Trojan War as remarkable individuals worthy of heroic status. So Simic's allusive opening is rather jarring.

Charles Simic (1938–   )

My Weariness of Epic Proportions (1982)

I like it when
Achilles
Gets killed
And even his buddy Patroclus—
And that hothead Hector—   5
And the whole Greek and Trojan
Jeunesse dorée
Are more or less
Expertly slaughtered
So there's finally   10
Peace and quiet
(The gods having momentarily
Shut up)
One can hear
A bird sing   15
And a daughter ask her mother
Whether she can go to the well
And of course she can
By that lovely little path
That winds through   20
The olive orchard

We don't normally like it when the heroes of a story are "Expertly slaughtered." Simic's poem puts itself in opposition to our usual reading experience from the very start: His speaker likes it when Achilles, Patroclus, Hector, and the whole mass of Greek and Trojan soldiers die in battle. Anyone who has read the *Iliad* can quickly grasp Simic's perspective: peace and quiet are indeed refreshing after widespread carnage—however heroic we might have taken that violence to be. Simic conveys through allusion at the start of the first stanza the overwhelming exhaustion that comes from reading the *Iliad*—an epic poem full of descriptions of relentless destruction. Simic's second stanza turns to very different matters: descriptions of simple, peaceful, ordinary events that don't belong to the world of the *Iliad*. Yet even as Simic claims to be weary of "epic proportions," the proportions and scale of the epic help reaffirm the value of the everyday, peaceful existence he champions. He intensifies our sense of the latter qualities by setting them against the action of Homer's epic.

REVISITING AND RENEWAL

The previous example clarifies another aspect of allusion. The allusion can work not only to enrich a new piece but to also encourage us to rethink a past literary experience. Simic's poem challenges us to consider what it means to read Homer in ways that many people have read Homer. He may make us more sensitive to suffering and less enamored of heroic deeds when we return to the *Iliad*. In this way, allusions can be critical and generative of new readings.

In "Up Home Where I Come From," the poet Dick Barnes presents an account of a hawk that a trapper caught accidentally. The first nineteen lines describe the hawk and its wild dignity. At line 19, Barnes offers an allusion. The allusion affects the meaning of Barnes's poem profoundly. It changes our understanding of what comes before and after it. This allusion also challenges us to think freshly about the source text. In other words, the allusion doesn't just use an older story; it challenges our conventional understanding of the older story.

Dick Barnes (1932–2000)

Up Home Where I Come From (2005)

Roy Smith ran traps for furs
but a hawk got caught in one of them

spreading its wings, there in the trap
turning its sharp beak toward him

as he came to get it out, its glaring eyes so deep   5
they seemed to open onto another world in there

and steady: thus the hawk in time past
came to be an image of aristocracy.

One leg hung by a tendon; with his sharp pocketknife
Roy cut it off and left it lay   10

but brought the hawk home
to feed it til it got well.

There in his basement, in a hutch built for rabbits,
it glared at us with its unfathomable eyes,

accepted the dead meat he brought it, even hamburger,   15
unquenched. That wildness

is what we can know of dignity.
We aspire to it ourselves but seldom—

seldom. Nailed to the tree
Jesus must have been as still as that,   20

as wild. And I'd say
that was the right way to be, there.

Later it got well and he let it go,
our hearts leapt up when we saw it

living somehow in the wild with its one leg: 25
in its life we felt forgiven.

Probably it learned to pin its prey to the ground
and eat there, running that risk.

Risen, that was one thing Jesus did too:
showed he was alive and could still eat.   30

Barnes expects his reader to have at least an elementary knowledge of the Christian story that tells of Jesus being nailed to a cross, dying, and being resurrected to continue his ministry. In this poem, though, the allusion is something of a surprise. The poet concentrates on the wildness of the hawk and its dignity even in captivity. Comparing that wounded hawk to Jesus creates a particular poetic experience in which the familiar story changes. The poet asks us to take the image of Jesus on a cross and to make his dignity akin to the wildness that we see in this injured hawk. With this allusion, we ask how that dignified wounded hawk compares to the crucified figure of Jesus

Leonardo da Vinci, *The Last Supper* (1496–1498)

on a cross that adorns so many Christian churches. The hawk is so powerfully established in particular detail that the allusion midway through the poem challenges any comfortable interpretation of the religious story. What happens when we place the Jesus commonly depicted eating in Leonardo da Vinci's *Last Supper* against the one-legged hawk that has learned to pin its prey to the ground? Barnes's allusion develops a complex image of both figures. When the poet ends by saying that Jesus "showed he was alive and could still eat," the comparison might seem to reduce the religious narrative to a story of simple survival. But the hawk's resilience in the face of the accidental trapping, its ability to reclaim its life and to adjust to the unwanted changes, offers a powerful natural lesson to the poet that echoes the story of Jesus. It is not the same story, but the poet shows us how the incident gives him insight into the more familiar religious narrative.

Barnes includes one more subtle allusion toward the end of the poem when the trapper lets the hawk go: "our hearts leapt up when we saw it." This seems to recall William Wordsworth's "My Heart Leaps Up."

William Wordsworth (1770–1850)

My Heart Leaps Up (1807)

My heart leaps up when I behold
    A rainbow in the sky:
So was it when my life began;
So is it now I am a man;
So be it when I shall grow old,   5
    Or let me die!
The Child is father of the Man;
And I could wish my days to be
Bound each to each by natural piety.

The natural piety that Wordsworth seeks here is a deep responsiveness to the power of natural things. Life for him isn't life without the intensity gained through that responsiveness. Is Barnes using Wordsworth to help us interpret the quality of "forgiveness" that he refers to in line 26? How does this forgiveness relate to the New Testament story that Barnes has alluded to?

Experiencing Film through Allusions

Legend has it that Quentin Tarantino trained to be a film director by working as a clerk in a video store where he immersed himself in countless old films. It is a plausible legend. As a director, Tarantino has created a fresh new film style that builds heavily upon allusions to old films and yet refuses to use the structures of the films he alludes to. His films make so many references to other movies that each of his films has inspired hundreds of web pages that document what goes on in every frame. But it's not just film buffs who are interested in Tarantino's work. *Pulp Fiction* (1994) in particular stands as a powerfully innovative and influential film. Understanding that film requires close attention not just to how many allusions Tarantino employs (a mere accounting of allusions); it requires careful thought on how allusions function. Consider, for example, the scene in which Mia insists that her escort Vincent join her in a dance contest. If John Travolta were not cast as Vincent, this scene might simply define the sort of playfully charged relationship that seems to be unfolding. But because John Travolta *is* cast as Vincent, viewers over forty will almost surely recognize an allusion and respond to the whole scene with that allusion in mind.

John Travolta and Uma Thurman in
Pulp Fiction (1994)

© Frank Trapper/Sygma/Corbis

© Bettmann/Corbis

John Travolta and Karen Lynn Gorney in
Saturday Night Fever (1977)

In the early 1990s, before *Pulp Fiction* came out, John Travolta was best known for having been a movie star in the seventies. When he, as Vincent Vega in *Pulp Fiction*, comes out on the dance floor with Mia Wallace (Uma Thurman), much of the original audience could not help but remember a younger, skinnier Travolta dancing in *Saturday Night Fever*—a tremendous hit in 1977. The reference does not necessarily change the meaning of the scene itself, but it deepens our reaction. We see the character in *Pulp Fiction* about to begin dancing, but we also see a familiar actor regaining his status as a movie star and commenting upon his past and potential within a notoriously fickle industry. These allusions to the old film and to the characters he used to play create a tension within us as we ask whether this newly old Travolta could go out and dance the way he used to. Which character are we responding to in this movie? The conflicted thoughts that we have about John Travolta, a public figure who has a life in our own experiences outside this particular film, bring us into an active engagement with the story.

There is clearly a way in which such allusions remind us of the fictionality of the entire enterprise; in this case, art refers us back to art, not to life. Is *Pulp Fiction* really about two hit men in Los Angeles? Or is it about the pleasure we've experienced watching movies about all sorts of things that would be very unpleasant in real life? *Pulp Fiction* is violent—brutally violent—profane, and oftentimes deliberately over the top, but viewers generally respond to all with a sense of exuberance. Tarantino's playful self-consciousness (his sense that in a movie anything can happen) comes through in the way he fractures the sequence of events so that Vincent Vega can stroll away coolly in the final scene after an earlier scene of his dismal death. The tendency to make transparent through allusion the unreality of art is characteristic of works we've come to label postmodern. The implications of **postmodernism** aren't necessarily light or purely comic; those qualities are more characteristic of the **absurd** (that is, characteristic of a vision that sees meaning drained from life). Postmodernism blurs distinctions between real and imagined. It suggests that in our commodified world—a world where everything becomes a product for sale and consumption—the reality of most people is a reality created by popular fictions (television, advertising, personality magazines, and so on). Perhaps allusions in works like *Pulp Fiction* center so heavily on pop culture because some have come to feel pop culture is what dominates our experience of the world.

IDENTIFYING AND RESPONDING TO ALLUSIONS

An allusion works only if we catch it, so we've attended mainly to fairly clear examples in this chapter. But once we know about allusions, we might become anxious as readers. Are we passing over important things because we don't share the author's aesthetic experience? Although most allusions are hardly hidden, they sometimes do restrict access to a text. The uninitiated, those who don't have particular experiences (like the new prisoner referred to earlier), are not allowed to share in the communal experience. The problem is compounded by the fact that many highly allusive texts arose out of societies that are far more homogeneous than any that exist today. John Milton could take it for granted that anyone who read his *Paradise Lost* in seventeenth-century England had a thorough knowledge of the Bible and could appreciate some subtleties of religious controversy. But far more people are exposed to *Paradise Lost* today than the narrow group of the educated elite that first appreciated its significance. And today's readers are hardly in the know about the theological concerns that occupy Milton. There are many such examples. James Joyce wrote as though his readers knew the details of the Catholic liturgy, the streets of Dublin, Irish music, and Irish politics. These texts are challenging for anyone, but non-Irish readers might find portions particularly obscure.

These problems lead us to a practical reflection. It is important to remember first of all that literary texts and films are rich works of art. Allusions may be *one* element in a complex system of meaning; in other words, you don't necessarily fail to read a work well because you've missed some allusions. And even when allusion is a main element, one need not catch every allusion (nor is one likely to catch every allusion) in any one reading/viewing. So one simple bit of advice is to read confidently and take the time to appreciate what you do catch (as opposed to having anxious concerns over what you don't). Patience, in this case, is a virtue. The more you read, the more receptive you'll be to allusion. And even though that may sound discouraging in the short term, it really should not be. The literary experience can be a lifelong experience. A sense of new discovery is part of what keeps the experience alive over time. So read and view boldly and trust that you'll find much that is rewarding and that you will keep finding more as you experience more.

There are, however, some shortcuts you should be aware of and use. In many cases, modern editions of older works point out important allusions for us. These as well as printed guides and web sources can help lead us through the thickest of allusive texts. For example, more than one modern paperback edition of Dickens's *Great Expectations* identifies the following allusion for us. Pip, the narrator, is reflecting on the startling news that the person who "made him a gentleman" is himself no gentleman. It is the criminal Magwitch, now returned illegally to England, who has set up Pip's expectations. Pip remarks on the feeling of being chased down: "The imaginary student pursued by the misshapen creature he had impiously made, was not more wretched than I, pursued by the creature who had made me, and recoiling from him with a stronger repulsion, the more he admired me and the fonder he was of me." In this line, we're told in notes of varying length that Pip compares himself to Victor Frankenstein pursued by the monster he has created.

Those who know Mary Shelley's novel might notice that Pip revises the roles between Victor and his monster. Pip doesn't claim the role of creator: he is himself the product of the creature and is pursued not out of a desire for revenge, but from admiration, even love. This variation on the Frankenstein/monster theme adds layers of complexity to Pip's character and situation. Pip seems still morally confused at this point. He hasn't quite realized that he is the monster, nor has he fully appreciated the admiration and fondness Magwitch has for him—however inconvenient those feelings may be. Yet Pip's self-confessed repulsion does anticipate the mature and responsible insight he ultimately must come to.

Our example of allusion here and the explanation that follows it is meant to suggest first that you do not need to resign yourself to missing out on allusions: help is available. But we also want to suggest that identifying allusions isn't finally the most important thing. This chapter has not concentrated on finding allusions (identifying, listing, etc.); our efforts are to show how allusions work and what purposes they serve. In other words, we have explored ways to approach, analyze, and understand allusions. Responding to an allusion is a far more substantial matter than merely finding or identifying one. Our poor prisoner from the story early in this chapter did not understand the difference.

A Note to Student Writers: Reference versus Allusion

Allusions are generally thought of as a tool for the creative writer to use and for the critical writer to avoid. That is not altogether bad advice. Allusions are suggestive more than directive. They invite the reader to draw upon experience from other texts but don't spell out fully what the reader should do with that experience. Dickens teases us into thinking about how the *Frankenstein* allusion works. He doesn't explain. Critical writers are, however, expected to explain. A brief allusion in an analytical essay to another critic or to a work of literature might well be seen as a kind of inappropriate showing off. Rather than being richly suggestive, such an allusion might seem superficial. It's usually important to thoroughly integrate references—to lead into them and to follow them out. Never "plug in" a source or simply "drop" a reference to meet a quota. Critical writers need to show why a reference appears in the text; readers need to grasp where that reference comes from and how it applies. An overly allusive style in a critic can quickly become mannered and exclusive. That is, such a critic implies there is a little club of experienced readers who will understand and a larger group of outsiders who need not bother.

Although all of this stands as good advice and useful commentary, nothing about writing is ever simple or absolute. As we've mentioned before, critical writing takes place in the context of an ongoing conversation. Critical writers seek to contribute to the conversation. On occasion, you may feel the conversation is so well established for the audience you write to that you can refer very briefly to a key critic or to an important line or scene in a well-known literary text. Just be sure that any quick reference you make has a clear function in the context of your larger discussion and that it draws from something your audience will recognize and apply easily. Also be sure that you do not assume a very brief reference will carry more weight than it can sustain; a well-placed allusion might highlight a point or signal your place in a community of writers, but it won't make an argument. Ultimately, to allude or not to allude is not the question; it's better to ask *whether* and *how* an allusion will work for a particular audience at a specific point in an essay.

MODELING CRITICAL ANALYSIS:
TOM STOPPARD, THE FIFTEEN MINUTE HAMLET

We normally think of allusions as short elements existing within texts; we don't think of them as constituting a whole text as they do in Tom Stoppard's *The Fifteen Minute Hamlet*. In the play, we get nothing but allusions—in this case, exact words lifted from Shakespeare and strung together to make what seems a brief highlight film of famous moments from this most famous of plays. Beginning with the title, Stoppard assumes we are familiar with Shakespeare's *Hamlet*—so familiar that we'll enjoy the radical cutting and splicing that he has done. But also beginning with the title, we might ask how much we have to know about the real *Hamlet* to appreciate the fifteen-minute version.

Shakespeare's play is longer than fifteen minutes—maybe about four hours longer! It is, in fact, the longest of Shakespeare's works. Efforts to trim the play into a manageable stage production or movie always ignite controversy among the Shakespeare purists. How could anyone be so brazen as to trim anything from this masterpiece? And yet, trimming is what has happened routinely in productions of the last few centuries. Stoppard takes the task of trimming to a whole new level. He boldly reduces every aspect of the play but still maintains the basic elements of the tragic plot. What are we to make of what is left? We have a series of familiar quotes strung together. It's almost as if Stoppard has lifted the yellowed-over lines from his old class text and made those lines his play.

One thing that is clearly lost is any sense of character development. Hamlet's most famous soliloquy becomes simply "To be, or not to be / that is the question" before he is interrupted by Ophelia. The speech has been replaced by its first line. **Synecdoche**, the rhetorical term for such an abbreviation, describes a situation in which the whole is represented by just a part. For instance, when a ship's captain orders "All hands on deck," he does not just want the hands, he wants the entire sailor even though it may be primarily the hands that will do the work. Similarly, in this version of the play the opening line stands in for the entire soliloquy; the wide familiarity with the whole makes this work—sort of. Obviously, mere recognition of the speech doesn't equal the impact of the whole in a conventional production. Just as the audience gears up for the famous speech, the speech is over and Hamlet has moved on to his next famous line "Get thee to a nunnery!" The tragic plot remains true to the original, but by eliminating any attempt to develop character or motive in the play, the impact becomes comic. We laugh at this Hamlet who doesn't bother to ponder about anything, not because he says or does anything that is funny, but because the juxtaposition of what little he says here and what we know he should really have said is so jarring.

There may be a subtler allusion to something not directly expressed in Stoppard's play. A longstanding critical argument concerns Hamlet's hesitation: why does he delay in acting upon the command of his father's ghost? Stoppard may be teasing those who obsess too much about this matter. If things move quickly, after all, we have an altogether different main character and an altogether different play. Hamlet is meditative, conflicted, a sensitive man in an insensitive world. When we rocket through the main points toward the general destruction at the end, we no longer have Hamlet, play or character, even though the lines are all taken directly from the original.

Using Allusions to Focus Writing and Discussion

A particular challenge with allusions is figuring out whether or not there is any reason to research them. Can we tell whether a name within a work, for instance, is just an author's arbitrary invention or whether it refers to some other character in some other work? Don't overdo your attention to allusions. When you see them, or when your professor or your footnotes point them out to you, try to establish how your attention to this allusion can help you engage with your analysis of this text.

- What is the specific reference?
- How can we tell that this is a reference to another text, to a historical event, or to some existence outside the text?
- How does the author introduce the allusion? How is it incorporated within this text? For instance, is the allusion something that the fictional characters in the story are conscious of or is it introduced by a third-person narrator?
- How does the author interpret the allusion? How does the text ask us to read this outside event?
- How does the allusion impact our understanding of or engagement in the present text? For instance, does it shape the text itself?

Anthology

TIME TRAVEL: A CRITIC WRITES ABOUT ALLUSIONS AND TIME TRAVEL

In his review of *Looper* (2012), Fergus engages in his own series of allusions to describe a genre of film that entertains the paradoxes that time travel engenders. He expects that his readers know enough about film to appreciate the various examples of time travel that he discusses (and the title, of course, is an allusion

Filmdistrict/The Kobal Collection/Picture Desk

Joseph Gordon-Levitt and Bruce Willis in *Looper* (2012)

to Eliot's Prufrock), and he reveals the central rule of this particular film: that the character who travels back in time only has blurred visions of what hasn't yet happened in the current world until it happens—at which point the memory becomes clear.

REVIEW

C. B. Fergus (1984–)

And indeed there will be time . . . (2012)

What is the appeal of time travel? Going back (or forward) as a time tourist is all well and good. But, as we have learned in Ray Bradbury's short story, "A Sound of Thunder," the rules are even more stringent than those set out by the

Sierra Club. "Take only pictures, leave only footprints" is not cautious enough of the environment of another time because a misplaced footstep can be amplified by millions of years and alter the course of evolution. Once people have gone to the trouble of travelling in time, though, they want to get off the path to start tinkering with things. Who will complain if I take out Hilter before he starts causing trouble in Europe or John Wilkes Booth before he gets to Ford's Theater?

This itch to get things right may have been played out most memorably in Harold Ramis's *Groundhog Day* (1993), where weatherman Bill Murray must relive the same day over and over again until he gets things right. Jake Gyllenhall and Tom Cruise find themselves in similar time loops, but with more specific missions in Duncan Jones's *Source Code* (2011) and Doug Liman's *Edge of Tomorrow* (2014), respectively. These soldiers have to go back again and again to the same time and place and die violently again and again in order to learn the intricacies of that moment and to finally prevent the explosion in which Gyllenhall dies or defeat the aliens who kill Cruise. Avoiding death ends the loop and allows time to move forward again.

Such heroics are admirable, but this time travel occurs in a storytelling vacuum. Only one or two characters are subject to the time loop. Everyone else involved experiences the scene only once. The time traveller gains a god-like knowledge of the scene through repeated exposure and knows what everyone else will do before they do it. He makes slight adjustments in order to achieve the result that he desires.

Another strand of time travel narrative is concerned with the consequences of this sort of tourism. When Michael J. Fox's Marty McFly brings his 1985 sophistication to bear upon 1955, in Robert Zemeckis's *Back to the Future* (1985), he threatens his own being. His mother is so attracted to his sense of fashion and his rock and roll sensibilities that she is falling for McFly rather than for his father, and McFly must undo the damage that has been done. The ultimate horror of time travel is that the traveler is always in danger of getting stuck, of losing the ability to get through whatever portal will take him home. The tension in the film comes from the possibility that history might change enough so that McFly himself would never have been born to go on this adventure. A good writer works through the head-scratching possibilities before rescuing the hero from the time-space continuum.

Thankfully, director Rian Johnson enters wholeheartedly into the complexity of the time travel puzzle that he sets up in *Looper* (2012). He entertains the possibility that these other sorts of films hint at but largely avoid: what if the time traveller meets himself? Marty McFly may watch himself from the other side of the parking lot, but in *Looper* Joe talks to himself in a diner. Old Joe (Bruce Willis) travels from 2074 to 2044 and sits across the

5

booth from his younger self (Joseph Gordon-Levitt) and says that he doesn't want to talk about time travel because if they do, they will be there all day making diagrams with straws. He does, however, set up the rules for his interaction with his younger self: "My memories aren't really memories; they are just one possible eventuality now, and they grow clearer or cloudier as they become more or less likely. But they get to the present moment, and they are instantly clear again. I can remember what you do after you do it."

To make this conversation possible, Old Joe has already hit his younger self in the face with a bar of silver because his younger self was standing ready with a shotgun to shoot Old Joe as soon as he materialized from the future. Both have the same word carved into their right arm and both carry the same watch. But the two aren't really all that pleased to be spending time together. Young Joe wants to be rid of Old Joe so that he can get on with his life, while Old Joe cannot get clear of the past, so they are stuck with each other for a time.

The two Joes are convincing versions of one another, and there's a father/son sort of tension between them. But that's not the only tension that Johnson gets right. The speed of the dark and gritty city that is Young Joe's home contrasts with the quiet light of the old farm house where the action plays out. In this world, time travel is used by the crime syndicates of the future as a means of disposing of bodies, and their greatest abuser may be the grownup version of the cherubic child, Cyd (Pierce Gagnon), who lives on this farm with his mother, Sarah (Emily Blunt). As Sarah and Young Joe grow closer, the action builds as Johnson shows how his puzzle fits together.

You won't leave the theater yearning to go back in time, but the past and present that come together in *Looper* create both an effective tale of suspense and a satisfying immersion into the paradoxes entertained by this particular version of the time traveler.

FICTION

John Crowley (1942–   )

Born in Presque Isle, Maine, John Crowley attended Indiana University. His first novels were speculative (or science) fiction. *Little, Big: or, The Fairies' Parliament* (1981) received the World Fantasy Award for best novel. It is a modern fantasy novel set in a countryhouse, somewhere north of "the City," and tells the stories of the Drinkwaters and their interactions with the Fairy world. He has also received the American Academy of Arts and Letters Award for Literature.

Snow (2011)

I don't think Georgie would ever have got one for herself: She was at once unsentimental and a little in awe of death. No, it was her first husband—an immensely rich and (from Georgie's description) a strangely weepy guy, who had got it for her. Or for himself, actually, of course. He was to be the beneficiary. Only he died himself shortly after it was installed. If *installed* is the right word. After he died, Georgie got rid of most of what she'd inherited from him, liquidated it. It was cash that she had liked best about that marriage anyway; but the Wasp couldn't really be got rid of. Georgie ignored it.

In fact the thing really was about the size of a wasp of the largest kind, and it had the same lazy and mindless fight. And of course it really was a bug, not of the insect kind but of the surveillance kind. And so its name fit all around: One of those bits of accidental poetry the world generates without thinking. O Death, where is thy sting? Georgie ignored it, but it was hard to avoid; you had to be a little careful around it; it followed Georgie at a variable distance, depending on her motions and the numbers of other people around her, the level of light, and the tone of her voice. And there was always the danger you might shut it in a door or knock it down with a tennis racket.

It cost a fortune (if you count the access and the perpetual care contract, all prepaid), and though it wasn't really fragile, it made you nervous.

It wasn't recording all the time. There had to be a certain amount of light, though not much. Darkness shut it off. And then sometimes it would get lost. Once when we hadn't seen it hovering around for a time, I opened a closet door, and it flew out, unchanged. It went off looking for her, humming softly. It must have been shut in there for days.

Eventually it ran out, or down. A lot could go wrong, I suppose, with   5
circuits that small, controlling that many functions. It ended up spending a lot of time bumping gently against the bedroom ceiling, over and over, like a winter fly. Then one day the maids swept it out from under the bureau, a husk. By that time it had transmitted at least eight thousand hours (eight thousand was the minimum guarantee) of Georgie: of her days and hours, her comings in and her goings out, her speech and motion, her living self— all on file, taking up next to no room, at The Park. And then, when the time came, you could go there, to The Park, say on a Sunday afternoon; and in quiet landscaped surroundings (as The Park described it) you would find her personal resting chamber, and there, in privacy, through the miracle of modern information storage and retrieval systems, you could access her, her alive, her as she was in every way, never changing or growing any older, fresher (as The Park's brochure said) than in memory ever green.

***

I married Georgie for her money, the same reason she married her first, the one who took out The Park's contract for her. She married me, I think, for my looks; she always had a taste for looks in men. I wanted to write. I made a calculation that more women than men make, and decided that to be supported and paid for by a rich wife would give me freedom to do so, to "develop." The calculation worked out no better for me than it does for most women who make it. I carried a typewriter and a case of miscellaneous paper from Ibiza to Gstaad to Bial to London, and typed on beaches, and learned to ski. Georgie liked me in ski clothes.

Now that those looks are all but gone, I can look back on myself as a young hunk and see that I was in a way a rarity, a type that you run into often among women, far less among men, the beauty unaware of his beauty, aware that he affects women profoundly and more or less instantly but doesn't know why; thinks he is being listened to and understood, that his soul is being seen, when all that's being seen is long-lashed eyes and a strong, square, tanned wrist turning in a lovely gesture, stubbing out a cigarette. Confusing. By the time I figured out why I had for so long been indulged and cared for and listened to, why I was interesting, I wasn't as interesting as I had been. At about the same time I realized I wasn't a writer at all. Georgie's investment stopped looking as good to her, and my calculation had ceased to add up; only by that time I had come, pretty unexpectedly, to love Georgie a lot, and she just as unexpectedly had come to love and need me too, as much as she needed anybody. We never really parted, even though when she died I hadn't seen her for years. Phone calls, at dawn or four A.M. because she never, for all her travel, really grasped that the world turns and cocktail hour travels around with it. She was a crazy, wasteful, happy woman, without a trace of malice or permanence or ambition in her—easily pleased and easily bored and strangely serene despite the hectic pace she kept up. She cherished things and lost them and forgot them: Things, days, people. She had fun, though, and I had fun with her; that was her talent and her destiny, not always an easy one. Once, hung over in a New York hotel, watching a sudden snowfall out the immense window, she said to me, "Charlie, I'm going to die of fun."

And she did. Snow-foiling in Austria, she was among the first to get one of those snow leopards, silent beasts as fast as speedboats. Alfredo called me in California to tell me, but with the distance and his accent and his eagerness to tell me *he* wasn't to blame, I never grasped the details. I was still her husband, her closest relative, heir to the little she still had, and beneficiary, too, of The Park's access concept. Fortunately, The Park's services included collecting her from the morgue in Gstaad and installing her in her chamber at The Park's California unit. Beyond signing papers and taking delivery when Georgie arrived by freight airship at Van Nuys, there was nothing for me to do. The Park's representative was solicitous and made sure I understood how to go about accessing Georgie, but I wasn't listening. I am only a child of my time, I suppose. Everything about death, the fact of it, the fate of the remains, and the situation of the living faced with it, seems grotesque to me, embarrassing, useless: And everything done about it only makes it more grotesque, more useless: Someone I loved is dead; let me therefore dress in clown's clothes, talk backwards, and buy expensive machinery to make up for it. I went back to L.A.

A year or more later, the contents of some safe-deposit boxes of Georgie's arrived from the lawyer's: some bonds and such stuff and a small steel case, velvet lined, that contained a key, a key deeply notched on both sides and headed with smooth plastic, like the key to an expensive car.

***

Why did I go to The Park that first time? Mostly because I had forgotten about it: Getting that key in the mail was like coming across a pile of old snapshots you hadn't cared to look at when they were new but which after they have aged come to contain the past, as they did not contain the present. I was curious.

10

I understood very well that The Park and its access concept were very probably only another cruel joke on the rich, preserving the illusion that they can buy what can't be bought, like the cryonics fad of thirty years ago. Once in Ibiza, Georgie and I met a German couple who also had a contract with The Park; their Wasp hovered over them like a Paraclete and made them self-conscious in the extreme—they seemed to be constantly rehearsing the eternal show being stored up for their descendants. Their deaths had taken over their lives, as though they were pharaohs. Did they, Georgie wondered, exclude the Wasp from their bedroom? Or did its presence there stir them to greater efforts, proofs of undying love and admirable vigor for the unborn to see?

No, death wasn't to be cheated that way, any more than by pyramids, by masses said in perpetuity. It wasn't Georgie saved from death that I would find. But there were eight thousand hours of her life with me, genuine hours, stored there more carefully than they could be in my porous memory; Georgie hadn't excluded the Wasp from her bedroom, our bedroom, and she who had never performed for anybody could not have conceived of performing for it. And there would be me, too, undoubtedly, caught unintentionally by the Wasp's attention: Out of those thousands of hours there would be hundreds of myself, and myself had just then begun to be problematic to me, something that had to be figured out, something about which evidence had to be gathered and weighed. I was thirty-eight years old.

That summer, then, I borrowed a Highway Access Permit (the old happy cards of those days) from a county lawyer I knew and drove the coast highway up to where The Park was, at the end of a pretty beach road, all alone above the sea. It looked from the outside like the best, most peaceful kind of Italian country cemetery, a low stucco wall topped with urns, amid cypresses, an arched gate in the center. A small brass plaque on the gate: PLEASE USE YOUR KEY. The gate opened, not to a square of shaded tombstones but onto a ramped corridor going down: The cemetery wall was an illusion, the works were underground. Silence, or nameless Muzak-like silence: Solitude—whether the necessary technicians were discreetly hidden or none were needed. Certainly the access concept turned out to be simplicity itself, in operation anyway. Even I, who am an idiot about information technology, could tell that. The Wasp was genuine state-of-the-art stuff, but what we mourners got was as ordinary as home movies, as old letters tied up in ribbon.

A display screen near the entrance told me down which corridor to find Georgie, and my key let me into a small screening room where there was a moderate-size TV monitor, two comfortable chairs, and dark walls of chocolate-brown carpeting. The sweet-sad Muzak. Georgie herself was evidently somewhere in the vicinity, in the wall or under the floor, they weren't specific about the charnel-house aspect of the place. In the control panel before the TV were a keyhole for my key and two bars: ACCESS and RESET.

I sat, feeling foolish and a little afraid, too, made more uncomfortable   15
by being so deliberately soothed by neutral furnishings and sober tools. I imagined, around me, down other corridors, in other chambers, others communed with their dead as I was about to do, that the dead were murmuring to them beneath the stream of Muzak; that they wept to see and hear, as I might, but I could hear nothing. I turned my key in its slot, and the screen lit up. The dim lights dimmed further, and the Muzak ceased. I pushed ACCESS, obviously the next step. No doubt all these procedures had been explained to me long ago at the dock when Georgie in her aluminum box was being off-loaded, and I hadn't listened. And on the screen she turned to look at me—only not at me, though I started and drew breath—at the Wasp that watched her. She was in mid-sentence, mid-gesture. Where? When? *Or put it on the same card with the others,* she said, turning away. Someone said something, Georgie answered, and stood up, the Wasp panning and moving erratically with her, like an amateur with a home-video camera. A white room, sunlight, wicker. Ibiza. Georgie wore a cotton blouse, open; from a table she picked up lotion, poured some on her hand, and rubbed it across her freckled breastbone. The meaningless conversation about putting something on a card went on, ceased. I watched the room, wondering what year, what season I had stumbled into. Georgie pulled off her shirt—her small round breasts tipped with large, childlike nipples,

child's breasts she still had at forty, shook delicately. And she went out onto the balcony, the Wasp following, blinded by sun, adjusting. *If you want to do it that way*, someone said. The someone crossed the screen, a brown blur, naked. It was me. Georgie said: *Oh, look, hummingbirds.*

She watched them, rapt, and the Wasp crept close to her cropped blond head, rapt too, and I watched her watch. She turned away, rested her elbows on the balustrade. I couldn't remember this day. How should I? One of hundreds, of thousands.... She looked out to the bright sea, wearing her sleepwalking face, mouth partly open, and absently stroked her breast with her oiled hand. An iridescent glitter among the flowers was the hummingbird.

Without really knowing what I did—I felt hungry, suddenly, hungry for pastness, for more—I touched the RESET bar. The balcony in Ibiza vanished, the screen glowed emptily. I touched ACCESS.

At first there was darkness, a murmur; then a dark back moved away from the Wasp's eye, and a dim scene of people resolved itself. Jump. Other people, or the same people, a party? Jump. Apparently the Wasp was turning itself on and off according to the changes in light levels here, wherever *here* was. Georgie in a dark dress having her cigarette lit: brief flare of the lighter. She said, *Thanks.* Jump. A foyer or hotel lounge. Paris? The Wasp jerkily sought for her among people coming and going; it couldn't make a movie, establishing shots, cutaways—it could only doggedly follow Georgie, like a jealous husband, seeing nothing else. This was frustrating. I pushed RESET. ACCESS. Georgie brushed her teeth, somewhere, somewhen.

I understood, after one or two more of these terrible leaps. Access was random. There was no way to dial up a year, a day, a scene. The Park had supplied no program, none; the eight thousand hours weren't filed at all, they were a jumble, like a lunatic's memory, like a deck of shuffled cards. I had supposed, without thinking about it, that they would begin at the beginning and go on till they reached the end. Why didn't they?

I also understood something else. If access was truly random, if I truly   20 had no control, then I had lost as good as forever those scenes I had seen. Odds were on the order of eight thousand to one (more? far more? probabilities are opaque to me) that I would never light on them again by pressing this bar. I felt a pang of loss for that afternoon in Ibiza. It was doubly gone now. I sat before the empty screen, afraid to touch ACCESS again, afraid of what I would lose.

I shut down the machine (the light level in the room rose, the Muzak poured softly back in) and went out into the halls, back to the display screen in the entranceway. The list of names slowly, greenly, rolled over like the list of departing flights at an airport: Code numbers were missing from beside many, indicating perhaps that they weren't yet in residence, only awaited.

In the Ds, three names, and DIRECTOR—hidden among them as though he were only another of the dead. A chamber number. I went to find it and went in. The director looked more like a janitor or a night watchman, the semiretired type you often see caretaking little-visited places. He wore a brown smock like a monk's robe and was making coffee in a corner of his small office, out of which little business seemed to be done. He looked up startled, caught out, when I entered.

"Sorry," I said, "but I don't think I understand this system right."

"A problem?" he said. "Shouldn't be a problem." He looked at me a little wide-eyed and shy, hoping not to be called on for anything difficult. "Equipment's all working?"

"I don't know," I said. "It doesn't seem that it could be." I described what I thought I had learned about The Park's access concept. "That can't be right, can it?" I said. "That access is totally random...."

He was nodding, still wide-eyed, paying close attention.   25

"Is it?" I asked.

"Is it what?"

"Random."

"Oh, yes. Yes, sure. If everything's in working order."

I could think of nothing to say for a moment, watching him nod reas-   30
suringly. Then, "Why?" I asked. "I mean why is there no way at all to, to organize, to have some kind of organized access to the material?" I had begun to feel that sense of grotesque foolishness in the presence of death, as though I were haggling over Georgie's effects. "That seems stupid, if you'll pardon me."

"Oh no, oh no," he said. "You've read your literature? You've read all your literature?"

"Well, to tell the truth..."

"It's all just as described," the director said. "I can promise you that. If there's any problem at all..."

"Do you mind," I said, "if I sit down?" I smiled. He seemed so afraid of me and my complaint, of me as mourner, possibly grief crazed and unable to grasp the simple limits of his responsibilities to me, that he needed soothing himself. "I'm sure everything's fine," I said. "I just don't think I understand. I'm kind of dumb about these things."

"Sure. Sure. Sure." He regretfully put away his coffee makings and sat   35
behind his desk, lacing his fingers together like a consultant. "People get a lot of satisfaction out of the access here," he said, "a lot of comfort, if they take in the right spirit." He tried a smile. I wondered what qualifications he had had to show to get this job. "The random part. Now, it's all in the literature. There's the legal aspect—you're not a lawyer are you, no, no, sure, no offense. You see, the material here isn't for anything, except, well, except

for communing. But suppose the stuff were programmed, searchable. Suppose there was a problem about taxes or inheritance or so on. There could be subpoenas, lawyers all over the place, destroying the memorial concept completely."

I really hadn't thought of that. Built-in randomness saved past lives from being searched in any systematic way. And no doubt saved The Park from being in the records business and at the wrong end of a lot of suits. "You'd have to watch the whole eight thousand hours," I said, "and even if you found what you were looking for there'd be no way to replay it. It would have gone by." It would slide into the random past even as you watched it, like that afternoon in Ibiza, that party in Paris. Lost. He smiled and nodded. I smiled and nodded.

"I'll tell you something," he said. "They didn't predict that. The randomness. It was a side effect, an effect of the storage process. Just luck." His grin turned down, his brows knitted seriously. "See, we're storing here at the molecular level. We have to go that small, for space problems. I mean your eight-thousand-hour guarantee. If we had gone tape or conventional, how much room would it take up? If the access concept caught on. A lot of room. So we went vapor trap and endless tracking. Size of my thumbnail. It's all in the literature." He looked at me strangely. I had a sudden intense sensation that I was being fooled, tricked, that the man before me in his smock was no expert, no technician; he was a charlatan, or maybe a madman impersonating a director and not belonging here at all. It raised the hair on my neck and passed. "So the randomness," he was saying. "It was an effect of going molecular. Brownian movement. All you do is lift the endless tracking for a microsecond and you get a rearrangement at the molecular level. We don't randomize. The molecules do it for us."

I remembered Brownian movement, just barely, from physics class. The random movement of molecules, the teacher said; it has a mathematical description. It's like the movement of dust motes you see swimming in a shaft of sunlight, like the swirl of snowflakes in a glass paperweight that shows a cottage being snowed on. "I see," I said. "I guess I see."

"Is there," he said, "any other problem?" He said it as though there might be some other problem and that he knew what it might be and that he hoped I didn't have it. "You understand the system, key lock, two bars, ACCESS, RESET..."

"I understand," I said. "I understand now." 40

"Communing," he said, standing, relieved, sure I would be gone soon. "I understand. It takes a while to relax into the communing concept."

"Yes," I said. "It does."

I wouldn't learn what I had come to learn, whatever that was. The Wasp had not been good at storage after all, no, no better than my young soul had been. Days and weeks had been missed by its tiny eye. It hadn't seen well, and in what it had seen it had been no more able to distinguish the just-as-well-forgotten from the unforgettable than my own eye had been. No better and no worse—the same. And yet, and yet—she stood up in Ibiza and dressed her breasts with lotion, and spoke to me: *Oh, look, hummingbirds.* I had forgotten, and the Wasp had not; and I owned once again what I hadn't known I had lost, hadn't known was precious to me. The sun was setting when I left The Park, the satin sea foaming softly, randomly around the rocks.

I had spent my life waiting for something, not knowing what, not even knowing I waited. Killing time. I was still waiting. But what I had been waiting for had already occurred and was past.

It was two years, nearly, since Georgie had died; two years until, for the first and last time, I wept for her—for her and for myself. 45

***

Of course I went back. After a lot of work and correctly placed dollars, I netted a HAPpy card of my own. I had time to spare, like a lot of people then, and often on empty afternoons (never on Sunday) I would get out onto the unpatched and weed-grown freeway and glide up the coast. The Park was always open. I relaxed into the communing concept.

Now, after some hundreds of hours spent there underground, now, when I have long ceased to go through those doors (I have lost my key, I think; anyway I don't know where to look for it), I know that the solitude I felt myself to be in was real. The watchers around me, the listeners I sensed in other chambers, were mostly my imagination. There was rarely anyone there.

These tombs were as neglected as any tombs anywhere usually are. Either the living did not care to attend much on the dead—when have they ever?—or the hopeful buyers of the contracts had come to discover the flaw in the access concept—as I discovered it, in the end.

ACCESS, and she takes dresses one by one from her closet, and holds them against her body, and studies the effect in a tall mirror, and puts them back again. She had a funny face, which she never made except when looking at herself in the mirror, a face made for no one but herself, that was actually quite unlike her. The mirror Georgie.

RESET.

ACCESS. By a bizarre coincidence here she is looking in another mirror. I think the Wasp could be confused by mirrors. She turns away, the Wasp adjusts; there is someone asleep, tangled in bedclothes on a big hotel bed, morning, a room-service cart. Oh, the Algonquin: myself. Winter. Snow is falling outside the tall window. She searches her handbag, takes out a small vial, swallows a pill with coffee, holding the cup by 50 its body and not its handle. I stir, show a tousled head of hair. Conversation—unintelligible. Gray room, whitish snow light, color degraded. Would I now (I thought, watching us) reach out for her? Would I in the next hour take her, or she me, push aside the bedclothes, open her pale pajamas? She goes into the john, shuts the door. The Wasp watches stupidly, excluded, transmitting the door.

RESET, finally.

But what (I would wonder) if I had been patient, what if I had watched and waited?

Time, it turns out, takes an unconscionable time. The waste, the footless waste—it's no spectator sport. Whatever fun there is in sitting idly looking at nothing and tasting your own being for a whole afternoon, there is no fun in replaying it. The waiting is excruciating. How often, in five years, in eight thousand hours of daylight or lamplight, might we have coupled, how much time expended in lovemaking? A hundred hours, two hundred? Odds were not high of my coming on such a scene; darkness swallowed most of them, and the others were lost in the interstices of endless hours spent shopping, reading, on planes and in cars, asleep, apart. Hopeless. ACCESS. She has turned on a bedside lamp. Alone. She hunts amid the Kleenex and magazines on the bedside table, finds a watch, looks at it dully, turns it right side up, looks again, and puts it down. Cold. She burrows in the blankets, yawning, staring, then puts out a hand for the phone but only rests her hand on it, thinking. Thinking at four A.M. She withdraws her hand, shivers a child's deep, sleepy shiver, and shuts off the light. A bad dream. In an instant it's morning, dawn; the Wasp slept, too. She sleeps soundly, unmoving, only the top of her blond head showing out of the quilt—and will no doubt sleep so for hours, watched over more attentively, more fixedly, than any peeping Tom could ever have watched over her.

RESET.

ACCESS.

"I can't hear as well as I did at first," I told the director. "And the definition is getting softer."

"Oh sure," the director said. "That's really in the literature. We have to explain that carefully. That this might be a problem."

"It isn't just my monitor?" I asked. "I thought it was probably only the monitor."

"No, no, not really, no," he said. He gave me coffee. We'd gotten to be friendly over the months. I think, as well as being afraid of me he was glad I came around now and then; at least one of the living came here, one at least was using the services. "There's a *slight* degeneration that does occur."

"Everything seems to be getting gray."

His face had shifted into intense concern, no belittling this problem. "Mm-hm, mm-hm, see, at the molecular level where we're at, there is degeneration. It's just in the physics. It randomizes a little over time. So you lose— you don't lose a minute of what you've got, but you lose a little definition. A little color. But it levels off."

"It does?"

"We think it does. Sure it does, we promise it does. We *predict* that it 65 will."

"But you don't know."

"Well, well you see we've only been in this business a short while. This concept is new. There were things we couldn't know." He still looked at me, but seemed at the same time to have forgotten me. Tired. He seemed to have grown colorless himself lately, old, losing definition. "You might start getting some snow," he said softly.

ACCESS RESET ACCESS.

A gray plaza of herringbone-laid stones, gray, clicking palms. She turns up the collar of her sweater, narrowing her eyes in a stern wind. Buys magazines at a kiosk: *Vogue, Harper's, La Mode. Cold,* she says to the kiosk girl. *Frio.* The young man I was takes her arm: they walk back along the beach, which is deserted and strung with cast seaweed, washed by a dirty sea. Winter in Ibiza. We talk, but the Wasp can't hear, the sea's sound confuses it; it seems bored by its duties and lags behind us.

RESET.

ACCESS. The Algonquin, terribly familiar morning, winter. She turns away from the snow window. I am in bed, and for a moment watching this I felt suspended between two mirrors, reflected endlessly. I had seen this before; I had lived it once and remembered it once, and remembered the memory, and here it was again, or could it be nothing but another morning, a similar morning. There were far more than one like this, in this place. But no; she turns from the window, she gets out her vial of pills, picks up the coffee cup by its body: I had seen this moment before, not months before, weeks before, here in this chamber. I had come upon the same scene twice.

What are the odds of it, I wondered, what are the odds of coming upon 70 the same minutes again, these minutes.

I stir within the bedclothes.

I leaned forward to hear, this time, what I would say; it was something like *but fun anyway,* or something.

Fun, she says, laughing, harrowed, the degraded sound a ghost's twittering. *Charlie, someday I'm going to die of fun.*

She takes her pill. The Wasp follows her to the john and is shut out.

Why am I here? I thought, and my heart was beating hard and slow. *What am I here for? What?*

RESET.

ACCESS.

Silvered icy streets, New York, Fifth Avenue. She is climbing, shouting from a cab's dark interior. *Just don't shout at me,* she shouts at someone; her mother I never met, a dragon. She is out and hurrying away down the sleety street with her bundles, the Wasp at her shoulder. I could reach out and touch her shoulder and make her turn and follow me out. Walking away, lost in the colorless press of traffic and people, impossible to discern within the softened snowy image.

***

Something was very wrong.   75

Georgie hated winter, she escaped it most of the time we were together, about the first of the year beginning to long for the sun that had gone elsewhere; Austria was all right for a few weeks, the toy villages and sugar snow and bright, sleek skiers were not really the winter she feared, though even in fire-warmed chalets it was hard to get her naked without gooseflesh and shudders from some draft only she could feel. We were chaste in winter. So Georgie escaped it: Antigua and Bali and two months in Ibiza when the almonds blossomed. It was continual false, flavorless spring all winter long.

How often could snow have fallen when the Wasp was watching her?

Not often; countable times, times I could count up myself if I could remember as the Wasp could. Not often. Not always.

"There's a problem," I said to the director.

"It's peaked out, has it?" he said. "That definition problem?"   80

"Actually," I said, "it's gotten worse."

He was sitting behind his desk, arms spread wide across his chair's back, and a false, pinkish flush to his cheeks like undertaker's makeup. Drinking.

"Hasn't peaked out, huh?" he said.

"That's not the problem," I said. "The problem is the access. It's not random like you said."

"Molecular level," he said. "It's in the physics."   85

"You don't understand. It's not getting more random. It's getting less random. It's getting selective. It's freezing up."

"No, no, no," he said dreamily. "Access is random. Life isn't all summer and fun, you know. Into each life some rain must fall."

I sputtered, trying to explain. "But, but..."

"You know," he said. "I've been thinking of getting out of access." He pulled open a drawer in the desk before him; it made an empty sound. He stared within it dully for a moment and shut it. "The Park's been good for me, but I'm just not used to this. Used to be you thought you could render a service, you know? Well, hell, you know, you've had fun, what do you care?"

He was mad. For an instant I heard the dead around me; I tasted on 90 my tongue the stale air of underground.

"I remember," he said, tilting back in his chair and looking else-where, "many years ago, I got into access. Only we didn't call it that then. What I did was, I worked for a stock-footage house. It was going out of business, like they all did, like this place here is going to do, shouldn't say that, but you didn't hear it. Anyway, it was a big warehouse with steel shelves for miles, filled with film cans, film cans filled with old plastic film, you know? Film of every kind. And movie people, if they wanted old scenes of past time in their movies, would call up and ask for what they wanted, find me this, find me that. And we had everything, every kind of scene, but you know what the hardest thing to find was? Just ordinary scenes of daily life. I mean people just doing things and living their lives. You know what we *did* have? Speeches. People giving speeches. Like presi-dents. You could have hours of speeches, but not just people, whatchacal-lit, oh, washing clothes, sitting in a park..."

"It might just be the reception," I said. "Somehow."

He looked at me for a long moment as though I had just arrived. "Anyway," he said at last, turning away again, "I was there awhile learning the ropes. And producers called and said, 'Get me this, get me that.' And one producer was making a film, some film of the past, and he wanted old scenes, *old*, of people long ago, in the summer; having fun; eating ice cream; swimming in bathing suits; riding in convertibles. Fifty years ago. Eighty years ago."

He opened his empty drawer again, found a toothpick, and began to use it.

"So I accessed the earliest stuff. Speeches. More speeches. But I found a 95 scene here and there—people in the street, fur coats, window-shopping, traf-fic. Old people, I mean they were young then, but people of the past; they have these pinched kind of faces, you get to know them. Sad, a little. On city streets, hurrying, holding their hats. Cities were sort of black then, in film; black cars in the streets, black derby hats. Stone. Well, it wasn't what they wanted. I found summer for them, color summer, but new. They wanted old. I kept looking back. I kept looking. I did. The further back I went, the more I saw these pinched faces, black cars, black streets of stone. Snow. There isn't any summer there."

With slow gravity he rose and found a brown bottle and two coffee cups. He poured sloppily. "So it's not your reception," he said. "Film takes longer, I guess, but it's the physics. All in the physics. A word to the wise is sufficient."

The liquor was harsh, a cold distillate of past sunlight. I wanted to go, get out, not look back. I would not stay watching until there was only snow.

"So I'm getting out of access," the director said. "Let the dead bury the dead, right? Let the dead bury the dead."

***

I didn't go back. I never went back, though the highways opened again and The Park isn't far from the town I've settled in. Settled; the right word. It restores your balance, in the end, even in a funny way your cheerfulness, when you come to know, without regrets, that the best thing that's going to happen in your life has already happened. And I still have some summer left to me.

I think there are two different kinds of memory, and only one kind 100 gets worse as I get older: the kind where, by an effort of will, you can reconstruct your first car or your serial number or the name and figure of your high school physics teacher—a Mr. Holm, in a gray suit, a bearded guy, skinny, about thirty. The other kind doesn't worsen; if anything it grows more intense. The sleepwalking kind, the kind you stumble into as into rooms with secret doors and suddenly find yourself sitting not on your front porch but in a classroom. You can't at first think where or when, and a bearded, smiling man is turning in his hand a glass paperweight, inside which a little cottage stands in a swirl of snow.

There is no access to Georgie, except that now and then, unpredictably, when I'm sitting on the porch or pushing a grocery cart or standing at the sink, a memory of that kind will visit me, vivid and startling, like a hypnotist's snap of fingers.

Or like that funny experience you sometimes have, on the point of sleep, of hearing your name called softly and distinctly by someone who is not there.

- What does the narrative tell us about the setting of this story? How is this world different from ours? What elements (if any) are fantastical?
- How does the story present the character's memories? How does the narrator learn the limits of The Park's memories?
- Why is this story called "Snow"?

James Joyce (1882–1941)

James Joyce was born in Dublin, Ireland. He was educated by Jesuit priests at Clongowes Wood College before entering the University of Dublin. He graduated in 1902 and moved to Paris but returned to Ireland a year later, where he began his career as a writer. Unfortunately, Dubliners were less than receptive to Joyce's work, so he and his wife, Nora Barnacle, moved to continental Europe. One of the first writers to employ the literary technique stream of consciousness, Joyce is remembered for his collection of short stories, *Dubliners*, as well as his novels, *A Portrait of the Artist as a Young Man, Ulysses,* and *Finnegans Wake.* Joyce's public and critical popularity improved as his career progressed, and he received grants from the Royal Literary Fund, the Civil List, and the Society of Authors. He is regarded today as one of the greatest of the modernists, and *Ulysses* as one of the period's undoubted masterpieces.

The Dead (1914)

LILY, the caretaker's daughter, was literally run off her feet. Hardly had she brought one gentleman into the little pantry behind the office on the ground floor and helped him off with his overcoat than the wheezy hall-door bell clanged again and she had to scamper along the bare hallway to let in another guest. It was well for her she had not to attend to the ladies also. But Miss Kate and Miss Julia had thought of that and had converted the bathroom upstairs into a ladies' dressing-room. Miss Kate and Miss Julia were there, gossiping and laughing and fussing, walking after each other to the head of the stairs, peering down over the banisters and calling down to Lily to ask her who had come.

It was always a great affair, the Misses Morkan's annual dance. Everybody who knew them came to it, members of the family, old friends of the family, the members of Julia's choir, any of Kate's pupils that were grown up enough, and even some of Mary Jane's pupils too. Never once had it fallen flat. For years and years it had gone off in splendid style, as long as anyone could remember; ever since Kate and Julia, after the death of their brother Pat, had left the house in Stoney Batter and taken Mary Jane, their only niece, to live with them in the dark, gaunt house on Usher's Island, the upper part of which they had rented from Mr. Fulham, the corn-factor on the ground floor. That was a good thirty years ago if it was a day. Mary Jane, who was then a little girl in short clothes, was now the main prop of the household, for she had the organ in Haddington Road. She had been through the Academy and gave a pupils' concert every year in the upper room of the Antient Concert Rooms. Many of her pupils belonged to the better-class families on the Kingstown and Dalkey line. Old as they were, her aunts also did their share. Julia, though she was quite grey, was still the leading soprano in Adam and Eve's, and Kate, being too feeble to go about much, gave music lessons to beginners on the old square piano in the back room. Lily, the caretaker's daughter, did house-maid's work for them. Though their life was modest, they believed in eating well; the best of everything: diamond-bone sirloins, three-shilling tea and the best bottled stout. But Lily seldom made a mistake in the orders, so that she got on well with her three mistresses. They were fussy, that was all. But the only thing they would not stand was back answers.

Of course, they had good reason to be fussy on such a night. And then it was long after ten o'clock and yet there was no sign of Gabriel and his wife. Besides they were dreadfully afraid that Freddy Malins might turn up screwed. They would not wish for worlds that any of Mary Jane's pupils should see him under the influence; and when he was like that it was some-times very hard to manage him. Freddy Malins always came late, but they wondered what could be keeping Gabriel: and that was what brought them every two minutes to the banisters to ask Lily had Gabriel or Freddy come.

"O, Mr. Conroy," said Lily to Gabriel when she opened the door for him, "Miss Kate and Miss Julia thought you were never coming. Good-night, Mrs. Conroy."

"I'll engage they did," said Gabriel, "but they forget that my wife here   5
takes three mortal hours to dress herself."

He stood on the mat, scraping the snow from his goloshes, while Lily led his wife to the foot of the stairs and called out:

"Miss Kate, here's Mrs. Conroy."

Kate and Julia came toddling down the dark stairs at once. Both of them kissed Gabriel's wife, said she must be perished alive, and asked was Gabriel with her.

"Here I am as right as the mail, Aunt Kate! Go on up. I'll follow," called out Gabriel from the dark.

He continued scraping his feet vigorously while the three women went   10
upstairs, laughing, to the ladies' dressing-room. A light fringe of snow lay like a cape on the shoulders of his overcoat and like toecaps on the toes of his goloshes; and, as the buttons of his overcoat slipped with a squeaking noise through the snow-stiffened frieze, a cold, fragrant air from out-of-doors escaped from crevices and folds.

"Is it snowing again, Mr. Conroy?" asked Lily.

She had preceded him into the pantry to help him off with his over-coat. Gabriel smiled at the three syllables she had given his surname and glanced at her. She was a slim, growing girl, pale in complexion and with hay-coloured hair. The gas in the pantry made her look still paler. Gabriel had known her when she was a child and used to sit on the lowest step nurs-ing a rag doll.

"Yes, Lily," he answered, "and I think we're in for a night of it."

He looked up at the pantry ceiling, which was shaking with the stamping and shuffling of feet on the floor above, listened for a moment to the piano and then glanced at the girl, who was folding his overcoat carefully at the end of a shelf.

"Tell me. Lily," he said in a friendly tone, "do you still go to school?" 15

"O no, sir," she answered. "I'm done schooling this year and more."

"O, then," said Gabriel gaily, "I suppose we'll be going to your wedding one of these fine days with your young man, eh?"

The girl glanced back at him over her shoulder and said with great bitterness:

"The men that is now is only all palaver and what they can get out of you."

Gabriel coloured, as if he felt he had made a mistake and, without looking at her, kicked off his goloshes and flicked actively with his muffler at his patent-leather shoes. 20

He was a stout, tallish young man. The high colour of his cheeks pushed upwards even to his forehead, where it scattered itself in a few formless patches of pale red; and on his hairless face there scintillated restlessly the polished lenses and the bright gilt rims of the glasses which screened his delicate and restless eyes. His glossy black hair was parted in the middle and brushed in a long curve behind his ears where it curled slightly beneath the groove left by his hat.

When he had flicked lustre into his shoes he stood up and pulled his waistcoat down more tightly on his plump body. Then he took a coin rapidly from his pocket.

"O Lily," he said, thrusting it into her hands, "it's Christmastime, isn't it? Just...here's a little..."

He walked rapidly towards the door.

"O no, sir!" cried the girl, following him. "Really, sir, I wouldn't take it." 25

"Christmas-time! Christmas-time!" said Gabriel, almost trotting to the stairs and waving his hand to her in deprecation.

The girl, seeing that he had gained the stairs, called out after him:

"Well, thank you, sir."

He waited outside the drawing-room door until the waltz should finish, listening to the skirts that swept against it and to the shuffling of feet. He was still discomposed by the girl's bitter and sudden retort. It had cast a gloom over him which he tried to dispel by arranging his cuffs and the bows of his tie. He then took from his waistcoat pocket a little paper and glanced at the headings he had made for his speech. He was undecided about the lines from Robert Browning, for he feared they would be above the heads of his hearers. Some quotation that they would recognise from Shakespeare or from the Melodies would be better. The indelicate clacking of the men's heels and the shuffling of their soles reminded him that their grade of culture differed from his. He would only make himself ridiculous by quoting poetry to them which they could not understand. They would think that he was airing his superior education. He would fail with them just as he had failed with the girl in the pantry. He had taken up a wrong tone. His whole speech was a mistake from first to last, an utter failure.

Just then his aunts and his wife came out of the ladies' dressing-room. 30 His aunts were two small, plainly dressed old women. Aunt Julia was an inch or so the taller. Her hair, drawn low over the tops of her ears, was grey; and grey also, with darker shadows, was her large flaccid face. Though she was stout in build and stood erect, her slow eyes and parted lips gave her the appearance of a woman who did not know where she was or where she was going. Aunt Kate was more vivacious. Her face, healthier than her sister's, was all puckers and creases, like a shrivelled red apple, and her hair, braided in the same old-fashioned way, had not lost its ripe nut colour.

They both kissed Gabriel frankly. He was their favourite nephew, the son of their dead elder sister, Ellen, who had married T. J. Conroy of the Port and Docks.

"Gretta tells me you're not going to take a cab back to Monkstown tonight, Gabriel," said Aunt Kate.

"No," said Gabriel, turning to his wife, "we had quite enough of that last year, hadn't we? Don't you remember, Aunt Kate, what a cold Gretta got out of it? Cab windows rattling all the way, and the east wind blowing in after we passed Merrion. Very jolly it was. Gretta caught a dreadful cold."

Aunt Kate frowned severely and nodded her head at every word.

"Quite right, Gabriel, quite right," she said. "You can't be too careful." 35

"But as for Gretta there," said Gabriel, "she'd walk home in the snow if she were let."

Mrs. Conroy laughed.

"Don't mind him, Aunt Kate," she said. "He's really an awful bother, what with green shades for Tom's eyes at night and making him do the dumb-bells, and forcing Eva to eat the stirabout. The poor child! And she simply hates the sight of it!...O, but you'll never guess what he makes me wear now!"

She broke out into a peal of laughter and glanced at her husband, whose admiring and happy eyes had been wandering from her dress to her face and hair. The two aunts laughed heartily, too, for Gabriel's solicitude was a standing joke with them.

"Goloshes!" said Mrs. Conroy. "That's the latest. Whenever it's wet 40 underfoot I must put on my galoshes. Tonight even, he wanted me to put them on, but I wouldn't. The next thing he'll buy me will be a diving suit."

Gabriel laughed nervously and patted his tie reassuringly, while Aunt Kate nearly doubled herself, so heartily did she enjoy the joke. The smile soon faded from Aunt Julia's face and her mirthless eyes were directed towards her nephew's face. After a pause she asked:

"And what are goloshes, Gabriel?"

"Goloshes, Julia!" exclaimed her sister "Goodness me, don't you know what goloshes are? You wear them over your...over your boots, Gretta, isn't it?"

"Yes," said Mrs. Conroy. "Guttapercha things. We both have a pair now. Gabriel says everyone wears them on the Continent."

"O, on the Continent," murmured Aunt Julia, nodding her head   45 slowly.

Gabriel knitted his brows and said, as if he were slightly angered:

"It's nothing very wonderful, but Gretta thinks it very funny because she says the word reminds her of Christy Minstrels."

"But tell me, Gabriel," said Aunt Kate, with brisk tact. "Of course, you've seen about the room. Gretta was saying..."

"O, the room is all right," replied Gabriel. "I've taken one in the Gresham."

"To be sure," said Aunt Kate, "by far the best thing to do. And the chil-   50 dren, Gretta, you're not anxious about them?"

"O, for one night," said Mrs. Conroy. "Besides, Bessie will look after them."

"To be sure," said Aunt Kate again. "What a comfort it is to have a girl like that, one you can depend on! There's that Lily, I'm sure I don't know what has come over her lately. She's not the girl she was at all."

Gabriel was about to ask his aunt some questions on this point, but she broke off suddenly to gaze after her sister, who had wandered down the stairs and was craning her neck over the banisters.

"Now, I ask you," she said almost testily, "where is Julia going? Julia! Julia! Where are you going?"

Julia, who had gone half way down one flight, came back and   55 announced blandly:

"Here's Freddy."

At the same moment a clapping of hands and a final flourish of the pianist told that the waltz had ended. The drawing-room door was opened from within and some couples came out. Aunt Kate drew Gabriel aside hurriedly and whispered into his ear:

"Slip down, Gabriel, like a good fellow and see if he's all right, and don't let him up if he's screwed. I'm sure he's screwed. I'm sure he is."

Gabriel went to the stairs and listened over the banisters. He could hear two persons talking in the pantry. Then he recognised Freddy Malins' laugh. He went down the stairs noisily.

"It's such a relief," said Aunt Kate to Mrs. Conroy, "that Gabriel is   60
here. I always feel easier in my mind when he's here...Julia, there's Miss
Daly and Miss Power will take so me refreshment. Thanks for your beautiful
waltz, Miss Daly. It made lovely time."

A tall wizen-faced man, with a stiff grizzled moustache and swarthy
skin, who was passing out with his partner, said:

"And may we have some refreshment, too, Miss Morkan?"

"Julia," said Aunt Kate summarily, "and here's Mr. Browne and Miss
Furlong. Take them in, Julia, with Miss Daly and Miss Power."

"I'm the man for the ladies," said Mr. Browne, pursing his lips until his
moustache bristled and smiling in all his wrinkles. "You know, Miss Morkan, the reason they are so fond of me is——"

He did not finish his sentence, but, seeing that Aunt Kate was out of   65
earshot, at once led the three young ladies into the back room. The middle
of the room was occupied by two square tables placed end to end, and on
these Aunt Julia and the caretaker were straightening and smoothing a large
cloth. On the sideboard were arrayed dishes and plates, and glasses and bundles of knives and forks and spoons. The top of the closed square piano
served also as a sideboard for viands and sweets. At a smaller sideboard in
one corner two young men were standing, drinking hop-bitters.

Mr. Browne led his charges thither and invited them all, in jest, to
some ladies' punch, hot, strong and sweet. As they said they never took anything strong, he opened three bottles of lemonade for them. Then he asked
one of the young men to move aside, and, taking hold of the decanter,
filled out for himself a goodly measure of whisky. The young men eyed him
respectfully while he took a trial sip.

"God help me," he said, smiling, "it's the doctor's orders."

His wizened face broke into a broader smile, and the three young ladies
laughed in musical echo to his pleasantry, swaying their bodies to and fro,
with nervous jerks of their shoulders. The boldest said:

"O, now, Mr. Browne, I'm sure the doctor never ordered anything of
the kind."

Mr. Browne took another sip of his whisky and said, with sidling mimicry: 70

"Well, you see, I'm like the famous Mrs. Cassidy, who is reported to
have said: 'Now, Mary Grimes, if I don't take it, make me take it, for I feel I
want it.'"

His hot face had leaned forward a little too confidentially and he
had assumed a very low Dublin accent so that the young ladies, with one
instinct, received his speech in silence. Miss Furlong, who was one of Mary
Jane's pupils, asked Miss Daly what was the name of the pretty waltz she had
played; and Mr. Browne, seeing that he was ignored, turned promptly to the
two young men who were more appreciative.

A red-faced young woman, dressed in pansy, came into the room, excitedly clapping her hands and crying:

"Quadrilles! Quadrilles!"

Close on her heels came Aunt Kate, crying: 75

"Two gentlemen and three ladies, Mary Jane!"

"O, here's Mr. Bergin and Mr. Kerrigan," said Mary Jane. "Mr. Kerrigan, will you take Miss Power? Miss Furlong, may I get you a partner, Mr.
Bergin. O, that'll just do now."

"Three ladies, Mary Jane," said Aunt Kate.

The two young gentlemen asked the ladies if they might have the pleasure, and Mary Jane turned to Miss Daly.

"O, Miss Daly, you're really awfully good, after playing for the last two   80
dances, but really we're so short of ladies tonight."

"I don't mind in the least, Miss Morkan."

"But I've a nice partner for you, Mr. Bartell D'Arcy, the tenor. I'll get
him to sing later on. All Dublin is raving about him."

"Lovely voice, lovely voice!" said Aunt Kate.

As the piano had twice begun the prelude to the first figure Mary Jane
led her recruits quickly from the room. They had hardly gone when Aunt
Julia wandered slowly into the room, looking behind her at something.

"What is the matter, Julia?" asked Aunt Kate anxiously. "Who is it?"   85

Julia, who was carrying in a column of table-napkins, turned to her sister and said, simply, as if the question had surprised her:

"It's only Freddy, Kate, and Gabriel with him."

In fact right behind her Gabriel could be seen piloting Freddy Malins
across the landing. The latter, a young man of about forty, was of Gabriel's
size and build, with very round shoulders. His face was fleshy and pallid,
touched with colour only at the thick hanging lobes of his ears and at the
wide wings of his nose. He had coarse features, a blunt nose, a convex and
receding brow, tumid and protruded lips. His heavy-lidded eyes and the disorder of his scanty hair made him look sleepy. He was laughing heartily in
a high key at a story which he had been telling Gabriel on the stairs and at
the same time rubbing the knuckles of his left fist backwards and forwards
into his left eye.

"Good-evening, Freddy," said Aunt Julia.

Freddy Malins bade the Misses Morkan good-evening in what seemed   90
an offhand fashion by reason of the habitual catch in his voice and then,
seeing that Mr. Browne was grinning at him from the sideboard, crossed the
room on rather shaky legs and began to repeat in an undertone the story he
had just told to Gabriel.

"He's not so bad, is he?" said Aunt Kate to Gabriel.

Gabriel's brows were dark but he raised them quickly and answered:

"O, no, hardly noticeable."

"Now, isn't he a terrible fellow!" she said. "And his poor mother made him take the pledge on New Year's Eve. But come on, Gabriel, into the drawing-room."

Before leaving the room with Gabriel she signalled to Mr. Browne by 95 frowning and shaking her forefinger in warning to and fro. Mr. Browne nodded in answer and, when she had gone, said to Freddy Malins:

"Now, then, Teddy, I'm going to fill you out a good glass of lemonade just to buck you up."

Freddy Malins, who was nearing the climax of his story, waved the offer aside impatiently but Mr. Browne, having first called Freddy Malins' attention to a disarray in his dress, filled out and handed him a full glass of lemonade. Freddy Malins' left hand accepted the glass mechanically, his right hand being engaged in the mechanical readjustment of his dress. Mr. Browne, whose face was once more wrinkling with mirth, poured out for himself a glass of whisky while Freddy Malins exploded, before he had well reached the climax of his story, in a kink of high-pitched bronchitic laughter and, setting down his untasted and overflowing glass, began to rub the knuckles of his left fist backwards and forwards into his left eye, repeating words of his last phrase as well as his fit of laughter would allow him.

Gabriel could not listen while Mary Jane was playing her Academy piece, full of runs and difficult passages, to the hushed drawing-room. He liked music but the piece she was playing had no melody for him and he doubted whether it had any melody for the other listeners, though they had begged Mary Jane to play something. Four young men, who had come from the refreshment-room to stand in the doorway at the sound of the piano, had gone away quietly in couples after a few minutes. The only persons who seemed to follow the music were Mary Jane herself, her hands racing along the key-board or lifted from it at the pauses like those of a priestess in momentary imprecation, and Aunt Kate standing at her elbow to turn the page.

Gabriel's eyes, irritated by the floor, which glittered with beeswax under the heavy chandelier, wandered to the wall above the piano. A picture of the balcony scene in Romeo and Juliet hung there and beside it was a picture of the two murdered princes in the Tower which Aunt Julia had worked in red, blue and brown wools when she was a girl. Probably in the school they had gone to as girls that kind of work had been taught for one year. His mother had worked for him as a birthday present a waistcoat of purple tabinet, with little foxes' heads upon it, lined with brown satin and having round mulberry buttons. It was strange that his mother had had no musical talent though Aunt Kate used to call her the brains carrier of the Morkan family. Both she and Julia had always seemed

a little proud of their serious and matronly sister. Her photograph stood
before the pierglass. She held an open book on her knees and was pointing out something in it to Constantine who, dressed in a man-o-war suit,
lay at her feet. It was she who had chosen the name of her sons for she was
very sensible of the dignity of family life. Thanks to her, Constantine was
now senior curate in Balbrigan and, thanks to her, Gabriel himself had
taken his degree in the Royal University. A shadow passed over his face
as he remembered her sullen opposition to his marriage. Some slighting
phrases she had used still rankled in his memory; she had once spoken of
Gretta as being country cute and that was not true of Gretta at all. It was
Gretta who had nursed her during all her last long illness in their house at
Monkstown.

He knew that Mary Jane must be near the end of her piece for she was   100
playing again the opening melody with runs of scales after every bar and
while he waited for the end the resentment died down in his heart. The
piece ended with a trill of octaves in the treble and a final deep octave in
the bass. Great applause greeted Mary Jane as, blushing and rolling up her
music nervously, she escaped from the room. The most vigorous clapping
came from the four young men in the doorway who had gone away to the
refreshment-room at the beginning of the piece but had come back when
the piano had stopped.

Lancers were arranged. Gabriel found himself partnered with Miss
Ivors. She was a frank-mannered talkative young lady, with a freckled face
and prominent brown eyes. She did not wear a low-cut bodice and the large
brooch which was fixed in the front of her collar bore on it an Irish device
and motto.

When they had taken their places she said abruptly:

"I have a crow to pluck with you."

"With me?" said Gabriel.

She nodded her head gravely.   105

"What is it?" asked Gabriel, smiling at her solemn manner.

"Who is G. C.?" answered Miss Ivors, turning her eyes upon him.

Gabriel coloured and was about to knit his brows, as if he did not
understand, when she said bluntly:

"O, innocent Amy! I have found out that you write for The Daily
Express. Now, aren't you ashamed of yourself?"

"Why should I be ashamed of myself?" asked Gabriel, blinking his eyes   110
and trying to smile.

"Well, I'm ashamed of you," said Miss Ivors frankly. "To say you'd write
for a paper like that. I didn't think you were a West Briton."

A look of perplexity appeared on Gabriel's face. It was true that he
wrote a literary column every Wednesday in The Daily Express, for which

he was paid fifteen shillings. But that did not make him a West Briton surely. The books he received for review were almost more welcome than the paltry cheque. He loved to feel the covers and turn over the pages of newly printed books. Nearly every day when his teaching in the college was ended he used to wander down the quays to the second-hand book-sellers, to Hickey's on Bachelor's Walk, to Web's or Massey's on Aston's Quay, or to O'Clohissey's in the by-street. He did not know how to meet her charge. He wanted to say that literature was above politics. But they were friends of many years' standing and their careers had been parallel, first at the University and then as teachers: he could not risk a grandiose phrase with her. He continued blinking his eyes and trying to smile and murmured lamely that he saw nothing political in writing reviews of books.

When their turn to cross had come he was still perplexed and inatten-tive. Miss Ivors promptly took his hand in a warm grasp and said in a soft friendly tone:

"Of course, I was only joking. Come, we cross now."

When they were together again she spoke of the University question 115
and Gabriel felt more at ease. A friend of hers had shown her his review of Browning's poems. That was how she had found out the secret: but she liked the review immensely. Then she said suddenly:

"O, Mr. Conroy, will you come for an excursion to the Aran Isles this summer? We're going to stay there a whole month. It will be splendid out in the Atlantic. You ought to come. Mr. Clancy is coming, and Mr. Kilkelly and Kathleen Kearney. It would be splendid for Gretta too if she'd come. She's from Connacht, isn't she?"

"Her people are," said Gabriel shortly.

"But you will come, won't you?" said Miss Ivors, laying her warm hand eagerly on his arm.

"The fact is," said Gabriel, "I have just arranged to go——"

"Go where?" asked Miss Ivors.   120

"Well, you know, every year I go for a cycling tour with some fellows and so——"

"But where?" asked Miss Ivors.

"Well, we usually go to France or Belgium or perhaps Germany," said Gabriel awkwardly.

"And why do you go to France and Belgium," said Miss Ivors, "instead of visiting your own land?"

"Well," said Gabriel, "it's partly to keep in touch with the languages 125
and partly for a change."

"And haven't you your own language to keep in touch with—Irish?" asked Miss Ivors.

"Well," said Gabriel, "if it comes to that, you know, Irish is not my language."

Their neighbours had turned to listen to the cross-examination. Gabriel glanced right and left nervously and tried to keep his good humour under the ordeal which was making a blush invade his forehead.

"And haven't you your own land to visit," continued Miss Ivors, "that you know nothing of, your own people, and your own country?"

"O, to tell you the truth," retorted Gabriel suddenly, "I'm sick of my own country, sick of it!" 130

"Why?" asked Miss Ivors.

Gabriel did not answer for his retort had heated him.

"Why?" repeated Miss Ivors.

They had to go visiting together and, as he had not answered her, Miss Ivors said warmly:

"Of course, you've no answer." 135

Gabriel tried to cover his agitation by taking part in the dance with great energy. He avoided her eyes for he had seen a sour expression on her face. But when they met in the long chain he was surprised to feel his hand firmly pressed. She looked at him from under her brows for a moment quizzically until he smiled. Then, just as the chain was about to start again, she stood on tiptoe and whispered into his ear:

"West Briton!"

When the lancers were over Gabriel went away to a remote corner of the room where Freddy Malins' mother was sitting. She was a stout feeble old woman with white hair. Her voice had a catch in it like her son's and she stuttered slightly. She had been told that Freddy had come and that he was nearly all right. Gabriel asked her whether she had had a good crossing. She lived with her married daughter in Glasgow and came to Dublin on a visit once a year. She answered placidly that she had had a beautiful crossing and that the captain had been most attentive to her. She spoke also of the beautiful house her daughter kept in Glasgow, and of all the friends they had there. While her tongue rambled on Gabriel tried to banish from his mind all memory of the unpleasant incident with Miss Ivors. Of course the girl or woman, or whatever she was, was an enthusiast but there was a time for all things. Perhaps he ought not to have answered her like that. But she had no right to call him a West Briton before people, even in joke. She had tried to make him ridiculous before people, heckling him and staring at him with her rabbit's eyes.

He saw his wife making her way towards him through the waltzing couples. When she reached him she said into his ear:

"Gabriel, Aunt Kate wants to know won't you carve the goose as usual. 140 Miss Daly will carve the ham and I'll do the pudding."

"All right," said Gabriel.

"She's sending in the younger ones first as soon as this waltz is over so that we'll have the table to ourselves."

"Were you dancing?" asked Gabriel.

"Of course I was. Didn't you see me? What row had you with Molly Ivors?"

"No row. Why? Did she say so?"   145

"Something like that. I'm trying to get that Mr. D'Arcy to sing. He's full of conceit, I think."

"There was no row," said Gabriel moodily, "only she wanted me to go for a trip to the west of Ireland and I said I wouldn't."

His wife clasped her hands excitedly and gave a little jump.

"O, do go, Gabriel," she cried. "I'd love to see Galway again."

"You can go if you like," said Gabriel coldly.   150

She looked at him for a moment, then turned to Mrs. Malins and said:

"There's a nice husband for you, Mrs. Malins."

While she was threading her way back across the room Mrs. Malins, without adverting to the interruption, went on to tell Gabriel what beautiful places there were in Scotland and beautiful scenery. Her son-in-law brought them every year to the lakes and they used to go fishing. Her son-in-law was a splendid fisher. One day he caught a beautiful big fish and the man in the hotel cooked it for their dinner.

Gabriel hardly heard what she said. Now that supper was coming near he began to think again about his speech and about the quotation. When he saw Freddy Malins coming across the room to visit his mother Gabriel left the chair free for him and retired into the embrasure of the window. The room had already cleared and from the back room came the clatter of plates and knives. Those who still remained in the drawing-room seemed tired of dancing and were conversing quietly in little groups. Gabriel's warm trembling fingers tapped the cold pane of the window. How cool it must be outside! How pleasant it would be to walk out alone, first along by the river and then through the park! The snow would be lying on the branches of the trees and forming a bright cap on the top of the Wellington Monument. How much more pleasant it would be there than at the supper-table!

He ran over the headings of his speech: Irish hospitality, sad memories,   155
the Three Graces, Paris, the quotation from Browning. He repeated to himself a phrase he had written in his review: "One feels that one is listening to a thought-tormented music." Miss Ivors had praised the review. Was she sincere? Had she really any life of her own behind all her propagandism? There had never been any ill-feeling between them until that night. It unnerved him to think that she would be at the supper-table, looking up at him while he spoke with her critical quizzing eyes. Perhaps she would not be sorry to see him fail in his speech. An idea came into his mind and gave him

courage. He would say, alluding to Aunt Kate and Aunt Julia: "Ladies and Gentlemen, the generation which is now on the wane among us may have had its faults but for my part I think it had certain qualities of hospitality, of humour, of humanity, which the new and very serious and hypereducated generation that is growing up around us seems to me to lack." Very good: that was one for Miss Ivors. What did he care that his aunts were only two ignorant old women?

A murmur in the room attracted his attention. Mr. Browne was advancing from the door, gallantly escorting Aunt Julia, who leaned upon his arm, smiling and hanging her head. An irregular musketry of applause escorted her also as far as the piano and then, as Mary Jane seated herself on the stool, and Aunt Julia, no longer smiling, half turned so as to pitch her voice fairly into the room, gradually ceased. Gabriel recognised the prelude. It was that of an old song of Aunt Julia's—Arrayed for the Bridal. Her voice, strong and clear in tone, attacked with great spirit the runs which embellish the air and though she sang very rapidly she did not miss even the smallest of the grace notes. To follow the voice, without looking at the singer's face, was to feel and share the excitement of swift and secure flight. Gabriel applauded loudly with all the others at the close of the song and loud applause was borne in from the invisible supper-table. It sounded so genuine that a little colour struggled into Aunt Julia's face as she bent to replace in the music-stand the old leather-bound songbook that had her initials on the cover. Freddy Malins, who had listened with his head perched sideways to hear her better, was still applauding when everyone else had ceased and talking animatedly to his mother who nodded her head gravely and slowly in acquiescence. At last, when he could clap no more, he stood up suddenly and hurried across the room to Aunt Julia whose hand he seized and held in both his hands, shaking it when words failed him or the catch in his voice proved too much for him.

"I was just telling my mother," he said, "I never heard you sing so well, never. No, I never heard your voice so good as it is tonight. Now! Would you believe that now? That's the truth. Upon my word and honour that's the truth. I never heard your voice sound so fresh and so…clear and fresh, never."

Aunt Julia smiled broadly and murmured something about compliments as she released her hand from his grasp. Mr. Browne extended his open hand towards her and said to those who were near him in the manner of a showman introducing a prodigy to an audience:

"Miss Julia Morkan, my latest discovery!"

He was laughing very heartily at this himself when Freddy Malins turned to him and said:

"Well, Browne, if you're serious you might make a worse discovery. All I can say is I never heard her sing half so well as long as I am coming here. And that's the honest truth."

"Neither did I," said Mr. Browne. "I think her voice has greatly improved."

Aunt Julia shrugged her shoulders and said with meek pride:

"Thirty years ago I hadn't a bad voice as voices go."

"I often told Julia," said Aunt Kate emphatically, "that she was simply 165 thrown away in that choir. But she never would be said by me."

She turned as if to appeal to the good sense of the others against a refractory child while Aunt Julia gazed in front of her, a vague smile of reminiscence playing on her face.

"No," continued Aunt Kate, "she wouldn't be said or led by anyone, slaving there in that choir night and day, night and day. Six o'clock on Christmas morning! And all for what?"

"Well, isn't it for the honour of God, Aunt Kate?" asked Mary Jane, twisting round on the piano-stool and smiling.

Aunt Kate turned fiercely on her niece and said:

"I know all about the honour of God, Mary Jane, but I think it's not 170 at all honourable for the pope to turn out the women out of the choirs that have slaved there all their lives and put little whipper-snappers of boys over their heads. I suppose it is for the good of the Church if the pope does it. But it's not just, Mary Jane, and it's not right."

She had worked herself into a passion and would have continued in defence of her sister for it was a sore subject with her but Mary Jane, seeing that all the dancers had come back, intervened pacifically:

"Now, Aunt Kate, you're giving scandal to Mr. Browne who is of the other persuasion."

Aunt Kate turned to Mr. Browne, who was grinning at this allusion to his religion, and said hastily:

"O, I don't question the pope's being right. I'm only a stupid old woman and I wouldn't presume to do such a thing. But there's such a thing as common everyday politeness and gratitude. And if I were in Julia's place I'd tell that Father Healey straight up to his face . . ."

"And besides, Aunt Kate," said Mary Jane, "we really are all hungry 175 and when we are hungry we are all very quarrelsome."

"And when we are thirsty we are also quarrelsome," added Mr. Browne.

"So that we had better go to supper," said Mary Jane, "and finish the discussion afterwards."

On the landing outside the drawing-room Gabriel found his wife and Mary Jane trying to persuade Miss Ivors to stay for supper. But Miss Ivors, who had put on her hat and was buttoning her cloak, would not stay. She did not feel in the least hungry and she had already overstayed her time.

"But only for ten minutes, Molly," said Mrs. Conroy. "That won't delay you."

"To take a pick itself," said Mary Jane, "after all your dancing."   180

"I really couldn't," said Miss Ivors.

"I am afraid you didn't enjoy yourself at all," said Mary Jane hopelessly.

"Ever so much, I assure you," said Miss Ivors, "but you really must let me run off now."

"But how can you get home?" asked Mrs. Conroy.

"O, it's only two steps up the quay."   185

Gabriel hesitated a moment and said:

"If you will allow me, Miss Ivors, I'll see you home if you are really obliged to go."

But Miss Ivors broke away from them.

"I won't hear of it," she cried. "For goodness' sake go in to your suppers and don't mind me. I'm quite well able to take care of myself."

"Well, you're the comical girl, Molly," said Mrs. Conroy frankly.   190

"Beannacht libh," cried Miss Ivors, with a laugh, as she ran down the staircase.

Mary Jane gazed after her, a moody puzzled expression on her face, while Mrs. Conroy leaned over the banisters to listen for the hall-door. Gabriel asked himself was he the cause of her abrupt departure. But she did not seem to be in ill humour: she had gone away laughing. He stared blankly down the staircase.

At the moment Aunt Kate came toddling out of the supper-room, almost wringing her hands in despair.

"Where is Gabriel?" she cried. "Where on earth is Gabriel? There's everyone waiting in there, stage to let, and nobody to carve the goose!"

"Here I am, Aunt Kate!" cried Gabriel, with sudden animation, "ready   195 to carve a flock of geese, if necessary."

A fat brown goose lay at one end of the table and at the other end, on a bed of creased paper strewn with sprigs of parsley, lay a great ham, stripped of its outer skin and peppered over with crust crumbs, a neat paper frill round its shin and beside this was a round of spiced beef. Between these rival ends ran parallel lines of side-dishes: two little minsters of jelly, red and yellow; a shallow dish full of blocks of blancmange and red jam, a large green leaf-shaped dish with a stalk-shaped handle, on which lay bunches of purple raisins and peeled almonds, a companion dish on which lay a solid rectangle of Smyrna figs, a dish of custard topped with grated nutmeg, a small bowl full of chocolates and sweets wrapped in gold and silver papers and a glass vase in which stood some tall celery stalks.

In the centre of the table there stood, as sentries to a fruit-stand which upheld a pyramid of oranges and American apples, two squat old-fashioned decanters of cut glass, one containing port and the other dark sherry. On the closed square piano a pudding in a huge yellow dish lay in waiting and behind it were three squads of bottles of stout and ale and minerals, drawn up according to the colours of their uniforms, the first two black, with brown and red labels, the third and smallest squad white, with transverse green sashes.

Gabriel took his seat boldly at the head of the table and, having looked to the edge of the carver, plunged his fork firmly into the goose. He felt quite at ease now for he was an expert carver and liked nothing better than to find himself at the head of a well-laden table.

"Miss Furlong, what shall I send you?" he asked. "A wing or a slice of the breast?"

"Just a small slice of the breast."

"Miss Higgins, what for you?"

"O, anything at all, Mr. Conroy."   200

While Gabriel and Miss Daly exchanged plates of goose and plates of ham and spiced beef Lily went from guest to guest with a dish of hot floury potatoes wrapped in a white napkin. This was Mary Jane's idea and she had also suggested apple sauce for the goose but Aunt Kate had said that plain roast goose without any apple sauce had always been good enough for her and she hoped she might never eat worse. Mary Jane waited on her pupils and saw that they got the best slices and Aunt Kate and Aunt Julia opened and carried across from the piano bottles of stout and ale for the gentlemen and bottles of minerals for the ladies. There was a great deal of confusion and laughter and noise, the noise of orders and counter-orders, of knives and forks, of corks and glass-stoppers. Gabriel began to carve second help-ings as soon as he had finished the first round without serving himself. Eve-ryone protested loudly so that he compromised by taking a long draught of stout for he had found the carving hot work. Mary Jane settled down quietly to her supper but Aunt Kate and Aunt Julia were still toddling round the table, walking on each other's heels, getting in each other's way and giving each other unheeded orders. Mr. Browne begged of them to sit down and eat their suppers and so did Gabriel but they said there was time enough, so that, at last, Freddy Malins stood up and, capturing Aunt Kate, plumped her down on her chair amid general laughter.

When everyone had been well served Gabriel said, smiling:

"Now, if anyone wants a little more of what vulgar people call stuffing let him or her speak."

A chorus of voices invited him to begin his own supper and Lily came   205
forward with three potatoes which she had reserved for him.

"Very well," said Gabriel amiably, as he took another preparatory draught, "kindly forget my existence, ladies and gentlemen, for a few minutes."

He set to his supper and took no part in the conversation with which the table covered Lily's removal of the plates. The subject of talk was the opera company which was then at the Theatre Royal. Mr. Bartell D'Arcy, the tenor, a dark-complexioned young man with a smart moustache, praised very highly the leading contralto of the company but Miss Furlong thought she had a rather vulgar style of production. Freddy Malins said there was a Negro chieftain singing in the second part of the Gaiety pantomime who had one of the finest tenor voices he had ever heard.

"Have you heard him?" he asked Mr. Bartell D'Arcy across the table.

"No," answered Mr. Bartell D'Arcy carelessly.

"Because," Freddy Malins explained, "now I'd be curious to hear your opinion of him. I think he has a grand voice." 210

"It takes Teddy to find out the really good things," said Mr. Browne familiarly to the table.

"And why couldn't he have a voice too?" asked Freddy Malins sharply. "Is it because he's only a black?"

Nobody answered this question and Mary Jane led the table back to the legitimate opera. One of her pupils had given her a pass for Mignon. Of course it was very fine, she said, but it made her think of poor Georgina Burns. Mr. Browne could go back farther still, to the old Italian companies that used to come to Dublin—Tietjens, Ilma de Murzka, Campanini, the great Trebelli, Giuglini, Ravelli, Aramburo. Those were the days, he said, when there was something like singing to be heard in Dublin. He told too of how the top gallery of the old Royal used to be packed night after night, of how one night an Italian tenor had sung five encores to Let me like a Soldier fall, introducing a high C every time, and of how the gallery boys would sometimes in their enthusiasm unyoke the horses from the carriage of some great prima donna and pull her themselves through the streets to her hotel. Why did they never play the grand old operas now, he asked, Dinorah, Lucrezia Borgia? Because they could not get the voices to sing them: that was why.

"Oh, well," said Mr. Bartell D'Arcy, "I presume there are as good singers today as there were then."

"Where are they?" asked Mr. Browne defiantly. 215

"In London, Paris, Milan," said Mr. Bartell D'Arcy warmly. "I suppose Caruso, for example, is quite as good, if not better than any of the men you have mentioned."

"Maybe so," said Mr. Browne. "But I may tell you I doubt it strongly."

"O, I'd give anything to hear Caruso sing," said Mary Jane.

"For me," said Aunt Kate, who had been picking a bone, "there was only one tenor. To please me, I mean. But I suppose none of you ever heard of him."

"Who was he, Miss Morkan?" asked Mr. Bartell D'Arcy politely.   220

"His name," said Aunt Kate, "was Parkinson. I heard him when he was in his prime and I think he had then the purest tenor voice that was ever put into a man's throat."

"Strange," said Mr. Bartell D'Arcy. "I never even heard of him."

"Yes, yes, Miss Morkan is right," said Mr. Browne. "I remember hearing of old Parkinson but he's too far back for me."

"A beautiful, pure, sweet, mellow English tenor," said Aunt Kate with enthusiasm.

Gabriel having finished, the huge pudding was transferred to the table.   225 The clatter of forks and spoons began again. Gabriel's wife served out spoonfuls of the pudding and passed the plates down the table. Midway down they were held up by Mary Jane, who replenished them with raspberry or orange jelly or with blancmange and jam. The pudding was of Aunt Julia's making and she received praises for it from all quarters. She herself said that it was not quite brown enough.

"Well, I hope, Miss Morkan," said Mr. Browne, "that I'm brown enough for you because, you know, I'm all brown."

All the gentlemen, except Gabriel, ate some of the pudding out of compliment to Aunt Julia. As Gabriel never ate sweets the celery had been left for him. Freddy Malins also took a stalk of celery and ate it with his pudding. He had been told that celery was a capital thing for the blood and he was just then under doctor's care. Mrs. Malins, who had been silent all through the supper, said that her son was going down to Mount Melleray in a week or so. The table then spoke of Mount Melleray, how bracing the air was down there, how hospitable the monks were and how they never asked for a penny-piece from their guests.

"And do you mean to say," asked Mr. Browne incredulously, "that a chap can go down there and put up there as if it were a hotel and live on the fat of the land and then come away without paying anything?"

"O, most people give some donation to the monastery when they leave." said Mary Jane.

"I wish we had an institution like that in our Church," said Mr.   230 Browne candidly.

He was astonished to hear that the monks never spoke, got up at two in the morning and slept in their coffins. He asked what they did it for.

"That's the rule of the order," said Aunt Kate firmly.

"Yes, but why?" asked Mr. Browne.

Aunt Kate repeated that it was the rule, that was all. Mr. Browne still seemed not to understand. Freddy Malins explained to him, as best he could, that the monks were trying to make up for the sins committed by all the sinners in the outside world. The explanation was not very clear for Mr. Browne grinned and said:

"I like that idea very much but wouldn't a comfortable spring bed do   235 them as well as a coffin?"

"The coffin," said Mary Jane, "is to remind them of their last end."

As the subject had grown lugubrious it was buried in a silence of the table during which Mrs. Malins could be heard saying to her neighbour in an indistinct undertone:

"They are very good men, the monks, very pious men."

The raisins and almonds and figs and apples and oranges and choco-lates and sweets were now passed about the table and Aunt Julia invited all the guests to have either port or sherry. At first Mr. Bartell D'Arcy refused to take either but one of his neighbours nudged him and whis-pered something to him upon which he allowed his glass to be filled. Gradually as the last glasses were being filled the conversation ceased. A pause followed, broken only by the noise of the wine and by unsettlings of chairs. The Misses Morkan, all three, looked down at the tablecloth. Someone coughed once or twice and then a few gentlemen patted the table gently as a signal for silence. The silence came and Gabriel pushed back his chair.

The patting at once grew louder in encouragement and then ceased   240 altogether. Gabriel leaned his ten trembling fingers on the tablecloth and smiled nervously at the company. Meeting a row of upturned faces he raised his eyes to the chandelier. The piano was playing a waltz tune and he could hear the skirts sweeping against the drawing-room door. People, perhaps, were standing in the snow on the quay outside, gazing up at the lighted windows and listening to the waltz music. The air was pure there. In the distance lay the park where the trees were weighted with snow. The Welling-ton Monument wore a gleaming cap of snow that flashed westward over the white field of Fifteen Acres.

He began:

"Ladies and Gentlemen,

"It has fallen to my lot this evening, as in years past, to perform a very pleasing task but a task for which I am afraid my poor powers as a speaker are all too inadequate."

"No, no!" said Mr. Browne.

"But, however that may be, I can only ask you tonight to take the will   245 for the deed and to lend me your attention for a few moments while I endeavour to express to you in words what my feelings are on this occasion.

"Ladies and Gentlemen, it is not the first time that we have gathered together under this hospitable roof, around this hospitable board. It is not the first time that we have been the recipients—or perhaps, I had better say, the victims—of the hospitality of certain good ladies."

He made a circle in the air with his arm and paused. Everyone laughed or smiled at Aunt Kate and Aunt Julia and Mary Jane who all turned crimson with pleasure. Gabriel went on more boldly:

"I feel more strongly with every recurring year that our country has no tradition which does it so much honour and which it should guard so jealously as that of its hospitality. It is a tradition that is unique as far as my experience goes (and I have visited not a few places abroad) among the modern nations. Some would say, perhaps, that with us it is rather a failing than anything to be boasted of. But granted even that, it is, to my mind, a princely failing, and one that I trust will long be cultivated among us. Of one thing, at least, I am sure. As long as this one roof shelters the good ladies aforesaid—and I wish from my heart it may do so for many and many a long year to come—the tradition of genuine warm-hearted courteous Irish hospitality, which our forefathers have handed down to us and which we in turn must hand down to our descendants, is still alive among us."

A hearty murmur of assent ran round the table. It shot through Gabriel's mind that Miss Ivors was not there and that she had gone away discourteously: and he said with confidence in himself:

"Ladies and Gentlemen,   250

"A new generation is growing up in our midst, a generation actuated by new ideas and new principles. It is serious and enthusiastic for these new ideas and its enthusiasm, even when it is misdirected, is, I believe, in the main sincere. But we are living in a sceptical and, if I may use the phrase, a thought-tormented age: and sometimes I fear that this new generation, educated or hypereducated as it is, will lack those qualities of humanity, of hospitality, of kindly humour which belonged to an older day. Listening tonight to the names of all those great singers of the past it seemed to me, I must confess, that we were living in a less spacious age. Those days might, without exaggeration, be called spacious days: and if they are gone beyond recall let us hope, at least, that in gatherings such as this we shall still speak of them with pride and affection, still cherish in our hearts the memory of those dead and gone great ones whose fame the world will not willingly let die."

"Hear, hear!" said Mr. Browne loudly.

"But yet," continued Gabriel, his voice falling into a softer inflection, "there are always in gatherings such as this sadder thoughts that will recur to our minds: thoughts of the past, of youth, of changes, of absent faces that we miss here tonight. Our path through life is strewn with many such sad memories: and were we to brood upon them always we could not find the heart to go on bravely with our work among the living. We have all of us living duties and living affections which claim, and rightly claim, our strenuous endeavours.

"Therefore, I will not linger on the past. I will not let any gloomy moralising intrude upon us here tonight. Here we are gathered together for a brief moment from the bustle and rush of our everyday routine. We are met here as friends, in the spirit of good-fellowship, as colleagues, also to a certain extent, in the true spirit of camaraderie, and as the guests of—what shall I call them?—the Three Graces of the Dublin musical world."

The table burst into applause and laughter at this allusion. Aunt Julia   255
vainly asked each of her neighbours in turn to tell her what Gabriel had said.

"He says we are the Three Graces, Aunt Julia," said Mary Jane.

Aunt Julia did not understand but she looked up, smiling, at Gabriel, who continued in the same vein:

"Ladies and Gentlemen,

"I will not attempt to play tonight the part that Paris played on another occasion. I will not attempt to choose between them. The task would be an invidious one and one beyond my poor powers. For when I view them in turn, whether it be our chief hostess herself, whose good heart, whose too good heart, has become a byword with all who know her, or her sister, who seems to be gifted with perennial youth and whose singing must have been a surprise and a revelation to us all tonight, or, last but not least, when I consider our youngest hostess, talented, cheerful, hard-working and the best of nieces, I confess, Ladies and Gentlemen, that I do not know to which of them I should award the prize."

Gabriel glanced down at his aunts and, seeing the large smile on Aunt   260
Julia's face and the tears which had risen to Aunt Kate's eyes, hastened to his close. He raised his glass of port gallantly, while every member of the company fingered a glass expectantly, and said loudly:

"Let us toast them all three together. Let us drink to their health, wealth, long life, happiness and prosperity and may they long continue to hold the proud and self-won position which they hold in their profession and the position of honour and affection which they hold in our hearts."

All the guests stood up, glass in hand, and turning towards the three seated ladies, sang in unison, with Mr. Browne as leader:

FOR THEY ARE JOLLY GAY FELLOWS,
FOR THEY ARE JOLLY GAY FELLOWS,
FOR THEY ARE JOLLY GAY FELLOWS,
WHICH NOBODY CAN DENY.

Aunt Kate was making frank use of her handkerchief and even Aunt Julia seemed moved. Freddy Malins beat time with his pudding-fork and the

singers turned towards one another, as if in melodious conference, while
they sang with emphasis:

UNLESS HE TELLS A LIE,

UNLESS HE TELLS A LIE.

Then, turning once more towards their hostesses, they sang:

FOR THEY ARE JOLLY GAY FELLOWS,

FOR THEY ARE JOLLY GAY FELLOWS,

FOR THEY ARE JOLLY GAY FELLOWS,

WHICH NOBODY CAN DENY.

The acclamation which followed was taken up beyond the door of the   265
supper-room by many of the other guests and renewed time after time,
Freddy Malins acting as officer with his fork on high.

The piercing morning air came into the hall where they were standing
so that Aunt Kate said:

"Close the door, somebody. Mrs. Malins will get her death of cold."

"Browne is out there, Aunt Kate," said Mary Jane.

"Browne is everywhere," said Aunt Kate, lowering her voice.

Mary Jane laughed at her tone.   270

"Really," she said archly, "he is very attentive."

"He has been laid on here like the gas," said Aunt Kate in the same
tone, "all during the Christmas."

She laughed herself this time good-humouredly and then added
quickly:

"But tell him to come in, Mary Jane, and close the door. I hope to
goodness he didn't hear me."

At that moment the hall-door was opened and Mr. Browne came in   275
from the doorstep, laughing as if his heart would break. He was dressed in a
long green overcoat with mock astrakhan cuffs and collar and wore on his
head an oval fur cap. He pointed down the snow-covered quay from where
the sound of shrill prolonged whistling was borne in.

"Teddy will have all the cabs in Dublin out," he said.

Gabriel advanced from the little pantry behind the office, struggling
into his overcoat and, looking round the hall, said:

"Gretta not down yet?"

"She's getting on her things, Gabriel," said Aunt Kate.   280

"Who's playing up there?" asked Gabriel.

"Nobody. They're all gone."

"O no, Aunt Kate," said Mary Jane. "Bartell D'Arcy and Miss
O'Callaghan aren't gone yet."

"Someone is fooling at the piano anyhow," said Gabriel.

Mary Jane glanced at Gabriel and Mr. Browne and said with a shiver: 285

"It makes me feel cold to look at you two gentlemen muffled up like
that. I wouldn't like to face your journey home at this hour."

"I'd like nothing better this minute," said Mr. Browne stoutly, "than a rattling fine walk in the country or a fast drive with a good spanking goer between the shafts."

"We used to have a very good horse and trap at home," said Aunt Julia sadly.

"The never-to-be-forgotten Johnny," said Mary Jane, laughing.

Aunt Kate and Gabriel laughed too. 290

"Why, what was wonderful about Johnny?" asked Mr. Browne.

"The late lamented Patrick Morkan, our grandfather, that is," explained Gabriel, "commonly known in his later years as the old gentleman, was a glue-boiler."

"O, now, Gabriel," said Aunt Kate, laughing, "he had a starch mill."

"Well, glue or starch," said Gabriel, "the old gentleman had a horse by the name of Johnny. And Johnny used to work in the old gentleman's mill, walking round and round in order to drive the mill. That was all very well; but now comes the tragic part about Johnny. One fine day the old gentleman thought he'd like to drive out with the quality to a military review in the park."

"The Lord have mercy on his soul," said Aunt Kate compassionately. 295

"Amen," said Gabriel. "So the old gentleman, as I said, harnessed Johnny and put on his very best tall hat and his very best stock collar and drove out in grand style from his ancestral mansion somewhere near Back Lane, I think."

Everyone laughed, even Mrs. Malins, at Gabriel's manner and Aunt Kate said:

"O, now, Gabriel, he didn't live in Back Lane, really. Only the mill was there."

"Out from the mansion of his forefathers," continued Gabriel, "he drove with Johnny. And everything went on beautifully until Johnny came in sight of King Billy's statue: and whether he fell in love with the horse King Billy sits on or whether he thought he was back again in the mill, anyhow he began to walk round the statue."

Gabriel paced in a circle round the hall in his goloshes amid the laugh- 300 ter of the others.

"Round and round he went," said Gabriel, "and the old gentleman, who was a very pompous old gentleman, was highly indignant. 'Go on, sir! What do you mean, sir? Johnny! Johnny! Most extraordinary conduct! Can't understand the horse!'"

The peal of laughter which followed Gabriel's imitation of the incident was interrupted by a resounding knock at the hall door. Mary Jane ran to open it and let in Freddy Malins. Freddy Malins, with his hat well back on his head and his shoulders humped with cold, was puffing and steaming after his exertions.

"I could only get one cab," he said.

"O, we'll find another along the quay," said Gabriel.

"Yes," said Aunt Kate. "Better not keep Mrs. Malins standing in the   305
draught."

Mrs. Malins was helped down the front steps by her son and Mr. Browne and, after many manoeuvres, hoisted into the cab. Freddy Malins clambered in after her and spent a long time settling her on the seat, Mr. Browne helping him with advice. At last she was settled comfortably and Freddy Malins invited Mr. Browne into the cab. There was a good deal of confused talk, and then Mr. Browne got into the cab. The cabman settled his rug over his knees, and bent down for the address. The confusion grew greater and the cabman was directed differently by Freddy Malins and Mr. Browne, each of whom had his head out through a window of the cab. The difficulty was to know where to drop Mr. Browne along the route, and Aunt Kate, Aunt Julia and Mary Jane helped the discussion from the doorstep with cross-directions and contradictions and abundance of laughter. As for Freddy Malins he was speechless with laughter. He popped his head in and out of the window every moment to the great danger of his hat, and told his mother how the discussion was progressing, till at last Mr. Browne shouted to the bewildered cabman above the din of everybody's laughter:

"Do you know Trinity College?"

"Yes, sir," said the cabman.

"Well, drive bang up against Trinity College gates," said Mr. Browne, "and then we'll tell you where to go. You understand now?"

"Yes, sir," said the cabman.   310

"Make like a bird for Trinity College."

"Right, sir," said the cabman.

The horse was whipped up and the cab rattled off along the quay amid a chorus of laughter and adieus.

Gabriel had not gone to the door with the others. He was in a dark part of the hall gazing up the staircase. A woman was standing near the top of the first flight, in the shadow also. He could not see her face but he could see the terra-cotta and salmon-pink panels of her skirt which the shadow made appear black and white. It was his wife. She was leaning on the banisters, listening to something. Gabriel was surprised at her stillness and strained his ear to listen also. But he could hear little save the noise of laughter and dispute on the front steps, a few chords struck on the piano and a few notes of a man's voice singing.

He stood still in the gloom of the hall, trying to catch the air that the   315
voice was singing and gazing up at his wife. There was grace and mystery in her attitude as if she were a symbol of something. He asked himself what is a woman standing on the stairs in the shadow, listening to distant music, a symbol of. If he were a painter he would paint her in that attitude. Her blue

felt hat would show off the bronze of her hair against the darkness and the dark panels of her skirt would show off the light ones. Distant Music he would call the picture if he were a painter.

The hall-door was closed; and Aunt Kate, Aunt Julia and Mary Jane came down the hall, still laughing.

"Well, isn't Freddy terrible?" said Mary Jane. "He's really terrible."

Gabriel said nothing but pointed up the stairs towards where his wife was standing. Now that the hall-door was closed the voice and the piano could be heard more clearly. Gabriel held up his hand for them to be silent. The song seemed to be in the old Irish tonality and the singer seemed uncertain both of his words and of his voice. The voice, made plaintive by distance and by the singer's hoarseness, faintly illuminated the cadence of the air with words expressing grief:

O, THE RAIN FALLS ON MY HEAVY LOCKS
AND THE DEW WETS MY SKIN,
MY BABE LIES COLD...

"O," exclaimed Mary Jane. "It's Bartell D'Arcy singing and he wouldn't sing all the night. O, I'll get him to sing a song before he goes."

"O, do, Mary Jane," said Aunt Kate.   320

Mary Jane brushed past the others and ran to the staircase, but before she reached it the singing stopped and the piano was closed abruptly.

"O, what a pity!" she cried. "Is he coming down, Gretta?"

Gabriel heard his wife answer yes and saw her come down towards them. A few steps behind her were Mr. Bartell D'Arcy and Miss O'Callaghan.

"O, Mr. D'Arcy," cried Mary Jane, "it's downright mean of you to break off like that when we were all in raptures listening to you."

"I have been at him all the evening," said Miss O'Callaghan, "and   325
Mrs. Conroy, too, and he told us he had a dreadful cold and couldn't sing."

"O, Mr. D'Arcy," said Aunt Kate, "now that was a great fib to tell."

"Can't you see that I'm as hoarse as a crow?" said Mr. D'Arcy roughly.

He went into the pantry hastily and put on his overcoat. The others, taken aback by his rude speech, could find nothing to say. Aunt Kate wrinkled her brows and made signs to the others to drop the subject. Mr. D'Arcy stood swathing his neck carefully and frowning.

"It's the weather," said Aunt Julia, after a pause.

"Yes, everybody has colds," said Aunt Kate readily, "everybody."   330

"They say," said Mary Jane, "we haven't had snow like it for thirty years; and I read this morning in the newspapers that the snow is general all over Ireland."

"I love the look of snow," said Aunt Julia sadly.

"So do I," said Miss O'Callaghan. "I think Christmas is never really Christmas unless we have the snow on the ground."

"But poor Mr. D'Arcy doesn't like the snow," said Aunt Kate, smiling.

Mr. D'Arcy came from the pantry, fully swathed and buttoned, and in a repentant tone told them the history of his cold. Everyone gave him advice and said it was a great pity and urged him to be very careful of his throat in the night air. Gabriel watched his wife, who did not join in the conversation. She was standing right under the dusty fanlight and the flame of the gas lit up the rich bronze of her hair, which he had seen her drying at the fire a few days before. She was in the same attitude and seemed unaware of the talk about her. At last she turned towards them and Gabriel saw that there was colour on her cheeks and that her eyes were shining. A sudden tide of joy went leaping out of his heart.

"Mr. D'Arcy," she said, "what is the name of that song you were singing?"

"It's called The Lass of Aughrim," said Mr. D'Arcy, "but I couldn't remember it properly. Why? Do you know it?"

"The Lass of Aughrim," she repeated. "I couldn't think of the name."

"It's a very nice air," said Mary Jane. "I'm sorry you were not in voice tonight."

"Now, Mary Jane," said Aunt Kate, "don't annoy Mr. D'Arcy. I won't have him annoyed."

Seeing that all were ready to start she shepherded them to the door, where good-night was said:

"Well, good-night, Aunt Kate, and thanks for the pleasant evening."

"Good-night, Gabriel. Good-night, Gretta!"

"Good-night, Aunt Kate, and thanks ever so much. Goodnight, Aunt Julia."

"O, good-night, Gretta, I didn't see you."

"Good-night, Mr. D'Arcy. Good-night, Miss O'Callaghan."

"Good-night, Miss Morkan."

"Good-night, again."

"Good-night, all. Safe home."

"Good-night. Good night."

The morning was still dark. A dull, yellow light brooded over the houses and the river; and the sky seemed to be descending. It was slushy underfoot; and only streaks and patches of snow lay on the roofs, on the parapets of the quay and on the area railings. The lamps were still burning redly in the murky air and, across the river, the palace of the Four Courts stood out menacingly against the heavy sky.

She was walking on before him with Mr. Bartell D'Arcy, her shoes in a brown parcel tucked under one arm and her hands holding her skirt up from the slush. She had no longer any grace of attitude, but Gabriel's eyes were still bright with happiness. The blood went bounding along his veins; and the thoughts went rioting through his brain, proud, joyful, tender, valorous.

She was walking on before him so lightly and so erect that he longed to run after her noiselessly, catch her by the shoulders and say something foolish and affectionate into her ear. She seemed to him so frail that he longed to defend her against something and then to be alone with her. Moments of their secret life together burst like stars upon his memory. A heliotrope envelope was lying beside his breakfast-cup and he was caressing it with his hand. Birds were twittering in the ivy and the sunny web of the curtain was shimmering along the floor: he could not eat for happiness. They were standing on the crowded platform and he was placing a ticket inside the warm palm of her glove. He was standing with her in the cold, looking in through a grated window at a man making bottles in a roaring furnace. It was very cold. Her face, fragrant in the cold air, was quite close to his; and suddenly he called out to the man at the furnace:

"Is the fire hot, sir?"

But the man could not hear with the noise of the furnace. It was just as 355 well. He might have answered rudely.

A wave of yet more tender joy escaped from his heart and went coursing in warm flood along his arteries. Like the tender fire of stars moments of their life together, that no one knew of or would ever know of, broke upon and illumined his memory. He longed to recall to her those moments, to make her forget the years of their dull existence together and remember only their moments of ecstasy. For the years, he felt, had not quenched his soul or hers. Their children, his writing, her household cares had not quenched all their souls' tender fire. In one letter that he had written to her then he had said: "Why is it that words like these seem to me so dull and cold? Is it because there is no word tender enough to be your name?"

Like distant music these words that he had written years before were borne towards him from the past. He longed to be alone with her. When the others had gone away, when he and she were in the room in their hotel, then they would be alone together. He would call her softly:

"Gretta!"

Perhaps she would not hear at once: she would be undressing. Then something in his voice would strike her. She would turn and look at him. . . .

At the corner of Winetavern Street they met a cab. He was glad of its 360 rattling noise as it saved him from conversation. She was looking out of the window and seemed tired. The others spoke only a few words, pointing out some building or street. The horse galloped along wearily under the murky morning sky, dragging his old rattling box after his heels, and Gabriel was again in a cab with her, galloping to catch the boat, galloping to their honeymoon.

As the cab drove across O'Connell Bridge Miss O'Callaghan said:

"They say you never cross O'Connell Bridge without seeing a white horse."

"I see a white man this time," said Gabriel.

"Where?" asked Mr. Bartell D'Arcy.

Gabriel pointed to the statue, on which lay patches of snow. Then he   365
nodded familiarly to it and waved his hand.

"Good-night, Dan," he said gaily.

When the cab drew up before the hotel, Gabriel jumped out and, in spite of Mr. Bartell D'Arcy's protest, paid the driver. He gave the man a shilling over his fare. The man saluted and said:

"A prosperous New Year to you, sir."

"The same to you," said Gabriel cordially.

She leaned for a moment on his arm in getting out of the cab and   370
while standing at the curbstone, bidding the others good-night. She leaned lightly on his arm, as lightly as when she had danced with him a few hours before. He had felt proud and happy then, happy that she was his, proud of her grace and wifely carriage. But now, after the kindling again of so many memories, the first touch of her body, musical and strange and perfumed, sent through him a keen pang of lust. Under cover of her silence he pressed her arm closely to his side; and, as they stood at the hotel door, he felt that they had escaped from their lives and duties, escaped from home and friends and run away together with wild and radiant hearts to a new adventure.

An old man was dozing in a great hooded chair in the hall. He lit a candle in the office and went before them to the stairs. They followed him in silence, their feet falling in soft thuds on the thickly carpeted stairs. She mounted the stairs behind the porter, her head bowed in the ascent, her frail shoulders curved as with a burden, her skirt girt tightly about her. He could have flung his arms about her hips and held her still, for his arms were trembling with desire to seize her and only the stress of his nails against the palms of his hands held the wild impulse of his body in check. The porter halted on the stairs to settle his guttering candle. They halted, too, on the steps below him. In the silence Gabriel could hear the falling of the molten wax into the tray and the thumping of his own heart against his ribs.

The porter led them along a corridor and opened a door. Then he set his unstable candle down on a toilet-table and asked at what hour they were to be called in the morning.

"Eight," said Gabriel.

The porter pointed to the tap of the electric-light and began a muttered apology, but Gabriel cut him short.

"We don't want any light. We have light enough from the street. And   375
I say," he added, pointing to the candle, "you might remove that handsome article, like a good man."

The porter took up his candle again, but slowly, for he was surprised by such a novel idea. Then he mumbled good-night and went out. Gabriel shot the lock to.

A ghostly light from the street lamp lay in a long shaft from one window to the door. Gabriel threw his overcoat and hat on a couch and crossed the room towards the window. He looked down into the street in order that his emotion might calm a little. Then he turned and leaned against a chest of drawers with his back to the light. She had taken off her hat and cloak and was standing before a large swinging mirror, unhooking her waist. Gabriel paused for a few moments, watching her, and then said:

"Gretta!"

She turned away from the mirror slowly and walked along the shaft of light towards him. Her face looked so serious and weary that the words would not pass Gabriel's lips. No, it was not the moment yet.

"You looked tired," he said.   380

"I am a little," she answered.

"You don't feel ill or weak?"

"No, tired: that's all."

She went on to the window and stood there, looking out. Gabriel waited again and then, fearing that diffidence was about to conquer him, he said abruptly:

"By the way, Gretta!"   385

"What is it?"

"You know that poor fellow Malins?" he said quickly.

"Yes. What about him?"

"Well, poor fellow, he's a decent sort of chap, after all," continued Gabriel in a false voice. "He gave me back that sovereign I lent him, and I didn't expect it, really. It's a pity he wouldn't keep away from that Browne, because he's not a bad fellow, really."

He was trembling now with annoyance. Why did she seem so   390
abstracted? He did not know how he could begin. Was she annoyed, too, about something? If she would only turn to him or come to him of her own accord! To take her as she was would be brutal. No, he must see some ardour in her eyes first. He longed to be master of her strange mood.

"When did you lend him the pound?" she asked, after a pause.

Gabriel strove to restrain himself from breaking out into brutal language about the sottish Malins and his pound. He longed to cry to her from his soul, to crush her body against his, to overmaster her. But he said:

"O, at Christmas, when he opened that little Christmas-card shop in Henry Street."

He was in such a fever of rage and desire that he did not hear her come from the window. She stood before him for an instant, looking at him strangely. Then, suddenly raising herself on tiptoe and resting her hands lightly on his shoulders, she kissed him.

"You are a very generous person, Gabriel," she said.   395

Gabriel, trembling with delight at her sudden kiss and at the quaintness of her phrase, put his hands on her hair and began smoothing it back, scarcely touching it with his fingers. The washing had made it fine and brilliant. His heart was brimming over with happiness. Just when he was wishing for it she had come to him of her own accord. Perhaps her thoughts had been running with his. Perhaps she had felt the impetuous desire that was in him, and then the yielding mood had come upon her. Now that she had fallen to him so easily, he wondered why he had been so diffident.

He stood, holding her head between his hands. Then, slipping one arm swiftly about her body and drawing her towards him, he said softly:

"Gretta, dear, what are you thinking about?"

She did not answer nor yield wholly to his arm. He said again, softly:

"Tell me what it is, Gretta. I think I know what is the matter. Do I   400
know?"

She did not answer at once. Then she said in an outburst of tears:

"O, I am thinking about that song, The Lass of Aughrim."

She broke loose from him and ran to the bed and, throwing her arms across the bed-rail, hid her face. Gabriel stood stock-still for a moment in astonishment and then followed her. As he passed in the way of the cheval-glass he caught sight of himself in full length, his broad, well-filled shirt-front, the face whose expression always puzzled him when he saw it in a mirror, and his glimmering gilt-rimmed eyeglasses. He halted a few paces from her and said:

"What about the song? Why does that make you cry?"

She raised her head from her arms and dried her eyes with the back of   405
her hand like a child. A kinder note than he had intended went into his voice.

"Why, Gretta?" he asked.

"I am thinking about a person long ago who used to sing that song."

"And who was the person long ago?" asked Gabriel, smiling.

"It was a person I used to know in Galway when I was living with my grandmother," she said.

The smile passed away from Gabriel's face. A dull anger began to   410
gather again at the back of his mind and the dull fires of his lust began to glow angrily in his veins.

"Someone you were in love with?" he asked ironically.

"It was a young boy I used to know," she answered, "named Michael Furey. He used to sing that song, The Lass of Aughrim. He was very delicate."

Gabriel was silent. He did not wish her to think that he was interested in this delicate boy.

"I can see him so plainly," she said, after a moment. "Such eyes as he had: big, dark eyes! And such an expression in them—an expression!"

"O, then, you are in love with him?" said Gabriel.   415

"I used to go out walking with him," she said, "when I was in Galway."

A thought flew across Gabriel's mind.

"Perhaps that was why you wanted to go to Galway with that Ivors girl?" he said coldly.

She looked at him and asked in surprise:

"What for?"   420

Her eyes made Gabriel feel awkward. He shrugged his shoulders and said:

"How do I know? To see him, perhaps."

She looked away from him along the shaft of light towards the window in silence.

"He is dead," she said at length. "He died when he was only seventeen. Isn't it a terrible thing to die so young as that?"

"What was he?" asked Gabriel, still ironically.   425

"He was in the gasworks," she said.

Gabriel felt humiliated by the failure of his irony and by the evocation of this figure from the dead, a boy in the gasworks. While he had been full of memories of their secret life together, full of tenderness and joy and desire, she had been comparing him in her mind with another. A shameful consciousness of his own person assailed him. He saw himself as a ludicrous figure, acting as a pennyboy for his aunts, a nervous, well-meaning sentimentalist, orating to vulgarians and idealising his own clownish lusts, the pitiable fatuous fellow he had caught a glimpse of in the mirror. Instinctively he turned his back more to the light lest she might see the shame that burned upon his forehead.

He tried to keep up his tone of cold interrogation, but his voice when he spoke was humble and indifferent.

"I suppose you were in love with this Michael Furey, Gretta," he said.

"I was great with him at that time," she said.   430

Her voice was veiled and sad. Gabriel, feeling now how vain it would be to try to lead her whither he had purposed, caressed one of her hands and said, also sadly:

"And what did he die of so young, Gretta? Consumption, was it?"

"I think he died for me," she answered.

A vague terror seized Gabriel at this answer, as if, at that hour when he had hoped to triumph, some impalpable and vindictive being was coming against him, gathering forces against him in its vague world. But he shook himself free of it with an effort of reason and continued to caress her hand. He did not question her again, for he felt that she would tell him of herself. Her hand was warm and moist: it did not respond to his touch, but he continued to caress it just as he had caressed her first letter to him that spring morning.

"It was in the winter," she said, "about the beginning of the winter 435 when I was going to leave my grandmother's and come up here to the convent. And he was ill at the time in his lodgings in Galway and wouldn't be let out, and his people in Oughterard were written to. He was in decline, they said, or something like that. I never knew rightly."

She paused for a moment and sighed.

"Poor fellow," she said. "He was very fond of me and he was such a gentle boy. We used to go out together, walking, you know, Gabriel, like the way they do in the country. He was going to study singing only for his health. He had a very good voice, poor Michael Furey."

"Well; and then?" asked Gabriel.

"And then when it came to the time for me to leave Galway and come up to the convent he was much worse and I wouldn't be let see him so I wrote him a letter saying I was going up to Dublin and would be back in the summer, and hoping he would be better then."

She paused for a moment to get her voice under control, and then 440 went on:

"Then the night before I left, I was in my grandmother's house in Nuns' Island, packing up, and I heard gravel thrown up against the window. The window was so wet I couldn't see, so I ran downstairs as I was and slipped out the back into the garden and there was the poor fellow at the end of the garden, shivering."

"And did you not tell him to go back?" asked Gabriel.

"I implored of him to go home at once and told him he would get his death in the rain. But he said he did not want to live. I can see his eyes as well as well! He was standing at the end of the wall where there was a tree."

"And did he go home?" asked Gabriel.

"Yes, he went home. And when I was only a week in the convent he 445 died and he was buried in Oughterard, where his people came from. O, the day I heard that, that he was dead!"

She stopped, choking with sobs, and, overcome by emotion, flung herself face downward on the bed, sobbing in the quilt. Gabriel held her hand for a moment longer, irresolutely, and then, shy of intruding on her grief, let it fall gently and walked quietly to the window.

She was fast asleep.

Gabriel, leaning on his elbow, looked for a few moments unresentfully on her tangled hair and half-open mouth, listening to her deep-drawn breath. So she had had that romance in her life: a man had died for her sake. It hardly pained him now to think how poor a part he, her husband, had played in her life. He watched her while she slept, as though he and she had never lived together as man and wife. His curious eyes rested long upon her face and on her hair: and, as he thought of what she must have been then, in that time of her first girlish beauty, a strange, friendly pity for her entered his soul. He did not like to say even to himself that her face was no longer beautiful, but he knew that it was no longer the face for which Michael Furey had braved death.

Perhaps she had not told him all the story. His eyes moved to the chair over which she had thrown some of her clothes. A petticoat string dangled to the floor. One boot stood upright, its limp upper fallen down: the fellow of it lay upon its side. He wondered at his riot of emotions of an hour before. From what had it proceeded? From his aunt's supper, from his own foolish speech, from the wine and dancing, the merry-making when saying good-night in the hall, the pleasure of the walk along the river in the snow. Poor Aunt Julia! She, too, would soon be a shade with the shade of Patrick Morkan and his horse. He had caught that haggard look upon her face for a moment when she was singing Arrayed for the Bridal. Soon, perhaps, he would be sitting in that same drawing-room, dressed in black, his silk hat on his knees. The blinds would be drawn down and Aunt Kate would be sitting beside him, crying and blowing her nose and telling him how Julia had died. He would cast about in his mind for some words that might console her, and would find only lame and useless ones. Yes, yes: that would happen very soon.

The air of the room chilled his shoulders. He stretched himself cautiously along under the sheets and lay down beside his wife. One by one, they were all becoming shades. Better pass boldly into that other world, in the full glory of some passion, than fade and wither dismally with age. He thought of how she who lay beside him had locked in her heart for so many years that image of her lover's eyes when he had told her that he did not wish to live. 450

Generous tears filled Gabriel's eyes. He had never felt like that himself towards any woman, but he knew that such a feeling must be love. The tears gathered more thickly in his eyes and in the partial darkness he imagined he saw the form of a young man standing under a dripping tree. Other forms were near. His soul had approached that region where dwell the vast hosts of the dead. He was conscious of, but could not apprehend, their wayward and flickering existence. His own identity was fading out into a grey impalpable world: the solid world itself, which these dead had one time reared and lived in, was dissolving and dwindling.

A few light taps upon the pane made him turn to the window. It had begun to snow again. He watched sleepily the flakes, silver and dark, falling obliquely against the lamplight. The time had come for him to set out on his journey westward. Yes, the newspapers were right: snow was general all over Ireland. It was falling on every part of the dark central plain, on the treeless hills, falling softly upon the Bog of Allen and, farther westward, softly falling into the dark mutinous Shannon waves. It was falling, too, upon every part of the lonely churchyard on the hill where Michael Furey lay buried. It lay thickly drifted on the crooked crosses and headstones, on the spears of the little gate, on the barren thorns. His soul swooned slowly as he heard the snow falling faintly through the universe and faintly falling, like the descent of their last end, upon all the living and the dead.

- How does Gabriel Conroy construct his own reality throughout this party? What indications do we get that others do not share his perception? How do other texts shape Gabriel's consciousness of his world?

- Look at Gabriel's speech at dinner—how has that speech developed over the course of the evening?

- Trace the various places where musical pieces shape events at the party.

- In what different ways does Gabriel travel through time within the story?

- Compare the snow at the end of this story to the snow in Crowley's story.

Ray Bradbury (1920–2012)

Born in Illinois, Ray Bradbury eventually settled in Los Angeles. He was an avid reader as a youth. Bradbury published his first science fiction story in 1938 and wrote prolifically for the rest of his life, writing 27 novels and over 600 short stories. He claimed that his only work of science fiction was his novel *Farenheit 451* (1953), about a future in which all books are burned, and that his other works, such as *Martin Chronicles* (1950), a series of stories about human civilization on Mars, were works of mythology.

A Sound of Thunder (1952)

The sign on the wall seemed to quaver under a film of sliding warm water. Eckels felt his eyelids blink over his stare, and the sign burned in this momentary darkness:

TIME SAFARI, INC.
SAFARIS TO ANY YEAR IN THE PAST.

YOU NAME THE ANIMAL.
WE TAKE YOU THERE.
YOU SHOOT IT.

Warm phlegm gathered in Eckels' throat; he swallowed and pushed it
down. The muscles around his mouth formed a smile as he put his hand
slowly out upon the air, and in that hand waved a check for ten thousand
dollars to the man behind the desk.

"Does this safari guarantee I come back alive?"

"We guarantee nothing", said the official, "except the dinosaurs." He
turned. "This is Mr. Travis, your Safari Guide in the Past. He'll tell you
what and where to shoot. If he says no shooting, no shooting. If you disobey
instructions, there's a stiff penalty of another ten thousand dollars, plus possible government action, on your return."

Eckels glanced across the vast office at a mass and tangle, a snaking and   5
humming of wires and steel boxes, at an aurora that flickered now orange,
now silver, now blue. There was a sound like a gigantic bonfire burning all of
Time, all the years and all the parchment calendars, all the hours piled high
and set aflame.

A touch of the hand and this burning would, on the instant, beautifully reverse itself. Eckels remembered the wording in the advertisements
to the letter. Out of chars and ashes, out of dust and coals, like golden
salamanders, the old years, the green years, might leap; roses sweeten the air,
white hair turn Irish-black, wrinkles vanish; all, everything fly back to seed,
flee death, rush down to their beginnings, suns rise in western skies and
set in glorious easts, moons eat themselves opposite to the custom, all and
everything cupping one in another like Chinese boxes, rabbits into hats, all
and everything returning to the fresh death, the seed death, the green death,
to the time before the beginning. A touch of a hand might do it, the merest
touch of a hand.

"Unbelievable." Eckels breathed, the light of the Machine on his thin
face. "A real Time Machine". He shook his head. "Makes you think, If
the election had gone badly yesterday, I might be here now running away
from the results. Thank God Keith won. He'll make a fine President of the
United States."

"Yes," said the man behind the desk. "We're lucky. If Deutscher had
gotten in, we'd have the worst kind of dictatorship. There's an anti everything man for you, a militarist, anti-Christ, anti-human, anti-intellectual.
People called us up, you know, joking but not joking. Said if Deutscher
became President they wanted to go live in 1492. Of course it's not our
business to conduct Escapes, but to form Safaris. Anyway, Keith's President
now. All you got to worry about is—"

"Shooting my dinosaur," Eckels finished it for him.

"A Tyrannosaurus Rex. The Tyrant Lizard, the most incredible monster   10
in history. Sign this release. Anything happens to you, we're not responsible.
Those dinosaurs are hungry."

Eckels flushed angrily. "Trying to scare me!"

"Frankly, yes. We don't want anyone going who'll panic at the first
shot. Six Safari leaders were killed last year, and a dozen hunters. We're here
to give you the severest thrill a real hunter ever asked for. Traveling you back
sixty million years to bag the biggest game in all of Time. Your personal
check's still there. Tear it up." Mr. Eckels looked at the check. His fingers
twitched.

"Good luck," said the man behind the desk. "Mr. Travis, he's all
yours."

They moved silently across the room, taking their guns with them,
toward the Machine, toward the silver metal and the roaring light.

First a day and then a night and then a day and then a night, then it   15
was day-night-day-night. A week, a month, a year, a decade! A.D. 2055. A.D.
2019. 1999! 1957! Gone! The Machine roared.

They put on their oxygen helmets and tested the intercoms.

Eckels swayed on the padded seat, his face pale, his jaw stiff. He felt
the trembling in his arms and he looked down and found his hands tight
on the new rifle. There were four other men in the Machine. Travis, the
Safari Leader, his assistant, Lesperance, and two other hunters, Billings
and Kramer. They sat looking at each other, and the years blazed around
them.

"Can these guns get a dinosaur cold?" Eckels felt his mouth saying.

"If you hit them right," said Travis on the helmet radio. "Some dinosaurs have two brains, one in the head, another far down the spinal column.
We stay away from those. That's stretching luck. Put your first two shots into
the eyes, if you can, blind them, and go back into the brain."

The Machine howled. Time was a film run backward. Suns fled and   20
ten million moons fled after them. "Think," said Eckels. "Every hunter
that ever lived would envy us today. This makes Africa seem like Illinois."

The Machine slowed; its scream fell to a murmur. The Machine
stopped.

The sun stopped in the sky.

The fog that had enveloped the Machine blew away and they were in an
old time, a very old time indeed, three hunters and two Safari Heads with
their blue metal guns across their knees.

"Christ isn't born yet," said Travis, "Moses has not gone to the mountains to talk with God. The Pyramids are still in the earth, waiting to be
cut out and put up. Remember that. Alexander, Caesar, Napoleon, Hitler—
none of them exists.'" The man nodded.

"That"—Mr. Travis pointed—"is the jungle of sixty million two thousand 25 and fifty-five years before President Keith."

He indicated a metal path that struck off into green wilderness, over streaming swamp, among giant ferns and palms.

"And that," he said, "is the Path, laid by Time Safari for your use."

It floats six inches above the earth. Doesn't touch so much as one grass blade, flower, or tree. It's an anti-gravity metal. Its purpose is to keep you from touching this world of the past in any way. Stay on the Path. Don't go off it. I repeat. Don't go off. For any reason! If you fall off, there's a penalty. And don't shoot any animal we don't okay."

"Why?" asked Eckels.

They sat in the ancient wilderness. Far birds' cries blew on a wind, and 30 the smell of tar and an old salt sea, moist grasses, and flowers the color of blood.

"We don't want to change the Future. We don't belong here in the Past. The government doesn't like us here. We have to pay big graft to keep our franchise. A Time Machine is finicky business. Not knowing it, we might kill an important animal, a small bird, a roach, a flower even, thus destroying an important link in a growing species."

"That's not clear," said Eckels.

"All right," Travis continued, "say we accidentally kill one mouse here. That means all the future families of this one particular mouse are destroyed, right?"

"Right."

"And all the families of the families of the families of that one mouse! 35 With a stamp of your foot, you annihilate first one, then a dozen, then a thousand, a million, a billion possible mice!"

"So they're dead," said Eckels. "So what?"

"So what?" Travis snorted quietly. "Well, what about the foxes that'll need those mice to survive? For want of ten mice, a fox dies. For want of ten foxes a lion starves. For want of a lion, all manner of insects, vultures, infinite billions of life forms are thrown into chaos and destruction. Eventually it all boils down to this: fifty-nine million years later, a caveman, one of a dozen on the entire world, goes hunting wild boar or saber-toothed tiger for food. But you, friend, have stepped on all the tigers in that region. By stepping on one single mouse. So the caveman starves. And the caveman, please note, is not just any expendable man, no! He is an entire future nation. From his loins would have sprung ten sons. From their loins one hundred sons, and thus onward to a civilization. Destroy this one man, and you destroy a race, a people, an entire history of life. It is comparable to slaying some of Adam's grandchildren. The stomp of your foot, on one mouse, could start an earthquake, the effects of which could shake our earth and destinies down through Time, to their very foundations. With the death of that one caveman, a billion others yet unborn are throttled in the womb. Perhaps Rome never rises on its seven hills. Perhaps Europe is forever a dark forest, and only Asia waxes healthy and teeming. Step on a mouse and you crush the Pyramids. Step on a mouse and you leave your print, like a Grand Canyon, across Eternity. Queen Elizabeth might never be born, Washington might not cross the Delaware, there might never be a United States at all. So be careful. Stay on the Path. Never step off!"

"I see," said Eckels. "Then it wouldn't pay for us even to touch the grass?"

"Correct. Crushing certain plants could add up infinitesimally. A little error here would multiply in sixty million years, all out of proportion. Of course maybe our theory is wrong. Maybe Time can't be changed by us. Or maybe it can be changed only in little subtle ways. A dead mouse here makes an insect imbalance there, a population disproportion later, a bad harvest further on, a depression, mass starvation, and finally, a change in social temperament in far-flung countries. Something much more subtle, like that. Perhaps only a soft breath, a whisper, a hair, pollen on the air, such a slight, slight change that unless you looked close you wouldn't see it. Who knows? Who really can say he knows? We don't know. We're guessing. But until we do know for certain whether our messing around in Time can make a big roar or a little rustle in history, we're being careful. This Machine, this Path, your clothing and bodies, were sterilized, as you know, before the journey. We wear these oxygen helmets so we can't introduce our bacteria into an ancient atmosphere."

"How do we know which animals to shoot?"

40

"They're marked with red paint," said Travis. "Today, before our journey, we sent Lesperance here back with the Machine. He came to this particular era and followed certain animals."

"Studying them?"

"Right," said Lesperance. "I track them through their entire existence, noting which of them lives longest. Very few. How many times they mate. Not often. Life's short, When I find one that's going to die when a tree falls on him, or one that drowns in a tar pit, I note the exact hour, minute, and second. I shoot a paint bomb. It leaves a red patch on his side. We can't miss it. Then I correlate our arrival in the Past so that we meet the Monster not more than two minutes before he would have died anyway. This way, we kill only animals with no future, that are never going to mate again. You see how careful we are?"

"But if you come back this morning in Time," said Eckels eagerly, you must've bumped into us, our Safari! How did it turn out? Was it successful? Did all of us get through-alive?"

Travis and Lesperance gave each other a look. 45

"That'd be a paradox," said the latter. "Time doesn't permit that sort of mess—a man meeting himself. When such occasions threaten, Time steps aside. Like an airplane hitting an air pocket. You felt the Machine jump just before we stopped? That was us passing ourselves on the way back to the Future. We saw nothing. There's no way of telling if this expedition was a success, if we got our monster, or whether all of us—meaning you, Mr. Eckels—got out alive."

Eckels smiled palely.

"Cut that," said Travis sharply. "Everyone on his feet!"

They were ready to leave the Machine.

The jungle was high and the jungle was broad and the jungle was the 50 entire world forever and forever. Sounds like music and sounds like flying tents filled the sky, and those were pterodactyls soaring with cavernous gray wings, gigantic bats of delirium and night fever.

Eckels, balanced on the narrow Path, aimed his rifle playfully.

"Stop that!" said Travis. "Don't even aim for fun, blast you! If your guns should go off—"

Eckels flushed. "Where's our Tyrannosaurus?"

Lesperance checked his wristwatch. "Up ahead, We'll bisect his trail in sixty seconds. Look for the red paint! Don't shoot till we give the word. Stay on the Path. Stay on the Path!"

They moved forward in the wind of morning. 55

"Strange," murmured Eckels. "Up ahead, sixty million years, Election Day over. Keith made President. Everyone celebrating. And here we are, a million years lost, and they don't exist. The things we worried about for months, a lifetime, not even born or thought of yet."

"Safety catches off, everyone!" ordered Travis. "You, first shot, Eckels. Second, Billings, Third, Kramer."

"I've hunted tiger, wild boar, buffalo, elephant, but now, this is it," said Eckels. "I'm shaking like a kid."

"Ah," said Travis.

Everyone stopped. 60

Travis raised his hand. "Ahead," he whispered. "In the mist. There he is. There's His Royal Majesty now."

The jungle was wide and full of twitterings, rustlings, murmurs, and sighs.

Suddenly it all ceased, as if someone had shut a door.

Silence.

A sound of thunder. 65

Out of the mist, one hundred yards away, came Tyrannosaurus Rex.

"It," whispered Eckels. "It . . .

"Sh!"

It came on great oiled, resilient, striding legs. It towered thirty feet above half of the trees, a great evil god, folding its delicate watchmaker's claws close to its oily reptilian chest. Each lower leg was a piston, a thousand pounds of white bone, sunk in thick ropes of muscle, sheathed over in a gleam of pebbled skin like the mail of a terrible warrior. Each thigh was a ton of meat, ivory, and steel mesh. And from the great breathing cage of the upper body those two delicate arms dangled out front, arms with hands which might pick up and examine men like toys, while the snake neck coiled. And the head itself, a ton of sculptured stone, lifted easily upon the sky. Its mouth gaped, exposing a fence of teeth like daggers. Its eyes rolled, ostrich eggs, empty of all expression save hunger. It closed its mouth in a death grin. It ran, its pelvic bones crushing aside trees and bushes, its taloned feet clawing damp earth, leaving prints six inches deep wherever it settled its weight.

It ran with a gliding ballet step, far too poised and balanced for its ten   70
tons. It moved into a sunlit area warily, its beautifully reptilian hands feeling the air.

"Why, why," Eckels twitched his mouth. "It could reach up and grab the moon."

"Sh!" Travis jerked angrily. "He hasn't seen us yet."

"It can't be killed," Eckels pronounced this verdict quietly, as if there could be no argument. He had weighed the evidence and this was his considered opinion. The rifle in his hands seemed a cap gun. "We were fools to come. This is impossible."

"Shut up!" hissed Travis.

"Nightmare."   75

"Turn around," commanded Travis. "Walk quietly to the Machine. We'll remit half your fee."

"I didn't realize it would be this big," said Eckels. "I miscalculated, that's all. And now I want out."

"It sees us!"

"There's the red paint on its chest!"

The Tyrant Lizard raised itself. Its armored flesh glittered like a thou-   80
sand green coins. The coins, crusted with slime, steamed. In the slime, tiny insects wriggled, so that the entire body seemed to twitch and undulate, even while the monster itself did not move. It exhaled. The stink of raw flesh blew down the wilderness.

"Get me out of here," said Eckels. "It was never like this before. I was always sure I'd come through alive. I had good guides, good safaris, and safety. This time, I figured wrong. I've met my match and admit it. This is too much for me to get hold of."

"Don't run," said Lesperance. "Turn around. Hide in the Machine."

"Yes." Eckels seemed to be numb. He looked at his feet as if trying to make them move. He gave a grunt of helplessness.

"Eckels!"

He took a few steps, blinking, shuffling.   85

"Not that way!"

The Monster, at the first motion, lunged forward with a terrible scream. It covered one hundred yards in six seconds. The rifles jerked up and blazed fire. A windstorm from the beast's mouth engulfed them in the stench of slime and old blood. The Monster roared, teeth glittering with sun.

The rifles cracked again, Their sound was lost in shriek and lizard thunder. The great level of the reptile's tail swung up, lashed sideways. Trees exploded in clouds of leaf and branch. The Monster twitched its jeweler's hands down to fondle at the men, to twist them in half, to crush them like berries, to cram them into its teeth and its screaming throat. Its boulder-stone eyes leveled with the men. They saw themselves mirrored. They fired at the metallic eyelids and the blazing black iris.

Like a stone idol, like a mountain avalanche, Tyrannosaurus fell.

Thundering, it clutched trees, pulled them with it. It wrenched and   90 tore the metal Path. The men flung themselves back and away. The body hit, ten tons of cold flesh and stone. The guns fired. The Monster lashed its armored tail, twitched its snake jaws, and lay still. A fount of blood spurted from its throat. Somewhere inside, a sac of fluids burst. Sickening gushes drenched the hunters. They stood, red and glistening.

The thunder faded.

The jungle was silent. After the avalanche, a green peace. After the nightmare, morning.

Billings and Kramer sat on the pathway and threw up. Travis and Lesperance stood with smoking rifles, cursing steadily. In the Time Machine, on his face, Eckels lay shivering. He had found his way back to the Path, climbed into the Machine.

Travis came walking, glanced at Eckels, took cotton gauze from a metal box, and returned to the others, who were sitting on the Path.

"Clean up."   95

They wiped the blood from their helmets. They began to curse too.

The Monster lay, a hill of solid flesh. Within, you could hear the sighs and murmurs as the furthest chambers of it died, the organs malfunctioning, liquids running a final instant from pocket to sac to spleen, everything shutting off, closing up forever. It was like standing by a wrecked locomotive or a steam shovel at quitting time, all valves being released or levered tight. Bones cracked; the tonnage of its own flesh, off balance, dead weight, snapped the delicate forearms, caught underneath. The meat settled, quivering.

Another cracking sound. Overhead, a gigantic tree branch broke from its heavy mooring, fell. It crashed upon the dead beast with finality.

"There." Lesperance checked his watch. "Right on time. That's the giant tree that was scheduled to fall and kill this animal originally." He glanced at the two hunters. "You want the trophy picture?"

"What?"   100

"We can't take a trophy back to the Future. The body has to stay right here where it would have died originally, so the insects, birds, and bacteria can get at it, as they were intended to. Everything in balance. The body stays. But we can take a picture of you standing near it."

The two men tried to think, but gave up, shaking their heads.

They let themselves be led along the metal Path. They sank wearily into the Machine cushions. They gazed back at the ruined Monster, the stagnating mound, where already strange reptilian birds and golden insects were busy at the steaming armor. A sound on the floor of the Time Machine stiffened them. Eckels sat there, shivering.

"I'm sorry," he said at last.

"Get up!" cried Travis.   105

Eckels got up.

"Go out on that Path alone," said Travis. He had his rifle pointed, "You're not coming back in the Machine. We're leaving you here!"

Lesperance seized Travis's arm. "Wait—"

"Stay out of this!" Travis shook his hand away. "This fool nearly killed us. But it isn't that so much, no. It's his shoes! Look at them! He ran off the Path. That ruins us! We'll forfeit! Thousands of dollars of insurance! We guarantee no one leaves the Path. He left it. Oh, the fool! I'll have to report to the government. They might revoke our license to travel. Who knows what he's done to Time, to History!"

"Take it easy, all he did was kick up some dirt."   110

"How do we know?" cried Travis. "We don't know anything! It's all a mystery! Get out of here, Eckels!"

Eckels fumbled his shirt. "I'll pay anything. A hundred thousand dollars!"

Travis glared at Eckels' checkbook and spat. "Go out there. The Monster's next to the Path. Stick your arms up to your elbows in his mouth. Then you can come back with us."

"That's unreasonable!"

"The Monster's dead, you idiot. The bullets! The bullets can't be left   115
behind. They don't belong in the Past; they might change anything. Here's my knife. Dig them out!"

The jungle was alive again, full of the old tremorings and bird cries. Eckels turned slowly to regard the primeval garbage dump, that hill of nightmares and terror. After a long time, like a sleepwalker he shuffled out along the Path.

He returned, shuddering, five minutes later, his arms soaked and red
to the elbows. He held out his hands. Each held a number of steel bullets.
Then he fell. He lay where he fell, not moving.

"You didn't have to make him do that," said Lesperance.

"Didn't I? It's too early to tell." Travis nudged the still body. "He'll live. 120
Next time he won't go hunting game like this. Okay." He jerked his thumb
wearily at Lesperance. "Switch on. Let's go home."

1492. 1776. 1812.

They cleaned their hands and faces. They changed their caking shirts
and pants. Eckels was up and around again, not speaking. Travis glared at
him for a full ten minutes.

"Don't look at me," cried Eckels. "I haven't done anything."

"Who can tell?"

"Just ran off the Path, that's all, a little mud on my shoes—what do you 125
want me to do—get down and pray?"

"We might need it. I'm warning you, Eckels, I might kill you yet. I've
got my gun ready."

"I'm innocent. I've done nothing!"

1999. 2000. 2055.

The Machine stopped.

"Get out," said Travis. 130

The room was there as they had left it. But not the same as they had
left it. The same man sat behind the same desk. But the same man did not
quite sit behind the same desk. Travis looked around swiftly. "Everything
okay here?" he snapped.

"Fine. Welcome home!"

Travis did not relax. He seemed to be looking through the one high
window.

"Okay, Eckels, get out. Don't ever come back." Eckels could not move.

"You heard me," said Travis. "What're you staring at?" 135

Eckels stood smelling of the air, and there was a thing to the air, a
chemical taint so subtle, so slight, that only a faint cry of his subliminal
senses warned him it was there. The colors, white, gray, blue, orange, in the
wall, in the furniture, in the sky beyond the window, were...were....And
there was a feel. His flesh twitched. His hands twitched. He stood drinking
the oddness with the pores of his body. Somewhere, someone must have
been screaming one of those whistles that only a dog can hear. His body
screamed silence in return. Beyond this room, beyond this wall, beyond
this man who was not quite the same man seated at this desk that was not
quite the same desk...lay an entire world of streets and people. What sort
of world it was now, there was no telling. He could feel them moving there,
beyond the walls, almost, like so many chess pieces blown in a dry wind....

But the immediate thing was the sign painted on the office wall, the same sign he had read earlier today on first entering. Somehow, the sign had changed:

TYME SEFARI INC.
SEFARIS TU ANY YEER EN THE PAST.
YU NAIM THE ANIMALL.
WEE TAEK YU THAIR.
YU SHOOT ITT.

Eckels felt himself fall into a chair. He fumbled crazily at the thick slime on his boots. He held up a clod of dirt, trembling, "No, it can't be. Not a little thing like that. No!"

Embedded in the mud, glistening green and gold and black, was a butterfly, very beautiful and very dead.

"Not a little thing like that! Not a butterfly!" cried Eckels.   140

It fell to the floor, an exquisite thing, a small thing that could upset balances and knock down a line of small dominoes and then big dominoes and then gigantic dominoes, all down the years across Time. Eckels' mind whirled. It couldn't change things. Killing one butterfly couldn't be that important! Could it?

His face was cold. His mouth trembled, asking: "Who—who won the presidential election yesterday?"

The man behind the desk laughed. "You joking? You know very well. Deutscher, of course! Who else? Not that fool weakling Keith. We got an iron man now, a man with guts!" "The official stopped. What's wrong?"

Eckels moaned. He dropped to his knees. He scrabbled at the golden butterfly with shaking fingers. "Can't we," he pleaded to the world, to himself, to the officials, to the Machine, "can't we take it back, can't we make it alive again? Can't we start over? Can't we—"

He did not move. Eyes shut, he waited, shivering. He heard Travis   145
breathe loud in the room; he heard Travis shift his rifle, click the safety catch, and raise the weapon.

There was a sound of thunder.

- What rules are established to govern this story of time travel? How are these rules presented in the story? Where are these rules violated? Think about the form of this story—would you describe it as a parable? What are the benefits and limits of such a classification?

- Compare this story to the mythic structure of the Orpheus story. What elements of this story emerge as you make this comparison? What elements of the story do you neglect with this comparison?

POETRY

Amy Clampitt (1920–1994)

The Dakota (1983)

Grief for a generation—all
the lonely people
gone, the riffraff
out there now mainly pigeons—
steps from its limousine   5
and lights a taper
inside the brownstone catacomb
of the Dakota. Pick up
the wedding rice, take out
the face left over from   10
the funeral nobody came to,
bring flowers, leave them woven
with the lugubrious ironwork
of the Dakota. Grief
is original, but it   15
repeats itself: there is nothing
more original it can do.

- How is the allegorical figure of Grief presented in this poem?
- How can we resolve the apparent contradiction in the final lines of the poem?

Czeslaw Milosz (1911–2004)

Orpheus and Eurydice (2004)

Standing on flagstones of the sidewalk at the entrance to Hades
Orpheus hunched in a gust of wind
That tore at his coat, rolled past in waves of fog,
Tossed the leaves of the trees. The headlights of cars
Flared and dimmed in each succeeding wave.   5

He stopped at the glass-paneled door, uncertain
Whether he was strong enough for that ultimate trial.

He remembered her words: "You are a good man."
He did not quite believe it. Lyric poets
Usually have—as he knew—cold hearts.   10
It is like a medical condition. Perfection in art
Is given in exchange for such an affliction.
Only her love warmed him, humanized him.
When he was with her, he thought differently about himself.
He could not fail her now, when she was dead.   15

He pushed open the door and found himself walking in a labyrinth,
Corridors, elevators. The livid light was not light but the dark of the earth.
Electronic dogs passed him noiselessly.
He descended many floors, a hundred, three hundred, down.

He was cold, aware that he was Nowhere.   20
Under thousands of frozen centuries,
On an ashy trace where generations had moldered,
In a kingdom that seemed to have no bottom and no end.

Thronging shadows surrounded him.
He recognized some of the faces.   25
He felt the rhythm of his blood.

He felt strongly his life with its guilt
And he was afraid to meet those to whom he had done harm.
But they had lost the ability to remember
And gave him only a glance, indifferent to all that.   30

For his defense he had a nine-stringed lyre.
He carried in it the music of the earth, against the abyss
That buries all of sound in silence.
He submitted the music, yielded
To the dictation of a song, listening with rapt attention,   35
Became, like his lyre, its instrument.

Thus he arrived at the palace of the rulers of that land.
Persephone, in her garden of withered pear and apple trees,
Black, with naked branches and verrucose twigs,
Listened from the funereal amethyst of her throne.   40

He sang the brightness of mornings and green rivers,
He sang of smoking water in the rose-colored daybreaks,
Of colors: cinnabar, carmine, burnt sienna, blue,
Of the delight of swimming in the sea under marble cliffs,
Of feasting on a terrace above the tumult of a fishing port,   45

Of the tastes of wine, olive oil, almonds, mustard, salt.
Of the flight of the swallow, the falcon,
Of a dignified flock of pelicans above a bay,
Of the scent of an armful of lilacs in summer rain,
Of his having composed his words always against death   50
And of having made no rhyme in praise of nothingness.

I don't know—said the goddess—whether you loved her or not.
Yet you have come here to rescue her.
She will be returned to you. But there are conditions:
You are not permitted to speak to her, or on the journey back   55
To turn your head, even once, to assure yourself that she is behind you.
And so Hermes brought forth Eurydice.
Her face no longer hers, utterly gray,
Her eyelids lowered beneath the shade of her lashes.
She stepped rigidly, directed by the hand   60
Of her guide. Orpheus wanted so much
To call her name, to wake her from that sleep.
But he refrained, for he had accepted the conditions.

And so they set out. He first, and then, not right away,
The slap of the god's sandals and the light patter   65
Of her feet fettered by her robe, as if by a shroud.
A steep climbing path phosphorized
Out of darkness like the walls of a tunnel.
He would stop and listen. But then
They stopped too, and the echo faded.   70
And when he began to walk the double tapping commenced again.
Sometimes it seemed closer, sometimes more distant.
Under his faith a doubt sprang up
And entwined him like cold bindweed.
Unable to weep, he wept at the loss   75
Of the human hope for the resurrection of the dead,
Because he was, now, like every other mortal.
His lyre was silent, yet he dreamed, defenseless.
He knew he must have faith and he could not have faith.
And so he would persist for a very long time,   80
Counting his steps in, a half-wakeful torpor.

Day was breaking. Shapes of rock loomed up
Under the luminous eye of the exit from underground.
It happened as he expected. He turned his head
And behind him on the path was no one.   85

Sun. And sky. And in the sky white clouds.
Only now everything cried to him: Eurydice!
How will I live without you, my consoling one!
But there was a fragrant scent of herbs, the low humming of bees,
And he fell asleep with his cheek on the sun-warmed earth.   90

- Trace the different sensory images throughout the poem.
- How does the poet modernize the descent into the underworld?
- How does the narrator justify the turning of the head?

Adrienne Rich (1929–   )

I Dream I'm the Death of Orpheus (1968)

I am walking rapidly through striations of light and dark thrown
under

an arcade.

I am a woman in the prime of life, with certain powers
and those powers severely limited
by authorities whose faces I rarely see.
I am a woman in the prime of life   5
driving her dead poet in a black Rolls-Royce
through a landscape of twilight and thorns.
A woman with a certain mission
which if obeyed to the letter will leave her intact.
A woman with the nerves of a panther   10
a woman with contacts among Hell's Angels
a woman feeling the fullness of her powers
at the precise moment when she must not use them
a woman sworn to lucidity
who sees through the mayhem, the smoky fires   15
of those underground streets
her dead poet learning to walk backward against the wind
on the wrong side of the mirror

- In what ways is the dead poet on the "wrong side of the mirror"?
- How does the narrator's voice contrast with that of "Death"? How does her "certain mission" relate to the Orpheus and Eurydice story?

Robert Pinsky (1940–   )

Keyboard (2003)

A disembodied piano. The headphones allow
The one who touches the keys a solitude
Inside his music; shout and he may not turn:

Image of the soul that thinks to turn from the world.
Serpent-scaled Apollo skins the naïve musician   5
Alive: then Marsyas was sensitive enough

To feel the world in a touch. In Africa
The raiders with machetes to cut off hands
Might make the victim choose, "long sleeve or short."

Shahid Ali says it happened to Kashmiri weavers,   10
To kill the art. There are only so many stories.
The Loss. The Chosen. And even before The Journey,

The Turning: the fruit from any tree, the door
To any chamber, but this one—and the greedy soul,
Blade of the lathe. The Red Army smashed pianos,   15

But once they caught an S.S. man who could play.
They sat him at the piano and pulled their fingers
Across their throats to explain that they would kill him

When he stopped playing, and so for sixteen hours
They drank and raped while the Nazi fingered the keys.   20
The great Song of the World. When he collapsed

Sobbing at the instrument they stroked his head
And blew his brains out. Cold-blooded Orpheus turns
Again to his keyboard to improvise a plaint:

Her little cries of pleasure, blah-blah, the place   25
Behind her ear, lilacs in rain, a sus chord,
A phrase like a moonlit moth in tentative flight,

O lost Eurydice, blah-blah. His archaic head
Kept singing after the body was torn away:
Body, old long companion, supporter—the mist   30

Of oranges, la-la-la, the smell of almonds,
The taste of olives, her woollen skirt. The great old
Poet said, What should we wear for the reading—necktie?

Or better no necktie, turtleneck? The head
Afloat turns toward Apollo to sing and Apollo,   35
The cool-eyed rainbow lizard, plies the keys.

■ How does the poem justify its final symbol of Apollo, the god of music, as a
"cooleyed rainbow lizard"? What relations does it draw between music and
death?

William Butler Yeats (1865–1939)

Sailing to Byzantium (1927)

I

That is no country for old men. The young
In one another's arms, birds in the trees
—Those dying generations—at their song,
The salmon-falls, the mackerel-crowded seas,
Fish, flesh, or fowl, commend all summer long   5
Whatever is begotten, born, and dies.
Caught in that sensual music all neglect
Monuments of unaging intellect.

II

An aged man is but a paltry thing,
A tattered coat upon a stick, unless   10
Soul clap its hands and sing, and louder sing
For every tatter in its mortal dress,
Nor is there singing school but studying
Monuments of its own magnificence;
And therefore I have sailed the seas and come   15
To the holy city of Byzantium.

III

O sages standing in God's holy fire
As in the gold mosaic of a wall,
Come from the holy fire, perne in a gyre,
And be the singing-masters of my soul.   20
Consume my heart away; sick with desire
And fastened to a dying animal
It knows not what it is; and gather me
Into the artifice of eternity.

IV

Once out of nature I shall never take   25
My bodily form from any natural thing,
But such a form as Grecian goldsmiths make
Of hammered gold and gold enameling
To keep a drowsy Emperor awake;
Or set upon a golden bough to sing   30
To lords and ladies of Byzantium
Of what is past, or passing, or to come.

■ What efforts does the poet describe to deny the fact that "That is no country for old men"?

■ Look carefully at the grammatical construction of the final stanza. Explain the significance of the last line: "Of what is past, or passing, or to come." How does this relate to the first line of the stanza?

John Keats (1795–1821)

Ode on a Grecian Urn (1819)

I

Thou still unravish'd bride of quietness,
   Thou foster-child of silence and slow time,
Sylvan historian, who canst thus express
   A flowery tale more sweetly than our rhyme:
What leaf-fring'd legend haunts about thy shape   5
    Of deities or mortals, or of both,
      In Tempe or the dales of Arcady?
What men or gods are these? What maidens loth?
    What mad pursuit? What struggle to escape?
      What pipes and timbrels? What wild ecstasy?   10

II

Heard melodies are sweet, but those unheard
   Are sweeter; therefore, ye soft pipes, play on;
Not to the sensual ear, but, more endear'd,
   Pipe to the spirit ditties of no tone:

Fair youth, beneath the trees, thou canst not leave   15
   Thy song, nor ever can those trees be bare;
      Bold lover, never, never canst thou kiss,
Though winning near the goal—yet, do not grieve;
   She cannot fade, though thou hast not thy bliss,
      For ever wilt thou love, and she be fair!   20

III

Ah, happy, happy boughs! that cannot shed
   Your leaves, nor ever bid the spring adieu;
And, happy melodist, unwearièd,
   For ever piping songs for ever new;
More happy love! more happy, happy love!   25
   For ever warm and still to be enjoy'd,
      For ever panting, and for ever young;
All breathing human passion far above,
   That leaves a heart high-sorrowful and cloy'd,
      A burning forehead, and a parching tongue.   30

IV

Who are these coming to the sacrifice?
   To what green altar, O mysterious priest,
Lead'st thou that heifer lowing at the skies,
   And all her silken flanks with garlands drest?
What little town by river or sea shore,   35
   Or mountain-built with peaceful citadel,
      Is emptied of this folk, this pious morn?
And, little town, thy streets for evermore
   Will silent be; and not a soul to tell
      Why thou art desolate, can e'er return.   40

V

O Attic shape! Fair attitude! with brede
   Of marble men and maidens overwrought,
With forest branches and the trodden weed;
   Thou, silent form, dost tease us out of thought
As doth eternity: Cold Pastoral!   45
   When old age shall this generation waste,
      Thou shalt remain, in midst of other woe
Than ours, a friend to man, to whom thou say'st,
   "Beauty is truth, truth beauty,"—that is all
      Ye know on earth, and all ye need to know.   50

■ Why does the poet describe the scene as "Cold Pastoral"?

■ How does the poem discuss the complications of reading allusions? What understanding is the poet able to achieve even without answering such questions as, "What men or gods are these?"

John Keats (1795–1821)

On First Looking into Chapman's Homer (1816)

Much have I traveled in the realms of gold,
        And many goodly states and kingdoms seen;
        Round many western islands have I been
Which bards in fealty to Apollo hold.
Oft of one wide expanse had I been told   5
        That deep-browed Homer ruled as his demesne,
        Yet did I never breathe its pure serene
Till I heard Chapman speak out loud and bold.
Then felt I like some watcher of the skies
        When a new planet swims into his ken;   10
Or like stout Cortez when with eagle eyes
        He started at the Pacific—and all his men
Looked at each other with a wild surmise—
        Silent, upon a peak in Darien.

■ Contrast the reaction to this version of Homer to the scene on the urn. How does the poet assert the value of Chapman's translation of Homer?

■ What is the significance of the silence that the poet describes in the final line?

Percy Bysshe Shelley (1792–1822)

Ozymandias (1818)

I met a traveler from an antique land
Who said: Two vast and trunkless legs of stone
Stand in the desert. Near them, on the sand,
Half sunk, a shattered visage lies, whose frown,
And wrinkled lip, and sneer of cold command,   5

Tell that its sculptor well those passions read
Which yet survive, stamped on these lifeless things,
The hand that mocked them, and the heart that fed;
And on the pedestal these words appear:
"My name is Ozymandias, king of kings: 10
Look on my works, ye Mighty, and despair!"
Nothing beside remains. Round the decay
Of that colossal wreck, boundless and bare
The lone and level sands stretch far away.

- How does "mocked" function within the narrative?
- How does the poem juxtapose the inscription on the pedestal with its current context?
- How does this poem illustrate the myth of cheating death?

Horace Smith (1779–1849)

Ozymandias (1818)

IN Egypt's sandy silence, all alone,
Stands a gigantic Leg, which far off throws
The only shadow that the Desart knows:—
"I am great OZYMANDIAS," saith the stone,
"The King of Kings; this mighty City shows   5
"The wonders of my hand." —The City's gone,—
Nought but the Leg remaining to disclose
The site of this forgotten Babylon.

We wonder,—and some Hunter may express
Wonder like ours, when thro' the wilderness   10
Where London stood, holding the Wolf in chace,
He meets some fragment huge, and stops to guess
What powerful but unrecorded race
Once dwelt in that annihilated place.

- Compare Smith's poem to Shelley's more famous version. Where do the two authors use the same images? Consider the impact of the different word and rhythm choices each author has made.

DRAMA

David Ives (1951–)

Playwright David Ives was born and raised in Chicago. He attended Northwestern University and Yale University School of Drama. Ives is primarily known for his one-act plays. His works include *All in the Timing: Fourteen Plays* (1995), *Mere Mortals: Six One-Act Comedies* (1998), *Lives of the Saints: Seven One-Act Plays* (2000), and *Time Flies and Other Short Plays* (2001). In 1995, he was awarded a Guggenheim Fellowship in playwriting.

Sure Thing (1988)

CHARACTERS

BILL *and* BETTY, *both in their late twenties*
SCENE: *A café table, with a couple of chairs*

(BETTY, *reading at the table. An empty chair opposite her.* BILL *enters.*)

BILL: Excuse me. Is this chair taken?
BETTY: Excuse me?
BILL: Is this taken?
BETTY: Yes it is.
BILL: Oh. Sorry.   5
BETTY: Sure thing. (*A bell rings softly.*)
BILL: Excuse me. Is this chair taken?
BETTY: Excuse me?
BILL: Is this taken?
BETTY: No, but I'm expecting somebody in a minute.   10
BILL: Oh. Thanks anyway.
BILL: Oh. Thanks anyway.
BETTY: Sure thing. (*A bell rings softly.*)
BILL: Excuse me. Is this chair taken?
BETTY: No, but I'm expecting somebody very shortly.   15
BILL: Would you mind if I sit here till he or she or it comes?
BETTY (*glances at her watch.*): They seem to be pretty late. . . .
BILL: You never know who you might be turning down.
BETTY: Sorry. Nice try, though.
BILL: Sure thing. (*Bell.*) Is this seat taken?   20
BETTY: No it's not.
BILL: Would you mind if I sit here?
BETTY: Yes I would.
BILL: Oh. (*Bell.*) Is this chair taken?
BETTY: No it's not.   25

BILL: Would you mind if I sit here?

BETTY: No. Go ahead.

BILL: Thanks. *(He sits. She continues reading.)* Everyplace else seems to be
    taken.

BETTY: Mm-hm.

BILL: Great place.   30

BETTY: Mm-hm.

BILL: What's the book?

BETTY: I just wanted to read in quiet, if you don't mind.

BILL: No. Sure thing. *(Bell.)*

BILL: Everyplace else seems to be taken.   35

BETTY: Mm-hm.

BILL: Great place for reading.

BETTY: Yes, I like it.

BILL: What's the book?

BETTY: *The Sound and the Fury*   40

BILL: Oh. Hemingway. *(Bell.)* What's the book?

BETTY: *The Sound and the Fury*

BILL: Oh. Faulkner.

BETTY: Have you read it?

BILL: Not...actually. I've sure read *about*...it, though. It's supposed to   45
    be great.

BETTY: It is great.

BILL: I hear it's great. *(Small pause.)* Waiter? *(Bell.)* What's the book?

BETTY: *The Sound and the Fury*

BILL: Oh. Faulkner.

BETTY: Have you read it?   50

BILL: I'm a Mets fan, myself. *(Bell.)*

BETTY: Have you read it?

BILL: Yeah, I read it in college.

BETTY: Where was college?

BILL: I went to Oral Roberts University. *(Bell.)*   55

BETTY: Where was college?

BILL: I was lying. I never really went to college. I just like to party.
    (Bell.)

BETTY: Where was college?

BILL: Harvard.

BETTY: Do you like Faulkner?   60

BILL: I love Faulkner. I spent a whole winter reading him once.

BETTY: I've just started.

BILL: I was so excited after ten pages that I went out and bought everything
    else he wrote. One of the greatest reading experiences of my life. I

mean, all that incredible psychological understanding. Page after page of gorgeous prose. His profound grasp of the mystery of time and human existence. The smells of the earth... What do you think?

BETTY: I think it's pretty boring. (*Bell.*)

BILL: What's the book?   65

BETTY: *The Sound and the Fury*

BILL: Oh! Faulkner!

BETTY: Do you like Faulkner?

BILL: I love Faulkner.

BETTY: He's incredible.   70

BILL: I spent a whole winter reading him once.

BETTY: I was so excited after ten pages that I went out and bought everything else he wrote.

BILL: All that incredible psychological understanding.

BETTY: And the prose is so gorgeous.

BILL: And the way he's grasped the mystery of time—   75

BETTY: —and human existence. I can't believe I've waited this long to read him.

BILL: You never know. You might not have liked him before.

BETTY: That's true.

BILL: You might not have been ready for him. You have to hit these things at the right moment or it's no good.

BETTY: That's happening to me.   80

BILL: It's all in the timing. (*Small pause.*) My name's Bill, by the way.

BETTY: I'm Betty.

BILL: Hi.

BETTY: Hi. (*Small pause.*)

BILL: Yes I thought reading Faulkner was... a great experience.   85

BETTY: Yes. (*Small pause.*)

BILL: *The Sound and the Fury*... (*Another small pause.*)

BETTY: Well. Onwards and upwards. (*She goes back to her book.*)

BILL: Waiter—? (*Bell.*) You have to hit these things at the right moment or it's no good.

BETTY: That's happened to me.   90

BILL: It's all in the timing. My name's Bill, by the way.

BETTY: I'm Betty.

BILL: Hi.

BETTY: Hi.

BILL: Do you come in here a lot?   95

BETTY: Actually I'm just in town for two days from Pakistan.

BILL: Oh. Pakistan. (*Bell.*) My name's Bill, by the way.

BETTY: I'm Betty.

BILL: Hi.

BETTY: Hi. 100

BILL: Do you come here a lot?

BETTY: Every once in a while. Do you?

BILL: Not much anymore. Not as much as I used to. Before my nervous breakdown. *(Bell.)* Do you come in here a lot?

BETTY: Why are you asking?

BILL: Just interested. 105

BETTY: Are you really interested, or do you just want to pick me up?

BILL: No, I'm really interested.

BETTY: Why would you be interested in whether I come in here a lot?

BILL: Just ... getting acquainted.

BETTY: Maybe you're only interested for the sake of making small 110
talk long enough to ask me back to your place to listen to some music, or because you've just rented some great tape for your VCR, or because you've got some terrific unknown Django Reinhardt record, only all you'll really want to do is fuck—which you won't do very well—after which you'll go into the bathroom and pee very loudly, then pad into the kitchen and get yourself a beer from the refrigerator without asking me whether I'd like anything, and then you'll proceed to lie back down beside me and confess that you've got a girlfriend named Stephanie who's away at medical school in Belgium for a year, and that you've been involved with her—*off and on*—in what you'll call a very "intricate" relationship, for about *seven* YEARS. None of which *interests* me, mister!

BILL: Okay. *(Bell.)* Do you come in here a lot?

BETTY: Every other day, I think.

BILL: I come in here quite a lot and I don't remember seeing you.

BETTY: I guess we must be on different schedules.

BILL: Missed connections. 115

BETTY: Yes. Different time zones.

BILL: Amazing how you can live right next door to somebody in this town and never even know it.

BETTY: I know.

BILL: City life.

BETTY: It's crazy. 120

BILL: We probably pass each other in the street every day. Right in front of this place, probably.

BETTY: Yep.

BILL *(Looks around.)*: Well, the waiters here sure seem to be in some different time zone. I can't seem to locate one anywhere... Waiter! *(He looks back.)* So what do you— *(He sees that she's gone back to her book.)*

BETTY: I beg pardon?

BILL: Nothing. Sorry. (*Bell.*)   125

BETTY: I guess we must be on different schedules.

BILL: Missed connections.

BETTY: Yes. Different time zones.

BILL: Amazing how you can live right next door to somebody in this town and never even know it.

BETTY: I know.   130

BILL: City life.

BETTY: It's crazy.

BILL: You weren't waiting for somebody when I came in, were you?

BETTY: Actually, I was.

BILL: Oh. Boyfriend?   135

BETTY: Sort of.

BILL: What's a sort-of boyfriend?

BETTY: My husband.

BILL: Ah-ha. (*Bell.*) You weren't waiting for somebody when I came in, were you?

BETTY: Actually I was.   140

BILL: Oh. Boyfriend?

BETTY: Sort of.

BILL: What's a sort-of boyfriend?

BETTY: We were meeting here to break up.

BILL: Mm-hm... (*Bell.*) What's a sort-of boyfriend?   145

BETTY: My lover. Here she comes right now! (*Bell.*)

BILL: You weren't waiting for somebody when I came in, were you?

BETTY: No, just reading.

BILL: Sort of a sad occupation for a Friday night, isn't it? Reading here, all by yourself?

BETTY: Do you think so?   150

BILL: Well sure. I mean, what's a good-looking woman like you doing out alone on a Friday night?

BETTY: Trying to keep away from lines like that.

BILL: No, listen— (*Bell.*) You weren't waiting for somebody when I came in, were you?

BETTY: No, just reading.

BILL: Sort of a sad occupation for a Friday night, isn't it? Reading here   155
all by yourself?

BETTY: I guess it is, in a way.

BILL: What's a good-looking woman like you doing out alone on a Friday night anyway? No offense, but...

BETTY: I'm out alone on a Friday night for the first time in a very long time.

BILL: Oh.

BETTY: You see, I just recently ended a relationship.   160

BILL: Oh.

BETTY: Of rather long standing.

BILL: I'm sorry. *(Small pause.)* Well listen, since reading by yourself *is* such a
sad occupation for a Friday night, would you like to go elsewhere?

BETTY: No...

BILL: Do something else?   165

BETTY: No thanks.

BILL: I was headed out to the movies in a while anyway.

BETTY: I don't think so.

BILL: Big chance to let Faulkner catch his breath. All those long sentences
get him pretty tired.

BETTY: Thanks anyway.   170

BILL: Okay.

BETTY: I appreciate the invitation.

BILL: Sure thing. *(Bell.)* You weren't waiting for somebody when I came in,
were you?

BETTY: No, just reading.

BILL: Sort of a sad occupation for a Friday night, isn't it? Reading here   175
all by yourself?

BETTY: I guess I was trying to think of it as existentially romantic. You
know—cappuccino, great literature, rainy night...

BILL: That only works in Paris. We *could* hop the late plane to Paris. Get on
a Concorde. Find a café...

BETTY: I'm a little short on plane fare tonight.

BILL: Darn it, so am I.

BETTY: To tell you the truth, I was headed to the movies after I finished   180
this section. Would you like to come along? Since you can't locate a
waiter?

BILL: That's a very nice offer, but...

BETTY: Uh-huh. Girlfriend?

BILL: Two, actually. One of them's pregnant, and Stephanie— *(Bell.)*

BETTY: Girlfriend?

BILL: No, I don't have a girlfriend. Not if you mean the castrating bitch   185
I dumped last night. *(Bell.)*

BETTY: Girlfriend?

BILL: Sort of. Sort of.

BETTY: What's a sort-of girlfriend?

BILL: My mother. *(Bell.)* I just ended a relationship, actually.

BETTY: Oh.   190

BILL: Of rather long standing.

BETTY: I'm sorry to hear it.

BILL: This is my first night out alone in a long time. I feel a little bit at sea, to tell you the truth.

BETTY: So you didn't stop to talk because you're a Moonie, or you have some weird political affiliation—?

BILL: Nope. Straight-down-the-ticket Republican. *(Bell.)* Straight-down- 195 the-ticket Democrat. *(Bell.)* Can I tell you something about politics? *(Bell.)* I like to think of myself as a citizen of the universe. *(Bell.)* I'm unaffiliated.

BETTY: That's a relief. So am I.

BILL: I vote my beliefs.

BETTY: Labels are not important.

BILL: Labels are not important, exactly. Like me, for example. I mean, what does it matter if I had a two-point at— *(Bell.)* —three-point at *(Bell.)* —four-point at college, or if I did come from Pittsburgh— *(Bell.)* —Cleveland— *(Bell.)* —Westchester County?

BETTY: Sure. 200

BILL: I believe that a man is what he is. *(Bell.)* A person is what he is. *(Bell.)* A person is...what they are.

BETTY: I think so too.

BILL: So what if I admire Trotsky? *(Bell.)* So what if I once had a totalbody liposuction? *(Bell.)* So what if I don't have a penis? *(Bell.)* So what if I once spent a year in the Peace Corps? I was acting on my convictions.

BETTY: Sure.

BILL: You can't just hang a sign on a person. 205

BETTY: Absolutely. I'll bet you're a Scorpio. *(Many bells ring.)* Listen, I was headed to the movies after I finished this section. Would you like to come along?

BILL: That sounds like fun. What's playing?

BETTY: A couple of the really early Woody Allen movies.

BILL: Oh.

BETTY: Don't you like Woody Allen? 210

BILL: Sure. I like Woody Allen.

BETTY: But you're not crazy about Woody Allen.

BILL: Those early ones kind of get on my nerves.

BETTY: Uh-huh. *(Bell.)*

BILL: Y'know I was headed to the— *(simultaneously.)* 215

BETTY: I was thinking about—

BILL: I'm sorry.

BETTY: No, go ahead.

BILL: I was going to say that I was headed to the movies in a little while, and...

BETTY: So was I.   220
BILL: The Woody Allen festival?
BETTY: Just up the street.
BILL: Do you like the early ones?
BETTY: I think anybody who doesn't ought to be run off the planet.
BILL: How many times have you seen *Bananas*?   225
BETTY: Eight times.
BILL: Twelve. So are you still interested? *(Long pause.)*
BETTY: Do you like Entenmann's crumb cake…?
BILL: Last night I went out at two in the morning to get one. *(Small pause.)*
    Did you have an Etch-a-Sketch as a child?
BETTY: Yes! And do you like Brussels sprouts? *(Small pause.)*   230
BILL: I think they're gross.
BETTY: They *are* gross!
BILL: Do you still believe in marriage in spite of current sentiments
    against it?
BETTY: Yes.
BILL: And children?   235
BETTY: Three of them.
BILL: Two girls and a boy.
BETTY: Harvard, Vassar, and Brown.
BILL: And will you love me?
BETTY: Yes.   240
BILL: And cherish me forever?
BETTY: Yes.
BILL: Do you still want to go to the movies?
BETTY: Sure thing.
BILL AND BETTY *(together.)*: Waiter!   245
(Blackout.)

■ What is the recurring structural device in this play? What defines the beginning and the end of each scene? How does the plot move forward by using
   this device?

■ How does this structure contribute to our understanding of the two characters? As they redo their scenes, to what extent do they remain true to their
   identities in previous scenes?

■ What do the characters resolve by the end of the play?

■ How does the play's structure help reveal the social constructs that govern
   interpersonal behavior?

Experiencing Literature through Writing

1. Choose a pair of texts that have some specific, stated connection. One may allude to the other, or both may allude to a common text. Identify the common element in the two texts.

    a. How important is that element in both of the texts? Does it hold the same place in both of the narratives?

    b. To what extent does each text treat the material in the allusion in the same manner as the original text? What sorts of changes do you see?

    c. How does the material in the allusion become more interesting within this new context?

    d. How does the "new" text become richer because of this particular allusion?

    e. How does the allusion add to our understanding of both of the texts involved in this shared element?

2. The texts here have a common theme of "The Myth of Cheating Death." How does the strategy of allusion serve the authors as they attempt to tackle a subject as perplexing as death? By appealing to an established myth, an author can, among other possibilities, make the experience of a single individual representative of a culture or make sense of individual experience by calling upon the collective experience that is represented in such myths. Look for examples in which the texts use allusions for each of these purposes. Explain how the particular texts illustrate each of these strategies and how this particular example fits into the myth.

3. It may be appropriate to treat the theme of death by thinking about the element of interruption. Death may seem like something more than an interruption, but often death intrudes on lives as an interruption, a reminder of mortality; everyone who is still living has in some way "cheated death." As you look at the readings in this section, discuss specific instances in which the texts treat the impact of some intruding death upon the worlds that these texts create. How does death interrupt in this specific instance? What is its impact? How does this create the given work? Where do other texts also intrude upon these narratives?

15

The Production and Reproduction of Texts

How Does Retelling and Revising Impact Our Experience of a Text?

How Can Literary Theory Clarify What Constitutes That Experience?

Whatever historical or social changes surround a work of art and however those changes influence our perception of the work, we tend to trust in the stable reality of a physical text. After all, words move from left to right across a page; pages are bound to turn in a fixed order. Film winds from one spool to another; the images pass across the projecting light in a set sequence. Given the arguments and ambiguities that are part of any serious reading, it's nice to think we have in hand a text—a single object—that grounds our study and gives us a common starting point for critical discussion.

But maybe that object isn't as stable as we usually assume. Given the labor William Blake put in to meld word and image onto an elaborately designed page, is it adequate to read just the poems themselves as they are presented in books like the one you are reading now? Charles Dickens first published all of his novels in weekly or monthly serial forms. What happens when the experience of those novels is no longer extended in small parts on a regular basis over a long period of time? Francis Ford Coppola ambitiously reedited *Apocalypse Now* years after its original release. Which version should command our critical attention? And is the experience of the film altered by its transmission to DVD and consequently from the theater to our living room?

Academic critics and scholars tend to be a fussy group. Some are especially devoted to the presentation of the truest text. But the most sophisticated textual critics understand that the notion of a single "best" text or "pure" text is problematic. Literature isn't merely an *object* of academic study. It's a human activity and experience that cannot be contained or bound within covers. And a literary text isn't created by an individual operating in a vacuum. Nothing stops a powerful producer from cutting a scene a director or screenwriter thought important, or an actor from improvising well beyond an author's stage directions, or a writer from revising an already published poem. These varied creative forces need not lead to crucial critical problems; after all, most people are focused on the actual text they encounter, not an idealized text someone thinks they "should" have. Throughout this book, we've been primarily interested in the literary experience, not the physical objects of literary study.

And yet it's also true that if we are oblivious to textual issues, we may fail to appreciate important aspects of an artist's craft. We may also remain insensitive to complex external forces that contribute to the shaping of a particular work. This chapter will emphasize critical issues concerning the production and reproduction of a text. We'll reflect upon how people have used—revised, abridged, and translated—literary texts and films. We'll explore how those uses matter, and we'll examine the underlying theoretical implications of choices we routinely (and often unconsciously) make as readers.

TEXTS AND TECHNOLOGY

Many people have observed that the development of the personal computer and of the World Wide Web make our age the "information age." It's often said that what is unfolding now compares in significance to the invention of movable type in the fifteenth century. Gutenberg's printing of the Bible had enormous implications. The ability to produce and distribute texts in great numbers changed notions of literacy and upset established bases of power. In arts, the primacy of spoken or performed works was overtaken by our modern notion of literature, which gave the printed word a privileged place.

In many ways, the computer further emphasizes the printed word. But some things about how words can be arranged and displayed have changed. A book (as we noted earlier) makes us turn pages. We read in a linear way, even when authors call into question notions of linear time or sequence. Words in an electronic space allow fresh design possibilities. Writers designing for e-books, especially those that artfully present book material in a tablet format, are liberated from the physical demands of paper and binding. An electronic manuscript can mix forms of presentation (moving images, sound,

Making Connections

As dramatic as recent developments in textual production seem, one could argue that there is still nothing new. Many writers from past decades or even past centuries have crafted forewords, prefaces, introductions, afterwords, postscripts, footnotes, and so on that frame the presentation of the main narrative in ways that keep readers conscious of the idea that conventional stories are made-up works of art. In the earliest days of film, images were sped up or run backward to achieve comic effects. As film matured as an art, directors employed styles of editing that made audiences aware of film as film (see Chapter 9). **Split-screen** techniques, for example, may be used to remind viewers that there is never only one thing happening at any one point in time. So hypertext could be seen as a new technology for the exploration of ideas and techniques that surfaced long ago.

and so on). Readers may feel liberated as well. The notion of **hypertext** puts the reader/user in a strong position. Hypertext allows readers to access on a screen any variety of linked documents, images, sound, and video instantly, at any time, and in any order. Writers have long challenged the idea that a story must be linear. Today, writers hoping to press the challenge further address the issue of linearity directly in the design of the page, as the spaces where we publish books are no longer confined to paper.

TEXTUAL FORM AND CONDITIONS OF PRODUCTION

There is a cliché often invoked when a good writer turns out an inferior bit of work: "even Homer nods." This cliché suggests that even a great writer can be sleepily inattentive to a line or a word, can "nod off" at one point or another in the writing process. It's a nice little saying, but it's also misleading. Homer, after all, wasn't a writer—at least not in the way we now think of what it is to be a writer. The great epics of ancient Greece were first delivered orally. No one lined up at the local bookstore to get copies of the next new big thing by Homer. The *Iliad* and the *Odyssey* as we know them were eventually written down, and the person (or persons) who did that writing had an extraordinary command of language. But the source materials were worked and reworked, revised, improvised, and elaborated upon over many years of oral performances.

Our current notions of poetry, drama, fiction, and film don't simply represent different forms of presentation that have always been available. These genres can be traced back to specific technologies and changing social conditions.

Before print, poets spoke or sung to audiences. Rhythmic devices and rhyming effects were used both to assist the memory of the performer and sustain attention of a listener. Early printed poems tended to circulate within a very narrow range of society. Live drama, of course, could not arise without a complex social structure to support it (if there were no theaters or no paying audience, would there be playwrights?). The novel emerged only when there was large middle-class readership; in fact, up until the early nineteenth century, novels were primarily aimed at women who had the time, the education, and the means necessary for sustaining a new form of entertainment and instruction. As for one of the latest "new forms" of entertainment, many observers of the film business believe that the growing popularity of streaming video and the installation of "home theaters" are redefining the moviegoing experience.

Experiencing Literature through Issues of Production

William Blake, as we mention earlier, designed pages as well as wrote poems. The interaction of word and image in his works offers an experience that conventional reprinting with words alone cannot match. One must even consider how and to what extent our interpretation of a given Blake poem may be controlled by the form we have of it. Consider, for example, "A Poison Tree"—one of the songs from his *Songs of Experience*.

The tree in the words of the poem is a tree of wrath—something that has grown from anger and hatred. It is the product of the speaker's experience. The words make for a powerful and fairly direct message: be open with your anger or it will become deadly. But our experience of the whole text is much broader and more subtly nuanced. In Blake's engraving, the fallen "foe" beneath the tree lies with arms open wide. He seems at peace in a sacrificial position. His long hair spreads upon the earth. The broad chest is foregrounded; the lower body melds with the landscape behind. There is an almost sensual quality to the presentation of the figure; if not for the accompanying poem, the figure could be seen as sleeping. The tree *drawn* on Blake's page seems part of a beautiful landscape. But the poem's title, "A Poison Tree," along with the fairly specific allegorical tree conjured by the words alone, jars against the image of the tree that so gracefully frames the whole composition. Blake had written of innocence and experience as qualities marking the "contrary states of the human soul." Viewing the whole page in this case (text and artwork) suggests he has encompassed that range. To put the point in a different way, the "experience" of the poem's speaker doesn't match Blake's complete vision or our own experience of the whole text.

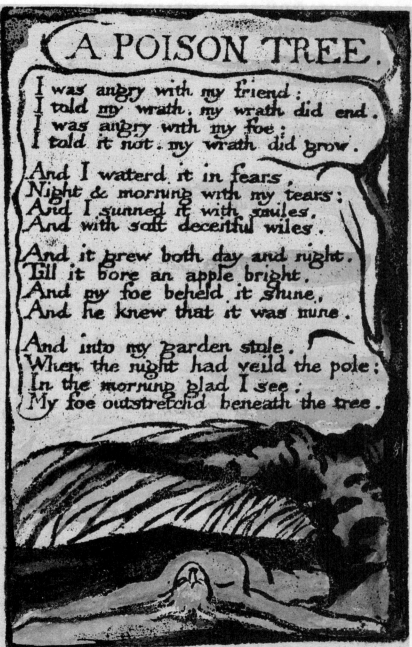

A POISON TREE.

I was angry with my friend :
I told my wrath, my wrath did end .
I was angry with my foe :
I told it not. my wrath did grow .

And I waterd it in fears,
Night & morning with my tears :
And I sunned it with smiles,
And with soft deceitful wiles .

And it grew both day and night.
Till it bore an apple bright,
And my foe beheld it shine,
And he knew that it was mine .

And into my garden stole .
When the night had veild the pole :
In the morning glad I see :
My foe outstretchd beneath the tree .

AN ORIENTATION TO CONTEMPORARY CRITICAL THEORY

Reading literature can be a challenge, but reading critical analyses of literature can seem impossible to a person unfamiliar with key ideas and assumptions. Not only is it easy to get lost amid the confusing names that signal the different angles critics take in studying literature and film, it can be hard to know what the angle is. Where is this critic coming from? What assumptions does she or he make about the critical task? If you are to tune in to conversations that occur in a college environment, you must acquire some understanding of common theoretical approaches to the literary experience.

New Criticism and *Auteur* Theory

We can get oriented to much current theory by knowing something about a critical movement that emerged in the middle of the twentieth century and that continues to influence much teaching. The name—**new criticism**—seems odd now, given that it's relatively old in context of recent schools of thought, but new criticism is the name that has stuck. The new critics were **formalists**; they argued that literary texts are the sole material of literary study. Literary criticism is *not* (the argument went) a branch of history, biography, psychology, or sociology, but a distinct discipline that must focus upon the structure, style, and language of a particular work of literary art. The "object itself" (a poem, story, or play) became the point of intense study for a generation of critics and scholars. **Explication** (the unfolding, the close reading, the analysis of the text) became the heart— indeed the end goal—of literary study. The best reading was the reading that accounted most fully for the work's complex features.

We've certainly assumed in this book that close attention to a work of art leads to a measure of exploration and discovery; but however valuable new criticism was as a disciplined method of analysis, it was ultimately narrow and arbitrary. The text, as we've suggested, can be in itself a problematic concept. And literature, like all human activities, is dynamic, changing, and messy. Both the strengths and the limitations of new criticism emerged quite clearly in the context of film studies. *Auteur* theory closely paralleled the new criticism (*auteur* is the French word for "author"). *Auteur* criticism assumed that if films were to be considered "art," they needed to be created by an artist (that is, the director). The focus on the director's management of the whole gave the critic a point of analytical focus. It led to serious and rigorous treatment of a film's structure and style. It worked from a sense that a single controlling creative force was shaping the whole work that unfolded. But *auteur* criticism also disregarded the social and economic processes that influenced the making of films. It also could not encompass the essentially collaborative nature of filmmaking.

Deconstruction

The limits of new criticism and *auteur* theory met progressively aggressive challenges beginning in the 1960s. The French philosopher Jacques Derrida in particular undermined some of the formalists' most basic assumptions. Derrida pointed out that no word has a fixed or "natural" meaning. He argued that a word takes on meaning only within a complex, arbitrary, and ever-changing structure of words. A word is used to *refer* to something or is *associated* with something; a word must not be mistaken for the thing it stands for and must not be read separate from a system of other words. *Carriage*, for example, in one text can refer to a fancy horse-drawn cart and in another to a push cart for babies. An automobile ad might use the word to suggest a substantial, expensive car. In still other contexts, *carriage* could refer to a loading mechanism for a gun or for the roller on a typewriter. Literary texts exploit (with or without the author's intention) such variable associations. It becomes the job of the critic to unfold a play of possible meanings that reveal multiple, even contrary messages. For Derrida, to read closely is to deconstruct, not interpret, the text. This line of thinking leads to the notion that literary texts are not great because of their wholeness or consistency (qualities new criticism would emphasize), but because of the irreducibly complex associations that they provoke. **Deconstruction,** then, is not a practice that seeks to make a work coherent or consistent. The deconstructionist would reveal inconsistencies and revel in them.

The American critic J. Hillis Miller attempted to clarify deconstruction's task by calling attention to the following description of Eve in John Milton's *Paradise Lost*:

> She as a veil down to the slender waist
> Her unadorned golden tresses wore
> Dissheveld, but in wanton ringlets wav'd
> As the vine curls her tendrils, which impli'd
> Subjection.

Miller notes Eve is at this point in Milton's story a free, yet unfallen, part of creation. Her place in nature is defined by her subjection to the authority of Adam and ultimately of God. Her loosely flowing hair is as natural as the growth of the garden that surrounds her. But however much Milton may stress Eve's innocence before the fall, "unadorned golden tresses" and "wanton ringlets" also achieve meaning in the context of a culture that sees a woman's loosely flowing hair as associated with sexuality and sin. It would seem the innocent Eve has already fallen or must necessarily fall by some flaw of her nature. But how can this be in a perfect creation? Perhaps Milton would tell us that his description of Eve's hair implies nothing more than "subjection" to God's perfect order ("As the vine curls her tendrils"), but would we be convinced by his authority?

How can we so limit our understanding of "wanton" or the general luxuriance that dominates Milton's description of nature and of Eve herself? Along these lines, Miller argues that there are associations conveyed by the words in Milton's lines that contradict one another. A rigorous deconstructive reading (unlike the interpretation of a new critic) would expose rather than explain those contradictions. Milton's orthodox theological system may collapse under such analysis, but from a deconstructionist's perspective, *Paradise Lost* is no less a poem for that. The richness of a literary text resides in the very complexity that makes final meaning impossible. To translate this into critical practice, a deconstructionist reading unfolds possible meanings rather than the correct meaning.

As you might imagine, deconstruction became highly controversial. Some people found it liberating. The new critical readings/interpretations that competed with one another for status as conclusive could now be seen as multiple and alternative lines of inquiry. New possibilities were opened and encouraged. Critics became strongly and self-consciously involved in the creative shaping of meaning because meaning was no longer assumed to be determined by the work of art. But as you might also imagine, many academics found deconstruction profoundly threatening: What do we have left if *meaning* cannot be determined? Did deconstruction send us down a path toward nihilism—the belief in nothing? Many other skeptics also pointed out that deconstruction in practice often led to trivial, self-absorbed, and overcomplicated essays. Still others suggested that deconstruction was merely new jargon for essentially old ideas, many of those ideas very well established.

New Historicism and Other Historically Grounded Approaches

Deconstruction itself no longer stands at the center of critical disputes. It is not so much that matters have been resolved, but that the grounds of discussion have shifted. Deconstruction's influence, for example, now shows in ways critics think of the relationship between history and literature. It is nothing new to observe that much can be learned about a given time by reading the literary works of that time. But in past decades, literary artists were given a special status as especially accurate mirrors or as particularly perceptive critics of their age. Advocates of **new historicism** don't give a poem or play a privileged place in the materials that make up a given culture. New historicists see systems of meaning as conditional and shifting, depending upon the interests the systems represent. In their view, literary artists are both caught in and contribute to the complex formation of ideas about power. From the perspective of a new historicist, a nineteenth-century American writer wouldn't merely take up the "frontier" as a subject, but would participate (perhaps unknowingly) in the formation of his culture's attitude toward the frontier. The very notion of "frontier" is, after all, conditioned by assumptions of forward movement and conquest that make sense only to those who move forward and conquer: the western frontier was no frontier for the Native Americans who lived on it.

New historicism had hardly had the chance to grow old before some academics began using the term **cultural poetics** (which accents the blurred distinctions among history, culture, and art); others adopted the term **postcolonial criticism** (which highlights a sense of power or authority imposed by one culture or system over another); and still more recently, **transnational criticism** (which accents interactions among countries without privileging any one country or culture). **Reader-response criticism** stands as yet another variant of new historicism that reflects the influence of deconstruction. As that name implies, reader-response critics shift emphasis from a text to how people read or use a text; the work of art is studied not through its own inherent qualities, but through the way readers of a particular time and place react to it. Any of these approaches can be taken from a distinct point of view. **Feminist criticism,** for example, seeks to gain insights largely obscured or bypassed by the men who have until recent decades dominated critical discussions. Feminists join the varieties of new historicists in assuming that a work of art is a product not only of an author, but of a specific culture. The "object of study" has shifted from the "text itself" that the new critics identified to a complex set of social/historical/linguistic contexts.

WHY DO WE STUDY THE TEXTS WE STUDY

Many people read Michael Crichton novels (*Congo, Jurassic Park,* among many), but relatively few people study them in literature classes. The distinction gets at the idea of the **canon.** The canon refers to those works considered appropriate for literary study. They are the durable works that a culture adopts and uses over time. Canonical works have achieved "classic" status. This seems simple enough: Great books find a secure place in the canon; books less than great find a temporary place on a sales chart. But value judgments are never as clear as this. Canonical works may indeed be great, but one must acknowledge that ideas of greatness change. And perhaps more important, one must acknowledge that literary/artistic greatness is usually defined by a very particular group of people: mostly college professors. That means that the interests, ethnicity, education, and class of a particular profession have great influence in determining what belongs or doesn't belong in the canon.

We've suggested in the previous section that challenges to the canon have been prepared for by the unhinging effects of contemporary critical theory, but this challenge has been even more strongly motivated by broad social changes. Literary theories relate to, but do not motivate, battles regarding the canon. Today's student and teaching population is more highly varied in age, ethnicity, gender, and race than ever before. The multicultural population has understandably inspired revisions of long-established course offerings and text selections. In fact, our perspective on entire genres or art forms changes as the surrounding world changes. For example, movies were once thought barely worth critical attention; they were seen as popular entertainments, not works of art. Although movies are still popular entertainment, the best of them claim attention and respect. Entire college courses are devoted to film (the change in name from *movie* to *film* or *cinema* suggests the higher status within the university). Film (and film studies) have been around long enough now that we can speak of certain movies/films as canonical.

Experiencing Literature through Theory

The following two passages are taken from the introduction of two very different (although both very large) anthologies of American literature. The first, *Major Writers of America*, was published in 1962—in the days when the new critics held sway in an institution that was still largely white and male. The second, from *The Heath Anthology of American Literature*, first appeared in 1990 and clearly sounded an early challenge to what were then conventional notions of "major" or canonical. The first focuses on concepts of quality that are presumed discernable through rigorous analysis. The second shifts attention to historical context and implies that quality is relative to the interests of the reader. As you read, identify how assumptions that govern the editors' principle of selection are signaled in specific words or phrases. Think, too, about how the editors define the audience or readership of their textbook. What can you learn about education in America or about the place literature takes in that education by reading these passages? And finally, where does it seem we've moved, nearly two decades after the first edition of *The Heath Anthology*?

from Major Writers of America (1962)

[W]hile the canon is at long last becoming established, a realization gradually forces itself upon us that, as the age of discovery and of elementary mapping closes, the era of evaluation opens. . . . [It] is incumbent upon us to make clear which are the few peaks and which the many low-lying hills. . . . We must vindicate the study of American literature because primarily the matter is literature, and only secondarily because it is American.

. . . The first requirement of the design, therefore, was inevitably that the authors so nominated be represented fully enough to testify to their superiority.[1]

---

1 *Major Writers of America* included substantial selections of twenty-eight writers. Only one (Emily Dickinson) was a woman. Dickinson, however, was in the majority on another count: nineteen of the authors included were, like her, from the northeastern United States.

from The Heath Anthology of American Literature (1990)

[A] major principle of selection has been to represent as fully as possible the varied cultures of the United States. American cultures sometimes overlap, sometimes differ, sometimes develop separately, sometimes in interactive patterns. To convey this diversity, we have included what is by far the widest sampling of the work of minority and white women writers available in any anthology of American literature. This selection includes material by 109 women of all races, 25 individual Native American authors (as well as 17 texts from tribal origins), 53 African-Americans, 13 Hispanics (as well as 12 texts from earlier Spanish originals and two from French) and 9 Asian-Americans. We have included significant selections from Jewish, Italian, and other ethnic traditions. ❖

These two selections represent radically opposed notions of what literary study involves. It's important that you understand that the arguments behind each position influence the education you now experience. Professors, after all, must decide on what texts to assign. Can you sense where your professors fit into the conversation about inclusion/exclusion (or "quality"/context) carried on by the two anthologies or how they may have moved beyond that conversation?

A Note to Student Writers: Using Theory to Develop Critical Analysis

Although it is important to reflect upon the theoretical implications that lie behind any paper we write, it is not necessarily good to work consciously from a set theoretical perspective. To think from the start "now I'm going to write as a deconstructionist" may be putting the cart before the horse. The cognitive activities that writing in response to a complex subject inevitably prompts should not be scripted in advance. Better to discover you've deconstructed a poem than to insist that deconstructing poetry is your job.

We suggest that you attend closely to the prompt your professor offers and begin to write without thinking too much about critical theory. Once you've worked through an argument very carefully and prepared an essay for submission, you can ask yourself: What characterizes my approach? What assumptions am I making about literary criticism? How do I look upon matters of interpretation or meaning? To what extent have I treated the text as an object of art? To what extent have I seen meaning as conditioned by things outside the text? From what perspective is my argument a strong one? If in answering these questions you achieve a clearer sense of the theoretical underpinnings of your work, you may be able to revise key points effectively. Theory may prove to enrich your reading and strengthen your analysis. But revision and development that bring theory forward happen after careful drafting. Don't allow theory to interfere with your powerful and immediate experience of a text. Don't allow theory to artificially force your writing in any particular direction. And don't assume that imposing a critical vocabulary will make your paper seem more sophisticated.

ABRIDGING, REVISING, AND REPACKAGING TEXT

For the most part in this book, we've offered "whole" works. But we haven't hesitated to use a fragment from a long novel or poem if we felt that that fragment helped illustrate a point. In relation to the subject of this chapter, it's important to also say that we don't assume fragments cease to be literature. The passage we excerpted from Milton's *Paradise Lost* in Chapter 7 no doubt functions fully only in context of the whole poem, yet it reads on its own very well as a short poem. We certainly don't want to disregard an author's carefully crafted whole work, but it's worth remembering that writers have made or approved abridgments of their own works in various forms (public readings, anthologies, translations, and so on). For that matter, individual readers may well choose to skip a chapter of the most meticulously prepared "critical edition." Such behaviors complicate our sense of what we study when we study literature and film. But these behaviors don't fundamentally change anything that we've addressed in other chapters. So rather than simply dismissing any abridgment as something less than literary, consider how an abridgment functions on its own terms. In other words, understand the limitations of an abridgment, but still critically attend to whatever you have before you.

An abridged work normally intends to represent fairly something of the whole from which it is taken. Or at least it shouldn't mislead one about the source text. But any substantial change presses a reader to experience a work of art as a new thing. Charles Dickens excerpted sections of his novels for his own

Oliver asking for more, from "The Adventures of Oliver Twist" by Charles Dickens (1812–70) 1838, published by Chapman & Hall, 1901 (engraving), Cruikshank, George (1792–1878)/Private Collection/The Bridgeman Art Library

Cruickshank's illustration from the first edition of *Oliver Twist*; a musical scene from Carol Reed's *Oliver!* (1968); Polanski's *Oliver Twist* (2005). *Oliver Twist* has been subject to very different treatments since its publication.

dramatic readings. Although he could expect his audience to know the complete novel, the readings inevitably had a strongly focusing effect. From *Oliver Twist*, Dickens selected and strung together passages that told of the murder of Nancy by Bill Sykes. His readings (by all accounts, brilliantly presented) inevitably concentrated attention in such a way as to change the original—or even displace the larger narrative. *Oliver Twist*, for those rapt by Dickens's readings, became an almost unbearably compelling story of a brutal murder. That was hardly the reaction that moviegoers had to the musical version *Oliver!* that appeared in 1968 (directed by Carol Reed). Nancy's murder remained an important part of the story, but elaborately staged musical/dance numbers gave the audience some distance from the most dramatic and melodramatic moments. Roman Polanski offered his own film version (*Oliver Twist*, 2005) that stripped away some of Dickens's elaborate side stories and concentrated heavily on a child's terrifying progress through a bitterly hard world. As often happens, an original work of art provides the occasion for variations upon a theme. Even though the new works reward attention to their own merits, it becomes necessary to think of film versions of novels or stage productions of plays as interpretations of a text. What does the director choose to foreground? Why does a casting choice matter? How does the look of a film or stage set (dark/light, elaborate/plain) have such an effect on our experience of the film or play?

Experiencing Literature through Issues of Production and Reproduction of Texts

No author has been subject to more interpretations than Shakespeare. Despite the rigorous efforts to establish the truest texts of his plays, there has never been a time when the texts were strictly honored in performance. Mark Twain has the bogus "king" from *Adventures of Huckleberry Finn* test out an especially corrupt version of "Hamlet's Immortal Soliloquy!!" on an unlettered audience. Twain's comedy doesn't pretend to say anything about Shakespeare, but it does say something about the breadth and variety of ways Shakespeare has been repackaged for innumerable audiences. In other words, it says something about the way people use literature.

Mark Twain (1835–1910)

from Adventures of Huckleberry Finn (1885)

To be, or not to be; that is the bare bodkin
That makes calamity of so long life;
For who would fardels bear, till Birnam Wood do come to Dunsinane,

But that the fear of something after death
Murders the innocent sleep,   5
Great nature's second course,
And makes us rather sling the arrows of outrageous fortune
Than fly to others that we know not of.
There's the respect must give us pause:
Wake Duncan with thy knocking! I would thou couldst;   10
For who would bear the whips and scorns of time,
The oppressor's wrong, the proud man's contumely,
The law's delay, and the quietus which his pangs might take,
In the dead waste and middle of the night, when churchyards yawn
In customary suits of solemn black,   15
But that the undiscovered country from whose bourne no traveler returns,
Breathes forth contagion on the world,
And thus the native hue of resolution, like the poor cat i' the adage,
Is sicklied o'er with care,
And all the clouds that lowered o'er our housetops,   20
With this regard their currents turn awry,
And lose the name of action.
'Tis a consummation devoutly to be wished. But soft you, the fair Ophelia:
Ope not thy ponderous and marble jaws,
But get thee to a nunnery—go!   25

The king's version manages to mix up sequence and phrasing, misuse words, and interject lines from other sources (most notably *Macbeth*). Twain teases our reverence to texts by making us see how easily and wildly we transform texts over time. For Huck, the king's soliloquy is a privileged discourse that gains its power from being so grandly unlike everyday speech. For educated readers of Twain's novel, the king's speech becomes a kind of game in which one tries to spot all the slips. Inevitably, those readers must think back (perhaps uneasily) on what they do *not* know when an error remains uncaught or is misidentified.

Twain may have left Shakespeare even further behind than Tom Stoppard does in his *Fifteen Minute Hamlet*, but Twain and Stoppard together remind us again that every play or filmed version must always be understood as a distinct interpretation of an original work. In fact, every time we read a text we necessarily interpret it anew. The text doesn't stay the same over successive readings. This may seem like a strange idea, but just reflect upon your own experience in rereading a poem or a story. Is the second reading just like the first? To take just one example: Reading a Sherlock Holmes story for the first time throws emphasis on the mystery Doyle conjures. Once we know "whodunit," we return to the story and note qualities of character or perhaps admire the complex storytelling strategies Doyle employs.

TRANSLATIONS, SUBTITLES, AND DUBBING

We don't read or speak Polish, but we've included English translations of several Polish poems in this book (see those by Wislawa Szymborska and Czeslaw Milosz). For practical purposes, we treat these poems (along with all translated works in this book) as we know them in the English language. Our practice requires an obvious concession: a translation is not the same work as the original. Translation isn't merely a matter of trading one word for another equal word. Those of you who know a language other than English know that there are words and phrases that do not easily translate. Specific idioms may be highly regional. And the sounds of one language will not be easily accommodated by another. Romance languages, for example, employ word endings that facilitate rhyming. An English translator approaching Dante is immediately faced with difficult choices: maintaining rhymes in English requires one to sacrifice much flexibility, yet dismissing rhyme changes a fundamental quality of the original poem's sound and rhythm.

A good translator then is not simply one who decodes a text, but one who grapples creatively with essential qualities of the text—one who seeks to catch and convey the spirit, sense, and tone of the original. A strong command of both languages (and cultures) is essential. Because we don't know Polish, we must trust the expertise and taste of those who have translated Szymborska and Milosz for us. And we feel the trust is rewarded if it results in a reading like the one we experience in, say, Szymborska's "The Courtesy of the Blind." We are forced to think of this poem to some degree as a new, independent work—one inspired by, but not equivalent to, the original piece. If you possess knowledge of a language other than English, we suggest you seek out original works and translations and read them consecutively. What differences do you notice? How does the translation not only translate, but *interpret* the original? Do you feel there are any subtle shifts in emphasis from one text to the other? Are there any points at which you feel that the translation has helped you read the original? Or is there anything in the original that you would want to explain to a reader who knew only the translation? Is there something in the translation that strikes you as effective, yet unwarranted by the original?

Issues of translation take on yet other dimensions in film, for there we do have visual cues that don't depend on words. For that matter, we have sounds (i.e., theme music, background noises like the roar of a crowd, the barking of a dog, the ringing of a bell) not tied to a specific language. Sometimes these elements are so richly textured and suggestive that we feel we experience the film without even keeping up with the subtitles. Other times, however, we're painfully aware of how much we must be missing. There is a clever scene in Sophia Coppola's *Lost in Translation* (2003) that gets at this difficulty. The protagonist, Bob Harris (an aging actor played by Bill Murray), listens without understanding to lengthy instructions offered in an energetic fashion by the director of a television commercial in the making. Bob turns to his translator, who offers the briefest of orders. The exchange that follows comically underscores a serious theme about human communication that runs through the whole film:

TRANSLATOR: He want you to turn, look in camera. OK?
BOB: That's all he said?
TRANSLATOR: Yes. Turn to camera.
BOB: Right. Does he want me to turn from the right or from the left?
(Another lengthy and animated exchange between the director and the translator leaves BOB *waiting for an answer.)*
TRANSLATOR: Right side. With intensity.
BOB: Is that everything? It seemed he said quite a bit more than that.

Bob is frustrated, for he knows that so many words spoken with such energy in one language cannot be reduced to the few words in the language he understands. He's left groping for something that is surely missing. He's left responding back with the most reductive phrases: "OK."

Bob's predicament is one many of us have shared in a very specific way while watching a film in a language we do not know. On occasion, after several lengthy lines of spoken dialogue that we cannot follow, we see a scant few words on the screen as subtitles. Like Bob, we believe there must be much we are missing. And it's likely we are right. But we should not give up on foreign films as unwatchable. Once again, we need to remember that we can deal only with what our education and experience allow us to deal with. We don't want to demand of the subtitles something they cannot supply. And in most films, we'll still have a great deal to respond to. In fact, sometimes our deficiencies in language force us to be especially attentive to an actor's physical gestures, expressions, or vocal tones. We also may appreciate matters of editing, cinematography, or dramatic structure that operate separate from dialogue. If you've ever watched a movie on an airplane flight without purchasing the headphones, you may have had this feeling that much can be learned about the art of film by experiencing a film in silence. So in dealing with works of art in a foreign language, don't too easily let yourself feel lost in translation.

Watching a dubbed film is another way around language problems, but dubbing presents its own difficulties. We've all seen how the words of one language just don't fit the vocalizations of another language; when the movements of the mouth are out of synch with the sounds we hear, the results are distracting. And there are the badly done dubbing jobs where the physical qualities of a voice simply don't match the physical presence of the person on-screen or voice tones are not matched with the performer's gestures. Dubbing perhaps lends itself best to comedy—oftentimes unintentional comedy. Woody Allen's first full-length film was, in fact, an extended play on bad dubbing. In *What's Up, Tiger Lily*, Allen simply took a hard-boiled B movie produced in China, threw out the original soundtrack, and imposed his own clumsily dubbed and ridiculous dialogue in English. In some ways, his film made points similar to Twain's appropriation of Hamlet's soliloquy. The ridiculous quality of *Tiger Lily* helps us understand something of the ridiculousness of all inept translations. More important, Allen (like Coppola with *Lost in Translation*) gets at the real difficulty of moving from one cultural framework to another.

MODELING CRITICAL ANALYSIS: TOM STOPPARD, THE FIFTEEN MINUTE HAMLET

William Shakespeare's *Hamlet* is a notoriously unstable text. Even though it is considered to be one of the greatest works by one of the greatest writers, no written record of Shakespeare's original work survives. What do we mean when we talk about *Hamlet* then? There is evidence that a play fitting *Hamlet*'s description was performed in about 1601. In 1603, a version of *Hamlet* appeared in print, apparently based upon an actor's memory of the lines. Some scholars believe that this actor played the minor part of Marcellus, because all of his lines are rendered perfectly and the text tends to vary considerably from other editions whenever Marcellus is not in the scene. As incomplete and imperfect as this text may be, it can't be dismissed. After all, we have no clearly authoritative alternative. And the 1603 version surely offers insight into the actual production of the play; this is how an original actor experienced *Hamlet*. What the actor from this early production of *Hamlet* thought to record in this first edition may not be a complete text, but it represents what stood out to him—a particular participant from a distant time we seek to recover as best we can.

It's important to remember that the entire process of recording a play in textual form is always problematic. A play is designed to be performed. Unlike a book, a play takes place on a specific stage with a specific set of actors performing to a specific live audience. Even when different productions use the same script (not by any means a given), every performance of the play is different from every other performance simply because it is live theater; actors forget lines or ad lib, the audience laughs in different places, and the weather outside changes the conditions in which this play occurs. Those in charge of a specific production don't necessarily see themselves obligated to the words the author gives them. Would a cut-down version of *Hamlet* command a bigger audience?

Later in 1603 or early in 1604, another version of the play appeared: the second quarto. This one was about twice as long as the previous edition and advertised itself as "according to the true and perfect coppie." If we are to believe this claim, this edition of the text comes from Shakespeare's own copy of the play. This may be a more accurate reflection of what the playwright wrote down, but it may not account for any changes to the play that came about as the play was actually performed. It would be naïve to assume that Shakespeare never revised a play after seeing how it unfolded on stage.

Another version of *Hamlet* appeared in the first complete works of Shakespeare in 1623: the first folio. This script apparently comes from the notes that the playhouse put together (but never used) to prompt actors who forgot their lines in production. It is shorter than the second edition but also includes some material that is not in that longer second edition.

Most modern editions of the play combine material from the second quarto and the first folio; as a result, we usually read a *Hamlet* that is longer than either of these editions. It is striking to realize we have no evidence that this *Hamlet* ever existed in Shakespeare's lifetime. A performance of this "complete" play lasts about four hours while the short first quarto lasts about two. Almost every production of the play edits the version we typically read in some way. Every staged or filmed version of the play must contend with critics who compare text to production and complain that a failure to adhere to the original somehow undermines the integrity of the work. Critics can and should complain about omissions or revisions that don't make dramatic or thematic sense. They shouldn't, however, be too quick to assume that there is a single true standard we can all refer to.

Tom Stoppard plays with these critical problems in *The Fifteen Minute Hamlet* by giving us a prologue that catches at bits and pieces of famous lines, a ten-act play that manages to cover essential actions, and then an encore that reduces *Hamlet* further still. Instead of one play in four hours, we have one play performed twice and what seems a "greatest hits" prologue thrown in for good measure. The effect is a frantic comedy that responds to a long-standing critical problem: What is it that makes *Hamlet Hamlet*? Huck Finn listening to the king's "Immortal Soliloquy!!" is satisfied with high-blown phrases that sound grandly important. Theater for Huck is all about posing. He doesn't bother to demand sense. He doesn't even demand plot. Stoppard is asking, What do we demand? Is it plot? Is it the characters? Is it the language? Is it some aura of specialness that is realized in performance? At what point do editorial changes make the play into something different? Something less? In the first quarto, for instance, Hamlet's famous soliloquy begins "to be or not to be, aye there's the point." Is this enough to destroy the play? It is possible that Shakespeare originally wrote the line that way; so what does it mean if we say that it doesn't sound Shakespearean?

Using the Production and Reproduction of Texts to Focus Writing and Discussion

As we study texts, we can keep in mind some general lessons from the various schools of criticism:

- What are the specific details of the language and structure of the text? How is our interpretation rooted in these details?

- How can we unlock meanings within a text rather than looking for a single definitive reading?

- What are the historical and cultural contexts of this text? How do these contexts lend to our understanding of this text and how does this text help us understand these contexts?

- What information do we have about the development of this particular text? How is the version that we are reading different from some original version of the text? How are these differences significant or interesting? Who has been responsible for the different versions? Can we trace some genealogy of the evolution of this text?

Experiencing Literature through Writing

1. How do the physical properties of a text shape our interpretation of that text? This is a comparative exercise. Find at least two versions of the same text. Blake's poem "A Poison Tree" (p. 1463) for instance, looks quite different on the page that he prepared than it would appear on a page in a textbook.

   a. Describe the specific differences that you see.

   b. How are these differences significant?

   c. How do they change the nature of the text? Remember that even a reproduction of Blake's page is out of context here—it is not surrounded by the rest of the pages that he created, and we have not reproduced the size and quality of the paper that Blake originally selected.

2. How is a particular text part of the culture that developed it? This question is one that works nicely for examining different productions of a particular play. Because each production begins with a script that is fairly stable, each difference within the production becomes material for our discussion. How do these differences help us make specific claims about the culture in which this play was produced? We must remember that every artist who is involved in any production has some individual artistic consciousness, but as we look at productions from different eras, we will identify specific details as representative of that era. The various

film images of *Oliver Twist* that we have included in this chapter offer an example of the sorts of comparisons that we might make within this question.

3. How does a particular cultural reading of a text contradict our close reading of that text? This is a more complex question, but working to explain the apparent contradiction here can result in a very rewarding discussion. In this question, we look for an interpretation of the text that we can support with specific details from within the text. Then we look at the cultural context of the work. For instance, a text that states "all men are created equal" becomes problematic when juxtaposed with the fact that the author was himself the owner of slaves. The goal in this paper is not simply to point out that there is a contradiction. We must explain why that contradiction is interesting. What does it tell us about this text or this culture that this apparent contradiction might be tolerated?

Appendix A

STUDENT MODEL ESSAY COLLECTION

Each of the essays on the following pages engages a literary text closely. Each grounds an argument in the evidence the text offers. Each may lead you back to your own reading with a richer sense of how the poem, play, or story works. But our main purpose here is not to supply still more critical commentary on texts. We want you to read these works from the perspective of a practicing (and perhaps inexperienced) critical writer. These essays then are offered as models of thoughtful critical analysis. Although we've stressed the importance of process throughout our book, it seems reasonable to display what product might result. After all, you'll be asked to write critically, and you'll be evaluated on your command of that task.

To learn from these models, you'll need to read carefully and actively. No model can or should provide a simple formula for success. How do these authors establish or define a topic? How do they signal the significance of their approach? How and why do they use the examples that they use? Do they explain carefully? How do they shape and follow an argument? Do you find the argument provocative or convincing? You'll also need to consider how you can achieve some of the qualities evident in these pieces (or how you can surpass any weaknesses you detect). How can you practice and build upon the strategies evident here as you write in response to a literary text?

We begin with the paper on "Harlem" by Langston Hughes by highlighting general organizational and argumentative qualities evident in some fashion in most critical essays. Observe a few very basic features as you read the model essay below:

- The title of the paper serves a purpose; it informs the reader of the broadly drawn subject (in effect, "this paper is about Hughes's 'Harlem'") and hints at the writer's insight regarding the subject (this poem moves from thinking to doing).

- The essay opens with a broad description of an important aspect of the poem and, thereby, establishes a topic.

- The essay moves toward an argument (the third, fourth, and fifth sentences) as the topic is more narrowly defined.

- The first paragraph ends with a thesis. The analysis will have a point to make, an argument to develop.

- The paragraphs that follow include evidence from the text to back up the thesis. Those paragraphs slow down our reading or unfold the text in relation to the thesis.

- The thesis serves as a controlling or leading idea; the writer's notion of how Hughes builds pressure, intensity, or tension can be charted in the first sentence of each paragraph. These sentences also provide a full sense of transition from one point to the next.

In the papers that follow the one on "Harlem," we call attention to more particular features evident in the specific model.

STUDENT MODEL ESSAY
LANGSTON HUGHES, HARLEM

Smith 1

Leslie Smith
Professor Jones
EN 112
September 25, 2014

From Thoughts to Deed in
Hughes's "Harlem"

Langston Hughes's "Harlem" opens by asking a big question that generates a number of what may seem very uncertain responses. The only sentence in the poem, after all, that does not end with a question mark begins with a "maybe." But "Harlem" ultimately moves well beyond uncertainty. The question that ends the poem builds

Smith 2

forcefully from the questions that precede it. Indeed, it seems more like a statement that implies a soon-to-be-realized event. In "Harlem," Hughes transforms passive speculation into a feeling of concrete and immediate action.

In the first stanza (or verse paragraph), which responds to the initial question ("What happens to a dream deferred?"), Hughes offers a series of similes as tentative possibilities. All are unpleasant possibilities. The likeness he draws makes us taste and smell frustration. Hughes links an abstract feeling to physical sensations, but the similes keep us aware of the mind's intellectual play. Similes, after all, clearly announce with "like" or "as" comparisons of things we don't usually place side by side; we are asked if a dream might dry up "like" a raisin, ooze "like" a sore, smell "like" spoiled meat, or crystallize "like" old syrup. The very fact that these possibilities are grouped together in one stanza strengthens the sense that they exist as possibilities. The speaker is thinking over feelings associated with deferred dreams; no one of those feelings seems any more likely or powerful than any other.

The collective force of these possibilities taken altogether, however, generates some sense of increasing intensity through sheer repetition. The four questions that pose themselves in such vivid physical images of death and decay come to a full stop at the end of the stanza. It seems that this line of possibilities must be exhausted, as dry and stuck as crusted sugar on the top of a syrup bottle.

The thinking process marked by similes and questions gathers great potential force in the next two lines; these lines are set off from the rest of the poem and express the burden of passive speculation. Again the possible result of deferring dreams is cast in the form of a simile. And again, there is a tentative quality to the idea. The "maybe" that begins the sentence keeps the reader in a state of uncertainty that seems appropriate for a poem largely about uncertainty. But here the separation of one possibility from the others as a group indicates that this feeling of weight is an inevitable result of the collected frustration. And for the first time, the tentative quality is not directly expressed as a question.

These shifts mark an increasing pressure in this two-line stanza. The pressure logically anticipates a breaking point. The first responses concerned taste and smell, but here the feeling is of sheer heaviness. At some point, something must happen. By setting off this simile in its own little stanza, Hughes makes the reader pause fully over it and sense the burden of oppression. And by separating this one simile, Hughes builds a greater sense of focus. No more are we quickly listing a series of possibilities. We are, on the contrary, moving to a point that seems too heavy to bear.

The closing line also ends with a question mark, but clearly we have arrived at something much closer to a flat statement of fact. We sense that this idea carries with it the force of an impending action. Hughes emphasizes the final line first of all by separating it from the rest of the poem. We have moved from the series of the first full stanza to the heaviness of the two-line load, to the focus of a single short line. Furthermore, that line is italicized. Its final word rhymes precisely with the last word of the line that precedes it (the other rhymes in the poem chime in on alternate lines). This nearness and the precision of this rhyme emphasize a kind of abrupt decisiveness.

But perhaps the most dramatic change in mood from tentative thoughts to substantial deeds is marked by a shift from simile to metaphor; in this final line, Hughes drops the "like" that has kept us speculating about possibilities. The final idea is expressed through metaphor. A deferred dream will not result in something "like" an explosion. Rather, it is a bomb that *will* explode. Hughes ends the poem by suggesting that violent revolution builds from frustration.

STUDENT MODEL ESSAY
SUSAN GLASPELL, TRIFLES

A major theme of Susan Glaspell's *Trifles* can be used to underscore an essential concern of critical writers: small things matter, or to put it another way, the "big picture" may obscure the significance of specifics. The paper that follows attends to small things to demonstrate how Glaspell leads the audience to sympathize with a character who never actually appears on the stage. For example, the writer notes Glaspell's title and explains how that title signals the play's central irony. The writer also pays attention to how the setting (the cold and depressing farmhouse) serves to clue us in on the quality of the lives lived there. So before moving to the first line of dialogue, a case is being made about how Glaspell controls the way we respond to her characters and to the distinct tone of specific words (think, for example, of the attitude behind the District Attorney's reference to Mrs. Peters as a "housekeeper").

Marquez 1

Joseph Marquez

Professor Wheeler

EN 101

October 9, 2014

Glaspell's Control of the Audience's
Sympathy in *Trifles*

Susan Glaspell's *Trifles* doesn't take long to get to a point where many murder stories end: the audience knows almost immediately "whodunit." The audience also knows "why" in a general sense (the murdered man was cruel to his wife). The only mystery involves the specific motive the District Attorney needs to discover so that he can aggressively pursue the case against his suspect, but this mystery doesn't really move the action forward. This play is more about character than plot.

Marquez 2

Ironically, the audience cares most about a murderer who never appears onstage, never speaks in her own voice, and never says a word in her own defense. Glaspell makes the absent Mrs. Wright the emotional center of the play.

The title of the play strongly directs the audience's sympathy. The "trifles" suggest a profound difference between the men who have power and the women who have no power. The County Attorney thinks that trifles are the concern of women. As a man, he believes he has really important matters to busy himself with. But as the action unfolds, we become aware that significance is a matter of imagination, sympathy, and intelligence. These are qualities that the male officials or authorities in this play do not possess.

The County Attorney, for example, is looking for something big but completely misses many leads. He abruptly cuts off Hale, the man who found the body, just as Hale begins to comment upon the relationship Mr. and Mrs. Wright shared. He also assumes that the dreary quality of the home (ill kept and gloomy) reflects directly upon the character of the "housekeeper," not upon the quality of life she had been forced to live. The Sheriff registers nothing beyond the County Attorney's narrow emotional limits; he merely reinforces the sense that authority either breeds insensitivity or grows from insensitivity.

Marquez 3

The women who come along with the County Attorney and the Sheriff supply a clear counterpoint. They are, no less than Mrs. Wright, subject to the condescending attitudes of those in charge. The official investigators find it amusing that Mrs. Hale and Mrs. Peters notice small things when something as important as a murder has happened. They seem to think that attention to small things indicates a woman's inability to deal with big concerns. The audience feels distant from this rude and self-satisfied attitude and sympathizes with the women.

Mrs. Hale and Mrs. Peters are the first characters the audience sides with, but Glaspell employs dramatic irony to extend sympathy to Mrs. Wright. The County Attorney and the Sheriff are totally oblivious to what the audience and the women know about Mrs. Wright's married life. The gloomy farmhouse does not reflect bad housekeeping but a miserable, cramped, and lonely existence. It is clear early on that Mr. Wright has controlled that existence. He doesn't want a phone because he doesn't want human contact. According to Mr. Hale (an apparently sensitive man, but not one in power), Wright never cared about what his wife might think or want. Wright doesn't want to talk to his wife any more than he wants to talk to anyone.

Marquez 4

For a time, Glaspell keeps the audience a small step ahead of Mrs. Hale and Mrs. Peters. They are in a way also controlled by the men around them. The women do not easily refute the assumptions the men make about their value. Mrs. Peters is, in fact, apologetic about the men's rudeness. She accepts their self-importance on their terms: "Of course they've got awful important things on their minds." Just at this point the audience is once again strongly cued to look for the importance of small things. Mrs. Hale notices the sewing Mrs. Wright had left unfinished and observes that the good stitching abruptly turns ragged. This small detail is evidence that Mrs. Wright became powerfully upset at a particular time. But Mrs. Hale keeps the insight to herself. Significantly, Mrs. Hale resews the bad portions to cover for Mrs. Wright. This act reveals the depth of her sympathy for the accused woman and the contempt she begins to feel for the Sheriff and the County Attorney.

From this point on, the audience participates with Mrs. Hale in her defiance of authority. And the stakes in that defiance grow ever higher, for the motif of the singing and silence brings Mrs. Wright forward as the real victim. Mrs. Hale had already remembered Mrs. Wright as the youthful Minnie Foster. Minnie once dressed in "pretty clothes," acted in a "lively" manner, and sang in the church choir; but that was thirty years ago (enough time for great rage to build over the loss of joy). After Mrs. Hale notices and repairs the ragged sewing, Mrs. Peters comes across the empty birdcage with the broken door: "Someone must have been rough with it." Mrs. Hale pursues her chain of memories: Mrs. Wright "used to sing real pretty."

All singing is in the past tense. Minnie Foster, Mrs. Hale tells us, was "like a bird." But the Wright home is marked by silence. The contrast foreshadows the dead bird the women discover in Mrs. Wright's sewing box. Its symbolic meaning is clear; Minnie Foster was like the singing bird, but John Wright had silenced her just as he had killed the bird. Mrs. Wright must have seen her fate in the dead bird and lashed out in her sense of loss.

All is in place in the closing scene for the audience to identify with the women's efforts to protect Mrs. Wright from further injustice. The audience is aligned in particular with the poised and able Mrs. Hale. Her final action (snatching the box from the stunned Mrs. Peters just before the officials arrive) speaks eloquently of her complete empathy with Mrs. Wright. By this final point, it is an empathy the audience shares with her.

STUDENT MODEL ESSAY ERNEST HEMINGWAY, HILLS LIKE WHITE ELEPHANTS

The essay that follows responds to Ernest Hemingway's "Hills Like White Elephants." Notice that the author shapes a fairly specific approach to the story: the way Hemingway establishes a perspective on his characters through their response to the environment. This kind of focus is essential; a writer cannot take on everything about any work. But notice, too, that the author does not artificially restrict the topic. Insights about point of view, imagery, symbolism, metaphor, and plot all support the thesis. Finally, observe how the author weaves in (and documents) relevant ideas of other critics.

Wright 1

Robin Wright
Professor Beiderwell
EN 110
October 16, 2014

Setting and Character in "Hills Like
White Elephants"

Ernest Hemingway's "Hills Like White Elephants" conveys in clipped dialogue and spare descriptions a conflict between an American man and his girlfriend, Jig. It would seem that the objective narrator gives the reader only the most impersonal glimpse at their relationship. Even the specific issue that generates the conflict, abortion, is only suggested indirectly. Yet Hemingway strongly guides the reader's sympathies. He contrasts the perspectives of his two main characters on the surrounding environment in order to define their moral substance.

The story opens with the couple seated in a shaded area at a train station; they stare across a hot, dry land. This is not a comfortable moment for either of them. When Jig states that the barren hills look like white elephants, the American retorts that he has never seen one. His answer is abrupt, and the girl's comment, "No, you wouldn't have," sets off a round of arguments. Something is going on here besides a dispute over the color of the mountain range.

After much frustrating, strained, and indirect discussion, the girl gets up and walks to the end of the station. From there she looks to the opposite side. By the river she sees trees, lush growth, and fields of grain. Her vision stands in sharp contrast to the dried landscape of the hills that were viewed from the other side.

Jig's fresh vision provides perspective on the man's persistent advice: "They just let the air in and then it's all perfectly natural" (726). The man presses Jig to have an abortion without any regard for what she may feel. His selfish manner hurts her more than the advice itself. He simply does not see the green world that she sees. Nor does he have a clue as to what Jig feels about the state of their relationship.

Wright 3

Jig and the reader understand what the American man misses. Mary Dell Fletcher argues that Jig's vision of the river Ebro aligns her with the forces of life:

> The life giving landscape is now associated in Jig's mind with . . . a fruitful life where natural relations culminate in new life and spiritual fulfillment, not barrenness and sterility, as represented by the dry hills. (17)

Fletcher may overestimate the importance Hemingway lends abortion itself; Hemingway seems more interested in a feeling than he is in the morality of a specific decision. But the contrasting attitudes toward abortion do reveal the general conflict Jig identifies in relation to her lover. One thing is clear: she feels lonely because she realizes how remote the man is from her.

By conveying the differing perceptions these characters have of the landscape, Hemingway helps the reader see each character fully. Gerry Brenner notes that Hemingway's use of the setting allows readers to "overhear" the dialogue correctly and note Jig's "depth of character and [the man's] shallowness" (198). Once we pick up the cues from the ways the characters see the world, we become alert to even the subtlest signs of the man's controlling

tendencies and Jig's more vital being. The following
dialogue illustrates the point:

> "Doesn't it mean anything to you? We
> could get along."
>
> "Of course it does. But I don't want
> anyone but you. I don't want anyone else. And
> I know it's perfectly simple." (728)

The man first claims that the child means something
but quickly shifts the plural pronoun "we" to the singular
forms "I" and "you" (Smiley 9). He refuses to accept the
implications of Jig's use of the plural pronoun.

This profound separation is also made plain in the
images Hemingway employs to mark off physical spaces.
The bead curtain in the bar, for example, forms a barrier
between the man (who stays inside) and Jig (who steps
outside and reflects upon the landscape). The curtain
emphasizes the perceptual differences between Jig and
her lover: the image of the curtain becomes, in effect,
a metaphor of all that divides them in their relationship.

The man's self-absorption is something Jig comes to
understand and accept. She sees things between her and
her lover plainly; there is no reason for her to talk to a
man who cannot listen. The climax of the story marks her

Wright 5

absolute recognition of the state her relationship has come to: "Would you please please please please please please please stop talking" (728). In light of this obvious anger, Jig's terse words at the story's conclusion must be read as ironic:

> "Do you feel better?" he asked.
>
> "I feel fine," she said. "There's nothing
>
> wrong with me. I feel fine." (728)

Obviously, she does not feel "fine," but she recognizes what is wrong. She has gained insight about herself and the man who has been her lover and understands very well that the man will not achieve any similar insight.

Jig even knows that the man will not understand the implications of her statement. He will take these words straight because he wants to believe that everything is fixed or "fine." The mysterious smile that precedes Jig's final words indicates her superior understanding. Perhaps this superior level of insight explains why it is that only Jig has a name; her lover is merely "the American." Everything is broken between these two characters, and only she and alert readers of Hemingway's story are in on that knowledge.

Works Cited

Brenner, Gerry. "A Semiotic Inquiry into Hemingway's 'A Simple Inquiry.'" *Hemingway's Neglected Short Fiction*. Ed. Susan F. Beegel. Ann Arbor: UMI Research P, 1989. 195–205. Web. 15 Oct. 2014.

Fletcher, Mary Dell. "Hemingway's 'Hills Like White Elephants.'" *The Explicator* 38 (1980): 16–18. *Proquest*. Web. 15 Oct. 2014.

Hemingway, Ernest. "Hills Like White Elephants." *The Complete Short Stories of Ernest Hemingway: The Finca Vigia Edition*. New York: Simon, 1987. 211–14. Print.

STUDENT MODEL ESSAY
EDNA ST. VINCENT MILLAY, I, BEING BORN A WOMAN AND DISTRESSED

The love sonnet by Thomas Wyatt that appears on page 721 raises some interesting issues regarding society's assumptions about gender roles. Wyatt's language is the language of battle. The man enters the fray of sexual warfare and seeks to win the prize of a woman's favor; the woman herself is essentially passive (if the man is the conqueror, the woman must be the conquered). Needless to say, Wyatt's notion of love is not, in the idiom of our own time, "politically correct." But his notions of love and of poetic conventions regarding love certainly have a substantial history.

Sonnet writing was in Wyatt's age a "gentleman's" endeavor. A woman writing (or at least publishing) a love sonnet in the sixteenth century would be a near impossibility. Things did not change much for generations. Given this background, one might understand how a woman writing a love sonnet in the early twentieth century would be conscious of the gender assumptions the form had acquired over time. Such a woman might, for example, write a sonnet that critiques the gender assumptions that sonnets had long perpetuated. The brief essay reprinted here arises from the context of this conversation on the sonnet and socially defined gender roles. The essay specifically addresses Edna St. Vincent Millay's sonnet "I, Being Born a Woman and Distressed."

Note how the writer pays close attention to the function of rhyme and how the rhyme scheme signals an underlying tension in the piece. Note also that the writer doesn't just say that Millay employs a conversational tone but explains how and for what purpose Millay creates a conversational tone. Notice also how the writer uses specific terms aptly (for example, *enjambs, turn, caesura, complication*).

Greene 1

Hunter Greene
Professor Smith
EN 102
October 30, 2014

Millay's Self-Assertive Sonnet

Edna St. Vincent Millay must have read many love sonnets by men and heard many proclamations of love by men. She must have become tired of such romantic expressions. Millay lived in an age when women were still usually portrayed as passive objects of men's desire. "I, Being Born a Woman and Distressed" suggests that she found these portraits one-sided, presumptuous, and stifling. Millay defies conventional ways of defining courtship roles by writing a sonnet about sexual desires from a woman's frank, self-assured perspective.

Millay raises in the octave what would be in the context of her time a shocking problem: the female speaker admits to experiencing sexual desires that occasionally overpower her rational faculties. Millay enjambs many of her lines to achieve a conversational tone, but the inner war between brain and body is highlighted by an intricate rhyme scheme that is not characteristic of everyday conversation. The "a" rhymes suggest qualities of thought or reason: "kind," "find," "designed," "mind." The "b" rhymes communicate physical, passionate impressions: "distressed," "zest," "breast," "possessed." The caesura before "possessed" (the last word of the octave) emphasizes the speaker's problem: the speaker feels desire but confesses that her desire often leaves her vulnerable.

The turn in this sonnet, however, is decidedly away from possession. The full pause that closes the octave allows the speaker to catch her breath and assert herself against any mistaken ideas the man (the implied audience) may have about her frank admission. The speaker does not regret her feelings but forcefully spells out what the audience should not think: don't think I have strong feelings still,

she states; don't think I have any pity for anything you
might feel now; don't even think I'm interested in anything
about you. Millay's speaker strongly dismisses any romantic,
soft conventions of love even as she admits to the power
of her own sexual nature.

Conventional poetic ideas of how a woman should
act, or what a woman should feel, have of course been
established and perpetuated by men. Millay's speaker
dismisses male attitudes in general and her former lover
in particular; the split personified by "stout blood"
and "staggering brain" is only one temporary, internal
breakdown. It does not mean that she will feel anything
like enduring love, respect, or even interest in the future
for the object of the passion.

The complication that loomed so large in the octave is
thus put in perspective in the sestet. The speaker accepts
her passion and will neither apologize for it nor be forever
ruled by it. Men have, after all, had the liberty of that "love
them and leave them" attitude all along. Millay announces
the final dismissal. She emphasizes the resolution by telling
the man that she will "make it plain."

The final two lines make the message very plain
indeed; in fact, these lines seem very unpoetic: "I find

Greene 4

this frenzy insufficient reason / For conversation when we meet again" (13–14). Millay conveys a mundane, spoken quality (the enjambment here is important); the word choice seems cold ("insufficient reason"); and no marked rhythm is discernible. But the matter-of-fact, conversational tone these lines express is in perfect accord with the poem's logic. The speaker acquires control by claiming her feelings and expressing her desires without apology.

Appendix B

ALTERNATE CONTENTS BY GENRE

FICTION AND PROSE

POETRY

DRAMA

CRITICAL REVIEWS

Glossary

Abstract: Describing an idea, concept, theme, or feeling as opposed to a thing or person. In literary texts, as in analytical essays, abstractions must occasionally be grounded by particular examples. See **concrete**.

Absurd: Characteristic of a vision in which meaning is drained from life. An absurdist work challenges the way we make sense of the world or the way we lend significance to events.

Aerial view: See **high-angle shot.**

Allegory: Serves to convey meaning through a narrative in which abstract notions are embodied and given life by concrete characters and actions. Usually, allegories set forth a lesson. See **didactic work.**

Alliteration: Refers to the repetition of consonant sounds at the beginning or in accented syllables of a sequence of words. For example, in Coleridge's "Rime of the Ancient Mariner": "The white foam flew,/The furrow follow'd free".

Allusion: A reference within a text to some other text or bit of knowledge outside the text. Allusion involves the author's play upon what is assumed the reader's literary experience; a brief reference in one work to a passage or scene from another work is an allusion.

Ambiguity: Uncertainty or multiplicity of meaning. Ambiguity involves suggestive qualities of expression as opposed to plainly directive statements. Ambiguity may also arise from statements in a single text that seem on the surface to possess contradictory implications or intents.

Analogy: A comparison used to make a point. An analogy uses the likeness of two things to build a forceful argument. If the comparison seems strained or if it does not apply clearly to the point made, the analogy breaks down.

Anapest: An anapest (anapestic foot) consists of two unaccented syllables followed by one accented syllable.

Antagonist: The character set in opposition to the **protagonist.**

Antistrophe: In classical drama, a part of the choral ode. While singing, the chorus would dance. According to some analysts, for the **strophe,** the chorus would move from left to right; for the antistrophe, they moved from right to left back to the original position. The two movements are identical in meter. See **strophe.**

Apostrophe: Refers to the speaker's direct address to an absent person or to some abstract idea or spirit.

Assonance: Consists of a similarity in vowel sounds, but the final consonants differ: *date/lake.* See **rhyme.**

Atmosphere: Feelings invoked in the reader or viewer through **setting.** Gothic works are said to be heavily atmospheric.

Auteur **theory:**   Closely parallels notions of **new criticism.** *Auteur* theory identifies the director of a film as the creative center (*auteur* is French for "author"). Such a focus on the choices of a single maker gave critics a point of analytical focus. But this focus necessarily disregarded the essentially collaborative nature of filmmaking.

Author: See **poet.**

Background: The physical elements against which characters are set. In Caspar David Friedrich's *Woman in the Morning Light* (p. 392), the rolling hills, spacious fields, and rising sun are the background. Background can also suggest information supplied about a situation or a character from outside the immediate narrative. For example, in *Oedipus the King* (p. 261) the *chorus*, along with Oedipus's opening speech, supply information about the past and Oedipus's current situation that helps us understand the action that unfolds.

Blank verse: Unrhymed verse in a prevailing **iambic pentameter.** Blank verse lends itself to serious subjects of lofty speech.

Blending: The thorough mixture of genres. The *Buffy the Vampire Slayer* episode "Once More, with Feeling" adopts many conventions of a traditional material but also plays out as a horror story; elements of comedy and tragedy unfold together as well in this episode.

Cacophony: A style marked by harsh, grating, hard sounds. Opposite of **euphony.**

Caesura: A pause within a line of poetry. The word may be used to suggest a pause in any text that has built some sense of rhythm. A caesura may suggest a shift in mood, a turn to another subject, a characteristic of common speech, or any number of effects. Oftentimes, a caesura serves to foreground a word, idea, or moment.

Canon: Refers to a body of works deemed (by experts/scholars) as worthy of critical study, as literature or art. Canonical works are seen as those works that a culture adopts and uses over time.

Catharsis: The release of strong emotions (pity and fear) inspired by *tragedy*. Catharsis is presented by Aristotle as purgation or a cleansing. The audience feels the terror associated with a tragic end yet finds in the action an affirmation of values or life.

Character: A person in a literary text/film/dramatic production.

Characterization: The method of creating **character.** Authors may, for example, create character through **dialogue,** description, or narration (revealing character through actions).

Chorus: A form of commentary in dramatic works that helps an audience contextualize, interpret, or judge the action that unfolds. In classical Greek drama, the chorus was sung by a group onstage in a highly formalized fashion.

Cliché: An expression that has been greatly overused and through overuse has lost its original force or meaning.

Climax: The turning point in a narrative. The point to which **tension** builds and at which it must be released.

Closed ending: An ending in which all the questions raised in the plot are answered. The reader senses that things have been neatly pulled together in a way that strongly ends the narrative. Detective stories typically are tightly closed.

Colloquial: Casual language that reflects common usage and informal conversation. The language of everyday life.

Comedy: At the simplest level, a work that ends in marriage (and thereby implies happiness, resolution, stability, continuity, and so on). Although comedies offer some sense of fulfillment, that fulfillment may be of a small sort. See **high comedy** and **farce.**

Comic relief: A form of mixing comic elements in the midst of a **tragedy.** The term is often misused, for most such mixing of comic with tragic provides no relief. Indeed, a surprising disruption of the comic into a tragic action may well intensify—not diminish—the action.

Common knowledge: Not what most people know, but what a reader or writer could acquire or confirm from any one of several accessible sources. Most people, for example, don't know the date of George Washington's death. But that date is common knowledge: several people could go to the library or look on the Internet and find the same information.

Complication: A problem, difficulty, or question raised in a literary text. See **sonnet.**

Composition: In film, the arrangement of objects within a frame seen from a particular **point of view;** more broadly, the arrangement of all elements within a single **scene** (lighting, movement, and so on). Composition can also refer to the arrangement of parts in a poem, play, fiction, or essay.

Concrete: Relating to some thing or person that has a physical presence, to something we can touch, see, or hear, to something we know through our senses. See **abstract.**

Concrete poetry: Poetry that is graphically set so that it takes the shape on the page of the thing it describes; in other words, the lines of the poem illustrate their own subject matter. Sometimes called **shape poetry.**

Conflict: That which creates the **tension** that moves a narrative forward to its **climax.** Conflict arises from opposing forces. A character might be set in conflict with another character, or perhaps a social condition, or nature itself. A conflict could even grow from a single character's inner struggle.

Connotation: What a word suggests that lies beyond what a word means in the strictest sense. Connotations may be complex, varied, and subtle, for they arise from a wide range of ever-changing associations. Compare **denotation.**

Consonance: Strikes a similarity in the sounds of the final stressed consonant, but the preceding vowel sounds differ: *date/rite.* See **rhyme.**

Context: Information from outside the text relevant to understanding the text. For example, it is important to know that Tennyson was Poet Laureate of Great Britain when he wrote "The Charge of the Light Brigade" (p. 1248).

He wrote, then, in an official position, not to question why the soldiers were asked to fight and die but to celebrate the fact that they did fight and die. The context for our own contemporary reading of this poem has changed dramatically.

Contextual or **situational irony:**　Contextual irony arises from circumstances or from coincidence (for example, a homeless person arrested for vagrancy on the street in front of a governmental housing and urban development office). See **irony.**

Convention:　An element that has become familiar through our reading or viewing experience.

Couplet:　A verse paragraph made up of two lines. See **stanza.**

Cultural poetics:　See **new historicism.**

Dactyl (dactylic foot):　Consists of an accented syllable followed by two unaccented syllables.

Deconstruction:　Posited notion that meaning is not fixed within a text but is both created and undone by a complex and ever-changing structure of words. Whereas new criticism sought a "best" or most complete reading of a text, deconstruction sought to revel in inconsistencies.

Deep focus:　In film/photography, a technique that allows all objects to remain clear—even those objects distant from the camera. Deep focus creates a sense of density, fullness, and sometimes activity; it does not direct or hold a viewer's attention to a particular place on the screen. See **shallow focus.**

Denotation:　The literal meaning of a word. The leading definition of a word one would find in a contemporary dictionary. Compare **connotation.**

Denouement:　Often suggests not only action that follows the **climax** but the explanation or resolution of what has happened. Denouement suggests an untying of a knot. See **falling action.**

Depth of field:　In film/photography, an extended range of focus. See **deep focus.**

Detached observer:　An observer who is not an active participant in the action he or she relates.

Dialogue:　Conversation between characters. Authors may, through dialogue, create the impression that characters reveal themselves in speech directly to the reader.

Diction:　Word choice. See **colloquial.**

Didactic work:　Literature intended to teach, to instruct readers in points of moral or social significance.

Displacement:　The overlaying of one generic mode upon another. See **blending.**

Disruption:　A break from what is expected; a deviation from an established convention. A familiar element that is revised or even reversed in a text; for example, Clint Eastwood disrupts the conventions of a western when he has his main character ride off not into the sunset but into a dark, rainy night.

Dramatic irony: Dramatic irony signals a distinction between what a character knows and what an audience understands. In other words, dramatic irony arises at moments when the audience knows more than the character or characters that are part of the action. See **irony.**

Dramatic monologue: A work in which a single speaker addresses an audience within a dramatic situation. Robert Browning's "My Last Duchess" (p. 406) is an especially good example of a dramatic monologue.

Dynamic character: A character who changes over the course of a story. The change might be fundamental (the result, for example, of a transformative experience) or superficial (the result of new information).

Editing: In film, the selecting, arranging, and organizing of **shots** to create desired effects. More broadly still, editing involves the integration of sound and image.

End rhyme: Rhyme that falls at the end of the poetic line, the most common place for rhyming words.

End stop: A full stop at the end of a poetic line.

English or **Shakespearean sonnet:**   A lyric poem of fourteen lines that lends itself to a tightly developed problem/response structure. The English sonnet often repeats the **complication** over the first twelve lines (three **quatrains**) and saves the **resolution** for the final two lines (**couplet**). See **sonnet.**

Enjambment: Literally, a striding over. Enjambment involves the running of one poetic line into the next without pause. A line that strides over is enjambed.

Epic simile: An extended and highly elaborate **simile.** Essentially, an epic simile carries on at length after the word *like* or *as* that introduces it.

Episode: Suggests a single, continuous, and brief action that either stands alone or could be detached from a larger narrative.

Episodic narrative/Episodic novel: An extended fiction made up of a **sequence** of episodes.

Epode: In classical drama, the third part of the ode (after the **strophe** and **antistrophe**), which completed the movement of the chorus with singing in unison at the center of the stage or altar. See **strophe** and **antistrophe.**

Euphemism: A deliberately indirect expression. A euphemism may arise from a sense of delicacy, politeness, or respect. Sometimes, however, a euphemism is employed to avoid truth or responsibility (for example, "collateral damage").

Euphony: A style marked by smooth, pleasing sounds. Opposite of **cacophony.**

Expectations: The result of a reader's previous literary experience. Someone, for example, who has seen many romantic comedies comes to expect the feuding couple to somehow realize at some point that they really can't live without each other. In conventional romantic comedies, the couple will indeed get together at the end—no matter how many misunderstandings they have along the way. In conventional works, expectations are met or satisfied.

Explication: Literally, an unfolding. Explication involves the close reading or analysis of a text. Through explication, one seeks to understand how a work achieves meaning and power, as well as what the meaning is. Explication can be thought of as a kind of slow-motion reading.

Exposition: A type of composition that centers on explanation (as opposed to argumentation, description, or narration). In relation to narrative works, exposition functions to introduce or contextualize the action that will unfold.

Extrametrical: Something that occurs within a **metric line** of poetry, like a pronounced pause, that is not accounted for by simple **scansion.**

Extreme high-level shot: See **high-angle shot.**

Eye-level shot: In film/photography, a **shot** taken from the same height as the subject. Such shots put the viewer on the same level as the subject.

Fable: A short story, usually with an explicit or implicit **moral,** that conveys some general truth through a fictional example. Talking animals are a frequent convention of the fable.

Falling action: The action that follows the **climax.** The action that releases **tension** built into the narrative and moves toward the work's conclusion. See **denouement.**

Falling meter: A foot in which the accent falls on the first syllable.

Farce: A form of **comedy** that sustains no **tension** that arises from the emotional complexities of **character.** A farce builds upon silly actions that require only superficial **resolution.** The complexities in farce are situational; complexities do not grow from depth or complexity of character. Television's *Seinfeld* is a good modern example of farce.

Feminine rhyme: A rhyme of two syllables, the second unstressed. Also called a double rhyme. Such rhymes tend to create a light, quick effect.

Feminist criticism: Seeks to gain insights largely obscured or bypassed by the men who have until recent decades dominated critical discussions. Feminists along with **new historicists** assume that a work of art (or a work of criticism for that matter) is a product not only of an author but of a specific culture.

Figurative language: Any language that is used in ways that deviate from standard significance, order, or meaning.

Figure of thought: See **trope.**

Filmic rhythm: Patterns of movement, **composition,** and sound that work together in a film for a particular effect.

First-person narrator: A story told from the perspective of one inside the story; that is to say, the narrator speaks as "I." A first-person narrator may be the **protagonist** of the story, but does not necessarily have that role. Dr. Watson in "A Scandal in Bohemia" (p. 218), for example, reports what he sees and hears of Sherlock Holmes's adventure, but Holmes himself is the protagonist.

Flashback: A return in a narrative to an action that occurred in the past (that is, before the present action of the story).

Flat character: A term used to describe a one-dimensional character. The term is often used negatively, but it is important to remember that characters have to be viewed in relation to how they function in the whole work. See **stock character.**

Foil: A minor character that functions in a narrative to highlight characteristics of more significant and complex characters.

Foot: The combination of one stressed and one or more unstressed syllables that constitutes the recurring rhythmic unit within the larger pattern of a poetic line.

Foreground: In film, that which is in front of the screen, closest to the audience; usually the space where the main action occurs. Foreground also signifies the front of the stage in a dramatic production. More broadly, foreground (used as a verb) may suggest the way an author has highlighted an element for the reader/viewer to note as important.

Foreshadowing: A hint about what will follow—a scene that prepares for action that is to come.

Formalist: See **new criticism.**

Formula: The strict adherence in all elements of a work to the established **expectations** of readers/viewers. See **convention.**

Fragment: A partial action. An action that suggests something larger left unexplored or unstated. A fragment could be a piece of a whole text, but it could also be an artistic device used to create feelings of mystery, for example, or to comment upon the impossibility of wholeness.

Frame: The smallest element of a film: a single photograph that, strung together with many other photos in **sequence,** creates the illusion of movement. Frame can also suggest the boundary that surrounds the image. In a literary context, frame may also refer to the way a narrative or argument is set up or introduced. For example, in the film *The Wizard of Oz*, the fantasy is framed by the mundane black-and-white world of Kansas.

Free verse: Poetry that is not marked by any regular metrical scheme or pattern of rhyme. Free verse may achieve coherence through repeated images or through purposeful variation of line length.

Full or **perfect rhyme:** Consists of the sameness of sounds in accented vowels and any consonants that follow: *date/fate*. See **rhyme.**

Genre: Literary/artistic type or kind. Genre suggests the grouping of individual works into larger categories. The grouping can be made in various ways. For the sake of convenience, for example, a teacher might treat poems, prose narratives, plays, and films as genres. But it is usually best to define genres on the basis of more particular **expectations** an audience brings to a work.

Haiku: A poetic form borrowed from a Japanese tradition. Haikus contain three unrhymed lines. The brevity serves to intensify emotions that find expression in what is usually a highly specific image.

Hero/heroine: Sometimes considered the same as **protagonist,** but that word more strictly signals the character's function to lead the action. Hero/heroine usually implies a moral prominence (the most admirable or sympathetic character in the narrative, the strongest force for good).

Hexameter: A line of poetry made up of six feet. See **metric line.**

High-angle shot: In film/photography, a **shot** taken from above the subject. A high-angle shot may be used to give the viewer a sense of power over the subject. Think, for example, of seeing a fallen boxer from the perspective of the boxer's opponent. An extreme high-level shot or an aerial view extends the logic of such shots further still by exaggerating the angle between camera above and subject below.

High comedy: Develops from the emotional substance of complex **characters.** Oftentimes, high comedies press toward tragic possibilities that are barely averted. They also genuinely suffer for the mistakes they make before achieving happiness at the end.

Hyperbole: Deliberate overstatement, exaggeration.

Hypertext: Allows readers to access on a screen any variety of linked documents instantly, at any time, in any order. Hypertext is not bound to a text laid out on a page.

Iamb: A metrical unit within a poetic line. An iamb consists of two syllables, the first unstressed and the second stressed. The iamb might consist of one word with multiple syllables (aTTEMPT) or multiple words (in LOVE).

Iambic: The most common standard rhythmic unit **(foot)** in English poetry. See **iamb.**

Iambic pentameter: A line consisting of ten syllables marked by prevailing **iambs.**

Identification: The effect of close sympathy and understanding with a character in a literary work. If we identify with a character, we see something of ourselves in the character.

Impersonal narrator: See **objective narrator** or **third-person narration.**

Impressionism: The invocation of an immediate, subjective feeling created by the conditions of a particular moment. An impressionist painter, for example, doesn't paint an idealized object but an object in specific conditions of light (not a church, but a church seen from a certain angle at a particular time of day in specific weather conditions).

Incident: A specific, small action that usually takes place within a more extended narrative.

Internal rhyme: Rhyme that occurs within a poetic line as opposed to the end of the line.

Introspection: A personal willingness to consider and reflect upon ideas that may seem to conflict or that may prove uncomfortable.

Intrusive narrator: A narrator who breaks into the story in order to offer judgment or guidance to the reader or to comment on the unfolding action.

Irony: A literary device that plays upon a gap between appearance and reality. Irony requires us to hold up two possible meanings simultaneously and to appreciate how the implied meaning overrides what seems apparent on the surface. There are many different types of irony. **Contextual irony** arises from circumstances or from coincidence (for example, a homeless person arrested for vagrancy on the street in front of a governmental housing and urban development office). **Dramatic irony** signals a distinction between what a character knows and what an audience understands. In other words, dramatic irony arises at moments when the audience knows more than the character or characters that are part of the action. **Verbal irony** (perhaps the most common ironic mode) suggests a deliberate play upon the difference between what is said and what is meant. **Sarcasm** is an especially blunt and aggressive form of verbal irony.

Italian or **Petrarchan sonnet:** A lyric poem made up of fourteen lines that lends itself to a tightly developed problem/response structure. It builds the **complication** (problem, question) in the first eight lines (**octave**), and the **resolution** (response, answer) is delivered after the **turn** in the final six lines (**sestet**). See **sonnet.**

Juxtaposition: A rhetorical technique of putting two (or more) things next to each other; the resulting contrast or similarity makes us see both objects differently than we saw them when each stood alone.

Limited narrator: See **limited omniscient narrator** and **third-person narration.**

Limited omniscient narrator: A narrator who knows most things but cannot relate selected bits of information or insight. See **third-person narration.**

Line break: The point at which a line of poetry breaks; the end of a line of poetry.

Low-angle shot: In film/photography, a **shot** taken from below the subject. A low-angle shot may be used to place the viewer in a weak position. For example, in the film *Rear Window*, Hitchcock uses a low-angle shot to have us look up at the murderer who is about to attack the wheelchair-bound hero. The viewer is, in effect, put in the wheelchair and feels the threat of the attacker.

Low comedy: A comedy that involves **characters** of little emotional or intellectual substance.

Masculine rhyme: A rhyme in which the rhyming syllable falls on the stressed and final syllable.

Metaphor: A joining of two qualities or things to create new meaning. For example, the phrase "love is a red rose" fuses two essentially unlike things to communicate something about the quality of love. Usually, metaphors build upon one concrete thing (like a rose) and an abstraction (like love). **Similes,** unlike metaphor, signal a comparison as opposed to a fusion (love is *like* a red rose).

Meter: The regular and therefore discernible rhythmic pattern of sounds that can be charted in poetry line by line.

Metric line: A line of poetry measured by the number of feet that compose it. The most common lines are **trimeter** (three feet), **tetrameter** (four feet), **pentameter** (five feet), and **hexameter** (six feet). See **iamb.**

Milieu: A French word that literally means "center" or "middle" and is used to designate particular social, temporal, and physical surroundings.

Mise-en-scène: A French term that indicates what is put into the scene. Mise-en-scène originally referred to the staging of plays: the arrangement and inclusion of furniture, backdrops, stray items, and props that make up the environment within which characters act. Film critics use the term to describe what is captured in a shot. The concept applies to any work of art that places objects in a scene. It's important to remember that if an item is in a scene, it's there because the author/director put it there.

Montage: From the French verb "to assemble." In film criticism, refers to a style of editing that uses sudden **juxtapositions** of images, surprising cuts, and radical shifts in **perspective.** Literary critics may use the word to describe dramatic contrasts of images, voices, or **genres.**

Moral: An explicit lesson oftentimes stated at the end of a narrative. An overt message signaled by the **author.** See **didactic work.**

Motif: A recurring element (an image, a key word, a **symbol,** a phrase, and so on) in a work of literature, film, or music. A motif may be analyzed in context of a group of works (that is, as a familiar element repeated in many different texts) or may be seen to operate within a single text.

Multiple plots: The weaving together of two or more plots in a single work; multiple plots suggest complexity or density of experience.

New criticism: A school of criticism that emerged in the middle of the twentieth century and continues to influence much teaching of literature and film. New critics were **formalists:** they argued that literary texts are the sole material of literary study. Literary criticism was seen as a distinct discipline that focused on the structure, style, and language of particular works.

New historicism: Views systems of meaning as conditional and shifting depending upon the interests the system represents. Literary artists are not free of the assumptions of power that are encoded in language. New historicism has also been called **cultural poetics** and **postcolonial criticism.** The former term puts emphasis on the cultural context that produces literary texts; the latter term calls attention to the ways in which language functions within a system of power.

Objective narrator: A narrator who reports from the outside what can be seen but makes no effort to get inside the minds of any character (sometimes called an **impersonal narrator**). See **third-person narration.**

Octave: A **stanza** of eight lines. An octave often constitutes the first part of an Italian sonnet. See **sonnet** and **sestet.**

Ode: A poem once structured in three parts that reflected their origins as public poems, performed by a **chorus** that moved in one direction as it delivered the first part (the strophe), moved in the opposite direction as it voiced the second part (the antistrophe), and stood still as it came to the final section (the epode). Those conventions of form and performance have worn away. Now odes are characterized more by elements of mood and subject; they are substantial poems of a meditative cast—serious and dignified.

Omniscient narrator: A narrator who knows everything about the characters' actions and thoughts. See **third-person narration.**

Open ending: An ending that prompts the reader to think, question, or project beyond the narrative. A reader might wonder after reading an open-ended novel, for example, what will happen to a character or might be left thinking about the implications of an action.

Pace: The relative speed of an unfolding action, presentation, or argument.

Paradox: An expression that seems to contradict itself but that actually realizes something genuine and deeply coherent. Paradox demands that we question common assumptions or understandings. Blake often plays upon paradox in his *Songs of Innocence* and *Songs of Experience* (p. 606–607, 607–608).

Paraphrase: Involves a superficial revision of the original text; the writer of a paraphrase stays close to the logic, length, and language of the original. See **summary.**

Parody: A comic imitation of a serious work or **genre.** Mel Brooks has made a career of making parodies of successful films or film genres (*Robin Hood* becomes *Men in Tights; Star Wars* becomes *Space Balls;* classic westerns become *Blazing Saddles,* and so on). **Self-parody** suggests an unintentional revelation of empty and tired formulas. Some critics would argue that Michael Bay's action films have descended into self-parody.

Particular: The specific and concrete illustration/image as opposed to the general and **abstract** idea. Authors often use the particular in order to ground more ambitious ideas and feelings—and make those ideas and feelings vivid and convincing. Note for example, Czeslaw Milosz's "A Song on the End of the World" (p. 1252).

Pastoral: Marked by setting in the quiet countryside amid a gently cultivated nature. Pastorals once had elaborate conventions (shepherds living the simple life upon nature's bounty), but the word has come to signal broader qualities: a peaceful and uncomplicated life away from the city can be called pastoral.

Pentameter: A line of poetry made up of five feet. See **metric line.**

Personification: Projecting animate (human or animal) qualities on an inanimate thing.

Perspective: See **point of view.**

Plagiarism: The inappropriate use of the words or ideas of another writer. Plagiarism is a form of theft. In its most extreme form, plagiarism involves lifting directly from a prior source and passing off the work as original. But inadequately acknowledged **summary** and/or an extended **paraphrase** (as opposed to straight copying) can also be deemed plagiarism and be subject to disciplinary or legal action.

Plot: A meaningful fabric of action. Plot suggests structure (a beginning, middle, and end). It suggests not only *what happened* but also *how what happened was conveyed.*

Poet: The source of the word suggests "maker." Poet can, of course, simply mean one who makes poetry. But oftentimes, the word is used more broadly. It can be important to distinguish the poet or **author** (the maker of any text you read) from the **speaker** or narrator (a voice created by the poet/author).

Poetic diction: The notion that the poetic words are necessarily different from everyday words.

Point of view: Strictly speaking, the point from which one sees. More broadly, point of view signals narrative perspective—the way a story is related. Thinking in terms of point of view involves considering who tells the story as well as how the teller's interests, personality, motives, and background influence what is observed and reported.

Postcolonial criticism: See **new historicism.**

Postmodernism: A highly self-conscious mode of expression that calls attention to the artifice of a work of art—the fictionality of a work of fiction. Postmodernism can be playful, but it also blurs distinctions between real and imagined in ways that challenge our conventional ways of understanding. *Pulp Fiction* has been called a postmodern film. The stories of Borges have also been called postmodern.

Prosody: The study of **meter** and verse.

Protagonist: From the Greek, "the first one to battle." The main or leading character. Although the protagonist is usually the **hero** of a story, the terms are not synonymous. See **antagonist.**

Pyrrhic: A foot that consists of two consecutive unstressed syllables; a **variant** or **substitution** of a standard rhythmic unit. That is, a pyrrhic foot may break a pattern, but it cannot be the pattern (a line cannot be made up of only unstressed syllables).

Quatrain: A verse paragraph made up of four lines. See **stanza.**

Reader-response criticism: A variant of **new historicism.** Reader-response critics shift emphasis from a text to how people read/use a text; the work of art is studied not through its own inherent qualities but through the way readers of a particular time and place react to it.

Realism: A mode of depiction that builds on close, accurate attention to specific historical and social conditions. Realism is a constructed illusion; it involves the author's efforts to convince the reader of the reality of a particular vision.

Reflexive plot (also reflexive or **self-conscious narrative**): A story in which the way a story is constructed becomes the very thing we are forced to think about.

For example, the film *Memento* makes questions of narration central to its theme. A self-conscious narrator is aware of the artfulness of the story he or she tells.

Refrain: A phrase, line, or **stanza** that recurs regularly throughout a poem or song.

Reliable narrator: A narrator who offers accurate information and a credible interpretation of action. A narrator who establishes and rewards trust.

Repetition: A means to foreground an image or theme.

Resolution: A satisfying explanation; the part of a **plot** in which problems are addressed. In a long Victorian novel, for example, the resolution might involve a final word on how all the characters turn out (who gets married and has children, who dies miserable and alone, and so on). In a **sonnet,** resolution suggests a response to the **complication** set forth in the first part of the poem.

Rhetorical figure: Uses a word or words in an unusual context or sequence but does not radically change the customary meaning of the word or words. See **trope.**

Rhyme: Consists of the similarity of the last stressed vowel of one word with the last stressed vowel of another. **Full** or **perfect rhyme** consists of the sameness of sounds in accented vowels and any consonants that follow: *date/fate*. **Assonance** also consists of a similarity in vowel sounds, but the final consonants differ: *date/lake*. **Consonance** strikes a similarity in the sounds of the final stressed consonant, but the preceding vowel sounds differ: *date/rite*. Such examples are often called **slant rhymes** or **off-rhymes.**

Riddle poem: A poem that leaves its subject unstated, that invites or requires readers to supply the missing subject. Emily Dickinson's "[A Route of Evanescence]" (p. 257), for example, describes something that it doesn't name: a hummingbird. Part of the fun is guessing the subject from the evidence supplied. See also Dickinson's "[I like to see it lap the Miles—]" (p. 257).

Rising action: The building part of a narrative that establishes, sustains, and intensifies a **conflict.**

Rising meter: A **foot** in which the accent falls on the last syllable.

Round character: A term used to describe characters that possess a complex psychology. A term used in opposition to **flat character.**

Sarcasm: An especially blunt and aggressive form of **verbal irony.** See **irony.**

Scan: To define by close metrical analysis the rhythmic pattern of poetic lines.

Scansion: The metrical analysis of a line of poetry.

Scene: In a dramatic work, may simply indicate the entrance and/or exit of characters from the stage. More broadly understood, a scene is an action within a larger narrative that has some thematic or dramatic function. A scene may be defined by mood, function, or place. It may convey a particular **conflict** that is subordinate to the larger conflict of the entire narrative.

Self-conscious narrative: See **reflexive plot.**

Self-parody: Self-parody suggests an unintentional revelation of empty and tired formulas. See **parody.**

Sequence: A series of actions or a list of points with no necessary logic; sequence alone implies no more than one thing after another.

Sestet: A **stanza** of six lines. A sestet often constitutes the second and final part of an Italian sonnet. See **sonnet.**

Sestina: A highly complicated, fixed poetic form. The sestina consists of six **sestets** (thirty-six lines) and a concluding **tercet** (three lines). The six words that close the first sestet must also appear (not necessarily in the same order) at the ends of the other sestets and then must appear in the final tercet. The **repetition** serves to foreground or develop **themes** and feelings central to the whole.

Setting: The total environment within which narrative actions take place. The characters' living conditions as well as the time and place in which they live constitute setting.

Shallow focus: In film/photography, a technique that brings a specific plane into clear focus and leaves the rest of the picture blurry. A director might use shallow focus to get us to look closely at the face of one character. See **deep focus.**

Shape poetry: See **concrete poetry.**

Shot: A single length of film that communicates a continuous action on the screen.

Shot analysis: A means to comprehend how a film communicates meaning and power. In shot analysis, one breaks a film down and assesses the relationship of shot to shot.

Simile: A comparison that links two things with *like* or *as.* Langston Hughes employs a series of similes in "Harlem" (p. xxxiii) to answer the question "what happens to a dream deferred": for example, it may dry up *like* a raisin. See **metaphor.**

Sincere: The antithesis of **irony;** the perfect correspondence between words and intended meaning. But it is important to remember that sincerity in a literary text may be a device used by an author as opposed to a quality the author actually possesses.

Slant rhyme or **off-rhyme:** Rhyme in which the sounds of the final stressed consonant are similar, but the preceding vowel sounds differ: *date/rite.* See **consonance** and **rhyme.**

Sonnet: A lyric poem of fourteen lines that lends itself to a tightly developed problem/response structure. The sonnet's opening section is often called the **complication;** the second part, the **resolution.** The brief transition that gives us pause just between these two parts is called the **turn.** The two most common forms are the **Italian** (or **Petrarchan**) sonnet and **English** (or **Shakespearean**) sonnet. The Italian sonnet builds the complication (problem, question, and so on) in the first eight lines (**octave**), and the resolution (response, answer, and so on) is delivered after the turn in the final six lines (**sestet**). The English sonnet often repeats the complication over the first twelve lines (three **quatrains**) and saves the resolution for the final two lines (**couplet**).

Speaker: Distinct from **poet** or **author.** The speaker is the voice created by the poet/author of a text. Robert Browning is the author/poet of "My Last Duchess," but the speaker is the duke (a character Browning has created).

Split-screen: A film-editing technique in which the screen space is split so that two or more film sequences run simultaneously next to each other. One of the more famous of these sequences shows a man and a woman talking on the phone with each other. Although they are in different places, the split screen allows us to see both sides of the conversation.

Spondee or **spondaic foot:**   Consists of two consecutive stressed syllables. A spondee is a **variant** or **substitution** of a standard rhythmic unit. That is, a spondee may break a pattern, but it cannot be the pattern (a line cannot be made up of only stressed syllables).

Staging: The elements that concern the physical production of a dramatic work: lighting, sound effects, costumes, mise-en-scène, and so on.

Stanza: A verse paragraph organized by a pattern of rhyme. The most common forms are the **couplet** (two lines), **tercet** (three lines), and **quatrain** (four lines). See also **octave** and **sestet.**

Stanzaic structure: The shape of a **stanza**, marked and knit together by a pattern of **rhyme.** Sometimes called **rhyme scheme.**

Static character: Character who does not change over the course of a story.

Stock character: Simple or **flat character** that is wholly defined by a familiar type or characteristic (for example, Nelson, the schoolyard bully in *The Simpsons* is a stock character).

Stream of consciousness: Direct access to the thoughts and feelings of a character as those thoughts and feelings unfold.

Strophe: In classical drama, a part of the choral ode. While singing, the chorus would dance. According to some analysts, for the strophe, they would move from left to right; for the **antistrophe**, they would move from right to left back to the original position. The two movements are identical in meter. See **antistrophe.**

Subplot: A secondary plot that runs parallel to the main plot. Subplots complement (reinforce, complicate, and deepen) the main plot. There may be more than one subplot in an extended narrative. See **multiple plots.**

Substitution: A break in the prevailing rhythmic pattern of a poetic line; a **foot** (oftentimes a **spondaic** or **pyrrhic** foot) that interrupts a pattern. Substitutions (also called **variants**) may be used to draw attention to a word or phrase. Substitutions/variants might be used to speed or slow the pace of a line.

Summary: Often used interchangeably with **paraphrase,** but a clear distinction between the two is useful. Paraphrase involves a superficial revision of the original text; the writer of a paraphrase stays close to the logic, length, and language of the original. Summary suggests a thorough rewriting and significant compression of the original. Whereas a summary may be appropriate when the source and the extent of the debt are clearly signaled and cited, an extended paraphrase should always be avoided.

Symbol: A type of **trope** in which an object or image comes to represent something more than or other than the object or image alone.

Synchronicity: Events that coincide in time and appear to be related but have no discoverable causal connection.

Synecdoche: A figure of speech in which a part represents the whole (for example, all hands on deck).

Synesthesia: The conflation or cross association of two or more of the five senses. For example, hearing a beautiful piece of music might lead one to feel a particular touch (perhaps a piercing pain or a soft caress).

Tension: A feeling (suspense, doubt, worry, puzzlement, and so on) that is sustained and released/resolved in a work. These feelings do not need to be the broadly drawn **conflicts** that press forward a narrative; many of Emily Dickinson's short poems, for example, are built upon a tension between highly specific words/images and cosmic associations/suggestions.

Tercet: A verse paragraph made up of three lines. See **stanza.**

Tetrameter: A line of poetry made up of four feet. See **metric line.**

Theme: A recurrent idea or feeling woven through a text. Although themes may be explicit (as in a moral to a **fable**), they are more often suggestive and open ended. See **motif.**

Thesis: An assertion that guides an argument, a main point, or a leading insight. A strong, clearly defined thesis underlies the development of a critical essay.

Third-person narration: A story told from outside; that is, the narrator refers to all characters as "he," "she," or "they." There are varied forms of third-person narration. An **omniscient narrator** knows everything about the characters' actions and thoughts. A **limited omniscient narrator** (as the name would suggest) knows most things but cannot relate selected bits of information or insight. Such a limited narrator might, for example, be able to report on the thoughts of all characters but one. An **objective narrator** (sometimes called an **impersonal narrator**) reports from the outside what can be seen but makes no effort to get inside the minds of any character.

Tragedy: At the simplest level, a work that ends in death. More particularly, tragedy involves a powerful sense of lost promise.

Trimeter: A line of poetry made up of three feet. See **metric line.**

Trochee: (trochaic foot) Consists of two syllables, the first stressed and the second unstressed.

Trope: From the Greek for a "turn" or "turning." Tropes use words to turn from conventional understanding; they significantly alter or enlarge meaning.

A trope is also called a **figure of thought** (as opposed to a **rhetorical figure**). **Metaphor, simile,** and **personification** are all tropes. A sarcastic statement (**sarcasm**) is also a trope (if one says, "thanks a lot" in response to an insult, no genuine thanks is intended).

Turn: Suggests a transition space between the **complication** and the **resolution** in a **sonnet.** More broadly, a turn can suggest a sudden movement against a main line of development in any literary work. It also suggests a break from the usual sense of a word or phrase. See **trope.**

Understanding: Grasping a key thought or feeling in a text. Understanding is distinct from knowing. Knowing suggests certainty and completeness (for example, we know Emily Dickinson is an American poet who lived in the nineteenth century). Conversely, one can attain a level of understanding or achieve an insight about an aspect of a text.

Universal: The belief that some ideas transcend historical or social **context** and apply across generations and cultures.

Unreliable narrator: A narrator who provides false leads or misinterprets important actions. Readers are forced to consider how the entire situation (not just what is related) helps establish a fair view of what unfolds.

Variant: See **substitution.**

Verbal irony: Perhaps the most common ironic mode; suggests a deliberate play upon the difference between what is said and what is meant. See **irony.**

Villanelle: A fixed and especially complex poetic form. A villanelle consists of nineteen lines. The first fifteen are made up of a series of five *tercets* (rhymed *aba*); a **quatrain** closes the poem (*abaa*). Dylan Thomas's "Do Not Go Gentle into That Good Night" (p. 753) is a famous example.

Visual image: The realization in words of something seen.

Credits

e. e. cummings

anyone lived in a pretty how town

E.E. Cummings, "anyone lived in a pretty how town" copyright 1923 1951, © 1991 by the Trustees for the E.E. Cummings Trust. Copyright © 1976 by George James Firmage from COMPLETE POEMS: 1904-1962 by E.E. Cummings, edited by George J. Firmage. Used by permission of Liveright Publishing Corporation.

i sing of Olaf glad and big

E.E. Cummings, "I sing of Olaf glad and big" copyright 1923 1951, © 1991 by the Trustees for the E.E. Cummings Trust. Copyright © 1976 by George James Firmage from COMPLETE POEMS: 1904-1962 by E.E. Cummings, edited by George J. Firmage. Used by permission of Liveright Publishing Corporation.

in Just

E.E. Cummings, "in Just" copyright 1923 1951, © 1991 by the Trustees for the E.E. Cummings Trust. Copyright © 1976 by George James Firmage from COMPLETE POEMS: 1904-1962 by E.E. Cummings, edited by George J. Firmage. Used by permission of Liveright Publishing Corporation.

David Denby

Anxiety Tests
David Denby/The New Yorker/© Conde Nast

Grand Scam
© The New Yorker Magazine/David Denby/Conde Nast

War Wounds
© The New Yorker Magazine/David Denby/Conde Nast

Emily Dickinson

The Brain—is wider than the Sky—
Reprinted by permission of the publishers and the Trustees of Amherst College from THE POEMS OF EMILY DICKINSON, edited by Thomas H. Johnson, Cambridge, Mass.: The Belknap Press of Harvard University Press, Copyright © 1951, 1955 by the President and Fellows of Harvard College. Copyright © renewed 1979, 1983 by the President and Fellows of Harvard College. Copyright © 1914, 1918, 1919, 1924, 1929, 1930, 1932, 1935, 1937, 1942, by Martha Dickinson Bianchi. Copyright © 1952, 1957, 1958, 1963, 1965, by Mary L. Hampson.

To make a prairie it takes a clover and one bee
Emily Dickinson

Chitra Banerjee Divakaruni
Indian Movie, New Jersey
Chitra Banerjee Divakaruni, "Indian Movie, New Jersey" Indiana Review, 1990. Copyright © 1990 Chitra Banerjee Divakaruni. Used with permission.

Emma Donoghue
Man and Boy
From Astray by Emma Donoghue. Copyright © 2012 by Emma Donoghue, Limited. Reprinted by permission of Little, Brown and Company. All rights reserved.

Rita Dove
Hattie McDaniel Arrives at the Coconut Grove
Rita Dove, "Hattie McDaniel Arrives at the Coconut Grove" from AMERICAN SMOOTH by Rita Dove. Copyright © 2004 by Rita Dove. Reprinted by permission of W.W. Norton & Company, Inc.

Arthur Conan Doyle
Scandal in Bohemia
Sir Arthur Conan Doyle, "A Scandal in Bohemia.© Courtesy of the Estate of Dame Jean Conan Doyle.

Theodore Dreiser
from *Sister Carrie*

Richard Eberhart
The Fury of Aerial Bombardment
Richard Eberhart, "The Fury of Aerial Bombardment," from Collected Poems. Copyright © 1960, 1976, 1987 by Richard Eberhart. Used by permission of Oxford University Press.

Jennifer Egan
Black Box
© 2012 by Jennifer Egan. Used by Permission. All rights reserved.

Desiderius Erasmus
Desiderius Erasmus, On Copia of Words and Ideas. (De Utraque Verborum ac Rerum Copia by Desiderius Erasmus of Rotterdam [1466-1536]) Translated from the Latin by Donald B. King and H. David Rix.

Frank X. Gaspar
It Is the Nature of the Wing
Frank X. Gaspar "It Is the Nature of the Wing" from Night of a Thousand Blossoms. Copyright 2004 by Frank X. Gaspar. Used with permission of Alice James Books.

Penelope Gilliatt
Peter Sellers in the Pink
© Penelope Gilliatt. Reprinted with permission from Angela Connor.

Allen Ginsberg
Supermarket in California
All lines from "A SUPERMARKET IN CALIFORNIA" FROM COLLECTED POEMS 1947-1980 by ALLEN GINSBERG. Copyright © 1955 by Allen Ginsberg. Reprinted by permission of HarperCollins Publishers.

H. D.
Helen
H.D., "Helen" by HD (Hilda Doolittle) from COLLECTED POEMS, 1912-1944. Copyright © 1982 by The Estate of Hlida Doolittle. Reprinted by permission of New Directions Publishing Corp.

Václav Havel
Temptation
"Temptation" by Václav Havel, translation by Ralph B Winn, copyright © 1989 by Marie Winn. Used by permission of Grove/Atlantic, Inc. Any third party use of this material, outside of this publication, is prohibited.

Robert Hayden
Those Winter Sundays
Robert Hayden, "Those Winter Sundays." Copyright © 1966 by Robert Hayden from ANGLE OF ASCENT: New and Selected Poems by Robert Hayden. Used by permission of Liveright Publishing Corp.

Ernest Hemingway
Excerpt from *Hills like White Elephants*
Ernest Hemingway, "Hills Like White Elephants"

Soldier's Home
Reprinted with the permission of Scribner Publishing Group from IN OUR TIME by Ernest Hemingway. Copyright © 1925 by Charles Scribner's Sons. Copyright renewed © 1953 by Ernest Hemingway. All rights reserved.

Nick Hornby
from *High Fidelity*
Nick Hornby, excerpt from HIGH FIDELITY.

Langston Hughes
Harlem
Used by permission of Alfred A. Knopf, an imprint of the Knopf Doubleday Publishing Group, a division of Random House LLC. All rights reserved.

Dream Boogie
"Dream Boogie" from THE COLLECTED POEMS OF LANGSTON HUGHES by Langston Hughes, edited by Arnold Rampersad with David Roessel, Associate Editor, copyright © 1994 by the Estate of Langston Hughes. Used by permission of Alfred A. Knopf, an imprint of the Knopf Doubleday Publishing Group, a division of Random House LLC. All rights reserved.

The Negro Speaks of Rivers
"The Negro Speaks of Rivers" from THE COLLECTED POEMS OF LANGSTON HUGHES by Langston Hughes, edited by Arnold Rampersad with David Roessel, Associate Editor, copyright © 1994 by the Estate of Langston Hughes. Used by permission of Alfred A. Knopf, an imprint of the Knopf Doubleday Publishing Group, a division of Random House LLC. All rights reserved.

Night Funeral in Harlem
"Night Funeral in Harlem" from THE COLLECTED POEMS OF LANGSTON HUGHES by Langston Hughes, edited by Arnold Rampersad with David Roessel, Associate Editor, copyright © 1994 by the Estate of Langston Hughes. Used by permission of Alfred A. Knopf, an imprint of the Knopf Doubleday Publishing Group, a division of Random House LLC. All rights reserved.

Zora Neale Hurston
from *Mules and Men*
Excerpt from pp. 26-8 from MULES AND MEN by ZORA NEALE HURSTON. Copyright 1935 by Zora Neale Hurston; renewed © 1963 by John C. Hurston and Joel Hurston. Reprinted by permission of HarperCollins Publishers.

David Ives
Sure Thing
Copyright © 1994, David Ives. Used by permission of Abrams Artists Agency.

Randall Jarrell
The Death of the Ball Turret Gunner
"Death of the Ball Turret Gunner" from THE COMPLETE POEMS by Randall Jarrell. Copyright © 1969, renewed 1997 by Mary von S. Jarrell.

James Joyce
The Dead
Published in "Dubliners" by James Joyce, 1914, by Grant Richards Ltd., London.

Joe Kane
The Boy Who Nearly Won the Texaco Art Competition
Joe Kane, "The boy who nearly won the Texaco Art Competition," New York Review of Books, 2/10/05. Copyright © 2005 Joe Kane. Used with permission.

Aron Keesbury
On the Robbery across the Street
Aron Keesbury, "On the Robbery Across the Street," College English, January 1998, Vol. 60, No. 1. Copyright © 1998 National Council of Teachers of English. Used with permission.

Jamaica Kincaid
Girl
Jamaica Kincaid, "Girl" from AT THE BOTTOM OF THE RIVER. Copyright © 1983 by Jamaica Kincaid. Reprinted by permission of Farrar, Straus & Giroux LLC.

Galway Kinnell
Shelley
"Shelley" from STRONG IS YOUR HOLD: Poems by Galway Kinnell Copyright © 2006 by Galway Kinnell. Reprinted by permission of Houghton Mifflin Harcourt Publishing Company. All rights reserved.

Yusef Komunyakaa
A Break from the Bush
Yusef Komunyakaa, "A Break from the Bush" from Pleasure Dome: New and Collected Poems © 2001 by Yusef Komunyakaa. Reprinted with permission of Wesleyan Univeristy Press.

Ted Kooser
A Hairnet with Stars
A Hairnet with Stars from Sure Signs: New and Selected Poems. by Ted Kooser, © 1980. Reprinted by permission of the University of Pittsburgh Press.

Wilfred Owen
Anthem for Doomed Youth
Wilfred Owen, "Anthem for Doomed Youth" from THE COLLECTED POEMS OF WILFRED OWEN. Copyright © 1963 by Chatto & Windus, Ltd. Reprinted by permission of New Directions Publishing Corp.

Dulce et Decorum Est
By Wilfred Owen, from THE COLLECTED POEMS OF WILFRED OWEN, copyright ©1963 by Chatto & Windus, Ltd. Reprinted by permission of New Directions Publishing Corp.

Dorothy Parker
One Perfect Rose
"One Perfect Rose", copyright 1926, renewed © 1954 by Dorothy Parker, from THE PORTABLE DOROTHY PARKER by Dorothy Parker, edited by Marion Meade. Used by permission of Viking Penguin, a division of Penguin Group (USA) LLC.

Penelope
"Penelope", copyright 1928, renewed © 1956 by Dorothy Parker, "Thought For a Sunshiny Morning", copyright 1928, renewed © 1956 by Dorothy Parker, from THE PORTABLE DOROTHY PARKER by Dorothy Parker, edited by Marion Meade. Used by permission of Viking Penguin, a division of Penguin Group (USA) LLC.

Thought for a Sunshiny Morning
"Penelope", copyright 1928, renewed © 1956 by Dorothy Parker, "Thought For a Sunshiny Morning", copyright 1928, renewed © 1956 by Dorothy Parker, from THE PORTABLE DOROTHY PARKER by Dorothy Parker, edited by Marion Meade. Used by permission of Viking Penguin, a division of Penguin Group (USA) LLC.

Suzan-Lori Parks
Topdog/Underdog
Topdog/Underdog by Suzan-Lori Parks. Copyright © 1999, 2001, 2002 by Suzan-Lori Parks. Published by Theatre Communications Group. Used by permission of Theatre Communications Group.

Linda Pastan
Ethics
Linda Pastan, "Ethics" from WAITING FOR MY LIFE by Linda Pastan. Copyright © 1981 by Linda Pastan. Used by permission of W.W. Norton and Company, Inc.

Muriel Rukeyser
Myth
Muriel Rukeyser, "Myth" from OUT OF SILENCE. Copyright © Muriel Rukeyser. Reprinted by permission of International Creative Management, Inc.

Salman Rushdie
The Courter
"The Courter" from EAST, WEST: STORIES by Salman Rushdie, copyright © 1994 by Salman Rushdie. Used by permission of Pantheon Books, an imprint of the Knopf Doubleday Publishing Group, a division of Random House LLC. All rights reserved.

On Leavened Bread
"On Leavened Bread" from STEP ACROSS THIS LINE: COLLECTED NONFICTION 1992-2002 by Salman Rushdie, copyright © 2002 by Salman Rushdie. Used by permission of Random House, an imprint and division of Random House LLC. All rights reserved.

Karen Russell
Haunting Olivia
Used by permission of Random House, an imprint and division of Random House LLC. All rights reserved.

Carl Sandburg
Grass
"Grass" from THE COMPLETE POEMS OF CARL SANDBURG, Revised and Expanded Edition. Copyright © 1969, 1970 by Lilian Steichen Sandburg, Trustee. Reprinted by permission of Houghton Mifflin Harcourt Publishing Company. All rights reserved.

Siegfried Sassoon
The Rear-Guard
Copyright Siegfried Sassoon by kind permission of the Estate of George Sassoon.

George Saunders
Escape from Spiderhead
Reprinted with permission from George Saunders.

Anne Sexton
Courage
"Courage" from THE AWFUL ROWING TOWARDS GOD by Anne Sexton. Copyright © 1975 by Loring Conant, Jr., Executor of the Estate of Anne Sexton. Reprinted by permission of Houghton Mifflin Harcourt Publishing Company. All rights reserved.

William Shakespeare
Much Ado About Nothing
The Wadsworth Shakespeare

Jim Shepard
Gojira, King of the Monsters
Published in "You Think That's Bad" (Knopf) 2011. Used by permission of Random House, an imprint and division of Random House LLC. All rights reserved.

David Shumate
High Water Mark
Published in "HIGH WATER MARK: Prose Poems" University of Pittsburgh, 2004

Charles Simic
My Weariness of Epic Proportions
Charles Simic, "My Weariness of Epic Proportions" from CHARLES SIMIC: SELECTED EARLY POEMS. Copyright © 1999 by Charles Simic. Reproduced by permission of George Braziller, Inc.

Horace Smith
Ozymandias
Published February 1, 1818 by The Examiner (London), p. 73.

Stevie Smith
Not Waving but Drowning
Stevie Smith, "Not Waving But Drowning" from COLLECTED POEMS OF STEVIE SMITH. Copyright © 1972 by Stevie Smith. Reprinted by permission of New Directions Publishing Corp.

Cathy Song
Picture Bride
Cathy Song, "Picture Bride" from PICTURE BRIDE. Copyright © 1983 Cathy Song. Reprinted by permission of Yale University Press.

Gary Soto
Black Hair
Gary Soto, "Black Hair" from NEW AND SELECTED POEMS. Copyright © 1995 by Gary Soto. Reprinted by permission of Chronicle Books, LLC, San Francisco.

Braly Street
Gary Soto, "Kearney Park" from NEW AND SELECTED POEMS. Copyright © 1995 by Gary Soto. Reprinted by permission of Chronicle Books, LLC, San Francisco.

Kearney Park
Gary Soto, "Braly Street" from NEW AND SELECTED POEMS. Copyright © 1995 by Gary Soto. Reprinted by permission of Chronicle Books, LLC, San Francisco.

Oranges
Gary Soto, "Oranges" from NEW AND SELECTED POEMS. Copyright © 1995 by Gary Soto. Reprinted by permission of Chronicle Books, LLC, San Francisco.

Michael Sragow
Getting Sherlock Holmes Right Onscreen
© The New Yorker/Mark Sragow/Conde Nast

William Stafford
Traveling through the Dark
William Stafford, "Traveling through the Dark" from The Way It Is: New and Selected Poems. Copyright © 1998 by the Estate of William Stafford. Reprinted with the permission of The Permissions Company, Inc. on behalf of Graywolf Press, Minneapolis, Minnesota, www.graywolfpress.org.

Bram Stoker
Dracula's Guest
"Dracula's Guest and Other Stories" was first published in the UK in 1914 by George Routledge & Sons, Ltd., London.

Tom Stoppard
The Fifteen Minute Hamlet
Tom Stoppard, FIFTEEN MINUTE HAMLET. Copyright © 1976 by Tom Stoppard. CAUTION: Professionals and amateurs are hereby warned that FIFTEEN MINUTE HAMLET being fully protected under the copyright laws of the United States of America, the British Commonwealth countries, including Canada, and the other countries of the Copyright Union, is subject to a royalty. All rights, including professional, amateur, motion picture, recitation, public reading, radio, television and cable broadcasting, and the rights of translation into foreign languages, are strictly reserved. Any inquiry regarding the availability of performance rights or the purchase of individual

copies of the authorized acting edition, must be directed to Samuel French Inc., 45 West 25th Street, NY, NY, 10010 with other locations in Hollywood and Toronto, Canada.

Robert Sward
For Gloria on Her 60th Birthday, or Looking for Love in Merriam-Webster
Robert Sward, "For Gloria on Her 60th Birthday, or Looking for Love in Merriam-Webster" from Four Incarnations: New and Selected Poems 1951-1991. Copyright © 1991 by Robert Sward. Reprinted with the permission of The Permissions Company, Inc., on behalf of Coffee House Press, www.coffeehousepress.org.

Wislawa Szymborska
ABC
"ABC" from MONOLOGUE OF A DOG: New Poems by Wislawa Szymborska, translated from the Polish by Stanislaw Baranczak and Clare Cavanagh. Copyright © 2002 by Wislawa Szymborska. English translation copyright ©2006 by Houghton Mifflin Harcourt Publishing Company. Reprinted by permission of Houghton Mifflin Harcourt Publishing Company. All rights reserved.

The Courtesy of the Blind
"The Courtesy of the Blind" from MONOLOGUE OF A DOG: New Poems by Wislawa Szymborska, translated from the Polish by Stanislaw Baranczak and Clare Cavanagh. Copyright © 2002 by Wislawa Szymborska. English translation copyright ©2006 by Houghton Mifflin Harcourt Publishing Company. Reprinted by permission of Houghton Mifflin Harcourt Publishing Company. All rights reserved.

James Tate
Shiloh
Printed in "Return to the City of White Donkeys," Ecco Press (HarperCollins imprint), 2004.

Henry Taylor
After a Movie
© Louisiana State University Press.

Dylan Thomas
Do Not Go Gentle into That Good Night
Dylan Thomas, "Do Not Go Gentle Into That Good Night" by Dylan Thomas from THE POEMS OF DYLAN THOMAS. Copyright 1952 by Dylan Thomas. Reprinted by permission of New Directions Publishing Corp.

Index of First Lines of Poetry

Index of Authors and Titles

Italics indicate a title of a work of art, film, or literature.